Yearbook on International Communist Affairs 1984

Yearbook on International Communist Affairs

1984

Parties and Revolutionary Movements

EDITOR: Richard F. Staar

ASSISTANT EDITOR: Margit N. Grigory

AREA EDITORS

Thomas H. Henriksen	•	Africa and the Middle East
William E. Ratliff	•	The Americas
Ramon H. Myers	•	Asia and the Pacific
Milorad M. Drachkovitch	•	Eastern Europe and the Soviet Union
Dennis L. Bark	•	Western Europe

HOOVER INSTITUTION PRESS
Stanford University, Stanford, California

The text of this work is set in Times Roman;
display headings are in Melior. Typeset by
Harrison Typesetting, Inc., Portland, Oregon.

Hoover Press Publication 303

First printing, 1984
Manufactured in the United States of America
88 87 86 85 84   9 8 7 6 5 4 3 2 1

International Standard Book Number 0-8179-8031-8
International Standard Serial Number 0084-4101
Library of Congress Catalog Card Number 67-31024

Contents

Preface ix

Register of Communist Parties x

Introduction xxv

AFRICA AND THE MIDDLE EAST

Introduction (*Thomas H. Henriksen*) 1
Algeria (*John Damis*) 7
Angola (*Richard E. Bissell*) 8
Bahrain (*Wallace H. Spaulding*) 12
Benin (*Michael S. Radu*) 13
Congo (*Michael S. Radu*) 15
Egypt (*Glenn E. Perry*) 18
Ethiopia (*Peter Schwab*) 21
Iran (*Joseph D. Dwyer*) 24
Iraq (*John F. Devlin*) 28
Israel (*Glenn E. Perry*) 30
    Palestine Communist Party (*Glenn E. Perry*) 34
Jordan (*Norman F. Howard*) 37
Lebanon (*Norman F. Howard*) 39
Morocco (*John Damis*) 45
Mozambique (*Thomas H. Henriksen*) 47
Nigeria (*Jack H. Mower*) 52
Réunion (*Joyce Myrick*) 53
Saudi Arabia (*Wallace H. Spaulding*) 55
Senegal (*Jack H. Mower*) 56
South Africa (*Sheridan Johns*) 57
Sudan (*Leif Rosenberger*) 61
Syria (*Glenn E. Perry*) 65
Tunisia (*John Damis*) 69
Yemen: People's Democratic Republic of Yemen (*John Duke Anthony*) 70
Zimbabwe (*Richard W. Hull*) 75

THE AMERICAS

Introduction (*William E. Ratliff*) 79
Argentina (*Mark Falcoff*) 82

Bolivia (*Robert J. Alexander*) 85
Brazil (*Carole Merten*) 88
Canada (*Alan Whitehorn*) 91
Chile (*Paul E. Sigmund*) 95
Colombia (*Daniel L. Premo*) 98
Costa Rica (*Lowell Gudmundson*) 105
Cuba (*George Volsky*) 110
Dominican Republic (*George Volsky*) 116
Ecuador (*David Scott Palmer*) 118
El Salvador (*Thomas P. Anderson*) 120
Grenada (*W. Raymond Duncan*) 124
Guadeloupe (*Brian Weinstein*) 129
Guatemala (*Daniel L. Premo*) 131
Guyana (*William E. Ratliff*) 138
Haiti (*Brian Weinstein*) 140
Honduras (*Thomas P. Anderson*) 141
Jamaica (*W. Raymond Duncan*) 144
Martinique (*Brian Weinstein*) 147
Mexico (*Wallace H. Spaulding*) 149
Nicaragua (*Thomas P. Anderson*) 154
Panama (*Christian V. Pascale*) 158
Paraguay (*Paul H. Lewis*) 162
Peru (*Sandra Woy-Hazleton*) 163
Puerto Rico (*George Volsky*) 170
Suriname (*William E. Ratliff*) 171
United States (*Harvey Klehr*) 173
Uruguay (*Martin Weinstein*) 176
Venezuela (*Carole Merten*) 177

ASIA AND THE PACIFIC

Introduction (*Ramon H. Myers*) 183
Afghanistan (*Richard P. Cronin*) 186
Australia 195
Bangladesh (*Walter K. Andersen*) 202
Burma (*Paul Belmont and Jon A. Wiant*) 204
China (*Stephen Uhalley, Jr.*) 209
India (*Walter K. Andersen*) 220
Indonesia (*Jeanne S. Mintz*) 226
Japan (*John F. Copper*) 230
Kampuchea (*William Scharf*) 235
Korea: Democratic People's Republic of Korea (*Tai Sung An*) 237
Laos (*Arthur J. Dommen*) 246
Malaysia and Singapore (*Jeanne S. Mintz*) 249
Mongolia (*Tania A. Jacques*) 255
Nepal (*Barbara Reid*) 257
New Zealand 259

Pakistan (*Walter K. Andersen*) 263
Philippines 266
Sri Lanka (*Barbara Reid*) 275
Thailand (*Clark D. Neher*) 277
Vietnam (*Douglas Pike*) 280

EASTERN EUROPE AND THE SOVIET UNION

Introduction (*Milorad M. Drachkovitch*) 287
Albania (*Nikolaos A. Stavrou*) 293
Bulgaria (*John D. Bell*) 302
Czechoslovakia (*Zdeněk Suda*) 312
Germany: German Democratic Republic (*David Pike*) 322
Hungary (*Bennett Kovrig*) 334
Poland (*Arthur R. Rachwald*) 343
Romania (*Walter M. Bacon, Jr.*) 360
Union of Soviet Socialist Republics (*R. Judson Mitchell*) 372
Yugoslavia 403
Council for Mutual Economic Assistance (*Aurel Braun*) 404
Warsaw Treaty Organization (*Aurel Braun*) 417
International Communist Organizations (*Wallace H. Spaulding*) 426
    World Marxist Review 426
    Front Organizations 427

WESTERN EUROPE

Introduction (*Dennis L. Bark*) 437
Austria (*Frederick C. Engelmann*) 443
Belgium (*Martin O. Heisler*) 446
Cyprus (*T. W. Adams*) 448
Denmark (*Eric S. Einhorn*) 452
Finland (*Leif Rosenberger*) 458
France (*Michael J. Sodaro*) 464
Germany: Federal Republic of Germany and West Berlin (*Eric Waldman*) . . . 470
Great Britain (*Richard Sim*) 478
Greece (*D. G. Kousoulas*) 481
Iceland (*Eric S. Einhorn*) 484
Ireland (*Richard Sim*) 487
Italy (*Giacomo Sani*) 489
Luxembourg (*Eric Waldman*) 496
Malta (*T. W. Adams*) 498
Netherlands (*Robert I. Weitzel*) 501
Norway (*Leif Rosenberger*) 505
Portugal (*H. Leslie Robinson*) 511
San Marino (*Giacomo Sani*) 513
Spain (*H. Leslie Robinson*) 514
Sweden (*Peter Grothe*) 519

Switzerland (*Eric Waldman*) 523
Turkey (*Frank Tachau*) 525

Select Bibliography 529

Index of Biographies 541

Index of Names 543

Index of Subjects 561

Preface

This eighteenth edition of the *Yearbook on International Communist Affairs* brought some changes in personnel. The area editorship for Latin America has been resumed by William E. Ratliff, who had filled this position for previous *Yearbook*s. Profiles were written by 71 scholars, some of whom prepared more than one. Names and affiliations appear at the end of the individual essays. Mr. John Ziemer prepared the subject index, and Mrs. Margit Grigory the customary name index. Area curators and librarians at the Hoover Institution contributed to the bibliography and located esoteric information.

The *Yearbook* provides data on the condition, organization, policies, activities, and international relations during calendar year 1983 of communist or Marxist-Leninist parties throughout the world. The volume covers these movements as completely as possible. Information is derived primarily from published sources, including local newspapers and radio broadcasts as reported by the U.S. Foreign Broadcast Information Service. This edition presents profiles on movements in 104 countries, two regional organizations, and ten international communist fronts.

The question of inclusion or exclusion of various parties and groups that espouse a quasi-Marxist-Leninist ideology, but are not officially recognized as being "communist," is difficult. This problem applies to certain among the so-called national liberation movements and, more important, even to some ruling parties. When considering the latter, the following aspects have been taken into account: rhetoric, nationalization of the economy, party organization, participation in international communist meetings and front organizations, and adherence to the foreign policy line of the strongest communist-ruled state, the USSR. It seems realistic to consider the governments of Nicaragua and Grenada (until October 1983) in the same category as that of Cuba. Algeria and Libya, despite their radicalism, are obviously less aligned. Ruling parties in the nine countries called "vanguard revolutionary democracies" by the Soviet Union seem rather clearly affiliated with the "world communist movement."

Finally, my personal expression of gratitude goes to Professor Robert Wesson for his outstanding editorship of the *Yearbook* during my recent leave of absence for public service.

Richard F. Staar

Register of Communist Parties

Status: * ruling   # unrecognized
                + legal   0 proscribed

AFRICA AND THE MIDDLE EAST (25)

Country: Party(ies)/Date Founded	Mid-1983 Population (est.)	Communist Party Membership (claim or est.)	Party Leader (sec'y general)	Status	Last Congress	Last Election (percentage of vote; seats in legislature)
Algeria Socialist Vanguard Party (PAGS), 1920	20,695,000	450 est.	Sadiq Hadjeres	0	Sixth Feb. 1952	n/a
Angola Popular Movement for the Liberation of Angola (MPLA), 1956 (MPLA-PT, 1977)	7,567,000	31,000 cl.	José Eduardo dos Santos	*	First Dec. 1980	(1980); all 203 MPLA approved
Bahrain Bahrain National Liberation Front (NLF/B), 1955	393,000	negligible	Yusuf al-Hassan al-Ajajai	0	unknown	n/a
Benin People's Revolutionary Party of Benin (PRPB), 1975	3,754,000	no data	Mathieu Kerekou	*	Second 13–15 Nov. 1979	(1979); all 336 PRPB approved
Congo Congolese Labor Party (PCT), 1968	1,694,000	7,000 est.	Denis Sassou Ngouesso	*	Third Aug. 1979	(1979); all 115 PCT approved
Egypt Egyptian Communist Party (ECP), 1921	45,851,000	500 est.	Farid Muhajid	0	First (NPUP) 10 Apr. 1980	n/a

Country / Party (founding)	Population	Party membership	Leader	Status	Last Congress	Elections / Notes
Ethiopia Commission to Organize the Party of the Working People of Ethiopia (COPWE), 1979	32,800,000	2,000 est.	Mengistu Haile Mariam	+	Second 3–6 Jan. 1983	no elections since 1974 revolution
Iran Communist Party of Iran (Tudeh Party), 1949 (dissolved May 1983)	42,490,000	2,000 est. (early 1983) (all subsequently executed, jailed, or in exile)	Nureddin Kianuri	0	1965 (party split)	3.0 (1980); none
Iraq Iraqi Communist Party (ICP), 1934	14,509,000	2,000 est.	Aziz Muhammad	+ (but repressed)	Third 4–6 May 1976	—(1980)
Israel Communist Party of Israel (CPI, "Rakah"), 1948 (Palestine Communist Party, 1922)	4,065,000	1,500 est.	Meir Vilner	+	Nineteenth 11–14 Feb. 1981	3.4 (1981); 4 of 120
Jordan Communist Party of Jordan (CPJ), 1951	3,436,000	200 est.	Faik Warrad	0	Conference Apr. 1970	n/a
Lebanon Lebanese Communist Party (LCP), 1924	2,598,000	15,000 est.	George Hawi	+	Fourth 1979	—(1972)
Morocco Party of Progress and Socialism (PPS), 1943	22,889,000	2,000 est.	'Ali Yata	+	Third 25–27 Mar 1983	2.31 (1977); 1 of 264
Mozambique Front for the Liberation of Mozambique (FRELIMO), 1962	13,047,000	35,000 cl.	Samora Moises Machel	*	Fourth 26–29 Apr. 1983	(1977); all 226 FRELIMO approved
Nigeria Socialist Working People's Party (SWPP), 1963	85,219,000	no data	(Idi)dapo Fatogun	0 (since Dec. 1983)	First Dec. 1965	—(1983)
Palestine Communist Party, 1982		200 est.	unknown	0	First 1982	n/a

Country: Party(ies)/Date Founded	Mid-1983 Population (est.)	Communist Party Membership (claim or est.)	Party Leader (sec'y general)	Status	Last Congress	Last Election (percentage of vote; seats in legislature)
Réunion Réunion Communist Party (PCR), 1959	531,000	10,000 cl.	Paul Vergès	+	Fifth 12–14 July 1980	32.73 (1983); 16 of 45 (local assembly); none in Paris
Saudi Arabia Communist Party of Saudi Arabia (CPSA), 1975	10,443,000	negligible	Abd-al-Rahim Salih	0	unknown	n/a
Senegal Independence and Labor Party (PIT), 1957	6,335,000	no data	Seydou Cissoko	+	Constituent Aug. 1981	0.0 (1983); none
South Africa South African Communist Party (SACP), 1921	30,938,000	no data	Moses Mabhida	0	Fifth Conference Dec. 1962	n/a
Sudan Sudanese Communist Party (SCP), 1946	20,585,000	1,500 est.	Muhammad Ibrahim Nugud Mansur	0	Fourth (legal) 31 Oct. 1967	n/a
Syria Syrian Communist Party (SCP), 1944	9,739,000	5,000 est.	Khalid Bakhdash	+	Fifth May 1980	0.0 (1981); none
Tunisia Tunisian Communist Party (PCT), 1920	7,020,000	100 est.	Muhammad Harmel	+	Eighth Feb. 1981	0.78 (1981); none

Country / Party (founded)	Population	Membership	Leader	Status	Last Congress	Parliamentary status
Yemen (Aden) Yemen Socialist Party (YSP), 1978	2,022,000	26,000 cl.	Ali Nasir Muhammad	*	Second Extraord. 12–14 Oct. 1980	—(1978); all 111 YSP approved
Zimbabwe Zimbabwe African National Union (ZANU), 1963	8,376,000	unknown	Robert Mugabe	*	Fourth 1979	62.9 (1980); 57 of 100
TOTAL	396,996,000	141,450				

THE AMERICAS (29)

Country / Party (founded)	Population	Membership	Leader	Status	Last Congress	Parliamentary status
Argentina Communist Party of Argentina (PCA), 1918	29,627,000 (1976 census)	70,000 est.	Athos Fava	+	Extraord. 5–6 Sept. 1983	1.3 (1983); none
Bolivia Communist Party of Bolivia (PCB), 1950	5,883,000	300 est.	Jorge Kolle Cueto	+	Fourth Apr. 1979	—(1980)
Brazil Brazilian Communist Party (PCB), 1960 (Communist Party of Brazil, 1922)	131,305,000	6,000 est.	Giacondo Dias	0 (but tolerated)	Seventh 13 Dec. 1982 (interrupted by police)	n/a
Canada Communist Party of Canada (CPC), 1921	24,882,000	2,500 est.	William Kashtan	+	Twenty-fifth 13–15 Feb. 1982	0.05 (1980); none
Chile Communist Party of Chile (CPC), 1922	11,486,000	20,000 est.	Luís Corvalán	0	Fifteenth Jan. 1971	16.0 (1973); 23 of 150
Colombia Communist Party of Colombia (PCC), 1930	27,663,000	12,000 est.	Gilberto Vieira	+	Thirteenth 7–11 Nov. 1980	1.2 (1982); 4 of 313

Country: Party(ies)/Date Founded	Mid-1983 Population (est.)	Communist Party Membership (claim or est.)	Party Leader (sec'y general)	Status	Last Congress	Last Election (percentage of vote; seats in legislature)
Costa Rica Popular Vanguard Party (PVP), 1931	2,599,000	3,500 est. 10,000 cl.	Humberto Vargas Carbonell	+	Third Extraord. 12–13 Nov. 1983	3.2 (1982); 4 of 57 (United People's Coalition)
Cuba Cuban Communist Party (PCC), 1965	9,852,000	434,143 cl.	Fidel Castro Ruz	*	Second 17–20 Dec. 1981	—(1981); all 499 PCC approved
Dominican Republic Dominican Communist Party (PCD), 1944	6,248,000	5,000 est. (30 leftist groups, Dominican Left Front)	Narciso Isa Conde	+	Third Nat'l Conf. Dec. 1976	7.1 (1982); none
Ecuador Communist Party of Ecuador (PCE), 1928	8,881,000	500 est.	René Mauge	+	Tenth 27–29 Nov. 1981	3.2 (1979); 1 of 71 (Popular Democratic Union)
El Salvador Communist Party of El Salvador (PCES), 1928	4,685,000	50,000 cl. (500 est.)	Shafik Jorge Handal	0	Sixth Aug. 1970	n/a
Grenada New Jewel Movement (NJM), 1973	111,000	unknown (30,000 cl. in 1983)	Maurice Bishop (shot 19 Oct. 1983)	*	unknown	Promised Nov. 1984 (first since 1976)
Guadeloupe Communist Party of Guadeloupe (PCG), 1958	320,000	3,000 est.	Guy Daninthe	+	Seventh 16–18 May 1980	22.6 (1983); 11 of 41 (local assembly); also 1 of 3 in Paris

Country / Party (founded)	Population	Membership	Leader		Last congress	Electoral data
Guatemala Guatemalan Party of Labor (PGT), 1950	7,714,000	750 est.	Carlos González	0	Fourth Dec. 1969	n/a
Guyana People's Progressive Party (PPP), 1950	900,000	100 est.	Cheddi Jagan	+	Twenty-first 31 July–2 Aug. 1982	19.5 (1980); 10 of 65
Haiti Unified Party of Haitian Communists (PUCH), 1968	5,666,000	350 est.	René Théodore	0	First 1979	n/a
Honduras Honduran Communist Party (PCH), 1954	4,276,000	1,500 est. (combined left)	Rigoberto Padilla Rush	#	Third Mar. 1977	(1981)
Jamaica Workers' Party of Jamaica (WPJ), 1978	2,335,000	50 est.	Trevor Munroe	+	Second 17–20 Dec. 1981	—(1983)
Martinique Martinique Communist Party (PCM), 1957	320,000	1,000 est.	Armand Nicolas	+	Eighth 12–13 Nov. 1983	9.07 (1983); 4 of 41 (local assembly); none in Paris
Mexico United Socialist Party of Mexico (PSUM), 1981	75,702,000	40,800 cl.	Pablo Gómez Alvarez	+	Second 9–14 Aug. 1983	4.3 (1983); 17 of 400
Nicaragua Nicaraguan Socialist Party (PSN), 1939	2,812,000	250 est.	Louis Sánchez	+	Tenth Oct. 1973	(1984) 90-member legislature promised
Panama People's Party of Panama (PPP), 1943	2,059,000	750 est.	Rubén Darío Souza	+	Sixth 8–10 Feb. 1980	—(1978)
Paraguay Paraguayan Communist Party (PCP), 1928	3,525,000	3,500 est.	Antonia Maidana (arrested 1980)	0	Third 10 Apr. 1971	n/a

Country: Party(ies)/Date Founded	Mid-1983 Population (est.)	Communist Party Membership (claim or est.)	Party Leader (sec'y general)	Status	Last Congress	Last Election (percentage of vote; seats in legislature)
Peru Peruvian Communist Party (PCP), 1930	19,161,000	2,000 est.	Jorge del Prado	+	Eighth Extraord. 27–31 Jan. 1982	2.8 (1980); 2 of 60
Puerto Rico Puerto Rican Socialist Party (PSP), 1971	3,196,520	150 est.	Juan Mari Bras (resigned)	+	Second 1979	0.3 (1980); none
Puerto Rican Communist Party (PCP), 1934		125 est.	Franklin Irrizarry	+	unknown	—(1980)
Suriname Communist Party of Suriname (CPS), 1981 (pro-Albanian)	356,000	25 est.	Bram Mehr	+	First 24 July 1981	n/a
Revolutionary People's Party (RVP), 1981		100 est.	Edward Naarendorp	+	First 1981	n/a
United States of America Communist Party USA (CPUSA), 1919	243,193,000	17,500 cl.	Gus Hall	+	Twenty-third 10–13 Nov. 1983	0.01 (1980); none
Uruguay Communist Party of Uruguay (PCU), 1920	2,916,000	7,500 est.	Rodney Arismendi	0 (since 1973)	Twentieth Dec. 1970	(1971); 2 of 99
Venezuela Communist Party of Venezuela (PCV), 1931	17,993,000 (1981)	4,000 est.	Jésus Faría	+	Sixth 8–11 Aug. 1980	2.0 (1983); 3 of 195
TOTAL	655,666,520	687,393				

ASIA AND THE PACIFIC (21)

Country / Party (founded)	Population	Membership	Leader		Congress / Conference	Election
Afghanistan People's Democratic Party of Afghanistan (PDPA), 1965	14,177,000	90,000 cl.	Babrak Karmal	*	Nat'l Conf. 14–15 Mar. 1982	(1978) (Revolutionary Council in power since 30 Apr. 1978)
Australia Communist Party of Australia (CPA), 1920	15,265,000	1,000 est.	Judy Mundey	+	Twenty-seventh 12–14 June 1982	—(1983)
Socialist Party of Australia (SPA), 1971		650 est.	Peter Dudley Symon	+	Fourth Oct. 1981	—(1983)
Bangladesh Communist Party of Bangladesh (CPB), 1948	96,539,000	3,000 est.	Muhammed Farhad	+	Third Feb. 1980	—(1981)
Burma Burmese Communist Party (BCP), 1939	37,061,000	3,000 cl.	Thakin Ba Thein Tin	0	Second 20 July 1945 (last known)	n/a
China Chinese Communist Party (CCP), 1921	1,059,802,000	40,000,000 cl.	Hu Yaobang	*	Twelfth 1–11 Sept. 1982	(1981); all 3,202 CCP approved
India Communist Party of India (CPI), 1925	740,009,000	470,000 cl.	C. Rajeswara Rao	+	Twelfth 21–28 Mar. 1982	2.6 (1980); 12 of 544
Communist Party Marxist (CPM), 1964		270,000 cl.	E. M. S. Namboodiripad	+	Eleventh 26–31 Jan. 1982	6.0 (1980); 36 of 544
Indonesia Indonesian Communist Party (PKI), 1920	160,932,000	200 est.	Jusuf Adjitorop	0	Seventh Extraord. Apr. 1962	n/a
Japan Japan Communist Party (JCP), 1922	119,400,000	400,000 est.	Tetsuzo Fuwa	+	Sixteenth 27–31 July 1982	9.43 (1983); 26 of 511

Country: Party(ies)/Date Founded	Mid-1983 Population (est.)	Communist Party Membership (claim or est.)	Party Leader (sec'y general)	Status	Last Congress	Last Election (percentage of vote; seats in legislature)
Kampuchea Kampuchean People's Revolutionary Party (KPRP), 1951	5,996,000	700	Heng Samrin	*	Fourth 26–29 May 1981	99.0 (1981); all 117
Democratic Kampuchea (DK), 1960		not available	Pol Pot	0	unknown	n/a
Korea (North) Korean Workers' Party (KWP), 1949	18,802,000	3,000,000 cl.	Kim Il-song	*	Sixth 10–15 Oct. 1980	100 (1982); all 615 KWP approved
Laos Lao People's Revolutionary Party (LPRP), 1955	3,800,000	35,000 est.	Kaysone Phomvihan	*	Third 27–30 Apr. 1982	(Dec. 1975); Supreme People's Assembly (all 45 appointed by LPRP)
Malaysia Communist Party of Malaya (CPM), 1930	14,995,000	1,100 est.	Chin Peng (if alive)	0	1965 (last known)	n/a
Mongolia Mongolian People's Revolutionary Party (MPRP), 1921	1,809,000	76,240 cl.	Yumjaagyn Tsedenbal	*	Eighteenth 26–31 May 1981	99.0 (1981); all 370 MPRP approved
Nepal Communist Party of Nepal, pro-Beijing (CPN/B), 1949	16,179,000	4,000 est.	Man Mohan Adhikari	0	Third 1968	n/a
New Zealand Communist Party of New Zealand (CPNZ), 1921	3,142,000	80 est.	Richard C. Wolfe	+	26–28 Jan. 1979 (first since 1966)	—(1981)
Socialist Unity Party (SUP), 1966		135 est.	George Jackson	+	Sixth 22–24 Oct. 1982	0.5 (1981); none

Country / Party	Population	Membership	Leader		Last Congress	Communist share of vote
Pakistan	96,876,000					
Communist Party of Pakistan (CPP), 1948		200 est.	Ali Nazish	0 (since 1954)	unknown	n/a
Philippines	53,162,000					
Communist Party of the Philippines, Marxist-Leninist (CPP-ML), 1968		7,500 est.	Rafael Baylosis	0	unknown	n/a
Philippine Communist Party (PKP), 1930		400	Felicismo Macapagal	0	Eighth 1980	n/a
Singapore	2,501,000					
Communist Party of Malaya, branch (CPM), 1930		200 est.	unknown	0	unknown	n/a
Sri Lanka	15,647,000					
Communist Party of Sri Lanka (CPSL), 1943		6,000 est.	Kattorge P. Silva	+	Eleventh 26–30 Mar. 1980	1.9 (1977); 1 of 168
Thailand	50,731,000					
Communist Party of Thailand (CPT), 1942		3,000 est.	unknown	0	Fourth Mar./Apr. 1982	n/a
Vietnam	57,036,000					
Vietnamese Communist Party (VCP), 1930		1,727,784 cl.	Le Duan	*	Fifth 27–31 Mar. 1982	97.9 (1981); 497 of 538, all approved by VCP
TOTAL	2,583,861,000	46,100,189				

EASTERN EUROPE AND USSR (9)

Country / Party	Population	Membership	Leader		Last Congress	Communist share of vote
Albania	2,845,000					
Albanian Party of Labor (APL), 1941		122,000 cl.	Enver Hoxha	*	Eighth 1–8 Nov. 1981	99.9 (1982); all 250 Democratic Front
Bulgaria	8,929,000					
Bulgarian Communist Party (BCP), 1903		825,876 cl.	Todor Zhivkov	*	Twelfth 31 Mar.–4 Apr. 1981	99.9 (1981); all 400 Fatherland Front

Country: Party(ies)/Date Founded	Mid-1983 Population (est.)	Communist Party Membership (claim or est.)	Party Leader (sec'y general)	Status	Last Congress	Last Election (percentage of vote; seats in legislature)
Czechoslovakia Communist Party of Czechoslovakia (KSC), 1921	15,420,000	1,600,000 cl.	Gustáv Husák	*	Sixteenth 6–10 Apr. 1981	99.0 (1981); all 350 National Front
Germany: German Democratic Republic Socialist Unity Party (SED), 1946	16,724,000	2,202,277 cl.	Erich Honecker	*	Tenth 11–16 Apr. 1981	99.9 (1981); all 500 National Front
Hungary Hungarian Socialist Workers' Party (HSWP), 1956	10,700,000	852,000 cl.	János Kádár	*	Twelfth 24–27 Mar. 1980	99.3 (1980); all 352 Patriotic People's Front
Poland Polish United Workers' Party (PUWP), 1948	36,556,000	2,327,349 cl.	Wojciech Jaruzelski	*	Extraord. Ninth 14–20 July 1981	99.5 (1980); all 460 Fatherland Front
Romania Romanian Communist Party (RCP), 1921	22,649,000	3,300,000 cl.	Nicolae Ceaușescu	*	Twelfth 19–23 Nov. 1979	98.5 (1980); all 369 Front of Socialist Democracy and Unity
USSR Communist Party of the Soviet Union (CPSU), 1898	272,308,000	18,331,000 cl.	Yuri Andropov	*	Twenty-sixth 23 Feb.–4 Mar. 1981	99.9 (1979); all 1,500 CPSU approved
Yugoslavia League of Communists of Yugoslavia (LCY), 1920	22,826,000	2,200,000 cl.	Mitja Ribičič	*	Twelfth 26–29 June 1982	—(1982); all 308 Socialist Alliance, all LCY approved
TOTAL	408,947,000	31,760,502				

WESTERN EUROPE (23)

Country / Party	Population		Leader	Membership	Last Congress	Election results
Austria Communist Party of Austria (KPO), 1918	7,574,000	+	Franz Muhri	16,000 est.	Extraord. 30 Jan. 1982 Twenty-fourth 6–8 Dec. 1980	0.66 (1983); none
Belgium Belgian Communist Party (PCB-KPB), 1921	9,865,000	+	Louis van Geyt	10,000 est.	Twenty-fourth Mar. and Dec. 1982 (two stages)	2.3 (1981); 2 of 212
Cyprus Progressive Party of the Working People (AKEL), 1941 (Communist Party of Cyprus, 1922)	653,000	+	Ezekias Papaioannou	14,000 cl.	Fifteenth 13–15 May 1982	32.8 (1981); 12 of 35 Greek Cypriot seats
Denmark Communist Party of Denmark (DKP), 1919	5,115,000	+	Poul Emanuel	10,000 est.	Twenty-seventh 12–15 May 1983	0.7 (1984); none
Finland Finnish Communist Party (SKP), 1918	4,850,000	+	Arvo Aalto	50,000 cl.	Extraord. 14–15 May 1982	14.0 (1983); 27 of 200
France French Communist Party (PCF), 1920	55,586,714	+	Georges Marchais	710,000 cl.	Twenty-fourth 3–7 Feb. 1982	16.2 (1981); 44 of 491
Germany: Federal Republic of Germany German Communist Party (DKP), 1968	61,543,000	+	Herbert Mies	48,856 cl.	Sixth 29–31 May 1981	0.2 (1983); none
Great Britain Communist Party of Great Britain (CPGB), 1920	56,078,000	+	Gordon McLennan	16,000 est.	Thirty-eighth 12–15 Nov. 1983	0.03 (1983); none

Country: Party(ies)/Date Founded	Mid-1983 Population (est.)	Communist Party Membership (claim or est.)	Party Leader (sec'y general)	Status	Last Congress	Last Election (percentage of vote; seats in legislature)
Greece	9,898,000					
Communist Party of Greece (KKE), 1921		27,500 est.	Kharilaos Florakis	+	Eleventh 15–18 Dec. 1982	10.9 (1981); 13 of 300
Communist Party of Greece–Interior (KKE-I), 1968		12,000 est.	Yiannis Banias	+	Third 17–23 May 1982	2.7 (1981); none
Iceland	236,000					
People's Alliance (AB), 1968		3,000 est.	Svavar Gestsson	+	Annual Meeting Nov. 1983	17.3 (1983); 10 of 60
Ireland	3,500,000					
Communist Party of Ireland (CPI), 1933		500 est.	Michael O'Riordan	+	Eighteenth 14–16 May 1982	—(1982)
Italy	56,353,000					
Italian Communist Party (PCI), 1921		1,670,000 cl.	Enrico Berlinguer	+	Sixteenth 2–6 Mar. 1983	29.9 (1983); 198 of 630
Luxembourg	366,000					
Communist Party of Luxembourg (CPL), 1921		600 est.	René Urbany	+	Twenty-third 31 May–1 June 1980	5.0 (1979); 2 of 59
Malta	364,000					
Communist Party of Malta (CPM), 1969		145 est.	Anthony Vassallo	+	Second Feb. 1979	1.0 (1981); none
Netherlands	14,374,000					
Communist Party of the Netherlands (CPN), 1909		14,000 est.	Elli Izeboud	+	Twenty-eighth 26–28 Nov. 1982	1.9 (1982); 3 of 150
Norway	4,131,000					
Norwegian Communist Party (NKP), 1923		500 est.	Hans I. Kleven	+	Seventeenth 4–6 Dec. 1981	0.3 (1981); none
Workers' Communist Party (AKP), 1973		1,000 est.	Paal Steigan	+	Third 4–5 Apr. 1983	0.7 (1981); none

Country / Party	Membership	Leader		Congress	Vote (%); Seats	Population
Portugal Portuguese Communist Party (PCP), 1921	187,000 cl.	Alvaro Cunhal	+	Tenth 8–11 Dec. 1983	18.0 (1983); 44 of 250	10,056,000
San Marino Communist Party of San Marino (PCS), 1941	300 est.	Ermenegildo Gasperoni	+	Tenth 1980	24.3 (1983); 15 of 60	22,000
Spain Spanish Communist Party (PCE), 1920	84,000 est.	Gerardo Iglesias	+	Eleventh 14–18 Dec. 1983	3.8 (1982); 4 of 350	38,234,000
Communist Party (PC) of Spain, 1984	25,000 est.	Ignacio Gallego	+	First 13–15 Jan. 1984	n/a	
Sweden The Left Party Communists (VPK), 1921	17,500 cl.	Lars Werner	+	Twenty-sixth 20–24 Nov. 1981	5.6 (1982); 20 of 349	8,331,000
Communist Workers' Party (APK), 1977	5,000 cl.	Rolf Hagel	+	Twenty-seventh ? 1983	0.1 (1982); none	
Switzerland Swiss Labor Party (PdAS), 1921	5,000 est.	Armand Magnin	+	Twelfth 21–22 May 1983	0.9 (1983); 1 of 200	6,463,000
Turkey Communist Party of Turkey (TKP), 1920	negligible	Haydar Kutlu	0	Fifth Oct. or Nov. 1983	n/a	45,155,000
West Berlin Socialist Unity Party of West Berlin (SEW), 1949	4,500 est.	Horst Schmitt	+	Sixth 15–17 May 1981	0.7 (1981); none	2,000,000
TOTAL	2,932,401					400,747,714
GRAND TOTAL	81,621,935					4,446,218,234

INTERNATIONAL FRONT ORGANIZATIONS

Organization (10)	Year Founded	Headquarters	Claimed Membership	Affiliates	Countries
Afro-Asian Peoples' Solidarity Organization	1957	Cairo	unknown	87	—
Christian Peace Conference	1958	Prague	unknown	—	ca. 80
International Association of Democratic Lawyers	1946	Brussels	25,000	—	ca. 80
International Organization of Journalists	1946	Prague	180,000	—	120 plus
International Union of Students	1946	Prague	10,000,000	117	109
Women's International Democratic Federation	1945	East Berlin	200,000,000	131	116
World Federation of Democratic Youth	1945	Budapest	150,000,000	ca. 270	123
World Federation of Scientific Workers	1946	London	450,000	ca. 33	70 plus
World Federation of Trade Unions	1945	Prague	ca. 206,000,000	90	81
World Peace Council	1950	Helsinki	unknown		142 plus

Introduction
The Communist World, 1983

An interview on Moscow domestic television offered a unique opportunity to obtain official figures on the number of countries in which movements recognized by the Communist Party of the Soviet Union (CPSU) operate and the approximate total membership worldwide. Vadim V. Zagladin, first deputy chief of the International Department in the Central Committee apparatus, gave these as 97 with "nearly 80 million" members. This represents an increase of 3 countries and an additional 3 million members over the figures announced in 1981 by the late CPSU leader Leonid I. Brezhnev at the last party congress. (Moscow television, 27 September; *FBIS*, 30 September; *Pravda*, 24 February 1981.)

Among these 97 countries, only 15 are recognized today as comprising the "socialist world"—that is, as having communist regimes in power. These 15 states include 75 of the 80 million communist party members, with the remaining 5 million in the other 82 countries. In this latter category, two communist parties are recognized in each of the following states: Australia, India, New Zealand, Spain, and Sweden ("The World Communist Movement: Yesterday and Today," *Socialism: Theory and Practice*, August, pp. 117–22).

The Register of Communist Parties, which precedes this Introduction, offers information on the official name of each communist movement and international front organization, its membership (claimed or estimated), name of the current leader, status (ruling, legal, not recognized, proscribed), dates of latest congress or national conference, and standing in the legislature. These last three items pertain to the parties only. Splits also exist in the communist movements of Greece and Finland, although the CPSU recognizes only one faction in each.

The *Yearbook* treats revolutionary movements in two categories: (1) the vanguard parties in Afghanistan, Angola, Bahrain, Benin, the Congo, Ethiopia, Kampuchea, Mozambique, and South Yemen; and (2) the ruling parties in "countries with a Socialist orientation," of which there are now twenty (Wallace Spaulding, "The Communist Movement and Its Allies," in Ralph M. Goldman, ed., *Transnational Parties*, Lanham, Md.: University Press of America, 1983, pp. 25–60). The former will be recognized as full-fledged communist movements sooner than the latter. Highlights of developments by geographic area and a section on front activities follow.

In *Africa and the Middle East*, there was a major setback for world communism. The regime in Iran disbanded the Tudeh Party during May, arresting more than a thousand members and reportedly executing 45 of its leaders. The following month, a meeting of delegations of communist parties from Arab countries voiced solidarity with their Tudeh comrades. At the end of the year, the official CPSU newspaper denounced the trials in Tehran as a farce and part of an anti-Soviet campaign. (For the full text of the statement by the Arab parties, see *Pravda*, 24 June; see also K. Vital'ev, "Komu eto nuzhno?" ibid., 31 December.)

The movements in Israel, Lebanon, and Syria by and large supported their mentors in Moscow. Not much was heard from the Palestine Communist Party in its second year of existence. Its name did appear on joint statements, like the one mentioned above, although control may be exercised by the movement in Jordan. The Party of Progress and Socialism in Morocco held its Third Congress during March.

Two congresses were held in other parts of Africa. The first in January 1983 laid the framework for transforming the Commission to Organize the Party of the Working People of Ethiopia into an Ethiopian communist movement. At the end of the year, a Soviet commentator suggested that the process "had entered its final stage." The other congress, in Mozambique, convened to approve the Central Committee's plans to shift the emphasis from state farms to small family ones and to large private agricultural enterprises. It also decided to return to colonial-type punishments, such as flogging for "economic crimes." The next congress, to be held in September 1984, is expected to ratify the transformation of the Front for the Liberation of Mozambique into a Marxist-Leninist party. (Radio Moscow, 23 December; *FBIS*, 28 December; *Tempo*, Maputo, 8 May.)

Country	Number	1983
Ethiopia (COPWE)	2nd	3–6 January
Italy	16th	2–6 March
Morocco	3rd	25–27 March
Mozambique (FRELIMO)	4th	26–29 April
Denmark	27th	12–15 May
West Berlin	6th	15–17 May
Switzerland	12th	21–22 May
Mexico (PSUM)	2nd	9–14 August
Argentina	Extraordinary	5–6 September
Turkey	5th	October or November
Iceland	Annual	November
United States	23rd	10–13 November
Costa Rica	Extraordinary	12–13 November
Martinique	8th	12–13 November
Great Britain	38th	12–15 November
Portugal	10th	8–11 December
Spain	11th	14–18 December

In the *Americas*, five party congresses were held, with the November one in the United States nominating communist party leader Gus Hall (73) and Central Committee member Angela Davis (39) for president and vice-president in the 1984 national election. In 1980, the CPUSA ticket ran in fewer than half the states and won 45,000 votes. However, three more important developments occurred in Central America, one of which had been resolved by year's end.

The United States, invited by six eastern Caribbean governments, joined them in sending troops on 25 October into Grenada, where Prime Minister Maurice Bishop and his pro-Cuban collaborators had been murdered six days earlier. A more radical, pro-Soviet group then seized power. Captured documents included the texts of secret treaties with Cuba, North Korea, and two with the USSR (U.S. Information Agency, *Documents Pertaining to Relations Between Grenada, the USSR, and Cuba*, Washington, D.C., December 1983, control nos. 000191–94), as well as lists of heavy military equipment to be provided by those three countries. Only 300 U.S. Army personnel remained on the island by early December.

Washington continued to isolate the repressive Sandinista regime in Nicaragua, which continues to funnel arms and ammunition from Cuba and the Soviet Union to the guerrillas of the Farabundo Martí National Liberation Front (FMLN) in El Salvador. Two FMLN leaders were murdered in Managua by political rivals, perhaps because of a dispute with the regimes supplying their movement with weapons. The Nicaraguan regime indicated it would hold elections in November 1984.

On 1 January 1984, Havana celebrated a quarter-century of rule by Fidel Castro. His government is able to survive only because of $4 billion per year in Soviet economic aid, which amounts to 25 percent of Cuba's GNP. Another billion dollars per annum in military assistance from the USSR permits its client state to have the most powerful armed forces in the region and fuel the insurgencies throughout Central America. Cuban mercenaries also serve Soviet foreign objectives in other parts of the Third World, primarily in Africa. (Free Press International, *International Report* 4, no. 2, 18 January 1984,

p. 3; for an eyewitness account, see William Ratliff, "Castro's Cuba Today," *Peninsula Times Tribune*, Palo Alto, Calif., 22–25 January 1984.)

The government of Peru declared a state of emergency in ten provinces by year's end due to Maoist guerrilla activities of the Shining Path (Sendero Luminoso) movement (Edward A. Lynch, "Is Peru Next?" *Heritage Backgrounder*, no. 314, 9 December). However, other pro-Chinese, Trotskyist, and pro-Moscow groups belong to the United Left, which received 30 percent of the vote during the 1983 municipal elections. Communists in Argentina joined an electoral alliance with Peronists for the December balloting. That same month, communists won seats in the national legislature of Venezuela.

Asia and the Pacific were dominated by events in China, where a "purification" campaign took place within the ranks of its 40 million–member communist movement ("The Purge: Why and How," *Inside China Mainland*, Taipei, November, pp. 5–8). The last two months of the year were devoted to eliminating "spiritual pollution"—that is, Western concepts of humanism, democracy, and capitalism. Thus, 1983 represented a year of emphasis on ideological orthodoxy. In their relations with Eurocommunist parties in Western Europe, the Chinese have been able to erode Soviet influence (D. J. Radenkovic, "Eurocommunists in Beijing," *Politika*, Belgrade, 3 September).

The murder on 9 October of seventeen high-ranking South Korean government officials on a visit to Thailand by army officers sent from North Korea represented a striking example of a communist regime employing assassination as an instrument of foreign policy. Other terrorists and infiltrators had been captured below the 38th parallel during the autumn. The shooting-down on 1 September of an unarmed Korean Air Lines passenger aircraft by a Soviet fighter plane gave the North Koreans an example to follow.

Across the sea, Japanese communists won less than 10 percent of the vote and lost three seats in the Diet after the December elections. Locally, the Japan Communist Party suffered even more, losing 37 positions in district assemblies. It appeared to be declining at both the national and the municipal level. The party now ranks fourth among Japanese parties.

The military stalemate continues in Afghanistan, where the puppet regime of Babrak Karmal would be swept away were it not for the 120,000 Soviet troops that have been in that country since December 1979. The situation is similar in Kampuchea, with 180,000 Vietnamese soldiers supporting the client government of Heng Samrin. An additional 200,000 civilian settlers occupy strategic areas. An unusual admission by two Vietnamese generals (Vo Nguyen Giap and Vo Bam) over French television revealed that a North Vietnamese communist party plenum had decided as early as 1959 to start armed activities in the South—that is, one full year before the National Liberation Front was established (*Economist*, London, 26 February).

In *Eastern Europe and the USSR*, neither elections nor party congresses were held during the year under review. CPSU leader Yuri Andropov did not appear in public after 18 August 1983, and his state of health became a mystery. An institutional triumvirate of top party bureaucrats, military officers, and economic planners seemed to be making decisions. Emphasis on labor discipline, improving industrial production, and streamlining party work represented domestic themes. Appointments of a new CPSU secretary, a candidate for Politburo membership, and promotions to full Politburo status for three others appeared in line with the foregoing. (*Pravda*, 16 June, 27 December.)

In foreign policy, decoupling the United States from Western Europe received top priority. Verbal and pictorial abuse of Ronald Reagan increased, especially after the first cartoon of the president appeared in *Pravda* on 15 October 1983. This apparently signifies that Soviet leaders had already decided at that time not to continue arms negotiations, which were indeed broken off in all three forums before the end of the year. On 30 January 1984, Tass even denounced the president's re-election bid.

Top officials of the Warsaw Treaty Organization met seven times during the year. In early December, the foreign ministers unanimously endorsed the Soviet decision to install new battlefield missiles in East Germany and Czechoslovakia to compensate allegedly for the nine Pershing II and 32 ground-launched cruise missiles deployed by the United States that same month in West Germany, Italy, and Britain. Bloc countries as a whole suffered from an economic slowdown. The USSR supplied less petroleum and natural gas at higher prices, causing resentment. A long-delayed summit of the Council for Mutual Economic Assistance was scheduled for February 1984, the first such high-level meeting since 1971 (*NYT*, 16 January 1984).

West European communist parties held seven congresses and participated in ten national elections. They registered between 1 percent or less in Austria, Denmark, West Germany, Britain, and Switzerland and from 14 to almost 30 percent in Finland, Iceland, Portugal, San Marino, and Italy. Externally, however, these movements seemed unable to achieve any significant unity of action among themselves.

One of the so-called Eurocommunist parties, that in Italy, held a congress, which a CPSU delegation, of distinctly lower rank than previous ones, attended. The Chinese also sent representatives, their first in some twenty years. The Spanish party's congress stressed Eurocommunist renewal during its mid-December deliberations. Only a month later, a new group calling itself the Communist Party of the Peoples of Spain formed a pro-Soviet movement, which claims 25,000 members, compared with 84,000 (down from 240,000 six years ago) for the Eurocommunist party. The new movement has been recognized by Moscow. (*Pravda*, 16 January 1984.) By contrast, the Portuguese party held a united congress, also in December, and claimed 200,000 members, up from 115,000 seven years earlier.

Communist parties in six NATO states of Western Europe joined their counterparts in the United States and Canada with an appeal for a nuclear freeze in early May. The leaders of the East German, West Berlin, and West German movements signed an appeal to prevent deployment in Europe of U.S. medium-range missiles (*Neues Deutschland*, East Berlin, 27 September). The former leader of the Finnish Communist Party, Aarne Saarinen, accused the Soviet Union of continuously interfering with party internal affairs, a most unusual charge (Stockholm radio, 6 December; *FBIS*, 8 December).

International front organizations orchestrate peace appeals that, usually, appear under the signatures of individuals without overt communist affiliation. The ten most important fronts are discussed in the *Yearbook*, with their claimed membership. Three of them, including the World Peace Council (WPC), have not revealed such figures. The WPC reported affiliates in seven additional countries. This organization has been more active than any of the others in the campaign against Euromissile deployment.

The World Federation of Trade Unions claimed an increase of 6 million members over the past two years, on the basis of organizations in ten additional countries. The World Federation of Democratic Youth also reported twenty more affiliates in as many new countries. The Women's International Democratic Federation added ten new affiliates. Otherwise, numbers remained static.

Richard F. Staar
Hoover Institution

*   *   *

The following abbreviations are used for frequently cited publications and news agencies:

CSM	*Christian Science Monitor*
FBIS	*Foreign Broadcast Information Service*
FEER	*Far Eastern Economic Review*
IB	*Information Bulletin* (of the *WMR*)
JPRS	*Joint Publications Research Service*
NYT	*New York Times*
WMR	*World Marxist Review*
WP	*Washington Post*
WSJ	*Wall Street Journal*
YICA	*Yearbook on International Communist Affairs*

ACAN	Agencia Central Americano Noticias
ADN	Allgemeiner Deutscher Nachrichtendienst
AFP	Agence France-Presse
ANSA	Agenzia Nazionale Stampa Associata

AP	Associated Press
BTA	Bulgarska telegrafna agentsiya
ČETEKA	Československá tisková kancelář
DPA	Deutsche Presse Agentur
KPL	Khaosan Pathet Lao
MENA	Middle East News Agency
MTI	Magyar Távirati Iroda
NCNA	New China News Agency
PAP	Polska Agencja Prasowa
UPI	United Press International
VNA	Vietnam News Agency

AFRICA AND THE MIDDLE EAST

Introduction

Nineteen eighty-three was a poor year for communist parties and revolutionary movements in Africa and the Middle East. The Tudeh Party in Iran, for example, was actively suppressed by the Khomeini regime after early years of toleration or benign neglect. In this forceful repression of the Tudeh Party, the Islamic regime in Tehran conformed to the policies of its Arab neighbors, who have long suppressed communist parties, even while the same governments were receiving large amounts of Soviet arms. The Palestine Liberation Organization (PLO), though not a communist party but a recipient of Soviet military and diplomatic assistance, suffered another year of serious setbacks when it was expelled from Tripoli, the port city of northern Lebanon, by PLO rebels and their Syrian mentors. The Iraqi Communist Party (ICP) suffered severe losses in its conflict with the government, which manipulates rivalries among the Kurds, some of whom collaborate with the ICP. The struggle among the Kurdish movements involved heavy ICP casualties.

Hard times also befell the beleaguered Marxist regimes in Angola and Mozambique at the foot of the African continent. Increasingly active guerrilla forces—at one time the almost exclusive instrument of communist-inspired movements—have pushed the Marxist-Leninist governments on the defensive and toward a more vigorous search for economic and military assistance from the West to combat their internal foes and restore their deteriorating economies.

A June meeting of communist and workers' parties in Arab countries was attended by representatives from the National Liberation Front of Bahrain, the Socialist Vanguard Party of Algeria, the Party of Progress and Socialism of Morocco, the Palestine Communist Party, and communist parties from Jordan, Tunisia, Saudi Arabia, Sudan, Syria, Iraq, Lebanon, and Egypt, but evidently not the Tudeh Party. The conference's statement criticized the "peace agreement" between Israel and Lebanon on 17 May as a continuation of the Camp David course and a "new step aimed at widening the American military presence in Lebanon." The statement also held that "Syria is taking legitimate defensive measures." It went on to advocate "the normalization of relations between countries of North West Africa (Maghreb) in the interest of intensifying the struggle against imperialism and for the liquidation of its military bases in the region." It declared solidarity with Kurdish national liberation movements in Iraq, Iran, and Turkey. The conference also approved a resolution "voicing solidarity with Iran's Tudeh Party." (*IB*, September.)

Communist parties continued to be repressed by Middle East governments or remained in a state of quasi acceptance or toleration by the ruling movements. Iran saw the greatest shift in communist fortunes in the Middle East. There, the fortunes of the Tudeh Party dramatically changed from uneasy toleration by the regime to active and systematic suppression.

The Syrian Communist Party (SCP) managed to retain its quasi-legal status as one movement in the ruling National Progressive Front by its strong support of the dominant Ba'th Party. The Syrian communists accomplished this end by vehement endorsements of the Ba'thist regime's expansionist foreign policy in Lebanon and by muted statements on domestic questions within Syria. As one of the many illustrations of the SCP's harmony with the Ba'thist regime's foreign policy, it described President Hafiz al-Assad's opposition to Israeli forces in Lebanon as a manifestation of "the Arab national liberation movement" (joint statement of the Syrian and Palestine communist parties in ibid., October).

Despite Moscow's differences with the Ba'thist government's support of the rebel challenge to Yassir Arafat's leadership of the PLO, the Soviet Union cooperated closely with Syria this year. Massive amounts of Soviet armaments went to Damascus. These cordial relations were not a result of the SCP's influence, but it benefited from them. The SCP made ambiguous statements about the internecine conflict among the Palestinians and Syria's backing of the anti-Arafat faction.

In nearby Lebanon, events swirled in a complex mix as a result of internal and external causes, at the center of which stood the peacekeeping forces from the United States, Britain, France, and Italy in Beirut. The Lebanese Communist Party (LCP) remained critical of the Israeli presence and the peacekeeping troops. The 17 May Lebanese-Israeli agreement setting forth the conditions for an Israeli withdrawal heightened concerns of the Lebanese communists. The LCP joined with the SCP in opposing this agreement as a threat to Syria and called on all Arabs to strengthen Arab-Soviet friendship. In June, the LCP joined with the Progressive Socialist Party, "other patriotic and progressive organizations," and a number of "distinguished politicians" to struggle for Israel's unconditional withdrawal and the restoration of Lebanese sovereignty.

Lebanese communist forces continued to be involved in the factional fighting in the country. The heavy fighting between the PLO and its rebel factions in northern Lebanon resulted in communist casualties. Various sources reported that a Muslim fundamentalist organization, the Islamic Unification Movement, executed a great number of communists in Tripoli. The LCP kept to its pro-Soviet position and to its anti-U.S. stance by holding the United States responsible for all Lebanese problems because it supported Israeli aggression (Moscow domestic television service, 14 July; *FBIS*, 15 July).

To the south of Lebanon, the Communist Party of Israel (CPI), made up mainly of Arabs who use it as an outlet for grievances of the Arab minority, kept up its criticisms of Israeli settlements on what had been Arab-occupied lands. Meir Vilner, secretary general of the party and a member of the Knesset, introduced a motion denouncing the proposal for the mass expulsion of Arabs from the Upper Nazareth region (*Jerusalem Post*, 6–12 and 13–19 November). Deputy Secretary General Tawfiq Tubi, an Arab who serves to balance the predominance of Jews in the top party organs, declared that the CPI "will support any initiative aimed to overthrow the government, disband the 10th Knesset, and hold new elections" (*al-Ittihad*, 19 June; *IB*, September). Later, when Prime Minister Menachim Begin announced his decision to resign, the CPI cited the resignation as evidence of the failure of his policies (Tass, 29 August; *FBIS*, 30 August).

The Palestine Communist Party (PCP) was formed in early 1982 from several communist organizations, including those in the Gaza Strip, West Bank, and Lebanon. Although the PCP has held a congress and has some of the standard organizational aspects of communist parties, little is known of its structure. The name of the secretary general, for instance, has not been publicly cited. Its membership is presumed to be no more than a few hundred. Yet its representatives did participate in meetings with other Arab communists in June and attended the international scientific convention "Karl Marx and Our Time—The Struggle for Peace and Social Advancement" in East Berlin in April along with delegations from many other communist parties and revolutionary movements. Together with strong condemnations of Israel, the PCP's statements on broader international questions closely paralleled the USSR's positions.

The Communist Party of Jordan (CPJ), which played the role of midwife to the PCP, continued to support Palestinian statehood and to endorse the PLO as the sole legitimate representative of the Palestinian people. The CPJ's support of the PLO, however, has been less than wholehearted; the party sees the PLO as the only way of achieving a Palestinian state in the West Bank. Secretary General Faik Warrad upheld the idea of a "confederative union of two independent states, the Palestinian and the Jordanian," but opposed plans for a "federal" relationship between the two as premature (*WMR*, May). Like other Arab communists, Warrad views recent U.S. foreign policy in Lebanon as "an attempt to assert U.S. hegemony in the region" by building military bases and by creating an anti-Soviet bloc (ibid.). In Warrad's opinion, the best means for attaining a just peace in the Middle East is to implement the Soviet proposal for an international conference open to the USSR as well as the PLO and the states of the Middle East.

The Iraqi Communist Party (ICP) received heavy blows from the central government, which it steadfastly opposes. Hard-pressed by its war with Iran, the Iraqi government successfully capitalized on Kurdish factions and turned Kurdish rivalries to its own good by enlisting the Patriotic Union of Kurdistan (PUK) against the ICP and its ally, the Kurdish Democratic Party of Iraq, which had formed the Democratic National Front (DNF) in 1980. In May, the ICP-DNF joint headquarters in northern Iraq were attacked by PUK forces, who inflicted heavy losses on the defenders. Soon after, Turkey, which had entered into an agreement with Baghdad, dispatched forces across their common border into an area about a hundred kilometers north of Mosul and caused the DNF further damage by killing or capturing its members. The Turks were moved by concerns that a Kurdish revolt in Iraq would spread to their Kurdish population.

Iraqi communists received another setback when a major opposition group, the Supreme Council of the Islamic Revolution (also known as *al-Da'wah*, "the Dawn"), refused to join them in a common struggle against the Ba'thist regime in Baghdad. Supported by Iran, these Iraqi Shi'ite Muslims hold to a creed that excludes communism and strive to establish an Islamic republic in Iraq. Syrian support for the ICP has not overcome these obstacles, and the Baghdad government continues to enjoy military assistance from Moscow. In fact, through its reliance on Syria, the ICP finds itself linked with a vehemently anticommunist Iran whose goal is to defeat Iraq and topple the government of President Saddam Husayn.

Much smaller but also firmly checked by the government is the Egyptian Communist Party (ECP), which kept to its customary low profile throughout the year. Unnamed representatives of the ECP attended the meeting of twelve communist and workers' parties of the Arab countries in June. Politburo member Michel Kamal attended the Karl Marx scientific convention in East Berlin. Communists outside the ECP seemed to have taken the brunt of the government's crackdown in 1983. The Egyptian government prosecuted 23 men—allegedly members of a communistic "popular movement"—for plotting a Guevara-style revolution among peasants and workers. The government also reported the uncovering of a clandestine communist Palestinian student organization after it tried to "infiltrate sectors of the Egyptian masses" (MENA, Cairo, 21 June; *FBIS*, 22 June).

The most severe setback to a communist movement in 1983 occurred in Iran. The Islamic revolutionary government of the Ayatollah Khomeini virtually annihilated the Tudeh Party. After the overthrow of the Pahlavi dynasty, the Tudeh Party had returned from 26 years of exile. Initially, the new Islamic republic allowed it to operate openly. But in February, the party's general secretary, Nureddin Kianuri, and several others were arrested. Mass roundups of Tudehis followed, amid reports of torture and executions carried out by the government, which charged the communists with being Soviet spies. In May, Iran expelled eighteen Soviet envoys for "interference in internal affairs and setting up links with mercenaries and traitors" (*WP*, 5 May). By midsummer, the Islamic Republican Party had become the only political force in Iran. The Mojahedin-e Khalq, which had led the armed struggle against Khomeini, was in disarray. Hundreds of its members were executed, jailed, or in hiding.

On the Arabian Peninsula, the Communist Party of Saudi Arabia (CPSA) was less active in participating in international communist meetings than in the previous two years. The CPSA did participate in the meeting of communist and workers' parties of Arab countries in June. The CPSA contended in an article that it was engaged in counterpropaganda against the government through its publications and its "influence in underground mass movements and in some governmental and other organizations" (*WMR*, April). But the extent of its activities within Saudi Arabia was not publicized.

In the People's Democratic Republic of Yemen (PDRY), the local communist party, the People's Democratic Union (PDU), maintained its low profile within the larger, ruling Yemen Socialist Party (YSP). PDU representatives continued to represent the PDRY within the Afro-Asian Peoples' Solidarity Organization and the World Peace Council. The PDU also continued to help in contacts between the PDRY and communist countries, which provide assistance and military aid (Soviet Union), defense cooperation (Ethiopia), and medical aid and paramilitary advisers (Cuba).

The Bahrain National Liberation Front (NLF/B), while in attendance at the convention on "Karl Marx and Our Time—The Struggle for Peace and Social Advancement" in East Berlin during April, proclaimed that Bahrain has "a labor class . . . that is engaged in a class struggle under the leadership of a communist party equipped with the Marxist-Leninist theory" (*Neues Deutschland*, 18 April). This statement indicates that the NLF/B considers itself a full-blown communist party. There appears to have been a change in the chief spokesman for the NLF/B. In 1982, Executive Committee member Abdallah Ali al-Rashid represented the front abroad; in 1983, another member of the Executive Committee, Aziz Mahmud, attended a number of international communist gatherings.

Of the three communist movements in the Maghreb, the party congress of Morocco's Party of Progress and Socialism (PPS) was the most newsworthy event. More than 1,200 delegates attended the Third National Congress in Casablanca from 25 to 27 March. 'Ali Yata was re-elected secretary general of the party, and the PPS reaffirmed its commitment to the ideals of scientific socialism and internationalism (*IB*, June). In its program, the PPS Central Committee demanded large-scale government intervention in the Moroccan economy, promotion of welfare programs, and price controls. The Central Committee's theses, which were adopted by the congress, called for making the PPS a mass party and for reaching out to other groups and classes to broaden support. In foreign affairs, the PPS continued its staunch backing of the Moroccan government's efforts to retain the Western Sahara.

The Tunisian Communist Party (PCT), a legal party since 1981, stood on the periphery of politics in the north African country. It did support the government of President Habib Bourguiba when it created a multiparty system by legalizing two opposition parties in November. But the PCT appeared distant from the riots that erupted at year-end in Tunisia over increases in food prices.

In neighboring Algeria, the Socialist Vanguard Party (PAGS) continued its low public profile while operating in a hostile political climate and lacking legal standing. Its view of President Chadli Benjedid's regime as more opportunist and reformist than the preceding one of Houari Boumediene remained unchanged. Instead of taking public positions, the PAGS concentrated its attention on infiltrating the mass organizations of the ruling National Liberation Front.

Below the Sahara, the most prominent event among communist parties and Marxist-Leninist movements took place this year in the People's Republic of Mozambique, where the Front for the Liberation of Mozambique (FRELIMO) held its Fourth Party Congress. Coming to power after a ten-year guerrilla war against Portuguese colonialism, FRELIMO in 1975 became a ruling movement in an independent country. Its Third Congress in 1977 approved the Central Committee's recommendation to transform FRELIMO into a "Marxist-Leninist vanguard party." During a four-year period of zealous implementation of what it believed to be a Marxist blueprint for development and egalitarianism, FRELIMO nationalized foreign enterprises, established state farms, seized control of the banking system, and intervened in most of the political and economic aspects of life in the southeast African country. These actions resulted in the flight of capital and skilled European laborers.

The Fourth Congress resulted, in part, from the recognition of past excesses, for it acknowledged serious errors in its economic policies. The congress approved the Central Committee's plans to switch the emphasis from state farms to small, family farms and to large private enterprises. In organization, the congress expanded the Central Committee's membership and approved numerous ministerial reshufflings. Citing antigovernment insurgency and a worsening economy, FRELIMO returned to the colonial-type punishment of flogging and added the death penalty for "economic crimes." It expelled from the cities thousands of "social parasites" who had left rural areas and settled in urban centers without work.

North of Mozambique in the Horn of Africa, the Commission to Organize the Party of the Working People of Ethiopia (COPWE) held its Second Congress, 3–6 January. COPWE adopted a resolution stating that "we have reached the last stage in the formation of the Ethiopian workers' party" (Addis Ababa domestic service, 6 January; *FBIS*, 7 January). The Second Congress laid plans for convening the Third Congress in September 1984 when the creation of a "vanguard party of working people" will be brought "to a successful conclusion" (*Pravda*, 8 January; *FBIS*, 10 January). In preparation for developing political structures, COPWE chairman and head of state Mengistu Haile Mariam reshuffled the Dergue (the ruling council) and COPWE's Executive Committee. COPWE's Central Committee was reduced from 123 to 117 members.

Across the border in Sudan, the Sudanese Communist Party (SCP) called for a united front to free the country from what it viewed as the corrupt military dictatorship of Jaafar Numeiri. With most SCP leaders in exile, party cadres within Sudan take orders from those outside the country and operate underground only. The SCP concentrates its efforts on intellectuals, students, railway workers, cotton growers, and sympathetic elements in the armed forces. It apparently accommodates itself to the religions of Sudanese society but lately seems to be focusing on the non-Muslim population in the southern region of the country. The SCP has taken a stand against the imposition of Islam or Arabic in the south, where an economic cleavage exists with the more wealthy northern sectors.

To the south in the landlocked country of Zimbabwe, the fragile unity between the two major parties unraveled in 1983. The ruling Zimbabwe African National Union (ZANU) is not an avowedly communist party, but it professes to be Marxist in ideology. Its rival, the Zimbabwe African People's Union (ZAPU), had been supported by Moscow during the long struggle for independence. The two organizations' common goals allowed them to form a coalition following independence, although ZANU had won a stunning landslide electoral victory in a pre-independence contest. Strains appeared in 1982 when Prime Minister Robert Mugabe sacked the head of ZAPU, Joshua Nkomo, from the cabinet. Anti-ZANU attacks by deserters from the National Army loyal to Nkomo followed. Ethnic factions inflamed political tensions.

In the first half of 1983, the ZANU government brutally retaliated, using the ill-disciplined North Korean–trained Fifth Brigade. In July, Mugabe withdrew the Fifth Brigade in the face of much international criticism for its atrocities. But by year-end, Mugabe's policy seemed a failure, for he had not lured key ZAPU leaders back in spite of intimidation or diplomacy. Angered by Zimbabwe's U.N. votes on the Soviet downing of the South Korean airliner, the Grenadian invasion, and Israel, Washington, which along with Britain was the main source of foreign aid, cut its fiscal 1984 aid almost in half, to $40 million (*NYT*, 28 December).

Off the coast on the island of Réunion, the Réunion Communist Party (PCR) participated in the regional elections held in February and municipal elections in March. Prior to these elections, the PCR made a temporary and unprecedented agreement with the Socialist Party (PS) in which offices would be shared by both parties, should they win the regional council elections. Left-wing candidates won over 50 percent of the votes cast in the elections for the regional council. PCR member Mario Hoarau became president of the regional council. Following the defeat of PCR candidate Bruny Payet in the September Senate elections, the two parties, however, accused each other of responsibility for the loss, and relations between the PCR and the PS again became strained.

At the toe of the continent, the South African Communist Party (SACP), the oldest communist organization in Africa, maintained its close alliance with the African National Congress. Together they have cooperated in staging sabotage attacks inside the Republic of South Africa, which occurred with some frequency in 1983. Both movements operate clandestinely within the country and maintain headquarters in exile.

The SACP chairman, Dr. Yusef Dadoo, died on 19 September in exile in London. The 74-year-old Indian medical practitioner had led the party since 1972; he had been a party member since 1939. He is survived by the general secretary, Moses Mabhida, a longtime African trade unionist who was awarded the Order of the Friendship of Peoples by the Soviet Union on his sixtieth birthday on 14 October. Mabhida delivered an address in East Berlin at the observation of the centenary of Karl Marx's death and at a special anniversary conference convened by the Communist Party USA in New York in March. In his speech to the U.S. conference, Mabhida reaffirmed his faith in the relevance of Marxism for Africa by stating that "Marxism has come to stay in Africa." Mabhida held that the Marxist-Leninist parties in power in Africa are "determined to solve the main problem of bringing about the transition from capitalism to socialism." (*African Communist*, no. 95, p. 26.) The SACP continued to identify itself fully with the Soviet Union and Eastern Europe, particularly the German Democratic Republic, but in contrast to previous years party publications were free from polemics against either the Chinese or Eurocommunism.

To the north in the People's Republic of Angola, the ruling Popular Movement for the Liberation of Angola–Labor Party (MPLA-PT) faced another year of a beleaguered economy and an ever-widening rural insurgency. The MPLA-PT's rival pre-independence organization, the National Union for the Total Independence of Angola (UNITA), kept up its successful attacks against government forces and their Cuban allies in much of the southeastern region and began penetrating other sections of the country. Partly as a result of these pressures, José Eduardo dos Santos, Angolan president and MPLA-PT chairman, came under criticism in late 1982 for being ideologically "soft" in domestic policy and international relations. Dos Santos countered with a purge. By the beginning of 1983, his housecleaning had prompted the suspension of 32 high officials. These party personnel changes were completed at an emergency meeting of the Central Committee in February.

Angola's domestic problems reinforced the pattern in turnover of individuals in ministerial and provincial positions throughout much of the year. In April, the post of minister of construction changed hands; in July, the deputy commissioner for the enclave of Cabinda was fired; and in August, dos Santos assumed more control of the ministries by arranging for the Secretariat of the Council of Ministers to report directly to the president. Dos Santos also made major changes in the government's operations in the country's provinces. Also changed was Angola's ambassador to its chief foreign backer—the Soviet Union. But Moscow reportedly stood steadfastly behind its African client, indicating to South Africa, which supports UNITA, that it would not tolerate the overthrow of the pro-Soviet Marxist government in Luanda (*Guardian*, London, 2 January 1984).

Much less activity characterized events in the People's Republic of the Congo—a newly added profile in the 1984 *YICA*. Despite its revolutionary claims and proclaimed allegiance to Marxism-Leninism, the ruling Congolese Labor Party, a self-styled "vanguard" party of the proletariat, governs in a generally nonradical fashion, judged by African standards. Some of its domestic and economic policies resemble capitalism far more than they do those of communism. Rhetorical attacks against "imperialism" and "neocolonial" influences continue to go hand in hand with legislation providing incentives for foreign investment. The Congo did sign a Treaty of Friendship and Cooperation with the USSR in May 1980, but remains oriented toward the West, particularly France, for trade and foreign aid.

A similar policy orientation delineates the government's activities in the People's Republic of Benin —another new profile in the 1984 *YICA*. In spite of its adoption of Marxism-Leninism and its fiery revolutionary rhetoric, the ideological stances of the ruling People's Revolutionary Party (PRPB) have been little more than an attempt to institutionalize military and personal rule. Independent from France since 1960, the small west African state of Dahomey changed its name to Benin and announced the establishment of the PRPB as a Marxist-Leninist "vanguard" party in 1975. But the PRPB has accepted the concept of compensation for the nationalization of assets of foreign companies. Furthermore, it permits the existence of small retail shops and, like the Congo, tends to encourage foreign, mostly French, investments.

Foreign aid sustains Benin's economy and the PRPB's bloated bureaucracy. But the country's foreign policy is marked by close alignment with the radical government of Libya and by support of the Libyan regime's activities on the continent. Security arrangements have been made with the USSR and East Germany. Yet Benin has avoided taking sides in the Sino-Soviet dispute.

Nigeria's Socialist Working People's Party (SWPP) played a very marginal role in the dramatic political life of Africa's most populous state in 1983. Once again, the SWPP failed to gain certification from the Federal Electoral Commission and so stood outside the November national elections that returned President Alhaji Shehu Shagari to office. The election, however, was nullified by a military coup on 31 December. The SWPP's main reported foreign venture apparently was Chairman Chaika Anozie's participation in the Karl Marx celebrations.

Further north on the west African coast, Senegal also held an election in 1983 and the ruling Parti Socialiste won an overwhelming victory, winning 111 seats in the National Assembly to the opposition's 9. The Independence and Labor Party (PIT), the only one of several parties claiming to be communist that is recognized by the world communist movement, played a minimal role in the February election, although it did complain of government harassment. Afterwards, the PIT pronounced that "while the masses were deeply shocked by what occurred on 27 February, they are not yet mature enough politically to break at once with the neocolonialist regime" (*IB*, July).

Thomas H. Henriksen
Hoover Institution

Algeria

Population. 20.7 million (estimate)
Party. Socialist Vanguard Party (Parti de l'avant-garde socialiste; PAGS)
Founded. 1920
Membership. 450 (estimate)
Secretary General. Sadiq Hadjeres
Politburo. Unknown
Secretariat. Unknown
Central Committee. Unknown
Status. Proscribed since December 1962
Last Congress. Sixth, February 1952
Last Election. March 1982; PAGS prohibited from participating
Auxiliary Organizations. Unknown
Publications. *Sawt al-Sha'b* (Voice of the people), issued clandestinely at infrequent intervals

The major event in Algerian politics in 1983 was the party congress of the National Liberation Front (FLN), the country's ruling and only legal political party, held in Algiers 19–21 December. The congress declared that top priority would be given to agricultural development, and it reduced the FLN Central Committee, the critical decisionmaking body in Algeria, from 200 to 160 members. The composition of the new Central Committee includes regional military commanders who enjoy the full confidence of President Chadli Benjedid, a former military commander. By contrast, several more militant FLN ideologues were excluded from the reduced Central Committee. The FLN congress marked the institutionalization of the regime and a further consolidation of Benjedid's power, a process begun at the June 1980 extraordinary party congress, which sharply reduced the size of the FLN Politburo, and continued during 1982 (see *YICA*, 1983, p. 5). The December congress renominated Benjedid as the party's candidate for president. Running unopposed, Benjedid won re-election for a second five-year term in the presidential election held on 12 January 1984. In foreign affairs, the Benjedid regime gave priority

in 1983 to promoting regional reconciliation by supporting efforts to build a Greater Arab Maghreb. This included a "historic" meeting with King Hassan of Morocco on 26 February, as well as meetings with the leaders of Tunisia, Libya, and Mauritania.

Leadership and Party Organization. Sadiq Hadjeres is first secretary of the party. Although the precise membership of the PAGS Politburo and Secretariat is not known publicly, other prominent members of the party in recent years are believed to include Larbi Bukhali, a former party secretary general, Bashir Hadj 'Ali, Ahmad Karim, and 'Ali Malki. Both Hadjeres and Malki have contributed to the *World Marxist Review* and the *Information Bulletin* on behalf of the PAGS.

Party Views, Positions, and Activities. PAGS generally has viewed the Benjedid regime as opportunist and reformist compared with the more militant regime of Houari Boumediene (1965–1978). Operating in a hostile political climate and without legal standing, PAGS prudently opted to maintain a low profile during 1983. The party did not take any public positions of note on either domestic or international issues. Instead, PAGS continued to focus its energies on the mass organizations of the ruling FLN. PAGS members worked to gain influence among the leadership of the National Union of Algerian Youth, and the party maintained its efforts to place cells in factories to compete with the units of the General Union of Algerian Workers, the government-sanctioned labor union.

John Damis
Portland State University

Angola

Population. 7.6 million
Party. Popular Movement for the Liberation of Angola–Labor Party (Movimento Popular de Libertação de Angola–Partido do Trabalho; MPLA-PT)
Founded. 1956 (renamed 1977)
Membership. Ca. 31,000
Chairman. José Eduardo dos Santos
Central Committee. 75 members (before December 1982 purges)
Status. Ruling party
Last Congress. First Extraordinary, 1980, in Luanda
Last Election. 1980; all 203 candidates MPLA-PT approved
Auxiliary Organizations. National Union of Angolan Workers (UNTA); Youth of the MPLA (JMPLA)
Publications. *A Jornal de Angola, Diario de Luanda* (both dailies). ANGOP is the official news agency.

The ruling Marxist-Leninist political party of Angola, the MPLA–PT, was founded as the MPLA in 1956 and adopted its present name in 1977 to reflect the institutionalization of workers' post-independence influence in the party.

The MPLA, one of three major parties leading the anticolonial fight against the Portuguese, was catapulted into power in 1974–1975 by virtue of being favored by significant factions in the ruling military junta in Lisbon. It also received massive external support from Cuba and the Soviet Union in the military showdown with the two other major parties in Angolan politics, the National Front for the Liberation of Angola (Frente Nacional de Libertação de Angola; FNLA) and the National Union for the Total Independence of Angola (União Nacional para e Independencia Total de Angola; UNITA). The latter party still holds between one-third and one-half of Angolan territory and remains an active competitor with the MPLA for political and military control of the entire country. Only the MPLA, however, claims to be a Marxist-Leninist party.

The MPLA has had some extraordinary leaders in its short history, often drawn from literary, urban-based elites. Active in the anti-Portuguese fight were Agostinho Neto, Viriato da Cruz, and Mario de Andrade, all alumni of the Portuguese Communist Party. Many important leaders have also been expelled from the MPLA, including

Gentil Viana, Joaquim Pinto de Andrade, and Daniel Chipenda; each took a faction of the party with him when expelled. With Neto's death in 1979, leadership passed into the hands of José Eduardo dos Santos.

Party Organization and Leadership. The MPLA–PT and its Central Committee monopolize political power in the areas of the country under the control of the central government. Decisionmaking is centralized in a much smaller group, the Politburo, headed by Chairman dos Santos. There also exists a broad structure (on paper only) of a People's Assembly, provincial assemblies, and other groups, but they are not functioning in the present civil war environment. Dos Santos is president, chairman of the MPLA–PT, and in late December 1982 was given broadened, but publicly undefined, powers by the Central Committee. A purge of his opponents resulted immediately.

Dos Santos came under attack from the "ideological wing" of his party in late 1982, for corruption and incompetence. The vehicle used for this dissent was a play by the writer Costa Andrade, ostensibly a recounting of Neto's life but transparently an attack on the current MPLA–PT leadership. Presentation of the play was authorized by Ambrosio Lukoki, Politburo member, who was dismissed on 8 December 1982, but dos Santos decided that a broader housecleaning was required. (AFP, 7 January; *FBIS*, 12 January.) Dos Santos requested special powers at an 8 December 1982 meeting of the Central Committee to deal with the challenge, and his proposal was accepted (Lisbon domestic service, 9 December 1982; *FBIS*, 9 December 1982). At a public rally for the twenty-sixth anniversary of the MPLA and fourth anniversary of the MPLA–PT on 10 December 1982, he signaled the centralization of power: "If there is no discipline, if the different echelons of the organizational structure do not function as one sole voice, under one sole command, the objectives of the revolution will not be logically implemented" (Luanda domestic service, 11 December 1982; *FBIS*, 13 December 1982). By the new year of 1983, the ax had fallen. Thirty-two high officials of the MPLA–PT were suspended, including Ruth Lara, head of MPLA political education and wife of Lucio Lara, number two in the MPLA–PT leadership (Lisbon domestic service, 30 December 1982; *FBIS*, 3 January). Playwright Andrade was arrested and kept in jail well into 1983, along with Vantagem

Lara, Lucio Lara's son, and two MPLA–PT officials, Simao Paulo and Raul Araujo.

The arrest of Araujo, deputy head of the party's education and ideology department and former head of the party school, indicated the depth of dos Santos's concern over dissent in the party (AFP, 10 January; *FBIS*, 11 January). Of particular importance were their charges that dos Santos was ideologically "soft," in terms of both domestic policy and international negotiations.

The party personnel changes were completed on 19 February, at an emergency meeting of the Central Committee. Roberto de Almeida was named secretary of the Central Committee for the Ideological Department, and Antonio Jacinto was brought in to be director of the Central Committee Secretariat. The Central Committee also ratified the measures taken by the "Central Commission of Control," a mystery organ that proposed "sanctions on party members who have violated discipline and abused the right to criticize," a reference to the purging of the Andrade-Lara faction (Luanda domestic service, 21 February; *FBIS*, 24 February). The director of the Department of Information and Propaganda, Manuel Miguel Carvelho Wadijimbi, was also dismissed by the Central Committee (AFP, 12 April; *FBIS*, 13 April).

During the remainder of 1983, Central Committee meetings were held quite routinely and without apparent controversy, in June and November (Luanda domestic service, 15 and 17 June, 17 November; *FBIS*, 16 and 20 June, 17 November).

Government Leadership. The domestic problems of Angola, whether of MPLA–PT origin or deriving from the military and economic hardships of civil war, wreaked continuing havoc on efforts to create stable public administration structures. The rotation of individuals through ministerial and provincial positions continued, with each apparently unable to deal with pervasive smuggling, the breakdown of collective economic efforts, larceny, and corruption. In April, Manuel Alves dos Passos Barroso Mangueira was replaced by Jorge Henriques Varrela de Melo Dias Flora as minister of construction (Luanda domestic service, 20 April; *FBIS*, 21 April). A number of deputy ministers were also relieved of their posts. In July, the deputy commissioner of Cabinda, Agostinho Miguel Francisco, was fired (Luanda domestic service, 13 July; *FBIS*, 15 July).

President dos Santos took more direct control of the ministries in early August, arranging for the Secretariat of the Council of Ministers to report directly to the president (Luanda domestic service, 5 August; *FBIS*, 8 August). The agenda for council meetings and responsibility for regulating the work of the ministries thus came under closer scrutiny of the president. He also undertook major changes in government operations in the provinces, in seven decrees replacing the leadership in Lunda Sul, Moxico, Luanda, and Cunene commissariats (Luanda domestic service, 12 August; *FBIS*, 12 August). Dos Santos also set up regional military councils in a number of central and southern provinces where control (to the extent Luanda retained any control at all over those provinces) was already effectively in the hands of the army authorities (*Pravda*, 15 September; *FBIS*, 20 September).

The shuffle of cabinet positions continued through the year, with a year-end effort including: at the ministry of agriculture replacing Artur Vidal Gomes with Evaristu Domingos Kimba, replacing Fernando Faustino Muteka with Manuel Bernardo de Sousa as minister of transport and communications, and in the key post of provincial commissioner of Luanda replacing Evaristu Domingos Kimba with Mariano Garcia Puku.

Domestic Economic Affairs. The Angolan economy continued to be plagued by endemic chaos. Virtually all supplies, including food beyond the subsistence level, had to be imported. If the port of Luanda had not continued functioning, starvation would have been a far greater problem. The West bought approximately 90 percent of Angola's exports, owing primarily to the continuing export of oil through a management contract with the U.S. Gulf Oil Corporation. Even that sector posed problems for the Angolan government in 1983; with the global oil glut, production peaked at about 180,000 barrels per day, as opposed to a production target of 250,000 barrels. (*WP*, 7 October).

Angola's ties with the Soviet Union yielded very limited benefits in the economic sector. The drafting of a fishing agreement was accomplished in the spring, and a major ceremony was held to honor the transfer of a fishing patrol boat from the Soviet to the Angolan government (ANGOP, Luanda, 2 May; *FBIS*, 4 May). The ceremony held some irony for Angolan observers since rumor in Luanda perpetuated the image of the Soviet fishing fleet as a band of looters in Angolan waters (*CSM*, 17 November). In April, an agreement on cooperation with the Soviet Union in agriculture was signed, small solace for the breakdown of that rich sector from pressures of civil war and collectivization (Luanda domestic service, 8 April; *FBIS*, 8 April; *WP*, 7 October).

International Relations. The MPLA–PT's foreign policy revolves, by choice, around the Cubans and Soviets; on the other hand, the South Africans, Portuguese, and Americans are, by imposition, also active participants in Angola's international relations. In the latter group, intermittent armed conflict with the South Africans continued, as did intermittent negotiations with the United States.

In core relations with the communist states, some personnel changes marked the conduct of foreign relations: the ambassador from Cuba, Francia Mestre, left Luanda in May after three years on duty, to be replaced by Rodolfo Quente Ferro (Luanda domestic service, 11 May, 19 July; *FBIS*, 13 May, 19 July). In November, a new Angolan ambassador to Moscow, José Cesar Augusto, arrived at his post (Tass, 5 November; *FBIS*, 7 November). And in December, the Soviet government replaced Vadim Petrovich Loginov as ambassador to Luanda with Arnold Ivanovich Kalinin (*Izvestiia*, 16 December; *FBIS*, 20 December).

Relations with Moscow continued to be governed by the network of treaties and agreements developed since the MPLA takeover of power in Angola. The seventh anniversary of the Treaty of Friendship and Cooperation with the Soviet Union was lauded in October, with particular emphasis on the economic cooperation said to be thereby developed, as well as the presence of Angolan youths in Soviet schools (Radio Moscow, 6 October; *FBIS*, 7 October). It was also said that 150 Soviet doctors were working in Angola in both hospitals and public health (ANGOP, 10 October; *FBIS*, 11 October). High-level representatives from Angola appeared at the major international communist party events, with Politburo member Pascual Luvualu at the sixtieth anniversary celebrations of the USSR (December 1982), and Roberto de Almeida, alternate Politburo member and rising star, at the Karl Marx anniversary celebrations in East Berlin (April 1983) (*Pravda*, 19–21 December 1982; *Neues Deutschland*, 11–14 April).

The main traffic of international affairs, of

course, was the unending flow of delegations to and from Angola, along with obligatory agreements in various fields that provide clues about the harmony of various visits. For example, a delegation from the Soviet Education and Science Union visited Angolan counterparts from the National Union of Workers of Education, Culture and Social Communication (ANGOP, 3 December 1982; *FBIS*, 6 December 1982). On 12 January, Angola formally established diplomatic relations with the People's Republic of China, reflecting movement on the part of the Beijing authorities (AFP, 12 January; *FBIS*, 13 January). The Leninist Komsomol sent a delegation for meetings with the Youth of the Popular Movement for the Liberation of Angola (JMPLA) in Luanda (Luanda domestic service, 27 January; *FBIS*, 27 January). In March, the control organs of the parties in Congo-Brazzaville, Angola, and Mozambique met to compare experiences, a timely concern for the MPLA–PT, which had just accomplished a major purge (Brazzaville domestic service, 3 March; *FBIS*, 9 March).

A serious crisis in intercommunist relations occurred in mid-March with the capture by UNITA of about 64 Czech technicians and family members from the Alto Catumbela paper mill project (AFP, 16 and 21 March; Prague domestic service, 17 March; Luanda domestic service, 22 March; [Clandestine] Voice of Resistance of the Black Cockerel, 28 March; *FBIS*, 16, 21, 23, and 30 March). The episode was serious in illustrating the inability of the Angolans to provide protection for civilian technicians giving assistance to the Luanda government and caused serious concern among other East Europeans with regard to their future ability to recruit their nationals to work in Angola. UNITA negotiated through various international organizations for a trade of the Czechs for prisoners held by the MPLA, with the result that at least twenty Czechs were held by UNITA into 1984 (AFP, 15 April, 7 May; *FBIS*, 19 April, 9 May). These developments were rather embarrassing to the Angolans, as President dos Santos was scheduled for an official visit to the Soviet Union and East Europe in May.

Before leaving for the Soviet Union, however, dos Santos hosted the Vietnamese foreign minister, Xuan Thuy, for several days; standard agreements for exchange of party delegations were signed (Luanda domestic service, 13–15 May; *FBIS*, 16 May). He also hosted the PRC vice-foreign minister, Gong Dafei, for four days, the only apparent outcome being an invitation to dos Santos to visit the PRC (Luanda domestic service, 13–15 May; *FBIS*, 16 May). Dos Santos then departed for his Soviet visit, held between 16 and 20 May, with several days spent in Moscow and several more in Kiev. Three public documents were signed: an agreement on cooperation between the Soviet party and the MPLA–PT, a plan for party ties, and a protocol on cultural and scientific cooperation between the USSR and Angola for 1983–84 (*Pravda*, 21 May; *FBIS*, 23 May; *IB*, July; Luanda domestic service, 16–19 May; *FBIS*, 18–20 May).

The summer and fall witnessed a return to more mundane diplomatic and political visits. The Czech deputy foreign affairs minister and the Tanzanian defense minister (with a delegation of five) came and went (Luanda domestic service, 19 July; *FBIS*, 19 July). A delegation of the Soviet Committee for Solidarity with African and Asian Countries arrived in July to talk with the Angolan Association for Friendship and Solidarity with Peoples (Luanda domestic service, 27 July; *Isvestiia*, 3 August; *FBIS*, 28 July, 10 August). An Algerian Politburo member and minister of foreign affairs, Ahmed Taleb Ibrahimi, visited Luanda as well (Algiers domestic service, 4 August; *FBIS*, 10 August). The chairman of the East German Friendship and Solidarity Committee, Kurt Scheidler, spend fifteen days in Angola in September, presenting a mobile cinema van to his hosts, the Angolan League for Friendship and Solidarity with Peoples (ANGOP, 29 September; *FBIS*, 30 September). Zinaida Kruglova, the chairman of the Union of Soviet Societies for Friendship and Cultural Relations with Foreign Countries spent two days in Luanda (Luanda domestic service, 5 October; *FBIS*, 6 October). The Cuban attorney general visited in October (Luanda domestic service, 8 October; *FBIS*, 11 October).

Several high-level Angolans were seen traveling abroad. The new secretary for ideology of the Central Committee, Roberto de Almeida, met with Boris Ponomarev, Soviet Politburo alternative member (Tass, 3 October; *FBIS*, 4 October) and Pascaul Luvualu, Politburo member, visited Romania and East Germany in a long tour (Agerpres, 10 October; *FBIS*, 12 October; East Berlin international service, 7 November; *FBIS*, 8 November). Finally, aside from the additional flow of Bulgarians, Tanzanians, and Yugoslavs, a particularly interesting visitor was the secretary general of the French Communist Party, Georges Marchais, who spend five days in Luanda in late October (Luanda domestic service, 21–25 October; *L'Humanité*, 25–26 October; *FBIS*, 17–21 October, 7 November). Tremendous publicity accompanied his time in Angola, an apparent attempt to focus French attention away from its traditional Central and West African preoccupation towards the more radical perspectives of the southern African states.

Publications and Information. The MPLA–PT faced continuing problems in controlling the flow of information among the people. The renewal of party discipline at the beginning of the year helped to intimidate part of the MPLA–PT back into using internal channels of dissent rather than cultural forms or the media. Measures taken included the replacement of the minister for in-

formation and propaganda. The task also continued to be of interest at the international level. In mid-October, Luanda signed an agreement on cinema cooperation with the Soviet government (*Izvestiia*, 15 October; *FBIS*, 20 October). Talks were also held with the Soviet party on cooperation in information and propaganda (Luanda domestic service, 20 December; *FBIS*, 22 December). A national assembly of coordinators of MPLA–PT party cells in the People's Defense Organization was held in October, to mobilize and give marching orders to the cadres necessary to maintain morale; public reports of the meetings indicated that monitoring of cultural expressions were essential, as well as "broad, dynamic propaganda activity" (Luanda domestic service, 2 October; *FBIS*, 4 October).

Richard E. Bissell
McLean, Virginia

Bahrain

Population. 393,000 (mid-1983)
Party. Bahrain National Liberation Front (NLF/B)
Founded. 1955
Membership. Unknown but believed to be negligible
Chairman. Yusuf al-Hassan al-Ajajai (1981)
Executive Committee. (Not necessarily complete) Aziz Ahmad Mudhawi (1982), Aziz Mahmud (1983), Jasim Muhammad (1981), Abdallah Ali al-Rashid (1982), Ahmad Ibrahim Muhammad al-Thawadi (presumed member) (1980)
Status. Illegal
Last Congress. Unknown
Last Election. Not applicable
Auxiliary Organizations. Bahrain Democratic Youth Union (affiliated with the World Federation of Democratic Youth), National Union of Bahraini Students (affiliated with the International Union of Students), Women's Organization of the NLF/B (affiliated with the Women's International Democratic Federation), Bahrain Workers' Union (?)
Publications. Unknown

The NLF/B report to the April Karl Marx celebrations in East Berlin, the only unilateral pronouncement of the organization noted during the year, states that Bahrain has "a labor class... which is engaged in a class struggle under the leadership of a communist party equipped with the Marxist-Leninist theory" (*Neues Deutschland*, East Berlin, 18 April). Here again, the NLF/B all but claims to be a full-blown communist party (see *YICA*, 1983, p. 10), even though the Soviets still officially categorize it as a "revolutionary democratic" one (*Socialism: Theory and Practice*, Moscow, August, p. 118). It would also seem that the Bahrain Workers' Union, about which little has been heard since the attendance of its representative at the Tenth World Trade Union Congress (Havana, February 1982), is at least theoretically playing an important role here.

The NLF/B statement also notes that "there are other national forces that confess Marxist ideas" (*Neues Deutschland*, 18 April). The Popular Front for the Liberation of Bahrain (PFLB) appears to remain in the forefront here (see *YICA*, 1983, p. 10). The latter's publication, *Fifth of March*, noted in its June issue that the Popular Front, the NLF/B, and other Arab revolutionary organizations had met together in Damascus the preceding month. Also in May, the NLF/B met separately with the Communist Party of Saudi Arabia, while in June both groups participated in a meeting of twelve communist and workers' parties of the Arab countries.

Executive Committee member Abdallah Ali al-Rashid remained the NLF/B's chief spokesman abroad through the end of 1982 (see *YICA*, 1983, p. 10), a year in which he represented the organization at the USSR's sixtieth anniversary celebration in Moscow in December. In 1983, however, that honor seems to have gone to fellow Executive Committee member Aziz Mahmud, who attended the September *L'Humanité* press festival (in a Paris suburb), the April Karl Marx celebrations in East Berlin, and the June World Assembly for Peace and Life, Against Nuclear War, in Prague. That Mahmud was listed as having attended the latter meeting in his capacity as an NLF/B leader rather than as a member of the Bahrain Peace and Solidarity Organization (see *YICA*, 1983, p. 10) indicates that the latter is probably defunct and that the NLF/B itself is the country's World Peace Council affiliate. Representatives of both the Bahrain Democratic Youth Union and the Women's Organization of the NLF/B also attended the June assembly in Prague (World Assembly for Peace and Life, Against Nuclear War, *List of Participants*, p. 25).

Wallace H. Spaulding
McLean, Virginia

Benin

The ruling People's Revolutionary Party (Parti de la révolution populaire du Bénin; PRPB) of this small West African state, known as Dahomey until 1975, was never more than an attempt to institutionalize military or personal rule. Despite its proclaimed allegiance to Marxism-Leninism and its fiery revolutionary rhetoric, the party is still little more than an ineffective instrument in the hands of a small clique of military and civilian individuals, with little impact on the national life and even less influence over actual decisionmaking.

After attaining independence from France in 1960, Dahomey was often called "Africa's Bolivia" because of its continuous chain of military coups and countercoups, briefly interrupted only by the shaky tenure of weak, corrupt, and incompetent civilian rulers with narrow ethnic bases of support. Dahomey appeared to experience another such episode of military interference when the 26 November 1972 coup took place. Led by then-captain Mathieu Kerekou, a leader of the paratroopers of the Ouidah base with a previous record of involvement in coups, that takeover by the military did not appear to be different from the eight previous army attempts to attain power. Of the three other captains leading the coup, Janvier Assogba was known to be a traditionalist, Michel Alladaye a moderate, and Michel Aikpe a favorite of the highly vocal urban Left and of Guinean President Sekou Touré. As for Kerekou, his political beliefs were unknown.

After more than two years of steady purging of the older senior officers, some of whom were retired and others jailed for plots (real or alleged), the initial group of four started falling apart. The jockeying for power led all of them to seek civilian support and to claim more or less coherent political ideas. The more radical group led by Aikpe, a dashing commando-paratrooper officer, appeared to have an early advantage by 1974, when on 30 November Kerekou proclaimed Dahomey's allegiance to Marxism-Leninism as its "ideological option." In January 1975, Assogba, accused of staging a coup, was imprisoned and died a few years later in jail. This appeared to encourage the radicals and thus to threaten Kerekou himself. Aikpe pushed for the creation of a "vanguard party," hoping to be able to control it, while uncommitted officers, including Kerekou, were reluctant to take such a risk. Interior minister since the 1972 coup, Michel Aikpe used his position to establish close ties with the radical student and intellectual groups of Cotonou and to undermine the influence of his competitors within the regime. On 21 June 1975, Aikpe was shot dead, apparently by one of Kerekou's closer military friends, Martin Azonhiho. Aikpe's death sparked student and radical union riots and demonstrations in Cotonou and the capital of Porto Novo. As a result, the regime undertook a number of measures, including nationalization (with compensation) of foreign companies and the creation of a "vanguard party," while at the same time turning up the volume of its anti-Western and anticapitalist rhetoric. On the other hand, with Alladaye at his side, Kerekou found himself in a position of unchallenged control over the regime.

On 30 November 1975, the official name of the country was changed to the People's Republic of Benin, after a precolonial African state that had existed in what is now Nigeria, and the PRPB was established as a Marxist-Leninist "vanguard" party. The new party's statutes were written with direct advice from the East Germans, and it had its first, extraordinary, congress on 15–17 May 1976. The second, and to this date the only, ordinary congress of the PRPB took place on 13–15 November 1979.

Party Leadership and Structure. Intended from the beginning to be only an institutionalization of military rule and its civilian supporters, the PRPB is structured along traditional Marxist-Leninist lines, including "democratic centralism" as its decisionmaking process, and the usual organisms and front organizations. The Central Committee is supposed to be the ruling body of the PRPB between congresses, but since congresses are only convened when the Politburo deems it necessary, the sixteen-member Politburo actually controls the country and policies of the government.

On the other hand, of the Politburo members, the Kerekou faction, including both military and civilian members, is by far the dominant one, with Kerekou himself, Alladaye, Information Minister Baba Moussa, Higher Education Minister (and former ambassador to East Berlin) Armand Monteiro, and Mass Education Minister Gratien Capo-Chichi, as well as Foreign Minister Tiamiou Adjibade, clearly in control. Since it is the Politburo that decides the candidates' list of the Central Committee, it is practically a self-defined and self-appointed group. Kerekou concentrates most of the national power in his own hands, as president, PRPB president, head of state, head of government, and national defense minister. In addition, he is the only Politburo member or minister who still retains an active command rank.

The PRPB decisionmaking process is defined as "democratic centralism," a principle also enshrined in the 1977 constitution, which proclaimed that "all state organs in the People's Republic of Benin are constituted and function according to the principle of democratic centralism" (text of the Benin constitution of 1977, *Afrique Contemporaine*, no. 93, September–October 1977, pp. 24–26).

Despite the fact that a majority of the PRPB

Politburo members are now civilians (mostly former student or union leaders), military control over the structure of power in the country, embodied by Kerekou himself, is still unchallenged. Moreover, the fact that such apparently influential leaders as Martin Azonhiho, former interior minister and information minister, were demoted, despite their military rank, to insignificant positions (in Azonhiho's case to that of governor of the marginal Mono department), indicates that Kerekou's personal control over the Politburo and, by implication, over the PRPB, is virtually total.

Domestic Attitudes and Activities. Internally, the PRPB, with only a few thousand members at most, is itself a front for the military-civilian radical coalition in power. Among the formal PRPB front organizations, all subsidized by the government, the Revolutionary Defense Organizations, the Youth Revolutionary Organization, and the Women's Revolutionary Committee are prominent, although quite irrelevant. On the other hand, the regime's attempts to control the trade unions in general and the teachers' union in particular seemed to have backfired, with the government forced to repudiate its rejection of independent teachers' unions and deal with their strikes during the 1980–1982 period.

Despite its revolutionary Leninist rhetoric, the PRPB did accept the concept of compensation for the nationalization of foreign companies' assets, it still allows the existence of small retail shops and tends to encourage foreign, mostly French, investments.

Foreign Policy. Despite Benin's complete dependence on Western (primarily French and West German) aid for the economic survival of both the country and the bloated bureaucracy traditionally characteristic of the country, PRPB foreign policy is characterized by close alignment with radical African causes. Strong ties with Libya are paralleled by security and ideological arrangements with communist countries, from China to the USSR, from North Korea to East Germany and Cuba. Benin, with Libyan encouragement, was instrumental in encouraging the radical military officers who took power in Ghana in December 1981 and in Upper Volta in August 1983 and supports the pro-Libyan faction in Chad. On the other hand, Kerekou has always avoided taking sides in the Sino-Soviet dispute and continues to draw aid from both China and the USSR.

Publications. The PRPB newspaper, *Ehuzu*, is the only national newspaper, despite its small circulation of about a thousand. The party also controls the national radio station, the Voice of the Revolution.

Michael S. Radu
Foreign Policy Research Institute

Congo

The Congo, formerly known as Congo-Brazzaville, is the oldest self-proclaimed Marxist-Leninist regime in sub-Saharan Africa. What was then defined as the Marxist-Leninist "option" was made public soon after the 13–15 August 1963 events that brought to power the radical group centered around Alphonse Massemba Debat. Since then, the pattern of Congolese politics has been characterized by a steady movement to the Left and by growing political and security ties with the Soviet bloc and China.

According to the present official mythology,

the events beginning on 31 July 1968, which resulted in the military coup led by Marien Ngouabi the following month, were the starting point of the present regime and of control by the ruling Congolese Labor Party (Parti congolais du travail; PCT).

Despite his coming into power by forcibly removing the radical regime of Alphonse Massemba Debat, then-captain Marien Ngouabi was forced, by the radicals within the military as well as by the strength of the urban Left of Brazzaville, to maintain and stress leftist rhetoric in order to strengthen and consolidate his own control over the government. In these circumstances, the establishment of the PCT on 31 December 1969, one day after the proclamation of the People's Republic of the Congo, was an attempt to placate the radicals within and outside the army. Ngouabi's problem, until his assassination on 18 March 1977, was that he was never able actually to control the PCT and was repeatedly forced to use his strength within the army in order to keep his ambitious and turbulent party colleagues under control. At times that had to be done by forcibly purging the PCT and thus reducing its numbers and influence to negligible levels. The most thorough of the Ngouabi purges took place after radicals in the army, led by Lt. Ange Diawara, attempted a coup in February 1972; they were defeated, and Diawara himself was killed the following year. The massive purge of the party at the time resulted in its practical dismantling, with the total membership falling to between 160 and 230, the Central Committee reduced to five members, and the Politburo to three members.

Attempts to reconstitute the PCT, particularly at the time of the Second Congress of 1974, were once again prevented by the use of union power against Ngouabi in 1975–1976. The outcome of the confrontation was yet another massive purge resulting in massive reductions in membership and influence of the party.

Ngouabi's assassination was, despite the mystery still surrounding it, another demonstration of the unstable and increasingly violent character of Congolese politics and the continuous strength of the military-civilian radical coalition. Although Ngouabi was succeeded as president by the most senior army officer, Yhombi Opango, the latter never attained control over the PCT, which became the vehicle for the military and civilian opposition to Opango's rule. On 5 Febru-

ary 1979, Opango was ousted by a coalition of military and party leaders led by his second in command and leader of the PCT at the time, Denis Sassou Ngouesso. The events of 1979 demonstrated that, unlike the period of Ngouabi, no Congolese leader could hope to retain power without the support of the dominant PCT faction and that the party has finally succeeded in becoming a real contender for power. On the other hand, however, Sassou Ngouesso's power was based on his military backing as much as bureaucratic party support, and a majority of the ten-member PCT Politburo are still military men.

One of Sassou Ngouesso's first acts was to convene the often postponed Third PCT Congress on August 1979, with the clear aim of consolidating his power base within the party.

Party Leadership and Structure. A self-proclaimed "vanguard" party of the proletariat, the PCT had about 7,000 members (*Kommunist*, Moscow, April 1982). Formally, the ruling body is the Congress, supposed to convene every five years. Between congresses the Politburo runs the country, as well as the party, and its membership is still far from homogenous, despite Sassou Ngouesso's apparently firm control over the majority faction. The major cleavages within the Politburo, as well as within the 30-member Central Committee, are ethnic as well as political, pitting the dominant northerners against the majority southerners, civilians against the military, and radicals against relative moderates. It appears that the president, who is also party chairman and chief of government, still has to cope with significant dissent from a largely civilian faction led by Foreign Minister Pierre Nze and, particularly, by party ideologue Jean-Pierre Thystere Tchikaya. Prime Minister Sylvain Goma, a southerner, is the only remaining member of the initial Politburo of 1969, and his powers are quite limited. Conflicts within the PCT leadership are generally solved by purging the losing members, such as former interior minister François Katali, expelled in 1982, and former information minister Florent Tsiba, one of the leaders of the February 1979 overthrow of Opango. Both were expelled from the Central Committee and from any position of influence, following clashes with Sassou Ngouesso's faction, under the pretext of their being unable to prevent terrorist actions in Brazzaville.

The major PCT front organizations are the

Congolese Trade Union Confederation (CSC), the Revolutionary Union of Congolese Women (URFC), and the Union of Congolese Socialist Youth (UJSC). Since membership in these organizations is compulsory, they have a very large nominal membership. The CSC and particularly the UJSC used to be quite powerful and independent during the late 1960s and early 1970s, providing a ready base for ambitious politicians challenging the regime, but since 1979 they both appear to be well under PCT control.

Domestic Policies. Despite its old revolutionary claims and allegiance to Marxism-Leninism, the PCT's domestic economic and social policies do not appear to be particularly radical by African standards. Under Ngouabi, massive nationalization took place but compensation was provided. Rhetorical attacks against "imperialism" and "neo-colonial" influences in the country went hand in hand with legislation providing incentives for foreign investments, particularly in the dominant oil industry. On the other hand, the growth of bureaucracy and of inefficient state companies draining the national economy were two problems no Congolese leadership has ever managed to solve, despite periodic official outbursts against "bourgeois tendencies" and corruption. The PCT's control over economic and political life is still far from total, as demonstrated by Sassou Ngouesso's mention of "irresponsibility, thoughtlessness, incompetence, confusion of roles, laziness, sabotage, and lack of modesty" as omnipresent in party activities (*FBIS*, 28 August 1979, p. C4).

On the other hand, the National Assembly, officially proclaimed an expression of democracy of a "new type," is only a rubber-stamp body, elected from the candidates' list provided by the party and seldom convened. In 1982, the PCT leadership decided to postpone national elections for another few years and therefore to eliminate even the appearance of any democratic legitimacy. In such circumstances and in light of the concentration of powers in the hands of the president, control over political change in the Congo remains, as always since 1963, in the hands of the military-radical coalition now controlling the PCT Politburo.

Foreign Policies. Congo's foreign policies since 1969 have been characterized by a sharp dichotomy between an economic and trade orientation toward the West, with France the largest trade partner and source of foreign aid, and regional and general political and security ties with the Soviet bloc and its African allies, particularly the Portuguese-speaking states. In May 1980, the Congo signed a treaty of friendship and cooperation with the USSR, and significant numbers of Cuban, East German, and Soviet military advisers are still present in the country. On the other hand, the PCT has consistently, and successfully, managed to avoid being involved in the Sino-Soviet dispute, and the Congo still receives significant Chinese aid, military as well as economic. At the Organization of African Unity, the Congo is generally supportive of the most radical group of states, has close ties with Libya, and even closer relations with Angola, dating from the 1975–1976 period, when the Congo provided logistical support for the Cuban intervention in that country.

Publications. All publications in the country are under direct or indirect PCT control. The party paper, *Etumba*, has a circulation of a few thousand copies.

Michael S. Radu
Foreign Policy Research Institute

Egypt

Population. 45.8 million (mid-June) (U.S. Census Bureau; *NYT* and AP, 4 September)
Party. Egyptian Communist Party (al-Hizb al-Shuyu'i al-Misri; ECP)
Founded. 1921; revived in 1972
Membership. 500 (estimate)
Secretary General. Farid Muhajid
Politburo. Michel Kamal, Najib Kamal (representative to the *WMR*); other names unknown
Secretariat. No information
Central Committee. The name of one member, Yusuf Darwish, has been mentioned.
Status. Proscribed
Last Congress. 1980
Last Election. 1979; no communist party candidates
Auxiliary Organizations. No information
Publications. Only sporadic pamphlets

The communist movement in Egypt dates back to the formation in 1921 in Alexandria of the Egyptian Socialist Party (al-Hizb al-Ishtiraki al-Misri) by Joseph Rosenthal and some former members of a more diverse group founded in Cairo the year before. With its name soon changed to the Egyptian Communist Party, it was admitted to the Comintern in 1923. Suppression by the authorities started almost immediately and has continued sporadically ever since.

The movement has also been highly subject to factionalism. It virtually disappeared during the late 1920s and 1930s. Numerous communist groups emerged during the early 1940s, and the two largest factions combined to form the Mouvement Démocratique de Libération Nationale (MDLN) in 1947. This group also splintered in the 1950s, with the formation of a Unified Egyptian Communist Party in 1958 soon giving way to so much splintering that for a while no one faction was important enough to be singled out for international recognition. At least two groups heeded Soviet instructions to cooperate with "progressive" single-party regimes by dissolving themselves in return for a commitment by the Egyptian government to tolerate indi-

vidual communists. Many of the latter occupied important positions in the Arab Socialist Union (ASU) and the mass media. But with President Anwar al-Sadat's shift to the right during the 1970s, a new ECP emerged in 1972.

The Egyptian communist movement remains as splintered as ever. Besides the ECP, several groups—including the Egyptian Communist Party-8 January, the Egyptian Communist Workers' Party, the Revolutionary Egyptian Communist Party, and the Revolutionary Current—have surfaced during recent years. Twenty-three men—allegedly members of a communist "Popular Movement"—were prosecuted on charges of planning a Guevara-style revolution after establishing a popular democratic front of peasants, workers, and members of the lower bourgeoisie (*al-Ahram*, 14 September; *FBIS*, 23 September). No allegation of any relationship to the ECP or other previously reported group was mentioned. The government also reported that it had "uncovered a clandestine communist Palestinian [student] organization consisting of twenty members [no relationship to the Palestine Communist Party was mentioned], after it attempted to infiltrate sectors of the Egyptian masses" and had deported them after allowing them to take their examinations (MENA, Cairo, 21 June; *FBIS*, 22 June).

Leadership and Party Organization. Little is known about the party's leadership and organization. The name of the secretary general has not been mentioned in any available publications. Official statements by ECP leaders published abroad are mostly notable for preserving their anonymity. The name most often mentioned is Politburo member Michel Kamal. Reports of arrests during previous years refer to the existence of party cells. All indications point to the typical pattern of "democratic centralism," but in a rudimentary form resulting from the group's small membership and clandestine character.

Domestic Party Affairs. There were no reports of ECP activities during 1983. Reports during previous years indicate that party activists were involved among university students and factory workers. Official suppression apparently makes the publication of a party newspaper impossible.

With the periodic occurrence of large-scale arrests, many party members are in prison or are repeatedly arrested and retried. An Amnesty International report entitled *Egypt: Violation of Human Rights* (London, 1983) and based on a memorandum of June 1982 to which the Egyptian government did not respond pointed to "hundreds of men and women [who], since 1971, have been imprisoned for their non-violent political beliefs or activities" without trial or with "trial before exceptional courts which deny them the right to appeal" and who have been subjected "to torture and ill-treatment" or executed (p. 3). Although such individuals represented "many different political persuasions and religious beliefs," the report concluded that "the overwhelming majority . . . belonged to illegal communist organizations or participated in their activities (p. 4). Among the examples cited were Farida Naqqash, a writer and member of the leftist National Progressive Unionist Party (NPUP), who was formerly in prison, though not at the time of the report; she was "facing trial with 29 others—her husband among them—on charges of participation in political activities connected with the [ECP]" (p. 7). Ali Sa'id Zahran, a furniture maker, had been in prison since 1978 for "membership in an illegal communist organization." Shihata Harun, a law-

yer and founding member of the NPUP, and Husayn Abd al-Raziq, a journalist, were charged with being members of the ECP (pp. 3–5). The report pointed to 176 defendants charged with instigating the food riots of 1977 (including 37 who were accused of membership in the ECP and 87 others accused of membership in the Egyptian Communists Workers' Party), proceedings against whom had not been completed.

Auxiliary and/or Front Organizations. No information has come to light about any auxiliary organizations of the ECP.

Much more important than the ECP is the broad, legal leftist oppositional front, the NPUP, whose secretary general is longtime Marxist Khalid Muhyi al-Din. (The deputy secretary general is Rif'at al-Sa'id.) Some of the members of the NPUP are Marxists, while some are Nasserites or other opponents of the nonsocialist, pro-Western direction of the regime. While some contacts with the ECP have been reported, the NPUP is not a front group for any organization per se.

The NPUP began in 1976 as the National Progressive Unionist Group (NPUG), one of the three "pulpits" (Left, Right, and Centrist) permitted to be formed within what was then the only legal political organization, the Arab Socialist Union (ASU). It soon became a full-fledged party. It publishes the weekly newspaper *al-Ahali*, edited by Muhyi al-Din. (See Yossi Amitay, "*Al-Ahali*: Profile of an Egyptian Left-wing Weekly," *New Outlook*, Tel Aviv, January/ February, pp. 46–50.) The party, which lost its three seats in the People's Assembly (parliament) in the 1980 elections, has often been harassed and some of its members arrested, while issues of *al-Ahali* have sometimes been confiscated. The paper has also periodically been forced to suspend publication, notably by Sadat in September 1981 (shortly before his assassination), but publication resumed in May 1982. According to one report, the paper is so popular that its 100,000 or more copies are completely sold out within three days (Roger Owen, "Egypt Gropes for Political Direction," *MERIP Reports*, Washington, July/ August, p. 25).

Muhyi al-Din spoke at an NPUP meeting in March with reference to the Camp David process about "the perfidious designs of Zionism and imperialism." Another speaker, M. al-Zayyat, explained the Camp David agreements as ensuring "U.S. and Israeli hegemony, with deals with Lebanon and other countries planned to widen the framework." (*Pravda*, 4 March; *FBIS*, 11 March.) An extraordinary congress of the NPUP was held in Cairo in late March and approved a report of the Central Committee. The report supported "positive steps" of the government away from Sadat's policies but proclaimed the goal of working for "fundamental changes in domestic and foreign policy," particularly "against the 'open doors' economic policy and the parasitic bourgeoisie engendered by it" and against the separate peace with Israel and "Egypt's being tied to military blocs and the granting of 'military privileges' on its territory" (*Pravda*, 28 March; *FBIS*, 1 April).

An article in *al-Ahali* by Dr. Fu'ad Mursi on 11 May (*FBIS*, 17 May) made ominous comparisons between the current situation and "the conditions or atmosphere of September 1981." Mursi also pointed to new restrictions on the Bar Association and to the newly proposed twenty-year ban on writing by certain former officials and warned that "the countdown may have started." In July, the NPUP joined with the Liberal and Socialist Labor parties to announce a boycott of local elections to be held in November. In October, Muhyi al-Din presented a report to the Central Committee that spoke of "positive changes" under President Mohammed Hosni Mubarak but also of doubts about the possibility of a return to nonalignment and Arabism alongside the Camp David agreements and pointed to joint U.S.–Egyptian military exercises and military facilities for the U.S. army as bases for pessimism (Radio Moscow, in Arabic to the Arab world, 28 October; *FBIS*, 31 October).

International Views, Positions, and Activities. Representatives of the ECP participated in a meeting of twelve communist and workers' parties of the Arab countries in June (the place was not mentioned). The meeting discussed regional and international problems and issued a joint statement. Leaders of the ECP and the Palestine Communist Party met in mid-September 1982 to discuss the situation resulting from the Israeli invasion of Lebanon. Central Committee member Darwish attended the sixtieth anniversary celebration of the USSR in December 1982, while Michel Kamal attended the international scientific convention on "Karl Marx and Our Time—The Struggle for Peace and Social Ad-

vancement" in April. The NPUP also had representatives at the latter two occasions.

In the joint statement issued with the Palestine Communist Party, the ECP declared that "the Israeli aggression against Lebanon...is part of the process of stepping up international tensions, a process led by the U.S. administration under President Reagan." The "unprecedentedly low level" of Arab solidarity was said to be "a result of collusion with the aggressors by right-wing, reactionary Arab regimes as well as of the vacillation shown by some contingents of the Arab liberation movement." Arab collusion with the aggressors was blamed on "class differentiation, a process sped up by the colossal incomes derived by reactionary regimes." The statement called for the creation of an independent Palestinian state in the territories occupied since 1967 and for the right of Palestinian refugees to return home. Israel's "attempts to impose a 'civil administration' on the territories preparatory to a definitive annexation" and "bloody terror campaigns" designed to expel the Palestinian population were deplored. The USSR was commended for its "principled attitude," and the "slander campaign" against it was emphatically condemned. (*IB*, January, pp. 26–29.)

The statement of the twelve Arab communist parties condemned the Reagan Plan, the Israeli–Lebanese agreement of 17 May, and "the growing danger of aggression against Syria." The "imperialist offensive" was said to be manifested in "the Israeli–U.S. alliance," the formation of the U.S. Central Command, and U.S. acquisition of "military bases and privileges." The "dangerous breach of the correlation of forces in the region" was said to have begun with "the reactionary Egyptian bourgeoisie's move to the road of alliance with imperialism" (Egypt was described as being "very close to losing its national sovereignty"), and further aided by the Iraq–Iran war. Support was declared for Western Saharan self-determination and for "the Kurdish national liberation movement in Iraq, Iran, and Turkey." "U.S. imperialism" was blamed for the "growing threat of nuclear war," while the Soviet record in promoting peace met with praise. (*IB*, September, pp. 24–26.)

Biography. *Khalid Muhyi al-Din.* Khalid Muhyi al-Din was born in 1922 into a prominent landowning family of Sharqiyya province in the Egyptian Delta. He was graduated from the Military Academy in 1940 and received a B.A. in commerce from Cairo University in 1951. He was associated with the MDLN during the late 1940s but may not have actually joined the group.

As an officer in the mechanized cavalry, Muhyi al-Din was closely associated with Jamal Abdul Nasser despite the latter's rejection of his Marxist ideas. Along with one other Marxist, he was one of the original ten members of the executive committee of the Free Officers in 1949. His cavalry force played an important role in the 1952 coup, and it is said that he was the author of a number of radical pamphlets distributed clandestinely by the officers beforehand. As one of the members of the Revolutionary Command Council (RCC), he is said to have been instrumental in drawing up the original "six principles" of the new regime.

Despite Muhyi al-Din's personal and family ties with members of the RCC (his cousin, Zakariya Muhyi al-Din, was reputedly one of the least radical and most "pro-American" members), he was ideologically at odds with the rest. He led the cavalry in a tactical alliance with President Muhammad Nagib in 1954 but was outmaneuvered by Nasser. He subsequently went into exile in Europe for over a year but was allowed to return in 1955 as editor in chief of the newspaper *al-Masa'*, which provided the Left a restricted base of activity. In 1959, at a time of deteriorating Egyptian–Soviet relations and of a general crackdown on communists, he was dismissed from his post but was one of the few leftists not arrested. He became editor of *Akhbar al-Yawm* and chairman of the Press Council in 1965 and was elected to the eight-member Executive Committee of the ASU in 1968.

Muhyi al-Din has been the leading leftist critic of the Sadat and Mubarak regimes, heading the NPUG (later NPUP) since its inception. He was one of the three NPUP deputies elected to the People's Assembly in 1976. His status as a former member of the RCC saved him from arrest in 1981, at the time other opposition figures were imprisoned. (Sources: numerous works on post–1952 Egypt, particularly P. J. Vatikiotis, *Nasser and His Generation*, New York: St. Martin's Press, 1978; and Robert Springborg, *Family, Power, and Politics in Egypt*, Philadelphia: University of Pennsylvania Press, 1982.)

Glenn E. Perry
Indiana State University

Ethiopia

Population. 32.8 million (1983 estimate, International Monetary Fund)
Party. Commission to Organize the Party of the Working People of Ethiopia (COPWE)
Founded. 1979
Membership. Uncertain; however, 2,000 COPWE representatives usually attend plenary sessions
Chairman. Mengistu Haile Mariam
Executive Committee. 7 members: Mengistu Haile Mariam, Legesse Asfaw, Berhanu Bayhi, Fikre-Selassie Wogderess, Tesfaye Gebre Kidan, Addis Tedlay, Fisseha Desta
Central Committee. 117 members
Status. Ruling party
Last Congress. Second, 3–6 January, in Addis Ababa

Last Election. Not applicable
Auxiliary Organizations. All-Ethiopian Peasant Association, Kebelles, All-Ethiopia Trade Union, Revolutionary Ethiopia's Women's Association
Publications. *Serto Ader, Addis Zemen, Ethiopian Herald, Negarit Gazeta*

The COPWE is apparently preparing to create a vanguard political party to reflect the conclusion of the first decade of the revolution. Because of the increasing stability of Ethiopia's international and regional relations, COPWE and the Provisional Military Administrative Council, or Dergue, have been able to make progress in moving from a pre-party to a vanguard political structure.

Leadership and Party Organization. After deliberating on 3–6 January, the Second Congress of COPWE adopted a resolution confirming "that we have reached the last stage in the formation of the Ethiopian workers party . . . which is the completion of work for the formation of the party" (Addis Ababa domestic service, 6 January). In commenting on the resolution, *Pravda* (8 January) maintained that it "reaffirmed the Ethiopian revolutionaries' loyalty to Marxism-Leninism [bringing] to a successful conclusion work on creating a vanguard party of working people [by] September 1984 . . . the Ethiopian revolution's 10th anniversary." According to COPWE chairman and head of state Mengistu Haile Mariam, the creation of such a party "is a necessary condition of the further progress of the Ethiopian revolution, which has proclaimed as its main goal the building of a socialist society" (*Pravda*, 5 January). In a radio commentary that reflected the official perception of the Soviet communist party (CPSU), Georgy Tanov maintained that the major result of the Second Congress was "the decision to summon in September of 1984 the third Congress of [COPWE], which will serve as the constituent congress of the country's vanguard Marxist-Leninist party . . . The second congress of COPWE served to draw this important political event nearer." ("Africa as We See It," Moscow, 8 January.)

Domestic Party Affairs. In preparation for the newly developing political structures, Mengistu reshuffled the Dergue and the Executive Committee of COPWE and altered somewhat COPWE's Central Committee. Lt. Col. Fikre-Selassie Wogderess, a pro-Soviet Dergue Standing Committee member and a member of the Executive Committee of COPWE, was made deputy chairman of the Dergue in April, and Taye Gurumu, director of COPWE's Cooperatives Department, and Tamirat Ferede of the Dergue were reported purged and removed from their positions in January. The overall COPWE structure was streamlined by Mengistu as he reduced representation on the Central Committee from 123 to 117; representation on the Executive Committee remained at 7 (ibid.).

Shortly after the conclusion of the Second Congress, Berhanu Bayhi, one of the most powerful members of both COPWE and the Dergue, began preparations for the new party. He led a delegation to Moscow on 9–20 March to discuss "questions of party work" with numerous representatives of the CPSU Politburo and Central Committee (*Pravda*, 23 March). The groundwork for this meeting had been laid at the congress and by Mengistu's limited restructuring of COPWE.

Auxiliary Organizations. Millions of Ethiopians were affected by the worst drought and famine to hit northern Ethiopia in a decade. While distribution of food was hampered by the low-keyed but continuing guerrilla war taking place in Eritrea and Tigre, two of the worst afflicted regions (Beghemdir and Wello were also affected), the All-Ethiopian Peasant Association and the kebelles (neighborhood political associations), along with Ethiopia's Relief and Rehabilitation Commission, were involved in trying to cope with the human aspects of this midyear disaster. Aided by Revolutionary Ethiopia's Women's Association, all three groups were prominent in trying to distribute millions in food and aid provided by Great Britain ($1 million), the United States ($9 million), the USSR (10,000 metric tons of rice), the World Food Program, the United Nations, the European Economic Community, and the U.S.-based Catholic Relief Services. The 4 million Ethiopians affected by the drought and famine rely on COPWE's auxiliary structures to a great extent. Whereas in 1973 Haile Selassie's government tried unsuccessfully to cover up a famine in order to maintain a positive image abroad, Mengistu's government "has sought to organize international aid" (*WP*, 26 June) and is utilizing COPWE's auxiliary party structures in this battle against nature.

International Views, Positions, and Activities. Twenty years after the founding of the Organization of African Unity (OAU) in Addis Ababa, Mengistu Haile Mariam was named its new chairman. In his first speech as chairman, Mengistu declared that U.S. involvement in the Horn of Africa was evidence of "the effort of the U.S. Administration to work against the forces of democracy and Socialism" (*NYT*, 14 June). In response to the U.S. announcement in June that 2,800 of its troops would engage in joint military exercises in and with Somalia, Ethiopia, in July, launched ground and air attacks against Somalia's invasion of the central part of the country. Although the Ethiopian forces were driven back, the attack was seen as a warning that Ethiopia would not continue to tolerate Somalia's growing dependency on the United States. From Mengistu's perspective, "The imperialists are promoting their strategic aims...It is enough to point out the military bases they have constructed and the military exercises they carry out [with] the reactionary Somali regime. We have to strengthen our unity and struggle for progress, prosperity, and the defense of the true independence of African people." (Addis Ababa domestic service, 13 September.)

In addition to Mengistu's selection as chair of the OAU, evidence of Ethiopia's growing international stability was seen in its international relations. In May, a three-year cooperation agreement was signed by COPWE and the Vietnamese Communist Party, while in September Fisseha Desta, assistant secretary general of the Dergue, traveled to Beijing from North Korea to meet with State Councillor Ji Pengfei. A statement was issued opposing hegemonism and agreeing to develop "exchanges" between the two countries. Also in September, the USSR sent a statue of Lenin to the people of Ethiopia in honor of the ninth anniversary of the revolution. It was unveiled in Lenin Square 13 September, and according to Zaudi Teklu, the mayor of Addis Ababa, it is the first monument to Lenin on the African continent (Tass, 13 September). In addition, Sharaf R. Rashidov of the CPSU Politburo led a sixteen-man delegation to attend the anniversary celebrations.

Relations with other socialist states were also developed. Late in the year, Legesse Asfaw, a member of COPWE's Executive Committee and a pro-Soviet figure, met in East Berlin with Erich Honecker. A program of "work for cooperation" was signed to cover 1983–84 (ADN international service, 12 October). Earlier in the year, Czech president Gústav Husák met with Ethiopia's minister of mines, Aytenfiso Tekeze-Shoa, and both reaffirmed the principles of the 1981 Treaty of Friendship and Cooperation (Prague domestic service, 30 March). The USSR maintained it would give the necessary material assistance for the implementation of Ethiopia's ten-year plan (Addis Ababa domestic service, 12 March), and an economic, scientific, and technical cooperation protocol was signed in Moscow in July by the Soviet Union and Ethiopia's minister of industry Hailu Yamanu. The Cuban-Ethiopian entente also continued to develop with numerous official visits between representatives of the two countries and the broadening of their educational programs. In Mito, Ethiopia, Cuban teachers, doctors, and nurses continue to provide services, and early in the year Ethiopia sent to Cuba for education 141 children orphaned in the Ethiopian-Somali wars. With little success, Ethiopia continued to prod the United States and Western Europe to advance it increased levels of economic aid.

In an indication of their weakened military and political position, a merger was once again agreed to in January among the factions of the Eritrean secessionists in the belief that one command and one army would aid them in their struggle to attain independence from Ethiopia. Ethiopia, in an effort once again to finally quell the secessionists in Eritrea and Tigre, issued a proclamation declaring all citizens between 18 and 30 eligible for conscription and those with previous military training or retired and aged up to 50 active reservists (Addis Ababa domestic service, 10 May). The decree states that six months of military training will be followed by two years of active service. In addition, in midyear Ethiopia initiated Operation Red Star II, a military operation in Eritrea and Tigre meant to dislodge the secessionists. Cuban and Soviet military advisers and Soviet helicopter gunships (used so effectively in Afghanistan) were put to use in the campaign. Although both the Eritrean and Tigrean secessionists and the Ethiopians claimed deaths in the thousands, it is evident that the war is presently at a stalemate, but with the secessionists more and more on the defensive. In August, while the Ethiopian military operation was being launched, a Nicaraguan delegation in Addis Ababa, led by Ernesto Aloma of the Africa and Nonaligned Movement Department, re-affirmed Nicaragua's support of the Ethiopian revolution.

Peter Schwab
State University of New York
College at Purchase

Iran

Population. 42.5 million (July 1983)
Party. Tudeh Party (Hazb-e Tudeh-ye Iran)
Founded. 1941
Membership. In early 1983, membership was estimated to be some 2,000 hard-core activists and over 10,000 sympathizers. By late 1983, virtually all of the hard core had been arrested, executed, or were outside Iran.
First Secretary. Nureddin Kianuri
Politburo/Central Committee. No exhaustive list of Politburo or Central Committee members is available, but the following persons are known to hold (have held) leading positions: Mohammad Ahmadi (Central Committee, in Europe), Mohammad Ali Amu'i (Politburo), Gagig Avanesian (Central Committee), Manuchehr Behzadi (Central Committee, Politburo, former editor of *Mardom*), Anushirvan Ebrahimi (Central Committee, Politburo), Ali Galavish (Central Committee), Shahrokh Jahangiri (Central Committee, candidate), Ali Khavari (Central Committee, in Europe), Nureddin Kianuri, Farajollah Mizani (Politburo), Raf'at Mohammadzadeh (Central Committee, Politburo), Gholamhassan Qa'empanah (Central Committee), Asef Ramazandideh (Central Committee), Ahmad Ali Rasadi (Central Committee), Reza Shaltuki (Central Committee), Ehsan Tabari (Central Committee, chief ideologist), Kiumars Zarshenas (Central Committee)
Status. Proscribed (4 May 1983)
Last Congress. 1965
Last Election. 1980, 3 percent, no representation
Auxiliary Organizations. Women's, labor and youth organizations existed between 1979 and 1983; now defunct
Publications. *Mardom* (daily), its supplements, *Donya* (weekly); all banned in 1982; *Rah-e Tudeh*, a new organ, is being published in West Berlin.

The year 1983 saw the virtual annihilation of the Tudeh Party. In mid-year 1981, the party enjoyed more strength and influence than it had since the early 1950s. Less than two years later, in early 1983, Ayatollah Ruholla Khomeini's Islamic revolutionary government turned on the Tudehis with a vengeance, arresting large seg-ments of the leadership and followers, executing a number of them, and rendering the party politically impotent.

The communist movement in Iran has had a checkered history. The roots of communism in Iran date to the Red Army's invasion of parts of the Caspian littoral in 1917–1918 and the short-lived Gilan Republic of 1920–1921 in the same area. Throughout the 1930s, the illegal Communist Party of Iran (Hezb-e Komunist-e Iran) operated clandestinely. Following the Soviet occupation of northern Iran in 1941, the movement reappeared as the Tudeh Party, or the "party of the masses." This regenerated group increased in strength until in 1944 the party claimed a membership of 25,000. Under Soviet aegis, independent and pro-Soviet republics were created in Azerbaijan and Kurdistan. At this time, the Tudeh Party was represented by three cabinet members in the Tehran government. With the pullout of Soviet troops in 1946 and the collapse of these republics, the power of the Tudeh Party began to decline. In February 1949, the Pahlavi government formally outlawed the Tudeh Party. During the oil crisis of 1951–1953, the party's strength again rose, and it supported Prime Minister Mohammad Mossadegh's National Front government. The pro-royalist coup of August 1953 ended not only the Mossadegh regime, but also the growing influence of the Tudeh Party. From 1953 until 1979, the Tudeh Party was centered in East Germany. Its leaders there consisted of exiled party figures, such as Dr. Iraj Eskandari, longtime party secretary.

The events of late 1978 and early 1979 that deposed the Pahlavi dynasty also led to the Tudeh Party's return to Iran. After 26 years in exile, the party returned as the only communist organization recognized and allowed to operate openly by the new Islamic Republic.

From 1980 on, the party, under the leadership of a new general secretary, Nureddin Kianuri, consistently supported the Islamic revolution and Ayatollah Khomeini, but nevertheless was forced to run a gauntlet of political ups and downs. The organization was legal, but its operations remained semiclandestine. Its Tehran headquarters were occupied by Hezbollahi religious extremists, and the party held no rallies or demonstrations. It seemed hesitant to anger the Islamic masses, who were anticommunist and anti-Russian for religious and historical reasons. Rather, it preferred to gain strength by infiltrating the ruling Islamic Republican Party. In July 1981, Ayatollah Mohammad Beheshti supposedly negotiated with the Tudehis and promised to appoint three pro-communist ministers in return for Soviet support. By August, there were said to be three communist ministers in the cabinet: the defense minister, the executive minister, and the minister for planning and budget. The Tudeh Party also had its problems. Khomeini said that communism was as bad as Western capitalism, prevented a Tudeh delegation from attending a party congress in Moscow, banned publication of the Tudeh's newspaper from June until September 1981, and declared Tudeh officials ineligible as candidates for the Majles. In spite of this, the Tudeh Party was in the strongest position it had known since the early 1950s.

In November 1981, Prime Minister Mir Hossein Musavi declared that members of the Tudeh Party and its ally, the majority faction of the Fedayin-e Khalq, had infiltrated the Revolutionary Guards and other fundamentalist organizations and warned that all infiltrators would be executed. At the end of November 1981, the Tudeh publication *Payam-e Mardom* was again banned. In March 1983, *Ettela'at*, the official Iranian newspaper, implied that the Tudeh Party was among those working against the interests of the Islamic Republic.

In August 1982, the Islamic government turned against a small group called the Union of Communists in Iran (Tashkilat-e Ettehadiye-ye Komunistha-ye Iran) after the group supposedly attacked a small city in Mazanderan. Revolutionary Guards counterattacked and arrested or killed more than a hundred members, including the entire leadership, and seized all equipment. This breakaway group no longer had any connection with the Tudeh Party; the fact that it called itself communist, however, was bound to have repercussions for the Tudehis. At about the same time, Khomeini learned that the communists were planning to foment several peasant revolts. The ayatollah moved immediately, banning all Tudeh publications and replacing Islamic government officials known to have communist leanings.

On 7 February, the Iranian Azadegan émigré press in Paris reported that the Tudeh leader Nureddin Kianuri and several others had been arrested two days earlier. The following day, *Ettela'at* announced the arrest of a number of persons on charges of spying for the Soviet KGB, and Interior Minister Ali Akbar Nateq-Nuri confirmed it (*FBIS*, 7 and 9 February). On 17 February, Prosecutor General Hoj. Musavi Tabrizi stated that the spies had made clear confessions. A Paris-based Iranian émigré newspaper, *Iran-e Azad* (26 February) also noted the arrest of some thirty Tudehis, including a number of officers in the Iranian military, but also added that both the

Iranian and Soviet governments stressed that this would have no impact on relations between the two nations.

Officially the Islamic government claimed there were three reasons for arresting the Tudeh members: (1) spying for the KGB, (2) forging passports, and (3) forging birth certificates (*Jomhuri-ye Eslami*, 15 March). In fact, there were probably three immediate causes for the government's move against the Tudeh Party. The party's position on the Iran-Iraq war, favoring cessation of hostilities and no invasion of Iraq (a position identical with that of the Soviet Union) angered the government. Second, in 1982 a Tehran-based Soviet diplomat, Vladimir Kuzich-kin, defected to the United Kingdom. His position while in Tehran had been liaison with the Tudeh Party. It is believed that information from him was "leaked" to the Iranian regime (*Soviet Analyst*, London, 22 June). Finally, Khomeini's government has two distinct factions, the "imamis" and the "hojjatiyehs." The attempt to crush the Tudeh Party must be seen as a victory for the "hojjatiyehs," conservative, traditional, anti-Marxist clergymen (ibid., 1 June).

A large amount of protest was quickly forthcoming from Tudeh members outside Iran, from the Soviet press, and from other fraternal parties around the world. It seemed to have no effect on the Iranian authorities, however. Instead, the government continued its prosecution, finding incriminating documents and weapons and declaring the Tudeh's intent to overthrow the Islamic regime (*FBIS*, 2 May).

In early May, interviews with Kianuri and other Tudeh Central Committee members were broadcast on Iranian domestic television (ibid., 2–3 May). Although denouncing the interviews and claiming the confessions had been extracted by torture, the *Intercontinental Press* (13 June) stated the following concerning the Kianuri interview: "Nureddin Kianuri, first secretary of the Tudeh Party Central Committee, testified, as did all the other prisoners, of being a 'Soviet spy' and traitor to the revolution. He said that 'due to the link between our party and the Communist Party of the Soviet Union...we went astray. Our activities in the political arena changed on occasion to espionage activities and hence treachery against the Islamic Republic.'

"He 'endorsed' the official government slogan 'Neither East Nor West,' and said the Iranian masses 'must avoid any contact with foreign powers or countries, be they Eastern or Western, the American or the Soviet superpower.'

"Kianuri said his party committed a crime because 'instead of dissolving we increased our membership and strenthened it,' including having members who were soldiers. He also claimed the party was stockpiling arms.

"He concluded with a message to young Tudeh Party leaders that 'no leftist trend should infiltrate into Iran, as it means affiliation to foreigners, to aliens. It is the mother of all treason and treachery.'"

On 4 May, Iran expelled eighteen Soviet diplomats for "interference in internal affairs and setting up links with mercenaries and traitors" (*WP*, 5 May). At the same time the Iranian regime officially dissolved and outlawed the Tudeh Party. Party members were ordered to turn themselves in by 15 June. On 10 May, the commander of the Islamic Revolutionary Guard Corps, Mohsen Reza'i, said more than a thousand Tudehis had been arrested (*FBIS*, 11 May). He also maintained that the roundup of Tudehis was a complete success and that no important leaders had escaped. The following week, the Iranian government declared that 1,500 party members would soon go on trial (*Radio Liberty Research*, 19 May).

A number of reports of brutal torture of Tudehis appeared in the communist press (*New Age*, New Delhi, 15 May) and the media, for example, Radio Moscow (*FBIS*, 22 June). On 7 June, a clandestine radio station carried a statement by a so-called foreign-based committee of the Tudeh Party, presumably based in East Berlin as in the pre-1979 period. The statement decried the authorities' treatment of the Tudeh Party and the torture of its members (ibid., 9 June). Radio Iran (clandestine) on 9 June reported the first death of a Tudehi in prison (ibid., 10 June).

As the summer progressed, an Iranian prosecutor said that the government had learned that the Tudeh Party had important contacts with the German Democratic Republic (GDR) and with Babrak Karmal's Afghan regime (ibid., 16 June). On 21 June, the *Daily Telegraph* (London) announced a report from Tehran that Nureddin Kianuri had been executed in Evin Prison. Radio Tehran reported that 4,000 people had been arrested for having links to the former Tudeh Party, among them a sizable number of army officers and air force pilots (*FBIS*, 27 June). On 3 July, the Tudeh External Committee (possibly based in the GDR) issued an appeal for the cessation of persecution of the Tudeh Party (*New Age*, 3 July). The clandestine radio Seda-ye Iran reported that the Khomeini regime's minister of health was on the list of those with ties to the Tudeh Party.

On 22 July, Iranian minister of foreign affairs Ali Akbar Vellayati said, "We have to separate the problem of the Tudeh from our relations with Moscow. We have to live in friendship and refrain from interfering in each other's domestic affairs." (*CMS*, 22 July.)

By midsummer, the Islamic Republican Party had become the only political force in Iran. The Mojahedin-e Khalq, which had led the armed struggle against Khomeini, was now in disarray. Hundreds of its members were executed, others are in jail or in hiding. In Paris, the leftist National Council of Resistance, headed by Massoud Rajavi, was torn by differences between its members. The Kurdish Democratic Party was isolated in a council whose majority supports a new centralized revolutionary power in Tehran. (Ibid.)

On 27 July, *Pravda* reported that one week after the arrest of Kianuri in February, members of the Tudeh Party and their allies in the Fedayin-e Khalq went underground. Despite the arrests of thousands of comrades, the party claimed to be continuing its activities.

An interview with a Mrs. Ruhi, wife of a Tudehi in hiding in Iran, revealed that the area of Kurdistan controlled by the Komeleh Party is the only real refuge for Tudehis still in Iran. She also spoke of the earlier cooperation between the Tudehis and Khomeini, and how they had aided in his coming to power (*FBIS*, 28 July).

On 30 July, the prosecutor of the Islamic Revolution's Court of the Armed Forces said that the former commander of the Iranian navy, Capt. Bahram Afzali, would be tried along with other military members of the Tudeh Party (ibid., 1 August).

A Tudeh member-in-exile told of funds received from sources in Eastern Europe, especially Bulgaria, the GDR, and the Soviet Union. The money was to be used to bribe Islamic officials to save crucially important Tudeh leaders (ibid., 5 August).

An interview with Kianuri was broadcast over Iranian television on 27 August—whether live or recorded is unknown. It was meant to show that he was still alive and to elaborate on his confession and crimes of the Tudeh Party (ibid., 1 September). In a similar interview, Manuchehr Behzadi, editor of the former Tudeh daily, *Mardom*, said that Tudeh's objectives were to mislead the peasants on land reform, agitate among youth, defend Soviet policies, widen internal rifts within the clergy, and prepare for the eventual toppling of the Islamic regime (ibid., 8 September).

According to a reliable diplomatic source in Kabul, on 14 September a bomb exploded in a building near the Soviet Embassy in Kabul. The building was occupied by members of the Tudeh Party who had fled to Afghanistan. Several of them were killed or wounded. (Ibid., 23 September.)

An article in the September issue of *African Communist* (London) discussed the survival and continuance of the Tudeh Party. It claimed preparations for the Eighteenth Plenum of the Tudeh were well under way. It also noted that a new weekly newspaper, *Rah-e Tudeh* (Way of the people), is being published in West Berlin and regularly smuggled into Iran.

On 3 October, another television interview was conducted with Tudeh leaders. Along with others, Kianuri again confirmed that he was still alive and that his confessions were true (*FBIS*, 4 October).

The clandestine radio Seda-ye Iran reported on 13 October that the External Committee of the Tudeh Party, headed by Ali Khavari, had expelled all 8,500 members of the Tudeh Party in Iran. This was certainly an unprecedented event (ibid., 14 October). On 15 October, the clandestine radio Free Voice of Iran announced that a new party, the Iranian Communist Party, had been set up to succeed the Tudeh Party of Iran. This party was also served by another clandestine radio station, the Voice of the Iranian Communist Party (ibid., 17 October). The 2 November issue of *Rudé právo* (Prague) quoted *Rah-e Tudeh* in describing the organization of the new party.

Iranian president Sayed Ali Khamene'i discussed this "revival" of the Tudeh Party in the GDR with the GDR's new ambassador to Iran on 6 November (*FBIS*, 9 November).

On 6 December, the trial of the leaders of the Tudeh Party began (*Neues Deutschland*, 7 December). At the end of December, as of the writing of this article, the final outcome of the trial is still unknown.

Joseph D. Dwyer
Hoover Institution

Iraq

Population. 14.5 million
Party. Iraqi Communist Party (ICP)
Founded. 1934
Membership. 2,000 (estimate)
First Secretary. Aziz Muhammad
Status. Legal, but repressed
Last Congress. Third, 4–6 May 1976
Last Election. June 1980; ICP prohibited from participating
Auxiliary Organizations. No information
Publications. *Tariq al-Sha'b* (People's road), clandestine

Nearly 50 years ago, half a dozen tiny groups banded together to form the Association Against Imperialism, the nucleus of the ICP. The party has for brief periods enjoyed great power, e.g., in the mid-1940s and in the years 1958–1960. Each of those eras was followed by great repression, and the very modest influence the party had in the 1970s has also been followed by years in the wilderness. They have not yet come to an end.

The activities of the ICP in 1983 can be characterized as continuity in leadership and dogged opposition to the Ba'thist regime in Baghdad. First Secretary Aziz Muhammad completed twenty years in office. Other long-timers continue in top offices; 72-year-old Zaki Khayri, a member of the Association Against Imperialism and a Politburo member since 1958, represented the ICP at the Karl Marx celebrations in East Germany in April 1983. Amir Abdallah, active in the party since the early 1950s, will complete twenty years on the Central Committee in 1984.

As it has for the past several years, the ICP continues to work for the downfall of the Ba'thist regime. Party headquarters are located in a remote area of the north, in that part of the country populated by Kurds. The ICP is allied with two Kurdish organizations in conducting guerrilla warfare against government positions in the area. However, the factionalism that characterizes

Kurdish politics hampers antiregime efforts. The Democratic National Front (DNF), formed in 1980 by the Kurdish Democratic Party/Iraq (DPK/I) and headed by sons of the late Mulla Mustafa Barzani continues to function, along with the United Socialist Party of Kurdistan and the ICP. There is also a DPK/Iran, engaged in fighting the Khomeini regime, and a tame, pro-Baghdad DPK. In the course of 1983, another opposition group, the Patriotic Union of Kurdistan (PUK), which has long fought the DPK/I and its allies, moved progressively closer to Baghdad. The central government, forced by the demands of war with Iran to draw on forces previously used for security in Kurdish areas, reverted to the time-honored custom of manipulating Kurdish rivalries. The PUK helped the DPK/Iran defend the bases in northeastern Iraq from which the latter supported anti-Khomeini activities against an Iranian attack in July. For this and its other acts of anti-DNF militancy, the Ba'thist regime came to terms with the PUK in December, promising to give it help "to protect Kurdistan against foreign enemies" (*NYT*, 4 January 1984). In Baghdad's view, those foreign enemies include the members of the DNF.

This agreement came at the end of a year of heavy loss and little success for the ICP and its associates. Although substantial areas of northern Iraq remain outside effective government control—and the regime is hard pressed by its inability to end the war with Iran—the scanty evidence available indicates that the DNF controlled less territory at the end of 1983 than a year earlier. The DPK/I did enjoy some success as a part of the Iranian-led forces that took some Iraqi territory in the Rayat–Hajji Umran area, but this was a temporary achievement. Improvement in relations between Baghdad and Moscow, signaled by increases in shipments of military supplies in early 1983 and an exchange of friendly messages on the eleventh anniversary of the Friendship Treaty in April (*World Affairs Report* 13, no. 2, p. 192), brought no betterment of the ICP's political position or in the lot of communists in Iraq.

ICP headquarters, apparently located with those of the DNF, fell to PUK forces on 1 May (Voice of Iraqi Kurdistan, 29 May; *FBIS*, 31 May). ICP losses were severe. The attack on "the headquarters of our party's CC Political Bureau. . .led to the loss of about 120 revolutionary fighters: more than 50 were killed, others were wounded, taken prisoner or disappeared without trace. The Voice of the Iraqi People, our party's radio station, is no longer on the air, and a number of ICP medical and information centres were destroyed." (*WMR*, August.) At the end of May, by agreement with the government in Baghdad, large Turkish forces crossed the border into Iraq in an area about 100 kilometers north of Mosul and inflicted substantial damage to the DNF's forces. Turkish spokesmen claimed that 1,500 to 2,000 "separatist adventurers" were caught. (*Gunes*, Istanbul, 30 May; *FBIS*, 1 June.) The DNF had chosen the area near the Turkish border for a safe haven, as far from the reach of Baghdad's troops as possible. But the Turkish government is concerned about the actual or potential effect of Kurdish insurgency in Iraq on its own Kurdish population. For its part, Baghdad was worried that its sole means of exporting oil—a pipeline along the edge of the Kurdish area and thence through Turkey to the Mediterranean—might be interdicted.

Although in February sixteen Iraqi opposition groups joined the DPK/I and the ICP in agreeing to establish a national front to overthrow the Ba'thist regime, true unity in the form of an effective front continues to elude the ICP. In addition to the Kurdish factions noted above, a major opposition organization, the Supreme Council of Islamic Revolution in Iraq (also known as al-Da'wah, or the Call), has rejected cooperation with communists. Its leaders, Iraqi Shi'ite Muslims, live in Iran, where they are building an organization dedicated to bringing Islamic government to Iraq. The following is a typical expression of the council's philosophy, which excludes communism: "We call on our brothers, the Muslim Kurdish people, to further adhere to their Islamic belief. . .and to coalesce with the Islamic Revolution" (Tehran international service, 21 March; *FBIS*, 24 March). Al-Da'wah, unlike the ICP, has some capacity to carry out attacks in Baghdad. Cumulatively these opposition forces do not affect Baghdad's control; Iranian military pressure is far more formidable.

Front Organizations. As a clandestine party fighting for the overthrow of the Ba'thist regime, the ICP directs its organizational efforts outside its own ranks chiefly toward aiding allies in the DNF. There are minor cooperative efforts elsewhere, such as the work of "democratic fighters, among them six of our (ICP) comrades" who were executed in Babylon during the first half of the year (*WMR*, August). Iraq's mass, or people's, organizations are exclusively in the hands of Ba'thists.

International Views. Externally, the ICP depended heavily on Syria in 1983 for material support in its struggle. First Secretary Aziz Muhammad was twice received by Syrian President Hafiz al-Assad in 1983, once in January and a second time after the conference of Arab Communist and Workers' Parties that was held in Damascus in June. On the latter occasion, he and Syrian communist leader Khalid Bakhdash, as members of a delegation representing the parties, praised Assad's efforts to redress the effects of Israel's 1982 invasion of Lebanon and noted that "the forces of liberation and progress in the region and the world must stand alongside Syria" (Radio Damascus, 30 June; *FBIS*, 1 July).

Through its reliance on Syria (and also through its ties with the DPK/I), the ICP finds itself linked to a vigorously anticommunist Iran. Syria, Iran, and Libya called for the overthrow of Saddam Husayn's regime in Baghdad in a statement issued on 23 January. Two weeks later, the Khomeini regime cracked down on the Tudeh Party, the Iranian communist party, arresting hundreds including much of the leadership. The

Tehran government has since extracted public confessions of spying for the USSR and of other anti–Islamic Republic activities from those arrested and has put them on trial. These actions have not changed the ICP's position. It and the Syrian Communist Party "strongly condemned the war which the dictatorship in Baghdad is waging against Iran" (Syrian Arab News Agency, 25 April; *FBIS*, 26 April).

Regionally, the ICP supported the Syrian position on Lebanon and strongly opposed U.S. moves with regard to the Persian Gulf. The ICP participated in the midyear meeting of communist and workers' parties in Arab countries, which regarded the 17 May Israeli-Lebanese agreement as nothing more than a continuation of the Camp David approach and not the comprehensive agreement that is needed (Radio Damascus, 6 June; *FBIS*, 8 June). The Arab parties' statement echoed that of the Syrian and Iraqi parties in April, which characterized "calls for a simultaneous withdrawal of the Israeli forces and the Syrian Arab forces" as "an excuse to prolong the Israeli occupation of Lebanon" (Syrian Arab News Agency, 25 April; *FBIS*, 26 April). Alternate Central Committee member Hamid Majid Musa denounced U.S. efforts to build military forces capable of operating effectively in the Persian Gulf and Red Sea areas in an article on the U.S. Central Command, which he said is "associated with the sharply increased danger of imperialist invasions...of Southwest Asia" (*WMR*, July).

John F. Devlin
Swarthmore, Pennsylvania

Israel

Population. Israelis: 4.06 million; Palestinians: 650,000 in Israel proper, 850,000 in Israeli-occupied West Bank (including 100,000 in East Jerusalem), 450,000 in Israeli-occupied Gaza Strip, 2 million outside boundaries of pre-1948 Palestine

Party. Communist Party of Israel (CPI); also called New Communist List (Rashima Kommunistit Hadasha; RAKAH)

Founded. 1922 (with a split in 1965)

Membership. 1,500 (estimate)

Secretary General. Meir Vilner (member of the Knesset [parliament])

Politburo. 9 members: David Burnstein, Benjamin Gonen, Wolf Erlich, Emile Habibi, David Khenin, Ruth Lublitz, Emile Tu'ma, Tawfiq Tubi (deputy secretary general and member of the Knesset), Meir Vilner; 4 alternates

Secretariat. 7 members: Yehoshua Irge (deceased in 1983), Zahi Kharkabi, Saliba Khamis, David Khenin, Jamal Musa, Tawfiq Tubi, Meir Vilner

Central Committee. 31 members; 5 candidates

Status. Legal

Last Congress. Nineteenth, 11–14 February 1981, in Haifa

Last Election. 1981, 3.4 percent of the vote (with Democratic Front for Peace and Equality allies), 4 seats (3 for the CPI and one for a Front partner, the Black Panthers)

Auxiliary Organizations. Young Communist League (Banki), Young Pioneers

Publications. *Al-Ittihad, Zo Ha-Derekh, al-Jadid*

The communist movement in Palestine began in 1920. Two years later, a Palestine Communist Party (Palestinische kommunistische Partei; PKP) was established; it joined the Comintern in 1924. Following the periodic appearance of factional divisions, the PKP split along ethnic lines in 1943. In October 1948, with the new state of Israel gaining control of most of Palestine, both groups reunited to form the Israeli Communist Party (Miflaga Kommunistit Isra'elit; MAKI).

The movement split again in 1965, partly along ethnic lines. RAKAH—pro-Moscow, strongly anti-Zionist, and primarily (at least 75 percent) Arab in membership, though with many Jewish leaders—soon eclipsed the almost completely Jewish and increasingly moderate MAKI. The latter's disappearance by the late 1970s left RAKAH (a name that is still widely used) as the undisputed communist party in Israel and the successor to the pre-1965 communist organizations. With Arab nationalist parties not permitted, it serves mainly as an outlet for the grievances of the Arab minority. Almost all of the party's vote comes from the Arab population, in both local and national elections (the CPI-dominated Democratic Front for Peace and Equality [DFPE] got 50 percent of the Arab vote in 1977 and 37 percent in 1981). The party has dominated most Arab town councils since the 1970s.

Leadership and Party Organization. The organization of the CPI is typical of communist parties in general. The Congress normally meets at four-year intervals and chooses the members of the Central Committee and the Central Control Commission (whose members attend the plenary meetings of the Central Committee), as well as a Presidium and a Secretariat. There are also regional committees, local branches, and cells (the latter based both on residence and place of work).

Although at least 75 percent of the members of the party are Arabs, Jews predominate in the top party organs. In recent years, the Jewish secretary general has been balanced by an Arab deputy secretary general.

Domestic Party Affairs. The fourteenth plenary session of the Central Committee met in October 1982. Another plenary meeting took place in Haifa in June to consider the CPI's preparation for local elections scheduled for October. In the October local elections, the DFPE lost control of five Arab local councils to the Labor Alignment.

In March, for the first time, over 60 Jewish and Arab chairmen of town councils in Galilee (including Mayor Tawfiq Zayyad of Nazareth, a member of the CPI and one of the CPI deputies in the Knesset) met in an attempt to improve Arab-Jewish relations. They agreed to promote interethnic friendship and to meet again soon in Acre or Shfaram to work out plans for municipal cooperation on a departmental level. But one Jewish chairman walked out when Zayyad accused the government of anti-Arab racism, of establishing settlements on land expropriated from Arabs, and of discriminating against Arab local councils in the allocation of funds. (*Jerusalem Post*, international edition, 6–12 and 13–19 March.) Zayyad told his colleagues that new sewage projects and roads are important but that "unless we build a future for the two peoples in their common land, all these roads will go nowhere." He singled out the Ministry of Tourism's failure to promote Kafr Kanna—"Yes, the very site where Jesus performed the miracle of turning water into wine"—as an example of neglect of Arab communities. (Ibid., 20–26 March.)

The seventh annual celebration of the Day of the Land was observed on 31 March in Arab towns and villages, with much participation by CPI leaders. Palestine Liberation Organization (PLO) flags and slogans were widespread, resulting in several arrests, but the occasion was quieter than in previous years, allegedly because of restraint shown by CPI and other Arab leaders (ibid., 3–9 April).

Expropriation of Arab land remained a major concern of the Arab community and of the CPI in particular. One specific concern, which resulted in the holding of a conference of Israeli Arab leaders in Shfaram in February, related to the decision of the Ministry of the Interior to turn over 37,000 acres of Arab-owned land in Galilee to a new Jewish regional council (ibid., 27 February–5 March).

Another issue—evoking protests from a broader spectrum that included the CPI—related to proposals to provide greater children's allowances to families of soldiers, in effect discriminating against Arabs, who normally do not serve in the military (ibid., 27 March–2 April and 31 July–6 August). A related issue concerned university tuition policies that involved discounts for veterans and students from development (i.e.,

Jewish) towns (but not from poor Arab villages) and those (again, almost exclusively Jewish) from families to whom veterans' benefits are due (ibid., 8–14 May).

In November, Vilner introduced a motion in the Knesset denouncing the highly publicized (and widely condemned) proposal of a Jewish citizen of Upper Nazareth for the mass expulsion of Arabs from the region and eventually from the whole country (ibid., 6–12 and 13–19 November). In December, the DPFE delegation in the Knesset introduced a motion of no confidence on the issue of U.S.-Israeli cooperation.

With reference to the violence used against Arab demonstrators in Nazareth in September 1982, the fourteenth plenary session of the Central Committee (October 1982) condemned "the police terror" and called for a "judicial commission...to inquire into...the criminal actions" (al-Ittihad, Haifa, 22 October 1982; IB, January, p. 20).

Deputy Secretary General Tawfiq Tubi declared that the CPI "will support any initiative aimed to overthrow the government, disband the 10th Knesset, and hold new elections" (al-Ittihad, 19 June; IB, September, p. 13). The CPI deputies in the Knesset introduced a no-confidence motion in February. The Politburo issued a statement in August hailing Prime Minister Menachim Begin's decision to resign as evidence of the failure of his foreign and domestic policies and "a sign of a deepening crisis" and "massive disillusionment" (Tass, 29 August; FBIS, 30 August) but declared that only a new government could save the country from "war" and "fascism."

In an interview, Politburo member Wolf Erlich provided a broad statement of his views on Israeli politics and society. He argued that Israel —particularly since 1977, with the Begin government "pushing the interests of the bourgeoisie" more than did its Labor predecessors— "has now reached the stage of monopoly capitalism," with the change "to direct bourgeoisie rule...a political reflection of this economic power of the bourgeoisie." He attacked the unprecedented rate of inflation, foreign trade deficits and massive foreign debt, and the alleged decline of "civilian industry and civilian agriculture" and—expressing a common CPI theme —declared that the solution is to "Stop the militarization of the Israeli economy, stop war and make the economy serve production and not ag-

gression." He declared that the trade union organization, the Histadrut, which is also an employer, is "in most cases on the other side of the barricades" from the workers. (Wolf Erlich, "Zionism and the Nature of Israeli Society," Political Affairs, New York, September, pp. 13–19.)

Auxiliary and Front Organizations. The CPI dominates the DFPE, which includes two noncommunist partners, the Black Panthers (an Afro-Asian, or Oriental, Jewish group protesting discrimination by Jews of European origin) and the Arab Local Council Heads. The DFPE delegation in the Knesset includes one member of the Black Panthers, Charlie Biton; it previously (1977–1981) included a representative of the Arab Local Council Heads as well. The DFPE is also organized on the local level, particularly in Arab towns and villages. Speaking to a June plenary meeting, Tubi stressed "the need to strengthen the local sections of the Front...and called on all CPI and Youth Organization members to join forces with their Front allies" (al-Ittihad, 19 June; IB, September, p. 13).

The CPI sponsors the active Young Pioneers and the Israeli Committee Against the War in Lebanon and participates in the Democratic Women's Movement, the Israeli-USSR Friendship Movement, and the Israeli Association of Anti-Fascist Fighters and Victims of Nazism. In September, the last group protested against Yitzhak Shamir's accession as prime minister, pointing to evidence that he tried to form an alliance with Germany during World War II (Benny Morris, "Shamir Steps out of the Shadows," Jerusalem Post, international edition, 18–24 September).

International Views, Positions, and Activities. In December 1982, Vilner attended the sixtieth anniversary celebration of the USSR. While there, he met with leaders of the Palestine Communist Party (including its unnamed secretary general)—said to be the first such meeting— "in an atmosphere of deep friendship and unity of opinions" (IB, March, p. 28). An Israeli delegation (consisting of Gonen, Biton, and others, including some members of the Labor Alignment) also visited Bulgaria during the same month.

In January, Biton attended a luncheon in New

York with Hatem Husayni, PLO deputy observer at the United Nations.

In March, a delegation of the CPI Central Committee headed by Khenin visited Sofia as guests of the Bulgarian Central Committee. Talks were held with top Bulgarian party leaders and information exchanged on party activities.

In April, Vilner and Kharkabi attended the international scientific convention on "Karl Marx and Our Times—The Struggle for Peace and Social Advancement" in East Berlin and also met with top party and state officials of East Germany. Vilner and other CPI leaders also visited Prague, where they met with a PLO delegation headed by Yassir Arafat and discussed Middle Eastern and international developments. (For their joint statement, see *IB*, July, pp. 10–11.) Another CPI delegation visited Moscow, Kiev, and Leningrad in July as guests of the Soviet Committee for the Defense of Peace. Tubi headed a delegation to Bulgaria in November (BTA, Sofia, 24 November; *FBIS*, 1 December).

On the Arab-Israeli conflict, CPI spokesmen continued to call for full Israeli withdrawal from the occupied territories and for the establishment of a Palestinian state under PLO leadership alongside Israel. The party also called for the convening of an international conference, with Soviet and U.S. participation, in which the PLO will be "the sole legitimate representative of the Arab Palestinian people" (statement of CPI Politburo, Tass, 29 August; *FBIS*, 30 August). Tubi demanded an urgent debate on reports of brutality against Palestinians in the West Bank (*Jerusalem Post*, international edition, 2–8 January).

The CPI demanded withdrawal from Lebanon, condemned "the aggressive war...unleashed against Lebanon" and praised "the heroic resistance put up by the Lebanese and the Palestinians and the mounting popular resistance in Israel...itself." Vilner condemned the Israeli–Lebanese agreement, particularly the provision for an Israeli security zone in Lebanese territory when in fact it is "the Lebanese and Palestinian peoples who need such zones, which should be located in Israel." (*Al-Ittihad*, 19 June; *IB*, September, p. 13.) Vilner spoke in the Knesset of Palestinian prisoners in the Ansar camp who, he said, were not being treated as human beings. Israeli and Bulgarian communist leaders condemned "the new aggression being prepared by the Israeli government against Syria" (BTA, Sofia, 4 April; *FBIS*, 5 April).

The few CPI statements on the broader world situation were all supportive of Soviet positions. Addressing the plenary meeting in June, Tubi described "the international situation [as] marked by the general crisis of capitalism and the USA's imperialist line aimed at frustrating international détente and intensifying the arms race, something which calls for special vigilance on the part of the world's peace forces led by the Soviet Union and the socialist community" (*al-Ittihad*, 19 June; *IB*, September, p. 13). The plenary meeting praised the Soviet Union for "doing everything possible to prevent another war in the Middle East and to establish a just peace for the good of all the peoples in that region" (Tass, 14 June; *FBIS*, 15 June).

Other Marxist Groups. For information on the Israeli Socialist Organization and breakaway organizations, including the Revolutionary Communist League (RCL), see *YICA*, 1982, p. 29. An editorial in *Matzpen*, published by the RCL, in March expressed happiness that "the Palestinian movement remained united" after the meeting of the Palestine National Council in February and that the meeting had not succumbed to "pressures...from the imperialist powers, and from the Arab bourgeoisie" to accept "dubious compromises." Yet the editorial expressed concern over potentially dangerous "retreats," including an opening to a modified Reagan Plan, and called for a redoubling of "solidarity with the Palestinian struggle." (*Intercontinental Press*, 2 May.)

During 1983, the RCL called for the establishment of a network of elected workers' committees to protest the government's economic policies (Michel Warschawski, "Bitter Medicine for Israeli Economy," *Intercontinental Press*, 12 December, p. 721). (For an exposition of RCL positions, see Leila Khatib, "'Bring the Boys Home': 15,000 at Israeli Antiwar Festival," *Intercontinental Press*, 12 December, pp. 721–722, originally published in the RCL Arabic publication, *Sharara*, October–November. See also "In Grenada as in Beirut: U.S. Go Home: Declaration of the LCR [RCL]," *Intercontinental Press*, 28 November, originally published in *Matzpen*.)

A notable development during 1983 was the appointment by the PLO of Ilan Halevi, an Israeli Jew who was active in the Israeli Socialist Organization during the mid-1960s, as its representative at the Socialist International meeting in Lisbon (*NYT*, 13 April).

The Sheli Party has represented the non-Marxist, dovish Left since the late 1970s. It is now divided into two groups: the Histadrut faction, which hopes to cooperate with elements of the Labor Alignment, and the Sheli-Alternativa, which has announced that it hopes to appeal to the Israeli Arab population and to work with the DFPE. (*New Outlook*, June/July, p. 50.)

The United Workers' Party (Mapam), a component of the Labor Alignment, has Marxist origins but no longer represents the far left. However, it has retained friendly ties with the Romanian Communist Party, as demonstrated by the "warm comradely greetings" extended by Romanian Politburo member Ion Coman in an address to the Mapam congress in June in Tel Aviv (Agerpress, Bucharest, 24 June; *FBIS*, 27 June).

Biography. *Felicia Langer.* Felicia Langer is a well-known member of the CPI, but—as a member of the Central Control Commission since 1972—is hardly among the inner circle of party leaders. Her importance is not the result of party activities per se but of her role as a capable, highly dedicated lawyer defending Palestinians accused of nationalist activity or striving to prevent their land from being expropriated.

Langer was born into a Jewish family in Poland in 1932. Her father was quite wealthy and a Zionist. During World War II, the now impoverished family took refuge in the USSR, and Langer says that she was deeply influenced by her stay there. Returning to Poland in 1945, she was married at eighteen years of age to another former Jewish refugee to the USSR who had joined the communist party. The couple emigrated to Israel in 1950 in order to join her mother, not because either was a Zionist. She worked in a factory at first and later as a clerk, and she and her husband knew considerable economic hardship until he received his indemnity from West Germany. (He is now a businessman engaged in trade with Eastern European countries.) Soon after arriving in Israel, they searched for and joined the communist party, hoping to find a link to a country in which they otherwise felt lost.

She eventually entered the Tel Aviv branch of the Hebrew University and became a lawyer in 1965. But her involvement in communist activities made it difficult for her to get a job; instead, she opened an office and began a career of helping underdogs, including Arabs. But it was not until 1967—when, as she relates, she was shocked by her fellow Israelis' "hysteria" and felt agony over the Arabs' suffering—that she opened an office in Jerusalem and came to specialize in helping the people in the occupied territories, and sometimes dissident Israelis. She has become well known in leftist and anti-Zionist circles in the Western world. She is the author of four books—translated into several languages— that relate a picture, based on the cases she has been involved in, of an occupation that is characterized by torture, expropriation, destruction of homes, and expulsion. (Sources: Felicia Langer, *With My Own Eyes*, London, 1974; idem, *These Are My Brothers*, London, 1970; "Felicia Langer: With Her Own Eyes" (interview), *MERIP Reports*, May 1977, pp. 14–16; and Joan Borsten, "A Lawyer Some Call 'Traitor,'" *Jerusalem Post*, international edition, 10–16 April 1983.)

PALESTINE COMMUNIST PARTY

Party. Palestine Communist Party (al-Hizb al-Shuyu'i al-Filastini; PCP)
Founded. 1982
Membership. 200 (estimate)
Secretary General. Not announced
Politburo. (Incomplete) Sulayman al-Najjab, Na'im Abbas Ashhab
Secretariat. No information available
Central Committee. (Incomplete) Dhamin Awdah, Mahir al-Sharif, Sulayman al-Nashshab
Status. Proscribed in Israeli-occupied areas and in most Arab countries
Last Congress. First, 1982
Last Election. Not applicable
Auxiliary Organizations. Unknown
Publications. *Al-Watan* (The homeland)

Several small communist groups have arisen among Palestinians, both inside and outside the territories now under Israeli occupation. A PCP leader has traced its lineage to several former organizations, including a post-1949 remnant in the Gaza Strip of the League for National Liberation (the Arab faction that had split off from the original Palestine Communist Party in 1943), which became the Gaza Strip Palestinian Communist Party in 1953. Other Palestinians joined communist parties in the various Arab countries in which they resided, particularly the Communist Party of Jordan (CPJ). In 1974, the section of the CPJ in the West Bank became the West Bank Communist Organization, with the goal of evolving into a separate party; with the addition of members from the Gaza Strip, the group became the West Bank and Gaza Strip Palestinian Communist Organization. Also, members of the CPJ in Lebanon became the Palestinian Communist Organization (PCO) in Lebanon. (Naim Ashhab, "Firm Principles, Flexible Tactics," *WMR*, February, pp. 29–30.) With the approval of the CPJ, the formation of a separate PCP was announced in February 1982, with the new party designed to include communists in the Gaza Strip and the West Bank, members of the PCO in Lebanon, and all Palestinian members of the CPJ except for those living in Jordan, i.e., the East Bank. (Galia Golan, "The Palestinian Communist Party," in *The Soviet Union and the Middle East*, vol. 7, Jerusalem: Soviet Union and East European Research Centre, Hebrew University, 1983.)

Leadership and Party Organization. Little is known about the organization of the PCP. It was announced that the First Congress, held in 1982, chose a secretary general, but his name was not mentioned. The PCP also has a Politburo, a Secretariat, and a Central Committee, all standard features of communist parties. It is not known whether other former Palestinian leaders of the CPJ hold positions in the PCP (see profiles on Jordan in earlier editions of *YICA*).

Domestic Party Affairs. Communist activity is banned in Israeli-occupied territories. Even CPI publications cannot be distributed there. *Al-Watan* is distributed clandestinely.

The PCP's membership is presumably no more than a few hundred. The average age of members is said not to be more than 24 years, and 45 percent of them are workers (Ashhab, "Firm Principles," *WMR*, February, p. 28). PCP members are said to be unique among those in "Palestinian political organizations...[in] that the main basis of their activities lies in the occupied territories...[into which] the center of gravity in the liberation battle increasingly moves" (ibid., p. 29).

Relations with Other Palestinian Groups. The communists have been peripheral to the overall Palestinian movement. Aside from such Marxist groups as the Popular Front for the Liberation of Palestine (PFLP) and the Popular Democratic Front for the Liberation of Palestine (PDFLP) (which are minority factions represented in the PLO), communist representation on PLO organs has been minimal. The Palestine National Front (PNF), organized in 1973 with CPJ participation, gained representation in the PLO and provided one minor communist component for the organization. The National Guidance Committee, set up in the West Bank in the late 1970s, failed to come under communist influence. Attempts to place other communists on the PLO Executive Committee in 1981 were unsuccessful (Golan, "The Palestine Communist Party"). (For further information on the PNF and other attempts to establish communist-led resistance groups, see John W. Amos II, *Palestinian Resistance: Organization of a Nationalist Movement*, New York: Pergamon Press, 1980, pp. 113–28.) It has been suggested that the formation of the PCP is partly designed to gain communist representation in PLO organs.

Not only has the PLO been dominated by Yassir Arafat's essentially conservative Fatah, but all indications point to overwhelming support for him in the occupied territories. A poll conducted in the West Bank during 1983 showed that Arafat had the backing of 93.4 percent of the population (*al-Fajr*, Jerusalem, 23 October; *FBIS*, 26 October). The former deputy mayor of Bethlehem, George Hazboun, described as the only leftist city council member and as "associated with" the PCP, was dismissed from his position in January (George Hazboun, "Palestinian Communism and the National Movement," *MERIP Reports*, June, p. 9). The PCP has recently been said to be the second strongest force (far behind Fatah) in the occupied territories, followed by the PFLP and the PDFLP (Sarah Graham-Brown, "Report from the Occupied Territories," *MERIP Reports*, June, p. 5).

International Views, Positions, and Activities. Leaders of the PCP and the Egyptian Communist Party met in September 1982 and issued a joint statement (for excerpts, see profile on Egypt). At the invitation of the Central Committee of the Cypriot party (AKEL), a PCP delegation headed by Na'im Ashhab traveled to Cyprus in November. In a joint communiqué issued at the end of the visit, Ashhab "expressed the full support and solidarity of the party (PCP) and Palestinian people with the struggle of AKEL and the people of Cyprus" to solve the Cyprus problem on the basis of relevant U.N. resolutions, to secure the independence, sovereignty, territorial integrity, and nonalignment of Cyprus, as well as the withdrawal of Turkish occupation troops, the liquidation of foreign military bases, and the demilitarization of the island (*IB*, February).

Al-Najjab attended the sixtieth anniversary celebration of the USSR in December 1982. (The PLO was represented by Mahmud Abbas of the Executive Committee.) While in Moscow, al-Najjab participated with Meir Vilner in a press conference on 23 December 1982 and issued a joint declaration said to have been adopted during a recent meeting between delegations of the two parties, the first ever held. Vilner and the unnamed secretary general of the PCP headed their respective delegations (ibid., March, p. 28).

Ashhab met with Abdullah al-Ahmar, assistant secretary general of the (Syrian) Ba'th Party to discuss recent developments in the area in January. Leaders of the PCP and the Syrian Communist Party convened at Damascus in August to discuss regional developments.

The PCP was represented by al-Najjab and al-Sharif at the international scientific convention in East Berlin on "Karl Marx and Our Time—The Struggle for Peace and Social Advancement" in April. (The PLO was represented by Abu Hatim of the Palestine National Council.) Representatives of the PCP participated in a meeting of twelve Arab communist and workers' parties in June (see profile on Egypt for a summary of the joint statement).

The PCP issued some strong statements on Israel during 1983. An "appeal" in July condemned "the bloody attack perpetrated by herds of Zionist settlers, dressed like the...Ku Klux Klan, against al-Khalil (Hebron) University" as "a clear example of the intensification of terror and murder" and as a part of "official policy" (*IB*,

October p. 25). The appeal further stated that policy is designed to force the Palestinian people "to leave their homeland" and that "it enjoys the open blessing of Washington." The passivity of "reactionary Arab regimes" was also blamed for the actions of "the criminal rulers of Israel, and behind them the rulers of Washington" (ibid.). The joint declaration of the PCP and the CPI declared that "the Israeli-U.S. aggression in Lebanon is a result of the Camp David Accords and strategic cooperation between Israel and the United States" and called for the withdrawal of "the aggressive forces" and an end to U.S. intervention (Tass, Moscow, 23 December 1982; *FBIS*, 28 December 1982).

The PCP calls for Israel's withdrawal from all occupied territories, removal of all Israeli settlements, self-determination for the Palestinians, settlement of the Palestinian refugee problem in accordance with U.N. resolutions, and the right of all states (including Israel and a Palestinian state in the West Bank and the Gaza Strip) to a secure existence (*IB*, March pp. 29–30).

Writing in the *World Marxist Review* (February, pp. 28–34), Ashhab analyzed the consistency of the Palestinian communists' "realistic" approach to the Palestinian problem, opposing "the imperialist-encouraged Zionist colonization" but also accepting a new demographic situation in 1947 that called for separate Jewish and Arab states. He blamed "the forces of imperialism, Zionism and local Arab reaction" for the failure of "the optimal solution" at that time. He condemned two current extremes—the rejectionist tendency that insists on the "liberation of the whole of Palestine" and the rejection of Palestinian self-determination and independence that is exemplified by the Reagan plan.

PCP statements on broader international questions closely paralleled Soviet positions. The joint PCP-CPI statement of December 1982 condemned the United States' "global policy directed against the freedom of peoples" and "the American strategy of aggression" and praised the "great achievements" of the USSR and its "Leninist peace policy"; the statement supported Soviet positions in Poland and Afghanistan (*IB*, March, p. 30).

Glenn E. Perry
Indiana State University

Jordan

Population. 3.4 million, including 850,000 in West Bank and East Jerusalem (precise figures not available from year to year)
Party. Communist Party of Jordan (al-Hizb al-Shuyu'i al-Urdunni; CPJ)
Founded. 1951
Membership. 200 (estimate)
Secretary General. Faik (Faiq) Warrad (for a list of other party leaders, see *YICA*, 1979, p. 413)
Status. Proscribed
Last Congress. Unknown
Last Election. 1967; CPJ held no seats
Auxiliary Organizations. Palestine National Front (PNF)
Publications. *Al-Jamahir, al-Haqiqah, Filastin* (PNF)

The CPJ was officially established in June 1951 and has operated under the guise of various popular front organizations since that time. Until the formation of the Palestine Communist Party (PCP) in 1982, its work centered on the West Bank, where it had drawn support from students, teachers, professional workers, and the lower middle class.

The CPJ has been illegal since 1957, although the government's normally repressive measures have been relaxed on occasion. At present, communist party membership is punishable by jail sentences of three to fifteen years. Israeli sources report that Jordan has promised the Soviet Union that it will permit the CPJ to operate openly, although not under its own name, within the framework of the Jordanian-USSR Friendship Society (*FBIS*, 2 July 1981). The Friendship Society was founded in 1968; in January 1983 it signed an agreement in Amman with its Soviet counterpart for cultural cooperation and exchange (Amman domestic service, 23 January; *FBIS*, 25 January). Few radical organizations are active in Jordan; however, some Palestinian groups, such as the Marxist-oriented Popular Front for the Liberation of Palestine (embittered by "repression" of the Palestinians during

1970–71), have urged the overthrow of King Hussein. They appear to have little overt influence in Jordan.

In late December 1981, the CPJ's Central Committee met in plenary session and agreed to authorize the leadership of the Palestine Communist Organization, based on the West Bank and the Gaza Strip, to conduct preparatory work for establishing an independent Palestinian communist party (*IB*, March 1982). The PCP, whose activities focus on the Israeli-occupied territories, was established on 10 February 1982 (*WMR*, February).

Leadership and Organization. The CPJ is said to be a tightly organized, well-disciplined network of small cells. (For a listing of Jordanian members of the World Peace Council, see *YICA*, 1983, pp. 26–27.) Palestinians have played a leading role in communist activities in Jordan and the West Bank. According to Na'im Ashhab, a member of the PCP's Politburo, Palestinian communists have carried on their struggle for nearly 60 years, during the British Mandate as the Communist Party of Palestine and the League of National Liberation and later in the CPJ; they reportedly did not join the refugees in flight after the 1948 Arab–Israeli war. Ashhab claims that "the communists represent the longest-standing political movement of the Palestinian people." (*WMR*, February.)

Auxiliary and Mass Organizations. The PNF is composed of professional and labor union representatives and "patriotic personalities." It was established in August 1973 on the West Bank, evidently on CPJ initiative, by Muhammad Abu Mayzar. A small organization with an estimated strength of 100–500 men, it is a resistance group reportedly containing communist exiles from Jordan, Syria, Iraq, and Lebanon. The PNF follows the Palestine Liberation Organization (PLO) line and advocates an independent Palestinian state comprising the West Bank and the Gaza Strip. Its program includes mass political struggle and armed resistance in the occupied territories. The PNF's precise relation to the CPJ or to the new PCP is unknown.

Party Internal Affairs. Prior to the formation of the PCP, the CPJ had been described officially as the working-class party of two fraternal peoples—Jordanian and Palestinian. Despite its support of Palestinian statehood, the CPJ traditionally has been somewhat suspicious of the PLO. According to Faik Warrad, the CPJ's first secretary, the party's central task is to effect the withdrawal of Israel from Palestinian land; to this end, the PLO must be helped to organize resistance from Jordanian territory (*WMR*, May).

Domestic Attitudes and Activities. The CPJ's leaders have consistently denounced the "reactionary regime" in Amman and its links with "imperialism." The CPJ's 1980 Central Committee report analyzes in some detail the party's attitudes toward the Jordanian government, the Palestinian revolution, and the PLO. (For further elaboration, see *YICA*, 1982, pp. 31–32.)

Recent public statements by CPJ officials on the Jordanian domestic situation reflect their concern with the Palestine problem. A May *World Marxist Review* article by Faik Warrad asserts that victory in the struggle for Palestinian rights would guarantee Jordan's security against Israeli expansion. He points out that the CPJ supports the Palestine National Council's February 1983 "decision" that there could be a "confederative union of two independent states, the Palestinian and the Jordanian." However, the CPJ opposes

plans for a "federal" relationship between the Jordanian kingdom and the proposed Palestinian entity because such plans are premature. Despite Israel's attempts to sow discord between Palestinians and Jordanian citizens, Warrad asserts that Palestinian-Jordanian ties remain close and—in apparent contradiction to the viewpoint of PCP leaders—that Palestinians in the East Bank "live in the same conditions" as Jordanians. However, some Palestinians are "justifiably dissatisfied with the discriminatory practices in Jordan, the despotic methods of government and the impingement of democratic freedoms." As a result of such internal conditions, these Palestinians are attempting to split the CPJ and the working class in Jordan and to fan regional fanaticism. Thus the CPJ strongly opposes any "tendencies toward fanatical sectarian insularity."

International Activities and Attitudes. In his May article, Warrad describes the growth of right-wing reaction in the Arab world, particularly Egypt, which has joined the "imperialist-Zionist camp." The forces of reaction have access to huge oil revenues, which they are using to influence events. Domestic spending by Arab governments has "promoted the growth of bourgeois strata," whose interests dovetail increasingly with those of world capitalism. Ashhab declares that bourgeois interests, together with Israel, desire to eliminate "the hotbed of revolutionary ferment in Lebanon." Most Arab countries are "continuing their policy of massive terror" and in some cases "brutal repression accompanied by bloodshed." The communist parties have persistently warned against the muzzling of democracy, which threatens the stability of "internal fronts" and weakens the Arabs' ability to repel aggression. Warrad also warns that the Middle East is being turned into a "war threat," which the Arab peoples must counter as their principal task, and notes in passing that the Iran-Iraq war is bringing only ruin to the two countries. He declares that "Arab solidarity was weak and pitiful" in reaction to Israel's 1982 invasion of Lebanon. The Front for Steadfastness and Confrontation has been ineffective, while the Soviets' willingness to help during the Lebanese war was not exploited. For more than three months after the Israeli invasion, the Arab states "maintained a helpless silence" and in some cases "acted as direct accomplices of the aggressors." Although Palestinian and Lebanese fighters displayed "unparalleled courage and heroism," the Lebanese national-patriotic movement was forced to confront Israel "single-handed." While the invasion did not achieve all its aims, Israel and the United States, acting in "strategic alliance," did make important gains.

Warrad asserts in the same article that President Reagan "categorically rejects the legitimate national rights of the Palestinian people." He describes the 1982 Reagan peace initiative as "an attempt to assert U.S. hegemony in the region" and to create an anti-Soviet military bloc. Specifically, the United States is accused of attempting to establish a military base in Lebanon and to widen the framework of the Camp David accords to include Lebanon and Jordan in order to impose "administrative autonomy" on the West Bank Palestinians in association with Jordan. Warrad approves aspects of the 1982 Arab summit in Fez, which proposed "realistic provisions that create the foundation for a just, sensible settlement of the Palestine problem." However, the summit failed to address what the Arabs should do if the United States and Israel rejected their plan. In Warrad's view, the best way to attain a just peace in the Middle East is through implementation of the Soviet proposal for an international conference open to the PLO, the USSR, the United States, and all other interested parties.

Little information is available on CPJ foreign travel in 1983. A CPJ delegation led by Abdul Aziz al-Uti, a member of the Central Committee's Politburo, met with Romanian communist officials in July to discuss concerns of the two parties and aspects of the international situation (Agerpress, 28 July; *FBIS*, 29 July).

Norman F. Howard
U.S. Department of State
Washington, D.C.

(Note: Views expressed in this article are the author's own and do not represent those of the State Department.)

Lebanon

Population. 3 million (estimate; last census 1932)
Party. Lebanese Communist Party (al-Hizb al-Shuyu'i al-Lubnani; LCP); Organization of Communist Action (OCAL)
Founded. Lebanese People's Party (predecessor of LCP), 1924; OCAL, 1970
Membership. LCP, 14,000–16,000 (*Monday Morning*, 8–14 June 1981)
Secretary General. George Hawi (LCP); Muhsin Ibrahim (OCAL)
Politburo. 11 members (LCP)
Secretariat. 7 members (LCP)
Central Committee. 24 members (LCP)
Status. Legal
Last Congress. LCP, Fourth, 1979; OCAL, First, 1971
Last Election. 1972; no representation
Auxiliary Organizations. Unknown, but various fronts, movements, or unions have communist representation
Publications. *Al-Akhbar* (weekly), *al-Tariq* (monthly), *al-Nida'* (daily)

The roots of the LCP are traceable to the establishment of the Lebanese People's Party in October 1924 by intellectuals and workers. The LCP's First Congress was held in December 1943–January 1944. Initially unresponsive to Arab nationalism, the party adopted a more sympathetic stance at its Second Congress in July 1968. According to Secretary General George Hawi, the party's membership remained stable at about 2,000 in the late 1960s but has increased seven to eight times since then (*Monday Morning*, 8–14 June 1981; *FBIS*, 17 June 1981). The greatest influx of new members took place in 1974 when the membership allegedly increased by more than 60 percent—all of them under age 25. Membership reportedly doubled during the 1975–1976 civil war, when the party was said to have about 5,000 volunteers under arms. In fact, membership is probably far less than the figures cited by Hawi. The communists traditionally have drawn much of their support from the Greek Orthodox community, although Shia Muslims are increasingly active in the party.

Leadership and Organization. The Congress, which is supposed to be convened every four years, is the supreme LCP organ. Owing to the instability in Lebanon, the Fourth Congress was not held until 1979 and was characterized by complete secrecy. During the congress, Niqula al-Shawi was elected to the new post of party president, an honorary position created for the longtime LCP leader. George Hawi, the effective leader of the party, was elected secretary general. The party's Central Committee announced the death of al-Shawi in February 1983 (Beirut domestic service, 17 February; *FBIS*, 18 February). (For a listing of Central Committee members, see *YICA*, 1981, p. 14; for members of the World Peace Council in Lebanon, see *YICA*, 1983, p. 29.) According to Rafic Samhoun, a member of the LCP Politburo, since the Second Congress in 1962, LCP "party life has been placed on the foundation of the Leninist principles of democratic centralism"; party committees were enlarged both to reinvigorate them and to improve leadership; party work in "large" factories, among agricultural workers, and poor peasants was intensified in order to increase the LCP's working-class component; and the party assigned members to work in trade unions and young people's associations, as well as student, intellectual, professional, and sports groups (*WMR*, February 1982).

Domestic Views and Activities. The LCP has taken an active role in Lebanese affairs.

Since late 1982, the LCP's public statements have focused on the political situation in Lebanon after the Israeli invasion and the imperative of ending the Israeli occupation. A Politburo statement issued in October 1982 (*al-Nida'*, 13 October 1982; *IB*, January 1983) noted that the forces of reaction are "fully mobilized" and that "the policy of securing communal hegemony is still being pursued." The statement reviewed Israel's aggressive designs as revealed by its intention to retain a 45-kilometer border strip in south Lebanon, its demand for open borders between Lebanon and Israel, its attempt to remove the Palestinian resistance from the Bekaa Valley and the north before withdrawing from Lebanon, and its "feverish activity" to sow discord throughout Lebanon. The Politburo accused the United States of protecting Israeli aggression and providing Israel with unlimited support. It asserted that the Lebanese government and army were looking in vain to the United States for salvation, insisting that "it is necessary to learn the lessons from the U.S. 'guarantees,' which never materialized, of safety for the refugee camps and from the assurances that the Israelis will not enter Beirut." However, despite U.S. actions in Lebanon, the LCP is not opposed to exploiting Lebanon's "traditional friendly ties" in order to secure national aims. The statement declares that a comprehensive program, including the use of armed force and the mobilization of international forces, would be necessary to effect Israel's unconditional withdrawal. The Politburo appealed for "an end to arbitrary actions, respect for democratic rights, resolute measures to disband the militia formations and confiscate their arms, liquidate the ghettos, wipe out every manifestation of unlawful self-rule at the ports and other public institutions throughout Lebanon, especially in East Beirut and the mountainous regions, and to reestablish the power of the state there." It denounced the practice of "forced mobilization" and the existence of "illegal wharves." It charged that "certain circles inside and outside the power apparatus" are "using the Israeli occupation to extend their positions" and to work against those resisting the occupation. Repression against residents of West Beirut was said to be continuing. The statement observes that the government's plan to disarm all factions was not being implemented in Christian areas. The Politburo discussed the consequences of the assassination of Bashir Gemayel, which it blamed on Israel, questioning why such a "serious matter" was being treated lightly. It suggested that the case should be submitted for consideration to the Council of Justice and urged that Lebanese involved in the "slaughter" at the Palestinian refugee camps be subjected to "an earnest investigation and impartial trial."

George Hawi elaborated on these and other themes during a visit to Paris in November 1982 (*Humanité Dimanche*, 26 November 1982; *IB*, January). He declared that Israel wants to justify its long-term occupation of Lebanon by reviving the religious and civil war. Tel Aviv desires to strengthen Lebanon's "fascist trends," to create Lebanese mini-states based on religion—i.e., Christian, Druze, Shia, and Sunni—as well as to divide Syria into Alawi and Sunni states, ultimately encompassing Iraq and the rest of the Middle East in these plans. According to Hawi, the LCP favors the withdrawal of all troops except the regular Lebanese army. The Palestinian presence should not be considered a pretext for continuing the Israeli occupation. The Lebanese government and the Palestine Liberation Organization (PLO) should hold direct talks concerning PLO troop withdrawal from the Bekaa and north Lebanon. In discussions between Hawi and Yassir Arafat, it was also agreed that the rights of Palestinian civilians should be guaranteed along with freedom of action for PLO political representatives in Lebanon.

In the same interview, Hawi referred to the LCP's "three inseparable slogans...independence, unity, democracy." The party leader asserted that Lebanese national unity and territorial integrity could be restored in the near future if the Lebanese bourgeoisie, "which always appeals to foreign countries to settle purely Lebanese problems," could be persuaded to abandon its policy. At present, however, the bourgeoisie was throwing itself into the arms of the United States. The LCP is described as the main force for Lebanese national liberation. The party is "deeply rooted" among the young and the most oppressed among the Lebanese. It "declares its readiness to accept the conditions of legal democratic struggle" provided that the bourgeoisie also accepts those conditions. The LCP's democratic struggle would be based on an "alliance of the left and a union of forces broader than that which exists today."

The LCP's Politburo met again in Beirut in March to review the domestic situation. A statement issued after the meeting (Tass, Moscow, 17 March; *FBIS*, 24 March) accused Israel of seeking to perpetuate the occupation through the use of terror, repression, blackmail, recruitment of traitors, and other forms of pressure. The statement denounced U.S. political maneuvers and efforts to impose an Israeli diktat on Lebanon. It claimed that the Reagan administration was using the "Lebanese card" to drag other Arab countries into the Camp David deal.

On 7 April, an LCP delegation led by Hawi and including Nadim 'Abd al-Samad and Khalil Na'us met with Lebanese Prime Minister Shafiq Wazzan. Hawi reported to the prime minister on his talks with leaders in Bulgaria, Czechoslovakia, Yugoslavia, Greece, Portugal, and Cyprus, and with Syrian officials and the PLO's Arafat. He stressed the need to guarantee Lebanon's independence and sovereignty (Beirut domestic service, 7 April; *FBIS*, 8 April). In a commentary in early May (Radio Moscow, 4 May; *FBIS*, 5 May), Hawi expressed optimism that the apparent success of the U.S.-Israeli design in Lebanon was only temporary and superficial. The Lebanese people and national forces led by the communists would not permit continued Israeli domination in Lebanon or the replacement of Israel by U.S. domination, "which is no less dangerous."

The 17 May Lebanese-Israeli agreement stipulating the conditions for Israeli withdrawal deepened LCP concerns. Hawi attended a meeting on 14 May at the residence of former president Suleiman Franjiyah along with representatives of the Ba'th, Syrian Social Nationalist, Progressive Socialist, and other parties, who denounced the draft agreement (Damascus domestic service, 14 May; *FBIS*, 17 May). Following a meeting between Hawi and Khalid Bakhdash, the Syrian communist leader, a joint statement was issued on 19 May attacking the agreement (*IB*, August; *al-Bayraq*, 21 May; *FBIS*, 23 May). The statement characterized the treaty as part of a plot orchestrated by the United States in order to establish its "complete political, economic and military domination in the region." The treaty "contradicts the will of the Lebanese people," obliges Lebanon's parliament to revoke within one year all treaties and agreements opposed to its terms, and contradicts U.N. resolutions requiring Israel to withdraw unconditionally from Lebanon. Moreover, the treaty provisions threaten freedom of speech and press in Lebanon and will increase Lebanon's internal divisions and strengthen "fascist separatist forces" attempting to impose their will on the entire country. Because the treaty allows Israel to use Lebanon's airspace and territorial waters, it also threatens Syria's security interests. Thus Lebanon is becoming a "U.S.-Israeli protectorate," a colonial base, and a base against Syria. Both the LCP and the Syrian Communist Party support Syria's opposition to the treaty and call on all Arab patriots to deepen Arab-Soviet friendship.

A plenary meeting of the LCP's Central Committee in Beirut in early June continued the attack on the Lebanese-Israeli agreement (al-Nida', 5 June; IB, October). According to the declaration adopted at the meeting, the agreement poses "an extreme danger" for Lebanon and the Middle East and for world peace. It provides Israel with "legal cover," creates conditions for Israel to usurp new areas in Lebanon—especially in the Bekaa, the Lebanese mountains, and in north Lebanon—promotes the U.S. solution to the Middle East crisis, and encourages Lebanon's pro-Israeli "racist subversive groupings" to consolidate their domination. Once again, the LCP called for the unconditional withdrawal of Israel and all non-Lebanese armed contingents so that "the authorities" will be able to exercise "sovereignty over every inch of the country's territory." The party supports barring the Phalangists from the levers of state government and state institutions and urges a national dialogue on the conditions for ensuring Lebanon's rebirth and democratic development. The declaration took note of increased resistance to Israeli aggression by the Lebanese patriotic front, assisted by the PLO, Syria, Soviet aid to Syria, and Soviet-Arab friendship, which had prevented Israel from achieving its main aims and led it into a "blind alley." A statement by Hawi in mid-June (Radio Moscow, 15 June; FBIS, 16 June) accused Israel of seeking to partition Lebanon and transform it into small, racist states in order to obtain secure borders. The Lebanese-Israeli agreement allegedly promotes such an outcome by placing "the entire south, and indirectly, all of Lebanon, under direct and indirect Israeli control," upsetting Lebanon's internal balance, and constituting an additional danger to Syria. Later in June, the formation of a "Progressive Independent Union of Lebanon" was announced in Beirut (Moscow domestic service, 21 June; FBIS, 22 June). The main task of the union, composed of the LCP, the Progressive Socialist Party, other "patriotic and progressive organizations," and a number of "dis-

tinguished politicians," is to struggle for Israel's unconditional withdrawal, the restoration of Lebanese sovereignty, and a just settlement of Lebanon's problems.

A statement following an LCP Politburo meeting in July (clandestine Voice of Arab Lebanon, 26 July; FBIS, 27 July) affirmed that the path to Lebanese sovereignty lies in canceling the Lebanese-Israeli agreement and in maintaining Lebanon's true affiliation in the Arab world. It blamed "the authority" and the Phalangists for leading Lebanon to the brink of civil war, disintegration, and partition. Karim Muruwwah, a member of the Politburo, called on "all the Arab nationalist forces and world public opinion" to help the Lebanese liberate their homeland (al-Bayraq, Beirut, 30 July; FBIS, 2 August). He noted the increasing dangers in south Lebanon since the Israeli decision to redeploy its forces from the Shuf region, blaming the Lebanese government for "the continuation and exacerbation of this plot against the South." A Politburo statement in September, following U.S. naval shelling of anti-government positions in Alayh province, called on world progressive and democratic forces to rebuff U.S. military interference in Lebanon and to foil the U.S. effort to transform Lebanon into a military base (Tass, Moscow, 21 September; FBIS, 22 September).

Communist forces continued to participate sporadically in Lebanon's factional fighting. In late 1982, "armed socialists and communists" were involved in clashes in the Lebanese mountains (Radio Free Lebanon, 19 December 1982; FBIS, 20 December 1982). In mid-1983, Sami Sariy, identified as a communist official and head of a band of gunmen, was slain in factional warfare (Voice of Lebanon, Beirut, 12 July; FBIS, 13 July). In August, diplomatic sources reportedly revealed that contacts took place between the Shia militia Amal, the LCP, and the OCAL, on the one side, and PLO officials, on the other, to obtain information on PLO arms caches left behind in Beirut; the contacts apparently failed because Arafat refused to turn over the arms (Voice of Lebanon, Beirut, 29 August; FBIS, 31 August). For many years, communists have been involved in Tripoli's communal warfare, which reached a peak in late 1983. According to one report, the October battles in Tripoli forced the communists to evacuate their positions in the city (Radio Free Lebanon, 15 October; FBIS, 18 October). This was denied by an LCP spokesman, who stated that the LCP presence in Tripoli, al-Mina, and the northern province was deeply rooted and that the party would remain there alongside the forces of the National Salvation Front and the "honest forces" of the Palestinian revolution (Radio Monte Carlo, Paris, 16 October; *FBIS*, 18 October). Tass reported that extremist elements belonging to the "Islamic Unity [Unification] Movement" in Tripoli attacked a party building in October, resulting in a large number of casualties (Tass, Moscow, 17 October; *FBIS*, 18 October). The report stated that "observers" associated the attack "with the intrigues of U.S.-Israeli agents" who were attempting to divert the Lebanese from the anti-imperialist struggle. The Voice of Lebanon (17 October) reported that on 17 October the Islamic Unification Movement executed 40 communists it had detained in Tripoli and was continuing to raid communists' homes (*FBIS*, 18 October). According to the *Washington Post* (10 December), more than 80 communists were killed by Muslim "fundamentalists" attempting to evict the communists from their stronghold in the Tripoli port. In the midst of these difficulties, Fatah's Central Committee wrote a letter to the LCP Politburo describing the clashes between the LCP and the Islamic Unification Movement (Radio Monte Carlo, 16 October; *FBIS*, 18 October). The letter reportedly expressed Fatah's regret over the LCP's "unfair and harmful" campaign, noting that the Palestinian commander in chief had helped to protect LCP offices, leaders, and fighters in Tripoli.

International Views and Activities. The LCP has maintained a consistently pro-Soviet posture, as revealed in its statements and activities over the years. In late 1982, the LCP professed to be encouraged by "the positive signs which have appeared in China's present policy," which will "have special weight on the international plane" (*Humanité Dimanche*, 26 November 1982; *IB*, February). In a 4 May statement broadcast from Moscow (*FBIS*, 5 May), George Hawi declared that Syria, with its improving defensive capability, is the "principal obstacle to the U.S. plan" to dominate the Middle East. He suggested that perhaps the most important factor in maintaining Arab steadfastness lies in the support given by progressive forces, particularly the attitude of the Soviet-led socialist countries. In a mid-July statement (Moscow domestic television service, 14 July; *FBIS*, 15 July), Hawi approved the Soviet plan for Middle East peace through the establishment of an international body "in whose framework the region's problems could be discussed with the participation of all sides concerned, including the PLO." He also thanked the Syrians for their efforts to restore Lebanese independence.

Official LCP travel was extensive during the year. A delegation headed by Hawi met in France with Secretary General Georges Marchais of the French Communist Party in December 1982 (*FBIS*, 8 December 1982) and in Belgrade with Yugoslav communist and government officials in early February (Tanjug domestic service, 3 February; *FBIS*, 7 February). The latter delegation included LCP Politburo member Rafic Samhoun and Central Committee member Suhayl Tawil. They discussed cooperation between the LCP and the Yugoslav League of Communists and stressed the importance of ending Israeli aggression and establishing a Palestinian state; the PLO's role as the sole legitimate representative of the Palestinian people was reaffirmed. Hawi visited Bulgaria on 8–12 March, meeting with Bulgarian Communist Party and government officials (BTA, Sofia, 12 March; *FBIS*, 16 March). The LCP delegation reported on the Lebanese struggle against Israeli aggression, Zionism, and imperialism, while the two sides expressed the view that events in Lebanon were the direct result of U.S.-Israeli strategic cooperation and the separate deal imposed by the Camp David accords. Hawi, accompanied by Nadim 'Abd al-Samad, visited Moscow in late June (Tass, Moscow, 29 June; *FBIS*, 1 July), where they met with Konstantin Chernenko, Boris Ponomarev, and Karen Brutents. The LCP representatives praised Soviet peace initiatives and thanked the Soviet party and the USSR for supporting Lebanon's struggle against imperialism. Both sides, among other things, demanded Israel's unconditional withdrawal from Lebanon and the evacuation of the multinational force, denounced Israel's alleged war preparations against Syria, and criticized U.S. and Israeli attempts to impose separate and unequal agreements on the Arabs.

Al-Samad visited South Yemen in early August, declaring on Aden television that Lebanese national resistance operations against Israel, conducted mostly in the south, were being increased and that Israeli redeployment would not reduce such activities (Aden domestic service, 2 August;

FBIS, 3 August). George Hawi conferred with Italian communist leader Enrico Berlinguer in Italy in September (*L'Unità*, 28 September; *FBIS*, 5 October), while al-Samad exchanged views on the Lebanese situation with the secretary of the BCP Central Committee in Bulgaria (BTA, Sofia, 10 October; *FBIS*, 13 October). Hawi journeyed to Moscow again in November (Tass, Moscow, 24 November; *FBIS*, 25 November), along with Abdel Karim Mrue, a member of the Politburo, for talks with Chernenko and Ponomarev. The LCP representatives praised Soviet peace policy and, in a joint statement with their Soviet hosts, denounced U.S. war preparations and deployment of new nuclear missiles in Europe and the U.S.-Israeli campaign of blackmail and provocation against Syria.

The LCP devoted some attention to the problems of Latin America. Maurice Nahra, identified as the LCP representative in Cuba, stated on Havana television (8 June; *FBIS*, 9 June) that both the LCP and the Lebanese people back the Salvadoran, Nicaraguan, and all other peoples fighting for national liberation. The LCP Politburo met to denounce the U.S. action in Grenada in October, declaring that the invasion was evidence of U.S. imperialist policy and of the Reagan administration's priority in supporting the interests of the U.S. war industry. The Politburo statement characterized U.S. policy as centering mainly on Cuba, which was described as "the first bastion of freedom" in the Americas. It asserted that U.S. policy was designed to deprive the Latin peoples of the right to select their own leaders and way of life. It detected increased U.S. hostility toward "victorious Nicaragua" and against those in El Salvador who were "struggling for deliverance from the Americans and their agents." The LCP noted that the Grenadian invasion took place as the United States was becoming more involved in Lebanon, which "implies grave dangers" for Lebanese sovereignty and existence. The statement called on the United States to leave the island immediately and to allow the Grenadian people to determine their own future.

Publications. The party's daily newspaper, *al-Nida'* (The call), celebrated its twentieth anniversary in 1979. It and *al-Akhbar* (The news) and the literary and ideological monthly *al-Tariq* (The road) serve as general information media for illegal communist parties in the Middle East.

The Organization of Communist Action. OCAL, composed mostly of students, was formed in May 1970 and held its First Congress in 1971. Like the LCP, it has drawn recruits from Shia migrants in Beirut. Its secretary general, Muhsin Ibrahim, is also secretary general of the National Movement. The OCAL has consistently supported the Palestinian resistance and has maintained close ties with the Democratic Front for the Liberation of Palestine. Since its First Congress, OCAL has moderated its strong support for China in the Sino-Soviet conflict; at present it rejects loyalty either to Moscow or Beijing. In recent years, the OCAL and the LCP have drawn closer.

Muhsin Ibrahim warned in mid-January of the danger of accepting Israel's conditions during the Israeli-Lebanese negotiations, stating that "the role of these [Lebanese] citizens today is to shoulder the burden of the struggle against the creeping Zionist domination of their country" (*al-Safir*, Beirut, 15 January; *FBIS*, 18 January). OCAL Politburo members Fawaz Tarabulsi and Nasir al-As'ad arrived in South Yemen on 22 June to discuss the critical situation in Lebanon following the Lebanese-Israeli agreement. Tarabulsi thanked Aden for its support and expressed satisfaction with the close relationship between OCAL and the Yemen Socialist Party (Aden domestic service, 22 June; *FBIS*, 23 June). In early July, Tarabulsi was awarded South Yemen's medal of courage (Aden domestic service, 4 July; *FBIS*, 8 July). Ibrahim met with Yemeni leader Ali Nasir Muhammad in Aden in October to discuss cooperation between the two parties as well as events in Lebanon (Aden domestic service, 22 October; *FBIS*, 25 October).

Norman F. Howard
U.S. Department of State
Washington, D.C.

(Note: Views expressed in this article are the author's own and do not represent those of the State Department.)

Morocco

Population. 22.9 million
Party. Party of Progress and Socialism (Parti du progrès et du socialisme; PPS)
Founded. 1943
Membership. 2,000 (estimate)
Secretary General. 'Ali Yata
Politburo. 'Ali Yata, 'Abd al-Wahid Suhail, others not known
Secretariat. 'Ali Yata, others not known
Central Committee. Unknown
Status. Legal since 1974
Last Congress. Third, 25–27 March 1983, in Casablanca
Last Election. 1977, 2.31 percent, 1 of 264 seats
Auxiliary Organizations. No information
Publications. *Al-Bayane* (daily), French and Arabic editions

Faced with a continuing conflict over the Western Sahara, Morocco sought in 1983 to undermine support for the independence struggle of the Polisario Front by improving relations with its major backers, Algeria and Libya. In pursuit of this aim, King Hassan held a "historic" meeting with Algerian president Chadli Benjedid on 26 February and met three times with Libyan leader Moammar Khadafy during the latter's visit to Rabat in late June. At the same time, the kingdom professed its willingness to go forward with the referendum in the Sahara called for by the Organization of African Unity (OAU), but it refused to negotiate directly with the Polisario. Domestically, Moroccans went to the polls for the first time since 1977 to vote in communal elections that were widely denounced as fraudulent by the political parties. Economically, a number of serious problems brought the country to the brink of a financial crisis, prompting the parliament in a special session in July to adopt an austerity budget for the year.

Leadership and Party Organization. The PPS held its Third National Congress in Casablanca from 25 to 27 March. 'Ali Yata was re-elected secretary general of the party. In addition to more than 1,200 PPS delegates, the congress was attended by representatives of several other Moroccan political parties, including the major left-wing organization and leading opposition party, the Socialist Union of Popular Forces (USFP). The foreign delegations attending included the Palestine Liberation Organization (PLO) and communist party members from the Soviet Union, Eastern Europe, France, Italy, Argentina, Chile, Tunisia, Jordan, Spain, Lebanon, Egypt, and the People's Democratic Republic of (South) Yemen. The Soviet delegation was headed by Aleksei V. Romanev, alternate member of the CPSU Central Committee and chief editor of the newspaper *Sovetskaya kultura* (*Pravda*, 1 April; *FBIS*, 7 April).

The congress aimed to assess the accomplishments of the party since its Second Congress in February 1979. The PPS asserted its character as the revolutionary vanguard in Morocco and declared the correctness of its general line in domestic affairs. On the ideological level, the congress reaffirmed the party's commitment to the ideals of scientific socialism and internationalism. (*IB*, June.) In a speech to the congress,

Soviet representative Romanev condemned the "militarism" of the United States and NATO and argued that whereas the United States was establishing military bases far from its own territory, the Soviet Union wanted to make the Mediterranean a "sea of peace."

Domestic Party Affairs. In the domestic field, the PPS at its party congress saw its main task as preventing foreign military presence on Moroccan territory and strengthening national independence and sovereignty (Tass, 27 March; *FBIS*, 29 March). In its program, the PPS Central Committee demanded the nationalization of the main sectors of the Moroccan economy; the consolidation of the public sector; the use of private capital in the interest of developing the national economy; agricultural reform measures; the promotion of the systems of social security and public health, education, and vocational training; and the freezing and control of prices (Radio Moscow, 24 March; *FBIS*, 25 March). On the organizational level, the theses adopted at the congress called for making the PPS a party of the masses; consolidating its relations with the working class, peasants, and progressive intellectuals; promoting action within the trade unions and among youth and women; and mobilizing the popular masses in the struggle for peace, détente, and disarmament and against the "intrigues of imperialism, Zionism, and neocolonialism." As evidence of concrete progress in broadening the party's links throughout Moroccan society, the theses cited the close coordination between the PPS and the USFP, including recent joint meetings of the politburos of the two parties. (*IB*, June.)

The PPS joined all other Moroccan political parties in denouncing various alleged irregularities in the 10 June balloting for communal and municipal councils. In its 15 June French-language edition, *Al-Bayane* decried the "elec-toral masquerade of 10 June" and called for the annulling of the results. It maintained that the redrawn electoral boundaries were never made public before the elections, that voters were arbitrarily stricken from the voting list, and that "thousands of candidacies" were disallowed on false pretexts. In the same edition, the PPS also alleged that certain people were allowed to vote without showing identification and that police were present inside the polling stations. Unlike all other Moroccan political parties, which stopped after a few days, the PPS maintained a litany of daily denunciations of the 10 June elections in *Al-Bayane*. The Moroccan government suspended publication of *Al-Bayane* for one day on 23 June and thereby issued a warning to the PPS that its patience with criticism of the government's performance in the elections had its limits.

International Views, Positions and Activities. The PPS continued its strong backing of the Moroccan government's international efforts to "recover" the Western Sahara. During 1983, those efforts centered around the summit meeting and deliberations of the OAU. Within the context of the Sahara issue, the PPS welcomed Morocco's rapprochement with Libya, which began following a visit to Rabat in late June by Libya's Colonel Khadafy. Noting that Moroccan-Libyan cooperation serves the greater Arab nation, *Al-Bayane* declared on 7 July that the rapprochement between the two brotherly Arab countries had become a necessity in view of "the serious situation prevailing in the Arab world, a divided and weakened world facing the imperialist-Zionist maneuvers." (Maghreb Arabe Presse, Rabat, 7 July; *FBIS*, 8 July.) Apart from this issue, the party focused its attention on a variety of domestic issues.

John Damis
Portland State University

Mozambique

Population. 13.0 million
Party. Front for the Liberation of Mozambique (Frente de Libertação de Moçambique; FRELIMO)
Founded. 1962
Membership. 35,000 (*Kommunist*, April 1982)
Secretary General. Samora Moises Machel
Politburo. 11 members: Samora Moises Machel, Marcelino dos Santos, Joaquim Alberto Chissano, Alberto Chipande, Armando Emilio Guebuza, Jorge Rebelo, Mariano de Araujo Matsinhe, Sebastião Marcos Mabote, Jacinto Soares Veloso, Mario de Graça Machungo, Jose Oscar Monteiro
Secretariat. 6 members: Samora Moises Machel, Marcelino dos Santos, Joaquim Alberto Chissano, Jorge Rebelo, Armando Panguene, Jose Luís Cabaço
Central Committee. 130 members
Status. Ruling party
Last Congress. Fourth, 26–29 April 1983, in Maputo
Last Election. 1977; won all 226 seats in the National People's Assembly
Auxiliary Organizations. Organization of Mozambican Women (Organização da Mulher Moçambicana); Mozambique Youth Organization
Publications. *Notícias* (daily); *O Tempo* (weekly); *Diario de Moçambique* (daily); *Domingo* (Sunday paper); *Voz da Revolução* (Central Committee organ)

FRELIMO has been in power in the southeast African country of Mozambique since 1975. The year 1983 witnessed the convening of FRELIMO's Fourth Party Congress amidst a deteriorating economy, food shortages, and continuing guerrilla warfare in the countryside. The Fourth Party Congress sought to deal with increasing problems faced by the ruling FRELIMO party.

Originally formed from three small movements in 1962, FRELIMO held its first congress in the same year. In 1964 it initiated a ten-year guerrilla war against Portuguese rule. (For more background on the early history of FRELIMO, see *YICA*, 1982, p. 37.) After Portugal's defeat, an independent People's Republic of Mozambique was proclaimed on 25 June 1975.

Organization and Leadership. FRELIMO's "struggle for national liberation" saw a steady drift leftward and a consolidation of the three movements into a Marxist-Leninist party. By its

second congress in 1968, FRELIMO had embraced many aspects of standard communist organizations, including democratic centralism, cell structure, self-criticism, and Marxian phraseology. Internal feuds marked this radicalization process and resulted in several assassinations within the leadership. FRELIMO's first president, Eduardo Mondlane, was the most prominent figure killed. After a six-month period of rule by a troika, Samora Moises Machel, who commanded the guerrilla army, emerged to become president as well.

The Third Congress in 1977 approved the Central Committee's recommendation to transform FRELIMO into a "Marxist-Leninist vanguard party." Even before this formal announcement, FRELIMO had erected many of the organizations typical of communist party structures. The Central Committee is approved by the Congress and is to carry out its policies. The policy-shaping body of FRELIMO is the Political

Bureau. Most of its members also hold ministerial positions in the government and sit on the Council of Ministers, the cabinet of the government. FRELIMO's constitution regards the People's National Assembly as the highest legislative organ. The National Assembly is made up of delegates from throughout the country chosen by an elaborate election process. The constitution provides that the president has the power to make many appointments. President Samora Machel, who is also president of FRELIMO, is empowered to appoint provincial governors and members of the Council of Ministers, among others. He has power to annul decisions of the provincial assemblies. The Third Congress abolished the office of vice-president.

The year under review witnessed the convening of the Fourth Party Congress, which presided over a confirmation of the leadership, expansion of the Central Committee, and a reshuffling of some responsibilities in the government. Over 600 delegates reportedly attended the congress. The Fourth Congress also "defined the defense of the fatherland and the fight against famine as our essential priorities" (Maputo domestic service, 29 May; *FBIS*, 1 June).

The Central Committee report noted serious errors in its own economic policy since the Third Congress. Economic and agricultural production grew more slowly than the population. This report laid the blame on investments in newer and bigger projects while existing equipment and ongoing efforts suffered neglect. Peasant agriculture and family farmers had received virtually no support because emphasis had been placed on state farms. The report called for support to small family farms and large private farms rather than to state farms, which must "reorganize and consolidate" (*Guardian*, London, 28 April). President Machel read the Central Committee's report to the Fourth Party Congress (Maputo domestic service, 28 April; *FBIS*, 11 May).

Pressing economic, agricultural, and military problems and delegate criticism were offered as an explanation in official FRELIMO communiqués for an almost doubling of the Central Committee's membership from 67 to 128 published names (*Notícias*, 1 May). Only twelve members of the old Central Committee were not reelected. By this membership expansion, FRELIMO reported that it sought to involve more workers and peasants in ruling the country and to give more power to the provinces. But how much actual investment will flow to small-scale agricultural and industrial enterprises and how much power will go to local authorities remain uncertain. The Maputo bureaucracy appears to be resisting the changes (*Guardian*, 3 May). One means to offset this seems to be the tactic of appointing members of the Political Bureau to manage directly "some of the provinces and decisive sectors which exercise sovereignty in the country" (Maputo domestic service, 29 May; *FBIS*, 1 June). For example, Political Bureau member and secretary of the FRELIMO Central Committee Marcelino dos Santos was placed in charge of Sofala province and Political Bureau member and Minister of National Defense Alberto Joaquim Chipande was placed in charge of Cabo Delgado province.

The Political Bureau remained unchanged by the Central Committee election except for the addition of an eleventh member, Oscar Monteiro (*Tempo*, special number, 8 May). Numerous reshufflings of ministerial posts were approved by the congress, which ended the communiqué announcing the change with "Long live the decisions of the fourth congress! The revolution shall win! The struggle continues." (Maputo domestic service, 30 May; *FBIS*, 1 June.)

Mass Organizations. In the course of the guerrilla struggle for independence, FRELIMO, like other political movements, made special appeals to various groups in the population. Women, for example, received much attention during the war. This trend continued into the post-independence period. The Organization of Mozambican Women, according to its pronouncements, seeks to liberate women from their traditional standing and increase their economic and political opportunities along with publicizing and implementing the party line in the country as a whole. FRELIMO also established the Mozambique Youth Organization and formed hundreds of production councils for factories, mills, and foundries. Much less well established are national organizations for artists and journalists.

The People's Forces for the Liberation of Mozambique (FPLM). The Mozambican army developed from the FRELIMO guerrilla force during the war for independence. Since 1975, the government has been attempting to remold the guerrillas into a conventional force with military vehicles and heavy weapons. The FPLM is estimated at 15,000 troops and is used both as a defense force and a mobilizing cadre to spread the party's message. At a celebration marking his fiftieth birthday, Machel, who holds the military title of field marshal, announced a five-year goal for the army. By 1988 the army "must be the most modern in Africa in terms of study, combat and production" (Maputo domestic service, 30 September; *FBIS*, 3 October).

Since 1982, the FPLM has been sorely tested by the increasing effectiveness and widening presence of an antigovernment insurgency, led by the Mozambique National Resistance (Resistencia Nacional Moçambicana; MNR). MNR guerrillas operate sabotage campaigns in much of the country, with varying degrees of success. But the counteroffensive launched by the FPLM seems to have decreased the antigovernment threat in the southern province of Gaza during the year. FRELIMO officials charge that the MNR is not a people's force but an externally directed bandit campaign from the Republic of South Africa, conducted in retaliation for Maputo's harboring of the African National Congress, which stages cross-border raids against Pretoria.

Although the MNR claims some 10,000 guerrilla fighters in Mozambique, its political philosophy is unclear beyond its opposition to Machel's Marxist government and its appeal to traditional ways. The guerrilla war has been highly effective in undermining economic development in Mozambique ("Pretoria-Backed Raids Bleed Destitute Country," *WP*, 6 April). In 1983, the MNR began moving toward a political structure within Mozambique by announcing that it was forming political cadres "as a complement to the military activity and as a guarantee of our victory and the security of our future" (Voice of Free Africa, 5 April; *FBIS*, 8 April). But the MNR suffered a setback with the assassination of its secretary general, Orlando Cristina, in April on a farm near Pretoria.

In an interesting development, the MNR criticized the United States for furnishing the "Maputo communist government" with military aid. It charged that the U.S. government provided financial and military aid to Portugal, which passes this assistance to FRELIMO. The MNR argued that Washington "intends to push Soviet influence aside by using the Portuguese." Its Voice of Africa radio station went on to comment that "the U.S. government's naivete and its stupidity regarding its African policy is well known" (Voice of Africa, 26 November; *FBIS*, 1 December).

Domestic Affairs. The continuation of a serious decline in some sectors of the Mozambican economy was reflected in the change of directions at the Fourth Party Congress. The economic deterioration also showed itself in the Maputo government's policy, begun two years ago, of seeking Western investment and aid. Abdul Magid Osman, secretary of state for coal and hydrocarbons, said: "There is no doubt here about the capacity and efficiency of American companies and there is no ideological obstacle" (Anthony Lewis, "Mozambique Seeks Western Investment," *NYT*, 5 February). FRELIMO is most interested in securing U.S. participation in energy development. Seismic studies along the coast indicated oil potential, and Mozambique has begun to extend invitations to Western companies for drilling concessions.

Although much of Mozambique's economy is below pre-independence levels, its coal production stands at 500,000 tons a year, which is about 150,000 tons above figures for 1974. East European assistance provides the major explanation for the increased production of coal. But the greatest failure of the Mozambican economy remains agricultural production. The severe drought, which hit most of southern Africa, exacted a heavy toll in Mozambique. The lack of rain and FRELIMO policies increased Mozambique's dependence on food aid. Commercial food imports were limited by the shortage of foreign exchange. A third factor limiting Mozambique's agricultural and industrial progress was the ongoing guerrilla warfare of the MNR.

The Central Committee's report to the Fourth Congress dwelled on the poor state of agriculture. Its recommendations were approved by the congress and represented by policy shifts from inadequate priority given to farming and from reliance on state farms rather than on family production. The congress placed a freeze on further capital expenditure on the state farm sector and appeared to move toward assisting the peasant sector by making consumer goods available in rural areas and by encouraging peasants to produce more for the urban market. Hence, much less emphasis was placed on collectivization of the peasant sector than in the ten-year plan initiated in 1981. But "socialization of the countryside" remains a goal of the Fourth Congress.

At year-end, government officials reported that "thousands of Mozambicans have starved to death and 700,000 are suffering from acute malnutrition as a result of Mozambique's worst drought in 50 years" (*NYT*, 4 December).

In line with the new agricultural policy, the FRELIMO party also adopted a strategy focusing on small local industries, using domestic resources, to raise production and satisfy basic consumer needs. The congress set goals of 12–15 percent production growth by 1985. The most serious industrial shortages are still in the production of cement, which is at less than half the pre-independence level of 600,000 tons. The scarcity of adequate cement has delayed construction projects and hurt industrial expansion.

In a May speech, Machel criticized "social parasites" who have left the rural areas and settled without jobs in the cities (Maputo domestic service, 8 June; *Facts and Reports*, 13, no. N, p. 7). During the following months, the government sent thousands of unemployed from Maputo and other cities to the countryside to grow food. It conducted house-to-house searches and checks on people walking the streets. Those without four cards—identity, work, residence, and national service—have been taken to "verification posts." Reportedly, many have been released, but there are estimates that thousands of others were shipped out of the city within a few days with only a few personal possessions. The government intends to reverse the migration to urban centers that has resulted in thousands of unemployed living off relatives or as "professional queuers, black-marketeers, petty thieves, or prostitutes" (*Guardian*, 19 July).

The Mozambican government also instituted the death penalty and public floggings for political and economic crimes. The People's Assembly Permanent Commission introduced the death penalty for crimes that seriously impact "the economic and political situation of our country. For example, hoarders and smugglers could be sentenced to death" (Maputo domestic service, 17 March; *FBIS*, 25 March). President Machel justified the reintroduction of public flogging, a colonial type of punishment, because of a "complacency and passivity among the people" in the face of antigovernment rebels and black marketeers. The new policy departed from FRELIMO's previous one of clemency and "reeducation." Both flogging and death sentences were meted out to those arrested and sentenced before the promulgation of the new laws (*Guardian*, 9 April).

International Affairs. The People's Republic of Mozambique theoretically adopted a policy of nonalignment. As with many Third World countries, FRELIMO's professed nonalignment meant a way to attract aid and trade from the West while siding with the Soviet Union or regularly criticizing, in the United Nations or other forums, the policies of Western nations, especially the United States. President Machel, in fact, stated at the Third Congress that Mozambique viewed "the socialist countries and the Marxist-Leninist Parties" as its "natural allies" (*Africa Contemporary Record*, 1976–77, p. B297). This compatibility with socialist states and Marxist-Leninist parties stems from the political orientation of the ruling FRELIMO party and its reliance on communist arms and assistance during the independence war. (For additional background, see *YICA*, 1982, p. 40.)

In 1981, Mozambique started to look to noncommunist states for assistance to bolster its sagging economy and deal with rising guerrilla opposition. In 1983, this search for aid from the West continued. FRELIMO also hoped that stronger ties with the West would help to restrain South Africa from its policy of retaliation against Mozambique for harboring guerrillas of the African National Congress. Additionally, Maputo sought Western pressure on Pretoria to negotiate the independence of Namibia (*WP*, 8 April).

FRELIMO's growing concern with the South African–backed MNR has strengthened its desire for Western diplomatic as well as financial assistance. But Maputo has refused to deny its territory to the ANC, which opposes the minority white rule in South Africa; it has stated officially that Mozambique would not be a staging area for guerrilla and sabotage attacks on South Africa. Pretoria, however, argued that Mozambican territory in fact serves as a launching pad for terrorist attacks within the republic. As in past years, South Africa struck back. In May, for example, South African warplanes rocketed and strafed an ANC headquarters in the suburb of Matola outside the capital in retaliation for a car bombing in Pretoria that killed eighteen people. Reports differed on the extent of civilian casualties, but South Africa claimed the death of 41 ANC guerrillas in the retaliatory air strike (*Washington Times*, 25 May). FRELIMO claimed that such raids were calculated to destabilize the government and weaken the Mozambican economic recovery (*WP*, 6 April). Despite these types of attacks and counterattacks, Mozambique and South Africa continued to cooperate on the economic level. South Africa uses the port of Maputo for export and import, and Mozambique relies on its southern neighbor for hard currency and expertise to maintain the railways and ports. Mozambique has a labor office in Johannesburg and South Africa keeps a trade commission in Maputo.

The most significant rapprochement with the West in 1983 entailed the improvement of relations between Mozambique and the United States. Relations had reached a low ebb in March 1981, when Maputo expelled three U.S. diplomats and their wives on charges of spying and the United States replied by ending all planned aid except emergency food assistance. Washington dispatched a new ambassador, Peter de Vos, to Mozambique, and Maputo appointed its first ambassador to the United States, Valerino Ferrao, formerly the Mozambican secretary of state for foreign affairs. Manuel dos Santos, former ambassador to Tanzania, became Mozambique's permanent representative to the United Nations (Mozambique Information Agency, 4 September).

Relations with Portugal, the former colonial power, continued to improve. Lisbon promised to return the remains of Gungunhana, a nineteenth-century tribal chieftain, to Mozambique. Gungunhana had successfully resisted the Portuguese military conquests of southern Mozambique for over a decade before being captured and transported to the Azores Islands, where he lived out his life in comfortable exile. He was buried on Teceira Island in 1906.

Still, FRELIMO's Fourth Party Congress was attended by delegations of most communist parties. The Soviet party delegation was led by Culture Minister Piotr N. Demichev. The Chinese Communist Party delegation was led by Wu Jinhua, member of the Central Committee and deputy chairman of the Chinese Nationalities Affairs Commission (Maputo domestic service, 26 April; *FBIS*, 29 April). Later, Machel stated that "Mozambique will work toward strengthening cooperation with the PRC to boost relations between the two socialist countries" (Maputo domestic service, 22 June; *FBIS*, 23 June). If

Machel follows through on this statement, this will represent a departure from the previous FRELIMO policy of maintaining close ties with Moscow.

As in previous years, Machel made visits to the USSR and Eastern Europe (ADN, East Berlin, 3 March; *FBIS*, 4 March). Soviet warships also continued to visit Mozambican harbors on a regular basis (Johannesburg international service, 29 November; *FBIS*, 30 November). A Soviet military delegation visited Mozambique's Military School at Nampula and other regions of the country in January (Maputo domestic service, 2 January; *FBIS*, 5 January). Additionally, Mozambique and the Soviet Union signed an agreement to double the value of bilateral trade by 1985. This agreement is to run for three years and stipulates that the Soviet Union is to supply Mozambique with machinery, raw materials, chemical products, animal feed, and consumer goods. Mozambican exports will include sisal, cashew nuts, and prawns.

FRELIMO also signed a cooperation agreement with the Soviet-backed People's Democratic Party of Afghanistan (Maputo domestic service, 3 May; *FBIS*, 5 May). President Machel also urged closer ties with Cuba to "strengthen the links of friendship and cooperation which bind the two peoples, parties, and states in the common struggle for economic, social and cultural development, and for peace among peoples" (Maputo domestic service, 26 July; *FBIS*, 27 July).

Publications. FRELIMO controls the media. Since gaining its independence from Portugal, FRELIMO has relied on two publications to carry its message to the Mozambican people —the daily paper *Notícias* and the weekly magazine *O Tempo*. To improve the popular appeal of the print media, the government launched two more national-circulation newspapers in 1981: *Diario de Moçambique* in Mozambique's second largest city, Beira, and the Sunday *Domingo*. (For additional background, see *YICA*, 1982, p. 41.) *Voz da Revolução*, an organ of the Central Committee, focuses on developing theoretical studies on Marxism and FRELIMO policies.

Thomas H. Henriksen
Hoover Insitution

Nigeria

Population. 85.2 million (*World Factbook*, 1983)
Party. Socialist Working People's Party (SWPP)
Founded. 1963
Membership. Unknown
Secretary General. (Idi)dapo Fatogun
Politburo. 4 members: Chaika Anozie (chairman), Wahab Goodluck (deputy chairman), Hassan Sunmonu (Presidium member and president of Nigerian Labour Congress), Lasisi A. Osunde
Secretariat. No information
Central Committee. No information
Status. Proscribed
Last Congress. First, December 1965
Last Election. November 1983 (SWPP ineligible)
Auxiliary Organizations. No information
Publications. *New Horizon*

The SWPP once again failed to receive certification from the Federal Electoral Commission and was thus unable to contest the November 1983 national election. The election was won by President Alhaji Shehu Shagari and the National Party of Nigeria with 47 percent of the vote. The results became meaningless on 31 December when the military took power in Nigeria and installed a new Federal Military Government. All political parties were banned, and the SWPP once again became a proscribed party.

The SWPP put much of its efforts during the year into the Nigerian Labour Congress (NLC).

Party Presidium member Hassan Sunmonu remained the head of the NLC and was successful in sending most NLC trainees to Eastern bloc countries and in keeping out Western labor influence.

SWPP chairman Chaika Anozie attended the Karl Marx celebrations in East Germany in April 1983. Little else was reported about SWPP activities, either internal or external.

Jack H. Mower
Washington, D.C.

Réunion

Population. 531,000 (July 1983)
Party. Réunion Communist Party (Parti communiste réunionnaise; PCR)
Founded. 1959
Membership. 10,000 claimed (September 1981); 2,000 (*YICA*, 1982, p. xvi)
Secretary General. Paul Vergès
Politburo. 12 members: Gervais Barret, Julien Ramin; remaining 10 members unknown
Secretariat. 6 members: Paul Vergès, Elie Hoarau, Jean-Baptiste Ponama; remaining 3 members unknown
Central Committee. 32 members: Bruny (Ary) Payet, Roger Hoarau, Daniel Lallemand, Hippolite Piot, Ary Yee Chong Tchi-Kan, Laurence Vergès; remaining 26 members unknown
Status. Legal
Last Congress. Fifth, 12–14 July 1980, in Le Port
Last Election. 1983, 32.7 percent, 16 of 45 (local assembly); none in Paris
Auxiliary Organizations. Anticolonialist Front for Réunion Autonomy, Réunion Front of Autonomous Youth, General Federation of Réunion Women, Réunion Peace Committee, Réunion General Confederation of Workers
Publications. *Témoignages* (daily); *Travailleur réunionnais* (semimonthly), published by Réunion General Confederation of Workers

The island of Réunion is a French overseas department—an integral part of the French Republic. The PCR was organized in 1959 when the Réunion federation of the French Communist Party became autonomous. The party is relatively small, with supporters primarily in the Le Port district. The left-wing parties of the island advocate increased autonomy, amounting to virtual internal self-government, but few advocate complete independence. As an overseas department, Réunion is governed by a Paris-appointed prefect who is the senior local official, an elected General Council of 36 members, and an elected Regional Council of 45 members. Réunion is represented by three deputies and two senators in the French parliament.

During 1983, the PCR continued its initiatives to revitalize the nation's economy. (Réunion has an agricultural economy based chiefly on sugar, which constitutes over 80 percent of the island's exports.) Unemployment and inflation are the major causes of discontent on the island. The basic difficulty with the island's economic system, according to the PCR, is that over centuries of French rule, Réunion has been turned too completely into an arm of the French economy. (Fredericka M. Bunge, *Indian Ocean: Five Island Countries*, Washington, D.C.: Government Printing Office, 1983.)

The party participated in the regional elections held on 20 February and municipal elections held in two rounds on 6 and 13 March. Prior to these elections, the Réunion Federation of the Socialist Party (SP) and the PCR signed an unprecedented agreement to share offices should they win the regional council elections (*Indian Ocean Newsletter*, 29 January). The two leftist parties also agreed on the manner in which candidates from both parties would run on a single ticket. The agreement also stipulated the terms under which other parties outside the traditional left-wing parties could participate in an alliance with them.

(The agreement between the two parties contrasted sharply with the 1977 municipal elections and the 1978 general elections when relations between the two parties were at a low point.) Left-wing candidates won over 50 percent of the votes cast in the elections for the regional council. PCR member Mario Hoarau subsequently became president of the regional council.

The rapprochement between the SP and the PCR increased on 5 August when a high-level meeting between the two parties was held. The two parties agreed that they wanted the Regional Council elected in February to be given wider powers in regard to establishing a new development policy for the island. During the four-hour meeting, a coordination committee composed of members of both parties was established to allow for daily contact to avoid future misunderstanding and lead to closer cooperation (*Ion*, 6 August). However, following the defeat of PCR candidate Bruny Payet in the 20 September Senate election, the two parties accused each other of responsibility for the defeat, and relations grew strained again (ibid., 8 October).

The conclusions reached by the PCR at a 2 October Central Committee meeting indicate that the party has hardened its positions toward the ruling left-wing government in France. In discussing a bill defining the powers of the Regional Council, the PCR stated that the range of those powers must be rather extensive in order to implement an economic and social development plan for the island (ibid., 8 October). PCR secretary general Paul Vergès had warned in July that if a development policy was not rapidly applied, a social explosion on the island seemed inevitable. The PCR, through affiliate organizations, has since the summer successfully mobilized the young and unemployed, in addition to women and plantation workers (ibid., 6 August).

In a move designed to defuse a social explosion, the PCR Central Committee embarked on a program of tasks in different areas to create conditions for economic revival on the island. The foundation of the PCR economic revival program is the shifting of government spending in Réunion from the most prosperous sectors to the productive forces. To support the revival program, the party set into motion a nationwide movement of internal solidarity.

Party Organization and Leadership. Paul Vergès, a member of the European Parliament since 1979, is secretary general and a member of the Secretariat of the PCR. He is also mayor of Le Port. Secretariat member Elie Hoarau serves concurrently as secretary of the Réunion Peace Committee, secretary general of the Réunion General Confederation of Labor, and a member of the World Peace Council. Central Committee member Bruny Payet serves concurrently as president of the Réunion Peace Committee and head of the Réunion General Confederation of Labor. Payet is also a member of the World Peace Council and the World Federation of Trade Unions General Council. Daniel Lallemand has been the party's major spokesman abroad since 1981. Ary Yee Chong Tchi-Kan was the secretary general of the communist youth in 1980. Other prominent members of the PCR are Jean-Baptiste Ponama, Gervais Barret, Julien Ramin, Roger Hoarau, Hippolite Piot, Laurence Vergès, and Lucet Langenier.

Domestic Policies and Activities. The major goal of the PCR, self-determination through democratic and popular autonomy, is the foundation of the party's domestic and international policies. The PCR contends that the neocolonial status of Réunion is the cause of the island's social and economic problems. The party continues to strive for a more balanced economy as a means of redressing the inequalities between social benefits in France and on the island.

In late summer, the PCR intensified its campaign to obtain the closure of the South African consulate in Saint-Dènis. The PCR held a demonstration in front of the consulate in July. On 6 August, a similar demonstration organized by the General Federation of Réunion Women drew a crowd of approximately 1,500 people (*Ion*, 20 August).

International Activities. Members of the PCR participate regularly in various international conferences and communist party activities and maintain close links with the communist parties of other French overseas departments. The PCR supports liberation struggles in South Africa and Namibia, endorses the Palestine Liberation Organization, and approves the Soviet occupation of Afghanistan. The party favors the creation of a zone of peace in the Indian Ocean and has repeatedly called for the removal of military forces from the region.

Joyce Myrick
Arlington, Va.

Saudi Arabia

Population. 10.4 million (mid-1983)
Party. Communist Party of Saudi Arabia (CPSA)
Founded. 1975
Membership. Unknown but believed negligible
Spokesmen. (Positions not identified) Abdullah Muhammad (1974, member of predecessor Saudi National Liberation Front), Abd-al-Rahman Salih (1980), Salim Hamid (1980), Hamad Mubarak (1982), Abu Abdullah (named as Saudi spokesman in July 1983 *World Marxist Review* but not specifically stated to be member of CPSA)
Status. Illegal
Last Congress. Unknown
Last Election. Not applicable
Auxiliary Organizations. Saudi Peace and Solidarity Committee (affiliate of the World Peace Council and, apparently, of the Afro-Asian Peoples' Solidarity Organization), Saudi Democratic Youth (affiliate of the World Federation of Democratic Youth)
Publications. Apparently exist (see below) but titles unknown

After participating in a spate of international communist meetings between October 1980 and July 1982 (see *YICA*, 1983, p. 40), the CPSA appeared inactive in this respect for almost a year, apparently missing both the December 1982 USSR sixtieth anniversary celebrations in Moscow and the April 1983 Karl Marx World Scientific Conference in East Berlin (both of which were attended by the vast majority of pro-Soviet communist parties). The organ of the illegal Popular Front for the Liberation of Bahrain, *Fifth of March*, noted in its June issue, however, that the CPSA along with the "Arab Socialist Work Party in [sic] the Arabian Peninsula" participated in a May meeting in Damascus of Arab revolutionary groups. Also in May, the CPSA met separately with the Bahrain National Liberation Front, and in June, the two groups participated in a meeting of twelve communist and workers' parties of the Arab countries. The French Communist Party's *L'Humanité* (10 September) cited the CPSA among the foreign organizations represented at its September press

festival (held in a Paris suburb). Also the Saudi Peace and Solidarity Committee sent Nasir Muhammad and Salim Ali (not further identified) to the June 1983 Prague World Assembly for Peace and Life, Against Nuclear War.

In the one unilateral CPSA policy pronouncement noted during the year, an unidentified spokesman cited an "Arab Socialist Labor Party" (believed identical to the Arab Socialist Work Party noted above) as one of the underground opposition forces with which his party was seeking cooperation; the other groups cited in this context were much less specific, i.e., "religious circles, and revolutionary elements of the petit bourgeoisie" (*WMR*, April). The article went on to state that the CPSA was opposing the government by engaging in counterpropaganda through its (undesignated) publications and by using its "influence in underground mass movements and in some governmental and other organizations."

Wallace H. Spaulding
McLean, Virginia

Senegal

Population. 6.3 million
Party. Independence and Labor Party (Parti de l'Indépendance et du Travail; PIT)
Founded. 1957
Membership. Unknown
Secretary General. Seydou Cissoko
Politburo. 5 members: Amath Dansoko, Semy Pathe Gueye, Maguette Thaim, Samba Diould Thaim, Makhtar Mbaye
Secretariat. Unknown
Central Committee. Unknown
Status. Legal
Last Congress. Constituent, August 1981
Last Elections. 27 February; 0 percent of the vote
Auxiliary Organizations. Unknown
Publications. *Ande Sopi*

On 27 February Abdou Diouf and the ruling Parti Socialiste won an overwhelming election victory. The Parti Socialiste now has 111 seats in the National Assembly versus 9 for the opposition.

Prior to the election, the PIT discussed the possibility of running in alliance with the main opposition party, the Parti Démocratique Socialiste. However, all parties had to run independently since coalitions were banned.

The PIT played a minimal role in the national election, and its activities, if anything, declined in the year under review. The political scene in Senegal is confusing, for there are now fifteen registered political parties. A number of these parties claim to be Marxist-Leninist or at least socialist, but the PIT is the party recognized by the world communist movement.

In December 1982 Seydou Cissoko attended the sixtieth anniversary celebrations of the founding of the USSR, and in April 1983 Amath Dansoko attended the Karl Marx celebrations in East Germany. Dansoko's statement on the elections complained about government harassment, but promised renewed efforts in the future. "Another lesson is that while the masses were deeply shocked by what occurred on February 27, they are not yet mature enough politically to break at once with the neocolonialist regime [which] . . . continues to fetter the people's thinking." (*IB*, October.) A statement by the PIT Politburo congratulated the party on its successes but called for more active efforts "to promote the further strengthening of our party as a party of struggle and initiative at the service of the working people of the country" (ibid.).

There is little additional information on the PIT's activities or its impact on the Senegalese scene.

Jack H. Mower
Washington, D.C.

South Africa

Population. 30.9 million (1980)
Party. South African Communist Party (SACP)
Founded. 1921
Membership. Unknown (not published)
Secretary General. Moses Mabhida
Politburo. Unknown (not published)
Secretariat. Unknown (not published)
Central Committee. Unknown (not published)
Status. Proscribed
Last Congress. Fifth Conference, December 1962
Last Election. Not applicable
Auxiliary Organizations. Not applicable
Publications. *African Communist* (in exile; quarterly)

Entering the fourth decade of its existence as the banned re-creation of the continent's first Marxist-Leninist party, the SACP maintained adherence to well-established policies linking it closely with the country's leading black nationalist organization, the African National Congress (ANC), which has also operated underground and in exile since its proscription in 1960. In the eyes of the Nationalist government of the country, both the SACP and the ANC are the linchpins of a Soviet-directed "total onslaught" against the existing established order.

Originally rooted in a small militant minority of primarily English-speaking white workers and professionals opposed to participation in World War I and drawn together by support for the Bolshevik Revolution, the party was formally established in 1921 as the Communist Party of South Africa. Although nonracial from its inception, the membership became predominantly African only in the late 1920s and early 1930s, at a time when the party's survival seemed threatened by simultaneous government persecution and debilitating internal factional disputes. Surmounting its sectarianism in the late 1930s and less harassed by a government increasingly preoc-

cupied with mobilizing for the war effort against the Nazis and containing Afrikaner Nationalist antiwar opposition, the party successfully extended itself to all segments of the country's population, drawing into its ranks Afrikaners as well as Indians and Coloureds. Party activists took leading roles in trade unions, organizing both white and black semiskilled and unskilled workers, and also participated in established African and Indian national political organizations. In the 1940s, the party selectively contested municipal, provincial, and parliamentary elections in the Cape and on Witwatersrand, succeeding only in the late 1940s when several white members gained election as representatives of the small number of African voters then enfranchised on a separate roll. Although the party's membership during this period of its legal existence never exceeded several thousand, its multiracial leadership and highly visible identification with labor militancy and black activism magnified its role as the country's first (and, at the time, only) nonracial political party. The Nationalist party government at the time of its unexpected electoral victory in 1948 spotlighted the small party as a major opponent and in 1950 passed the Suppression of Communism Act. Ill-prepared for il-legality, a majority of the party's Central Committee hastily voted in Cape Town to dissolve the 29-year-old party shortly before the act took effect.

Three years later, dedicated cadres meeting secretly in Johannesburg reconstituted the party as the SACP. Throughout the 1950s, its members participated actively in the expanding campaigns of the harassed, but grudgingly tolerated multiracial extraparliamentary Congress Alliance, headed by the ANC. A central event was the 1955 Congress of the People, at which the Freedom Charter, a generally worded statement demanding the dismantling of apartheid, full democratic rights for all South Africans, and major economic reforms including limited nationalization of some major industries, was accepted. In the aftermath of Sharpeville and the banning of the ANC in 1960, the SACP publicly revealed its underground existence; shortly thereafter it joined with leaders of the ANC to form a new clandestine organization, Umkhonto we Sizwe, dedicated to selected sabotage (initiated in December 1961) and eventually to guerrilla activity. The switch from the nonviolent tactics previously practiced by both organizations came amid accelerating government legislation and crackdowns designed to thwart all radical opposition, "a ferocity of reprisal which almost decimated the movement, which smashed the Party headquarters and penetrated deeply into its membership cells; and which finally made the retreat of the Party and the ANC leadership into temporary exile abroad essential if anything was to be saved for rebuilding" (*African Communist*, no. 86, p. 44). With many of its established leaders, as well as more recent recruits, imprisoned, the SACP directed most of its remaining longtime activists into exile in friendly African countries and Europe. Thrown into enforced proximity with fellow ANC exiles of all political persuasions, the SACP cooperated with the ANC to craft new methods and structures to cope both with exile and the rebuilding of an effective underground in their distant homeland. Despite sometimes sharp differences and unrelenting government antagonism, the exiled organizations have established underground beachheads from which militants, trained both outside and inside the country, have, with increasing effectiveness and visibility since the late 1970s, escalated armed attacks on selected military, admin-istrative, and industrial targets as a counterpoint to efforts by party activists and ANC supporters to spur further mass political challenges to the government and to extend worker solidarity in the exploding black trade union movement.

In the present situation of continuing exile and clandestineness, coupled with widening internal ferment, it is impossible to determine party membership or its racial composition. Yet it is clear that the SACP has been successful in attracting younger blacks from the ranks of the youth mobilized by the 1976 Soweto demonstrations and subsequent militancy; they swell clusters of older party members concentrated in the major exile headquarters and training centers where the bulk of the senior leadership lives and works. Internal membership is almost certainly centered in the largest urban centers at the hubs of the most intense political and trade union activity.

Organization and Leadership. The SACP suffered a major loss on 19 September when Dr. Yusef Dadoo, a 74-year-old Indian medical practitioner, who had been party chairman since 1972 (and a party member since 1939), died in exile in London. He is survived by the general secretary, Moses Mabhida, a longtime African trade unionist who was awarded the Order of the Friendship of Peoples by the Soviet Union on his sixtieth birthday on 14 October. Like Dadoo, Mabhida joined the party in its legal period (1942) and went into exile in the early 1960s. He occupied a full-time post with Umkhonto we Sizwe from 1963 until his election as general secretary in 1979. Other members of the Political Bureau and Central Committee have not been publicly named; most writers for the party press contribute under a nom de plume.

A major focal point for SACP activity is the ANC, which from its foundation in 1912 was open to Africans of all political persuasions. Although for a brief period in the 1930s communists were unwelcome and subsequently in the late 1940s and late 1950s the often intertwined questions of the roles of communists and non-Africans became contentious, the ANC continued to accept communist participation at all levels. In the harsh underground and exile environment shared by the SACP and the ANC since the banning of the latter in 1960, the two organizations grew even closer, with a major turning point being the decision of the ANC in 1969 to admit non-Africans to membership; immediately prominent non-African communists were made members of key ANC bodies. In the 1980s, according to Oliver Tambo, president of the ANC, "the relationship between the ANC and the SACP is not an accident of history, nor is it a natural and inevitable development. For, as we can see, similar relationships have not emerged in the course of liberation struggles in other parts of Africa . . . our alliance is a living organism that has grown out of struggle. We have built it out of our separate and common experiences . . . Our organizations have been able to agree on fundamental strategies and tactical positions while retaining our separate identities . . . Within our revolutionary alliance each organization has a distinct and vital role to play. A correct understanding of these roles and respect for their boundaries has ensured the survival and consolidation of our cooperation and unity." (*Sechaba*, September 1981, pp. 4–5.) In the perspective of Dr. Dadoo (in his last published analysis), "the ANC and the SACP personify the two complementary streams of revolutionary consciousness and revolutionary organization. They are complementary because in South Africa the struggle for national liberation insistently requires organized participation by the working class and its political vanguard, the Communist Party, and the struggle for socialism just as insistently requires a powerful movement for the freedom of the oppressed nations and races, a movement led by the ANC . . . The front of the fighters for the victory of the national-democratic revolution is led by the . . . ANC . . . a vanguard movement which includes Africans, coloureds, Indians, and the most courageous, farsighted and increasingly democratic-minded section of the White community," while "the South African Communist Party expresses the interests of the proletariat, which acts not only within the national-democratic front, but also carries on its own class struggle. Its goals do not conflict with the goals of the national-democratic revolution, but go beyond these, to the prospect of a radical restructuring of the society on socialist lines." (*WMR*, December 1982.)

To advance its goals, the SACP keeps itself separate and independent within the national liberation movement; in the formulation of Mabhida, "we are autonomous in all respects, having our own structure, leadership, information and communication services, finances and officials. It would not be possible for us to make a proper contribution to the struggle if we lost any piece of our independence and capacity for self-determination." (*African Communist*, no. 92, p. 82.)

Domestic Activities and Attitudes. Dadoo's and Mabhida's characterizations of the SACP and its relationship to the ANC are fully consistent with the tenor of the party's program, The Road to South African Freedom, adopted at an underground national conference in 1962 and reiterated at an augmented meeting of the Central Committee held in exile in 1979 and then further elaborated by the Political Bureau and Central Committee in 1980 and 1981. The South African system is diagnosed as "colonialism of a special type," "internal colonialism" in which the oppressors and oppressed live within the same territory, one in which capitalism has assumed highly developed forms such that bases exist for transition to a higher level of social organization. In this setting there is an organic connection between the struggles for national liberation and socialism in which the former takes priority, yet only with simultaneous attention to how the latter may be achieved once racial oppression is ended and national democracy is realized. As Joe Slovo, a prominent white SACP member, put it: "There is no Chinese Wall between the stages of our revolution . . . What will happen after the ANC is in Pretoria will depend on which class plays the dominant role *now* at *this* stage of the fight for liberation. It is at this stage that we need not just a mass national movement, but also an independent class party of workers which plays a significant role in the liberation alliance. If we wait for the working class to organize itself only after the liberation flag is raised in Pretoria, we will be in the same unfortunate position as 90 percent of Africa found itself after independence." (Ibid., no. 95, p. 87.)

The present conjuncture is seen as particularly promising. "Against the background of the deep economic, political and ideological crisis, which is rocking the very foundations of the existing system," the strategic initiative has passed to the oppressed as manifested "in the blend and close interlacing of various forms of struggle; armed operations by the combat Umkhonto we Sizwe (Spear of the Nation) contingents, the mounting strike movement, mass action by students, protests by the dispossessed in the poor Black townships and locations, and organized political campaigns" (*WMR*, December 1982). Buoyed psychologically, especially by the victories of the liberation movements in Angola and Mozambique, and then subsequently by the transition to majority rule in Zimbabwe, blacks are no longer willing to accept the existing order at the same time that rifts within the ranks of the white minority are deepening. Yet crisis does not mean imminent collapse.

The SACP sees no immediate hopes in the reforms either of the "moderates" of the Nationalist Party or in the proposals of the "pseudo-liberals" of the white opposition Progressive Federal Party. The government's "total strategy" is "essentially a strategy of total war against our people, a strategy of genocide" in which South Africa, able to survive only because of support of the major imperialist powers, "constitutes a real threat to the independence and peaceful life of the newly free African countries, especially the frontline states." (Ibid.) Nevertheless, a frequent contributor to the party journal contended that although differences between the Nationalists and its right-wing Afrikaner opponents are small, "the outcome of this conflict is not a matter of indifference to the people's movement. If the existing constellation of ruling forces can be broken, if the most reactionary among them can be isolated, if movement of the political situation can begin, the people have the strength to ensure that such movement will go on, much further than its initiators dream. The liberation movement must therefore be alert to seize every chance of advantage that the new developments offer...the Congress movement must remember the mission which it undertook, through the formation of the Congress of Democrats [in 1953], to the white population as a whole. That mission is an honorable one and one which deserves to succeed—to point out that broad circles of the white population, workers, intelligentsia, middle classes, have a genuine interest in changing direction and accepting the results of liberation for the oppressed majority. There is a purpose to be served by bringing this message even to those whites who refuse to listen...the white population must be made conscious, not of an enemy which threatens them with more radical change, but of a leadership which can become their own and lead them to a better future for the whole South African people." (*African Communist*, no. 92, p. 32.)

Yet "within the broad bloc of forces opposing the racist autocracy, the leading role objectively belongs to the working class, the chief motive force of the revolutionary process in South Africa and the mightiest adversary of racism." It is recognized that "the overwhelming majority of white workers are, unfortunately, infected with racial prejudice...the struggle to clear their minds of the poisonous fumes of chauvinism will be long and hard." But the SACP is heartened by the steady upsurge in trade union activity and militance among the black majority of the proletariat in which "effective support of militant working-class action by broad strata of the population is a relatively new and highly effective factor." (*WMR*, December 1982.) Taking note of calls for unity from all quarters of the emerging black trade union movement as well as continuing divisions over registration, industrial councils, appropriate types of unions, affiliations with international federations, and everyday strategies and tactics, a party analyst stated: "So much is at stake, so much to be gained by the formation of a single united trade union federation, that every effort must be made to remove all obstacles from the path of unity" (*African Communist*, no. 95, p. 35). To achieve this end, both registered and nonregistered unions should be accepted, affiliation with any international trade union center should presently not be attempted, and efforts should be made to encourage general workers' unions to give way to single unions for each industry.

The core of the struggle against apartheid remains the national liberation movement as a whole. In the estimation of Dr. Dadoo, it "largely owes its present scope and clarity of perspectives to our party's tireless activity in the organizational, political and ideological spheres. The well-thought and clear-cut concepts and tenets based on the theory of scientific socialism are now no longer the exclusive asset of the communist, but have been variously spread to broad sections of the fighters for liberation." (*WMR*, December 1982.)

International Views and Activities. The SACP continues to identify itself fully with the Soviet Union and its East European allies, particularly the German Democratic Republic, but in contrast with previous years, the party press was free from polemics against either the Chinese or Eurocommunism. Special attention was given to observations of the centenary of Karl Marx's death, with Mabhida delivering addresses at both the international conference organized by the Socialist Unity Party in East Berlin in April and at a special anniversary conference convened by the Communist Party of the United States in New York in March (a special delayed session of which was held to accommodate Mabhida's late arrival due to his inability to receive a U.S. visa in time). In his speech to the American conference, Mabhida articulated his faith in the relevance of Marxism for Africa: "Twelve Marxist-Leninist Parties have taken shape in different countries of Africa. A minority of these are in power, constituting islands of socialism in an underdeveloped and technologically backward continent. But they are Marxist-Leninist in outlook and organization; determined to solve the main problem of bringing about the transition from capitalism to socialism. Marxism has come to stay in Africa. Its immediate future depends on the determination of the vanguard parties and scattered groups of intellectuals, workers and peasants throughout the continent who recognize that socialism alone provides a satisfactory and lasting solution to the continent's problems of ignorance, illiteracy, disease, poverty, technological backwardness and imperialist exploitation." (*African Communist*, no. 95, p. 26.)

Publications. Since 1959 the SACP has published its quarterly, *African Communist*, "in the interests of African solidarity, and as a forum for Marxist-Leninist thought throughout our Continent." It is presently printed in the German Democratic Republic but distributed from an office in London that also sells other party publications. A similar arrangement is utilized by the ANC for publication of its monthly journal, *Sechaba*, which is directed to members and overseas supporters.

Both the SACP and the ANC smuggle their publications into South Africa to supplement internally produced literature that is circulated underground, as are banned Marxist-Leninist classics. Other publications are produced by the ANC and allied organizations in European and African exile centers.

The written word is complemented by Radio Freedom, Voice of the African National Congress and Umkhonto We Sizwe, The People's Army, which broadcasts on shortwave frequencies for several hours daily on the transmitters of the state-owned radios of Angola, Ethiopia, Madagascar, Tanzania, and Zambia.

Sheridan Johns
Duke University

Sudan

Population. 20,585,000 (*World Factbook*, 1983)
Party. Sudanese Communist Party (al-Hizb al-Shuyu'i al-Sudani; SCP)
Founded. 1946
Membership. 5,000–10,000 members before 1971; present number estimated at 1,500
Secretary General. Muhammad Ibrahim Nugud Mansur
Politburo. 6 members: Muhammad Ibrahim Nugud Mansur, Ali al-Tijani al-Tayyib Babikar (number two leader, arrested November 1980), Dr. Izz-al Din Ali Amir, Sulayman Hamid, Al-Gazuli (Jizuli) Said Uthman, Muhammad Ahmad Sulayman
Secretariat. 7 members: Muhammad Ibrahim Nugud Mansur, Ali al-Tijani al-Tayyib Babikar, Dr. Izz-al Din Ali Amir, Abu al-Qasim (Gassim) Muhammad, Sulayman Hamid, Al-Gazuli Said Uthman, Muhammad Ahmad Sulayman

Additional Central Committee Members. Sudi Darag, Khad(i)r Nasir, Abd-al-Majid Shakak, Hassan Gassim al-Sid (World Peace Council Presidential Committee member and World Federation of Trade Unions [WFTU] staff member), Ibrahim Zakariya (secretary general of WFTU)

Other Prominent SCP Members. Sharif Dishoni (1978 party spokesperson), Ahmad Salim (SCP Economic Commission member and member of Prague-based Editorial Council of *World Marxist Review*)

Status. Illegal

Last Congress. Fourth, October 1967, in Khartoum

Last Election. Not applicable

Auxiliary Organizations. Democratic Federation of Sudanese Students (DSFS, affiliated with International Union of Students), Sudanese Youth Union, Sudan Workers' Trade Union Federation (SWTUF, operates with quasi-official standing), Sudanese Defenders of Peace and Democracy (presumably a World Peace Council affiliate)

Publications. No formal newspaper, although SCP propagates its views through clandestinely distributed leaflets

A small group of intellectuals at Khartoum University founded the SCP in 1946. Communist elements soon infiltrated the White Flag League (the first modern expression of Sudanese nationalism), and the SCP broadened its appeal to include railway workers and peasants. On the basis of its ties with railway workers, the SCP made inroads into the SWTUF, which was set up in 1950. In 1951, the SCP was a leading force, along with the SCP-influenced Gezira Tenants' Union, in the Anti-Imperialist Front, the leader of the popular struggle for Sudanese independence.

In the stormy period following the declaration of Sudanese independence, the SCP made its presence felt in Sudanese politics. SCP activism was especially apparent after plummeting cotton prices triggered socioeconomic discontent and political chaos in 1958. The SCP was the only political party in Sudan to oppose the military regime that seized power in a coup d'etat in November 1958. The SCP could not make much immediate political capital from its opposition, however. Gen. Ibrahim Abbud promptly arrested all Sudanese communist leaders he could find. He also banned all trade unions, some of which were rallying points for the SCP.

The first Sudanese military regime foundered in 1964 when its inability to handle an increasingly expensive war in the south sparked a popular revolt and a general political strike. The SCP played a major role in this political instability by organizing workers, peasants, students, professionals, and intelligentsia of the Muslim north.

SCP officials were elected to parliament in 1965 as part of the second parliamentary government that replaced the junta. But the ruling coalition viewed the SCP members of parliament as a threat. The communist members were shortly thereafter denied their seats in parliament and eventually forced underground again.

Deteriorating economic conditions (especially the bottoming out of the cotton market) created another political crisis and still another opportunity for the SCP to enter the political scene. On 25 May 1969, Col. Jaafar Numeiri seized control of Sudan in a virtually bloodless coup d'etat. The SCP supported Numeiri and became the only legal party. The victory of Numeiri and his SCP allies was a decisive victory for the Left against powerful economic interests in Sudan and foreign capital.

Never was the popularity of the SCP so high as it was in 1970. At that time, the SCP had somewhere between 5,000 and 10,000 members, making it the strongest and best-organized communist party in the Middle East and Africa. But its popularity and strength were short-lived.

Numeiri's dream of a socialist paradise never materialized. The reality of Sudan's dependence on cotton and Sudan's inability to generate sufficient local capital to replace the departure of foreign capital prompted Numeiri to move to the right economically, thus sparking political differences between himself and the SCP. Numeiri's decision to veer from leftist economic policies also created a split in the SCP.

The SCP's call for "revolution by stages"—first "national democratic" and then socialist—encouraged the moderate faction to support Numeiri's drift to the right and Numeiri's eagerness to dissolve the SCP into the newly created Sudan Socialist Union (SSU). However, the more radical faction of the SCP (strongly represented by pro-communist army officers) opposed Numeiri's moves to the right. The abortive 1971 coup d'etat attempt—apparently the doing of leftist army officers who wanted to reverse Numeiri's shift to the right—pushed Numeiri even further away from his former SCP allies. Numeiri rounded up and liquidated most of the SCP leaders; others were forced into exile. The party was declared illegal, thus forcing it to operate mainly in exile.

By about 1970, the SCP consisted of roughly three factions: the orthodox Moscow-oriented faction (under Abdal-Khaliq Mahjub until his execution in 1971), a Chinese-oriented revolutionary communist faction, and a group professing "local Sudanized Marxism" without ties to any external powers (previously identified with cabinet members Ahmed Sulayman and Farouq Abu Issa).

Following the 1971 coup attempt, two distinct wings of the SCP emerged. A split developed over the proper role of the army in a revolution. One faction argued that the army must have the leading role in a revolution against the government. Followers of former secretary general Abd al-Khaliq Mahjub disagreed, arguing that to start a revolution with only the army ready to act would be to guarantee failure, that a successful revolution in Sudan must be led by the working class.

The Mahjub thesis stressed the staggering obstacles to a successful revolution in Sudan: the economic dominance of "Western imperialism"; the enormous strength of counterrevolutionary, traditionalist forces; and the factional divisions among the geographic regions of the country, which were exploited by the imperialists and Sudanese reactionary groups. Only a revolution led by the working class but with a strong organization of democratic-revolutionary forces from all Sudanese groups could overcome existing social and economic obstacles. A revolution with only the support of the army was not a real revolution and thus would fail.

The Mahjub faction appears to be the most dominant SCP group today, especially on the international stage. For instance, at the Karl Marx centenary in East Berlin in mid-April, Ahmad Salim, the SCP delegate to the *World Marxist Review*'s Editorial Council, stated that Marxism-Leninism arises from the efforts of "the most avant-garde class of our time, namely the working class" (*Neues Deutschland*, 16–17 April).

Domestic Issues. The SCP now calls for a united front of all progressive, democratic groups to free the country from the government of Numeiri, which it feels is an unjust, corrupt military dictatorship (interview with Fatimah Ibrahim, *Al-Yasar al-'Arabi*, Paris, no. 58, October, pp. 12–13). In this regard, the SCP is making every effort to forge alliances with other political groups in Sudan. During 1983, however, there was no indication that the SCP was enjoying any success. Most of the traditional political groups in Sudan are still suspicious of the communists. The SCP is not without supporters, but no formal bonds have been formed with other political parties. As a result, SCP cadres inside Sudan are forced to operate underground, taking orders from exiled leaders.

The SCP has considerable influence among intellectuals, students, railway workers, sympathizers in the armed forces, and cotton growers. The SCP is especially strong in the trade unions. Communist inroads are also visible among 2–3 million disgruntled refugees in Sudan. The SCP also has links with some Sudanese refugees in Ethiopia. In this regard, the SCP reportedly has been aided by Addis Ababa; it is not certain, however, whether this Ethiopian assistance is continuing in the wake of improved relations between Khartoum and Addis Ababa. (Harold D. Nelson, *Sudan: A Country Study*, p. 283.)

The SCP takes a predictable Third World Marxist line on what ails the Sudanese economy. Numeiri has allowed foreign capitalists to capture the Sudanese economy. These foreign capitalists have co-opted and corrupted the Numeiri government, making it an accomplice in the crime of amassing riches at the expense of the downtrodden Sudanese people. In a late 1983 interview, SCP member Fatimah Ibrahim referred to Numeiri as the "10 percenter," because he skims 10 percent off all state revenues and commercial transactions for himself. She also criticized Numeiri's wife for being a "millionairess." (*Al-Yasar al-'Arabi*, no. 58, October, pp. 12–13.)

The SCP also charges that the "new administrative bourgeoisie" in Khartoum has caved in to the International Monetary Fund's demands for austerity policies in Sudan. These policies, in turn, have caused the standard of living of the workers and peasants to plummet.

To rid the country of those responsible for the current economic malaise in Sudan, the SCP calls for "revolution by stages"—first a "national democratic" revolution and then a truly socialist revolution. As a first step in the quest for a national democratic revolution, Sudanese communists are calling for a national congress of all elements opposed to the Numeiri government. The congress would analyze the causes of the Sudanese economic disorder and come up with proposals to improve matters. This SCP proposal is seen in Sudan as a rather transparent attempt to establish some legitimacy. So far, the SCP has had no takers.

The SCP understands and accommodates itself to the fundamental religious nature of Sudanese society and maintains a rather flexible attitude toward ideology and religion. Unlike some more rigid communist parties, the SCP does not reject Islam. In fact, according to the SCP, communism and Islam are natural allies, both fighting against imperialism.

But while Islam may not contradict communism, Islam does not occupy a central political role for the SCP, and this fact puts the communists at a disadvantage vis-à-vis the religious political parties in Sudan—the Ansar and the Khatmiyya.

However, the SCP can and does appeal to the three most important sectors of Sudanese society where traditional religious, tribal, or sectarian loyalties have been increasingly undermined by the economic, cultural, and social impact of modernization. The cotton growers, the railway workers, and the intelligentsia have all been penetrated, to a greater or lesser extent, by the SCP. The SCP is the only communist party in the Arab world that regards the peasants (the cotton growers) as a potentially important ally.

But while modernization and the concomitant economic grievances provide a link between the SCP and elements within these groups, the majority of these groups still support the traditional parties in Sudan. In short, the SCP has yet to find a satisfactory way to overcome the inherent contradictions between communism and Islam.

On the fundamental dispute in Sudan between the rich north and the poor south, the SCP was the first and only Sudanese party to propose regional autonomy for the south. The SCP has consistently and firmly supported this position since 1954. According to the SCP, the unity of the country is endangered unless its plan for the south is implemented. And as long as this is not realized by the northern parties, the south will be a lightning rod to be exploited by external powers.

While the SCP has never succeeded in becoming a major force in Sudan, its impact on Sudanese politics has been significant, especially during periods of crisis. In difficult periods, the SCP poses at least a potential danger as a divisive factor in Sudanese society. In particular, the SCP tries to exploit the problems of the south and of sectarian politics in order to enhance its status.

From 1972 until 1980, north-south relations were relatively calm. But after 1980, relations deteriorated markedly. In the past year or two, an upsurge of violence in the south indicates that the north-south issue may be reaching crisis proportions. During this troubled period, the SCP can be counted on to try to exploit the situation in hopes of strengthening its position.

In an interview in late 1983, SCP official Mohammad Mahjub revealed that the SCP is now focusing its activities on the "southern problem." He defined the problem as an ethnic one (between the blacks of the south and the Arab Muslims of the north) as well as a socioeconomic one. He maintained that Numeiri had no concept of the problem in the south, and he blasted Numeiri for repression in the region. Mahjub said that the south should maintain its own ethnic identity and stressed that the SCP opposed any integration of the south by coercion. He also stated that the SCP is against the imposition of Islam or the Arabic language on the south. (Ibid., pp. 14–15.)

The SCP denounces Numeiri's plan of regional autonomy for the south as another "northern bluff." According to Mohammad Mahjub, SCP is the only party in Sudan that calls for a radical solution of the southern problem. Toward this end, Mahjub notes that the SCP is actively working with trade unions in the south as well as student, youth, and women's organizations to advance the democratic movement in the south. This movement calls for equal pay for equal work and overall social and economic equality for workers in the south. Mahjub stresses that this is the only way to lessen the disparity in wealth between the rich northerners and the poor southerners. (Ibid.)

So long as the economic disparity between the north and the south continues, the potential for the SCP to exploit the issue and sectarian politics in order to enhance its own image exists. This is especially true so long as the economy as a whole remains weak.

International Views. The SCP closely parrots the radical Arab communist line on Middle East politics. "U.S. imperialism" and the "Zionist aggression" of Israel are responsible for the instability in Lebanon and the insecurity of the Palestinian people. The communists in Sudan also condemn moderate Arab countries such as Egypt for siding with the U.S.-Israeli "strategic alliance." The SCP blasts the United States for its arms sales to Sudan and criticizes both the Numeiri government and the United States for making threats against Libya. The SCP echoed

these views in June at a meeting of twelve communist and workers' parties of the Arab countries (*IB*, September, pp. 24–28).

On almost all foreign policy issues, the SCP dutifully supports the "peace-loving policies" of the Soviet Union. In this role, the SCP attended a pro-Soviet conference in East Berlin in April commemorating the centenary of Marx's death. Ahmad Salim, the Sudanese representative on the Editorial Council of the *World Marxist Review*, gave a speech espousing the relevance of the ideas of Marx to the world today (*Neues Deutschland*, 16–17 April).

Leif Rosenberger
Washington, D.C.

Syria

Population. 9.7 million (estimate) (Population Bureau, *1983 World Population Data Sheet*)
Party. Syrian Communist Party (al-Hizb al-Shuyu'i al-Suri; SCP)
Founded. 1925 (as a separate party in 1944)
Membership. 5,000 (estimate)
Secretary General. Khalid Bakhdash (deputy secretary general: Yusuf Faysal)
Politburo. 6 members: Khalid Bakhdash, Ibrahim Bakr, Khalid Hammami, Maurice Salibi, Umar Siba'i, Daniel Ni'mah
Secretariat. Information unavailable
Central Committee. Information unavailable
Status. Component of the ruling National Progressive Front
Last Congress. Fifth, May 1980
Last Election. 1981. No seats (6 out of 175 in the 1977 elections); no information on the percentage of the vote
Auxiliary Organizations. No information
Publications. *Nidal al-Sha'b*

Several Marxist or quasi-Marxist groups appeared in Syria and Lebanon during the early 1920s. Three groups united in 1925 to form the Communist Party of Syria and Lebanon (CPSL). The Syrian and Lebanese parties separated in 1944, soon after the two countries were officially

declared independent, but maintained close ties with each other. The CPSL and the subsequent Syrian Communist Party (SCP) underwent alternate periods of toleration or legality and of suppression. The SCP often emphasized nationalism and reform and played down revolutionary ideology. It gained a considerable following and a membership that may have reached 10,000 by 1945. The party became quite influential during 1954–1958 but suffered a serious blow with the creation of the United Arab Republic and the subsequent suppression. Seemingly no longer a serious threat and following a foreign policy that often paralleled that of the Ba'thist regime, it gained a quasi-legal status after 1966 and finally joined the Ba'th-dominated National Progressive Front (NPF) in 1972.

The Syrian communist movement has undergone several schisms in recent years. Riyad al-Turk was chosen as secretary general of one breakaway group in 1974; according to some reports, this group has more supporters than the internationally recognized SCP (R. D. McLaurin, Don Peretz, and Lewis Snyder, *Middle East Foreign Policy: Issues and Processes*, New York: Praeger, 1982, p. 253). Yusuf Murad, a former member of the SCP Central Committee, formed another group, the Base Organization, in 1980. (For information on other breakaway factions, see Thomas Mayer, "Syria," in Colin Legum, ed., *Middle East Contemporary Survey, 1980–81*, New York: Holmes and Meier, 1982, pp. 792–93.)

Leadership and Party Organization. Little is known about the dynamics of the SCP's leadership except for the fact that Secretary General Khalid· Bakhdash has long been the dominant figure. There have been some divisions among the top leadership; for example, Politburo member Daniel Ni'mah (now a representative of the SCP on the Central Command of the NPF) broke with the party for a while during the early 1970s.

The SCP is organized like other communist parties. The Fifth Party Congress met in 1980. There are a Central Committee (a plenary session was reported in February), a Secretariat, and a Politburo.

Domestic Party Affairs. Although SCP statements emphasized international issues, there was strong support for the Syrian regime, which was described as a manifestation of "the Arab national liberation movement" (joint statement of the Syrian and Palestinian communist parties, *IB*, October, p. 33). A joint statement of the Syrian and Iraqi communist parties "expressed their firm belief that the consolidation of the [Syrian] Progressive National Front's political and organi-

zational role" would protect the country from "aggression," "reactionaries," and "imperialism" and called for "the broadening of the activity of the progressive parties within this front on the popular level" (Syrian Arab News Agency, Damascus, 25 April; *FBIS*, 26 April). Bakhdash explained that "generally speaking, we support Syria's policy" because of its "attitude toward imperialism" but that the party has a duty to fight "for the interests of the broadest strata of the population"; describing the situation as "difficult," he proclaimed the party's dedication to "improv[ing] the living standard of the masses" (*Rudé právo*, Prague, 13 September; *FBIS*, 15 September). On the thirteenth anniversary of President Assad's Corrective Movement, Ni'mah hailed the regime's achievements but pointed to dangers posed by Israel and imperialism (*al-Ba'th*, 16 November; *FBIS*, 30 November).

An Amnesty International report issued in 1983 described severe violations of human rights in Syria during recent years (*NYT*, 16 November). There is no indication, however, that members of any communist group are among the victims. The main threat to the regime—and·one that has been violently suppressed—is that of the "fundamentalist" Muslim Brethren.

Auxiliary and Front Organizations. Little information on auxiliary organizations is available. The Writers' Association and the Peasants' Organization were described as "front organizations" in past decades. It is likely that the SCP participates in such groups as the Arab-Soviet Friendship Society, the Syrian Committee for Solidarity with Asian and African Countries, the National Council of Peace Partisans in Syria, and the Syrian-Bulgarian Friendship Society.

The present Syrian regime is based on the National Progressive Front (NPF), which includes the SCP, the Arab Socialist Union, the Socialist Union, and the Arab Socialist Party, in addition to the dominant Ba'th Party (non-Marxist). In an evaluation that seemed to remain accurate during 1983, the role of the SCP in the NPF was recently described as "seeking legitimacy, getting accepted in the Syrian political arena, and influencing events by propaganda and example" (John Devlin, *Syria*, Boulder, Colo.: Westview, 1983, p. 113). In fact, the existence of the NPF has "brought into the governing system some useful people and deflected them from notions of active opposition" (ibid., p. 66). Another assessment of the SCP's role as "weak, third fiddle, strictly controlled and circumscribed" also remains valid (Arnold Hottinger, "Arab Communism at Low Ebb," *Problems of Communism*, July–August, 1981, p. 25).

However, cooperation between Syria and the USSR reached new heights during 1983, particularly in the military sphere. As of October, the value of Soviet military equipment transferred to Syria during the year was estimated at $2.5 billion (*NYT*, 8 October). Not only had Syrian losses in the 1982 war with Israel been fully replaced, but more sophisticated, up-to-date weapons were also transferred — including SAM-5 and SAM-10 antiaircraft missiles that had never before been deployed outside the Warsaw Pact countries. Late in 1983, the Soviets also deployed SS-21 ground-to-ground missiles. An estimated 7,000 Soviet military advisors and infantrymen were in Syria, with some of the new missiles allegedly under exclusive Soviet control. According to military correspondent Drew Middleton (*NYT*, 19 November), the new supply of Soviet armaments is of such scope that military analysts believe that Syria is overtaking Egypt as the leading power in the Arab world.

Also reflecting the intensified Soviet-Syrian relationship were numerous amicable exchanges of visits between Syrian party (Ba'th) and state officials and their counterparts in the USSR and other communist countries. Statements of solidarity in confronting Israel and U.S. imperialism followed each meeting.

There were similar exchanges with communist leaders from several Middle Eastern countries. These included a visit of a Palestinian Communist Party delegation to Ba'th Party Assistant Secretary General Abdullah al-Ahmar in January; separate meetings between Lebanese Communist Party Secretary General George Hawi (and other members of the Lebanese Politburo) on the one hand and Ahmar and President Hafiz al-Assad on the other hand in December 1982; a visit by Hawi to Muhammad Haydar, a member of the Ba'th Party National (i.e., pan-Arab) Command in January; and a visit of Iraqi Communist Party Secretary General Aziz Muhammad to President Assad in January. Assad also met with a delegation of "leaders of Arab countries' communist and workers' parties" headed by Bakhdash and including Aziz Muhammad (*Pravda*, 1 July; *FBIS*, 5 July).

Still, knowledgeable observers seem to be unanimous in rejecting allegations that Syria has become a mere Soviet proxy. The Syrian regime is pragmatic in accepting Soviet assistance but is not pro-Soviet per se. Both President Assad and his influential brother Rif'at al-Assad are said not to trust the Soviets (McLaurin, Peretz, and Snyder, *Middle East Foreign Policy*, p. 265). From a Soviet point of view, the Assad regime has been a "client" that has been notoriously willing to follow its own interests whenever they do not parallel those of the "patron." (See articles by Trudy Rubin in *CSM*, 29 April; by Thomas Friedman in *NYT*, 25 September; and by Flora Lewis in *NYT*, 30 October.) Even now, with Syria so dependent on Soviet aid (and also getting Saudi aid and allied with anti-Soviet—and anti-U.S.—Iran) for the pursuit of its own regional goals, the USSR is also highly dependent on its relationship with Syria as a window of influence in the area. In any case, the current Syrian-Soviet alliance is hardly the result of the influence of Syrian communists in the NPF.

International Views, Positions, and Activities. The SCP participated in a meeting of the communist and workers' parties of twelve Arab countries in June (see the profile on Egypt for a summary of the joint statement). There were also meetings between (and joint statements of) Bakhdash and Lebanese Secretary General Hawi (May), Iraqi Secretary General Muhammad (June), and (South) Yemeni Socialist Party Secretary General Ali Nasir Muhammad (February); the last meeting was also attended by George Habash, secretary general of the Popular Front for the Liberation of Palestine (PFLP), and Yasir Abd Rabbuh, assistant secretary general of the Popular Democratic Front for the Liberation of Palestine (PDFLP). Assistant Secretary General Yusuf Faysal also met with Ali Nasir Muhammad in Aden in March. Meetings between leaders of the SCP and the Palestine Communist Party were reported in April and August.

As for contacts outside the Arab world, Bakhdash and Politburo member Hammami visited Czechoslovakia at the invitation of the Central Committee in September, and Bakhdash was presented with the Order of Friendship by Czechoslovak Communist Party secretary general Gústav Husák in recognition of his contribution to friendly ties between the two countries. Bakhdash also visited Sofia in September and met with Bulgarian secretary general Todor Zhivkov, who awarded him the Order of Georgi Dimitrov on the occasion of his seventieth birthday for his contribution to the struggle against imperialism and Zionism, to the international communist movement, and to Bulgarian-Syrian friendship. Deputy Secretary General Faysal visited Azerbaijan in August as a guest of the CPSU Central Committee. Politburo member Salibi headed an SCP delegation to Romania in April. Bakhdash attended the celebration of the sixtieth anniversary of the USSR in December 1982; the Syrian Ba'th Party National Command was represented by Jabir Bajbuj. Bakhdash and Politburo member Ibrahim Bakr—along with a separate Ba'thist delegation headed by Deputy Secretary General al-Ahmar—also attended the Karl Marx World Scientific Conference in East Berlin in April.

The SCP emphasized its opposition to U.S. and Israeli plans in the area. In an interview broadcast from Prague, Bakhdash explained that the "complicated and dangerous" situation in the Middle East is mainly a result of "the efforts of American imperialism which, in alliance with Israel and certain other reactionary circles, is striving to establish its military, political, and economic hegemony in the entire Mideast area" and to "achieve the liquidation of [Arab] independence" (*Rudé právo*, 13 September; *FBIS*, 15 September). The SCP Politburo described the Lebanese-Israeli agreement as "a writ of submission imposed on Lebanon by force" and supported the Syrian government's opposition to it (Damascus domestic service, 17 May; *FBIS*, 18 May). The Central Committee warned of "preparations for an armed strike against Syrian troops . . . in full accordance with the strategic agreement concluded between Washington and Tel Aviv" (*Pravda*, 23 February; *FBIS*, 1 March).

Bakhdash made ambiguous statements about the intra-Palestinian and Syrian-Palestinian conflict. He stated the SCP's support for "a united Fatah organization" and for resolution of conflict "through democratic dialogue" (ibid.). In a joint SCP-Palestine Communist Party statement in August, "the fratricidal clashes between Palestinians in el-Fateh, and the contradictions artificially stirred up between Syria and the Palestinian revolution" were deplored as benefiting "only the enemies of the Palestinians and those of Syria and the Arab liberation movement." The statement called for the "necessary democratic reforms" as "a reliable base for ensuring the unity of el-Fateh and the Palestine Liberation Organization." (*IB*, October, p. 33.)

The SCP stated its support for "liberating the . . . occupied Arab territories" and the Palestinians' right to return and establish an independent state under PLO leadership (joint SCP-Yemeni Socialist Party communiqué, Aden domestic service, 17 March; *FBIS*, 18 March). Syria's "steadfastness" against "the Reagan plan, and [against] the rehabilitation of the Mubarak regime" were praised in a Central Committee statement (Damascus domestic service, 21 February; *FBIS*, 24 February).

A joint statement of the Iraqi and Syrian communist parties "denounced the alliance among Baghdad, Cairo, Amman, and Khartum." It "condemned the war which the dictatorship in Baghdad is waging against Iran" and Iraq's "joining . . . the Camp David camp." Israel's "aggression against Lebanon" was made possible, the statement explained, by Iraq's war against Iran. (Syrian Arab News Agency, 25 April; *FBIS*, 26 April.)

The Soviet Union was praised for "supporting all peoples who are fighting for their independence" (Syrian Arab News Agency, 14 September; *FBIS*, 15 September). Bakhdash joined Czechoslovak Communist Party secretary general Gústav Husák in denouncing "the aggressive policy of imperialist circles, especially the U.S., and their attempts to deploy new U.S. medium range missiles in Western Europe" and in praising the USSR for its "consistent peace policy" and "initiative aimed at halting feverish armament" (ČETEKA, 8 September; *FBIS*, 9 September).

Biography. *Khalid Bakhdash.* Kahlid Bakhdash is widely regarded as the grand old man of Arab communism, although he is not an Arab himself. He was born in 1912 into a poor Kurdish family in the Kurdish quarter of Damascus. Following extensive involvement in political activities during his high school days, he became a member of the CPSL soon after his eighteenth birthday. It has been suggested that the international character of the communist movement made it an attractive alternative to the predominant Arab nationalist movement in which he, as a Kurd, could not fit and that the party was eager to recruit such a person—of Muslim background—into a movement that was isolated from the mainstream by its then almost exclusively Christian membership.

Bakhdash soon became the secretary of the party's Syrian branch. He was arrested in 1931 and again in 1933. During the latter stay in prison he produced the first Arabic translation of *The Communist Manifesto*. He subsequently studied communist theory in Moscow, where he also mastered the Russian language before returning to Syria around 1936, soon thereafter to become secretary general of the CPSL (and, since 1944, of the SCP, a position he has held virtually uninterrupted ever since). With his party embracing the Popular Front government of France, Bakhdash helped to conclude the 1936 Franco-Syrian treaty. He and other communists were arrested again in 1939, after the beginning of World War II. But he was released after the Free French took control of Syria in 1941, and he called for support for the Allied cause. For a while he acted as the coordinator of all Arab communist parties, and he was officially appointed by the Cominform in 1948 as party director of Arab countries.

With his major base of support in his native Kurdish quarter, where he drew extremely large crowds, Bakhdash gained the distinction in 1954 of being the first communist ever elected to an Arab parliament. But, after four years of unprecedented communist influence, he left the country when the United Arab Republic was established in 1958 and proceeded to attack Nasser from exile in Prague. It was not until 1966 that he was able to return to Syria, with his still officially outlawed activities tolerated as a prelude to the official cooperation that emerged in 1972. (Sources: Majid Khadduri, *Arab Contemporaries*, Baltimore: Johns Hopkins University Press, 1973; and M. S. Agwani, *Communism in the Arab East*, Bombay: Asia Publishing House, 1969.)

Glenn E. Perry
Indiana State University

Tunisia

Population. 7.0 million (estimate)
Party. Tunisian Communist Party (Parti communiste tunisien; PCT)
Founded. 1920
Membership. 100 (estimate)
Secretary General. Muhammad Harmel
Politburo. 6 members: Muhammad Harmel, Muhammad al-Nafa'a, 'Abd al-Hamid ben Mustafa, Hisham Sakik, 'Abd al-Majid Tariki, Salah al-Hajji
Secretariat. 3 members: Muhammad Harmel, Muhammad al-Nafa'a, 'Abd al-Hamid ben Mustafa
Central Committee. 12 members: Ahmed Brahim, 'Abd al-Hamid ben Mustafa, 'Abd al-Majid Tariki, Hisham Sakik, Muhammad Su'id, 'Abd al-Wahhab 'Abassi, Habib Kazdaghli, Mahdi Mas'udi, Muhammad al-Nafa'a, Salah al-Hajji, Muhammad Harmel, Bu Jama'a Ramili
Status. Legal (since July 1981)
Last Congress. Eighth, February 1981, in Tunis
Last Election. November 1981; 0.78 percent of the vote; no seats
Auxiliary Organizations. No information available
Publications. *Al-Tarik al-Jadid* (The new path), weekly

The major event in Tunisian politics in 1983 was the move by President Habib Bourguiba to transform the country's political system from a virtual one-party system to a multiparty system. On 19 November, Bourguiba legalized two opposition parties, the Socialist Democratic Movement and the Popular Unity Movement II. Prior to this move, the Socialist Destour Party (PSD), founded in 1934 by Bourguiba as the Neo-Destour Party, had a virtual monopoly on Tunisian political life. The small exception to this monopoly was the legalization of the PCT in July 1981. The government's move to broaden political participation did not prevent a serious outbreak of domestic violence at the end of the year. A cabinet decision to double the price of bread and flour touched off riots in provincial towns in southern Tunisia that soon spread throughout the country. The resultant clashes between angry demonstrators and the army and police left about seventy dead and hundreds injured during eight days of food riots that ended only in the first week of January when Bourguiba announced the cancellation of price increases. In foreign affairs, Tunisia gave priority in 1983 to pursuing regional reconciliation by substantially improving and strengthening relations with neighboring Libya. Building on initial steps toward a rapprochement taken in 1982 (see *YICA*, 1983, p. 49) and the work done by a joint preparatory committee in January and April, the Tunisian and Libyan cabinets held their first joint session in Tripoli on 19–20 July. The session approved a comprehensive cooperation program that emphasized economic integration and called for coordination of the two countries' foreign policies.

Leadership and Party Organization. The PCT's Eighth Congress (February 1981) reelected Muhammad Harmel as secretary general and elected a three-member secretariat, a six-member politburo, and a twelve-member central committee (see *YICA*, 1983, p. 48).

Domestic and International Views, Positions, and Activities. Enjoying the status of a legal party, the PCT operated in 1983 as a loyal opposition. During a July 1982 meeting with Prime Minister Muhammad M'zali, PCT Secretary General Muhammad Harmel had pressed the government to move toward a multiparty system (see *YICA*, 1983, p. 48), and the party then supported the government when it legalized two opposition parties in November. In general, the small and aging membership of the party remained quiet during 1983, and the PCT leadership did not take any public positions of note on either domestic or international issues. The party had little impact on the political scene in Tunisia during the past year, and the move to a multiparty political system is expected to push the PCT further into the shadow.

John Damis
Portland State University

Yemen:
People's Democratic Republic
of Yemen

Population. 2.0 million
Party. Yemen Socialist Party (YSP)
Founded. 1978

Membership. 26,000 (claim)
Secretary General. Ali Nasir Muhammad
Politburo. 5 members
Central Committee. 47 members
Status. Ruling party
Last Congress. Second extraordinary, 12–14 October 1980
Last Election. 1978, all candidates YSP approved

The People's Democratic Republic of Yemen (PDRY) has been governed by a militant, Marxist-oriented regime since June 1969. Although a local communist party, the People's Democratic Union (PDU), has existed for two decades, the party has never been the dominant power in South Yemeni (PDRY) politics. The PDU's status and role in national affairs have been highly circumscribed by the practical necessity, both legal and political, for it to operate in close association with a substantially larger organization.

In 1982, the PDU enjoyed official status in the prevailing, larger organization, the YSP. PDU members held one of five posts in the YSP's Politburo—both the YSP's and the government's highest policymaking body—and several seats on the YSP's 47-member Central Committee. In addition, PDU representatives sat in the nonparty 111-member Supreme People's Council, which served as a consultative body and debating forum for the government. These positions, in addition to other, less formal ones within the national power structure, have accorded the PDU a degree of influence in PDRY politics far beyond what its limited membership (estimated at less than 500) would suggest. (For a history of the PDU, YSP, and PDRY, see *YICA*, 1982, pp. 56–59.)

Although the global orientation of the PDRY regime remained unchanged, the flux in regional alignments was sufficient to at least confound certain Soviet objectives in Aden. Moscow remained mildly supportive of Yemeni unity but monitored developments in this direction with a view to detecting whether such a merger might undo gains it had acquired because of the two countries' separate status.

The bilateral discussions that took place in the early period following the 1979 unity agreement between Aden and Sana'a confronted several formidable barriers. One was Sana'a's relationship with the conservative Gulf states and several important Western countries versus Aden's predominant reliance on the Soviet bloc, Cuba, and Arab states deemed sympathetic to the Soviet Union—Syria, Libya, and, to a lesser extent, Algeria. Another impediment was that North Yemen's traditional economic and social system remained largely intact while South Yemen's had been thoroughly purged. Even so, the movement toward integrating the two Yemens had by the end of 1983 proceeded substantially beyond slogans and hopes of earlier years.

Throughout the year, there were frequent meetings and high-level visits, the upgrading of a joint ministerial committee to the status of a secretariat, with a branch in each capital, and further discussions on the draft constitution of the year before. In addition to these developments, the agenda for unity discussions was broadened substantially, with joint subcommittees being authorized to deal not only with political, social, educational, and health questions but also with more contentious topics such as foreign policy and economic relations.

Regarding the last two areas, it was a source of some concern among their northern neighbors that officials of both countries spoke in rather negative terms about what portions of their citizenry characterized as the Balkanization of the Arabian Peninsula through the Gulf Cooperation Council (GCC). The GCC, in this view, showed signs of an exclusive rich man's club. Comprising oil-producing countries, most of which were less populous and further away from possessing a quantity of native manpower commensurate to their national development goals than either of the Yemens, the GCC, in this view, was also on ethnic and nationalist grounds, far less homogeneous.

In addition to the interplay of these external variables pressuring the YSP-dominated regime to adopt a less doctrinaire approach to regional affairs, internal fissures produced other changes in PDRY politics. Just as the PDU's position and role in PDRY society remained as contingent as ever on its relationship with the YSP, so, too, did the YSP's status and function continue to be determined in part by the nature of its relationship with the country's armed forces. A key development in this regard was the surfacing in late 1982–early 1983 of a long-simmering dispute between YSP secretary general and head of government Ali Nasir Muhammad and the head of PDRY's armed forces, Brig. 'Ali Ahmad Nasir Antar.

The problem, insofar as the YSP was concerned, was rooted not so much in the kinds of asymmetry often manifested in civil-military relations as in the fact that Antar, though himself a YSP stalwart, was a renowned ex-guerrilla from the pre-independence era. Antar, for two decades an immensely popular figure in his own right, drew support from substantial segments of the armed forces who, in the eyes of many YSP leaders, were as loyal to him as they were to the party. The removal of Antar from his post at the beginning of this period occasioned a certain uneasiness in the relationship between the YSP and the country's regular armed forces. This constituted still another reason for the regime to adopt a more subdued approach to controversial foreign and domestic policies than in previous years. Antar was replaced as minister of defense in February by Salih Muslih Qasim, a member of the YSP Central Committee. Antar himself remained a member of the YSP's important Politburo, as well as the party's Central Committee. In addition, his removal from the defense portfolio was cushioned by his appointment to two prestigious posts in the government: deputy chairman of the Supreme People's Council and first deputy chairman of the Council of Ministers.

The dispute between the former defense minister and the YSP leadership centered in part around the national division of labor that had evolved between the regular armed forces, which numbered some 32,000, and the popular militia groups, of whom some 20,000 were regarded as an arm of the YSP. Other differences centered around the extent to which the army ought to remain engaged as a supplier of weaponry and other support to guerrilla groups anxious to continue subversive activities against North Yemen and Oman.

Throughout 1983, the continuing domestic debate over the proper orientation of PDRY foreign policy notwithstanding, both the YSP and the government continued along their previous pragmatic course of improving relations with neighboring countries. The most compelling evidence of this fundamental realignment in intra-regional relations were the facts that support for insurgent activities in North Yemen remained at a standstill and the 27 October 1982 agreement with Oman was upheld.

The PDRY-Oman agreement, mediated by Kuwait and the United Arab Emirates (UAE) on behalf of the GCC, stipulated that each side work toward normalizing relations, exchanging diplomats, ending South Yemen's support for insurgent activities in Oman, and ceasing hostile propaganda. During 1983, propaganda attacks and insurgent activities did in fact cease, a joint committee undertook to establish a means for demarcating borders, and a proclamation marking the official establishment of diplomatic relations between the two states was announced on 27 October, on the occasion of the agreement's first anniversary.

The Soviet Union had its own reasons for wanting the Aden regime to be more accommodating in its relations with neighboring countries. Throughout 1983, Moscow manifested a decreasing interest in what had begun to be an increasingly widespread image of South Yemenis, many of whom had seen military service in Afghanistan and Ethiopia, as "Arab Cubans"— Soviet proxies—in Muslim countries. In particular, Moscow believed that the prolongation of Aden-sponsored subversive activity in either North Yemen or Oman—and most certainly were the PDRY to aid such activity in both countries simultaneously—would prod these regimes into closer relationships with Saudi Arabia and the United States, a contingency that Moscow was anxious, even if at considerable costs, to avoid. Even worse, the continuation of such activities would almost certainly have been used by U.S. military planners to justify yet another development that Moscow hoped to forestall: the U.S. military buildup in the Indian Ocean and the forging of closer U.S. security and defense ties with a number of Gulf states.

Although the YSP sought to refurbish its regional relations with neighboring states, further afield and with assistance from PDU leaders and local pro-Syrian Ba'thists, the party's ideological and international wings retained links with the several factions of the Palestine Liberation Organization as well as with leading leftists in Syria, Libya, Ethiopia, and the Lebanese Nationalist Movement. PDU officials, although maintaining a low profile throughout the period, continued to represent the PDRY within the Afro-Asia Peoples' Solidarity Organization and the World Peace Council and remained as involved as before in cementing relations between the PDRY and those countries of socialist orientation that provided educational assistance, military aid, and ideological indoctrination (Soviet Union), defense cooperation (Ethiopia), and medical aid and paramilitary advisers (Cuba).

There was also evidence during the year that the image and role of a leading PDU stalwart, Ali Abd al-Razzaq Ba Dhib, younger brother of the party's secretary general, who had fared poorly in the last elections for the Supreme People's Council, was being resuscitated. Among his several titles and functions are deputy premier, chairman of the State Information Committee, chairman of the Yemen Council for Peace and Solidarity, PDRY representative to the Committee for Solidarity with African and Asian Peoples, and one of several secretaries on the YSP's Central Committee.

The Soviet leadership's emerging view of its relationship with the PDRY less in terms of the Horn of Africa than of the Persian Gulf resulted from several factors. First, Moscow had ample reason to feel relatively secure in terms of retaining a firm presence in southwest Arabia. Giving added reason for such assurance was the prominence that both governments had come to attach to the 1979 Soviet-PDRY Treaty of Friendship. The document rather pointedly made reference to their "coordination of positions in the interest of eliminating threats" and their "cooperation in strengthening defense capabilities." Further provisions calling for the "preservation of the people's social and economic gains" appeared to lay the base for potential Soviet intervention in the event of an internal threat to the PDRY regime. Moreover, added reasons for Moscow to believe that its relationship with the YSP and the Aden government would continue to be reliable and long-term were that the PDRY remained one of the few socialist-oriented Third World countries with a Soviet-style ruling party; there was an ongoing, large contingent of Soviet advisers and a growing number of Soviet loyalists with a vested interest in maintaining the status quo; and should miscalculation occur and an outside threat present itself, there was the reassurance of a Cuban force nearby in Ethiopia that could be moved in quickly.

The second reason was Moscow's increasing concern that a continuation of business as usual in its relationship with the PDRY might undermine important Soviet interests further north. The PDRY, by far the poorest Arabian Peninsula country and the one with the least potential in terms of natural resources, stood in marked contrast to the Gulf states, with their substantial petroleum reserves and financial holdings. In this context, the PDRY's reputation for supporting Soviet-backed revolutions was a potential liability to important Soviet interests elsewhere. In light of changed regional conditions, the fact that the PDRY was the only Arabian Peninsula state to elect not to condemn the Soviet invasion and occupation of Afghanistan was eclipsed by events. Moreover, continued close identification of Moscow with the PDRY, the only radical state in the peninsula, and retention of its own close ties with national liberation movements in North Yemen, Oman, and Bahrain could only serve to continue to prevent Moscow from achieving normal relations with most of the conservative oil states, including the establishment of embassies and trade missions. While it remained unclear when the Soviet Union would have to import oil, there seemed little doubt that the necessary political and diplomatic groundwork for such an eventuality would have to be laid during the 1980s.

If petroleum and financial considerations helped explain the altered relationship between Moscow and Aden, a more immediate factor was Moscow's strategic interest in preventing further expansion of the U.S. military presence in the Gulf, especially in the form of joint military maneuvers, access to defense facilities, and the pre-positioning of supplies. Soviet propaganda toward this end—emphasizing U.S. support for Israel; propounding the view that U.S. Central Command forces could be used to intervene in the internal affairs of the Gulf states as well as deployed to protect the region's petroleum resources and maritime routes; and promising that the Soviet Union would stay out of the Gulf if the United States agreed to do the same—were powerful arguments aimed at a sympathetic audience. Even so, they were doomed to yield little more than uncontested debating points in the absence of comparably altered acts on the ground. It was in this context that one could see more clearly the rationale behind the changed circumstances in Moscow's relationship with the PDRY during much of 1983.

The prospects for Soviet policy in both the PDRY and the Gulf thus remained heavily influenced by local and regional conditions, most of which were not under Soviet control. Certainly this was the case with respect to the outcome of the Iraq-Iran war and Kuwait-UAE mediations between Aden and Muscat and the GCC states, not to mention the results that might ensue from direct relations between South Yemen and Oman. These issues and events, far more than any of Moscow's own choosing, remained of prime significance in determining the ultimate outcome of Soviet efforts to make political and diplomatic headway among PDRY's northern neighbors.

Even so, nothing had altered the PDRY's overall strategic value to Moscow, which derived from its location adjacent to the Bab al-Mandab Strait, the Gulf of Aden, and the Arabian Sea and comprised the northwest quadrant of the Indian Ocean. Nor was there any lessening of Aden's role vis-à-vis larger Soviet interests, e.g., airfield facilities for regional reconnaissance missions over the Indian Ocean and the need for a staging post for Soviet flights to Africa. These roles, combined with the use of Aden's port facilities, remained crucial not only for Soviet regional projections of power by air but, also, for Soviet naval activities in the Indian Ocean, which continued to evince a need for shore-based air support.

In February, the fourth annual session of the Joint Permanent Committee for Technical and Economic Cooperation between the PDRY and the Soviet Union placed special emphasis on enhancing the country's transportation and communications systems. Joint economic cooperation between Aden and Moscow was strengthened across the board, with the Soviet Union continuing to play a greater role than any other country in helping the government to fulfill the objectives of the 1980–1985 five-year plan. The fields of planning, education, and youth continued to receive special Soviet attention, with Soviet instructors serving on the faculties and as tutors in several institutions of higher learning. With project finance being provided through the Soviet Standing Committee for Foreign Economic Relations, the Soviet Union was the principal foreign power assisting in the construction, administration, and maintenance of the PDRY's schools, roads, factories, and medical centers.

Most Soviet assistance was rendered through the 1979 Soviet–South Yemen Treaty of Friendship and Cooperation. On various public occasions during the year when the merits of PDRY-Soviet cooperation were extolled, treaty supporters claimed that the treaty had helped to strengthen Aden's position and role within the region while accentuating political, economic, and social cooperation and, increasingly, military cooperation to protect the revolution's achievements.

At a slightly lower level of cooperation, YSP ties to the Communist Party of the Soviet Union deepened as additional delegations of YSP members traveled to the Soviet Union to learn from Soviet leaders how the YSP might play a more effective leadership role in the activities of the PDRY's various administrative organs. Toward this end, the YSP's political directorate made further progress during the year toward assuring the neutralization of the military, adhering closely in this regard to Soviet practice.

John Duke Anthony
National Council on U.S.-Arab Relations

Zimbabwe

Population. 8.4 million (*The World Factbook*, 1983)
Party. Zimbabwe African National Union (ZANU)
Founded. 1963
Membership. No information available
Secretary General. None since the purging of Edgar Tekere in 1981; Robert Mugabe is president, prime minister, and minister of defense.
Central Committee. 33 members
Status. Ruling party
Last Congress. Fourth, 1979
Last Election. 1980, 62.9 percent, 57 of 100 seats
Auxiliary Organizations. People's Militia
Publications. *Moto*; ZANU also has strong influence in all Zimbabwan media.

ZANU is the ruling party of the Republic of Zimbabwe. Though not an avowedly communist party, it professes to be Marxist in ideology. It was formed in 1963 by the African nationalist Ndabaningi Sithole after he split from Joshua Nkomo's Zimbabwe African Peoples' Union (ZAPU). Robert Mugabe, a Marxist, became ZANU secretary general under Sithole's presidency. In the late 1960s, ZANU launched a guerrilla war against the white-dominated Rhodesian government of Prime Minister Ian Smith. Much of ZANU's logistical and training support came from the People's Republic of China. After a bitter power struggle in 1974, Mugabe was elected to replace Sithole as party president. Internal leadership struggles continued, but by the time of the peace negotiations in Geneva in 1976, Mugabe had gained almost complete control. At the Geneva conference, the front-line states forced Moscow-supported Nkomo and his ZAPU into a Patriotic Front (PF) alliance with Mugabe and ZANU in order to present a stronger, more united opposition to the Rhodesian regime.

This fragile fabric of unity began to unravel in February 1980 when Nkomo-led ZAPU contested the pre-independence elections as a sepa-

rate party. ZANU won a stunning landslide, gaining 57 of the 100 parliamentary seats to ZAPU's 20. Mugabe emerged as prime minister when Zimbabwe achieved independence from Britain in 1980. ZANU's strength derives mainly from the majority Shona people, while ZAPU's support comes overwhelmingly from the Ndebele, who constitute only 18 percent of the population.

After independence, the two parties formed a coalition government, but this collapsed in early 1982 after Nkomo spurned Mugabe's call for a merger into a single party. In February, Mugabe sacked Nkomo from his cabinet post, along with other ZAPU ministers, accusing them of stockpiling arms in preparation for a coup. ZAPU and ZANU have since been in an adversarial relationship.

Organization and Leadership. ZANU is directed by a 33-member Central Committee, under the presidency of Robert Mugabe, who is also the country's prime minister and minister of defense. Simon Muzenda is vice-president. No secretary general has been named since the purging of Edgar Tekere in 1981. No party congress has been convened since 1963 for fear it might lead to party factionalization. However, a congress is scheduled for May 1984. ZANU has not yet established an ideological institute, but is in the process of forming a People's Militia, its first auxiliary mass organization.

Nearly 80 percent of the Central Committee members have been elected to parliament, and the majority of cabinet portfolios are held by committee members. The committee meets occasionally, usually at least six times annually. Leadership is collective, and decisions are by consensus. Alongside the Central Committee is the National Executive, which rarely meets. Both organs are overwhelmingly Shona in ethnic composition but are divided ideologically. Many of the most fervent Marxists are drawn from the Ndebele minority. But the party itself is torn by considerable ethnic and ideological rivalry. ZANU's professed Marxism has been substantially diluted since the end of the liberation struggle and its elevation as the ruling party. Mugabe has become more cautious and pragmatic in his policies. He is committed to a mixed economy, has refrained from expropriating private property, and pays fair market prices for all government acquisitions. ZANU tolerates the white-dominated private sector because it is so vital to the economy. The highly influential agricultural minister is a prominent, nonideological white farmer. The country is in desperate need of foreign capital and has therefore permitted considerable foreign equity control over locally based enterprises. However, ZANU seeks greater state control and the progressive expansion of the state in economic development. Toward that end, the government has purchased the major newspapers, a large bank, and a pharmaceutical company and has created a state-owned minerals marketing board. But the drought and lack of capital have stalled its program to resettle 165,000 families on two-thirds of the commercial land presently under white ownership. Also, modest efforts to form agricultural cooperatives have been blocked by prominent civil servants who have a stake in the private sector. In the area of social services and education, the government has introduced free health care for people on low incomes and free education at the primary school level. State agricultural, industrial, and trading schemes have been delayed because of high capital costs. Indeed, the drought, a costly guerrilla war in Matabeleland, and declines in world min-

eral and commodity prices have caused a deterioration in public revenue and forced severe cuts in socialist programs. This has heightened the power struggle between the fiscal conservatives, or pragmatists, and the "scientific socialist" radicals. The former remained in control of economic matters, but the radicals' influence over purely political questions grew. This conflict over national policies exists within the party's Central Committee and in the cabinet. There is also a subtle power struggle between the cabinet and the Central Committee over their respective roles in administrative decisionmaking.

ZANU's major publication, *Moto*, tends to reflect the more militant Marxist wing. The government-owned radio and television services have recently come under ZANU party domination. The country's major dailies, once privately held by a South African–based conglomerate, are also falling under strong ZANU editorial influence. The government is increasingly sensitive to negative reporting by foreign correspondents and recently expelled several Western journalists. Zimbabwe led several southern African nations into the Kadoma Declaration, banning all South African–based foreign correspondents. It also broadened its news links with the East by signing agreements with the Soviet, Bulgarian, and East German news agencies. The government is also extending its influence over organized labor. A new labor bill will make strikes illegal and will give the government power to control the movement and employment of workers. (*African Business*, November.)

Domestic Affairs. Zimbabwe's population is deeply and bitterly divided over fundamental questions of power and of national purpose and direction. This is reflected in ambivalence and contradictions in economic theory, development strategy, and in dealings with foreign diplomats and business people. The whites, numbering approximately 160,000, are generally against ZANU's socialist policies but grudgingly cooperate. They are less active in parliament, which itself is becoming less relevant as political power and decisionmaking shift to Mugabe and the ZANU Central Committee. However, key white farmers and industrialists still exert considerable behind-the-scenes influence in the economic realm.

Most of the Ndebele resent Shona political

domination and remain in ZAPU as an implacable opposition. They and the whites oppose the creation of a one-party state, and Mugabe has pledged that this will not occur before the 1985 elections. Nevertheless, mutual suspicions and recriminations run deep and tend to impair the overall functioning of the state machinery. Zimbabwe has already become a de facto one-party state, but not one based on a broad national consensus.

Anti-ZANU activity has greatly escalated since Nkomo's removal from the cabinet in early 1982. Nearly 15 percent of the 35,000-strong National Army (mostly ZAPU supporters) have deserted and returned to bush guerrilla warfare. Military armories have been attacked, farms have been burned, whites as well as blacks have been killed or kidnapped, and nearly a quarter of the air force was destroyed by a guerrilla raid on a major air base. In the first half of 1983, the government retaliated brutally, using the ill-disciplined, North Korean–trained Fifth Brigade. Numerous ZAPU officials in Matabeleland were detained, several thousand Ndebele villagers and ZAPU functionaries were killed or wounded, and in March Nkomo and nearly a hundred ZAPU officials fled into voluntary exile in Great Britain. (*Economist* Intelligence Unit, Quarter II.) After severe criticism and accusations of atrocities by the clergy and foreign press, the violence subsided, and in July the Fifth Brigade was withdrawn. Nkomo returned in August to retake his parliamentary seat. But the violence in Matabeleland placed enormous constraints on the ability of ZAPU and ZANU, Ndebele and Shona, to deal with each other on economic and political levels. The hostility was exacerbated by the government's redetention of two popular ZAPU military heroes after their acquittal by the High Court. All pretense at unity talks between the two parties had disappeared by late 1983. Mugabe had failed, first through diplomacy and then by intimidation, to lure key ZAPU leaders into the ZANU fold. The strife in Matabeleland had left ZAPU's 150-member Central Committee bitter, confused, fearful, and paralyzed. (Frost and Sullivan, *World Political Risk Forecast: Zimbabwe*, January.) Also, ZANU's relations with the tiny opposition party, the United African National Congress (UANC) deteriorated following the detention in late October of its leader, Abel Muzorewa, Zimbabwe's former prime minister (*New African*, December).

International Positions. ZANU and the Zimbabwe government officially adhere to a policy of nonalignment. The government actively seeks loans from such multinational agencies as the World Bank and the International Monetary Fund (IMF). In March, the IMF approved a $381 million loan in support of economic and fiscal programs (*African Business*, April). The World Bank has added more than $400 million in soft loans for the private sector and for a massive hydroelectric facility (*Africa Report*, September). The assistance of such Western international lending institutions has given the capitalist countries considerable leverage over the direction of Zimbabwe's fiscal and monetary policies. Aid from Marxist countries has been meager by comparison.

Since independence, the United States and Great Britain have been Zimbabwe's largest donors. However, relations with the United States became strained in 1983, despite Prime Minister Mugabe's September visit with President Reagan in Washington. The administration resented Zimbabwe's votes in the United Nations on such issues as the Soviet downing of the South Korean airliner, the Grenada invasion, and Israel. In reaction, the Reagan administration cut its fiscal 1984 aid almost in half to $40 million. (*NYT*, 28 December.)

There was little indication in 1983 that Zimbabwe was moving diplomatically or economically closer to the Soviet Union. Since independence, ZANU has rejected the Soviet ties cultivated by Nkomo and ZAPU over the past two decades. But some members of ZANU's Central Committee would like to see stronger links with the Marxist governments of Central Europe.

Mugabe's visit in June to East Germany, Hungary, and Czechoslovakia failed to produce substantial economic assistance (African Consulting Associates).

On the other hand, Zimbabwe continues to enjoy warm relations with the People's Republic of China, its long-standing ally. Chinese premier Zhao Ziyang made an official visit in January, on his tour of eleven African countries (*New African*, November). This was followed by an interest-free loan of approximately $32 million and assistance in training armored military units and in the construction of a 60,000-seat stadium (*Africa News*, 17 October).

On the African continent, Zimbabwe continues to support the South-West Africa People's Organization (SWAPO) and its Soviet-supported effort to achieve Namibian independence. It plays leading roles in the Southern African Development Coordination Conference and the Preferential Trade Agreement with central and eastern African countries. Zimbabwe is a member of the Organization of African Unity and supports movements aimed at establishing a multiracial socialist government in South Africa.

Richard W. Hull
New York University

THE AMERICAS

Introduction

The overlying communist-related issue in Latin America during 1983 was the conflict between Marxist-Leninist governments and movements supported by Cuba and its Soviet-bloc allies, on the one hand, and those noncommunist or anticommunist governments and organizations in the Caribbean Basin backed in varying degrees by the United States, on the other. The major focal points were Grenada, El Salvador, and Nicaragua. In addition, significant levels of Marxist-Leninist activities occurred in other countries throughout the hemisphere.

The 25 October intervention in Grenada by the United States and six eastern Caribbean governments reflects a shift in U.S. willingness to respond directly with military force in the Caribbean Basin when Washington concludes that lives of Americans and security interests are threatened. And the U.S. action caused revolutionary governments and organizations in the region to have to reconsider their own political strategies.

Even before arriving in Washington, Ronald Reagan had made public his concern over Grenada's close ties with Cuba and the Soviet Union, a concern that eventually became associated largely with the construction of a strategically significant airfield on the eastern Caribbean island. In June 1983, Grenadian prime minister Maurice Bishop, who had seized power in a 1979 coup, visited the United States and after talks with top U.S. officials concluded that the groundwork had been laid for renewing bilateral relations. But Bishop's opening to the United States coincided with serious problems at home. Since late 1982 he had been under fire in his own New Jewel Movement for alleged ideological, organizational, and tactical deficiencies. In September, Bishop was effectively ousted from power by his opponents, led by Bernard Coard, his more doctrinaire, pro-Soviet second in command. Bishop was arrested on 13 October and murdered along with several of his cabinet ministers and others on 19 October. A period of unrest followed and led to the intervention on 25 October.

Occupying forces found almost 900 Cuban, Soviet, North Korean, Libyan, East German, and Bulgarian personnel, including permanent military advisers; antiaircraft weapons, armored personnel carriers, and rocket launchers; and thousands of infantry weapons, with millions of rounds of ammunition. There were hundreds of pounds of documents, including five secret military agreements, three with the Soviet Union and one each with North Korea and Cuba; written indications of additional military agreements with Bulgaria and Czechoslovakia; and extensive evidence of the internal workings of the New Jewel Movement.

In the wake of this event, the government of Suriname, which had come under increasing Cuban influence since a military coup there in 1980, expelled the Cuban ambassador and more than a hundred other Cuban personnel in order to "control" Cuban influence in the country. Cuban president Fidel Castro stated at a press conference in Havana that his government could not practically assist either the Coard government—which he said had killed the Grenadian revolution along with Bishop and provoked a U.S. response—or other allies, such as Nicaragua, in the Caribbean Basin.

The Nicaraguan government, under growing domestic and international pressure, increasingly expressed concern that the United States would similarly intervene in Nicaragua, despite U.S. assurance that the Grenadian incident was unique. It pointed out that the United States was already conducting large-scale military maneuvers in the region and giving "covert" aid to guerrillas trying to overthrow the Sandinista government from bases in Honduras and Costa Rica and within Nicaragua itself. In the meantime, pressures were building on the Managua government from thwarted democrats at home, who have now been promised that elections will be held in 1984. While the Nicaraguan government maintained that the Reagan administration was interfering in its domestic affairs, Washington maintained, in part through its special Central American peace-negotiating envoy Richard Stone, that U.S. concerns were threefold: the Nicaraguan domestic situation, the increasing level of Cuban–Soviet bloc influence in the country, and the use of Nicaraguan territory as a center for undermining other governments in the region.

The civil war continued in El Salvador between the U.S.-supported Salvadoran government and the Cuban-supported Farabundo Martí Front of National Liberation (FMLN). The guerrillas, with an estimated force of 9,000 regulars, hold substantial territory in several provinces. Government military forces of more than 39,000 include many inexperienced, impressed peasants. Americans and some Salvadorans argue that the level and quality of U.S. military aid is not sufficient to meet the guerrilla challenge. But Reagan administration efforts to increase military and economic aid have been hampered by congressional and other concerns over thousands of murders by right-wing death squads and by fears that Central America could become "another Vietnam." A major event during the year was the mysterious "suicide" in Nicaragua of the oldest and toughest Salvadoran guerrilla leader, Salvador Cayetano Carpio (see below).

Cuba itself planned for the celebration of the twenty-fifth anniversary of the Cuban revolution on 1 January 1984. This celebration came in the wake of the first open military conflict between U.S. and Cuban troops, in Grenada, and an unprecedented deterioration in already low bilateral relations. As Cuba approached its quarter-century anniversary, government leaders noted achievements in making health services, education, and other social services available across the board in Cuban society. The economy had become increasingly dependent on the Soviet Union through $4 billion in economic aid annually, more than 25 percent of the Cuban GNP. The Soviet Union also provides approximately $1 billion annually in military aid, enabling Cuba to have a military second only to Brazil in Latin America. In exchange for this aid, Cuba provides troops for Soviet international objectives in the Third World, particularly Africa.

Cuban international policies at the end of 1983 ranged from maintaining nearly 40,000 military personnel abroad—up to 30,000 of them in Angola—and an estimated 4,000 military advisers in Nicaragua to economic assistance worth $63 million to Grenada before, in Castro's words, "hyenas emerged from the revolutionary ranks [of the New Jewel Movement] . . . and objectively destroyed the revolution and opened the door to imperialist aggression." Cuban relations with the United States fell to an all-time low after military forces of the two nations clashed in Grenada. Although both sides professed to be interested in improved relations, neither seemed to feel this would be possible as long as the current administrations remained in the two countries.

But relations with the Soviet Union seemed to deteriorate as well by the end of the year, despite continuing Cuban dependence on Soviet aid. (Among other things, the Soviet Union pays Cuba above-market prices for sugar and sells Cuba oil at less than the market rate.) In 1982, Cuban vice-president Carlos Rafael Rodríguez had said, "The Soviet Union is the basic element in Cuba's economic development," but no such statements emerged during the twenty-fifth anniversary celebrations in late 1983 and early 1984: the Soviet Union was not mentioned in official slogans nor thanked in Castro's anniversary speech or the Cuban Communist Party's anniversary communiqué. Conversely, Cuba has received little attention from Soviet diplomats or in the Soviet press in recent months. This situation may be the result of Soviet frustration over Cuba's continuing domestic economic stagnation, of the Soviet refusal to pledge full support in defense of Cuba in the event of a U.S. attack, or of differences over Grenada and other foreign policy issues.

Guerrillas were active during the year in Guatemala, although a government "pacification" program there weakened the cooperation of revolutionary forces and forced a reconsideration of strategic objectives. Activities of the Maoist Shining Path (Sendero Luminoso) guerrillas in Peru resulted in the government's declaring seven provinces under a state of emergency by the beginning of 1983 and ten by the end of the year. The Communist Party of Chile, once the foremost advocate of peaceful revolution in Latin America, has turned increasingly to support of confrontational revolution in its bid to return to more active participation in Chilean affairs. In May, the party and other groups began conducting antigovernment protests. The communists have been removed from the Democratic Alliance, which coordinates democratic opposition to the Pinochet government, but in September formed their own Popular Democratic Movement with the participation of some members of the Socialist Party.

Communists in some countries participate actively in their national government. Many leftists in Peru are members of the United Left (IU), an extraordinarily broad opposition front, founded by the Peruvian Communist Party, that includes pro-Soviet, pro-Chinese, Trotskyist, and other groups. The IU received 30 percent of the vote in the 1983 municipal elections and took nineteen mayoral seats, in contrast to six in 1980. The most important victory was the mayor's seat in the capital of Lima. Two important Trotskyist groups have not joined the IU. The Communist Party of Argentina was legalized in 1983 and formed an informal electoral alliance with the Peronists in that country's December election.

Two members of the pro-Soviet Communist Party of Bolivia held cabinet positions in Bolivia throughout the year and went along with virtually every program of President Hernán Siles Suazo, including his adherence to a program imposed by the International Monetary Fund. A wide variety of Venezuelan Marxist groups won seats in the December elections, the most successful being the Movement Toward Socialism, which returned two senators and ten deputies. Communists in two French overseas departments won regional council seats in February: 11 of 41 seats in Guadeloupe and 4 of 41 in Martinique. The Communist Party USA reportedly had its most successful membership campaign in many years during 1983 and set its organization in motion for the 1984 U.S. presidential elections. The party's Young Workers Liberation League was abolished in favor of a new Young Communist League, among other organizational changes. The new youth group, like the party as a whole, pledged to rally opposition to President Ronald Reagan's re-election. Throughout the year, the party, in particular through its U.S. Peace Council, devoted much of its attention to supporting the nuclear-freeze movement.

The prospects for revolution have improved greatly in parts of the Western Hemisphere in recent years. Although a number of factors lie behind this change, not least the declining influence of the United States in the region and the tyranny of fluctuating international markets, shifts in the revolutionary strategies of the Soviet Union and Cuba have been equally important. Both Cuba and the USSR have revised their positions on revolution in Latin America, and these revisions, though simple, have made Marxist-Leninist groups a potent force for change in the region.

In short, the Soviet Union has turned increasingly toward supporting or even engaging in armed struggle to achieve revolutionary objectives in many countries around the world, from Afghanistan, Ethiopia, and Angola to portions of Central and South America. And Cuba, which has long supported armed struggle, has abandoned its suicidal divisive policies of the late 1960s, policies that reached their peak in 1967 during the Latin American Solidarity Organization (OLAS) Conference in Havana and Che Guevara's abortive adventure in Bolivia. Fidel Castro, now backed by the Soviet Union, refuses to assist the squabblers he nurtured fifteen years ago—so long as they keep squabbling. Cuba played a leading role in the overthrow of Somoza in Nicaragua by helping to pull the fratricidal Sandinista factions together, with the backing of broadly based national and international fronts, for a final drive to power. In El Salvador, the same policy led to the formation of the FMLN guerrilla front, with the backing of the less-radical, nonmilitary FDR, and to the level of success the dissident forces had achieved there by the beginning of 1984.

Of course, cooperation in a war against an existing government does not mean real unity of strategy and objectives has been achieved. The Sandinistas did not maintain their unity after the overthrow of Somoza. And, in El Salvador, important differences remain. These differences emerged clearly in 1983 within the Salvadoran Popular Liberation Forces (FPL), when Mélida Anaya Montes was brutally murdered and Cayetano Carpio, the most experienced and in many respects most radical of the Salvadoran guerrillas, reportedly committed suicide, although few who have followed Cayetano Carpio's career think he is likely to have killed himself. Both died in Managua, and it is probable that the issues involved touched on FMLN strategy generally, including the level of influence exercised on the Salvadorans by Cuba and Nicaragua. The FPL itself soon split with the splinter group, maintaining what it believes to be the spirit of the deceased founders.

And though open disputes continue in some other countries—such as between the communist party and the Movement Toward Socialism in Venezuela—efforts to achieve revolutionary unity have never been so great among so many Marxist-Leninist organizations, particularly in the Caribbean Basin. The result has been an expanding level of Marxist-Leninist influence in the region.

William E. Ratliff
Hoover Institution

Argentina

Population. 29.6 million
Party. Communist Party of Argentina (Partido Comunista de la Argentina; PCA)
Founded. 1918
Membership. 70,000 (estimate)
Secretary General. Athos Fava
Politburo. 6 members: Athos Fava, Jorge Pereira, Fernando Nadra, Pedro Tadioli, Irene Rodríguez, Rubens Iscaro
Status. Legal
Central Committee. 92 members, 33 alternates
Last Congress. Extraordinary, 5–6 September 1983
Last Elections. 30 October 1983, 1.3 percent, no representation
Auxiliary Organizations. Communist Youth; local branch of the World Peace Council; the party effectively controls the Argentine Permanent Assembly on Human Rights.
Publications. *Qué Pasa?* (weekly)

In elections held in October—the first after more than six years of military rule—Dr. Raúl Alfonsín of the moderate Radical Civic Union (UCR) emerged the decisive victor, with 52 percent of the popular vote. The Justicialist (or Peronist) party came in second with 40 percent—its first electoral defeat in nearly forty years of existence.

The PCA had supported the Peronist presidential ticket and Peronist gubernatorial candidates, presenting its own list of candidates for parliament and the municipal councils.

In general, the Left did poorly in the elections; votes for all its parties—including the communists—amounted to less than 5 percent of the total. The best performance was turned in by the Intransigent Party, whose candidate, Dr. Oscar Alende, obtained 344,434 votes.

Alfonsín captured much of the traditional constituency of the Left by promising a thorough investigation of events under the various military juntas that had ruled the country since 1976, with particular attention to corruption, mismanagement, and the prosecution of the war against urban terrorism, in which 6,000 Argentines are thought to have "disappeared." He also preempted the ground on international issues by loudly denouncing the Reagan administration and promising an "independent" foreign policy, with full participation in the Nonaligned Movement and the various organisms designed to promote Latin American integration.

On the other hand, Alfonsín was actually less left-wing than he appeared, a fact recognized by many conservative voters who also deserted their traditional parties to vote for the Radicals, in this case, as a way of getting rid of Peronism once and for all. Peronism remains the most important single factor in Argentine politics. At issue is its continuing control of the country's large labor movement—seen as corrupt and insufficiently radical by the Left and corrupt and excessively powerful by the Right. How Peronism will be integrated into the new political system as an ordinary opposition party remains to be seen, particularly in the context of a severe economic recession. Nor is it clear who will benefit most from this situation: the PCA (and other parties of the Left) who still dream of capturing the labor movement; the Radicals, who plan to depoliticize it; or the military, which in the past has alternatively exploited Peronism both as an ally and as an adversary.

Membership and Party Organization; Domestic Affairs. The most recent party congress reconfirmed Athos Fava as secretary general, but one concession to new cultural trends was the elevation of a woman—Irene Rodríguez—to the Politburo and her subsequent nomination as vice-presidential candidate. (Both she and presidential nominee Rubens Iscaro subsequently withdrew from the race when the party decided to back the Peronist slate of Italo Luder and Deolindo Bittel.)

In July, a federal judge officially recognized the juridical personality of the PCA, lifting what little remained of the mild ban on party activity that had prevailed in the late years of military rule (see YICA, 1983, p. 56). The party weekly, *Qué Pasa?*, circulated freely, and communist television advertising for party candidates—in frequency, length, and professional quality—rivaled that of the two major parties. This lent credibility to the frequent allegation that the PCA receives a 5 percent royalty on all Argentine commercial transactions with the Soviet Union (see below). Whatever the case, the party indisputably possesses financial resources far out of proportion to its actual membership.

The PCA's informal electoral alliance with

Peronism in 1983 seemed a bit strange in view of the long history of mutual hostility and (in the mid-1940s) rivalry for control of the labor movement. One theory holds that the PCA initially hoped to sponsor (and presumably control) what Rubens Iscaro called "a large democratic and popular front" in which Peronists (and others) would subsume themselves. (ATC, 23 April; *FBIS*, 27 April.) When this failed, so the reasoning runs, the communists attached themselves to the Peronist presidential ticket, hoping that their local candidates would benefit from an expected landslide. Another speculation—which need not exclude the first altogether—is that by supporting the Peronists at the national level, the party's operatives would have greater freedom of movement within Peronist-controlled locals in factories and industrial plants, positioning themselves for maximum benefit in the future. According to a left-wing British source (often guilty of wishful thinking), this process is already well under way. Thus it reported at midyear that the PCA had established a "presence" in the Syndicate of Light and Power Workers ("always considered out of bounds for non-Peronist groups") and a "small but significant" representation within the metallurgical, construction, transport, port, railway, bank, and state employees unions. (*Latin America Weekly Report*, 6 May.)

International Views, Positions, and Activities. The close commercial relationship between Argentina and the Soviet Union (see *YICA*, 1983, pp. 57–58) continued and intensified. The Soviet Union remained the leading purchaser of Argentine cereals (nearly 50 percent of all exports in the first half of 1983) followed at some distance (14.5 percent) by the PRC (Noticias Argentinas, 21 September; *FBIS*, 27 September). Aeroflot began regular commercial service to Buenos Aires (via East Berlin and Dakar) in March. The Soviets were reportedly supplying turbines for the Salto Grande dam and unspecified equipment for a similar project at Piedra de Aguila (Noticias Argentinas, 31 May; *FBIS*, 1 June). Under study were a concession to a Soviet consortium to electrify the Buenos Aires–Rosario branch of the General Mitre Railway (Noticias Argentinas, 13 July; *FBIS*, 18 July), the acquisition of one million cubic meters of Soviet oil (Noticias Argentinas, 26 May; *FBIS*, 1 June), and the exchange of military commissions (*Buenos Aires Herald*, 24 November; *FBIS*, 26 November). During the year, both countries exchanged high-level trade and technical delegations; a Soviet oceanographic vessel bound for the Antarctic put in at Buenos Aires; and there was a significant increase in cultural exchange programs (TELAM, 24 May; *FBIS*, 26 May).

To some degree, the Argentine-Soviet relationship has operated in isolation from local political conditions; that is, it derives from geo-economic necessities and Argentina's shrinking place in Western grain markets. On the other hand, in recent months it has drawn additional sustenance from the drastic shift in Argentine foreign policy following the military defeat in the Falklands/Malvinas war. Since then, Argentines have been vociferously anti-Western and particularly anti-American, exemplified by renewed participation in the Nonaligned Movement and a degree of rapprochement with Cuba and Nicaragua.

The PCA has tried to make the most of this turn of events. For example, *Qué Pasa?* (May) echoed and embroidered on an Argentine charge at the United Nations that NATO was constructing "a gigantic military base with launching pads for nuclear missiles" in the Malvinas (Noticias Argentinas, 10 May; *FBIS*, 2 June). But it still labors under the disability of being associated with the Soviet-Argentine entente during the years of military rule. During the campaign, Athos Fava found it necessary to protest to a popular weekly that his party had "never supported" the military government and even claimed for the PCA a share of the "disappeared" —but the figure he gave (105 persons) was so low as to confirm rather than allay the widespread suspicions of collusion or, at least, preferential treatment. Revealing, too, was his insistence even at that late date on dividing the military into "patriotic, democratic, and anti-imperialist sectors" and those who were not. (*La Semana*, 28 October.)

In 1983, Fava traveled as a guest of local communist parties to France, Czechoslovakia, Poland, and the USSR. A delegation from the French party visited Argentina in July.

Other Leftist Groups. Of the three urban guerrilla groups active in Argentina during the 1970s, only one—the Montoneros—continues to exist, directed by an exile leadership based in Havana, Mexico City, and occasionally, Managua. Since 1980, the Montoneros have experienced serious setbacks: a split into rival factions, a steady loss of membership (once estimated at 15,000), and—according to one report—a cooling of relations with host nations such as Cuba and Libya (as well as with silent partners in the Eastern bloc) following the shifts in Argentine foreign policy outlined above (*Somos*, 10 June; *JPRS*, July).

Within Argentina itself, there were current reports of resurgent Montonero activity, but it was difficult to know to what degree they reflected actual fact or merely the exaggerated claims of security forces needing justification for the rough handling or occasional murder of leftist or dissident elements. In 1983, authorities arrested two alleged members of the movement's top leadership in Misiones and killed a purported Montonero in Córdoba and yet another in Buenos Aires. The best-documented incidents involved the periodic interruption of the audio portion of TV broadcasts to read Montonero communiqués.

The wide political opening that followed the junta's call for elections in 1982 encouraged the appearance of new leftist parties and the revival of many old ones. The former included the Movement Toward Socialism and the Labor Party; the latter, the Intransigent Party, Front of the Popular Left, Revolutionary Communist Party, Popular Socialist Party, and Party of the National Left. Almost all of these could be described as Peronist-Trotskyist, and in fact most supported the Peronist presidential ticket. Before the elections, the Labor Party claimed 70,000 members (DYN, 19 April; *FBIS*, 5 May), and the British source cited above generously attributed to it and the Movement Toward Socialism significant inroads into the labor movement; nonetheless, apart from the Labor Party all of these parties together managed to poll only 109,000 votes.

An attempt by Vicente Leonidas Saadi to reintroduce a quasi-Marxist line within Peronism (the so-called Intransigence and Mobilization movement) was a signal failure, and this in spite of its launching a major new daily, *La Voz*. Authorities accused Saadi of Montonero connections and financing; this he heatedly denied. (*NYT*, 21 May.) His paper, however, survived without any advertising at all.

Mark Falcoff
American Enterprise Institute

Bolivia

Population. 5.9 million
Party. Communist Party of Bolivia (Partido Comunista de Bolivia; PCB)
Founded. 1950
Membership. 300 (estimate)
Secretary General. Jorge Kolle Cueto
Status. Legal
Last Congress. Fourth, April 1979
Last Election. 1980; the People's Democratic Union, the electoral coalition supported by the PCB, won 47 of the 130 seats in the lower house; these elections were nullified by a military coup; in October 1982, the parliament was allowed to meet; the PCB holds 2 cabinet posts, Labor and Mines.
Auxiliary Organizations. Communist Youth of Bolivia

The democratic regime of President Hernán Siles Suazo, which came into office in October 1982, continued in power throughout 1983. Through several changes in the cabinet during the year, the Partido Comunista de Bolivia (PCB), the pro-Moscow Communist Party of Bolivia, continued to hold two ministries in the Siles cabinet, those of Labor and of Mines.

Virtually all far-left parties and tendencies in Bolivia originated in one of five original groups: (1) the pro-Stalinist Party of the Revolutionary Left (Partido de Izquierda Revolucionaria), established in 1940, whose heirs include the pro-Moscow PCB and the pro-Beijing Marxist-Leninist Communist Party of Bolivia (Partido Comunista de Bolivia Marxista-Leninista); (2) the Trotskyist Revolutionary Workers' Party (Partido Obrero Revolucionario; POR), organized in the mid-1930s, the ancestor of several other parties, most still using the same name; (3) the National Liberation Army (Ejército de Liberación Nacional), a guerrilla group organized by Ernesto "Che" Guevara in 1966, which in 1975 established the Revolutionary Party of Bolivian Workers (Partido Revolucionario de Trabajadores de Bolivia); (4) the middle-of-the-road Christian Democratic Party, which gave birth to

the Movement of the Revolutionary Left (Movimiento de Izquierda Revolucionaria; MIR) in 1971; and (5) the center-left Nationalist Revolutionary Movement (Movimiento Nacionalista Revolucionario), in power from 1952 to 1964, which gave rise to a dissident left-wing group that formed the Socialist Party (Partido Socialista de Bolivia) in the early 1970s, which was in 1983 the fourth largest political group in the country, at least in terms of parliamentary representation. The total membership of these factions is probably less than 10,000.

At the beginning of the year, the three principal parties that belonged to the Popular Democratic Union (Union Democratica Popular; UDP), which had elected President Siles, were represented in his cabinet. These were Siles's own Left National Revolutionary Movement (Movimiento Nacionalista Revolucionario de Izquierda; MNRI), the MIR, and the PCB.

The first cabinet crisis occurred in January when the six MIR cabinet ministers resigned over a disagreement with President Siles's economic policies. After long negotiations, the MIR refused to rejoin the government, although Vice-President Jaime Paz Zamora, head of the MIR, denied that this meant that the MIR was leaving the UDP or withdrawing support from the Siles government. The PCB ministers remained in the government.

A second major reorganization of the cabinet came in August. Although efforts had been made to bring the MIR back into the government, these were of no avail; but the Christian Democratic Party did enter the cabinet for the first time. The PCB continued to hold the ministries of Labor and of Mines.

The persistence of the pro-Stalinist party in the cabinet provoked claims from the opposition press that the PCB in fact dominated the Siles government. The La Paz daily *El Diario* editorialized on 16 March that "the Communists practically control the entire sphere of social influence both inside and outside of the government." Three months later, on 13 June, *El Diario* maintained that "in a very curious and certainly unexpected manner, one of the various communist party factions has climbed to power in Bolivia, despite the fact that voters did not support their presence in the executive branch in the 1980 elections." It claimed that after the exit of the MIR from the Siles regime, the PCB "assumed control of the government and had rapidly expanded its influence and power."

With one exception, the PCB, as a coalition partner in the cabinet, vocally supported the Siles government and its policies. It continued to remain in the regime even though the Siles government first sought help from the International Monetary Fund (IMF) to deal with the country's critical economic situation and then agreed to accept the IMF's terms for giving such aid. In June, a PCB leader commented on a television program that "we are not in favor of a break with the IMF; what we want is that no impositions affecting our sovereignty be accepted; that is to say, the authority that a country has to adopt its own policy in a sovereign manner" (*El Diario*, 22 June).

Three months later, Deputy Marco Domic of the PCB said that the party supported negotiations with the IMF, "although the negotiations must respect national sovereignty." He argued that the IMF had to "take into account the poorest sectors of our country," which he said "will suffer the consequences of this sort of measure" (AFP, 15 September).

A few days later, Minister of Labor Ramiro Barrenechea, of the PCB, said, "I would like to affirm categorically that this is a UDP government, with a UDP program and popular support. Those of us who joined this cabinet are fully aware that this is a UDP government with a UDP economic, political, social, and cultural program, and I reiterate that this is a popular program." (Cadena Panamericana, 20 September; *FBIS*, 21 September.)

Even after the Siles government fully accepted the IMF's terms in November, involving drastic devaluation of the peso from 200 to 500 to the U.S. dollar, a 200 percent increase in the price of gasoline, and elimination of most subsidies of prices of essential foodstuffs, the PCB did not abandon the Siles government (*Latin America Weekly Report*, 25 November).

The only issue on which the PCB publicly questioned the policies of the Siles government was that of the Soviet invasion of Afghanistan. When Foreign Minister Mario Velarde "repudiated the occupation of Afghanistan by foreign troops" (AFP, 10 February), Senator Jorge Kolle Cueto, secretary general of the PCB, claimed that this statement "misinterprets the UDP nonaligned position." Kolle claimed that the PCB "cannot agree with the statement issued by the foreign minister" and argued that since the constitution authorized only the president to determine foreign policy, Foreign Minister Velarde's statement did not constitute the policy of the UDP government. (Cadena Panamericana, 11 February; *FBIS*, 15 February.)

The second source of influence of the PCB during 1983 was its power in the organized labor movement, particularly in the Miners' Federation (FSTMB). Although Juan Lechin, leader of the Partido Revolucionario de la Izquierda Nacionalista, remained executive secretary of both the FSTMB and the Central Obrera Boliviana (COB), the pro-Moscow communists constituted the single largest political element among the miners. Near the end of the year, labor protests against the austerity program of the Siles government intensified. They culminated in a 24-hour strike in November. However, these protests did not convince the PCB to abandon the government.

The PCB leaders of the Mineworkers participated in seizure of control of the Mining Corporation of Bolivia by the Miners' Federation, which took place in April. This seizure was later legalized by the Siles government.

At the time of the August ministerial crisis, President Siles invited the COB to participate in the government. However, when the COB submitted a list of demands as its price for participation, which included majority representation in the cabinet, majority workers' representation on boards of directors of all government-owned enterprises, and "workers' control" of all large private enterprises, Siles rejected these demands. In spite of this, the PCB continued to remain in President Siles's cabinet.

The PCB maintained its contacts with the pro-Moscow international communist faction during the year. In January it was announced that the party had participated in a conference of South American communist parties, including those of Argentina, Brazil, Chile, Paraguay, Peru, and Uruguay, held in Lima in November 1982, which had pledged support for the struggle against "enslavement of our countries by U.S. imperialism" (*FBIS*, 19 January).

In February, a delegation from the Soviet party visited Bolivia on the invitation of the PCB. It not only went to La Paz, but also visited several mining areas, where the PCB had a following (*El Diario*, 23 February). In the following month, a delegation of Soviet trade union leaders also visited the country and was officially received by leaders of the COB (Radio Fides, 16 March; *FBIS*, 17 March). The PCB undoubtedly gained prestige from the fact that in January the Siles government for the first time in two decades extended diplomatic recognition to the Castro government of Cuba (*FBIS*, 9 September). Much later in the year, in October, Ivan Kalin, deputy chairman of the Soviet Presidium, visited Bolivia for three days. He met with President Siles and Vice-President Jaime Paz Zamora and attended special sessions of the parliament. However, extensive expansion of Soviet aid did not result from the visit.

Throughout the year, the Maoist communists of the PCB (Marxista-Leninista) continued to be in the opposition, aligned with the faction of the Movimiento Nacionalista Revolucionario headed by ex-president Víctor Paz Estenssoro. It accused the pro-Moscow party of seeking to undermine the influence of Congress in the re-established democratic regime (*Los Tiempos*, 9 October 1982). The Maoists held a Special National Conference in Cochabamba late in July. Those attending included representatives of fourteen regional committees and members of the Central Committee. *El Diario* (19 August) reported that "the conference reaffirmed the determination of the party to defend its political, ideological, and organizational unity against the attempt by the government and international revisionism to divide it."

The Socialist Party was apparently considered for inclusion in the government during the various cabinet crises. In June, it urged the unification of all of the leftist parties and the inclusion of the Peasants' Confederation in the Siles government (AFP, 9 June; *FBIS*, 13 June). Two months earlier, it had announced that it would not participate in the administration "because this government shows a gap between programs and ideology" (EFE, 6 April; *FBIS*, 7 April).

Several Trotskyist factions continued to be active during the year. The POR-Combate, the faction affiliated with the United Secretariat of the Fourth International, had at least one member on the Executive Committee of the FSTMB (*Intercontinental Press*, 16 May). In July, two Trotskyist factions, POR-Combate and the Vanguardia Comunista–POR, combined to form the POR-Unificado. The new organization publishes the periodical *Bandera Socialista*. It has some following in several mining sectors and among some peasant groups. (Ibid., 7 November.)

Robert J. Alexander
Rutgers University

Brazil

Population. 131.3 million
Party. Brazilian Communist Party (Partido Comunista Brasileiro; PCB); originally Communist Party of Brazil (Partido Comunista do Brasil; PCdoB); name changed in 1960
Founded. 1922
Membership. 6,000 (estimate)
Secretary General. Giocondo Dias
Central Committee. Now called National Leadership Collective; members include Geraldo Rodríguez dos Santos, Regis Frati, Teodoro Mello, Luis Tenorio de Silva, Salomão Malina, Givaldo Siqueira, and Lindolfo Silva
Status. Illegal
Last Congress. 1967; planned 1982 congress interrupted by police
Publications. *Voz da Unidade*

The PCB directed all its efforts in 1983 to the campaign to obtain legal recognition of the party. With this aim in mind, it eschewed any participation in the waves of social disturbances that affected most of the large cities. The originally pro-Chinese, now pro-Albanian, Communist Party of Brazil (Partido Comunista do Brasil; PCdoB) had no such compunctions; a 1961 splinter of the PCB, the PCdoB was implicated in the initial organization of unemployment protests that led to two days of the worst rioting ever seen in São Paulo. Two Trotskyist groups, Libelu and Socialist Youth Foundation, also helped to radicalize those protests. Another 1960s breakaway from the PCB, the 8 October Revolutionary Movement (Movimento Revolucionario 8; MR–8), seems to be returning to the party fold. The MR–8 was apparently the last of several armed resistance movements active through the early 1970s.

Domestic Activities. Charges were dropped and then reinstated against 67 persons accused of attempting to hold the Seventh Congress of the illegal PCB in December 1982 (see *YICA*, 1983, p. 61). The indictments were the result of a July review of the case that coincided with a growing momentum in the campaign for PCB legalization. Among those indicted, Secretary General Giocondo Dias contends that the question of legalization would have been discussed at the interrupted meeting (not congress) and "the repression of the communists, opening up a possible witch hunt, delays and complicates political normalization" (*O Estado de São Paulo*, 18 January). In fact, the arrests, plus the confiscation of a March issue of *Voz da Unidade* defending legalization, probably generated new sympathies for the PCB cause. All legal opposition parties support legalization of the PCB, and the São Paulo state assembly approved a motion calling for its recognition. Some anticommunist sectors, such as *O Estado de São Paulo*, favor legalization so that "the monster can be seen for the dwarf that it is ... according to the most optimistic forecasts, its electoral support may reach 3% ... Legalization would put an end to communist infiltration of other parties ... and a democracy must in any case be able to absorb anti-democratic minorites" (*O Estado de São Paulo*, 15 December 1982; *FBIS*, 22 December 1982).

The Catholic church is divided on the question. The leaders of the National Bishops Conference (CNBB)—Dom Ivo Lorscheider, Dom

Benedito Ulhoa, and Dom Luciano Mendes—have spoken out against legalization, while some members of the Pastoral Episcopal Commission, a dependency of the CNBB, have declared in favor (*Folha de São Paulo*, 27 May; *JPRS*, July). The military hierarchy continues to reject the idea of a legalized PCB, and President João Figueiredo recently confirmed his opposition (*Diario Las Américas*, Miami, 29 November).

The tactics of the National Collective, seeking support from all sectors, including the government party (Partido Demócrata Social; PDS), have caused some rifts within the PCB. Eleven members of the São Paulo state collective, oldtimers like David Capistrano Filho among them, were expelled when they dissented. Founder and former secretary general Luiz Carlos Prestes said, "it is not by petitioning the dictatorship that the PCB will obtain legal status, which must be won in the streets" (*Jornal do Brasil*, 16 May; *JPRS*, 14 June). The National Collective would reportedly have invited Prestes, who broke with the PCB last year, to assume the presidency of the party if he agreed to sign the petition for legalization; Prestes refused (ibid.).

In January, Dias said the petition for legalization will be presented to the Supreme Electoral Council only when it is "politically opportune." At the same time, he spoke of a "Brazilian socialism, different from the models of the Soviet Union and China." (*O Estado de São Paulo*, 18 January.) A document containing drafts of the PCB manifesto, program, and statutes was distributed in Congress at the time of Dias's visit to that body in May to enlist support. The manifesto states: "We plan to organize, in accordance with legal norms, an autonomous national party that will assume the full defense of human rights, of ideological, political, and party pluralism and autonomy of the mass movements, as well as respect for the representative forms of expression of popular sovereignty." (*Jornal do Brasil*, 12 May; *JPRS*, 9 June.)

Auxiliary and/or Front Organizations. The disruptive strikes led by the PCB-dominated General Labor Command (CGT) in the early 1960s were among the decisive factors leading to the overthrow of President João Goulart. After the 1964 revolution, the CGT was abolished and the unions stripped of all power. The 1978–1980 metalworkers' strikes in São Paulo tested the new democratic opening and discovered its limits;

their leader, Luis Inácio da Silva ("Lula") was barred from union activity but went on to form the Workers' Party (Partido dos Trabalhadores; PT), with support from the Basic Christian Communities (CEBs) of the Catholic church, students and intellectuals, and two Trotskyist groups. The PT won 10 percent of the vote in São Paulo but had no impact elsewhere.

In the recent trend toward nationwide labor union organization, the PT has become a serious rival of the PCB for control of the movement's left wing. An August, PT-dominated National Congress of the Working Class (Congreso Nacional da Classe Trabalhadora; CONCLAT) created a Single Labor Central (Central Unica dos Trabalhadores; CUT), claiming support from some 900 organizations. These included some civil servants' groups prohibited by law from forming unions, as well as community and church organizations. The PT effort was boycotted by an alliance of PCB, PCdoB, and conservative unions, which convened its own CONCLAT in November and formed the National Coordination of the Working Classes (Coordenação Nacional das Classes Trabalhadores; CNTC). About 1,200 strictly labor organizations have joined the CNTC. Both the CNTC and the CUT have their power base among the metalworkers of São Paulo and have tentatively planned a joint congress for some time in 1984. Existing legislation prohibits the confederation of unions from involvement in more than one industry or activity, but no action has been taken against either group. (*O Estado de São Paulo*, 10–31 August; *Latin America Weekly Report*, 18 November.)

International Positions and Activities. The PCB attended a meeting of Southern Cone communist parties in Lima in November 1982. A joint declaration noted the growing successes of the anti-imperialist movement in South America: "The democratic struggle" against U.S. warmongering "is expressed through solidarity with Cuba, Nicaragua and Grenada, and the peoples of Guatemala and El Salvador." The "explosion of anti-imperialist feeling" provoked by the Malvinas conflict showed that the "master-slave" basis of inter-American relations can be changed. The communist parties can help bring this about by working for a unified Left, particularly in the labor movement, in individual countries, and on the continent; the fronts created should also include peasants, students, intellectuals, church, and certain circles of the upper class and military. The communist parties must also fight the imperialistic campaigns that belittle socialist accomplishments and foster anti-Sovietism. The document "reaffirms the creative vigor of Marxism-Leninism," rejects "alleged modernizations" intended to disguise reformism, and "confirms the Havana declaration of 1975." It "absolutely endorses the unity of the international communist and workers' movement." (*Horizont*, East Berlin, no. 10; *FBIS*, 19 January.)

Giocondo Dias met with Czechoslovak Central Committee secretary Vasil Bil'ák during a working visit to Czechoslovakia in March. Among the congratulations received by Dias on his seventieth birthday was one from the East German party's secretary general, Erich Honecker. The East German leader praised Dias's work and said that "the Brazilian communists are in line with all those forces in your country supporting basic democratic rights of working people, including the right of the PCB to operate legally" (*Neues Deutschland*, East Berlin, 18 November; *FBIS*, 30 November).

PCdoB. The 71-year-old João Amazonas still heads the illegal PCdoB, which now has four deputies in Congress, elected on the ticket of the Brazilian Democratic Mobilization Party (PMDB, originally the MDB, the only legal opposition party before the 1978 reforms). "An open secret," according to the newsweekly *Veja*, the PMDB also harbors deputies from the PCB and the MR-8. The PCdoB controls the São Paulo Committee Against Unemployment, responsible in April for the original protest march that degenerated into two days of the worst riots and looting ever seen in the city, with damages estimated at $5 million. (*Vega*, 13 April.) The PCdoB is also credited with provoking disturbances on 15 March in São Paulo and 21 September in Manaus, both involving destruction of large numbers of city buses (*O Estado de São Paulo*, 22 September). The Trotskyist wing of the PT has a few

seats on the unemployment committee and was active in the São Paulo protests. No real action has been taken against the parties because the scope of the riots clearly went far beyond their powers of organization. (In the same way, often well-founded suspicions of political manipulation in the sporadic waves of supermarket lootings in several cities seemed to lose importance when police were faced with genuinely hungry prisoners.) The PCdoB publishes the newspaper *Tribuna da Luta Operária*.

Trotskyist Groups. Two Trotskyist organizations form the left wing of the PT. Freedom and Struggle (Liberdade e Luta; Libelu) is headed by architect Clara Ant, a defeated candidate for the state assembly of São Paulo. Socialist Youth Foundation (Alicerce da Juventude Socialista) is the result of a recent merger of Alicerce with the Convergencia Socialista. Eduardo de Almeida, speaking for Alicerce, absolved the PT of any responsibility for the group's activities. (*Veja*, 13 April.)

MR-8. The Central Committee and a majority of state leaders and members decided at the Fourth Congress in June to dissolve the MR-8 and return to the PCB. Members made a radical self-criticism of their "anti-Soviet and leftist" positions and chose the "party's main fold" as the "true and only center" of the Brazilian communist movement. The only condition imposed by the PCB is that the dissidents should join the party individually, in keeping with party statutes. Frictions have arisen nonetheless between PCB and MR-8 members, particularly in Rio de Janeiro and São Paulo; some members were directly involved in mutual accusations and personal confrontations and are still distrustful of the reunification process. (*Folha de Sao Pāulo*, 18 September; *FBIS*, 22 September.)

Carole Merten
Miami, Florida

Canada

Population. 24.9 million

Parties. Communist Party of Canada (CPC); Workers Communist Party (Marxist-Leninist) (WPC); Communist Party of Canada (Marxist-Leninist) (CPC-ML); Revolutionary Workers' League (RWL)

Founded. CPC: 1921; WCP: 1979; CPC-ML: 1970; RWL: 1977

Membership. CPC: 2,500 (estimate); WCP: a few hundred; CPC-ML: 500–1,000; RWL: several hundred

Secretary General. CPC: William Kashtan; CPC-ML: Hardial Bains; RWL: John Riddell

Central Committee. CPC: 20 members

Status. Legal

Last Congress. CPC: Twenty-fifth, 13–15 February 1982, in Toronto; WPC: Second, 22–23 January 1983, in Montreal; CPC-ML, Fourth, 3 April 1982, in Montreal; RWL, 27 December 1983–1 January 1984

Last Election. 1980; CPC: 0.5 percent; CPC-ML 0.1 percent; RWL: ran 4 candidates; no party has representation

Auxiliary Organizations. CPC: Canadian Peace Congress, Conseil Québecois de la Paix, Association of United Ukrainian Canadians, Congress of Canadian Women; CPC-ML: People's Front Against Racist and Fascist Violence, Revolutionary Trade Union Opposition, Democratic Women's Union of Canada, East Indian Defence Committee, West Indian People's Organization, Communist Youth Union of Canada (M-L); RWL: Young Socialist Organizing Committee

Publications. CPC: *Canadian Tribune, Pacific Tribune, Combat, Communist Viewpoint, Communist, New Horizons, Jeunesse militante, Nouvelle revue internationale*; WPC: *Forge, La Forge, October, Octobre*; CPC-ML: *People's Canada Daily News, Le Quotidien du Canada* (both to be replaced on 1 January 1984 by *The Marxist-Leninist* and *Le Marxiste-Leniniste*), *Voice of the Youth, Voice of the People, West Indian, Lok Awaz, Etincelle, Bulletin de nouvelles, Femmes démocratiques, Non aux coupures, Revolutionary Trade Union Opposition of Canada, BC Worker*; RWL: *Socialist Voice, Lutte ouvrière, New International* (copublished with U.S. counterpart)

Several Marxist-Leninist parties and groups operate legally in Canada. The oldest and largest is the CPC. Since its founding in 1921, the CPC has been consistently pro-Moscow in alignment. The WCP was founded in 1979 and until its demise this year was pro-Beijing. The CPC-ML, founded in 1970, is pro-Albanian. Several Trotskyist groups exist, including the RWL, Groupe socialiste des travailleurs (GST), Trotskyist League (TL), and Forward Readers Group (FRG).

In the last federal election (1980), the com-

bined vote for all communist parties was less than 0.2 percent of the vote. Communist candidates ran in the 1983 provincial election in British Columbia. No candidates were elected. The parties have been increasingly active in municipal elections, notably in Vancouver, Winnipeg, and Toronto, and several members have won election.

The Canadian economy, mired in its worst recession since the Great Depression of the 1930s, has a record 1.5 million unemployed (12.5 percent of the labor force). In an effort to control inflation and the deficit, the federal government, along with most provincial governments, continued to legislate limits on salary increases for public employees.

In addition, proposals for government cutbacks in social services, welfare programs, and the size of the civil services have generated discussions within the labor movement about the need for a general strike, particularly in Quebec and British Columbia. Over 200,000 workers walked out in protest in Quebec (*Globe and Mail*, 27 January) and over 80,000 struck in British Columbia (*Canadian Tribune*, 21 November).

International affairs grew in importance as Canadians became increasingly concerned about the arms race, Reagan's foreign policy, and the dangers of nuclear war. A majority of Canadians (52 percent) opposed the testing of cruise missiles in Canada (ibid., 14 February). The peace movement, rallying behind the slogan of "Refuse the cruise," and reminiscent of the Ban the Bomb movement of the early 1950s, continued to grow in size, with the *Toronto Star* (16 October) reporting as many as 500 different peace and disarmament organizations now in Canada, most notably a Canadian version of the Green Party. Over 80,000 Canadians participated in peace demonstrations on 23 April. Even Prime Minister Pierre Trudeau embarked late in the year on a much publicized odyssey for peace.

Communist Party of Canada. Headquartered in Toronto, the CPC ran four candidates in the British Columbia provincial election and received a total of 693 votes. Gordon Massie was officially elected leader in Ontario, as was Kimball Cariou in Saskatchewan. Sam Walsh is president of the Parti communist du Québec. In May, William Kashtan, CPC general secretary, met in Ottawa with Mikhail Gorbachev, USSR Politburo member (*Canadian Tribune*, 30 May). John Hanley Morgan, president of the Canadian Peace Congress, received the Lenin Peace Prize (ibid., 9 May). Alfred Dewhurst, Central Executive Committee member, and John Weir, both columnists for the *Canadian Tribune*, died. Fred Rose, former member of Parliament and convicted spy, also died in exile in Poland (ibid., 21 March). In party educational affairs, an effort is being made to expand the size of the *Canadian Tribune* and have it distributed in more bookstores (ibid., 2 May, 19 December). The USSR has agreed to publish 50,000 copies of *Canada's Party of Socialism*, the official party history (ibid., 5 December).

The CPC notes that Canada, severely affected by the economic crisis, has seen an intensification of the class struggle and that efforts are required to prevent a turn to the right (ibid., 27 June, 21 November). New antilabor legislation and government cutbacks in social services, particularly in Quebec and British Columbia, should be opposed under the slogan "No to concessions" (ibid., 18 July, 5 September). The "attack" on universal medical care must be repulsed by banning extra-billing and user fees (ibid., 7 March, 11 April). While initially cautious about demands for general strikes in Quebec and British Columbia (ibid., 21 February, 8 August), the CPC finally embraced such "mass struggle" (ibid., 31 January, 7 November, 22 August) as being preferable to the New Democratic Party's (NDP) electoral politics. Increasingly, there was a call for a "united front" among the "genuine left forces" and the need "to bridge the gaps in creed and orientation" (ibid., 28 March, 20 June, 26 December). Sectarianism was to be avoided (*Communist Viewpoint*, June). The Catholic church is seen to be capable of being "progressive" (*Canadian Tribune*, 7 February, 18 April). The CPC observes that most "progressive and socialist-minded Canadians" are NDP supporters, thus its "relationships with the NDP [are] ...of major importance" (*Communist Viewpoint*, December). While critical of past NDP provincial governments' antilabor legislation and the NDP's recent drift to the political center, the CPC calls for cooperation with the NDP, particularly in municipal politics (*Canadian Tribune*, 7 March, 18 April, 21 November). Members are encouraged "to exert all efforts" in this domain (ibid., 6 June). Accordingly, communists ran under the label of the Committee of Progressive Electors in Toronto and Vancouver and the Labour Election Committee in Winnipeg. Some were successful in the last two cities. Canada's most successful communist municipal politician, Joe Zuken of Winnipeg, retired after 42 years of elected office. Several Canadian cities, most notably Toronto and Vancouver, declared themselves nuclear-weapons-free zones in 1983 (ibid., 31 January, 2 May).

The CPC has given priority to party building among industrial workers (ibid., 12 December). This has included efforts to organize the unemployed, often in communist-front organizations.

During the past year key labor conventions passed resolutions opposing cruise missile testing in Canada (ibid., 21 February, 28 February), a theme vigorously pursued by party activists. The CPC calls on labor to stress "unity, not raiding" and to seek a wider redefinition of collective bargaining to include issues such as technological innovation (ibid., 21 November, 12 December). While extensive "nationalization under democratic control" is posited, the CPC nevertheless calls for the defense of the small farmer and businessman (ibid., 16 May). Youth is seen as bearing the burden of unemployment (ibid., 3 October), and recent proposals to induct youth into the military are condemned (ibid., 17 January).

Viewing the discontent with the Parti Québecois (PQ) government in Quebec, the CPC suggests "a new political situation" has arisen and calls for a "mass labor" party in the province (ibid., 14 February).

The CPC points out that Canadian economic woes are accentuated by Canada's dependence on the United States (ibid., 7 February). It notes U.S. pressures to keep Canada as a "resource hinterland" (ibid., 19 September; *Communist Viewpoint*, June) and calls for exchange controls to stop the outflow of Canadian capital (*Canadian Tribune*, 2 May). The CPC warns: "We have entered a more critical stage of development internationally and we should have no illusions . . . [the] United States has shifted its strategy, has abandoned détente and gone over to a cold war, confrontationist policy and material preparations for war. Its aim is clear: achieve military superiority so as to destroy socialism as a world system." (Ibid., 17 October.) The CPC suggests that "world peace, more than ever before, is a priority task" (ibid., 19 December) and observes the growing size of the peace movement. The recent addition of key Canadian labor bodies to the peace cause is welcomed (ibid., 18 April, 2 May). The party urges that the peace movement's ranks be enlarged still further and contain a broad spectrum of views (ibid., 14 February, 2 May). Such a united front can focus on opposition to cruise missile testing (ibid., 19 December) and efforts to have regions of Canada declared nuclear-weapons-free zones. The CPC calls for an independent foreign policy and Canadian withdrawal from NATO, NORAD, and the Defense Production Sharing Agreement. While the CPC was initially extremely critical of Trudeau's deci-

sion to test the cruise missile (ibid., 28 March, 4 and 25 April), the prime minister's peace initiative has received increasing praise (ibid., 31 October, 28 November, 5 December). In general, the CPC continues to echo Soviet positions in foreign affairs.

Workers Communist Party. The turmoil that engulfed the WCP in 1982 continued. The eve of the party's Second Congress, held in Montreal 22–23 January, saw the party with half of its national membership and two-thirds of its Quebec base lost, most of its party structures "paralyzed," and the former leadership "almost completely discredited" (*Forge*, April). The WCP's past lack of commitment to intraparty democracy, workers' power, feminism, and sensitivity to the Quebec nation continued to fracture both the leadership and the membership. The result was, in the words of one member, "chaos and hysteria" (ibid.). Still, 150 delegates gathered and amid "often heated debates" voted to "revoke the WCP Central Committee" and "continue as a revolutionary organization (81 for, 39 against, 17 abstentions)." They also voted (48 for, 44 against) to "look to Marxism as their ideological base," "maintain . . . a minimal form of organization," publish the *Forge* as finances permit, and "suspend the ex-members of the PB [Political Bureau] from the organization," at least until a referendum could determine their status. A new, more balanced coordinating committee was elected, equally represented by men and women, Québecois and English Canadians, and with workers represented in proportion to their membership. The months of turmoil had produced "enormous financial difficulties." After not being printed for several months, the weekly *Forge* reappeared in mimeographed form. As before, the pages were opened to a great outpouring of divergent viewpoints. By June, even the *Forge* officially ceased publication, while a few flyers were being circulated on an ad-hoc basis by several regional caucuses.

Communist Party of Canada (Marxist-Leninist). The CPC-ML, headquartered in Montreal, perceives that the "capitalist-revisionist crisis" has deepened (*People's Canada Daily News*, 28 January, 23 February) and that the bourgeoisie have launched an all-out ideological attack against the workers. The CPC-ML believes that while objective conditions are ripe for revolution, subjective conditions lag (ibid., 7 April). Since there can be no third road between the dictatorship of the bourgeoisie and the dictatorship of the proletariat, the party calls on workers to reject the "class-collaborationist" schemes of "labour-aristocrats" and to reject all demands for concessions in salaries and services (ibid., 31 January, 17 February, 7 July). Efforts should be made to resist the shifting of the burden of the crisis onto the backs of the working class. The CPC-ML rejects pressure to unite with revisionists. The NDP is portrayed as a bourgeois party with a "socialist mask" that, when in power, fosters "state monopoly capitalism." The PQ is characterized as seeking to split people along "reactionary narrow nationalism and chauvinism." Increased restrictions on immigration and student visas, police harassment of minorities, and "super exploitation" of immigrants provide evidence, according to the CPC-ML, that there is a growing tendency toward fascism and state-fostered racism. (*Lok Awaz*, 29 January; *People's Canada Daily News*, 12 April, 18 June.) Canada is portrayed as becoming increasingly a "military-bureaucratic state machine" (*People's Canada Daily News*, 25 April, 24 August) that is escalating its attacks on "progressive and democratic organizations." Such circumstances necessitate that the "people" militantly defend themselves against such assaults. The CPC-ML asserts that fascists and racists have no right to speak or organize and has blocked several pro-Israeli speaking engagements and Defence Department recruitment meetings at several universities (ibid., 22 March, 30 June, 22 September). The CPC-ML has also organized "militant pickets" around visiting warships, military recruiting centers, and military tatoos (ibid., 30 June, 4 and 5 July). CPC-ML militancy has frequently led to scuffles, arrests, and fines (ibid., 28 and 29 April, 25 May). Responding to the party's call on activists "to step up the mass struggle" (ibid., 25 May, 30 June), a growing number of members have been arrested. While several incidents of property damage occurred, the arson attack on the party's headquarters and bookstore in British Columbia caused the most serious damage (ibid., 15, 22, and 29 August). The party nevertheless remains resolute in its call for "revolutionary violence" as the means for establishing a communist regime (ibid., 31 January).

On the international scene, the CPC-ML sees inter-imperialist contradictions as sharpening and says the "imperialist" United States and the "social-imperialist" USSR are "preparing for war to redivide the world" (ibid., 11 February, 11 July). The CPC-ML dismisses disarmament talks as "fraudulent" and maintains they will not lessen the arms race. Both superpowers are seen as endeavoring to intimidate smaller states into joining the "aggressive" military blocs (ibid., 19 February). The CPC-ML calls on Canada to regain its sovereignty (ibid., 30 June) by reducing the "U.S. imperialist domination of Canada," by withdrawing from NATO and NORAD, by refusing to test cruise missiles, and by declaring "neutrality" (ibid., 4 April, 23 July, 24 August). Canada should also desist from efforts to transform the Caribbean states into "neo-colonies of Canadian imperialism" (ibid., 23 February). Albania is held up as the only state pursuing a proper course of action.

Revolutionary Workers' League. The RWL belongs to the Trotskyist Fourth International. While on the whole supporting the union-based reformist NDP in English Canada, the RWL is nevertheless critical of the "pro-capitalist" NDP leadership (*Socialist Voice*, July) and calls for the NDP to take a more socialist and pro-Quebec position. Recently several RWL members were expelled from the NDP. The RWL sees Quebec as an oppressed nation and while conceding some positive role for the "bourgeois-nationalist" PQ, the RWL now calls for a new Quebec labor party (ibid., 7 February, 7 March). The RWL supported the general strikes in Quebec and British Columbia.

According to the RWL, the danger of war is caused, not by the USSR, but by U.S. imperialism (ibid., 30 May). The real danger to peace at the moment is from U.S. involvement in a regional war in Central America to thwart the revolutionary regimes of Cuba, Nicaragua, and Grenada (ibid., 21 February, 30 May).

Other Marxist Groups. The Groupe socialiste des travailleurs (GST), which is affiliated with the Fourth International (International Committee), is estimated to be the second largest Trotskyist organization. The GST favors Quebec independence and the creation of a workers' party in Quebec. It publishes *Tribune ouvrière*.

While critical of the Stalinist degeneration of the USSR caused by a parasitic leadership caste, the Trostkyist League (TL) claims that the USSR and Cuba, nevertheless, should be defended from attacks. It sees Central America as being "red hot" (*Sparticist Canada*, June). Believing in "permanent revolution," it calls for a military victory in El Salvador and an extension of the revolution in Nicaragua, and anticipates unrest in Mexico (ibid., March). While conceding Quebec's right to independence, it is critical of the alleged progressive character of Québecois nationalism and instead favors "bi-national class unity" within Canada and joint "U.S./Canadian working class unity" towards a "continental socialist revolution" (ibid., March, Fall). The TL denies that the RWL is revolutionary, noting that the RWL is unwilling to use violence and supports the "ultra-reformist" NDP. In recent months, several TL members have been charged with assault (ibid., Fall). The TL supported the general strike in British Columbia but chastised the "pro-capitalist" labor leadership (ibid., June, Fall). The TL publishes *Sparticist Canada*.

The Forward Readers Group (FRG) chooses to operate within the NDP. Despite the deficiencies of the NDP, the FRG sees the NDP as the only mass labor vehicle capable of coming to power (*Forward*, June/July). The FRG suggests that the growing malaise in the NDP is an indication of rank-and-file discontent with NDP leaders' attempts to push the party into a rightist electoral stance. The FRG calls on the NDP to become bolder in its commitment to socialism, to a program of class struggle, and demands for Canada's withdrawal from NATO and NORAD. It sees opposition to cruise missile testing as a rallying point for the mounting antiwar movement (ibid.). It notes the "collapse of Maoism" in Canada and is critical of expulsions of RWL members from the NDP (ibid.).

The Socialist Challenge Organization, a pro-Fourth International group, publishes *Socialist Challenge*. Despite the demise of two Marxist-Leninist parties within two years, there have been calls for a new party. The Ottawa Committee for Labour Action, which publishes the journal *Labour Focus*, organized a May conference in Ottawa to determine the level of support for a new organization. Among those attending were ex-members of In Struggle and the WCP. Most delegates, however, expressed opposition at this time to building a new party.

Alan Whitehorn
Royal Military College of Canada

Chile

Population. 11.5 million
Party. Communist Party of Chile (Partido Comunista de Chile; CPC)
Founded. 1922
Membership. 20,000 (estimate)
Secretary General. Luís Corvalán
Politburo. 20 members (clandestine and in exile)
Secretariat. 5 members (clandestine)
Central Committee. 100 plus members (clandestine and in exile)
Status. Illegal, but operates through Popular Democratic Movement

Last Congress. Fifteenth, January 1971; clandestine Central Committee plenums held subsequently
Last Election. 1973, 16 percent, 23 of 150 seats
Auxiliary Organizations. Communist Youth (illegal); National Trade Union Coordinating Committee (CNS; headed by a Christian Democrat); Popular Democratic Movement (MDP; organized in September 1983)
Publications. *El Siglo* (clandestine), appears sporadically

During 1983, the Communist Party of Chile, still officially outlawed, emerged from clandestinity to take an active public role in the process of repoliticizing the country. It formed its own front group, the Popular Democratic Movement (MDP), but was excluded from the broad-based Democratic Alliance that coordinated the opposition to the Augusto Pinochet dictatorship.

This is the third time that the party has emerged from clandestinity (it was outlawed between 1927 and 1931 and again from 1948 to 1956). The government claims that there are 50,000 communists, organized into five-person cells in a hierarchical structure through Chile's communes, provinces, and regions up to the Central Committee and secretary general (*Que Pasa*, 28 August–3 September), but most estimates of current party strength are much lower. Its top leadership from the pre-1973 period is in exile in Moscow or Eastern Europe, but it has maintained an internal organization and has even held national meetings within Chile.

Since September 1980, when Luís Corvalán, party secretary general, endorsed an anti-Pinochet strategy employing "all forms of combat, including acute violence," the party has been committed to popular rebellion as the way to remove Pinochet. However, it has also called for collaboration with centrist groups, especially the Christian Democrats, in a common opposition program against the dictatorship. Exile leaders of the extreme leftist Movement of the Revolutionary Left (MIR), the Almeyda faction of the Socialist Party, and the former secretary general of the Radical Party have issued joint declarations with the communists endorsing the *violentista* position, but the *via armada* has been opposed within Chile, publicly by the Radicals and the other Socialist Party factions, and more discreetly by a number of communists. In March 1983, Corvalán, Clodomiro Almeyda, leader of the left wing of the Socialist Party, and Andres Pascal Allende of the MIR once again joined to issue a statement in Mexico City favoring strikes and worker action against the Pinochet regime. Within Chile, the MIR carried out bombings of

power pylons and rail lines in June, July, and December, and it took public responsibility for the assassination of Carlos Urzua, a retired general and the governor of Santiago, at the end of August. Because of the alliance of the MIR and the communists, the Pinochet government was able to exploit the actions of the *violentistas* as evidence of a continuing threat from communist extremism.

The violence issue had an effect on the realignment of parties in Chile that took place during 1983. It provided the principal justification for the exclusion of the communists from the opposition coalition that emerged. The first effort at coordination of the opposition had taken place in December 1982 when several centrist politicians announced the formation of the Project for National Development (PRODEN), a private group dedicated to promoting the return of democracy and civilian rule. Then in March, a broad spectrum of political leaders ranging from the Socialist Party on the Left to several former representatives of the old Liberal and Conservative parties on the Right, and including the leaders of the Christian Democratic, Radical, and Social Democratic parties, published a Democratic Manifesto calling for the election of a constituent assembly to write a new constitution to replace the constitution that went into effect in March 1981. That document, approved by a two-thirds vote in a manipulated plebiscite in September 1980, had given Pinochet the presidency until 1989 with the possibility of re-election to a second term until 1997. It also postponed congressional elections until 1990 and, under its transitional powers, gave the government power to exile and expel political leaders, impose states of emergency, prohibit political activity, and impose censorship on publications and the media.

The communists were not involved in the preparation or signing of the manifesto, and when the signatories later created the Democratic Alliance to coordinate their efforts, they were again excluded. The Socialists were represented by three former party leaders, but the party itself was so split into rival factions that it was difficult to say who spoke for the party. By September, however, most of the factions of the Socialist Party had reunited in the Socialist Bloc, which also included the former leaders of several Catholic leftist groups that had split from the Christian Democrats in 1969 and 1971. The Bloc was committed to democratic socialism and supported the Democratic Alliance in its efforts to promote a nonviolent transition to democracy, although the Socialists stated that they would favor the admission of the communists to the Alliance if they indicated a desire to join. The differing policies of the two groups, however, was a further indication of the growing rift between the Socialist and the communist parties, who had been electoral allies before the 1973 coup, when the communists favored the *via pacifica* and the Socialists were critical of the institutions of "bourgeois democracy."

Since May, Chile has been rocked by monthly antigovernment protests, first called by the copper workers' union under Rodolfo Seguel, then by the National Workers' Command, a new coordinating body of Chile's trade unions, and subsequently sponsored by the political leaders of the Democratic Alliance. Each month the protests grew larger, until August, when Pinochet called out 18,000 troops to keep order, and 30 people were killed. During the August protest, Pinochet appointed as minister of interior an old-time right-wing professional politician, Sergio Onofre Jarpa, who announced the adoption of several liberalization moves, including the ending of censorship, the return of a number of prominent exiles who had been expelled from the country, and the initiation of a dialogue with the opposition concerning the possibility of holding congressional elections before the constitutionally fixed 1990 date. Three dialogues were held in August and September, but they were undercut by Pinochet's insistence that his own continuation in office until 1989 was not negotiable and by his ambiguity about the proposed congressional elections. In addition, the Socialists were dubious about the wisdom of discussions with what they saw as an illegitimate government, and their representatives participated only in a personal capacity.

Jarpa exploited the communist issue in two ways. Knowing that the Socialist Party differed from the other parties on the question of communist participation, he kept pressing the Alliance for a public declaration on the issue. In addition,

the government publicized incidents of violence and vandalism in the shantytowns as preludes to communist-led uprisings of the type endorsed earlier by the party. The government tactic had some results both in winning back a part of Pinochet's right-wing support and in promoting disunity among the opposition. The non-Socialist members of the Alliance, however, continued to oppose communist participation on the ground that their commitment to violence was antithetical to the democratic and peaceful methods of the Alliance.

The communists themselves took advantage of the political opening to come out of clandestinity and enter the political fray. In early September, they held a public press conference for the first time since the 1973 coup, calling for the establishment of a civilian provisional government and a national agreement of all democratic parties on the principles of a new constitution (*Chile-America*, Rome, no. 88–89). Later in the month they formed a front group, the Popular Democratic Movement (MDP), that also included members of the Almeyda faction of the Socialists. In October when the Alliance decided to call off the monthly demonstration, the MDP and PRODEN ran their own protests, and the unions also called a strike for the end of the month. In November, however, all the opposition groups were able to support a massive anti-Pinochet rally in a public park, called by the Alliance, which turned out an estimated 200,000 people.

The issue of communist participation was bypassed in December when the Alliance called for a series of local town-meeting (*cabildo abierto*) discussions in which anyone could participate— and hinted at new tactics, perhaps involving a general strike, at the end of the summer vacation period in March 1984. Reviewing the year's developments, political observers called the contest between the Pinochet government and the opposition a "political draw" (*un empate politico*) since the opposition had demonstrated a broad mass following and the possibility of a viable alternative to the military junta, but Pinochet still had the support of the armed forces, especially the army—the leadership of which he continued to manipulate with great skill. Of special importance in maintaining military support was the communist issue, since Pinochet and his supporters argued that a too rapid transition to democracy would result in communist domination of

Chile and swift reprisals against the military for past repression. In turn, the members of the Democratic Alliance led by the Christian Democrats, called for an immediate return to democracy in order to avoid Nicaragua-style polarization and violence that could only benefit the extreme left.

The future role of the communist party remains a problem for any peaceful transition to democracy, since the 1980 constitution permits the Constitutional Tribunal to outlaw persons or groups who propagate "totalitarian doctrines" or those "based on the class struggle." In addition, the constitution establishes a National Security Council that is dominated by the military commanders and can make public declarations addressed to any organ of the government concerning possible threats to national security—which might well include the activities of the commu-

nists and the MIR. The MIR represents a minuscule number of Chileans, and its leadership has been decimated by government persecution, but the communist party has in the past received 10 to 15 percent of the vote, and it retains considerable influence among organized workers, especially through the (illegal) National Trade Union Coordinating Committee (Coordinadora Nacional Sindical). The question of the relation of the military to the communist party thus complicates any scenario for a possible return to democracy, but the year's developments—especially the protests, the creation of the Democratic Alliance, and the formation and democratic orientation of the Socialist Bloc—make the future prospects for democracy in Chile considerably brighter.

Paul E. Sigmund
Princeton University

Colombia

Population. 27.7 million
Party. Communist Party of Colombia (Partido Comunista de Colombia; PCC)
Founded. 1930
Membership. 12,000 (estimate)
General Secretary. Gilberto Vieira
Executive Committee. 14 members
Central Committee. 54 members
Status. Legal
Last Congress. Thirteenth, 7–11 November 1980
Last Elections. 1982; presidential, 1.2 percent; congressional, 1.2 percent, 1 of 114 senators, 3 of 199 representatives
Auxiliary Organizations. Trade Union Confederation of Workers of Colombia (CSTC), claims 300,000 members; Federation of Agrarian Syndicates; Communist Youth of Colombia (JUCO), claims 2,000 members
Publications. *Voz Proletaria* (weekly), 45,000 circulation; *Documentos Políticos*, theoretical journal, 5,000 circulation; Colombian edition of *World Marxist Review*, 7,500 circulation; JUCO publishes a monthly supplement to *Voz Proletaria*.

The communist movement in Colombia has undergone various transformations in both name and organization since the party's initial formation in December 1926. The PCC was publicly proclaimed on 17 July 1930. In July 1965, a schism within the PCC between pro-Soviet and pro-Chinese factions resulted in the latter's becoming the Communist Party of Colombia, Marxist-Leninist (PCC-ML). Only the PCC has legal status. It has been allowed to participate in elections under its own banner since 1972. In 1982, the PCC participated in congressional elections as the leading member of a leftist coalition.

According to U.S. intelligence sources, the PCC has 12,000 members. Although the party contends that its ranks have increased in recent years, the 1982 elections suggest that the party's growth has been less rapid than its leaders had hoped, especially in the larger cities. The PCC exercises only marginal influence in national affairs.

The highest party authority is the Congress, convened at four-year intervals. Gilberto Vieira, the general secretary of the PCC, is 74. Other important members of the Central Committee are Jesús Villegas, Alvaro Vásquez, Manuel Cepeda, Teofilo Forero, Roso Osorio, Pástor Pérez, Carlos Romero, Jaime Caycedo, Hernando Hurtado, Mario Upegui, and Alvaro Mosquera. A major source of the party's influence is its control of the CSTC, which is a member of the Soviet-front World Federation of Trade Unions. The PCC attempts to influence the CSTC through the Federation of Agrarian Syndicates, which functions as a part of the CSTC.

The PCC's youth organization, the JUCO, operates through the National Youth Coordinating Committee, where it plays an active role in promoting party policy among university and secondary school students.

Guerrilla Warfare. Although not a serious threat to the government, guerrilla warfare has been a feature of Colombian life since the late 1940s; the current wave began in 1964. The four main guerrilla organizations are the Revolutionary Armed Forces of Colombia (FARC), long controlled by the PCC; the M-19, a guerrilla organization that began as the armed hand of the National Popular Alliance (ANAPO); the pro-Chinese People's Liberation Army (EPL), which is the guerrilla arm of the PCC-ML; and the Castroite National Liberation Army (ELN). The small, urban Trotskyist-oriented Workers' Self-Defense Movement (ADO) was dismantled in June 1982 with the capture of its principal leaders in Bogotá. A sixth group, the Revolutionary Organization of the People (ORP), emerged in 1982 as the armed branch of the National Association of Land Users (ANUC), Sincelejo line. It revealed itself with the kidnapping and subsequent murder of the director of Colombia's Community Action program. In its only major operation in 1983, the ORP kidnapped and ransomed the American explorations manager for the Texas Petroleum Company (*El Espectador*, 15 April).

According to intelligence estimates, the FARC has expanded its areas of influence in recent years to include portions of the departments of Huila, Caquetá, Tolima, Cauca, Boyacá, Santander, Antioquia, Valle, Meta, and Cundinamarca and the intendancy of Arauca. According to the FARC's principal leader, Manuel Marulanda Vélez, the movement has 5,000 combatants operating on 25 fronts. In addition to Marulanda, other members of FARC's central staff are Jacobo Arenas, Jaime Guaraca, Alfonso Plana, and Román Reyes. The central staff oversees the operations of a 22-member high command. The FARC's general headquarters is located somewhere in the border zone between Caquetá and Huila. Each FARC unit (or squad) consists of a minimum of twelve members. Two units constitute a guerrilla cell. Four units, with an equal number of replacements, make up a column. Each of the FARC's rural fronts is composed of two columns, numbering about 200 men. The leadership mechanisms and general policy of the FARC are determined by the PCC's bylaws and political resolutions emitted at various party congresses and plenums and presumably transmitted to the fronts through Marulanda's directives.

In its first operation in 1983, a 120-man column from the FARC's 8th front attacked the town of Toribio in the Cauca valley, killing a local government official and police chief (*El Tiempo*, 14 January). FARC units were also active in Caquetá, Meta, and Santander, prompting the military high command to commit additional helicopters and special counterinsurgency forces to combat the unexpected outbreak of violence (*El Siglo*, 19 February). While troops succeeded in preventing FARC's effort to create a new front on the eastern plains, at least ten soldiers were killed in February during armed clashes with FARC units in Caquetá and Arauca intendancy (*El Espectador*, 27 February).

Members of FARC's high command met with leaders of Colombia's Peace Commission in early February somewhere in Huila. Marulanda praised President Belisario Betancur's effort to establish the conditions for an amnesty and agreed to hold future meetings to "help consolidate the peace programs and encourage proposals for social and economic change" (*El Tiempo*, 6 February).

During counterinsurgency operations in March and April, troops discovered several FARC training camps in Huila and dismantled an urban network that had been operating in various parts of Santander (ibid., 31 March, 1 May). FARC guerrillas were also active in the middle Magdalena region, ambushing military patrols, attacking police outposts, and temporarily occupying villages. In a letter addressed to the president of Colombia's Peace Commission, FARC's high command instructed its followers and asked other guerrilla groups to release all kidnapped persons under their control. A high-ranking government official accused the FARC of widespread kidnapping and extortion of wealthy landowners and cattlemen, especially in the Magdalena region (*El Espectador*, 25 March; *El Tiempo*, 6 April). In June, the commander of FARC's 4th front met with the governor of Santander to discuss ways to end the armed struggle in the middle Magdalena region (EFE, 19 June).

In July, FARC leaders operating in the western and southern sectors of the country met with the bishop of Caquetá, who conveyed their satisfaction with the government's announcement of a development plan for areas affected by guerrilla violence. According to the bishop, the guerrillas emphatically condemned kidnappings as a means of financing their movement and voiced their willingness to hold another conference with the Peace Commission and other guerrilla leaders in efforts to advance toward peace (*El Siglo*, 22 July). In an interview in September, Marulanda raised the need for a high-level dialogue to secure a cease-fire between the military and the FARC. In a message to the Chamber of Representatives, he blamed the army "for abetting the private bands of killers financed by cattlemen who are sowing terror among the peasants" (ibid., 7 September). In testimony before the Chamber, Defense Minister Gen. Fernando Landazábal Reyes said that the military would not withdraw from the rural areas "because we are not going to hand power over our territory to the subversives; and we are not going to hold a dialogue with the guerrillas because that is the reason for the amnesty." Landazábal directly accused the PCC and "its armed wing," the FARC, of being responsible for the violence in the middle Magdalena region. He charged that part of the money obtained from the kidnappings carried out by the FARC "goes to the coffers of the PCC's Central Committee." (*El Espectador*, 9 September.) For his part, Gilberto Vieira accused General Landazábal of "rejecting the dialogue between the Peace Commission and the guerrilla groups" and of "vetoing a cease-fire proposed by the FARC." He added that the PCC is not in a position to heed the defense minister's "ill-intentioned" call to demobilize guerrilla groups since the guerrilla movement "is not an instrument subordinate to any political party." (*Voz Proletaria*, 15 September; *El Tiempo*, 19 September.)

In October, the PCC asked the government for a truce in the armed forces' military operations against the FARC in various parts of the country. The party urged the government to initiate a dialogue with the FARC, within the framework of the peace talks it had reportedly begun with other guerrilla organizations (*Voz Proletaria*, 13 October). In late October, the FARC sent a peace plan to President Betancur proposing a cease-fire and a truce until 20 January 1985 to permit the guerrillas' integration as a political group and to allow for the withdrawal of army troops from areas considered combat zones. The document, signed by Marulanda, called for political reform and major changes in the country's socio-economic structure. (EFE, 30 October.) FARC commanders in Caquetá submitted a new proposal in November calling for a broad amnesty law, a democratic opening, and an effective cease-fire through direct dialogue with the government (*El Espectador*, 14 November).

Members of the FARC's 4th front and peasants of the middle Magdalena region's self-defense groups met on 19 November for the first time with the Peace Commission. The guerrillas asked the government for the demilitarization of the peasant areas and the lifting of the military siege against guerrilla groups. They also insisted on the dismantling of the armed bands, such as the Death to Kidnappers squad (MAS), "the Crickets," and "the Smudged Ones," which are accused of murdering scores of persons suspected of helping the guerrilla groups. (*El Tiempo*, 21 November.) In a surprise attack employing helicopters, the army subsequently occupied the FARC camp visited by the Peace Commission, killing one guerrilla and capturing five. According to a communiqué issued by the Defense Ministry, captured documents disclosed plans for terrorist actions, lists noting contributions to the guerrillas from farmowners in the region, and instructions on the assistance that the FARC is giving the PCC in its recruitment activities (AFP, 26 November). Members of the Peace Commission reportedly met with Marulanda at an undisclosed location in November.

In December, military sources reported various successful operations against FARC guerrillas in Cauca, Santander, and Arauca intendancy (*El Tiempo*, 16 December). On 21 December, the FARC and the M-19 announced that they had reached "a complete political and military agreement" at a recent guerrilla "summit." In a joint communiqué, the principal leaders for the two movements claimed to have unified their views on peace. They insisted that a cease-fire is "a necessary step for developing a dialogue for peace" and announced plans to coordinate their efforts to conclude a negotiated truce with the government. (EFE, 21 December.)

The president of the Peace Commission affirmed that a peace agreement between the government and leading guerrilla groups is "imminent." In its early stages, the agreement would be signed with the FARC because of its conduct in condemning the kidnapping of President Betancur's brother and because of its "call to other groups to release kidnapped persons." (DPA, 13 December; *FBIS*, 15 December.)

Domestic Attitudes and Activities. The PCC recognizes the experience of the Communist Party of the Soviet Union as an ideological source, but it also takes "maximum account of the national characteristics and revolutionary and democratic traditions of the Colombian people." This has enabled the party to devise its own tactics, which combine diverse forms of struggle ranging from electoral campaigns to guerrilla warfare. According to Gilberto Vieira, "We communists want to advance by democratic means, by what we call action and the mass

struggle, and not only by means of elections, which are only one part of the process." Vieira claims that the PCC has failed to become an important factor in the electoral process because of Colombia's deeply rooted bipartisan tradition. He admits that in the past, specifically since 1948, the party has found itself obliged to "take part in the armed resistance against institutionalized violence." The FARC was formed in 1964 as an answer to the military offensive against regions colonized by former guerrilla fighters. Vieira contends, however, that the PCC "has never regarded the FARC as its armed branch." The party does not take responsibility for the FARC's actions, although it vigorously defends the justice of the movement's cause. (*Cromos*, 23 November 1982.)

Various PCC leaders from the Valle region, including former Central Committee member José Cardona Hoyos, were expelled in 1983 after open disagreement over the party's "permanent support" for the FARC. Cardona, who joined the PCC in 1946, charged that the Central Committee is the "main promoter of guerrilla warfare in the country." Referring to the proposals of the Thirteenth Congress (1980), he urged the Central Committee to concentrate on the work of mass action and organization as the "main form of struggle" and to abandon the belief that "there are conditions for extending the guerrilla movement until it becomes a power alternative." (*El Tiempo*, 7 June; *Cromos*, 14 June; *El Siglo*, 21 December.)

The Thirteenth Congress reaffirmed the party's commitment to the creation of a broad antimonopoly and anti-imperialist front. As a basis for forming this front, the party approved a program aimed at combating inflation, increasing wages, nationalizing oil and coal resources, and providing free health, education, and social assistance programs. In recent years, the PCC has pursued a policy of fostering unity between urban workers and the peasantry. The party is actively engaged in efforts to organize peasant unions, including the organization of the Indian population in Cauca, where the PCC supports the Regional Indian Council. The party considers itself the vanguard in pursuing "democratic agrarian reform" and a fundamental change in the system of land tenure.

According to the Executive Committee, the forms of struggle in Colombia cannot be changed without modifying the "antidemocratic structure" of the political system. PCC statements criticize "adventurist and terrorist practices" that militate against the unity of the masses and weaken the prospects of the popular movement. Early in 1983, the party called on "all democratic and popular currents" to work in common for (1) an end to military operations and the withdrawal of all troops from combat zones; (2) a dialogue between the government and the guerrilla movement; (3) the liquidation of MAS and the adoption of legal sanctions against the assassins of popular leaders; and (4) a radical reform of the political system, particularly the abolition of the bipartisan system and full guarantee of political and trade union rights (*IB*, February).

The PCC joined other leftist groups in a joint communiqué in November rejecting the government's statute on parties on the grounds that it "perpetuates the monopoly held by liberals and conservatives" and is, therefore, "antidemocratic" (*El Tiempo*, 11 November). In December, the Central Committee renewed its rejection of anarchy, supported actions that lead to democratic political reforms, stressed that kidnappings are "an abominable disgrace," and maintained that terrorism "has no bearing on the proletarian idea of struggle for change in society" (ibid., 22 December). In reviewing the prospects for an end to guerrilla strife in 1984, Vieira stated that the military hierarchy's "excessive influence" on the government is "hindering the dialogue for civil peace" (*FBIS*, 3 January 1984).

International Views and Positions. The PCC faithfully follows the Soviet line in its international positions. According to Vieira, the party is engaged primarily in the struggle to emancipate the Colombian people. However, the PCC insists that it is impossible to remain neutral in the "great international struggle" between socialism and capitalism. The party therefore "enthusiastically" supports the socialist countries and particularly the Soviet Union "because it defends genuine socialism, despite its imperfections" (*Cromos*, 23 November 1982). At the same time, the party claims that it is not dependent on Moscow, Havana, or "any foreign place," nor does it serve as the agent for the international policy of any foreign country. The PCC wants a Colombian international policy that is "independent and autonomous." Party statements in 1983 were highly supportive of Colombia's entrance into the Nonaligned Movement, its active participation in the Contadora group, and President Betancur's position on the problems of peace and disarmament (*El Tiempo*, 7 August). The PCC vigorously condemned the "interventionist policy" of the United States in Grenada and organized a series of street protests in solidarity with the people of Grenada.

A delegation of the PCC headed by Gilberto Vieira attended a meeting in Costa Rica in June for the purpose of exchanging views on the political situation in Central America and the Caribbean with representatives of the communist parties of Mexico, Venezuela, Panama, and Costa Rica (*IB*, August). Party members also visited Cuba, various European countries, and the Soviet Union during the year. While in Cuba, Manuel Cepeda reaffirmed the party's support for the Cuban revolution as an example of "dignity, patriotism and sovereignty" (Havana international service, 25 October).

The Maoists. The PCC-ML is firmly pro-Chinese. Its present leadership hierarchy is not clearly known. The PCC-ML has an estimated membership of one thousand. Unlike the PCC, it has not attempted to obtain legal status, and its impact in terms of national life is insignificant. Its official news organ is *Revolución*. The Marxist-Leninist League of Colombia publishes the monthly *Nueva Democracia*. PCC-ML statements are sometimes found in Chinese publications and those of pro-Chinese parties in Europe and Latin America.

The PCC-ML's guerrilla arm, the EPL, was the first to attempt a revolutionary "people's war" in Latin America. The EPL has conducted only limited operations since 1975, although according to Colombian intelligence it still has an estimated 250 guerrillas organized into four fronts. The EPL operates primarily in the departments of Antioquia and Córdoba, with urban support networks in Bogotá, Medellín, Montería, Bucaramanga, Barrancabermeja, Cali, and Florencia (*El Tiempo*, 27 June). The EPL is headed by Francisco Caraballo. In June, the EPL denounced the government's amnesty law and censured those FARC and M-19 members who accepted it, "despite orders from Moscow to seek the unification of all guerrilla groups in the country" (*FBIS*, 15 June). The Defense Ministry reported in August that the army had captured the leader of an EPL front operating in Caquetá (EFE, 31 August). Authorities arrested five members of an EPL urban command involved in a payroll robbery in Medellín (AFP, 6 September). The EPL took part in an outbreak of kidnappings during September and October. According to a military spokesman, twelve people, primarily ranchers, were kidnapped by guerrillas operating in Antioquia (*El Siglo*, 1 November). Earlier, police reported having killed an EPL guerrilla and capturing another involved in the extortion of money from landowners (*El Espectador*, 15 October).

The Independent Revolutionary Workers' Movement (MOIR) has aspired since 1971 to become the first mass-based Maoist party in Latin America. Its leadership and organization are independent of those of the PCC-ML. The MOIR has no military branch and has been unable to strengthen its political position in recent elections. The MOIR's general secretary is Francisco Mosquera. Other prominent leaders are Marcelo Torres and Avelino Niño. In June, MOIR leaders complained about the government's "increasingly slanderous campaign intended to link the name of MOIR to various acts of violence and to certain armed groups with which we have never agreed either politically or ideologically" (*Excelsior*, Mexico City, 28 June). A delegation headed by Mosquera visited the People's Republic of China in May. The MOIR's official newspaper is *Tribuna Roja*.

The M-19. The M-19, which first appeared in January 1974 as the self-proclaimed armed branch of ANAPO, takes its name from the contested presidential election of 19 April 1970. Since 1976, the M-19 has been actively involved in Colombia's guerrilla movement, pursuing "a popular revolution of national liberation aimed toward socialism." Estimates on the movement's size range from 800 to 5,000. According to an alleged M-19 defector, the M-19 operates in columns of 70 men and has 22 combat fronts located in over a dozen departments. The largest concentration of M-19 guerrillas, an estimated 2,500, is found in Caquetá and in the Putumayo intendancy area in southern Colombia (*El Tiempo*, 9 September).

The M-19's national directorate confirmed in a communiqué dated 18 July that its principal leader, Jaime Bateman Cayón, died in an airplane crash on 28 April. Conrado Marín, former head of the M-19's southern front, also died in the accident. The communiqué, signed by eighteen

commanders of the "military force and regional command," stated that Bateman had been succeeded by his second in command, Iván Marino Ospina. Marino, 38, joined the M-19 in 1971 and was captured in the abortive "invasion" of Putumayo in March 1981. After two years in prison, he was amnestied in November 1982 and rejoined the M-19 as leader of the front operating in Caqueta. (*El Espectador*, 20 July; *El Siglo*, 22 July.) Other prominent leaders are Alvaro Fayad, Gustavo Arias Londoño, Rosemberg Pabón, Germán Rojas Niño, Marcos Chalista, Ramiro Lucio, Andrés Alvarales, and ex-ANAPO congressman Carlos Toledo Plata.

In September, a communiqué attributed to the M-19's high command denounced the government's "democratic opening" as a "sophism of deceit" and declared that the M-19 would increase its military actions and efforts to achieve an alliance with other guerrilla groups (AFP, 30 September). On 11 October, however, a presidential spokesman confirmed that President Betancur had met with Iván Marino and Alvaro Fayad in Madrid "to perfect political mechanisms that will facilitate a more effective reconciliation between the government and the guerrillas" (*El Espectador*, 12 October). According to the M-19, the conclusions reached in their "historic" meeting with the president included an agreement to hold further talks in early 1984 to negotiate a cease-fire. Ospina and Fayad praised President Betancur for understanding "with political realism" the essential factors that led to the revolutionary struggle. They reiterated the M-19's willingness to hold a dialogue "as long as there are minimum guarantees." (EFE, 15 December.)

The ELN. The ELN was formed in Santander in 1964 under the inspiration of the Cuban revolution. It undertook its first military action in January 1965. Once recognized as the largest and most militant of the guerrilla forces operating in Colombia, the ELN has never recovered from the toll exacted on its leadership and urban network in recent years by government forces, including the defection in 1976 of its principal founder and maximum leader, Fabio Vásquez Castaño. According to Colombian intelligence, the ELN has approximately 200 men organized into four fronts. It operates mainly in Arauca intendancy and the northeastern sector of Caquetá. The ELN intensified its urban operations in 1983, especially through holdups, dynamite attacks, and occasional kidnappings in the Medellín and Bucaramanga areas. The ELN's principal leader is Nicolás Rodríguez Bautista. It is one of the few subversive groups believed by some to have increased in strength (*El Siglo*, 11 November).

According to Colombian sources, the ELN appears to be working in concert with the Pedro León Arboleda (PLA) group in the Medellín area. In February, the PLA and the ELN took joint credit for the murder of a high-ranking police official. A PLA informer revealed that the PLA had begun a "harassment campaign" against the government, taking advantage of its recent "political unity" reached with the ELN (*El Tiempo*, 24 February). In May, police in Bucaramanga captured the leader of the ELN's urban network in Santander (ibid., 25 May).

In July, the ELN carried out a series of dynamite attacks against entities linked with the United States. It also occupied radio stations and wire service offices in several cities to protest "Yankee imperialism" in Central America and "administrative graft and drug trafficking" among the Colombian political class (*El Espectador*, 2 July; EFE, 8 July). Bogotá police reported that ELN activists were responsible for violent disturbances at the National University on 7 October in which eleven persons were injured (*El Siglo*, 9 October).

In its most spectacular operation of 1983, the ELN kidnapped President Betancur's brother on 22 November. Among the conditions listed for his release, the ELN demanded a general salary increase, the release of political prisoners, a freeze on the price of food staples, demilitarization of the peasant areas and allocation of funds for their rehabilitation, and the immediate arrest and prosecution of members of MAS (*El Espectador*, 26 November). Mr. Betancur was released unharmed on 7 December. According to the president, "there were no negotiations, either official or secret, with the kidnappers" (EFE, 7 December).

Guerrilla Prospects. By year's end, it was confirmed that the Peace Commission was holding talks with the M-19 and the FARC. The EPL, which had previously opposed the government's amnesty and pacification initiatives, officially announced its willingness to hold talks with government representatives in January. With the recent disclosure by the ELN that it, also, was willing to participate in talks, all of Colombia's major guerrilla groups appeared ready to discuss a possible cessation of their revolutionary activities. With talks between the Peace Commission and various guerrilla leaders well under way, there exists the basis for genuine optimism about the future pacification of the regions currently affected by armed insurrection. As Peace Commission president John Agudelo Ríos stated, "the country now has the right to believe not only that peace is possible, but also that it is not as far off as some tend to believe" (*El Espectador*, 22 November).

The ultimate solution and durability of any peace settlement depends on the cooperation of the Colombian military. Thus far, General Landazábal has given no indication that the armed forces are prepared to accept guerrilla demands for the demilitarization of the countryside, which would seriously impinge on the military's self-perceived role as a national institution. In a New Year's message to the Colombian people, General Landazábal stated that the military "respects" President Betancur's efforts to establish peace talks with the guerrillas, but it does not support a cease-fire. He warned that the "subversive movements" were preparing to launch new actions in 1984 and emphasized that the military would continue to use force in dealing with subversion. He affirmed that the armed forces "will never allow communism to take over through violence" (AFP, 26 December). In a document delivered to President Betancur in early January, the top commanders of the armed forces, including six generals, expressed support for General Landazábal's position on the need to take stronger action against the guerrilla threat (*FBIS*, 10 January 1984).

The friction that surfaced in early 1983 between military and civilian authorities over alleged links between MAS and senior army officers is likely to intensify in 1984 as the Peace Commission moves forward in its talks with guerrilla leaders. The military contends that its troops were ambushed 144 times by guerrilla forces in 1983. It is also aware that several score of the guerrillas amnestied since November 1982 have rejoined guerrilla ranks. Given the usual ups and downs of civil-military relations in Colombia, it will be difficult for President Betancur to persuade the military high command that it is in the military's interest to accept a cease-fire, much less to withdraw from combat zones as a precondition set by guerrillas for negotiations that might lead to a meaningful and lasting peace.

Daniel L. Premo
Washington College

Costa Rica

Population. 2.6 million
Party. Popular Vanguard Party (Partido Vanguardia Popular; PVP)
Founded. 1931
Membership. Variously estimated at 3,500 (*YICA*, 1983) or 5,000 "cells" with over 10,000 members (*La Nación*, San José, 27 December)
President. Manuel Mora Valverde (honorific post created for and later rejected by Mora, December 1983)
Secretary General. Humberto Vargas Carbonell
Under–secretary General. Eduardo Mora Valverde (resigned December 1983)
Central Committee. 35 members (*La Nación*, 6 December 1983)
Status. Legal
Last Congress. Third Extraordinary Congress, 12–13 November 1983; last ordinary congress; thirteenth in 1980; all congresses in San José
Last Election. 1982, United People's coalition, 3.2 percent of presidential vote, compared with 2.7 percent in 1978; elected 4 of 57 national deputies, up from 3 in 1978
Auxiliary Organizations. General Workers' Confederation (Confederación General de Trabajadores); National Peasant Federation (Federación Campesina Nacional); Costa Rican Peace and Solidarity Council (an umbrella group made up of some 50 union and solidarity committees)
Publications. *Libertad* (weekly); *Trabajo*

The PVP was founded in 1931 as a group of students, intellectuals, and workers by Manuel Mora Valverde. While originally a splinter group of Jorge Volio's Reformist Party of the 1920s, the PVP gained its limited prominence in national politics from the 1934 Atlantic banana workers' strike against United Fruit Company. Although an economic failure, the strike achieved political gains that led to organization of the banana workers' union, which the PVP still controls. During the administrations of Rafael Calderón (1940–1944) and Teodoro Picado (1944–1948) the PVP and Mora, in league with the then archbishop, claimed credit for those administrations' achievements in progressive labor legislation and social reform. Although defeated and subsequently outlawed by José Figueres in the 1948–49 Revolution, the PVP was able to wrap itself in the flag of the labor code and social security legislation and today still claims primary authorship.

Since its founding, the PVP has won a small number of deputyships in the national congress, often held by leading professionals and academics whose legislative concerns have anticipated major party initiatives in health, education, and housing. The party's public popularity and ideological influence is broadest on the general issues of social services, land reform, and anti-imperialism, as portrayed in the major national media and the party weekly *Libertad*. However, a rigid hierarchy within the party (a veritable gerontocracy until recently) and its boundless devotion to the Soviet line have fatally limited its political appeal. What organizational support the PVP enjoys comes overwhelmingly from the banana workers and various public employees' unions, as well as from students and intellectuals.

In the past two electoral campaigns (1978 and 1982), the PVP has fielded a People's Unit (Pueblo Unido; PU) candidate, Dr. Rodrigo Gutiérrez, in coalition with two smaller leftist parties, the Costa Rican Socialist Party (Partido

Socialista Costarricense; PSC) and the Revolutionary People's Movement (Movimiento Revolucionario del Pueblo; MRP). In the 1982 election, the PU won only 3.2 percent of the vote, but 4 of 57 national deputyships. Those originally elected were the PVP's Eduardo Mora Valverde (brother of the party leader), Arnoldo Ferreto, and Freddy Fernández, as well as the MRP's leader Sergio Erick Ardón, who gained international recognition by his interruption of President Ronald Reagan's address in San José in December 1982. Subsequently, Mora resigned his seat as part of a coalition trade-off, allowing the PSC's public employee union leader, Alvaro Montero Mejía, to hold office after November 1982.

The two junior members of the coalition are outgrowths of early 1970s university radical movements, with little if any mass base of support. The MRP and its leader, the architect Ardón, are most at odds with the PVP leadership and most eclectic in revolutionary doctrine, resisting any designation as Marxist-Leninist and criticizing the PVP's "permanent alliance with the Soviet Union" (*La Nación Internacional*, 24–30 November). The PSC is a small party of public employees and intellectuals, founded in 1972 in the aftermath of the university student movement against a proposed (1970) contract with the ALCOA aluminum company. The PSC considers itself more flexible in its Marxist-Leninist analysis and, in practice, has been much less critical of the PVP. Internally, however, the PSC has suffered the recent defection of ex-deputy and state electrical employee union leader Mario Devandas and nineteen of his followers, who claimed that the party had been reduced to "a circle of intimates which does not represent any popular sector" (ibid.).

The PU coalition has been plagued by internal divisions. In its very founding in January 1980, this was expressly recognized in the proviso that each of the three parties would "maintain its own identity, its own organic unity, and complete independence as a political force . . . and no organization is obliged to follow policies which it does not share" (ibid.). During 1982 and 1983, the PSC and MRP complained of the PVP's "dogmatism, sectarianism, and lack of comprehension and dialogue." The PVP and MRP publicly differed over whether the two major Costa Rican parties were "bourgeois parties" (the PVP view) or simply ones in which bourgeois interests were "prevalent" (the MRP position). Such hairsplitting reflected the PVP's disenchantment with Ardón's collaboration with major party deputies on specific legislation involving foreign loans. A further reflection of the PVP's frustration with its coalition partners could be seen in Ferreto's year-end and probably accurate claim that the PVP represented more than 90 percent of the PU's 1982 electoral strength and 99 percent of campaign financing, while the MRP and PSC received half of the legislative seats (ibid.).

Leadership and Organization. During the year, two issues dominated the party. Most important was a year-end shakeup of party officialdom in which the first and only party secretary general, Manuel Mora Valverde, was "elevated" to the newly created and honorific presidency after 53 consecutive years as head of the party. Mora was replaced by the leader of the younger generation, ex-deputy Humberto Vargas Carbonell. This passing of the mantle, described in greater detail below, came after a year of intense debate over the Left's alleged links to terrorism (increasingly frequent) and plans for internal armed conflict and the Left's own view of the issue as a pretext for U.S.-sponsored militarization of local politics.

The removal of Mora from the post of secretary general was initiated, paradoxically, with the drafting of new party statutes at the extraordinary congress (12–13 November) called by Mora himself. The creation of a new post of president, with which Mora concurred, set the stage for his removal. At its eighteenth plenary session, 3–4 December, the 35-member Central Committee "overwhelmingly" accepted these changes and proceeded to replace Mora with Vargas Carbonell and, ignoring the former's protests, appointed him party president. (*La Nación*, 2 and 6 December.) However, this overwhelming majority was later reported by Mora supporters to have been only a 20 to 15 vote (ibid., 24 December).

Mora, who at the time was in Nicaragua, left for Cuba shortly after the early December vote without making any official statement. He did send a letter to the Central Committee in which he denounced the move, resigned the presidency (his brother Eduardo, the party's under–secretary general, also resigned), and implied that hard-liners and hotheads were employing a bureaucratic ruse to deprive him of the leadership that his popularity with the party bases would reconfirm at the upcoming Fourteenth Congress 13–15 September 1984 (ibid., 27 and 30 December). Consultation with party militants by Ferreto and Vargas demonstrated a degree of hostility toward the move and support for Mora, which led Vargas to travel to Cuba to meet with the latter in an attempt to head off a public division of the party (ibid., 30 December). At this writing, both leaders remain in Cuba, with Mora supporters planning a public reception for their leader on his return, 9 January 1984, as a demonstration of his continuing popularity and power (ibid., 4 January 1984).

Within the party, the Ferreto-Vargas faction had taken control of the weekly *Libertad* in 1982 when Francisco Gamboa, a Vargas supporter, replaced Eduardo Mora as editor (ibid., 30 and 31 December). They forced the issue on the Central Committee after having gained control of its security (now called "military") and organizational commissions (under Ferreto's control as senior party deputy). Mora retained control over party finances and a minority of the Central Committee, and enjoyed vastly greater popularity within and outside the party (ibid., 1 January 1984).

The major national media, in particular the conservative and stridently anticommunist daily *La Nación*, repeatedly suggested, quoting various pro-Mora party members, that the change represented the triumph of younger hard-liners disenchanted with what they considered a "soft and complacent" leadership and exploiting both the creation of a party presidency and the secretary's advanced age to effect his removal (ibid., 2, 24, 27, and 30 December; 1 and 4 January 1984). An intriguing twist to this interpretation was added by *La Nación*, whose editorial analyst portrayed Mora's trip to Cuba, oddly enough, as an attempt to marshal the moderating influence of Fidel Castro in his favor, against what he considers Soviet-backed advocates of anti-U.S. armed adventurism throughout Central America (ibid., 1 January 1984). Although Mora has been a faithful Soviet supporter for half a century, unlike Vargas he had no firsthand formative experience in that country and was known to be working with both Castro and the Costa Rican government toward a peace plan for Central America acceptable to the United States (ibid.).

While Vargas may well represent somewhat more radical party elements, it is equally clear that generational conflict played an important part in the change as well. Moreover, the support of the Central Committee majority and legislative leader Ferreto for Vargas indicates something other than a simple "hard-line" takeover. Vargas took a leading role in party affairs as a deputy from 1978 to 1982. He and Ferreto were largely ineffective in organizing strike activities while deputies during this period, but Vargas was known as a serious and capable legislator who played a major role in resolving problems of university and public sector finance. In any event, the only official party statement on the affair was a repetition of Ferreto's claim that there had been no internal divisions, no change in policy, no reduction in Mora's powers, and that the party was the victim of a defamatory publicity campaign that painted it as advocating violence, thus justifying its repression (ibid., 7 December). Barring any early compromise, the September party congress promises to be contentious.

Domestic Affairs. Fear of being identified with terrorism and internal armed violence increased as the events of 1983 unfolded. In late March, the deputy government minister claimed to have seized an "arsenal of M-14 and M-1 rifles, 8,600 rounds of ammunition, and grenade launchers" from an unnamed brother of a "communist deputy" (ibid., 28 March; *FBIS*, 4 April). At the same time, the "infiltration" of the newly created 10,000-man paramilitary Organization for National Emergencies (OPEN) by the Left was being denounced by members of the government and a leading editorial commentator (*La Nación*, 30 March, 3 June; *JPRS*, 16 May, 12 July; *La Prensa Libre*, San José, 2 June; *FBIS*, 14 June); this in spite of the PVP's strident denunciations of OPEN as a rightist protomilitary establishment since its initial proposal in 1982. Leftist leadership of widespread community demonstrations and roadblocks to protest spiraling electrical rates was alleged by President Luís Alberto Monge in June (Radio Reloj, San José, 10 June; *FBIS*, 14 June), while similar unsubstantiated charges were made by lesser officials regarding the proposed "occupation" of the Atlantic province of Limón (*La República*, San José, 11 July; *FBIS*, 26 July) and the agitation for land invasions in several locations (Radio Reloj, 29 July; *FBIS*, 2 August).

Two serious incidents of terrorism further inflamed local public opinion and were widely perceived as linked to leftist extremism. The late June dynamiting in San José of a car in which two Nicaraguan citizens were killed and several onlookers injured was widely reported to have been a bungled attempt at assassinating anti-Sandinist leader Alfonso Robelo, in coordination with Basque separatists (*La Nación*, 30 June; Latin-Reuters, Buenos Aires, 14 September; *FBIS*, 15 September). Later, in October, the home of the British ambassador in Costa Rica was attacked, allegedly by Basque militants with the possible collaboration of local elements from the National Patriotic Committee, a leftist splinter group (Radio Reloj, 3 October; *FBIS*, 4 October). Also in September, the trials of fifteen terrorists involved in the 17 March 1981 attack on U.S. marines and the Honduran embassy were concluded; sentences ranged from three to fifteen years' imprisonment (*La Nación*, 3 September; *FBIS*, 14 September).

By year's end one local daily known for its sensationalism even claimed that a "communist training camp" for terrorists was being operated in northern Costa Rica by North Koreans and possibly Basque militants (*La Prensa Libre*, 21 November; *FBIS*, 30 November). Why such a shocking revelation should be relegated to a minor notice near the sports pages was not explained, but may well have been an indication that the story was based on something less than unimpeachable sources. Given this state of affairs, it should come as no surprise that as early as 1982, in a poll commissioned by *La Nación*, some 54.2 percent of respondents felt there was a link between "terrorists and domestic communist groups" (*La Nación*, 19 December 1982).

The only instance of armed conflict directly linked to PVP sympathizers, victims in this case, was the midyear fighting and deaths between pro- and anti-Sandinista Costa Ricans along the border in the Upala region. As the Nicaraguan rebels led by Edén Pastora increased their operations in the area, Costa Rican supporters and opponents began to choose sides. This led to the death-squad style murder of at least six, and possibly twenty, local peasants (four claimed to have been PVP members) who were thought to have passed information on Pastora's forces to the Sandinista army. In retaliation, leftist members of the local branch of the PVP-affiliated National Peasant Federation attacked and burned a row of shops and a light plane owned by wealthy residents supportive of Pastora. (*El Nuevo Diario*, Managua, 23 July; *La Nación*, 26 and 27 July; *JPRS*, 29 August; *NYT*, 31 October.) The government's reaction was one of genuine concern and led initially to reinforcement of the Civil Guard contingent in Upala (AFP, Paris, 4 August; *FBIS*, 5 August). Fear of a Central Americanization of Costa Rica's border region and its internal politics no doubt contributed to the increased emphasis on neutrality and the interdiction of rebel operations since September.

During 1983, the Left consistently maintained its opposition to armed action within local politics, but Deputy Ferreto insisted that he could not "rule out the possibility that this course might change" owing to "North American imperialist" pressures (*La Nación Internacional*, 24–30 November). Expanding on this somber assessment, Ferreto revealed that the PVP had some one hundred fighters in Nicaragua and would send a thousand or more if need be. Deputy Ardón added that while he did not advocate violent change, this was "not a question of wills but of situations." (Ibid.)

Foreign Affairs. The overwhelming party concern internationally was the Central American crisis and the Nicaraguan border clashes. Moreover, the Left actively opposed and denounced both U.S. actions throughout the area and alleged Costa Rican governmental cooperation with the United States during the first half of the year. Complicating these issues even further were the multifaceted relations of the party and the Costa Rican government with Cuba, as well as the latter's often distorted international reporting of local events.

Border clashes, arms trafficking, and alleged Costa Rican governmental complicity, or at least insouciance, were denounced by PVP and PU leaders throughout 1983. Loud protests were repeatedly made over border clashes during the first half of 1983. With the August bombing of the airport in Managua by a light plane thought to have taken off from San José, and the *contra* attack on the Peñas Blancas border post in September, a high point of official recriminations was reached (Radio Reloj, 8, 16, and 18 September; Radio Impacto, San José, 28 and 30 September; *FBIS*, 9, 19, 29, and 30 September, 3 October).

Fernando Volio, the Costa Rican foreign minister at the time, missed no opportunity to denounce the Sandinista regime as totalitarian and expansionist, while criticizing the local Left's support of it. President Monge also referred to the Left as a potential "fifth column" in the event of war with Nicaragua (*La Nación Internacional*, 24–30 November) and disparagingly went to the source when he addressed his pleas for restraint to the Soviet Union and Cuba rather than to the Sandinistas or the PVP (*La Nación*, 24 December 1982; ACAN-EFE, Panama City, 12 January; *FBIS*, 5 and 14 January).

During the second half of the year, the Monge government shifted away from this overtly conflictive rhetoric and policy, first with its declaration of "active and permanent neutrality" in September (Radio Reloj, 15 September; *NYT*, 20 September; *La Nación*, 22 September; *FBIS*, 16 and 30 September) and then with the replacement of Volio as foreign minister (Radio Reloj, 15 November; Havana international service, 14 November; *FBIS*, 16 November) and the reaffirmation of neutrality in November (*FBIS*, 18 November). The ostensible reason for Volio's resignation was the U.N. vote cast against the U.S. invasion of Grenada by Costa Rica's delegate, contrary to Volio's instructions to him to abstain. Needless to say, this realignment met with PVP approval. At the same time, a march was organized on the U.S. Embassy in downtown San José to protest the invasion of Grenada, while the National Assembly was debating and subsequently condemning U.S. actions there (Radio Reloj, 26 October; *FBIS*, 27 October).

Further fuel was added to the fire of anti-U.S. feeling when some seventeen Cuban-American mercenaries were deported in September (*NYT*, 20 September); another report mentioned some one hundred armed U.S. citizens "invited to leave the country" (AFP, Paris, 7 September; *FBIS*, 9 September). Moreover, at year's end a much publicized U.S. offer of several hundred combat engineers to build roads and bridges along the northern border was ultimately rejected by the Monge administration, which then was forced to ask that Ambassador Curtin Winsor clarify the issue publicly (ACAN-EFE, Panama City, 15 November; Radio Reloj, 16 November; *FBIS*, 16 and 17 November). The ambassador further infuriated the Left when he stated that the United States did not rule out an invasion of Nicaragua, as it could not live with an active, subversive, Marxist-Leninist regime in the region (Havana international service, 21 November; *FBIS*, 22 November, quoting *La Nación*). Earlier, the

PVP had criticized Winsor's "interventionism" in a lengthy and combative statement from Eduardo Mora, then traveling in Cuba (Havana international service, 26 October; *FBIS*, 2 November).

Other international gatherings and issues of relevance to the Costa Rican Left included the Fourth Congress of the Costa Rican Peace and Solidarity Council, 18–20 March in San José (*Libertad*, San José, 25–31 March; *FBIS*, 4 April) and a meeting in San José in early June of the PVP and the communist parties of the four Contadora group nations.

A final topic of continuous controversy was the status of Costa Rican–Cuban relations and Cuban reporting of local political events. In March, rightist groups in Costa Rica denounced alleged governmental and private contacts designed to establish full diplomatic relations (*La Nación*, 22 March; *FBIS*, 30 March). This came in the wake of the January visit to Cuba of a large delegation of national deputies. Some favorable comments on the experience had led to renewed speculation regarding a thaw in bilateral relations (Havana international service, 21 January; *FBIS*, 25 January; *Central American Report*, 28 January). Costa Rica continued to receive a substantial number of Cuban émigrés and political prisoners throughout the year, and relations remained generally cool.

Cuba's international news service reported extensively on Costa Rica and its Central American affairs. This reporting was challenged several times by governmental officials, and on one occasion by the PVP itself. When Havana alleged the existence of political prisoners and a 30,000-man army in Costa Rica, PVP Deputy Ferreto issued a public disclaimer (*La Nación*, 29 December 1982). Additional reports focused upon the alleged arrival in Costa Rica of U.S. military personnel for road building in the north, and still later interpreted the brief suspension of the flow of U.S. AID funds as punishment for the government's reversal of course, declaration of neutrality, and rejection of U.S. troops (Havana domestic service, 17 November; Havana international service, and 18 November; *FBIS*, 18 and 21 November). Such reports, and Costa Rican denials, in themselves suggest a much higher profile for future Costa Rican–Cuban relations, albeit without necessarily increased cordiality.

Lowell Gudmundson
Florida International University

Cuba

Population. 9.8 million (estimate)
Party. Communist Party of Cuba (Partido Comunista de Cuba; PCC)
Founded. 1965
Membership. 434,143 (including candidates; *WMR*, July 1981)
First Secretary. Fidel Castro Ruz
Politburo. 14 full members: Fidel Castro Ruz, Raúl Castro Ruz (second secretary), Juan Almeida Bosque, Ramiro Valdés Menéndez, Guillermo García Frías, José Ramón Machado Ventura, Blas Roca Calderío, Carlos Rafael Rodríguez, Pedro Miret Prieto, Sergio del Valle Jiménez, Armando Hart Dávalos, Jorge Risquet Valdés, Julio Camacho Aguilera, Osmany Cienfuegos Gorrián; 11 alternate members
Secretariat. 9 members: Fidel Castro Ruz, Raúl Castro Ruz, Pedro Miret Prieto, Jorge Risquet Valdés, Antonio Pérez Herrero, Lionel Soto Prieto, José Ramón Machado Ventura, Jesús Montana Oropesa, Julián Rizo Alvarez
Central Committee. 148 members, 77 alternates (*Granma*, 5 April 1981)
Status. Ruling party
Last Congress. Second, 17–20 December 1981
Last Election. 1981; all 499 representatives PCC approved
Auxiliary Organizations. Union of Young Communists (Unión de Jovenes Comunistas; UJC), Union of Cuban Pioneers (Unión de Pioneros de Cuba; UPC), Federation of Cuban Women (Federación de Mujeres Cubanas; FMC), Committees for the Defense of the Revolution (Comités de Defensa de la Revolución; CDR), Confederation of Cuban Workers (Confederación de Trabajadores de Cuba; CTC), National Association of Small Farmers (Asociación Nacional de Agricultores Pequeños; ANAP)
Publications. *Granma* (six days a week), official organ of the Central Committee of the PCC; *Juventud Rebelde* (daily), organ of the UJC

In 1983 the Cuban leadership came under strong external and internal pressures. Externally, the loss of a friendly regime in Grenada as a result of the U.S. military action there was a telling blow to the regime of President Fidel Castro. Equally damaging was Castro's inability to foresee and prevent a deadly internecine power struggle in Grenada's Marxist New Jewel Movement in which its top leader, Maurice Bishop, was first deposed and later assassinated by his erstwhile colleagues. Nor were things going well for Castro's friends in Nicaragua, and he was forced to admit that, as in the case of Grenada, he would not be able to offer them much assistance in the

hour of need. Castro was more defensive and somewhat less stringent in his pronouncements, which were no longer extemporaneous as before but read from prepared text, and he appeared to be playing down, at least in public, his country's military role in Central America and Africa.

Internally, a period of economic austerity persisted. The country produced less in 1983 than in the preceding year despite claims to the contrary. The low world price of sugar, Cuba's main export, adversely affected the country's trade with the West and its ability to pay foreign hard-currency obligations. As a result, the Soviet Union continued to subsidize the Cuban economy. If anything, that aid had to be increased. The delivery of Soviet goods to Cuba increased by 19 percent over 1982. Trade with the Soviet Union alone amounted to 70 percent of Cuba's total trade. (Havana domestic radio, 5 August.)

Leadership and Party Organization. There were no changes in the composition of the Cuban communist leadership in 1983. Two Politburo members died and were not replaced: in June, Osvaldo Dorticós Torrado, 64, who committed suicide; and in July, Arnaldo Milián, 70, of cancer. Activities of PCC organizations were reported very infrequently. There were no announcements in 1983 of any formal meetings of the party's Central Committee or Politburo, and a couple of informal ones that did take place were mentioned briefly after the fact. The Sixth Plenum of the Central Committee, some of whose resolutions were summarized in January, apparently took place late in 1982. (There was a "joint meeting" of the PCC and the government on 15 December.) The Central Committee called for "greater efficiency in the fulfillment of production and service programs in the economic field and savings in fuel, electric energy, lubricants, and raw and other materials, particularly those from the capitalist countries . . . thousands of tons of oil must be saved." (Havana domestic radio, 4 January.) As before, Fidel Castro dominated the party and the government. But the fact that his statements were carefully prepared seemed to underline a subtle emphasis on the principle of collective leadership.

After 25 years in power, the Cuban leadership has remained virtually unchanged. By Cuban standards—Havana reported recently that half of Cuba's population had been born after 1 January 1959, the day Castro came to power—it is an aging group, with most members in their mid-fifties. The 56-year-old Castro has not been challenged since 1967, when an old-guard communist "microfaction" tried unsuccessfully to replace him or at least to reduce his then predominant position. While there appears to be no one in the Cuban governing group to cast a shadow on the "maximum leader," it is reasonable to assume that the longevity of the Cuban leadership has given its members an opportunity to develop a system of internal discussion and decisionmaking, hence a formal or de facto collective leadership. Indeed, the phrase "our party leadership" has become standard in the official

Cuban vocabulary. So is the sentence "we shall take this up" ("*vamos a elevar esto*"), now a routine reply by Cuban officials when asked for a decision on any issue. As the institutionalization of collective decisionmaking progressed, the Cuban revolutionary process became fossilized and lost a sense of purpose.

Domestic Affairs. The Cuban Revolution was 25 years old on 1 January 1984. It was less than a happy anniversary. The prime accomplishment of the Cuban revolutionary government might well have been that it was able to survive that long. But this was probably due as much to the ruthless exercise of police power by Castro and to the internal propaganda apparatus and massive Soviet assistance as it was to the shortsightedness and indecisiveness of Castro's domestic and foreign adversaries.

In the president's anniversary speech, delivered to a small, invitation-only crowd of some 4,000 in Santiago de Cuba, Castro read a list of the Revolution's achievements and cited some of the problems, especially what he said was a threat from President Reagan's "warlike hysteria." In the last 25 years, he said, Cuba has greatly improved health and education, has built roads and ports, and made other economic and social gains. He claimed the Cuban economy has grown at an average annual rate of 4.5 percent despite what he called the "brutal economic blockade" by the United States. He said that his government had kept all the promises it made to the Cuban people in 1959. He predicted that in the coming years other revolutionary governments would emerge in Latin America, pledged to continue assisting revolutionaries around the globe, and said that his government has sent Cuban personnel to work in 30 developing countries and had received 30,000 young people from those nations to study in Cuba. (*NYT*, 3 January 1984.)

In what was the first such top level exchange in Cuban-U.S. relations, President Castro's speech was refuted four days later by President Reagan. "Twenty-five years ago, during the early January days, you were celebrating what all of us hoped was the dawn of a new era of freedom," Reagan told Cubans over the Voice of America. "Most Cubans welcomed the prospects for democracy and liberty which the leaders of the Cuban Revolution had promised . . . But, tragically, the promises made to you have not been kept. Since 1959, you've been called upon to make one sacrifice after another. And for what? Doing without has not brought you a more abundant life. It has not brought you peace. And most important, it has not won freedom for your people—freedom to speak your opinions, to travel where and when you wish, to work in independent unions and to openly proclaim your faith in God and to enjoy all these basic liberties without having to be afraid."

Reagan said that political prisoners continued to languish in Cuban jails and that "others" convicted of political crimes last year could expect to remain imprisoned well into the twenty-first century "if the present system in Cuba survives that long."

"Never in the proud history of your country have so many been imprisoned for so long for so-called crimes of political dissent as during these last 25 years." (*Miami Herald*, 6 January.) The president also announced that a new radio system, Radio Martí, would begin in the spring to "tell the truth about Cuba to the Cuban people."

The exchange was one of several in 1983 between the two countries, which led Cuban vice-president Carlos Rafael Rodríguez to declare in June that Cuban-U.S. relations were at the lowest point since 1959, with the possibility of the United States using military force against Cuba much closer than at any time in the past.

Even though Castro claimed some advances in the economy, U.S. specialists estimated that the 1983 annual growth was under 2 percent rather than the 5 percent envisioned by the 1981–1985 plan. Havana announced a 15 percent cut in food consumption in schools and work centers and a price increase for many consumer goods, including gasoline. Strict rationing remained in force, apparently a permanent feature of the Castro revolution. In June, Cuba imposed new restrictions on small individual entrepreneurs, permitted to operate in 1982 to ease shortages in food supply and the lack of services, apparently because the private sector grew much faster than Cuban planners foresaw. Havana conceded internal opposition. Roberto Veiga, secretary general of the Cuban Confederation of Labor, in a May letter to the communist-oriented World Federation of Trade Unions, headquartered in Prague, Czechoslovakia, said that 33 workers had been jailed, accused of sabotage, including burning crops, work centers, and transportation vehicles, and setting fires in Havana. Five workers received death sentences, later commuted to 30 years in jail. (*WP*, 7 June.)

In the spring, as Havana reported, prolonged inclement weather inflicted "serious damage" on agriculture, caused widespread electric power outages, and reduced industrial output. Torrential rains and tornadoes lasting almost 80 days swept the western half of the island, virtually destroying the export tobacco harvest and reducing the sugar crop, the country's principal product, by one million tons (*Granma*, 3 April). Although Havana has not announced 1983 figures on sugar production, it was estimated by Western specialists to be under 7 million metric tons, about 1.2 million less than in 1982. Because the low world price of sugar, about 9 cents a pound, is below Cuban production costs, estimated at 14 cents a pound, the treasury's reserves of foreign exchange diminished drastically. In 1983, according to the Central Planning Board, Cuba had hard currency to pay for only 63 percent of its essential Western imports. With fewer imports of those raw materials, output in many industries declined. In 1983, Cuba twice obtained deferment of interest payments on its $3.5 billion debt to some 150 Western banks, mostly in Europe.

Soviet aid to Cuba in 1983 was estimated at over $3.5 billion and there were no indications that the burden would diminish in the foreseeable future. If anything, it would be much more costly for Moscow in 1986 when under the existing treaties Cuba is supposed to begin repaying the $9 billion Soviet debt accrued as of 31 December 1976. The total of what Cuba now owes the Soviet Union, military assistance excluded, is believed to be more than $22 billion.

Havana did not concede any major economic problems, only minor inconveniences. At the 21–22 December regular session of the National Assembly of People's Power, the Cuban parliament, the government said the economy grew 5 percent in 1983 and the budget registered a surplus of 383 million pesos. (The Cuban peso, not listed on the international monetary markets, is pegged to the Russian ruble, and tourists visiting Cuba get 80 cents for U.S. $1.) For 1984, according to an economic plan presented to the assembly, growth is estimated at 4.5 percent, with an increase of 4 percent in trade and 2.5 to 3 percent in productivity, with income estimated at 11,471 million pesos and expenditures at 11,249 million.

While claiming a 5 percent growth in 1983, Humberto Pérez, president of the Central Planning Board and vice-president of the Council of

Ministers, did not give any figures to corroborate his assertion. Other data presented to the assembly seemed to indicate serious problems in many important economic sectors. Because of bad weather, Pérez said, 89 percent of the sugar production goal was attained. In housing construction 56 percent of the plan was fulfilled, and there were difficulties in the transportation sector. (Ibid., 1 January.)

The 1983 National Assembly was composed of 499 deputies representing the country's 169 municipalities. The assembly, elected for a period of five years, holds two 2-day sessions a year and approves, with a minimum of discussion, laws and reports presented to it by the Council of Ministers and the party, including the state budget.

There were no indications that the Cuban regime would adopt any innovative measures to stimulate the economy. On the contrary, Havana made it clear that the small-farm sector, which several years ago occupied about 20 percent of the arable land and produced a much larger part of the nonsugar agricultural output, would be progressively collectivized. Cuba reported that by August 50.3 percent of small individual farms had merged into cooperatives. The new cooperatives are closely controlled by the government, which purchases their production and regulates all their activities. (Ibid., 28 August.)

Auxiliary Organizations. Cuban mass and auxiliary organizations were either less active in 1983 or were kept out of the limelight by the regime. However, by all indications the CDR were as busy as ever performing block-by-block surveillance for counterrevolutionary activity, their principal task since their creation in 1960.

International Activities and Positions. For the Cuban leaders, the year started with a flurry of activities. In January, Gen. Raúl Castro, first vice-president and minister of defense, saw Soviet president Yuri Andropov in Moscow. Other Cuban officials traveled wide and far, and Havana received dignitaries from foreign lands. Cuba and Bolivia re-established diplomatic relations. In February, Carlos Rafael Rodríguez visited India prior to the March meeting of the Nonaligned Movement in New Delhi, which ended Fidel Castro's chairmanship of the Third World movement, which he had assumed at the Sixth Summit in Havana, September 1979.

From April on, relations with the United States occupied and preoccupied Havana. Cuba reacted sharply to the 6 April statement by President Reagan that he would try to prevent a "proliferation of Cuban-model states in Central America." Shortly afterwards, two Cuban officials at U.N. headquarters in New York were accused of spying by U.S. authorities and ordered to leave the country.

On 24 May, the Reagan administration asked Cuba to take back several thousands of the 125,000 Mariel boatlift refugees, some of whom were common criminals placed on U.S.-bound boats by Cuban authorities. Washington, which wanted to send home about 800 Cubans held in the Atlanta Federal Penitentiary and described as hardened criminals, told Cuba that until these men were repatriated the U.S. Interests Section in Havana would not issue U.S. visas to any Cubans except immediate relatives of American citizens. On 17 June, the Cuban Government replied that it would discuss the Mariel repatriation issue only as part of the overall conversation on the "normalization of migration" between the two countries. On 7 July, a spokesman for the State Department stated that the United States did not want to broaden the Mariel refugee discussion, thus appearing to reject the Cuban note.

A rash of airplane hijackings to Cuba in mid-1983 also prompted an exchange of notes between Havana and Washington. The treatment of hijackers arrested in Cuba has been one of many long-standing disputes between the two countries, which signed an antihijacking treaty in 1973. In 1976, Cuba repudiated the treaty but a year later declared it would abide by its provisions. In reply to suggestions in the United States that Cuba by lenient treatment was encouraging hijackers, on 15 June Havana delivered a note to the United States detailing punishment given to such transgressors. The note said that whereas prior to 1981 hijackers received sentences ranging from two to five years in prison, after that date fifteen-year prison sentences were the average. (*NYT*, 28 June.)

Cuban military and political activities in Nicaragua, Grenada, and Africa were also a bone of contention in Cuban-U.S. relations. In June, the number of Cuban civilians in Nicaragua was placed at about 4,000, with an additional 2,000 working with the Nicaraguan army and the Ministry of Interior. Cuban ambassador Julián López was said to be the most influential diplomat in

Managua. At the same time, Gen. Arnaldo Ochoa, deputy to General Castro, was reported to have spent at least a month in Nicaragua. General Ochoa, one of Cuba's top commanders, saw action in Angola in 1976 and a year later in Ethiopia, where Cuban forces defeated their allies' adversaries. (Ibid., 19 June.) A month later, President Castro, commenting on U.S. policy in Central America, said that the Reagan administration was trying to create an "atmosphere of terror" around Nicaragua. Struggle in Central America, he stated, was "not local, but worldwide." (Ibid., 27 July.) A few days later, he said Cuba would halt military aid to Nicaragua if an agreement could be reached for all countries to stop sending arms and advisers to Central America (ibid., 30 July). One of the unexplained episodes of Havana's Nicaraguan involvement was a report, confirmed by Cuba, that a senior official of the Castro government held a series of meetings with dissident anti-Sandinista commander Edén Pastora, who is engaged in an armed struggle against the Managua government (ibid., 6 October).

The U.S. military landing on Grenada on 25 October was a surprise to the Castro government, which appeared to have committed a major political blunder and an intelligence disaster. Cuba, which had been helping the revolutionary Marxist regime of Premier Maurice Bishop economically, militarily, and politically, was ignorant until the very last moment that its ally, and Castro's protégé, was threatened with overthrow by fellow Marxist and his deputy Bernard Coard. "It is difficult to understand with all our [Cuban] Embassy personnel there that we didn't know the split was taking place. That's our biggest criticism against our political staff, our diplomatic staff and our military-cooperation staff. They had absolutely no idea of what was happening." (*Newsweek*, 9 January 1984.) When Bishop was arrested and later killed by his erstwhile comrades, Cuba declared official mourning for the slain Grenadian premier and called the killing a "cold-blooded execution" for which the guilty "should receive exemplary punishment" (Radio Havana, 20 October). A day later, Lieut. Col. Pedro Tortoló Comas arrived in Grenada on a "working visit" and "took command of all Cuban personnel." According to some reports, the commander's role was to overthrow the regime headed by Bishop's enemies and place in power the pro-Bishop faction of the Grenadian Marxist movement. Colonel Tortoló did not, or could not, act in time, and a Cuban military contingent surrendered shortly after the invading force landed in Grenada. (On the same day, 25 October, Lieut. Col. Desi Bouterse, the leftist leader of Suriname, who had friendly relations with Havana, expelled all Cuban diplomats.)

Castro, faced with a considerable loss of prestige, moved at home and abroad to contain the damage, save face, and recoup influence. When initially the U.S. and world press were not allowed to enter Grenada, Castro invited every newsman who wanted to do so to go to Havana to hear the Cuban side of the conflict. After the repatriation from Grenada of 784 Cubans, including 59 wounded and bodies of 24 men killed there, Castro delivered a clever panegyric in which he launched a verbal counteroffensive against the Reagan administration. (The text of the speech was printed as an advertisement in several American newspapers.) Cuba, Castro said, gave Grenada economic assistance worth $63 million, or over $540 per inhabitant. But "hyenas emerged from the revolutionary ranks . . . were they simply a group of ambitious, opportunistic individuals, or were they enemy agents who wanted to destroy the Grenadian revolution?" Castro asked rhetorically. "In our view, Coard's group objectively destroyed the revolution and opened the door to imperialist aggression." Taking advantage of several misstatements, errors, and confusion by the White House, the Pentagon, and the State Department, Castro enumerated what he called "19 lies told by the U.S. Government to justify its invasion of Grenada and its subsequent actions." He said the action reminded him of the methods Adolf Hitler used invading small countries prior to World War II. Taking note that between 65 and 71 percent of Americans supported the invasion, Castro said that "if a poll had been taken in Hitler's Germany at the time, in the midst of the chauvinistic wave unleashed by the Nazis, around 80 or 90 percent of the people would have approved of those aggressions." The Grenadian action, he continued, "if anything, was a pyrrhic victory and a profound moral defeat . . . The imperialist government of the United States wanted to kill the symbol of the Grenadian revolution but the symbol was already dead . . . The United States killed a corpse and brought the symbol back to life at the same time." Speaking about the future and indicating a revision of his strategy of "internationalism," Castro said, "The experiences of Grenada will be examined in detail to extract the utmost benefit from them for use in case of another attack against a country where there are Cuban cooperation personnel or on our own Motherland." (*NYT*, 20 November.)

Several weeks after the Grenadian invasion, it was reported that about a thousand Cubans working in Nicaragua returned to their homeland. Apparently military personnel were not involved in the early departure of the Cubans, scheduled for rotation in January, and it was not known whether they would be replaced later in 1984. (Ibid., 23 November.) Speaking about Cuban involvement in Nicaragua, Castro told a U.S. journalist: "We give them [the Sandinistas] moral support and we have never denied that we have military advisers in Nicaragua. I don't want to help the aggressive plans of the U.S. Administration by mentioning figures. For the same reason I will not discuss arms supplies to Nicaragua." (*Newsweek*, 9 January.)

Part of Cuba's effort to repair political fences in the post-Grenada period was a move to improve relations with Argentina and other Latin American countries. Early in December, Carlos Rafael Rodríguez traveled to Buenos Aires to attend the inauguration of President Raúl Alfonsín and met with a group of senior officials from Latin America and Western Europe. They reportedly discussed the situation in Central America and Latin America's external debt. (*Granma*, 25 December.) After a long period of cool relations and less than friendly criticism of the Beijing government, Havana improved its ties and trade with China, which in 1983 was to be twice the 1978 total (ibid., 27 November).

Cuban troops continued to be stationed in Angola and Ethiopia, although the latter country is reportedly sending some of these troops back home. Both South Africa and the Reagan administration maintain that the presence in Angola of Cuban military units, estimated at between 25,000 and 30,000 (*NYT*, 14 January 1984) is the main obstacle to the settlement of the issue of Namibia. Both Cuba and Angola deny this assertion. Late in December, when a South African force launched a pre-emptive strike into southern Angola against camps of the South-West Africa People's Organization, the South African government said that its soldiers had directly engaged Cuban troops and scored a major victory over them (ibid., 7 January 1984). There were no immediate comments from Havana on the South African reports, which mentioned battles against Cuban regular forces in three places some 100 miles inside Angola.

Since the late 1970s, Cuban troops have served as a prop of the government of Lieut. Col. Mengistu Haile Mariam. Western sources have reported that Cuba plans to cut its troop strength in Ethiopia from its present 10,500 to fewer than 3,000 by June. The cuts reportedly reflect Ethiopian and Cuban convictions that Somalia will not attack the disputed Ogaden territory as well as the need to cut Ethiopia's defense costs. The Cuban forces are said to cost the Addis Ababa government approximately $6 million a year. (ibid., 25 January 1984.)

George Volsky
University of Miami

Dominican Republic

The leftist movement in the Dominican Republic, as divided as ever, played an insignificant part in the country's political life in 1983. Leftists took to the streets in Santo Domingo late in October to protest the U.S. military intervention in Grenada and, in general, protested against the policies of the Reagan administration in Central America. But their effectiveness was diminished by the fact that President Salvador Jorge Blanco was the leader of the ruling left-of-center Dominican Revolutionary Party (PRD), whose current secretary general, José Francisco Peña Gómez, mayor of Santo Domingo, is a vice-president of the Socialist International. The government, while generally pro-American, maintains close relations with Nicaragua. In July, Nicaraguan foreign minister Miguel d'Escoto visited and, with his Dominican counterpart, Augusto Vega Imbert, expressed a desire to strengthen relations and their support for the Contadora group's efforts to find a peaceful solution in Central America and for the "democratic and pluralistic system" of government. (EFE, Madrid, 12 July.) Various Marxist leaders, complaining of a brief jailing in August of some fifty activists from the Dominican Left Front (Frente de Izquierda Dominicana; FID), declared in an open letter to President Jorge Blanco and Dr. Peña Gómez that the PRD administration has moved to the right and become too pro–United States. They also charged that antileftist security agencies have manufactured details of a destabilizing plot that Marxists were supposed to be preparing. At the time of the arrest of the leftists, Dominican police expelled from the country two Cuban sociologists who had been attending a seminar on the life of women in the rural areas of the Dominican Republic. The two were accused of engaging in activities incompatible with their tourist visa status.

President Jorge Blanco accused the FID of "organizing strikes and occupations of land and churches" and of "mounting demonstrations throughout the country with the aim of destabilizing" the government. Dr. Peña Gómez charged that the leftist organizations were preparing for guerrilla warfare by setting up a military training school for guerrillas. (*Intercontinental Press*, 5 September.)

The recently created FID is a coalition of ten of the principal leftist organizations in the country. Even though there are perhaps thirty such groups in the Dominican Republic, their combined membership totals only some 5,000 persons, and they have no congressional representation. Politically, the Left covers the entire ideological spectrum: from pro-Soviet and pro-Cuban to Maoist and Trotskyist. The Dominican Communist Party (Partido Comunista Dominicano; PCD), is pro-Soviet and pro-Cuban. Its secretary general is the veteran communist activist Narciso Isa Conde. In 1983, Isa Conde traveled to the Soviet Union, where he was treated as *the* leader of the Dominican Left. His views and statements are frequently aired by Radio Havana's international service, and they usually coincide with those of the Cuban government and communist party. There are also, among other groups, the Communist Party of the Dominican Republic (Partido Comunista de la República Dominicana; PACOREDO), and the Labor Communist Party of the Dominican Republic, whose secretary general is Rafael Chaljub Mejía. Chaljub Mejía is a friend of Albania, which he visited in July as an invited guest of that country's communist party.

In March, Claudio Tavárez, a leader of the Revolutionary Workers' Party (Partido Revolucionario de Trabajadores; PRT), gave his version of the disintegration of the Dominican Left:

"After the crushing of the April 1965 insurrection through the U.S. intervention, the strongest left currents in the Dominican Republic were the Maoists. There were various organizations that professed Maoism, as well as organizations that held to a guerrilla-warfare strategy. The latter included one of the most important revolutionary figures of recent times, Col. Francisco Caamaño Deño. He had led the April 1965 revolution; after it was defeated, he had to flee the country. He went to Cuba and returned from there with a small group of followers at the beginning of the 1970s. In 1972 Caamaño was captured and murdered by the repressive forces, aided by the Central Intelligence Agency. He died in much the same way that Che Guevara had in Bolivia.

"That was another big setback for the revolutionary movement—losing a young leader who was among the most respected figures in the country. It was of course a limitation of Caamaño's part not to have seen that more than a guerrilla force was necessary to overthrow the dictatorship. Not only was Caamaño killed. A whole group of leaders who had come out of the 1965 upsurge were also killed. They had participated with him in the founding of the Latin American Solidarity Organization (OLAS) in Havana in 1967.

"Later the popular movement focused mainly around the fight for democratic rights against the Balaguer dictatorship. Once Balaguer was ousted through the 1978 elections, fresh debates and discussions arose around questions of strategy and the character of the Dominican revolution. As a result, the organizations that had held to a guerrilla-warfare policy abandoned it. The most important of these was the Camilo Torres Revolutionary Committees [CORECATO], which split into two tendencies, the Socialist Party [PS] and the Socialist Workers Movement [MST].

"The Maoist currents also underwent splits and regroupments. The main organizations from this background today are the Communist Workers Nucleus [NCT], the Dominican Workers Party [PTD], and the Dominican People's Movement [MPD]. Out of a series of discussions on how to unite in action against the Guzmán government's policies and how to orient to the May 1982 elections, various coalitions arose. One of these is the Socialist Bloc, made up of the NCT, the MST, and the PS. These three groups and seven others—including our own, the PRT—joined to present candidates in the elections as the United Left, confronting the capitalist parties.

"Another bloc, involving the Communist Party, the Movement for Socialism, and the Socialist Unity Movement, also presented candidates in the elections under the name Socialist Unity. As a product of common experiences in the election and in other mass activity, a wide-ranging political discussion has opened up among the various organizations over points of agreement, disagreement, and convergence of program, strategy, and orientation. As part of this process, the MST and PRT have deepened their political collaboration—for example in common work in solidarity with the Nicaraguan and Salvadoran revolutions—and have adopted a perspective of fusion. They are pursuing discussions to bring about such a fusion in the near future." (Ibid., 14 March.)

George Volsky
University of Miami

Ecuador

Population. 8.9 million (*IADB Annual Report*, 1983)
Parties. Communist Party of Ecuador (PCE, pro-Moscow); Communist Party of Ecuador, Marxist-Leninist (PCE-ML, pro-Beijing); Revolutionary Socialist Party of Ecuador (PSRE, pro-Havana)
Founded. PCE: 1928; PCE-ML: 1972; PSRE: 1962
Membership. PCE: 500; PCE-ML: 100; PSRE: 200 (all estimates, *World Factbook*, 1982)
Secretary General. PCE: René Mauge
Central Committee. PCE: 8 members: Milton Jijón Saavedra (secretary), José Solís Castro, Efraín Alvarez Fiallo, Bolívar Bolanos Sánchez, Ghandi Burbano Burbano, Xavier Garaycoa Ortíz, Alfredo Castillo, Freddy Almeidau
Status. Legal
Last Congress. PCE: Tenth, 27–29 November 1981, in Guayaquil
Elections. In national elections, August 1979, PCE electoral organization, the Popular Democratic Union (UDP), received 3.2 percent of the vote and one seat in the 71-member one-chamber legislature. The PCE-ML electoral organization, the Democratic Popular Movement (MPD), received 1.5 percent of the vote and one seat in the legislature. In the December 1980 local elections, the Marxist parties received no seats on the Provincial Councils.
Auxiliary Organizations. PCE: Ecuadorean Workers' Confederation (CTE); PCE-ML: Ecuadorean University Students' Federation (FEUE)

In the midst of Ecuador's worst year economically in memory, caused by the lingering effects of the world recession, debt repayment problems, and severe weather, the political process remained in civilian hands in 1983, and a record number of political parties prepared for national and local elections in 1984. Although isolated incidents were attributed to armed groups of both Marxist and non-Marxist orientation, the most important developments related to the communist parties and organizations of Ecuador in 1983 involved their expansion and proliferation in the rather open and tolerant political climate of the country. Important strikes, including a national stoppage in March for two days, helped maintain the organizational momentum of the Marxist unions (*YICA*, 1983, p. 86).

In an event of primary importance to the electoral future of the Marxist-Leninist parties, the national legislature reinstated those that had been ordered disbanded by the Supreme Electoral Tribunal for failing to get at least 5 percent of the vote in three successive elections (*FBIS*, 24 May). As the 29 January 1984 elections approached, however, the electoral organizations of the various communist parties of Ecuador demonstrated, by participating in three different electoral alliances, their inability to consolidate the Marxist vote.

With a 3.2 percent economic decline in Ecuador (due partially to $600 million in agricultural and infrastructure losses due to severe flooding), a doubling of food prices, an overall inflation rate of about 50 percent, and over $1 billion falling due on the foreign debt, increased social and economic tensions were to be expected. A general strike was called for 23–24 March by the United Workers' Front (*YICA*, 1983, p. 86) to protest a 27 percent currency devaluation, fuel price increases, and a rise in interest rates. With the support of all the Marxist political and labor organizations, the strike was almost 100 percent effective. Although it did not succeed in rolling back the government's economic adjustments, Congress and the president did approve a minimum-wage increase in June (*El Universo*, 3 June, p. 1). A month-long strike by the 60,000-member National Union of Teachers in June and July forced Congress into a special session, resulting in the passage of a salary adjustment of over 25 percent spread over a six-month period (*El Comercio*, 6 July, p. A-1).

Government Minister Galo García Feraud suggested that some activities connected with the March general strike "may have a terrorist character," including the destruction of property and commercial establishments, a bomb explosion at the home of a television news director, the dynamiting of an electrical substation, and the machine-gunning of the Israeli Embassy (*FBIS*, 25 and 31 March, 4 April). Other incidents during the year suggested that subversive elements might be becoming active in Ecuador. In August, the government broke up a ring of international thieves believed responsible for a rash of bank robberies in Ecuador, the proceeds of which were being sent to Peru to support Shining Path guerrillas there (ibid., 31 August). Government ministry officials reported in October the capture of members of an organized armed band originally reported active in northern Esmeraldas province in July (ibid., 21 July, 13 October). In August, another new organization, claiming historical ties to the Montonero guerrillas who led the successful Liberal Revolution of 1895, stole the swords of Liberal Party forebears Eloy Alfaro and Pedro Montero from a Guayaquil museum; in November, the organization briefly occupied a news agency to publicize its cause (ibid., 19 August, 29 November). While its statements admitted the validity of the electoral process, they also urged the need for unity with Marxist organizations to accomplish the organization's goals. Government Minister Vladimiro Alvarez termed the situation a case of "latent insurgency." (Ibid., 24 August, 13 September.)

As the Marxist parties prepared for the 1984 elections, their distinctive ideological tendencies and leadership personalities became more evident. With the rescinding by Congress of the section of the Law of Parties designed to eliminate from electoral politics those organizations unable to muster 5 percent of the vote in three successive elections, these and some of the smaller non-Marxist parties lost part of their in-centive to merge for the elections (ibid., 24 May). What eventually emerged were three distinct groupings of the more progressive parties, roughly along ideological lines. In August, the 1,130 delegates to the Fourth National Congress of the UDP, electoral organization of the pro-Moscow PCE, unanimously selected Dr. René Mauge as their presidential candidate. At the same time, the delegates voted to change their organization's name to the Broad Left Front (FADI). (Ibid., 19 August.) Efforts by the non-Marxist Democratic Party led by Dr. Francisco Huerta Montalvo to build a unified center-left coalition that included FADI came to naught, but Huerta left open the possibility of Marxist party support in the event that he is one of the runoff candidates in May 1984 (*El Comercio*, 17 October). Given the presence of ten presidential contenders with no clear front runner, the 6 May 1984 runoff was almost inevitable.

The pro-Havana PSRE eventually formed part of the Socialist Front, composed of the Socialist Party of Ecuador and the Ecuadorean People's Party, in addition to the PSRE (*FBIS*, 3 November). Their candidate was Manuel Salgado Tamayo. The Maoist MDP selected maverick congressional deputy Jaime Hurtado as its candidate (*Visión*, 5 December, p. 16). The strategy of the Marxists appeared to be to remain separate for the first electoral round, when they would have no chance for the presidency but might well be able to elect a handful of deputies to the 71-member unicameral legislature and some share of provincial and local officials as well. Then they could throw their support to the more progressive of the two presidential finalists for the May 1984 runoff in exchange for as yet unspecified rewards.

International Activities. In international affairs, the PCE, meeting in Lima with other South American communist parties in November 1982, supported a joint declaration roundly denouncing "the pilferage and enslavement . . . by U.S. imperialism and its regional accomplices which are responsible for the serious economic crisis from which our continent suffers," and supporting "the anti-imperialist movement'[s] . . . stubborn struggle . . . waged by the democratic workers and people's forces . . . In order to achieve this," the joint manifesto continues, "the unity of the forces of the Left is indispensable, . . one of the fundamental aims of the communist parties" (*Horizont*, no. 10, p. 10). Among the declarations adopted by the PCE Central Committee meeting in Guayaquil in August was, "a resolution of solidarity with the people of revolutionary Nicaragua" (*Pravda*, 15 August). Ecuadorean Marxist party declarations seldom criticized the foreign policy of the current elected government, which regularly declared its commitment to an independent position in international affairs, sent ministers to Eastern European countries to improve relations, and agreed to resume relations at the ambassadorial level with Cuba (*FBIS*, 26 September, 4 January 1984).

David Scott Palmer
Foreign Service Institute

El Salvador

Population. 4.7 million
Party. Revolutionary Coordination of the Masses (Coordinadora Revolucionario de Masas; CRM) is composed of five Marxist-Leninist groups. The Democratic Revolutionary Front (Frente Democrático Revolucionario; FDR) comprises the CRM and two social-democratic groups. The FDR is a virtual government-in-exile and meets chiefly in Mexico City.
Founded. CRM, 1980; FDR, 1980
Membership. Not applicable
Member Organizations. CRM: National Democratic Union (Unión Nacional Democrática; UDN), a Moscow-oriented communist group headed by Mario Aguiñada Carranza; Popular Revolutionary Bloc (Bloque Popular Revolucionaria; BPR), the largest of the movements with some 50,000 adherents, headed by Facundo Guardado y Guardado; Unified Popular Action Front (Frente de Acción Popular Unificada; FAPU), under Alberto Ramos; Popular Leagues of 28 February (Ligas Populares 28 de Febrero; LP-28), commanded by José Leoncio Pinchinte; Popular Liberation Movement (Movimiento de Liberación Popular; MLP), a small, radical Marxist movement led by Dr. Fabio Castillo Figueroa. FDR: CRM and National Revolutionary Movement (Movimiento Nacional Revolucionario; MNR) of Dr. Guillermo Manuel Ungo; Popular Social Christian Movement (Movimiento Popular Social Cristiano; MPSC) under Rubén Ignacio Zamora Rivas
FDR President. Guillermo Manuel Ungo
Political Action Committee. 7 members: Guillermo Manuel Ungo (chairman; MNR), Fabio Castillo (MLP), Mario Anguiñada Carranza (UDN), Rubén Ignacio Zamora Rivas (MPSC), José Napoleón Rodríguez Ruiz (FAPU), Ana Guadalupe Martínez (LP-28), Salvador Samayoa (BPR)
Status. Illegal

The oldest Marxist-Leninist movement in El Salvador is the Communist Party of El Salvador (Partido Comunista de El Salvador; PCES), which was founded in 1928. But the brutal massacre that followed the abortive rising of Farabundo Martí in 1932 drove the movement underground, and radical activity did not re-emerge in El Salvador on a large scale until 1970, with the founding of the Popular Liberation Forces (Fuerzas Populares de Liberación; FPL). The establishment of massive peasant movements, such as the BPR in 1975, gave added weight to the Left. When a reformist junta failed to move rapidly enough in late 1979 to satisfy the demands of the peasants, a civil war broke out in this desperately poor country. This war has now dragged on for almost four years, totally disrupting the already shaky economy and causing an estimated half million Salvadoreans to flee into exile. Despite the re-establishment of constitutional government in 1982, the state has been powerless to stop the activities of the right-wing death squads, which continually add fuel to the rebellion.

The Armed Rebel Movement. The military force of the BPR is called the Farabundo Martí Front of National Liberation (Frente Farabundo Martí de Liberación Nacional; FMLN) and comprises an armed component of each organization in the CRM. The BPR is represented by the FPL, headed, until his death in April, by Salvador Cayetano Carpio, who also headed the Unified Revolutionary Directorate (Directorio Revolucionario Unificada; DRU), which directs the war. The FAPU armed forces are the Armed Forces of National Resistance (Fuerzas Armadas de Resistencia Nacional; FARN—sometimes referred to simply as Resistencia Nacional; RN), led by Fermán Cienfuegos. The LP-28 has the Trotskyist movement called the Popular Revolutionary Army (Ejército Popular Revolucionario; ERP), commanded by Joaquín Villalobos with Ana Guadalupe Martínez as second-in-command. The UDN's military arm is the PCES, led by Shafik Jorge Handal, and the MLP uses the group known as the Central American Revolutionary Workers' Party (Partido Revolucionario de Trabajadores Centroamericanos; PRTC) commanded by Roberto Roca.

The Death of Carpio. Overshadowing even the war itself were the mysterious circumstances surrounding the suicide of Salvador Cayetano Carpio, known as "Comandante Marcial" and considered to be the grand old man of the Left (see biography, *YICA*, 1983, pp. 89–90). These events began on 9 April when the second-in-command of the FPL, Mélida Anaya Montes ("Comandante Ana Maria") was brutally assassinated in her Managua apartment by a dissident group within the FPL led by Rogelio A. Bazzaglia Recinos. He and a number of confederates were rounded up by Nicaraguan authorities. Carpio and his wife flew at once to Managua for the

funeral. According to official reports, "depressed and dismayed" by the treason within his group, at 9:30 P.M. on 12 April, Carpio shot himself in the house where he and his wife resided (*Barricada Internacional*, 25 April). Though suicide seems an unlikely recourse for one who had survived prison, torture, and years of guerrilla life, no satisfactory alternate explanation has been forthcoming. More important is the significance in terms of the internal politics of the FPL and FMLN. According to one report, Carpio and Mélida Anaya had been working to strengthen the unity of the FMLN, a move opposed by Bazzaglia, who wanted a more independent role for the FPL (*Intercontinental Press*, 27 June). However, another version says that Carpio and Anaya had been at odds in this matter, Carpio refusing to integrate the FPL into the larger movement (*NYT*, 25 September). In September, the FPL chose an ex-schoolteacher and protégé of Anaya, Leonel González, to replace Carpio and Dimos Rodríguez to take Anaya's position. Rodríguez, who commanded rebel forces in Chalatenango department, will assume military command of the FPL. Both are regarded as seeking closer cooperation within the FMLN.

The Civil War. The war, which began in earnest in March 1980, appears interminable. Government casualty figures are fragmentary, but piecing together a number of sources of information suggests that about 5,000 troops have been killed in the fighting. The rebels have probably lost half that number, while civilian deaths from bombing, random massacres, and death-squad activities stand at about 40,000. The government has 25,000 men in its army, with another 6,000 in military police units. The rebel regular forces are generally estimated at about 7,000, but are supplemented by the local People's Militia and guerrilla bands behind enemy lines. Most of the department of Morazan, the northern half of Chalatenango, the Guazapa volcano region in San Salvador and Cuscatlán, and large stretches of the departments of Usulután and San Vicente were in rebel hands at the beginning of the year. A government drive in midsummer made considerable inroads into Usulután and San Vicente, but by December not only had the rebels won back all this territory, but they enjoyed control of a large stretch of the Pacific coast and of the cathedral city of Jucuarán. On the other hand, no departmental capitals have passed permanently into rebel hands. Despite U.S. aid and training, the government is handicapped by having to fight its battles using impressed peasants, who leave as soon as their term is up, if not before, whereas the rebels are battle-hardened professionals. The FMLN policy of turning most prisoners over to the Red Cross for repatriation (and dismissal from the army) has caused whole units to surrender and turn over their weapons to the rebels (*Time*, 12 December).

The year opened inauspiciously enough for the government side when its commander in Cabañas department, Col. Sigifredo Ochoa Pérez, went into open revolt, protesting against the lackluster performance of Defense Minister Gen. José Guillermo García. Ochoa was dismissed from his command and sent abroad, but the handwriting was on the wall for García, whom the United States considered uncooperative, and he was replaced on 17 April by Col. Carlos Eugenio Vides Casanova. At the time of the Ochoa revolt, the FMLN was in the midst of an offensive launched in October 1982, and by the middle of January it controlled all of Morazán north of the Torola River, an area containing some 100,000 persons (*Central America Report*, 21 January). The FMLN also demonstrated its firm hold of the Guazapa region by setting up a new radio station on the volcano, Radio Guazapa, to supplement Radio Venceremos in Morazán. Even the capital was not spared; heavy fighting broke out in San Salvador around the San Carlos Barracks on 28 January. On 1 February, Berlín, a city of 30,000 in Usulután, was seized by the FMLN. Devastating air strikes followed, and by the time the rebel forces left on 7 February, the city was reduced to rubble (*Los Angeles Times*, 7 February). The FMLN forces from Guazapa surrounded Suchitoto, only a few miles north of the capital, and cut it off for twelve days in February, although they were unable to take this strategic highway center.

The United States urged a new strategy on the government forces. A great number of small battalions would be created, which would fan out across designated departments in sweeps of about 10,000 men. Behind the troops would come civic action teams that would set up strategic hamlets along the lines of the Civic Operations and Rural Development Support program (CORDS) used in Vietnam. The first major offensive launched under this new plan began in April against the deeply entrenched rebel positions in the Guazapa region. The drive, unlike a previous effort in February, made some headway and even succeeded in taking the FMLN "capital" of Palo Grande (Radio YSU, San Salvador, 1 June; *FBIS*, 3 June), although the army was unable to hold it. The drive lingered on until 1 August, but the FMLN remained in control of this vital region only 25 kilometers north of the capital.

An even more ambitious government drive was launched on 9 June. Called "Well-Being for San Vicente," it was designed to incorporate rural pacification techniques on the CORDS model. The goal was to take Chichontepec volcano, from which the rebels had been able to dominate the main east-west route across the country. Using tanks and heavy artillery as well as air strikes, the government forces took the volcano against surprisingly light resistance, the FMLN simply melting away as the army approached. While fighting continued throughout the country, the FMLN stepped up an assassination campaign in the capital. On 30 May, Lt. Cmdr. Albert Scheufelberger, USN, second-in-command of the U.S. advisory mission, was gunned down. On 28 June, René Barrios Amaya, first secretary of the Constituent Assembly and a leader of the right-wing ARENA party, was also assassinated. The FPL took responsibility for these acts.

By the end of July, the government had occupied most of Usulután and San Vicente and even made headway against the enemy in Morazán and Chalatenango, although suffering heavy casualties in some areas (*This Week Central America and Panama*, 1 August). Then, on 4 September, the rebels launched a counterattack on a nationwide scale, even briefly overrunning the departmental capital of San Miguel (ibid., 12 September). This last attack was personally led by Joaquín Villalobos of the ERP, and for the first time the FMLN made extensive use of heavy artillery, including 120-mm mortars. As the FMLN reconquered Usulután and San Vicente, the pacification program collapsed (*Latin America Update*, September/October). In the former department, the major city of Jucuapa fell to the FMLN, was retaken, and then fell again in early October (UPI, 9 October). Chichontepec volcano again passed into rebel hands, as did Cacahuatique volcano in San Miguel. By early November, U.S. advisers in El Salvador reported that in the preceding two months the FMLN had killed 800 soldiers and captured 400 more (to be turned over to the Red Cross). Vast quantities of arms had been taken, and a north-south route had been opened up to connect rebel forces in Morazán with those in Usulután. So bold had the rebels become that their truck convoys moved openly in daylight. (*This Week Central America and Panama*, 14 November.) Apparently, only fear of direct U.S. military intervention dissuaded the FMLN from launching a "knockout blow" (ibid., 28 November). Not only had the FDR-FMLN set up schools, hospitals, local governments, and civil registries in the area under their control, but a "regional governing junta" was created in Chalatenango, possibly as a first step to setting up an opposition government on Salvadorean soil.

Efforts at Negotiation. The sticking point in negotiations to end the war has been over the question of whether the rebel forces should be given a share of power prior to any elections, as the FDR wishes, or whether they should simply be free to participate in the elections of March 1984, with appropriate guarantees of safety, as the government wants. Shafik Handal of the PCES declared in Havana in April that the FDR could never participate in such elections as were now being prepared (Havana international service, 2 April; *FBIS*, 5 April). A few days later, in San José, Costa Rica, Mario Aguiñada Carranza and Jorge Villacorta made a proposal for the FDR: immediate talks with an open agenda and the presence of representatives from the Contadora group (Mexico, Panama, Colombia, and Venezuela) as well as, if possible, from the United States. Seeing the key role of the United States, FDR president Ungo announced in Washington that "the United States has the right to stop the spread of communism. . . We believe the best way to be secure is, in a respectful way, to accept political pluralism" (*Los Angeles Times*, 3 May). During the summer and early fall, talks did occur between the FDR and the Peace Commission of the Salvadorean government and between the FDR and U.S. special envoy Richard Stone. After several attempts at a meeting had failed,

Stone met with Rubén Zamora at Bogotá on 31 July and 1 August. Zamora hailed the talks as "a positive step" (*WP*, 2 August), but apparently there was no agreement on substantive points. On 30 August, an FDR delegation including Dr. Ungo, Zamora, and Aguiñada again met with Ambassador Stone at San José, but again little was decided except that talks should continue. Simultaneously, an FDR delegation met with the Salvadorean Peace Commission at Bogotá. A second attempt at dialogue with the Peace Commission at Bogotá was made on 29 September, but, said commission head Francisco Quiñónez, it failed because of FDR insistence on "restructuring power" (*This Week Central America and Panama*, 3 November). Talks with Stone likewise broke off, but Ungo met in Washington with Henry Kissinger, head of the Special Bipartisan Commission on Central America, in late October (*Time*, 31 October).

Foreign Contacts. The FDR busied itself about the world as usual. Rubén Zamora traveled to Belgium in March to enlist the aid of that country in starting negotiations. August found him in West Germany, where he conferred with high officials and urged the German government not to supply arms to the government side in the civil war. Guillermo Ungo and Salvador Samayoa visited Paris in April to confer with French Communist Party leaders and government members. They also visited Portugal and Sweden, where Samayoa met with Premier Olof Palme, generally regarded as sympathetic to their cause. Managua was a frequent meeting site for the FDR until Zamora, Aguiñada, Samayoa, and other leaders were asked to leave in early December; the Nicaraguan government evidently feared that their presence might seem a provocation to the United States, which had just invaded Grenada and might attack Nicaragua.

Thomas P. Anderson
Eastern Connecticut State University

Grenada

Population. 110,000 (estimate)
Party. New Jewel Movement (NJM), until U.S. invasion of 25 October
Founded. 1973
Membership. Information unavailable
NJM Chairman. Maurice Bishop, until his assassination on 19 October
NJM Government Cabinet. (Until coup of 13 October) Maurice Bishop (prime minister), Bernard Coard (deputy prime minister but not a member of the Central Committee), Unison Whiteman (minister of foreign affairs), Kendrick Radix (minister of industrial development, labor and legal affairs), Norris Bain (minister of housing), Jacqueline Creft (minister of education), Chris ("Kojo") de Riggs (minister of health), George Louison (minister of agriculture, rural development and cooperatives), Selwyn Strachan (minister of national mobilization), Gen. Hudson Austin (chief of the army)
Central Committee. 14 members: principally cabinet members named above
Status. Ruling party until October
Auxiliary Organizations. National Youth Organization, National Women's Organization, Young Pioneers, Peasants' Organization, Workers' Parish Councils, People's Militia
Publications. *Free West Indian*, *New Jewel Movement* (both weeklies)

In a virtually bloodless coup on 13 March 1979, the New Jewel Movement came to power under the leadership of Maurice Bishop. ("Jewel" is an acronym for "Joint Endeavor for Welfare, Education, and Liberation.") Grenada's new prime minister was a Marxist, London-trained lawyer influenced by the black civil rights movements of the 1960s, who promised to forge a truly democratic system and a new postcolonial society geared toward meeting basic human needs. With its goal of a corruption-free and constitutional society, the NJM found a receptive audience. Critics had described the preceding regime of Eric Gairy as extremely dishonest and ruthless, both before and after Grenada's independence from Great Britain in February 1974. Gairy is known to have frequently ignored constitutional procedures. He surrounded himself with bodyguards, the so-called Mongoose Gang, who beat up opposition leaders, including Bishop. Bishop's father, Rupert, was killed by this group during anti-Gairy strikes in 1974. Against this

backdrop, Bishop adopted the slogan "Forward ever, backward never." (*NYT*, 21 October.)

After Gairy's overthrow, the NJM set about major revolutionary changes along a socialist path that would transform the political system and class structure. The NJM, which its leaders described as "the vanguard capable of directing the actions of the people," quickly formed a Central Committee and Political Bureau, established a People's Revolutionary Government (PRG) and a People's Revolutionary Army (*WMR*, September 1980). During the following years, Grenada became clearly aligned with Cuba and the Soviet Union, which led to deteriorating relations with the United States. By the end of 1982, a number of Soviet- and Cuban-backed projects were under way in Grenada, including a $71 million international airport with a 9,000-foot runway (*YICA*, 1982, p. 104). Both Presidents Jimmy Carter and Ronald Reagan perceived this airport to be of high strategic significance for the Soviet Union and Cuba, given its proximity to the shipping lanes utilized by oil tankers bound for the United States.

Grenada's domestic policies increasingly mirrored those found in Cuba. This is not surprising because Bishop had received Cuban backing in the 1960s and eventually became a close personal friend of Fidel Castro (*WP*, 9 November). Soon after the March 1979 coup, Grenada established diplomatic relations with Cuba and created a series of mass organizations like those found in Cuba (*YICA*, 1983, p. 91). No elections were held, the constitution was eliminated, and mass meetings became the principal form of communication between the leaders and the led. Despite these socialist manifestations and the rhetoric of Marxism-Leninism, over half of the economy remained in private hands, and Bishop seemed less inclined to move the country toward a more pronounced version of Marxist principles than did other members of the NJM, such as Bernard Coard, the deputy prime minister. These differences among the NJM leadership set the scene for the dramatic events that unfolded in October.

Leadership and Party Organization. A major rift among NJM leaders began to surface in late 1982. The central figures in the drama appear to have been Bishop, Coard, and Coard's wife, Phyllis. Both Deputy Prime Minister Coard and his wife are known to have been more doctrinaire Marxists than Bishop. They split with Bishop over his leadership and his direction of domestic policies, including his support of private industry as a means of strengthening the economy (*NYT*, 21 October). This was an important split because Coard also held the critical position of finance minister. By July 1982, Coard had resigned from the Central Committee because of dissatisfaction with Bishop's leadership and his belief that Bishop could never build a truly Marxist-Leninist party (*WP*, 9 November). He accused Central Committee and Political Bureau members of coming to meetings with "hands and minds swinging" (ibid.). The Central Committee met during 14–16 September, according to Donald McPhail, first secretary of the Grenadian embassy in Cuba, in order to "analyze the state of the Revolution," which "had reached a point of stagnation" (*NYT*, 30 October). By a vote of nine to one with three abstentions (one member of the Central Committee was ill), the committee voted on 14 September to allow Bishop to continue as head of state, but to have Coard privately take over control of the economy and party affairs. Bishop abstained from the vote, because he "needed time to think about it," even though the vote was binding. (Ibid.)

The source of discontent behind this September Central Committee meeting lay in Bishop's continuing leadership problems, the weak functioning of the Central Committee and the Political Bureau, and Bishop's apparent lack of commitment or ability to transform the NJM into a truly Leninist party. Among the documents captured after the U.S. invasion of Grenada on 25 October was a typewritten summary, dated 20 September, of the October 1982 plenary meetings of the NJM Central Committee. This document emphasized that the previous four and a half years had "proven that Comrade Bishop lacks the precise qualities and strengths...to transform the Party into a Leninist one." Bishop lacked "(1) a Leninist level of organization and discipline; (2) great depth in ideological clarity; (3) brilliance in strategy and tactics; and (4) the capacity to exercise Leninist supervision, control and guidance of all areas of work of the party." The document concluded that "the only comrade with precisely these strengths is Comrade Bernard Coard." (Ibid., 7 November.)

Events proceeded rapidly after the September meeting. On 27 September, just prior to his visit to Czechoslovakia and Cuba, Bishop apparently accepted the notion of joint leadership of the NJM. When he returned on 8 October, he was no longer in favor. This produced the train of events that led to his arrest on 13 October, and his death on 19 October, the day he was shot in a crowd that had released him from house detention. When the armed forces killed Bishop, they also shot Unison Whiteman, foreign minister and cofounder of the NJM; Norris Bain, housing minister; Jacqueline Creft, education minister; and two union leaders, Vincent Noel and Fitzroy Bain.

The collapse of the NJM came swiftly. When Bishop returned from his trip to Czechoslovakia and Cuba, he apparently started a rumor that the Coards were plotting to kill him. This rumor caused major tension within the Central Committee. When Bishop, at a special Central Committee meeting of 13 October called to discuss the issues of joint leadership and the alleged plot, failed to deny that he had instigated the rumor, the meeting ended with Bishop being placed under house arrest. On 14 October, the official

Grenadian radio reported that Coard had resigned to end the leadership struggle, but other reports indicated that Coard had taken power (Congressional Research Service, 9 November). On 16 October, Radio Free Grenada announced that the army had assumed control of the island and indicated that Bishop had been deposed (*NYT*, 17 October). On 17 October, General Austin announced that Bishop was "at home and quite safe," but that he would be turned out of office unless he agreed to share power with his deputy. "The main problem," Austin stated, "is that Comrade Bishop had allowed his power and authority to go to his head." (Ibid., 18 October.) Reportedly on 18 October, the NJM formally asked Bishop to continue as prime minister; Bishop replied that "he would consider that offer but was not willing to talk" (ibid., 30 October). The next day brought his death.

After the deaths of 19 October, the Grenadian military, under the leadership of General Austin, emerged as the dominant power group. By 20 October, a 24-hour curfew had been imposed by the Grenadian army, which announced that it would govern by a military council, headed by Austin. Cuba condemned Bishop's killing in strong terms; Soviet criticism was less vociferous. By 21 October, the whereabouts of Coard was reported to be unknown, and the Grenadian military expressed great concern over a possible attack by U.S. forces. The members of the thirteen-nation Caribbean Community agreed on 23 October to cancel trade agreements with Grenada and to expel it from the Community, and the Organization of Eastern Caribbean States requested help from the United States. These events, in addition to the 24-hour "shoot on sight" curfew imposed by Grenada's military council, led U.S. forces, along with the troops of six Caribbean states, to invade Grenada on 25 October in order to protect the lives of some one thousand U.S. citizens on the island and to restore the island's democratic institutions. Bernard Coard and Gen. Hudson Austin were eventually captured and turned over to Grenada's new security forces. (Ibid., 7 November.)

Domestic Party Affairs. Under NJM leadership, the economy continued to reflect both a socialist and private-sector orientation. This mixed economy contained both positive and negative features. On the positive side, Deputy

Prime Minister Coard announced at a national conference organized by the PRG in February to discuss the proposed 1983 budget that the island's economic growth during 1982 had reached a record 5.5 percent (*FBIS*, 25 February). Tourism Minister Lyden Ramdhanny stated in August that tourism was up 35 percent during the first five months of 1983 over 1982, a bad year in the tourist industry (*Los Angeles Times*, 5 August). In August, the Grenada Beach Hotel reopened, and during the celebration of the event Bishop stressed the important role that tourism would have to play in providing foreign exchange earnings and creating new jobs (*FBIS*, 3 August). As some observers noted, the Grenadian economy had improved considerably since the revolution: 45 miles of badly needed roads had been completed, fruit and vegetable exports had tripled, dependence on food imports had dropped by 12 percent (*Time*, 2 May). Food imports, for example, fell from $4.2 million in January to $2.8 million in February. The NJM had also achieved a 50 percent increase in fresh water production. (*JPRS*, 27 June.) Grenada also had a $2.5 million surplus in 1982; half of this was used to repay the country's outstanding debts. Prime Minister Bishop, meanwhile, continued to stress that the PRG would emphasize human resources, suggesting labor-intensive over capital-intensive growth formulas (*FBIS*, 10 March).

Yet critics of the NJM's economic leadership noted in July that economic conditions were by no means completely positive (*JPRS*, 1 September). High inflation, unemployment, low productivity in the agricultural and industrial sectors, and the emigration of professionals and skilled workers plagued the economy. Despite the drop in food imports, the overall value of imports rose in early 1983, leaving Grenada with a balance of trade problem (*St. George's Free West Indian*, 14 May). The NJM claimed to have reduced unemployment on the island from 49 to 14 percent, but critics noted that the decline resulted from the shifting of the unemployed into the People's Militia, which was to be expanded from 4,000 to 8,000 during 1983. This doubling of the militia tended to inflate the PRG's payroll while lowering unemployment statistics. (Ibid.) And despite the rise in tourism, the overall low rate of tourism, which used to produce 60 percent of the island's hard currency revenues, continued to undermine the PRG's growth potential.

The PRG's economic performance during 1983 reflected other problems, which undoubtedly were a source of great dissatisfaction to Coard and, consequently, of his opposition to Bishop's leadership. In March, Coard described productivity in the PRG's state-run enterprises as low, noting that 50 percent of them had not achieved their targets. Eight had showed a loss of $2.2 million, among them the National Fisheries Company, which fell 82 percent short of its 1982 objectives. The state-run Grenada Farms Corporation (GFC), which operated 23 government-owned farms comprising 3,967 acres, also fared poorly in 1982. It lost $1.5 million, or 176 percent of its output of $851,500. Coard attributed the GFC's problems to "poor organization and management"; other sources stated that lack of worker incentives was another major problem (*FBIS*, 23 March). Coard cited motivation as a huge problem for the PRG's agricultural workers, noting that wages averaged $8.50 per day, while the workers produced $3.00 to $4.00 a day in agricultural output (*Daily Gleaner*, Kingston, 16 July). In a related matter, the National Cooperative Development Agency reported in March that four cooperatives, a sector that had expanded significantly since 1979 and a major pillar of the economy, had closed down as a result of the poor academic level of cooperative members (*St. George's Free West Indian*, 13 March).

In March, the NJM began to shift leftward on economic matters. A new investment code moved the government into infrastructure and most foreign trade and gave private capital incentives to invest in new tourist hotels or factories. In effect, the code prohibited the private sector from investing in utilities, radio and television stations, infrastructural activities of all types, national airlines, and telecommunications and from trading in certain strategic and basic commodities. (*FBIS*, 5 April.) Several businessmen doubted the ability and willingness of the private sector to invest in Grenadian industry because the island was so small and the other Caribbean islands were more developed and competitive. The business sector also noted that tourism was not an attractive growth sector, given the low rate of hotel occupancy (running at about 25 percent), which was in part a result of the NJM's political style and reactions in the United States. (Ibid.) The business sector continued to criticize government officials at all levels for their lack of

qualifications, something revolutionary enthusiasm cannot replace (*WP*, 22 April). The PRG's principal sources of foreign aid continued to be communist countries.

On the political front, the PRG continued to receive criticism for the absence of elections and a constitution and for the high number of political detainees. Bishop promised elections, but refused to be pinned down specifically (ibid.). In an effort to ease these criticisms and to establish a base for the rapprochement with the United States, the PRG announced the release of several political prisoners in late December 1982 (*FBIS*, 27 December). Criticism of the PRG's violation of human rights nevertheless continued (*Daily Gleaner*, 20 July). As for possible elections, the prime minister's more flexible approach was offset by Phyllis Coard at a press conference in Port-of-Spain on 27 May when she remarked that the Grenadians were not discussing holding a general election (ibid., 18 July). Earlier, on 4 June, the PRG announced the appointment of a five-member commission to draft a new constitution; the prime minister pointed out that this new constitution would "pave the way" for general elections (*FBIS*, 7 July). The differences between Bishop and Mrs. Coard in interpreting the meaning of the new constitution illustrate the rising tensions within the leadership that led to the October coup, for with Bishop's announcement came his prediction that elections would follow within eighteen months to two years (ibid., 7 June). The announcement of the new constitution coincided with Bishop's visit to Washington, during which he sought to ease the PRG's strains with the United States. Some observers believe the visit displeased the Coards and other radicals, especially because Bishop was largely unsuccessful in his efforts (*NYT*, 21 October).

Bishop's overthrow and the subsequent U.S. invasion led to the formation of a nine-member "advisory council," appointed by Sir Paul Scoon, the governor general. A principal mandate of the advisory council is to prepare Grenada for elections, which could include participation by the NJM. By year's end, elements of the NJM were meeting and considering the possibility of resurrecting the party (ibid., 26 December). But the NJM's turbulent history had left it in great disarray, with its members feeling leaderless and betrayed. Yet they were sufficiently in agreement to call for a full trial of Bernard and Phyllis Coard,

Selwyn Strachan, and Chris de Riggs. Riggs was arrested in late November when he returned from New York, where he had been sent by the Revolutionary Military Council to attempt to rally support among the Grenadian community (*Latin America Regional Report*, 9 December). The problem in bringing these individuals to trial lay in insufficient admissible evidence that they and the army officials conspired to murder Bishop and the other NJM leaders (ibid.).

Auxiliary or Front Organizations. Little information is available on the PRG's auxiliary or front organizations. A Grenada-USSR friendship society was launched in Grenada in January (*FBIS*, 17 January), and the Grenada Peace Council was elected to the Bureau of the World Peace Council in July (ibid., 21 July).

International Views, Positions, and Activities. The PRG, under Bishop's leadership, relied heavily on Cuban, East German, and Soviet economic aid, although it also received support from the European Economic Community and Canada (*WP*, 24 April). Cuban assistance included help in organizing the people's militia; teachers, doctors, and dentists in the countryside; and construction workers for the new international airport, which was due to open in 1984. At the time of the U.S. invasion, 784 Cubans were in Grenada, of whom 636 were construction workers, with others in public health, education, fishing, transport, trade, culture, and communications (*NYT*, 31 October). Among the 784 Cubans, 43 were members of the armed forces; of these 22 were officers and the rest translators and other support personnel. Part of the work of the Cuban military contingent lay in training the militia. (Ibid.) The Cubans were reputed to be financing as much as half of the $71 million cost of the new airport, in addition to supplying construction workers, and they had contributed a large new antenna for Radio Free Grenada (*Los Angeles Times*, 5 August). Additional Cuban aid came in the form of 10,000 units of furniture (*FBIS*, 17 February) and housing facilities for members of Grenada's armed forces (ibid., 18 January).

As might be expected, these economic ties were paralleled by close diplomatic and political relations between the PRG and Cuba. Examples include Prime Minister Bishop's attendance at celebrations in Cuba of the thirtieth anniversary of Castro's 1953 attack on the Moncada Army Barracks, which marked the beginning of the Fidelista revolution (ibid., 2 August). Bishop also strongly supported Cuba's leadership of the Nonaligned Movement. Cuba, in return, backed the PRG's foreign policy, including Bishop's attempt to establish better relations with the United States (ibid., 2 June) and the PRG's emphasis on a possible U.S. invasion throughout the early months of 1983 (ibid., 6 April).

The Soviets signed contracts with the PRG in June, in keeping with the Grenada-Soviet agreement on economic and technical cooperation reached in 1982, to facilitate joint efforts in education, communications, water supply, and seaport development (ibid., 17 June). Specific projects involved a satellite earth station, to be financed under a $7.5 million line of credit, a three-month feasibility study on the water supply system, a seaport development project, and sixteen Soviet educators to teach science and math (ibid., 5 July). The Soviets also gave the PRG some small arms and a crop duster (*Time*, 2 May). The East Germans offered to build a new telephone system (ibid.). Grenada's diplomatic relations with the USSR remained close until Bishop's overthrow and the U.S. invasion. Bishop visited the USSR in April, meeting with Soviet Foreign Minister Andrei Gromyko (*FBIS*, 18 April). Both parties expressed concern over developments in Central America.

The U.S. invasion of Grenada uncovered documents indicating five secret military cooperation agreements between the Bishop government and Cuba, the Soviet Union, and North Korea. The agreements would have provided $37 million in additional military equipment to Grenada, plus a permanent delegation of 27 Cuban military advisers. The Soviets planned to ship $27 million in military equipment and North Korea $12 million. The Cubans would have provided training for the armed forces. (*NYT*, 6 November.) At the time of the coup, there were 49 Soviet personnel on the island (ibid., 30 October).

The Cubans probably did not participate in the coup against Bishop. The Castro government, long a Bishop ally, denounced his overthrow in clear terms, and some members of the Cuban Politburo argued strongly that Cuba should break relations with Grenada's new Revolutionary Military Council (ibid., 28 October). Soviet reactions to the Bishop overthrow were less clear. A flurry of activity occurred between Soviet embassy personnel and Bishop's opponents in the days before the coup (*CSM*, 2 November). A trip to the Soviet Union by Bishop's opponents was called off three weeks before the coup, suggesting that the Soviets may have known what was happening to Bishop. And official Soviet condemnation of the U.S. invasion was made at a relatively low level. The Cubans voiced deep concern at the highest government levels (*NYT*, 26 and 27 October).

Prior to the U.S. invasion in October, the PRG established economic and political ties with other communist countries. The East Germans provided $4 million worth of vehicles in July (*FBIS*, 26 July), and the North Koreans agreed to cooperate in the fields of irrigation and agriculture (ibid., 21 April). In addition to visiting North Korea during 1983, Prime Minister Bishop also traveled to Hungary, Vietnam, and Yugoslavia. Ten Grenadian youth departed the island for one-year leadership training courses in the Soviet Union, East Germany, and Cuba (ibid., 16 September), and the five best workers in the PRG were awarded a one-month holiday in the USSR (*JPRS*, 11 July).

Prime Minister Bishop stressed the need for normal diplomatic relations with the United States and toward that end paid a visit to Washington in June. He met with National Security Council chief William Clark and Deputy Secretary of State Kenneth Dam (*Latin America Regional Report*, 17 June). Although the contents of the meetings remained secret, Bishop described them as successful in laying the groundwork for renewed bilateral relations (*FBIS*, 10 June). At the same time, the PRG continued its criticism of U.S. policy in the Caribbean and Central America, especially U.S. hostility toward Nicaragua and the exclusion of Grenada from the U.S. Caribbean Basin aid and trade program (ibid., 6 April). It is likely that Bishop's moderate policies, including his attempt at rapprochement with the United States contributed to his downfall.

W. Raymond Duncan
State University of New York
College at Brockport

Guadeloupe

Population. 320,000 (estimate, French embassy)
Party. Communist Party of Guadeloupe (Parti Communiste Guadeloupéen; PCG)
Founded. 1944 as a section of the French Communist Party; 1958 as an independent party
Membership. 3,000 (estimate, Hoover Institution)
Secretary General. Guy Daninthe
Politburo. 12 members
Status. Legal
Last Congress. Seventh, 1980
Last Elections. 1981 French National Assembly elections, 38.6 percent, 1 of 3 deputies (Ernest Moutoussamy); 20 February 1983 Conseil Régional elections, 22.6 percent, 11 of 41 seats; 1983 municipal elections, 6 of 34 mayors

Auxiliary Organizations. Union of Guadeloupan Communist Youth (UJCG), General Confederation of Labor (CGT), Union of Guadeloupan Women (UFG)
Publications. *L'Etincelle* (weekly); *Madras* (published by UFG)

The PCG was founded in 1944 as a section of the French Communist Party (PCF). Fourteen years later it transformed itself into an independent party with very close ties with the PCF. In 1983, it celebrated the twenty-fifth anniversary of its independence. The pleasures of the occasion were nonetheless diminished by a difficult economic situation, including an unemployment rate of almost 30 percent, an increase in anonymous violence, including attacks from noncommunist supporters of independence, and growing disappointment with the Socialist government in Paris.

Leadership and Party Organization. Celebrations of the twenty-fifth anniversary of the founding in 1958 of the PCG were led by Guy Daninthe, general secretary, Christian Céleste, secretary of the Central Committee, Jean-Claude Lombion, general secretary of the UJCG (which had celebrated its fifteenth birthday in December 1982), and Daniel Génies, chairman of the eleven-member PCG delegation in the Conseil Général. Joining them was Claude Morvan, CGT general secretary, and the UFG. Congratulations came from communist parties of Vietnam, USSR, France, Japan, and Italy, and from the Democratic Revolutionary Front of El Salvador and elsewhere.

Ernest Moutoussamy emerged as an important spokesman for party interests. He received more coverage in the party newspaper than did any other single member. As a deputy in the French National Assembly, he raised many questions concerning Guadeloupe and the other overseas departments. Party members also paid tribute to Gerty Archimède, a PCG leader who died in 1980, by setting up a committee to establish a museum in her honor at Basse-Terre, the capital, where she practiced law.

On 20 February, elections were held for the Conseil Régional, created by the law of 31 December 1982. It may become more important than the Conseil Général because it suggests ways to adapt French legislation to Guadeloupan realities, and it must be consulted about proposed agreements between France and other Caribbean states. For purposes of the single-round election, the PCG reaffirmed its support for the French alliance between the French Socialist Party (PS) and the PCF. It put forward 41 candidates.

Although all parties of the Left won 50.19 percent of the vote (*L'Etincelle*, 26 February), the presence of small parties and groups prevented the PCG and PS from gaining a majority of seats. The PCG won 11 out of 41 and the socialists 9. The opposition Rassemblement pour la République (RPR) and Union for French Democracy (UDF) won 21, giving them the majority and thus the presidency of the council.

Less than a month later, on 6 and 13 March, municipal elections were held, and the communists presented lists of candidates in nineteen towns. The voters re-elected the communist councils in the six towns where they were already in power and also elected combined PCG and PS lists in two other towns. Four more PCG members were elected to the councils as minority representatives. As a result, out of 34 mayors, who are elected by the councils, 6 are PCG, 5 PS, and 6 RPR. Several other groupings control the remaining positions.

Simmering tensions between the PCG and the PS came further into the open at Bouillantes, where a communist who expected to be supported by the PS for mayor claimed he was doublecrossed by the PS council members.

Domestic Party Affairs. The anger over the Bouillantes election stoked the growing PCG criticism of the Socialist government of François Mitterrand. Secretary General Daninthe and others said they were beginning to believe the Socialists in power would betray the workers. Prime Minister Pierre Mauroy visited the islands as did Georges Lemoine, the state secretary responsible for the overseas departments. Party members complained to them about the economic situation.

Guadeloupe's economy was threatened by a recommendation, made by a government committee, to close the Beauport sugar mill, a major purchaser of sugarcane. The PCG organized protest meetings as did other political organizations. The concerted action helped convince the government to keep the mill in operation for another three years. As the government prepared its ninth development plan, the PCG also made suggestions about increased aid to Guadeloupe's economy.

The party continued to resist and to criticize proponents of immediate independence. It condemned explosions in May and in November that killed people and damaged property. These acts of terrorism, allegedly the work of independence groups, could never help Guadeloupe, party leaders said.

International Views, Positions, and Activities. The PCG supported the actions in El Salvador of antigovernment groups such as the Democratic Revolutionary Front. In April, Ramón Cardona, a Front representative, gave a press conference at Pointe-à-Pitre, Guadeloupe's economic capital, and the youth group UJGC showed a film on El Salvador.

To permit closer ties with other nearby states, Ernest Moutoussamy, PCG member and the is-

land's deputy to the French National Assembly, requested that the government permit Guadeloupe sports organizations to enter into direct relations with other Caribbean sports associations. He also requested permission for Guadeloupe groups to join international sports organizations separately from France.

Moutoussamy and other members of the PCG criticized France for its involvement in Chad but reserved their strongest denunciations for the U.S. invasion of Grenada. In full-page articles in the party newspaper and in speeches given before special public meetings, "USA Go Home" was the loudest and most popular slogan. The communists steadily condemned deployment of new U.S. missiles in Western Europe and circulated a petition to strengthen the anti-missile effort. The party lent its complete support to the antinuclear peace movement.

Brian Weinstein
Howard University

Guatemala

The communist party in Guatemala, renamed the Guatemalan Party of Labor (Partido Guatemalteco del Trabajo; PGT) in 1950, originated in the predominantly communist-controlled Socialist Labor Unification founded in 1921. The PGT operated legally between 1951 and 1954, playing an active role in the administration of President Jacobo Arbenz. Outlawed in 1954 following the overthrow of Arbenz, it has since operated underground. Internal disagreements over the proper role of armed struggle culminated in a major party schism in 1978 and the formation of a Leadership Nucleus Cell that carries out independent guerrilla actions. Although the PGT has

some influence among students, intellectuals, and workers, its role in national affairs is insignificant. According to U.S. intelligence sources, the PGT's several factions contain about 750 members.

The Year in Brief. The Guatemalan political scene was dominated in 1983 by the continuing struggle between various Marxist-led guerrilla groups and counterinsurgency operations by the military. General Efraín Ríos Montt's government began the year confident that Guatemala's guerrilla movement was virtually dead. The systematic repression used to control the guerrilla threat following Ríos Montt's accession to power in March 1982 gave way to a program of resettlement and pacification in the Indian highlands, with "security" organized by the armed forces and guaranteed by local civil defense militia. After less than a year in power, Ríos Montt was considered by many observers to be "the success story" of Central American politics (*CSM*, 23 February). Although estimates of the number of people killed in political violence in 1982 ranged from 1,300 to 5,000, with another 35,000–40,000 persons displaced in refugee camps in Mexico, the Guatemalan army appeared to have succeeded in winning the war against a powerful Marxist insurgency involving an estimated 4,000 guerrillas and their supporters (*Time*, 23 May).

Despite evidence of guerrilla activity in January, high-ranking military officers insisted that insurgents' actions were "sporadic" and that the situation throughout the country was "under control" (AFP, 30 January). The guerrilla organizations comprising the Guatemalan National Revolutionary Unity (Unidad Revolucionaria Nacional Guatemalteca; URNG)—a guerrilla alliance proclaimed in February 1982—declared a "military truce" during the pope's visit to Guatemala in March. On 23 March, Ríos Montt lifted the state of siege, marking the first anniversary of the coup that put him in power. URNG spokesmen predicted that the Ríos Montt program of "democratic restoration" would fail and that conditions favorable to "a definite reaffirmation of the people's revolutionary war" were appearing (*Libertad*, San José, 25–31 March). In June, Guatemala's foreign minister told special U.S. envoy Richard Stone that dialogue with guerrilla groups was "not viable, significant or necessary for Guatemala, particularly as subversion here has been defeated and has largely disappeared" (ACAN, 13 June).

On 8 August, Ríos Montt was replaced by Gen. Oscar Humberto Mejía Víctores as head of state. According to military spokesmen, the removal of Ríos Montt was "not a coup d'etat" but "a change of authority at the highest level" (ibid., 10 August). The new government confirmed that guerrilla activity had been "practically eliminated" by the previous government and was "only a nuisance" to the armed forces.

In September, guerrilla leaders met "to reorient their future action and launch a new offensive." According to the army's information chief, the rebels transferred their major operations from the highland departments of Quiché, Huehuetenango, San Marcos, and Quetzaltenango to the country's northern region, especially the Petén area, "due to the armed forces' strict control over the highlands" (*El Imparcial*, 23 September). Military sources reported "increased guerrilla activity" at a press conference on 4 October. An army spokesman admitted that the guerrillas still had support bases, but civilian self-defense patrols, currently 50,000 strong, had been created "to defend the civilian population" and "to neutralize those who sympathize with the rebel groups" (ACAN, 4 October).

Guatemala experienced an escalation of violence during the latter part of the year. Military sources reported in October that during Mejía Víctores's first two months in power, 180 guerrillas had been killed in skirmishes; the government admitted to 30 casualties among security forces. Human rights organizations reported that over 50 people were kidnapped in various parts of the country during the same period (*Prensa Libre*, 16 October). As of early December, the official death toll for 1983 was 472 guerrillas, 90 members of the armed forces (including nine officers), 32 civil defense patrolmen, and 60 civilians (*Diario el Gráfico*, 9 December). These figures contrast markedly with those provided by nongovernmental sources, which place the figure in excess of 1,000, excluding noncombatants. During December, various guerrilla forces staged effective military and political operations in the capital, Quiché, San Marcos, Huehuetenango, Chimaltenango, Alta and Baja Verapaz, and Petén. At year's end, the Guatemalan military's counterinsurgency plan, Firmness '83, appeared to have fallen short of reducing in quantifiable terms the size of Guatemala's guerrilla forces or the areas in which they effectively operate.

Politically, Mejía Víctores has pledged to legalize political parties, although he stated in August that "the communist party is still prohibited from functioning by law" (*Prensa Libre*, 27 August). In December, the Supreme Electoral Tribunal announced that elections for a constituent assembly had been tentatively set for 1 July 1984.

Guerrilla and General Violence. As part of their counterinsurgency strategy, recent military governments in Guatemala have downplayed the importance of guerrilla and communist operations. Press censorship continued in 1983. Apart from official army communiqués and local press reports, in which guerrilla groups are not identified by name, news about guerrilla and clandestine party activity is found in bulletins and political manifestos issued by the various guerrilla organizations and opposition movements and infrequent statements by church and human rights groups.

Four guerrilla groups have been active in Guatemala in recent years. The Revolutionary Armed Forces is the military arm of the PGT (see below). The Rebel Armed Forces (Fuerzas Armadas Rebeldes; FAR) was a military commission of the PGT when it was originally formed in 1962. Three fronts were established, one made up of PGT members, one led by rebel army officers from an abortive 1960 uprising, and one made up of student (mostly PGT) youth. The FAR split in 1965. The army officer front left, and the student front disintegrated. In 1966, the remainder of the FAR split from the PGT, taking with it most of the party's youth. In the late 1970s, FAR developed considerable influence in the trade union movement, and its activists played a key role in the formation of the Central Nacional de Trabajadores and the broad-based National Committee for Labor Unity, both of which have been subjected to heavy repression since 1978. Former FAR members have provided the founding nucleus for Guatemala's other major guerrilla groups. FAR was active in 1983 primarily in Guatemala City, Chimaltenango, and the remote Petén region. It is believed to have fewer than 200 members, plus several hundred sympathizers. According to the FAR's principal commander, Pablo Monsanto, the revolutionary movement in Guatemala requires separate but complementary military and political organizations (*Intercontinental Press*, 31 January). In an analysis of the August coup, the FAR predicted that the Mejía Víctores government "will be just another dictatorship...whose goals include a continued effort to annihilate revolutionary organizations and to participate, together with the Honduran and Salvadoran armies, in Reagan's warmongering adventure in Central America" (AFP, 10 August). In its most spectacular actions of 1983, the FAR kidnapped the sisters of Ríos Montt (29 June) and Mejía Víctores (10 September). In a manifesto published as a condition for their release, the FAR called for the working masses to "assert themselves against imperialist intervention...and join the process of popular

revolutionary war" (*Prensa Libre*, 19 October). FAR fronts attacked military patrols, occupied villages, conducted sabotage missions, and carried out propaganda activities, especially in the departments of Chimaltenango and Petén. In December, FAR units claimed to have inflicted 86 government casualties, including 45 dead, in various operations in the Petén. A FAR communiqué declared that the intensification of its activity coincided with the United Nations' condemnation of human rights violations in Guatemala (ACAN, 23 December).

A third guerrilla organization is the Armed People's Organization (Organización del Pueblo en Armas; ORPA), many of whose founders split from FAR in 1972. ORPA prepared for eight years before launching its first military actions in September 1979. ORPA's principal leader is Gaspar Ilón, one of the few survivors of a PGT rural guerrilla front smashed in 1961. Unlike the Guerrilla Army of the Poor, ORPA has no mass organizations and operates primarily as a military entity. Other guerrilla leaders have criticized ORPA's lack of political organization, which they claim has reduced its overall effectiveness. Although ORPA claimed credit for various attacks in the capital in February, May, and July, the movement has never fully recovered from the destruction of its urban network in late 1981. ORPA's rural fronts continue to operate in the southwestern part of Guatemala, especially in the departments of San Marcos, Quetzaltenango, Sololá, Totonicapán, Chimaltenango, and Retalhuleu.

In April, ORPA claimed credit for inflicting 154 casualties during guerrilla encounters with troops in various parts of the country in March and April, including skirmishes in the western departments of Quiché and Huehuetenango. ORPA also interrupted twenty radio stations and several television broadcasts in a propaganda campaign intended to "break the wall of silence about guerrilla accomplishments the government tries to maintain by censoring the press" (*Excelsior*, Mexico City, 30 April).

In an interview commemorating the fourth anniversary of ORPA's operations, Ilón contended that the movement "has made great strides in carrying out its objectives." He claimed that through September ORPA's operations against army and government installations had resulted in over 244 casualties, including dead and wounded, and "severe" economic losses for the government. He added that ORPA had inflicted over 600 casualties in rural areas, occupied 73 sites, and carried out "hundreds" of military harassing operations (*FBIS*, 29 September). On 7 December, ORPA guerrillas carried out simultaneous attacks on five police posts in Guatemala City, killing one inspector and wounding six policemen. In leaflets distributed to the media, ORPA implied that it would be launching new attacks on security forces and warned people to stay away from military installations (ACAN, 15 December). On 23 December, urban guerrillas belonging to ORPA attacked the government's public relations office in Guatemala City. ORPA spokesmen claimed that the equipment destroyed was being used by the army to "prepare misinformation and psychological warfare material" (*FBIS*, 27 December). ORPA publishes the clandestine newspaper *Erupción*.

The largest and most active of Guatemala's guerrilla organizations is the Guerrilla Army of the Poor (Ejército Guerrillero de los Pobres; EGP). The EGP's founders broke from FAR in the 1960s mainly because of differences over policy toward the Indian population. The EGP proper was formed in 1972. After a long period of only sporadic operations, the EGP began its phase of "continuous military actions" in 1980. It now operates on seven fronts and is the only guerrilla group to have a truly national organization. The EGP has an estimated 1,500 combatants, although some of its leaders claim as many as 3,000. The EGP operates primarily in the Indian highland departments of Quiché, Huehuetenango, Alta and Baja Verapaz, and Chimaltenango. The EGP's major activities in 1983 are discussed below.

In February 1982, Guatemala's four major guerrilla groups proclaimed the URNG. The URNG's political platform promised to end repression, racial discrimination, and economic domination by the rich; guaranteed the establishment of a truly representative government; and adopted a nonaligned foreign policy. There is less agreement among the groups on the question of how to combine political and military work. The URNG declared that the only path open to the Guatemalan people was a "revolutionary people's war." To this end, they called for the formation of "a great front of patriotic unity." In response to the URNG's request, Guatemalan exiles in Mexico City organized the Committee of Patriotic Unity (Comité Guatemalteco de Unidad Patriótica; CGUP). The CGUP is headed by Luís Tejera Gómez and contains representative leaders from the primary opposition political forces in Guatemala, including the United Revolutionary Front, the Democratic Front Against Repression, and the Directorate of the National Committee of Labor Unity.

In a communiqué released in Havana on the first anniversary of its creation, the URNG reiterated its intent to "qualitatively strengthen the struggle for the people's national liberation" (Havana international service, 6 February). The URNG's annual report claimed that the Guatemalan government has employed "all sorts of Israeli, U.S., and Argentine counterinsurgency techniques, including genocide, the scorched earth policy, and various kinds of psychological warfare." According to the URNG, the government lost 1,489 men and considerable military equipment through the combined operations of the FAR, ORPA, and the EGP in 1982 (*Excelsior*, 14 February).

Following Mejía Víctores's accession to power, the URNG met to rechart its strategy. Sources admitted that the leadership also reviewed the internal divisions that have persisted within the organization and the appearance of other new, small guerrilla movements (ACAN, 19 August). In September, the URNG charged that Guatemala had become "a docile instrument of U.S. military intervention in Central America," and that Gen. Mejía Víctores was "beginning to play an active military and political role in defense of the Reagan administration's policy and in pursuit of U.S. interests" (*Barricada*, Managua, 19 September; Havana international service, 20 September). URNG spokesmen called the U.S. military action in Grenada "a flagrant violation of international law," and "an arrogant implementation of the U.S. government's interventionist plans to intimidate Cuba, reverse the Sandinist people's revolution, and exterminate the revolutionary processes in El Salvador and Guatemala." The organization called for "the elimination of any extremist or sectarian deviation" and "a broad and flexible policy of alliances at the national and international levels." (AFP, 7 November.)

Politically motivated killings involving leftist groups and right-wing paramilitary organizations have been a common feature of Guatemalan life since the mid-1960s. Political life became increasingly violent after Gen. Romeo Lucas

García assumed the presidency in 1978. The systematic assassination of people in opinion-making positions by self-proclaimed death squads, such as the Secret Anticommunist Army, has decimated university faculties, student associations, rural cooperatives, trade unions, peasant leagues, and the leadership of moderate and left-of-center political organizations. Assassinations and "disappearances" continued in 1983, although it is generally agreed that urban death squad activity, which church and human rights organizations have charged is directly controlled by the government, declined somewhat after Ríos Montt came to power. Groups such as Guatemala's Human Rights Commission, the Peasants' Unity Committee (CUC), and the Democratic Front Against Repression issued communiqués periodically in 1983, charging the government with mass murders, attacks on refugee camps, kidnappings, and increased repression in general. In September, the auxiliary bishop of Guatemala denounced the worsening of repression, charging that in the first 40 days of the Mejía Víctores government, 75 civilians were killed in politically related incidents and another 35 were "missing" (Havana international service, 22 September). The Democratic Front accused Mejía Víctores of engaging in "some sort of macabre competition with his predecessors," and peasant spokesmen for the CUC charged the army with unleashing "a chain of persecution" against Indian peasants in Alta Verapaz (El Día, Mexico City, 25 October). Kidnappings and "disappearances" continue to be a disturbingly common occurrence in Guatemala. The rector of Sán Carlos University announced in December that two professors were missing, presumably among sixteen persons abducted during the final days of the year (Havana international service, 27 December). For its part, the government claimed that some 700 guerrillas, most of them reportedly "active fighters," took advantage of the amnesty decreed in August by the new government (Times of the Americas, 21 December).

Leadership and Organization. Little information is available on PGT leaders or structure. Since 1972, two general secretaries and nineteen ranking members of the Central Committee have "disappeared," apparently the victims of assassination. In 1978, the leadership split over the question of the proper role of armed struggle in the revolutionary process. The dissident faction,

known as the PGT–Leadership Nucleus (PGT–LN), is headed by Mario Sánchez. According to Sánchez, the party itself must become the communists' organ for armed revolutionary struggle (El Nuevo Diario, Managua, 6 October 1982). The PGT–LN is a member of the URNG. The Moscow-oriented faction of the PGT is headed by Carlos González. Other prominent members of the PGT's Central Committee are Antonio Castro, Otto Sánchez, Daniel Ríos, José Cardoza Aguilar, A. Bauer País, Antonio Fuentes, Pedro González Torres, and Pablo Hernández.

The PGT has a youth auxiliary, the Patriotic Youth of Labor (Juventud Patriótica del Trabajo; JPT). Student agitators are active at the secondary and university levels but disclaim direct affiliation with the PGT. Student leaders supported by the PGT have been unsuccessful in recent years in gaining control of the influential Association of University Students (AEU), although the AEU's statements on domestic issues tend to be strongly critical of the government and its inability to control right-wing extremists. Members of the JPT are believed to be active in the Robín García Student Front and other student organizations involved with the 31 January People's Front (FP–31), created in 1981 to combat the government at the political level. At a plenary meeting of the Central Committee in April, it was announced that the leader of the JPT had been killed "at the hands of henchmen of the military dictatorship" (IB, July).

The PGT also controls the clandestine Guatemalan Autonomous Federation of Trade Unions (FASGUA), an umbrella organization of some fifty small unions before the government drove it underground. FASGUA became an affiliate of the communist-front World Federation of Trade Unions in October 1974. Manuel Contreras, a founder of FASGUA and its representative to the National Committee for Labor Unity (CNUS) and to the Democratic Front Against Repression, was kidnapped on 2 June, according to the FP–31 (El Nuevo Diario, 24 June). The CNUS, which had the support of some seventy member unions, was the most important voice for organized labor in Guatemala until the late 1970s. Some observers believe that its militant activities resulted from increasing PGT influence within its ranks.

Domestic Attitudes and Activities. It is difficult to determine whether the PGT's Central Committee met on a regular basis during 1983.

Similarly, there are few sources that reveal the content of any political resolutions that may have been adopted. In order to characterize the PGT's attitudes on domestic and foreign issues, it is necessary to rely on statements of party leaders made in foreign publications or in occasional interviews published abroad. Clandestine bulletins attributed to the PGT appear occasionally in Guatemala, but their authenticity is questionable.

For over 26 of the party's 33 years of existence, it has been forced to work underground and subjected to varying levels of persecution. Despite such adverse conditions, the party claims a steady increase in influence among the masses, especially among workers, peasants, and other sectors of the population that it says are "suffering from capitalist oppression and exploitation."

Since its Fourth Congress in 1969, the PGT has adhered to the position that the revolution can triumph only through the use of force. Until May 1981, however, the party did not commit itself fully to armed struggle. The Political Commission of the Central Committee viewed as an important step the formation of the URNG and declared that no political-military organization on its own can achieve a revolutionary war of the people as a whole against the military (*IB*, May 1982). PGT leaders' unwillingness to devote themselves exclusively to developing the military potential of the party has been the source of internal dissension and has led to a number of splits in recent years. No faction is strong militarily, although the group headed by Carlos González maintains international ties with the Soviet bloc and residual influence in the trade union and student movements.

Although generally supportive of the URNG's efforts to achieve a revolutionary alliance, the PGT fears that the revolutionary movement is in danger of becoming isolated from the masses. González feels that a broad initiative is required to overcome "existing shortcomings and mistakes" connected with the political leadership of the armed struggle, especially the failure to involve the masses within the frame work of their own organizations (*FBIS*, 18 March). This task is closely linked to the settlement of problems pertaining to the development and consolidation of the party itself. According to González, the PGT is not yet part of the URNG, but "talks are taking place and a favorable atmosphere, aimed at expanding the process of building an alliance has been established" (ibid.).

At a plenary meeting in April, the PGT acknowledged the "considerable contribution" of the various guerrilla movements and the URNG as a whole to the development of the revolutionary process. However, the party favors the formation of "a single revolutionary front" and "renewed efforts to achieve tactical and strategic unity in order to work out a single plan and create a single leadership of the armed operations." The URNG has created the foundations for an even broader movement. Now, says the Central Committee, it is the PGT's task to "consolidate the relations between the party and the people's masses and to establish an alliance of all revolutionary forces." (*IB*, July.)

Not surprisingly, PGT leaders chose not to respond to the Guatemalan interior minister's announcement in April that the PGT and other leftist parties would have "full guarantees" to exercise their rights to participate in politics and elections (*Prensa Libre*, 8 April). According to the Political Organizations Statute promulgated on 23 March, the PGT would have to prove that it had at least 4,000 literate members and had party organizations in at least 50 towns and cities. Moreover, to register officially, the party would have to reveal the names of its principal leaders and its members. (*El Imparcial*, 3 May.)

The Central Committee has determined that "the political and military activity of the party, its armed formations and youth organization must be directed primarily against the reactionary army, which is the armed support of the dictatorship." According to the party, the army is becoming "more and more an instrument of repression" and, according to the military leaders themselves, sees its tasks as those of: (1) "defending the population, (2) "winning over the misled," and (3) "annihilating those who disagree" (*IB*, July). In Antonio Castro's view, Guatemala under Mejía Víctores's leadership has "once more elevated political terrorism to the level of state policy, with death squads regularly committing murders" (*FBIS*, 6 December). For his part, Mejía Víctores has denied the existence of death squads. In September, he charged that incidents of violence were "due to the fact that the PGT was celebrating its anniversary . . . and wanted to indicate that it is still operating" (ACAN, 29 September).

International Positions and Contacts. The PGT's positions on international issues follow those of the USSR closely. According to Otto Sánchez, Guatemalan communists view strengthening the party's solidarity with the Soviet Union and other socialist countries as their primary international duty. The party maintains that by steadfastly supporting the USSR, the international working class "strengthens its solidarity with all the peoples fighting for political emancipation, economic independence, democracy, peace and socialism" (*WMR*, April 1979).

The party's Central Committee declared in April that the principal danger in Central America is "that of direct military aggression by imperialism against Nicaragua and the spreading of the Salvadoran conflict throughout the region as a result of foreign intervention." It proclaimed that "militant, moral and material solidarity" with revolutionary peoples in the region must continue to be a central task of the party (*IB*, July). In a statement commemorating the party's founding, Carlos González denounced the "slavish behavior' of Mejía Víctores in providing his "unconditional support to the aggressive, adventurous, and provocative plans of the Americans in Central America." He reaffirmed the party's commitment to fight for world peace in the face of Washington's "insane policy." (Havana international service, 29 September.) Antonio Castro characterized the Grenadian operation as "a warning" to Cuba, Nicaragua, and the revolutionary forces in El Salvador and Guatemala (*FBIS*, 6 December).

The Guerrilla Army of the Poor. The EGP emerged out of discussions among former FAR members in exile. The first contingent of the EGP entered Guatemala in January 1972, and military operations began in November 1975. The EGP's membership is believed to have increased from an initial 300 to an estimated 1,500 in 1983. Six independent commands operate in the countryside, and one is active in Guatemala City. The movement's rural fronts were most active in the mountainous regions of Quiché and Huehuetenango in northwestern Guatemala; in Chimaltenango, Sololá, and Alta and Baja Verapaz in the central highlands; near Escuintla, along the tropical Pacific Coast; and to a lesser extent, in the department of Zacapa, where the guerrillas had their strongest support in the late 1960s. The EGP's commander in chief is Rolando Morán, 51, whose revolutionary career began in the ranks of the PGT. He later joined the FAR and then helped found the EGP.

The EGP's principal thesis is that the revolutionary war in Guatemala cannot be conceived without the mass participation of the people. In the absence of legal means for change, EGP leaders believe that securing the support and active participation of Guatemala's Indian population is decisive. The incorporation of the Indians into the people's war and the promotion of guerrilla methods of struggle by Indians in an effort to achieve their liberation is viewed by EGP theorists as Guatemala's fundamental contribution to revolution in Latin America.

According to EGP leader Carmelo Díaz, the EGP does not have separate political and military organizations. The movement consists of groups that conduct political work and also serve as combat units. According to Díaz, guerrillas operate in urban areas in commando-type combat groups in detachments of 20 to 30 men. For attacks on military barracks and rural operations, the EGP has specially trained groups numbering about 80 men. The EGP's rural fronts rely heavily on peasants to supply food and provide information concerning troop movements and actions taken by local civil militia. (*Latinskaia Amerika*, May 1982.)

EGP leaders now admit to making tactical errors in 1981 and early 1982. The movement's support in the Indian highlands in 1981 led it to believe that it could move quickly from the propaganda-harassment stage to one of general insurrection against the isolated Lucas García regime. In addition, the guerrilla offensive in El Salvador and the U.S. campaign against Nicaragua influenced the leadership to accelerate the pace of the "popular revolutionary war." The EGP admits that it was caught off guard by the 1982 coup and the effectiveness of the subsequent counterinsurgency campaign launched by the Ríos Montt government. The EGP was poorly prepared to defend its rural support bases or to evacuate peasants from the main areas of conflict. Guerrilla strategy now is to concentrate on "the annihilation of army units and the recovery of weapons" (*Latin America Regional Report*, 25 March). According to Morán, the EGP is in the stage of spreading the guerrilla war throughout the country. In terms of tactics, this means "harassment, attacks on local government, and the execution of enemy cadres." The EGP does not yet consider itself prepared to challenge the army over terrain and control of the masses. Previous plans to establish liberated zones in areas of long-standing guerrilla strength, such as the Ixil triangle in Quiché, are now seen as premature (*El Nuevo Diario*, 6 October 1982).

In a communiqué issued in San José in June, the EGP claimed that its various units carried out 78 operations during the first three months of 1983 in Quiché and Huehuetenango, inflicting 158 casualties on government forces. Most of these actions allegedly occurred "during repressive raids carried out by government troops against civilians" (Havana international service, 24 June). The EGP announced that the army lost 66 men in clashes between 1 June and 18 July (ibid., 26 August). The movement reported in August that "approximately 6,000 ground and air troops" had been mobilized in the central highlands to deny guerrilla forces access to key towns in the area (*La Razón*, 17 August). In October, an EGP bulletin issued in Managua charged that an Israeli weapons factory is being established in Guatemala to supply the armies of the region. The bulletin also stated that 300 Israeli advisers are working in Guatemala with the army and security forces (AFP, 10 October).

In November, Rolando Morán claimed that despite the Guatemalan military's efforts to achieve greater organization and technical expertise, it is "deeply corroded by its own contradictions, undermined by struggles among cliques, and demoralized by a lack of real prospects." According to Morán, the army is losing an average of a hundred men per month and is "resentful and frustrated" at not being able to eliminate the guerrilla movement (*FBIS*, 18 November).

On balance, the military's pacification program (Firmness '83) had some success in 1983. However, the guerrillas are not yet at the point of defeat and their combined forces continue to represent a serious threat to Guatemala's stability. The URNG forces are experienced and still enjoy the advantages of favorable terrain and supply routes through Mexico that are almost impossible to detect. On the other hand, guerrilla organizations have been obliged to rethink their strategy. The disagreements evident among different leaders indicate that the revolutionary movement in Guatemala has not yet achieved complete unity. At this moment, no clear advantage lies with either side.

Daniel L. Premo
Washington College

Guyana

Population. 900,000
Party. People's Progressive Party (PPP); Working People's Alliance (WPA)
Founded. PPP in 1950; WPA organized in 1973, became formal party in 1979
Membership. PPP: 100 leaders and several hundred militants above non-Marxist rank and file (estimated); WPA: 30 leaders (estimated)
Politburo. PPP: Cheddi Jagan (general secretary), Janet Jagan, Ram Karran, Feroze Mohamed, Pariag Sukhai, Clinton Collymore, Narbada Persaud, Isahak Basir, Rohit Persaud, Cyril Belgrave, Reepu Daman Persaud, and Harry Persaud Nokta; WPA: Clive Thomas, Walter Omawale, Moses Bhagwan, Eusi Kawayana, and Rupert Roopnarine
Status. Legal but harassed
Last Congress. PPP: Twenty-first, 31 July–2 August 1982

Last Election.   1980: PPP received 19.46 percent of vote and 10 of 65 seats in national assembly, and 35 of 169 seats in regional democratic councils. The WPA boycotted the elections.

Auxiliary Organizations.   PPP: Progressive Youth Organization (PYO), Women's Progressive Organization (WPO)

Publications.   PPP: *Mirror* (weekly) and *Thunder* (quarterly); WPA: *Dayclean* and *Open Word* (weeklies)

Guyana remains under the rule of Forbes Burnham and his People's National Congress (PNC), both overwhelmingly returned to power in the fraudulent 1980 elections. The depressed economy continued to deteriorate during 1983. Political opposition to the government came chiefly from the PPP, secondarily from the WPA and several other small parties, despite harassment by the government.

Cheddi Jagan remained the dominant opposition voice in Guyana, and the PPP was still primarily (but not exclusively) the party of the nation's Indo-Guyanese population. (The PNC is largely, but not entirely, the political organization of the Afro-Guyanese population.) The PPP, founded in 1950, has only been a professed Marxist-Leninist party since 1969 and now is "in the process of transforming from a mass but organizationally loose party into a Leninist party of the new type." One of the distinguishing characteristics of the PPP is the relatively disciplined Marxism-Leninism of the small number of top leaders and the ignorance of and indifference to that ideology of most Indo-Guyanese.

Jagan and the PPP receive strong backing from the PYO, which is described as a "training ground for young Communists" (*Mirror*, Georgetown, 12 September 1982). The PYO, under the leadership of First Secretary Navin Chandarpal, is a member of the Executive of the Soviet-front World Federation of Democratic Youth. The WPO is led by Janet Jagan, Gail Teixeira, and Indra Chandarpal. Both PPP auxiliaries focus on problems of employment and education, among other issues.

The PPP maintained its ongoing critique of the PNC, charging that the latter "is incapable of finding a solution to the grave social and economic crisis; production and productivity are decreasing instead of increasing" (ibid., 31 July). According to the PPP, "the core of the problem" in the nation's major and increasingly run-down and depressed industries—sugar and bauxite, hard hit by strikes during the year—is mismanagement (ibid., 24 July). "The blame rests with the incompetence, mismanagement, lack of

planning and corruption of the PNC regime" (ibid., 14 August). Jagan and his party repeatedly accused the PNC of indifference to the hunger, employment, safety, and human rights of the Guyanese people (ibid., 22 May, 1 May, 19 July; CANA, Bridgetown, 15 December). At one point, when condemning the government's inability or unwillingness to import food for the people, Jagan suggested that the PNC ought to let the private sector do it (*Mirror*, 26 June). One of the PNC's problems, according to the PPP, is its subservience to the United States, despite the fact that Burnham's party, with periodic anti-American campaigns, tries to fool people into thinking "the PNC concubine has turned around to fight its imperialist master" (ibid., 14 August). Repeatedly the PNC was attacked for giving in to the dictates of the International Monetary Fund. The only solution to Guyana's problems, as the PPP Central Committee concluded (once again) in December, is the formation of a broad government, a National Patriotic Front (CANA, Bridgetown, 28 December; *FBIS*, 29 December). "Unity without struggle and struggle without unity are both intellectual and fruitless," the *Mirror* editorialized on 31 July. "A principled, united struggle must be mounted for a free Guyana, for bread and social justice." The PPP regretted that "the WPA, which had first advocated socialism, anti-imperialism and democracy, has now gone back on those commitments and joined right-wing forces" (*Mirror*, 14 August).

The PPP is most active in the labor movement, particularly in the Guyana Agricultural and General Workers' Union (GAWU), headed by Ram Karran, the largest union in the country. In recent years the PPP-controlled GAWU has worked closely with three other smaller unions—the National Association of Agricultural, Commercial and Industrial Employees, the Clerical and Commercial Workers' Union, and the University of Guyana Staff Association—to protest what they considered the subservience to the government of the national Guyana Trades Union Congress (TUC). By September, the PPP reported three other unions had joined the dissidents, among them the Guyana Mine Workers Union (ibid. 11 September). The TUC congress in May took some "steps in the right direction," the PPP admitted, though much remains to be done (ibid., 29 May).

The PPP consistently adopted international positions that paralleled those of the Soviet Union. The world is "teetering on the brink of a nuclear cataclysm," because of the United States and the Reagan administration in particular (ibid., 19 June). The party condemned the U.S. intervention in Grenada and claimed that the action had created "an explosive situation in the Caribbean Basin" (Havana television, 19 December; *FBIS*, 20 December). During a visit to Caracas in June, Jagan told journalists that Guyana and Venezuela should "discuss programs and projects for mutual development" of their disputed Essequibo territory (Havana radio, 29 June; *FBIS*, 1 July).

The WPA. The WPA also called for unity in the struggle against "the illegal and tyrannical Burnham regime that has brought starvation and beri-beri sickness to Guyana" (*Caribbean Contact*, Bridgetown, March). According to the WPA, "the ruling party has succeeded in transforming the bauxite industry of Guyana from a branch plant of multinationals into a bauxite slum" as a result of "12 years of ill-informed political interference" (*Open Word*, Georgetown, 22 August). The party called on the PNC to import food, drugs, and other items needed to sustain the Guyanese people in these hard times (*Barbados Advocate*, Bridgetown, 17 May; *JPRS*, no. 2698). Increasing PNC repression of WPA activities led the party to charge there is "an undeclared state of emergency in Guyana" (*Barbados Advocate*, 8 August; *JPRS*, no. 2740). The WPA was particularly critical of PPP willingness to cooperate with the government on some issues and its failure to give adequate attention to multiracial labor developments that were not dominated by the PPP itself (*Open Word*, 6 June). As an advocate of unity against the Burnham government, the WPA was repeatedly critical of PPP efforts to brand the WPA as "just another right-wing party," although even some outside observers have noted a recent moderation in WPA positions "where a moderate, social-democratic wing seems to be now in control" (*Latin America Caribbean Report*, 23 July, 9 December). The WPA condemned the U.S. intervention in Grenada.

William E. Ratliff
Hoover Institution

Haiti

Population. 5.7 million in Haiti; about 1 million outside Haiti
Party. United Party of Haitian Communists (Parti Unifié des Communistes Haïtiens; PUCH)
Founded. 1934; transformed into PUCH in 1968
Membership. 350 (estimate)
Secretary General. René Théodore
Status. Illegal and proscribed. Membership and activity labeled communist is punishable by death.
Last Congress. First, 1979
Last Election. Not applicable
Publications. Ephemeral

The PUCH was originally founded in 1934 by intellectuals, particularly writers and poets such as Jacques Roumain. The government of Dumarsais Estimé banned all parties in 1949, and the government of Dr. François Duvalier added the death penalty for suspected communist activity in 1969. Noncommunist parties have been created since the advent of Jean-Claude Duvalier, but the extreme antagonism toward communism has continued to the present.

The party operates in extreme secrecy even outside Haiti. During 1983, a Dominican newspaper, *El Sol*, printed an alleged communication from the party that René Théodore, who has indicated he is secretary general, wished to refute. He or his representative hand-delivered the refutation to one Haitian newspaper in New York, *Le Progrès*, and arranged to have it sent over the telex to another, *Haïti-Observateur*.

Members are probably still drawn from a group of writers, poets, and teachers. They have received modest support from Cuba, which has also used its resident Haitian population to produce films based, for example, on Jacques Roumain's novels. Interestingly, the Cubans prudishly removed meaningful sexual sequences from their production.

In the course of 1978, the PUCH claims to have held a congress within the borders of Haiti, but it is likely that more important meetings take place in Havana, Montreal, and Paris.

The several other Haitian political movements outside Haiti ignore or denounce communism. Movements in Haiti dare not mention its name.

The PUCH condemns the life presidency and calls for elections and the release of political prisoners. The man calling himself secretary general, René Théodore, denies the PUCH believes it is the only organization that can transform Haiti (*Le Progrès*, 27 May–2 June).

Internationally, the PUCH blames the United States for the continuing survival of the Duvalier regime. In 1983, René Théodore wrote to French prime minister Pierre Mauroy to protest the French government's decision to return the ashes of revolutionary leader Toussaint L'Ouverture to Port-au-Prince because he said such an act helps glorify the Duvalier regime. He also blames other foreign interests for maintaining Duvalier and giving him prestige. (Ibid., 3–9 June.)

The several recent initiatives taken from within and without Haiti to change the regime have not been influenced by the PUCH, an insignificant organization. Calls by the PUCH to unite the opposition with the PUCH go unheeded, as it is disdained. (Such a call was issued in 1983; see *IB*, January.)

Brian Weinstein
Howard University

Honduras

Population. 4 million (estimate)

Major Marxist-Leninist Movement. Honduran Revolutionary Movement (Movimiento Hondureño Revolucionario; MHR)

Governing Body. National Unified Directorate (Directorio Nacional Unificado; DNU) of the MHR is composed of representatives of the following small parties: Honduran Communist Party (Partido Comunista Hondureño; PCH), Secretary General Rigoberto Padilla Rush; Revolutionary Party of Central American Workers (Partido Revolucionario de Trabajadores Centroamericanos; PRTC), led until his death in September by Dr. José María Reyes Matos; Lorenzo Zelaya People's Revolutionary Front (Frente Popular Revolucionario; FPR-LZ), under Efraín Duarte; Movement of Revolutionary Unity (Movimiento de Unidad Revolucionario; MUR); Popular Liberation Movement (Movimiento de Liberación Popular; MLP), commonly known as the Cinchoneros, led by Raul López; and Morazanista Front of Honduran Liberation (Frente Morazanista de Liberación Hondureña; FMLH), whose spokesman is Fernando López. These organizations are all clandestine, and their size and, in general, their leadership remains unknown.

The most significant trend among the Honduran Left this year has been the move toward greater coordination and centralization, following the example of the Salvadorean Left several years earlier. The PCH is the oldest group, tracing a checkered history back to the year 1927. The MLP dates back to 1978 and the FMLH, in its present form, only to 1979. The other groups are even smaller, and some are likely to prove ephemeral.

There are two major aspects of Marxist activity in Honduras. One is the ongoing effort of indigenous groups to topple, or at least destabilize, the current constitutional government of President Roberto Suazo Córdova. The other aspect is the aid that Honduran Marxists are able to give to the rebel forces in El Salvador by acting as a conduit for aid from Marxist-led Nicaragua. The Honduran Left also seeks to disrupt the activities of the counterrevolutionary Nicaraguans (the *contras*) who use Honduras as a base for raids into Nicaragua. Two of the groups that comprise the MHR have strong links to movements in neighboring countries. The PRTC is the Honduran branch of the organization of the same name in El Salvador that is one of the five rebel movements locked in civil war with the government, while the FPR-LZ is considered an adjunct of the ruling Sandinista party of Nicaragua (see *YICA*, 1983, pp. 107–8).

Domestic Activities. Things had not gone well for the forces of the Left during 1982. Dr. Padilla Rush of the PCH had been forced to go underground in July and the seizure of the Chamber of Commerce in San Pedro Sula in September by the Cinchoneros had ended in the rejection of most of their demands and the flight of the terrorists into exile. Then on 30 January, the prominent PCH leader Herminio Deras, who had just returned from a visit to Cuba, was shot dead in San Pedro Sula in a bungled abduction attempt by a death squad (AFP, Paris, 30 January; *FBIS*, 2 February). In Havana, Ana María Rodríguez, head of the permanent PCH mission in Cuba,

accused the Honduran government of having been responsible.

During the first months of the year, the two major armed groups of the Left, the FPR-LZ and the MLP Cinchoneros, remained quiet. In February, they were reported to have abandoned many of their hideouts and safe houses in an apparent effort to cut the risk of discovery (*Latin America Regional Report*, 18 February). A series of terrorist bombings began again in the summer, two major blasts being set off by the Cinchoneros, one near the cathedral of San Pedro Sula on 23 August and another at the office of the Costa Rican airline on 13 September, apparently in retaliation for use of a Costa Rican field for a bombing strike against Managua's Sandino airport.

General Gustavo Alvarez Martínez, the chief of the Honduran military, announced in August that the MHR had formally divided the country into four combat zones, in the manner of the Salvadorean rebels, and that some 300 rebels had slipped into Olancho, the vast and rugged northern province of the country, from Nicaragua after having been trained in Cuba. General Alvarez further stated that an additional 2,000 Hondurans were being trained in Nicaragua. (*This Week Central America and Panama*, 22 August.) The supposed leaders of the guerrillas in Olancho were Dr. José Reyes Matos, a biochemist who had trained in Cuba and had worked in Salvador Allende's Chile, and Father James Carney, a North American–born naturalized Honduran who had worked in the country for eighteen years until his expulsion in 1979. Father Carney was known by the revolutionary code name of "Padre Guadalupe." Reyes Matos and his band were hunted by the army command in Olancho, and it was reported that he was killed along with seven other guerrillas on 18 September on the banks of the Patuca River (*Tiempo*, San Pedro Sula, 22 September). On the whole, the government sweep through Olancho and the easternmost department of Gracías a Díos proved very successful. Twenty-six insurgents were reported captured, and another ten were said to have died of starvation while fleeing the troops. Among the latter group was said to be Father Carney. (*Washington Report on the Hemisphere*, 15 November.) Two captured members of the rebel band, Mario Rodríguez and Miguel Hernández, were said to have confessed to security forces that the Nicaraguan and Cuban governments had been behind the guerrilla incursion into northeastern Honduras (*Honduras Update*, October). After the death of Reyes Matos, it was stated that Teofilo Martínez, as former head of the National Peasants' Union (Union Nacional de Campesinos), would take over as the top guerrilla commander of the PRTC and that he was hiding in the Agalta Mountains of Olancho with a small band (ACAN, Panama, 21 September). However, the San Pedro Sula paper *Tiempo* had previously reported him killed on 11 September, a report that has not been substantiated. No accurate reports of the numbers of Honduran government forces killed in the September clashes have been released, but word came from Managua that a U.S. Green Beret, Eddy Gear, was killed fighting the guerrillas on 3 September (Managua, Radio Noticias, 29 September; *FBIS*, 30 September). This has not been confirmed by Washington. On the whole, the government appeared to have successfully blunted the guerrilla thrust, although in October, Foreign Minister Edgardo Paz Bárnica warned that hundreds of Honduran rebels were poised in Nicaragua for a new invasion (EFE, Madrid, 3 October; *FBIS*, 4 October).

The September campaign pointed up two important weaknesses of the radical Left in Honduras. Its inability to establish training centers within Honduran territory forces them to rely on the hard-pressed Managua government for training and equipment. This weakness was itself due to a more important failure on the part of the guerrillas: their inability to find a mass base of popular support similar to that of the Salvadorean rebels. In an effort to remedy this defect, both the MLP Cinchoneros and the FPR-LZ group began to infiltrate peasant and industrial unions early in 1983 (*Latin America Regional Report*, 18 February). But industrial unionism and peasant associations have long been legal and encouraged in Honduras, and they do not have the incentive to ally themselves with radical movements in the same manner as the more oppressed workers' groups in El Salvador.

Not only does Honduras have the problem of domestic insurgency, but it is caught between the more active struggles in Nicaragua and El Salvador. The Honduran Left has consistently denounced the activities of the Nicaraguan *contras* and sought to disrupt them whenever possible. Rigoberto Padilla Rush of the PCH warned in April that Honduran support of the Nicaraguan rebels would lead to disaster and a general Central American war, and the PRTC announced its "total disapproval of the criminal attacks" of the *contras*, accused the United States of turning Honduras into a vast military encampment, and called for popular rebellion (Havana international service, 21 April; *FBIS*, 25 April). In March, the Honduran army announced that it had captured a shipment of arms destined for the Salvadorean rebels and killed two members of a Sandinista band who were with the supplies (Cadena Audio-Video, Tegucigalpa, 5 April; *FBIS*, 6 April). The prospects for an increasing role for the Marxists in Honduras appear very strong as the Central American situation continues to deteriorate.

Thomas P. Anderson
Eastern Connecticut State University

Jamaica

Population. 2.3 million
Party. Workers' Party of Jamaica (WPJ); Jamaican Communist Party (JCP)
Founded. WPJ, 1978; JCP, 1975
Membership. Information unavailable
Party Chairman. Trevor Munroe (WPJ); Chris Lawrence (JCP)
Status. Legal
Last Congress. 17–20 December 1981 (WPJ)
Last Election. December elections boycotted (only 20 percent of Jamaica's eligible voters cast ballots)
Auxiliary Organizations. Principal WPJ organizations are the Young Communist League, the Committee of Women for Progress, the University and Allied Workers' Union, and the National Union of Democratic Teachers
Publications. *Struggle* (WPJ)

The emergence of Jamaica's two communist parties occurred as Jamaica's rapid economic growth of the 1950s and 1960s came to an end in the 1970s. The economic problems leading to their emergence included Jamaica's deep recession during the 1970s, increasing foreign debt, declining production in the bauxite industry, a fall in tourism, and a rise in unemployment from 12 to 24 percent during 1962–1972. During these years, the relative and absolute income of the poorest 30 percent of the population declined. As the decade of the 1960s ended, these economic conditions spawned large-scale political alienation from Jamaica's two party system—consisting of the conservative Jamaica Labor Party (JLP) and the democratic socialist People's Nationalist Party (PNP). Edward Seaga is the leader of the JLP, and Michael Manley heads the PNP. Jamaica's economic and political problems led to widespread unrest and new currents of leftism, represented by the formation of the JCP in 1975 and the WPJ in 1978.

Of the two communist parties, the WPJ became the more influential. It is a pro-Moscow party and at the outset aligned itself with Michael Manley's PNP, which ruled Jamaica during 1972–1980. During the Manley years, relations between the WPJ and the PNP remained relatively amicable, owing in part to the appointment of leftist ministers within the PNP. Close relations between the WPJ and the PNP also were stimulated by specific policies pursued by the PNP. While Manley followed a moderate and orthodox approach to the politics of economic development during 1972–1974, he moved toward a more leftist direction during 1974–1977, largely under pressure from leftists within the PNP, such as D. K. Duncan, Hugh Small, and others. Manley returned to a more orthodox approach during 1977 and 1978, but shifted back to leftism in 1980. The PNP's leftist formulas included programs to expand youth employment, food subsidies, and equal pay for women; increased state control over the foreign-dominated bauxite industry; expanded government power to redistribute land, and popular ownership through cooperatives and community enterprises.

The Manley era, with its democratic socialist ideology, produced much closer relations with Cuba and the Soviet Union, a trend welcomed by the WPJ and the JCP. Jamaica's top leaders exchanged visits with those of Cuba. A number of

Cuban-inspired projects appeared in Jamaica. Cuba provided about a hundred doctors, nurses, school-building teams, and mini-dam construction workers by 1978, the year the WPJ was formed. The number of Cubans in Jamaica grew to 450 by 1979 and 600 by 1980. Cuba became visibly active in Jamaica during the Manley years, aiding the country in water supply problems, housing, schools, agriculture, fishing, medical facilities, culture, and sports training. These close ties with Cuba, combined with a growing association with the Soviet Union—supported by the WPJ and influenced by leftists within the PNP—led the JLP to accuse the PNP of seeking to make Jamaica "another Cuba" (*Weekly Gleaner*, 28 October 1977).

Strains began to develop between the moderate PNP membership and its left-wing group during the late 1970s. The PNP's middle-class supporters became disenchanted with the party's radical leftist orientation, and the leftists criticized PNP moderates for leaning toward Western capitalist economic solutions such as borrowing from the International Monetary Fund (IMF). It was in part this type of dispute that led to the formation of the WPJ under Trevor Munroe in 1978. When the PNP lost the national elections to the JLP in 1980, the rift between the PNP and the WPJ widened even more.

Leadership and Party Organization. Following the bitterly contested 1980 general elections, which brought Edward Seaga and his JLP to power, the PNP increasingly distanced itself from the WPJ. In late December 1981, the PNP went so far as to declare that its identification with the WPJ had been a key cause of its losing the 1980 elections (Caribbean News Agency [CANA], Bridgetown, 17 December 1981). Meanwhile, the coming to power of the conservative JLP in 1980 produced a distinctly different political climate for the WPJ, compared to the halcyon days of the late 1970s under PNP leadership. In March 1983, Trevor Munroe stated that JLP's "pro-imperialist path" was accompanied by "repression against the communists and left activists and communities, strict censorship of party statements and the intensified cold war anti-communism" (*WMR*, March). As to the WPJ's association with the PNP by late 1982 and early 1983, Munroe stated that because of its "class character," the PNP "is supportive of working class interests only in a limited way.

Therefore the WPJ will have to fill the gap in championing the interests of the working class and moving the country in the direction of social progress." (*Georgetown Mirror*, 14 November 1982.)

The WPJ continues to deny that its active role in the 1980 elections contributed to the PNP's defeat (*WMR*, March). Rather, it attributes Manley's defeat, and consequently the undermining of WPJ power, to the destabilization efforts of the United States, the power of Jamaica's "national bourgeoisie" within the liberation movement to "water down" firm resistance to the JLP's "reactionary" force, and insufficient strength of the WPJ and the leftists within the PNP to "overcome the vacillations" in the PNP leadership (ibid.). Munroe stated in early 1983 that the PNP had "compromised its position" and had "become a centre party." The PNP was removing from leadership positions those individuals who defended the leftist alternative and "was now depending on imperialism and parliamentary democracy in Jamaica." According to Munroe, the PNP leadership had "lost much of the presence within it of those individuals who defended the poor people." (*Trinidad Guardian*, 3 February.)

The WPJ sees its immediate tasks as expanding its membership, strengthening its ties with the working class, and unifying other leftist groups in Jamaica (ibid.). The leadership remains active in calling attention to Jamaica's continuing economic difficulties, which they allege include high levels of corruption and mismanagement (*Georgetown Mirror*, 14 November 1982). The WPJ focuses on Jamaica's unemployment, which grew by 19,200 people between October 1981 and April 1982, increasing even more since April 1982 due to the entry of approximately 30,000–35,000 young people into the labor market (*Trinidad Guardian*, 4 February). The WPJ emphasizes these and other economic and political conditions in its pursuit of greater cooperation between WPJ communists and different sections of the people: youths, students, workers, professionals, farmers, and small-business people (ibid.).

Domestic Party Affairs. Although promising signs of economic recovery marked the early months of 1983, Seaga's JLP faced mounting difficulties toward the end of the year. On the positive side, tourism had improved, construction had recovered, and hopeful signs had emerged in the manufacturing sector (*CSM*, 4 March). At the same time, Seaga negotiated over $1 billion in loans, much of which was applied toward Jamaica's debts and industrial revitalization (*San Francisco Chronicle*, 16 October).

But on the negative side, serious economic trends also plagued the country. Unemployment was indeed high, 20 percent officially and 30 percent unofficially; and a worldwide drop in demand for bauxite deeply hurt the important mining industry (*CSM*, 8 March). The inflation rate began to rise, foreign exchange shortages developed, and growth in the gross domestic product began to lag (ibid.). A three-day strike by civil servants in April suggested the depth of discontent with economic conditions in Jamaica (*Latin America Weekly Report*, 29 April). The political dimension of economic unrest was reflected in a poll published by the *Gleaner* in April that gave Seaga's JLP only 38 percent compared with 41 percent for the opposition PNP, with additional evidence that the majority of those polled believed that conditions had worsened under JLP leadership (ibid.).

In mid-December, Seaga called for a national election, which gave the JLP all 60 seats in parliament. The PNP and WPJ boycotted these elections, and the PNP argued that elections should not have been held until voter lists were revised in 1984 (*CSM*, 18 December). Voter lists used in the mid-December 1983 election did not include Jamaicans who were under age when the list was constructed in 1980, but who were eligible to vote in 1983. An updated list presumably would include younger, and potentially more radically leftist voters, which could work in favor of the PNP and WPJ (ibid.). Critics of the election argue that Seaga called for them in the wake of popular support for Jamaica's role in the U.S.-led invasion of Grenada in October as a means of gaining backing at a time when attention was diverted from domestic economic issues (ibid., 19 December). These observers also note that Seaga was worried that his popularity would probably slip even more, relative to the PNP, under economic hardships expected to follow the devaluation of the Jamaican dollar (ibid.). But critics of the PNP argue that it boycotted the elections less because of the voter list situation than because of its continuing disarray, inherited from the late 1970s, and simply could not have won the election (ibid.).

Throughout 1983, the WPJ remained highly critical of the JLP leadership in economic and political matters. It centered criticism on the JLP's pro-IMF policies, which the WPJ argued had led Jamaica into the trap of debt, deregulation, and devaluation. In the words of Trevor Munroe, such policies had "never solved Jamaica's problems in the past and [would] lead to further economic ruin for nearly all classes of Jamaicans except a tiny minority of merchants and financiers." The results of the JLP's pro-IMF policies, according to the WJP, would be further price increases, production cuts, layoffs, raw material shortages, and superprofits for the banks. The WPJ also criticized the JLP's restriction of the press, notably the refusal of Jamaica's only newspaper, the *Daily Gleaner*, to accept statements and analyses from the WPJ. (*IB*, October.) Other setbacks for the leftists in Jamaica included the electoral defeat of left-wing leadership of the Press Association of Jamaica, when a communist, Ben Brodie, who had led the association for six years, was defeated by the assistant news editor of Radio Jamaica, Clifton Seagree, in August (*FBIS*, 31 August). Also in August, John Haughton, general secretary of the National Union of Democratic Teachers in Jamaica and an executive member of the WPJ, was detained in Miami under a U.S. immigration law (ibid., 9 August).

International Views, Positions, and Activities. When Prime Minister Seaga broke relations with Cuba in October 1981, he fulfilled a campaign promise that ended the pro-Cuban era of Manley, backed by the WPJ in 1978–1980. Both the PNP and the WPJ condemned Seaga's action, which in no way altered the JLP's course. Indeed, following the U.S. invasion of Grenada, which the JLP strongly supported, Seaga expelled four Soviet diplomats and a Cuban journalist for purportedly spying and conspiring to kill a Foreign Ministry official (*NYT*, 2 November). Trevor Munroe described the Cuban and Soviet threat to the Caribbean Basin as "mythical" (*WMR*, March).

The WPJ is sharply critical of U.S. foreign policy. It denounces the U.S. Caribbean Basin Initiative, first proclaimed in February 1982, as a plan to strengthen the oligarchy and to defend the interests of U.S. imperialism (ibid.). It opposes the IMF as an institution that "makes the rich richer and the poor poorer" because of the conditions it imposes for loans to countries like Jamaica (*IB*, October). Special targets of WPJ opposition include U.S. multinational corporations and military bases in the Caribbean (*WMR*, March). In characterizing the nature of the present epoch, the WPJ continued to stress the theses established in the 1981 Report of the Central Committee to the Second Party Congress: (1) "The great danger from the extraordinarily aggressive but vain effort by imperialism to turn back the gains made by the progressive forces around the world and, in particular, to upset the equality of military strength between imperialism and socialism—an equality which remains a powerful guarantee that imperialism will not start a world war"; (2) the "need to strengthen existing ties with the working people and to strengthen the unity of the entire left"; (3) "the ever more inspiring influence of the socialist countries on the working masses"; (4) the "growing unity around anti-imperialism"; and (5) "the Cuban Revolution is, as always, a beacon light for the Caribbean and Latin America, despite all the efforts of imperialism to put out that light" (ibid.). By year's end, the WPJ remained convinced that the "system of imperialist domination in the Caribbean is experiencing an acute crisis caused...by the people's invincible striving for a better future" (ibid.). Nevertheless, the WPJ's own political role in Jamaica remained greatly limited throughout the year and the WPJ's view of Cuba contrasted with those of many other Caribbean groups that supported the U.S. invasion of Grenada, in part because of the substantial Cuban presence.

W. Raymond Duncan
State University of New York
College at Brockport

Martinique

Population. 320,000 (estimate, French embassy)
Party. Martinique Communist Party (Parti Communiste Martiniquais; PCM)
Founded. 1921 as a section of the French Communist Party; 1957 as an independent party
Membership. Probably less than 1,000
General Secretary. Armand Nicolas
Politburo. 3 members
Secretariat. 4 members
Central Committee. 33 members
Status. Legal
Last Congress. Eighth, 12–13 November 1983
Last Elections. 1981 French National Assembly elections, 6.4 percent, no representation; 20 February 1983 Conseil Régional elections, 9.1 percent, 4 of 41 seats
Auxiliary Organizations. General Confederation of Martinican Labor (CGTM), Martinican Union of Education Personnel (SMPE-CGTM), Union des Femmes de la Martinique–Union of Women of Martinique, Martinican Committee of Solidarity with the Peoples of the Caribbean and of Central America
Publications. *Justice* (weekly)

The PCM, which was founded in 1921 as a section of the French Communist Party and transformed itself into an independent party in 1957, suffered from disunity and disappointment in 1983. Party leaders complained about discipline problems within the party because individual members and the allied trade union CGTM seemed to feel free to comment independently on political events and goals. Disappointments came with the apparent decline of communist influence in France as a whole and with the anti-Soviet position of the government of François Mitterrand.

Economic difficulties resulting from unemployment, strikes, the general decline of sugar prices, and an outburst of violence and terrorism, attributed to independence supporters, troubled the party. The PCM continued to reject outright independence, asserting in the words of the general secretary a preference for "national and social liberation, socialism, and, for the time being, democratic and popular autonomy in order to run our own affairs in our country" (*Justice*, 14 July).

Leadership and Organization. Armand Nicolas continued his long tenure as general secretary. As usual, the party took a backseat to Aimé Césaire's Progressive Martinique Party (PPM) with which it tried in vain to ally itself for the elections. In the elections to the newly created Conseil Régional on 20 February, the PCM won only 10,255 votes out of 113,061 valid ballots (9.07 percent), while the PPM won 31,443 (27.81 percent) and the Socialists won 14,029 (12.41 percent) (ibid., 24 February). Because seats are allocated to each party in proportion to the popular vote, the PCM only 4 out of the total of 41, but the combined votes of the three parties of the Left gave them majority control, or 21 of 41 seats. Aimé Césaire, PPM leader, mayor of Fort-de-France, deputy, and world-famous writer, was elected president of the Conseil Régional.

Municipal elections were held on 6 and 13 March in 34 towns. The PCM ran lists in only 15, carefully avoiding Fort-de-France, which is PPM-held territory. Of the 3 towns the PCM controlled before the elections, it won only 2, but it sent representatives to town councils in 9 other municipalities.

Weakened by the voters' rejection, the PCM nonetheless pressed on with its active but highly regularized program. It sponsored a bicycle race,

organized a meeting in honor of Karl Marx, the centenary of whose death was noted, and held its Eighth Congress.

Over 40 percent of the 205 delegates to the November congress were civil servants (including teachers) (ibid., 17 November). This fact is one reason for the party's ambivalence about independence, which would cut off civil servants from the French treasury. A majority favored autonomy over independence. They agreed that the party has had some problems, including the discipline of party members in the CGTM trade union. Robert Ebion, a member of the Central Committee, also complained about lethargy: "It is practically impossible for our party to mobilize in ten or fifteen days 200 to 300 militants for any action" (ibid., 15 September). There was no unanimity about the political course to follow.

Domestic Party Affairs. Reservations about the ruling Socialists were less muted. The party complained that devaluation of the French franc would damage Martinique's ability to import oil, but it hoped for more tourists from Paris because of currency restrictions. The party complained that the Socialists were doing little to help the sugar industry and, sensing a rise in anti-Semitism in France, exploited economic fears by claiming Jews were becoming too important in Martinique's economy.

Loyal to Moscow, the PCM complained about the expulsion of 47 Soviet spies from France. It had many questions about the ninth development plan that the government is preparing, but was pleased by the decision to introduce the Creole language into schools, at least as a subject of study. Five explosions in Martinique set by independence groups disturbed party leaders who denounced violence and terrorism, but they blamed the "colonialists" for creating a situation that encouraged such actions.

Auxiliary Organizations. The most important auxiliary organization is the labor union, the CGTM, whose leaders met in Paris with CGT members from Guadeloupe, Guyana, Réunion, and France.

In an attempt to unify the party, leaders created an Association of Communist and Democratic Elected Officials of Martinique. All elected officials of the Left were invited to join this effort to establish a front. Emile Capgras took the post of president. The Union of Women of Martinique continued under the leadership of Solange Fitte-Duval.

Due to lack of funds, Radio Kônn Lanbi, created in May 1982, had to shut down. It reopened in 1983 with the help of the Association for the Promotion of the Martinique Culture. The latter collected money for the radio station. Hervé Florent, former general secretary of the communist youth organization, served as program director for Radio Kônn Lanbi.

The communist-led Martinique Committee of Solidarity with the Peoples of the Caribbean and of Central America (Comité martiniquais de solidarité avec les peuples de la Caraïbe et de l'Amérique Centrale) denounced the government of neighboring Dominica for the death sentences passed on some criminals.

International Views. Dominica seemed at times more important to party leaders than other countries in the area, but the PCM welcomed Ramón Cardona, itinerant representative of the Democratic Revolutionary Front of El Salvador. The PCM demonstrated against the U.S. government for its policies in Central America and for its invasion of Grenada. It criticized the French government for apparently following the U.S. lead at the Williamsburg summit meeting on economic questions. French action in Chad was crit-

icized, and, again promoting Soviet views, the PCM blamed the CIA for the Soviet destruction of the Korean civilian airliner.

Nicaragua's government sent a note of thanks to the PCM for the verbal support offered, and similar messages were received from the New Jewel Movement of Grenada (before the U.S. intervention) and the National Joint Action Committee of Trinidad and Tobago. Four PCM members traveled to the Soviet Union, and the party welcomed observers from the USSR, France, Guadeloupe, Guyana, and Réunion for its Eighth Congress.

Publications. The 63-year-old weekly newspaper, *Justice*, continued to be the party's major organ of information. In July, thousands of nonparty members joined the PCM to participate in the annual festival and fair of *Justice*, an important social event in Martinique. *Kon-Lanbi* is published monthly by the PCM section in Paris (whose members are immigrants from Martinique). Armand Nicolas's brochure, *La Révolution antiesclavagiste de Mars 1848 à la Martinique*, was reissued.

Brian Weinstein
Howard University

Mexico

Population. 75.7 million (*World Factbook*, 1983)
Party. Unified Socialist Party of Mexico (Partido Socialista Unificado de Mexico; PSUM)
Founded. Mexican Communist Party, 1919; PSUM, 1981
Membership. 40,800 (*IB*, no. 15, p. 21; *Uno Mas Uno*, 14 September)
Secretary General. Pablo Gómez Alvarez
Political Commission. 17 members: Pablo Gómez Alvarez, Sabino Hernández Tellez, Gilberto Rincon Gallardo Meltiz, Manuel Stephens García, Jorge Alocer Villanueva, Rolando Cordera Campos, Ivan García Solis, Arnaldo Martínez Verdugo, Eduardo Montes Manzano, Pablo Pascual

Moncayo, Marcos Leonel Posadas Segura, Gerardo Unzueta Lorenzana, Miguel Angel Velasco Muñoz, Leopoldo Arthur Whaley Martínez, Valentin Campa Salazar, Eduardo González Ramírez, Adolfo Sánchez Rebolledo

Secretariat. 7 members: Pablo Gómez Alvarez, Sabino Hernández Tellez, Gilberto Rincon Gallardo Meltiz, Manuel Stephens García, Jorge Alocer Villanueva, Jesús Sosa Castro, José Woldenberg Karakowsky

Central Committee. 75 members

Status. Legal

Last Congress. Second, 9–14 August 1983

Last Elections. 1982. 3.5 percent of the vote for president; 4.3 percent of the vote for, and 17 of 400 seats in, the legislature

Auxiliary Organizations. Youth/Student Section of the PSUM, Independent Center of Agricultural Workers and Peasants (CIOAC), Sole National Union of University Workers (SUNTU), Single Union of Workers of the Nuclear Industry

Publications. *Asi Es* (weekly), Mexico City

The PSUM, recognized by the Soviets as the official communist party of the country, was formed in 1981 as a result of the fusion of the Mexican Communist Party (Partido Comunista Mexicano; PCM) and four smaller groups: the Popular Action Movement (Movimiento de Acción Popular; MAP), the Mexican People's Party (Partido Popular Mexicano; PPM), the Revolutionary Socialist Party (Partido Socialista Revolucionario; PSR) and the Socialist Action and Unity Movement (Movimiento de Acción y Unidad; MAUS). During 1982, the dominant PCM faction within the PSUM was reportedly continuing the Eurocommunist orientation it had prior to the merger, and it was said to have been allied to the similarly "anti-Soviet" "national socialists" of the MAP (*El Dia*, 30 June). These two groups were said to have been pitted against the other three (ibid.). (Note that at least the PSR had been slavishly pro-Soviet, supporting the latter's position on both Poland and Afghanistan [*YICA*, 1982, p. 123] and the PPM had supported the Soviets on Afghanistan [ibid., 1981, p. 91].)

Domestic Party Affairs. It appears that the right wing of the PSUM, as represented by the Eurocommunist faction of the PCM and the even more rightist MAP contingent, increased its relative strength within the party during 1983. A spokesman for the more orthodox communist elements claimed in March that some 20,000 persons of his persuasion had withdrawn from the PSUM since its formation, leaving it with only 40,000 members (*Excelsior*, 4 March). This defection apparently should not be confused with the refusal of a large part of the PCM to join the

PSUM in the first place. That party was estimated to have had 100,000 members at the time of the merger (*YICA*, 1981, p. 123). This group (or part of it at least) appears to constitute the Communist Libertarian Movement led by Evaristo Pérez Arreola (*Uno Mas Uno*, 17 March 1982; *Nexos*, no. 54, June 1982, p. 31) and did not seem very active politically during 1983.

It has been suggested that the mass defection from the PSUM had been triggered when MAP leaders successfully outmaneuvered traditional communists for leadership positions in the new party (*Excelsior*, 11 June). Presumably this was done with Eurocommunist help; but in any case, the PSUM Political Commission elected in March 1982 had 4 ex-MAP leaders (out of 21), giving that group the second highest of any party contingent (*El Dia*, 17 March 1982). Thus, as a result of the defection, the right wing increased its relative strength at a great cost, a one-third loss in party membership. Ironically, the PSUM's February Central Committee Plenum, which incidentally confirmed the 40,000 membership figure, came out strongly for forming "a large and broad-based revolutionary socialist organization" (*IB*, August, p. 13); the PSUM has been looking for new groups to latch on to ever since.

The Eurocommunist PCM/MAP again increased its relative strength at the leadership level as a result of the August (Second) PSUM Congress, for the PPM, PSR, and MAUS lost one representative each from the new (and smaller) Political Commission, while the PCM retained its ten and the MAP its four slots (*Uno Mas Uno*, 17 August). It appears that at least one member of the PCM group, however, was disturbed that former PPM Secretary General Alejandro Gascon Mercado did not take his position on the Political Commission again (he refused the office after losing to Pablo Gómez Alvarez for the secretary generalship of PSUM) (*Proceso*, 22 August). This same PCM spokesman had quite a different attitude toward the extremely pro-Soviet former PSR secretary general, Roberto Jaramillo Flores, however, attacking him for officially retaining the identity of his organization (the PSR was still registered as a political association with the government) and for speaking about the "dictatorship of the proletariat" (ibid.). (True to its presumed Eurocommunist orientation, the PSUM uses the term "democratic worker government" to characterize its goals; it feels that the "dictatorship of the proletariat" has gotten a bad name due to Stalinist "distortions" [ibid.].) A further difference in treatment of the two parties is seen in the PPM retention of two seats on the new Political Commission (three if Gascon had accepted the invitation) and the PSR's loss of representation with the exit of Jaramillo.

Just as the right wing's capture of the PSUM seemed to be complete, that dominant faction appears to have moved toward a more pro-Soviet position. Included in the Soviet delegation to the Second Congress were those party officials most concerned with Mexico, Karen N. Brutents, International Department (ID) deputy chief concerned with Latin America, Mikhail F. Kudachkin, ID Latin America sector chief, and Konstantin N. Kurin, ID Mexican specialist (*Asi Es*, 12–18 August). This is an unusually high amount of area expertise for the Soviets to invest in such a meeting, and things do seem to happen after such a crew visits a country. For example, these same three visited Mexico in August 1981, leaving just days before the PSUM fusion plan was finally announced (*Oposición*, 9 August 1981); and Brutents (also responsible for the Middle East) headed a Soviet delegation that left Beirut on the eve of the February 1982 announcement of a Palestine Communist Party in that city (*Pravda*, 28 January 1982). In this case, the change seen was the new emphasis the PSUM placed on supporting efforts to keep U.S. intermediate-range missiles out of Western Europe, the major Soviet concern in the propaganda field during the year. While the Eurocommunist position is to oppose the U.S. missiles as well, it is usually coupled

with at least a pro forma appeal to the Soviets to dismantle their SS-20s (a line not noted in PSUM statements on the subject). Besides, no more complaints about Poland or Afghanistan have been noted on the PSUM's part.

Soviet concern over the new missiles was evident at the Second Congress (*Uno Mas Uno*, 10 August) and even more so during and just after the visit of a PSUM delegation led by Secretary General Pablo Gómez Alvarez to Moscow in October (Tass, 25 October; *FBIS*, 26 October; *Népszabadság*, Budapest, 20 November). This might help explain why the Soviet press was so uncritically supportive of the Second Congress (*Pravda*, 16 August) even when that meeting saw the downgrading of Roberto Jaramillo, one of the USSR's most consistent and stalwart supporters. The change in emphasis can be seen in the January establishment by the PSUM, in true Eurocommunist fashion, of relations with the Chinese Communist Party.

In contrast with the attitude of the dominant PSUM faction toward Jaramillo's PSR, the PSUM has continued its efforts to incorporate the Mexican Workers' Party (Partido Mexicano de los Trabajadores; PMT) during the year. Although it is more proletarian than the largely white-collar PCM/MAP component of the PSUM and revolutionary and class-oriented in spirit, the PMT is not even clearly Marxist (*Excelsior*, 11 June). In fact, the reasons given by the PMT for its failure to unite with the PSUM are the latter's refusal to change its name (by deleting the word "socialist") and to give up its hammer and sickle symbol (*Uno Mas Uno*, 9 September). What the PMT has to offer the PSUM are numbers (on the eve of its September [Third] National Assembly, it claimed 36,602 members plus over 20,000 unprocessed applications [*Proceso*, 29 August]) and its chairman, Herberto Castillo Martínez, is probably the most attractive figure in all of the Mexican Left (*YICA*, 1982, p. 123). Ironically, it is generally believed that it is Castillo's ego, his refusal to take second place to anyone, that caused the negotiations with PSUM to break down (*Excelsior*, 11 June). These negotiations had begun again in June and appear to have been officially suspended only when it was so announced at the PMT's September assembly. The PMT's number two leader, organization secretary Demetrio Vallejo Martínez, however, withdrew from the party with 800 followers just before this meeting and joined the PSUM (*Pro-*

ceso, 29 August; *Uno Mas Uno*, 14 September). Vallejo claimed that this action took away 80 percent of the PMT's "active militants" (ibid., 26 August). In spite of the failure to coalesce, the PSUM and PMT did cooperate during the year in the National Committee to Defend the People's Economy, playing the dominant role in this grouping set up to oppose the government's austerity program and its allegedly related ties to Western economic interests. The two also cooperated in the Mexican Peace Movement (MOV-PAZ), the local affiliate of the international Soviet-line World Peace Council (WPC), and, to a very limited extent, in the municipal and state electoral campaigns.

The PSUM cooperated more indirectly, and mostly at the international level, with the Popular Socialist Party (Partido Popular Socialista; PPS). Like the MAP component within the PSUM, the PPS has close ties with the left wing of the ruling Institutional Revolutionary Party (Partido Revolucionario Institucional; PRI) (*Nexos*, no. 52, June 1982, p. 29), and like its PSR component it has been extremely pro-Soviet (e.g., it supported the Soviet position in both Poland and Afghanistan) (*YICA*, 1982, p. 123). At least as of 1978, the PPS's General Union of Workers and Peasants of Mexico paralleled the PCM's CIOAC in being affiliated with the Permanent Committee for Latin American Trade Union Unity (CPUSTAL) (*Boletin del CPUSTAL*, March/April 1978, p. 15), de facto regional affiliate of the international Soviet-line World Federation of Trade Unions (WFTU). Similarly, both the PCM's youth organization and the Popular Socialist Youth were, at least as of 1981, affiliated with the Soviet-line World Federation of Democratic Youth (WFDY) (World Forum of Youth and Students, *For Peace, Detente, Disarmament*, January 1981, p. 59). And currently the PPS's Adriana Lombardo de Silva is more visible than any PSUM leader in both the WPC and WFTU, being one of four Mexicans on the former's Presidential Committee (as well as MOVPAZ coordinator). Through her Vincente Lombardo Toledano Workers' University, she serves as Latin American distribution point for the WFTU's *World Trade Union Movement* monthly (*World Trade Union Movement*, Prague, no. 10, inside back cover). In addition, PPS secretary general Jorge Cruickshank García was the only Mexican other than the PSUM's Arnaldo Martínez Verdugo (former PCM secretary general and 1982

PSUM presidential candidate) to have addressed the East Berlin Karl Marx anniversary celebrations in April (*Neues Deutschland*, East Berlin, 15 and 18 April). Despite all this activity and a more satisfactory ideological history, the PPS nevertheless does not seem to be the Soviet-approved communist party of the country. There are two reasons, historical and political: the PPS splintered from the PRI some 28 years after the PCM had been founded, and it is a small and weak party compared to PCM/PSUM, although it did manage to elect ten deputies in the 1982 elections.

The Socialist Workers' Party (Partido Socialista de los Trabajadores; PST) similarly appears to have a relationship to the PSUM primarily indirectly and through the front organization mechanism (e.g., PST secretary general Rafael Aguilar Talamantes and two of his followers sat on the 1980–83 WPC, as did at least seven current members of the PSUM Central Committee, including the ex–secretaries general of four of its five component parties (WPC, *List of Members 1980–1983*, pp. 94–95). Like the PPS, the PST is close to the PRI Left, has about half of the voting strength of the PSUM (it elected eleven deputies in 1982), and supported rather than criticized the Soviet invasion of Afghanistan (*YICA*, 1981, p. 91). With its stress on total nationalization, with worker-council control of the industries so expropriated, and its somewhat anti-Soviet attitude, it may have a somewhat Yugoslav orientation (Robert J. Alexander, ed., *Political Parties of the Americas*, pp. 526, 528). It is said to be very antibourgeois (as distinct from antigovernment) and in this respect somewhat similar to the PMT in orientation.

Another arm's-length relationship exists between the PSUM and the left wing of the PRI, a relationship facilitated by the general convergence of Mexican government, Mexican communist, and to some extent Soviet interests in Latin American international political affairs (e.g., the PSUM along with the communist parties of Colombia, Costa Rica, Panama, and Venezuela met in February to support efforts of the Contadora group (Mexico, Colombia, Panama, and Venezuela) to settle Central American problems (*IB*, August, p. 40). The Soviet Union has taken a similar line (*Pravda*, 27 October). Such cooperation again is indirect and at the international front level. The PRI's Luís Echeverria Alvarez (a former Mexican president), as a WPC vice-president, is Mexico's most important member of that organization. The PRI youth organization, like those of the PSUM and the PPS, was, at least as of 1981, an affiliate of the pro-Soviet WFDY rather than of its pro-Western counterpart. Furthermore, these three Mexican youth organizations, together with a Soviet one they were hosting at the time, issued a joint statement in November attacking the U.S. position on Nicaragua as well as the stationing of U.S. intermediate-range missiles in Western Europe (*Excelsior*, 30 November).

The PRI-controlled Workers' Congress and National Trade Union of Educational Workers participated at least nominally in the WFTU's 1982 Tenth World Trade Union Congress (along with the PSUM's CIOAC and SUNTU (Tenth World Trade Union Congress, *List of Participants*, pp. 44–45). Parenthetically, it should be noted that the PRI-led Mexican government sees fit to allow to operate in Mexico City not only the aforementioned Workers' University and CPUSTAL headquarters but also the headquarters of the Federation of Latin American Journalists, the de facto regional affiliate of the Soviet-line International Organization of Journalists.

Unlike any of the aforementioned groups, the Revolutionary Workers' Party (Partido Revolucionario de los Trabajadores; PRT) of José Manuel Aguilar Mora is not known to participate in the peace movement or any other Soviet-line front activity, which is logical in view of this party's status as Mexico's most important Trotskyist organization. The PRT is rather flexible for such a group, however, and has probably had a closer relationship with the PSUM this year than has any other party other than the PMT. In fact, according to *El Dia* columnist Héctor Ramírez Cuellar, the PSUM and PRT share in the control of the Workers', Peasants', and Students' Coalition of the Isthmus (COCEI) in Oaxaca (*El Dia*, 30 June 1982). In any case, COCEI's electoral successes, among other things, allowed it to run the city administration of Juchitan (although the latter was ousted by the PRI-controlled state government late in the year on the grounds that it was not keeping order). The two

parties also cooperated in a few other areas during the municipal and state elections during the year (e.g., in Morelos, where the PMT was included as well). Interestingly, it has been alleged that it is specifically the dominant Eurocommunist PCM/MAP faction of the PSUM that has pushed for cooperation with both the PMT and the PRT over the objections of the minority PPM/PSR/MAUS grouping (ibid.).

The PSUM Second Congress's Political Resolution. This document called for replacing the government's present economic policy with one that would allow for periodic increases in the wages of workers and in guaranteed prices for agricultural goods, for nationalization of (unspecified) enterprises with worker participation in the decisionmaking for these enterprises, for a moratorium on Mexico's foreign debt, and for the implementation of (again unspecified) industrial and rural production programs. It also called for the replacing of economically oriented and government-controlled trade unions with politically oriented ones that express class interests (all, however, to be combined under "a single organizational form"). Politically, the program calls for replacing the present government with a left-revolutionary one via the electoral process. To this end, the PSUM favors merger of revolutionary-left parties with the same political programs, an alliance of the entire Left, and even cooperation with non-leftist groups where there is agreement on specific goals. It also favors the supremacy of the legislature over the executive level of government (replacing "presidentialism" with true parliamentary democracy at the top) and a system of proportional representation. At the international level, the document calls for Mexico to ally itself with other "backward capitalist states" and expresses the party's intent to cooperate with "like-minded...communist, revolutionary, and socialist" parties as well as with additional pacifist and anti-imperialist groups. (*Asi Es*, 23–29 September.)

Wallace H. Spaulding
McLean, Virginia

Nicaragua

Population. 2.8 million
Party. Sandinista Front of National Liberation (Frente Sandinista de Liberación Nacional; FSLN)
Founded. 1961
Membership. 200,000 (estimate)
National Directorate. 9 members (all participate equally): Humberto Ortega Saavedra, Daniel Ortega Saavedra, Tomás Borge Martínez, Jaime Wheelock Román, Henry Ruiz Hernández, Bayardo Arce Castano, Carlos Núñez Téllez, Luís Carrión Cruz, Víctor Manuel Tirado López
Central Government Leadership Committee. 9 members: Dora Maria Téllez (political secretary), Sergio Ramírez Mercado, Lourdes Girón, Carmen Moreno, Pablo Cuca, Nelly Castillo, Elias Nieves, Pedro Hurtado, Damaso Vargas
Status. Ruling party
Main State Organs. National Junta of Government, 3 members: Daniel Ortega (coordinator and chief of state), Sergio Ramírez, Rafael Córdova Rivas; Rodrigo Reyes is secretary to the Junta. Cabinet includes Humberto Ortega (defense), Tomás Borge Martínez (interior), Fr. Miguel d'Escoto Brockman (foreign affairs), Jaime Wheelock Román (agrarian reform), Joaquín Cuadro Chamorro (finance), Carlos Tunnerman Bernheim (education), Alejandro Martínez Cuenca (foreign trade), Henry Ruiz Hernández (planning)
Auxiliary Organizations. Sandinista Defense Committees (Comites de Defensa Sandinista), the most important mass organization, exist from the neighborhood to the national level, secretary general Leticia Herrera; Sandinista Youth (Juventud Sandinista, 19 de Julio), under Carlos Carrión; Association of Nicaraguan Women (Asociación de Mujeres Nicaraguenses), led by Glenda Monterrey; Sandinista Workers Central (Central Sandinista de Trabajadores), secretary general Lucio Jiménez; Association of Farmworkers (Asociación de Trabajadores del Campo), under Edgardo García.
Other Marxist Parties. Several parties of the Left combine with the FSLN to form the Patriotic Revolutionary Front (Frente Patriotico Revolucionario; FPR). These include the small, Moscow-oriented communist movement known as Nicaraguan Socialist Party (Partido Socialista Nicaraguense), Luis Sánchez secretary general. This is the oldest Marxist organization, having been founded in 1937. Also participating are the Popular Christian Socialist Party (Partido Popular Social Cristiano), the Popular Action Movement (Movimiento de Acción Popular), and the Independent Liberal Party (Partido Liberal Independiente). None of these groups is allowed any real share of power. There is also a radical Trotskyist party, the Communist Party of Nicaragua (Partido Comunista Nicaraguense), headed by Eli Altamirano, which is not in the FPR.

The Sandinista movement seized power in July 1979, after a year and a half of civil war against the dictatorship of Anastasio Somoza. Since that time, the FSLN and its government have moved continuously to the left and alienated many former supporters, who have gone into exile.

Domestic Problems. After two years of economic growth, the economy sagged in 1982; this continued into 1983. Nevertheless, the coffee harvest that concluded in February was a record 140,000 metric tons (*Latin America Weekly Report*, 4 February). Food production remained a problem, and in June, the USSR donated 15,000 metric tons of wheat. In that same month, the government announced that it would suspend indefinitely payment of $900 million to foreign banks; Central Bank President Enrique Figueroa blamed this on floods, drought, and the border war with counterrevolutionaries (Latin-Reuters, 15 June; *FBIS*, 16 June). In economic moves against the counterrevolutionaries (*contras*), the Sandinista government confiscated the estates of sixteen large landholders said to be supporters of the *contras* and also seized the assets of the leader of the largest *contra* group, Aldolfo Calero. These included his Coca-Cola bottling business, his Datsun agency, land, and hotel interests. (*This Week Central America and Panama*, 28 March, 3 May). Much confiscated land was to be put into the agrarian reform, which intended to turn over 350,000 hectares (870,000 acres) to peasants during the course of 1983 (*La Prensa*, 25 February). Many of the Sandinistas' economic problems were not of their own making. In May, the United States slashed the Nicaraguan sugar export quota to the United States by 90 percent. The next month, the Nicaraguan airline, Aeronica, lost its permission for six weekly flights to Miami. But even more important than the actions of the North Americans was the growing oil shortage, which was due both to *contra* activity and Nicaragua's insolvency. On 1 November, the government cut the fuel ration for private cars from twenty to two gallons a month and slashed bus rations by a third. Nor was fuel the only thing in short supply. Earlier in the year, the government had nationalized the distribution of soap, oil, and flour and then in November rationed newsprint, cutting out Sunday papers and limiting each paper to eight pages a day.

Church and state continued to clash. The papal visit in March was seen as a gesture of support for the conservative archbishop, Miguel Obando y Bravo, who, like the pope, deplores the authoritarianism of the government and wants the several priests in the government to get out. Although there was talk of a "people's church," there was no real schism, but rather a polariza-

tion of elements within Catholicism. Occasional violence of Sandinista groups against conservative churchmen continued to occur, and in November two priests, a Spaniard and a Costa Rican, were expelled, leading Obando to charge "open persecution" of the church (*This Week Central America and Panama*, 7 November).

One area where progress was evidently being made was toward holding elections. The Council of State, a consultative body composed of various elements loyal to the regime and headed by Carlos Núñez, completed its draft of a political parties law on 17 August; it was accepted by the Junta on 2 September. The law creates a National Assembly of Political Parties that would in turn send delegates to a National Council of Political Parties, which would also include three members of the Council of State and a Junta member. This National Council would then supervise all activities of political parties. Parties already having legal status include those in the FPR and three antigovernment parties belonging to the Nicaraguan Democratic Coordination (Coordinadora Democrática Nicaraguense; CDN). There are several other small parties that could receive legal status. Parties are guaranteed the right to organize, publicize, and run candidates, but must pledge to "promote and support national unity and consolidate and defend revolutionary conquests" (*Barricada International*, 29 August). The next phase is to draft the actual electoral law, and a committee under Carlos Núñez hopes to have completed this work by the spring of 1984. Núñez promised that the elections would be held in 1985 even if the violence of the *contra* groups increased, but predicted that the Sandinistas would win "because the masses are on the side of those who have liberated them" (AFP, Paris, 20 August; *FBIS*, 22 August). Carlos Tunnerman, on the other hand, cautioned that violence might delay the elections, and certain members of the National Directorate, especially Tomás Borge and Humberto Ortega, seemed to have reservations about any elections that might reverse the revolution or give power to some group outside the Sandinista circle (*NYT*, 7 July). (In February 1984, the elections were rescheduled for November 1984.)

If the prospect for elections suggested the possibility of a trend toward more democratic forms, the continued censorship of the opposition paper, *La Prensa*, the closure of several radio stations, and, above all, the establishment of the anti-Somocista People's Tribunals in April suggested that authoritarianism was still the rule. Like other emergency measures, these courts were declared necessary due to the incessant attacks of the *contras*. "The emergency situation," explained the government, "requires swift-acting judicial bodies" (Managua Radio Sandino, 11 April; *FBIS*, 12 April). The courts were to be composed of one lawyer and two nonlawyers who would be empowered to try "war criminals" without benefit of jury, or much legal machinery of any kind. Eduardo Rivas, chairman of the CDN, charged the government was thus creating "totalitarian structures of a Marxist-Leninist tendency" (*This Week Central America and Panama*, 8 August).

The Nicaraguan Military Buildup. Feeling threatened by both external and internal enemies, Nicaragua continued to build up its military forces. Although plans to procure MiG-21 jets from the USSR were evidently dropped, arms continued to flow in. An international sensation was created in April when Libyan planes bringing arms to Nicaragua were turned back in Brazil after being detained by the Brazilian government. In late July, the Pentagon announced that it had evidence that Soviet cargo ships bringing helicopters, tanks, artillery, rockets and electronics were nearing Nicaragua (ibid., 1 August). One Russian freighter was intercepted by a U.S. destroyer 30 miles off the Nicaraguan coast, but allowed to proceed to its destination. France also announced plans in July to sell two patrol boats to Nicaragua. There were persistent reports of an international brigade forming in Nicaragua, and the Marxist United Socialist Party of Mexico announced that it was sending volunteers.

Nicaragua itself made two important military reforms during the year. One was to reorganize the Popular Sandinista Militia on a regional basis to make it, for the first time, a really effective fighting force. The first three regional battalions were formed in July (*Barricada Internacional*, 11 July, 1 August). In August, Defense Minister Humberto Ortega appeared before the Council of State to request that it draft a military conscription law. The draft initially called for the registration of all males between 17 and 50 and females from 18 to 40, although it was later modified so that the men's registration ages matched those of the women. In actuality, only males in the youngest draft-age category could expect to be called

up, and those probably in small numbers. The conscription act, therefore, was more a symbolic gesture of defiance than an attempt to create a huge military force. Although many Latin American nations theoretically have universal military service, the new law received harsh condemnation from the CDN parties and the hierarchy of the Catholic church. On 31 August, the Episcopal Conference of Nicaragua branded the measure "an attack on freedom." The Sandinista People's Army (Ejercito Popular Sandinista; EPS) now numbers 25,000 effectives, with a similar number of reservists and 80,000 militia. There may be as many as 2,000 Cuban and Eastern bloc military advisers. (*Washington Report on the Hemisphere*, 20 September.)

Border War with the *Contras*. In 1983, the EPS and militia faced opponents on both borders. On the Honduran border operate the Nicaraguan Democratic Front (Frente Democratica Nicaraguense; FDN) of Adolfo Calero as well as smaller groups, largely led by former Somoza officers; on the Costa Rican frontier, ARDE, the force led by former Sandinista commander Edén Pastora and ex-Junta member Alfonso Robelo opened operations in April. The FDN was quite openly receiving millions of dollars in U.S. aid from the CIA and operating with the full cooperation of the Honduran government. Costa Rica appeared to ignore the operations of ARDE. Serious FDN incursions occurred in March, with heavy fighting in Nueva Segovia and Matagalpa against a *contra* force estimated at more than a thousand (*WP*, 22 March). Humberto Ortega accused the Honduran army of actual participation in this drive and warned of the possibility of war between the two countries (*NYT*, 22 March). On 30 April, the first clashes between the EPS and ARDE occurred (ibid., 1 May). On 6 May, there was again heavy combat in the northwest, with a major action at Jalapa, Nueva Segovia. The FDN force, which Managua put at 1,200, was repelled; over sixty *contras* were killed (Managua Radio Sandino, 6 May; *FBIS*, 9 May). The EPS also clashed with Pastora's forces along the Rio Maiz, with some sixty being killed on either side (*This Week Central America and Panama*, 16 May). The EPS won back all lost territory in the north by the end of May and was then accused of violating Honduran national territory near Cifuentes in Paraiso department. The fighting in that area went on through June. On 21 June, two foreign newsmen were killed on a Honduran road; each government accused the other of responsibility. On 23 June, Edén Pastora mysteriously called a "truce," saying his forces were exhausted, but by 28 June they were back fighting. It has been suggested that the pause was an effort to convince the CIA to aid his cause, although he steadfastly denied taking money from any such source. In July, ARDE forces invaded across the San Juan River and seized San Juan del Norte, only to be thrown back. August saw an FDN drive into Jinotega and northern Zelaya, where many Miskito Indians were sympathetic to the *contra* cause, but by mid-month the offensive had run aground (*Newsweek*, 22 August). October saw the heaviest fighting with the FDN since May, centering around Ocotal, Nueva Segovia (*Time*, 10 October). In the meantime, ARDE was resorting to more imaginative tactics —bombing Managua's Sandino airport and the oil storage facilities at the port of Corinto in September and then attacking the port in October by speedboat and destroying 3 million gallons of fuel. The oil storage facilities at Puerto Benjamin Zelaya were similarly attacked. But while the *contras* continued to prove a nuisance, it was plain by December that they had little popular support and even less chance of toppling the Sandinista government. The United States even appeared to be considering abandoning its support (*This Week Central America and Panama*, 12 December).

A bizarre footnote to the strained relations between Washington and Managua was provided by the Miguel D'Escoto poison plot. On 4 June, the FSLN alleged that three staff members of the U.S. embassy in Managua had attempted to have the foreign minister poisoned by a member of his staff, who was in fact a double agent and betrayed the plot to the Nicaraguan government. The three officers were named and expelled from Managua. In retaliation, Washington, denying the plot, closed the six Nicaraguan consulates in the United States. The consul in New Orleans thereupon sought political asylum rather than return to Managua.

Efforts Toward Negotiations. Throughout the year, efforts were under way to improve U.S.–Nicaraguan relations and end the border war. In May, Managua called for direct talks with Washington aimed at ending the fighting on the Honduran border, but the United States dismissed the idea. Nicaragua, a member of the U.N. Security Council, asked in May for an urgent meeting to discuss the Honduran border situation, but little came of these discussions. In June, Tomás Borge was denied an entry visa into the United States, where he had planned to present his government's views to a number of university audiences. Perhaps the best hope for a solution lay in the proposal of the Contadora group (Mexico, Panama, Colombia, and Venezuela) for a demilitarization of Central America, but the United States appeared cool to the proposal. U.S. special envoy Richard Stone met with Miguel d'Escoto in July and August, and although characterized as positive, the talks had no immediate results. In October, d'Escoto delivered a note to the State Department, offering to cease support for the Salvadorean rebels if the United States would cease to aid the *contras*, but this was rejected (*Time*, 31 October). In July, *contra* leader Edén Pastora went to Cuba and was cordially received by Fidel Castro, leading to speculation that he might be about to rejoin the Sandinistas, but at year's end ARDE was still opposing the government (*NYT*, 6 October). At the end of November, the Sandinistas declared a policy of "national conciliation." Talks were opened with the leaders of the Catholic church to improve relations, over 300 Miskito prisoners were freed, and all *contras* were to be allowed to return and have full civil rights and their property restored, save for former Somoza officers and a few of the leaders. (*WP*, 4 December.) As many as 2,000 Cubans were sent home. These measures, coupled with the promise of free elections in 1985, appeared to have impressed even the U.S. government that the FSLN really wanted a détente (*Time*, 12 December).

Other Foreign Contacts. Ninety-seven nonaligned nations held their fifth special ministerial meeting in Managua in January to prepare for the full-scale meeting of the nonaligned bloc in New Delhi in March (*NYT*, 15 January). They formulated the "Managua Declaration," which declared that the region was not the strategic preserve of any power and that its countries should be left to solve their own problems. On his way to the New Delhi gathering, Miguel d'Escoto stopped on 6 March in Moscow for talks with Kremlin leaders. In April, Henry Ruiz conferred in Mexico City with President Miguel de la Madrid, and Bayardo Arce visited Spain for talks with Premier Felipe

González. June saw Arce heading a delegation to Eastern Europe, speaking in Moscow with principal Soviet ideologist Konstantin Chernenko. At the same time, Sergio Ramírez, Carlos Tunnerman, and other leaders were in Caracas to celebrate the bicentennial of Simon Bolivar's birthday with the Venezuelan government. Another important celebration, Cuba's thirtieth 26 July holiday, brought Henry Ruiz and a delegation to Havana. He also met in Mexico with President de la Madrid. Sergio Ramírez was in North Korea in September and in Yugoslavia in October. Seeking support for Nicaragua's position on the border war, Tomás Borge toured Europe in September, speaking with Premier Pierre Mauroy in Paris and Premier Bettino Craxi in Rome. The secretary general of the Soviet Foreign Ministry, Yuri Fokin, came to Managua in August and held two days of talks with Miguel d'Escoto, following which the Soviet Union and Nicaragua issued a joint declaration condemning the *contras* and praising the Contadora plan (Moscow world service, 3 August; *FBIS*, 5 August).

Thomas P. Anderson
Eastern Connecticut State University

Panama

Population. 2.1 million (*World Factbook*, July)
Party. Panamanian People's Party (Partido del Pueblo; PPP or PDP)
Founded. 1943
Membership. 500–1,000 militants (*Statistical Yearbook*). The party gathered 34,990 signatures in its legalization campaign (Panama TV 2, 20 June). Some sources cite this number as membership.
Secretary General. Rubén Darío Sousa (alternate spelling Souza) since 1951
Politburo. (Incomplete) César Agusto De Leon Espinosa, Miguel Antonio Porcella Peña, Anastacio E. Rodríguez, Clito Manuel Souza Batista, Ruperto Luther Thomas Trottman (international secretary). Other prominent members are Felix Dixon (Editorial Council representative) and Carlos Chang Marin (a high-ranking leader) (*Critica*, April 1980)
Central Committee. 26 Members
Status. Legal
Last Congress. Sixth, 8–10 February 1980
Last Election. 1978, no representation
Auxiliary Organizations. Panama Peace Committee, People's Party Youth, National Center of Workers of Panama, Union of Journalists of Panama, Federation of Panamanian Students, and National Union of Democratic Women
Publications. *Unidad* (weekly)

Although communism has never found very fertile soil in Panama, the use of common front tactics and a commitment to Panamanian nationalism have allowed the PDP to play a role in national politics that at times has been far greater than its numerical strength. One of the PDP's predecessors, the Partido Laborista, founded in 1930, began as a laborite party affiliated with the Communist International. The original Panamanian party, the Partido Comunista de Panama, was formed by members of the Partido Laborista who broke away from that party on Moscow's orders. In order to increase its popular appeal, the Partido Comunista renamed itself the Partido del Pueblo in 1943.

Although the PDP was able to gain a strong position in organized labor in the 1940s, it was unable to elect candidates to office. (In 1947, for example, the PDP presidential candidate received only a thousand votes.) In 1953, the PDP was declared illegal, and it remained so until 1968. However, it continued to operate with varying degrees of openness, depending on the existing government's policy. In the 1960s, its cooperation with revolutionary student groups (in the 1964 Panama Canal Zone riots) enabled the PDP to exert an influence disproportionate to its size. Its membership increased by only 300 (from about 150 to about 450) during this period.

With the military coup in 1968, the PDP, as well as all other political parties, was officially dissolved. The party's labor arm, the Federación Sindical de Trabajadores (FST), was closed down, and its leader, Angel Gómez, was imprisoned along with other PDP leaders who were not exiled. By August 1970, Gen. Omar Torrijos, the military strong man, had declared an amnesty. Although the PDP was denied formal recognition, certain members participated in the Torrijos government. The PDP had originally labeled the Torrijos government as "petty bourgeois," but by the early 1970s it began to speak of a new "balance of forces" that had dealt a blow to the "oligarchy" and "U.S. imperialism." Torrijos needed the party's support, and an accommodation was reached. Most of the PDP's activities in the mid- and late 1970s centered around the "struggle for national liberation," which concretely took the form of a campaign to win back the Panama Canal Zone. The PDP supported the Torrijos-Carter treaties of 7 September 1977 but demanded that all territory be returned to Panama immediately.

Two events were central to a more recent decline in PDP influence in the Panamanian government: the new civilian government of 1978 and the death of Torrijos in 1981. The PDP's influential position in the government began to erode when Torrijos opened the political system to political parties; created a new official government party, the Democratic Revolutionary Party (DRP); and appointed a civilian president, Arístides Royo. The PDP was allowed to present candidates in the September 1980 elections as "independents" since it was unable to secure the required 30,000 signatures for registration. With Torrijos no longer in direct control of the government and after a shift toward more conservative domestic economic policies by Royo, the government began to view close ties with the ideologically oriented PDP as a liability. In the party's Sixth Congress resolution (Political Bureau statement, 5 April), however, the PDP established a political line that called for a democratic front of national liberation as part of a transitional stage to socialism. This stage would include a progressive democracy, a mixed economy, and an alliance with the National Guard and the DRP.

In July 1981, the same month that Torrijos was killed in a plane crash, the PDP was able to gather the necessary 30,000 signatures to achieve legal status and participate in the presidential elections of 1984 under its own name. The party spent most of fall 1981 and 1982 adjusting to its new legal status and reacting to the power struggle that was unleashed after Torrijos's death. It sought to expand its traditionally narrow organizational base by developing a new outreach program and an ideological education campaign in February 1982. President Royo ostensibly retired for health reasons, but in reality his desire for diplomatic relations with communist countries and his criticism of the United States made him a liability to the National Guard. General Rubén Darío Paredes became the leader of the Guard after Torrijos's death, and Ricardo de la Espriella replaced Royo as president. The PDP tried to maintain good relations with the DRP and the National Guard, but this became increasingly difficult in late 1982 and early 1983 as certain members of those groups sought to win U.S. approval by verbally demonstrating their anticommunism.

Party Organization. The PDP supreme authority is the National Congress, which is supposed to meet every four years. (This process was abandoned between 1968 and 1980.) The Congress elects a Central Committee, which in turn elects a Secretariat and Political Bureau.

Auxiliary Organizations. On 3 September 1982, Panamanian President Espriella granted legal status to the Panama Peace Council. At its most recent congress (23 September 1982), Dr. Camilo O. Pérez (a World Peace Council [WPC] vice-president) was appointed president, and a presidium of 33 members was reappointed. It included "representatives of political parties, mass organizations, and the regional presidents of this organization" (*Peace Courier*, September 1982). Influential members of the Peace Council include Nathaniel Hill Arboleda (a WPC secretary) and Luther Thomas Trottman (international secretary of the PDP). The PDP is also very influential in an affiliate of the Women's International Democratic Federation, the National Union of Democratic Women; a PDP official, Marta Matamoros, is international secretary of this organization. Matamoros is also international secretary of the Panamanian Women's Committee for the Defense of the Rights of Women and Children (*Quien es Quien en Panama*, 18 May 1982). Although the PDP lost its complete control over the International Union of Students affiliate, the Federation of Panamanian Students (Federación des Estudiantes de Panama; FDP) in the late 1960s, it still remains very influential in this organization, which is active at the University of Panama. As of 1978, the PDP had its own student affiliate, the Frente Reformista Universitaria. The party's youth affiliate is called the People's Party Youth and is affiliated with the World Federation of Democratic Youth. Its trade union affiliate, the Federación Sindical de Trabajadores, was disbanded by Torrijos in 1968. However, the party is influential in the World Federation of Trade Unions affiliate, the Central Nacional de Trabajadores.

Other Leftist Parties. In 1975, a group called the Tendencia or Fracción was formed by PDP youth leaders and members of the leadership of the FDP. This organization held its first congress in 1978. Although little is known about its recent activities, it had as of early 1983 about 1,500 members (*World Factbook*, 1983). Another party that was not very active in 1983 was the Maoist Communist Party/Marxist-Leninist. During 1982, this party launched a violent attack on the pro-Moscow PDP, accusing it of being nonrevolutionary, collaborationist, and acting against the interest of the people. A third party of the non-PDP left, the Socialist Workers' Party (PST), was officially recognized on 26 September after it had gathered 30,382 signatures. Virgilio Arauz was recognized as the party's legal representative. The PST was the only major party that opposed the constitutional referendum

of 29 April (*Critica*, 26 September). This party opposed the Torrijos-Carter treaties, calls for social revolution, accuses the United States of being responsible for Central American problems, and calls for an "electoral front" against "Yankee imperialism." It wants to solve the unemployment problem, defend the rights of the working class, and achieve national independence. It supports the revolutions in El Salvador and Nicaragua. (*La Prensa*, 14 September.) In May, the PST opposed the candidacy of General Paredes for the presidency in 1984 and called on the PDP to break with the National Guard and the DRP presidential candidate and form a left-wing coalition. The PST called for a joint PST-PDP presidential candidate. (*Critica*, 26 May.) A fourth party, the Workers' Revolutionary Party (PRT), was declared legal in October after gathering 31,059 signatures. The party's legal representative is its president, Graciela J. Dixon; its secretary general is Dr. Egbert Wetherborne. The party nominated Dr. José Renan Esquivel as its presidential candidate and formed an alliance with several trade union groups under the name Frente Electoral del Pueblo Unidos. It hopes to attract the PDP and PST (*Latin America Weekly Review*, 23 September). The Trotskyist PRT has accused Paredes of deviating from Torrijist goals (*FBIS*, 13 September) and in a 4 July letter told the PDP that it would be "nearsighted and opportunist" if the PDP supported Paredes. Secretary General Wetherborne called on the PDP to discuss an alternative to Paredes (*Ya*, 6 July). Finally, several far-left groups were also active in 1983. The Revolutionary Student Front stoned the U.S. Embassy on 15 September and in October participated along with other groups including the Guaykudo-NIR, the People's Revolutionary Youth, and the PST in a demonstration in front of the U.S. Embassy to protest the invasion of Grenada (*Critica*, 16 September; *La Prensa*, 16 October).

Constitutional Reform and Paredes's Candidacy. On 28 October 1982, the Panamanian legislative body, the National Assembly of Corregimiento Representatives, authorized the executive branch of the Panamanian government to proceed with the revision of the 1972 constitution. Under cabinet resolution no. 148 (19 November 1982), a commission was appointed to make a reform proposal. This committee was composed of nine representatives from the 505

Corregimiento members, four representatives from the DRP, and one representative from the PDP, as well as representatives from the other parties. The draft amendment approved by President Espriella on 31 March included a proposal for a new national legislative branch and the relegation of the corregimientos to local responsibility only. Members of this new assembly would be nominated by the political parties and elected by direct popular vote, one member for each province and additional members for each 30,000 individuals. This put smaller parties like the PDP at a disadvantage.

The PDP Central Committee and Political Bureau issued two statements (5 and 16 April) concerning the constitutional reform proposal. They stated that the primary need was to defend the Torrijist process. Although they had originally felt that the present was not the time to reform the 1972 constitution, they called for a yes vote. The party had originally feared that the "oligarchic forces" would completely destroy the gains of 1972. The PDP delegate, for example, had voted against the relegation of the corrigimientos to local-level authority. However, the party was willing to accept this and other changes as long as the spirit of Torrijism—popular power, worker rights, and the role of the National Guard in the political process—were not destroyed. Although the reforms were not satisfactory, the PDP said they were not a "surrender to imperialism." (*IB*, July; PDP Manifesto, 16 April.)

The results of the 29 April referendum were 476,716 yes and 66,447 no votes. The new constitution took effect on 20 May. (*FBIS*, 29 April.) Elections for president, vice-president, and members of the National Assembly were scheduled for 6 May 1984 and those for mayors, municipal councillors, and corregimiento representatives for 3 June 1984.

General Paredes's candidacy for president of Panama was proposed by the DRP (20 March) and by the Agrarian Labor Party (17 May). The two parties set up a united action campaign on 23 May. The PDP originally viewed this candidacy in a positive light. However, in July during a news conference in Costa Rica, Paredes stated that "the democratic countries of Central America cannot tolerate the belligerent stance taken by Cuba and Nicaragua. Should this situation continue, Panama might break off relations with these two governments, which are fostering nothing but instability, violence, and death in the

area." (ACAN, 1 July; *FBIS*, 5 July.) The PDP leadership was unhappy with this stand by Paredes, and they held a meeting with Paredes's successor as National Guard head, Manuel Antonio Noriega (*FBIS*, 12 July). On 12 August, Paredes resigned from the National Guard in order to pursue legally his presidential aspirations, and Noriega took his place. During a Telemetro interview (22 August), Paredes stated, "I think it would be wrong to promote relations with the PRC or USSR. We are on the side of the Western world, whose leader is the U.S." (*FBIS*, 22 September.) For whatever reason, probably to encourage U.S. support for his candidacy, Paredes was taking positions that were anathema to the PDP.

Paredes withdrew his candidacy on 6 September, claiming that it was divisive and not in the best interests of the country. He had expected that Noriega and Espriella as well as the political parties would not accept his resignation. Instead, Noriega sent a telegram approving his decision, and several hours later Espriella replaced Paredes's supporters and overtly pro-U.S. elements in a major cabinet reshuffle. On 12 September, Paredes accused Noriega of "high treason" and "betrayal of commitment." Government spokesmen responded that Paredes had demanded "total and absolute support," which could not be given. (*Ya*, 12 September; *Latin America Regional Report*, 23 September; *Latin America Weekly Report*, 23 September.)

The PDP had begun to reconsider seriously its support for Paredes's candidacy in August, before his withdrawal. On 29 August, Sousa told *La República* that the PDP was "analyzing the situation, but if we reach the conclusion that Paredes is not following Torrijos—the Torrijos program —we cannot support him. Our party is assessing Paredes's overt and irate anticommunism." The day after Paredes withdrew, the PDP Political Bureau issued a statement that said that Paredes's candidacy had been an attempt to create a convergence of forces based on "rightist concessions." The effort had failed, the PDP said, because the masses had rejected the effort to abandon Torrijism. After Paredes withdrew, the PDP proposed a presidential candidacy based on the following principles: national liberation; defense of health, housing, social security, and labor systems; economic independence; protection of the state sector of the economy and of cooperatives; and collective use of Panama Canal

Zone land returned by the United States (*La Prensa*, 16 September).

Secretary General Sousa stated on 12 September that the PDP would support a candidate committed to Torrijist ideals. Although Carlos del Cid, PDP legal adviser, had his candidacy put forth by the National Federation of Workers, it is probable that the PDP will support a candidate proposed by National Guard leader Noriega (ibid., 17 July; *Latin America Weekly Report*, 23 September).

PDP's International Positions. During a speech at the Karl Marx conference held in April in East Germany, Sousa stated that the PDP was linked by its Marxist-Leninist heritage to the "democratic struggle of the international labor class," the "national liberation movement," and the "defense of world peace." Sousa called the USSR the "vanguard" of this struggle. The Reagan government, he said, through its "bellicose" policies was attempting to circumvent the Torrijos-Carter treaties and promote U.S. imperialism in Central America (*Neues Deutschland*, East Berlin, 14 April). The PDP Political Bureau (7 September) pledged to continue Torrijos's efforts to achieve "diplomatic independence," "internationalism," and "nonalignment." The Political Bureau affirmed PDP solidarity with Nicaragua and the revolutionary struggle in El Salvador, Guatemala, and other Central American nations. It approved the Contadora group's principles of "self-determination," "peace," and "nonintervention" (*La Prensa*, 16 September).

Concrete positions taken by the party in 1983 include opposition to the U.S. Kindle Liberty project, opposition to the continued existence of the School of the Americas (a U.S. military school that Paredes decided should be turned over to Panama in 1984 rather than closed down as agreed in the Torrijos-Carter treaties), a declaration of full solidarity with Cuba, and solidarity with the USSR concerning the Korean airliner incident (ibid., 25 October; *FBIS*, 27 July; Political Bureau statement, 15 September). On the occasion of his sixtieth birthday, Secretary General Sousa received the Soviet Order of Friendship and a medal from the Bulgarian Communist Party.

Christian V. Pascale

Paraguay

Population. 3.5 million (estimate)
Party. Paraguayan Communist Party (Partido Comunista Paraguayo; PCP)
Founded. 1928
Membership. 3,500 (approximate)
First Secretary. Antonio Maidana
Politburo. Unknown
Secretariat. Unknown
Central Committee. Unknown
Status. Illegal
Last Congress. Third, 10 April 1971
Last Election. Not applicable
Auxiliary Organizations. No information
Publications. *Adelante* (daily underground newspaper)

In February, Gen. Alfredo Stroessner was elected to a seventh presidential term, which set a Paraguayan record for longevity in power and made him the most durable of Latin America's contemporary dictators. Stroessner pledged to continue the tough line against Paraguay's communists he has followed since coming to power in 1954. Other opposition groups have been accorded amnesty over the past 29 years and allowed to return from exile, but never the communists. Indeed, Stroessner's secret agents are known to be active among exile communities in neighboring countries, and more than one important communist party official has been kidnapped and brought back to Paraguay to be tortured for information. For example, the PCP's first secretary, Antonio Maidana, was seized by Stroessner's police in downtown Buenos Aires in 1980 and has since been held incommunicado. According to the PCP, Maidana is still alive and is currently being moved from one remote military outpost to another in order to keep him hidden from inquiring human rights groups. Another PCP leader, Emilio Roa, is being held under similar conditions (*New Times*, Moscow, October 1982).

The Paraguayan government considers the PCP to be very much of a threat. The Ministry of Interior claims that the communists are behind a guerrilla movement called the Politico-Military Organization (OPM) that is trying to infiltrate student, labor, and peasant groups (*Patria*, 3 May; *FBIS*, 6 May). Using this as a justification, the police made several raids on alleged subversives during May, June, and July. The chief targets were the Movement for University Reorganization, the Inter-Union Committee of Solidarity, the Central Confederation of Peasants, the Banco Paraguayo de Datos (a human rights information center), and various student publications (*Patria*, 3 May; *FBIS*, 6 May; *Latin America Weekly Report*, 27 May, 23 and 29 July).

Although the government claimed the OPM terrorists had planned a massive disruption of the presidential inauguration on 15 August, Paraguay's noncommunist opposition dismissed such allegations as constituting an excuse to silence any dissent (*Hoy*, 24 May; *FBIS*, 26 May). The leading opposition newspaper, *ABC*, argued that deteriorating economic conditions—30 percent inflation, 15 percent unemployment, and production idling at 80 percent of capacity—were making Stroessner especially sensitive to any criticism. Soon after writing this Aldo Zucolillo, *ABC*'s editor and publisher, was arrested.

Meanwhile, the PCP's underground daily, *Adelante*, continued to call for the formation of a popular front to combat Stroessner and U.S. imperialism. Nevertheless, it remains excluded from the National Accord, a coalition of four noncommunist parties opposed to the dictatorship. The PCP had to settle for participating, in late 1982, in a meeting of Latin American communist parties held in Lima, Peru. There it joined with the others in promising to carry on the struggle for "national and social liberation" after the examples of Cuba, Nicaragua, and Grenada (*Horizont*, no. 10; *FBIS*, 19 January).

Paul H. Lewis
Tulane University

Peru

Population. 19.2 million
Party. Peruvian Communist Party (PCP)
Founded. 1930

Membership. 2,000

Secretary General. Jorge del Prado

Central Committee. 15 members: Gustavo Espinoza Montesinos, Guillermo Herrera, Asunción Caballero Méndez, Jorge del Prado, Olivera Vila, Isidoro Gamarra, Roberto Rojas, Valentín Pacho, Julián Serra, Jaime Figueroa, Victor Checa, Antonio Torres Andrade, César Alva, Carlos Bonino, and Alfonso Barrantes

Status. Legal

Last Congress. Eighth extraordinary, 27–31 January 1982, in Lima

Last Election. 1980; PCP and other Marxist parties won 9 of 60 seats in Senate and 10 of 180 Chamber of Deputies seats, receiving 15.6 percent of the votes for president, 21.8 percent of the votes for the Senate

Auxiliary Organizations. General Confederation of Peruvian Workers (CGTP), Peruvian Peasant Confederation (CCP)

Publications. *Unidad*, newspaper of the PCP; *El Diario*, leftist newspaper

Other Marxist Parties. Peruvian Communist Party–Red Fatherland (PCP-PR), f. 1969, Maoist; Peruvian Communist Party–Red Flag (PCP-BR), f. 1969, pro-Albanian; Revolutionary Vanguard (VR), f. 1965; Revolutionary Movement of the Left (MIR-PERU), f. 1965, refounded in 1977; Revolutionary Communist Party (PCR), 1974 split from VR; Revolutionary Socialist Party (PSR), f. 1976, Velasquista; Worker, Peasant, Student, and People's Front (FOCEP), f. 1978, Trotskyist; Popular Democratic Union (UDP), f. 1978, Maoist front; Union of the Revolutionary Left (UNIR), f. 1980, pro-Chinese front; Marxist Revolutionary Workers'–Socialist Workers' Party (POMR-PST), f. 1968–1974, Trotskyist; Revolutionary Workers' Party (PRT), f. mid-1970s, Trotskyist

The PCP, as part of the United Left (IU) parliamentary and electoral coalition, participated as an important member of the legal opposition in Peru in 1983. As the nation faced economic collapse and a mounting terrorist campaign, the political opposition of IU and the non-Marxist American Popular Revolutionary Alliance (APRA) consistently fought the policies of President Fernando Belaúnde Terry's Popular Action (AP)–Popular Christian Party (PPC) administration. Their success was registered in a resounding triumph over the governing coalition in the November municipal elections in which mayors and councilmen were chosen in 1,517 districts nationwide. The most important victory was that of Alfonso Barrantes Lingán (IU) who, as mayor of Lima, became the first freely elected Marxist mayor of any South American capital. The PCP stated that IU's victory was a great historic event for the left and progressive sectors. Describing the elections as a "plebiscite of the Peruvian people," the Central Committee said the results were "an emphatic rejection of the current regime and its policies, especially the mismanaged economic policy" (*FBIS*, 13 December).

Political Parties. The PCP, under Secretary General Jorge del Prado, is the foundation of the IU; it provides the most local bases and the best organization, but it does not provide the most militant leadership. The smaller parties continually strive to maintain their ideological independence while benefiting from the advantages of unity on the national scene. The IU has been a loosely but consistently united coalition since 1980. Its heterogeneous membership consists of two fronts, the Maoist UDP and the pro-Beijing UNIR, and four parties, the pro-Soviet PCP, the Velasquista PSR, the PCR, and the Trotskyist FOCEP. In March, the National Executive Committee of the IU (composed of Alfonso Barrantes, president; Genaro Ledesma, FOCEP; Jorge del Prado, PCP; Manuel Dammert, PCR; Edmundo Murrugarra, UDP; Luís Benitez, UDP; Jorge Hurtado, UNIR; Juan Sánchez, UNIR; and Alfredo Filomeno, PSR) presented a draft program for a "popular and sovereign democratic state that opens the way towards socialism." The joint program called for (1) mobilization to defend and fulfill democratic liberties; (2) respect for political liberties and human rights and lifting of the state of emergency; (3) creation of provisional emergency governments in zones affected by disasters or subject to military control; (4) realization of the accords of the Unified National Agrarian Congress; and (5) reaffirmation of the principles of nonintervention and self-determination "being violated by the Reagan administration" (*Resumen Semana*, 10–16 June, p. 2).

The most important groups on the Marxist left

that are represented in parliament yet do not participate in the IU are the Trotskyists—the POMR-PST and Hugo Blanco's PRT—which have been a problem for the IU since its founding. They criticize the coalition as an "electoralist" front and charge that the orthodox communist labor confederation is too reformist to launch a generalized fight against the government (*Intercontinental Press*, 11 July, p. 384). And yet, after the November victory for the IU, Blanco announced that he wanted to be incorporated into the coalition. Barrantes was not too conciliatory: "I cannot realize an alliance with those who have always tried to divide us" (*Resumen Semana*, 25 November–1 December, p. 4). Disagreement exists even among the Trotskyist parties, as is evident in their positions regarding Nicaragua. While Blanco's PRT supports the Sandinista struggle as part of a larger fight against North American imperialism and talks of recruiting international brigades to assist Nicaragua, the POMR-PST accuses the Sandinista leadership of being "bureaucrats and capitulators" (*Intercontinental Press*, 11 July, p. 386).

Domestic Affairs. The strength of the IU-APRA victory (64 percent) in the municipal elections was testimony to the grave problems that Peru faced in 1983. The economy was at its worst in a century, natural disasters had destroyed 60 percent of the nation's agricultural production, and the population suffered under the greatest revolutionary guerrilla challenge ever launched against a Peruvian government.

The administration's economic policy consisted of monetarist stabilization policies dictated by the International Monetary Fund, reprivatization of the economy, and liberalization of trade. But the promised economic growth and increased employment were not forthcoming. During most of 1983, inflation was over 100 percent, unemployment and underemployment topped 59 percent, exports declined in value, and growth was −6 percent. (*NYT*, 24 July; *Latin America Weekly Report*, 2 September, p. 1.) Although much of Peru's $12 billion foreign debt was refinanced, the loans went to pay off old obligations rather than to provide funds for new development (*NYT*, 24 July). At the end of the year, the nation's deficit was 10 percent of gross domestic product, and most of this was due to military and domestic security outlays (*Latin America Weekly Report*, 2 December, p. 1). Military acquisitions

during the year, including French Mirage jets, Soviet helicopters, and German submarines, cost over $4 billion and were said to account for one-third of the budget (ibid., 14 October, p. 1).

In response to these policies, there was considerable labor and social unrest. During January and February, man-hours lost to strikes reached a new high, and in March the orthodox communist Confederation of Peruvian Workers (CGTP), the largest Peruvian labor organization, led its most successful stoppage since Belaúnde took office. All the other labor confederations—the Velasquista Confederation of Workers of the Peruvian Revolution (CTRP), the Aprista General Confederation of Labor (CTP), and the Christian Democratic National Workers Central (CNT)—participated. The 10 March general strike took place despite a state of emergency declaration that made public assemblies illegal and suspended personal liberties. CGTP Secretary General Eduardo Castillo said 34 percent of the workers participated in Lima, with total success in Arequipa, Ica, Marcona, San Martin, Chimbote, Iquitos, and Trujillo. Four persons died, however, in clashes with the police in Lima. (*Resumen Semana*, 4–10 March, p. 1, 11–17 March, p. 1; *Latin America Weekly Report*, 18 March, p. 7.)

The pro-Soviet group retained its influence in the CGTP leadership after its Seventh National Congress, ratifying Isidoro Gamarra as president and electing Valentín Pacho as the new secretary general (*Resumen Semana*, 15–21 July, p. 3). In the Bank Workers Federation, however, the new leader is Edgardo Cubas, an independent leftist from Arequipa. He won over Antonio Zúñiga, who became a member of the directorate along with former CGTP leader Eduardo Castillo. The directorate includes independents, pro-Soviet PCP members, Trotskyists, and members of the Maoist-led UNIR (*Resumen Semana*, 20–26 May, p. 4).

In other efforts to influence government policy, the PCP acted with the major opposition groups. Jorge del Prado (PCP), Alfonso Barrantes (IU), Enrique Bernales (PST), and Alan Garcia (APRA) were all participants in the first Unified National Agrarian Congress in early May. Over 800 delegates from all the agrarian organizations met to discuss the regime's agricultural policy. Although opened by Minister of Agriculture Mirko Cuculiza and closed by President Belaúnde, the congress was severely critical of the current policies and presented numerous demands (*Resumen Semana*, 6–12 May, p. 2).

The second general strike of the year, the eighth since 1977, was preceded by serious union unrest. The 30,000 members of the Bank Workers Federation had struck for one week, 4,700 miners were out of work, fishermen were fighting closure of processing plants, and the state doctors were off duty. The CGTP had originally planned a 48-hour stoppage to demand price controls on food and gasoline, but the second largest confederation, the Aprista CTP, pulled out because of internal problems. But the 24-hour general strike on 27 September was successful in Cuzco, Puno, and Juliaca and in banks nationwide. Secretary General Valentín Pacho said 100 percent of the CGTP bases adhered to the strike, as it paralyzed the textile and metalworking industries in Lima and most industry and commerce in Arequipa. (*Latin America Weekly Report*, 30 September, p. 7.) During the strike, however, 150 persons were arrested, and one student died (*Resumen Semana*, 23–29 September, p. 1). The increased violence in labor demonstrations was a result of the government's fear that uncontrolled protest in the cities would only add to the mounting unrest in the countryside.

Terrorism. The terrorism that gripped Peru in 1983 was the work of the PCP–Sendero Luminoso (Shining Path). The group's leader and cult hero, Dr. Abimael Gúzman (Comrade Gonzalo), was a member of the PCP-BR but split off in 1970. Sendero's philosophy is Mariateguista-Maoist and its message is that Peru's reality is similar to what it was in the 1930s and the only model for change is that of the Maoist protracted struggle in the countryside. This is described in the two pamphlets, *The New Government and Prospects for Economics, Politics, and Class Struggle in General* (1981), and *Let Us Develop Guerrilla Warfare* (1982). (Cynthia McClintock, *Problems of Communism*, September-October, p. 23.) For close to twenty years, followers of Gúzman recruited, trained, and organized cadres in the isolated Andean highlands. In 1980, as democracy was restored to Peru, Sendero began its activity. They first created the social bases of a people's army, then collected material and made their organization known through symbolic attacks on public buildings. In 1982, they launched their so-called third stage, which was to initiate

an armed struggle in the rural areas and gradually move into urban areas to create the conditions for the fourth stage—a people's war. (*Oiga*, 29 November 1982, pp. 20–34.) Throughout 1983, disruptions spread from Ayacucho to interior regions previously untroubled and to the urban areas of the coast, specifically Lima.

Despite the creation of a military zone in Ayacucho, Sendero was able to paralyze the departmental capital of 80,000 people twice during the month of January. On 25–26 July, it shut down the city to the point that outside airline and telephone services were terminated. It repeated this feat for three days during the municipal elections. (*Resumen Semana*, 22 July–4 August, p. 1; *FBIS*, 14 November.)

Sendero was able to completely disrupt normal civic activities in Ayacucho and parts of Huancavelica and Apurimac by intimidating bankers and merchants to close when strikes were called and to give them money and lower prices on essential goods at other times (*Resumen Semana*, 11–17 March, p. 3; *Expreso*, 9 July). Death lists, warnings, and murders were effective in forcing government authorities, teachers, and priests to leave their jobs, schools, and churches (*Resumen Semana*, 25 February–3 March, p. 7). Individuals who informed or cooperated with the authorities were dealt with harshly. Sometimes whole villages were punished, as on 3 April when 45 peasants, including ten children, were assassinated in Lucanamarca by Senderistas. Among the dead were leaders recently appointed by the military (ibid., 1–7 April, p. 2; *FBIS*, 6 April).

Sendero's activities in urban areas expanded greatly by midyear. On 27 May, in the most spectacular assault yet, ten high-tension towers were downed, plunging all of Lima into darkness for 90 minutes. At the same time, the Bayer Acrylic Fiber Factory, one of the most modern in South America, was destroyed. Dynamite blasts were heard throughout the city, and a fire in the shape of a hammer and sickle appeared on San Agustín hill (*Latin America Weekly Report*, 3 June, p. 7). Twice in June Lima was rocked by a series of explosions, causing extensive property damage (*Resumen Semana*, 17–23 June, p. 2). In July, the headquarters of the AP party was dynamited; 2 persons died, and 30 were injured. At the same time, power outages occurred elsewhere in the city (ibid., 8–14 July, p. 1).

The final major offensive of the year for Sendero preceded the municipal elections. In mid-October, Lima suffered a 30-minute blackout during which police posts came under attack. In the aftermath, 270 persons were arrested, although most were later released (*FBIS*, 19 October). On 29–30 October, there were nine synchronized bombings whose targets included a police station, a factory, a town hall, barracks, a civil guard station, a bank, the offices of the CGTP and *Caretas*, and AP headquarters, where one person was killed. (*Latin America Weekly Report*, 11 November, p. 1; *FBIS*, 3 November.) On 10 November, the U.S. and Honduran Embassies were hit, and on 12 November various political party headquarters were dynamited (*FBIS*, 14 November). Three policemen were killed and AP candidates were murdered in Cerro de Pasco, Huanta, and Huamangilla; at least 46 others resigned out of fear. (*Resumen Semana*, 4–11 November, p. 4; *FBIS*, 14 and 29 November.)

On the occasion of the AP headquarters blast, spokesmen of the Left made clear their disagreement with Sendero. CGTP leader Isidoro Gamarra said, "The attack contributed nothing to the working class struggle, in fact it makes the oppression against workers and peasants worse" (*El Observador*, 13 July). Barrantes (IU) expressed the hope that the perpetrators would be caught, but asked that the regime "act calmly and not prejudice democracy in the process" (*Resumen Semana*, 8–14 July, p. 1). The leftist paper *El Diario* criticized Sendero for this "new provocation" that helps to "legitimize the dirty war in Ayacucho" and "put into second place the concern with the regime's economic policies" (ibid.). A political commentator noted that "this brought about a new stage of terror, the loss of a civic treasure: liberty and daily peace" (ibid.). The deprivation of liberty and the threat to peace were seen to come not only from the terrorist campaign but also from the government's response.

The year began with seven provinces, all in Ayacucho, under a state of emergency and ended with ten, as provinces in Huancavelica and Apurimac were later included. For a period of 100 days, from 30 June to 9 September, there was a nationwide emergency during which all civil liberties were suspended. On 1 January, the province of Ayacucho was placed under the political-military command of Gen. Roberto Clemente Noel y Moral. The armed forces were to provide only logistical support, but they soon became actively involved in the struggle, and the number of incidents and victims drastically increased. Early estimates placed the number of rebels in the area at 500–700, but by May, the death toll of alleged Senderistas had exceeded 700, six times the number for the previous two years. (*Latin America Weekly Report*, 27 May, p. 3.) By August, Interior Minister Luí Percovitch said 1,033 Senderistas and 465 campesinos had been killed. Some noted with skepticism that this would make it the best-organized political party in the country (*Latin America Weekly Report*, 23 September, p. 10). Despite the unreliability of these statistics, at the end of 1983 it was likely that more than 2,000 persons had been killed in three and a half years of guerrilla activity (*FBIS*, 12 December).

The military's authority was increasingly undermined by charges of "Southern Cone tactics" (kidnapping, torture, illegal interrogations, helicopter strafing) and disclosures that counterinsurgency forces dressed as peasants were responsible for some Senderista deaths (*Resumen Semana*, 17–23 June, p. 2; *Peru Update*, July, p. 3).

Perhaps the greatest embarrassment for the regime was the massacre of eight journalists on 26 January by the peasants of Uchurracay. Initial accounts that they were mistaken for Senderistas were soon disproved. Police complicity in the affair was denied by a Special Commission Report that blamed "all official Peru." (*Resumen Semana*, 29 January–4 February, pp. 1–3, 29 April–5 May, p. 2; *Latin America Weekly Report*, 11 March, p. 5; *NYT Magazine*, 31 July, pp. 18–23.) The attitude that indiscriminate killing was "inevitable" in a situation of guerrilla warfare was not accepted by the IU-APRA opposition or by some members of the ruling coalition. Attempts by the nation's attorney general, Miguel Cavero Egúsquiza, to "avoid a bloodbath" were rebuffed, and he was censured for his efforts. (*Resumen Semana*, 26 September, p. 1; *FBIS*, 8 September.)

The hard-line approach was evident in Belaúnde's Independence Day speech when he asked for a reinstatement of the death penalty for treason (*Resumen Semana*, 22 July–4 August, p. 1). The administration's frustration with the lack of success on the military and economic fronts vented itself in attacks not only on all domestic political opposition, including peasant and trade union leaders, ex-military officers (ibid., 19–25 August), and university officials

(*FBIS*, 25 July), but also on research organizations in Peru funded by foreign sources (*Resumen Semana*, 1–7 July, p. 2), international organizations investigating human rights violations such as Amnesty International, and the international press, which Belaúnde claimed had launched a "campaign to discredit Peru." Throughout the year, the government struggled to eliminate the elusive terrorists while at the same time protecting political freedom and human rights. (*Latin America Weekly Report*, 26 August, p. 2.)

A major concern of the Left was harassment of political, labor, and peasant leaders. Examples included a campaign against schools run by unions, popular groups, or municipalities (*Resumen Semana*, 25 February–3 March, p. 7), and the detention of persons who organized or participated in strikes or meetings critical of the regime or even possessed "subversive material" such as books by Marx, Mariategui, or Lenin (*El Diario*, 27 June; *Resumen Semana*, 24–30 June, p. 5). In June, more than 15,000 police were mobilized in Lima, and 500 people were arrested; although most were freed when no evidence of terrorism could be found, for many this meant months of detention (*NYT*, 14 July). Communist labor leader Isidoro Gamarra was arrested as he was leaving for Prague to attend an antinuclear congress. Strong pressure from the CGTP brought about the release of the 78-year-old leader, who was held for one week, forced to sleep on the floor, and given no food. The charges against him were "disturbing the peace" during the 10 March national strike. (*FBIS*, 1 July; *CSM*, 27 June, p. 7.)

The IU opposition steadfastly denounced repression in Ayacucho also. Javier Diaz Canseco (UDP) and others charged General Noel with assassination, kidnapping, violating his constitutional obligations, and organizing paramilitary bands (*Resumen Semana*, 1–7 July, p. 3). By the end of the year, Noel had been replaced by Gen. Adrian Huaman Centero (*FBIS*, 12 December), and Minister of Justice Ernesto Alayza resigned after eight unarmed inmates and a nun they had taken hostage were killed in an escape attempt at Lurigancho Prison (ibid., 20 December).

Despite government attempts to link the Marxist parliamentary Left with the guerrillas, there is more evidence that Sendero believes the majority of the Left are not real Marxists because they will not accept violence as a means of revolution. It ridicules the IU as a "servant of reactionary opportunism" (*Caretas*, 22 December 1981, no. 629, p. 30). In addition, it has termed the Soviet Union and other Marxist countries "cruel deceptions" (*CSM*, 3 June). Apparently, the closest ties Sendero has domestically are with the PCP-Pucallacta, formed in 1979 to promote worker-peasant alliances in the mining sector, and the Huaccaycholo subversive groups created by former VR leader Julio César Izaguirre in Ongoy, Andahuylas (*Oiga*, 29 November 1982, pp. 20–23; *FBIS*, 5 August). There is some evidence, from a Colombian M-19 defector, that Sendero is in contact with other guerrilla movements in Latin America (*Free Press International*, 28 September; *FBIS*, 13 September). Important ties may also exist, as President Belaúnde has claimed, with drug traffickers. It appears likely that Sendero has financed its activities by charging the dealers for uninterrupted operation in Ayacucho, which is the third-largest coca paste producer in Peru (*FBIS*, 13 December).

Most important for the guerrilla group's survival, however, is popular support, and that appears to be diminishing with a backlash against their tactics in the countryside. In addition, the organization was weakened by the capture of more members as they moved into a less hospitable urban setting (*FBIS*, 1 July; *Expreso*, 16 June, p. 4). Rumors persisted all year that leaders Julio César Mezzich and Emilio Antonio Diaz Martínez had been captured, and it may be true that Diaz was taken in late December (*FBIS*, 20 December, p. 4). But perhaps the major challenge to the guerrillas is the popularity of the legitimate left, which was demonstrated in the November election.

Despite attempts to have the government cancel the elections and to intimidate the population into boycotting them, Sendero was able to affect only four Ayacuchan provinces, where no candidates would run for election, and turnout nationwide was approximately 70 percent (*Resumen Semana*, 4–11 November, p. 4). APRA was the overall winner, taking 34 percent of the vote to control more municipal councils than any other group; the center-left party is in a good position for the 1985 presidential elections. The IU won 30 percent nationwide and obtained the most votes in Lima. There, the IU elected 19 mayors in comparison to the 6 they won in 1980. The IU also won in major departments, including Puno, Cuzco, Huaraz, and Pucallpa (*Latin America*

Weekly Report, 16 December, p. 5; *Resumen Semana*, 4–11 November, p. 4). Their most significant victory was that of Alfonso Barrantes in Lima. His campaign focused on local issues of improving food distribution and basic services, but he seized on the national importance of the opposition victory and demanded the cabinet be changed in accordance with the people's wishes. He was not alone, and there was an immediate, unanimous vote in the Chamber of Deputies to bring about an administrative change (*NYT*, 17 November). Barrantes is well aware, however, that it will not be so easy to address the economic and social problems that face Peru in 1984. He asked for party unity and talented people to help the city and the nation (*Resumen Semana*, 4–11 November, p. 5).

International Relations. Peru's relations with the Soviet Union continued to be good. Outside of Cuba, Peru has the largest Soviet military presence in the Western Hemisphere. Although much of this was inherited from the military regime, the current government has allowed Soviet fishing within the 200-mile limit and continues military purchases. This was made possible by a refinancing of the Peruvian debt to the USSR in November. The agreement extended the repayment period for $519.5 million and allowed 75 percent of the debt to be paid with nontraditional products for the Soviet market and 25 percent to be paid with surplus traditional exports (*FBIS*, 21 November, 1 December). In other developments, Anatoly Filatov, the new ambassador from the Soviet Union, indicated a willingness to discuss the stalled Olmos project (ibid., 2 November). On a visit to the Peruvian legislature, Ivan P. Kalin, the vice-president of the Supreme Soviet of the USSR, rejected any ties with the Sendero Luminoso group, saying,

"There are many groups who call themselves communists because it serves their purposes. It is not enough to say one is a communist for it to be so." (*Resumen Semana*, 16–24 November, p. 3.)

Representatives of the People's Republic of China also repudiated the conduct of the terrorists in a meeting with Senate president Javier Alva Orlandini (ibid., 2–8 December, p. 4). China's relations with Peru are improving, as demonstrated by the designation of Lima and Beijing as sister cities on 21 November. Mayor Chin Xindong attended a special session of the Provincial Council, at which Mayor Eduardo Orrega gave him the traditional baton of Peruvian mayors—a varayoc. The visitor then met with Mayor-elect Alfonso Barrantes (*FBIS*, 22 November).

Trade relations with Cuba entered their third round of negotiations since 1972. Agreements were discussed on the purchase of textiles and mining, fishing, and agricultural products by Cuba in exchange for sugar, beef, and technical assistance for the dairy industry (ibid., 8 November). But relations were strained by charges that Havana had been broadcasting commentaries in Quechua to incite the Indians to violence (ibid., 8 September).

Peru's foreign policy orientation is decidedly supportive of the principles of nonintervention. The IU, APRA, and government parties deplored the U.S. invasion of Grenada (*Resumen Semana*, 16–24 November). On 2 December, President Belaúnde met with Daniel Ortega of Nicaragua, and both agreed to support the Contadora group's efforts to negotiate the problems in Central America and to condemn terrorism and subversion from the outside.

Sandra Woy-Hazleton
Miami University

Puerto Rico

Puerto Rico's Marxist organizations, both legal and clandestine, continued to be a minute factor in the otherwise lively if not agitated political life of the island. The principal revolutionary group is the Puerto Rican Socialist Party (Partido Socialista Puertorriqueño; PSP), a pro-Cuban Marxist-oriented organization that has some 150 members. It was headed for many years by Juan Mari Bras, a frequent visitor to Cuba and personal friend of Fidel Castro. However, late in 1982 Mari Bras, 56, resigned as secretary general. The PSP is to hold a congress soon (the last took place in 1979) to reorganize its leadership. In the November 1980 elections, the PSP candidate for governor, the highest office in Puerto Rico, received 0.3 percent of the vote. The PSP publishes the newspaper *Claridad*. The party's program calls for the establishment of a socialist state.

The Puerto Rican Communist Party (Partido Comunista Puertorriqueño; PCP) has some 125 members and is a pro-Moscow group closely tied to the Communist Party USA. There are also two Trotskyist parties, the International Workers' League and the Puerto Rican Socialist League, both even smaller than the PSP and the PCP.

There are several clandestine, Marxist-oriented terrorist groups that operate more on the U.S. mainland than on the island. The main group is the Armed Forces of National Liberation (Fuerzas Armadas de Liberación Nacional; FALN), which demands independence for Puerto Rico and has claimed responsibility for 120 bombings that have killed five people and caused damage in New York and other cities since 1974. Investigators estimate that FALN has no more than twenty members. Its leader, William Morales, who escaped from a hospital prison ward in New York City in 1979, was recaptured in Mexico City in May after a gun battle with Mexican police in which two persons were killed (*NYT*, 28 May). The FALN is re-grouping and shifting tactics, according to experts on terrorism. The group is now targeting government buildings rather than public facilities such as airports for their bombings. According to FBI figures, the frequency of FALN attacks has generally declined over the last several years along with the decline in overall domestic terrorist incidents. (*CSM*, 7 January.)

The Puerto Rican Independence Party, which, like FALN, favors independence for the island, is categorically opposed to urging violence to achieve its aim. The party, led by Ruben Berrios Martínez, is legal and non-Marxist, and it usually gets about 5 percent of the vote in Puerto Rican elections. In May, the party was accepted as member with consultative status by the Socialist International, an action that the State Department considered inappropriate interference in the internal affairs of the United States (*NYT*, 7 May).

Economic problems in Puerto Rico, accentuated by cuts in federal social programs, did not have an appreciable impact on the political life of the island in 1983. But a split in the governing New Progressive Party and a Watergate-type scandal that involved the administration of Gov. Carlos Romero Barceló, occupied the attention of the public more than any other issue. Even though the primary to choose gubernatorial and other candidates for the November 1984 elections will be held on 10 June 1984, almost feverish campaigning started more than a year ago. Governor Romero Barceló, running for a third four-year term, was initially opposed by San Juan mayor Hernán Padilla, also a leader of the pro-statehood New Progressive Party. But in August, Padilla, realizing that Romero Barceló would be difficult to beat, abandoned, along with thousands of his followers, the New Progressive Party and formed a new one, the Puerto Rican Renewal Party. Thus Padilla undercut the base of support of the governor, who in 1980 was re-elected with a small, 3,600 vote margin. The governor's opponent then, and assuredly in 1984, Rafael Hernández Colón, is watching the Progressives' wrangling with satisfaction. Leader of the Popular Democratic Party, which supports the present commonwealth status of the island, Hernández Colón was governor until 1976 when his re-election bid was defeated by Romero Barceló.

But more than by the division in his party, Romero Barceló was wounded politically by the so-called Cerro Maravilla case. According to the version of the governor's administration, on 25 July 1978 two members of a little-known group called the Armed Revolutionary Movement went to the top of Cerro Maravilla mountain, a 4,000-foot peak, to sabotage a TV tower there. They were confronted by a police force and started shooting. The policemen fired back and killed the two. The governor called the policemen heroes and the account remained unchallenged for four years. When early in 1983 serious doubts about the killing emerged, Romero Barceló blamed them on a "campaign of vilification" launched against him by the opposition.

Despite the governor's opposition, his opponents, who control the Puerto Rican Senate, voted to investigate the case and retained as chief counsel Sam Dash, the Washington attorney who held the same position with the U.S. Senate Watergate committee. Under questioning by investigators, several police and Justice Department officials admitted that documents related to the Cerro Maravilla case had been destroyed. Finally, other witnesses testified that the two youths had been lured into a police ambush, had raised their hands, and were on their knees pleading for mercy when they were killed. In December, the federal government initiated a new investigation to determine whether perjury or obstruction of justice had occurred in 1979. (Ibid., 21 December.)

The case, according to reports from San Juan, could not only affect the governor's re-election chances but also the island's political status. Romero Barceló had announced plans for holding a referendum in 1985 on statehood, which he supports. Mayor Padilla's Renewal Party favors delaying the vote. And the Popular Democratic Party does not want any change in the current status. If its candidate wins in November, the statehood issue could be postponed indefinitely.

George Volsky
University of Miami

Suriname

Population. 356,000
Party. Communist Party of Suriname (CPS), pro-Albanian; Revolutionary People's Party (RVP, by its Dutch initials), pro-Cuban
Founded. CPS: 1981; RVP: 1981
Membership. CPS: 25 (estimated); RVP: 100 (estimated)
Leadership. CPS: Bram Mehr; RVP: Edward Naarendorp, Glenn Sankatsingh, and Lothar Boksteen
Status. All regular party activity has been suspended since 1980 coup, though the Progressive Workers and Peasants Union (PALU) and the RVP participate in the government through the Revolutionary Front. The RVP received two cabinet positions early in the year.
Last Congress. CPS: First, 24 July 1981

Suriname gained independence from the Netherlands in 1975. On 25 February 1980, the country's democratic government was overthrown by a military coup that brought Lt. Col. Desi Bouterse to power. After a moderate beginning, Bouterse adopted a leftist line and proved adept at maintaining himself in political power. Several reported coup attempts against Bouterse in the period of one year—in December 1982, and January and November 1983—have resulted in scores of arrests and the murders of at least two dozen prominent Surinamese intellectual, political, and labor leaders. Bouterse charges that the Dutch government, the CIA, and Surinamese exiles are behind the attempted coups. (*Bohemia*, Havana, 25 March; *Soberania*, Managua, February–March; *FBIS*, 19 April.) Foremost among the exile groups is the Suriname Liberation Council, set up in the Netherlands by former Surinamese president Henk Chin-a-Sen after he was removed from office in early 1982.

By 1982 Soviet-bloc influence was expanding rapidly in Suriname. The Soviet Union sent a full-time ambassador in August, and Cuba sent one a month later. The Cuban ambassador was Oswaldo Cardenas, head of the Caribbean–Central American section of the Americas department of the Cuban Communist Party and one of the few blacks to hold a top-level position in Havana (*Daily Gleaner*, Kingston, 10 February; *FBIS*, 18 February; *WSJ*, 26 January). Political and military leaders, and at least 150 students, were sent to Cuba for training; diplomatic sources reported that the Cubans trained commando teams and personal bodyguards for Bouterse in addition to giving advice on assorted Surinamese programs (*WP*, 13 October). Among the Cuban programs is the people's militia, which was established in May. According to one report from the Surinamese capital, there were 1,500 militia members in training in Cuba (*WSJ*, 7 December). When Surinamese president Chin-a-Sen warned about increasing Cuban influence, he was removed from office; in mid-1983, by then in exile, he warned there was the "not unlikely possibility" that Cuban leaders would remove Bouterse whenever it suited their purposes (*WSJ*, 26 January: *Elseviers Magazine*, Amsterdam, 23 July; *JPRS*, no. 84252). Former Surinamese prime minister Andre Haakmat said the Cuban influence was a catalyst for the bloody events of December 1982 (see *YICA*, 1983, p. 125) and charged that Cubans were playing the "prompter's role" in Surinamese politics (*Daily Gleaner*, 10 February; *FBIS*, 18 February).

Bouterse also developed close ties to the Maurice Bishop government in Grenada, which is several hundred miles northwest of Suriname. After the October 1983 coup in Grenada, which left Bishop and several of his ministers dead, and the subsequent move by the United States and several Caribbean governments on 25 October to eliminate Cuban influence on the island, Bouterse expelled the Cuban ambassador and more than a hundred advisers and embassy personnel from Suriname. At a press conference on 25 November, Bouterse said the action was to "control" Cuban influence in Suriname, although he added that there is no question of his breaking all ties with Havana (*Latin America Caribbean Report*, 9 December; *WSJ*, 7 December).

Just months before the reduction of the Cuban presence, Chin-a-Sen had warned that "if the Cubanization continues, Brazil will annex Suriname" (*De Volkskrant*, Amsterdam, 7 July; *FBIS*, 15 July). Indeed, Brazilian leaders, who have long looked askance at the prospects of a "Cuba" on their northern border, in Suriname or Guyana, have tried to woo Bouterse away from Havana. In 1983, they offered military and economic aid to Suriname, which, by the end of the year, amounted to some U.S. $15 million annually (*WSJ*, 7 December). According to the Brazilian paper *O Estado de São Paulo* (29 December), the military exchange will be "intensified" in 1984 (*FBIS*, 4 January 1984).

William E. Ratliff
Hoover Institution

United States

Population. 243 million
Party. Communist Party USA (CPUSA)
Founded. 1919
Membership. 17,500 (claim)
Secretary General. Gus Hall
Politburo. 9 members: Henry Winston, George Meyers, Charlene Mitchell, James Jackson, Arnold Bechetti, Mike Zagarell, Helen Winter, John Pittman, James West
Central Committee. 83 members
Status. Legal
Last Congress. Twenty-third Convention, 10–13 November 1983, in Cleveland, Ohio
Last Election. 1980 presidential election, Hall-Davis ticket 45,023 votes, less than 0.1 percent of the total
Auxiliary Organizations. U.S. Peace Council, National Alliance Against Racist and Political Repression, Trade Unionists for Action and Democracy, National Congress of Unemployed Organizations
Publications. *Daily World*, *Political Affairs*, *People's World*

The CPUSA remains the largest and most influential Marxist-Leninist organization in the United States. During 1983, party membership grew substantially for the first time in many years. Gus Hall, the general secretary, claimed that "we are experiencing the most successful period of Party building in many, many years." Hall has led a drive to make the CPUSA more visible and forceful, urging party clubs to work openly as communists and combat the "right opportunism" that is their greatest internal danger. (*Political Affairs*, July–August.) Unnamed party members were accused of minimizing the leading role of the working class and too often engaging only in "reformist" activities (*Daily World*, 2 June, 11 November).

Among the party's prominent leaders, in addition to Hall, are Henry Winston (national chairman), Arnold Bechetti (national organizational secretary), Sid Taylor (treasurer), Si Gerson (political commission), Charlene Mitchell (Afro-American affairs), George Meyers (labor), Mike Zagarell (editor, *Daily World*), James Jackson, and Victor Perlo. Party leaders in important states include Jarvis Tyner (New York), Rick Nagin (Ohio), Sam Webb (Michigan), Helui Savola (Minnesota), and Charles Wilson (Illinois).

The party held its Twenty-third National Convention in Cleveland from 10 to 13 November. Five hundred delegates and guests from 48 states attended. They heard Hall boast that the party's influence "has grown tremendously . . . the Party is a political power in its own right" (ibid., 15 November). At least some of Hall's confidence could be explained by the ability of the party's auxiliaries to attract prominent noncommunist support.

As part of its desire to expand its public presence, the party eliminated the Young Workers Liberation League (YWLL), its de facto youth arm for the past twelve years. Meeting in Cleveland from 29 April to 1 May, 375 delegates from 30 states founded a Young Communist League (YCL). The delegates, 60 percent of whom were under 25, 56 percent workers, 21 percent unemployed, 47 percent students, and 50 percent minorities, elected James Steele, former head of the YWLL, national chairman. The YCL, which publishes *Dynamic*, decided to focus on registering 100,000 new anti-Reagan voters and on the peace struggle. (Ibid., 24 September; *Political Affairs*, June.)

Another new auxiliary organization is the National Congress of Unemployed Organizations, formed at a congress in Chicago on 2–3 July. The party gave the gathering its complete support and many party members were active "in organizing participation." The 490 delegates, 30 percent black, 20 percent Latino, 25 percent women, from 81 cities, chose John Lumpkin national chairman and Scott Marshall national organizer. Among the speakers were Chicago's new mayor, Harold Washington, and Charles Hayes, who succeeded Washington in Congress. (*Political Affairs*, September.) One of the party's older auxiliaries, the National Alliance Against Racist and Political Repression, held its Tenth Anniversary Conference in Chicago in May. Charles Hayes served as chair, and the guests included Boston mayoral candidate Mel King and Gus Eugene Newport, the mayor of Berkeley, California. The major speaker was Congressman John Conyers. Charlene Mitchell was succeeded as National Alliance director by Frank Chapman, who defined the group's major targets as repressive immigration laws and the government "attack" on elected black politicians. (*Daily World*, 6 May, 18 May.) Still another auxiliary, the Labor Research Association, heard speeches by new United Mine Workers president Richard Trumka and a new congressman from New York, Major Owens, at its annual dinner in November (ibid., 29 September).

One of the most visible party auxiliaries was the U.S. Peace Council, an affiliate of the World Peace Council. Its cochairmen are Frank Rosen, a union official, and Mark Solomon, a professor. The executive director is party member Michael Myerson. The Council, which is active in the nuclear-freeze movement, was attacked as a tool of Soviet manipulation. In response, it insisted it was not pro-Soviet, but that "Russia's foreign and military policies most closely resemble those we'd like our own country to adopt" (ibid., 17 November). At its Third Conference in Chicago in October, 200 delegates and observers from 50 chapters heard speeches from Georgia

state senator Julian Bond and Southern Christian Leadership conference chairman Joseph Lowry (ibid., 29 September, 19 October).

The party announced that it will field a presidential ticket in 1984. Its major focus will be on defeating Ronald Reagan, and it is willing to cooperate with all "progressives" to achieve that end. It believes that a new antimonopoly people's party will soon emerge in which it can play a role. Among the encouraging signs the party saw were the election of Harold Washington in Chicago, Mel King's getting into a Boston mayoral runoff, and congressional victories by Charles Hayes and Major Owens. The party also welcomed Jesse Jackson's presidential candidacy, "whatever weaknesses he may have," because of his positions on issues and because he will contribute to the anti-Reagan effort and ultimately an independent party (ibid., 4 November).

On foreign policy issues, the CPUSA is one of the more slavishly pro-Soviet parties in the world. When Korean Air Lines flight 007 was shot down, the *Daily World* at first called it a jet crash and denied that the Soviets were responsible. An editorial said that "the apparent deaths" of passengers was a source of sorrow. Politburo member James Jackson angrily charged that "no slander has been too slimy, no abuse too beastly . . . to spew forth upon the head of the Soviet Union." Gus Hall later charged that the plane was used for spying and that the Reagan administration was responsible for the deaths of its passengers. (Ibid., 3 and 9 September.)

On other foreign policy issues, the CPUSA was no less hostile to the Reagan administration. It denounced the Grenada invasion as "a crime against peace and humanity," charged that "the White House and its allies in Israel [were] responsible" for the Marines killed in Beirut and that Reagan's actions in Central America "warrant his impeachment" (ibid., 3 August, 25 and 27 October). The party also withdrew its support of the Khomeini regime in Iran, denouncing its "brutal" treatment of the Tudeh Party as "part of the anti-revolutionary, anti-Soviet, pro-war policy of the Reagan administration" (ibid., 6 May).

Socialist Workers' Party. The largest of several Trotskyist parties in the United States is the Socialist Workers' Party (SWP), founded in 1938. Although not formally affiliated to the Fourth or Trotskyist International because of the Voorhis Act, it cooperates with it. The SWP publishes the *Militant* and has around 2,000 members.

A thousand people attended the SWP's yearly conference in Oberlin, Ohio, in August. Party leaders, including National Secretary Jack Barnes and National Chairs Barry Sheppard, Malik Miah, and Mary-Alice Waters, argued that "we are in a preparatory period prior to the working class challenging the imperialists for power." The convention urged concentration of party forces on nine key unions and, in particular, garment and textile workers. Half of all party members are currently in industry and a fourth are unemployed. (*Militant*, 2 September.) The Young Socialist Alliance (YSA) gathered 850 people to its Twenty-second National Convention in Chicago early in January and selected a new national chairman, Mac Warren, and national secretary, Andrea Gonzalez (ibid., 21 January).

The SWP is scornful of the "reformist" politics practiced by the CPUSA. It refused to support Harold Washington for mayor of Chicago; an SWP candidate got 4,000 votes. While rejecting work in the Democratic Party, it admitted that supporters of Jesse Jackson were seeking new directions. It urged recruiting them for independent politics when Jackson was defeated (ibid., 18 November).

The SWP has become more unabashedly pro-Soviet in its foreign policy positions. It opposed a nuclear freeze because that policy implied that the United States and the USSR were equally guilty in the arms race. It supported the Vietnamese occupation of Kampuchea and insisted that charges of chemical or biological warfare were "a fake from start to finish" (ibid., 1 July). The SWP called for an end to U.S. aid to "ultra-rightist" Afghan rebels and insisted that the Soviet invasion was designed to forestall a U.S. invasion (ibid., 27 May). The charges that there was a plot to kill the pope were a "frame-up" (ibid., 1 July). The party insisted that the "hysteria" over Flight 007 was part of Washington's "war drive" and accepted the Soviet Union's explanations for why it shot down the plane (ibid., 16 September, 22 September). Finally, while agreeing that Lech Walesa had fought for independent and democratic unions, the SWP charged he had received the Nobel Peace Prize "to add fuel to the reactionary anti-communist propaganda campaign of the imperialist governments and their apologists" (ibid., 21 October).

Other Marxist Parties. There are a variety of other Marxist-Leninist organizations in the United States. The Workers World Party, led by Sam Marcy, the Sparticist League, and the Workers League are all Trotskyist. The last group has been linked to charges by Alan Gelfand, a dissident SWP member expelled in 1979, that the SWP leadership is composed of U.S. government agents. Gelfand's lawsuit, seeking reinstatement in the SWP and charging most of its leaders with being agents, was thrown out of a federal court early in 1983. The Communist Party (Marxist-Leninist), which had supported the Chinese government, disbanded late in 1982 and was succeeded by the United States League of Revolutionary Struggle, which publishes *Unity*. The Revolutionary Political Organization (Marxist-Leninist) supports secession from the United States by blacks. The Revolutionary Communist Party, one of the largest of these tiny Maoist sects, is led by Bob Avakian, currently in exile in France, and facing a long prison sentence if he returns to the United States. There are other shadowy avowedly communist groups that have been linked to armed robberies and "expropriations," including the May 19th Communist Organization, several of whose members were apparently involved in the holdup of a Brinks armored car and the murder of three policemen and guards in New York.

Harvey Klehr
Emory University

Uruguay

During June 1983, Uruguay's armed forces celebrated their tenth anniversary in power. However, as the year unfolded, many observers began to feel that it could be their last. The year began with the overwhelming rejection of the military in the November 1982 internal party elections still fresh in everyone's mind. The military, taking advantage of the Southern Cone summer, did not begin negotiations with party representatives over a new constitution until the second quarter of the year. It soon became apparent that despite the people's rejection of the "National Security" constitution, the military high command was still determined to impose it on Uruguay and continue to keep the Left—in all its manifestations—illegal.

During the first week of July, talks between the armed forces and the legalized opposition parties collapsed. As expected, the negotiations broke down over national security issues. The military continued to insist that the security services should be able to hold suspects incommunicado for fifteen days as opposed to the 48 hours provided in the 1967 constitution. They insisted on military trials for future cases of subversion and demanded a "state of subversion" constitutional clause that would go far beyond the limits placed on the police and military under the emergency powers granted by the prompt security measures (medidas prontas de seguridad) found in the last constitution. Enrique Tarigo of the Colorado Party complained that the armed forces look at the constitution "only through the keyhole of subversion" (*Latin America Weekly Report*, 15 July, p. 9).

In early September, the military responded to the breakdown in negotiations by decreeing a ban on all political activity. By late October, Gen. Julio Rapela, head of the Armed Forces Political Commission (COMASPO), announced that the military, even without negotiations, would submit a new constitution to the people and hold to its promise of elections in November 1984. Apparently these elections would take place with continued restrictions on the Left and a ban on important figures of the traditional parties. The opposition vowed to oppose this caricature of democracy.

The Interpartidaria, as the coalition of the three legalized parties (Blancos, Colorados, and Unión Cívica) called themselves, now moved to a position of "civic action" against the regime. As in Chile, demonstrations were organized around such activities as honking horns, banging pots, and turning off lights at indicated times. Demonstrations took place on dates of national significance, 18 July, 25 August, and 25 September. On the last Sunday of November, the traditional election day in Uruguay, one of the largest demonstrations in the history of the country took place. Some 300,000 Uruguayans marched to demand a quick return to democracy.

In November, Amnesty International reported that some two dozen young people had been tortured after being involved in antigovernment demonstrations. Amnesty also indicated that hundreds of political prisoners continued to languish in their cells. The year ended with more government repression. On 30 December, riot troops and mounted police charged a group of demonstrators, beating many in the crowd and arresting over a hundred people. The crowd had gathered in front of the home of the owner of a small radio station that had been closed after it broadcast the proceedings of the Blanco Party convention. The demonstrators, as usual, had called for an end to military government.

The economic situation remained bleak during 1983. Unemployment climbed to an official historic high of 16–17 percent. Inflation rose to

40 percent. Although the government managed to renegotiate part of its foreign debt, the country was burdened with a total debt of over $4 billion, an extraordinary amount for a nation of only 3 million people.

The Communist Party of Uruguay (PCU), still able to operate only in exile, continued to call for the restoration of constitutional government. Its leader, Rodney Arismendi, and Leopoldo Bruera, a member of the PCU Central Committee, spoke at various forums in Europe and Cuba. Their constant themes were the increased isolation of the armed forces in Uruguay; a call for an amnesty; and the earliest possible restoration of democracy. Perhaps their greatest success during the year was the release from prison of one of the party's most prominent figures, Rita Ibarbaru.

On the labor front, a new umbrella organization called the Workers' Syndicate (Plenario Intersindical de Trabajadores) emerged. This organization supported the various demonstrations that took place, organized work stoppages, and demanded better salary adjustments than the government had granted, and, of course, supported the right of workers to organize. In apparent economic (and political) desperation, the government recalled one of its brightest civilian technocrats, Alejandro Vegh Villegas, from his ambassadorship in Washington. Vegh took his old job as head of the Ministry of Economy, where the armed forces hoped he could do something about the economic situation and rebuild some bridges to civilian sectors.

Finally, 1983 saw an event take place that, although outside its borders, could have important political consequences for Uruguay. In fact, the election of Raúl Alfonsín of the Partido Radical in Argentina had immediate repercussions in Uruguay. Alfonsín lost no time in signaling his Uruguayan neighbors that he would like to see the restoration of democracy there. Many of Uruguay's civilian opposition leaders, including the exiled head of the Blanco Party and its designated candidate for the promised November elections, Wilson Ferreira Aldunate, were invited to the inauguration of the Argentine president. When the principal Colorado newspaper, *El Día*, took the opportunity to interview the Blanco leader, it was hit with a three-day suspension by the government. The atmosphere in Argentina, coupled with the increased isolation of the military in Uruguay, has led many of Uruguay's exiles in Europe, Mexico, and elsewhere to plan a move to Buenos Aires with the expectation that they will be able to return to Montevideo before the end of 1984. As 1984 began, the military, although not budging from their public position, was meeting with civilian leaders, but no one could be sure that the exiles' expectations would be fulfilled.

Martin Weinstein
William Paterson College of New Jersey

Venezuela

Population. 18 million
Party. Communist Party of Venezuela (Partido Comunista de Venezuela; PCV)
Founded. 1931
Membership. 4,000 (estimate)
Secretary General. Jesús Faría

Politburo. 18 members, including Hector Mujica, Radamés Larrazábal, and Eduardo Gallegos Mancera; president and founder Gustavo Machado died 17 July in Caracas
Status. Legal
Last Congress. Sixth, 1980
Last Election. December 1983; all leftist parties, presidential vote: 7 percent; legislative vote: 12 percent; elected 2 senators and 22 deputies
Auxiliary Organizations. United Central of Venezuelan Workers (Central Unitaria de Trabajadores Venezolanos; CUTV), Communist Youth (Juventud Comunista; JC)
Publications. *Tribuna Popular* (weekly)

The performance of the Left as a whole in the 4 December presidential and congressional elections, down slightly from the 1978 results, frustrated expectations aroused by favorable early polls and well-attended rallies. Economic stagnation and rising unemployment had seemed to augur well for proponents of change in the status quo. Rather than diminishing as predicted, however, polarization between the major Social Democratic (AD) and Social Christian (COPEI) parties increased, and the landslide victory of the AD candidate drew votes away from the Left. Postmortems among the divided Marxist parties will be painful in some cases, particularly so in the Movement to Socialism (Movimiento al Socialismo; MAS), whose presidential candidate, Teodoro Petkoff, polled substantially fewer votes than predicted. He was supported by the Revolutionary Left Movement (Movimiento de Izquierda Revolucionaria; MIR) and independent groups.

Independent José Vicente Rangel became the candidate of the multiparty coalition, Alliance for the Unity of the People (Alianza para la Unidad del Pueblo; AUP). Members included the PCV, the New Alternative (Nueva Alternativa, a new group comprising the United Communist Vanguard [VUC] and the Américo Martín faction of the MIR), the Socialist League (Liga Socialista; LS), Revolutionary Action Group (Grupo de Acción Revolucionario; GAR), The People Advance (El Pueblo Avanza; EPA), and some smaller groups.

Differences between the PCV and the anti-Soviet Petkoff made presentation of a unity candidate impossible. It remains to be seen whether those differences can be papered over in time for the municipal elections expected in June. Petkoff's first postelection statement makes this seem unlikely: "We will speak of unity if only to preserve the ritual. Personally, I am not interested in the rest of the Left, I am interested in the MAS." (*El Universal*, 7 December.)

Radical Cause (Causa R) candidate Andrés Velásquez did not win even enough votes to become the party's first representative in Congress. Essentially a regional movement, Causa R was hurt by the death this year of its founder, Alfredo Maneiro, followed by the resignation of its first, and unlikely, presidential candidate, Jorge Olavarría. The Red Flag (Bandera Roja) guerrilla organization remained active in the Venezuelan-Colombian border region even though police continued to roll up its political cells in major cities.

PCV. Successive divisions over the years have greatly diminished the size and resources of the PCV, but it is not without influence among the leftist parties. In the prolonged unity talks preceding the electoral campaign, the PCV was able to prevent the Petkoff candidacy from gaining control of the Left. The PCV could enthusiastically join the AUP and support Rangel's candidacy, "even though it differs both with him and the groups supporting him" (Jesús Faría, *WMR*, January), but could not tolerate Petkoff's attacks on the Soviet Union. The Sixth PCV Congress classed the MAS as a leftist force, although opinions varied. Now, according to Faría, "Reality has fully borne out the fears of doubters. . . What prevents the MAS from being considered Left is above all the violent anti-Sovietism of some of its leaders." (Ibid.) Nonetheless, the PCV apparently does not intend to relinquish its objective of a Left front, including the MAS, in the municipal elections. In response to Petkoff's undiplomatic postelectoral statement, Politburo member Eduardo Gallegos warned that "Teodoro was and is the principal obstacle to the unity of the Left that is now more than ever necessary. The other MAS leaders must reconsider the problem." (*El Nacional*, 9 December.)

The financially strapped party made no television appearances during the campaign but, as the best organized party of the AUP, contributed much to the coordination and legwork of Rangel's campaign. Despite the lack of publicity, the PCV was one of the few leftist parties increasing its share of the vote, from 1 percent in 1978 to almost 2 percent, and elected three deputies compared with one in 1978.

The principal center of PCV activity in the labor movement is the United Workers' Central of Venezuela (Central Unitaria de Trabajadores de Venezuela; CUTV). It has little influence but keeps the PCV name before the public. CUTV secretary general Hemmy Croes was an invited orator at the traditional 1 May rally of the Confederation of Venezuelan Workers (Confederación de Trabajadores Venezolanos; CTV), the principal labor confederation. By participating in the winning MAS–MIR slate in the Central University elections, the PCV was able to send one representative to the Executive Committee of the Federation of Student Centers (Federación de Centros Universitarios; FCU).

Jesús Faría visited Erich Honecker, chairman of the East German State Council, in East Berlin in September. Both leaders were concerned with the "confrontation course of imperialism" and considered Soviet initiatives on arms limitation significant for the improvement of the international situation. Faría and Honecker condemned U.S. interference in Central America and declared their solidarity with the struggle of the people of Nicaragua. They praised the efforts of the Contadora group of states to find a political solution to the tensions of this region. Faría reported on the struggle of Venezuelan communists to defend the interests of the workers under conditions of heightened capitalist crisis and spoke of the readiness of the Venezuelan communists to contribute actively on a national and international level to the union of all anti-imperialist and peace-loving forces. (ADN, East Berlin, 2 September; FBIS, 7 September.)

In San José, Costa Rica, a PCV delegation met with representatives of the communist parties of Coast Rica, Colombia, Mexico, and Panama. The delegates from the countries of the Contadora group expressed their solidarity with the People's Vanguard Party and "other democratic institutions of Costa Rica that are opposed to the stationing of foreign military forces in Costa Rica, demanding an end to the actions of Nicaraguan counterrevolutionaries from Costa Rican territory against the Sandinista people's revolution, and urging truly friendly and peace-

ful relations between the governments and peoples of Costa Rica and Nicaragua." The five parties agreed that the efforts of the Contadora group constitute a positive diplomatic and political initiative aimed at developing a peaceful and just settlement of Central America's problems "without the provocative and aggressive interference of the U.S. government." (IB, August.)

A delegation from the Cultural Workers Union of the USSR visited Venezuela at the invitation of the National Federation of Industrial Workers and met with leaders of the CUTV, and press, graphics, and radio/TV unions (Tribuna Popular, 17/23 June).

MAS. The MAS grew out of a 1970 split in the PCV and soon became the most important force of the Left. Long-standing rivalries between founders Pompeyo Márquez and Teodoro Petkoff were laid to rest in 1980, but the party's refusal to accept a compromise candidate for the presidential election led to new divisions. Deputy Secretary General Tirso Pinto resigned in March together with 300 regional directors protesting "rightist tendencies in the party directorate" (El Universal, 21 March). Postelectoral debates in the MAS are expected to be intense, moving from campaign critiques to major ideological definitions. The MAS percentage of the vote was down slightly from 1978, but the party returned two senators and ten deputies.

Petkoff's approach to the immediately critical economic issues dominating the campaign differed little from that of the major candidates. He rejected the idea of solutions imposed by the International Monetary Fund but said "unavoidable austerity measures would be adopted" (ibid., 19 October). Although "multilateral Latin American initiatives for restructuring foreign debt will be studied," refinancing must be negotiated immediately with the foreign banks (ibid., 28 September).

According to youth secretary Felipe Mujica, the new MAS–MIR youth organization, "Fuerza Joven," was created specifically to attract sympathetic independents to extraparty activities. A MAS–MIR–PCV ticket won first place in this year's Central University elections, and Julio Casas of MAS is the new president of the FCU. The party has been criticized for joining AD slates in the elections of several professional associations.

The MAS has one seat on the Executive Committee of the CTV. In the wake of scandals involving labor directors of the huge Venezuelan Workers' Bank (BTV; 60 percent controlled by the CTV), the MAS took an unpopular stand, asking that implicated former bank directors be suspended from all CTV posts until investigations are completed. At the same time, it ratified support for the CTV policy of increased joint management but noted that policies should be revised to improve labor leadership and effectively safeguard labor interests.

The MAS continued to espouse the principle of "active nonalignment," and Petkoff worked it into his condemnation of the U.S. invasion of Grenada: "The intervention of one of the superpowers stimulates the appetite of the other, and the victims are always the small nations of the Third World." He had previously condemned the murders of Prime Minister Maurice Bishop and his cabinet but said this in no way justified the invasion, which was "unacceptable from any angle." (Ibid., 26 October.) The MAS platform envisages relations with the United States based on "mutual respect, reliable petroleum supplies at fair prices, and cultural exchange." It also calls for an end to the blockade of Cuba; Cuban entry into inter-American forums; solidarity with the Nicaraguan revolution; and support for the Contadora group negotiations in Central America. (Ibid., 19 October.) Germán Lairet, head of the MAS fraction in Congress, considered the postponement of Venezuelan admission to the Nonaligned Movement a diplomatic setback; Guyana's opposition to Venezuelan entry was able to succeed because of Venezuela's long neglect of the movement and the pro-U.S. position in Central America of the Luís Herrera government.

MIR. The MIR's fortunes have fluctuated violently since its creation as an AD splinter in 1960. When it abandoned the armed struggle in 1969, only a handful of members remained; by 1978, it had become the country's fourth-largest party. A 1980 split and subsequent adjudication of the party name to the Moisés Moleiro faction deprived the MIR of the charismatic leaders of the Américo Martín faction. It dropped to sixth place in the December elections and lost two of its four deputies. The court awarded the party name to the Moleiro faction because it appeared to better represent the orthodox Marxist-Leninist

position of the MIR, advocating dictatorship of the proletariat.

The MIR opposes the concept of "broad unity" with nonsocialist sectors. According to national organizer Segundo Meléndez, elections involving the overwhelming majority of the nation are important for expanding the Left's sphere of influence and establishing contact with the masses, thus hastening the transformation of their revolutionary potential into a real force capable of effecting fundamental changes. (*WMR*, January.)

AUP. The AUP is an unlikely electoral alliance hastily assembled to oppose MAS pretensions to hegemony in the Left. Credit for its relative success is usually given to the appeal of its presidential candidate, José Vicente Rangel, an independent who headed MAS tickets in 1973 and 1978. Anti-Sovietism aside, his ideological position closely resembles that of the MAS: a "Venezuelan socialism" absorbing all democratic sectors dissatisfied with the status quo (*El Universal*, 29 November). In addition to the PCV, the most important groups supporting his candidacy were the following:

New Alternative. The Américo Martín faction of the MIR and the VUC joined forces in 1981 to create this first vehicle for Rangel's candidacy. Guillermo García Ponce's VUC, a PCV splinter, lost its national registration after failing to attract the required 1 percent of the vote in 1978. PCV leaders had frequently questioned the professed Marxism-Leninism of the VUC. Former guerrilla leader Américo Martín was presidential candidate of the MIR in 1978, the year of the party's comeback. Soon after, however, he opted for "Venezuelan socialism" and unsuccessfully tried to change the party's statutory description from Marxist-Leninist to Marxist. Two MIRs, the MIR–Américo and the MIR–Moleiro, existed until the court awarded the name to the Moleiro faction in 1982. (See above.) New Alternative elected two deputies.

MEP. A 1968 breakaway from AD, the democratic socialist MEP has the strongest labor sector of the Left, with two representatives on the Executive Committee of the CTV. It was this sector, however, that caused major desertions from the party this year. The National Council not only refused to temporarily suspend MEP labor leaders implicated in the BTV scandals (see above), but censured the authors of the proposal. This led to the resignation of directors Salom Meza, Luís Salas, Isaac Olivera (president of the teachers' federation), and others, who all took large followings with them. Salom Meza joined a new group, Apertura, which he hopes will become a "truly revolutionary party" (*El Universal*, 13 October). Acting Secretary General Adelso González was apparently correct in saying that "the MEP is not going to disappear" (ibid., 15 March); the MEP elected four deputies in spite of the division. Secretary General Angel Paz Galarraga took leave of absence to manage Rangel's campaign. (Charges were dropped against Salom Meza for presumed participation in the William Niehous kidnapping [see *YICA*, 1977, p. 512]. He did not run for Congress this year and would otherwise have returned to prison when his present parliamentary immunity expires in February 1984.)

Socialist League. The Marxist-Leninist LS headed by Secretary General Julio Escalona and President Carmelo Laborit, obtained legal recognition in 1978 after a long history of guerrilla activity. It duplicated its 1978 vote in the December elections and returned one deputy, David Nieves, to Congress. The favorable vote probably reflected solidarity with Nieves—who would have otherwise gone back to prison on charges in the Niehous case—rather than any growing influence of the LS. (*El Nacional*, 9 December.)

Guerrillas. Extracting reasonably hard data from press accounts of guerrilla activity has always been tricky. Difficulties increased this year, particularly in the Venezuelan-Colombian border zone, where apparently combined attacks of subversives from both countries became confused with the possible involvement of Venezuelan security forces in the area's active narcotics traffic. José Vicente Rangel credibly denounced drug dealings by some members of the National Guard (GN), army, and intelligence police (DISIP) and questioned the identification of

"guerrillas" given to peasants killed by the GN (*El Universal*, 19 and 20 October, 11 November).

The Colombian armed forces reported that delegates from guerrilla groups of four countries met in Esmeraldas, Ecuador, to discuss joint strategies for expanding revolutionary action in Latin America. Represented were Red Flag (Bandera Roja; BR) of Venezuela, the Colombian National Liberation Army (Ejército de Liberación Nacional; ELN), Shining Path (Sendero Luminoso) of Peru, and the Farabundo Martí National Liberation Front of El Salvador. Shortly after, a 17 September attack on a Venezuelan GN outpost at Cutufí was described by the Colombian army as a combined BR-ELN operation, but Venezuelan authorities attributed it solely to the ELN. (*El Universal*, 19 and 23 September.) The ELN reportedly "protects" the narcotics route to Venezuela, and the Cutufí attack may have been a reprisal for GN confiscation of a large cocaine shipment a few days earlier (ibid.). The same confusion exists with regard to the origins of the continuing and highly profitable kidnappings of Venezuelan ranchers in the border region. Victims are taken to Colombia to await payment of ransom, and bodies are returned—with ELN propaganda—if ransom is not paid. In Maracaibo, the DISIP arrested Asdrúbal Cordero, putative successor of Gabriel Puerta Aponte in the BR. (Puerta Aponte has been in prison since 1981.) He reportedly carried plans for combined BR-ELN operations in the frontier region (ibid., 15 April). Security forces continued to make large-scale arrests in the BR political cells of Puerto Ordaz and Caracas. In an unrelated but highly publicized security operation, thirteen "international terrorists," Uruguayan Tupamaros among them, were arrested in October and charged with a series of spectacular bank robberies and holdups using machine guns and hand grenades. A new wave of bank robberies with the same characteristics took place in November.

Carole Merten
Miami, Florida

ASIA AND THE PACIFIC

Introduction

Communist activity in the Asia and Pacific region can be differentiated according to three kinds of state and communist party behavior: states with ruling communist parties, states with legal communist parties in opposition, states with banned communist parties. When looked at in this way, communist party activity in 1983 in the region closely resembled that of previous years. But in two countries in particular, the People's Republic of China (PRC) and North Korea, several events dramatized more sharply than ever the unique behavior of communist parties in general: an obsession with maintaining thought and behavior control of party members and a reliance on terror as a tactic to weaken enemy states.

In the PRC, the regime, currently led by the troika of Deng Xiaoping, Hu Yaobang, and Zhao Ziyang, initiated policies to rid the party of cadres suspected of deviant party behavior, e.g., ultra-leftist thinking and activities, and to reassert thought conformity over urban intellectuals. In North Korea, the leadership resorted to terror and infiltration: North Korean terrorists exploded a bomb at a ceremony in Rangoon, killing seventeen high-ranking South Korean government officials, and numerous North Korean agents landed on the coast of South Korea to carry out espionage and to foment incidents in cities to embarass and weaken the central government.

These tactics of periodically cleansing the party to improve party efficiency and engaging in terror and infiltration have been standard tactics of communist parties in the region as well as elsewhere in the world. They represent nothing new in the communist movement and are activities regarded as normal by the leaders of communist parties.

States with Ruling Communist Parties. The leaders of the seven countries ruled by communist parties continued to search for ways to ensure communist party dominance over society. In large part, the leaders' concern with appropriate cadre behavior originated from their perception that the dysfunctions in the economy and polity could be solved only by more effective implementation by cadres of the party's basic policies. Even in a country like Afghanistan, where the ruling communist regime controlled only the major cities, their environs, and the central road system, this was the case.

Throughout 1983, the military stalemate continued in Afghanistan, with over 100,000 Soviet troops, armor, and support forces trying to shore up a beleaguered communist government and its security forces. Fighting raged throughout the year, as Soviet search and destroy missions were matched by Afghan guerrillas retaliating at night in the cities and ambushing Soviet convoys along key transportation arteries.

The Afghan communist party tried to pay more attention to party recruitment and to make cadres comply with party policies. Without a firm party organization, even Soviet military intervention would prove inadequate to save the regime. Therefore, when on 3 July 1983 at the Twelfth Plenum of the People's Democratic Party of Afghanistan's Central Committee, Babrak Karmal delivered his report on conditions in the country and on party tasks, it came as no surprise that he stressed the critical importance of improving the party's networks of control and cadre training, especially of the young with good records of political work, to go into different localities to mobilize various ethnic groups to support the regime.

In Communist China, too, the leadership gave priority to purifying the ranks of the party. When Deng Xiaoping's selected works appeared in July, they became the standard reading text for cadres' study sessions. In the fall, the party announced a three-year plan of party cleansing with the goal of trying to remove at least 400,000 undesirable cadres from the party (about 1 percent of the party's membership). Later in the year, the party launched a campaign to stop the spread of "spiritual pollution" in the cities among the more educated, but in January 1984 this campaign was downgraded to focus only on pornography and intellectuals publishing underground circulars attacking the regime and its policies. Meanwhile, the government announced the creation of a new Ministry of State Security to watch over state secrets and guard against foreign spies.

Strong as the troika leadership of Deng, Hu, and Zhao appeared, there still were signs of factional infighting between those supporting the Deng faction's pragmatic policies for modernizing the country and those opposing such policies. In December, the *Liberation Army Daily* stressed the importance of Mao Zedong's thought and criticized individuals close to the Deng faction. The paper singled out three people in particular for criticism: Zhou Yang, the party's cultural commissar; Wang Ruoshui, deputy editor in chief of the *People's Daily*; and Hu Jiwei, director and former editor in chief of the *People's Daily*. Wang and Hu were removed from their posts, but Deng remained silent while his policies were ridiculed and his loyal backers accused.

Factional struggle is endemic in communist-ruled countries, and it was only natural that factional struggle continued over who would succeed Kim Il-song in North Korea. But all signs pointed to Kim's son, Kim Chong-il, who is the second most powerful man in the country and the most likely successor to his father. North Korea's Politburo was expanded by three members, to 39, and a new premier elected in January 1984. Whether such shuffling of individuals truly consolidated Kim Chong-il's position is difficult to say, but it is very likely they were carried out to ensure the younger Kim's smooth accession to power.

Nowhere was the hand of North Korea more evident than in the terrorist bombing attack in Rangoon on 8 October, when three North Korean naval intelligence officers exploded a huge bomb that took the lives of seventeen South Korean officials and four Burmese dignitaries. Although Pyongyang denied responsibility for the incident, Burmese authorities captured two of the agents alive and collected enough evidence to prove beyond doubt that North Korea had sanctioned this terrorist act.

In Vietnam, communist party factional infighting continued between those urging more collective control over the society and economy and the more pragmatic-moderate wing, which argues for a mix of policies flexible enough to revive the economy while consolidating collectivist control. In mid-June, the Fourth Plenum of the party's Central Committee seemed to indicate that the doctrinaire faction was in ascendancy again, but as is typical of such plenums, most attention was still devoted to party political work and organizational activities at the grass roots to maintain control and demand citizen loyalty to the regime.

The communist state of Laos continued to remain fully within Vietnam's orbit of control and influence, and Vietnam continued to impose its military and political control over Kampuchea, except for those jungle-mountain regions still occupied by Khmer Rouge guerrilla forces committed to driving the Vietnamese out of the country.

In the sparsely inhabited Mongolian People's Republic (MPR), the most significant event in the communist party was the removal of Sampilyn Jalan-Aajav from his posts on the Politburo and Secretariat. At the same time, Moscow replaced its longtime ambassador, which strongly suggests Soviet desires to improve and strengthen relations with the MPR and to influence political affairs in that country more to its own interests.

States with Legal Communist Party Opposition. In the six states where communist parties continue to enjoy legal status, communists sought to ally with left-wing political interest groups wherever possible and campaign on issues that might discredit and undermine the leading parties and the central government. Nowhere was this more apparent during 1983 than in Japan.

The Japan Communist Party (JCP), which has been critical of both Moscow and Beijing, attacked corruption in the Liberal Democratic Party by calling on the government to insist that Kakuei Tanaka resign from office because of his conviction by the Supreme Court for receiving bribes from the Lockheed Corporation in 1976. The JCP also attacked the Yasuhiro Nakasone government for trying to increase defense expenditures. Even so, that strategy did not seem to win support from the voters at the polls; in the 10 April local elections the JCP lost 37 seats, and in the December national elections the party lost 3 seats in the House of Representatives.

In Australia and New Zealand, the communist parties continued to work within the labor union movement and focused on bread-and-butter issues for the working class, such as demanding that the government impose price controls, protect industry, create more jobs, and introduce a medicare system. In India, the two communist parties prepared for the 1984 national elections and campaigned on popular issues likely to elicit voter support against the government. In Sri Lanka, the party was banned for several months for its alleged role in fomenting ethnic unrest, but had been reinstated by year's end. In Bangladesh, the pro-Soviet communist party continued to infiltrate other political parties by carrying out a united-front campaign to cooperate with them while at the same time making efforts to unify the different Marxist splinter groups in the country.

States with Banned Communist Parties. The countries of Pakistan, Nepal, Burma, Thailand, Malaysia, Singapore, Indonesia, and the Philippines have banned communist parties. Even so, these sanctions have not completely stifled communist activities.

In Pakistan, communists participated in antigovernment demonstrations in the southern province of Sind in the fall of 1983.

In Burma, communist guerrillas continued their sporadic attacks against the government but without any success. In Thailand, however, the large defection of cadres and leaders, the loss of guerrilla bases, and the reduction of support from China and Vietnam reduced the size of communist guerrilla forces to only 3,000—the lowest level in decades—and greatly restricted their activities. In fact, in October, the Thai government even went so far as to boast of a "total victory" over the Communist Party of Thailand, a claim that might well be premature. In Singapore and Indonesia, the governments continued to maintain a strict vigilance and communist activity continued to remain dormant if not nonexistent in these two countries. In the Philippines, there were isolated cases of communist guerrilla attacks on small towns and several kidnappings, but these incidents indicated no increase in activity.

Soviet Activity in the Region. Soviet naval and air military activity was very conspicuous in the region, especially during September after the Soviets shot down an unarmed South Korean commercial jet aircraft flying from Anchorage to Seoul. Soviet military advisers continued to support the Vietnamese government, and Soviet ships made effective use of that country's large harbor and port facilities at Cam Ranh.

The Thai government reported in September that 33 Soviet officials left Bangkok of their own volition rather than being declared persona non grata by the Thai government. In fact Soviet espionage activities in that country had so alarmed Thai officials that in October the foreign minister called on both the United States and Thailand's allies in the Association of Southeast Asian Nations to maintain a "large balance of power" along the strategic ring from the Persian Gulf through the southeast Asian straits to Japan in response to the huge Soviet military buildup in the region in the past few years.

Ramon H. Myers
Hoover Institution

Afghanistan

Population. 14.2 million
Party. People's Democratic Party of Afghanistan (Jamiyat-e-Demokratiki Khalq-e-Afghanistan; PDPA)
Founded. 1965
Membership. Officially, more than 90,000 in "over 2,000 primary party organizations" of whom "more than half" are candidates (Radio Kabul, 5 July; *FBIS*, 8 July). These figures are almost certainly inflated. Western estimates range down to 11,000 full members, including 3,000 Parchamis and 8,000 Khalqis (*NYT*, 18 March 1982).
Secretary General. Babrak Karmal
Politburo. 9 members: Babrak Karmal, Sultan Ali Keshtmand (prime minister), Dr. Najibullah (chief of the State Information [security] Service, KHAD), Nur Ahmad Nur (member, Revolutionary Council Presidium), Ghulam Dastigir Panjsheri, Maj. Gen. Mohammed Rafi (deputy prime minister), Dr. Anahita Ratebzad (Presidium member and head of the Democratic Women's Organization of Afghanistan), Lt. Col. Mohammed Aslam Watanjar (minister of communications), Dr. Saleh Mohammed Zeary (Presidium member); 4 alternate members: Gen. Abdul Qader (minister of defense), Abdul Zahoor Razmjo (secretary, Kabul city committee), Mahmoud Baryalai, Mohammed Ismail Danesh
Secretariat. 7 members: Babrak Karmal, Mahmoud Baryalai, Dr. Niaz Mohammed Mohmand, Nur Ahmad Nur, Dr. Saleh Mohammed Zeary, Gen. Mohammed Yaseen Sadeqi (army chief of political affairs), Mir Saheb Karwal (administrator of Central Zone). (Of those mentioned above, only Danesh, Qader, Watanjar, and Zeary are believed to have been associated with the Khalq faction at one time or another. All appear to have downplayed their Khalqi affiliation since the Parchamis took over. All others listed appear to be Parchamis.)
Central Committee. 46 identified full members, 27 identified alternates
Status. Ruling party
Last Congress. First, 1 January 1965, in Kabul
Last Election. Not applicable
Auxiliary Organizations. National Fatherland Front (NFF, membership unknown), Saleh Mohammed Zeary, chairman; Central Council of Trade Unions (claims 94,000 members), Abdus Sattar Purdeli, president; Democratic Youth Organization of Afghanistan (DYOA, claims 90,000 members), Burhan Ghiyasi, secretary; Democratic Women's Organization of Afghanistan (DWOA, claims 50,000 members), Anahita Ratebzad, chairman
Publications. *Haqiqat-e-Enqelabe Saur* (The truth about the Saur Revolution), Central Committee daily organ; *Haqiqat-e-Sarbaz* (The soldier's truth); *Dehqan* (Peasant); *Darafshe Djavanan* (The banner of youth), a weekly in Pashtu and Dari; *Kar* (Labor); *Kabul New Times*, English-language daily. The official news agency is Bakhtar.

In 1967, two years after its founding, the PDPA split into opposing Parcham and Khalq wings. Both kept the PDPA name and both were loyal to Moscow, but each maintained a separate organization and recruitment program. Khalq, led by Nur Mohammed Taraki, the PDPA's founder, depended for support on the relatively poor rural intelligentsia and recruited almost solely among

Pushtuns, the dominant (55 percent) Afghan ethnic group. Parcham, less numerous but more broadly representative ethnically, was urban oriented and appealed to a wealthier group of educated Afghans. It was led by Babrak Karmal, son of an Afghan general. Both groups focused their initial recruitment efforts on intellectuals, media employees, and especially teachers. When President Mohammed Daoud overthrew the Afghan monarchy in 1973, the Parchamis at first collaborated with him, but the Khalqis remained in opposition and began an intensive clandestine recruitment effort among the military in preparation for the PDPA coup that was to follow five years later.

Under Soviet pressure, Parcham and Khalq formally reunited in mid-1977, and their combined strength was enough to overthrow Daoud and inaugurate the Democratic Republic of Afghanistan (DRA) in April 1978. They almost immediately fissioned again, however, with Taraki sending the most prominent Parchamis into diplomatic exile as ambassadors and jailing or demoting most of those who remained in Afghanistan. When a Parchami plot to unseat Taraki was uncovered in the summer of 1978, the ambassadors were recalled but disobeyed the order and fled into exile in Eastern Europe.

Meanwhile, popular resistance to Khalq's rigidly Marxist-Leninist rule grew rapidly and soon threatened to topple the new regime in spite of massive Soviet military aid. In September 1979, the Soviets attempted to force another artificial reconciliation between Parcham and Khalq, but their plan to place all blame for the schism on Taraki's deputy, Hafizullah Amin, backfired when Amin himself seized power and murdered Taraki. Amin, however, could not pacify his rebellious people, and on 27 December 1979, Soviet troops invaded, shot Amin, and restored the Parchamis to power. Babrak (he affects the surname Karmal, "friend of labor" or "Kremlin," for political purposes) became the new leader and tried to heal the breach with the Khalqis on the one side and the Afghan population on the other. In neither effort was he successful, and the regime maintained a tenuous hold on power only in a few main Afghan towns and only thanks to Soviet combat troops protecting them.

Party Developments. During 1983, the PDPA apparently increased its numerical base but almost certainly diluted the quality and intensity of commitment of its membership. In an April speech to the Kabul Military Academy, Babrak Karmal claimed that party membership had grown from 18,000 at the time of the 1978 revolution to over 85,000 full and candidate members, of whom more than 50 percent were military personnel (Radio Kabul, 16 April; *FBIS*, 19 April). By July, Karmal reported to a PDPA Central Committee plenum that party strength had grown by nearly 35 percent from March 1982 to March 1983 to over 90,000. Of the 31,000 new candidates, 16.9 percent were workers and 33.2 percent peasants. Overall, these classes still represented only slightly more than one-fourth of the party, whose average age was now under 30. (Radio Kabul, 5 July; *FBIS*, 8 July.)

The party's success in recruiting from the military may be exaggerated. Although the highest command positions are held by party members, an Afghan army colonel who defected claimed that most lower-ranking officers refuse to join the party. Those who join normally adhere to the predominantly Pushtun Khalq faction. (AFP, 3 January; *FBIS*, 4 January.) The army's rank and file, who are overwhelmingly conscripts, are generally illiterate and politically unaware.

The Parcham-Khalq rivalry continued unabated. Even the Soviet media acknowledged that the split, which mirrors historical tribal, ethnic, and ideological conflicts in Afghan society, was deep and unresolvable in the short term. The factionalism is especially evident in the military, where the Khalqis remain more numerous but lack political power. Numerous reports indicate that the more doctrinaire Khalqis are resentful of Soviet domination and favoritism toward the Parcham and frequently aid or maintain tacit truces with the *mujahidin*. In May, Defense Minister Abdul Qader, formerly associated with the Khalq but now close to Babrak Karmal, was reportedly hospitalized for several days after being assaulted by his deputy, General Khalilullah, a member of the Khalq who was angered by the promotion of a number of Parcham supporters (AFP, 24 May; *FBIS*, 24 May; U.S. Department of State, *Afghanistan: Four Years of Occupation*, Special Report no. 112, Washington, D.C., December). Subsequently, Khalilullah was forcibly retired and placed under house arrest (Radio Karachi, 22 June; *FBIS*, 22 June). Factional opponents also may have killed the head of Ariana Airline, Capt. Sayed Baba, a Parchami and a relative of Babrak

Karmal, whose death was reported in March (U.K. Foreign and Commonwealth Office, *Background Brief*, August). A Parcham-Khalq confrontation near Herat on 17 August reportedly resulted in the death of more than a hundred army and police personnel (*NYT*, 7 September). During the summer, posters in Qandahar reportedly placed by Khalq adherents demanded the resignation of Babrak Karmal and the withdrawal of Soviet forces (*Jasarat*, Karachi, 11 August; *FBIS*, 16 August).

Factional rivalry in the PDPA extended beyond the Parcham-Khalq split. The Parcham itself was reportedly divided into two groups, one consisting of Karmal, his half-brother Mahmoud Baryalai, and Dr. Anahita Ratebzad, the other consisting of Prime Minister Sultan Ali Keshtmand, Deputy Prime Minister Maj. Gen. Mohammed Rafi, and Nur Ahmad Nur (U.K. Foreign and Commonwealth Office, *Background Brief*, August). Rafi's unexpected return from a military training course in the Soviet Union in the summer touched off rumors of sweeping changes in top personnel (AFP, 31 August; *FBIS*, 31 August). Keshtmand has been mentioned as a possible successor to Karmal, but his status as a member of an ethnic minority appears to limit his prospects. Defense Minister Qader also figured in reports of personnel changes. In May, Qader demanded a special session of the cabinet to complain about a statement by Keshtmand on the occasion of the fifth anniversary of the revolution that acknowledged mujahidin successes against Soviet and Afghan troops. According to reports, after inflammatory accusations by both sides, the meeting broke up amid confusion and disorder. (Radio Karachi, 4 May; *FBIS*, 4 May.)

At its Eleventh Plenum in May, the Central Committee, for the first time, focused on the country's economic problems (Bakhtar, Kabul, 17 May; *FBIS*, 17 May). The session apparently took place without the turmoil that had marked earlier plenums, such as the semiannual meeting in March 1982 that broke up amid severe and violent dissension (*Defense and Foreign Affairs Daily*, 30 March, 2 June 1982; *FEER*, 26 March 1982). Prime Minister Keshtmand indicated that a basic goal of the plenum—whose timing followed introduction of the new budget—was to raise production above the pre-revolutionary level (Bakhtar, 17 May; *FBIS*, 17 May).

The Twelfth Plenum, in July, addressed a wide range of issues relating to the political and security situation, the tasks of the party and state, and party organizational issues. Babrak Karmal's opening speech of 3 July, which was broadcast two days later by Radio Kabul, emphasized that the "counterrevolutionaries" had failed to stop the progress of the revolution and that a spreading network of party committees was broadening popular support and solving "the most important issues of the provinces, cities, districts, and sub-districts." Having put a positive face on the situation and accomplishments of the regime, Karmal emphasized that "all necessary actions have not been taken" and that "many times" more effort was needed, including full execution of party decisions and resolutions of earlier plenums. Although Karmal cited a number of causes for failure, his prominent mention of factors such as "lack of unity, fatalism," and "signs of clan loyalty, tribal loyalty, loyalty to material gains, to family, group and rank, and the lack of mutual trust" indicated that the party's deep divisions remain. He acknowledged that many had failed to heed the resolutions of the Tenth Plenum on party unity and that "the situation has either not improved in principle" or improved slowly at best. Karmal admonished the plenum that "without unity the party does not exist." (Radio Kabul, 5 July; *FBIS*, 8 July.)

The PDPA continued to have little success in promoting its front groups. During 1983, groups like the DYOA and DWOA received frequent publicity in the Kabul press, largely in connection with visits from delegations of sister organizations from abroad. In early 1983, a Politburo member claimed 100,000 members for the DYOA (*Rudé právo*, Prague, 20 January; *FBIS*, 25 January).

The PDPA continued to publicize the NFF, but failed to attract any significant noncommunist participation. Despite the avowed purpose of uniting Afghans from all sectors of society, the NFF demonstrated its identity as a tool of the party by giving high priority to coordinating activities of local bodies to celebrate the nineteenth anniversary of the founding of the PDPA, carrying out "propaganda and popularization duties," and explaining "the solid stand of the PDPA and the DRA government." The resolution of the Third Plenum of the NFF noted major deficiencies in the collection of dues and writing letters and reports. The resolution also noted serious shortcomings regarding tribal affairs and support for recruitment for the armed forces. (Radio Kabul, 15 June; *FBIS*, 16 June.) Overall, the gulf between party activists and the population appeared to widen rather than to narrow.

Despite factionalism and rumors of personnel changes, the lineup at the top remained essentially the same. The Twelfth Plenum promoted five candidate members of the Central Committee to full membership and elevated five new full members and 16 new candidate members to the body. Most of those promoted or appointed already held high government positions, including three corps commanders (one in each promotion list above) and the commander of the air force, who was made a candidate member of the Central Committee. (Radio Kabul, 3 July; *FBIS*, 6 July.)

Domestic Affairs. The year saw no decisive change in the struggle between the Afghan resistance and the regime and its Soviet allies, which foreign observers continued to characterize as a "standoff." Intensified combat caused the population of Kabul and other principal towns to swell further, while the flow of refugees to Pakistan stabilized at a lower rate than in the past. At year-end, official Pakistani sources claimed some 2.9 million refugees, while the U.S. government estimated another 1.5 million in Iran, including some 850,000 living there before 1979 (U.S. Department of State, *Afghanistan*, December).

During the year, the Afghan army may have achieved some limited gains in rebuilding its strength through the expedients of reducing deferments, increasing the military obligation of conscripts from two to three years and retaining some troops even beyond this period. The army still fights a constant struggle to gain more conscripts than it loses to defections and losses. Defections in some units are claimed to run as high as 80 percent, and whole units continue to melt away in the course of combat operations. (Ibid.) The retention of soldiers beyond their legal obligation period probably led to the mutiny of part of the garrison of Khost, headquarters of the Afghan 25th Division, in January (AFP, 18 January; *FBIS*, 19 January). Almost every male high-school graduate was expected to be drafted in 1983. As a result, the regime permitted only female and "special" students—presumably young party members—to sit for the university entrance examinations in February (AFP, 18 Jan-

uary; *FBIS*, 19 January).

Early in 1983, high-ranking military defectors claimed the army had as few as 15,000–20,000 troops, but the former commander of the 7th Division, who fled to Pakistan late in the year, estimated the army's strength at about 35,000 (AFP, 6 December; *FBIS*, 7 December). The discrepancies may reflect the conscription/release cycle more than anything else. At year-end, the U.S. Department of State estimated the Afghan army at 40,000–50,000, up from an estimate of 30,000–40,000 for the previous year (U.S. Department of State, *Afghanistan*, December). Defectors noted that most of the army's foreign-trained doctors had fled and that wholesale promotions intended to bolster morale had led to situations such as that of a Kabul-based supply unit that had twenty brigadier generals for 400 men (AFP, 11 January; Radio Karachi, 17 January; *FBIS*, 12 and 19 January). Even the Karmal government claims only that the army is near "normal" strength, which was given as 60,000 in 1978, a figure far below that needed to combat the insurgency (*FEER*, 23 December).

One obvious source of weakness for the army was the continuing alienation of the Pushtun tribes, who traditionally have dominated Afghan politics. Pushtuns make up the vast bulk of the refugees in Pakistan. By custom many of the border tribes such as the Shinwari are exempt from military service, and efforts by the regime to reverse this policy have been rebuffed violently. Conscripts are drawn largely from the ranks of town and city dwellers, who are more susceptible to coercion. Efforts to recruit the tribes into frontier militias by cash bribes or arms generally have not been successful. Either the offers are refused, or the tribes are bought off only to go over to the resistance at a later date.

The regime appreciates the importance of the tribes, especially since its own small base lies among the urban, secularized, educated classes. Tribal affairs are coordinated by Suleiman Laeq, minister of tribes and nationalities, who also has broad powers to direct security and political cadres in badly disaffected Paktia and Paktika provinces astride the Afghan-Pakistan border (*FEER*, 29 December). Staged meetings with purported tribal leaders and elders, especially under the banner of the NFF, and so-called *jirga*s (council meetings), received heavy play in the media. The meetings are invariably begun with ostentatious deference to Islam and Afghan traditions. However, even non-Western journalists deemed safe enough to be allowed into Afghanistan have observed that the participation by tribal representatives in such meetings cannot be assumed to signify loyalty to the regime (ibid.).

During 1983, the regime put increasing emphasis on building up the secret police (KHAD) and paramilitary forces such as the Sarandoy. The U.S. government estimates the strength of KHAD, which is headed by Dr. Najibullah, at 15,000–20,000. However, many of its members are thought to be opportunists seeking a less dangerous and more remunerative alternative to military service. KHAD is organized along KGB lines and is under heavy Soviet control. Although torn by party factionalism and inefficiency, the KHAD is credited with having increasingly effective intelligence on mujahidin operations and with fomenting strife in the refugee camps. (*U.S. News & World Report*, 12 December.)

Following the Twelfth Plenum, the regime decreed a new law on the Sarandoy, the interior ministry's paramilitary force, apparently aimed at correcting abuses. In a speech to the Council of Ministers, Prime Minister Keshtmand stressed the role of the Sarandoy in winning over the country's "toilers," rather than alienating them through abuses of power. Keshtmand implicitly criticized the new law as too closely resembling those of the pre-revolutionary era, where regulations supported "the class interests of the exploiting circles," and he admonished the ministers to take a direct hand in drafting legislation. (Radio Kabul, 3 October; *FBIS*, 4 October.)

The economy continued to be severely distorted by regime policies, a focus on the needs of the Soviet occupation forces, and the effects of the ongoing guerrilla war. So far as state and private economic activity in the organized sector —largely Kabul and a few other large towns— the economy continued to suffer from the poor security situation and mujahidin attacks on the country's meager infrastructure. In a 6 October address to the U.N. General Assembly, Foreign Minister Shah Mohammed Dost claimed that "counterrevolutionary bands, mainly sent in from Pakistani territory," had destroyed 50 percent of the country's schools, 14 percent of its hospitals, 75 percent of public transport, all communication cables, a number of hydroelectric and thermal installations, and other public installations. He put the losses at 24 billion Afghanis

(about \$287 million) or "half the total development investment in the 20 years prior to the April revolution." (Radio Kabul, 17 October; *FBIS*, 18 October.)

Faced with serious economic problems, the PDPA regime continued to emphasize coexistence between the state and the private sector. It also continued to move slowly on land reform, acknowledging that past errors had resulted in unfair confiscation of land from middle peasants, while corruption, bribery, and "counterrevolutionary" attitudes among the bureaucracy had left many large estates untouched (Radio Kabul, 21 May; *FBIS*, 23 May).

After an acknowledged decline in GNP from 1978–79 through 1981–82, the regime projected 4.4 percent growth for 1983–84. The unbalanced budget for 1983–84 "envisioned" 253 projects, including 181 continuing and 36 new ones. Prime Minister Keshtmand acknowledged that a number of projects "where the progress of work in 1983–84 is not feasible" would be closed. The Soviet Union expanded its dominance of the economy. Western and multilateral aid, which made up 14 percent of the development budget in 1978–79, now accounts for 2 percent. In his budget address, Keshtmand credited the USSR and other countries in the Council for Mutual Economic Assistance with unspecified "disinterested assistance" to offset the loss of other foreign aid. (Radio Kabul, 17 March; *FBIS*, 21 March.)

The budget's focus on mines, energy, transport, and communications reflects the continuing integration of the economy of northern Afghanistan into that of the Soviet Union. The development budget, whose 36 percent increase barely compensated for inflation, allotted 36 percent of the total to mines, industry, and energy, 27 percent to transport and communications, and only 12 percent to agriculture (Bakhtar, 17 May; *FBIS*, 17 May). The regime also emphasized increasing gas production and further developing nascent oil production—both primary exports to the USSR (Radio Prague, 1 April; *FBIS*, 6 April). Kabul acknowledges that 40 percent of its export earnings come from the sale of gas to the Soviet Union, but given the severe drop in Afghanistan's other exports and former sources of hard currency such as tourism, the figure is almost certainly much higher. More than half of state sector products are being produced in factories or institutions built with Soviet aid (Radio Kabul, 16 April; *FBIS*, 19 April).

While even the government's description of the small organized sector of the economy was negative, the condition of the countryside, where the majority of Afghanistan's remaining population lives, was grim by nearly all independent accounts. Although many areas are said to be relatively untouched by the war (*Foreign Affairs*, Winter 1983–84), the general depopulation of the countryside in areas deemed of strategic importance by the Soviets, such as the Shomali Plain—once Afghanistan's "breadbasket"—and other areas along contested communications routes has sharply curtailed agricultural output (U.S. Department of State, *Afghanistan*, December). As the Soviets rely increasingly on massive air and artillery bombardment to break the will of the Afghan resistance, output in areas that formerly supplied food for Kabul and other population centers has declined sharply. One study by a former Kabul University agronomist estimated wheat, corn, rice, and barley production at only a fraction of the 1978 level (*FEER*, 16 January).

Primarily to make up for this shortfall and to feed the growing population of Kabul and other urban areas, the Soviet Union, in late 1982, agreed to supply 100,000 tons of wheat as grant-in-aid and another 110,000 tons of wheat and flour under a barter arrangement during 1983 (Radio Kabul, 22 December 1982; *FBIS*, 27 December 1982). Reports on the availability and prices of goods indicate relatively low prices for luxury imported goods and items used by the Soviet military forces, but high prices for food and other domestically produced essentials (*Foreign Affairs*, Winter 1983–84).

The PDPA leadership kept up an extensive program of travel, inadvertently adding new grist for Kabul rumor mills. Travel focused on the USSR and Eastern bloc countries, attendance at U.N. and Nonaligned Movement sessions, and a visit to Mongolia by Karmal and a very high-level delegation in July. Before returning from Mongolia, Karmal himself visited the Soviet Union for "medical examinations." Anahita Ratebzad attended the World Assembly for Peace and Life, Against Nuclear War in Prague, a Soviet-sponsored propaganda extravaganza. Mohammad Khan Jalalar, commerce minister, attended a meeting of the U.N. Conference on Trade and Development in Belgrade in June and went to the USSR to conclude a trade agreement in December. Foreign Minister Dost participated in a new round of U.N.-sponsored Geneva talks in June and headed a delegation to Cuba and to the U.N. session in September–October. Defense Minister Abdul Qader visited the USSR for consultations. Keshtmand and Dost attended the Delhi meeting of the Nonaligned Movement and Brig. Gen. Sayed Mohammed Gulabzoy, the interior minister, visited the USSR at the invitation of his Soviet counterpart.

The year saw an accelerating series of military confrontations between the mujahidin and Soviet/regime troops. The resistance was active throughout the country and dominated perhaps 75–80 percent of the provinces. In many parts of the country, the mujahidin constituted the local government, collecting taxes, operating schools, courts, and other public services. The central Hazara region was perhaps the most free of any Soviet or regime presence. Leaders of the predominantly Shi'ite Hazara resistance claim to control 24 of 26 districts, collect taxes, carry out administrative functions, and hold regular sessions of *shura* ("local assembly") (*Jasarat*, Karachi, 22 December 1982; *FBIS*, 30 December 1982). Other resistance strongholds included Paktia, Logar, and Kabul provinces (*WP*, 10 December 1982).

The most notable change in the situation was the increased activity of the resistance in urban areas. In early 1983, the resistance repeatedly cut electrical power to Kabul by destroying pylons and generating facilities and caused severe fuel shortages well into March by cutting pipelines and attacking fuel convoys (*Los Angeles Times*, 4 February; *NYT*, 16 March). Urban guerrilla warfare also including the detonation of a number of bombs at places frequented by Soviet and regime security forces. Three bombs in late January were noted by the Soviet military publication *Krasnaia zvezda*, an early instance of Moscow's decision to prepare the public for a long struggle (*CSM*, 28 February).

In mid-June, coincident with the Id holiday and the beginning of a new round of talks in Geneva, the resistance carried out a series of spectacular attacks on Soviet-occupied Bala Hissar Fort, Kabul Radio, and the Microrayan housing area, home of Soviet advisers and regime officials (*WP*, 22 June). The resistance carried out even more extensive attacks in mid-August against the same targets (AFP, 16 August; *FBIS*, 17 August).

The resistance also undertook more coordinated offensive operations in provinces bordering on Pakistan, including attacks on Jalalabad airport and a major effort in Paktia and Paktika provinces involving the cooperation of both moderate and fundamentalist factions.

The Soviets responded with an intensified military campaign to clear and protect key cities, base areas, and communication links between Kabul and the Soviet-Afghan border. This included a severe and prolonged bombardment of Herat in April–May, which failed to dislodge the resistance from the western suburbs of the city but did great damage and caused heavy civilian casualties (AFP, 3 May; *FBIS*, 4 May), and the summer-long pounding of the Shomali Plain, north of Kabul. A concentration of Soviet attention on the northern parts of the country appears to have improved security on the road links to Kabul, but press reports continued to cite incidents in Mazar-e Sharif throughout the year.

In the south and southwest, the security situation deteriorated markedly. Throughout the summer, the resistance built up its strength in Paktia and Paktika provinces around the military cantonments of Khost, Urgun, and Jaji Maidan, astride key infiltration routes from Pakistan. By September, the resistance claimed to have 10,000 fighters in "tribal battalions" around Khost (*London Daily Telegraph*, 15 September; *FBIS*, 16 September). At year-end, all of these towns and their garrisons were beseiged and cut off except by air (AFP, 2 December; *FBIS*, 6 December).

The truce in the Panjsher Valley between the Soviets and the resistance apparently held throughout 1983, despite its formal lapse in July and frequent reports of an imminent breakdown. Reportedly the young Jami'at-e Islami leader, Ahmad Shah Mahsud, rejected Soviet overtures for an extension, but neither side reopened large-scale conflict. Mahsud's reputation for effectiveness continued to grow as he expanded his organization further into northern Afghanistan and carried out operations outside the valley itself (*WP*, 18 October).

A strong Soviet show of force kept Kabul relatively quiet for the 27 April anniversary of the Marxist coup, although a series of bomb blasts and assassinations claimed numerous re-gime supporters, and the electricity was again knocked out for several days (ibid., 4 May).

In May, the Soviets sought to reduce the threat to the capital with their heaviest military operations since the 1979 invasion, through ground, air, and artillery actions directed at the Shomali Plain area. The operations caused as many as 3,000 casualties and a new flood of refugees into Kabul, but failed to capture or destroy the resistance forces. (AFP, 10 May; *FBIS*, 11 May.) The operations did not eliminate the danger to Kabul, and the resistance conducted a series of attacks in late May.

In March and April, the Soviets conducted major sweeps in Qandahar, Gazni, and Paktia, involving 10,000–15,000 troops, in an effort to relieve pressure on garrisons and close resistance infiltration routes from Pakistan (AFP, 10 March; *FBIS*, 11 March). These operations resulted in heavy fighting around Khost, when troops moved out of the garrison in an effort to break a long siege (AFP, 23 March; *FBIS*, 23 March).

In May, the resistance achieved its most dramatic victory in the war by decimating the elite, Soviet-trained 38th Commando Brigade in an operation in Paktia. The resistance killed up to 200 Afghan and Soviet troops in an ambush near Urgun, while the remainder defected (BBC, 31 May; *FBIS*, 1 June; U.S. Department of State, *Afghanistan*, December).

The conflict claimed a number of senior Soviet and Afghan military personnel, as well as Soviet civilian advisers during the year. The U.S. government estimated total Soviet killed and wounded at 17,000–20,000 as of the end of 1983 (U.S. Department of State, *Afghanistan*, December). Afghan military casualties are not known, but are almost certainly much higher. Deaths attributed to resistance action during the year included the chief of the Soviet intelligence department in Zabol province, whose death was reported in August (Radio Karachi, 9 August; *FBIS*, 9 August) and Gen. Vlady Anitnov (also reported as Vlado Arokov) and other senior Soviet and Afghan army personnel, who died when their helicopter was shot down in the Logar Valley in November (AFP, 3 December; Radio Karachi, 4 December; *FBIS*, 6 December). Losses among the leadership of the Afghan army included Maj. Gen. Mohammed Abdul Azim, commander of the 8th Division, who died in the same helicopter crash, and the head of military intelligence, Colonel Khudadad, shot to death by mujahidin outside his Kabul residence (Saudi Press Agency, Riyadh, 3 October; *FBIS*, 4 October).

Although overall losses are uncounted, the intensified combat during 1983 also claimed a number of important guerrilla commanders, including Mohammed Ibrahim, who died in an attack on a Soviet convoy near the Afghan-Soviet border (AFP, 6 January; *FBIS*, 7 January), and Pehalawan Mohammed Jan, whose death was mourned as a "big loss to Jihad" (AFP, 1 August; *FBIS*, 2 August).

While the resistance was widely reported to be stronger and better equipped and showed better coordination and cooperation in its military operations, it remained split politically. Personal, ethnic, ideological, and territorial rivalries continued to prevent the emergence of a unified leadership. The political groups based in Peshawar, Pakistan, continued to be divided between seven rival "fundamentalist" groups on the one hand and three "moderate" or "traditionalist" groups on the other. With strong encouragement from their friends in the Islamic world, the fundamentalists agreed in May to unite under the leadership of Prof. Abdul Sayyaf, the leader of one of the smallest groups, who would serve for a two-year term. (U.S. Department of State, *Afghanistan*, December.) The major rivalry was that between Gulbuddin Hekmatyar, an admirer of the Ayatollah Khomeini and leader of the Hezb-e Islami, and Burnhanuddin Rabbani's Jami'at-e Islami. These antagonisms have taken their toll. In August, a clash in Wardak province involving Gulbuddin's forces and those loyal to Sayyaf reportedly claimed 250 lives (AFP, 14 August; *FBIS*, 15 August). Other reported instances of cooperation, especially in the siege of Khost and Urgun, offered encouragement that the resistance groups may be learning to bury their differences in the interest of the common objective of freeing the country from Soviet domination.

A possibly promising note was sounded by the June initiative by former king Zahir Shah to offer himself as a rallying point for coordinating the resistance and better representing it internationally. In August, the leaders of the three moderate factions met in Rome to offer a mandate to the king, who has disavowed any desire to reintroduce the monarchy (ANSA, Rome, 22 August; *FBIS*, 23 August). While the king's initiative has been favorably received by many of the refugees, fundamentalist leaders have expressed various degrees of reservation or, in the case of Gulbuddin Hekmatyar, adamant opposition. Gulbuddin and others charge that Zahir Shah's reign created the conditions that led to the Soviet domination of the country (*CSM*, 24 August), and they are suspicious over reports that the Soviets are also interested in the king as a possible basis for a political settlement involving a secular, noncommunist but pro-Soviet Afghanistan (*Middle East*, December).

Foreign Affairs. Since the Soviet invasion, Afghanistan has had no independent foreign policy. The most publicized diplomatic exchanges were with the USSR and Eastern bloc countries and participation in international meetings. The Afghan role in the U.N.-sponsored indirect talks on Afghanistan was totally determined by the Soviet Union.

The Geneva process failed to achieve any concrete progress toward a political settlement. The Soviets and the DRA placed primary stress on ending "interference" in Afghanistan's internal affairs and gaining recognition of the Kabul regime. Prior to a February shuttle-round by the U.N. negotiator, Diego Cordovez, Afghan foreign minister Shah Mohammed Dost told a Hungarian interviewer that "we hope that as a result of this mission direct talks may take place with Iran and, above all, with Pakistan." Dost explained that "if the representatives of Pakistan and Iran are prepared to sit at the same table with the representative of the current Afghan government, this would amount to recognition" of the DRA and acknowledgment "that the presence of Soviet troops in Afghanistan is a matter exclusively for the Afghan and Soviet governments." (Radio Budapest, 25 January; *FBIS*, 26 January.)

From 21 January to 7 February, Cordovez conducted a round of talks in Islamabad and Kabul to refine a draft negotiating text along lines agreed on in 1982. The main areas of agreement included withdrawal of foreign forces, noninterference and nonintervention, external guarantees of a settlement, and voluntary return of the refugees.

In March, Cordovez and U.N. secretary general Javier Pérez de Cuellar met with Soviet officials in Moscow and obtained assurance of support for the U.N. effort. During 11–22 April, Cordovez conducted a new round of indirect talks in Geneva. These included daily meetings with Soviet advisers, as well as negotiations with the Pakistani and Afghan representatives. He also kept Iran informed of developments. At the conclusion, all of the parties expressed optimism and a desire to continue the round in June. (U.S. Department of State, *Afghanistan*, December.)

Although the Soviets rejected a Pakistani demand for a timetable for withdrawal of their forces, Pakistani foreign minister Yaqub Khan, expressed satisfaction with "substantial progress" (AFP, 7 May; *FBIS*, 9 May). Cordovez went further and claimed that an agreement, including a timetable for withdrawal of Soviet forces, was "95 percent" complete (Radio Karachi, 11 May; *FBIS*, 12 May).

The continuation of the second round in Geneva in during 12–24 June failed to achieve significant progress on key issues, especially that of a specific timetable for a Soviet troop withdrawal. Although all parties expressed interest in continuing the talks, Pérez de Cuellar decided to cancel an intended visit to the area in September by Cordovez on grounds that the nature of the impasse did not offer much hope for progress.

Informal discussions continued at the fall session of the General Assembly, which passed for the fifth time and by the largest majority yet (116–20 with seventeen abstentions) a resolution calling for the withdrawal of foreign troops from Afghanistan. On 30 November, the United Nations announced that a new shuttle-round would be initiated at a time mutually agreeable to the parties (U.S. Department of State, *Afghanistan*, December). Despite this glimmer of life, the prospect for a political settlement involving a firm commitment by Moscow to withdraw its forces remained dim at year-end.

Outside the Soviet bloc, Afghanistan's closest ties were with India. In January, Indian deputy foreign minister Natwar Singh visited Kabul for routine talks on the March meeting of the Nonaligned heads of state in Delhi (Radio Kabul, 31 January; *FBIS*, 1 February). An Indian parliamentary delegation attended celebrations of the April Revolution (Radio Kabul, 25 April; *FBIS*, 3 May). Prime Minister Keshtmand and Foreign Minister Dost met Prime Minister Indira Gandhi and senior Indian Foreign Ministry officials in conjunction with the Nonaligned session (Radio Kabul, 4 March; *FBIS*, 7 March). Indo-Afghan trade continued to expand, even as the economic situation deteriorated. Afghanistan imports In-

dian tea, textiles, spices, and industrial goods in exchange for dried fruit and medicinal herbs (Radio Delhi, 10 October; *FBIS*, 12 October), but the trade was heavily in India's favor. The Indian-Afghan Joint Commission met in October in Kabul. Agreements covered trade, agriculture, and health services. (Radio Delhi, 12 October; Radio Kabul, 12 October; *FBIS*, 12 October.)

Relations with Pakistan remained strained despite considerable official trade and illegal smuggling across the common frontier. New irritants arose in the form of Soviet and Afghan violations of Pakistan's airspace and territory, countercharges of border violations by the Afghans, and reports of an increased flow of arms to the resistance through Pakistan. Following the failure of the June talks in Geneva and the summer visits to Pakistan by the U.S. secretaries of state and defense, the Soviet and Afghan media stepped up their criticism of Pakistan and the United States. A series of overflights and air attacks on Pakistani territory in the late summer coincided with intensified fighting in Paktia province (Radio Karachi, 18 September; *FBIS*, 19 September), but may also have been intended to demonstrate a tougher stance. Foreign Minister Dost complained to the U.N. General Assembly that "armed intervention against the DRA from Pakistani territory is the root cause of the Afghan problem" (Radio Kabul, 17 October; *FBIS*, 18 October).

The DRA stepped up its criticism of Iran, especially after Tehran's crackdown on the communist Tudeh Party in the spring, and continued fighting in Herat, near the Iranian border. Iran may have increased its support to the resistance, though the primary recipients of Iranian aid are thought to be the Shi'a groups in western Afghanistan and the central Hazara region (U.S. Department of State, *Afghanistan*, 1983). The DRA continued to criticize Iran's nonparticipation in the Geneva talks. Tehran refuses to participate until representatives of the resistance are included (*Muslim*, 12 February; *FBIS*, 7 March.)

U.S.-Afghan relations further deteriorated as a result of the overall hardening of U.S.-Soviet relations and the deportation of three embassy officials on spying charges. The United States, which has not designated an ambassador since the killing of Ambassador Adolph Dubs in February 1979, maintains a small embassy headed by a chargé d'affaires. It regards the present regime as Soviet-imposed and deals with it only at the consular and administrative level. In May, the DRA expelled one U.S. official on 48 hours' notice for allegedly corrupting Afghan youth by circulating pornographic magazines (Radio Kabul, 8 May; *FBIS*, 9 May). The United States retaliated by expelling the Afghan second secretary in Washington (*WP*, 10 May). In September, in the wake of the Korean Air Lines incident and a series of expulsions of Soviet diplomats around the world, the DRA expelled two additional embassy officials on spying charges based on "confessions" of foreign national employees of the embassy who had been in Afghan police custody for several months (ibid., 16 September).

At year's end, all sides in the Afghanistan dispute seemed prepared for a long struggle. Having failed to gain easy concessions from Pakistan that would have given international legitimacy to the Karmal government and reduced the problem of resistance sanctuaries and supply routes across the border, the Soviets seemed determined to follow their established strategy. Soviet troop levels, estimated by the U.S. government at about 105,000 in the country plus an additional 30,000 in reserve on the Soviet side of the border, appeared relatively unchanged throughout the year. An inspection visit to Afghanistan during the summer by Marshal S. L. Sokolov, the first deputy minister of defense, led to no apparent increases either in the level of Soviet forces or the tempo of operations. (U.S. Department of State, *Afghanistan*, December.) However, some European sources believe troop levels are well over the U.S. estimates. Press reports suggest continued Soviet efforts to refine counterinsurgency tactics and use their forces more efficiently (*NYT*, 23 January; *U.S. News & World Report*, 12 December).

The long-term Soviet strategy still appears to be one of transforming Afghanistan into a Soviet-bloc model with a minimum investment of resources. This involves concerted efforts to build up the DRA military, maintain minimum security needs, gain access to the country's resources, and train thousands of Afghans each year in Soviet military and educational institutions.

For the time being, the Soviets appear to have given up any effort to put together a more palatable or effective Afghan government. Many observers see the increased use of air and artillery attacks on Afghan villages as terror tactics that reflect a determination to break the will of the population rather than gain its support. Pakistan also may come under increased Soviet pressure to close off resistance sanctuaries and supply routes.

The resistance gave a good account of itself on the battlefield during 1983 but failed once again to find a formula for unity and cooperation. As a result, it diluted its power and spent much of its energy in internecine conflict. The year confirmed that there would be no quick or easy solutions to the Afghan conflict, either political or military, but failed to establish any clear sense of its longer-term direction.

Richard P. Cronin
Annandale, Va.

Australia

Population. 15.3 million (*World Factbook*, July 1983)

Parties. Communist Party of Australia (CPA); Socialist Party of Australia (SPA); Communist Party of Australia (Marxist-Leninist) (CPA-ML); Socialist Workers Party (SWP); Socialist Labor League (SLL); Spartacist League of Australia and New Zealand (SLANZ)

Founded. CPA: 1920; CPA-ML: 1964; SPA: 1971; SLL: 1972

Membership. CPA: 1,000+; SPA: 650; CPA-ML: 300; SWP, 200; SLL: 100; SLANZ: 50

Leadership. CPA: Judy Mundey, general secretary; SPA: Peter Dudley Symon, general secretary, John Leslie McPhillips, chairman, Alan Miller, secretary; CPA-ML, Edward Fowler Hill, chairman; SWP: Jim Percy, national secretary

Status. Legal

Last Congress. CPA: Twenty-seventh, 12–14 June 1982; SPA: Fourth, October 1981; SWP: 5–11 January 1983

Last Election. 5 March 1983, negligible vote for Marxist parties, no representatives

Auxiliary Organizations. CPA: Australian Peace Liaison Committee; SPA: Young Socialist League, Australian Peace Committee

Publications. CPA: *Tribune* (weekly); SPA: *Socialist* (fortnightly); CPA-ML: *Vanguard* (weekly), *Australian Communist*; SWP: *Direct Action* (weekly)

The numerous communist parties operating legally within Australia's federal parliamentary democracy include the Eurocommunist-oriented CPA, the pro-Moscow SPA, and the Beijing-aligned CPA-ML. Dissident elements within these organizations recently organized the Australian Marxist Forum (AMF) and the Maritime Unions Socialist Activities Association (MUSAA); each seeks to broaden the base of the Left and to reduce sectarian quarrels among the SPA, CPA, and CPA-ML. There are also three Trotskyist parties in Australia, the SWP, which is affiliated with the United Secretariat of the Fourth International; the SLL, which is affiliated with the International Committee of the Fourth International; and the SLANZ, which is affiliated with the International Spartacist Tendency. Although their combined membership is approximately 3,000 out of Australia's total population of 15 million, these parties generally are able to exert a disproportionate influence due to their heavy concentration in the trade unions. In some instances, it is not unusual to find members of the several parties vying for power within the same trade union.

Communist Party of Australia. The CPA claims to have more than 2,000 members, but it probably has only slightly over 1,000 members; nonetheless, it is still the largest of the communist parties in Australia. It has concentrated its efforts in the trade union movement and has influence in the Amalgamated Metal Workers and Shipwrights Union, the New South Wales Teachers Federation, the Federated Engine Drivers and Firemen's Association, the Transport Workers Union, the Waterside Workers Federation, some districts of the South Coast Miners' Federation, the Federated Miscellaneous Workers Union,

and the Australasian Meat Industry Employees' Union. The CPA, through its influence in these unions, has some voice in the councils of the ruling Australian Labor Party (ALP).

On 9 February, the CPA's newspaper, *Tribune*, noted that the defeat of the government of Malcolm Fraser and the election of a Labor government in the 5 March federal elections was the overriding task before the labor movement and the progressive social movements. The CPA ran candidates in New South Wales and South Australia and encouraged its members to vote for Labor elsewhere (*Tribune*, 2 March). The CPA's campaign stressed the issues of providing jobs through creating new manufacturing industries; opposition to Fraser's economic restructuring to suit large local and foreign corporations; the need for a comprehensive incomes policy in the interests of working people and broader "social agreements" that extend workers' rights; and the need for economic policies that challenge the domination of big business over economic and social affairs (ibid., 9 February). The CPA received a negligible number of votes in the election.

After the Labor victory, the CPA's National Committee saw implementation of the Australian Council of Trade Unions–ALP accord on economic policy as a major concern. The committee indicated that the main issues arising from the accord were (1) achieving a centralized wage-fixing system; (2) increasing spending on social wages, especially through the early introduction of Medicare; (3) introducing a more equitable tax system and collecting evaded taxes; (4) developing effective price controls; (5) creating jobs, especially through the protection and regeneration of manufacturing industries; and (6) expanding trade union rights by involving unions in economic decisionmaking, as a first step toward democratic control of investment (ibid., 30 March).

In addition to its work in the trade unions and on economic issues, the CPA is active in promoting peace issues. It has organized the Australian Peace Liaison Committee, a loosely organized umbrella peace organization, to further the CPA's peace policies, which include opposition to the ANZUS (Australia, New Zealand, United States) Security Treaty, uranium mining, the presence of U.S. military bases on Australian territory, and nuclear proliferation (ibid., 9 March). According to the *Tribune* (2 March), the CPA planned a five-part lecture series in Melbourne during March and early April entitled "Wednesday Night at the CPA: Australia and the Movement for Disarmament." Additional peace activities were given extensive coverage in *Tribune* throughout the year.

CPA leaders made several international trips during the year. Rob Durbridge, member of the CPA National Executive and CPA national organizer, attended the Italian Communist Party's congress in Milan during early March (ibid., 11 April).

Significantly, for the first time in almost twenty years, a CPA delegation visited China at the invitation of the Central Committee of the Chinese Communist Party. The CPA delegation, which consisted of Mark Taft, member of the National Executive Committee, and Eric Aarons, former joint national secretary of the CPA, arrived in Beijing on 11 May. During their stay in Beijing, the delegates held talks with Zhu Liang, deputy head of the International Liaison Department, and other departmental officials on both domestic and international questions and on party-to-party relations. Differing assessments of the Indochina situation were also discussed. A banquet for the delegation was hosted by Ji Pengfei, state councilor and member of the Standing Committee of the Chinese party's Central Advisory Commission (ibid., 1 June).

Two CPA members, Warwick Neilly and Betty Blears, visited the Democratic People's Republic of Korea during July and held talks with representatives of the International Affairs Committee of the Korean Workers' Party (ibid., 31 August).

Elliott Frank Johnston, a CPA member for forty years, became the first party member to be appointed a judge. Before presenting his commission to the South Australia Supreme Court on

30 June, Johnston resigned from the CPA (ibid., 20 July).

One CPA member was cleared for access to information at the "secret" level after a hearing before the Security Appeals Tribunal. In June 1982, the Australian Security and Intelligence Organization (ASIO) had recommended that such access not be granted on the grounds that the CPA was a subversive organization. In June, the Security Appeals Tribunal apparently ruled that the CPA is not a subversive organization and that individuals could not be denied "security clearances" because of membership in the CPA (ibid., 22 June).

After twenty years of radio silence, the CPA began producing a weekly half-hour program entitled "Red All Over," aired in Sydney and Canberra (ibid.). In addition, the CPA's *Tribune* celebrated its sixtieth anniversary this year.

Communist Party of Australia (Marxist-Leninist). Since the mid-1960s, the CPA-ML has kept its membership secret and has functioned underground. It has influence in some labor unions, primarily the Builders Laborers Federation under Norm Gallagher. The CPA-ML denounces the ALP as traitors, unlike the CPA, which has advocated a coalition of the Left. The CPA-ML also has some influence among young leftist students on university campuses. It has an estimated membership of 300.

Edward Fowler Hill, chairman of the Central Committee of the CPA-ML, held talks on 20 October in Beijing with Ji Pengfei and Qian Liren, head of the International Liaison Department of the Chinese Central Committee. After the meeting, Ji Pengfei hosted a dinner in honor of Hill and his wife. (NCNA, Beijing, 20 October; *FBIS*, 21 October.)

The CPA-ML produces the weekly newspaper *Vanguard* and the theoretical journal *Australian Communist*. It also produces and distributes publications through party-operated bookshops in various Australian cities.

Socialist Party of Australia. The pro-Soviet SPA was formed on 5 December 1981, by a group that split away from the CPA after the latter became increasingly critical of Moscow. Its current membership is estimated to be 650. The SPA is the largest, best organized, and most influential of the two pro-Soviet parties in the South Pacific region. At the SPA's Second National Congress (October 1975), it was formally announced that the Communist Party of the Soviet Union had recognized the SPA as the only Marxist-Leninist party in Australia. The SPA has been quite effective in using its position in the labor movement to operate as a pro-Soviet pressure group within Australia and to spread the influence of the Soviet-front World Federation of Trade Unions (WFTU) throughout the nascent labor unions of the South Pacific region. This equation may have been significantly altered, however, by the increasing dissension within the party over the past several years, which resulted in the recent expulsion of leading members from the party's trade union wing, including Patrick Martin Clancy, founder and former president of the SPA and federal secretary of the important Builder Workers' Industrial Union (BWIU). The dissension was primarily between party bureaucrats, such as John Leslie McPhillips and Peter Dudley Symon, on the one hand, and the trade union wing of the party led by Clancy, on the other. The two factions have divergent interpretations of what the party's relationship should be with its members who work full-time in the trade union movement, the degree to which the party should dictate policy to the trade unions, and also the type of party best suited to promote Soviet objectives within Australia. The SPA bureaucrats have been highly critical of the leading members of the trade union wing, whom they believe give their allegiance first to their trade unions and operate independently of the party. Clancy noted in an interview with the *Tribune* (19 October) that "we weren't prepared to allow our work in the union to be directed by officers of the SPA." He added that the SPA national leadership had adopted a dogmatic approach to the Labor Party and the trade union movement and sought to apply Marxism to political life in a mechanical way. The major task of the working class in the March elections was the defeat of the Fraser government and the election of a Labor government. By its portrayal of itself as the only real alternative, the SPA, Clancy claims, "gave the impression that it did not really understand the significance of the need to defeat the Fraser government." Despite their differences, however, both factions remain loyal to the USSR.

The dissension was initially aired during February 1981, when a booklet entitled *Strategy for Workers Action, 1981* was published by the SPA's New South Wales Industrial Committee.

Articles representing the differing views were then featured in the *Socialist*. During the SPA's Fourth Congress (October 1981), much of the debate was devoted to promoting or opposing one of the two factions. Expulsions from the party started taking place. As Clancy noted in the *Tribune* interview, "every meeting of the central committee was punishing someone." Clement Thomas Supple, a leading member of the trade union wing and now president of the Waterside Workers Federation, was expelled from the SPA in early February 1982. On 30 March, the *Socialist* reported that the SPA had abolished the position of the president of the party, which Clancy occupied. It was later announced that Clancy had been expelled, along with several other Central Committee members, including the BWIU's assistant national secretary, Tom McDonald, and New South Wales secretary, Stan Sharkey. According to the *Tribune* (19 October), all three had submitted their resignations to the party several months previously, but these were rejected and the unionists were expelled instead. Besides the complaints against them by the party bureaucrats, another bone of contention apparently was the expelled unionists' membership in the Australian Marxist Forum (AMF) and the Maritime Unions Socialist Activities Association (MUSAA).

According to the *Socialist* (20 July), the SPA Central Committee noted that for several years the SPA had suffered some division and disruption and suggested that all members who may have been misled into resigning or who may have reconsidered their positions take the necessary steps to rejoin the party, which is the "only party which bases its activities on an application of Marxism-Leninism and working class internationalism."

Clancy was instrumental in forming the AMF in June 1982. The AMF promotes a broad coalition of the Left in the trade union movement and has the active support of the CPA. It is open to members of the CPA, the SPA, the CPA-ML, Trotskyist groups, and anyone else who is interested, particularly members of trade unions. It has the potential to influence a wide section of the Australian labor movement. On 29 May, the AMF presented a seminar "The Left and the Labor Government," which featured Pat Clancy, Rob Durbridge of the CPA, and Jim Percy of the SWP as speakers (*Tribune*, 25 May).

Before the dissension, among the most important unions the SPA controlled was the 55,000-member BWIU. The SPA may continue to have some influence in the Australian Federated Union of Locomotive Enginemen, the National Miners Union, some branches of the Amalgamated Metal Workers and Shipwrights Union, and the Sydney branch of the Waterside Workers Federation. As previously noted, the SPA has been particularly active in promoting the WFTU among the young and growing trade unions of the South Pacific region. This has been accomplished primarily through the WFTU-affiliated Committee for International Trade Union Unity (CITUU), which has sponsored WFTU-organized seminars, schools, and conferences for trade unionists of the region. According to its literature, the CITUU "was formed in September, 1978, with the objective of working for the strengthening of trade union unity and solidarity in the Asian and Pacific region, as part of the work for world-wide trade union unity." Patrick Martin Clancy played a leading role in the establishment of the CITUU, of which he is the national convenor. The assistant federal secretary of the BWIU, Ernest Albert Boatswain, also a SPA member, is assistant national convenor of the CITUU. WFTU control of the CITUU is assured since Clancy is a WFTU Executive Bureau member and Boatswain is an alternate member of the WFTU Bureau.

The highest authority in the SPA is its National Congress, which meets triennially. The SPA's founding congress was held in October 1972; its last, the fourth, met in Sydney in October 1981. The Central Committee is elected by the National Congress and, in turn, elects a Central Committee Executive, which is responsible for party leadership between Central Committee meetings. The party Secretariat, which coordinates party activity at the national level, is also appointed by the Central Committee. Members of the party Secretariat reside in Sydney, where the party's national headquarters is located. Other organizations on the local, district, and state level are established as needed. The party branch, which can vary in size, is the basic unit of the party. The principal officers of the Central Committee are Peter Symon, general secretary; John Leslie McPhillips, chairman; and Alan Miller, secretary.

A meeting of the Central Committee Executive on 17–18 December 1982 set party objectives for 1983. It was decided that the SPA should organize the strongest possible participation in the 27 March peace mobilization, the Hiroshima Day demonstrations on 6 August, and the U.N. International Women's Peace Day activities in October. It also resolved that all party organizations should step up activities designed to strengthen and build the party in workplaces. Special attention was to be given to assisting the development of the Young Socialist League (YSL), with particular emphasis on building YSL branches next to branches of the party. In addition, the SPA was to do all it could to help make the YSL National Congress scheduled for June an outstanding success. The Central Committee Executive also placed before the membership the responsibility in 1983 of maintaining attention to party work among women, including maximum party participation in International Women's Day on 8 March (*Socialist*, 19 January).

The SPA supports Soviet policy on peace and disarmament largely through the Australian Peace Committee (APC), which is affiliated with the Soviet-front World Peace Council (WPC). The SPA's Fourth Party Congress concluded that "the building of the broadest and strongest peace movement in our history in support of policies of peaceful coexistence, detente, and disarmament is the most urgent task before everyone. A mighty and broad front embracing all men and women who are for peace and not for war, for relaxation of tension and not confrontation, for disarmament and not a nuclear missile race, can stop the present drift toward catastrophe." (Ibid., 2 February.) The SPA supports calls for the removal of all U.S. bases from Australian soil and the refusal of facilities for naval vessels and aircraft associated with the use of nuclear missiles. It claims that the very presence of U.S. bases threatens Australia and its people with nuclear devastation; their removal is a matter of highest priority. The SPA believes a nonaggression pact should be signed between Australia and the Soviet Union and that Australia urgently needs to break with the ANZUS (Australia, New Zealand, United States) Pact and to adopt a policy of nonalignment. The SPA hailed the decision of the Labor government to appoint an ambassador for disarmament. (Ibid., 16 February, 20 July.)

Spearheading the SPA's peace efforts has been Pat Clancy's assistant in the BWIU, Ernest Albert Boatswain, who boasts the following credentials: assistant national convenor of the WFTU-affiliated CITUU, WFTU Bureau alternate member, cochairman of the WPC-affiliated APC, and WPC Presidential Committee member.

Members of the APC protested outside U.S. Navy headquarters in Perth against the arrival of the USS *Enterprise*, the cruiser *Bainbridge*, and the attack submarine *Los Angeles* (ibid., 2 February). The *Socialist* (20 July) reported that some 9,000 people demonstrated in Fremantle, Western Australia, against the visit by the USS *Carl Vinson* and thirteen other ships accompanying it. This demonstration was followed by a 24-hour strike by waterside workers and seamen on the Brisbane wharves. A large demonstration in the Brisbane city square protested the visit by the nuclear-powered USS *Texas*.

In addition to working through the APC, SPA members are urged to participate in other peace organizations, such as the Association for International Cooperation and Disarmament in Sydney, the Congress of International Cooperation and Disarmament in Melbourne, Australians for Nuclear Disarmament, People for Nuclear Disarmament, and People for Peace, to name a few (ibid.).

The political resolution adopted by the SPA's Fourth Congress described the YSL as "a youth organization having fraternal links and a special relationship with the SPA. While being organizationally independent, its program and activities are determined on the basis of a Marxist-Leninist approach." The SPA document pointed out that the YSL accepts the political leadership of the SPA, whose policies it takes in an appropriate form to the young people of Australia. (Ibid., 11 May.)

The YSL held its Fourth Congress in Sydney on 10–13 June under the theme of "Youth forward for peace, jobs, and a new way of life." The leader of the Soviet Komsomol, Vladimir Fedosor, attended the YSL Congress and received the YSL's highest award, the Australian Youth Award for Peace and Friendship, on behalf of his organization. Other foreign guests at the Congress included Triantafyllos Travaliaris, who represented the Communist Youth of Greece; Miklós Barabás, general secretary of the World Federation of Democratic Youth (WFDY); and Hoang Thuy Giang, vice-president of the WFDY. (Ibid., 8 June.) Spiro Anthony, YSL national secretary, is a member of the SPA Central Committee. The YSL publishes *Youth Voice*.

In April, Alan Miller, SPA Central Committee secretary, traveled to East Berlin to attend the international theoretical conference on Karl Marx (ibid., 13 April). Miller's speech to the conference was reprinted in German in *Neues Deutschland* (12 April). Miller then traveled to Poland, where he had discussions with Polish party leaders (*Socialist*, 25 May).

SPA general secretary Peter Symon attended the World Assembly for Peace and Life, Against Nuclear War, in Prague, 21–26 June (ibid., 20 July). In December 1982, Symon also attended both the sixtieth anniversary celebrations of the USSR and addressed the Eleventh Congress of the Communist Party of Greece. He presented a check for $4,000 to the Greek party (ibid., 19 January).

The SPA produces the *Socialist*, a fortnightly newspaper with inserts in both Arabic and Greek aimed at recent immigrants from those areas. Although there is no Australian representative to the *World Marxist Review* in Prague, the *Socialist* does maintain a correspondent in Moscow. The party runs New Era Books and Records as a propaganda outlet and source of revenue.

None of the SPA's electoral bids during the 5 March national elections were successful. The SPA ran seven candidates for the Senate and three for the House of Representatives.

The Trotskyist Parties. It is estimated that the SWP has a membership of slightly less than 200; the SLL around 100, and the SLANZ less than 50. Each party adheres to the founding theses of the Fourth International but differs in the interpretation and implementation. All criticize the United States and USSR for being imperialistic and expansionary but clearly consider the United States to be the greater of two evils.

The primary objective of the SLANZ, according to its constitution, is to achieve "communism over the whole earth by means of proletarian, revolutionary internationalist class struggle."

The SLL aims to prepare and mobilize the working class for the overthrow of capitalism, the establishment of working class power, and the building of a socialist society.

The SWP believes that the working class will be the power base of the revolution and that it will be led by a vanguard of politically educated workers. The SWP exerts a great deal of effort on support for revolutionary movements in Central

America. An article in the *Australian* (July) reported a potential split within the SWP and potential ostracism of the SWP by other leftist parties because of the SWP's espousal of the cause of the Croatian Movement for Statehood.

The influence of the Trotskyist parties is practically nil.

The SWP held its national conference in Sydney from 5–11 January (*Intercontinental Press*, 28 February). The conference was attended by approximately 300 people, including numerous foreign guests who gave presentations on the class struggle in their respective countries. An article on the conference in the SWP's weekly newspaper, *Direct Action* (25 January), noted the attendance of guests from the United States, New Zealand, Hong Kong, Sri Lanka, and Melanesia. A member of the International Executive Committee of the Fourth International was to have presented three talks but did not receive a visa until it was too late for him to fulfill his speaking commitments.

The SWP decided during the late 1970s to base itself in the industrial working class, and most of the members are industrial workers. Previously the party had subscribed to the view that revolutionaries should seek to take leadership positions in the trade unions only after a significant rise in the consciousness of workers. In September 1982, the SWP leadership decided that this view had been incorrect and that revolutionaries should participate actively in the trade unions, up to and including struggle for control of the union apparatus itself. The January conference adopted a resolution entitled "Revolutionary Strategy and Tactics in the Trade Unions" that outlined this new approach (*Intercontinental Press*, 28 February).

Discussion at the conference centered on SWP members' participation in struggles and union election campaigns in the car and steel industries and on the railways. The conference also assessed the party's work in the growing antinuclear movement and resolved that the party should increase its participation and attempt to have the movement adopt an anti-imperialist, class-struggle approach. (Ibid.)

The conference decided to run 38 candidates in the 5 March federal elections. To finance this and other projects, including the purchase of a new three-story building for the Melbourne branch, the conference decided to launch the biggest fund appeal in its history—A\$80,000 (U.S. \$76,800). Utilizing Australia's system of ranked voting, the SWP called on working people to vote for the SWP as their first preference and the ALP as their second. Under this system, if the first-preference candidate fails to win a sufficient number of votes, those for the second are the ones that are actually counted. (Ibid., 28 February, 2 May.) *Direct Action* (15 March) reported that the party had received a total of 41,803 votes, or 0.5 percent of the total cast nationally. In those electorates where it ran candidates, it received an average of 1,000 votes, or about 1.5 percent of the votes for those seats. The SWP produced more than half a million national campaign leaflets and printed 80,000 posters.

The SWP claims to have grown significantly —16 percent in 1981 and 35 percent in 1982. The SWP's national secretary and most influential member is Jim Percy.

Bangladesh

Population. 96.5 million
Party. Communist Party of Bangladesh (CPB)
Founded. 1948 (as East Pakistan Communist Party, banned in 1954, re-emerged in 1971 following the establishment of Bangladesh)
Membership. 3,000
Secretary General. Muhammed Farhad
Secretariat. 10 members
Central Committee. 26 members
Status. Legal
Last Congress. Third, February 1980
Last Election. 1981 national election; CPB ran no candidates, though it did support candidates of other leftist parties
Auxiliary Organizations. Trade Union Centre, Cultural Front, Bangladesh Student Union, Khetmozdur Samiti
Publications. *Sangbad* (in Bengali)

The pro-Soviet Communist Party of Bangladesh (CPB) is the successor party of the pre-independence East Pakistan Communist Party. There are over a dozen parties in the country that also claim to be Marxist. These parties, while small and largely limited to urban centers, possess cadres willing to exploit any sign of discontent against the martial law government of President Hussain Mohammed Ershad. They charge that he has guided Bangladesh closer to the West in both his foreign and domestic policies.

During the year, President Ershad gradually unfolded his plans for returning Bangladesh to civilian rule. He also laid the groundwork for a future political role for himself after the lifting of martial law. In March, he announced an eighteen-point program that virtually amounted to a political manifesto. Four months later, the government began establishing local eighteen-point implementation committees that could also serve as the nucleus of a new official political party. On 1 April, Ershad lifted restrictions on "indoor" political activities and resumed a politi-

cal dialogue to discuss the restoration of democracy. On 14 November, he lifted the ban on "outdoor" politics and committed himself again to a dialogue with opposition politicians. He also announced that presidential elections would be held in May 1984 and parliamentary elections in November 1984. Both would build on local elections scheduled for 27 December 1983–10 January 1984. On 27 November, his new political party vehicle—the Janadal—was formed, and in early December he assumed the presidency. Despite widespread protest demonstrations on 28 November that resulted in a reimposition of curbs on political activity, Ershad affirmed that the electoral schedule would not be altered.

Almost all of Bangladesh's seventy-odd political parties demanded an immediate end to martial law and immediate elections, with parliamentary elections to precede the presidential. Their first major confrontation of the year occurred on 14 February at Dhaka University. The student affiliates of many parties took part in the anti-government demonstrations. Some thirty political leaders, including Sheikh Hasina Wajed of the Awami League (Hasina), the largest component of the fifteen-party center-left alliance, were arrested, as were several leaders of the CPB and other Marxist parties. (*FEER*, 24 February.) Following a number of demonstrations in mid-1983, on 28 November a broad ideological spectrum of parties staged a large-scale rally calling for immediate elections. A small contingent, reportedly led by Marxist cadres, broke off from the main body and smashed its way into the Government Secretariat. The resulting confrontation with security forces resulted in a reimposition of the ban on political activities and the detention of Wajed and Begum Khalida Zia, widow of late president Zia-ur Rahman and the de facto leader of the seven-party center-right alliance. (Ibid., 8 December.) They were quickly released, perhaps because the government recognized that the 28 November violence was the work of the radical left.

The CPB and other Marxists exercised influence out of proportion to their popular following in large part because of their participation in the fifteen-party center-left combine. Besides the CPB, the radical grouping in this alliance includes the Awami League (Razzak), the Jatiya Samajtantrik Dal, the Workers Party, the National Awami Party (Muzzaffar), and the National Awami Party (Harun). The government charged that they had a major role in the 14 February student demonstrations. Major General Abdur Rahman, commander of the Ninth Division Garrison at Dhaka reportedly cautioned those with "pro-China" and "pro-Russian" views to "mend themselves or they would be eliminated from politics" (AFP, Hong Kong, 27 February). Matiur Rahman, secretary of the CPB Central Committee, in turn claimed that "the military regime is spreading reactionary ideas in the ideological and cultural spheres" (*Rudé právo*, Prague, 4 May). The Marxist groups were also blamed for the violence during the 28 November rioting in Dhaka.

The CPB pursued a two-track tactical line during the year. Matiur Rahman noted that the CPB intends to build "unity" of the Left and "broader unity" among "democratic forces" (ibid.). The Bangladeshi press reported increased cooperation among the Marxist parties, although there are continuing tactical and policy differences between them and the larger and

more moderate parties of the fifteen-party combine. One sign of the tension within the alliance was the split that occurred within the Awami League. The dominant, moderate faction of the Awami League, led by Sheikh Hasina Wajed, suspended several followers of the Marxist faction led by General Secretary Abdur Razzak. The Razzak group in turn announced a formal separation in September, advised Wajed to come "out of the clutches" of "imperialist agents," and to uphold "progressive politics" (*Bangladesh Observer*, 9 September).

The CPB itself has limited popular appeal and has never won a seat in parliament. The party claims about 3,000 activists, but as events during the year demonstrated, they can make an impact during demonstrations. The CPB student front, the Bangladesh Student Union, has some influence at Dhaka University and other campuses. The peasant front, the Khetmozdur Samiti, conducted a number of demonstrations during the year. Other fronts are the Trade Union Center and the Cultural Front. Among the more outspoken leaders of the party are Moni Singh (president), Abdur Salam (secretary, agricultural affairs), Saifuddin Ahmed Manik (secretary, labor and industry), and Muhammed Farhad (general secretary).

On the foreign policy front, Bangladesh maintains cool, but correct, relations with the USSR. A long-standing concern of the Bangladeshi authorities was the presence of an exceptionally large Soviet establishment in Bangladesh. After the 28 November riots, in which it was widely believed that the Soviets had a role, the government ordered the Soviet ambassador to cut his staff by one-half and to close a new cultural center in Dhaka (*NYT*, 1 December). Responding to such actions, a Soviet commentator stated that "despite more than one statement by the Bangladeshi authorities regarding their interest in strengthening and expanding bilateral relations between our two countries, they are willingly or unwillingly providing scope to hurt the constructive foundation of Soviet-Bangladeshi relations . . . This tendency can harm our bilateral relations." (Radio Moscow, 15 December; *FBIS*, 19 December.) Despite this coolness, the two states signed a new barter agreement increasing the volume of trade some 12 percent and a new scientific and cultural accord. The USSR also entered into an agreement for the construction of a 210-megawatt generator, the fourth unit of the Soviet-aided Ghorasal Thermal Power Station, which will be the largest in Bangladesh when completed.

Relations with China remained very good. The two sides signed an agreement in November establishing a joint economic commission and providing for Chinese construction of a bridge across the Buriganga River at Dhaka. The PRC also remained Bangladesh's largest supplier of military equipment.

Walter K. Andersen
University of California, Berkeley

Burma

Population. 37.1 million
Name. Burmese Communist Party (BCP)
Founded. 1939
Membership. 3,000 (1979)
Chairman. Thakin Ba Thein Tin
Politburo. 7 members: Thakin Ba Thein Tin, Pe Tint, Khin Maung Gyi, Myo Myint, Tin Yee, Kyaw Mya, Kyin Maung
Central Committee. At least 20 members
Status. Illegal
Last Congress. Second, July 1945 (last known)
Last Election. Not applicable
Auxiliary Organizations. None known
Publications. None; broadcasts over Voice of the People of Burma (VOPB), located in Yunnan province in southern China

The BCP was a leading part of the nationalist coalition that led the struggle for Burmese independence. At the end of World War II, many of Burma's nationalists thought of themselves as communists or at least professed a belief in Marxism-Leninism. Differences over the "road to power" and questions of continued cooperation with British colonial authorities split the nationalist movement along communist-socialist lines. Further ideological schisms plagued the BCP. A Trotskyist group broke with the party mainstream in 1947. In March 1948, three months after Burma gained independence, the BCP broke completely with the parliamentary socialist government and went underground. Outlawed, the party has been in insurrection ever since. Periodic attempts to bring the BCP into the government fold have been unsuccessful. Some of the wartime Burmese communists have defected from the party, and several have become influential figures in the military-socialist government that has ruled Burma since 1962. Most of these, however, were purged from the government's Burma Socialist Program Party (BSPP) when it jettisoned its more radical programs in the mid-1970s.

Since the early 1960s, the BCP has been avowedly and unswervingly pro-Chinese, characterizing itself as a party guided by Marxism-Leninism–Mao Zedong Thought and adapting its line to the shifts in Beijing's ideological course. Pro-Soviet communists were purged from the party in a paroxysm of ideological infighting that nearly destroyed the BCP when China's Great Proletarian Cultural Revolution spilled over into Burma in the mid-1960s.

Leadership and Organization. For more than a decade, the party has been led by Central Committe Chairman Thakin Ba Thein Tin, a veteran (thought to be in his mid-seventies) of BCP struggles who has resided in Beijing since fleeing Burma in 1953. The Central Committee is believed to have at least twenty members. A 14 April *Far Eastern Economic Review* article identified the other members of the Politburo as Pe Tint, an old-guard communist organizer from Pyinmana, Burma, who fled to Beijing with Ba Thein Tin in 1953; Khin Maung Gyi, BCP second vice-chairman, reportedly Moscow-educated, and at 43, the youngest member; Myo Myint, an activist with long experience in the Shan state of eastern Burma; Tin Yee, political commissar of the BCP's Northeast Command, the party's principal military command, and former adviser to the Yang family, once the feudal rulers of Burma's defunct Kokang state; Kyaw Mya, an Arakenese communist who was the chairman of the regional party organization in Arakan until he joined the Politburo in 1980 (his successor in Arakan state rallied to the Rangoon government with over a hundred followers later in 1980); and Kyin Maung, a Burma-born Chinese.

The Central Committee oversees a party Military Commission, which includes the seven-member Politburo plus Kyaw Zaw, a retired Burmese army officer who defected to the BCP in 1976 (*FEER*, 14 April).

Theoretically the party is organized along Leninist lines, but in practical terms its principal organization is the military-administrative region. The largest of these is the Northeast Military Region, which covers much of Burma's northern Shan state in the area east of the Salween River to the Sino-Burmese border. Party organizations have also been identified in the territory adjacent to the Laotian border (the 815th Military Region) and in eastern Kachin State. Some party activity has also been reported in lower Burma,

particularly in Arakan state and the Tenasserim division. Little, however, is known about any BCP organization beyond the Northeast Military Region.

The BCP's size is difficult to determine. In 1979, the BCP claimed some 3,000 members, including candidate members (see *YICA*, 1983, p. 152), but the party has not published any membership figures subsequently. Party organization is the strongest in the Northeast Military Region, where in BCP-controlled areas, party organizations operate at the village level.

The size of the BCP's military force remains problematical. Estimates of its armed strength range from 8,000 to 15,000, but the provenance of these figures is unclear (see ibid., pp. 151–52). Journalists' accounts as well as battle reports broadcast over the party's clandestine radio station, Voice of the People of Burma (VOPB), frequently refer to BCP brigades. Several have been identified by unit designation; the size of these brigades, however, is unknown. In the past, Burmese troops have engaged at least battalion-size BCP formations, but since the BCP shifted its military line in 1979–1980 (see ibid., 1981, pp. 130–31), the insurgents have relied primarily on small-unit guerrilla tactics—hit-and-run raids, ambushes, and mines. BCP forces have been reported operating side by side with a number of ethnically based insurgent groups, some of which from time to time have been incorporated into the BCP command (see below).

The BCP forces are under the command of Zaw Mai, a Kachin rebel. According to the *Far Eastern Economic Review* (14 April), the real power in the BCP military rests with Taik Aung, nominally vice-chief of the Northeast Command. He has responsibility for the 683rd Brigade, a strategic unit, and reportedly commands the security forces around the BCP headquarters in Pang Hsang, a small village on the Sino-Burmese border. Another important BCP commander recently identified is Peng Chia-Shin (variously Fung Kya-Shin), also identified as vice-commander of the Northeast Command. Peng once served as a key lieutenant to the former Golden Triangle opium warlord Lo Hsing-han when Lo was associated with Kokang leader Jimmy Yang. Peng controls the BCP's narcotics activities, an increasingly important source of revenue for the party. Peng has also figured as a key player in fashioning alliances with other Golden Triangle narcotics-trafficking organizations.

Party Internal Affairs. Party propaganda organs seldom discussed ideological issues or party organizational matters in 1983. Whereas the abortive 1980–81 peace talks with the Ne Win government were the subject of much commentary in 1982, only passing reference was made to them in 1983. An unattributed article commemorating the thirty-fifth anniversary of the revolution (VOPB, 27 March; *FBIS*, 29 March) repeated the Central Committee's statement issued in May 1981 when Rangoon suspended the talks (see *YICA*, 1982, pp. 169–71, 1983, pp. 152–53). While noting that the BCP is still prepared to resume negotiations in the future "if the opportunity arises," the article claimed that the "military government of Ne Win–San Yu has called off the talks for good . . . This means that [Rangoon] will never again negotiate on ending the civil war and will only wage the reactionary civil war whether it wins or loses." This will not deter the BCP, the article concluded: "Our party, while counterattacking the reactionary civil war with the revolutionary war, has gradually gained the fruits of the revolution. As long as the reactionaries continue to wage the anticommunist and antipeople civil war, the communists will counter with a revolutionary war of self-preservation. They are also determined to wage the revolutionary war until victory is attained. As long as the revolutionary war is waged resolutely and correctly, more fruits of the revolution will grow for the plucking. Ultimately, the reactionaries will not only not achieve what they expected, but they will be drowned in the revolutionary sea of flames."

Apparently the internal debates that plagued the party in the late 1970s and early 1980s have been resolved since there was no reflection of the past contentious issues in VOPB broadcasts. One tantalizing glimpse of a potential ideological issue—broadening the united front—however, surfaced in regard to the Kachin insurgency. A "knowledgeable source" claimed that the Chinese, longtime backers of the BCP, thought that "the Kachin, without foreign aid, had been far more successful in organizing people than the BCP" (*FEER*, 18 August).

Party leaders have tried to keep the party line consistent with that of their mentors in Beijing, but the pressure for broadening the united front through alliances with ethnic insurgent groups may increasingly call into question the leadership of the Ba Thein Tin "old guard." Younger leaders like Tin Yee, Taik Aung, and Peng Chia-Shin have been more adept at forging alliances than has the old guard, but their success appears to rest more on pragmatism than on adherence to the party's ideological line.

Domestic Activities. While Burma suffered some wracking economic disappointments during 1983—petroleum shortages and increasingly serious debt-servicing problems being among the most troublesome—there was little economic criticism on the VOPB. Rather the commentary on Burma's domestic situation focused on the travails of Ne Win's inner circle provoked by the June sacking of Brigadier Tin U, Ne Win's right-hand man and heir apparent, and Home Minister U Bo Ni on charges of corruption. As Rangoon tried to sort out the implications of this crisis, arguably the most serious rupture in Ne Win's ranks since the 1962 coup, the BCP sought to gain maximum propaganda advantage from the government's troubles. The party's anniversary statement, issued while rumors of trouble in the government's inner circle floated through Rangoon, presaged the problem of high-level corruption that was to be aired in the government press in the weeks ahead: "The only people who have become richer and richer in the 35 years of civil war are the members of the military clique who have used the mercenary army to do whatever they please. They control the entire country's economic and financial lifeline and work to further their own interests. All key economic enterprises in the country have become the family business of this handful of members of the military clique. These people practice the one-party dictatorship system to ensure that their next generations enjoy their power and sham socialism to further their own interests. As a result of the military clique's one-party dictatorship and sham socialism, the clique members have become richer. However, the food, clothing and shelter of the majority—the people of all nationalities—have become worse with time." (VOPB, 27 March; *FBIS*, 29 March.)

The downfall of Tin U, who had developed and controlled Burma's security services over the past decade and made significant gains in controlling both the military and the BSPP, provided a ready target for BCP propaganda. The VOPB attacks took two forms over the summer months. First, party propaganda organs sought to demonstrate that the corruption charges brought by the government against Tin U were indicative of a power struggle over the succession to Ne Win. In a statement broadcast on 30 May (*FBIS*, 7 June), a party commentary argued that the formal charges leveled against Tin U—covering up the illegal importation of goods by Bo Ni—merely masked more serious struggles in Ne Win's inner circle. The statement concluded that Tin U's sacking shattered Ne Win's dreams of an orderly succession. The current problems were indicative of the "contradictions within the military clique," which must be exploited: "It will be necessary to take advantage of these contradictions to further the interests of the people's democratic armed revolution. Only when all the people concertedly fight to destroy the military government—the government that has gagged the people and committed the bloody massacre of students, workers, peasants and people of all nationalities—will they be able to attain a bright future."

On a second front, the VOPB used the Tin U affair to argue the extent to which Burma had become a police or intelligence state. In a series of articles broadcast in July and August, the VOPB examined the development of Burma's security service. Variously comparing Tin U's use of the intelligence service for political ends to Goering's use of the Gestapo or to Andropov's climb to power through the KGB, BCP propaganda claimed that Tin U "transformed the intelligence branch of the mercenary armed forces into the most important pillar of state power and made this branch, relatively for a semicolonial and semifeudal country like Burma, equal to the Gestapo, the [Japanese] Kempetai and the KGB" (VOPB, 25 July; *FBIS*, 26 July). According to the VOPB, Tin U's agents pervaded the country from privates in the army to the State Council.

In other articles, the VOPB painted a graphic picture of how Tin U's service relied on torture to maintain its control. A five-part presentation entitled "Hells in Burma" (VOPB, 16, 17, 20, and 22 July, 22 August; *FBIS*, 19 and 28 July, 25 August) presented case after case of the torture of BCP members and others suspected of anti-government activity. The party vowed to continue its fight even in the face of this "brutality." The VOPB concluded the series with the observation that revolutionary consciousness is being shaped by the government's reliance on torture.

The Insurgency. BCP guerrilla forces were

considerably more active during 1983 than in the previous two years. Much of the BCP campaigning was in response to Burmese army offensives aimed at BCP enclaves in central and northeastern Shan state, the BCP's primary area of operations. Elements of five Burmese divisions, supported by air power and heavy artillery, were employed in two major anti-BCP drives—termed Min Yan Aung II and III ("King Conquerer")—during the annual dry-season fighting from December 1982 until May 1983. In an unusual move, the government reported the campaigns in its controlled press, claiming 345 battles—including twelve major clashes—had taken place (*Guardian*, Rangoon, 5 and 6 April). Several regimental-sized engagements occurred. Burmese attempts to penetrate and secure BCP domains resulted in heavy casualties on both sides. The BCP claimed to have inflicted 400 casualties on a Burmese division in a battle in January (VOPB, 11 April; *FBIS*, 14 April). This massive commitment of resources did not, however, bring significant BCP areas under government control. The Burmese army still appears handicapped in such campaigns by its lack of mobility, inferior armaments, and local support for insurgents in minority areas.

While the BCP battled government forces to a stalemate in the northeast, the BCP appeared to make some gains in the central regions of Shan state through alliances with ethnic insurgencies in the area. Both the government press and the VOPB reported that the Red Pa-O (Shan State Nationalities Liberation Organization) and elements of the Shan State Army conducted extensive joint military operations with the BCP. BCP expansion in central Shan state is in line with its ambition to gain access to population centers in the Burmese heartlands, from which the communists were expelled in the early 1970s. BCP gains in this central region may have been further facilitated by April government campaigns that weakened one of the BCP's chief rivals in the area, the Shan United Revolutionary Army drug-trafficking organization.

In contrast with 1982, there was little mention in 1983 by the VOPB of joint BCP operations with its ally in the northern Kachin state, the Kachin Independence Organization (KIO). This omission suggests an easing of military cooperation between the BCP and the noncommunist, Christian KIO. A possible decrease in BCP-supplied Chinese arms for the KIO may have persuaded the KIO to scale down its operations with the BCP. Arms aid is the BCP's primary attraction, in fact, for many ethnic insurgencies, illustrating the pragmatic, ephemeral nature of most BCP alliances with such groups.

There were continuing indications during 1983 that the BCP was becoming increasingly reliant on the narcotics trade for revenue, probably to supplant a decline in Chinese assistance. The BCP, in fact, controls some of the most important opium-growing areas in the Golden Triangle region encompassing Burma, Laos, and Thailand. A significant development in this regard was the apparent BCP effort to establish bases along the Thai-Burmese border (*Bangkok Post*, 1 January 1984), where the major heroin-refining centers are located. This move would increase BCP narcotics revenues and perhaps enable the BCP to enter large-scale heroin refining.

Despite the apparent gains in territory and influence during 1983, the long-term prospects for the BCP remain dim. A major obstacle is the predominance of hill-tribe minorities in the BCP's rank and file but of Sino-Burmese among the leadership cadre. This ethnic mix would severely restrict the BCP's appeal in ethnic Burmese population centers. Any increase in association with narcotics, which also is identified with hill-tribe cultures, will further tarnish the BCP's image and, perhaps, create resentment among hard-line Marxist ideologues within the BCP. Finally, the socialist model employed by the central government dilutes the BCP's ideological appeal, particularly since Rangoon's socialist programs are unpopular and generally ineffective.

International Views and Contacts. BCP statements on international matters continued to mirror those espoused by its Chinese Communist Party patron. Strong anti-Soviet themes, criticism for superpower military rivalry, and identification with Third World revolutionary movements dominated VOPB commentary. The VOPB's New Year's message (VOPB, 1 January; *FBIS*, 4 January) gave a representative summary of the BCP current worldview. The VOPB broadcast attacked Moscow's occupation of Afghanistan and its support for "puppet" regimes in Indochina and assailed USSR-Vietnamese "hegemonism" in Southeast Asia. VOPB tirades against Vietnamese actions in Southeast Asia were even more venomous than those directed against Soviet machinations in the region. Hanoi was singled out for particularly pointed criticism regarding its military occupation of Laos and Kampuchea, as was the United States for its "blatant aggression" in Nicaragua and Grenada. The VOPB pronouncement repeatedly scored Moscow and Washington for their dangerous global arms race, noting especially, new Soviet SS-20 missile emplacements and naval bases in East Asia, U.S. Pershing missile deployments in Europe, and the arming of surrogates in the Middle East. The BCP also expressed its solidarity with fellow "wars of liberation" in Southeast Asia (Maoist guerrillas in Thailand, Malaysia, and the Philippines), "revolutions against reactionary regimes" in El Salvador and Namibia and "people's wars" in Kampuchea, Afghanistan, and Nicaragua. The comprehensive VOPB commentary commented briefly on economic matters, characterizing the capitalist world as remaining in deep recession and plagued by high unemployment. This observation presented an opportunity to laud the Chinese model: "China proved again in 1983 that the socialist system is superior to the capitalist system."

Despite Beijing's official policy of providing only moral support to the BCP, China continues to provide weapons, medical facilities, and other material aid (*FEER*, 14 April). BCP-controlled towns along the China border facilitate such aid and are protected from Burmese attacks by Rangoon's fear of provoking Beijing. China has gradually decreased its aid to the BCP in line with its desire to improve relations with Burma and other noncommunist Southeast Asian nations and counter Vietnamese expansionism. Beijing is hesitant to abandon the BCP, fearing the Burmese communists might turn to Hanoi or Moscow. China values the BCP as a pro-Chinese presence along its rugged border with Burma and is unlikely to end all material support. Local Chinese officials and military commanders may, in fact, independently aid the BCP, given their long personal and working relationships with BCP leaders.

Paul Belmont
Jon A. Wiant
U.S. Department of State
Washington, D.C.

(Note: Views expressed in this article are the authors' own and do not necessarily reflect those of the U.S. Department of State.)

China

Population. 1,059.8 million
Party. Chinese Communist Party (Zhongguo gongchan dang; CCP)
Founded. 1921
Membership. Over 40 million (*Renmin Ribao*, 27 June; *FBIS*, 29 June)
General Secretary. Hu Yaobang
Standing Committee of the Politburo. 6 members: Hu Yaobang, Ye Jianying, Deng Xiaoping, Zhao Ziyang (premier), Li Xiannian (president, PRC; chairman, National People's Congress [NPC]), Chen Yun
Politburo. 24 full members (listed in order of number of strokes in their surname): Wan Li (vice-premier), Xi Zhongxun, Wang Zhen, Wei Guoqing (vice-chairman, NPC), Ulanfu (vice-president, PRC), Fang Yi (state councillor), Deng Xiaoping, Deng Yingchao, Ye Jianying, Li Xiannian, Li Desheng, Yang Shangkun, Yang Dezhi, Yu Qiuli (state councillor), Song Renqiong, Zhang Tingfa, Chen Yun, Zhao Ziyang, Hu Qiaomu, Hu Yaobang, Nie Rongzhen, Ni Zhifu, Xu Xiangqian, Peng Zhen (chairman, Standing Committee, NPC), Liao Chengzhi (deceased 10 June); 3 alternate members (listed in order of number of votes): Yao Yilin (vice-premier), Qin Jiwei, Chen Muhua (state councillor)
Secretariat. 9 full members: Wan Li, Xi Zhongxun, Deng Liqun, Yang Yong, Yu Qiuli, Gu Mu (state councillor), Chen Pixian, Hu Qili, Yao Yilin; 2 alternate members: Qiao Shi, Hao Jianxiu
Military Commission. Chairman: Deng Xiaoping; 4 vice-chairmen: Ye Jianying, Xu Xiangqian, Nie Rongzhen, Yang Shangkun (permanent vice-chairman)
Central Advisory Commission. Chairman: Deng Xiaoping; 4 vice-chairmen: Bo Yibo (state councillor), Xu Shiyou, Tan Zhenlin, Li Weihan
Central Commission for Discipline Inspection. First secretary: Chen Yun; second secretary: Huang Kecheng; permanent secretary: Wang Heshou; 5 secretaries: Wang Congwu, Han Guang, Li Chang, Ma Guorui, Han Tianshi
Central Committee. 348 full and alternate members
Last Congress. Twelfth, 1–11 September 1982, in Beijing
Last Election. 1981, all 3,202 candidates CCP approved
Auxiliary Organizations. All-China Women's Federation, led by Kang Keqing; Communist Youth League of China (50 million members), led by Wang Zhaoguo; All-China Federation of Trade Unions, led by Ni Zhifu
Publications. The official and most authoritative publication of the CCP is the newspaper *Renmin Ribao* (People's daily), published in Beijing. The theoretical journal of the Central Committee, *Hongqi* (Red flag), is published approximately once a month. The daily paper of the People's Liberation Army (PLA) is *Jiefangjunbao* (Liberation Army daily). The weekly *Beijing Review* (BR), published in English and several other languages, carries translations of important articles, editorials, and documents from these three publications and from other sources. *China Daily*, the first English-language national newspaper in the PRC, began official publication in Beijing and Hong Kong on 1 June 1981. It began publishing an edition in New York in June 1983. The official news agency of the party and government is the New China News Agency (Xinhua; NCNA).

Leadership and Party Organization. According to the party constitution, the National Congress of the party is the "highest leading body" of the CCP. Normally, the National Congress is held once every five years. However, except for the most recent congress, the twelfth, which met in September 1982, all previous ones were convened early or postponed. The congress elects a Central Committee, which governs when the congress is not in session. The Central Committee elects the Political Bureau (Politburo), the Standing Committee of the Politburo, the Secretariat, and the general secretary of the Central Committee. The Politburo and its Standing Committee act for the Central Committee when it is not in session. The Secretariat handles the day-to-day work of the Central Committee under the direction of the Politburo and its Standing Committee. The general secretary of the Central Committee convenes the meetings of the Politburo and presides over the work of the Secretariat. In September 1982, the CCP abolished the post of chairman. The Central Committee also decides on the members of the Military Commission of the Central Committee, whose chairman is a member of the Standing Committee of the Politburo. There is also a Central Advisory Commission, created in September 1982, which "acts as political assistant and consultant to the Central Committee." Members of this commission must be party members of at least 40 years' standing who have rendered considerable service. Finally, there is a Central Commission for Discipline Inspection, which functions under the Central Committee.

The Twelfth Party Congress elected the Twelfth Central Committee in September 1982. Of its 348 full and alternate members at the time, 211, or more than 60 percent, were elected to the Central Committee for the first time, and two-thirds of these new members were under 60, the youngest being 38. As many as 59 of the 211 are professional and technological cadres; 17 percent of the Twelfth Central Committee have such expertise compared with only 2.7 percent of the Eleventh Central Committee (*BR*, 20 September 1982).

Primary party organizations are found in factories, shops, schools, offices, city neighborhoods, people's communes, cooperatives, farms, townships, towns, companies of the People's Liberation Army (PLA), and other basic units where there are three or more party members. The PLA's General Political Department is the political-work organ of the Military Commission, and it directs party and political work in the armed forces. According to the newly revised party constitution (Article 23), the organizational system and organs of the party in the PLA are to be prescribed by the Military Commission.

The highest organ of state power in the PRC is the National People's Congress (NPC). The NPC is elected for a term of five years and holds one session each year, although both of these stipulations are subject to alteration. The first session of the Sixth NPC was held 6–21 June.

The NPC elects a Standing Committee composed of a chairman, vice-chairman, the secretary general, and other members. The officers and members of the Sixth NPC Standing Committee were elected on 18 June.

The 1982 PRC constitution restored the post of president (previously translated as chairman) of the PRC. The president represents the state in its domestic affairs and in its relations with foreign states. A vice-president assists him in his tasks. Both are elected for five-year terms and may not serve more than two consecutive terms.

The State Council is the Central People's Government of the PRC and as such is the executive body of the NPC and the NPC's Standing Committee; it is the highest organ of state administration. The State Council was extensively reorganized in 1982. It consists of the premier, vice-premiers, the state councillors, the ministers in charge of ministries and of commissions, the auditor-general, and the secretary general. (For a list of members, see *BR*, 27 June.)

The People's Political Consultative Conference (CPPCC) is the official organization of the PRC's united front policy. The CPPCC is organized into a National Committee, which holds plenary sessions and elects the CPPCC's Standing Committee. At its first session in June, the current Sixth National Committee had 2,039 members (ibid., 13 June). Deng Yingchao is chairperson of the CPPCC's National Committee. The CPPCC also has local committees at the provincial, autonomous region, municipal, and other levels.

The PLA includes the Chinese navy and air force. It numbers over 4 million men, but is cutting back. Its political influence is also being reduced. The 1982 PRC constitution established a Central Military Commission, which is to direct the armed forces of the country. From 1978 to 1982, the chairman of the CCP (a post now abolished) was commander in chief of the armed forces. The constitution says little of the specific responsibilities of the Central Military Commission or of its relationship to the CCP Central Committee's Military Commission. However, on 20 January—46 days after the constitution was adopted—*Renmin Ribao* said that the state commission as the "top-most military organization of the country, leads and directs all the armed forces of the country" (*FEER*, 7 April). Deng Xiaoping is chairman of both commissions.

Domestic Affairs. The year under review was marked by continuing efforts to consolidate Deng Xiaoping's power and to implement policies associated with him since the Third Plenum in December 1978 and reaffirmed by the Twelfth Party Congress in September 1982. The most important meetings of 1983 marking these processes were the First Session of the Sixth National People's Congress in June and the Second Plenary Session of the Twelfth Central Committee in October. At the latter meeting, the leaders decided to launch the major three-year party consolidation campaign announced at the Twelfth Party Congress more than a year earlier. As was the case in 1982, considerable attention was given during the year to the crackdown on criminals of various kinds, especially those accused of economic crimes, and on "spiritual pollution" or "cultural contamination," even as the policies that seem to facilitate behavior regarded as manifestations of such phenomena proceeded apace. Also continuing from the previous year was the program to retire and otherwise weed out party and government cadres.

On 25 January, the sentences of the two principal Gang of Four members, Jiang Qing and Zhang Chunqiao, were reduced from death with a two-year reprieve to life imprisonment. The two continue to be deprived permanently of political rights. (*BR*, 7 February.) This reduction was widely expected; few believed that the former party chairman's widow, however recalcitrant and unpopular she might be, would be executed. In April, an erstwhile supporter of the Gang of Four, former sports minister Zhuang Zedong, was reported officially rehabilitated (AFP, Hong Kong, 30 April; *FBIS*, 2 May).

The twenty-sixth meeting of the Fifth NPC Standing Committee, held 28 February– 5 March, was notable on two counts. Premier

Zhao Ziyang reported on his visit to eleven African countries (see below), and aged NPC chairman Ye Jianying announced that he did not wish to be nominated or elected to the forthcoming Sixth NPC (*BR*, 14 March).

The Central Committee held a mass rally on 13 March in Beijing to mark the centenary of the death of Karl Marx. Party General Secretary Hu Yaobang's report acknowledged that without Marx's theory, "China could not possibly have become what she is today." Hu disputed the contention that recent agricultural policies represent a retreat from socialism: "Far from losing its foothold or slipping back as some half-baked critics have claimed, socialism has become greatly consolidated and is taking big strides forward in our rural areas." (For the full text, see ibid., 21 March.)

The Central Committee announced that the curricula of party schools are to be reorganized in order to provide full-scale training to leading cadres at all levels, thus breaking from the tradition of short-term rotational training only. There are more than 2,000 party schools run by the Central Committee and party committees at lower levels. Cadres will enroll in the new programs for two or three years and take courses in various subjects well beyond the exclusively political courses of the past. (Ibid., 4 April.)

A third national symposium on party-building education in party schools met for ten days in Zhengzhou, Henan, in April. It set the orientation of reforms, publicized the new party constitution, and made preparations for the party rectification campaign expected later in the year. (*FBIS*, 22 April.)

A February publication entitled *Questions and Answers About the Party's Organizational Work*, compiled by the Research Office and the Organizational Bureau of the Central Committee Organization Department, reportedly expounds on the basic tasks of the party's organizational work; the main functions and responsibilities of the Organization Department; cadre policy and requirements; the transfer, appointment, and removal of cadres; work among old cadres; the organizational system; leading bodies; supervision of party members; and recruitment of new party members "in the new period" (Xinhua, Beijing, 27 February; *FBIS*, 4 March).

The year saw continued efforts to bring the PLA in line with the new policies, specifically to eliminate leftist elements and to raise its educational and professional level. Perhaps most notable was an article by Gen. Li Desheng, formerly known as somewhat leftist himself, opposing ideological thinking. Li said that 1983 is the "first year of creating a new situation in armed forces building." He acknowledged that in carrying out leftist policies in the past, "we often also said it was the mass line," but "in reality" it was "'canvassing the masses' based on our subjective will." Policies "were not created by the masses or based on the consciousness of the masses," he said, but "exactly the reverse." (*Renmin Ribao*, 13 April; *FBIS*, 14 April.) In July, Yu Qiuli, director of the PLA's General Political Department, called for a "shake-up" in the PLA and put forth ten guidelines for the military based on Deng Xiaoping's theories (Xinhua, Beijing, 26 July; *FBIS*, 26 July). Meanwhile, the system of war academies, destroyed in the Cultural Revolution, is being restored. By 1984, 70 percent of all officers, from the rank of platoon commander up, will be expected to have attended one of these. Nor will officers be promoted unless they have attended an academy. (*FEER*, 22 September.)

The First Session of the Sixth NPC was held 6–21 June at the Great Hall of the People in Beijing. A total of 2,978 deputies were elected to the Sixth NPC; 76 percent of them are new faces. Compared with the Fifth NPC, there has been a great increase in the number of intellectuals among the deputies, and they are now said to account for 41.5 percent of the total. Also, the number of CCP members has decreased, so that the noncommunist deputies now comprise 37.5 percent of the total, a 10 percent increase over the previous congress. (*BR*, 30 May.) Premier Zhao delivered a report on the work of the government. The NPC elected new state officers and its 133-member Standing Committee. It also approved reports by Vice-Premier Yao Yilin on the 1983 plan for national economic and social development, Minister of Finance Wang Bingqian on the final state accounts for 1982, Vice-Chairman of the Fifth NPC Standing Committee Yang Shangkun, President of the Supreme People's Court Jiang Hua, and Procurator-General of the Supreme People's Procuratorate Huang Huoqing. Li Xiannian, newly elected president of the PRC, spoke at the closing ceremony, as did Peng Zhen, newly elected chairman of the NPC Standing Committee. (Ibid., 27 June.) Other newly elected officers included Deng Xiaoping as chairman of the Central Military Commission of the PRC, Ulanfu as vice-president of the PRC, Zheng Tianxiang as president of the Supreme People's Court, and Yang Yichen as procurator-general of the Supreme People's Procuratorate. (For a complete list of state leaders and ministers under the State Council, see ibid.)

Premier Zhao's 25,000-word, two-part report reviewed the past five years (1978–1982) and outlined the main tasks for the next five (1983–1987). (For the full text, see ibid., 4 July.) Zhao, concerned about falling state revenues, advocated measures to raise them, although less than a week earlier a new tax system designed to allow state-owned enterprises to keep a share of their own profits had come into being (*Asian Wall Street Journal* [*AWSJ*], 7 June). In his report, Vice-Premier Yao Yilin noted that the combined value of heavy and light industrial production had risen 7.7 percent over the previous year, exceeding the 4 percent target. However, heavy industrial output had risen 9 percent, exceeding by far its 1 percent target, while light industrial output had fallen short of its 7 percent target by 1.3 percentage points. (AP–Dow Jones, Beijing; *AWSJ*, 8 June.) Keeping the lid on heavy industry continued to be a problem. The target for growth of heavy industry for 1983 was placed at 3.9 percent, but by the first half of the year it had already grown 12 percent (*CSM*, 15 July). Wang Bingqian in his report to the Sixth NPC revealed that in 1982 China had its fourth consecutive budget deficit and would have another one in 1983 because revenue trailed behind production growth (AP–Dow Jones; *AWSJ*, 8 June). At the end of September, China's outstanding foreign debt amounted to U.S. $3 billion. This was the first official debt figure ever released by China, and it generally agrees with estimates of foreign analysts. China's net foreign currency assets other than gold were U.S. $11 billion. (*FEER*, 22 December.)

Zhao Ziyang also announced to the Sixth NPC that a Ministry of State Security would be established, a move that seemed out of keeping both with efforts to streamline the bureaucracy and with the more open and liberalizing characteristics of Deng's policies. Subsequently, Ling Yun, a deputy minister of public security since 1964, was named head of the new ministry. In a Xinhua interview, Ling explained: "To ensure the security of our state we will take effective measures and forcefully exercise the functions of dictatorship in striking at espionage and other counterrevolutionary activities to undermine and subvert China's socialist system" (Xinhua, Beijing, 20 June; *FBIS*, 21 June).

On 1 July, the sixty-second anniversary of the CCP, the *Selected Works of Deng Xiaoping* went on sale throughout China. The volume contains 47 of Deng's speeches and talks (39 of them published for the first time) given between January 1975 and September 1982. Twelve days later, the Central Committee issued a circular enjoining the entire party to study the book earnestly, indicating that it "is an important ideological preparation for an overall party consolidation to be started this fall and winter." The aim of this "ideological consolidation" is to achieve a "common understanding. . .along the Marxist lines" established at the Third Plenary Session of the Eleventh Central Committee and the Twelfth Party Congress. (Xinhua, Beijing, 12 July; *FBIS*, 13 July.) From 7 to 17 July, the Central Committee's Propaganda Department sponsored a national conference on propaganda in Beijing. The conference decided that the *Selected Works of Deng* "is the grand program for national construction and for building socialism with distinctive Chinese features as well as the theoretical basis for formulating the party's lines, principles, and policies." It decided that the focal point of propaganda work henceforth would be to study and publicize the book. (Xinhua, Beijing, 24 July; *FBIS*, 25 July.) Over the following weeks and months, the media in China were filled with excerpts from and commentaries on Deng's thoughts. By year-end, there was even talk of a low-key Deng cult, despite an explicit prohibition against personality cults in the 1982 party constitution (see, e.g., *NYT*, 20 November).

During the summer, the Central Committee's Organization Department held a national organization work discussion meeting. The meeting "stressed speeding up, in the spirit of reform, the process of leading bodies' becoming more revolutionary, younger in average age, better educated and more professionally competent so as to guarantee organizationally the fulfillment of the task of socialist modernization." It was reported at the meeting that as of the end of 1982, "unjust and erroneous cases involving some 3 million cadres were redressed, more that 470,000 party members were reinstated with their party membership, erroneous judgments and actions against some 120,000 party members were revoked, and the problems of millions of innocent cadres and masses who were linked to those cases were solved." Also, since 1979 "over 317 million cadres" were trained in political and professional affairs as well as given "general education." Finally, since 1979 over 4 million individuals, including more than 460,000 professionals and technicians, have become new party members. (Xinhua, Beijing, 21 July; *FBIS*, 22 July.)

The campaign against crime continued throughout 1983. In March, the Central Committee's Central Discipline Inspection Commission issued an open letter to the whole party calling for firm efforts to check "the unhealthy practices of party members in housing construction and distribution," a recognition of the serious abuses by cadres in this regard (Xinhua, Beijing, 13 July; *FBIS*, 14 July). On 25 July, Han Guang, secretary of the commission, in a report on economic crimes to an informal meeting of the NPC Standing Committee, revealed that such crimes have grown to a record high since 1949. He said that by the end of April, 192,000 crimes had been investigated, more than 131,000 of which had been resolved. More than 30,000 criminals were sentenced, and 8,500 persons were expelled from the party. More than 24,400 persons had voluntarily surrendered and confessed their crimes. (*BR*, 15 August). On 2 September, Peng Zhen delivered "an important speech" on "the question of severely punishing criminal offenders" to the closing meeting of the Second Session of the Sixth NPC Standing Committee. The Standing Committee accordingly approved decisions on severely punishing criminals who seriously jeopardize public security, on the procedure for swiftly trying criminals who do so, and on the functions and powers exercised by state security organs to conduct investigations, detentions, pretrial hearings, and arrests. (Xinhua, Beijing, 2 September; *FBIS*, 6 September—includes texts of the decisions.) The tough line on criminals became apparent during the year as tens of thousands of accused persons, many of them young people, were arrested; more than a thousand have been executed (AFP, Hong Kong, 21 October; *FBIS*, 25 October). Some executions were performed publicly. There were rumors that provinces and cities were given quotas of arrests, convictions, and even executions. One Chinese commentator pointed out a connection that many suspected: "The struggle to deal hard blows at criminal offenses, which is now being carried out throughout the country, is a serious struggle against the enemies in the political realm" (*Hongqi*, 16 September, pp. 2–8; *FBIS*, 21 October).

The theme of patriotism received notable attention during the year, perhaps as another means of compensating for heavy foreign influences during this period of open-door policies and as a means of buttressing the more independent foreign policy line pursued since 1982. In February, for example, a commentator in *Hongqi* pointed out, "Every Chinese, whether living on the mainland or in Taiwan, Hong Kong, Macao or elsewhere, is faced with this choice: are you patriotic?" The article went on to reply, "The answer can only be in the affirmative." (*FBIS*, 17 February.) At midyear, a lengthy party circular stressed the desirability of education in patriotism. It held that constant propaganda and education on patriotism among the people, "in order to foster their patriotic spirit and enhance their patriotic awareness, is an important task in building a socialist spiritual civilization with communist ideology as its core" (Xinhua, Beijing, 15 July; *FBIS*, 18 July).

Contact with foreigners continued to be discouraged by regulations imposing barriers, by cautioning articles in the media (e.g., a lecture on treason in *Renmin Ribao*, 11 May; *FBIS*, 17 May), and by the Ministry of Public Security's practice of investigating almost any Chinese seen associating informally with foreigners (*FEER*, 6 October). The establishment of the new Ministry of State Security only intensified the care taken by Chinese in dealing with foreign contacts.

The Second Plenary Session of the Twelfth Central Committee was held in Beijing 11–12 October, preceded by a two-day preparatory session. It was attended by 201 members and 136 alternate members, 150 members of the Central Advisory Commission, 124 members of the Central Commission for Discipline Inspection, and 11 leading members of central organs and local party committees as observers. Hu Yaobang, Ye Jianying, Deng Xiaoping, Zhao Ziyang, Li Xiannian, and Chen Yun presided. Deng Xiaoping and Chen Yun spoke on party consolidation, and Deng raised the question of improving ideological work. The committee decided to hold a meeting in the winter or the following spring to discuss this issue and to make appropriate decisions. The session issued a communiqué on 12 October announcing a 13,000-word decision on party

consolidation. A central commission was created to ensure day-to-day leadership in the conduct of this campaign, with Hu Yaobang as its chairman. (*BR*, 17 October.)

The party consolidation campaign is aimed at two categories of problem members: (1) those who, because of difficulties comprehending the current line due to leftist or rightist influences, have adopted a passive attitude; and (2)—to be dealt with more severely—those who rose to prominence under the Gang of Four and those who are guilty of serious economic crimes and other criminal offenses. The campaign is to be completed in three years, beginning in winter 1983–84, in two stages. During the first stage, work will concentrate on leading body party organs at the central, provincial, municipal, and autonomous region levels and the leading party organs in the PLA. The second stage, which will begin one year later in the winter of 1984–85, will consolidate all remaining party organizations. The documents for study during the campaign consist of the *Selected Works of Deng Xiaoping* and three forthcoming books entitled *A Must Book for Party Members*; *A Concise Edition of Important Documents Since the Third Plenary Session of the Eleventh Party Central Committee*; and *Comrade Mao Zedong on the Party's Style of Work and Party Organization*. The Central Committee's decision made it clear that "on no account should the past erroneous practice of 'letting the masses consolidate the party' or letting nonparty members decide issues in the party be repeated." (For full text of the decision, see ibid.)

During a meeting in late October to which the Central Committee invited more than 200 nonparty public figures to discuss documents of the Second Plenary Session of the Twelfth Central Committee, mainly relating to party consolidation, Peng Zhen gave a talk that stressed the current problem of "spiritual contamination" (Xinhua, Beijing, 23 October; *FBIS*, 24 October). After this, the media initiated a secondary campaign against such "spiritual contamination" or "spiritual pollution," and this became intermixed with the party consolidation campaign. On 28 October, Deng Liqun, head of the Propaganda Department, explained the interconnection: clearing away cultural contamination was necessary to achieve the unity of thinking that is the first task of party consolidation (Xinhua, Beijing, 1 November; *FBIS*, 2 November). One of the first victims of this new campaign was Zhou

Yang, chairman of the China Federation of Literary and Art Circles, who had discussed the concepts of humanism and "alienation" during the observation of the centenary of Marx's death earlier in the year (*Ming Pao*, Hong Kong, 29 October; *FBIS*, 3 November). Hu Yaobang and others criticized Zhou, who subsequently made a self-criticism (*BR*, 12 December). Also victimized were Hu Jiwei, director of *Renmin Ribao*, and Wang Ruoshui, the paper's deputy editor in chief. Hu was replaced by editor in chief Qin Chuan. Qin's former position was taken by one of his deputies, Li Zhuang. (AFP, Hong Kong, 14 November; *FBIS*, 14 November.)

From 5 to 12 November, a national symposium on Mao Zedong Thought sponsored by the Party History Research Center of the Central Committee and by the National Party History Society (which has a membership of 10,000) met in Nanning, Guangxi. About 500 theoreticians attended, and more than 300 papers were presented. The participants were said to have agreed that Mao's thought is the "crystallization of the collective wisdom of the Chinese Communists" (*BR*, 28 November). Mao's mausoleum was reopened on 26 December, the ninetieth anniversary of his birth, amid much fanfare commemorating the day.

Auxiliary and Front Organizations. There were several important meetings of the more significant auxiliary organizations, beginning with the Eleventh National Congress of the Chinese Communist Youth League, which concluded an eleven-day meeting on 30 December 1982. This congress revised and adopted a new constitution. It also elected the league's Eleventh Central Committee, which held its first plenary session on 31 December 1982, at which time Wang Zhaoguo was elected first secretary (ibid., 10 January).

A notable trend during 1983 was the reduction of the percentage of communist party members who participated in nonparty organs. Thus, on 25 April, Yang Jingren, head of the Central Committee's United Front Work Department, announced that the percentage of communists in the upcoming CPPCC Sixth National Committee would drop from 60 to 40 percent (ibid., 9 May). Similarly, the number of noncommunist deputies elected to the Sixth NPC increased by 10 percent over the previous NPC, while the number of communist party members decreased (ibid., 30

May). Earlier in the year, the Shanghai Municipal CCP Committee's United Front Committee decided to withdraw communist party members gradually from the various democratic party organizations in that city (*Wen Hui Bao*, Shanghai, 13 March; *FBIS*, 21 March).

The First Session of the 2,039-member Sixth National Committee of the CPPCC was held 4–22 June in Beijing. Members of this committee also attended the Sixth NPC as observers. The First Session elected Deng Yingchao chairperson of the Sixth National Committee, along with 29 vice-chairmen (listed in *BR*, 27 June) and 297 Standing Committee members.

The Fifth National Women's Congress, held in Beijing 2–12 September, was attended by more than 2,000 representatives. The congress revised the constitution of the Women's Federation and elected its new leadership, re-electing Kang Keqing as chairwoman (for a list of new federation leaders, see *FBIS*, 13 September). Kang's report reviewed major achievements of the past five years, described major problems still confronting women in China, and outlined tasks for the next five years (*BR*, 19 September).

The Tenth National Trade Union Congress was held in Beijing, 18–29 October, with 2,326 participants (representing 110 million nonagricultural workers and staff). The meeting adopted a new constitution for Chinese trade unions. It also elected the Tenth All-China Federation of Trade Unions (ACFTU) Executive Committee. The first meeting of this committee elected a Presidium of 34 members. Ni Zhifu was re-elected president of the Executive Committee and first secretary of the Secretariat of the ACFTU. (Ibid., 7 November.) In a work report to the congress, Ni said that by the end of 1982 there had been 430,000 grass-roots trade union organizations, with 73.31 million members (ibid., 31 October).

In late October, the Central Committee sponsored a six-day forum for more than 270 leading nonparty figures representing the eight democratic parties. Deng Yingchao presided over the forum. Hu Yaobang addressed the group and said that he hoped nonparty public figures would help the party's consolidation campaign by making comments and criticisms (ibid., 7 November).

International Views and Positions. The PRC continued to maintain a very active foreign policy in 1983. Its determined commitment to economic modernization was visible in the continued expansion of foreign trade and in the evolving arrangements to attract foreign capital and expertise as well as to secure connections with international financial institutions and other organizations. This open-door policy line remained ascendant, and notable efforts were under way to underpin it further by means of party and bureaucratic reform, although the disquieting strictures on Chinese relationships with foreigners and the campaign against "cultural contamination" underscored the regime's concern about undue foreign influence. Premier Zhao and General Secretary Hu continued to travel abroad. On 17 January, Zhao concluded an eleven-nation African tour, begun with a visit to Egypt on 20 December 1982, when he left Kenya for Beijing. He also visited New Zealand (13–17 April) and Australia (17–23 April). Hu Yaobang visited Romania (5–10 May), Yugoslavia (10–15 May), and Japan (23–30 November).

In December, the PRC and Great Britain concluded their seventh round of talks on the question of Hong Kong's reversion to China in 1997. However, even though the talks were scheduled to continue in January 1984, Beijing had already indicated in November that if no accord resulted from the talks, China would announce its position on Hong Kong "no later than next September" (AFP, Beijing, 14 November; *FBIS*, 14 November).

China's excellent relations with Japan resulted in Hu Yaobang's week-long visit to that country in November. The relationship with Vietnam remained tense and on hold, largely because of continued Vietnamese occupation of Kampuchea, although Hanoi appeared to be more disposed to negotiate (*FEER*, 15 December). Relations with South Korea warmed unexpectedly with the hijacking of a Chinese plane, which landed in Korea in May, and the expeditious return of the plane and its crew and passengers to China (ibid., 19 May). However, Beijing was upset at the lenient sentences subsequently meted out by Korean authorities to the hijackers (*BR*, 5 September).

The PRC's renewed interest in courting the Third World remained apparent in Premier Zhao's African visit and in the number of prominent Third World visitors to China (see below). Beijing hosted a four-day South-South conference (4–7 April), attended by 68 scholars and statesmen (ibid., 18 April). Vice-Premier Yao

Yilin addressed the Sixth Session of the U.N. Conference on Trade and Development in Belgrade on 10 June, calling for a new international economic order (ibid., 27 June).

Among the prominent visitors to China, in rough chronological order, were U.S. secretary of state George Schultz, Japanese special envoy Susumu Nikaido, Nigerian vice-president Alex I. Ekwueme, Belgian foreign minister Leo Tindemans, Egyptian president Mohammed Hosni Mubarak, Ecuadorean foreign minister Luís Valencia Rodríguez, Swedish Left Party chairman Lars Werner, Indian Communist Party (Marxist) general secretary E. M. S. Namboodiripad, Seychelles president France Albert René, French president François Mitterrand, Rwandan president Juvenal Habyarimana, U.S. secretary of commerce Malcolm Baldrige, Mauritian prime minister Aneerood Jugnauth, Central African president André Kolingba, Vanuatu prime minister Walter Hadye Lini, Antigua and Barbuda prime minister Vere Cornwall Bird, Burundi foreign minister Laurent Nzeyimana, Zimbabwan president Canaan S. Banana, U.S. senator Henry Jackson, Italian Communist Party secretary general Enrico Berlinguer, Jordan's King Hussein, U.S. senators Orrin Hatch and Edward Zorinsky with Anna Chennault, U.S. secretary of defense Caspar Weinberger, Yugoslav vice-president Vidoje Žarković, Iranian foreign minister Ali Akbar Vellayati, Mozambican foreign minister Joaquim Alberto Chissano, Tanzanian Revolutionary Party general secretary Rassidi Mfaume Kawawa, Japanese Socialist Party general secretary Masashi Ishibashi, Gabon president Hadj Omar Bongo, Botswanan president Quett K. J. Masire, Romanian premier Constantin Dascalescu, Peruvian vice-president Javier Alva Orlandini, and Democratic Kampuchea coalition leaders Prince Norodom Sihanouk, Son Sann, and Khieu Samphan (Khmer Rouge representative).

The PRC established diplomatic relations with Antigua and Barbuda on 1 January, with Angola on 12 January, with the Ivory Coast on 2 March, and with Lesotho on 30 April (ibid., 10 and 24 January, 14 March, 23 May).

The *Beijing Review* (25 April) featured an article by Li Ji and Guo Qingshi on the "Principles Governing Relations with Foreign Communist Parties." The authors held that there should be no "centre of leadership" or "leading party" in the international communist movement.

Foreign Minister Wu Xueqian provided an overview of China's views on international issues in his address to the U.N. General Assembly session of 27 September (for text, see ibid., 10 October). During the year Wu held press conferences in Beijing; the first of these in February was the first by a Chinese foreign minister in seventeen years (*WP*, 11 February); he held others in August and September.

The PRC applied for membership in the Asian Development Bank (ADB) on 10 February, arguing that Taiwan should be expelled. However, the ADB's charter ignores the political status of members, and the United States refused to agree to the expulsion (*BR*, 16 May). The PRC participated in an International Labor Organization meeting in Geneva on 6 June, its first such participation ever (ibid., 20 June). The World Bank expects to lend China about $2.4 billion in fiscal years 1984 and 1985, adding to the nearly $900 million it has provided China thus far (ibid., 13 June).

The PRC was admitted to the International Atomic Energy Agency on 11 October, was elected a member of the United Nations' International Maritime Organization on 11 November, and became a full member of the World Energy Conference in September (ibid., 3 and 24 October, 28 November).

Relations with the USSR. China did not send a delegation to the sixtieth anniversary of the founding of the USSR in Moscow in December 1982, but it did send warm congratulations, reflecting the modest improvement of relations in the preceding months. At the end of 1982, the Bank of China and the USSR's Bank for Foreign Trade signed an agreement in Beijing on settling accounts in the border trade between the two countries (Tass, Beijing, 24 December; *FBIS*, 29 December).

The year began with a mild polemical exchange. On 14 January, the Soviet magazine *Novoye vremya* (New times) broke months of silence on the Russian side by accusing Beijing of undermining the effort to normalize relations by continuing to claim that the present border had resulted from unequal treaties and that vast territories of the USSR belong to China. The article also said that China was using this issue as a ready-made expedient for retarding the process of normalization. A week later, the Chinese journal *Shijie Zhishi* (World knowledge) replied, saying that "China has no territorial claims whatsoever on the Soviet Union. . . but stands for an overall solution to the border issue through peaceful negotiations" by taking into consideration actual conditions and the unequal treaties (Xinhua, Beijing, 22 January; *FBIS*, 24 January).

The second round of the resumed talks, called "consultations," on a vice-ministerial level took place in Moscow on 1–15 March. The Chinese continued to maintain that real improvement depends on the USSR's withdrawal of troops from the border and from Afghanistan and the ceasing of assistance to the Vietnamese occupation of Kampuchea, to which the Soviets again replied that the talks cannot involve the affairs of a third country. A Xinhua commentator pointed out that the USSR had already discussed "the affairs of a third country" with other countries and had done so at least seven times with the United States between 1959 and 1977 (Xinhua, Beijing, 6 March; *FBIS*, 7 March). During the March consultations, Moscow reportedly proposed a mutual nonaggression treaty and a mutual reduction of border forces (NHK Television, Tokyo, 19 March; *FBIS*, 21 March). The two countries did agree to exchange experts in the fields of agriculture, science, and technology (Kyodo, Tokyo, 23 March; *FBIS*, 23 March). The Chinese called the talks "useful" and their atmosphere "frank and calm" but rejected the offer of a nonaggression treaty.

On 10 March, the new trade agreement for 1983 was signed and promised an increase from the $300 million mutual trade of 1982 to $800 million in 1983 (*CSM*, 28 March). On 10 April, Heilongjiang province and the Soviet Far East signed a border trade agreement (*FBIS*, 11 April). This trade was to take place at Heike, Heilongjiang. Two additional trading stations were to be opened at Korgas and at Turugart in Xinjiang province (*AWSJ*, 5–6 August). The Korgas post was opened in mid-November (Xinhua, Beijing, 17 November; *Honolulu Advertiser*, 18 November), becoming the first trading station in the northwest in twenty years.

Between early March and late May, between 8,000 and 10,000 Chinese were forcibly expelled from Mongolia, eliciting an official protest from Beijing on 3 June (*BR*, 13 June).

In an interview with *Pravda* on 27 August, Soviet general secretary Yuri Andropov appealed explicitly for better ties with China.

Less than two weeks later, Soviet deputy foreign minister Mikhail Kapitsa was in Beijing for a week-long working visit at China's invitation. He was the highest Soviet official to be invited in over twenty years. (AFP, Beijing, 12 September; *FBIS*, 12 September.)

The third round of talks between Deputy Foreign Minister Leonid Ilyichev and Vice–Foreign Minister Qian Qichen was held in Beijing 6–29 October. There were no breakthroughs on the major outstanding issues, but the atmosphere continued to improve and there were some new agreements. These included the renewed decision to continue inceasing trade and cultural ties and to resume technical cooperation. The USSR will help modernize a factory it built in Manchuria in the 1950s. The Soviets also offered "confidence-building" proposals, including a freeze on their military buildup on the frontier, removal of nuclear weapons from border areas, and a Moscow–Beijing hotline. The Soviets also renewed the offer of a nonaggression pact and suggested that first the foreign ministers, then the premiers, meet to lay a firm foundation for relations. This time the Chinese did not reject the proposals out of hand but agreed to consider and discuss them. (*Los Angeles Times* service, Beijing; *Honolulu Advertiser*, 28 October.)

China sent an entry to the Moscow Film Festival in July and for the first time participated in the Moscow International Book Fair. A delegation of the Chinese People's Association for Friendship with Foreign Countries visited the USSR in July. In September, the two countries exchanged ten students each for study in Moscow and Beijing, another first since the early 1960s. Sports exchanges were also resumed: a Soviet soccer team played in China and a Chinese women's volleyball team played in the USSR in August. The first group of Soviet tourists, led by sinologist S. L. Tikhvinsky, was scheduled to begin in China on 6 October, the opening date of the third round of the normalization talks (Radio Liberty, 9 September).

One of the dilemmas in Sino-Soviet relations was underscored by the celebration in Hanoi on 2 November of the fifth anniversary of the Soviet-Vietnamese treaty. On this occasion, Soviet Politburo member Geidar Aliev signed a new treaty of long-term economic and technical cooperation and affirmed Moscow's "unbreakable friendship" with Hanoi. With China obviously in mind, Aliev stated: "Let no one have any illusion about it if he wants to test this friendship or use it for political bargains." On the other hand, Vietnam undertook to continue its efforts to improve relations with China. (*FEER*, 17 November.)

Relations with the United States. This was a turnaround year in relations between the United States and the PRC. Relations were already strained at the beginning of the year because of differing interpretations of the 17 August communiqué of the preceding year (which was to have temporarily resolved the Taiwan arms sales issue) and a number of other nagging issues. Prominent among these were the Hu Na defection, the Qing Huguang railway bonds case, and disagreements over textile import quotas and the transfer of high technology. These differences occurred as China was pursuing a consciously independent foreign policy line and responding positively, if cautiously, to Soviet initiatives to improve relations. Similarly, the United States appeared to be clearly less attentive to the China connection.

The United States tried to improve relations with the visit of Secretary of State George Shultz to Beijing on 2–6 February. The low-keyed Shultz patiently explained U.S. positions and listened carefully to Chinese representations. Restored at this time was the U.S.-PRC dialogue on international issues. Undoubtedly this visit had a favorable long-term impact, although shortly afterward in an interview with the weekly *Human Events* President Reagan made a comment regarding the 17 August communiqué, to which Beijing took exception (*BR*, 7 March). On 5 March, Secretary Shultz suggested to a San Francisco audience a new U.S. orientation that regarded Asia as a whole, with less emphasis on a strategic relationship with China, although he discussed the desirability of aligning the United States with China's modernization program (*FEER*, 21 April).

The outstanding aggravating differences seemed to come to a head in the spring and summer in a way that made relations appear worse than they actually were. Estimates that arms sales to Taiwan for the next year would actually increase rather than decline as outlined in the 17 August agreement brought sharp criticism from Beijing, regardless of the explanation that projected inflation accounted for the increase. Even worse seemed to be the decision on Hu Na, the defected tennis star, over which Beijing may have believed it "lost face." The Chinese

Foreign Ministry charged that this incident was "long premeditated and deliberately created" by the United States (*WP*, 6 April). The PRC canceled nineteen government-sponsored sports and cultural exchange programs in retaliation. This was done, coincidentally, on the same day that the new PRC ambassador, Zhang Wenjin, presented his credentials to President Reagan.

The direction changed in May, with the visit to Beijing of Secretary of Commerce Malcolm Baldrige, who brought the message that restrictions on exports of high technology to China were to be significantly liberalized (*FEER*, 16 June). This assurance probably strengthened the hand of Deng Xiaoping in a timely fashion. Afterward, many of the outstanding differences and some new ones were quickly resolved or placed on the back burner and handled less stridently. A new textile agreement was signed on 19 August, to run retroactively from 1 January 1983 to 31 December 1987 (*BR*, 29 August). With regard to the perplexing Huguang railway bonds case, the Chinese seem to have decided to pursue it in the courts and Secretary Schultz asked that the default judgment be set aside for foreign policy reasons and that China be allowed to appear in court (*AWSJ*, 5–6 August). Meanwhile, although Beijing objected to the decision by Pan American to resume flying to Taiwan in June, it made only token retaliation.

Senator Henry Jackson delivered a letter from President Reagan to Deng Xiaoping in August. Deng responded by telling Jackson that relations had improved significantly. Relations improved even further with the visit to China of Defense Secretary Caspar Weinberger in late September. Weinberger assured Deng Xiaoping that about three-quarters of China's shopping list of 65 weapons and military-related technology had been approved and that there was hope that some of the remaining items might be approved during discussions by military specialists on both sides in the months ahead (*FEER*, 13 October). Weinberger was able to announce that Premier Zhao would visit the United States in January 1984 and President Reagan would visit China in April 1984. During Foreign Minister Wu Xueqian's visit to Washington in October, progress apparently was made toward settling differences regarding three principal items: arms sales; the transfer of peaceful nuclear technology; and the transfer of dual-use technology (ibid., 27 October).

On 18 November, U.S. ambassador Arthur Hummel was summoned to the Ministry of Foreign Affairs to receive a strong protest against a Senate Foreign Relations Committee resolution on "Taiwan's future" (*BR*, 28 November). On 25 November, Ambassador Hummel again received a strong protest from the Chinese government against an alleged "two Chinas plot" in an appropriations bill passed by the U.S. Senate and House of Representatives a week earlier. At issue was a subsection of the bill that held that "Taiwan, Republic of China, should remain a full member of the Asian Development Bank, and that its status within that body should remain unaltered no matter how the issue of the People's Republic of China's application is disposed of" (ibid., 5 December). However, President Reagan issued a personal statement on 30 November repudiating this pro-Taiwan formulation and reaffirming the position of four successive administrations that the PRC "is the sole legal government of China" (*FEER*, 22 December).

The Reagan administration's guidelines governing sensitive "dual-use" technology were finally published on 21 November, after the PRC had agreed to obtain U.S. permission before transferring technology of U.S. origin to third countries (ibid., 1 December).

Because of the dispute over textile import quotas earlier in the year, which entailed the imposition of arbitrary quotas by the United States and retaliatory Chinese halting of purchases of U.S. agricultural products, U.S. exports to China fell by 40 percent in the first nine months of 1983 (AP–Dow Jones, Beijing; *AWSJ*, 14 November). It is expected that trade will improve as relations have improved; this expectation is particularly evident among U.S. electronics manufacturers (*AWSJ*, 30 September–1 October).

However, the Reagan administration tightened textile import controls in December as part of a compromise with U.S. textile manufacturers, who are to drop charges of unfair trade practices by China (*FEER*, 22 December). Also in December, negotiations on a new U.S.-PRC shipping agreement broke down in Washington (*Honolulu Advertiser*, 19 December).

Stephen Uhalley, Jr.
University of Hawaii

India

Population. 740 million
Party. Communist Party of India (CPI); Communist Party of India–Marxist (CPM)
Founded. CPI: 1925; CPM: 1964
Membership. CPI: 470,000; CPM: 270,000
Secretary General. CPI: C. Rajeswara Rao; CPM: E. M. S. Namboodiripad
Politburo. CPI: Central Executive Council, 11 members; CPM: 9 members
Central Committee. CPI: National Council, 124 members; CPM, 45 members
Status. Legal
Last Congress. CPI: Twelfth, 21–28 March 1982, at Varanasi; CPM: Eleventh, 26–31 January 1982, at Vijayawada
Last Election. 1980: CPI: 2.6 percent, 12 seats; CPM: 6 percent, 36 seats of 544
Auxiliary Organizatons. CPI: All-India Trade Union Congress, All-India Kisan Sabha, All-India Student Federation; CPM: Centre for Indian Trade Unions, All-India Kisan Sabha, Students' Federation of India
Publications. CPI: *New Age*, *Party Life*, dailies in Kerala, Andhra Pradesh, West Bengal, Punjab, and Manipur; CPM: *People's Democracy*, dailies in Andhra Pradesh, Kerala, and West Bengal

The major Indian communist parties—the pro-Soviet CPI and the more independent CPM—were caught up in the pre-election maneuvering that gripped Indian politics in 1983. While elections are not scheduled until early 1985, the communists and the other opposition parties, if not the ruling Congress (I) Party, acted as if elections would be called earlier. The two communist parties cooperated more closely and on more issues, although they are far from merger. The pre-election maneuvering also exacerbated the divisions within the CPI between those supporting a "patriotic national front" (re-establishing links with Prime Minister Indira Gandhi) and those favoring a "left and democratic front" (cooperating with other opposition parties to defeat Mrs. Gandhi).

Mrs. Gandhi's Congress (I) Party continued to dominate the Indian political scene during the year. It controls over two-thirds of the seats in parliament, and it dominates 14 of the country's 22 state assemblies. (The communists control the assemblies of two northeastern states and have 48 of the 544 seats in the Lok Sabha, the lower house of parliament.) Yet, for a second year, the Congress (I) did poorly in state elections, losing the two large and former Congress strongholds of Andhra Pradesh and Karnataka to noncommunist opposition parties.

The apparent loss of popular support for the Congress (I) has encouraged the opposition parties to work more closely with each other as they detect a potential victory at the next general elections. The need to cooperate was given added impetus by the pervasive view that Mrs. Gandhi would call early general elections, although the significant divisions among the opposition parties remain one of Mrs. Gandhi's major political assets. Two opposition alliances—the right-of-center National Democratic Alliance (NDA) and the left-of-center United Front (UF)—were formed, and the communists, while not members of either, agreed to work closely with the UF. The communists in effect have developed into a third opposition grouping. The opposition parties, including the communists, also met at three national conclaves in an effort to work out a consensus on major issues facing the country. The one issue that received broad support was a proposed redistribution of power that would grant the states greater control over the allocation of financial resources.

The communists, for their part, made no major electoral gains during the year, and both the CPI and CPM reluctantly concluded that the Left is not yet a viable alternative to Congress (I). As a result, each moved more vigorously to forge a "left and democratic front." Each also shifted away from its earlier hostility toward regional political parties, which made major electoral gains during the year.

Foreign policy received considerable attention in 1983. In part, this was due to India's assumption of the presidency of the Nonaligned Movement in March and its hosting of the Commonwealth heads of state meeting in November. The increasing intensity of communal tension in the northeastern state of Assam and the northwestern state of Punjab, as well as communal riots elsewhere, led to charges of a "foreign hand" in Indian affairs. Many politicians, including the prime minister, occasionally blamed Pakistan for exacerbating the situation. The communists tried to exploit such suspicions by blaming the West.

The communists generally characterize Prime Minister Gandhi's foreign policy as progressive, but they also criticize her for continued Indian borrowing from multilateral lending agencies and for blaming both superpowers for the growing tensions in Asia. They are much more critical of her continued efforts to reduce bureaucratic controls over the economy and to ease regulations that impede foreign investment in India. The dominant faction of the CPI stepped up its criticism of Mrs. Gandhi's domestic policies and brought the party close to the vociferously anti-Gandhi stand of the CPM.

Communist Party of India–Marxist. During 1983, the CPM again demonstrated that it was far more successful than the CPI in mobilizing electoral support, but the voting also showed that both parties are not able to break out of regional pockets of strength. CPM front groups have also grown more rapidly than CPI-affiliated groups. The CPM claims some 11 million members in its various front groups, and the CPI, about 5 million. The CPM controls 36 parliamentary seats, the largest single opposition group, to

12 for the CPI. The CPM also has a majority position in two state assemblies—West Bengal and Tripura.

The CPM (and the CPI) performed poorly in the 5 January assembly elections in the two southern states of Andhra Pradesh and Karnataka, winning 9 (of 294) in Andhra Pradesh and 6 (of 224) in Karnataka. The victories were divided about evenly between them. They demonstrated an equally poor drawing power in the subsequent assembly elections in the Delhi Union Territory and in Assam, both won by Congress (I). The CPM's only consolation was its expectedly strong showing in Tripura, where a CPM-led front won 39 (of 60) seats, a repeat of its 1978 showing. In West Bengal, the party also repeated its 1978 victory in a majority of the local council elections. In both cases, however, the leftist fronts lost some ground to the Congress (I). In a review of the elections, the CPM's Central Committee pronounced that the Left had failed to capitalize on the significant shift of voter support away from the Congress (I) (*People's Democracy*, 6 February). It issued a communiqué noting that the CPI and CPM had misjudged the shifting of voter sentiment. In the case of Andhra Pradesh, where the Left had expected to make major gains, the leadership criticized the party for cooperating with two "declining bourgeois parties" (the Janata Party and the Lok Dal) and suggested that a better associate would have been the newly founded Telegu Desam, a regional party that won a solid majority on a state's rights platform. The Central Committee argued that the CPM must view the Telegu Desam as a "new positive factor in the countrywide struggle against the monopoly rule of the congress." (Ibid., 13 March.)

Nonetheless, the CPM had no coherent theoretical base to reconcile Marxist class theory with the rising regional nationalism in parts of India. The party seriously misjudged the growing popular support for "sons-of-the-soil" movements in Andhra Pradesh as well as in Punjab and Assam. In the case of Assam, a six-party leftist front, including the CPI and the CPM, supported Mrs. Gandhi's decision to hold the long-delayed state assembly elections, even though Assamese agitators were strongly opposed and the Assamese-speaking population largely boycotted the poll. The CPM's decision to back the elections may have been influenced by its efforts to mobilize support among minority groups, particularly the Bengali-speaking population, in Assam. An editorial in the party's national news organ suggested that the Assamese agitators used the election controversy to instigate trouble againt the linguistic and religious minorities in Assam (ibid., 16 January). In the wake of post-election riots there, the Central Committee blamed Mrs. Gandhi for the violence, charging that she had failed to mobilize the population against "terror groups" (ibid., 17 April). There was almost no serious analysis of the socio-economic causes of the violence or of solutions acceptable to the various protagonists. In any case, the party's stand earned it little support from the minorities, who looked to Mrs. Gandhi for protection and voted for the Congress (I).

In the case of Punjab, the party adopted a more favorable stand toward the majority Sikh community and the actions of its political arm, the Akali Dal. CPM representatives in parliament blamed the violence in the state on Mrs. Gandhi's "inordinate delay" in settling the Punjab issue (ibid., 20 February). The Central Committee, however, did appeal to the Akali Dal to avoid violence and to disassociate itself from an extremist fringe demanding independence for the state (ibid., 10 April). In Punjab, as in Assam, the CPM was unable to come up with any political formula capable of mobilizing support for itself among either the majority or minority communities. The latter in both instances turned to the Congress (I) and the majority community to regionally based movements.

As a result of its poor electoral showing, the CPM (like the CPI) moved away from a largely "left front" line to a tactical line calling for links among "democratic bourgeois" parties. In September, General Secretary E. M. S. Namboodiripad pledged CPM support to the five-party UF, although the party rejected a UF appeal to join the alliance (*Statesman*, Calcutta, 23 September). This move may have been coordinated with CPI leaders since they, too, came to the same decision and at about the same time. Both communist parties blasted the two-party NDA because of the inclusion of the Hindu nationalist Bharatiya Janata Party (BJP) in it. The BJP announced its refusal to have any electoral adjustments with the communists or any alliance that works with the communists (ibid., 1 October), thus underscoring the continuing inability of the opposition to work together against Mrs. Gandhi.

The CPM was generally pleased with the expansion of front groups. However, at least in the case of the labor affiliate, party leaders criticized the loose integration of new units into the parent body. Apparently, many units had failed to pay dues or to record affiliation with the national organization. (*People's Democracy*, 10 April.) The party's major front organizations are its agricultural workers' affiliate, the All-India Kisan Sabha (5.7 million); the Students' Federation (714,000); and the Centre for Indian Trade Unions (1.5 million). The CPM sanctioned increased cooperation between these fronts and their CPI counterparts. It also allowed CPM cadres to participate for the first time in the activities of the CPI-affiliated All-India Peace and Solidarity Organization, which sponsored over 200 seminars and demonstrations in advance of the March Nonaligned Summit to publicize the message that the USSR is the natural friend of the nonaligned and that the West is their enemy.

The CPM remained faithful to the pro-Soviet line on international issues adopted at the 1982 congress. The March Nonaligned Summit in New Delhi provided an opportunity for the party to reaffirm its support for Soviet positions. The CPM, along with the CPI, generally praised Mrs. Gandhi's handling of issues, but it did criticize the draft political document as "retrogressive" in places, largely because of the blame it placed on both superpowers for the deterioration in international relations. In contrast, the party's national news weekly claimed that "it is the Soviet Union and Socialist countries that have staunchly and consistently given support to the position of the Nonaligned Movement." (Ibid., 27 February.)

Party leaders, however, toned down their criticism of China, echoed at the 1982 congress, and made only muted references to those issues (e.g., Afghanistan and Kampuchea) where its views differed from those of the Chinese. This shift may have been dictated in part by the moves of the Chinese Communist Party (CCP) and the CPM to re-establish fraternal links after a sixteen-year hiatus. (The CCP was the only communist party to establish fraternal links with the CPM when the CPI split in 1964.) Pramode Das Gupta, general secretary of the West Bengal unit and advocate of a policy of equidistance between the PRC and the USSR, laid the groundwork for renewed ties during a late 1982 visit to Beijing. Following Das Gupta's death in November in Beijing, Politburo member A. Basavapuniah carried out advance planning on behalf of the CPM. The CPM leadership chose three Politburo members to visit

China in April—Namboodiripad, Basavapuniah, and H. S. Surjeet. All three are considered sympathetic to the pro-Soviet line. This choice may have been deliberate. The CPM side would not be prone to agree to any decisions that might embarrass the party at home or undermine the ongoing talks for establishing fraternal relations with the Communist Party of the Soviet Union (CPSU).

The Chinese rolled out the red carpet for the Indian delegation, providing extensive media coverage and frequent opportunities for meetings with senior Chinese officials. This included three rounds of meetings between Namboodiripad and Hu Yaobang, general secretary of the CCP. The Chinese accepted blame for the 1967 rift in relations, blaming it on the Gang of Four. The CPM delegation publicly accepted this minimal loss of face for the Chinese side. The Indian side also accepted the Chinese party's four principles for fraternal relations: party autonomy, complete equality, mutual respect, and noninterference. (NCNA, Beijing, 26 April.) The Indian delegation even agreed to language in the joint statement that took an indirect swipe at the CPSU by criticizing advocates of "one road to socialism." The joint statement also came out strongly for improved Sino-Indian relations.

The CPI, reflecting comments in the Soviet press, criticized the lack of any reference to "proletarian internationalism" in the public statements of the two delegations. Indradeep Sinha, editor of the official CPI news organ, wrote that the CCP is a "disruptive" element in the international communist movement and that the CPM's negotiations with it on its terms suggested an "erosion of proletarian internationalism in the CPI (M) itself." (*New Age*, 26 June.) General Secretary Namboodiripad responded to such criticism with a strong defense of independence in fraternal relations. He pointed out that the CPM could function without a patron. (*People's Democracy*, 5 June.)

Nonetheless, the CPM national leadership acted quickly to put in motion negotiations with the CPSU. The Politburo met on 1–2 June and selected Jyoti Basu, chief minister of West Bengal and a Politburo member, to visit Moscow to discuss the establishment of fraternal ties with the CPSU. While the CPSU has not yet made a decision, there are signs that Moscow is giving favorable consideration to the question. The August issue of the Soviet journal *Socialism: Theory and Practice* noted in an article on the CPM that both the CPI and CPM were legitimate communist parties. While not predicting whether the CPSU would establish links with the CPM, the article did mention that several communist parties (e.g., the Yugoslav, Vietnamese, Romanian, Laotian, Korean, Kampuchean, and Cuban) already have fraternal ties with both the CPI and CPM.

Moscow's willingness to discuss fraternal links with the CPM suggests that Moscow wants the CPI and CPM to work more closely with each other. Soviet leaders, who may already be looking to the post-Gandhi period, would find it in Moscow's interest to have a strong pro-Soviet movement to represent its interests in Indian politics.

Communist Party of India. The CPI, at least its dominant element led by General Secretary Rajeswara Rao, maneuvered to align itself with a broad anti–Congress (I) constellation of parties. To do so, Rao had to beat back an effort from within to make up with Mrs. Gandhi and to abandon the "left and democratic front" line adopted at the party's 1978 congress and affirmed at the 1982 congress. Indeed, the controversy seemed to strengthen Rao's hand and resulted in the party's strongest denunciation yet of Mrs. Gandhi.

The apparent shift in political trends suggested by the off-year voting sparked an internal CPI debate over tactics. In April, the National Council warned that the erosion of Congress (I) support could result in some "bourgeois alternative" in the next general election. The party explicitly recognized that by itself the Left was too weak to fill this role. (*New Age*, 17 April.) While there was little argument with these conclusions, there was a heated debate over what tactical line to adopt in response to the new situation. The pro–Congress (I) faction led by National Council members Mohit Sen and Yogendra Sharma argued that the danger of "right reaction" could be met effectively only by re-establishing a "national patriotic front" with the Congress (I). They pointed to apparently supporting arguments in the Soviet press that seemed to say that Mrs. Gandhi's leadership is necessary to keep the Right out of power. This argument was exhaustively developed by Rostislav A. Ulyanovsky, a member of the CPSU Central Committee, in the November 1982 issue of *Asia and Africa Today*. This prescription is often referred to in the Indian press as the "alternate line," and about one-fourth of the National Council's 124 members reportedly are sympathetic to it, as are a large number of state council members.

General Secretary Rao vehemently rejected the "alternate line." He had been instrumental in orchestrating the shift in party tactics at the 1978 congress, pointing out then (and after) that association with Mrs. Gandhi had isolated the CPI politically and had seriously eroded its support base. He convinced a majority of the National Council to brand Ulyanovsky's article as "merely" the opinion of an academician and not the considered view of the CPSU. (*New Age*, 2 January.) The council conceded that the Soviet leadership "respects" Mrs. Gandhi because she "is broadly pursuing our country's progressive foreign policy." However, it also noted that "the USSR does not interfere in the internal affairs of other countries and political parties," that "there is no international Communist guiding centre," and that the CPI is an "independent" political party. (Ibid.) At the important April National Council meeting, Rao's views were again affirmed, and the council called for "temporary combinations" with "democratic" parties to "pave the ground" for a "left and democratic alternative" to the Congress (I) and a "positive approach" to the UF in an effort to strengthen the influence of the Left and isolate the Right (ibid., 17 April). Rao, for his part, developed the theme that Mrs. Gandhi was herself a part of the "rightist" danger as evidenced by her "appealing to the prejudices of Hindus," and "joining forces" with the Hindu nationalist BJP and its affiliated organization, the Rashtriya Swayam Sevak Sangh. Perhaps because of the controversy that this theme generated, a clarification was issued pointing out that Rao had not called Mrs. Gandhi a Hindu communalist, but "she is now skillfully using Hindu communal sentiments for preserving her own power." (Ibid., 3 July.)

Consistent with this tactical approach, the party agreed to participate in an opposition conclave in Vijayawada and two subsequent meetings in New Delhi and Srinagar. These meetings brought together a broad spectrum of opposition parties. The BJP even participated in the first two and was invited to attend the third, though it declined because of the BJP's disagreement with certain items on the agenda.

Then, in one of the more bizarre episodes of Indian politics, the pro-Gandhi section tried to take its case to the CPSU. In June, on the occasion marking the anniversary of the German attack on the USSR, Mrs. Gandhi transmitted a letter to General Secretary Yuri Andropov, in which she reportedly complained that the CPI was "conspiring" with the Right in ways that made it difficult for her to resolve domestic problems, a complaint she had raised publicly with Brezhnev on two earlier occasions. In both cases, the Soviets refused to take any action to discipline the CPI, arguing the dubious case that the CPSU does not interfere in the domestic affairs of fraternal parties. Yogendra Sharma, a leading advocate of the "alternate line" in the National Council, a leader of the CPI parliamentary delegation, and editor of two CPI journals, agreed to take the letter to Moscow. Sharma did not seek party approval, though he claims to have given a copy of the letter to N. K. Krishna, who heads the Foreign Department of the CPI. (*India Abroad*, 14 October.) While it is unclear whether Andropov received the letter, it seems clear that the CPSU informed the CPI leadership of its contents. The Soviets thus implicitly made clear that Brezhnev's refusal to take the CPI to task on the Gandhi question remains CPSU policy.

A firestorm then erupted within the CPI. The National Council met in New Delhi 17–20 September. After a heated debate, the party overwhelmingly decided to censure Sharma after he refused to apologize for his action. He was stripped of all posts. Sharma's blatant refusal to act through party channels on this question apparently undermined whatever support he might have expected from supporters of the "alternate line" in the National Council. Rao told reporters that only 2 of the 124 sitting members of the council voted against the censure (*Times of India*, 23 September).

The Gandhi letter to Andropov and Sharma's handling of the issue strengthened Rao's position considerably. The council solidly backed his "left and democratic front" approach. While it turned down a request to join the UF, the council did adopt a "positive approach" to it (*Statesman*, 23 September). The council also issued its harshest criticism of Mrs. Gandhi. Rao, in explaining the council's decisions to reporters, came very close to calling Gandhi a Hindu communalist. He also refuted the notion that her leadership was necessary to keep Indian foreign policy progressive, a direct refutation of the Ulyanovsky thesis (*Times of India*, 23 September).

Regarding the CPSU, Rao objected to its being "dragged into an internal matter of the party. We do not want outside interference in our internal matters." (Ibid.) West Bengal CPI secretary Biswanath Mukherjee reportedly stated at the time that the CPI's anti-Gandhi stand would not affect relations with the USSR (*Statesman*, 23 September).

Although CPI-CPM links were strengthened, two problems persist. First, there is considerable fear at the grass-roots level that the stronger CPM organization will overwhelm the CPI. This fear emerged in West Bengal, where party activists grumbled openly about the "miserly" attitude of the CPM in allocating seats to it during the local council contests. Supporters of the "alternate line" can benefit from these apprehensions. Rao's presently unchallenged position is due in large part to the clumsy tactics adopted by some national leaders supporting the "alternate line." The fast-moving pace of Indian politics could undermine his position.

A second source of tension between the two communist parties can be traced to the establishment of fraternal relations between the CCP and the CPM at a time when the CPI was blaming China for the failure of the Sino-Soviet talks to produce results. N. K. Krishna, a National Council member, charged that China in the 1–5 March Sino-Soviet talks adopted a "totally negative" attitude, that China was still "nudging" the United States and NATO to oppose the USSR, and that it was seeking to create divisions within national communist parties. He even saw a "deplorable comity of approach" between the United States and China on Afghanistan and Kampuchea. (*New Age*, 1 May.) Still another National Council member wrote that the CPM was not sufficiently sensitive to the question of "international proletarianism," the code word for the leading role of the USSR in foreign affairs (ibid., 26 June). This issue will likely fluctuate in intensity with the state of Sino-Soviet relations. It is also likely to affect the CPSU decision regarding ties with the CPM.

The CPSU continued to take a dual approach to Mrs. Gandhi throughout the year. On the one hand, favorable items continued to appear in the Soviet press. For example, just at the time the National Council was meeting in September to censure Sharma and to criticize Mrs. Gandhi, a Soviet foreign affairs weekly suggested that "progressive forces" in India support the prime minis-

ter to "enable the Indira Gandhi government to pursue an anti-imperialist foreign policy" (reported in *Times of India*, 23 September). However, the CPSU is unwilling to put sufficient pressure on the CPI to drop its anti-Gandhi line. Such an effort would sabotage the rapprochement between the CPI and the fiercely anti-Gandhi CPM. It would also lose the USSR the sympathy of the opposition, who may succeed Gandhi.

This caution is dictated by the Soviet Union's desire to maintain good bilateral relations with India. Relations remained very cordial this past year. Rajiv Gandhi, Mrs. Gandhi's son and Congress (I) general secretary, visited the USSR in June–July, and Soviet first deputy prime minister I. V. Arkhipov conferred with Indian leaders in May and December. Arkhipov, the first senior Soviet official to visit India since the death of Brezhnev, promised India additional assistance in steel making, power generation, oil exploration, and the exchange of technological information. He confirmed the Soviet offer to set up two nuclear plants, each of 440 megawatts capacity, and to provide credits for the Visakhapatnam Steel Plant. (Delhi domestic service, 12 May.) India's foreign minister announced to parliament on 31 March that Andropov had agreed in principle to visit India, at some unspecified date (AFP, Hong Kong, 31 March). However, Andropov turned down an invitation to attend an informal heads of state meeting in New York in September that Mrs. Gandhi sponsored as president of the Nonaligned Movement.

Smaller Communist Parties. A number of small communist groups have split off from the CPI and the CPM over the past fifteen years. None has gained significant popular support, and none won seats in the various elections during the year.

The All-India Communist Party of India (AICP), founded by former CPI chairman S. A. Dange in 1980 to protest General Secretary Rao's anti-Gandhi line, was unable to sustain the minor gains it made during 1982 and probably lost support in 1983. While there is much grass-roots support for Dange's views within the CPI, the defeat of the "alternative line" approach did not result in any significant losses to the AICP. Rao even claimed that many who defected to the AICP were trying to get back into the CPI.

The press reported a number of violent incidents between the police and the various revolutionary groups associated with the radical Marxist-Leninist movement. Some four dozen groups have split off from the CPM because of its insufficiently revolutionary program. Some estimates claim that they have about 30,000 activists. The major revolutionary groups are the Provincial Central Committee of the Communist Party of India–Marxist/Leninist (CPI-ML), the Communist Party of India–Marxist/Leninist (Reddy) group, the Anti–Lin Biao group of the CPI-ML, the Unity Committee of the Communist Revolutionaries of India, and the CPI-M/L People's War group. The center of their activities remains West Bengal and Kerala, two states with strong communist roots. Several armed revolutionary groups in seven northeastern states reportedly joined forces in early 1983. According to the press, this Mao-inspired front, the Marxist National Socialist Council, met in Assam to lay a plan of coordinated attack against the Indian military and will next consider the question of leadership. However, there is no evidence linking the council to Marxist-Leninist groups or even to other non-Maoist insurgency movements in the northeast. (AFP, Hong Kong, 16 August.)

Walter K. Andersen
University of California at Berkeley

Indonesia

Population. 160.9 million
Party. Indonesian Communist Party (Partai Komunis Indonesia; PKI)
Founded. 1920
Membership. Pro-Chinese faction: 200; pro-Soviet faction: 50
Secretary General. Pro-Chinese faction: Jusuf Adjitorop; pro-Soviet faction: Satiadjaya Sudiman
Status. Illegal
Last Congress. Seventh Extraordinary, April 1962
Last Election. Not applicable
Front Organizations. None active in Indonesia
Publications. None known in Indonesia

The PKI was once the largest communist party outside the USSR and the PRC. It is now reduced to a few hundred members living abroad and is split between pro-Moscow and pro-Beijing factions. There is no way of judging whether there is any connection between these exiled and scattered party figures and any remaining pockets of sympathy within the country. The only visible manifestation of the PKI's existence is the participation of a handful of those exiles in international communist activities.

Leadership and Party Organization. Neither leadership nor party organization are particularly meaningful concepts when dealing with an outlawed party whose pro-Moscow faction numbers perhaps 50 members and its pro-Beijing faction possibly 200. Although more PKI exiles are in or affiliated with Beijing, they tend to be less visible than their Moscow-linked comrades. Jusuf Adjitorop remains the leader of the pro-Beijing faction, but little is known of his activities or those of his fellow party members in China. At present, this may be because of the current Chinese line playing down support for regional communist insurgent groups. It may also be that their activities are well concealed but more significant than those of the exiles in the USSR. Since 1971, Indonesians have been free to travel to the PRC. Large numbers of those travelers, many of them students, return to Indonesia after several years in Chinese universities. Since returning nationals are required only to show a proper Indonesian identity card, the droves of returnees are regarded with suspicion by some Indonesian officials, who refer to a "sea of IDs" flooding the ports of entry. These officials claim that even if only 5 percent of the returnees are communist agents, this could still mean thousands of potential subversives entering the country. There are no solid data to show whether these suspicions are grounded in fact or if the PKI exiles in China are actually engaged in propagandizing visiting Indonesians.

The much smaller pro-Moscow faction has far more public visibility, sending representatives to a variety of international communist gatherings and appearing on the boards of various front organizations and publications. For example, since October 1979 Satiadjaya Sudiman, chairman of the pro-Moscow wing of the party, has been listed as the PKI representative on the Prague-based staff of *World Marxist Review*. He also attended the commemoration of the centenary of Karl Marx's death in East Berlin in April (*Neues Deutschland*, East Berlin, 12 April) along with Tomas Sinuraya, secretary of the Overseas Committee of the PKI.

Sjahrul Munir, president of the Indonesian Peace Committee (IPC), attended the World Assembly for Peace and Life, Against Nuclear War in Prague in June. Munir and four other members of the IPC are listed in the *World Peace Council List of Members, 1980–1983* (Information Center of the World Peace Council, Helsinki). Mera Surya, president of the All-Indonesian Federation of Trade Unions (SOBSI), and S. P. Suwardi, a member of SOBSI's national council, were present at the Tenth World Trade Union Congress in Havana in February 1982. SOBSI, the PKI trade union front organization, was of course banned in 1965 along with the PKI.

The party's slogans for the continuing struggle in Indonesia, as provided by the Central Committee of the pro-Soviet PKI, were "to improve the standard of living; guarantee all Indonesians political and other civil rights; democratize public life; carry on an independent and active foreign policy and establish control over the activity of multinationals in Indonesia; unite all patriots and democrats in action to put the above demands into practice" (*IB*, August).

Domestic Party Affairs. There is no domestic party as such, and whether any fragment of the PKI is still functioning within the country is a matter for speculation. It is unlikely that domestic political unrest is directly linked to remnants of the PKI since released former political prisoners are under close surveillance. However, from time to time press reports contain references to official allegations of resurgent PKI activities in Indonesia.

In early January, following reports in several Jakarta newspapers of the circulation of calendars showing a hammer and sickle emblem on a T-shirt, the commander of the Security and Order Restoration Command, Admiral Sudomo, ordered the calendars confiscated. Most of the hundred thousand calendars printed were destroyed, and members of the public holding the remaining calendars were asked to surrender them to their local military or police station. (Jakarta domestic service, 6 January; *FBIS*, 6 January.) There was no indication of the source of what the papers referred to as "leftist calendars."

Indicative of some official concern over domestic unrest, Admiral Sudomo asked that public gatherings connected with political activities be postponed during the period from mid-February until the end of the People's Consultative Assembly (MPR) general session, scheduled for March. The eleven-day general session proceeded smoothly, returning President Suharto to office for a fourth five-year term. One of the session's principal achievements was to make Pancasila—belief in God, the sovereignty of the people, national unity, social justice, and humanity—the sole political principle for all social-political organizations, effectively minimizing the future political role of the "radical" Muslims (*FEER*, 24 March).

In his acceptance speech to the MPR, President Suharto spoke of disturbances to the peace "which have been settled with the help of the military" (Jakarta domestic service, 1 March; *FBIS*, 4 March).

Some of the reported unrest had to do with

Muslim dissidents rather than communist groups. The Legal Aid Institute, Indonesia's principal human rights organization, in its 1981 report (which appeared in the spring of 1983), estimated that as of the time of the report at least 400 Muslims from various groups had been detained and warned of a "new form of judgment"—political disappearances (AFP, 28 March; *FBIS*, 1 April). A Darul Islam leader, whose trial received major public attention, was sentenced to a twenty-year term for attempting to set up an Islamic state and replace the Pancasila state ideology with another (Antara, 21 April; *FBIS*, 26 April).

It was reported that the government released 3,198 prisoners and reduced the sentences of 14,000 others in an amnesty celebrating Indonesia's national day, in August (*Facts on File*, 18 August), but what proportion of the released prisoners were political detainees is not clear.

In September, an official report to a committee of the House of Representatives disclosed activities of a new-style PKI and referred to former PKI members who had succeeded in becoming a chairman of a cooperative in one case and a village chief in another (*Berita Buana*, 9 September). Former PKI members released from detention are enjoined from any political activity or from holding any community office.

The governor of West Java asked society to guard against Marxist-Leninist pamphlets called *Tekad Rakyat* (People's determination) sent from the Soviet Union, India, and Australia (*Pelita*, 9 September). Later that month, the chief of the Intelligence Coordination Department told a parliamentary committee hearing that the internal security situation in the country was stable, although there remained some problems centered on religion and the state ideology (AFP, 23 September; *FBIS*, 23 September).

More and more public attention, however, has been directed to a wave of mysterious killings that began in Java in April but spread rapidly across the country. General Ali Murtopo, vice-chairman of the Supreme Advisory Council, told reporters in July that the killings (then unofficially counted at 553) were justified and "in line with the rules governing the implementation of the duties of the armed forces." The purpose of the killings is to eradicate crime, and the killings would stop, he said, "when the mission is over." Opposition groups, including the Legal Aid Institute, called for an end to the murders. (AFP, 25

and 28 July; *FBIS*, 28 July.) The killings began following a reported rise in robberies and public disorder that some observers linked to the gradual disappearance of government subsidies for food, kerosene, and other basics and the resulting economic pressure on the bulk of the people. Other recent fundamental changes in the economy have also had at least a temporary destabilizing effect, as, for example, the government's permitting local Chinese business development in sectors from which Chinese had heretofore been excluded, such as agriculture, where they are now permitted to invest for a maximum of ten years.

International Views, Positions, and Activities. As a party of exiles, the PKI's visible activities are exclusively overseas. Overall, these activities are small-scale and low-key for a party that was once the leader among Third World parties.

It is not surprising that the Beijing faction is particularly soft-spoken, given the overtures that its host country has been making to the Indonesian government. In a laudatory article marking President Suharto's re-election, *Beijing Review* (11 April) praised his achievements in markedly lowering the inflation rate, adding substantially to the country's foreign reserves, boosting the growth of its GNP, expanding per capita GNP to six times the 1966 figure, and making Indonesia basically self-sufficient in rice. The country's remaining problems, according to the article, are the result of the Western economic recession. The article made a delicate reference to Suharto's rise to power "after the September 30 incident" of 1965 but said nothing of communist activity in the country before or after the incident.

The PRC is in agreement with the Indonesian government, as well as with the other member-states of the Association of Southeast Asian Nations (ASEAN), in its approach to the Kampuchean situation. However, China flunks the current litmus test applied by Indonesia because the PRC has not supported the Indonesian government on the subject of East Timor (Antara, 11 January; *FBIS*, 14 January).

In any case, in President Suharto's view, "the time is not yet ripe to normalize diplomatic relations with the PRC," as long as the PRC "has not yet convinced us that it will not assist the remnants of communist parties in Southeast Asian countries" (Jakarta domestic service, 1 March;

FBIS, 4 March). He specifically stated that normalization depends on the PRC's attitude toward the remnants of the banned PKI (Jakarta domestic service, 1 May; *FBIS*, 2 May). Despite overt moves by China to re-establish diplomatic relations and despite Malaysia's, Thailand's, and the Phillippines' re-establishment of ties in the mid-1970s following the Sino-American détente, Indonesia has steadily refused to do so (*FEER*, 2 June). Influencing this decision may be the fact that, as an official of the Foreign Affairs Department told newsmen, "experience shows that the PRC continues to support the communist movements in Malaysia, Thailand, and the Philippines" (Jakarta domestic service, 22 March; *FBIS*, 24 March).

In early December, the Indonesian government confiscated the Chinese diplomatic property in Jakarta, evoking protests from Beijing. In response to journalists' queries whether the PRC was willing to meet the Indonesian requirement that it publicly state that it would suspend material and moral support to the PKI, the Chinese spokesman said that China never intervened in the internal affairs of other countries. He added that China was ready to "develop its relations with the communist parties of other countries on the basis of complete equality, freedom, mutual respect and non-intervention in each other's internal affairs." (UPI, 7 December; BBC, 13 December.)

The much smaller but more visible pro-Moscow faction of the PKI generated angry reaction in Indonesia when the speech by its principal delegate, Tomas Sinuraya, to the Karl Marx conference in East Berlin was given broad coverage by East German newspapers, radio, and television. The speech included the standard attack on the Indonesian government and accused anticommunists of trying to use Indonesia as a silent partner in the preparation of a war against the USSR. As for the PKI, Sinuraya said that "the experiences of our party give us the moral right to conclude that most of the time or perhaps even all of the time, the source of our difficulties lies in our own inability to measure politics according to Marxist-Leninist standards, to apply the Marxist-Leninist method appropriately, and to find the right solution." (*Neues Deutschland*, 13 April.) The foreign minister called in the East German ambassador to protest the wide publication of Sinuraya's remarks, and there were parliamentary hearings on the event (Antara, 23 June; BBC, 27 June). Indonesia's Muslim leaders condemned the PKI presence at the conference and called on the Indonesian people to heighten vigilance against efforts now being made abroad to revive the banned PKI (Antara, 25 May).

The event did little to improve the Indonesian government's relations with the USSR, which were influenced by allegations of another possible Soviet spy scandal. The vice-speaker of the House of Representatives called on the government to pay serious attention to a report alleging that a Soviet spy network was operating in Southeast Asia under diplomatic cover. The Jakarta correspondent of *Asiaweek Magazine* said he had been offered money by the assistant Soviet military attaché to provide information on Indonesia (Antara, 23 April; *FBIS*, 25 April).

This occurred while Indonesians were reacting angrily to Soviet deputy foreign minister Mikhail Kapitsa's statement in Singapore that the infrastructure of the ASEAN countries would erode if ASEAN continued its confrontation with Vietnam and its allies, a statement taken as a threat of Vietnamese support for domestic insurgents in the ASEAN countries (*Kompas*, 13 April; *FBIS*, 21 April).

In September, the foreign minister warned that the Soviet consulate in Medan might be closed down "if its existence was no [longer] relevant." The Indonesian military had been pushing for closure of the Medan consulate, which it feared was spreading communist propaganda in an area previously known for its many communist sympathizers. The Soviet consulate in Banyermasin had been closed in 1982 after the discovery of a Soviet spy ring, leaving only the Medan and Surabaya consulates. (AFP, 19 September; *FBIS*, 20 September.)

Jeanne S. Mintz
Washington, D.C.

Japan

Population. 119.4 million (*Monthly Statistics of Japan*, 1983)
Party. Japan Communist Party (Nihon Kyosanto; JCP)
Founded. 1922
Membership. 500,000 (claimed); probably somewhat over 400,000
Chairman of Central Committee. Kenji Miyamoto
Chairman of Presidium. Tetsuzo Fuwa
Central Committee. 189 regular and 22 candidate members
Status. Legal
Last Congress. Sixteenth, July 1982
Last Election. December 1983, 9.43 percent, 26 of 511 seats in House of Representatives
Auxiliary Organizations. All-Japan Student Federations, New Japan Women's Association, All-Japan Merchants Federation, Democratic Federation of Doctors, Japan Council of Students, Japan Peace Committee
Publications. *Akahata* (Red banner), daily; *Zen'ei* (Vanguard), monthly theoretical journal; *Gekkan gakushu* (Educational monthly), education and propaganda; *Gikai to jichitai* (Parliament and self-government), monthly; *Bunka hyoron* (Cultural review); *Sekai seiji shiryo* (International politics); *Gakusei shimbun* (Students' gazette), weekly

Party Internal Affairs and Leadership. The JCP regards itself as independent, and since the 1960s, its relations with the Soviet and Chinese parties have been poor.

Kenji Miyamoto remained chairman of the party's Central Committee and announced most party policies throughout 1983. Tetsuzo Fuwa retained the position of chairman of the Presidium and ran the party on a day-to-day basis, taking over additional duties from the aging Miyamoto. Central Committee Chairman emeritus Sanzo Nosaka, at age 92, was still active during the year, attending party meetings and helping campaign for party candidates.

In July, the *Okinawa Times* reported that Presidium Chairman Tetsuzo Fuwa and Vice-Chairman Koichiro Ueda had written articles for the party's theoretical journal that contained self-criticism. Their self-abnegation focused on a history of the party the two had jointly written 27 years earlier. They confessed that they had committed errors in overestimating the importance of relations with China and the USSR and by publishing in a non-JCP publication internal JCP polemics. Fuwa subsequently said in connection with his self-criticism that the party was "conducting an in-depth review of its history" and that he "wanted to clarify his responsibility for something that occurred in the past." (*FBIS*, 26 July.) However, the self-criticism may relate to differences with Central Committee Chairman Miyamoto, who noted at the Fifth Plenum on 11 July that there was a "tendency toward bourgeois individualism" in the party and "a need for mutual criticism." Miyamoto may have been displeased with the decline in subscriptions to the party's paper, *Akahata*, which he noted at the same meeting had fallen below 3 million subscriptions—compared with 3.5 million, according to Miyamoto's count in 1982. *Akahata* subscriptions are a mirror of party strength and a harbinger of the party's fortunes in elections.

The JCP held its Third, Fourth, Fifth and Sixth plenums of the Sixteenth Central Committee in January, May, July, and November, respectively. At the first meeting, party leaders proposed a Great Special Emergency Campaign aimed at improving the party's position in upcoming local elections throughout Japan. This decision was made in the context of an announcement of a decline in *Akahata* readership for the preceding five months. A goal of a 30 percent increase and a target of 4 million readers was announced.

Party leaders also labeled the Nakasone cabinet the "worst of all postwar cabinets" and explained the JCP's differences with the Liberal Democratic Party and the government, as well as its platform for the coming elections. Party leaders also discussed the JCP's relationship to the other opposition parties in Japan, which recently have not been good. JCP leaders portrayed the Democratic Socialist Party and the Komei (Clean Government) Party as having moved from the opposition to join the Diet majority. They characterized the Japan Socialist Party as having "moved to the right following these other parties." (*Akahata*, 21 January.) JCP leaders expressed concern over the anticommunist stances of the other parties and the isolation of the party.

At the Fourth Central Committee Plenum in May, party leaders focused on the recent local elections and the lessons to be learned from them. Preparations for the upcoming upper house (House of Councillors) elections were also discussed. Chairman Miyamoto characterized the local elections as the first nationwide local elections since the "rightward degeneration" of the Japan Socialist Party. He hit at the anticommunism of the other parties and explained the basis for a joint campaign with the Japan Socialist Party in the Tokyo gubernatorial election. He observed that the JCP had gained in voting strength in the prefectural elections, but that overall the elections ended in "bitter results in the number of party seats gained." He presented more analysis than solutions, stressing hard work and continuing the present party line.

The Fifth Plenum convened in July for three days. At this meeting the results of the House of Councillors election and "future tasks" of the party were the main agenda items. Miyamoto characterized JCP gains in the elections as a "historic victory," although he was careful to qualify this. He also talked about "party building," the need for ideological construction, preparation for a general election, and needed improvements in intermediate-level organs. Re-

garding the House of Councillors election, Miyamoto noted that 4.2 million people had written the name of the party on the ballot and that the JCP won a victory in spite of the new proportional representation system in the national constituency election, which favored the Liberal Democratic Party and the Japan Socialist Party. The JCP had increased its representation in the national constituency, which no other party did. Concerning party reconstruction and ideological training, Miyamoto announced that during the summer the party would hold study meetings and that correspondence courses would be prepared by the party center in which ideological awareness would be stressed. (Ibid., 13 July.)

At the Sixth Plenum in November the agenda issues were the pending House of Representatives election and the bombing in Rangoon, which killed seventeen South Korean leaders, for which the JCP blamed the government of North Korea. JCP leaders expressed concern that both the downing of Korean Air Lines flight 007 and the massacre in Burma would have adverse effects on the party at the polls, notwithstanding the party's tough stand on both issues. (*FBIS*, 14 December.)

Political, Economic, and Military Issues. The main political issues discussed by the party during the year were former prime minister Kakuei Tanaka's continued role in Japanese politics, constitutional revision, taxes, the government's increasing debt, environmental issues, welfare, and several defense-related issues. JCP leaders also engaged in polemics with the Chuch'e Society, formed by Koreans in Japan in 1978 to create a cult of Kim Il-song.

The JCP took a strong stand on the "Tanaka affair" throughout the year, claiming to have been the first party to call for his resignation, when Tanaka first came under indictment in 1976 for receiving bribes from Lockheed to help in selling aircraft in Japan. JCP leaders called on the Cabinet to demand Tanaka's resignation from the Diet and for a closer examination of the "scandal" by summoning high-ranking "gray" officials as witnesses before a Diet committee. When the other parties joined to issue a resolution demanding Tanaka's resignation after his conviction was announced in October, the JCP made a separate, stronger resolution asking for Tanaka's expulsion. The JCP, in its own investigation, exposed Tanaka's influence in construction contracts in

Niigata Prefecture, which the JCP said reflected illegal activities (*Japan Times*, 15 February).

JCP leaders assailed the Nakasone government on the issue of constitutional revision, which they said Nakasone wants, notwithstanding his statements that he would not initiate constitutional changes (*Akahata*, 21 January). JCP criticism focused on statements Nakasone made while in the United States, primarily relating to altering the no-war provision in the constitution to pave the way for a greater Japanese role in defending Northeast Asia.

The party continued to advocate enhanced welfare and social benefits for the poor, but focused more on tax reduction—a new and generally unique position for the JCP. Party leaders advocated a bigger tax reduction than the Nakasone government planned, saying taxes would probably have to be increased later and that waste, inefficiency, and corruption in various areas of national administration were the main causes.

The JCP also used the issue of the budget deficit to attack the Liberal Democratic Party and particularly Prime Minister Nakasone. Party leaders noted that the government's debt had risen from 6 percent of GNP in the 1970s to 33 percent and concluded that the government was following outdated policies, that big business and arms expansion were the cause, and that fundamental changes were required in economic policy.

The party also assailed the government for relaxing environmental protection standards in the name of "administrative reforms" and budget cuts. The JCP called these moves "new reactionary measures" that relaxed controls on big business and reflected regression in conservation measures. (Ibid.)

More attention was given to defense matters, with the JCP attacking changes in Japan's defense posture and a closer defense relationship with the United States. On almost every available occasion, the party underscored its opposition to the U.S.-Japan Security Treaty—even though it is supported by all of the other political parties in Japan and favored by public opinion. Criticism centered on Prime Minister Nakasone's statements about a "common community" and a "common destiny," Japan's being an "unsinkable aircraft carrier" and a "bulwark" against an invasion by Soviet bombers, Japan's responsibilities in controlling the straits around the Japanese ar-

chipelago, and its need to defend the sea-lanes in Northeast Asia.

JCP leaders also charged that Japan's three non-nuclear principles were being ignored, stating that the Liberal Democratic government had been allowing nuclear weapons to be brought into Japan, and called for a "declaration" that would strengthen these principles.

Party spokesmen also chided the government for small increases in social security (0.6 percent) and decreases in spending on education (1.1 percent) while military appropriations were raised by 6.5 percent.

Party strategy seemed to center on joining hands with the antinuclear forces in Japan and winning more voter support on an issue the JCP has been identified with for some time. In so doing, the party seemed to seek to separate itself from the other opposition parties by taking an even firmer line than in the past, even if it contradicted its hostile policies toward the Soviet Union and its tough stand on what it claims to be Japanese territory—the Northern Islands—still held by the USSR.

In June, the JCP issued a statement calling for a "true nuclear weapons zero"—asking the United States and the Soviet Union, in open letters to the heads of state of each, to reduce the number of nuclear weapons in the world to zero (ibid., 19 June). At the same time, JCP leaders reiterated their call for Japan to become a non-nuclear zone.

Subsequently, the JCP took the government to task for the Japanese Self-Defense Forces' use of Japanese communications satellites, claiming this violated an agreement against the militarization of outer space. At almost the same time, the party expressed its dismay that the White Paper on Defense (a semi-official defense publication), which had just been published, mentioned Japan's role in blockading nearby straits for the first time. (*Japan Times*, 21 and 27 August.)

During the December election campaign, the party restated its position on defense in even stronger language, formally calling for an end to the U.S.-Japan Defense Treaty and a specific government declaration that Japan is a non-nuclear nation (even though it has signed and ratified the Nuclear Nonproliferation Treaty). It also called for a democratic coalition to adopt nonaligned policies and suggested that Japan should have no military except the police. (*FBIS*, 13 December.)

Elections. Nineteen eighty-three was an unusual year in that Japan held nationwide local elections and elections for both houses of parliament all in the same year. The JCP fared poorly in the first, won marginally in the second, and lost marginally in the third. Overall it was not a good year for the party at the polls.

The 10 April elections ended in a resounding victory for the ruling Liberal Democratic Party and a defeat for almost all of the opposition parties, but chiefly for the JCP—which wound up with 85 seats in local assemblies, for a loss of 37. Although JCP–Japan Socialist Party candidates won only two of the thirteen governorships contested (in Hokkaido and Fukuoka prefectures), these two victories were interpreted by some as constituting a problem for Prime Minister Nakasone since the opposition had not been in power there for 24 years. Still, the election was called one of the JCP's worst defeats in local elections in recent years because of the number of local assembly seats lost and the large margin of defeat by the JCP–Japan Socialist Party candidate for governor of Tokyo—usually a JCP–Japan Socialist Party stronghold (*NYT*, 12 April). JCP spokesmen, while disappointed, optimistically noted that the JCP had won more votes in almost all prefectures (*Japan Times*, 12 April). The JCP's losses resulted primarily from bad election planning and lack of cooperation with other opposition parties. The second part of the nationwide local elections (24 April) also resulted in a conservative victory. JCP–Japan Socialist Party cooperation eroded in local assembly and mayoral races, resulting in a number of defeats for both. On the other hand, JCP leaders could claim some evidence of victory: an increase of 30 seats in local assemblies despite the anticommunist campaigns of the other parties (ibid., 26 April).

In the June election for the House of Councillors, the JCP fared much better, winning 5 seats in the national constituency and 2 in local constituencies for a total of 7, or a gain of 2 seats. This made the JCP the fourth largest party in the upper house, with a total of 12 representatives compared with 137 for the Liberal Democratic Party, 44 for the Japan Socialist Party, and 14 for the Komei Party. Prominent JCP winners included Central Committee Chairman Kenji Miyamoto and Shoichi Ichikawa, JCP Diet Policy Committee chairman.

The JCP victory can probably be attributed mainly to the JCP's generally pragmatic campaign, its stress on non-nuclear issues, and disputes that plagued the other opposition parties. Little stress was placed on ideology. JCP candidates were also generally successful in shedding the party's image as a dangerous party. Liberal Democratic Party problems also contributed. So did voter apathy and a low voter turnout.

In December, elections were called for the lower and more important house of the Diet. The results were disastrous for the ruling Liberal Democratic Party and favorable for most of the opposition parties, but not the JCP. The JCP lost 3 seats, ending up with 26 seats in the House of Representatives. Its popular vote fell from 9.83 percent in 1980 to 9.34 percent. This setback seemed attributable primarily to anticommunist campaigns by the other opposition parties and public abhorrence of communism as a result of the Soviet downing of Korean Air Lines flight 007 and the North Korean assassination of South Korean leaders in Rangoon, both of which received much publicity in Japan.

Foreign Relations and Ties with Other Communist Parties. During 1983, the JCP maintained its cool attitude toward the communist parties of the Soviet Union (CPSU) and China (CCP). It maintained good relations with several European "Eurocommunist" parties and with a number of other communist parties throughout the world. However, there were no significant meetings with any foreign party during the year.

There had been speculation during the course of the past several years concerning a rapprochement with the CPSU, but events of 1983 indicate this is unlikely. In January, *Akahata* published an article entitled "The Japanese Communist Party and the Brezhnev Era of the Soviet Union" that was quite uncomplimentary of Moscow's policies and the JCP-CPSU relationship. This article subsequently became recommended reading. In September, the JCP strongly condemned the Soviet Union for shooting down Korean Air Lines flight 007. Miyamoto referred to the shooting-down as an "uncivilized, barbarous act" (*Akahata*, 11 September). Almost immediately, the JCP sent an open letter to the CPSU refuting and criticizing Moscow's interpretation of the event and its reply to Miyamoto's statements (ibid., 22 September). In October, the JCP sent another open letter to the CPSU that was highly critical of the Soviet Union's arms reduction proposals, its military buildup, and its behavior toward other nations, particularly that relating to national self-determination. Specifically mentioned in this context were the Soviet "invasion" of Czechoslovakia and the "military intervention" in Afghanistan (ibid., 4 October).

Relations also remained strained with Beijing. Early in the year, a member of the CCP Central Committee stated that JCP demands for reconciliation constituted "unjustifiable interference," a reference to the JCP's demand that the CCP admit its errors regarding the causes of the rupture and sever relations with the "anti-JCP factional elements in Japan" (referring to Kiyoshi Inoue and Torao Miyagawa—pro-Chinese leaders of communist "factions" in Japan) (Jiji Press, 21 February). On 29 April, *Akahata* published a long article charging the CCP with interference and noting that the CCP had already admitted to mistakes during the Cultural Revolution that were tantamount to recognizing errors in its relations with the JCP. The article went on to delineate CCP efforts to improve relations with other communist parties (but not the JCP) and its support of anti-JCP factions in Japan—including Hiroshi Noma, who visited China in December 1982 and who had joined the Yoshio Shiga "clique" against the JCP. In September, Chinese president Li Xiannian said the People's Republic of China had no intention of trying to repair relations with the JCP—severed for seventeen years (*Sankei*, 30 September).

The JCP condemned the government and the communist party of North Korea for the bombing in Rangoon, which killed seventeen South Korean officials. Presidium Chairman Fuwa stated that such terrorist acts had nothing to do with socialist or communist movements. He also noted that the export of terrorism to a foreign country, no matter what country may be responsible, is an "unforgivable act." He went on to assert that the evidence confirms that it was not simply a criminal act performed by reckless elements, but was carried out on the orders and with the participation of North Korea's public officials. (*FBIS*, 14 December.)

Following U.S. actions in Grenada, the JCP accused Washington of "imperialist aggression in classic form" on the pretext of protecting Americans. JCP officials further charged that U.S. aggression was not limited to Grenada. The party subsequently introduced to the Japanese press the Cuban Communist Party's account of the event (ibid., 28 October).

In October, the JCP officially opposed the visit of President Ronald Reagan to Japan because, it said, the United States had "interfered in Japan's internal affairs and had forced Japan into a military buildup." (Ibid.) JCP representatives boycotted the session when Reagan addressed the Diet.

On an unrelated issue, the JCP declared it would cooperate in the Levchenko case (a spy scandal involving a number of Japanese leaders), averring that it was a "conspiracy of the U.S. CIA" (Kyodo, 1 May). The JCP reaction was probably related to the implication in the affair of several members of the Japan Socialist Party, along with some other Japanese leaders with whom the party was not on good terms.

John F. Copper
Heritage Foundation
Washington, D.C.

Kampuchea

Population. 5.9 million (1983 estimate)
Party. Kampuchea People's Revolutionary Party (KPRP)
Founded. 1951 (offshoot of the Indochinese Communist Party)
Membership. 700 (1983 estimate)
Secretary General. Heng Samrin
Politburo. 7 members: Heng Samrin (chairman, Council of State), Chan Si (premier), Say Phuthang (vice-chairman, Council of State), Chea Sim (chairman, National Assembly), Bou Thang (defense minister), Hun Sen (vice-chairman, Council of Ministers; foreign minister), Chea Soth (minister of planning)
Secretariat. 7 members: Heng Samrin, Say Phuthang, Chan Si, Bou Thang, Hun Sen, Chea Soth, Chan Phin
Central Committee. 18 full and 2 alternate members
Status. Ruling party
Last Congress. Fifth, in Phnom Penh
Last Election. 1981, 99 percent, all 117
Auxiliary Organizations. Kampuchea Front for National Construction (KNUFNS), Kampuchea Women's Association, Kampuchea Youth Association
Publications. *Kampuchea*, *Kaset Kantoap Padivoat* (Revolutionary army)

During 1983, Kampuchea remained a cockpit of Sino-Vietnamese and Sino-Soviet rivalry. The country was occupied by about 160,000 Vietnamese troops, with most of the country at least nominally governed by the KPRP government known as the People's Republic of Kampuchea (PRK). The PRK remained closely allied to Vietnam and the Soviet Union and responsive to the advice of several thousand Vietnamese advisers. Resistance to the PRK was provided by the Coalition Government of Democratic Kampuchea (CGDK). This was a very loose and brittle alliance composed of the communist Party of Democratic Kampuchea (PDK), supported by China, and two noncommunist resistance groups, which were supported by the Association of Southeast Asian Nations. Perhaps the most noteworthy change in this whole series of relationships during 1983 was a growth in animosity between the Cambodian people (including some elements of the PRK) and the occupying forces.

Leadership and Party Organization. In the PRK, Heng Samrin remained the senior figure in both party and government as secretary general of the KPRP and the chairman of the Council of State. A colorless figure who defected from Pol Pot's PDK army in the late 1970s, he has been described as an ideal puppet leader. From Hanoi's perspective, this means he shows no signs of developing nationalistic tendencies. Nor has he tried to gain any freedom of action by playing off his Vietnamese and Soviet patrons against each other.

The half-dozen or so other figures, mostly trained in Vietnam, who form the KPRP Politburo and appeared to run the PRK's affairs, have formed a fairly stable group since they were put in place by the Vietnamese in 1979. (The exception was Pen Sovan, who was ousted in 1982, apparently for efforts to move the PRK closer to the Soviet Union. See *YICA*, 1982, p. 196.) Most members of this group hold government portfolios, and these have been reshuffled periodically, quite possibly at Vietnam's initiative. Judging from radio comments from Phnom Penh and Hanoi, Bou Thang's responsibilities may have increased since he was named defense minister as well as vice-chairman of the Council of Ministers. Bou Thang is plainly regarded by Hanoi as one of the key figures in the PRK, as is Chan Si, chairman of the Council of Ministers, who formerly held the defense portfolio. The two most important economic ministries—Finance and Planning—are now held by Chan Phin and Chea Soth. Increasing publicity for their activities undoubtedly reflects Hanoi's desire to improve production, particularly of rice and other food crops, to help offset the deficit in "fraternal" Vietnam.

The Chinese-supported PDK (formerly called the Khmer Communist Party) was also quite stable during 1983. Since the party was under some pressure from its patrons (Thai as well as Chinese) to cooperate with the noncommunist resistance, there was probably a tendency to elevate or advance cadres with suitable political skills. Khieu Samphan, who served as vice-president of the coalition government, was apparently able to work smoothly with Prince Norodom Sihanouk, the president of the coalition (though neither of them had an easy relationship with Premier Son Sann). Other PDK cadres were being chosen to set up joint administrative committees and information offices with the noncommunist resistance.

Auxiliary and Front Organizations. Both the KPRP and the PDK maintained a range of auxiliary and front organizations, though some undoubtedly existed only on paper. For the KPRP, the purpose was mainly to try to mobilize public support for the PRK regime—or to prevent disaffection from reaching dangerous levels. For the PRK, a major purpose of maintaining at least the fiction of mass organizations was probably to impress foreign visitors to their enclaves. For example, one group of Japanese journalists was reportedly impressed to find that Buddhist religious activity of a sort takes place in the PDK-controlled camp they visited. The PDK maintains its membership in a large number of U.N.-affiliated and other international organizations.

International Views and Activities. The question of Vietnamese settlement in Kampuchea was raised in many forums during 1983 by the opponents of the PRK and Vietnam. The CGDK and its Thai and Chinese supporters charged that Vietnam was colonizing Kampuchea with hundreds of thousands of Vietnamese and forcing the Khmers to make a place for them. A growing tendency for Vietnamese forces in Kampuchea to torture and intimidate the local people was also alleged. These charges drew considerable international attention and may have reached some people in Kampuchea.

The PRK's response was to deny and attempt to refute the charges—often with support from Vietnam. At the same time, the PRK regime concluded a formal agreement with Hanoi on principles for settlement of border questions. According to Radio Phnom Penh, this pact was ratified by Kampuchea in August and by Vietnam in September. The pact provided that both governments would have to approve any further movement of peoples into Kampuchea. The PRK broadcast a lengthy defense of its policies over Radio Phnom Penh, claiming that there were only about 40,000 Vietnamese in the country, whom it described as former residents who had been expelled by Lon Nol or Pol Pot in the 1970s. It compared this number with the 400,000 who are believed to have resided in Kampuchea before 1970. By way of contrast, it noted that there are now at least 60,000 ethnic Chinese living in Kampuchea. While it was not possible to verify the conflicting reports of Vietnamese immigration into Kampuchea, the fact that growing numbers of Cambodians sought refuge in the Thai border areas during 1983 lent credence to the charge that a new, more repressive policy may have been instituted by Vietnamese forces in Kampuchea.

William Scharf
Marlboro, Md.

Korea: Democratic People's Republic of Korea

Population. 18.8 million
Party. Korean Workers' Party (Choson Nodong-dang; KWP)
Founded. 1949
Membership. 3 million
General Secretary. Kim Il-song
Presidium of the Politburo. 5 members: Kim Il-song (DPRK president), Kim Il (DPRK vice-president), Kim Chong-il (Kim Il-song's son and designated successor), O Chin-u (minister of People's Armed Forces), Yi Chong-ok (premier)
Politburo. 20 full members: Kim Il-song, Kim Il, Kim Chong-il, O Chin-u, Yi Chong-ok, Pak Song-chol (DPRK vice-president), Yim Chun-chu (DPRK vice-president), So Chol, Kim Chung-nin, Kim Yong-nam, Yon Hyong-muk, Kim Hwan, O Paek-yong, Chon Mun-sop, Kang Song-san (DPRK first deputy premier), O Kuk-yol, Paek Hak-im, Choe Yong-nim, So Yun-sok, Ho Tam (DPRK deputy premier, foreign minister); 19 alternate members: Hyon Mu-kwang, Yun Ki-pok, Cho Se-ung, Yi Kun-mo, Choe Kwang (DPRK deputy premier), Chong Chun-ki (DPRK deputy premier), Kong Chin-tae (DPRK deputy premier), Kye Ung-tae (DPRK deputy premier), Choe Chae-u (DPRK deputy premier), Chong Kyong-hui, Kang Hui-won, Kim Kwang-hwan, Yi Song-sil, Hong Song-nam, Chon Pyong-ho, Kim Tu-man, An Sung-hak, Hong Song-yong (DPRK deputy premier), Kim Pok-sin (DPRK deputy premier)
Secretariat. 11 members: Kim Il-song, Kim Chong-il, Kim Chung-nin, Kim Yong-nam, Yon Hyong-muk, Hyon Mu-kwang, An Sung-hak, Hwang Chang-yop, Ho Chong-suk, So Kwang-hui, Chae Hui-chong
Central Committee. 145 full and 103 alternate members
Status. Ruling party
Last Congress. Sixth, 10–15 October 1980, in Pyongyang
Last Election. 1982, 100 percent, all 615 candidates KWP approved
Subordinate and Auxiliary Organizations. Korean Social Democratic Party, Young Friends' Party of the Chondogyo Sect, General Federation of Trade Unions of Korea (2 million members), League of Socialist Working Youth of Korea (2.7 million members), Union of Agricultural Working People of Korea, Korean Democratic Women's Union, General Federation of the Unions of Literature and Arts of Korea, Korean Committee for Solidarity with the World People, United Democratic Fatherland Front (united front organization)
Publications. *Nodong Sinmun* (Workers' daily), KWP daily; *Kulloja* (Workers), KWP monthly; *Minchu Choson* (Democratic Korea), organ of Supreme People's Assembly and cabinet; *Choson Inminkun Sinmun* (Korean People's Army news). English-language publications are the *Pyongyang Times*, *People's Korea*, and *Korea Today*, all weeklies. The Korean Central News Agency (KCNA) is the official news agency.

The Korean Communist Party (KCP) was formed in Seoul in 1925, but ceased to function in 1928 because of Japanese suppression. Shortly after World War II, a revived KCP appeared briefly in Seoul, but the center of the communist movement suddenly shifted to the Soviet-occupied northern zone, where the North Korean Central Bureau of the KCP was formed in October 1945 under Soviet auspices. Three major factions of Korean communists who had been in China, the Soviet Union, and Korea merged and on 24 June 1949 formed the KWP. Kim Il-song, Korean-born but Soviet-trained, who had been an anti-Japanese communist guerrilla leader in southern Manchuria in the 1930s, consolidated his dictatorial power by eliminating rival factions, and today his Manchurian partisan group (the Kapsan faction) rules the Democratic People's Republic of Korea (DPRK).

Leadership and Organization. The KWP Presidium of the Politburo, the Politburo, and the Secretariat decide policy in the DPRK and dominate the Central Committee. The present central government structure consists of three pillars: the Central People's Committee, a policymaking and supervisory body under KWP guidance; the State Administration Council, an organ to execute policies already decided by the Central People's Committee; and the Standing Committee of the Supreme People's Assembly (SPA), a symbolic, honorific body that allegedly functions as the legislative branch.

The cult of the North Korean dictator and his family members (especially his son and heir-designate, Chong-il) continued unabated in 1983. DPRK mass media constantly stressed that loyalty to Kim Il-song and his ideology of *chuch'e* (self-identity or national identity) should continue from generation to generation, and the Pyongyang regime continually waged an intensive campaign to solidify the younger Kim's position. Radio Pyongyang (15 June) broadcast a special program on a monument to Kim Il-song erected in Samchiyon, a mountainous town located in northern Korea near Mt. Paiktu (the highest mountain in Korea, located on the North Korean–Chinese border). In August, the DPRK regime built a "grand museum" on Mt. Paiktu to immortalize the battles Kim Il-song allegedly fought against the Japanese colonialists. On 9 September, the DPRK observed its thirty-fifth anniversary; various events throughout the country stressed the "wise leadership" of President Kim.

Kim Chong-il acted virtually as the second-most powerful man in North Korea in every public event during 1983, and there were signs that he was preparing to assume authority in the not-too-distant future. Foreign dignitaries visiting Pyongyang now routinely toast both Kims at formal banquets. *Nodong Sinmun* (28 April) called on the North Korean people to further enhance the spirit of unconditional obedience to Kim Chong-il's ideological guidance. A radio commentary broadcast by the North Korean Central Broadcasting Station on 10 October, on the thirty-eighth anniversary of the KWP, emphasized that the party had already "resolved the problem of succession" and was ready to carry on "the revolutionary task initiated by great leader Kim Il-song under the leadership of his successor."

As the evidence of Kim Chong-il's further consolidation of power became firmer in 1983, the tempo of the DPRK regime's image-building for the junior Kim quickened and accelerated. On 17 January, Radio Pyongyang claimed that President Kim's son was now held in high esteem by the people of the world as a great genius of communist revolution and construction. The radio added that "the esteemed leader" had achieved such miracles in various fields of communist revolution and construction that complimentary messages regarding his performance were pouring into Pyongyang from all parts of the world.

On 15 February, *Nodong Sinmun* carried a special article entitled "Let Us Inherit the Chuch'e Lineage" in commemoration of Kim Chong-il's forty-first birthday.

The junior Kim published a treatise "Let Us March Under the Banner of Marxism-Leninism and the Chuch'e Idea" in the May issue of *Kulloja*, on the occasion of the 165th birthday of Karl Marx and the centenary of his death. Thereafter, the DPRK carried out an intense campaign at home and abroad to propagandize this treatise. During May, for example, North Korean mass media carried a series of commentaries on the treatise, saying that "it clarifies the truth of Marxism-Leninism and chuch'e thought and gives a definite answer to the question of how to carry on communist revolutionary work," and that "the treatise is a piece of eternal literature that substantiates the theory of revolutionary leadership." Following publication of the treatise, Pyongyang accorded Kim Chong-il unsparing respect as a prominent Marxist-Leninist, the most acceptable legitimizing qualification for a leader of a communist nation.

Kang Yang-uk, 80-year-old vice-president of the DPRK, who was concurrently chairman of the Social Democratic Party, passed away on 9 January. Kim Il-tae, 52-year-old president of the Academy of Sciences, who was concurrently a member of both the Central Committee of the KWP and the Standing Committee of the Seventh SPA, died on 25 September.

The second session of the Seventh SPA, held on 5–7 April, named former secretary of the Central People's Committee (CPC) Yim Chun-chu, 71, to succeed the deceased vice-president. Yi Yong-ik, member of the Central Committee of the KWP and concurrently chairman of the Central Broadcasting Committee as well as an SPA member, was elected secretary and member of the CPC. Choe Yong-nim was elected a member of the CPC.

The session also elected a new chairman and vice-chairmen of the SPA. Yang Hyong-sop, director of the Social Science Academy, was elected chairman (replacing Hwang Chang-yop); Son Song-pil, member of the SPA Standing Committee, and Yo Yong-ku, director of the Secretariat of the Democratic Front for Reunification of the Fatherland, were elected vice-chairmen. Kim Il-tae was elected a member of the SPA Standing Committee.

The seventh plenary session of the Sixth KWP Central Committee, held 15–17 June in Pyongyang, elected An Sung-hak secretary of the party Central Committee in charge of light industry and Chae Hui-chong secretary of the party Central Committee in charge of planning and finance. Kim Hwan and Yun Ki-pok were removed from the Secretariat and named deputy premier and chairman of the People's Committee of Pyongyang City, respectively. (Kim Hwan's assumption of deputy premiership brought the total number of deputy premiers to thirteen.) The plenary meeting elected Kim Nam-yun and Pak Song-pong members of the party Central Committee to fill vacancies.

At the eighth plenary session of the KWP Central Committee, which met 29 November–1 December in Pyongyang, Ho Tam, a deputy premier and foreign affairs minister, was promoted to full membership on the party Politburo. The session also made party secretary An Sung-hak and Deputy Premiers Hong Song-yong and Kim Pok-sin candidate members of the party Politburo. (These appointments raised the membership of the Politburo to 39 from 36.) Chon Ha-chol, who ranked seventy-third on the list of candidate members of the Central Committee, was elected a full member.

Domestic Attitudes and Activities. President Kim Il-song's New Year's address, which lasted 27 minutes, concentrated on economic problems. He put little emphasis on politics, diplomacy, or the reunification issue. Kim pointed out that many sectors of the current Seven-Year Economic Plan (1978–1984) had been completed two years ahead of schedule, thanks to the "strenuous efforts made by revolutionary workers." Major achievements in 1982 included the construction of "monumental structures and new streets in Pyongyang, an increase in production capacity of nonferrous metals, and bumper crops." He indicated that industrial output in 1982 increased 16.8 percent over 1981, but did not disclose any other economic indicators.

As for the 1983 economic program, President Kim gave guidelines for various industrial sectors, including mining, electricity, chemicals, metals, nonferrous metals, machinery, manufacturing, transportation, and farming. But, "the first priority objective for 1983 is to boost coal production." Coal was the key to solving the shortage of fuel, energy, and raw materials, he emphasized.

The Speed of the 1980s drive to attain ten economic goals for the decade and the four-point Nature-Remaking Program were to be continued in 1983 so as to complete the current economic plan ahead of schedule. (The ten economic goals are to reclaim 300,000 *jongbo*, or 735,000 acres, of land and to produce 100 billion kwh of electricity, 120 million tons of coal, 15 million tons of steel, 1.5 million tons of nonferrous metals, 20 million tons of cement, 7 million tons of chemical fertilizer, 1.5 billion meters of cloth, 5 million tons of marine products, and 15 million tons of grain.)

The seventh plenary session of the Sixth KWP Central Committee in mid-June dealt with two main economic items: increasing production of chemical goods to achieve the goal of 15 million meters of cloth and improving the railway transportation capacity.

Meanwhile, depressed world commodity

prices seemed to have dampened economic progress in North Korea during 1983, and its reliability as a trading partner remained tarnished by its periodic rescheduling of foreign debts, estimated at U.S. $2–3 billion.

On 6 March, North Korea elected a total of 24,562 members of municipal and county people's assemblies. (According to the DPRK constitution, such elections are to be held every two years.) The number of assembly members increased by 371 over the 1981 elections.

Nodong Sinmun (5 March) carried an article praising Joseph Stalin on the thirtieth anniversary of his death. (North Korea did not follow the Soviet Union and China in degrading Stalin.) The article called him a faithful Marxist-Leninist who had carried on Lenin's great work and a prominent activist who had led the Comintern as well as the labor movement in his lifetime. North Koreans would long remember Stalin as their closest friend, who recognized North Korea as an independent country and greatly contributed to the strengthening of mutual relations between the Soviet Union and North Korea.

On 5 April, the DPRK regime fixed its budget for fiscal 1983 at 24.3 billion won (U.S. $11.5 billion). The budgetary action came during the three-day second session of the Seventh SPA, which opened on 5 April. The budget for fiscal 1983 showed an increase of 7.3 percent in revenues and a 9.6 percent rise in spending over 1982. Of this year's expenditures, 62.5 percent ($7.2 billion) was allotted to the people's economy sector, 20.2 percent ($2.3 billion) to social welfare, and 14.8 percent ($1.7 billion) to the military. (The actual defense expenditure is no doubt higher because Pyongyang hides defense expenditures in other sectors.)

South Korea. Relations between North and South Korea were very tense during 1983, due chiefly to Pyongyang's bellicosity. The DPRK stepped up its harsh propaganda and other attacks on the Seoul government under President Chun Doo-Hwan, calling him the head of a "despicable fascist clique" to be overthrown by force, if necessary.

On 1 February, the DPRK put its entire armed forces on what it called "a quasi-war state" after the United States and South Korea started an annual joint military exercise (called Team Spirit) involving 188,000 troops in the South. (The exercise ran until mid-April.) This was the first time North Korea called a general alert to coincide with this annual military exercise.

North Korean attempts to infiltrate the South have long been routine, but they seemed to have increased considerably during 1983. South Korean forces sank North Korean spy boats and killed or captured armed North Korean agents in April, June, August, and December.

Nodong Sinmun (10 July) leveled criticism at Seoul's nationwide televised campaign to help families separated during the Korean War find their lost members, saying that "the campaign was nothing but a premeditated drama staged by the South Korean government" solely to escalate the anticommunist mood among the people under the pretext of humanitarianism. In mid-July, the DPRK rejected Seoul's bid of 6 July to discuss a family-reunion program throughout the Korean peninsula.

Pyongyang countered Seoul's continued bid to resume the South-North dialogue with a joint statement issued on 18 January in the name of the KWP and twenty other organizations. The statement made it clear that North Korea would not talk with the Chun government of South Korea but it would meet with any of those, including members of South Korean political parties, who were willing to discuss the withdrawal of U.S. forces from the South. The statement also urged that the withdrawal should come before reunification talks, saying that Seoul's South-North reconciliation formula was aimed at perpetuating the division of the Korean peninsula.

Both Pyongyang and Seoul sent delegates to the Twenty-third Asian-African Legal Consultative Conference held in Tokyo in mid-May. But both delegates failed to have any contact, except for the exchange of cold stares.

The DPRK regime vehemently denounced and even tried to abort the Seventieth International Parliamentary Union Conference held in Seoul in early October, saying that the meeting was aimed at perpetuating the "two-Korea policy" of the United States and providing momentum for promoting the idea of "cross-recognition" among the participating nations. (Despite Pyongyang's obstructive tactics, some 600 persons from 67 member-countries and representatives from twenty international organizations participated in the conference.)

The most audacious of North Korea's relentless anti-Seoul acts during 1983 was a terrorist bombing attack in Rangoon, Burma, on 9 October that killed 21 people, including seventeen visiting South Korean government officials. The incident took the lives of four South Korean cabinet ministers and narrowly missed killing Chun Doo-Hwan. According to Foreign Minister Yi Won-kyung of South Korea, North Korea had planned a coordinated military and diplomatic drive to take advantage of the confusion that would have resulted from the terrorist bombing (*WP*, 2 December).

The Burmese government announced on 4 November that its four-week investigation had "firmly established" that North Korean commandos were responsible for the bombing. (Burma put two captured North Korean officers on trial—a third had been killed—and the prosecution's case against them documented the DPRK regime's wide-ranging plot.) At the same time, Rangoon broke diplomatic relations with North Korea.

On 5 November, Pyongyang dismissed as "sheer fabrication" an official Burmese finding that the DPRK was responsible for the 9 October incident and said that the Burmese decision to sever diplomatic ties was an "unjustifiable act." It reiterated its allegation that the Rangoon explosion had been staged by Seoul and Washington as part of their scheme to escalate tension on the Korean peninsula and said that Burma's "unjust" action would only further their vicious plot.

International Views and Positions. During 1983, Pyongyang mounted an intensive diplomatic offensive against South Korea to undermine the international position of the Seoul regime and to develop world support for its own reunification policy. Parliamentary, trade, and goodwill missions were dispatched abroad or invited to North Korea. Numerous friendly diplomatic gestures and offers of economic and technical aid were made, especially to Third World countries, which increasingly dominate the United Nations. In particular, the DPRK sought to prevent recognition of the "two Koreas" concept by the world community; to isolate South Korea from the Third World, the communist bloc, and even the Western world; and to drum up diplomatic support for its demand to remove U.S. forces from South Korea.

On 28 February, the DPRK established diplomatic ties with Bolivia.

In a bid to boost its standing in the Nonaligned Movement and win friends in developing countries, North Korea is believed to have recently stepped up its activities to supply some twenty Third World countries (mostly in Africa and Latin America) and various guerrilla movements with arms and military advisers (*NYT*, 29 November). Evidence that Pyongyang had extended its military activities overseas came in October when U.S. forces occupying Grenada reported finding 24 North Koreans, along with a treaty agreeing to provide automatic weapons and ammunition worth U.S. $12 million.

Kim Pyong-il, the second son of President Kim Il-song, was reportedly in Malta to learn English (*Korea Herald*, Seoul, 20 March). Earlier it had been reported that it was Kim Chong-il who was in the Mediterranean country. Pyong-il was believed to be with his wife and some bodyguards. It was not known what he did in Malta besides learning English.

During 1983, a number of heads of Third World countries visited North Korea, including President France Albert René of the Seychelles, President Mohammed Hosni Mubarak of Egypt, Prime Minister Maurice Bishop of Grenada, President Juvenal Habyarimana of Rwanda, Prime Minister Joshua Lebua Jonathan of Lesotho, Ethiopian head-of-state Mengistu Haile Mariam, and Prime Minister Mir Hossein Musavi of Iran.

In early July, North Korea hosted 163 delegations from 113 countries and sixteen nonaligned organizations at the World Meeting of Journalists for Anti-Imperialism, Friendship and Peace. The delegations were mostly from African, Latin American, and other Third World countries.

The first meeting of the Nonaligned Nations' education and culture ministers was held 24–28 September in Pyongyang in accordance with a decision taken by the Seventh Nonaligned Summit of March 1983 in New Delhi. The meeting was attended by delegations from 72 nonaligned and developing countries and nineteen international organizations.

Indications are that the DPRK has become increasingly frustrated in its Third World diplomatic contest against South Korea. The Nonaligned Movement no longer appears to be an arena exclusively for North Korea's political maneuvers against South Korea. The Nonaligned Summit in New Delhi adopted a "mild" Korean clause despite a North Korean push for a strongly worded resolution against Seoul and Washington. Diplomatically, South Korea has made considerable progress in the past few years in outdistancing the North in the race for international recognition. Several experts on world affairs and Asia viewed the October bombing in Rangoon as a desperate reprisal against Seoul because of the stability and international recognition it has gained.

The Rangoon bombing incident, especially Burma's subsequent severing of diplomatic relations, was a blow to North Korea in its intense rivalry with the South for the sympathy of Third World countries. In protest against the bloody terrorist bombing in Rangoon, Costa Rica (2 December) the Comoros (3 December), and Western Samoa (22 December) broke diplomatic relations with North Korea. Pakistan, once a close friend of the DPRK, seems to have decided to distance itself from Pyongyang by establishing ambassador-level relations with South Korea in the light of the bombing incident. Thailand expressed its "outrage" at the bombing and decided in mid-December to reject indefinitely a North Korean request to open a permanent embassy in Bangkok. A North Korean cargo ship reported to have been in Burmese waters just before the October bombing was refused docking facilities in Singapore.

The Soviet Union and China. During 1983, Pyongyang continued to maintain its middle-of-the-road position in the Sino-Soviet rift, although it moved slightly closer to China. Moscow and Beijing competed with verbal assurances and material support for North Korea's friendship. Both countries urged the prompt withdrawal of U.S. troops from South Korea and supported Pyongyang's formula for reunification and its demand for direct U.S.-DPRK contacts to settle the Korean problem.

Najin port in Hamgyong province, some 40 kilometers south of Soviet territory, became an important port for Soviet transit cargoes. (On 31 December 1978, North Korea and the Soviet Union signed a protocol authorizing Moscow to use Najin to export goods to Pacific nations, including Vietnam and Kampuchea.) Radio Moscow (11 May) reported that the Soviet freight handled at Najin port was increasing in quantity every year.

North Korea and China signed an agreement authorizing Beijing to use Chongjin port on the northeastern coast of North Korea about 70 kilometers south of Najin, as a transit port in its trade with Japan (Radio Beijing, 2 July). Export and import goods to and from Manchuria would be transported through the port under the agreement.

President Kim Il-song was rumored to have made clandestine visits to China in August and November, presumably to discuss the high level of tension on the Korean peninsula (*Nihon Keizai Shimbun*, 7 October; *NYT*, 8 November). This rumor was not confirmed by either Beijing or Pyongyang.

The North Korean Central Broadcasting Station (2 September) said that Kim Chong-il had visited China on 2–12 June at the invitation of Hu Yaobang, general secretary of the Chinese Communist Party's Central Committee. The radio reported that the junior Kim met with Hu and such top Chinese leaders as Deng Xiaoping and Zhao Ziyang and toured various places, including a naval base and a number of factories. This visit indicated China's official recognition of Chong-il as successor to his father as North Korean leader.

On 8 September, the Central Broadcasting Station reported that a Chinese mission, led by Peng Zhen, chairman of the Standing Committee of the National People's Congress, was greeted on its arrival in Pyongyang on 7 September by Kim Chong-il and other high-ranking DPRK officials. The Chinese mission visited North Korea to join in the celebration of the thirty-fifth anniversary of the DPRK. It was the first time that the junior Kim was reported to have officially received a foreign delegation at the airport.

The hijacking of a Chinese airliner across North Korea into South Korea in the spring of 1983 and the subsequent "friendly negotiations" between China and South Korea in Seoul about the return of the airliner and its crew and passengers clearly (and not surprisingly) angered North Korea. Chinese foreign minister Wu Xueqian's hasty visit to Pyongyang on 20 May was probably undertaken to allay North Korea's concern that Beijing's contacts with Seoul over the hijacking did not mean a thaw in relations. Wu reaffirmed China's continued support of Pyongyang's position on the Korean question. Noteworthy is the fact that Wu proposed a toast to both Kim Il-song and his son. Wu's visit was followed by Kim Chong-il's visit to China.

North Korea kept silent for three weeks on the shooting-down of a South Korean Air Lines jetliner by a Soviet fighter on 1 September, in contrast with the deep concern Beijing showed over the mishap. Radio Pyongyang (23 September) strongly supported the Soviet position on the shooting incident. The radio shifted responsibility for the killing to the United States and South Korean authorities, repeating the Soviet claim that the South Korean commercial jetliner had deliberately intruded into Soviet airspace for spying.

Radio Moscow (10 October) reported the Rangoon bombing incident without comment, but two days later denounced the United States, Japan, and South Korea for scheming to form a "tripartite military alliance" and added that Washington and Seoul were using the bombing incident to escalate tension on the Korean peninsula. On 24 October, Radio Moscow, quoting an article in *Izvestiia*, said that Seoul had launched a nationwide anti-Pyongyang campaign to shift responsibility for the Rangoon incident to the DPRK and asserted that the move was orchestrated by Washington. On 5 November, Radio Moscow briefly reported both the Burmese decision to sever relations with North Korea and Pyongyang's dissatisfaction with the Burmese action. This report touched more on North Korea's announcement than that of the Burmese government, but made no comment.

China remained publicly neutral on the Rangoon bombing incident. Privately, however, Chinese officials were known to be upset by evidence suggesting that North Korea was responsible for the blast and were believed to have sought an explanation from Pyongyang. Reliable diplomatic sources said that Beijing was "deeply concerned" about the incident, which undermined a Chinese effort to encourage contacts between North Korea and Western countries, especially the United States and Japan. It was especially embarrassing to China because shortly before the bombing, Chinese leader Deng Xiaoping had personally raised the Korean question with visiting U.S. defense secretary Caspar Weinberger. Deng suggested that the United States and China could cooperate to ease tension on the Korean peninsula. (Deng's overture was the first Chinese effort to play an active role in resolving the Korean dispute.) Two days later, the United States responded by relaxing a ban on informal contacts with North Korean diplomats.

In the course of an official visit to Japan in late November, General Secretary Hu Yaobang of the Chinese Communist Party indirectly condemned the Rangoon bombing attack, saying that "generally speaking, terrorist activities in any country in the world should be opposed." He told Japanese leaders that his government had twice advised North Korea to avoid raising tensions with South Korea. He also said that Kim Il-song had personally assured him that he would not invade the South.

Europe. On 14 April, the Finnish government ordered the expulsion of the North Korean ambassador for allegedly attempting to bribe Finnish politicians to drop Seoul as the site of the International Parliamentary Union meeting.

An article in the 25 June issue of *Vjesnik*, a Yugoslav party organ, said that North Korea had begun the Korean War, thereby denying the long-standing North Korean allegation that the war began with an attack from the South.

Major newspapers in Western Europe gave prominent coverage to news concerning Burmese measures against North Korea regarding the 9 October bombing in Rangoon. Both the French and British governments publicly rebuked North Korea for the bombing incident.

Japan. Relations between the DPRK and Japan have never been cordial. In Pyongyang's view, Japan is excessively partial to Seoul, pursues a policy of "two Koreas," and is hostile toward North Korea, as exemplified by the Japanese government's strong opposition to a drastic reduction of U.S. ground forces in South Korea. North Korean media continued to denounce growing Japanese "imperialism" in South Korea and the alleged collusion between Tokyo and Washington to preserve their mutual "colonial interest" in the Korean peninsula.

The Japanese government has never had political or diplomatic ties with the DPRK regime, limiting itself to low-level cultural and economic exchanges to maintain a pipeline into North Korea. Due to combined pressures from Japanese business and trading interests and left-wing political and labor groups, nongovernmental contacts are expected to continue to increase during the 1980s, although official exchanges between Pyongyang and Tokyo appear unlikely. Officially the expanding nongovernmental contacts with the DPRK are presented as Japan's contribution to easing tensions between the two Koreas.

The Tokyo government allowed a five-member North Korean delegation to enter Japan to attend the mid-May meeting of the Asian-African Legal Consultative Conference. At the same time, it re-emphasized that there was no basic change in Japan's policy toward North Korea.

In early July, Chuji Kuno, president of the Dietmen's League for Japan–North Korea Friendship and a senior member of the ruling Liberal Democratic Party, visited North Korea. His main purpose was to renew a bilateral private fishery agreement between Japan and North Korea that had expired in 1982. During his stay, he proposed to the DPRK regime that trade offices be established in Tokyo and Pyongyang and that a reporter-exchange program be initiated. (The Dietmen's League for Japan–North Korea Friendship was in danger of being dissolved, according to the *Asahi Shimbun* [25 December], as a result of the defeats suffered by Kuno and Vice-Chairmen Koken Nosaka and Kazuo Shioya in the December parliamentary elections and the recent retirement of Togo Yoneda, secretary general of the league.)

In late July, the Tokyo government turned down a request from the Japan Socialist Party to ease restrictions imposed on a North Korean delegation to an antinuclear meeting in Japan in early August. The Liberal Democratic government made it clear that it would not allow anyone ranking higher than a member of the KWP Central Committee to participate in the rally and those allowed to participate would be barred from political activities in Japan.

Japan Communist Party Executive Committee vice-chairman Tomio Nishizawa said, in a press conference held on 9 December in Tokyo, that there was no evidence that U.S. forces were responsible for the outbreak of the Korean War. He also criticized North Korea, saying that "the North Korean leadership system is similar to Japan's Meiji monarch system with its emperor and his subjects, and it is far from being a legitimate, constructive monarchy."

During 1983, the DPRK stepped up its propaganda attacks against the Tokyo government under Prime Minister Yasuhiro Nakasone, whose attitude and policies seemed to be more pro-U.S., pro-Seoul, and pro-rearmament than any of his predecessors. For example, *Nodong Sinmun* (10 January) harshly attacked Nakasone for planning a two-day official visit to South Korea for summit talks with President Chun Doo-Hwan by saying that Nakasone was making a "war-mongering pilgrimage" to Seoul. The paper labeled the Nakasone cabinet "a product of the U.S. imperialists' Asian policy" and said that it was persisting in Japan's military expansion and revision of the no-war constitution. North Korean mass media condemned joint U.S.-Japan military exercises during 1983, and *Nodong Sinmun* (6 May) warned bluntly that the Nakasone government was walking a dangerous road, again pushing Japan into a war. The same paper (25 August) accused the United States of hurrying the formation of a U.S.–Japan–South Korea military alliance in Asia and Japan of stepping up its remilitarization.

The Tokyo government assailed North Korea for the Rangoon bombing incident and said that it would take a "stern stance" toward the DPRK in the aftermath of the bombing. Japanese Foreign Ministry officials indicated later that Japan's stern stance toward North Korea would mean tighter controls over contacts between their officials in third countries and over entry permits to North Koreans wishing to visit Japan. They also indicated to Japanese reporters that the government might also call on private interests to restrain economic and people-to-people exchanges between Tokyo and Pyongyang. Four North Korean social scientists, who were scheduled to visit Japan on 17 October, became the first victims of the Japanese government's decision to restrict exchanges with the DPRK when the Japanese Justice Ministry withdrew permission for entry.

In early December, the DPRK regime apparently decided to reciprocate. On 10 December, a North Korean patrol boat captured two Japanese fishing boats, and in mid-December, the Pyongyang regime decided to hold a Japanese freighter, which had entered Nampo port on the west coast on 15 November, and four crewmen hostage until Tokyo handed over a North Korean soldier who had defected to Japan in September by stowing away on the boat during a September visit. Otherwise, the government announcement said, Pyongyang would detain the ship and its crew indefinitely.

The United States. During 1983, the DPRK increased its hostility toward the United States. Pyongyang condemned the United States for supporting Chun Doo-Hwan's "fascist" regime in Seoul and repeatedly urged Washington to withdraw all U.S. troops and lethal weapons from

South Korea. It renewed its call for direct talks with the United States to replace the 30-year-old Korean armistice with a peace agreement.

On 24 June, Pyongyang issued a special statement to begin the annual "month for the joint anti-U.S. struggle," saying that "the U.S. imperialists were the sworn enemy" of the North Korean people. North Korean mass media joined in the campaign, and anti-U.S. rallies were held throughout the country. *Nodong Sinmun* (4 October) denounced Washington and Seoul for escalating tension on the Korean peninsula by introducing such highly sophisticated weapons as nuclear and neutron bombs in the South. On 27 October, the DPRK Foreign Ministry denounced the U.S. action in Grenada. Pyongyang's anti-U.S. propaganda reached a climax on 15 November when it said that President Reagan's visit to South Korea had pushed the Korean situation to the brink of war.

On 1 March, the U.S. State Department said that applications from North Korean citizens for U.S. visas would be considered on a case-by-case basis and reaffirmed that this was not a change in policy. A spokesman said that issuance of visas was determined by applicable law and worldwide regulations and that "our policy remains that we would have discussions with North Korean authorities only with a full and equal participation" of South Korea.

On 14 February, the U.S. State Department reaffirmed that it would maintain its policy against issuing re-entry visas to members of the North Korean observer mission to the United Nations as long as the DPRK sheltered one of its diplomats, accused of attempting to rape an American woman, from the U.S. justice system. The North Korean diplomat, who had avoided arrest for eleven months by hiding in his nation's mission, surrendered on 26 July and pleaded guilty to third-degree sexual abuse, ending the prolonged dispute between Pyongyang and Washington. Shortly afterwards, he was expelled from the United States.

In mid-November, U.S. diplomats were ordered to suspend all contacts with North Korean envoys because of the Rangoon bombing incident. In early 1983, the State Department told the diplomatic corps that it was permissible to have limited or low-level contact with North Korean diplomats at receptions, parties, or official functions hosted by other countries.

United Nations. As in preceding years, the Korean question was absent from the agenda of the annual session of the U.N. General Assembly.

On 17 February, the governing council of the U.N. Development Program approved the DPRK's application for a loan of U.S. $18.4 million for development.

On 6 December, North Korea came under attack in the U.N. General Assembly's Legal Committee for the bombing incident in Rangoon. Forty-three Western and Third World delegations condemned the Rangoon incident in speeches before the committee. None of North Korea's allies rallied to its defense. In short, the DPRK suffered a sharp political setback.

Tai Sung An
Washington College

Laos

Population. 3.8 million (estimate)
Party. Lao People's Revolutionary Party (Phak Pasason Pativat Lao; LPRP)
Founded. 1955
Membership. 35,000 (estimate)
General Secretary. Kaysone Phomvihan (premier)
Politburo. 7 members: Kaysone Phomvihan, Nouhak Phoumsavan, Souphanouvong (president), Phoumi Vongvichit, Khamtai Siphandon, Phoun Sipaseut, Sisomphon Lovansai
Secretariat. 9 members: Kaysone Phomvihan, Nouhak Phoumsavan, Khamtai Siphandon, Phoun Sipaseut, Sisomphon Lovansai, Sali Vongkhamsao, Sisavat Keobounphan, Samon Vi-gnaket, Maichantan Sengmani
Central Committee. 48 full members, 6 alternate members (for names, see *FBIS*, 30 April 1982)
Status. Ruling party
Last Congress. Third, 27–30 April 1982, in Vientiane
Last Election. 1975, all 46 candidates LPRP approved
Auxiliary Organizations. Lao Front for National Construction
Publications. *Pasason* (The people), LPRP central organ, published in Vientiane (daily); *Vientiane Mai* (daily); *Kong Tap Pasason Lao* (weekly); *Noum Lao* (weekly); *Heng Ngan* (monthly); *Megning* (monthly); *Yaowachon* (monthly); *Suksa Mai* (monthly); *Wannasin* (monthly); *Sathalanasouk* (quarterly). Khaosan Pathet Lao (Pathet Lao News Agency; KPL) is the official news agency.

The year 1983 was marked in Laos by a reshuffle of the government organization of the Lao People's Democratic Republic (LPDR), the holding in Vientiane of the first Indochinese summit conference since the war years, continued strict adherence to the Vietnamese line on all major foreign issues, and hints of a desire for some improvement in relations with the United States.

Leadership and Party Organization. The only significant change in party leadership was the death from a heart attack on 7 February of Central Committee member Souk Vongsak, 68 (Radio Vientiane, 8 February; *FBIS*, 8 February). A veteran party member who had served in a number of capacities in the party's "legal" activities prior to the seizure of power in 1975, he was elected a deputy to the National Assembly from Luang Prabang, his home, in the 1958 election and became secretary of state for public works

and transport in the tripartite coalition of 1962 and remained in Vientiane after the more important party representatives in the coalition withdrew to their base area in Sam Neua in the spring of 1963. He was a close friend of the former prime minister, Prince Souvanna Phouma.

On the government side, in a cabinet reshuffle in January, virtually all former ministers were promoted or retained their portfolios. The LPDR now has five vice-premiers under Kaysone Phomvihan; all are high-ranking LPRP leaders. Six departments were raised to ministerial rank. (For a complete listing, see AFP, Bangkok, 12 January; *FBIS*, 13 January.)

Domestic Affairs. The LPRP observed the twenty-eighth anniversary of its founding on 22 March. Instructions for the celebration of this event were signed by Khamtai Siphandon on behalf of the Secretariat (Radio Vientiane,

17 March; *FBIS*, 18 March). On this occasion the name of the party newspaper was changed from *Siang Pasason* (Voice of the people) to *Pasason* (The people) (KPL, 22 March; *FBIS*, 23 March).

Among statistics on the economy released by the LPDR was the number of agricultural cooperatives: 1,943 such cooperatives covering 86,490 hectares (20 percent of all rice fields) and including 86,490 [*sic*] families (17.5 percent of all peasant families) had been formed by year-end 1982 (Radio Vientiane, 1 January; *FBIS*, 4 January). A Western observer reported that the 1983 paddy crop totaled 1.2 million tons, bearing out official forecasts and seeming to confirm that the government is moving slowly to extend state control over the largely agricultural economy and has learned to use free-market incentives to boost production after previous experiments with rapid cooperativization in the 1970s led to near disaster (*Time*, 18 July 1983).

The LPDR has also successfully pushed a nationwide literacy campaign and has raised attendance at primary and secondary schools from 350,000 in 1979 to 600,000 (ibid.).

Auxiliary Organizations. The Lao Front for National Construction, the successor front organization to the dissolved Neo Lao Hak Sat (Lao Patriotic Front), held a meeting in Vientiane on 7 May to review its past year's work and was addressed by Souphanouvong. The first Lao National Youth Congress was held in Vientiane on 27–29 April and was addressed by Kaysone; several foreign youth delegations attended.

International Views, Positions, and Activities. The LPDR continued to follow a Hanoi-dictated line on such major foreign issues as the legitimacy question in Kampuchea and the presence of Vietnamese troops in that country, diplomatic interchanges with the Association of Southeast Asian Nations, "collusion" between China and the United States, and perspectives on the nonaligned movement and the world at large.

Such a line was evident in the statements that emerged from the first summit meeting of Indochinese leaders in Vientiane on 22–23 February. The summit was preceded by a meeting of the foreign ministers of Laos, Vietnam, and Kampuchea. Party and government leaders attending the summit were Le Duan and Pham Van Dong for Vietnam; Heng Samrin and Chan Si for Kampuchea; and Kaysone and Souphanouvong for Laos. (Radio Vientiane, 23 February; *FBIS*, 23 February.) In their final statement, the leaders pledged to hold further summits at unspecified intervals and semiannual meetings of their foreign ministers "to deal with all problems concerning relations among the three countries," to establish committees in each country to promote economic cooperation and coordination of national economic development plans, and to establish joint commissions for cooperation among the three countries in specific areas of activity (KPL, 23 February; *FBIS*, 23 February). The summit also issued a statement on the presence of Vietnamese "volunteer" troops in Kampuchea (VNA, 23 February; *FBIS*, 23 February).

Another important visitor to Laos during 1983 was General Van Tien Dung, Vietnam's defense minister, at the head of a military delegation that visited from 3 to 8 January. Speaking at a banquet on 3 January in Vientiane, General Dung hailed the solidarity of the communist movements in the two countries and declared: "The historic Ho Chi Minh trail is a brilliant symbol of the close solidarity between the fraternal Vietnamese and Lao peoples in the national liberation struggle against the U.S. imperialists" (Radio Vientiane, 4 January; *FBIS*, 5 January). The following day he spoke about the communist victories of 1975 and praised the LPRP for having grasped the "strategic opportunity" to seize power (Radio Vientiane, 5 January; *FBIS*, 7 January). Finally, at a farewell reception he thanked the people of Laos for their "support and assistance to the Vietnamese volunteer army in the past and to Vietnamese cadres and combatants who are currently carrying out their internationalist duties in Laos" (Radio Vientiane, 8 January; *FBIS*, 10 January). There are currently an estimated 50,000 Vietnamese troops in Laos.

Other visitors to Laos included delegations from Grenada and Nicaragua.

LPRP leaders who traveled abroad during 1983 were Kaysone, who was reported to have left "for rest" in the Soviet Union in September (Radio Vientiane, 6 September; *FBIS*, 6 September); Souphanouvong, who was in New Delhi from 5–12 March for the Seventh Nonaligned Summit Conference (Radio Vientiane, 6 March; *FBIS*, 7 March) and on a visit to Cuba in July (Radio Vientiane, 20 July; *FBIS*, 21 July); Phoumi Vongvichit, who was in East Germany in April (Radio Vientiane, 7 April; *FBIS*, 14 April) and again in July and August (KPL, 12 August; *FBIS*, 18 August); and Phoun Sipaseut, who was in Mongolia in May (Radio Vientiane, 26 May; *FBIS*, 3 June) and in Kampuchea in July (Radio Vientiane, 20 July; *FBIS*, 21 July).

The final statement of the Indochina summit conference in February included a paragraph about relations of the three countries with the United States, which said: "The three countries . . .express their desire to have normal relations with the United States on the basis of equality, respect for independence, sovereignty and territorial integrity, and non-interference in each country's internal affairs" (KPL, 23 February; *FBIS*, 23 February). Laos is the one country in Indochina in which the United States continued to maintain an embassy following the communist takeover in 1975, and statements by LPDR spokesmen over the years have suggested that an inprovement in bilateral relations would be welcomed.

In February, for the first time since the war, the LPDR allowed a four-man team from the U.S. Joint Casualties Resolution Center in Hawaii to visit Laos to discuss the question of information about U.S. servicemen missing in action in Laos. The delegation stayed in Laos for two days and had consultations with LPDR authorities. An LPDR statement said: "Following the exchange of views, both sides have come to understand each other's interest and concern" (Radio Vientiane, 15 February; *FBIS*, 16 February).

The LPDR may have hoped that this gesture would lead to a lifting of the U.S. restriction on aid (other than for humanitarian purposes). If so, Vice–Foreign Minister Soubanh Srithirath expressed his country's official disappointment in an interview published in August; he suggested that only if U.S. aid were forthcoming would it be possible to get cooperation from villagers to search for remains of missing servicemen (*FEER*, 18 August).

A May report quoting administration officials in Washington as saying talks were under way with the LPDR concerning the raising of the rank of diplomatic missions to ambassadorial level, as well as the lifting of the aid ban, was not followed by any concrete action (*NYT*, 17 May). However, Hanoi severely limits the LPDR leaders' room for negotiations on the question of improving relations with the United States. Thus, while such a move remains a possibility, it is a fragile

one and could easily be reversed by a change in circumstances.

As may be indicated by Soubanh's interview, LPDR propaganda organs emit a hard, pro-Hanoi line on all questions, but the actual attitudes of Laotian leaders on specific issues of immediate concern to their country may be somewhat softer. Thus, LPDR behavior toward China and Thailand, especially, seems to be much more flexible than the ideological statements issued by *Pasason* and the KPL would suggest. While the LPDR officially shares the Vietnamese view that China is not socialist, in practice the Chinese embassy in Vientiane deals with the department in the Foreign Ministry that is in charge of socialist countries. The LPDR has also allowed the Chinese embassy to issue 4,000 passports to Chinese residents in Vientiane, who still dominate the free market there. A private Chinese school has also been allowed to operate. In spite of periodic references to the Chinese threat on the northern border in the official press, the LPDR has made no serious effort to bar trade and other contacts between minorities in northern Laos and Yunnan Province of China. (*FEER*, 18 August.) The impression given is that China is reluctant to use its vast potential for stirring up trouble along its mountainous border with Laos, even though this would in all likelihood embroil Vietnamese forces in an exhausting conflict, because it judges the damage this might do to its relations with Laos as too high a price to pay for getting at Vietnam.

Neither Laos nor Thailand has allowed the continuation of shooting incidents along the Mekong River border to disrupt working relations. Whatever the origins of these incidents (and some of them appear to be related to the activities of armed resistance bands of Laotian émigrés based on the Thai side of the river), and whatever the inflammatory tone of the reports they give rise to, the two governments appear to desire a peaceful relationship.

The two countries share considerable economic advantages from normal relations with one another. About one-half of total Laotian imports in 1982 came from Thailand. According to the Thai embassy in Vientiane, about 200 Thai firms are registered to trade with the state-owned Société Lao Import-Export, in such goods as rice, cement, construction materials, textiles, fabrics, and other consumer goods. Aside from the high-value official trade, there is a considerable local barter trade between towns along the Mekong.

Moreover, in political terms, while the large influx of refugees from Laos has certainly caused strains in relations in the past, the present governments of the two countries see the benefit of avoiding direct conflict. Thailand is heavily preoccupied with the situation along its border with Kampuchea. The LPDR is intent on the economic rehabilitation of its own country after the disastrous war, which inflicted tremendous damage on all areas except for the large towns.

Again, however, the dominance of Hanoi may lead the LPDR into a situation that the LPDR leaders would wish to avoid. Hanoi, with its hegemonistic view of an Indochina that includes not only Kampuchea and present-day Laos, but also the "lost" Lao-speaking territory on the right bank of the Mekong, may be willing to go further in provoking the present government in Bangkok than may LPDR leaders. Laos and Thailand reached an agreement during Thai prime minister General Kriangsak Chamanan's January 1979 visit to Vientiane regarding harboring of insur-

gents. Thailand promised not to support anti-LPDR insurgents, and Laos promised not to support the insurgents of the strongly pro-Chinese Communist Party of Thailand, many of whose supporters had taken refuge in Laos following the coup d'etat in Thailand of October 1976.

By 1979, in any case, China had good reason to befriend Thailand, which represented the only secure route for shipping arms and supplies to the remnants of the Pol Pot regime in Kampuchea still resisting the Vietnamese invaders. Thus, China ceased support for the CPT, which rapidly disintegrated. Asked in an interview about reports from Thailand about a pro-Soviet party known as the Pak Mai (New party), backed by Laos and presumably Vietnam, Soubanh said, "The Thai Government is increasing its support for the reactionaries who come into Laos to attack us. This could be harmful for Thailand." (Ibid., 18 August.)

Arthur J. Dommen
Bethesda, Maryland

Malaysia and Singapore

Population. Malaysia: 15 million; Singapore: 2.5 million
Party. Communist Party of Malaya (CPM)
Founded. 1930
Membership. 1,100 in Malaysia, 200 in Singapore (estimate)
Secretary General. Chin Peng (?)
Status. Illegal
Last Congress. Not known
Last Election. Not applicable
Auxiliary Organizations. Malayan People's Army (NPA), Malay Nationalist Revolutionary Party of Malaya (MNRPM), Islamic Brotherhood Party (Paperi), Singapore People's Liberation Organization
Publications. None known. Principal means of communication remains the Voice of Malayan Democracy (VOMD), which reportedly broadcasts from southern China.

The banned and enfeebled CPM remained a minor factor in the Malaysian political landscape in 1983. Nevertheless, the party and its factional offshoots continued to be a source of concern to the government. Although identifiable communist activities were limited largely to sporadic guerrilla attacks and aggressive statements over the party's clandestine radio station, there was the suspicion that elements of the CPM and its front organizations were infiltrating the growing fundamentalist Islamic movement. Estimates of the number of communists remained relatively low —from 2,000 to 4,000 (see below for details)— but Malaysian prime minister Datuk Mahathir Mohamed and other government officials expressed concern over the communist threat on a number of occasions.

In addition to terrorist attacks, sniper fire and apparent sabotage incidents added to the impression of domestic unrest (AFP, 13 December 1982; *New Straits Times*, 17 January; *FBIS*, 15 December 1982, 19 January). This was underlined when Prime Minister Mahathir said the government would eschew the development of nuclear energy because of internal security problems (*FBIS*, 11 March). Later in the year, he told a group of lawyers critical of the government's continued reliance on the emergency powers first introduced in the 1960s not to forget that there was a "real emergency" in Malaysia (*New Straits Times*, 1 November; *FBIS*, 2 November).

Apparently of greater concern than guerrilla attacks and isolated terrorist incidents were reports that the CPM was working with some leaders of an opposition party—presumably the Partai Islam (PI)—to recruit supporters. Government officials charged that the CPM was trying to win over dissident Muslim groups by claiming that communism and Islam are compatible ideologies. Deputy Prime Minister Datuk Musa Hitam warned that the CPM could exploit the fundamentalist Islamic movement, with its potential appeal to large segments of the Muslim population, and the inspector general of police said that although there had been no direct links between the banned CPM and Muslim extremist groups in the country, the party "is trying hard to win over Moslem groups who are opposed to the government." (*FBIS*, 24 January, 11 March, 13 June.)

Adding to government disquiet was alleged Iranian support for Muslim dissidents. Malaysians have been prominent in a variety of special conferences in Iran and on occasion have formed the largest foreign delegation at these meetings. The deputy prime minister accused an unidentified foreign country of trying to export its Islamic revolution to Malaysia, citing the active participation of opposition party members and leaders in seminars and visits organized by the country in question. He said the foreign power concerned was also trying to influence government officials, teachers, and professionals and seeking to win over Malaysian students overseas. There were reports in the press that an Islamic republic in West Asia had been actively funding the participation of these groups at meetings in Malaysia and abroad. The deputy prime minister said that the Malaysian government was not stopping anyone from attending meetings or seminars overseas, but added that "when the nation organizing the seminar or meeting concerned makes an arrogant declaration that only revolution and force can solve the problem of Muslims, the government should and will oppose them." Datuk Musa then went on to say that Malaysia had diplomatic relations with many countries, including communist nations, although it disagreed with the communist system of administration, but the Malaysian government and its people would fight any attempt by communist countries to interfere with internal Malaysian affairs or export communism. He added that this would include prohibiting visits to such communist countries. (AFP, 7 November; *FBIS*, 9 November; *New Straits Times*, 11 November.) This juxtaposition of charges left open whether the deputy prime minister was in fact equating the Iranians' fishing in troubled Malaysian waters with the communists' activities.

While these events increased government uneasiness about Iran's role in Malaysian political movements, the government continued to perceive China as the primary threat in the region. One source of great concern to both the Mahathir and Lee Kuan Yew regimes was that while a rapprochement between the Soviet Union and the PRC might bring about a solution to the dangerously unsettling Kampuchean situation, it also raised the specter of possible new communist inroads in the region. The Malaysian government in particular looked askance at the possibility of a regime in Phnom Penh open to Chinese influence (*FEER*, 20 October). At the same time, both the Singapore and the Malaysian governments were uneasy about the increase in Soviet naval forces in nearby waters and the attendant possibility of arms being smuggled to rebel groups (*New Straits Times*, 1 October; *FBIS*, 7 October).

Leadership and Party Organization. Information about the current size and strength of the CPM is necessarily tentative, but at the beginning of 1983 the deputy prime minister estimated that there were some 1,120 members of the CPM, 605 Communist Party of Malaya—Marxist-Leninist (CPM/M-L), and 113 Communist Party of Malaya—Revolutionary Faction (CPM/RF) at the Thai border, as well as 356 communist terrorists still in the country. A total of 40 terrorists had surrendered in Peninsular Malaysia during 1982, 10 were killed and 1 captured, while in Sarawak, 3 had surrendered and 2 were captured. (*FBIS*, 26 January.) In July, the inspector general of police estimated that 273 communist terrorists were operating in western Malaysia, and the deputy prime minister said 98 guerrillas were active in Sarawak. Some military personnel have questioned these figures and claim that there are still about 4,000 guerrillas in the Thai border area (*FEER*, 20 October). Given the elusive nature of guerrilla forces, the precision of these official estimates may appear surprising. The explanation presumably lies in the Malaysian forces' heavy reliance on police methods of detailed record keeping, the tactic that served so well to isolate and defeat the earlier communist insurgency.

Communist activity in Singapore has virtually disappeared under the government of Lee Kuan Yew and his People's Action Party (PAP). Nevertheless, it is evident that the government continues to harbor some concern about the possibility of renewed activity supported by the PRC and the CPM, with which Singapore's communists have always been affiliated. There are believed to be about 200 party members. (For background, see *YICA*, 1980, p. 295.) The name Communist Party of *Malaya* represents the party's refusal to accept the existence of Malaysia and Singapore as two separate entities.

Virtually no information is available about the Communist Party of North Kalimantan beyond the details noted above of clashes with guerrilla units in Sarawak. A key question about CPM leadership is who will succeed the party's long-time secretary general, Chin Peng, who has held that position for over thirty years. Although there have been unconfirmed reports of his death for

several years, the party's traditional New Year's message, delivered over its clandestine radio station, referred to him as chairman of the Central Committee. His name was invoked in other broadcasts later in the year. (*FBIS*, 6 January).

The question of his replacement is critical because the party has never developed a Malay leadership. Indeed, the CPM has always suffered from a failure to attract broad Malay support at any level. Despite its espousal of Maoist precepts of people's war and armed struggle as the path to power, its emphasis on a base among the peasants, and rejection of urban warfare, the CPM remains a largely Chinese-led party seeking to appeal to a peasant population that is overwhelmingly Malay (Shee Poon Kim, "Insurgency in Southeast Asia," *Problems of Communism*, May–June).

In Malaysia, the party has sought to garner popular support by building up Malay, and in particular Muslim, front organizations, principally the Paperi and more recently the MNRPM (see below). Current official statements by these front organizations focus largely on the interests of the Muslim community. Recent MNRPM broadcasts, for example, castigated the Mahathir government for its failure to carry out true Islamic precepts (*FBIS*, 14 July). The government, for its part, accused the CPM of teaming up with the leaders of the Muslim opposition parties to win broad support from the Muslim masses (ibid., 13 June). Nevertheless, the majority of Malays still see the CPM as a Chinese party, dominated by ethnic Chinese and tied to China.

Along with its failure to develop broad popular appeal among rural Malays, the party has difficulty recruiting Chinese support in urban communities. The most likely explanation is that a majority of Malaysia's town-dwelling Chinese population find their present economic situation more satisfactory than any promises of rewards to come after the revolution. Also, with memories of the race riots of 1969, it can be assumed that most Chinese are not eager to risk increasing tensions between Chinese townspeople and Malay farmers by rallying to the CPM.

Doubtless, much of the failure of the CPM to attract large numbers of followers in Singapore can be attributed to the booming economy, which has spurted ahead since Lee Kuan Yew first took office. Coupled with this is the highly pragmatic outlook of Singapore's tradespeople, whose increasing share in Singapore's boom would be threatened by political unrest and revolutionary activity. The government's very effective public housing program has removed a potential major source of discontent. Finally, the CPM persists on its course as a classic Maoist peasant-based party, eschewing the base among urban labor that might give it some appeal in Singapore. Even the appeal of altruistic political action that the CPM might be expected to offer students and discontented intellectuals has been largely co-opted by the PAP.

There are reports that some CPM leaders on the Thai border might be willing to defect if they could keep their arms—which the Thais will not permit—and become Thai citizens. However, these same reports indicate that the lower ranks are less willing to consider defection. (*FEER*, 10 November.)

In general, defections from the CPM appear to be in small numbers, not whole units. Those who do defect, in the view of many Malaysian officials, are doing so because the PRC currently advocates that communists in Southeast Asia should channel their opposition through legitimate political activities (ibid.).

Whatever the uncertainties about the current leadership of the CPM, still less is known about the present leadership of the party's two factional offshoots, the CPM/RF and the CPM/M-L. The CPM/RF came into existence in February 1970 when 200–300 members of the CPM's 8th Regiment, defying a Central Committee directive to liquidate alleged government infiltrators who had joined the party since 1962, challenged the committee's directive and fled to Sadao in southern Thailand. The CPM/M-L was formed in August 1974 by a group of guerrilla fighters who broke away from the CPM's 12th Regiment. At the time of its founding, the CPM/M-L was headed by a member of the State Committee of the CPM, Yat Kong. Neither the CPM/RF nor the CPM/M-L appears to have grown, and both remain far weaker militarily than their parent organization, the CPM. Nevertheless, some Malaysians consider the CPM/M-L members to be younger, tougher, and more dedicated fighters than those in the CPM mainstream (ibid.).

CPM/M-L guerrillas are believed to be the principal faction in the jungle sanctuaries in Yala province of Thailand, bordering Malaysia, and it is now thought that they are the group that has been particularly active in the province's Betong salient, the traditional home of the CPM's 12th Regiment. Many of the CPM/M-L forces are believed to be Thai (ibid.).

Domestic Party Activities. As a proscribed party, the CPM's activities are largely carried on through its front organizations and attacks by its principal military auxiliary, the MPA. While the party's front organizations may be having some success in penetrating the increasingly important fundamentalist Islamic movement, the party's military affiliates apparently have, if anything, lost ground over the past few years. Despite glowing accounts of the victories of the MPA in "foiling the enemy's large-scale encirclement and suppression campaign against base areas and guerrilla zones" (VOMD, 31 December 1982; *FBIS*, 6 January), the fact that the Malaysian army now devotes only about 25 percent of its resources to counterinsurgency (*FEER*, 20 October) suggests that the MPA threat has dwindled significantly. This is attributed in part to the effectiveness of the coordinated military operations conducted with Thailand in Peninsular Malaysia and with Indonesia in East Malaysia (*FBIS*, 8 December 1982; *WP*, 29 December). Some observers also credit cooperation among the intelligence services of the member-states of the Association of Southeast Asian Nations (ASEAN), which have been sharing information on internal and external threats since the mid-1960s (*Economist*, London, 24 December).

Throughout the year, there were numerous reports suggesting a decline in CPM military strength. In May, for example, the chief minister of Perak reported that guerrilla units there, deprived of food and other supplies by the success of government forces, had turned to terrorizing rubber tappers and the forest people. In the course of government operations, five armed and uniformed guerrillas had been killed, including the leader of the 6th Assault Unit. (Kuala Lumpur domestic service, 10 May; *FBIS*, 17 May.)

Measured solely by government claims of communist terrorist casualties, it was clear that CPM guerrilla strength had declined. Certainly the level of activity was down markedly from the period of CPM resurgence in the mid-1970s. A government announcement in January justifying the need for continued reliance on internal security measures stated that whereas 85 communist terrorists had been killed in 1974, only 6 had been killed in 1982 (Kuala Lumpur international service, 13 January; *FBIS*, 19 January). In June, government sources reported an overall decline in CPM strength, and defections from the CPM and the CPM/M-L military organizations were reported throughout the year (*FBIS*, 1 June). A communist recruiting campaign in eastern Malaysia, planned for the area around the Indonesian border, was reportedly unsuccessful (Kuala Lumpur domestic service, 14 and 15 November), and the deputy prime minister said that the number of terrorists along the Sarawak-Kalimantan border had been reduced to 100, compared with 1,800 ten years before (*FBIS*, 16 November).

CPM political activities may be enjoying greater success than military efforts, although information on this is largely inferential. Party manifestos continued to emphasize the need to broaden the base of support, and there were continuous appeals addressed to people of all nationalities. The party's goals for 1983 remained much as in the past and stressed the link between the revolutionary armed struggle and the revolutionary people's movement. The task of that war is to "oppose the reactionary clique's policy and rule . . . and to fight imperialism, especially Soviet and Vietnamese hegemonism, to safeguard the nation's interests." The MNRPM was praised for its achievements in promoting political consciousness among the Malay population and "for its cooperation with political parties of all nationalities regardless of their faith and ideology" and encouraged to new successes in that area. The party's appeals were directed to the usual congeries of hoped-for supporters, including peasants, fishermen, smallholders, farm workers, city squatters, small- and medium-scale traders, vendors, workers in industrial and commercial enterprises, and lower-level civil servants. There were also special appeals to educated youths and to members of the activist religious student movements. (VOMD, 31 December 1982; *FBIS*, 11 January.)

Auxiliary and Front Organizations. It is difficult to determine the extent of auxiliary and front organization activities from the available evidence, although something of their nature can

be gleaned from official party statements, generally broadcast over the VOMD.

The 34th Army Day salute to the CPM's principal auxiliary, the MPA, paid the customary tributes to that force's past achievements, denounced the "hypocrisy of parliamentary democracy," and pledged the MPA's "support to implement the party line and program." Despite the CPM's failure to resolve ethnic problems in its recruitment, the statement stressed that the military arm of the CPM is "the people's army of all nationalities in Malaya." (VOMD, 31 January; *FBIS*, 9 February.) Both the Army Day statement and the CPM Central Committee's New Year's Day message a month earlier made reference to a 20 June 1982 joint communiqué issued by the Central Committee and the Supreme Command of the Malayan National Liberation Army (Tentera Pembebasan Nasional Malaya; MNLA) changing the MNLA's name to Tentera Rakyat Malaya (MPA). In a "solemn oath-taking ceremony" at the time of that change, MPA commanders and combatants pledged their support to "the party Central Committee headed by Comrade Chin Peng," another reference to the continued leadership of the longtime secretary general of the party (VOMD, 31 January; *FBIS*, 9 February).

The MNRPM, founded in 1981, remains the CPM's principal front organization and is designed to capture the allegiance of the Muslims of Malaysia. As with the party's military arm, the amount of MNRPM activity is not necessarily commensurate with its public claims. In a New Year's message, D. C. Abdullah, chairman of the MNRPM, speaking on behalf of the party's Central Committee, said the party was "launching a series of meaningful activities . . . consolidating patriotic and democratic forces . . . and enhancing the consciousness of the broad Malay masses" and denounced the Kuala Lumpur and Singapore governments for "using force to suppress those patriotic fighters who were fighting for the complete independence of the fatherland." The appeal was addressed to "all MNRPM members and supporters, Islamic scholars and broad Malay nationalists, socialists and communist masses" and contained a strong attack on the principal Malay party in the ruling government coalition, the United Malays National Organization (UMNO) for "meddling in and undermining" the religious practices of Muslims who did not support them, thus "splitting the unity" of Muslims. (VOMD, 31 December 1982; *FBIS*, 6 January.)

Abdullah used the occasion of the Muslim religious holiday of Id Al-Fitr to accuse the government of ignoring Muslim sensibilities by permitting the use of English as the medium of instruction at the Islamic University and for permitting gambling in the interests of the huge state revenues derived from taxes on it. He charged that the government had only recognized the Palestine Liberation Organization because it had been forced to by strong and incessant demands over a long time by the country's Muslims. (VOMD, 11 July; *FBIS*, 14 July.)

The older CPM front, the Paperi, founded in 1965, which had been somewhat subdued in recent years, re-emerged to take a more vigorous role as the government tried to cope with pressure from fundamentalist Muslim groups. Paperi attacked "the hypocrisy of Mahathir and Musa Hitam" for "launching a large-scale campaign to slander Paperi" (VOMD, 28 February; *FBIS*, 11 March). Both Paperi and the MNRPM have focused on the battle between UMNO-backed and PI-supported religious leaders (VOMD, 11 July; *FBIS*, 14 July), which has led to the "two-imam" problem (rival religious leaders preaching to split congregations). It is possible to overstate the ideological significance of this split, however, since voters appear to sway between UMNO and PI rather easily. There is apparently a substantial reservoir of opposition sentiment in the Malay community waiting to be tapped, but it is not at all clear that the CPM or its fronts will necessarily reap the benefits of that opposition (*FEER*, 31 March).

International Views and Positions. The CPM remains staunchly committed to the PRC. This has led to some anomalies, given China's current policy of wooing the governments of the ASEAN states and renouncing all but moral support for the region's communist insurgents (see Harry Harding, "Change and Continuity in Chinese Foreign Policy," *Problems of Communism*, March–April; *FEER*, 20 October). Thus, while Kuala Lumpur and Singapore were negotiating improved trade relations with the PRC, the MNRPM was broadcasting attacks on both governments for their disastrous economic policies over the CPM's clandestine radio station (VOMD, 11 July; *FBIS*, 16 July).

Another area in which the CPM is squeezed by the improving relationship between Beijing and the ASEAN governments is the question of Kampuchea. The ASEAN states and the PRC are in accord in their support for the anti-Vietnamese, anti-Soviet tripartite coalition of Democratic Kampuchea, as is, perforce, the CPM. The party vociferously endorses the Kampuchean people's efforts to evict the Vietnamese aggresssors and even more strongly condemns Soviet-Vietnamese hegemonism. To escape from the dilemma of finding itself on the same side as the Kuala Lumpur and Singapore governments, the party stated that these two "ruling cliques" have "not abandoned their compromising stand of seeking peace with the Soviet-Vietnam axis." Claiming that fear of China motivates Kuala Lumpur and Singapore, the party charged that both governments were secretly encouraging Vietnam to turn its aggression and rebellion against China. (VOMD, 13 January; *FBIS*, 18 January.)

Both China and Vietnam have renounced aid to communist insurgencies in Southeast Asia (Shee, "Insurgency"), but this was of little interest to the anti-Vietnamese CPM. Public opinion in Malaysia and Singapore was aroused when a Soviet deputy foreign minister repeated the Vietnamese threat to support insurgent movements in ASEAN countries if the governments of those countries were to confront the Indochinese states.

Singapore's deputy prime minister, S. Rajaratnam, pointed out that since subversive groups in ASEAN were pro-Chinese and not pro-Vietnamese, the threat was merely Vietnamese propaganda (Singapore domestic service, 6 April; *FBIS*, 7 April). The Malaysian prime minister characterized the threat as an open admission of Soviet ambitions in the region, the Soviets hoping to find an excuse to use Vietnam as a proxy to send its troops into the region as they had their own in Afghanistan and some African countries (Kuala Lumpur international service, 11 April; *FBIS*, 14 April). The Soviets shortly thereafter disclaimed the threat, but not before youth groups in both Malaysia and Singapore had held rallies denouncing Soviet imperialism.

CPM members do not figure importantly in the numerous international communist-front conferences, which are sponsored principally by Moscow. However, the general secretary of Malaysia's Transport Workers' Union, V. David, is listed as a member of the World Peace Council and two Malaysians attended the World Assembly for Peace and Life, Against Nuclear War in Prague, in June. Both delegates, Dewa Abu Bakar and Nazri Aziz Mohamed, were identified as representatives of the Afro-Asian Peoples' Solidarity Organization.

Jeanne S. Mintz
Washington, D.C.

Mongolia

Population. 1.8 million
Party. Mongolian People's Revolutionary Party (Mongol Ardyn Khuvagalt Nam; MPRP)
Founded. 1921
Membership. 76,240 (June 1981)
Secretary General. Yumjaagyin Tsedenbal
Politburo. 8 full members: Yumjaagyin Tsedenbal (chairman, Presidium of People's Great Hural), Bat-Ochirym Altangerel (chairman, People's Great Hural), Jambyn Batmonkh (premier), Damdinjavyn Maidar (first deputy premier), Tumenbayaryn Ragchaa (first deputy premier), Damdiny Gombojav, Sampilyn Jalan-Aajav (until 19 July), Demchigiyn Molomjamts; 4 candidate members: Bujyn Dejid, Nyamin Jagvaral, Sonomyn Luvsangombo, Choijilsuren
Secretariat. 7 members: Tsedenbal, Gombojav, Jalan-Aajav (until 19 July), Molomjamts, Gelegiyn Adyaa, Paavangiyn Damdin, Mangaljavyn
Central Committee. 91 full and 71 candidate members
Status. Ruling party
Last Congress. Eighteenth, 26–31 May 1981, in Ulan Bator
Last Election. 1981, 99 percent, all 370 seats in Great Hural
Auxiliary Organizations. Mongolian Revolutionary Youth League (over 200,000 members), Lodongiyn Tudev, first secretary; Central Council of Mongolian Trade Unions (400,000 members), Luvsantseren, chairman; Committee of Mongolian Women, Pagmadula, chairman
Publications. *Unen* (Truth), MPRP daily organ, published Tuesday–Sunday. Montsame is the official news agency.

Organization and Leadership. The only significant change in the leadership of the MPRP during 1983 occurred on 19 July, when the Sixth Plenum of the Central Committee removed Sampilyn Jalan-Aajav from membership in the Politburo and the Secretariat. A week later he was dismissed as deputy chairman of the People's Great Hural.

A Politburo member since 1972, Jalan-Aajav apparently became the scapegoat for the dismal performance of the country's livestock industry, and the decision to relieve him seems to have been taken in haste. Indeed, on 18 June, he had received the Labor Red Banner Order in connection with his sixtieth birthday. In making the award, the party Central Committee and the Presidium of the People's Great Hural expressed collective wishes to Jalan-Aajav for "great success in his work, good health and long life" (Montsame, 18 June; *FBIS*, 1 July). Earlier, between 30 May and 7 June, he had led a Mongolian People's Republic (MPR) delegation to Moscow for talks on interparty cooperation. Central Committee members Tsendiin Molom and N. Sereenendorj were also removed along with Jalan-Aajav.

New appointments in 1983 included those of Lhaghbajabyn Dzantav as chairman of the State Committee for Information, Radio, and Television (16 March) and Buralyn Jadambaa as MPR first deputy procurator (26 July).

Domestic Affairs. The MPR celebrated the ninetieth birthday of its founder, Damdiny Sukhe Bator, in 1983, which was also proclaimed the Year of the Schoolchild. A new law on public education was adopted, replacing the 1963 law. It extended, for the first time, the right of education to foreign citizens resident in the MPR.

The economy of Mongolia continued to benefit from aid from the member-states of the Council for Mutual Economic Assistance (CMEA), especially the Soviet Union, which alone has donated some 480 national economic projects to the MPR over the past decade (Montsame, 1 February; *FBIS*, 2 February). In 1983, the USSR gave Mongolia a house-building combine with a construction capacity of 140,000 square meters of living space annually (Montsame, 31 October; *FBIS*, 10 November). Among the several other economic projects are a Bulgarian agroindustrial complex to be built in the Sharyngol Valley and a furniture and cardboard factory established with Romanian assistance. As the result of increased aid from other CMEA members (which account for 97 percent of Mongolia's foreign trade), the share of industry in Mongolia's GNP rose to a projected 44 percent in 1983 (Montsame, 1 February; *FBIS*, 2 February). Mongolia's deepening commitment to the CMEA is further evidenced by the fact that during 1983 Ulan Bator played host to CMEA conferences on transportation, agriculture, water cooperation, prices, and jurisprudence.

Livestock breeding, the principal agricultural activity as well as the source of the country's chief export commodity, continued to perform dismally. Tsedenbal expressed serious concern over "the unfavorable situation in livestock breeding"

(Montsame, 19 July; *FBIS*, 21 July). His concern was merited. Although capital investment in livestock breeding during the first three years of the Seventh Five-Year Plan (1981–1985) increased by 24 percent, the number of livestock raised in 1983 increased only by a fraction of a percentage over the 1981 figure of 9.1–9.4 million head (compare *Unen*, 13 December 1982; *FBIS*, 16 December 1982 with Montsame, 20 July; *FBIS*, 29 July). The problems plaguing livestock breeding were detailed by Politburo member Tumenbayaryn Ragchaa at the Sixth Plenum of the Central Committee, which was convened on 19 July specifically to address the crisis in livestock breeding. This meeting passed a special resolution obliging "party and state organs and agricultural organizations to realize urgent and effective measures to replace lost livestock" (Montsame, 19 July; *FBIS*, 28 July). The poor showing of Mongolian livestock breeding was an important item on the agenda of the thirty-sixth session of the MPR-USSR Intergovernmental Commission for Economic and Scientific and Technological Cooperation, held 31 October–2 November in Ulan Bator.

International Views and Contacts. Support for Soviet interests and activities among the countries of the Third World is the essence of MPR foreign policy. Accordingly, the USSR embassy in Ulan Bator plays an important role in influencing the direction and tone of Mongolia's foreign relations. For this reason, the replacement in 1983 of A. I. Smirnov after nearly a decade as Soviet ambassador to the MPR must be seen as an event significant not only to bilateral Soviet-Mongolian relations but also to the MPR's foreign policy as a whole. The new Soviet ambassador to the MPR is S. P. Pavlov.

Sino-Mongolian relations descended to a new low in May, when several hundred (perhaps thousand) Chinese workers were forcibly repatriated to the People's Republic of China (*NYT*, 26 May). Claiming that "the overwhelming majority [of Chinese residents in the MPR] avoid socially useful work and live on unearned income," the Mongolian government attempted to resettle the Chinese in a northern province of the country. The Chinese refused resettlement and were "voluntarily repatriated" (Montsame, 1 June; *FBIS*, 2 June). On 6 June, the PRC embassy protested the expulsion as illegal; the MPR government rejected the protest. Strains between the two countries intensified when, in commemorating the PRC's National Day, the 1 October issue of *Unen* accused Chinese leaders of "reluctance to abandon anti-Sovietism," "Great Han expansionism," and of having a "negative attitude toward correctly combining national and international interests" (*FEER*, 10 November).

Other noteworthy developments in the MPR's relations with Asian countries during 1983 included a consular agreement with Laos, a friendship treaty with Kampuchea, and trade agreements with Vietnam and North Korea. The search for supporters among Asian states of a proposal for a convention on mutual nonaggression and nonuse of force among the states of Asia and the Pacific Ocean, adopted by the 1981 MPRP congress, continued.

In 1983, the MPR expanded its contacts with the Middle East and Latin America. Politburo member Nyamin Jagvaral participated in the sixteenth session of the Palestinian National Council and held talks with Palestine Liberation Organization chairman Yassir Arafat. In May, a Ba'th Party delegation from Syria came to Ulan Bator. Politburo member Tumenbayaryn Ragchaa traveled to Kabul in April and discussed the forthcoming trip to the MPR by Babrak Karmal. The first visit by a party and state delegation from Afghanistan to Mongolia, the occasion (July) was marked by the signing of a treaty of friendship and cooperation, a consular agreement, and an agreement on trade and payments. A protocol on cooperation in sports was subsequently concluded.

Daniel Ortega Saavedra, member of the Sandinista National Liberation Front leadership, led a Nicaraguan delegation to Ulan Bator at the invitation of the MPRP Central Committee and the MPR government in March. A second delegation, headed by Sergio Ramírez Mercado, arrived in the Mongolian capital in September. A number of official visits between the MPR and Cuba were exchanged during the year.

The MPR also sought closer ties with African countries during this period. Mongolia signed a protocol on cultural cooperation with Angola, and Deputy Foreign Minister Jambalyn Banzar headed a goodwill delegation to Mozambique. A delegation from the People's Republic of the Congo visited the MPR.

In April, Jambyn Batmonkh, chairman of the MPR Council of Ministers, made an official visit to the German Democratic Republic, which was reciprocated in September. Tsedenbal visited Romania in June and signed a friendship treaty, which was ratified by the MPR People's Great Hural on 17 October.

Tania A. Jacques
Washington, D.C.

Nepal

Population. 16.2 million (estimate)
Party. Communist Party of Nepal, pro-Beijing Adhikari Faction (CPN/B) (Maoist elements are divided); Communist Party of Nepal, pro-Moscow (CPN/M)
Founded. 1949
Membership. 4,000 (estimate), with pro-Chinese factions probably accounting for all but a few hundred members
Leadership. CPN/B: secretary general, Man Mohan Adhikari; CPN/M: secretary general, Bishnu Bahadur Manandhar, president, Keshar Jung Raimajhi

Status. Proscribed
Last Congress. Third, 1968
Last Election. Not applicable
Auxiliary Organizations. CPN/B: All-Nepal National Independent Students' Union; CPN/M: National Student Union
Publications. CPN/M: *Samiksha* (weekly)

All political parties have been illegal in Nepal since 1960, but there has been some liberalization in recent years under King Birendra. The leftist movement is quite fragmented, with various Maoist elements commanding much stronger support than the pro-Moscow communist party faction.

The first elected prime minister under Nepal's partyless Panchayat system was ousted in mid-1983 after a long period of widespread criticism. There were initial indications of unification efforts by the factionalized communists, who continued to show strength among students.

Prime Minister Surya Bahadur Thapa, elected by the National Assembly in 1981 following constitutional changes, faced mounting opposition at the beginning of the year, both inside and outside the government. In February, more than half the National Assembly representatives called for his cabinet's dissolution. Their spokesman, former Assembly chairman Lokendra Bahadur Chand, cited severe problems of corruption, inflation, unemployment, and nepotism. (*FBIS*, 3 February.) Lower-level government workers staged a series of protest rallies during the spring. Several former prime ministers supported the rallies, at least partly motivated by personal rivalries. The leftists criticized price increases for consumer goods.

In July, nearly two-thirds of the cabinet ministers resigned, and a motion of no-confidence was passed by the National Assembly. Even members appointed by the king voted against Thapa. Chand, another supporter of the Panchayat system and one of Thapa's leading opponents, was elected by the National Assembly to succeed him. Chand promised to give priority to economic problems, eliminate corruption, and release political prisoners.

As the new government was taking office, a leader of the major democratic opposition party, the Nepali Congress, renewed the call for abolition of the Panchayat system and the holding of general elections. Ganesh Man Singh said, however, that the party still favors reconciliation and cooperation with King Birendra. (Ibid., 14 July.)

The Chand government came under attack almost immediately from National Assembly members, including Thapa, for failing to keep campaign promises and for leniency toward the Nepali Congress. These opponents proposed a no-confidence motion, but in August the National Assembly chairman declared it unconstitutional.

Opposition has also developed among the banned political parties. Nepali Congress leaders traveled throughout the country to propagate their views, insisting that the Panchayat system had failed (*FEER*, 19 January 1984). In September, 300 Nepali Congress student supporters were arrested, apparently for violating bans on political meetings (ibid., 13 October).

The pro-Soviet CPN/M stepped up its opposition activities, campaigning against Chand for failing to control corruption and help the poor. Recently, it was reported that the communist splinter groups had decided to merge into a pro-Soviet faction under the leadership of Man Mohan Adhikari. Adhikari was a leader of pro-Chinese elements, but has changed political alignments in the past. The communists hope to launch a political movement demanding the restoration of political rights, control of administrative corruption, and a faster pace of economic development. Adhikari appealed to the democratic parties to cooperate in a combined movement to recover democratic rights. (Ibid., 19 January 1984.) It remains to be seen, however, whether greater communist unity, if genuine, would result in significantly increased influence.

Leftist students also attacked the Panchayat system and called for freedom of speech and an independent judiciary. The pro-Chinese All Nepal National Independent Students' Union observed a successful one-day token strike in December, protesting the government's indifference to popular suffering caused by the economic situation as well as corruption and "political anarchy." The leftist All Nepal High School Teachers' Union lent its support, objecting to the government's decision to remove leftist-oriented teachers from schools. (Ibid.)

Internationally, the Nepalese government

continues to pursue its nonaligned policy and its proposal to make Nepal a "zone of peace." King Birendra received an endorsement of this proposal during his visit to the United States (ibid., 22 December). The king visited Spain and Egypt in September and received visits from the presidents of France and Pakistan in May. A Chinese economic delegation to Nepal announced further development aid, and in late 1982 Nepal signed its first trade and payments agreement with Czechoslovakia.

Barbara Reid
Earlysville, Virginia

New Zealand

Population. 3.1 million (*World Factbook*, July 1983)
Parties. Communist Party of New Zealand (CPNZ); Socialist Unity Party (SUP); Workers Communist League (WCL); Socialist Action League (SAL); Preparatory Committee for the Formation of the Communist Party of New Zealand
Founded. CPNZ: 1921; SUP: 1966; WCL: 1980; SAL: 1969; Preparatory Committee: 1978
Membership. CPNZ: 80; SUP: 135; WCL: 130; SAL: 60; Preparatory Committee: 12 (author's estimates)
Leadership. CPNZ: Richard C. Wolfe; SUP: Gordon Harold Andersen, national president, George Edward Jackson, national secretary; WCL, SAL, Preparatory Committee: not known to author
Status. All legal
Last Congress. SUP: Sixth, 22–24 October 1982, in Wellington
Last Election. 1981, 0.5 percent (total all Marxist parties), no representatives
Auxiliary Organizations. SUP: maintains close ties with the New Zealand–USSR Friendship Society, New Zealand Council for World Peace, Union of New Zealand Women, Young Workers' Alliance
Publications. CPNZ: *People's Voice* (weekly); SUP: *New Zealand Tribune* (fortnightly), *Socialist Politics* (quarterly theoretical journal); WCL: *Unity* (monthly newssheet); SAL: *Socialist Action* (fortnightly); Preparatory Committee: *Struggle* (bimonthly)

Although communism has little appeal as an ideology or way of life to the average New Zealander, several minuscule communist parties of varying ideological orientation may be found on this island-nation. They include the pro-Moscow SUP; the Beijing-oriented Preparatory Committee; the Beijing-leaning but more independent WCL; the Trotskyist, Havana-oriented SAL; and the pro-Tirana CPNZ.

All of these organizations function legally but are closely watched by the government. Their combined strength is now slightly over 400, excluding sympathizers and associated youth groups. The influence New Zealand's communist parties wield, however, is greater than their small numerical strength and tiny electoral support would otherwise merit, due primarily to their concentration of effort in the trade union movement and the media coverage generated by their activities regarding local and topical issues such as Maori land rights and visits by nuclear-powered ships. With the exception of the SUP, their influence on the public life of New Zealand is negligible.

The Communist Party of New Zealand (CPNZ) was formed in Wellington during 1921, making it the second oldest political party in New Zealand. The CPNZ is unusual for a Western communist party in that it was first aligned with the USSR, then with China, and, since 1978, with Albania. The CPNZ has an estimated membership of eighty and is headed by Richard C. Wolfe. The party's headquarters is located in Auckland, New Zealand's second-largest city. The CPNZ is equally anti-U.S., anti-USSR, and anti-PRC.

During January 1966, six leading members of the CPNZ, including a former national chairman, resigned to form a Moscow-oriented communist organization. This body was named the Socialist Unity Party (SUP) at its first conference (1966). With approximately 135 members, the SUP is the largest, best organized, and most active of the communist parties in New Zealand. It has the further distinction of being the only communist party in the country officially recognized and supported by the Soviet Union. The SUP is headquartered in Auckland, where approximately 60 percent of its membership resides.

The major Trotskyist group in New Zealand is the Cuban-oriented SAL, which originated in the radical student movement during 1969. Also based in Auckland, the SAL has steadily declined in membership the past several years and is now believed to have approximately sixty members. As in 1982, the SAL appears to have engaged in little activity in 1983, although it continues to publish the fortnightly *Socialist Action*. SAL member Mike Tucker attended the Socialist Workers Party of Australia's National Conference in Sydney in January.

During the 1970s, particularly with the purge of the Gang of Four in the PRC, a schism developed within the CPNZ, which resulted in the Albania-oriented faction's retaining the CPNZ title and pro-Beijing elements forming several offshoots. In 1978, one group led by former longtime CPNZ general secretary V. G. Wilcox, announced the formation of the Preparatory Committee for the Formation of the CPNZ (Marxist-Leninist). Other pro-Beijing groups included the Wellington Marxist-Leninist Organization (WMLO), the Northern Communist Organization (NCO), the Marxist-Leninist Workers'

Group (MLWG), and a group formed around the theoretical journal *Struggle*. During 1980, however, the pro-Beijing groups consolidated their forces and reduced their number from five to two. In January 1980, the WMLO and NCO combined to form the present-day Workers' Communist League (WCL). During February 1980, the group around the theoretical journal *Struggle* joined the Preparatory Committee. The small MLWG was absorbed by the WCL in July 1980.

The Preparatory Committee stresses its adherence to Marxism-Leninism–Mao Zedong Thought and is totally committed to the support of Chinese policies. Although it is the only communist party in New Zealand officially recognized by the PRC, the Preparatory Committee has dwindled down to some dozen members.

The WCL proclaims its adherence to Marxism-Leninism–Mao Zedong Thought but, since the death of Mao Zedong, has adopted a more independent stance, particularly as PRC foreign policy has shifted. The WCL keeps its membership secret and is more radical and conspiratorial than the other communist parties. It is composed primarily of young, university-educated ideologues who are strongly committed to revolutionary change. It is active in the trade union movement, particularly in the Wellington Trades Council, and among university students and unemployed workers, especially in the Wellington Unemployed Workers' Union. The WCL is the only communist party which seems to have experienced any growth during the year, due primarily to its success in recruiting among unemployed workers. Its current membership is believed to be 130 (up from an estimated 70 members in 1982). Based in Wellington, the WCL also has members in Auckland and other areas of the nation. Although the New Zealand government describes the WCL as a "revolutionary communist party dedicated to the violent overthrow of the state" (*YICA*, 1982, p. 218), there is no evidence to date that suggests the party has engaged in any acts of violence.

Socialist Unity Party. The SUP's National Conference, held triennially, is the highest decisionmaking body in the SUP and elects both the ten-member National Committee, which governs the party between conferences, and the National Appeals Committee, which functions as the party auditor. According to press reports (*Dominion*,

26 October 1982; *Evening Post*, 25 October 1982; *Christchurch Press*, 25 October 1982), the following individuals were elected to the National Committee during the Sixth National Conference, held in Wellington 22–24 October 1982: Gordon Harold Andersen, George Edward Jackson, Eleanor Matilda Ayo, Marilyn Gay Tucker, Kenneth George Douglas, Aubrey Bruce Skilton, Kenneth William Perrott, Francis Edward McNulty, John Leslie Marston, and Richard Edward Gillespie.

A great deal of concern was expressed at the SUP's Sixth National Conference over the aging of its leadership (both Jackson and Andersen, for example, are 75, and Ayo is in her late sixties). For this reason, four younger party members were subsequently named as alternate members of the National Committee: Warwick James Armstrong, David George Arthur, Bernard Noel O'Brien, and Jackson Smith.

The National Appeals Committee, also elected during the Sixth National Conference, consists of Herbert Leonard Spiller, Mavis Laura Hepburn, and Aubrey Bruce Skilton.

The SUP National committee also elects the National Executive, which is responsible for the party's day-to-day affairs. At an 11–12 December 1982 meeting of the National Committee, five individuals were chosen to constitute the National Executive: Gordon Harold Andersen (national president), Eleanor Matilda Ayo (national vice-president), George Edward Jackson (national secretary), Kenneth William Perrott (national organizer), and Marilyn Gay Tucker. The SUP National Executive meets weekly and is the real seat of power in the party. Despite the presence of two women on the National Executive, it appears that women in general do not rise to positions of leadership within the party.

Policy. In addition to concern over the age of the party's leadership, the Sixth National Conference discussed peace issues and industrial policies, the bread-and-butter issues of the SUP. According to a party publication entitled *Our Country, Our Future*, the SUP looks forward to a New Zealand with full employment; a living wage; decent housing for all; technology that raises living standards, improves jobs, and provides more leisure time; free job training and retraining; a cheap, efficient public transport system; a strong, healthy trade union movement; a good, free health system; cheap, high-quality childcare; equal opportunities for women and for Maori and Pacific Island people; and a firm anti-nuclear peace policy. The party claims these goals can be reached through (1) nationalization of financial houses, banks, insurance companies, and key industries; (2) a planned economy controlled by representatives of trade unions, working farmers, small businessmen, consumers, professionals, and other antimonopoly social groups; (3) independent trade and foreign policies, including development of industries to process New Zealand's primary produce, equal trade and political relations with the South Pacific nations, nonalignment, withdrawal from the ANZUS pact (Australia, New Zealand, United States) and the International Monetary Fund, and zones of peace in the Pacific and Indian Ocean.

The SUP is totally subservient to the Soviet party and does nothing to conceal that fact. In return for Soviet support, the SUP directly endorses Soviet foreign policy initiatives, including the extension of Soviet "fraternal aid" to Afghanistan. The SUP particularly supports Soviet proposals regarding disarmament, including the concept of a nuclear-free zone in the Indian Ocean and South Pacific, and calls for unilateral disarmament on the part of New Zealand and the disbanding of the ANZUS Security Treaty because membership means that New Zealand is integrated into the U.S. military-industrial complex and makes New Zealand a nuclear target (*Tribune*, 25 July).

Domestically, the SUP has had a very successful policy of working through the trade union movement, concentrating on obtaining leadership positions. Approximately half of the SUP's members are involved in trade unions, with the large majority holding positions of responsibility. SUP members hold office in the New Zealand Federation of Labor (FOL), the country's principal national union organization (almost 440,000 members). They also hold office in four of the regional trade councils, including the major ones of Auckland and Wellington, and in a number of individual unions. Kenneth George Douglas, SUP National Committee member and president of the N.Z. Drivers' Federation and Wellington Trades Council, is now secretary-treasurer of the FOL and responsible for its day-to-day operations. In fact, his position is second in importance only to the FOL presidency, for which it is said he will be a major contender in the May 1984 elections. Gordon Harold "Bill" Andersen, SUP national president and well-known labor leader, serves as secretary of the Northern Drivers' Union and president of the Auckland Trades Council (which alone has one-quarter of the FOL's membership) and is a member of the FOL National Executive Board. The SUP has two of the eleven seats on the powerful FOL National Executive Board. FOL president Walter James Knox, although not a SUP member, is often seen as a captive of Andersen and Douglas and is heavily influenced by them (*Business Week*, 7 June 1982, p. 52). Several other members of the FOL National Executive Board, although not members of the SUP, endorse positions consistent with those of the SUP and the Soviet-front World Federation of Trade Unions (WFTU). Included among them is Sonya Davies, FOL vice-president, who has been closely associated with Andersen and Douglas.

Past FOL resolutions have attacked U.S. activities, supported the nuclear-free zone concept in the South Pacific, and protested visits by U.S. nuclear-powered vessels. The FOL's preoccupation with peace issues is not surprising. Andersen and Knox are New Zealand's representatives to the Soviet-front World Peace Council. Knox is patron of the National Committee and vice-president of the Wellington Committee of the New Zealand Council for World Peace (NZCWP). At the same time, Andersen and Douglas attempt to limit FOL resolutions critical of the Soviet Union and its allies. Not surprisingly, the Soviet Union often sends observers to FOL conferences.

Although there are no WFTU-affiliated unions in New Zealand, the SUP actively participates in WFTU activities in the region and has played an active role in WFTU efforts to penetrate the young and growing trade union movement in the South Pacific. Jackson Smith, SUP National Committee alternate member, Wellington Drivers' Union official, head of the New Zealand Committee for International Trade Union Unity, and prominent Maori trade unionist, appears to be a leading member in these WFTU efforts. Several WFTU officials visited New Zealand under the sponsorship of Kenneth George Douglas for meetings with FOL and SUP members in 1983.

SUP influence in the trade union movement has been of great concern to the government of New Zealand. In 1980, Prime Minister Robert David Muldoon publicly named 32 prominent trade unionists who were members of the SUP (*FBIS*, 21 March 1980). The New Zealand government, however, is faced with a dilemma since many of the issues the SUP pushes in the FOL have a large degree of support among rank-and-file unionists. Andersen and Douglas have done such a good job of convincing everyone that they are trade unionists first and communists second (i.e., can separate their union duties from their communist affairs) that any attack on them is perceived as an attack on organized labor and only serves to strengthen the degree of support they receive from the rank and file.

In addition to actively supporting the WFTU, the SUP maintains close ties with the New Zealand–USSR Friendship Society; the NZCWP, an affiliate of the Soviet-front World Peace Council; and the Union of New Zealand Women, an affiliate of the Soviet-front Women's International Democratic Federation. It also supports activities of the Women's Action for Nuclear Disarmament, which sponsored an International Women's Day for Nuclear Disarmament on 24 May (*Tribune*, 2 May). The SUP also maintains close ties to the Young Workers' Alliance.

Early in the year, the National Committee called for the broadening of activity to prevent visits by U.S. nuclear-powered warships and for enlarging the nuclear-free zone campaign to include demands for a nuclear-free South Pacific (ibid., 21 March). SUP members supported and participated in protests against visits by the USS *Hoel* in March, the USS *Texas* in August, and the USS *Phoenix*, USS *Marvin Shields*, and the USS *Lynde McCormick* in November (ibid., 21 March, 25 July, 31 October).

Party representatives were active in attending conferences, congresses, and official events held abroad. Andersen attended the sixtieth anniversary celebrations of the USSR and presented a speech on the international significance of the USSR and the difficulties created by counterrevolution and wars of imperialist intervention afterwards (ibid., 7 February). Andersen sometimes visits the USSR for up to three months at a time, claiming his trips are paid for by the Soviets in the same manner the U.S. State Department gives travel grants to other New Zealanders (*Business Week*, 7 June 1982, p. 52).

In April, George Jackson traveled to East Berlin to attend the international theoretical conference on Karl Marx (*Tribune*, 2 May). Jackson's speech to the conference was reprinted in German in *Neues Deutschland* (13 April).

Other party members attended conferences on peace and security in Asia and the Pacific (Ulan Bator, 26–28 April) and trade unions in the chemical industry against chemical and bacteriological weapons (Ho Chi Minh City, 24–26 May), as well as the World Assembly for Peace and Life, Against Nuclear War (Prague, 21–26 June).

Occasionally, the SUP sponsors training seminars and schools. The SUP Auckland Regional Committee sponsored a school 25–27 February to study the "national question" (*Tribune*, 7 February). Considered to be a success, the topics the school dealt with included the emergence of nations, the Soviet experience, an examination of the historical and present-day Maori experience, and the Samoan experience (ibid., 7 March).

The SUP held a political seminar in Wellington 20–24 August that focused on philosophy, political economy, and the important role and workings of a Marxist-based political party (ibid., 5 September).

George Jackson was awarded the Gold Star of Friendship by the Central Committee of the Socialist Unity Party of the German Democratic Republic and the Order of Friendship Between Nations from the Soviet Central Committee (ibid.).

Pakistan

Population. 96.9 million
Party. Communist Party of Pakistan (CPP)
Founded. 1948
Membership. Under 200 (estimate)
Secretary General. Ali Nazish
Leading Bodies. No information available
Status. Illegal

The CPP was banned in 1954, and no formal communist party has functioned aboveground since then. However, Marxists—some pro-Soviet and some pro-Chinese—have established a number of political groupings, none very large, or worked through larger political parties, student groups, and trade unions. Leftists do not now represent a threat to the government of President Mohammad Zia-ul Haq, though they have a disproportionate influence in the major opposition grouping, the Movement to Restore Democracy (MRD), an eight-party alliance representing a wide ideological spectrum. Marxists played a significant role in antigovernment demonstrations in the southern province of Sind during the fall. Generally, leftist cadres will take to the streets to exploit signs of discontent.

During the year, President Zia's martial law government gradually unfolded its plans for Pakistan's political future. That framework was spelled out most completely in Zia's address to the nominated Federal Advisory Council on 12 August. He informed the council that he envisaged "the restoration of the 1973 constitution with the creation of a balance between the powers of the president and the powers of the prime minister, making it conform with Islamic principles." To ensure such a balance, the president would appoint a prime minister who, "in the president's view," had a majority in the National Assembly; call for new elections; and serve as supreme commander of the armed forces as well as appoint the military chiefs of staff. Zia also called for a two-stage electoral process to restore democracy, with local elections on a nonparty basis in late 1983 and national and provincial elections to be completed no later than 23 March 1985. (Karachi domestic service, 12 August; *FBIS*, 15 August.)

In response, the MRD launched a civil disobedience campaign in all four of Pakistan's provinces, demanding immediate elections and an end to martial law. The campaign, however, had significant popular support only in Sind, where it was fueled by Sindhi nationalism. The campaign there was backed by several non-MRD Sindhi parties, including the Maoist Sindhi Awami Tehrik (SAT), founded by Bux Pallejo in the late 1960s. The well-organized SAT, which up till then had focused its efforts on tenant-farmer grievances, moved to the front ranks of agitation in rural Sind. As a consequence, it could pose a major challenge to Sind's landlord-dominated Pakistan People's Party (PPP), the largest political organization in Sind and in Pakistan. Ali Nazish, the general secretary of the banned and tiny CPP, used the occasion to issue a statement calling for the "overthrow of the military rule, transfer of power to a civilian representative government and holding of general elections" (*New Age*, New Delhi, 9 October).

Nonetheless, the campaign lost momentum in the late fall, even in Sind. Despite the boycott of the local elections by most parties, incuding the MRD alliance, the turnout equaled that of the 1979 local elections, except in Sind, where it was only about 10 percent in the rural areas. The turnout was much higher in Sind's urban centers, which contain large non-Sindhi populations. Because of the failure of traditional political parties to mobilize support, the focus of protest shifted to students, lawyers, and low-level civil servants.

Throughout the year, the small leftist partners of the MRD—the Quami Mahaz-e-Azadi and the Mazdoor Kisan Party—exercised a disproportionate influence on the MRD, perhaps because so many of the MRD's moderate political leaders were either out of the country or under arrest. The first has a following among leftist circles in Karachi and the latter in Northwest Frontier Province. Their representatives on the MRD executive—Meraj Mohammad Khan and Fatayab Ali Khan—assumed a leading role. Their influence showed up most clearly in the foreign policy stands of the MRD. On the eve of the Nonaligned Movement's meeting in New Delhi, for example, the MRD executive issued a press release charging that the improvement in Pakistan-U.S. relations had undermined Pakistan's nonaligned credentials and that the government was converting Pakistan into a front-line state at the behest of the United States. On 14 March, it released a "briefing to the press" charging the CIA with propping up dictators in Pakistan and elsewhere. The leftists also called for a more permanent structure for the MRD and for its transformation into an electoral alliance. The larger and more moderate parties, including the PPP, successfully resisted both moves, affirming that the MRD is an alliance with the sole goal of ending martial law. (*Dubayy Khaleej Times*, 19 June.) Such disagreements underscore the disarray among the members of the MRD and its lack of a sense of direction. The weakness of the anti–martial law agitation in the fall, especially in Punjab, the most populous province, also revealed the difficulties the MRD encounters in building a public following.

Al-Zulfikar, the revolutinary terrorist organization led by Murtaza Bhutto, son of late president Zulfikar Ali Bhutto, appeared less active during the year. However, the group did claim responsibility for some scattered acts of violence in 1983. The government also blamed al-Zulfikar for some bombing incidents in Lahore (*Jang*, 12 October). Murtaza confirmed rumors that al-Zulfikar had shifted its base from Kabul to some undisclosed location (*Pakistan Times*, 23 October). This move may indicate a weakening of Soviet and Afghan support. In any case, al-Zulfikar again failed to elicit popular support anywhere in the country.

The most significant Marxist groups are those like the SAT that have a regional nationalist component. In Sind, this would include the Jiay Sind and the Jiay Sind Student Federation. In the neighboring province of Baluchistan, it would include the Baluchi People's Liberation Front and the Baluchi Student Organization.

Foreign Policy. The government of President Zia wants to preserve its nonaligned credentials and maintains a correct, if sometimes cool, relationship with the USSR. During the year, two rounds of U.N.-sponsored talks were held in Geneva (19–22 April and 16–24 June) involving delegates from Afghanistan and Pakistan. Consistent with U.N. resolutions sponsored by Pakistan, Islamabad insisted on four key points: withdrawal of all foreign troops, the voluntary return of some 3 million Afghan refugees, a nonaligned Afghanistan, and a representative government.

In late 1982, President Zia expressed the hope, based on conversations with General Secretary Yuri Andropov, that the Soviets were looking for some acceptable formula that would enable them to withdraw from Afghanistan. After the April U.N.-sponsored talks, Zia stated in a television interview that "the Soviets, in my opinion, are in difficulty and they feel the pinch of their difficulties. Whereas they may not be able to take positive steps in other parts, I think there is enough for us to believe that they might be able to compromise—if I can use the word—on Afghanistan." (London ITN Television Network, 10 May; *FBIS*, 11 May.) U.N. secretary general Javier Pérez de Cuellar's special representative, Diego Cordovez, publicly stated before the third round of talks that the draft treaty is "95 percent" acceptable to the parties (*Guardian*, 15 June.)

However, the remaining 5 percent apparently included the most intractable issues, such as who would take over the government after Soviet troops left and who would guarantee noninterference in Afghanistan (*WP*, 21 May). The second round of talks ended with no substantive progress on the most difficult issues. An editorial in the government-owned *Pakistan Times* (31 July) noted that the "truth of the matter" is that Moscow "has not given assurance on the timing of withdrawal of troops from Afghanistan," but rather has continued to insist that Islamabad recognize the regime of Babrak Karmal.

The Soviets for their part were suspicious of Pakistan's good faith in the bargaining. Andropov, in a *Der Spiegel* interview published in *Pravda* (25 April), stated that the talks "were going on with difficulty, with the Pakistanis, one may say, being held by their sleeve by their overseas friends." On several occasions, Soviet officials stated that the major problems could be resolved if Pakistan recognized the Karmal government and negotiated directly with it, moves

Pakistan has not taken since such steps would not necessarily give Pakistan what it wanted (i.e., conditions in Afghanistan that would permit the 3 million refugees in Pakistan to return).

As a result of the apparent inability to resolve the outstanding issues on the Afghan question, the Soviets took a more critical public line toward Pakistan. *Izvestiia* (3 October), for example, blamed the "country's authorities for taking steps to militarize the economy." The USSR downgraded the pre–U.N. General Assembly discussions from the ministerial to the deputy level. In late September, the Pakistanis announced that Afghan war planes were increasingly violating Pakistan's airspace. Pakistan claimed that these violations were "deliberate," involving more aircraft and for longer periods than before. (Karachi domestic service, 20 September; *FBIS*, 21 September.)

Reflecting the apparent impasse on the Afghan deliberations, Cuellar canceled Cordovez's summer consultations with the involved parties. The secretary general noted that "I cannot conceal . . . my deep concern at the slow pace of the negotiations and at the difficulties encountered in overcoming existing obstacles. It would indeed be regrettable if the solid work that has been done were to be wasted." ("Report of the Secretary General," 28 September.)

Nonetheless, the USSR and Pakistan retained formally correct bilateral relations. In some areas there were even advances. Moscow and Islamabad signed a commodities exchange agreement in April and a cultural cooperation agreement in July. In addition, Soviet construction minister Boris V. Bakin visited Pakistan in early March to participate in the dedication of two more units of the massive Soviet-assisted Pakistan Steel Mill. Bakin announced that Soviet economic cooperation would continue, if not increase. (Karachi domestic service, 19 March; *FBIS*, 21 March.) In September, the USSR agreed to sell Pakistan ten deep drilling rigs (Karachi domestic service, 12 September; *FBIS*, 13 September.)

In contrast, relations with China remained very good. China is Pakistan's most trusted ally, and Islamabad values Beijing's diplomatic support. Pakistan's economic relations with China are the most extensive Pakistan maintains with any communist state. In 1983, the foreign ministers of the two sides exchanged visits, as did high-level military figures. The first plenary session of the Pakistan-China Joint Economic Committee was held in April, resulting in protocols setting up subcommissions to consider trade, industry, joint ventures, and science and technology exchanges. In February, China signed a contract to supply and install a 210-megawatt steam turbo set at the Guddu power station.

Walter K. Andersen
University of California, Berkeley

Philippines

Population. 53.2 million (*World Factbook*, 1983)
Parties. Communist Party of the Philippines (Partido Komunista ng Pilipinas; PKP); Communist Party of the Philippines (Marxist-Leninist) (CPP-ML)
Founded. PKP: 1930; CPP-ML: 1968
Membership. PKP: 400 (author's estimate); CPP-ML: 7,500 (estimates range from 3,000 to 14,000)
Leadership. PKP: Felicismo C. Macapagal, secretary general; CPP-ML: Rodolfo Salas, chairman, Rafael Baylosis, secretary general, Juanito Rivera, commander of New People's Army (NPA)
Status. Proscribed
Last Congress. None known
Last Election. Not applicable
Auxiliary Organizations. PKP: National Association of Workers (Katipunan), Democratic Youth Council of the Philippines, Philippine Committee for Development, Peace, and Solidarity (PCDPS), Association of Philippine Women Workers, Philippine Printers Union, Agricultural Workers Union; CPP-ML: May First Movement (KMU), Nationalist Youth (KM), League of Filipino Students (LFS), Youth for Nationalism and Democracy (YND), New People's Army (NPA), National Democratic Front (NDF), Christians for National Liberation (CNL), Nationalist Health Association (MASAPA), Nationalist Teachers' Association (KAGUMA), Union of Democratic Filipinos (KDP)
Publications. PKP: *Ang Komunista* (The communist), irregular; CPP-ML: *Ang Bayan* (The nation), monthly; NDF: *Liberation*, monthly, *NDF-Update*, bimonthly, published in the Netherlands, *Ang Katipunan*, published in Oakland, California

There are two communist parties of note in the Philippines. The smaller, pro-Soviet PKP has an estimated membership of 400. Membership figures for the much larger CPP-ML are not available and difficult to estimate due to overlapping membership between the party and its two major auxiliary organizations, the NPA and the NDF. Membership estimates for the NPA vary between 3,000 and 14,000, although it is widely believed that NPA strength stands at 7,000, of which approximately 5,000 may be armed. The NDF claims to have one million adherents, but this probably is an exaggeration.

Both parties have been officially proscribed since 1957. Because of its moderate position, however, the PKP functions virtually unmolested. The PKP's primary emphasis is on "legal" and "parliamentary" forms of struggle, and it maintains a policy of cautious and critical collaboration with the government of Ferdinand Marcos. By presenting itself as a mature and responsible party, nonviolent and reform-minded, the PKP hopes to obtain legal status. PKP leaders have served as informal contacts for the Marcos government with the Soviet bloc and have even attended functions at the presidential palace.

For public consumption, the PKP rejects a pro-Moscow label, but it supports the "Soviet point of view" because the USSR takes a "progressive and principled position" (Justus M. van der Kroef, *Communism in Southeast Asia*, Berkeley, University of California Press, 1980, p. 217). The PKP has received "limited funds" from the Soviet Union in the past and presumably does so today (*FEER*, 7 August 1981). Because of its "collaboration" with the Marcos government and its identification with Soviet interests, the PKP is largely ineffective within the Philippine environment.

While the PKP favors the process of "peaceful revolutionary change," primarily through front building, the CPP-ML combines guerrilla warfare with peaceful united front tactics aimed at the forceful overthrow of the "U.S.-Marcos dictatorship." The year under review saw an increase in the quality and quantity of military/terrorist operations carried out by the CPP-ML through its military arm, the NPA, particularly on the island of Mindanao. As in the past, much of this activity was geared toward obtaining additional weapons. Due to their armed struggle policy, the CPP-ML and NPA are subject to a vigorous counterinsurgency campaign by the Philippine military establishment.

Hand in hand with its focus on armed struggle, the CPP-ML seeks to forge a "united front" of the "national bourgeoisie," "petty bourgeoisie," and "workers and peasants," which it plans to lead in the "revolutionary struggle" against the "U.S.-Marcos dictatorship" (ibid., p. 137). This broad-based mass movement is being developed through the NDF, an umbrella organization that seeks to unite "all forces that are opposed to the "fascist dictatorship of the U.S.-Marcos clique." Specific target groups for the NDF include labor, the church, students, and professionals. The existence of the NDF makes it easier for noncommunists to participate in the CPP-ML's political activities.

Initially pro-Beijing in orientation, the CPP-ML received considerable moral and some financial support from the PRC during the early years of the party's existence. The PRC, however, established diplomatic relations with the Philippines in June 1975, and there has been no evidence of any direct Chinese support for the CPP-ML since that time.

Discomfort among CPP-ML members about the "Maoist" appellation appears to be growing and in practice, the party has gradually moved away from Maoism. The CPP-ML's shift was accelerated by Beijing's withdrawal of support from most national liberation struggles in Southeast Asia and its support for a continued U.S. military presence in the Philippines, on which the Chinese appear to place a higher priority than aid to a "fraternal party" (*The Bulletin*, 6 September, p. 100). While the PRC views retention of U.S. military bases in the Philippines as a necessary counterweight to Soviet "expansionism," the CPP-ML adamantly campaigns for their removal (*Ang Katipunan*, April).

Several CPP-ML statements and actions in recent years attest to the shift in allegiance. The CPP-ML has hailed the Nicaraguan and Iranian revolutions, which were seen by the current Beijing leadership as victories for "Soviet social-imperialism" (*Intercontinental Press*, 28 February; *NDF-Update*, March–April). The CPP-ML labor front, the KMU, participates in a leftist labor umbrella grouping known as "Solidarity." The other major participants in Solidarity are unions affiliated with the Soviet-front World Federation of Trade Unions and include the PKP's Katipunan labor grouping.

The year proved to be turbulent. Numerous issues that were exploitable by the communists arose in 1983. President Marcos's major political rival, former senator Benigno S. Aquino, Jr., was assassinated on 21 August while under escort of the Philippine Aviation Security Command minutes after his arrival at Manila Airport following a three-year self-imposed exile in the United States. Suspected government complicity in the assassination led to massive antigovernment demonstrations throughout the country, with many of the protesters calling for Marcos to resign. Following the assassination, numerous protest groups were spawned, providing communists with additional infiltration targets and many opportunities for front-building activities.

The Aquino assassination led to a massive wave of capital flight. The central bank's foreign reserves dropped rapidly from $2.28 billion on 30 June to $430 million on 17 October. The balance of payments deficit rose sharply, from $600 million at the end of June to more than $2 billion as of 17 October. (*NYT*, 1 November.) The soaring trade deficit forced foreign debt rescheduling and led to two devaluations of the peso and corresponding commodity and fuel price increases. Both communist parties protested what they perceived as U.S. economic domination of the country.

The U.S.-Philippines Military Bases Agreement, opposed by both communist parties, was reviewed and signed this year, providing additional grist for the communists' propaganda mill. The communists claim that the U.S. bases symbolize the continuing colonial status of the Philippines, that the "rent" paid for the bases is being used to acquire more guns and weapons for the suppression of the Filipino people, and that the U.S. presence makes the Philippines a nuclear target.

Organization and Leadership. *PKP.* The PKP central organization follows that of the typical communist party. According to its constitution, the highest authority in the party is the National Congress, which decides the party's general political line, tactics, and organization. The National Committee elects the Central Committee, which is in charge of the party's finances and establishes and supervises the different departments and committees. The Central Committee also elects the secretary general and members of the Politburo. The Politburo has the authority to carry on the work of the Central Committee when it is not in session. The current secretary general of the PKP is Felicismo C. Macapagal. José Lava, former PKP secretary general and current PKP representative to the *World Marxist Review*, has been listed in that journal as a member of the PKP Politburo. Both Macapagal and Lava are in their seventies. Merlin Magallona, PKP secretary for political affairs and the party's leading theoretician, has been mentioned as the most likely successor to Macapagal.

CPP-ML. Organizationally, the CPP-ML is distinctive for its combination of "democratic centralism" and "territorial organization" made necessary by the Philippines' archipelagic nature. Despite its hierarchical structure, the party is decentralized, with regional and provincial units exercising a high degree of autonomy. This has played a key role in the survival of the party despite what the Philippine government has labeled "crippling blows"—the arrest or killing of high-level CPP-ML cadres, such as Bernabe Buscayno, former commander of the NPA, who was arrested in August 1976, and José Maria Sison, former secretary general, who was captured in 1977.

The highest organ of the CPP-ML is the National Congress, which is convened every five years by the Central Committee, unless it is deemed necessary to hold it later or earlier. The National Congress hears reports of the Central Committee, decides the party's general political line, and elects members and candidate members of the Central Committee and other central organs.

The Central Committee elects members of the Politburo, the Secretariat, the Central Committee chairman and his deputies, the secretary general, and other secretaries of the Central Committee. Functions and powers of the Central Committee are carried out between plenums by the Politburo and its Executive Committee. The Secretariat takes charge of the administration and day-to-day activities of the party under guidance from the Politburo. The Secretariat also controls the National Finance Bureau, National Liaison Bureau, and the International Liaison and Propaganda Commission.

According to the Philippine Ministry of Defense, Rodolfo Salas (alias Commander Bilog) is the current CPP-ML Central Committee chairman, Rafael Baylosis is the CPP-ML secretary general, and Juanito Rivera (alias Commander Juaning) is the CPP-ML Military Commission chairman and NPA commander (*FBIS*, 28 September 1982; *Bulletin Today*, 24 September). The Philippine Ministry of Defense has offered substantial rewards to anyone who can provide information leading to the capture, dead or alive, of these individuals—250,000 pesos for Salas and 200,000 pesos each for Baylosis and Rivera.

The CPP-ML currently divides the Philippines into fifteen regions, each serviced by a regional party committee whose basic purpose is to facilitate party activities at that level. In addition to the fifteen regional committees, the CPP-ML has established five party commissions whose purpose is to direct and coordinate political and military activities across regional party committee lines.

NPA. During the course of fighting its protracted people's war, the NPA is to create and employ four types of fighting units: regular mobile forces, guerrilla forces, militia and self-defense corps, and armed city partisans (*The Maoist Communist Party of the Philippines*, SEATO short paper, no. 52, Bangkok, SEATO Research Office, 1971, p. 24). Each type of unit has a specific type of task to perform. The armed city partisans are to disrupt governmental activities and assassinate individuals considered to be traitors in the cities. Militia and self-defense corps are to defend the masses in local areas without separating themselves from daily productive work. Guerrilla zones are defended by guerrilla forces, who are also to create new guerrilla zones and prepare for the emergence of regular mobile forces. The regular mobile forces are to defend the rural bases and destroy government forces on a large scale. The regular mobile forces are to be organized into battalions, companies, platoons, and squads. Based on press reporting, it appears that the size of regular mobile force units is still at the company level.

NDF. Little is known about the leadership and organization of the NDF, which was headed by Horatio "Boy" Morales until his arrest on 21 April 1982. The NDF umbrella includes organizations of peasants, women, students, health workers, teachers, lawyers, and journalists (*Intercontinental Press*, 28 February, p. 117). Known groups belonging to the NDF include the KM, the KMU, the CNL, the MASAPA, and the KAGUMA. The largest among the NDF forces are said to be the Revolutionary Movement of Peasants, which allegedly had 800,000 members by March 1980, and the Revolutionary Movement of Workers, which achieved a membership of several hundred thousand by the end of 1980 (*NDF-Update*, March–April).

During 1977, the NDF initiated international work in Europe. Luís Jalandoni, a former priest, serves as the NDF international representative and is located in Utrecht, Holland. The NDF has developed extensive support networks in Western Europe, the United States, Canada, and Southeast Asia. The Union of Democratic Filipinos (Katipunan Democraticong Pilipino) is the major NDF front in the United States.

Auxiliary Organizations. *Labor.* After the lifting of martial law in January 1981, strike activities and labor agitation increased rapidly in the Philippines. Despite ideological differences, leftist unions allied with PKP and CPP-ML formed a loose alliance called Solidarity (PMP). At its May Day 1981 rally, attended by some 20,000 workers, Solidarity vociferously called for the removal of U.S. bases and an end to "imperialist control." By early summer 1982, radical labor groups led by the KMU were becoming active in leading strikes and organizing workers in factories, particularly in the Bataan Export Processing Zone, where 20,000 workers went on strike in June (*Intercontinental Press*, 28 February). During early June 1982, President Marcos claimed the existence of a conspiracy, "Operation Skylark," by communist insurgents, Muslim terrorists, radical labor leaders, and opposition politicians and businessmen to paralyze the economy and embarrass the government before and during the Marcos visit to the United States during September 1982. Marcos asserted that nationwide strikes, bombings, and assassinations of government officials were planned. As a consequence, a number of prominent labor leaders were arrested, including Felixberto Olalia, head of the KMU, and Bonafacio Tupaz, head of the Trade Unions of the Philippines and Allied Services (TUPAS). Both Olalia and Tupaz were released to "house arrest" by President Marcos on 1 May (Manila Far East Broadcasting Company, 1 May; *FBIS*, 3 May).

Felixberto Olalia died on 4 December of a heart ailment and pneumonia. During the five-hour-long funeral procession, about 5,000 mourners sang protest songs, and some marchers carried a banner saying, "Oust the U.S.-Backed Marcos Regime." Many others wore red arm bands carrying the same message. (*WP*, 12 December.)

There are three labor groups in the Philippines associated with the Soviet-front World Federation of Trade Unions: TUPAS, the National Association of Trade Unions, and the PKP's Katipunan. Neither Bonafacio Tupaz nor TUPAS is known to be directly affiliated with either of the Philippine communist parties.

Students. The Democratic Youth Council of the Philippines, associated with the Soviet-front International Union of Students, is believed to be sponsored by the PKP. The PKP, however, is a weak force among youth and students.

The case is quite different with the CPP-ML,

which is actively involved with youth through its youth wing, the KM. The KM played a central role in the student radicalization and violence of the later 1960s and early 1970s prior to the declaration of martial law. With the advent of martial law, the KM was dissolved, and many of its members went underground and joined the NPA. The KM was reinstituted by the CPP-ML in early 1977 in order to provide an organizational framework for inter-university political work in the underground network (*Southeast Asia Chronicle*, no. 62, p. 12). The KM has controlled or strongly influenced the University of the Philippines student council through its political front, the Samasa Party. The KM was also instrumental in founding the radical LFS. The LFS led a three-hour, 5,000-person demonstration on 18 November that protested government "repression and economic exploitation" and condemned the United States for its support of Marcos (AFP, Hong Kong, 18 November; *FBIS*, 21 November). On 29 November, police forcibly dispersed about 200 LFS militants before they could march to the U.S. Embassy to protest Washington's policies (AFP, Hong Kong, 29 November; *FBIS*, 30 November). The Youth for Nationalism and Democracy is also believed to have been infiltrated by the CPP-ML.

Peace. The PKP is an active participant in activities of the Soviet-front World Peace Council through one of its fronts, the PCDPS. The PCDPS consists of an umbrella grouping of PKP auxiliary organizations, including Katipunan, the Association of Philippine Women Workers, the Philippine Printers Union, and the Agricultural Workers Union. Pedro Baquisa, chairman of the PCDPS and the Democratic Youth Council, attended the WPC-sponsored World Assembly for Peace and Life, Against Nuclear War, held in Prague in June. During 1983, the PCDPS organized a campaign to oppose the continued presence of U.S. military facilities in the Philippines. Also, approximately one hundred members of the PCDPS and Katipunan held a demonstration on 4 July in front of the U.S. Embassy to denounce the International Monetary Fund and World Bank and to charge the United States with dictating the peso's devaluation (AFP, Hong Kong, 4 July; *FBIS*, 6 July). A conference on "Asia as a nuclear-weapons-free zone" was hosted on 20 October by the Philippine Peace and Solidarity Council (PPSC). The conference bitterly criticized U.S. foreign policy and demanded the removal of U.S. bases. The meeting was held to mark U.N. disarmament week. The PPSC is probably a PKP front and may represent either a supplementary or successor organization to the PCDPS.

Domestic Activities. *PKP.* The PKP was active during the year opposing the continued presence of U.S. military bases in the Philippines, advocating making Southeast Asia a nuclear-weapons-free zone, criticizing the United States for its alleged economic subjugation of the Philippines, and chiding the Marcos government regarding the assassination of Benigno Aquino. Other aspects of the PKP program can be seen in a "letter to the editor" of the *Metro Manila Times* (1 October) written by PKP secretary general Macapagal. According to Macapagal, in order to regain the confidence of the people, the Marcos regime needed to respond to the question of responsibility for the assassination of Aquino and effect several "democratic changes," including restoration of the privilege of the writ of habeas corpus; rescinding of constitutional amendment no. 6 (1976), which gives the president extraordinary powers inimical to democratic rights; removal of restrictions on accreditation of political parties; the release of all political prisoners; the strengthening of legal protection for mass organizations; removal of restrictions on workers' basic rights, especially the right to strike; suspension of increases in tuition fees in all schools, public and private; interest-free amortization payments for family farms; cooperative farms for landless rural workers and marginal farmers; a comprehensive price control system in coordination with mass-based consumer organizations; and a rollback in water and power rates to at least 1982 levels.

"These are the minimum demands," write Macapagal, "that will immediately alleviate the difficulties which the broad ranks of the people experience." Macapagal noted that since the present administration had "incapacitated itself" by its "surrender to the dictation of foreign financial and political agencies," there was no illusion that it could deal with the demands "without the mobilization of the people." By understanding their "exploited position in a neocolonial society," it is the organized masses who must solidify their strength and "bring about decisive political

action to realize these minimum demands."
(*FBIS*, 20 October.)

CPP-ML. According to the December 1982 edition of *Ang Bayan*, the CPP-ML and NPA suffered numerous setbacks during 1982, including the incarceration, torture, and killing of top CPP-ML and NPA leaders, members, and sympathizers; the arrest and imprisonment of top union officers; a lack of new recruits and an apparent lack of effort in the penetration of legal organizations for use as fronts and in the development of alliance work; and the utilization by the government of former CPP-ML and NPA members to combat the propaganda efforts of the party and to analyze CPP-ML and NPA methods to develop counterinsurgency strategies.

Ang Bayan then outlined the following CPP-ML plans for 1983: (1) an expansion of front organizations in and out of the Philippines against the "U.S.-Marcos dictatorship"; (2) a more aggressive information drive for the masses in order to advance their struggle against government suppression; (3) help for the advanced section of the masses in forming a revolutionary coalition government to change the "U.S.-Marcos dictatorship"; and (4) consolidation and augmentation of the underground movement in a safe and cohesive manner and integration of members on the periphery into the party.

The party advised its members to continue propaganda work, explore issues indigenous to their area of responsibility, and strengthen their hold on legal organizations already infiltrated by underground elements of the party. They were also instructed to infiltrate and/or organize more organizations to be used as fronts for teach-ins, symposiums, rallies, and similar activities for the masses to make them aware of issues of concern to the CPP-ML. The party expressed its intentions to re-educate elements of the NDF and to expand guerrilla zones of the NPA.

NPA. CPP-ML guerrilla units, particularly those in Mindanao, greeted 1983 with a series of assaults, raids, and ambushes. In the month of January alone, the NPA launched 28 "tactical offensives" in various parts of the country, including the dramatic capture of the town of Mabini in Davao del Norte, Mindanao, on 12 January. During the capture of Mabini, which has about 35,000 inhabitants, an estimated 200 guerrillas struck simultaneously at the town hall, police headquarters, Philippine Constabulary headquarters, and the office of a logging company. An additional 50 guerrillas held the road to the town (*Ang Katipunan*, April). The guerrillas seized rifles from the constabulary, held political meetings, and departed without incurring any losses. Moving to the hills above Mabini, the guerrillas trained 45 new recruits in the use of the newly seized weapons (*WP*, 14 January).

The NPA as yet is no match for the Armed Forces of the Philippines, which are numerically superior, better trained, and better equipped. Not all raids are as dramatic or successful as the one at Mabini. Most NPA operations are small-scale armed operations or ambushes designed to obtain enough weapons and military supplies and equipment to permit an expansion of its armed units. *Bulletin Today* (5 February) reported that "50 NPA guerrillas" led by a female former political detainee had raided a lumber mill at Anticala, Butuan City, on 2 February. According to the account, the NPA "disarmed a squad of constabulary soldiers" guarding the mill. No casualties were reported, but the NPA allegedly carried off an M-60 machine gun, a Browning automatic rifle, a shotgun, three pistols, 2,000 rounds of ammunition, two-way radios, and office equipment. Mines and lumber mills have been frequent targets of the NPA because they are often in isolated areas and because they sometimes are repositories for sizable stocks of weapons.

The NPA is also known to punish its enemies and traitors through liquidations carried out by "sparrow" units. For example, the NPA killed the mayor of Luba Town, Abra province, allegedly because he was cooperating with the military in an anti-NPA campaign (AFP, Hong Kong, 3 November; *FBIS*, 4 November).

During a speech commemorating the Philippine army's eighty-sixth anniversary, President Marcos revealed that in 1982 and the first four months of 1983, the military had arrested or "neutralized" 37 top leaders of the CPP-ML. He noted that this included Carlos Gaspar, the CPP-ML's link in "international funding support" (AFP, Hong Kong, 27 April; *FBIS*, 28 April).

Carlos Gaspar, alias Karl Gaspar, 36, an anthropologist and church lay worker, was arrested by a military intelligence team raid on a suspected underground house of the CPP-ML Mindanao regional party committee in Davao City, the Philippines' third-largest city. Gaspar was identified as head of the Resources Development Foundation, a legal institution suspected of being a CPP-ML front. Gaspar was thought to be head of the Mindanao United Front Commission. Confiscated documents indicated he had traveled regularly to Europe, North Africa, the United States, Nicaragua, El Salvador, and Bangladesh to contact various groups. The documents also indicated the CPP-ML maintained links with solidarity groups in foreign countries through its International Liaison Committee (*Bulletin Today*, 3 April).

Philippine military authorities believe the CPP-ML receives about 80 percent of its agitation and propaganda funds from international funding institutions (ibid.). The *Manila Times Journal* (29 March), citing captured documents, noted that the communists were using humanitarian organizations in the Netherlands and West Germany as a source of funds for fronts known as "legal institutions." The CPP-ML and NPA are also capable of obtaining considerable funds domestically. During 5–7 April, a series of articles in *Bulletin Today* detailed the NPA's "progressive taxation system." According to the series, NPA fund-raising appeared to fall into two broad categories: taxes on families in areas under its control and the extortion of money from vulnerable business concerns.

Families in areas under NPA control are asked to contribute approximately 2–5 pesos per week (20–50 cents) or its equivalent in rice or other foodstuffs. Taxes are levied on a "progressive basis," with poor families asked for little while more prosperous families are expected to pay more. Teachers reportedly had to contribute 10 percent of their salaries; the tax rate for farm and plantation products is said to be 25 percent of the crop.

As in the case of personal taxation, the NPA base business taxes on the size of a company's operations and its ability to pay. Captured NPA tax collectors claimed that the typical logging firms in the Davao del Norte area of Mindanao pay from 10,000 to 60,000 pesos ($1,000–6,000) monthly. The NPA tax rates appear to fluctuate from area to area and probably depend on the extent of control the NPA has in each area.

The Muslim Revolt. Since the late 1960s, the island of Mindanao has been the scene of a Muslim revolt, waged by the independence-seeking Moro National Liberation Front (MNLF) under the leadership of Nur Misuari. At the height of the revolt in the mid-1970s, over 60 percent of the Philippine armed forces were estimated to have been committed to fighting the MNLF (*CSM*, 5 January). In December 1976, Misuari signed an agreement in Tripoli under Libyan auspices with the Philippine government that was to have granted full autonomy to thirteen southern provinces in Mindanao (*FEER*, 22 December). Misuari now believes that the Philippine government unilaterally abrogated the 1976 Tripoli agreement, and he is continuing to fight for full independence for the entire southern region. The MNLF revolt, however, has been on the wane for several years. Sources of foreign support, notably that of Libya, have tapered off, and the MNLF has been seriously split with one faction under the leadership of Hashim Salamat breaking away. Nonetheless, the MNLF has developed a great deal of expertise in weapons smuggling and fighting, and these factors have made Muslims attractive to the NPA.

According to the *Christian Science Monitor* (5 January), an NPA spokesman stated that the NPA was trying to establish firm links with the MNLF. "When the Moros were at the height of the revolt, they were rather patronizing to us," he said. "They used to say 'you handle Luzon and the Visayas (the northern and central Philippines), we'll take Mindanao.' Now they are more willing to talk . . . Progress in the relationship has been slow but steady. Perhaps by the mid-1980s we'll have a formal agreement."

Speaking to local newsmen on 27 January, President Marcos stated that there was no evidence that the NPA and MNLF were operating together in any serious way. He noted that in some cases they had joint training but staged different operations. "In some instances they may exchange intelligence information, but that's about all," he added. (AFP, Hong Kong, 27 January; *FBIS*, 28 January.) While addressing a Philippine Constabulary–Integrated National Police seminar on 14 March, President Marcos acknowledged that in some areas of the south, the MNLF and NPA had joined forces and were exerting efforts to strengthen themselves further. He noted, however, that their efforts did not pose a threat to the stability of the country. (*Manila Times Journal*, 15 March; *FBIS*, 16 March.)

For years, the NPA has been anxious to link up with the MNLF. Although the Muslims view communism as a "godless" ideology, there have been documented reports of on-the-ground cooperation between the MNLF and NPA in Mindanao on the basis that the Marcos government is the common enemy (*FEER*, 22 December).

As far as future relations between the MNLF and NDF, the *Southeast Asia Chronicle* (no. 62) noted, it is important to remember that "Misuari and many of the core leaders of the MNLF have personal and political ties with the NDF leadership." Many of them worked together "in progressive student organizations like the KM while they were undergraduates at the same universities."

The *NDF-Update* (March–April) claims that the NDF and MNLF have developed good relations, resulting in tactical cooperation between the NPA and the MNLF's Bangsa Moro Army. It also noted that the NDF was exerting an effort to develop a dialogue with other underground opposition groups such as the 6 April Liberation Movement and the Philippine Liberation Movement.

The Church. Church-state relations continued to deteriorate during 1983 over the "rebel priest" controversy and other issues. In an effort to resolve points of difference, during December 1982 a dialogue between the Catholic Church and the armed forces was initiated after security forces cracked down on militant priests and nuns accused of working for the CPP-ML, NPA, and NDF—a campaign described by some bishops as "persecution" of the clergy (AFP, Hong Kong, 25 January; *FBIS*, 26 January). The dialogue proved futile and the bishops withdrew from it.

On 15 June, Defense Minister Juan Ponce Enrile said that rebels had infiltrated the Catholic church in the Davao region by making use of certain programs to their advantage. He did not state which church programs were being used but noted the military had records of certain church people in the region who were consorting with the rebels (*Bulletin Today*, 16 June; *FBIS*, 17 June).

On 18 July, three priests, two nuns, and three other persons were arrested in Surigao del Sur for seditious activity. They had allegedly helped ignite rebellion in Surigao, where NPA rebels were reportedly active (*Bulletin Today*, 20 July; *FBIS*, 21 July).

During August, the military raided a Catholic church, the residence of a Catholic bishop, and a convent of teaching nuns, searching for suspected dissident priests, two alleged women communist guerrillas, pistols, ammunition, and subversive documents. One of the individuals being sought was Father Conrado Balweg, alleged military head of the NPA in the northern Philippines, for whom a 200,000 peso reward has been offered. None of the persons or articles being sought was found (AFP, Hong Kong, 26 August; *FBIS*, 2 September).

On 8 October, President Marcos granted amnesty to Father Edgardo Kangleon, who, following his arrest by military authorities on 10 October 1982, made a well-publicized confession admitting his involvement in the communist movement. Father Kangleon headed the Paul VI Social Action Center in Catbalogan, where, during a raid by military authorities, "subversive" documents and a firearm were seized. The government used Kangleon's confession to show the extent to which communists had infiltrated Catholic church organizations. During an interview on 14 December, Kangleon said that he was able to use church-related documents as propaganda material. He was also able to donate money from church-related projects to the underground movement and claimed that he had given 60,000 pesos to the movement for various projects (Manila domestic service, 14 December; *FBIS*, 15 December).

The Government Response. While the NPA has grown steadily, so, too, has the Philippine military establishment. In 1972, the combined manpower of the armed forces and the paramilitary constabulary totaled 54,000. They currently stand at 156,000. A decade ago, they were backed by 400 village-based home defense volunteers; today, there are more than 60,000 home defense force volunteers throughout the country. (*CSM*, 14 June.)

To date, the Philippine military establishment has failed to find an effective counter to the growing NPA insurgency. Last year's strategy for Mindanao, "strategic hamleting" or "grouping," was a dismal failure. In towns where the NPA was alleged to have gained a strong foothold, villagers were summarily moved to closely controlled settlements in an effort to cut all lines of communication between them and guerrillas and to deprive the guerrillas of food and shelter. A prime example was the municipality of San Vicente, an alleged NPA-influenced municipality whose 30,000 inhabitants were "grouped" into a military supervised settlement (ibid., 5 January). While the strategic hamlets may have temporarily limited NPA activities in the region, the forced resettlement generated numerous complaints of military abuses and in some instances led to a greater degree of cooperation between the population and guerrillas (ibid., 17 May).

Late in 1982, Gen. Fabian C. Ver, armed forces chief of staff, head of the Presidential Security Command, director of the National Intelligence Board, and reputedly an uncle of President Marcos's, announced the government's counterinsurgency plan for 1983, code-named "Operation Katatagan," a new strategy to neutralize the insurgent leadership and political structure and to deny them access to manpower and material resources (*Bulletin Today*, 25 December 1982; *FBIS*, 29 December). Operation Katatagan was designed to gain popular support by more closely linking counterinsurgency strategies with rural development projects and by coordinated and integrated employment of all defense forces in national security efforts (Manila Far East Broadcasting Company, 6 January; *FBIS*, 7 January). Ver said civil relations were to be the most important facet of Operation Katatagan. It also involved medical-dental services, information campaigns, and an intensified drive against abusive law enforcers and military personnel.

Faced with an increase in NPA activities, the government reorganized the armed forces and committed elite units to affected areas. On 7 February, in response to the large number of military casualties inflicted by the NPA in Mindanao during January, President Marcos ordered the deployment of more battle-tested troops and field commanders, heavy armaments, and helicopters to spearhead a government offensive in northern and eastern Mindanao (AFP, Hong Kong, 8 February; *FBIS*, 10 February).

Lieutenant General Fidel Ramos, the Philippines' second highest general and purportedly a cousin of Marcos's, flew to Mindanao on 8 February to supervise personally an intensified drive against the communists. Radio Manila (10 February) reported that Ramos had disclosed that seven crack battalions had been sent to northern and eastern Mindanao to arrest the growing insurgency in those two regions. Ramos said the troops would be backed by ten helicopter gunships and two battleships to patrol the coastline. (*FBIS*, 10 February.) The chief of the Philippine navy said that an additional seven combat ships and a Marine brigade had been dispatched to the area to complement government forces already there (Manila Far East Broadcasting Company, 10 February; *FBIS*, 11 February). The seven combat ships were to be deployed as a blocking force in strategic locations surrounding the Davao Gulf to seal off possible entry of supplies for the insurgents.

On 14 March, President Marcos ordered a purge of "scalawags and rotten apples" in the Philippine Constabulary–Integrated National Police who, he said, "have obstructed the fight against subversion and criminality." He also urged closer cooperation between soldiers and policemen and local civilian authorities to make the peace and order campaign more forceful. (*Manila Times Journal*, 15 March; *FBIS*, 16 March.)

Other Opposition. A new leftist opposition party called the Nationalist Alliance for Justice, Freedom, and Democracy held its first formal gathering on 5 November in the Manila suburb of Araneta (*NYT*, 5 November). Believed to be a CPP-ML front, the organization, which has strong anti-U.S. overtones, is headed by 85-year-old former senator Lorenzo Tanada. The Nationalist Alliance purportedly brings together many small nationalist groups from throughout the Philippines that advocate expulsion of the U.S. military bases, curbs on multinational companies, and other left-wing causes. The principal target of Tanada and other speakers at the gathering was what they referred to as the "U.S.-Marcos dictatorship." Organizers of the group described it as "a nonviolent alternative to the CPP-ML and NDF." Approximately 15,000 persons attended the gathering. (*Link*, 4 December.)

Sri Lanka

Population. 15.6 million (estimate)
Party. Communist Party of Sri Lanka (CPSL)
Founded. 1943
Membership. 6,000 (estimate)
Secretary General. Kattorge P. Silva
Political Bureau. 14 members: K. P. Silva (secretary general), Pieter Keuneman (president), M. G. Mendis (trade union leader), A. Vaidyalingam (the only Tamil representative), H. G. S. Ratnaweera (former Education and Publications Bureau chairman), L. W. Panditha (trade union activist), D. W. Subasinghe, D. E. W. Gunasekara (foreign affairs expert), Jayetilleke de Silva (national organizer), J. A. K. Perera (trade union activist), Sarath Muttetuwegama (member of parliament), Peter Jayesekara (Friendship League coordinator), Leslie Gunawardene (university history professor), A. G. Jayasena
Central Committee. 50 members
Status. Legal
Last Congress. Eleventh, 26–30 March 1980, in Colombo
Last Election. 1977, 1.9 percent, 1 of 168 representatives
Auxiliary Organizations. Ceylon Federation of Trade Unions, Youth League, Women's Organization
Publications. *Aththa, Mawbima, Deshabimani, Forward* (journal)

In mid-1983 Sri Lanka suffered one of its worst outbreaks of communal violence since independence, and three leftist parties were banned for alleged direct involvement in it.

Early in the year before the ethnic violence escalated, the pro-Moscow CPSL and other parties opposing the conservative United National Party (UNP) government were concerned with the December 1982 referendum approving an extension of the parliament's term. Several of the parties claimed this action did not have the support of a majority of the people and unsuccessfully demanded a general election within the year.

In May, parliamentary by-elections were held in eighteen districts, and all the major parties competed. A poor showing by the UNP would not have threatened its overwhelming majority in parliament; in fact, President J. R. Jayewardene's party won fourteen of the seats. Former prime minister Sirimavo Bandaranaike's Sri Lanka Freedom Party (SLFP) won three, and the small People United Party took the other. Failing to win any seats were the CPSL, the Trotskyist Lanka Sama Samaja Party (LSSP), and the Marxist-Leninist Janatha Vimukthi Peramuna (JVP). Opposition spokesmen charged the government with illegal election tactics, but the leftists' failure to unite against the UNP undoubtedly contributed to the losses. The Marxist groups held discussions with each other and with the SLFP about electoral arrangements, but in the end most fielded their own individual candidates. (*FEER*, 19 May.) The by-elections also appeared to be a setback for the JVP, whose strength had been increasing in recent years.

Soon after the by-elections, the government faced the country's most severe communal rioting in decades. The deep-seated mistrust and rivalry between the Sinhalese majority and the

Tamil minority is a chronic problem. During the past few years, young Tamil extremists have carried out a terrorist campaign against the government in pursuit of their goal of a separate state. In July, Jayewardene was making plans for an all-party conference to discuss the growing terrorism when the killing of a dozen soldiers by insurgents on 23 July triggered widespread Sinhalese retaliation. Days of intense rioting left hundreds dead (mostly Tamil) and tens of thousands of Tamil refugees. Tamil properties and factories were also burned.

A week after the rioting began, the president proscribed the CPSL, the JVP, and a Trotskyist faction headed by V. Nanayakkara and closed their printing operations. CPSL leaders arrested included Secretary General K. P. Silva, H. G. S. Ratnaweera, L. W. Panditha, and D. E. W. Gunasekara. Leaders of the other two groups, including Rohan Wijeweera and Lionel Bopage of the JVP, reportedly went underground. (*FBIS*, 1 and 3 August.)

According to President Jayewardene, the three leftist parties had exploited the ethnic tension to cause violence as a cover for a government takeover. He charged that army supporters of the JVP were also involved. (*WP*, 8 August.) Other government officials alleged the involvement of a foreign power, widely assumed to be the Soviet Union. No conclusive proof appeared, at least in the case of the CPSL; CPSL members were released in September, and the ban on the party lifted.

In an interview with *Le Matin*, CPSL parliamentary deputy Sarath Muttetuwegama claimed the government had made his party a scapegoat and in turn alluded to collusion in the rioting by high government officials. According to Muttetuwegama, the CPSL regards the Tamils as a nation. "But we do not advocate the creation of a separate state. That would be completely contrary to the workers' interests." (*FBIS*, 18 August.) In early August, the government passed a constitutional amendment requiring parliamentary members to take an oath not to support separatism, and the CPSL member was one of those who did so.

After the security situation had improved, Jayewardene renewed a call for a multiparty meeting on the Tamil issue. Four parties were invited to an October meeting, but only the People United Party attended. Responding to the invitation, the CPSL said every effort should be made to convene a "conference of all recognized political parties without exceptions and preconditions." It also stated that the party did not have sufficient time for preparation because of the ban. (Ibid., 20 October.) The SLFP and LSSP were also absent. By the end of the year, however, due largely to mediation efforts by the Indian prime minister's special envoy, prospects appeared good for a conference that would include the major Tamil political parties as well as the leftist and democratic parties.

International activities were overshadowed by the domestic crisis, but the CPSL secretary general did attend the sixtieth anniversary celebrations of the USSR in December 1982 and the Karl Marx celebrations in East Berlin in April.

Barbara Reid
Earlysville, Virginia

Thailand

Population. 50.7 million
Party. Communist Party of Thailand (CPT)
Founded. 1942
Membership. 3,000 (estimate)
Secretary General. Unknown
Politburo. Unknown
Secretariat. Unknown
Central Committee. Unknown
Status. Illegal
Last Congress. Fourth, 1982
Last Election. Not applicable
Auxiliary Organizations. Unknown
Publications. None

The CPT continued to decline in 1983: the united front collapsed, cadres and leaders defected, government forces captured guerrilla bases, and China and Vietnam reduced their support. From the CPT's peak five years ago, when some 12,000 insurgents required the attention of tens of thousands of government troops and caused the deaths of about 500 civilians, soldiers, and officials each year, the number of insurgents had been reduced to 3,000 by year-end 1983.

The CPT was founded in 1942 by ethnic Chinese and slowly evolved into a rural movement with Thai membership but with Chinese-Thai leadership. In 1975, following the change of governments in Vietnam, Laos, and Kampuchea, Thai and U.S. insurgency experts had predicted that Thailand would be the next Southeast Asian nation to become communist controlled. Moreover, the repressive policies of the ultra-right-wing government that came to power in Thailand in 1976 caused several thousand university students to join the insurgents in the mountainous jungles of the kingdom. However, since 1980, communist insurgents and their supporters have defected en masse. The loss of support, when rural-based revolutionary movements have been

thriving in other parts of the world, stems from both internal and external conditions. Thailand's consistent and booming economic growth rate and the clear improvement in the living conditions of the rural Thai have undercut support for the party. In the past decade, per capita income has increased from $300 to $800 per year. Moreover, the governments of Prime Ministers Kriangsak Chamanan and Prem Tinsulanond have initiated a number of rural development projects, particularly in those areas where insurgency has been the greatest. More important, in 1977 the government began offering amnesty to insurgents who would defect from the communist cause. Some 8,000 insurgents took advantage of the amnesty program. The Thai government allocated a 140 million baht budget for defectors who desired to start a new life. The plan calls for the distribution of farmland to defectors, who are called *phu ruam pattana chat Thai* ("participants in Thai national development") instead of the more perjorative term "defector." The deaths of the country's top three counterinsurgency specialists in a tragic helicopter crash in June created a temporary setback for the government's program to encourage defectors. The three had negotiated a series of mass CPT defections that had undermined party structure in the northeast. At the end of the year, defectors and government officials expressed concern over the welfare of defectors as the resettlement projects bogged down in interagency rivalries.

Rivalries internal to the CPT also contributed to the demise of party strength. At the party's Fourth Congress (1982), a major schism centering on ideological differences became evident. The doctrinaire Maoist leadership posited that Thailand was "semifeudal" and "semicolonial," whereas, younger CPT leaders argued that Thailand was a "rapidly advancing capitalist" country —"semicolonial" and "semicapitalist." When the former view prevailed, many of the activists defected, including Udom Srisuwan, the chairman of the Coordinating Committee for Patriotic and Democratic Forces and a prominent Politburo member. The party was unable to heal the rift in 1983 or to fashion an essentially Thai road to revolution.

Counterinsurgency specialists in Thailand credited the demise of the CPT to the government's strategy of "politics over military." The strategy is part of Order no. 65/2525, decreed by Prime Minister Prem Tinsulanond in May 1982. The order calls for an end to corruption among officials, a pledge to rely on persuasion rather than combat in counterinsurgency strategy, and a far-reaching development program for the major poverty areas of the country. In describing his reasons for defecting, Udom Srisuwan stated that policy 65/2525 put the CPT on the defensive politically and militarily. He added that the causes for the CPT's defeat are "erroneous theory (dogmatism, formalism), political mistakes (wrong assessment of Thai society), military mistakes, and wrong organization (patriarchy, favoritism)." (*Matichon Sutsapda*, 23 October; *FBIS*, 27 October.) Udom Srisuwan also referred to the leadership's unwillingness to listen to the voice of the majority at the party's Fourth Congress.

External variables also contributed to the demise of the CPT. Vietnam cut off financial support to the party after being invaded by Chinese forces in 1978. China withheld funds after establishing diplomatic relations with Thailand in 1979. China now attaches greater weight to its relations with the government of Thailand than to its relations with the CPT. For example, China's support of Khmer resistance forces in Kam-

puchea requires the cooperation of Thai officials. In the northeast, refugees pouring into Thailand with horror stories of life under communist rule in Laos and Kampuchea undermined much of the support Thais might have given to communist insurgents in their own country. Kampuchea's and Laos's current inaccessibility has cut Thai insurgents in the northeast off from their previous sanctuary and source of supplies.

In October, the Thai government proclaimed a "total victory" over the CPT. The Internal Security Operation Command (ISOC), the principal counterinsurgency agency of the government, reduced the number of "most sensitive zones" from 12 to 4 provinces. The ISOC classifies the strength of communist insurgency throughout the country into four levels, depending on the degree of activity. The 4 provinces where communist insurgency remains most active are Nan and Mukdahan in the north and Surat Thani and Nakhon Sri Thammarat in the south. Areas where the degree of communist activities was ranked at the second level were reduced from 22 to 19 provinces, while areas in the third degree increased from 16 to 26 provinces. Areas with the least activity (the fourth degree) increased from 18 to 20 provinces.

Despite the official declaration of victory, not all Thai government officials were sanguine about the status of the CPT in 1983. One classified document allegedly written by CPT leaders and published in the *Nation Review* (10 August) called on party cadres to pay more attention to political, economic, and other forms of struggle in both rural and urban areas. In the past, the CPT has not been involved significantly in urban political and economic struggles. Some fear that the large number of defectors in Bangkok, if still committed to the revolutionary aims of the party, could become the nucleus of an urban guerrilla strategy. The same document called on party operatives to step up efforts to recruit members among workers. The document reaffirms that the "composition and powers of capitalists in this country have grown considerably over the past years." (*FBIS*, 11 August.)

No evidence was presented by government officials to indicate that such an urban strategy was actually being carried out or that defectors were involved in insurgency activities. Army Commander in Chief Arthit Kamlangek stated: "Now that the Communist returnees have trusted us and surrendered, we should not be too suspicious. Be watchful, not doubtful." (*Asiaweek*, 8 April.)

As the CPT lost influence in the north, party leaders attempted to seek support from the stronger Burmese Communist Party (BCP), which has an estimated 15,000–20,000 armed guerrillas. However, senior army officials in Bangkok stated that the prospect of joint CPT and BCP operations along the Thai-Burmese border is remote. The BCP itself poses no direct threat to Thailand's security, although it could serve as an indirect threat by providing aid to the declining CPT.

In 1978, the Thai government rated the north as a "most sensitive zone" because of the high level of CPT activity. In 1983, however, only some 500 insurgents were active in the north, and they were virtually cut off from outside aid. The security situation in Chiang Mai province, for example, has improved so much that the province dropped from "security risk level 2" to "security risk level 3." The only northern province remaining at the sensitive "level 1" is Nan on the Laotian border, where small groups of CPT guerrillas still attack villages and government development projects. The insurgency in Nan was significantly undermined when more than 5,000 communist guerrillas and their sympathizers surrendered to the authorities on 22 December (*NYT*, 22 December).

In the northeast, Thai security officials reported the emergence (or re-emergence) of an insurgent group called the Green Star Movement (named after the color of the star on the caps of the insurgents). Thai security officials believe that the group is pro-Soviet, is at the recruitment stage, and has attracted about 200 guerrillas. Although the government of Vietnam denies any involvement with the group, Thai authorities claim that the Green Star Movement is being trained in Laos with support from the 45,000 Vietnamese troops stationed there.

The Green Star Movement may consist of remnants of the Pak Mai (New party), which split from the CPT in 1979. Thus far, there is little concrete evidence about the identity of the members of the group, their political stance, or their weaponry. One report theorized that the new movement replaced a red star with a green star to create a fresh image following the failure of CPT operatives to expand influence in the northeast. An estimated 300–400 communist guerrillas now operate in the northeast.

A deputy leader of Pak Mai reported in November that Soviet support for the underground party included study tours in the Soviet Union for Pak Mai leaders and ten military trucks given through Laotian authorities. He also disclosed that the party, whose headquarters and "forward command" are in Vientiane and Khveng Khammouane, Laos, respectively, had set up three operational zones in Thai border provinces covering Chiang Rai in the north to Ubon Ratchathani in the northeast. (*Nation Review*, 8 November; *FBIS*, 8 November.)

In the south, the Thai government's amnesty and "hearts and minds" approach proved successful throughout the year as insurgents continued to surrender to the authorities. The Thai military had been carrying out operations aimed at flushing out insurgents for over two years. These military operations are followed by political teams, who provide political education and military protection for villagers. The mass surrender of 680 bandits and communist insurgents in an official ceremony in Pattani province on 2 November was presided over by Gen. Arthit Kamlangek. The Thai state radio announced that 471 Muslim separatists, 165 communist insurgents, and 44 members of the Communist Party of Malaya from five southern provinces surrendered, making it the largest defection in the southern region. The defectors were promised land and money to build homes. Approximately 1,700 unreconstructed insurgents are said to be active in the southern provinces of the country.

Thai officials saw Soviet influence in a new threatening light because of the Soviet Union's position in the former Indochinese states. In October, Foreign Minister Sitthi Sawetsila called on the United States and Thailand's Association of Southeast Asian Nations allies to maintain the "larger balance of power" along the strategic ring from the Persian Gulf through the Southeast Asian straits to Japan in the wake of the Soviet military buildup in the region. In return for its support for the three former Indochinese regimes, he said, the Soviet Union has gained access to several military facilities in Vietnam, in particular Cam Ranh Bay, where Moscow has established a facility with improved communications and intelligence collection capabilities to support operations in the South China Sea and the Pacific and Indian oceans. The foreign minister said that with the presence of about 250,000 Vietnamese troops in Laos and Kampuchea,

Thailand is forced to share more than two thousand kilometers of border with Vietnam. Since 1979, he said, the Soviet Union has channeled more than $2 billion of military aid into the three Indochinese countries, where about 2,500 Soviet military advisers are stationed. (*Nation Review*, 7 October; *FBIS*, 12 October.)

In September, a total of 33 Soviet officials left Bangkok. The officials were allegedly connected with espionage activities and were known to be agents of the KGB, the Soviet state security organization. These officials had been attached to the Soviet embassy, assigned to the Soviet trade mission, or had held positions in Aeroflot. The agents left Bangkok to avoid being declared persona non grata by the Thai government. The Soviet Union did not want a repetition of the incident involving Viktor Baryshev, a Soviet trade official who in May had been caught taking documents from a Thai agent. These incidents, in addition to the downing of Korean Air Lines flight 007, in which Thai passengers were killed, exacerbated relations between Thailand and the Soviet Union.

Clark D. Neher
Northern Illinois University

Vietnam

Population. 57 million (1983 estimate)
Party. Vietnamese Communist Party (Dang Cong San Viet Nam; VCP)
Founded. 1930 (as Indochinese Communist Party)
Membership. 1,727,784 (March 1982)
Chairman. Vacant (since death of Ho Chi Minh)
Secretary General. Le Duan
Politburo. 13 full members: Le Duan, Truong Chinh (president, Council of State), Pham Van Dong (premier), Pham Hung, Le Duc Tho, Sen. Gen. Van Tien Dung (defense minister), Sen. Gen. Chu Huy Man (vice-president, Council of State), To Huu, Vo Chi Cong, Vo Van Kiet, Do Muoi, Le Duc Anh, Nguyen Duc Tam; 2 alternate members: Nguyen Co Thach (foreign minister), Dong Sy Nguyen
Secretariat. 10 members: Le Duan, Le Duc Tho, Vo Chi Cong, Nguyen Duc Tam, Nguyen Lam, Le Quang Dao, Hoang Tung, Nguyen Thanh Binh, Tran Kien, Tran Xuan Bach
Central Committee. 116 full and 36 alternate members
Status. Ruling party
Last Congress. Fifth, 27–31 March 1982, in Hanoi
Last Election. 1981, for Seventh National Assembly, 97.9 percent, 496 of 538, with all candidates VCP approved
Auxiliary Organizations. Fatherland Front, Huynh Tan Phat, president; Ho Chi Minh Communist Youth Union, Dang Quoc Bao, secretary general
Publications. *Nhan Dan* (The people), VCP daily; *Tap Chi Cong San* (Communist review), VCP theoretical monthly; *Quan Doi Nhan Dan* (People's Army), army newspaper

Vietnamese society appeared to experience somewhat less trauma in 1983 than in recent years. Food production was up, and some shortages of consumer goods eased slightly. Outside observers argued over probable trends. All agreed that socioeconomic conditions had tended downward since the end of the Vietnam war in 1975. Some held they had finally reversed direction in 1983 and had started moving upwards; others maintained that the decline had been halted but the upturn had not yet begun. In any event, it appeared that for the first time in nearly a decade the people of Vietnam did not end a year in worse condition than they began it. This relatively encouraging assessment did not extend to the VCP itself. For the most part, 1983 was another beleaguered year for the party.

Leadership and Party Organization. No significant change in the top party leadership occurred during 1983, either in personnel or in terms of the basic operational principle of collective leadership with Le Duan as "first among equals" of the "inner circle" (the other four being Truong Chinh, Pham Hung, Pham Van Dong, and Le Duc Tho). This small group of absolute rulers, of course, grew a year older. Its average age was now 74; the average age of the Politburo was about 72. Le Duan again went to Moscow (in June) for "a rest," but by all evidence both he and the other top figures were in good physical condition for their age.

In the never-ending factional infighting that marks the Hanoi scene, the struggle during the year appeared to be mainly between the ideologues and the pragmatists. The pendulum swung away from the pragmatists, who have tended to be pre-eminent in the past several years, back to the ideologues. The tone of the directives coming out of the Fourth Plenum (18–23 June) seemed to indicate that the ideologues were again in the ascendancy. The plenum's political report, for instance, spoke of the preceding few years as being marked by "delay" in collectivizing southern agriculture and of general "laxity" in the drive to create a full-scale collectivist economy for all of Vietnam. This delay and laxity, it suggested, were the cause of Vietnam's present socioeconomic difficulties. Such, of course, is the ideological faction's standard position; the pragmatists contend that overzealous efforts to ram through immediate establishment of a collectivist economy, especially the decision to collectivize

southern agriculture quickly, were the original causes of the socioeconomic decline that began soon after the war ended. Ironically, it appears that the gathering strength of the ideologues is traceable to the success of the pragmatist solution. The October 1982 rice crop was the best on record and resulted in part from a lessening of central controls on agriculture, as the pragmatists had predicted. But success in the face of (or due to) minimal party involvement raises the specter of an irrelevant party and thus rearms the ideologues as defenders of party jobholders and party perquisites.

The Fourth Plenum issued a sober communiqué that said Vietnam remained locked in a "very arduous, complex, and fierce struggle between socialist and capitalist ways." Most of the plenum was devoted to "organizational"—that is, administrative—problems and to devising ideological explanations for Vietnam's present economic condition. The plenum seemed in agreement that the central problem was economic stagnation and that the major causes were China's "multifaceted long-term war of economic sabotage" and ineffectual party cadres (see below). Most of the directives that emerged dealt with domestic trade and production problems. The communiqué also referred to Vietnam's "internationalist duties in Kampuchea," but indicated no new strategic, diplomatic, or administrative change of direction. Tass termed the plenum "a routine affair," which it was.

In terms of high-level party politics, probably the most significant development of the year, certainly the most interesting, was the Ho Chi Minh City Municipal Party Congress (7–11 November), at which certain issues came to a head.

The root of the trouble was the North-Center-South geographic regionalism that has cursed all twentieth-century Vietnamese political movements. The perceptions, self-images, and contentions involved here are more or less the same as the north-south divisions found in most larger societies; the three-way split in Vietnam merely complicates matters. During 1983, the strain between the party apparat in the South and the party center in Hanoi increased. Some of it was due to the usual factional infighting and the politics of entourage, which of course divided the center itself. Some was due to the center's view that the party leadership in the south had been touched by the southern "yellow wind," the softer influences of southern living as compared to the more spartan North, which produced sloth and casual administrative practices if not outright corruption. Party leaders in the South claimed Hanoi simply did not understand southern ways.

A doctrinal dimension involving economic problem solving also divided the Politburo. This was not simply a North-South issue. For several years, party officials in the South had been experimenting with new methods of increasing agricultural production and improving domestic trade, chiefly incentives and initiative-encouraging techniques. While they could be justified ideologically, having been drawn from neo-Marxist examples in Eastern Europe, the fundamentalists at the center disliked them. Nevertheless the experiments did work better than previous methods and were tolerated for a period. But their very success triggered the showdown at the Ho Chi Minh City Congress. The attack by party organs in Hanoi on southern party leadership, which began early in the year, dealt with administrative shortcomings and the tendency of party leaders in the South to ignore Politburo instructions, but clearly the truly important criticism was the erroneous ideological approach—it was not enough to solve the country's economic problems, they must be solved in ideologically correct ways.

Le Duan attended the Ho Chi Minh City meeting, an unusual development in itself, as did Pham Hung, the leading "southerner" in the Politburo, and Vo Van Kiet, Vietnam's economic development czar and former secretary of the Ho Chi Minh City Municipal Party Central Committee. Since all three have extensive southern connections, they would be the disciplinarians sent to reassert Politburo authority. The action was directed chiefly against Nguyen Van Linh and Mai Chi Tho, the top southern leaders. Changes in southern methods, as well as possible changes in personnel, resulting from the Ho Chi Minh City Municipal Congress, if any, will surface gradually throughout 1984.

Hanoi held the other major municipal-level party congress of the year on 16–21 June. It was attended by some 600 delegates representing 150,000 party members in the city. Le Van Luong was elected secretary general, along with a 55-member Central Committee. Most major Politburo figures, including Le Duan, attended. The extensive public attention given to a city-level party meeting suggested a new outbreak of factional infighting at the party leadership level,

probably involving improvement of the economy and relations with China. Le Duan's speech concerned these two topics as well as his favorite—"collective mastery," a code phrase meaning ensuring the centrality of the party in all things.

Domestic Party Affairs. No event on the party's calendar during 1983 was comparable to the previous year's Fifth Congress. Much of the day-to-day party activity during the year was devoted to developing and implementing the many instructions that came out of that congress.

The year began with a meeting of party organizational cadres, attended by some 300 top personnel. Nguyen Duc Tam, chief of the Central Committee Organizational Department, announced plans for the newest round of the never-ending internal party rectification program, which is part purge, part reorganization, and part moral exhortation. Five programs were mapped out, and these largely consumed the attention of party cadres and the rank and file throughout the year. The five were (1) the weeding out and expulsion of unqualified persons; (2) a series of local level party congresses "to raise the sense of organization and discipline among cadres and members"; (3) a round of new training and retraining programs for cadres with a view to "building a pure and solid corps of party cadres"; (4) a revamping of party organization at all levels, largely a consolidation effort in which functions are combined in the name of efficiency; and (5) a strengthening of the party administrative system at the top by applying the principle of the dictatorship of the proletariat and at the lower levels by tightening the control and inspection mechanism (*Nhan Dan*, 15 March). Little of this was new.

Much of the year was given over to intensive emulation campaigns in the form of "second-stage" party congresses. These follow-ons to the Fifth Party Congress were designed to motivate members to continue implementing the various instructions that emerged from the congress or to bolster interest where necessary. Focus at the sessions was heavily, if not entirely, economic. Every provincial central committee staged a congress; many of these were attended by Politburo members.

In a further effort to increase its internal control, this one party-wide, the Politburo created a new mechanism in September, apparently as a new Central Committee department. Called the

Party Central Organ Internal Affairs Department (Dang Bo Khoi Co Quan Noi Chi Chinh Truong Uong), it is run by a veteran party figure from the south, Vo Chi Cong. Press references did not make clear the department's precise mission. The monitoring of internal party affairs is now apparently divided between the Central Committee's Internal Affairs Department and the new department; the former deals with personal behavior or individual senior cadres and officials, and the latter monitors the activities and performance of upper-level party institutions. The presence of Cong as its chief executive suggests that the new department may be concerned chiefly with monitoring party organs in the South.

The party's internal training system was reorganized during the year in accordance with a 2 January Central Committee order restructuring the party school system. Under the new arrangement, certain intermediate and specialized party schools were abolished or consolidated into other schools. The highest, most prestigious school remains the Nguyen Ai Quoc Central Party School in Hanoi. Newly created, as an integral part of it, are three additional "center" schools: the Nguyen Ai Quoc Party School no. 1 in Hanoi, no. 2 in Ho Chi Minh City, and no. 3 in Da Nang. These are directly supervised by the Secretariat and offer year-round coursework. Under them is a system of subordinate party schools in provincial capitals and in some district capitals and other towns. These are under the control of their respective party central committees and offer mostly short-term, ad hoc courses.

The underlying objective in the overhaul of the party's educational system, as well as the inspection and control mechanisms introduced during the year, is to improve the overall quality of party cadres. "We must build a pure and solid cadre corps," said a *Nhan Dan* editorial. No activity could be more important to the VCP. Its cadre corps is the central dynamic in its entire governing system and largely accounts for the party's various successes over the years, including its victory in the Vietnam war. The party in the future will stand or fall on what the cadre system becomes.

Two overriding concerns with respect to the party cadre, the so-called negative cadre phenomena, although not new, have assumed new importance since the end of the Vietnam war. Both are regarded as nearly intractable and have been the subject of endless official statements and

uncounted hours of labor over the years. Both to date have defied solution.

The first has to do with cadre performance. It is assessed variously, by the leadership in Hanoi, by the cadres themselves, and by the onlooking Vietnamese population. However it is perceived, it is inadequate. To the Politburo, the problem is cadre indiscipline—a failure by cadres, for whatever reason, to meet the demands of the leadership as set down in basic party directives. To the cadres themselves, recipients of these directives, the failure to perform as ordered is due to the impossibility of the demands placed on them, including no small amount of foolish, unfulfillable orders. Rank-and-file Vietnamese, not fully aware of these crosscurrents, simply see party cadres as having lost their long-standing image of omnipotence and their reputation for infallibility. They are not solving the existing economic and other problems and have not fulfilled Ho Chi Minh's promise to make postwar Vietnam "ten times as beautiful."

The second negative cadre phenomenon is the less than exemplary behavior of the party cadre, who is expected at all times to be a model of social deportment, neither succumbing to life's many temptations nor coping with life's many problems in anything but a doctrinally correct manner. While the earlier wartime cadres probably were never the superhuman figures of the official portrayals, there is no doubt that their performance throughout the war was generally consistently high. There is also no doubt that cadre quality grievously declined after 1975.

Most current cadre sins and shortcomings involve economic behavior that elsewhere might be explained away as a victimless crime by one economically beset. A *Nhan Dan* editorial described it as "cadres engaged in smuggling, cadres in collusion with decadent business elements, cadres engaged in exploitation in various forms, cadres illegally earning a living." While party by-laws clearly state (Art. 1) that "party members do not exploit others . . . and no one who does can be qualified as a member," there is no precise definition of "exploitation." It does not appear that the cadres involved consider themselves stigmatized in the manner they would be if they engaged in embezzlement or outright corruption; rather they rationalize their actions as merely trying to cope with personal economic problems, which would not be necessary if the party could end the country's economic malaise.

An illustration of the conflicting views of cadre behavior can be found in the Central Committee campaign, launched in midyear, against continued ownership of land by party cadres in the South. *Nhan Dan* (2 May) reported that 22 percent of all cadres in the South (at the district level or higher) still held title to land "for exploitive purposes." Their guilt was only made more apparent by "backward and reactionary explanations such as 'The land belonged to my ancestors.'" For the cadres involved, morality becomes a tug of war between cultural heritage and revolutionary ethics.

While blame for party failures during the year was heaped entirely on the cadres and none of it was assumed by the Politburo, the fact is that many instructions to cadres are not obeyed because they are unobeyable. The cadre's fate for the most part is to stand as mute whipping boy since the organs of assessment are monopolized by the center.

Party recruitment during the year focused on the young, specifically on the Ho Chi Minh Youth Union. Party documents said that in the four-year recruiting campaign that ran from 1979 to the end of 1982, ten times as many Youth Union members were admitted as in the previous four-year period. Some 85 percent of the new party members in 1983 came out of Youth Union ranks.

The last official tabulation of party strength came at the Fifth Congress, when membership was set at about 1.7 million. During the remainder of 1982, an additional 60,000 were admitted, and an estimated 50,000 new members were added in 1983. These were recruited unevenly in geographic terms; party journals reported that many grass-roots level units, especially in the South, recruited few or no new members. At the same time, significant numbers of party personnel have been expelled each year through the mechanism of not issuing them current party cards. In recent years, this has ranged from 2 to 5 percent of the total membership. It appears therefore that the size of the party did not increase appreciably during 1983.

Auxiliary and Front Organizations. The Second Congress of the Vietnam Fatherland Front, the party's omnibus mass organization, convened in Hanoi on 12 May for a routine meeting. It was chaired by outgoing president Hoang Quoc Viet and attended by some 500 delegates representing member-organizations. Pham Van Dong delivered the keynote address. The two-day session consisted of numerous speeches by high-level state and party officials. Huynh Tan Phat, a major party figure in the South during the Vietnam war, was elected the organization's new president.

The Ho Chi Minh Youth Union's Central Committee's Sixth Plenum in August proved to be a routine meeting largely devoted to what were called organizational and ideological tasks.

International Views, Positions, and Policies. The party's external relations, policies, and day-to-day activities during the year were monopolized by the ever more intimate association with the USSR, the continuing cold war with China, and the stalemate in Kampuchea.

Vietnam's close relationship with the USSR is inadvertent rather than deliberate, the result of leadership blunders that made the country dependent on Moscow for food, other material necessities, and military hardware. While improved agricultural performance reduced if not eliminated the need for Soviet food shipments, dependency continued for oil, chemical fertilizers, and other commodities and for military equipment and supplies. Vietnam in effect remained on the international socialist dole for another year.

Late in the year, Vietnam and the USSR announced far-reaching plans for the joint economic development of Vietnam, the full scope of which was not clear at year's end. On 31 October, the two sides signed a Long-Term Agreement on Economic Development and Scientific Cooperation. It was in effect the initial draft of the next Vietnamese five-year plan, or at least the plant development aspects of the plan. The agreement seeks to establish "priority areas" for all developmental work. The principal ones are (1) developing and mechanizing Vietnamese agriculture; (2) fostering industrial support of agriculture (with increased steel production and machine tool manufacture capacity); (3) increasing energy and fuel production; (4) expanding the transportation and communication sectors (more rolling stock, improved maintenance); (5) increasing production of chemical fertilizers, and (6) increasing exports, primarily to the USSR (based on "mutually beneficial compensation for the USSR," i.e., meeting Soviet needs more closely). There was no indication in the document of the costs involved, which must be borne almost entirely by the USSR, but such an ambitious undertaking, involving massive plant investment, certainly will range in the tens of billions of dollars.

Throughout the year, Hanoi fully embraced the USSR's international position. A typical gesture was the 2 July Central Committee statement (also issued by the Council of State and Council of Ministers) supporting the final communiqué of the Warsaw Treaty summit meeting, which the Vietnamese statement endorsed without reservation.

The only other country in the socialist world to which Vietnam exhibited what might be called public warmth during the year was Cuba.

Relations with China remained frozen throughout 1983, with a great deal of verbal abuse hurled in both directions. Hanoi continued to blame Beijing for the continued suffering in Kampuchea and for conducting what it called a "multifaceted war of sabotage" against Vietnam. Periodically it listed astronomical statistics on the number of shellings, incursions, and other Chinese-initiated border incidents, and China replied in kind. Late in the year, there was a spate of foreign press speculation that Vietnam had quietly embarked on a campaign to establish a limited rapprochement with China.

The war in Kampuchea slogged along for another year with no significant progress toward Vietnam's two major objectives: pacifying the countryside by driving the Coalition Government of Democratic Kampuchea forces into the Cardamom mountains and making the People's Republic of Kampuchea government in Phnom Penh (under Heng Samrin) a viable entity.

The seventh conference of the foreign ministers of Vietnam, Laos, and Kampuchea met in Phnom Penh 19–20 July and issued a five-point statement that in effect reiterated their public stance on the nature of the war in Kampuchea and the outcome acceptable to them. Essentially it offered to "open a dialogue" with the Association of Southeast Asian Nations (but not China), but indicated no willingness on Hanoi's part to compromise in creating a new governing system in Kampuchea.

Biography. *Truong Chinh.* Throughout his party career, Truong Chinh has sought the role of scene shifter, highest-level adviser, and general *éminence grise.* His ventures into positions of operational command have generally been unsuccessful. Exactly how influential he has been as backstage manipulator is impossible to determine with any precision. He also is generally considered to be chief party theoretician, if anyone can claim that title. However, with few exceptions, his writings are restatements of existing dogma and break no doctrinal ground.

Because his alias or "revolutionary name" *truong chinh* ("long march") is an obvious reference to the heroic 1930s episode in Chinese communist history, he has been considered by outsiders to be pro-Chinese, a belief reinforced by the clear Chinese influences in his early writings. In terms of overt behavior over the years, however, Truong Chinh has been no more sympathetic to China than was Ho Chi Minh or any other early party figure.

Truong Chinh's contribution, for which he is held in high regard by older party members and does deserve credit, was to hold the party together during the difficult 1930s, when Ho had vanished from the scene and Comintern orders were to cooperate with the hated *colon* in the name of the united front.

Truong Chinh was born (as Dang Xuan Khu) in 1908 in what was then Nam Dinh province (now part of Nam Ha province) into a village gentry family. His father was a schoolteacher. He was educated at Lycée Albert Sarraut in Hanoi, the most prestigious of all French-operated secondary schools in Vietnam at the time, and later attended a commercial college. He participated in the activities of revolutionary organizations in Vietnam and China in the late 1920s and was one of the founding members of the Indochinese Communist Party in 1930. He was jailed by the French in the early 1930s, released under the Popular Front amnesty, and then went to China. He became secretary general of the party in the revival of activities in 1940 when the party began operating out of Kuangxi province in China. He served in that position throughout the Viet Minh war.

In 1956, Truong Chinh was ousted from the secretary general's post because of the party's failure in implementing the agricultural collectivization program, which resulted in peasant uprisings and much harsh repression. However, he maintained his other party posts, and his removal was more of a political maneuver than a disgrace.

Truong Chinh's political base within the factional system of the party is the National Assembly, and his constituency is drawn from mass organizations, principally the Fatherland Front.

His major works are *The Resistance Will Win* and *The August Revolution* (both 1946).

Douglas Pike
University of California at Berkeley

EASTERN EUROPE AND THE SOVIET UNION

Introduction

The death of Yuri Andropov on 9 February 1984 gave to the event-laden year of 1983 a stamp of inconclusiveness. Its essential characteristic was the discrepancy between the aims and the results of Andropov's performance at both the domestic and the foreign policy levels. Complementing each other, two noted American Kremlinologists opined that there was "no Andropov era" and that he "may be remembered best for what he didn't do." And yet Andropov did accomplish a certain number of things, nationally and internationally, of more than fleeting importance.

Soviet Union. The agenda of Andropov's exceptionally brief tenure was crowded from 12 November 1982, the day he replaced Leonid Brezhnev as general secretary of the Communist Party of the Soviet Union (CPSU). He wanted above all to replace the social flabbiness, economic inefficiency, and public apathy of the last years of Brezhnev's rule by a new style and substance of governance that would galvanize the country and impress the world. It soon became evident, however, that contrary to the earliest, optimistic expectations, Andropov was not a "closet liberal" bent on opening and reforming Soviet society and pursuing genuine détente with the West, but a ruthless and determined Leninist who wanted to discipline society and make the Soviet Union fit to win the global struggle against imperialism headed by the United States.

Depending on the field of application, Andropov's activism bore uneven fruits. (His relentless dynamism was particularly remarkable since his debilitating and in the end fatal kidney disease began to handicap him as early as February 1983, only three months after he succeeded Brezhnev.) Andropov's longest professional experience was as head of the Committee for State Security (KGB), whose head he became in May 1967 on Brezhnev's initiative. The new KGB under Andropov became the "eyes of the Kremlin" (the title of a well-informed and perceptive article published in *Time*, 14 February 1983), and its numerous and well-trained agents performed various duties at home and abroad. But the KGB emblem—sword and shield of the party—indicated that the organization had a much loftier function than that of an intelligence-gathering and spy/counterspy institution. When in his famous speech before the CPSU Central Committee on 22 November 1982, Andropov extolled the Soviet people's "utter devotion to the ideas of Marxism-Leninism, their deepest respect and love for their own party, a high degree of organization, endurance, and confidence in their strength," he unmistakably arrogated to himself the role of the guardian of the CPSU's ideological purity. He succeeded (not without resistance) in placing his loyalists in key KGB, militia, party, and state administration posts. At the June 1983 meeting of the Central Committee, Andropov invoked the "subversive imperialist propaganda both in the world arena and inside our country" and then insisted on the systematization of the CPSU's counterpropaganda in a "battle for the hearts and minds of the billions of people on this planet . . . the future of mankind depending to a large extent on the outcome of this ideological struggle." Konstantin Chernenko, Andropov's rival for Brezhnev's position, addressed the same plenum along identical lines. He assailed practically every group in Soviet society (branches of the USSR Academy of Sciences, other research institutions, especially in the field of social sciences, the press, television, radio, filmmakers, musical performers, and youth in general) for not adequately implementing the party line. Reminding the audience of the "Leninist principle that ideological work is the business of the entire party," Chernenko emphasized the necessity of refining the "technology" of ideological work. The Andropov-inspired hardening of the ideological struggle was reflected in a tough speech made on 5 November by Grigory Romanov, Politburo member and Central Committee secretary, at the solemn meeting devoted to the sixty-sixth anniversary of the October Revolution at the Kremlin's Palace of Congresses.

The insistence on ideological purity and militancy went hand in hand with a process of partial re-Stalinization of the Soviet regime. Without assuming the terrorist aspects of Stalin's rule, Andropov's repression consisted of a reintroduction of judicial practices reminiscent of the "monster trials" of the Stalin era; of systematic persecution of dissidents and other advocates of human rights, including the enhanced use of psychiatric asylums for political purposes; of clearly anti-Semitic emigration policies; and last but not least, of official rehabilitation of Stalin, which tended to overshadow Khrushchev's revelations about Stalin's crimes, which in the late 1950s and early 1960s had a traumatic impact on world opinion and on many communists in the Soviet Union.

Andropov's novel policies tending to KGBize Soviet society and to infuse into it a new ideological fervor and behavioral discipline, including his attempts to make the regime more responsive to the plight of the popular base, will leave marks on Soviet domestic history despite the shortness of his reign. The question remains, however, of the application and continuity of his endeavors under his successor(s).

With regard to the state of the economy he inherited from Brezhnev, Andropov appeared a candid, even brutal, critic and the corrector of evil practices. In his 22 November speech, he denounced, among other things, the slow growth rate of labor productivity; "shoddy work, inactivity, and irresponsibility" in many enterprises; and interruptions in the supply of some food products. Admitting that he did not have remedies for the problems afflicting the economy, he still offered pointers for change. The workers' remuneration, official status, and moral prestige should be improved at the factory level, a resolute struggle against mismanagement and wastefulness should be waged, the independence of amalgamations, enterprises, and collective and state farms should be extended, and new technology and work methods should be advanced. All this sounded both promising and vague, but it was such a contrast to the empty official terminology and the corrupt economic practices of the last years of Brezhnev's era that Andropov's approach attracted immediate interest and caused inflated expectations.

Indeed, early in 1983, spectacular police crackdowns hit absentee workers and employees as well as alcoholics in factories, and the KGB Lefortovo prison received as new inmates former executives, ranking militia officers and procurators, customs officers, party functionaries, and black marketeers. Store managers who diverted for fraudulent purposes hard-to-find products and foreign trade officials caught accepting bribes or opening Swiss bank accounts were executed. All this had a sobering influence. According to Marshall I. Goldman, a leading U.S. expert on the Soviet economy, productivity and production rose sharply, and the output of most products improved measurably in 1983. By the middle of the year, however, the essential question of the nature of Andropov's economic innovations was resolved in a way that deeply disappointed experts and people who expected structural reforms of the Soviet economy. The target of resolutions passed by the Politburo and the Supreme Soviet between mid-July and early August relating to the rights of enterprises and labor discipline was the improvement of economic mechanisms but not their reform. Innovations that may expand the rights of individual enterprises with respect to planning and economic activity had a strictly experimental and geographically limited character. Ernst Kux, a noted Swiss Kremlinologist, said of Andropov's handling of the economy: "It has nothing whatever to do with liberalization, decentralization, the requirements of the market and of modern management or the expansion of private-sector production and private consumption . . . It is far more reminiscent of Stalin's method of achieving discipline by intimidation. Andropov has not the slightest intention of meddling with the principle of party control over the economy and its central planning and controls, for it is the interplay of these that ensures that power stays in the Kremlin. All he is aiming to do is to make the existing system more efficient by eliminating its rigidities, revivifying it, and relieving it of some of the immobilizing burden of bureaucracy."

The hybrid character of Andropov's economic initiatives was apparent in other actions. On the one hand, by the combined effect of crackdowns against the lower strata of producers and the purge of some 20 percent of local party chiefs, he re-established to a certain degree and for the time being both labor discipline and economic production. On the other hand, as a shrewd political maneuverer, he refrained from initiating and trying to implement structural changes that might negatively affect the vested interests of the military, central planning, and heavy industry establishments (the support of top-ranking military officers was a key factor in his political infighting). Moreover, even if he wanted to go beyond the limits of political prudence, his declining health would have commanded otherwise. He left therefore an ambiguous legacy to his heir, Chernenko, once the mainstay of Brezhnev's economics against which Andropov initially rebelled. The title of a column by Marshall Goldman in the *New York Times* (14 February 1984) contains a legitimate question: "Chernenkonomics—Back to Stagnation?"

Foreign policy was the third field in which Yuri Andropov left an inconclusive and perplexing record. A reading of his speeches, public statements, and interviews regarding world affairs invariably suggests relations with the United States were uppermost in his mind. Henry Kissinger's words in a memorandum prepared for Richard Nixon prior to a summit meeting with Leonid Brezhnev in 1973 appear remarkably applicable ten years later to Andropov's motivations and policies: "Like all Soviet postwar leaders, Brezhnev [read Andropov] sees the US at once as rival, mortal threat, model, source of assistance and partner in physical survival. These conflicting impulses make the motivations of Brezhnev's policy toward us ambivalent. On the one hand, he no doubt wants to go down in history as the leader who brought peace and a better life to Russia. This requires conciliatory and cooperative policies toward us. Yet, he remains a convinced Communist who sees politics as a struggle with an ultimate winner: he intends the Soviet Union to be that winner. His recurrent efforts to draw us into condominium-type arrangements—most notably his proposal for a nuclear non-aggression pact—are intended both to safeguard peace and to undermine our alliances and other associations."

This dual interest in preserving peace and in maintaining and extending communist domination, an interest shared by Brezhnev and Andropov alike, was of a pure Leninist vintage. There was a difference, however, between the two leaders about the most effective way of avoiding war while advancing the interests of the Soviet Union and of the CPSU-led part of the international communist movement. Intellectually sharper than Brezhnev, especially during his last years, Andropov, the man in a hurry, believed that he had found the right formula for waging the anti-imperialist struggle. While maintaining the threatening presence of the Red Army and supplementing it with sophisticated nuclear weaponry, Andropov played the card of peace, arms control negotiations, and ultimately of universal disarmament with a skill that at first appeared consummate. Almost all Western experts agree that the military might of the Soviet Union serves as a backdrop for a gigantic political and psychological operation of intimidating, paralyzing, and ultimately dividing the Western alliance. One may assume that one of Andropov's basic convictions was that the combination of military pre-eminence, skill in psychological warfare, and the contribution of KGB specialists in above- and underground assignments around the world, will decisively affect the global correlation of forces in favor of the Soviet Union. As it happened, international events did not unfold according to Soviet expectations.

During 1983, the confrontation between the two superpowers reached a level of hostility never attained under Leonid Brezhnev and the Nixon, Ford, and Carter administrations. But it was not a uniform and even process. It corresponded instead to the Kissinger formula of the Soviets' viewing the United States as "rival, mortal threat, model, source of assistance and partner in physical survival." In 1983, relations between the two powers fell into these five distinct categories of behavior. The cooperative high was reached during the summer, following the 28 July decision to lift the U.S. grain embargo and the readiness of both sides to sign a new five-year grain agreement. Prospects for increased industrial trade also brightened, prompting the chief U.S. trade negotiator to express hopes of further moves to "improve business relations, political relations, diplomatic relations across the board." This superoptimism was soon shattered, and a new bout of hostile acts and mutual recriminations ensued. The central element in the new East-West confrontation was NATO's deployment, scheduled for early December, of new intermediate-range nuclear missiles. The centrality of that issue should be viewed within the context of other notable occurrences in different parts of the world, some connected with the U.S. policies, others happening independently. Their impact on Soviet-U.S. relations was considerable, and they left their imprint on Yuri Andropov's record in foreign affairs.

The prevention of the deployment of intermediate-range nuclear missiles in Western Europe was from the outset the dominating item on the agenda of Andropov's foreign policy. All the means of Soviet diplomacy and propaganda were used to influence Western European governments and public opinion. The decision of these governments to favor the deployment, despite or perhaps because of Soviet pressure, reflected the disposition of the popular majority and signified a defeat for the Kremlin. The Soviet suspension of arms control talks in Geneva and Vienna and Andropov's statement of 25 November announcing the accelerated deployment of operational-tactical missiles of increased range in East Germany and Czechoslovakia meant that the Soviets had concluded that political negotiations over military matters with the United States were futile and that new methods for dealing with the West should be devised. At the end of the year, no one imagined that Yuri Andropov would depart within weeks in such an atmosphere of uncertainty.

The failure to prevent the deployment did not exhaust the list of Andropov's foreign political worries in 1983. The Red Army's massive intervention in Afghanistan showed no signs of leading to a prompt and effective termination. The June visit of Pope John Paul II to Poland testified that to his "divisions" belonged the overwhelming majority of the population and that the pontiff was in fact a formidable potential adversary. The shooting-down of an unarmed Korean passenger plane by a Soviet pilot near Sakhalin Island on 1 September, causing the loss of 269 lives, and the subsequent inadequate and contradictory official explanations and justifications for the incident created a worldwide outcry, detrimental at least temporarily to the Soviet peace campaign.

On a deeper level of political realities, the electoral victories of conservatives in the most industrialized countries of the world (Great Britain and West Germany in Europe and Japan in Asia), with the most numerous and best-educated working classes, offered no encouragement to the Soviet Union. Even the behavior of France, governed by a socialist-communist coalition, toward the Soviet Union must have made Moscow nostalgic for the policies of François Mitterrand's conservative predecessor, Valéry Giscard d'Estaing. Another political novelty that the Kremlin certainly did not appreciate was the emergence and persistence of anticommunist insurgencies, on three continents and on territories supposed to be under full control of pro-Soviet regimes (Kampuchea, Angola, Nicaragua).

But the greatest source of worries for Yuri Andropov was the United States under Ronald Reagan. First and worst of all was the systematic U.S. policy of rearmament, enhancing defense efforts whose aim is to prevent the Soviet Union from gaining the upper hand militarily and thus being in an unassailable position to dictate its political will without risking nuclear confrontation. Soviet military experts must have followed with concern the development by U.S. specialists of a new breed of non-nuclear weapons known as "deep strike" or ET (emerging technology), which could stop waves of a Warsaw Pact attack in Central Europe without risking nuclear annihilation. In fact, the functioning of an effective non-nuclear deterrent would have extremely important political and psychological consequences and would deprive the Soviet Union of using the prospect of a nuclear war to frighten and morally disarm especially the West Germans.

There were other aspects of U.S. activism in 1983 that Moscow regarded with disapproval. One of these was the new content of broadcasts aimed at Soviet and East European listeners, which censured the worst features of communist regimes and extolled the virtues of pluralistic Western democracies. The U.S. military intervention in Grenada in October and other political and military pressures against Cuba and Nicaragua were vehemently attacked in official Soviet statements and in the Soviet press, but besides trying to aggravate anti-U.S. feelings, no concrete action in support of friendly "progressive" regimes that would risk a military confrontation with the United States was ever contemplated. Ronald Reagan, criticized whether he was verbally aggressive or accommodating, must have particularly puzzled Soviet leaders. It is impossible to say whether Moscow has written him off as a serious negotiating partner or might try to strike a deal with him if he is re-elected.

For his part, Yuri Andropov must have watched with alarm some of the U.S. policies destined, as they must have appeared in his eyes, to weaken if not to destroy the Soviet Union. He certainly approved and encouraged the resourceful Soviet-inspired anti-U.S. campaigns in Western Europe, the Third World, and the United States itself. The Soviet engagement in Syria suggests a potentially rich field for the Kremlin to reassert its prestige and to complicate the already weakened U.S. position in the Middle East. And one may be certain that if his physical condition had allowed, Yuri Andropov would have reacted much more forcefully to U.S. "provocations."

To sum up these observations on Andropov's foreign policies, his legacy, again, is ambiguous. With him at the helm, the Soviet Union has conserved its status as a major and strong world power. Some of his own moves, however, along with unpredictable U.S. actions, have resulted in confusion that his heirs will have to dispel.

Eastern Europe. In 1983, a series of small changes, but no precedent-shattering event, characterized the situation of the states that through their membership in the Warsaw Treaty Organization (WTO) and the Council for Mutual Economic Assistance (CMEA) belong to the Soviet bloc. It should be noted from the outset that the domination of the bloc by the Soviet Union was distinctly more complete in the military than in the economic field. Some of the ambiguities of Yuri Andropov's rule in the USSR were also perceptible in Eastern Europe.

Reviewing the Soviet Union's foreign policy before the Supreme Soviet on 16 June, Foreign Minister Andrei Gromyko made two apodictic statements with regard to Eastern Europe. He warned the West that it should have no doubt about the Eastern bloc's resolve to "uphold the inviolability of our borders, to ensure the safety of all members of the commonwealth, and to defend socialist gains." This confirmation of the Brezhnev Doctrine (first enunciated in November 1968, after the invasion of Czechoslovakia) was now made regarding Poland. After assailing the West for ideological sabotage and subversive political and economic actions against the Polish People's Republic, Gromyko asserted that in the eyes of the Warsaw government and its allies in the WTO, "Poland has been and will remain an integral part of the socialist commonwealth."

To fully consolidate control over Eastern Europe, more specifically to include their governments in the fulfillment of the central foreign political task of the Andropov administration—preventing the deployment of Pershing II and cruise missiles in Western Europe—the Soviet Union set the WTO a hectic pace. The military and political components of this activity were indistinguishable. Several joint maneuvers throughout the region, especially within the WTO's northern tier (East Germany, Poland, and Czechoslovakia), were held. The commander in chief of the WTO, Marshal Viktor G. Kulikov, was in charge of the operations and practiced the "intimidation through maneuver" ploy fully. Ten meetings between the first week in January and the first week in December were held in various WTO capitals (Moscow, Prague, Sofia) and at different levels. Prague and Moscow (January and June respectively) hosted summit meetings attended by Yuri Andropov. Other meetings included separate gatherings of prime, defense, and foreign ministers of the member-states, of the WTO's Military Council (chaired by Marshal Kulikov), and of parliamentary presidents. The final communiqués of these meetings contained proposals for solving disagreements between the two blocs (NATO and WTO) and were usually couched in relatively moderate terms, but none failed to denounce the danger of the U.S. missile deployment. Conversely, they approved in advance the necessity of a Soviet counterdeployment of missiles as an element of legitimate collective defense. It was certainly not coincidental that although the communiqués were destined for foreign media and public opinion as instruments of the WTO's "peace offensive," top Soviet marshals concurrently made tough speeches essentially for domestic consumption. A multiplicity of factors pointed to the actual strength and the potential weaknesses of the WTO, but it is probably a fair conclusion that the organization played a positive role in safeguarding Soviet imperial interests in that part of the world.

Being topically and structurally different, the CMEA has played a distinctive role in East European history. Although its function is to oversee the organization's economic problems, it also serves the foreign policy purposes of the Soviet Union. Thus a statement of the heads of government of the member-states of the CMEA, signed on 20 October in East Berlin, argued that "preventing a further escalation of the arms race is the most important task of our time." Formal unanimity on that issue, however, did not correspond to unanimity on some basic economic problems. All CMEA members were aware of the conflicts of interest existing within it, and many hoped that a meeting in Moscow at the highest level, planned for the end of May (the first summit since 1971) would find solutions to intra-CMEA disputes. To everyone's embarrassment, a preparatory meeting in Moscow in early May could not agree on the summit's agenda, and the meeting was postponed. In the meantime, the procedural problems within the CMEA were settled. In East Berlin on 18–20 October, the thirty-seventh meeting of the chief CMEA decisionmaking body, the Council, composed of the prime ministers of the member-states, agreed to hold the summit meeting in Moscow during early February 1984.

The basic issues of disagreement between the Soviet Union and its CMEA partners (who were not unanimous in their dissenting views; some followed the Kremlin line unconditionally) can be reduced to three points. One was the degree of economic integration. The Soviets favored greater self-sufficiency, a "qualitatively new level" of integration, "increasingly deep, comprehensive, and effective," as Andropov put it in June. The others favored looser ties within the CMEA that would permit an opening to and wider economic cooperation with the West. The second issue revolved around Soviet supplies of energy and raw materials to Eastern Europe and the quantitative and qualitative aspects of intra-bloc trade relations. National economic discrepancies made agreement extremely difficult. The non-Soviet states needed larger supplies of Soviet energy sources, especially oil, and at lower prices; Moscow was cutting supplies and asking for price increases. It particularly wanted to orient its oil exports to hard-currency countries, to the detriment of its disadvantaged allies. Moreover, Moscow was displeased with the quality of manufactured goods it imported from Eastern Europe. At the East Berlin meeting, Soviet premier Nikolai Tikhonov declared that the Soviet ability to supply raw materials "largely depends on the extent to which the other CMEA countries are able to supply products which the USSR's national economy needs." The third basic issue of contention was the problem of economic reforms. Many East Europeans saw structural changes in the established centralized system as the precondition for increasing the efficiency of their economies. But they knew—especially after the Soviet decision in the summer not to proceed with structural economic changes—that they could not hope to obtain anything more than improvements in the existing system. It was natural therefore that the unanimously adopted final declaration of the East Berlin meeting was, in the words of one Soviet bloc economist, an "anodyne, a compromise on just about everything." Hopes rested with the problem-solving wisdom of the February summit.

As for the overall economic situation of Eastern Europe during 1983, at the beginning of the 1980s, all the East European members of the CMEA faced an economic slowdown unprecedented in the postwar period. The essential factors causing the slowdown were failure to carry out effective economic reforms; huge borrowings from Western banks and governments; the Western economic recession, which lowered the demand for East European exports; and the drastic deterioration in the area's terms of trade with the Soviet Union. Given this gloomy background, the limited recovery at the end of the year was good news indeed. The central element was the reduction of indebtedness to the West. The region's financial problems looked less serious for several reasons: the progress in rescheduling debts and obtaining new credits; the decline in interest rates, which permitted savings; hard-selling tech-niques aimed at a post-recession West interested again in imports; and a certain debureaucratization of the Eastern European trade system. The list of remaining problems, as enumerated in a report issued by the Economic Commission for Europe, shows that the 1983 recovery involved only minor economic problems. Major remaining ones are a sharp fall in the growth of labor resources, fewer possibilities for attracting agricultural workers into industry, varying improvements in productivity, substantial cost increases in exploiting natural resources, higher raw material and energy import costs, economic bottlenecks, structural imbalances, and a move away from material- and energy-intensive production, especially in the smaller East European countries.

To return to the central problem of this essay—the meaning and results of Yuri Andropov's tenure—he brought little change to Eastern Europe, but he maintained firm control over the area. In Eastern Europe, as in the Soviet Union and in the West, Andropov had elicited high expectations of qualitative changes. By the middle of the year, it was clear, however, that the reformer was only a piecemeal innovator. And yet, as every profile in this section shows, the realization that the Soviet overlordship is presently unchallengeable does not mean that the region is listless. On the contrary, the amount of movement under the surface of imposed conformity is remarkable, even within communist parties and *a fortiori* outside of them. In this sense, for Eastern Europeans Andropov's reign was essentially an inconclusive interlude.

Milorad M. Drachkovitch
Hoover Institution

Albania

Population. 2.8 million
Party. Albanian Party of Labor (Partia e Punës e Shqipërisë; APL)
Founded. 8 November 1941
Membership. (Approximate) 122,000 full and 22,363 candidate members; workers and peasants 66 percent; office workers and "intellectuals" 34 percent; women, 30 percent of full and 40 percent of candidate members
First Secretary. Enver Hoxha
Politburo. 10 full members: Enver Hoxha (chairman of Democratic Front); Ramiz Alia (president of the republic), Adil Çarçani (premier), Hejredin Çeliku (minister of industry and mines), Lenka Çuko, Hekuran Isai (minister of internal affairs), Rita Marko (vice-president), Pali Mishka, Manush Myftiu (deputy premier), Simon Stefani; 4 alternate members: Besnik Bekteshi (deputy premier), Foto Çami, Llambi Gjegprifti, Qirjako Mihali
Secretariat. 6 members: Enver Hoxha, Ramiz Alia, Vangjel Çerava, Lenka Çuko, Hekuran Isai, Simon Stefani
Central Committee. 80 full and 38 alternate members
Status. Ruling party
Last Congress. Eighth, 1–8 November 1981, in Tirana
Parliamentary Elections. All candidates run unopposed on the ticket of the Democratic Front. In the elections of 14 November 1982, only one voter voted against the front's candidates.
Auxiliary Organizations. Trade Union Federation of Albania (UTUA) (610,000 members), Sotir Koçallari, chairman; Union of Labor Youth of Albania (ULYA), Mehmet Elezi, first secretary; Women's Union of Albania (WUA), Lumturi Rexha, president; Albanian War Veterans, Shefqet Peci, chairman; Albanian Defense of Peace Committee, Musaraj Shefqet, acting chairman
Main State Organs. Council of Ministers (20 members). The People's Assembly (250 members) is constitutionally the leading body of the state, but in reality it rubberstamps decisions reached at the party Politburo and Central Committee levels.
Publications. *Zëri i Popullit*, organ of the APL Central Committee, daily; *Bashkimi*, organ of the Democratic Front, daily; *Zëri i Rinisë*, organ of ULYA, semiweekly; *Puna*, organ of UTUA, weekly; *10 Korik*, organ of Ministry of Defense, biweekly; *Laiko Vema*, organ of the Greek minority, semiweekly. The Albania Telegraphic Agency (ATA) is the official news agency.

The Albanian Communist Party was founded in Tirana on 8 November 1941 on the initiative of Josip Broz Tito, who was implementing a Comintern directive to activate and control anti-German resistance in the Balkans. Prior to 1941 there was no significant communist movement in Albania. Three loosely organized groups of communists existed in the cities of Korçe, Tirana, and Shkoder, but their followers had different interpretations of what communism meant or what it could do for a society still in the grips of feudalism.

The dominant group, located in the city of Korçe, was initially led by Pillo Peristeri and Koce Xoxe. Peristeri sponsored Enver Hoxha's admission to the communist cell of the city, which at the time had close ties with the Greek Communist Party. The second group, located in the northern city of Shkoder, was under the influence of Yugoslav and Austrian communists. Elements of these two groups formed the Tirana cell, which by 1941 had come under the control of Enver Hoxha.

Two Yugoslav emissaries, Miladin Popović and Dušan Mugoša, who arrived in Tirana in early November 1941, managed to unite these three groups under a single leadership with Enver Hoxha as the provisional first secretary. The newly founded party was then charged with the simultaneous tasks of organizing armed resistance against the occupation forces and conducting a domestic class struggle.

At the First Party Congress (1 November 1948), the party was renamed the Albanian Party of Labor (APL) and Hoxha was elected first secretary, a post he still holds. A permanent characteristic in the life of APL is its instability at the highest ranks. Since 1948, the party has been subjected to four major purges, and the country has suffered the consequences. In all instances, purges preceded or followed major foreign policy reorientations, and predictably all were managed by Enver Hoxha.

During 1983, the Albanian Party of Labor appeared to regain a degree of normalcy following the massive upheavals of the previous year and the astonishing revelation by Enver Hoxha that Mehmet Shehu, his premier for 28 years, was in fact a triple agent (of Yugoslavia, the USSR, and the United States). After the dramatic changes in the cabinet and party bodies that commenced with the apparent assassination of Shehu on 18 December 1981 and concluded with the November 1982 parliamentary elections, the party and state organs were spared additional changes at the top. At lower levels, however, purges continued, and the process of rooting out pro-Shehu elements was far from over at year-end. Reliable information reaching the West confirms earlier rumors that a number of high-level officials of the Shehu regime have been physically eliminated. Among them are former defense minister Kadri Hazbiu, former minister of health Llambi Ziçishti, former interior minister Feçor Shehu (Shehu's nephew), and the Sigurimi (security police) chief of Vlore (AFP, 3 November; *FBIS*, 4 November; *Makedonia*, Salonica, 4 November).

Parallel with efforts to cleanse the party of pro-Shehu elements, a concerted campaign to legitimize a new hierarchical order, with Ramiz Alia as heir apparent to Hoxha, was under way during 1983. Implicit in this process is the likelihood of wider changes at the top at some future date and readjustment of the distribution of power among several key institutions. At present, the Politburo functions with ten full members, and the Central Committee has not taken formal action to fill several vacancies created by the removal of Hazbiu, Fiqret Shehu (Mehmet Shehu's wife), and several other key individuals. Presumably, alternate Central Committee members have been elevated to full membership, but no information is available.

Party Internal Affairs. *Reconstructing the Hierarchy.* Two mutually reinforcing trends were apparent in the APL during 1983: first, a sustained and carefully coordinated campaign on the part of key Central Committee members to restructure the hierarchy with Alia as the number two man and Hoxha as the elder statesman; and second, a systematic effort to rearrange the distribution of power in the executive branch so as to place the Shehu-created bureaucracy under firmer party control. Parallel to these two trends is a grass-roots campaign to legitimize the new pecking order in Albanian politics.

If public exposure is a measure of political status, Ramiz Alia can be considered the upcoming strong man in Albanian politics. His fortunes took a distinct upward turn with the demise of Shehu and his election in November 1982 as chairman of the Presidium of the People's Assembly and president of the republic. During 1983, Alia appeared at all major public events and formal gatherings as the undisputed heir apparent to Hoxha. His "theoretical knowledge" and expertise were offered on all issues dealt with by party organs, auxiliary organizations, and mass movements. Public appearances by Alia were coupled with more concrete efforts on his part to shift power away from known Shehu power bases (i.e., the military and the Sigurimi) and to create adequate substitutes without raising undue suspicions among the top leaders or appearing to undermine Hoxha's status. As in previous internal upheavals in Albania, Alia's efforts to consolidate his position were conducted in an artificially created climate of external and internal "threats" and enemies. With the applause of Vito Kapo (wife of the late theoretician Hysni Kapo), Alia made a major appearance at a conference on the national economy that had the dual purpose of identifying problems in fulfilling the Seventh Five-Year Plan and of attacking all enemies of the "socialist order" as well as the remnants of the Shehu regime (*Zëri i Popullit*, 12 April; *FBIS*, 15 April). Speaking in his capacity as secretary of the Central Committee, Alia pointed to serious shortcomings in the economy, all of which, in his view, were ideologically related and point to a "failure to consolidate the cooperativist order" (ATA, 13 April; *FBIS*, 15 April). In October, Alia gave a similar speech at a conference on Marxism-Leninism held in Tirana under the auspices of the Institute for Marxism-Leninism, whose director is Nexhmije Hoxha, wife of the first secretary. His message, there, was also in a hard-line mold, and he reserved most of his attack for Serbian chauvinism and modern revisionism (ATA, 4 October; *FBIS*, 6 October).

It is apparent from press coverage and the content of his addresses that Alia's activities have the approval of Enver Hoxha, who now seeks to affirm in the eyes of his people an image of elder statesman, eager to do everything possible to assure the perpetuation of his policies and ideological viewpoint after he is gone. Toward that end, Alia visited most major cities as Hoxha's emissary during 1983, but paid particular attention to the regions close to the Yugoslav border and to the southern part, where a sizable Greek minority resides. In his visit to the north, Alia attacked the Yugoslav revisionists with unusual ferocity and in a rather paternalistic way pledged Albania's assistance to the Albanian "brethren across the borders in Kosovo," whose demand for

"republic status" is, in his view, legitimate (*Zëri i Popullit*, 23 June). As an afterthought, he declared Albania's desire to have good relations with "its neighbors, including Yugoslavia."

In the southern districts of Gjirokaster and Sarande, Alia sought to reassure the Greek minority of its rights and to guarantee its "equality within the Albanian socialist system" (ATA, 4 November; *FBIS*, 8 November; *Laiko Vema*, 8 November).

Besides these public appearances that had the general purpose of legitimizing Alia's status as heir apparent, he made careful use of administrative and legislative structures to broaden his power base and to re-establish the party's preeminence in public life.

Administratively, Alia secured his flanks against the powerful Sigurimi. The People's Assembly, over which Alia presides, rubber-stamped a legislative decree separating the Office of Public Investigator from the Ministry of Interior (*Zëri i Popullit*, 30 June). The declared purpose of this "innovation" was to render the Office of Public Investigator "more objective" in its tasks. The real objective, however, seemed to be to curb the power of the security forces, which had been the main power base of Shehu and his brother-in-law, Kadri Hazbiu. Under the new arrangement, the office comes under the jurisdiction of the People's Assembly.

The second change was the restructuring of the State Planning Commission, which is headed by Harilla Papajorgji, a person often mentioned as having higher ambitions. Under its new charter, the State Planning Commission becomes de jure a super-ministry, with powers to question ministerial decisions, to seek and receive all pertinent information from the ministries, and to advise the People's Assembly in its tasks. The chairman of the State Planning Commission is now to be assisted by several deputy chairmen appointed by the Council of Ministers and fifteen to seventeen "specialists." To elevate the status of the commission, its chairman has ministerial rank and is responsible to the assembly (read Alia). (*Gazeta Zyrtarë*, 1 January; *JPRS*, 26 May.)

Making maximum use of his positions as head of the Assembly and of the republic, Alia activated all special committees of that body, which pursued their tasks of overseeing ministries with zeal and, apparently, with strong party approval. In a rather novel practice, most ministers were called on to report to the parliamentary committees prior to the convening of the parliament, thus de facto extending Alia's control over the executive in a more concrete way (ATA, 20–22 June; *FBIS*, 24 June).

Characteristic of the efforts to restructure the hierarchy is the relative prominence given to the newest member of the party Secretariat, Vangjel Çerava, who was elevated to the party Secretariat from the obscure post of candidate member of the Central Committee (*YICA*, 1983, p. 240). Çerava was singled out to give the main report at the September meeting of the Central Committee, which was presided over by Hoxha and dealt with "problems in the construction industry" (ATA, 21 September; *FBIS*, 22 September). Throughout the year, Çerava was prominently mentioned in party organs and at meetings of mass organizations and received foreign visitors in his capacity as a member of the Secretariat.

Party Rejuvenation and Control of the Military. In addition to efforts at the top to consolidate the image of the post-Shehu hierarchy and to secure Alia's base in Albanian politics, lower party organizations were equally active throughout the year. Two areas of concern were party rules governing admission and criteria for judging performance.

Major editorials in the party daily were critical of sloppy party work and pointed to the need to "link party admission to productivity" (*Zëri i Popullit*, 16 April). Alia and Çerava also referred to this problem in their remarks to a three-day ideological conference held in Tirana in early October. Both leaders pointed to the reluctance of cadres to "be involved directly in production," an attitude that, in their view, is inevitable given the overrepresentation in party ranks of office workers and intellectuals (ATA, 5 October; *FBIS*, 6 October). Criticism of poor "party work at the base level" is usually followed by large turnover in the party membership.

The civilian segment of the party was not alone in being scrutinized rather carefully during 1983: the military, too, came under a renewed examination and occasional criticism for weak party-army links.

Although the current minister of defense, Prokop Mura, has given every indication of being submissive to the party line (*Rruga ë Partisë*, July), it appears that Hoxha and Alia have some concern about the military's tendency to empha-

size professionalism at the expense of ideology. Both men were active during the year in military matters, seeking to impress on the army in particular the "need for better party work." *Zëri i Popullit* (11 August) noted certain problems "in the coordination of party work and that of the professional soldier." Underscoring the party's interest in the military, Alia appeared at the graduation ceremonies of the military academy in his capacity as party secretary rather than president of the republic (ATA, 28 July; *FBIS*, 29 July). On 10 July, Hoxha as commander in chief issued an order of the day on the occasion of the fortieth anniversary of the founding of the Albanian People's Army (*Zëri i Popullit*, 10 July), a task traditionally performed by the minister of defense. Finally, Alia personally handed decorations to 1,400 officers and implored them to eliminate the remnants of the Kadri Hazbiu–Mehmet Shehu gang (ibid., 11 July), which was accused of undermining the country's defense with the strategy of "inland deployment of the bulk of the armed forces" instead of coastal deployment (ibid., 18 May). Party concern for the situation in the military is not fully unjustified, given the fact that four of the six defense ministers since 1948 were either purged or fled to Yugoslavia.

Auxiliary and Mass Organizations. Most mass organizations held routine gatherings of congresses during 1983, and predictably they dealt with basically the same topics as in the past —namely, how to serve the party and its leader, Enver Hoxha, and how to perform their main task as the party's transmission belts. The WUA held its Ninth Annual Congress in the city of Durres on 1–5 June. Several foreign delegations, the largest being the Vietnamese, attended the proceedings (ATA, 27 May; *FBIS*, 6 June). The surprise "guests" this year were "Albanian women from the United States." No details were given as to who they were or what organization they represented. The Central Committee's report to the WUA gathering was given by Pali Mishka. Predictably Lumturi Rexha was reelected chairperson and Eleni Selenica secretary general.

The ULYA Central Committee met in Tirana to discuss the defense duties of the younger generation and to better link the "party's work, the youth, and the defense tasks" of the armed forces (*Zëri i Popullit*, 10 October). The ULYA closely follows the party's emphasis on defense matters, and in a sense it seeks to play a role in expanding "Marxist influence" in the armed forces. Simon Stefani delivered the report of the party's Central Committee to the gathering and conveyed the "personal greetings of the first secretary." Mehmet Elezi, ULYA first secretary, delivered the main address and stressed the "need for defense preparedness" in accordance with the often repeated slogan "Defense is a duty above all duties." (*Bashkimi*, 11 October.) The addresses by Elezi and Stefani were less militant in their references to the Kosovo situation and Serbian chauvinism compared with the preceding year's presentations.

The Democratic Front, the main organization to which all eligible voters belong, was active in preparing for municipal and district council elections in April. As is the rule, the Democratic Front, in cooperation with local party organizations, prepared the slates and saw to it that all voters participated. A total of 1,635,838 voters cast ballots for people's councils and judges (ATA, 24 April; *FBIS*, 27 April). However, in comparison with the 1982 parliamentary elections, a larger number of voters rejected the proposed candidates—110 voted against candidates for municipal councils, and 15 against the proposed judges. In the 1982 parliamentary elections only one voter had objected to the party's candidates.

Domestic Affairs. *Administrative and Political Changes.* Changes in the distribution of power continued in Albania during 1983, and all indications were that the aim was to stabilize the Hoxha-Alia coalition at the expense of Premier Adil Çarçani. As stated earlier, of significance is the separation of the Office of Public Investigator from the Ministry of Interior, bringing it under the direct control of Ramiz Alia (*Zëri i Popullit*, 29 June). The expressed purpose of this administrative separation was to "render it more objective." But the net result could be a check on the powers of the Sigurimi and the creation of a new power structure under the direct control of Alia. The Sigurimi was the main power base of the Shehu-Hazbiu group (*RFE-RL Report*, 11 and 13 July), and it is more than likely to still have among its ranks sympathizers of the late premier. Although the separation of the Office of Public Investigator may suggest "relaxation" of domestic oppression, other trends and indications point in the opposite direction. *Zëri i Popullit* carried a

number of articles and editorials during the year that implored the people and the party cadres to intensify the class struggle at all levels and to forfend against all sorts of enemies. Specifically, the trend is to expand the "exclusion" from the Democratic Front not only of "Kulaks, but also of their children and relatives because of the latter's inability or unwillingness to reform." Party cadres and officials are instructed to place as "much trust as control" over suspected class enemies. "It is not necessary to suspect everybody," a signed article states, "but to keep your eyes closed is a dangerous thing." (*Zëri i Popullit*, 21 April.)

Lawbreaking and Social Reform. In an unusual appearance before the People's Assembly's Judiciary Committee, Aranit Cela, the president of the Albanian Supreme Court, demanded new measures to "prevent lawbreaking" in Albania (ATA, 20 June; *FBIS*, 24 June). Following the chief justice's appeal, Rrapo Mino, the prosecutor general, presented to the same committee several proposals to streamline law enforcement and to educate the masses "in the need to respect socialist judicial order" (ibid.).

The main area in which lawbreaking occurs, according to published accounts, seems to be in what the regime calls "socialist property abuses," or expropriation of common property for private use (*Bashkimi*, 26 May). In a frank admission, the government sought to define this problem and to isolate those who consistently engage in such practices. In the government's view, those who engage in "antisocial practices" are "ideologically uninformed, or ill-meaning people who wish to damage our socialist order and economy" (*Puna*, 10 May; *FBIS*, 26 May). The proposed remedy is more "ideological work and police effectiveness." Besides the problems of lawbreaking and abuse of socialist property, the persistence of excessive "bureaucratization and formalism" occupied the party and the mass organizations. The failure of some "comrades to pay attention to the demands of the people" and their callous responses to personal issues are seen by officials as a minor but contributing cause of lawbreaking or creation of anti-state feelings (*Zëri i Popullit*, 10 October). Albanian authorities routinely attribute even ordinary crimes to "domestic and foreign enemies." *Zëri i Popullit* (10 October) linked this problem to "hidden enemies" but promised that they will fail in their "effort to destroy the magnificent victories that the Albanian people have scored."

The Shehu Affair. The Shehu affair continues to serve as an excuse for the Hoxha regime to settle political scores. Information reaching the West confirms earlier analyses that the late prime minister was the victim of foul play. Following his demise, Feçor Shehu (minister of interior) disappeared. A year later, several ministers, including Minister of Defense Kadri Hazbiu, were eliminated. According to recent accounts by Albanian refugees, at least thirty high-level officials and ministers of the Shehu cabinet have been eliminated (*NYT*, 23 October). During 1983, secret trials involving "followers of Shehu" were conducted in Vlore, Gjirokaster, and Elbasan (*Makedonia*, 4 November). Among those tried, according to the Greek Foreign Ministry, were the two sons of the late prime minister and his wife, all of whom received long sentences. Posthumously, Shehu is accused of undermining the defense of the country and of "weakening the links between army and party" (*Zëri i Popullit*, 11 July). Specifically, Shehu is accused of permitting a previous minister of defense (Beqir Baluku) to leave the sea coast unprotected by devising an inland defense (ibid., 21 April). Implicit in all these accusations is the broader issue of cleansing the military of remnants loyal to Shehu and his brother-in-law, Kadri Hazbiu.

Human Rights Violations. During 1983, Albania became the target of extensive criticism in the Western press for human rights violations involving regime opponents and leaders of the Greek minority in the south (*Sunday Times*, London, 14 August). Twenty-one Albanian refugees who reached Greece in 1983 told of a new wave of political arrests and activation of labor camps (*NYT*, 23 October). Similar accounts were given by four Albanian political refugees who sought asylum in Yugoslavia, all of whom stated that the benefits of the 11 November 1982 political amnesty have been canceled by a new wave of arrests (*Oslobodjenje*, Sarajevo, 28 April).

At least two international organizations have studied Albania's violations of human and civil rights: the U.N. Commission on Human Rights (Geneva) and the European Parliament (*Acropolis*, Athens, 17 August; *Sunday Times*, 14 August). The U.N. body has scheduled a discussion for its spring 1984 session, and the Europarlia-

ment requested the assistance of the Greek government in influencing Albania to relax its harsh domestic policies (*Mesimvrini*, Athens, 11 August). Finally, the Subcommittee on Human Rights of the U.S. House Committee on Foreign Affairs scheduled hearings on the same topic for January 1984, at the request of the Panepirotic Federation of America and Canada.

The Albanian government, apparently disturbed by external criticism, reacted with a massive propaganda effort to assure the Greek minority that its rights are "guaranteed, like those of the majority." Ramiz Alia conducted two extensive tours of the south and pledged among other things "the party's determination to assure the cultural identity of the Greeks." For propaganda purposes, Vitoria Çuri, a Gjirokaster deputy representing the Greek minority, was given prominence during the June session of the Albanian parliament (ATA, 30 June; *FBIS*, 1 July) and, as expected, expressed her satisfaction over the government's treatment of the Greek minority.

The Economy. The Albanian economy was the subject of several conferences and high-level scrutiny by party and state organs. A major conference on the economy, organized by the Institute of Marxism-Leninism, was held in Tirana to discuss problems affecting productivity and organization of social forces. Nexhmije Hoxha, wife of the first secretary, gave the keynote address and identified the main problem affecting the country's economy as inadequate "utilization of productive forces, their extension and [state] of their modernization" (ATA, 11 April; *FBIS*, 12 April). Piro Dode, former director of the State Planning Commission and now a party functionary in Shkoder, pointed to problems of "imbalance in the availability of raw materials" and the slow pace of "discovering new sources" of such materials. However, in a more detailed analysis of economic problems, Vangjel Çerava, the newest member of the party Secretariat, blamed the economic problems on bad management and failure to "use scientific approaches" in the disposition of the work force. Çerava singled out two regions, Vlore and Burrel, for failure to meet their production quotas for 1982 and the first quarter of 1983 (*Rruga ë Partisë*, March). Quotas for the production of three items critical to maintaining a credible export trade, chrome, copper, and oil, have not been met, and steel production for domestic use lags behind expectations, according to Çerava. Whether politically explainable or not, there is evidence that a large number of workers failed to meet their quotas in 1983. According to Çerava, no less than "100,000 workers did not fulfill their norm." (Ibid.)

Two other problems affected the Albanian economy during 1983: a massive and poorly planned transfer of the work force from agricultural production to other areas and a badly planned reorganization of agriculture. Approximately 13,000 workers were removed from productive agricultural jobs and transferred to nonexistent industrial projects. This was the result of a new attempt to "consolidate agricultural plots" and to create larger production units (minimum 100,000 hectares) in which new "methods were to be tested," particularly in lowlands; the mountainous areas were to revert to livestock production. Apparently the experiment was badly implemented, and the work force from the mountainous areas had been shifted to other areas. In addition, Albania faced the problem of absorbing approximately 40,000 new entrants into the labor market annually (*JPRS*, 2 May) and the reluctance of party cadres to engage in manual labor. To correct the behavior of bureaucratized party cadres, the higher authorities proposed that all office employees (who as a rule are overrepresented in party ranks) be required to work 15–30 days annually in production (*Zëri i Popullit*, 16 April; *JPRS*, 16 June).

The problems of productivity and evasion of tasks were discussed more forcefully by UTUA chairman Sotir Koçollari in his May Day speech (*Zëri i Popullit*, 2 May; *FBIS*, 2 May). Because of past problems, he promised "forceful work and production" to make up for the shortcomings of the previous year, most of which he blamed on Shehu's perfidy.

In foreign economic relations, Albania followed its previous practice of signing or renegotiating trade protocols and barter agreements. The surprise this year was the revival of Chinese-Albanian economic ties and the visit to Albania of a high-level Chinese delegation to patch up differences (*WSJ*, 18 May). Protocols were signed for barter exchanges with all East European states, Cuba, Vietnam, and Korea. In addition, trade agreements were also signed with France and Belgium (ATA, 10 October; *FBIS*, 11 October), and relations with Italy were expanded in several areas, including transportation. In all

trade agreements with Western countries, the main import item is machinery, and for good reason. Western accounts of Albanian industry document a deplorable state of repair in almost all areas and a dire need for spare parts (*JPRS*, 25 May; *Esprit*, Paris, March).

Trade agreements with Yugoslavia, Greece, Austria, and Denmark were renewed, and a transportation agreement with Finland was signed (ATA, 7 June; *FBIS*, 8 June).

Foreign Affairs. Albanian foreign policy during 1983 was characterized by cautious yet sustained steps to expand Tirana's contacts with the noncommunist world, without giving the appearance of compromising its rhetorical militancy or its opposition to the two superpowers. Indicative of the regime's willingness to leave its isolationist bunker has been a relative openness to Western journalists. For the first time, major news organizations, including the *Wall Street Journal* and the *Manchester Guardian*, were permitted to send correspondents. In the past, only pro-communist news outlets were invited, and even their reporters were subjected to intense police surveillance during their stay.

Despite the new approach toward Western news media, the top leaders maintained the same anti-Western rhetoric and vowed to go it alone. In a major speech in the northern town of Tropoje, Ramiz Alia repeated the familiar Albanian position of "no relations with the two superpowers" (ATA, 23 June; *FBIS*, 28 June). The same theme was repeated by Minister of Defense Prokop Mura in a speech before the Central Committee and the High Command on the occasion of the fortieth anniversary of the founding of the Albanian People's Army (ATA, 10 July; *FBIS*, 11 July) and by Foreign Minister Reiz Malile in his U.N. address (PSRA/U.N. Mission, text of speech, 5 October).

The rhetoric of key regime figures, however, contrasts sharply with several steps taken by Albania during 1983 that suggest that most, if not all, militant pronouncements may have been intended for their own captive audience.

In a surprise move, Albania and China reestablished economic relations and a high-level Chinese delegation visited Tirana to settle past differences and institute "correct relations" (*WSJ*, 18 May; *Economist*, London, 23 April). A trade protocol was signed with Beijing, and a new

Chinese ambassador was sent to Tirana (ATA, 5 October; *FBIS*, 6 October).

In an even more dramatic way, Albania broadened its relations with Italy in several areas. Foreign Minister Malile paid an official visit to Rome, the net result of which was "an expansion of cultural and economic relations" (ANSA, Rome, 12 October; *FBIS*, 13 October). Following the visit, Albania and Italy signed a transportation agreement linking the ports of Trieste and Durres via ferryboat.

In another direction, Sokrat Pliaka, the deputy foreign minister, visited Sweden for the purpose of increasing trade with that Scandinavian country (ATA, 6 December; *FBIS*, 7 December), and Themie Thomai, minister of agriculture, visited Turkey for the second time in as many years (ATA, 7 June; *FBIS*, 8 June).

Yugoslavia. Relations between Tirana and Belgrade showed no sign of improving during 1983. Although the two countries signed a trade protocol (ATA, 8 October; *FBIS*, 10 October) and Yugoslavia remains Albania's number one trading partner, the Hoxha regime did not relent in its attacks on "Serbian chauvinism and modern revisionism." In a major speech at Diber in northern Albania, Ramiz Alia repeated the usual grievances against "Stambolić and Company" and accused the Yugoslav government of denying elementary rights to the Kosovo Albanians (ATA, 19 June; *FBIS*, 20 June). More specifically, Albania accused Yugoslavia of "procrastinating" in building its part of the railroad linking Shkoder and Titograd. *Zëri i Popullit* interpreted the failure of Yugoslavia to complete its part of the line on time as a deliberate attempt to harm Albania's economy and an effort to reinforce the perception of "Albanian isolationism" (ATA, 19 April; *FBIS*, 22 April).

Attacks on "Greater Serbian chauvinism" were a recurring theme of the Albanian press during 1983, suggesting continuation of Tirana's efforts to serve as the "cultural beacon" for the Albanian minority in Kosovo. In a major editorial, *Zëri i Popullit* (1 November) attacked the "so-called Yugoslav communists who imposed on schoolchildren books about [Saints] Cyril and Methodius" (converters of the Slavs), as well as other Serbian chauvinist writers. *Rruga ë Partisë* (March), on the other hand, revived the accusation that Tito had doublecrossed the Albanian minority who joined his forces believing

in his promise of national liberation at the end of the war.

Finally, Albania took notice of the visits to Yugoslavia of Soviet premier Nicolai Tikhonov and U.S. vice-president George Bush (ATA, 19 September; *FBIS*, 19 September) and concluded that Belgrade was ready to make concessions to the superpowers in order to save itself from the "bankruptcy of the self-management system" (*Zëri i Popullit*, 2 April). Another issue between Albania and Yugoslavia was the latter's military maneuvers near Albanian borders and Macedonia. Although the Yugoslav government invited Albania to send observers, in accordance with the provisions of the Helsinki accords, Tirana preferred to denounce the exercise as an "attempt at intimidation" (ATA, 25 August; *FBIS*, 26 August).

Greece. Formal relations between Greece and Albania remained satisfactory in 1983. However, several issues suggest a possible deterioration. First is the issue of violations of the human rights of the Greek minority—an issue brought before the U.N. Commission on Human Rights in Geneva (*Mesimvrini*, 11 August). The Greek representative to the subcommittee of experts voted with the majority to have the matter discussed by the entire commission during its spring 1984 session. Second, Albania's rejection of Prime Minister Andreas Papandreou's invitation to participate in a conference on a nuclear-free Balkan zone chilled relations between Tirana and the Greek socialist government (ATA, 12 June; *FBIS*, 13 June). Third, the Albanian press criticized the Greek government sharply for "failing to protect its embassy in Athens" from a terrorist attack by "reactionary forces." Tirana demanded total censorship of all those who have, for many years, criticized the Albanian regime and demanded "freedom for northern Epirus." (*Zëri i Popullit*, 28 June.) Finally, on 10 November, *Zëri i Popullit* unleashed an unprecedented, personal attack against Archbishop Serafim of Athens and all Greece, on the occasion of his visit to Belgrade. The Greek government protested to the Albanian ambassador, and several Athens dailies demanded his expulsion from the country (*Mesimvrini*, 16 November). To counter anti-Albanian feelings in Athens, Tirana invited correspondents of leftist dailies to visit the country, who, on their return, wrote glowing accounts about life in Albania (*Ethnos*, 23 October).

Eastern Europe. Albania's relations with the Eastern bloc remained correct and proper, with only occasional ideological objections on the part of Tirana against certain nonsocialist features in the satellite countries. Poland came under severe criticism for continuing business as usual with the Catholic church and for accepting the pope as a "partner in seeking solutions to its domestic problems" (ATA, 15 June; *FBIS*, 16 June). Similarly, the Hungarian economic model became the subject of press criticism (ATA, 14 November; *FBIS*, 15 November), and Bulgaria was singled out for permitting an "expansion of the private holding of land," reversing a long process of collectivization (ATA, 4 August; *FBIS*, 6 August). Regardless of ideological objections, however, Albania signed trade protocols with all Eastern bloc countries in 1983. In most instances, the agreements were signed by third-level bureaucrats in the Ministry of Foreign Commerce. But in the case of Romania, its minister of foreign trade ventured to Tirana for the occasion and was received, rather warmly, by high-level party officials (ATA, 1 November; *FBIS*, 4 November). Relations with Vietnam, too, have been conducted at a higher level than usual. Foreign Minister Malile held private meetings with his Vietnamese counterpart in New York, and Deputy Foreign Minister Sokrat Pliaka traveled to Hanoi for the signing of trade and cultural agreements (ATA, 30 November; *FBIS*, 2 December).

Western World. During 1983, Tirana undertook several steps that, if continued, could pave the way for improved relations with selected Western countries. Notable were the broadened relations with Italy discussed above and Albania's improved relations with Turkey, a cultural mentor of the small, predominantly Muslim country. Several Turkish delegations visited Tirana in 1983, culminating in an official visit by the Turkish under secretary of state (ATA, 20 October; *FBIS*, 26 October) and the signing of cultural and economic agreements. The Turkish foreign minister was among those with whom Malile conferred privately in New York; Malile reported on this contact to the "Foreign Relations Committee of the Albanian parliament" (ATA, 12 November; *FBIS*, 14 November). Austria, Belgium, France, Finland, and Malta also maintained close contacts with Albania and signed trade protocols during 1983.

Although Albania has intensified relations with most Western European countries, there are no signs of its seeking to establish relations with the United States or Great Britain. If anything, Tirana's rhetoric against the Reagan administration became rather more strident. Albania considers the two superpowers as "having parallel interests" and implicitly accuses them of being in collusion at the expense of small nations (*Zëri i Popullit*, 15 September). Relations with Great Britain and West Germany remained at the same level as in 1982. Nevertheless, Marxist delegations from both of these countries visited Albania in 1983, and in both instances they were received by members of the Central Committee. The West German delegation, led by Ernst August, was received by Ramiz Alia and the chairman of the Committee for Relations with Foreign Communist Parties, Agim Popa (ATA, 31 March; *FBIS*, 1 April). The British delegation, which was led by David Williams (leader of the "Marxist-Leninist party"), visited Albania at the invitation of the APL Central Committee and was given a tour of major industrial cities (ATA, 13 October; *FBIS*, 14 October).

China. Relations with China improved substantially, and state-to-state relations have in essence been normalized. Although Albania did not reverse itself on the ideological questions that arose between it and China and continues to view the Beijing regime as "revisionist," it nevertheless received a high-level delegation in Tirana and restored normal trade and economic relations (*WP*, 2 June). A new Chinese ambassador was appointed to Tirana and was received by several high-level officials, including Reiz Malile and Besnik Bekteshi (alternate Politburo member). No information on the level of the new trade agreement or its implementation is available (ATA, 13 September; *FBIS*, 15 September).

USSR. It would be fair to say that Albania reserved the highest level of hostility for the Soviet Union. All major leaders made it part of their rhetorical menu to single out the Soviet Union and the United States as the two "evils" in the world. Albania sees the USSR as a greater danger than the United States simply because of its expansionist policies. In a series of articles in newspapers and journals on the anniversary of the Czechoslovak invasion, Albanian leaders attacked Moscow for its "systematic enslavement of people." "Soviet foreign policy," an editorial in *Zëri i Popullit* (21 August) stated, "has gradually assumed a pronounced militaristic character, which is expressed in the use of force to realize its expansionist aims." Besides Soviet expansionism, Albanian leaders zeroed in on the Soviet military threats in Europe and attacked the Kremlin's "missile blackmail" (ATA, 28 November; *FBIS*, 30 November). The Albanian press attacked Andropov's "missile speech" and dismissed the Geneva talks as a "farce" (*Bashkimi*, 27 November). Finally, the Soviets received extensive criticism for their occupation of Afghanistan and for their "exploitation of the Eastern European" peoples.

International Party Contacts. Several Third World communist delegations visited Tirana at the invitation of the APL Central Committee. Among them were delegations from Brazil (ATA, 7 July; *FBIS*, 8 July), Portugal, West Germany, and Great Britain. In addition, several delegations from Third World communist parties, including the North Korean and Vietnamese, attended the WUA congress.

Nikolaos A. Stavrou
Howard University

Bulgaria

Population. 8,929,000 (1 January; *Rabotnichesko delo*, 29 January)

Party. Bulgarian Communist Party (Bulgarska komunisticheska partiya; BCP)

Founded. Bulgarian Social Democratic Party founded in 1891; split into Broad and Narrow factions in 1903; the Narrow Socialists became the BCP and joined the Comintern in 1919.

Membership. 825,876; 42.7 percent industrial workers

Secretary General. Todor Khristov Zhivkov

Politburo. 10 full members: Todor Zhivkov (chairman, State Council), Milko Balev (head of Zhivkov's personal secretariat), Todor Bozhinov (first deputy prime minister, minister of metallurgy and mineral resources), Ognyan Doynov (member, State Council), Tsola Dragoicheva (member, State Council; honorary chairman, Soviet-Bulgarian Friendship Society), Gen. Dobri Dzhurov (minister of national defense), Grisha Filipov (prime minister), Pencho Kubadinski (member, State Council; chairman, Fatherland Front), Petur Mladenov (minister of foreign affairs), Stanko Todorov (chairman, National Assembly); 3 candidate members: Petur Dyulgerov (chairman, Central Council of Trade Unions), Andrey Lukanov (deputy prime minister), Georgi Yordanov (chairman, Committee on Culture)

Secretariat. 9 members: Chudomir Alexandrov (first secretary, Sofia city party committee), Georgi Atanasov (chairman, Committee for State Control), Milko Balev, Ognyan Doynov, Stoyan Mikhailov, Misho Mishev, Dimitur Stanishev, Vasil Tsanov, Kiril Zarev

Central Committee. 193 full and 138 candidate members

Status. Ruling party

Last Congress. Twelfth, 31 March–4 April 1981, in Sofia; next congress scheduled for 1986

Last Election. 7 June 1981. All candidates run on ticket of Fatherland Front, an umbrella organization (4.4 million members) comprising most mass organizations. Fatherland Front candidates received 99.9 percent of votes cast. Of the National Assembly's 400 members, 271 belong to the BCP and 99 to the Agrarian Union; 30 are unaffiliated (some 20 of these are Komsomols). The Bulgarian Agrarian National Union (BANU, 120,000 members) formally shares power with the BCP, holds 4 of the 29 places on the State Council, the ministries of justice, public health, communications, and forestry, and about one-sixth of local people's council seats. BANU leader Petur Tanchev's post as first deputy chairman of the State Council makes him Todor Zhivkov's nominal successor as head of state.

Auxiliary Organizations. Central Council of Trade Unions (CCTU, about 4 million members), led by Petur Dyulgerov; Dimitrov Communist Youth League (Komsomol, 1.5 million members), led by Stanka Shopova; Civil Defense Organization (750,000 members), led by Col. Gen. Tencho Papazov, provides training in paramilitary tactics and disaster relief; Committee on Bulgarian Women (30,000 members), led by Elena Lagadinova, no real significance

Publications. *Rabotnichesko delo* (*RD*; Workers' cause), BCP daily; *Partien zhivot* (Party life), BCP monthly; *Novo vreme* (New time), BCP theoretical journal; *Otechestven front* (Fatherland Front), front daily; *Durzhaven vestnik* (State newspaper), contains texts of laws and decrees. Bulgarska telegrafna agentsiya (BTA) is the official news agency.

Todor Zhivkov seemed completely recovered from the previous year's illness, resuming an active schedule of domestic appearances and international travel, including a state visit to India at the end of the year. In the one high-level political change, Alexander Lilov was suddenly removed from the Politburo and Secretariat. Government leaders expressed general satisfaction with the performance of the economy, but drought followed by heavy late-summer rains created problems in agriculture. On the international scene, Bulgaria continued to receive uncommon and unwanted attention owing to the alleged "Bulgarian connection" in the attempt on the life of the pope.

Leadership and Party Organization. On 28 September, a plenum of the Central Committee relieved Alexander Lilov of his positions on the Politburo and the Secretariat "at his own request . . . because of his transfer to other work" (*RD*, 29 September; *FBIS*, 30 September). No mention was made of his membership on the State Council. Lilov had been a Central Committee secretary since 1972 and a Politburo member since 1974. The party's chief ideologist, he was generally included in the small circle of possible successors to Zhivkov. No reasons were given for his dismissal, which came unexpectedly since he had been visibly active in party and public affairs. Less than a month earlier, he had been awarded the Order of Georgi Dimitrov on the occasion of his fiftieth birthday; at that time he was called an "inspired builder of socialist society, and an en-

thusiastic fighter for Bulgarian-Soviet friendship" (Sofia domestic service, 30 August; *FBIS*, 31 August). Speculation on the cause of his downfall centered on possible conflicts over ideological and cultural policies. Lilov was believed to have been a strong supporter of Liudmila Zhivkova's efforts, before her death in 1981, to bring a more liberal and more nationalistic approach to Bulgarian culture (see *YICA*, 1982, p. 378). Since that time, there has been increasing evidence that proponents of a more orthodox party line on culture have gained greater influence. (*RFE Situation Report*, 18 October, item 1.) Milko Balev, who joined the Politburo in 1982 (see *YICA*, 1983, p. 251) and has been a Central Committee secretary since 1977, seemed to take over Lilov's role as chief spokesman on ideological issues, chairing a national meeting of ideological cadres on 31 October (BTA, 31 October; *FBIS*, 2 November).

Four provincial party first secretaries were replaced during the year owing to their "transfer to other work." Velichko Karadzhov, first secretary of the Smolian provincial BCP committee, was replaced by Atanas Atanasov, chairman of the Smolian People's Council. Atanasov's old position was taken by Asen Yankov, a member of the provincial party committee secretariat. (Sofia domestic service, 12 April; *FBIS*, 13 April.) In Vratsa province, Nano Lalov, party committee first secretary since 1976, was replaced by Lazar Petrov, chairman of the Vratsa People's Council. No replacement for Petrov was announced. (Sofia domestic service, 18 May; *FBIS*, 20 May.)

Vasil Nedev, first secretary of the Stara Zagora BCP committee since 1979, was replaced by Georgi Georgiev (Sofia domestic service, 24 October; *FBIS*, 26 October). In 1981, Georgiev had been appointed "second secretary" in charge of cadres in the Varna party committee after the old leadership of that organization was purged (see *YICA*, 1982, p. 380). His promotion indicates that he probably succeeded in putting the situation in Varna in order. Penko Gerganov, first secretary of the Pleven party committee since 1965, resigned owing to his election as first deputy chairman of the Soviet-Bulgarian Friendship Society and was replaced by Stefan Manov, head of the Pleven People's Council (Sofia domestic service, 6 July; *FBIS*, 7 July). Gerganov's career seems to have been boosted by the marriage of his daughter to Todor Zhivkov's son Vladimir in 1979. Georgi Stankov, a member of the BCP Central Committee and a secretary of the Varna provincial party committee, died 25 December (Sofia domestic service, 26 December; *FBIS*, 27 December).

The career of Vladimir Zhivkov (see *YICA*, 1983, p. 252) advanced another step with his election to the National Assembly on 30 January in a by-election to fill the seat made vacant by the death of former Politburo member Army Gen. Ivan Mikhailov in 1982 (Sofia domestic service, 30 January; *FBIS*, 1 February). The election "campaign" provided a few biographical facts about the younger Zhivkov, who had played no visible role in public life before the death of his powerful older sister in 1981. Vladimir Zhivkov was born on 5 June 1952 and joined the Komsomol in 1966 and the BCP in 1971. He completed military service in the Pleven School for Reserve Officers and graduated from the Sofia University law school in 1978. (*RFE Situation Report*, 11 February, item 1.) In May, Vladimir Zhivkov was also elected a deputy chairman of the Committee on Culture, the organization his sister had headed (Sofia domestic service, 26 May; *FBIS*, 31 May).

Domestic Affairs. *Economy.* On 11–12 February, the BCP Central Committee, the Council of Ministers, and the governing bodies of the major mass organizations held a conference to assess the results of the December 1972 Central Committee plenum on living standards and to update its provisions for the future. Prime Minister Grisha Filipov delivered the major address, reporting that in the decade since 1972 the average gross monthly wage had grown from 125 to 197 leva and that the average worker's real income had increased about 4 percent annually. The average annual per capita consumption of certain categories of food had grown appreciably: meat and meat products from 41.4 kg to 67 kg; milk and milk products from 152.1 liters to 206 liters; eggs from 122 to 214; and fruits from 148.2 kg to 227.0 kg. He promised that the minimum monthly wage would be raised from 100 to 120 leva before the end of the current five-year plan (1981–1985), that entry-level wages for various categories of workers would also increase, and that real income would grow at an average of about 3 percent annually in coming years. Filipov also discussed Bulgaria's demographic problems, which had emerged as a focus of concern the preceding year (*YICA*, 1983, pp. 254–55). He proposed that individuals who without valid reason do not form families should be barred from leading posts. Moreover, couples who fail to have children should pay higher taxes and not be eligible for state-owned housing. He added that older workers should not automatically be pensioned off, but that a system of incentives should be developed to keep them in the labor force for a longer time. (BTA, 12 and 13 February; *RD*, 14 February; *FBIS*, 15 February.)

According to the report of Stanish Bonev, chairman of the State Planning Committee, most of the targets of the 1982 plan were met or exceeded. Bonev did not, however, give specific information except for the category of industrial production, which grew 5.3 percent (target of 4.5 percent), preferring instead to give average approximations for 1981 and 1982 together. The 1983 plan called for increases of 3.8 percent in the country's domestic net material product; 3.9 percent in labor productivity; 4.8 percent in industrial production; 2.7 percent in agricultural production, and 2.8 percent in real per capita income. These goals were in harmony with those announced in 1981 at the beginning of the current five-year plan. (*RFE Situation Report*, 19 January, item 2.)

The economic plan for 1984 was adopted by the National Assembly on 29–30 September, two months earlier than had become customary. The plan targets for 1984 were nearly identical to those for 1983. Stanish Bonev's report was again lacking in specific information, but expressed general optimism that the overall goals of the five-year plan would be fulfilled (Ibid., 18 October, item 2.)

Housing construction represents one area in which the state's targets are perennially unfulfilled. Only 352,000 housing units of a planned 420,000 were actually built during the 1976–1980 five-year plan; reports indicated that construction in 1981 and 1982 had also fallen short of targets. In an effort to deal with this problem, the Council of Ministers jointly issued a decree with the CCTU in August calling on enterprises to assume responsibility for alleviating the housing problems of their workers and employees. Crediting Todor Zhivkov with providing the inspiration, the decree "permits" enterprises to build housing with their own funds and using the labor of their employees. On the other hand, this must not interfere with the enterprise's fulfillment of its economic plan. The decree does not make clear where the resources for housing construction are to come from. (Ibid., 12 September, item 1.)

Although party officials expressed general satisfaction with the quantitative increases in production, they showed increasing concern with the problem of quality. In May, the BCP Central Committee announced that a national party conference would be convened in March 1984 to discuss this issue. On 30 May, Todor Zhivkov addressed a meeting devoted to this subject in Varna, giving a very blunt and critical assessment of Bulgaria's manufactures. Admitting that Bulgarians preferred imported goods to domestic ones, that poor quality had caused the loss of some foreign markets during 1982, and that during the same year losses from claims made by foreign customers had grown by 68 percent, he stated that even goods manufactured under foreign license were "Bulgarized"—that is, marked by the country's poor level of production. Among the causes of this state of affairs, he cited the economic system's lack of incentives for quality as opposed to quantity, poor quality control and inspection during the manufacturing process, and the low level of labor discipline. To correct these problems, Zhivkov called for changes in the New Economic Mechanism to encourage concern for quality, "cooperation with firms from the developed countries of the West," and a greater effort on the part of individual workers. (Sofia domestic service, 30 May; FBIS, 2 June.) Later in the year, the press began to publish letters from citizens

complaining of the poor quality of domestic consumer goods. Numerous examples were given of shoddy workmanship, inadequate repair facilities, and indifference on the part of retail and manufacturing enterprises. (RFE Situation Report, 18 October, item 5.) To encourage enterprises to innovate, the government announced that they would be required to establish a "risk fund," to which 2 percent of "profits" annually would be contributed, to cover the costs of lost production time during the introduction of new technology and to cushion the enterprise in case the innovation proved unsuccessful (BTA, 22 August; FBIS, 23 August).

Bulgarian agriculture suffered from drought during the first half of the year and from extremely heavy rains during the harvest season. In May, the drought was used to justify a series of price increases. Citrus fruits rose 30 percent in price, pork 21.4 percent, poultry 23 percent, and ground meat 18.7 percent, although lamb fell 15 percent. At the same time, the price of imported beverages was increased 30 percent and the price of taxi fares 50 percent. (Sofia domestic service, 29 May; FBIS, 31 May.) Human inefficiency was also blamed for the problems in agriculture. The director of the Bulgarian fruit trust and several lower-ranking officials were fired for gross violations of legality, and their cases were turned over to the judicial authorities for prosecution. (Sofia domestic service, 3 October; FBIS, 4 October.)

On 3 December, the State Council and the Council of Ministers issued a decree criticizing administrative and judicial services. It complained that the ordinary citizen wastes too much time with paperwork and bureaucracy in dealing with government agencies and called for a simplification of procedures, streamlining of bureaucracy, and computerization to reduce the problem. (BTA, 3 December; FBIS, 5 December.)

Elections. On 4 December, elections were held for provincial, district, and municipal people's councils and for village mayors and deputy mayors. Some 6,564,000 people, or 99.96 percent of those eligible, voted. The candidates of the Fatherland Front received over 99.9 percent of the votes cast, and all were elected. Of the 54,475 candidates elected, 54.9 percent belonged to the BCP and 14.6 percent to the BANU; 30.5 percent were described as nonparty, although this group includes Komsomols.

Compared with the last local elections in 1979 (see *YICA*, 1980, p. 13), the results show a slight decline in the proportion of BCP members, a somewhat larger decline for the BANU, and a corresponding rise in the nonparty category. It was also reported that 31.9 percent of those elected were industrial workers (34.1 percent in 1979), 25.2 percent were agricultural workers (21.7 percent in 1979), and 37 percent (31.4 percent in 1979) were women. (BTA, 5 December; *FBIS*, 7 December.)

Cultural Affairs. The Fourth Congress on Bulgarian Culture was held 25–27 May. It was attended by 2,000 delegates including Zhivkov and Piotr Demichev, the Soviet minister of culture. Georgi Yordanov, chairman of the committee and a candidate member of the Politburo, delivered the main address, surveying developments in the cultural sphere since the last congress in 1977. He concentrated on the material indexes of progress—the number of museums opened, exhibitions held, etc.—but also indicated that the party was not satisfied with the direction taken by some Bulgarian artists and writers. He stressed the need for "party spirit" to be the guiding force in creative work and called on the country's writers to give the public "positive, enthusiastic, socialist heroes." At the close of the congress, Yordanov was re-elected chairman of the committee. Of the 217 sitting committee members, 147 were re-elected; 127 new ones were chosen, bringing total membership to 274. First Deputy Chairman Svetlin Rusev was re-elected, as were most of the deputy chairmen. Todor Zhivkov's son Vladimir was also made a deputy chairman of the committee by virtue of his role as head of the Banner of Peace children's international assembly (*RD*, 25 May; Sofia domestic service, 26 May; *FBIS*, 31 May.)

During the year, government representatives called on cultural workers (publishers, editors, theater managers) to exercise greater vigilance to prevent the appearance of works that "distort reality." They were encouraged to work more closely with the creative artists and inform them of the themes and ideas that the public would find most useful. (*RFE Situation Report*, 11 February, item 2, 18 November, item 1.)

A new series of scandals focused national attention on the state of Bulgarian soccer. According to the press, bribery of players and referees, the falsification of results and standings, and

abuses of power by sports administrators are rampant. The weekly cultural paper *Literaturen front* described the situation as being marked by "the foul stench of immorality and the corruption of even the most elementary principles of socialist legality." (Ibid., 24 August, item 5, 18 November, item 2.)

Auxiliary Organizations. On 25–27 October, the CCTU hosted an international conference devoted to the theme of Peace and the Trade Unions. CCTU Chairman Petur Dyulgerov gave the opening address, depicting the United States as the chief threat to peace. The conference was also addressed by Zhivkov, who warmly recalled the 1970s as an era of détente and peaceful coexistence, a demonstration that international problems could be settled peacefully. He urged the trade union leaders to struggle against the deployment of new medium-range missiles in the NATO countries. (BTA, 25 October; *RD*, 28 October; *FBIS*, 3 November.)

Foreign Affairs. The efforts of Italian prosecutors to establish a conclusive case against Sergei Antonov (see *YICA*, 1983, p. 256) and other Bulgarians arrested in connection with the 1981 attempted assassination of Pope John Paul II seemed to lose momentum during the year as several, sometimes sensational charges failed to be substantiated. In March, French intelligence sources announced confirmation of the "Bulgarian connection" by a defector, Yordan Mantarov, who allegedly had highly placed connections within Bulgaria's state security organization (*NYT*, 29 March). Further investigation, however, seemed to cast doubt on his story, and CIA director William Casey and other sources in the Western intelligence community dismissed his testimony as "not credible" (*Los Angeles Times*, 29 May; *WP*, 7 July). On 8 July, authorities of the Italian Justice Ministry placed would-be assassin Mehmet Ali Agca in proximity to a group of newsmen. Although Agca stated for an international television audience that "the attempt on the pope was done by the Bulgarian secret services" and "I have been trained specially by the KGB international terrorists," this episode served mainly to raise questions of judicial propriety. The Italian minister of justice promised a full investigation of the circumstances that led to the "press conference," and the judge in charge of the investigation apologized to a Bulgarian interviewer for this breach of ethics. (*WP*, 10 July; BTA, 17 July, transcript released by the Bulgarian embassy in Washington.) Agca's credibility was further eroded by the discrediting of much of his earlier testimony that had been leaked to the press (Paul B. Henze, *The Plot to Kill the Pope*, New York, 1983; Luigi Barzini, "The Gunman in Saint Peter's Square," *Washington Post Book World*, 11 December). On 12 December, the Italian judge completed his investigation and forwarded his results and recommendations to the state prosecutor's office, but without revealing them to the public (*WP*, 13 December). Nine days later, Antonov was allowed to leave prison owing to his deteriorating health. Although Antonov was warned that he could still be brought to trial and ordered not to leave Italy, his release from prison so soon after the completion of the investigation fueled end-of-year speculation that the charges would be dropped. (Ibid., 22 December.)

For their part, Bulgarian authorities conducted an energetic campaign to discredit the accusations and to win sympathy for the jailed Antonov. Boyan Traykov, director general of the BTA, emerged as the principal spokesman for the Bulgarian side, depicting the case against Antonov and the others as the product of an anti-Bulgarian, anti-Soviet conspiracy designed by Western intelligence organizations, and comparing Antonov's plight to the prosecution of longtime BCP leader Georgi Dimitrov by the Nazis. At the same time, Bulgarian authorities claimed to be cooperating fully in the investigation by making figures in the case who are Bulgarian citizens or Turks held in custody available for questioning by the Italians. (BTA and Sofia Press Agency, *A Subversion of the Neo-Crusaders*, Sofia, 1983; idem, *Free Antonov*, Sofia, 1983; Iona Andronov, *On the Wolf's Track*, Sofia, 1983.)

The Soviet Union. As in the past, Bulgarian leaders continued to emphasize their loyalty to the Soviet Union and to support Soviet positions on all major international questions. There was some indication, however, of a rift between Zhivkov and the new Soviet leadership. Zhivkov was believed to have favored Konstantin Chernenko over Yuri Andropov in the competition to succeed Brezhnev. According to intelligence sources, Andropov sharply criticized Zhivkov during the latter's visit to Moscow for Brezhnev's

funeral in November 1982. Some confirmation of this report can be found in the scant attention the Soviet press gave to Zhivkov's meeting with Andropov compared with the more extensive coverage devoted to his meetings with other East European leaders and in the fact that Viktor Chebrikov, Andropov's successor as head of the KGB, led a large delegation to Sofia for talks with Zhivkov in May (Sofia domestic service, 16 May; *FBIS*, 17 May). The cause of Soviet displeasure was said to be either the unwelcome publicity given terrorism in Western Europe and Turkey by the Bulgarian connection or the possibility that Bulgaria's state security has become corrupt and out of control owing to its involvement in clandestine drugs and arms traffic. If the latter is the case, Zhivkov might well stand accused of "lack of vigilance." (*Los Angeles Times*, 29 May.) Andropov was scheduled to visit Bulgaria some time in late October, but this trip was canceled, presumably because of Andropov's health problems. Marshal Dimitri Ustinov, Soviet defense minister and Politburo member, was the highest-ranking Soviet visitor during the year. He was lavishly welcomed by Zhivkov and the entire BCP Politburo during his stay 8–10 December. (*RD*, 10 December; *FBIS*, 12 December.)

The Soviet-Bulgarian Friendship Society held its Fifth Congress on 9–10 July. Chairman Nacho Papazov reported on the society's activities in the organization of celebrations of Soviet holidays, the mastering of "Soviet experience" in areas of technology and production, and establishment of courses in Russian-language instruction. Most of the society's leadership was re-elected, including Papazov. A new addition to the leadership was Penko Gerganov (see above). (*RFE Situation Report*, 7 July, item 2.) Shortly after the congress, a new Soviet ambassador, Leonid Grekov, was appointed. He replaced Nikita Tolubeyev, who had been the USSR's envoy to Bulgaria since 1979. (Sofia domestic service, 20 July; *FBIS*, 21 July.)

Other East European and Balkan Countries. In April 1981, some six months before the victory of the Panhellenic Socialist Movement in the Greek elections, Todor Zhivkov revived the idea of a Balkan "nuclear-free zone" and suggested a Balkan summit conference to discuss the issue (see *YICA*, 1982, pp. 386–87). Greek Prime Minister Andreas Papandreou endorsed the idea and in May of this year proposed a series of preliminary meetings to discuss denuclearization, the first of which was scheduled for 15 January 1984. Bulgaria accepted this proposal with enthusiasm, as did the Romanian government, which had originated the idea in the 1950s. Neither the Turkish nor the Yugoslav government, however, has been enthusiastic, and both have questioned the relevance of the idea in an era of intercontinental missiles. (*WP*, 25 February; *RFE Situation Report*, 1 March, item 1, 25 March, item 3, 7 July, item 7.) There were some indications that Bulgaria may have begun to back away from the idea, particularly in view of the possibility that the USSR will respond to NATO's deployment in Eastern Europe. On 29 July, Zhivkov told a delegation from the Central Committee of the Fighters Against Fascism and Capitalism that although the other Balkan leaders had expressed interest in a Balkan nuclear-free zone, as yet little progress had been made (BTA, 29 July; *FBIS*, 9 August).

Although the Bulgarian government has repeatedly stated its acceptance of the borders established after World War II, Yugoslavia regards its refusal to admit the existence of a distinct Macedonian nationality as a denial of the legitimacy of the Yugoslav Macedonian Republic and as an implicit claim on Yugoslav territory. This year, several officially sponsored events underscored Bulgaria's insistence that the inhabitants of Macedonia are historically and culturally Bulgarian. On 23–24 March, the Ministry of National Defense, the army's Political Directorate, and the Institutes of History and of Party History organized a conference devoted to the seventieth anniversary of the First Balkan War. Military spokesmen, particularly Col. Gen. Kiril Kosev, head of the army's Political Directorate, stated that the war, in the past regarded as an episode of bourgeois imperialism, was progressive and a manifestation of Bulgarian national patriotism both in Bulgaria proper and in Macedonia and Thrace. (*Narodna armiya*, 26 March.) This theme was continued later in the year in connection with the celebration of the Ilinden (St. Elias's Day) uprising in Macedonia against Ottoman rule. Academician Khristo Khristov, who frequently speaks for the regime on historical issues, wrote that Ilinden was a *Bulgarian* national revolt and that the demands of its leaders for Macedonian autonomy were merely tactical ma-

neuvers. He added that in only one-tenth of Macedonia, the Pirin region belonging to Bulgaria, do the people live under conditions of freedom, while the remaining Macedonians live under "foreign rule." Yordan Yotov, editor in chief of *Rabotnichesko delo*, added that the Macedonian problem should have been settled in a Marxist-Leninist way through free self-determination, implying that the population would have chosen to be united with Bulgaria. The Yugoslavs noted the Bulgarian claims, but made only token responses, probably because of preoccupation with the Albanian nationality problem. (*RFE Situation Report*, 24 August, item 1.) On the positive side, friendship rallies attended by thousands from both sides were held along the border on 3 July (BTA, 3 July; *FBIS*, 5 July), and Foreign Trade Minister Belcho Belchev reported that trade between the two countries has continued to expand despite "certain difficulties" in their relations. In 1971–1975, it amounted to $667 million; in 1976–1980 to $1.25 billion; and is expected to reach $3.1 billion during 1981–1985. (BTA, 10 August; *FBIS*, 11 August.)

Although Bulgaria's relations with Albania have not been close, the two countries signed a protocol calling for a 25 percent increase in trade in 1984 (BTA, 21 September; *FBIS*, 22 September).

Despite Romania's more independent foreign policy, Romanian-Bulgarian relations have for some years been very cordial. Zhivkov and Nicolae Ceauşescu exchanged visits, the Romanian leader visiting the town of Burgas 24–26 February, where he was given a decoration in honor of his sixty-fifth birthday, and Zhivkov going to Bucharest 6–8 October. Following this second meeting, it was reported that the two countries had agreed to enter into projects for the joint production of computers, farm machinery, and naval equipment. No mention was made of the large-scale joint projects for generating hydroelectric power along the Danube that had been discussed in the past or were actually under way. These were rumored to have been delayed or suspended owing to Romania's recent economic difficulties. (*RFE Situation Report*, 1 March, item 1; *RD*, 8 October; *RFE Background Report*, 9 December.) At the conclusion of meetings between Constantin Dascalescu, Romania's prime minister, and his Bulgarian counterpart, Grisha Filipov, in Sofia 22–23 December, the two signed a protocol calling for an increase of 11 percent in trade during 1984 (BTA, 24 December; *FBIS*, 28 December).

Zhivkov paid a visit to Turkey 6–9 June as a guest of the Turkish president. Both sides expressed satisfaction with the state of relations, but little substantive information was reported. One issue that apparently arose concerned the right of ethnic Turks to emigrate from Bulgaria to Turkey. In 1978, a ten-year treaty between the two countries permitting this emigration lapsed, after which its level fell sharply. After Zhivkov's visit, the Bulgarian government issued a statement that no change of policy was contemplated, but that it would permit emigration to Turkey for the purpose of reuniting families. (*RFE Situation Report*, 7 July, item 1; *RD*, 10 June.) Bulgaria "viewed with concern" the establishment of the "Northern Turkish Cypriot Republic" on the island of Cyprus, calling it a unilateral act that might complicate international relations and recommending that the Cyprus problem be solved in an international context with the help of the United Nations (BTA, 17 November; *FBIS*, 18 November).

Relations between Bulgaria and Greece remained good. Greek president Constantin Karamanlis visited Bulgaria 25–27 April, and Prime Minister Papandreou 11–13 November. On both occasions, official statements stressed the absence of any divisive problems. (Sofia domestic service, 25 April; BTA, 11–13 November; *FBIS*, 3 May, 18 November.) The two countries also signed an agreement on cooperation in the fields of science and technology, covering electronics, fish breeding, and projects involving solar and wind energy (BTA, 6 January; *FBIS*, 10 January).

Bulgaria has always stressed its loyal and active participation in the Warsaw Pact and the Council for Mutual Economic Assistance (CMEA), which in 1982 accounted for 74 percent of the country's foreign trade (BTA, 16 February; *FBIS*, 18 February). Zhivkov led a delegation to Prague to take part in the meeting of the Warsaw Pact Political Consultative Committee 3–5 January (Sofia domestic service, 3 January; *FBIS*, 4 January). Defense Minister Dobri Dzhurov stated that the "Bulgarian people's army is ready to meet its national and international obligations" by participating in a Warsaw Pact response to the deployment of new medium-range missiles by NATO, but did not describe specific measures (*RD*, 9 March). During the year, Zhivkov paid official visits to Hungary 14–16 July and the German Democratic Republic 21–23 June. On both occasions, the major topic of discussion was economic cooperation and coordination of economic planning within the CMEA structure. (Ibid., 15 June; Sofia domestic service, 23 June; *FBIS*, 21 and 24 June.)

The Third World. Libya is the largest of Bulgaria's Third World trading partners. Libyan head-of-state Moammar Khadafy visited Bulgaria for meetings with Zhivkov 17–21 January. The two leaders reportedly discussed economic and technological cooperation and at the conclusion of their talks signed a ten-year treaty of friendship and cooperation. (Sofia domestic service, 17 January; *FBIS*, 18 January.)

Palestine Liberation Organization chairman Yassir Arafat met briefly in Sofia with Zhivkov on 15 April, after which the usual condemnation of U.S. and Zionist imperialism was issued (Sofia domestic service, 15 April; *FBIS*, 15 April; *RD*, 16 April). Bulgarian leaders and the press took no position on the conflict between Arafat and his Syrian-backed opponents that broke out later in the year.

Zhivkov also played host to a delegation from the Arab League, headed by its secretary general, Chedli Klibi. The two leaders condemned Israeli aggression and the U.S. "occupation" of Lebanese territory (BTA, 19 August; *FBIS*, 22 August). Ali Nasir Muhammad of the People's Democratic Republic of Yemen visited Zhivkov in Sofia on 3 October (BTA, 3 October; *FBIS*, 4 October). The press reported little except their mutual support for the Syrian position in Lebanon, although Bulgaria is believed to be one of Yemen's major arms suppliers. A Syrian military delegation, led by Defense Minister Mustafa Talas, also visited Bulgaria, but no information of substance was made public (BTA, 8 November; *FBIS*, 10 November).

Bulgaria continued its efforts to strengthen relations with several African states. During February, Foreign Minister Petur Mladenov visited Malta, Morocco, and Tunisia (BTA, 15 February; *FBIS*, 18 February). An agreement on trade and scientific and technological cooperation was signed by the Rwandan foreign minister in Sofia on 12 April (BTA, 12 April; *FBIS*, 13

April). The prime minister of Lesotho, Joseph Lebua Jonathan, visited Bulgaria 20–23 May for meetings with Zhivkov, which were also concluded by the signing of agreements on trade and scientific and technological cooperation (*RD*, 24 May). President Ahmed Sékou Touré of Guinea spent four days in Bulgaria 19–22 July and signed an agreement on economic cooperation for the 1983–1987 period that would "intensify cooperation in agriculture, industry, prospecting, and the exploitation of mineral resources" (ibid., 24 July; *FBIS*, 1 August). An agreement on economic cooperation focusing on fishing, water management, and prospecting was reached with Mauritania, whose president, Lt. Col. Mohamed Khouna Ould Haidalla, was in Bulgaria 19–21 November (*RD*, 21 November; *FBIS*, 1 December).

Japanese foreign minister Shintaro Abe was in Bulgaria 5–6 August for meetings with Zhivkov and his counterpart Mladenov. Although the two sides disagreed on the causes of the nuclear arms race, they both favored expanded trade and cultural exchanges. (BTA, 5 and 6 August; *FBIS*, 5 and 8 August.) Politburo member Ognyan Doynov signed a trade protocol during a visit to India on 10 September (BTA, 10 September; *FBIS*, 14 September). His visit was also intended to pave the way for the meeting between Zhivkov and Indira Gandhi in New Delhi 12–15 December. According to the official protocol, the two leaders were satisfied with the cultural exchange programs, but believed that economic relations could be expanded. Although international questions were discussed, little agreement was reported beyond a mutual desire for reductions in world tensions. (*RD*, 14 and 18 December; *FBIS*, 20 December.)

Bulgaria signed a trade agreement with Vietnam, according to which Bulgaria will export chemical products, electronics, and medicines and will import tea, tin, rubber, and handicrafts (BTA, 10 February; *FBIS*, 15 February). A trade agreement was signed with Afghanistan, calling for Bulgaria to export textiles, medicines, tires, and consumer goods in return for cotton, wool, dried fruit, and leather (BTA, 12 February; *FBIS*, 15 February). Bulgaria signed a trade agreement with Cuba 17 May (Sofia domestic service, 17 May; *FBIS*, 18 May) and an agreement on cultural exchanges with Ecuador during a visit to Bulgaria by the Ecuadorean foreign minister 17–21 September (*RD*, September 22).

Western Europe and the United States. Although in recent years Bulgaria has enjoyed generally cordial relations with West European countries, the alleged Bulgarian connection in the attempt on the life of Pope John Paul II caused some deterioration. This was most serious with regard to Italy, which had been one of Bulgaria's most active trade partners in the West. According to a report in the Bulgarian press, trade between the two countries was almost entirely halted as credits were frozen, markets closed, and meetings of joint commissions suspended (*Zemedelsko zname*, 27 November; *FBIS*, 28 November). Also clouding Bulgaria's relations with Italy was the trial in Sofia of two Italian citizens, Gabriella Trevisin and Paolo Farsetti, for espionage. Trevisin, who pleaded guilty, was sentenced to three years' imprisonment; Farsetti, who denied guilt, received ten years and six months. (BTA, 14 April; *FBIS*, 14 April.)

Italian investigations produced several accusations that Bulgaria was involved in the smuggling of narcotics from Asia and the Middle East to Western Europe. The Bulgarian government took pains to deny these charges, to publicize the arrests of smugglers, and to cooperate with Western drug enforcement agencies. On 19–20 October, Bulgaria hosted an international seminar on measures to combat drug smuggling that was attended by representatives of 37 states, the European Economic Community, and Interpol, many of whom praised Bulgaria's efforts to halt the flow of drugs through its territory (BTA, 20 October; *FBIS*, 21 October).

In March, Bulgaria signed a finance and credit agreement with France aimed at implementing existing long-term agreements on economic, technological, and industrial cooperation (BTA, 23 March; *FBIS*, 24 March). A trade protocol was signed with Great Britain on 25 March (BTA, 25 March; *FBIS*, 29 March). West German foreign minister Hans-Dietrich Genscher visited Bulgaria 14–17 July. Although he sharply disagreed with Bulgarian leaders on NATO defense policy, he stated that since relations between West Germany and Bulgaria were established ten years before, they had become firm and rested on "a broad basis of trust." (BTA, 17 July; *FBIS*, 18 July.)

Relations between Bulgaria and the United States remained formally correct, but reflected the growing hostility in East-West relations. Statements by Bulgarian leaders and in the press accused the United States of escalating the arms race and of seeking new military confrontations with the socialist camp and in the Third World. In a speech in Vienna on 21 September, Vice-President George Bush referred to Bulgaria as a "closed society" with a "belligerent foreign policy," which both denies its own people the most basic human rights and acts "as proxy for the Soviets in the training, funding, and arming of terrorists." Bulgarian commentary on this speech referred to Bush's "pathological hatred" and challenged him to prove his charges. (*RFE Situation Report*, 18 October, item 3.) Penyu Kostadinov, an assistant counselor for the Bulgarian commercial office in New York, was arrested on 24 September and charged with espionage. According to FBI spokesmen, Kostadinov was a high-ranking officer in Bulgaria's state security and sought to acquire classified information on nuclear energy. The Bulgarian government called the charges "groundless" and "a crude and premeditated provocation against Bulgaria." (*WP*, 25 September.) On a more positive note, Bulgaria and the United States signed a treaty on fishing rights in U.S. waters (BTA, 23 September; *FBIS*, 27 September), and the Bulgarian public responded enthusiastically to an exhibition of paintings from Armand Hammer's collection. Hammer, president of Occidental Petroleum Corporation, was warmly welcomed to Bulgaria by Zhivkov. (BTA, 12 August; *FBIS*, 16 August.)

International Party Contacts. Politburo member Milko Balev led a Bulgarian delegation to the German Democratic Republic 11–17 April to participate in an international conference devoted to the centennial of the death of Karl Marx (*RD*, 17 April). Zhivkov received George Hawi, secretary general of the Lebanese Communist Party, 8–12 March (BTA, 12 March; *FBIS*, 16 March) and Khalid Bakhdash, secretary general of the Syrian Communist Party, on 21 September (BTA, 21 September; *FBIS*, 22 September). For several years Zhivkov has invited party leaders to vacation at Bulgaria's Black Sea resorts. This year's summer visitors included Yumjaagyin Tsedenbal of Mongolia, Georges Marchais of France, Rodney Arismendi of Uruguay, and Herbert Mies of West Germany. Zhivkov met with all these leaders, and the usual statements on solidarity and friendship were issued.

During the year, the BCP sent delegations to participate in congresses, celebrations, or other events sponsored by communist or leftist parties in the USSR, the German Democratic Republic, Denmark, Italy, Luxembourg, Portugal, Spain, Switzerland, the People's Democratic Republic of Yemen, Ethiopia, Benin, Mozambique, Libya, Afghanistan, Cuba, Nicaragua, Mexico, and the United States. Bulgaria was visited by communist party delegations from the USSR, the German Democratic Republic, Hungary, Poland, Czechoslovakia, Yugoslavia, Greece, Portugal, Spain, France, the Netherlands, Norway, Switzerland, Israel, Lebanon, Guinea, Benin, Ethiopia, Mozambique, Vietnam, North Korea, Cuba, Nicaragua, and Chile, and also from the British Labour Party.

This year's recipients of the Order of Georgi Dimitrov included Gústav Husák of Czechoslovakia; Soviet Politburo members Grigori Romanov and Dimitri Ustinov; Soviet ambassador Nikita Tolubeyev on the occasion of the conclusion of his tour of duty; Rodney Arismendi, first secretary of the Uruguayan Communist Party; Khalid Bakhdash, secretary general of the Syrian Communist Party; Ezekias Papaioannou, general secretary of the Progressive Party of the Working People of Cyprus; and Alexander Lilov, shortly before he was purged.

John D. Bell
University of Maryland Baltimore County

Czechoslovakia

Population. 15.4 million (1 January 1983)
Party. Communist Party of Czechoslovakia (Komunistická strana Československa; KSČ)
Founded. 1921
Membership. 1,600,000 (May 1983)
Secretary General. Gustáv Husák
Presidium. 12 full members: Vasil Bil'ák, Petr Colotka (deputy prime minister), Josef Haman, Karel Hoffman (chairman, Revolutionary Trade Union Movement), Gustáv Husák (president of the republic), Alois Indra (chairman, Federal Assembly), Miloš Jakeš, Antonín Kapek, Josef Kempný, Josef Korčák (deputy prime minister), Jozef Lenárt, Lubomír Štrougal (federal prime minister); 2 candidate members: Jan Fojtík, Miloslav Hruškovič
Secretariat. 10 full members: Gustáv Husák, Mikuláš Beňo, Vasil Bil'ák, Jan Fojtík, Josef Haman, Josef Havlín, Miloš Jakeš, Josef Kempný, František Pitra, Jindřich Poledník; 1 member-at-large: Marie Kabrhelová
Central Committee. 123 full and 55 candidate members
Status. Ruling party
Last Congress. Sixteenth, 6–10 April 1981, in Prague; next scheduled for 1986
Slovak Party. Communist Party of Slovakia (Komunistická strana Slovenska; KSS); membership: 400,000 full and candidate members; Josef Lenárt, first secretary; Presidium: 11 members; Central Committee: 91 full and 31 candidate members
Parliamentary Elections. All candidates run on the ticket of the National Front, an umbrella organization comprising the KSČ, four other political parties, and several mass organizations. In the National Front, 66 percent of seats are reserved for candidates of the KSČ. In the last elections (1981), the front polled 99 percent of the vote.
Auxiliary Organizations. Revolutionary Trade Union Movement (Tenth Congress, April 1982), Cooperative Farmers' Union, Socialist Youth Union (Third Congress, October 1982), Union for Collaboration with the Army, Czechoslovak Union of Women, Union of Fighters for Peace
Main State Organs. The executive body is the federal government, which is subordinate to the 350-member Federal Assembly, composed of the Chamber of the People (200 members) and the Chamber of the Nations (150 members). The assembly, however, merely rubber-stamps all decisions made by the KSČ Presidium and Central Committee.
Publications. *Rudé právo*, KSČ daily; *Pravda* (Bratislava), KSS daily; *Tribuna*, Czech-language ideological weekly; *Predvoj*, Slovak-language ideological weekly; *Život strany*, fortnightly journal devoted to administrative and organizational questions; *Práce* (Czech) and *Práca* (Slovak), Trade Union Movement dailies; *Mladá fronta* (Czech) and *Smena* (Slovak), Socialist Youth Union dailies; *Tvorba*, weekly devoted to domestic and international politics; *Nová mysl*, theoretical monthly. Československá tisková kancelář (ČETEKA) is the official news agency.

Historically, the KSČ developed from the left wing of the Czechoslovak Social Democratic Party, having co-opted several radical socialist and leftist groups. It was constituted in September 1921 at a merger congress in Prague and admitted to the Communist International the same year. Its membership in the Comintern, however, was an uneasy one until in 1929 the so-called bolshevization process was completed and a leadership of unqualified obedience to the Soviet Union assumed control. During the First Czechoslovak Republic (1918–1939), the KSČ enjoyed legal status, but it was banned after the Munich Agreement. After the war, it emerged as the strongest party in the postwar elections of 1946, although it did not poll the majority of votes. In February 1948, the KSČ seized all power in a coup d'etat and transformed Czechoslovakia into a communist party-state of the Soviet type. The departure from Stalinist practices started later in Czechoslovakia than in other countries of Central and Eastern Europe, but it led to a daring liberalization experiment known as the Prague Spring of 1968. A Soviet-led military intervention by five Warsaw Pact countries in August of the same year ended the democratization course and imposed on Czechoslovakia the policies of so-called normalization—a return to unreserved subordination to the will of the Soviet Union and the emulation of the Soviet example in all areas of social life.

Party Internal Affairs. The KSČ Central Committee met in two plenary sessions during 1983: the Eighth Plenum (counting from the committee's election at the Sixteenth Congress in 1981) took place 15–16 June, the Ninth Plenum 23–24 November. The former was preceded by party conferences called by KSČ regional organizations in all ten regions of the country. It dealt chiefly with the problem of securing in Czechoslovakia the conditions of scientific and technological progress. A new Federal Commission for Scientific, Technical, and Investment Development was established, with subordinate state commissions in each of the two ethnic republics, replacing the Federal Ministry for Technical and Investment Development with state ministries in Prague and Bratislava (Radio Prague, 16 June; *FBIS*, 17 June; *Rudé právo*, 17 June). The November plenum focused on international politics and planned deployment of U.S. and Soviet missiles in Europe. The Central Committee unreservedly endorsed the Soviet position on this matter and decreed an unspecified increase in military expenditure (Radio Prague, 24 November; *FBIS*, 25 November).

Both sessions made several personnel changes. The June plenum appointed, among

others, Zdeněk Hoření, Central Committee candidate member, to the post of editor in chief of *Rudé právo* to succeed the late Oldřich Švestka and raised him to full membership on the Central Committee (*Rudé právo*, 18 June). On the other hand, it was not disclosed whether or to whom the seat on the Presidium made vacant by the death of Václav Hůla, deputy prime minister and chairman of the State Planning Commission, would be assigned. The November session released Eugen Turzo from his duties on the Central Committee to allow him to assume the post of deputy chairman of the Control and Auditing Commission, but the death, soon after the plenum, of the commission's chairman, Miroslav Čapka, created new problems that had not been resolved by the time of this writing (ibid., 25 November). Furthermore, the party may soon have to look for a replacement for Federal Prime Minister Lubomír Štrougal, whose illness had long been a public secret in Czechoslovakia before it was officially confirmed (Czechoslovak Television, 30 April; *FBIS*, 2 May). According to informed sources, Jaromír Obzina, the present federal minister of interior, may be the most likely choice (AP, London, 22 February). Obzina's appointment as deputy prime minister in June seemed to substantiate this hypothesis (BBC, London, 21 June).

In 1983, Gustáv Husák, KSČ secretary general and president of the republic, celebrated his seventieth birthday. Carefully edited articles and programs in the media, both in Prague and in Moscow, avoided the details of Husák's persecution during the years of Stalinist terror and of his active participation in the 1968 reform movement (Radio Moscow, 9 January; *Rudé právo*, 10 January). Husák has been in control since the ouster of Alexander Dubček in April 1969, but rumors about a possible change of course under some more dogmatic leader have never ceased. In 1983, contrary to previous years, it was speculated that an attempt may be soon made to accommodate the widespread desire for liberalization in Czechoslovakia by co-opting some of the protagonists of the Prague Spring. There were unconfirmed reports that Soviet party boss Yuri Andropov had unofficial talks with several former party members prominent in the Prague Spring, among them Oldřich Černík, Čestmír Císař, and Alexander Dubček, during his stay in Czechoslovakia in January (see *Tagebuch*, Vienna, no. 6, June). Whether or not these rumors have substance, the need for greater freedom seems indisputable. The unsatisfactory record of present policies in solving the country's major problems, especially economic problems, has been discouraging large strata from any form of participation. This also appears to be true of the younger generation of party members. Although the age composition of party ranks has improved of late (the average age is now 44 years, compared with 49 in 1970; *Život strany*, no. 10), regime media admit that young communists are "not mature enough and firm in their convictions" and that they are often heard "complaining that they see no prospects for their future" (*Rudé právo*, 9 June). To party leaders, the most alarming aspect was that "the young people are neither blind nor deaf" and that they "attribute the shortcomings of a single party member or one party group to the whole of the party" (ibid., 7 July).

Domestic Affairs. The year brought anniversaries of several important events in the history of the party and of the country: 65 years from regaining of national independence, 35 years from the seizure of power by the KSČ, 15 years since the Prague Spring and the Soviet military intervention. The original Independence Day, 28 October, has under the communist regime always been observed as the Day of Nationalization (of industrial enterprises in 1945, actually only the first stage of it). The anniversary of the 1948 coup d'etat was this time remembered mostly in mass media. The events of 1968, with their dramatic climax in August, on the other hand, were barely mentioned by party and government spokesmen. It was the domestic opposition, represented by various dissident groups, that reminded the population of this date in clandestine (*samizdat*) publications. The disastrous legacy of the Soviet intervention did not need to be emphasized to anyone. According to official statements, "the social climate that currently prevails is one of increasing feelings of hopelessness. Many people are losing hope in the future." (*Hospodářské noviny*, no. 47, 26 November.) Lack of interest, motivation, and responsibility, as well as corruption, has been rife, and "a reinforcement of discipline and order" is "the fundamental task before the entire society" (*Rudé právo*, 19 February). The general demor-

alization is to a large extent a direct consequence of the forcible suppression of the reform movement and of the repressive policies of the postinvasion regime in many areas of social life. Some of the conditions prevailing in Czechoslovakia since the Soviet-led invasion of 1968 were in 1983 objects of international attention and criticism. The Committee on Application of Standards of the International Labor Organization stated that discriminatory practices in the area of employment against political opponents in Czechoslovakia constituted a continuing cause for concern (AFP, Geneva, 14–15 June). Czechoslovak federal minister of labor and social affairs Michal Šturcl rejected this statement as "antisocialist propaganda and interference with the internal matters of the socialist nations" (Radio Hvězda, 11 June).

Another complaint, not so easy for Czechoslovak authorities to dismiss, concerned the treatment of the Hungarian-speaking minority in Slovakia. Some spokesmen of the minority objected to the cultural and educational policies pursued in areas inhabited by Hungarian speakers; sufficient schools and teachers able to ensure elementary education in Hungarian were not available, and everything seemed to point to "assimilation efforts on the part of the government." One of these spokesmen, Miklós Duray, had been arrested in November 1982 and kept in custody until February 1983, when his scheduled trial was suddenly canceled and he was freed (Reuters, Prague, 28 February). The treatment of the Hungarian minority has been a delicate matter because it might adversely influence relations between Czechoslovakia and its southern communist neighbor and the climate in the Soviet bloc in general. Another ethnic group, about 300,000 strong, which has been causing problems of an entirely different kind, is the gypsies. It appears that it has been extremely difficult to integrate the gypsies into the normal life of an industrial society like Czechoslovakia. Their crime rate is very high, and working morale very low (*Smena*, Bratislava, 7 March).

There is growing environmental concern in Czechoslovakia. Successful actions at the grassroots level against ecological disruptions caused by housing construction and mass transit were reported from Prague (*Rudé právo*, 17 and 28 February). The "ecological lobby," however, is only just beginning; experts, such as members of the Czechoslovak Scientific and Technical Society, believe that the "potential ecological consequences of large-scale pollution are still being underestimated at all levels of the government" (Radio Hvězda, 12 April).

The Economy. The most urgent problems in 1983 were economic: low efficiency; poor-quality goods and services; shortages of manpower with special skills, paralleled by a surplus of workers who cannot find employment in the area for which they have been trained; stagnation of research and development; spreading economic crime in the form of petty theft, embezzlement, and misuse of public resources for private ends. None of these is new. One considerable worry is the large number of investment projects that are either far behind schedule or have had to be discontinued altogether; in 1982 there were about 25,000 such projects, worth 482 billion Kcs, or about $75 billion (Radio Prague, 29 January; *FBIS*, 1 February). In addition, the continuing world recession has been affecting the foreign balance of payments and thus restraining access to important raw materials and technological know-how, which must be purchased with convertible currency. In 1982, for example, exports to the West dropped by 1.4 percent (Radio Prague, 29 June). The semiannual report on the performance of the economy published in summer 1983, the third year of the Seventh Five-Year Plan, showed few signs of an upward trend; 16.8 percent of industrial enterprises did not meet their planned production targets. Although total industrial output increased, official commentators conceded that the increase "was not directed to areas where the interest of society would require" (*Rudé právo*, 27 July), a reference to shortages of consumer goods and consumer discontent. This discontent was hardly mitigated by a two-stage rise in the cost of services, carried out in February and in October; on average, the cost of services increased by 17.5 percent (Radio Prague, 27 January; *FBIS*, 28 January; Radio Hvězda, 29 September).

The energy sector has been in a state of crisis for many years, the crisis being compounded by the failure of an ambitious nuclear development program. Of the five nuclear power stations started between 1956 and 1980, only two have thus far been commissioned and only partially at

that. A conference of ministers holding portfolios relating to energy, held in Prague 18 July, was supposed to solve these problems (*Rudé právo*, 19 July).

In order to improve the state of the economy, two reforms have been introduced since the beginning of the 1980s: the so-called Set of Economic Measures in 1981 (in 1982 in agriculture), and the Amendment to the Economic Code, enacted at the end of 1982. Both assign greater powers and responsibilities to the managers of individual enterprises, which constitutes a departure from the rigid economic centralism of the Stalinist era, reintroduced after the Soviet military intervention in 1968. However, according to the media, this limited reform met with hostility from many people and therefore could not be fully implemented (*Nové slovo*, 23 June; Czechoslovak Television, 4 July). Opposition has originated from two sources: those who believe the reform not to be radical enough, and those who would like the economy to return to pure and simple centralism. At any rate, the Set of Economic Measures and the Amendment to the Economic code have not as yet notably improved the Czechoslovak economy.

Agricultural production has been stagnating, and the target figures of the five-year plan have not been reached in any of the previous years of the plan; nor were they in 1983. Owing to drought, the 1983 harvest, especially in Slovakia, was again an average one. Increasing dependence on food imports will further aggravate the already sizable food deficit (*Rol'nícke noviny*, 6 September).

The growth of economic crimes in 1983 prompted action by both the party and the government. It became an important subject of deliberations of the Ninth Joint Session of the Federal Assembly (counting from the last parliamentary elections in 1981). The "war on economic crime" declared on this occasion is to be waged mainly by mobilizing public opinion and strictly enforcing the existing legislation, although the session did consider changes in the criminal code (*Rudé právo*; *Pravda*, Bratislava; *Večerník*; and many other dailies, 15 June). It has been officially estimated that prosecuted economic offenses— 30,651 cases involving losses for the national economy of 151 million Kcs ($23.5 million)— represent only a fraction of the actual total (*Práca*, 10 June). Opinion surveys have shown that although another vice—bribery—is very widespread, a large proportion of the population does not view it as a truly criminal act (*Nové slovo*, 9 March; Radio Prague, 9 June).

Culture, Youth, and Religion. One important cultural event in 1983 was the opening of the renovated National Theater in Prague, on the centenary of its construction. In acknowledgment of this anniversary, 1983 was proclaimed the Year of Czech Theater. This reminder of the long and rich tradition of Czech dramatic art emphasized the poverty of contemporary drama and literature. This poverty has been admitted and decried even by official critics (e.g., *Tvorba*, no. 4, 26 January; *Kmen*, no. 9, 3 March; *Rudé právo*, 26 March). Fifteen years of "normalization" seem to have stifled all initiative and original thinking and forced genuine art and artists into the underground. Indeed, the number of books and periodicals produced and circulated without official permission, especially in the Western part of the country, has increased so much recently that it is difficult to keep count of them. At least five *samizdat* periodicals appear, despite great difficulties (George Moldau, *Samizdat Periodicals in Czechoslovakia*, Prague, August 1983).

The barrenness of the cultural scene has had a negative effect on youth. Young people shun official art and prefer either foreign literature and music or much earlier literary productions. It is characteristic of their mood that the novel *The Petroleum Prince* by Karl May sold 95,000 copies in Slovakia alone, while works of "socialist realism" could not find buyers (e.g., the book by Miloslav Hruškovič, candidate member of the KSČ Presidium, *Zápas o socialistický charakter kultury* [The struggle for the socialist character of culture], Bratislava, 1981). Regime commentators complained that the mass media failed to neutralize "dangerous hostile ideology that is deliberately focusing on culture for young people" (*Rudé právo*, 29 April) and urged reforms of radio and television programs in order "to arouse young people's socialist awareness" (ibid., 17 May). The call for these reforms was accompanied by repressive measures against "undesirable elements" that allegedly have penetrated the world of young culture, especially against some popular music groups. In January, the Prague rock group Selection was repeatedly attacked in the press and eventually banned (*Tribuna*, no. 7,

16 January). Later in the year, the same fate befell the group Patent, which had earned an "honorable mention" at the National Festival of Political Song in early spring; it was disbanded in June for "two-faced behavior" (*Rudé právo*, 24 June). It is estimated that no less than thirty rock groups have thus far been forbidden to appear in public (AP, Prague, 24 June).

The educational system is found wanting by students and the population at large. The prevailing view is that the educational reform of the 1970s, which was intended to link education more closely to occupational careers, has "failed completely" (Radio Prague, 7 April).

The uneasy coexistence of the regime and the Christian churches, owing to antireligious campaigns resumed after the Soviet intervention in 1968, continued throughout 1983. Catholics, by far the largest group, were the principal target of the regime's offensive. But it appears that despite these efforts, religiosity remains strong. Investigations undertaken by the Institute of Scientific Atheism indicate that 5,633,000 Czechoslovaks, or about 37 percent, maintained "religious attitudes of some kind or other" (*Ateizmus*, Brno, no. 1, 1983). In Slovakia, at the beginning of the 1980s, 45 percent were believers, about a third reported themselves to be agnostics or atheists, and about a fourth had "no crystallized world outlook" (*Smena*, 8 September). In 1983, the strength of religious beliefs was demonstrated by, among other events, the extent of participation in the traditional pilgrimage to the Holy Shrine of the Virgin Mary near Levoča in eastern Slovakia. No less than 150,000 pilgrims turned up, 50,000 more than in 1982, among whom young people prevailed (Kathpress, Bratislava, 1 August).

Observers speculated whether the appointment of Vladimír Janků, former deputy head of the International Department of the KSČ Central Committee, to succeed Karel Hrůza as head of the State Office for Church Affairs would bring any change in the regime's policies; however, no such change was perceptible. Legal and administrative restrictions of religious activities continued. From an internal document of the State Office for Church Affairs, published in the *samizdat* periodical *Informace o Církvi* (no. 9, September), it appears that progressive liquidation of all religion remains the KSČ's final objective. The police and the judiciary continued to serve this purpose. Frequent raids on the homes of priests and laymen known for their religious activism took place all over the country. Several persons were arrested for "impeding state supervision of churches," which usually means performing rites in private without a valid state permit. In Easter week, twenty Franciscan monks were detained on the charge that they "had acted as the fifth column of the Vatican, against the security and integrity of the state" (*Tribuna*, no. 13, 30 March). These arrests prompted a protest from the Franciscan superior general in Rome to Husák (*Times*, London, 7 April). They also led to a protest action in Czechoslovakia, on a scale not seen since the Soviet military intervention in August 1968: over 3,000 Christians, Catholic as well as Protestant, signed a letter dated 23 April and addressed to František Cardinal Tomášek expressing indignation at the treatment of the friars (AP, Prague, 7 June). The cardinal himself, who in 1982 had withdrawn his sponsorship of *Katolické noviny* for its continuing support of the pro-regime organization of priests Pacem in Terris and had been attacked for this step in the regime media, became the subject of a new controversy when a letter originally attributed to him and addressed to Czechoslovak authorities, containing a protest against the persecution of believers, was published in the West (Kathpress, Vienna, 24 August). Regime media claimed that the letter was "a forgery, a shameless attempt to drag a high church official into a filthy game" (Radio Prague, 31 August; *FBIS*, 1 September). Later the actual writer of the letter, Catholic theologian Dr. Josef Zvěřina, clarified the issue, but the suspicion remained that Czechoslovak police had deliberately placed an unsigned copy of the letter into the hands of Kathpress to mislead and discredit this news agency (AFP, Vienna, 18 September). Cardinal Tomášek for his part complained publicly about discrimination against Christians in Czechoslovakia in his address to the World Peace Assembly in Prague in June. Recalling the words of the late Pope John XXIII, he emphasized that "he who threatens basic human rights, including religious freedom, threatens peace." Not surprisingly, the media did not broadcast this part of his address (cf. *Rudé právo*, 25 June).

This treatment only worsened the already strained relations between Czechoslovakia and the Vatican in 1983. The hostility of Czechoslovak communists toward the "Polish pope" became manifest on several occasions. The visit of John Paul II to Austria in September, for example, unleashed a campaign in the media to present the trip as "an attempt to disrupt socialism" and to "instigate counterrevolution" (Radio Prague, 12 September; *FBIS*, 13 September). The Czechoslovak government reacted very sharply to the pope's appointment of Czech and Slovak exile prelates to titular bishoprics, although John Paul II expressly defined their duties as spiritual work among Czech and Slovak exiles (*Rudé právo*, 21 January).

Perhaps to alleviate these tensions, Czechoslovak foreign minister Bohuslav Chňoupek, during an official trip to Italy in December, requested and obtained a private audience with the pope and conferred at length with Vatican secretary of state Agostino Casaroli. In reporting these two meetings, regime media admitted that "tense relations" existed between the two governments (Radio Prague, 1 December; *FBIS*, 5 December); Western commentators characterized the climate of the audience granted to Chňoupek by John Paul II as "chilly" (*Messagero*, Rome, 1 December).

Mass Movements: Peace Rally, 1983. The World Assembly for Peace and Life, Against Nuclear War, held in Prague from 21 to 26 June, was organized by the Czechoslovak Peace Committee, executive organ of the Union of the Fighters for Peace, and cosponsored by the National Front. It was attended by 3,625 delegates from 132 countries. President Husák and Federal Assembly chairman Alois Indra opened the rally on 21 June. Because of the truly international participation—only 20 percent of delegates came from socialist countries—the assembly could not escape the disputes and disagreements dividing the various peace groups in the world. The presence of a large number of Western visitors provided an opportunity for opponents of the regime, organized as well as unorganized, to express their views on the official peace propaganda. A group of young people demonstrated on the evening of 22 June for "peace in freedom," which ultimately led to the arrest of several demonstrators by the police (*NYT*, 23 June). At the same time, the police dispersed a French peace group that wanted to protest the exclusion of the well-known dissident group Charter '77 from the rally (*DPA*, Prague, 22 June). Representatives of Charter '77 signed a joint manifesto with Western peace activists in Prague, 23 June, stating that "peace and human rights belong together" (*NYT*, 24 June).

Dissidence. The regime has been able to contain the dissident movement, but it cannot eradicate it completely. Spokesmen for Charter '77 made statements and issued documents on several important issues or anniversaries. In a letter dated 30 May, the group asked the secretary of the World Assembly for Peace, Tomáš Trávníček, for admission to the peace rally (*RFE Situation Report*, 24 June), a request that was denied. The group then circulated an open letter among the participants of the assembly, pointing out that the repressive policies of the regime were a threat to peace. A meeting with Western delegates took place on 22 June, and informal contacts with various foreign peace activists occurred throughout the rally (AFP, Prague, 21 June).

On 12 May, the group issued an extensive assessment of the dangers to the environment in Czechoslovakia (ibid., 12 May). Later that same month, Charter '77 protested to the International Labor Organization in Geneva about political discrimination in the workplace (Charter Document no. 18; AP, Prague, 24 May). Charter Document no. 26 (1 July) dealt with ecological and social devastation of northern Bohemia (*DPA*, Prague, 1 July). On 13 August, an open letter to the Federal Assembly, signed by Charter spokespersons Jan Kozlík, Maria Rut Křížková, and Anna Marvanová, recalled the Soviet military intervention fifteen years earlier and stressed the connection between the major crisis in Czechoslovak society and the forcible stopping of the reform movement of 1968 (AP, Prague, 13 August). In Document no. 37 (24 October), the same three representatives sent a letter to Gustáv Husák appealing for amnesty—on the occasion of the sixty-fifth anniversary of Czechoslovak independence—for "prisoners of conscience" (Reuters, Prague, 24 October). Charter Document no. 38 reported the taking into custody of citizens who expressed views contrary to the official position on the deployment of Soviet missiles in Czechoslovakia. Finally, Charter Document no. 39 (14 November) reproduced an open letter addressed to the president of the republic, the prime minister, the chairman of the Federal Assembly, and the prosecutor general in which the signatories stated that "the government's attempts to stifle all domestic discussion on the missile redeployment in East and West under-

mines its own credibility with Western peace movements and does nothing to dispel the justified apprehensions at home or to advance the cause of the peace in general" (AP, Prague, 14 November).

The persecution of dissidents continued throughout 1983. On 3 March, the regional court in Ostrava sentenced two Charter signatories— former World War II Resistance member and KSČ member of long standing Vladimír Liberda and Jaromír Šavrda, already jailed for another political crime—to 20 and 25 months in prison respectively (*samizdat* report, April). Another prominent Charter spokesman, Ladislav Lis, who had joined the underground KSČ during World War II and later became chairman of the Youth Union, was tried by the district court in Česká Lípa, in northern Bohemia, for "incitement against the socialist order and dissemination of unathorized literature" and condemned to fourteen months in prison plus a further three years of police surveillance (UPI, Prague, 21 July). Lis has not only been an active member of Charter '77, but also worked as an official of the Committee for the Defense of Unjustly Persecuted Persons (VONS), for which activity, he had been jailed twice prior to the current sentence. Military tribunals tried several cases of conscientious objectors during 1983, evaluating their offense mostly as a form of high treason (*Rol'nícke noviny*, 3 May). On the other hand, well-known playwright Václav Havel, who had been incarcerated since 1979, was released and hospitalized in the spring. He gave an interview about the state of Czechoslovak culture to the French daily *Le Monde* (9 April) and appeared on West German television at the end of the year (Bavarian TV and Radio, 19 December). Havel pointed out that unofficial cultural productions have long been taken quite seriously by representatives of the official culture. In April, Jiří Hájek, minister of foreign affairs in the Dubček government in 1968 and later chief spokesman of Charter '77, was interviewed by the Italian paper *La Repubblica* (16 April). He spoke about the enormous difficulties dissent in Czechoslovakia has been encountering, especially since the crisis in Poland.

Foreign Affairs. At the start of 1983, foreign ministers, and subsequently the heads of state, of the Warsaw Pact countries met in Prague for a three-day conference. This trip was Yuri Andropov's first travel abroad as Soviet party head. The conference, in the words of the Czechoslovak foreign minister Bohuslav Chňoupek, "started a peace offensive of great style" (Rudé právo, 21 February). The heads of state of the Warsaw alliance issued a declaration that later was frequently quoted by many diplomats of the Soviet bloc in official representations (ČETEKA, 6 January).

The most significant event involving relations with other Central and East European countries in 1983 was the visit paid by Husák to neighboring Poland in November to reciprocate the visit to Prague in 1982 of General Jaruzelski (YICA, 1983, p. 268). During his stay in Poland, Husák addressed workers at a tractor factory and gave an interview to the Polish party daily, Trybuna Ludu. On both occasions he assured the present Polish regime of "full support from the KSČ in the efforts to build socialism, consolidate society, and strengthen the country, both politically and economically." He also discussed the decisions of the 1981 KSČ congress and the danger to peace caused by "militant policies of imperialism" and endorsed Soviet plans to install operational-tactical missiles on Czechoslovak territory. (PAP, Warsaw, 29 November.) Earlier in November, Prague's unqualified support for the Soviet position on this issue was reiterated at a comparably high level, during the visit to Prague of Hungarian leader János Kádár. Kádár came to Czechoslovakia to present Gustáv Husák with a diamond-studded Order of the Hungarian People's Republic, in recognition of his responsibility "for all the important achievements of Czechoslovakia under socialism" (Radio Hvězda, 10 November).

Foreign Minister Bohuslav Chňoupek met with Andrei Gromyko in Moscow, 26 and 27 September. The deployment of U.S. missiles in Europe and the Soviet reaction were the main topics of discussion. The joint communiqué by the two foreign ministers repeated known Soviet positions on this matter (Tass, Moscow, 27 September).

In 1983, Chňoupek also undertook several official trips both to the West and to Third World countries. In April, he traveled to Tokyo, where he had talks with Japanese prime minister Yasuhiro Nakasone. Official coverage of the visit stressed the "lively political dialogue between the two countries" and the need for further expansion of economic cooperation (Radio Prague, 23 April; FBIS, 25 April). In May, during Chňoupek's visit to Madagascar, he and his host, Foreign Minister Christian Remi Richard, condemned U.S. plans for rearmament in Europe (ČETEKA, 29 May). In the fall, the Czechoslovak foreign minister visited Italy. He was received by his Italian counterpart and other cabinet ministers (Radio Prague, 1 December; FBIS, 2 December) and also stopped at the Vatican (see above). In the spring, Chňoupek had to appeal to U.N. secretary general Javier Pérez de Cuellar for help in obtaining the release of Czechoslovak citizens kidnapped by the Angolan guerrilla group UNITA (Radio Prague, 12 April; FBIS, 13 April). Husák sent a cable to Ethiopian president Mengistu Haile Mariam asking for his assistance in obtaining the liberation of the kidnapped experts (ibid., 1 April; FBIS, 4 April). Chňoupek's deputy, Stanislav Svoboda, went to Luanda to discuss the subject with the Angolan government and with the International Committee of the Red Cross (Radio Bratislava, 5 April; FBIS, 6 April). Svoboda also participated in interministerial consultations with the Libyan government in Tripoli (Pravda, Bratislava, 2 June).

An important event in the area of the relations with Western Europe was the visit to Prague in February of West German foreign minister Hans-Dietrich Genscher. It was Genscher's second official trip to Czechoslovakia since 1980. Czechoslovak and West German positions on the missile controversy, as well as possible coordination between the two countries in the protection of the environment against pollution originating in the industrial regions of Czechoslovakia, were the principal points on the agenda (DPA, 31 January; Frankfurter Rundschau, 3 February).

Czechoslovakia was represented by Richard Nejezchleb, the deputy chairman of the Federal Assembly's Chamber of the People, at the Palestine Liberation Organization's congress in Algiers in February (Pravda, Bratislava, 16 February). In March, Ethiopian minister of mines, energy, and water resources Aytenfiso Tekeze-Shoa came to Prague and met with Husák (Radio Prague, 30 March; FBIS, 31 March). In May, a party and state delegation from Zimbabwe, headed by Robert Mugabe, arrived in Czechoslovakia and was received with great pomp at Ruzyně airport (Radio Prague, 23 May; FBIS, 24 May). A parliamentary delegation from India, led by Shyam Lal Yadav, vice-chairman of the Indian Council of States, paid a visit to Czechoslovakia in July (Radio Prague, 6 July; *FBIS*, 7 July).

Foreign Trade and Foreign Debt. In early 1983, Czechoslovakia's foreign balance of payments was in the red by roughly $3.5 billion to the dollar and other hard-currency areas. This debt, to which the deficit of payments with the Council for Mutual Economic Assistance (CMEA) countries has to be added, was reduced by an unspecified amount during the year. Regime sources reported that Czechoslovakia had made payments to all its foreign creditors amounting to the equivalent of 9 billion Kcs ($1.4 billion at the official exchange rate). Sometimes the reduction was achieved, as these sources admitted, "at the price of cutting back imports" (*Život strany*, no. 1, 1983). Czechoslovakia's foreign debt is rather modest in comparison with that of some other CMEA countries, especially Poland.

The principal cause of foreign payments problems has been Czechoslovakia's dependence on imports of raw materials, above all oil. The new contract with the Soviet Union, signed in Moscow 13 January, provides for imports of crude oil and oil products to the total value of more than 2 billion rubles (*Rudé právo*, 14 January) or 23 percent more than in 1981 (see *Statistická ročenka ČSSR*, 1982, p. 480). More advantageous to Czechoslovakia appear to be the deliveries of natural gas from the Soviet Union, via the recently completed Urengoi-Uzhgorod pipeline. The gas is sold to Czechoslovakia at only 75 percent of the world price. In addition, Czechoslovakia is to receive 23 billion cubic meters of gas in lieu of payment for the transit fees resulting from the use of the pipelines on Czechoslovak territory (Czechoslovak Television, 28 January).

Czechoslovak party and government spokesmen often voiced the hope that a meeting of the signatories of the CMEA would improve the economic situation of the member-nations and enhance their mutual cooperation. In this context, significant changes in the system of industrial management of the individual Soviet bloc countries, defined as the "completion of reforms of economic mechanisms pursued since the middle of the 1960s" were suggested (Radio Hvězda, 6 April); in the case of Czechoslovakia this unequivocally would mean the reforms carried out by the protagonists of the Prague Spring. How-

ever, the CMEA summit, originally scheduled for 24–26 May 1983 in Bucharest (DPA, Vienna, 3 May), was not held. It has been assumed that disagreement over the summit's agenda, particularly between the USSR and Romania, was the major obstacle (AFP, Moscow, 3 May), but the possibility of a change in the economic course being fostered by the new Soviet leadership cannot yet be dismissed. Czechoslovak media reported in the fall that the summit would take place in 1984 (*Rudé právo*, 22 October). Bilateral trade agreements and projects between Czechoslovakia and other CMEA members, especially the USSR, however, have been in existence a long time. Negotiations with the Soviet Ministry of Aviation Industry resulted in an increase in cooperation in this field, determined by an agreement signed in the summer of 1983 (ibid., 3, 14, and 16 July). More intensive economic cooperation in the framework of the CMEA was called for during the visit of Hungarian prime minister György Lázár in Prague in October (Radio Hvězda, 10 October).

Next to import savings and promoting cooperation with the CMEA area, Czechoslovak economic policymakers tried to improve the economic situation by introducing "a new experiment" in the field of foreign trade. The experiment consists in closer linkage between production and foreign trade, which hitherto have been operated separately under the supervision of two different ministries (*Hospodářské noviny*, 4 March). Among the foreign trade agreements concluded or renewed during 1983, the protocol with the People's Republic of China, signed in January, called for the volume of trade to increase by 50 percent over 1982 (*Rudé právo*, 11 January).

Reaction to Polish Events. The prolonged social and economic crisis in neighboring Poland gave the Czechoslovak regime reasons for continuing and serious concern. The fear that the Polish popular movement, although stifled by martial law between 1981 and 1982, might become "contagious" inspired a number of preventive steps by the party and the government. Czechoslovak leaders seemed particularly apprehensive about the impact of the second papal visit to Poland on their population, especially the Catholics. However vehemently it may have been denied by official spokesmen (e.g., Radio Prague, 12 September; *FBIS*, 13 September), it is probable that the authorities prevailed on Cardinal Tomášek not to meet the pope while he was in Poland or, later, in Austria. In an unprecedented move, they also suspended the issuance of Czechoslovak transit visas from Austria to Poland during the stay of John Paul II (*Die Presse*, Vienna, 16 June). The pope's visit itself was first ignored by the Czechoslovak media and then commented on, after a considerable delay, in a hostile, almost venomous tone (e.g., *Rudé právo*, 18 and 20 June). The commentators, however, did not dissimulate that what they termed "outdated and obscurantist clericalism" was able "to govern the behavior of a not small part of the population of Poland" and that the Polish government "had no other choice but to face this reality" (*Tribuna*, no. 29, 20 July). The stiffening of the regime's attitude toward believers in Czechoslovakia in 1983 can also, at least partly, be explained by the scare created by the overwhelming reception of John Paul II by the Polish population. Despite attempts to isolate it, the Czechoslovak public was informed in great detail about events in Poland, thanks, in large measure, to underground publications. The leaders of Charter '77 sent a letter of congratulations on 5 October to Solidarity leader Lech Walesa when he was awarded the Nobel Peace Prize (AP, Prague, 5 October). The official media recorded this event only belatedly and called it "a mere gesture of political provocation" (*Rudé právo*, 6 October). It can be assumed that the bilateral talks on ideological questions held in Prague between the members of the Institute of Basic Problems of Marxism-Leninism in Warsaw and the workers of the KSČ Central Committee's Institute of Marxism-Leninism, in March, also served the purpose of mutual help in the fight against the forces of reform. On the agenda of these talks there was "an exchange of experience acquired in the post-crisis period"—during "normalization" in Czechoslovakia and the rule of martial law in Poland (*Pravda*, Bratislava, 31 March).

International Party Contacts. Since the Soviet military intervention of 1968, Czechoslovak party officials and spokesmen have used every opportunity of contact with other communist and radical left parties to demonstrate their full support for all policies and professed views of the USSR. In 1983, the major issue receiving unreserved endorsement was the Soviet deployment of long-range missiles in Europe. This theme was contained in virtually all communiqués or joint statements made by the Czechoslovak party delegations abroad, as well as by KSČ officials when they hosted party delegates from other countries. It was included in the message of the KSČ Presidium to the Sixteenth Congress of the Italian Communist Party (*L'Unità*, Rome, 6 March) and recalled by the Presidium member Vasil Bil'ák in Lisbon when he met with General Secretary Alvaro Cunhal of the Portuguese Communist Party (ČETEKA, 8 June). Similar occasions were provided by the visits of party leaders from Iraq, Tunisia, Brazil, and Uruguay.

Relations with some communist parties continue to be disturbed by disagreements about the present political course in Czechoslovakia and the legitimacy of the Soviet-led intervention in 1968 against the reformist leadership of Alexander Dubček. This is the case in relations with the communist parties of Italy and of Spain. The interparty climate between the KSČ and the League of the Communists of Yugoslavia became tense in 1983. KSČ spokesmen and media attacked Yugoslav communists for the support they had lent to the émigrés of 1968, former members and functionaries of the KSČ. They objected to the publicity Yugoslav media and publishing houses gave to Antonín Liehm, former editor of *Listy*, and Jiří Pelikán, former director of Radio Prague, by interviewing them on radio and television or by printing their works or Serbo-Croation translations of their books originally published in the West (*Tribuna*, no. 36, 7 September).

The dissatisfaction in the KSČ with the position of some "fraternal" parties on such issues as unconditional obedience to the USSR, considered vital by the present KSČ leadership, prompted repeated expressions of enthusiastic sympathy for the idea of a new international conference of all communist and workers' parties on the model of the Moscow meetings of 1957 and 1960, so that ideological differences could be settled and the world communist movement would emerge as a homogeneous body, capable of better promoting the cause of Soviet-style communism (*Rudé právo*, 6 May, 19 July).

Zdeněk Suda
University of Pittsburgh

Germany:
German Democratic Republic

Population. 16.7 million
Party. Socialist Unity Party of Germany (Sozialistische Einheitspartei Deutschlands; SED)
Founded. 1918 (SED, 1946)
Membership. 2,202,277 (ADN, 3 October; *FBIS*, 3 October); workers, 57.7 percent; production workers, 37.5 percent
Secretary General. Erich Honecker
Politburo. 17 full members: Erich Honecker (chairman, State Council), Hermann Axen, Horst Dohlus, Kurt Hager (member, State Council), Joachim Herrmann, Werner Felfe (member, State Council), Heinz Hoffmann (defense minister), Werner Krolikowski (first deputy chairman, Council of Ministers), Erich Mielke (minister of state security), Günter Mittag (member, State Council), Erich Mückenberger (member, Presidium of People's Chamber), Konrad Naumann (first secretary, Berlin regional party executive), Alfred Neumann (deputy chairman, Council of Ministers), Horst Sindermann (member, State Council; member, Presidium of People's Chamber), Willi Stoph (deputy chairman, State Council), Harry Tisch (member, State Council; chairman, Free German Trade Union Federation), Paul Verner (deputy chairman, State Council); 8 candidate members: Werner Jarowinsky, Günther Kleiber (deputy chairman, Council of Ministers), Egon Krenz (member, State Council), Ingeborg Lange, Margarete Müller (member, State Council), Günter Schabowski, Gerhard Schürer (chairman, State Planning Commission), Werner Walde (first secretary, Cottbus regional party executive)
Secretariat. 11 members: Erich Honecker, Hermann Axen (international relations), Horst Dohlus (publications), Werner Felfe (agriculture), Kurt Hager (culture and science), Joachim Herrmann (agitprop), Werner Jarowinsky (commerce and welfare), Günter Mittag (economic affairs), Ingeborg Lange (women's affairs), Paul Verner (security), Egon Krenz
Central Committee. 156 full and 51 candidate members
Status. Ruling party
Auxiliary Organizations. Free German Trade Union Federation (FDGB, 9.1 million members), led by Harry Tisch; Free German Youth (FDJ, 2.3 million members), led by Eberhard Aurich; Democratic Women's League (DFB, 1.4 million members), led by Ilse Thiele; Society for German-Soviet Friendship (DSF, 3.5 million members)
Main State Organs. Council of State, chaired by Erich Honecker; Council of Ministers (45 members, all but 4 belong to SED), chaired by Willi Stoph; both constitutionally answer to People's Chamber
Parliament and Elections. All candidates run on ticket of National Front, an umbrella organization comprising the SED, 4 smaller parties, and other groups. The 500 seats in the People's Chamber are distributed as follows: SED 127, 52 to each of 4 smaller parties, FDGB 68, FDJ 40, DFB 35, Cultural League 22.
Publications. *Neues Deutschland (ND)*, official SED daily; *Einheit*, SED theoretical monthly; *Neuer Weg*, SED organizational monthly; *Junge Welt*, FDJ daily; *Tribüne*, FDGB daily. The official news agency is Allgemeiner Deutscher Nachrichtendienst (ADN).

Party Internal Affairs. The SED Central Committee met for its customary two plenums in 1983: the sixth was held on 15–16 June (Horst Dohlus read the Politburo report), and the seventh convened on 24–25 November (with Werner Felfe delivering the main address). As usual, these meetings were not the occasion for any startling new policy announcements; occasional comments about domestic matters and foreign affairs contained some hints and allusions that supplemented what was otherwise known or suspected about internal developments in the German Democratic Republic (GDR) in 1983 and SED intentions for the immediate future. No fundamental alterations in the broad contours of GDR foreign or domestic policy, however, came to light. The only personnel change of importance was the promotion of Egon Krenz, the former first secretary of the FDJ's Central Council, to the post of Central Committee secretary. Krenz, who had been a candidate member of the Politburo since May 1976, also joined that group as a co-opted full member. (*Informationen*, no. 23, p. 19.) A short time later, Krenz received the GDR's highest medal, the Karl-Marx-Orden, for his "meritorious service in the cause of the communist education of young people, the creative application of Marxism-Leninism, and in recognition of his work over many years as first secretary of the Central Council of the FDJ" (*ND*, 3–4 December).

SED party elections for 1983 and 1984 began in early October, implementing a decision taken at the Sixth Plenum. The stated "main purpose" of the elections, which took place in 92,000 party groups and more than 83,000 basic and regional party organizations, was "to put into effect all the advantages and driving forces of socialism for the continuation of the policy of the main tasks in its unity of economic and social policy and to mobilize Communists and all citizens for the political mass struggle in the all-round strengthening of the GDR and making peace secure" (ADN, 3 October; *FBIS*, 3 October).

On the occasion of Walter Ulbricht's ninetieth birthday, *Neues Deutschland* and most other GDR dailies carried commemorative articles, continuing the incremental rehabilitation of Ulbricht begun five years ago. Following his ouster as secretary general in 1971 and death two years later, Ulbricht had been handled virtually as a nonperson. Even though not a single street or square in the GDR is named after him, however, the SED's general neglect of Ulbricht has slowly turned into a cautious and restrained "appreciation" of his historical services. "As an eminent leader of the German working class, an exemplary proletarian revolutionary and statesman with close ties to the people," read the article originally published in *Neues Deutschland*, Ulbricht occupies a "permanent place in the history of our party and of the German Democratic Republic." The formation of the SED and the development of the GDR, the paper went on to say, were intimately associated with Ulbricht's activity. (*Frankfurter Allgemeine Zeitung* [*FAZ*], 1 July.) An authoritative biography of Ulbricht that appeared in 1983 was written by the head of the SED's Institute for Marxism-Leninism and contained a restrained but positive appraisal of Ulbricht that contrasts vividly with the hagiographical biographies published during his lifetime. Ulbricht's main "service" was his development of "a collective, unified, and resolute leadership within the party." (Ibid., 28 December.)

Domestic Affairs. *Peace Movement.* The year under review was one of frequent and often ugly confrontations between the authorities and members of the unofficial peace movement in the GDR, who took the SED's peace rhetoric other than it was intended, namely not hypocritically, and tried to apply it to circumstances in the GDR. Other than calling attention to the SED's double standard in its policy of "safeguarding" the peace in general and its opposition to the stationing of intermediate-range missiles in Western Europe in particular, the nonregime peace activists in the GDR celebrated few meaningful successes. By the end of the year, in fact, many of the leaders found themselves either in West German exile or under East German arrest following various waves of repression. Hopes for any improvement in the general situation are bleak. Seventeen young people were arrested in Jena, for instance, when they attempted to hold a symbolic moment of silence for peace on Christmas Eve, 1982. Western reports on their arrest, on the eve of the GDR's Luther-year commemorations in 1983, evidently concerned the GDR enough for the responsible authorities to issue a statement through ADN stating that "in the GDR, not a single citizen, critical artist, or worker, let alone young people, has been arrested because he was working for peace." Of course the statement, which was not carried in any GDR publication, was true as far as it went: the seventeen young people were naturally not charged with offenses related directly to their peace activity; rather, they were accused of defaming or wishing to defame the GDR with actions that had an objectively antisocialist content. In late February, however, all seventeen were released from jail. (*RAD Background Report*, no. 76.) In early summer, there was another incident in Jena (in general a hotbed of antiregime peace activism); this one ended with the expulsion from the GDR of some twenty Jena peace adherents who were simultaneously deprived—"released" is the East German euphemism—from their state citizenship. (Ibid., no. 128.)

Later in the summer, a group of East Germans fasting for peace urged the SED to renounce the threatened stationing of Soviet tactical missiles on East German soil in the event that the Geneva negotiations ended unsuccessfully. The strikers, who had just completed a week-long fast in the Church of the Redeemer in East Berlin coinciding with hunger strikes in Bonn, Paris, and California, addressed their appeal directly to Erich Honecker and explained their goal as the exertion of "pressure in a nonviolent fashion on those holding power, in order to further the continuing political negotiations." Politics was not of preeminent importance because the question was simply not one of the survival of either capitalism or socialism; rather, no less than the continued existence of human civilization in dignity and justice was at stake. Referring to themselves and their hunger strike, the protestors added: "We appeal to your conscience and to the conscience of the political leadership of the GDR not to allow 10 people to die in the coming weeks as representatives of the fate that threatens mankind. Their deaths would strengthen our fears that the deaths of many might become reality...The government of the GDR could declare, in the case of a further delay in or even collapse of the Geneva negotiations, that it is not willing to allow nuclear missiles to be stationed in its territory...In our opinion, this would in no way endanger its security, since the deterrent potential of the Warsaw Pact states is already sufficient to make any attack an act of suicide." (Ibid., no. 206.)

The atmosphere in the GDR worsened considerably following the decision by the West German parliament to begin deployment of NATO medium-range missiles and especially with the relatively successful completion of the official Luther-year celebrations. In mid-December, Bärbel Bohley and Ulrike Poppe were arrested by the East German security police. Both belonged to the independent peace movement in the GDR, and both were leading members of the Women for Peace coalition. More arrests followed in Weimar, Potsdam, and Leipzig. The official reason given for the arrest of Bohley and Poppe was their violation of paragraph 99 of the GDR penal code, which prohibits the "treasonous dissemination of information" to foreigners (the two had talked with Western peace activists). The pair had also attracted attention by protesting the new GDR military service law passed in March 1982 (see *YICA*, 1983, p. 275), which stipulates that women can be drafted. They had also angered authorities by opening up their own kindergarten as a protest against the mounting level of militarization in the public schools. On 16 December, following the women's arrest, the kindergarten was shut down and the entire entrance way bricked shut. (*FAZ*, 23 December; *Der Spiegel*, 26 December.)

Several other incidents occurred late in the year. In Potsdam, some thirty protesters met in November for a silent vigil; two were arrested. In Weimar, a number of teenagers sprayed slogans protesting Soviet SS-20 missiles on walls, and six arrests followed. In Leipzig, four young people were accused of asocial behavior, group-building hostile to the state, and public denigration of the GDR. (*FAZ*, 23 December.) Just a week before Christmas, East Berlin photographer Harald Hauswald was picked up by security police and detained for seven hours. For Hauswald, this was the fourth detention since 1978 and the second house search. The authorities were particularly anxious to trace the source of stickers showing up on numerous house or apartment doors reading "Atomic-Free Zone," one of which had decorated Hauswald's door. (Ibid., 28 December.)

Religion. Since its inception, the unofficial peace movement in the GDR has been closely linked with the Protestant church, which—especially in a year commemorating the 500th anniversary of Luther's birth—has developed into a source of real aggravation to the regime. At the fall synod of the Federation of Evangelical Churches in the GDR, for instance, one resolution called on NATO and the Soviet Union to do everything in their power to arrive at an understanding that would make the stationing of new missiles unnecessary. The resolution urged the United States to display greater flexibility and encouraged the Soviet Union to begin immediate destruction of its SS-20 missiles. The synod, which closed with a statement renouncing the "spirit and logic of deterrence," also appealed to the GDR to take certain concrete steps, specifically to work for the establishment of an "instrument of international law" that would make the possession and use of atomic weapons a crime against humanity and to exercise its influence in the Warsaw Pact to prevent the stationing of new nuclear missiles on East German territory. The synod also appealed to the government to recognize the right of conscientious objectors to refuse military service and for a form of nonviolent alternative service. (Ibid., 21 September.)

Less than a month later, a synod of local churches in Mecklenburg, representing 350 parishes, likewise voiced its concern over plans to station tactical nuclear missiles in the GDR and asked that the government reconsider its decision. The synod also criticized state actions against autonomous peace initiatives, the new military service law that permits the conscription of women, and the artificial state-sponsored signature campaigns carried out in schools and factories intended to make a show of "mass support" for the deployment of new missiles in the GDR. (Ibid., 15 November.)

The church has not always been so willing to advocate controversial measures that risked a direct confrontation with the authorities. When the seventeen young people were arrested in Jena in December 1982, the church hierarchy in Thuringia went to some lengths to dissociate itself from the circumstances surrounding the arrests. In response to detailed Western press coverage, the press office of the Lutheran church in Thuringia addressed a letter to all accredited Western correspondents in the GDR asking for more objectivity in the treatment of the events in Jena and understanding for the position of the church. No activities, the letter stated, "took place outside of the Church and Church facilities for which the Church would have to assume responsibility." Soon after this statement became known, however, the Western press published a letter from eighteen young Christians from Thuringia who expressed their "shame" at the church hierarchy's action. There had been "no room" for the arrested within the church, "so therefore their place is now in the detention center of the security police . . . There is a point after which silence becomes complicity. In our recent past, Christians have already been faced with this painful question." The church, in turn, responded by emphasizing that it also supported those in need, "even if we don't share their motivations and convictions." (*RAD Background Report*, no. 76.)

One of the more unusual events of the year relating to church-state affairs was the publication in *Neues Deutschland* (22–23 October) of two letters to Erich Honecker written by an Evangelical church congregation in Dresden-Loschwitz, East Germany, and by a congregation in Hausen-Pohlheim, West Germany. The letter from the East German church congregation voiced the parishioners' general fear in the face of an escalating arms race. The very thought that the deployment of U.S. missiles, which the church deplored, might be followed by the positioning of corresponding weapons "on our territory" and the unavoidability of having to live directly with atomic weapons filled the church with despair. Speaking to Honecker personally, the letter repeated his frequent comment that an accelerated military buildup offered no assurance of greater security. The letter closed with the argument that the only way to maintain peace lay in unilateral measures, that is, in forgoing the temptation to respond to missiles with more missiles. There were two unusual aspects to the publication of the letter, apart from the fact that it appeared in *Neues Deutschland* at all. First, it was printed in a space normally reserved for official commentaries; and, second, it was the first expression of nonofficial peace sentiment to be published in an official GDR organ. The letter from the West German church was more succinct. The most important passage read simply: "The leadership of the Evangelical church in Hausen-Pohlheim is *for* peace in the world and *against* weapons of mass destruction in East and West" (ibid.). But the very mention of such weapons in *East* and West was unusual for the GDR, not to say for *Neues Deutschland*.

The reasons for the publication of the two letters were unclear; perhaps it was an attempt on the part of the SED to demonstrate its awareness of public concern over the countermeasures that it was threatening to take at the time if NATO proceeded with the deployment of Pershing II and cruise missiles (*RAD Background Report*, no. 254). If so, this particular event is a prime illustration of how the GDR's peace rhetoric has actually led to an unintended, heightened sensitivity within the country over this issue, a concern that is becoming increasingly difficult for the SED to manage. The publication might also have been planned as the more standard trick of preparing the way for a later announcement that the GDR shared the concerns of those who wrote the letters, but that due to NATO policies, countervailing measures had regrettably become necessary. In fact, *Neues Deutschland* (25 October) reported on the front page a few days later that the GDR's National Defense Council had announced preparatory work for the installation of new tactical missiles in the GDR and in Czechoslovakia as a response to the deployment of Pershing II and cruise missiles.

Following a year of commemorations and festivities, the GDR closed out the 500th anniversary of Martin Luther's birth with an official celebration in November. Shortly before, Erich Honecker granted an interview to the West German *Lutherische Monatshefte*, and segments of the conversation were published in *Neues Deutschland* (6 October). In the interview, Honecker said that cooperation between the two official Luther committees, sponsored by the church and by the state, had exercised a "stabilizing effect on church-state relations" (*Informationen*, no. 19, p. 9). As for the SED's historical assessment of Luther, Honecker said that a Marxist understanding of Luther stressed his role as an intellectual initiator for the early bourgeois revolution and his important role in the development of language and culture. Luther's "tragedy" lay in the contradiction between his actions as an initiator of a great movement and his inability to understand fundamental social progress. With regard to the general SED policy of appropriating major German historical figures, Honecker said that the GDR did not need to integrate German history; it came from it, was part of it, and was the continuation of it. (*DPA*, 30 September; *FBIS*, 3 October.) In an interview carried in *Neues Deutschland* (14 November), the deputy chairman of the state Luther committee added a more contemporary note. The commemoration of Luther in the GDR was an important contribution to the struggle for peace and security, against the imperialist military buildup and policy of

confrontation, which, after all, also called the future existence of Luther's legacy into question and threatened the lives of millions of Luther's followers.

Military. At the Seventh Plenum, which convened just a few days after the West Germans approved the deployment of new U.S. missiles, GDR defense minister Heinz Hoffmann announced that in view of the devastating weapons in the hands of the "enemies of peace and progress," the socialist states were obliged to do everything in their power "to prevent war." Those who were planning new acts of aggression had to be confronted with the threat of their own certain destruction and were to be given no reason to think victory might be possible in any kind of war. Hoffmann also announced that preparations were already under way for the stationing of new operational-tactical missile systems in the GDR. These systems, considering their range and accuracy and combined with weapons systems in Czechoslovakia and the Soviet Union, would create "a counterbalance to the stationing of Pershing II and cruise missiles in the Federal Republic [FRG]." Hoffmann added that "socialist military instruction, premilitary training, and the civil defense of the GDR," as well as the supplementation of the country's armed forces and instructional institutions with "physically and mentally healthy, morally resolute, and capable young people," was to be guaranteed at a high level. (*FAZ*, 26 November.)

The March issue of the monthly *Junge Generation* (*JPRS*, 16 June) had earlier reported on what Hoffmann meant about premilitary training, specifically in the so-called Society for Sports and Technology (GST). FDJ activists in the GST had established for themselves a "clear position" on the military class mission and the function of the "socialist armed forces as a factor in securing peace" and developed a class-conscious attitude toward training in the GST. It was not enough merely to "rehash" material from civics lessons or to leaf through occasional newspapers; rather, members of the FDJ were to devote themselves early on, "systematically and purposefully," to questions of the party's military policy so as to understand better the military contexts of world events and to strengthen basic convictions. This understanding was contingent on loyalty to the party of the working class and to the "workers' and peasants' state"; on the strengthening of friendship with the Soviet Union and other countries of the socialist community; on a greater hatred of imperialism; and on the recognition of NATO's intentions, "which endanger peace." The activists thus helped to demonstrate why one later bore arms as a soldier in the National People's Army (NVA) and what the very purpose of being a soldier in socialism meant. Strong socialist armed forces as organs of working-class power were the "best protection against all imperialist intrigues."

Economy. The economic highlight of the year was the announcement in late June that a one billion mark banking credit had been granted to the GDR by a West German banking consortium. The loan, the first non-trade-related credit that West German banks had ever granted the GDR (guaranteed by the West German government), is repayable over five years at an interest rate of 1 percent over the London inter–bank office rate. The GDR apparently approached the West German government after having unsuccessfully courted Swiss and Austrian financial circles. (*RAD Background Report*, no. 217.) Next to the fact that the Christian Democratic government even supported the bank deal (as an opposition party, the Christian Democrats had constantly criticized the Social Democrats for their concessions to the GDR and had always insisted on quid-pro-quo dealings with the East Germans), the biggest surprise was that Franz-Josef Strauss had played a leading role in arranging for the credit. The Bavarian minister-president had long been an opponent of liberal policies toward the GDR. The credit was also unusual because West German government officials admitted that the East Germans had made no specific promises in connection with the loan.

The credit came as a major relief to the GDR because the country faces heavy financial obligations in hard currency, and a large portion of the GDR's debts are in short-term maturities that must be repaid over the next two years. Western experts expect the GDR to use the credit to meet interest payments and a portion of the maturing principle due in 1984. (Ibid.; *FAZ*, 9 September.) The GDR in general has accumulated an indebtedness to the West that is causing the SED leadership increasing problems. The latest figures available from the Basel Bank for International Settlements indicate that the GDR had gross liabilities to Western banks in the amount of $8.8

billion, not counting supplier credits of $1.9 billion. Nor does this figure include GDR debts in the inner-German clearing system. Counting these, total GDR indebtedness to Western creditors amounts to about $12.5 billion. According to some estimates, debts of about $3.5 billion will come due in 1984, as well as interest amounting to $1.1 billion. In inner-German trade, the GDR had gross liabilities by the end of 1983 that came to $1.7 billion. (*FAZ*, 29 June.)

The GDR's interest payments were estimated for 1983 at approximately $1 billion with payment on the principal amounting to $3 billion (lower than in 1982). Available statistics for 1982 disclose that the GDR was forced to use about one-half of its export profits in hard currency for interest payments in that year. The GDR is absolutely dependent on new credits, and it is unclear how willing Western banks are to offer them. Compounding the problem is the necessity to supply more and more products to the Soviet Union in order to obtain an unchanging quantity of raw materials. As for the improvement of the balance of trade vis-à-vis the Western industrial states, this was arrived at more by throttling imports than by raising exports. (Ibid., 21 September.) Nor is the situation expected to improve much in 1984. One report spoke of an interest payment of over $1 billion and repayment or renegotiation of 30 to 40 percent of the GDR's entire indebtedness (ibid., 9 September). Some bank analysts acquainted with the GDR's situation predict that East Berlin, taking all sources of hard currency and maturing loans into account, will still be confronted with a shortage of $1.2–1.5 billion by 31 March 1984. The need to obtain further credit, probably from the West Germans, may help to explain the GDR's unexpected interest in the continuation of good relations with the FRG in spite of the West German decision to deploy new missiles; and it may even account in part for Soviet acquiescence to a special kind of German-German cordiality at a time of high tension between the two superpowers: the GDR also owes the USSR some 3 billion transfer rubles. (Ibid., 16 December.)

In some other respects, however, 1983 was not an especially poor year. "The GDR economy will complete the year 1983, too, with a good overall record of accomplishment," said Honecker at the Seventh Plenum (*ND*, 26–27 November). Other speakers confirmed that 1983 had ended better than expected, though a 119 percent increase in exports to the USSR reveals how disproportionate the GDR's foreign trade is becoming and the extent to which the country's economic output is being taken over by exports to the East. Honecker claimed that trade with the "nonsocialist" countries brought a considerable surplus in 1983, but he failed to note that the surplus was caused by a sharp restriction on imports. The GDR was expected to continue this policy as long as necessary to convince Western banks that it is capable of controlling its economic difficulties and that it is a good credit risk. (Ibid.; *FAZ*, 27 November.)

Dissent and Repression. Figures released by the Association of Victims of Stalinism (VOS) in September disclose that West Germany has purchased the freedom of some 20,000 political prisoners from East German jails over the past 21 years. The VOS also estimated that around 2,000 political prisoners were currently in GDR prisons. Between 1,200 and 1,300 inmates are released into West Germany annually. (*FAZ*, 14 September.) In a related matter, the Working Group 13 August revealed in October that about 200 political prisoners who had been serving sentences in GDR labor camps had been released to West Berlin over the preceding two months. Some 4,000 political prisoners remain in the GDR, according to the Working Group, which also claimed that about 50,000 GDR citizens carry a special identity card given to those suspected of harboring the intention of escaping to the West or for any past actions that indicate opposition to the regime. The "PM-12 replacement identity card" requires that a citizen register constantly with the police, ties the holder to his job, and places restrictions on visits. (DPA, 21 October; *FBIS*, 24 October.)

Evidently as part of the "repayment" of the one billion mark credit granted the GDR, East German authorities ordered the removal of automatic firing and explosive devices from a fourth of the German-German border. But there was much speculation in the West that they might merely be replaced with more effective devices or that the GDR would establish barriers further back of the border, beyond the view of Western observers. (*FAZ*, 29 September.) In any case, the effectiveness of the devices may have struck the GDR as disproportionate to the damage inflicted on the country's prestige every time reports reached the West of a new death or disfiguration caused by

the explosions. In early October, Austrian journalists asked Honecker whether the devices would be removed entirely and along the entire length of the border, and he answered in the affirmative. "The responsible offices here have decided to remove these things, and, yes, they are being removed. But then there is a slight difference between an automatic firing device and a cruise missile and Pershing II." (*Informationen*, no. 19, p. 19.) By the end of the year, however, West German authorities confirmed that only about a tenth of the devices had, in fact, been removed. Observations along the border confirm that the GDR has tightened the belt of mines in the actual border region, erected higher barriers in select areas, and installed new warning systems designed to trap would-be escapees some 500–800 meters from the actual border (*Süddeutsche Zeitung*, 4 January 1984).

Culture. At a press conference in Leipzig, Deputy Cultural Affairs Minister Klaus Höpcke confirmed indirectly that East German writers would be fined if they read from their works in private circles or in private homes without reporting the readings beforehand to authorities. Not surprisingly, reports out of the GDR soon confirmed that young writers who had applied for permission to give private readings were rarely granted permission. (*JPRS*, 13 April.)

The Ninth Congress of the GDR Writers' Union met in East Berlin from 31 May to 2 June, and many of the speeches given there centered on the peace issue. Hermann Kant, the president of the union, said that the struggle for peace had always been an integral part of the history of East German literature and that it was natural for the issue to come up at the congress because world peace was endangered at the time. Kant went on to say that 1983 was an especially crucial year because of the NATO twin-track decision, which called for the deployment of "first strike weapons and plans for the decapitation" of the political leadership in the Warsaw Pact countries. The NATO decision was, in fact, "nothing less than an attack on the continuation of mankind." As for the indigenous East German peace movment, "There is no need to get overly excited about one individual or another who knows how to attract attention [to himself] or to mime the traveling drama critic with his horror stories about persecuted catacomb-Christians in the GDR"; but the attempts to unsettle the GDR peace movement with anticommunism had to be opposed. (*RAD Background Report*, no. 133.) Stephan Hermlin, on the other hand, called for more tolerance toward those whose views on how to work for peace did not always match the party's: "Among the populace there is immense untapped energy calling for liberation, for unfurling, when it comes to peace, that most ancient of dreams. It is precisely among the young that such energy rests. One should encourage them to make their contribution, even if one cannot agree with every idea they might express. Nothing is more liberating than the feeling of having done something for a great cause. I know and never forget that there are some who say 'peace' and mean something entirely different. I same 'some' because they are a small minority, the only minority that does not deserve respect. But revolutionary vigilance must not paralyze, must not diminish, the existing high degree of trust, if we want to preserve peace." (Ibid.)

Following the "rehabilitation" of Martin Luther and in line with general attempts to claim the great personalities of German history for the GDR, "cultural authorities" gradually began laying the groundwork in 1983 for the incorporation of Otto von Bismarck into their historical outlook. In June, for instance, an FDJ publication called Bismarck a "statesman of great importance," and the surprise that this assessment evoked in the Western press precipitated an East German attempt to show that an appreciation of Bismarck had been a "component of our historical outlook for a long time." (*Informationen*, no. 14, p. 9.) In mid-December, Kurt Hager went into far greater detail. History knew of examples where representatives of the exploiting classes had managed to maintain an eye for reality. Some of these specific figures in German history were Yorck von Wartenburg, Bismarck, Walter Rathenau, and Claus von Stauffenberg and other "personalities of the conspiracy of 20 July 1944." Certainly Bismarck deserved no praise in GDR historiography for his enactment of antisocialist legislation and for his policy of Germanization of the *Kaiserreich*. "But the political course being followed by the confrontation politicians in the United States, which threatens mankind and is supported unconditionally by leading circles in the FRG, calls for the consideration of other sides of [Bismarck's] politics and his personality." For Bismarck had made it a political principle to deal with realities and not fictions. His sense of reality

thus placed him in a position to calculate soberly, especially in foreign policy, and to advocate "good relations with Russia." In February 1888, for instance, he warned against a preventive war. Hager concluded that "no one should be surprised when we call attention to such positions, arrived at from entirely different class interests, at a time when much depends on whether a sense of reality and reason within the ruling circles of imperialist states prevails over adventurism and military delusions of grandeur." (*FAZ*, 17 December.)

Writer Anna Seghers died on 1 June at the age of 82. Seghers had long been active in the Writers' Union and the World Peace Council.

Foreign Policy. *The West.* In a speech delivered to "leading cadres" of the NVA early in the year, Defense Minister Heinz Hoffmann attacked the Reagan administration and NATO and issued strong warnings about countermeasures to be taken should the deployment of medium-range missiles proceed at the end of the year according to plan, assuming that the Geneva negotiations ended unsuccessfully. "As the outlines of the course chosen by the USA and NATO become increasingly evident, it has become clear that what we have to deal with is not merely a gradual hardening of the previous policy toward the Soviet Union and other Warsaw Pact states." Hoffmann went on to explain: "We are being confronted with a dangerous turn in imperialist policy, with an open challenge to socialism, above all in the military field. With its policy of armament, the USA wishes to exhaust the socialist states through a new round of the arms race and to force them to their knees . . . The American leadership has thereby radically broken with the policy of peaceful coexistence and the obligations of the Helsinki conference and is now pursuing a policy with the more or less publicly proclaimed goal of decisively weakening socialism as a world system and of smashing it, even at the price of a nuclear war. We must draw the appropriate conclusions for the increase in our fighting and mobilization preparedness and, among other things, must be prepared to make our contribution to timely reconnaissance and an effective defense against the new fighting capabilities of NATO." (*RAD Background Report*, no. 30; *ND*, 5–6 February.)

At the Seventh Plenum in November, Hoffmann's rhetoric was among the toughest. The U.S. government and the highest representatives of the leading NATO countries, by beginning the deployment of medium-range missiles, had "to all practical purposes declared war against the socialist community. They are in the process of developing broadly conceived war preparations against the states of the Warsaw Pact." (*FAZ*, 26 November.)

Dr. Gerhard Herder was named ambassador to the United States in July. From 1975 to early 1979, Herder had represented the GDR in the Geneva Conference on Disarmament; since then, he had been the GDR's permanent representative to the United Nations and to other international organizations in Geneva.

Following the U.S. intervention in Grenada, Harry Ott, deputy minister of foreign affairs, declared at the U.N. General Assembly: "With the naked aggression in Grenada, the undeclared war against Nicaragua, and the threat of military intervention against other states of the region, the United States has . . . made terrorism its state policy." *Neues Deutschland* (4 November) also made an unflattering comparison of the United States with Nazi Germany: "The GDR knows from historical experience that such pretexts as the 'protection of compatriots in foreign countries,' used by the United States in the Grenada case or so-called preventive measures, were also used another time when, as a consequence, the European continent was engulfed by the flames of World War II." Maurice Bishop had been in East Berlin on a stopover in early October, where he was received by Ernst Mecklenburg, deputy chairman of the GDR State Council, and by Deputy Minister for Foreign Affairs Bernhard Neugebauer (ADN, 6 October; *FBIS*, 7 October).

Intra-German Relations. Throughout 1983, the East Germans took advantage of every opportunity to warn the West German government that "certain measures" would be taken if the country went ahead with the deployment of new U.S. nuclear missiles. In an editorial in *Neues Deutschland* (3 May), the GDR responded to the concern over the deaths of three West German visitors to the GDR over a three-week period. All had suffered heart attacks, in two cases while being questioned by GDR border guards. As a result of the tension caused by these incidents and related speculation (Franz-Josef Strauss spoke of "murder" in one case), Honecker canceled a trip to West Germany originally scheduled for late 1983 "because of the situation brought about by

West Germany in relations between the two German states" (*NYT*, April 29). In the May editorial, *Neues Deutschland* accused "certain circles" in West Germany of using the deaths as a pretext for "destroying" continuity in West Germany's *Ostpolitik* and introducing a change in the country's policy with regard to the GDR. "It is a part of the offensive of untruths when attempts are now made to turn matters completely around, all the more so because it is necessary to deceive the citizens of the Federal Republic and, in 1983, to station the new U.S. medium-range missiles in spite of the express will of the majority." The important passage read: "It is not the goal of the GDR to loosen the FRG's ties to the NATO alliance. But it would behoove Bonn not to forget that the GDR is likewise firmly anchored in its alliance. Thus, the stationing of new U.S. nuclear missiles . . . would not contribute at all to the establishment of normal, to say nothing of good neighborly, relations with the GDR. Just the opposite." But the article went on to point out that, all in all, the development of ties between the two countries since 1971, especially considering all the impediments, was quite impressive.

The practice of issuing warnings to the West Germans combined with positive observations about past relations and the expression of hope for future satisfactory ties continued throughout the year. At the Sixth Plenum, Dohlus noted that in the event of the "stationing of new nuclear U.S. first-strike weapons in Western Europe," the USSR would have to take "prompt effective countermeasures" in order to maintain the continuation of military-strategic parity and to provide effective protection for socialism and peace. But Dohlus also spoke of the "continuity, predictability, and reliability" of the SED's German policy and made it clear that the GDR was interested in maintaining good relations. (*ND*, 16 November; *Deutschland Archiv* [*DA*], no. 8, p. 840.)

In October, Honecker granted an interview to a Western publication (*Stern*) for the first time in five years. On the subject of FRG-GDR relations, he said that a worsening of the international situation would not be conducive to good relations between the two countries. The GDR would do everything in its power to continue the process of normalization because a "correct" relationship between the GDR and FRG "exerts a positive influence on the overall system of relations in Europe." (*ND*, 4 November.)

Several months later, at the Seventh Plenum,

Honecker reacted with surprising moderation to the West German Bundestag's decision to proceed with the deployment of Pershing II and cruise missiles. The European system of treaties, including the basic treaty regulating relations between the GDR and the FRG, had suffered serious damage because of this decision, Honecker said. But, he added, "we are in favor of limiting the damage as much as possible." The situation had changed once the deployment began, but it was better to negotiate ten times than to shoot once, and it was not unthinkable that the negotiations would be continued and lead eventually to positive results. The GDR would examine carefully every reasonable suggestion made by the West Germans to re-establish normality in relations between the two German states, although all attacks on the sovereignty of the GDR would be repelled. As for the Soviet announcement that new nuclear weapons would be deployed in Czechoslovakia and the GDR, Honecker noted openly: "Of course these steps, which are unavoidable in order to thwart U.S. military strategical superiority, cause no outbreak of joy in our country." (Ibid., 25 November.)

In related matters, *Neues Deutschland* carried a cover story on 1 November reporting on the visit of a delegation of the West German Green Party, which was received by Honecker. The Greens gave Honecker a list of 24 East Germans who had been arrested because of their peace activism, and Honecker approved the release of one of them, which followed the next day. He also promised to have the other cases reopened. (*Informationen*, no. 21, p. 8.) Following the visit, the Greens began planning a joint protest with members of the unofficial peace movement in the GDR, intending to deliver disarmament appeals to the U.S. and Soviet embassies in East Berlin. Several hundred East Germans, among them numerous members of Women for Peace, planned to participate. Evidently, Honecker had already encountered trouble within the Politburo for his cordial reception of the Greens, and this time the treatment of the West Germans was different. A Central Committee member appeared the day before the scheduled protest at the Greens' office in Bonn and warned them that the protest could not take place. The next day, two of the Greens made it across the border, but they were immediately picked up by the police and expelled as "undesirable persons." The rest of the Greens were denied permission to cross the border. The police had detained many of the East German protesters the night before. (*Der Spiegel*, 7 November.) Petra Kelly and Gert Bastian, who had earlier been received so cordially, voiced strong criticism of the SED's policy with respect to peace protests not directly sanctioned and controlled by the state. Kelly accused the East Germans of hypocrisy when GDR police confiscated Green peace pamphlets and other materials from various East Germans arrested for their activism, the same material that the Green delegation had given Honecker. Bastian called for "mass outrage" in the West over the arrests of East Germans working independently for peace. (*FAZ*, 23 December.)

In response to the billion-mark credit to the GDR by West German banks, the East German government announced in late September that it would free children under the age of fifteen from the mandatory exchange of currency when visiting the GDR. In addition, the GDR enacted a new statute affecting the reunification of families divided by the wall and marriages between GDR citizens and "foreigners." Because the GDR regards the Federal Republic as a foreign country, the new statute will theoretically make these matters easier to resolve in the future. Spokesmen for the West German parties expressed only restrained approval because these steps fell far short of what was expected from the GDR in response to the bank credit. In the case of the family measures, the GDR really did little more than bring itself closer into line with the Helsinki agreements. (Ibid., 28 September.)

On 26 December, *Der Spiegel* reported that Honecker was interested in rescheduling his canceled trip to West Germany for the second half of 1984. He apparently felt that the timing would be more appropriate once the Americans and the Soviets had met at a conference on environmental protection scheduled for early summer and assumed that he would be in a better position then to grant the West Germans additional concessions in return for the billion-mark credit. Besides, as one West German minister put it, if Honecker wanted a second billion-mark credit, which he badly needs, he would have to come to get it himself.

China. The gradual process of improving relations between China and the GDR begun in 1982 (see *YICA*, 1983, pp. 281–82) continued this year. In May, Chinese deputy foreign minister Qian Qichen visited three countries of the Warsaw Pact, among them the GDR, where he held talks with Herbert Krolikowski, the first deputy minister for foreign affairs, and paid a "courtesy call" on GDR foreign minister Oskar Fischer. Neither the Chinese nor the East Germans made the subject or results of the talks public. (*DA*, no. 7, p. 687.) A number of less visible steps were also taken in 1983. For instance, Chinese films and television programs were shown on East German television, and a Chinese delegation representing Central Chinese Television visited the GDR in March and April for negotiations on expanding cooperation between Chinese and East German television stations. In other cultural affairs, a delegation representing the GDR's League for Friendship Among the Peoples journeyed to China in May at the invitation of the Society for Friendship of the Chinese People with Foreign Countries. On the other hand, Chinese authorities stressed that the modest progress in all these areas represented an improvement in the relations between the two states, not between the two communist parties. No relations exist between the SED and the Chinese Communist Party, and the Chinese evidently have no immediate intention of establishing them. Also, the Chinese emphasized that China's good relations with the Federal Republic remain unaffected by the improvements in GDR–Chinese relations. (Ibid., pp. 687–91.)

Soviet Union. Piotr Abrasimov, who had served as ambassador to the GDR for a total of seventeen years, was unexpectedly "released" from his duties—as the official announcement put it—in order to assume the post of chairman of the Soviet State Committee for Foreign Tourism. The move was generally regarded as a demotion, although the reasons behind it remain the subject of speculation. Some suggested that his removal was linked to his close association with Leonid Brezhnev and the personnel changes made since Brezhnev's death. Others felt that the change adumbrated a general switch in the Soviet Union's approach to relations with West Germany. (*Der Spiegel*, 6 June; *RAD Background Report*, no. 136.)

Eastern Europe. Throughout 1983, East German state and party leaders exchanged visits with their counterparts within the Warsaw Pact and the Council for Mutual Economic Assistance

(CMEA), as well as with Yugoslavia. On 16 August, Erich Honecker arrived in Warsaw for a three-day state visit, the first to Poland by a Warsaw Pact leader since 1980. Honecker was accompanied by Prime Minister Willi Stoph, and East Germany's top economist, Günter Mittag. *Zycie Warszawy* said of GDR-Polish relations, "Much remains to be done, particularly in economic cooperation and tourist exchange." The most important factor, however, was that the will to continue relations existed and that possibilities to do so existed. "Poland has again become a reliable political partner, and it is also becoming an economic one, albeit slowly. That is why both countries set such great store to the visit." (*RAD Background Report*, no. 202.) A joint communiqué following the meeting stated that the two sides intend to reach agreement by the end of 1983 on long-term economic cooperation. There has already been some coordination of the two countries' plans for 1984 and 1985, but the two sides are looking for closer collaboration in the 1986–1990 period.

An earlier official visit of a Bulgarian party and state delegation, headed by the Bulgarian party's general secretary, Todor Zhivkov, demonstrated in Werner Felfe's words, "the close internationalist militant alliance between our parties and states." Similar terms were used to characterize the encounter between Honecker and Gustáv Husák, the Czechoslovak leader, during Honecker's visit to Prague. Finally, János Kádár of Hungary journeyed to East Berlin at the end of the year for discussions and used the opportunity to decorate Honecker with a Hungarian medal ("with diamonds") for his "services to the cause of friendship between the two peoples, for socialism and peace" (*ND*, 1 December).

Third World. The past year was not an especially active one for the GDR in Third World affairs. Among the highlights was the May arrival of Robert Mugabe, prime minister of Zimbabwe, in East Berlin for talks with Honecker, which were held, as such talks always are, "in an atmosphere of mutual understanding and friendship." At a news conference, Mugabe called his visit to the GDR a "study trip" that had provided him with the chance to learn about the GDR's experience in constructing socialism and to study how "socialist theory is implemented, how the role of the state developed, and how the relationship between people and state is structured."

The trip resulted in one agreement on economic, industrial, and scientific-technical cooperation and a second accord arranging for scientific-technical cooperation. (ADN, 26 and 27 May; *FBIS*, 27 and 31 May.) In September, Honecker and Sam Nujoma, president of the South-West Africa People's Organization, exchanged views "on current international issues" (ADN, 9 September; *FBIS*, 12 September). Later in the month, Luís Valencia Rodríguez, Ecuadorean minister of foreign affairs, paid an official visit to the GDR (*ND*, 17 September).

International Party Contacts. High party dignitaries represented the SED at the congresses of two of the staunchest pro-Soviet communist parties, the British and the Portuguese. Günter Schabowski, candidate member of the SED Politburo, used the November congress of the Communist Party of Great Britain to link the revolutionary traditions of the German and British working classes and to criticize the United States for its warmongering nuclear culpabilities and to praise the pacific attitudes and constructive arms control proposals of the Soviet side at the Geneva talks. (ADN, 13 November; *FBIS*, 14 November.) Hermann Axen, member of the SED Politburo and secretary of the Central Committee, headed the delegation that attended the congress of the Portuguese Communist Party a few days later. Axen followed a script similar to Schabowski's. He claimed that the socialist states, led by the Soviet Union, the international workers' movement, and national liberation movements, were able to check the most aggressive circles in the United States and the other NATO countries. He hailed "the upswing and the successful advance of the heroic Portuguese party" and assured congress participants that the SED "will do everything to deepen the close fraternal relations between the two parties." (*ND*, 17/18 December; *FBIS*, 21 December.)

David Pike
University of North Carolina (Chapel Hill)

Hungary

Population. 10.7 million
Party. Hungarian Socialist Workers' Party (Magyar Szocialista Munkáspárt; HSWP)
Founded. 1918 (HSWP, 1956)
Membership. 852,000 (1983); workers and farmworkers 44.6 percent; women 28.3 percent; average age 45.5; 74 percent joined after 1956 (1980 statistics)
First Secretary. János Kádár
Politburo. 13 full members: János Kádár, György Aczél, Valéria Benke, Sándor Gáspár (secretary general, National Council of Trade Unions), Ferenc Havasi, Mihály Korom, György Lázár (prime minister), Pál Losonczi (president), László Maróthy (first secretary, Budapest party committee), Lajos Méhes (minister of industry), Károly Németh, Miklós Óvári, István Sarlós
Secretariat. 7 members: János Kádár, György Aczél (culture and ideology), Ferenc Havasi (economic policy), Mihály Korom (party, mass organizations, and military), Károly Németh (youth and party building), Miklós Óvári (agitprop and cultural policy), Mátyás Szürös (foreign affairs)
Central Committee. 127 full members
Status. Ruling party
Last Congress. Twelfth, 24–27 March 1980, in Budapest; next congress scheduled for 1985
Auxiliary Organizations. National Council of Trade Unions (NCTU, 4.5 million members), led by Sándor Gáspár; Communist Youth League (874,000 nominal members), led by György Fejti
Main State Organs. Presidential Council; Council of Ministers (18 members); both constitutionally responsible to the National Assembly (352 deputies)
Parliament and Elections. Elections are administered by the Patriotic Peoples' Front (PPF). In 1980, PPF candidates received 99.3 percent of the vote. A majority of members of parliament do not belong to the HSWP.
Publications. *Népszabadság* (People's freedom), HSWP daily; *Társadalmi Szemle* (Social review), HSWP theoretical monthly; *Pártélet* (Party life), HSWP organizational monthly; *Magyar Hirlap*, government daily; *Magyar Nemzet*, PPF daily; *Népszava*, NCTU daily. The official news agency is Magyar Távirati Iroda (MTI).

The Hungarian Section of the Russian Communist Party (Bolshevik) was founded in Moscow in March 1918 by Béla Kun (1886–1939) and a few other Hungarian former prisoners of war. The Communist Party of Hungary came into being in Budapest in November 1918. Kun was the dominant figure in the communist–left socialist coalition that proclaimed the Hungarian Soviet Republic on the collapse of Mihály Károlyi's liberal-democratic regime. The red dictatorship lasted from March to August 1919.

During the interwar period, the party functioned as a faction-ridden movement in domestic illegality and in exile. The underground membership numbered in the hundreds. With the Soviet occupation at the end of World War II, the Hungarian Communist Party (HCP) re-emerged as a member of the provisional government. Kun had lost his life in Stalin's purges, and the party was led by Mátyás Rákosi (1892–1971). Although the HCP won no more than 17 percent of the vote in the relatively free 1945 elections, it continued to exercise a disproportionate influence in the coalition government. Thanks largely to Soviet-backed coercive tactics, the HCP gained effective control of the country in 1947. In 1948, it absorbed left-wing social democrats into the newly named Hungarian Workers' Party.

Rákosi's Stalinist zeal was exemplified by the show trial of József Cardinal Mindszenty and the liquidation of the alleged Titoist László Rajk. The New Course of 1954–1955 offered some relief from economic mismanagement and totalitarian terror; inspired by some of Stalin's successors, it was represented in Hungary by the moderate communist Imre Nagy. De-Stalinization undermined the party's power and unity, and the replacement of Rákosi by Ernö Gerö (1898–1980) could not halt the rising tide of popular opposition. Following the outbreak of revolution on 23 October 1956, Imre Nagy became prime minister for the second time and eventually headed a multiparty government that withdrew Hungary from the Warsaw Pact. On 25 October, János Kádár became leader of the renamed party, the HSWP. The Nagy government was overthrown by the armed intervention of the Soviet Union on 4 November.

Since the end of the revolution, the HSWP has ruled unchallenged as the sole political party, firmly aligned with the Soviet Union. After an initial phase of repression that culminated in the final collectivization of agriculture (1959–1960), Kádár's rule came to be marked by his conciliatory "alliance policy" and by pragmatic reforms, most notably the New Economic Mechanism (NEM) launched in 1968.

Party and Government. An unusually important meeting of the Central Committee was held 12–13 April to conduct a midterm review, between the HSWP's last (1980) and next (1985) congresses, of the party's achievements and problems. The Politburo report, delivered by First Secretary János Kádár, generally endorsed the principles and application of the 1980 program (*Pártélet*, May). The report's most critical elements dealt with the economy and with culture and ideology.

According to Kádár's report, the economic crisis had imposed a "severe test" on Hungarian society. Parasitism and corruption were spreading, as was a cynical passivity among young people. Because productivity had not improved sufficiently, economic stability had been maintained at the cost of investment and personal consumption. Nevertheless, the HSWP was in-

tent on maintaining and developing the NEM. Somewhat paradoxically, Kádár also warned against the arrogant view that only the Hungarians knew how to build socialism.

The report's harshest words were reserved for the cultural-ideological sphere. The party, said Kádár, had failed to adjust to the ideological and cultural impact of hard times and the resultant social tensions. Oppositional elements, encouraged by Western "propaganda outlets," had become more aggressive in seeking a public platform, but "we will not legalize hostile endeavors in the framework of the People's Front or of the peace movement, or in any other area, and will not tolerate the establishment of bases of opposition." Kádár claimed that there was no censorship in Hungary but warned against the publication of radical commentaries on the economy and other issues. In this connection, he deplored the Western disposition to equate with capitalism the new Hungarian experiments with small-scale privatization, and he urged the Hungarian media to withhold comment on the experiments for the time being. In regard to the Hungarian minorities in neighboring countries, Kádár observed that it was natural to sympathize with them, but their problems had to be solved through socialism and not by imperialist-incited nationalism. The report demanded a stronger Marxist presence in culture to combat bourgeois and nationalist views, conservatism, pessimism, and a distorted image of socialism.

Kádár reported HSWP membership had risen by a net 40,000 since the 1980 congress to 852,000. Recruitment among young people and certain intellectual strata was inadequate. There was also some evidence of uncertainty and weakness in members' support for HSWP policy. Critical and self-critical analysis of party work was necessary at all times.

The economic crisis had stimulated criticism from both egalitarian and dogmatic elements in the party and labor and from experts urging more rapid reform (see below). The image of the Hungarian economic system in the West (generally positive) is, moreover, not necessarily helpful in Hungary's relations with the East. In a rare radio-television interview (Radio Budapest, 29 April), Kádár tried to strike a balance between these extremes. The party, he recalled, had to be innovative and flexible in the aftermath of the 1956 revolution. The introduction of the New Economic Mechanism in 1968 had created a certain anxiety among Hungary's socialist friends, but practice showed that the Hungarian model worked. He insisted that socialist principles were in no way compromised or jeopardized by the reforms, pointing out that in 1982 the private sector accounted for only 1.3 percent of industrial production, while in agriculture private farms produced 1.1 percent of total output, household plots 4.9 percent, state farms 16 percent, and cooperatives 68 percent. There was to be, on the other hand, no further radical reform of the existing "socialist management system."

In its usual methodical fashion, the regime has been moving toward what it calls an "expansion of democracy." On 11 November 1982, the Central Committee had invited the PPF to develop proposals for "further development of the electoral system" (*Népszabadság*, 13 November 1982). In a Christmas message, PPF Secretary General Imre Pozsgay called for more democracy to help cope with the economic crisis (*Magyar Nemzet*, 24 December 1982). Rezsö Nyers, the father of the economic reform, former Politburo member, and currently a deputy and economic adviser, also lent his voice to the campaign. He conceded that in the period of "revolutionary transformation," the parliament's role had to be restricted but argued vigorously that now the National Assembly should play an active role in debating planning alternatives. Nyers deplored the official and unofficial intolerance that frequently greets dissenting views (*Magyar Hirlap*, 27 January). Later in the year, at the annual meeting of economists, Nyers outlined conditions for effective government in Hungary: a more open process of medium-term planning and regulation, decentralization of authority in the counties, and expanded cooperation between government agencies and other representatives and specialized organizations (*Müszaki Élet*, 16 June). Early in the year, Pozsgay had deplored secrecy in political decisionmaking and argued that dialogue was particularly important in a one-party system (Radio Budapest, 28 February). Mihály Korom, party secretary in charge of public administration, conceded in another interview that in the existing system, "elections don't have much political significance" (ibid., 9 May).

This buildup culminated in a Central Committee resolution of 6 July regarding changes in the electoral law. Henceforth at least two candidates must be nominated in each parliamentary constituency (currently 352 seats) and in local council elections (59,270 seats). The PPF would continue to manage the nomination process. Candidates could be nominated by at least one-third of those attending a nomination meeting, but individuals opposed to socialism or to the PPF platform would not be eligible. Runners-up who obtained at least 25 percent of the votes would become alternative deputies or councillors. At least 10 percent of the National Assembly would be elected by all eligible voters from a national list nominated by the PPF. The Central Committee also proposed modifications in the representation of administratively linked small localities (*Népszabadság*, 9 and 16 July). The minister of justice thereupon produced a draft bill that was submitted by the PPF for public discussion in September.

The latest experiment in token pluralism will presumably govern the conduct of the 1985 elections. Indeed, multiple candidacies may become the new norm. A perhaps not coincidental milestone was the two-candidate contest for the post of first secretary of the Somogy county party committee (Radio Budapest, 15 September). In a move designed to "bring administration close to the people," the Central Committee at its 12 October session approved the abolition of districts (*járás*) as state administrative units. District party committees would also disappear. The district administrative functions will be assumed by borough councils and by new "regional centers" created from towns and large boroughs.

The presumably Soviet-inspired tendency toward ideological-cultural retrenchment was in evidence at the party's national conference on agitprop and cultural policy, held 11–12 January in Budapest (*Népszabadság*, 15 January). The veteran György Aczél delivered the main report on the party's ideological work and issued a call for ideological activism to address the new problems and adverse conditions in Hungarian society. Aczél reminded his audience of the tragic consequences of "distortions" in the Stalinist 1950s and anticipated expansion of socialist democracy to encompass the "various differing and even contradictory interests and views in society." He reiterated the notion that the HSWP was intent on assuring the hegemony, not the monopoly, of Marxism in Hungary, but noted that even this modest objective was challenged in some intellectual circles. He criticized negativism and nihilism in the cultural sphere and those cosmopolitan and populist writers who indulged in cheap and simplified depictions of political problems. The party's alliance policy regarding non-Marxists retained its validity, he said, but it did not extend to the so-called democratic opposition. Persuasion rather than more "administrative intervention" was the party's response to these ideological transgressions. Aczél reflected on the continuing difficulty faced by Marxist instructors in explaining to young people the apparent discrepancy between Marxist ideology and reality, notably with regard to recent economic experiments. On the burning issue of Hungarian minorities, Aczél referred elliptically to chauvinism and oppression without naming Romania.

The Hungarian socialist system bears a heavy burden of myths and historical falsifications that confuse and alienate the population, particularly young people. Pressures for a more objective reevaluation of national history, in particular of the precommunist period, have been growing along with a wave of nostalgia for the popular culture of those times. The party's ideological monthly, *Társadalmi Szemle*, has been running a series of brief biographical sketches of postwar political figures, including noncommunists and discredited communists, in an unconvincing attempt to display historical objectivity. But even official histories run into unexpected trouble. Party historian György Borsányi's biography of Béla Kun was withdrawn shortly after publication, presumably because of Soviet displeasure.

The year 1983 saw important personnel changes in the foreign affairs administration. At its 6 July meeting, the Central Committee approved the appointment of Péter Várkonyi as foreign minister, replacing Frigyes Puja. Várkonyi, aged 52, has long experience in foreign relations. He joined the party in 1948 and has been a foreign policy specialist in the Foreign Ministry and the Central Committee apparatus since 1951. He was head of the Council of Ministers Information Office from 1969 to 1980, editor in chief of *Népszabadság* from 1980 to 1982, and most recently Central Committee secretary in charge of international relations. He resigned as secretary but remains a member of the Central Committee, to which he was elected in 1975. Mátyás Szürös, aged 50, replaces Várkonyi as secretary responsible for international relations.

A party member since 1951 and on the Central Committee since 1978, Szürös has served as ambassador to East Germany and to the Soviet Union. Gyula Horn, aged 42, replaces Szürös as head of the Central Committee's Foreign Affairs Department. A specialist in interparty relations, Horn had been deputy head of the same department since 1974.

Other personnel changes include the transfer of Sándor Rácz from the head of the Central Committee's Public Administration and Administrative Department to the post of deputy minister of defense. Rácz has a police background and has been a member of the Central Committee since 1975. Pál Varga, former first secretary of the Somogy county party committee, was appointed to replace Rácz. In the cultural field, Richárd Nagy, president of Hungarian television since 1974, was demoted to the post of deputy chairman of the Budapest Municipal Council, reportedly because of the controversy over a program on World War II (see below). He was replaced by the former head of the Central Committee's Science, Public Education, and Cultural Affairs Department, the ideologically conservative Dr. Mihály Kornidesz. The post vacated by the latter was filled by a chemist, Dr. Pál Tetényi.

Economic Affairs. Hungary's economy performed at the low end of official projections in 1982. Economic planners had responded to the protracted slump by trimming targets to a very low level, but even this proved unrealistic in light of the unfavorable price trends for Hungarian agricultural, aluminum, and chemical products. National net material product ("distributed national income") fell by over 3 percent in 1982. The overall trade balance, however, was positive for the first time since 1973. By importing less and aggressively promoting exports, Hungary achieved a surplus in nonruble trade with socialist countries, although trade with the West remained in deficit. There was a small deficit in the ruble account. (*Magyar Hirlap*, 26 January; *Statisztikai Havi Közlemények*, no. 1.) The National Bank managed to overcome the liquidity crisis of early 1982, and in December of that year the bank and the International Monetary Fund concluded an agreement on drawing rights of approximately $600 million. In the course of 1983, Hungary borrowed $385 million on the Euromarket. The country's outstanding foreign debt was estimated at $8.5–9.0 million (*Financial Times*, London, 1 February).

The 1983 budget promised more belt-tightening to reduce the foreign debt burden. Investment was slashed, consumption was to decline by 0.5–1.0 percent, and real wages were to fall 3.7 percent. Despite talk of greater enterprise autonomy, subsidies to enterprises were projected to rise over 1982. The domestic net material product (roughly equivalent to GNP) was expected to increase by only 0.5–1.0 percent (*Magyar Hirlap*, 17 December 1982). Even these modest expectations proved to be optimistic. Ferenc Havasi, HSWP secretary in charge of economic policy, reported in September that industrial production was lagging behind plan; a severe drought had set back agricultural production; only one-third of the planned foreign trade surplus had been achieved in the first seven months; and the consumer price index had risen 8.2 percent in the first half, followed closely by a rise in personal income (Radio Budapest, 5 September). The Central Committee noted at its 6 July session that the industrial sector was in deep trouble, with the number of unprofitable enterprises growing steadily. Gross industrial production in Hungary grew more slowly in the first half of 1983 than in the corresponding period in 1982, reversing the pattern in other Eastern bloc countries. This dismal record impelled the government to order substantial increases in food prices, effective 19 September, in order to reduce subsidies and save commodities for export.

Fearing a potential social as well as economic crisis, a number of economists have been pressing for a second reform in the direction of greater decentralization and privatization (e.g., Márton Tardos in *Közgazdasági Szemle*, June 1982; and *Mozgó Világ*, March). Tibor Liska's ingenious schemes for avoiding orthodox capitalism while recapturing its benefits attracted attention at home and abroad (*Economist*, London, 19 March). The Soviet Union reportedly protested the criticism of the Council for Mutual Economic Assistance (CMEA) in Tamás Bauer's reformist essays (*Mozgó Világ*, November 1982). The party has rejected more radical economic reforms (see above), but incremental tinkering with the system continues.

Since provision was made in 1982 for various types of small independent business ventures, several thousand have been established, mostly in the service and retail sectors (*Népszabadság*, 17 August). Private enterprise accounts for 40 percent of housing construction. New decrees were issued in July and September to facilitate and regulate the rental and lease of small enterprises to private individuals.

The new wage regulation system that came into effect 1 January linked increases more closely to productivity. Recognition that the drive for efficiency could lead to plant closures and unemployment inspired a new program, which came into effect 1 June, providing a state subsidy for the retraining of redundant and otherwise unemployable workers (*Népszava*, 14 May). A joint resolution by the Council of Ministers and the NCTU on the development of enterprise democracy provides for the appointment of directors (general managers) by the relevant ministry and the director's council, which along with the enterprise control committee has the right to comment on enterprise plans (*Magyar Hirlap*, 26 November 1982). The party has conceded that its presence in factories had not always been constructive. The matter was discussed at the 12 October Central Committee meeting, and Politburo member Károly Németh indicated that it was necessary to "raise the standard of party guidance" to facilitate trade union independence. He also reported that in 1982 trade union committees had exercised their veto right regarding norms and wages some 170 times, "mostly with justification" (*Népszabadság*, 15 October).

A recent and noteworthy instance of decentralization was the breakup of the Csepel Iron and Metal Works Trust into some fifteen units on 1 July. The subdivision of the chronically unprofitable conglomerate essentially restored the pattern that obtained in the early years of the NEM, from 1968 to 1972. Of the 60 large industrial units that have come under review since 1979, over half have been subdivided.

An innovation in economic restructuring was the purchase of an unprofitable knitwear factory by a successful cooperative purchasing-marketing enterprise. The new owner evidently expects to be able to improve productivity and profits. The media took pains to stress that this shift from state to cooperative property was not retrogressive since both were socialist forms of ownership (*Népszava*, 29 July). Another first was the issue in March of "communal bonds" by the State Development Bank and by the Petroleum and Gas Industry Trust (for a pipeline). The bonds are for sale to financial and economic institutions as well as to foreign individuals and are evidently designed to mop up idle capital and increase its mobility.

The consumption of oil and oil products was reduced by 20 percent between 1979 and 1982, but Hungary is still inefficient compared with Western Europe in its use of energy in production. The first Hungarian nuclear reactor, planned (with Soviet technology) since 1966 and intermittently under construction since 1969, was phased into service in late December 1982.

Culture and Dissent. The Hungarian regime's reputation for relative liberalism and tolerance took a beating in 1983. The shift to a harder line was signaled in an article by *Népszabadság*'s deputy editor, Péter Rényi (11 December 1982). He denounced the intellectuals of the "democratic opposition" as witting or unwitting agents of imperialism. Rényi reserved his harshest words for the writer György Konrád, whose praise of the Polish Solidarity movement had been quoted in Western media. A few months later, Konrád was again denounced, this time for his evenhanded criticism of the superpowers and for urging the West to demand at least neutrality for Eastern Europe (*Magyar Nemzet*, 29 May). On 14 December 1982, the police raided László Rajk's apartment, which for two years had served as a *samizdat* shop, as well as other dissidents' homes. Written material and duplicating machines were seized. Later in December, a British academic with dissident contacts was expelled from the country. Rajk's apartment was raided again on 26 January and was in effect seized. On 29 March, police again raided dissidents' homes and confiscated *samizdat* material.

Rajk reopened his *samizdat* shop in another apartment and resumed publication of the opposition review *Beszélő*. The issue (no. 5–6) contained an exposé of the censorship system, in which certain authors are put on a special "consultation list," which means they cannot publish without explicit party permission; the account also relates cases of articles being excised after printing and of books withheld from distribution. A recent case in point was that of Sándor Csoóri, a leading literary figure who was put on the "consultation list" for one year. He had written the introduction to a book by Miklós Duray (see below) that concerned the Hungarian minority in Slovakia and was published in the United States; Csoóri excoriated the superpowers and blamed the one-party system for the neglect of minority problems of Eastern Europe.

In May, the editors of *Beszélő* formally petitioned for a publishing license but were ignored by the authorities. Despite official harassment, the journal appeared again (no. 6) during the summer. Meanwhile, in June, the government issued a decree, effective 1 September, that increased fines for printing and publishing unauthorized material. On 24 September, a well-known dissident and *samizdat* publisher Gábor Demszky was severely beaten by the police in course of a search of his car.

The dissidents view these events as a turning point in the regime's policies. It is also true that intellectuals have become bolder and more outspoken over the past few years on a wide range of politically sensitive issues. The party has not forgiven the Hungarian Writers' Union for rejecting six party nominees at its December 1981 general meeting, and periodic organized debates on literature reveal a deepening gulf between cultural administrators and intellectuals (see *Alföld*, no. 2).

A major television series on the Hungarian army in World War II was abruptly canceled, evidently because of Soviet displeasure. Reference to this project and other material on the war appeared in *Mozgó Világ* (September), a periodical that regularly carries controversial literary and critical articles. The journal had links with the Attila József Circle of young writers and had been temporarily suspended in 1981. Miklós Veress, the editor, had been dismissed on that occasion; now his successor, Ferenc Kulin, suffered the same fate. Dezső Tóth, a deputy minister of culture, declared that certain periodicals had become the mouthpiece of non-Marxist views and that, as was made clear in the Central Committee's April resolution, a "politically pluralized literary life" was unacceptable (*Élet és Irodalom*, 23 September). The spirit of confrontation spread. On 23 September, a meeting of the Attila József Circle passed a resolution protesting official obstruction of a planned conference, of various publication projects, and of planned visits to Hungarian minority districts in neighboring countries. The resolution also protested official measures taken against Kulin and *Mozgó Világ* and the censorship of writers such as Csoóri, calling such practices "incompatible with cultural freedom and dignity." (*RFE Research*, 8 November.) The resolution also demanded a public accounting for these measures and threatened a boycott of a "normalized" *Mozgó Világ*. In mid-October, students at several Budapest university faculties passed similar resolutions, signed petitions, and confronted Deputy Minister Tóth in heated debate.

An autonomous pacifist movement has emerged in Hungary, and gatherings several hundred strong have called for a nuclear-free Europe and for military disengagement by the two alliances. The official National Peace Council initially accommodated itself to the self-styled Peace Group for Dialogue, which was in contact with Western peace groups. By the turn of the year, the regime no longer concealed its aversion to grass-roots pacifism, and the official media took to denouncing the "naive" equation of Western and Soviet nuclear weapons and to reminding Hungarians that the arms race was entirely the fault of the West (*Népszabadság*, 15 January). The National Peace Council suddenly professed concern over the appearance of disunity and created a Youth Peace Council in an attempt to draw young pacifists to the orthodox fold.

May was proclaimed the official month of peace, and hundreds of propaganda events were organized, including a mass peace march on 7 May, at which time the Peace Group for Dialogue demonstrated separately. Official harassment escalated. Dissident peace group members were prevented from attending a Berlin peace meeting that was officially boycotted by the Soviet bloc. The Communist Youth League's György Fejti accused the independent peace groups of being manipulated by the enemy (ibid., 14 May). The Peace Group for Dialogue had planned an international peace camp for July, but administrative obstruction prevented the event from being held. The handful of Western pacifists who did reach Budapest were expelled, and police warned Peace Group members that they were engaging in antistate activities. The group formally disbanded, but police harassment of individual pacifists continued.

Pacifism has also inspired the autonomous Roman Catholic "basic communities," for which the prime proselytizer has been the activist priest Father György Bulányi. These groups have been encouraging conscientious objectors, several of whom are serving jail sentences. The church hierarchy has received the Vatican's guarded support for constraining Bulányi's activities, and indeed church-state relations remain stable. Recent official media commentary has reflected favorably on the socially progressive activities of the church in precommunist times, and the regime appears disposed to exploit the church's potential for dealing with social problems such as divorce and alcoholism.

Foreign Affairs. Hungary is steadfast in its endorsement of the Soviet position on international issues. The Budapest regime missed no opportunity in 1983 to praise Soviet peace and disarmament proposals and to accuse the United States and the other NATO powers of heightening international tensions. Within these constraints, the Hungarians try to tailor their policies to please various interests and not incidentally improve commercial prospects. For allies of the United States, the Hungarian line is one of shared concerns by smaller members of alliances and of economic pragmatism. For the Third World, the line is anti-imperialism mixed with socialist commerce.

Western States. Hungarian-U.S. relations were marked by frequent and on balance positive contacts in 1983. A congressional delegation led by Tom Lantos (D.-Calif.) visited Hungary 12–13 January. Lantos expressed satisfaction with domestic liberalization and support for the notion of multiyear most-favored-nation status for Hungary (now requiring annual approval by Congress). He met with dissident intellectuals, including László Rajk and Gyula Illyés. In Romania the delegation had reportedly raised the problem of discrimination against the Hungarian minority. Back in Washington, three members of Congress responded to pleas by Hungarian Americans to ask the Hungarian ambassador to request of his government the identification of the unmarked graves of the victims of the 1956 revolution, notably those of Imre Nagy and Pál Maléter, who were executed in 1958. The embassy refused to forward their request.

Vice-President George Bush paid a one-day visit to Budapest in September. He described Kádár as "a man of enormous capacity and leadership capability" and praised Hungary's human rights record, its spirit of enterprise, and the sound state of Hungarian-U.S. relations. The next day, in Vienna, Bush declared that because of its liberal social and economic policies Hungary benefited from Washington's policy of differentiation among East European states (Reuters, 19 and 21 September). The compliment did not go down well in Budapest, and in referring to the Bush visit the Central Committee's 12 October resolution pointedly rejected all attempts to drive a wedge between Hungary and its allies. While Bush was in Hungary, Foreign Minister Várkonyi was meeting in Washington with Secretary of State George Shultz and Secretary of Commerce Malcom Baldrige in quest of trade expansion and multiyear most-favored-nation status.

France's inclination to foster a special relationship with Hungary, already displayed in 1982 when President François Mitterrand visited Budapest, was confirmed by the visit 10–12 July of a delegation led by Premier Pierre Mauroy. He met with László Cardinal Lékai as well as with Kádár, engaging in talks that were said to be cordial and constructive. Differences of opinion on international issues could not be concealed any better than they were on the occasion of Foreign Minister Puja's visit to Paris in February. An agreement was signed on economic and scientific-technical cooperation in energy and raw material management, and talks on cultural and educational cooperation were held by György Aczél and Education Minister Alain Savary. A tangible gesture of support came Hungary's way at the Madrid review of the Conference on Security and Cooperation in Europe (CSCE). The East European participants had pressed to have at least one of the interim meetings (prior to the next CSCE review at Vienna in 1986) to be held in their region. France agreed to transfer to Budapest a cultural forum that the French had originally proposed and was to be held in Paris in 1985.

Other notable international contacts included the visit of West German foreign minister Hans-Dietrich Genscher on 26–27 November 1982, of New Zealand prime minister Robert Muldoon on 12–15 May, of Zimbabwan prime minister Robert Mugabe on 18–22 May, of Greek prime minister Andreas Papandreou on 23–25 May, of Turkish prime minister Bülent Ulusu on 29 June– 1 July, and of the British and Indian foreign ministers in September. Papandreou signed a long-term development program for economic, technical, and scientific cooperation and for joint manufacturing projects. The communiqué at the conclusion of his visit reported agreement on the idea of a nuclear-free zone in the Balkans, on the withdrawal of all foreign military forces from Cyprus, and on Israeli withdrawal from all Arab territory occupied since 1967 (*Népszabadság*, 26 May). János Kádár paid a three-day visit to Finland in September; he described Hungarian-Finnish relations as traditionally friendly and problem-free and expressed the wish that nuclear weapons not be stationed in countries where they did not previously exist.

The European Economic Community (EEC) accounts for 60 percent of Hungary's nonsocialist trade, and Budapest has long complained of discriminatory trade policies. After consultations with the French and West Germans, exploratory talks were held in April by Foreign Trade Minister Péter Veress and EEC external affairs commissioner Wilhelm Haferkamp with a view to a general agreement on trade in agricultural and industrial products. At their meeting in July, the EEC foreign ministers gave approval to formal negotiations on the question.

Communist Relations. The Hungarian party's preference in the realm of interparty relations is for orderly diversity, for a system that guarantees the security of communist regimes while allowing them a certain latitude in handling their affairs. Thus the HSWP's Mátyás Szürös argued that Hungary, like the other socialist states, was building socialism within a national framework; that sovereign socialist states pursued separate and diverse national interests, notably in economic development, that were harmonized voluntarily; and that national characteristics and interests had to be respected, notably within an open and flexible CMEA framework (ibid., 26 February). It was with evident caution that at the April meeting of the Central Committee Kádár endorsed the idea of an international conference of communist and socialist parties as long as it was properly prepared and organized around a unifying theme, to wit, the defense of peace.

Kádár led a delegation to the Soviet Union 18–23 July. The group included Prime Minister György Lázár, Deputy Prime Minister József Marjai, Foreign Minister Várkonyi, and Central Committee secretaries Havasi and Szürös. The last visit of similar caliber occurred in September 1974. The joint communiqué expressed agreement on all points. In particular, Kádár and

Andropov agreed "to bring ideological and educational activities of the fraternal parties closer to the requirements of the resolute struggle against bourgeois ideology" (Tass, 19 July). At a gala dinner, Andropov hailed Kádár as the "tested leader of socialist Hungary and a good friend of the Soviet Union." Kádár in turn praised the Soviet party, but stressed that each socialist country was making its own contribution to the theory and practice of socialism (ibid., 20 July). Four economic agreements were signed on the occasion of the Moscow visit: on cooperation in alum earth and aluminum production; on a pilot project to introduce integrated corn-growing systems in the Ukraine; on a poultry farm in Azerbaijan, to be installed by the successful Bábolna Agricultural Combine; and on the technical modernization of a Soviet shoe factory. It is noteworthy that these last three projects represent the second stage of technology transfer, the original know-how coming from the United States (corn), West Germany (poultry), and Italy (shoes). The Soviet Union remains Hungary's largest trading partner, taking (in 1982) 33.4 percent of Hungary's exports and providing 30.1 percent of its imports. Ninety percent of Hungary's oil supplies, 95 percent of natural gas, 93 percent of iron ore, and 85 percent of lumber come from the Soviet Union.

Other Hungarian-Soviet contacts included the visit of Warsaw Pact commander in chief Marshal Viktor G. Kulikov in September (a Warsaw Pact civil defense exercise involving all seven members took place in Hungary that month). In October, Soviet Politburo member Mikhail Gorbachev visited Budapest for talks with Kádár. Pozsgay led a PPF delegation to Moscow 16 November, at which time András Gyenes (chairman of the Central Control Commission of the HSWP) was awarded the Order of Friendship of Peoples for his contribution to Hungarian-Soviet amity.

The problems of Hungarian minorities surfaced again in relations with neighboring socialist countries. Aczél and Várkonyi reportedly received a chilly reception on a visit to Bucharest in November 1982, and the Romanian communiqué, unlike the Hungarian version, made no mention of minorities. The visit to Budapest of Romanian Foreign Minister Stefan Andrei 28 February–2 March was apparently equally unproductive on the minority issue. *Magyar Hirlap* (1 March) referred to "open and unsolved questions" and to unfulfilled aspects of the 1977 agreement between Kádár and Romanian leader Ceauşescu. The fate of the Transylvanian Hungarians remains an explosive topic in intellectual circles and popular opinion in Hungary; the controversial book by Ion Lancranjan (see *YICA*, 1983, p. 290) was attacked again in *Élet és Irodalom* (13 May).

With regard to Czechoslovakia, it was the case of Miklós Duray that aroused public concern. Duray is a member of the Hungarian minority in Slovakia, a geologist who has written about the cultural and educational problems of the 600,000 Magyars there and had communicated their grievances to the Charter '77 group and to the West. He was arrested in Bratislava 10 November 1982 and charged with slander. His trial, which opened 2 February, was attended by three members of the Hungarian Writers' Union Presidium. Sentencing was postponed, and Duray was provisionally set free. The minority problem was apparently discussed at lower official levels in the spring and came up again on the occasion of Prime Minister Lázár's visit to Prague 10–11 October. That visit produced agreement on completion of the trouble-ridden joint hydroelectric project on the Danube. Kádár's one-day visit to Prague 10 November gave rise to a routine statement of agreement on international issues.

The Hungarian minority in Yugoslavia was the subject of critical media commentary. There are some 425,000 Hungarians in Yugoslavia, 390,000 of them in Vojvodina. A Yugoslav article in March accused Hungarian minority intellectuals of nationalism and irredentism. In May, the editors of a Hungarian-language youth magazine were dismissed for ideological transgressions. More criticism of Hungarian nationalist views was published in June. (*RFE Research*, 2 March, 11 July.)

Poland's protracted political and economic crisis has intensified contacts between the two countries. The more notable high-level visits were those of Deputy Prime Minister Mieczyslaw Rakowski and Trade Union Minister Stanislaw Ciosek 16–20 February to study Hungarian trade unions, of Foreign Minister Stefan Olszowski 21–23 February, of Deputy Prime Minister József Marjai 11 January to sign the 1983 trade protocol, and of János Kádár at the end of October. The visits normally produce fulsome statements of traditional fraternal friendship and socialist solidarity. Trade between the two countries has been expanding rapidly since 1982. Hungary has also given some substantial economic aid to the Jaruzelski regime, giving rise to some popular concern that Hungary's hard-earned new Western credits may be channeled to this purpose.

Todor Zhivkov, the Bulgarian party leader and head of state, led a mixed delegation to Budapest 14–16 June. The two parties voiced full unanimity on all bilateral and international issues, and the Hungarian media lauded Sofia's economic reforms, which in some respects emulate the Hungarian NEM.

Although Hungary has had no formal inter-party relations with the Chinese People's Republic for many years, there were signs in 1983 of a progressive normalization of bilateral relations, including a tourism agreement in April; a visit by Chinese vice–foreign minister Qian Qichen in May; the arrival of a delegation of Chinese economists to study the Hungarian management system in June; the visit of the Chinese minister of machine industry in August to discuss bilateral cooperation; and the visits to China in October of Foreign Trade Minister Veress, an economists' delegation headed by Rezsö Nyers, and a Hungarian National Bank delegation. China reportedly provided financial credits to Hungary in 1982–83 (*Le Monde*, 20 October).

Bennett Kovrig
University of Toronto

Poland

Population. 36.6 million
Party. Polish United Workers' Party (Polska Zjednoczona Partia Robotnicza; PZPR)
Founded. 1948
Membership. 2,327,349 (31 December 1982), a 20 percent decline since 1978; workers, 40 percent, or 12.6 percent of all "workers" employed in national economy (*Polityka*, 30 July)
First Secretary. Army Gen. Wojciech Jaruzelski
Politburo. 15 full members: Wojciech Jaruzelski, Kazimierz Barcikowski, Tadeusz Czechowski, Jozef Czyrek, Zofia Grzyb, Stanislaw Kalkus, Hieronim Kubiak, Zbigniew Messner, Miroslaw Milewski, Stefan Olszowski, Stanislaw Opalko, Tadeusz Porebski, Jerzy Romanik, Albin Siwak, Marian Wozniak; 5 candidate members: Stanislaw Bejger, Jan Glowczyk, Czeslaw Kiszczak, Wlodzimierz Mokrzyszczak, Florian Siwicki
Secretariat. 9 members: Kazimierz Barcikowsi, Jozef Czyrek, Jan Glowczyk, Manfred Gorywoda, Zbigniew Michalek, Miroslaw Milewski, Wlodzimierz Mokrzyszczak, Marian Orzechowski, Waldemar Swirgon
Central Committee. 200 full and 70 candidate members
Status. Ruling party
Last Congress. Extraordinary Ninth, 14–20 July 1981, in Warsaw
Last Election. 1980, 99.5 percent (Fatherland Front), all 460 seats
Publications. *Trybuna Ludu*, party daily; *Nowe Drogi* and *Ideologia i Polityka*, party monthlies; *Zycie Partii*, fortnightly party organ; *Zolnierz Wolnosci*, army daily. Polska Agencja Prasowa (PAP) is the official news agency.

This profile focuses on the major organized forces—the party, the church, the military, and the unions—and how they behaved in the context of their own aims and ideologies in reaction to social and economic developments. Unlike some preceding years, 1983 was not a particularly dramatic period. Its importance should be measured by actions taken to overcome the crisis and redesign the political superstructure of the Polish state.

The Party. A paramount task for the ruling oligarchy remains the construction of a viable Polish model of socialism, one that reconciles the requirements of a Leninist state with the pluralistic traditions and aspirations of the Polish people. After two years of "normalization," the results are ambiguous. The situation continues to be unstable, a case of neither war nor peace, resulting from the indecisive and contradictory nature of General Jaruzelski's policy of "class struggle and class alliance" (*Trybuna Ludu*, 15/16 October).

In a sense, Poland today resembles the Poland of 1945, when a militarily superior foe imposed communism on an exhausted nation. The fact that the communist authorities are forced to repeat this system-building phase after 40 years testifies to their lack of political competence. But since there is no realistic alternative to a Soviet-style system for Poland, the present circumstances offer an opportunity to create a political framework that will eliminate Poland's cyclical pattern of revolt.

During 1983, the primary concern of the oligarchy was restoration of the leading role of the party. Involved in this was an attempt to develop a new ideological profile, an exercise that might appear vain for a party whose leadership had to be supplanted by military-security forces. The purpose of the ideological debate was to regain the initiative and re-establish the legitimacy destroyed by Solidarity and the imposition of martial law. The party not only had to repair its image, it also had to deal with such fundamental questions as whether the socioeconomic conditions for sustaining socialist construction even existed in Poland. Another reason for the ideological focus was to regain Moscow's confidence.

In his attempts to explain the 1980–1981 crisis, General Jaruzelski appeared to choose a dogmatic approach, one that avoided condemnation of the system itself. The crisis was brought on, he argued, not by too much socialism, but by too little. There was, he said, a "disregard for the role of ideology, treating it as a kind of decoration for political and economic practice" (ibid.). This inadequate ideological vigilance enabled class enemies from the West to penetrate the Polish intelligentsia and neo-bourgeoisie, who smuggled counterrevolution to the workers.

Still, Jaruzelski promised implementation of the 1980 Gdansk agreement, greater democracy, self-management, economic reform, a revised electoral law, and, above all, a broad partnership with the Catholic church. In a way, he adopted the Hungarian formula of "whoever is not against us is with us" by proclaiming that "there will be no pacts with the enemy, with pupils of imperialist subversion. But we hold out our hands to those who have gone politically astray." (Ibid., 17 October.)

His political platform attempts to combine tough ideological rhetoric with a conciliatory, pragmatic, and patriotic appeal to the nation and to define the limits of "socialist" renewal in Poland. The country is a dictatorship of the proletariat. Demands for spontaneity and pluralism are "tantamount to asking the captain to throw his compass and navigational gear into the high seas." (Ibid., 15/16 October.) "Poland's place in Europe and in the world is unambiguous and permanent. We are a socialist state fulfilling its political, economic, and defense aims within the allied unity of the Warsaw Pact and within the partnerlike cooperation of the Council for Mutual Economic Assistance [CMEA]. Our party was, is, and will be the chief guarantor of the inviolability of this historic choice. No one can perform this duty for us. Our party combines its responsibility for the interests of the working class and the Polish people and for the sovereign and secure existence of our socialist fatherland with its responsibility for the universally understood cause of socialism and peace. This is in fact the same responsibility." (Ibid., 3 June.)

Jaruzelski's message was directed to all interested parties: the Polish nation, Polish communists (liberals and dogmatists), and Moscow. The Soviet uneasiness with Jaruzelski's political moderation was voiced by *Novoye vremya*, the foreign affairs weekly, which criticized several officials believed to be members of the general's kitchen cabinet. In particular, the Soviets attacked Mieczyslaw Rakowski, the deputy prime minister, for describing the party as "intellectually and politically bankrupt," and Daniel Passent for his allegation that eventually "the Yalta civilization" (the Pax Sovietica) will share the fate of the Vienna and Versailles treaties, which "disintegrated, although those who signed them believed they were decreeing order for eternity" (*Polityka*, 14 May).

This indirect attack on Jaruzelski was probably unauthorized since the general later received the Order of Lenin. In any event, it helped him shake his reputation as "a Russian general in a Polish uniform" and strengthened his position against factional opponents. Despite the official ban on partisan activities imposed in December 1982, the party continues to be riven by bitter public disputes between liberals and neo-Stalinists. Jaruzelski has accused the liberals of questioning "the basic principles of the party" and the neo-Stalinists of being incapable of "understanding new phenomena" (*Trybuna Ludu*, 15/16 October).

Party factionalism seems to be less the result of personalities than ideological differences. The liberals, or realists, pay only lip service to Marxism-Leninism. Their motive for accepting —or feigning to accept—the ideology is the necessity of coming to terms with the Yalta accords and Poland's geostrategic position. Masquerading behind a mask of communist rhetoric, they continue to support the Solidarity slogan "Let Poland be Poland," that is, institutionalize political and economic pluralism.

The so-called conservative sectarians claim to be the only true militant proletarians faithful to Marxist-Leninist dogma. They reject compromise with noncommunists and strongly favor repressive administrative methods of government. They view the 1956 deviation from the Stalinist path in Poland as the main source of instability, allowing too much autonomy to the church, private farmers, unruly intellectuals, and Western influence. For them the solution is to re-emphasize discipline, ideological orthodoxy, and other absolutist methods. As a Polish commentator observed, they "need the workers only as performers in a given scenario. They are ready to do battle for socialism down to the last worker, to destroy anything and anyone that stands in their way." (Stanislaw Kwiatkowski, *Tu i Teraz*, no. 35, 31 August, p. 8.)

The numerically smaller neo-Stalinist wing of the party owes its survival to strong Soviet support. Its members are unquestionably loyal to Moscow and serve as a check on nationalistic Polish communists. Owing to Soviet sponsorship, representatives of this group can question Jaruzelski's program with impunity.

At the center of the political spectrum are General Jaruzelski and his associates. They assume that it is possible to overcome the present crisis and erect a strong state founded on socialism and patriotism. This program is a hybrid containing both neo-Stalinist and liberal-realist elements. It supposes a decisive party leadership to protect Poland's pro-Soviet profile, and it appears to leave plenty of room for genuine pluralism. Thus, a hard, unconditional rejection of institutionalized pluralism has been softened somewhat, primarily by a de facto alliance with the Catholic church.

As approved by the thirteenth ideological plenum (14–15 October) of the Central Committee, this form of socialism does not consist of a grand coalition between two partners of equal political status, nor is it an Italian-style historic compromise on ideological and political matters. Relations between the party and the church in Poland have been defined as antagonistic and openly confrontational, especially in matters of ideology. However, the party's lack of moral and political authority forces its leadership into businesslike cooperation with the class enemy on a few selected issues related to national sovereignty, internal order, and economic well-being. (*Ideologia i Polityka*, April.) The party hopes to use the moral force of the church to consolidate and revitalize the communist state. The party has not renounced its dictatorial ambitions, as the official endorsement of pluralism would imply. While the class struggle and eventual elimination of all opposition continues to be the long-range goal (*Polityka*, 24 October), the short-range solution for the transitional period is that of selectively applied class alliances.

The invitation extended to the church to take an active part in Polish politics has no constitutional mandate and does not include participation in the governmental process. The church's political status has received no official recognition, although the party has conceded that the church speaks for the great majority of Poles. A semi-independent political organization acting outside the official structure has been designated as a forum for the church's political activities. The Patriotic Movement of National Rebirth (PRON) claims to be a broad social framework uniting

Poles on the basis of universal humanitarianism, the only common denominator between Marxism and Christianity and a proper ground for the church to express its political opinions (*Trybuna Ludu*, 13 June).

The regime established the PRON in recognition of the pluralistic essence of Polish society. This pluralism, though, is to have limits. Most important, it cannot be allowed to conflict with the leading role of the communist party. Though not a political party, the PRON received constitutional recognition in a July amendment that called the PRON "a platform of unity for the nation's patriotic forces . . . and also a platform of joint activity by the political parties, social organizations and associations, and citizens, *regardless of their outlook*, on matters concerning the functioning of the socialist state and the country's comprehensive development" (ibid., 23/24 July).

Acceptance of constitutional principles and patriotic inspiration are sufficient for membership. Catholics and former Solidarity activists are made particularly welcome in order to convince the nation that national reconciliation and dialogue remain prominent in Polish politics and are not tactical concessions. Jan Dobraczynski, a Catholic writer, was named chairman of the PRON's first National Council. The National Council's composition was intended to eliminate fears of a procommunist bias: only 30 percent belong to the communist party, 20 percent were members of two other parties, and fully 50 percent had no party affiliation. However, the powerful secretary of the National Council is Marian Orzechowski, a determined communist hard-liner and a member of the PZPR Secretariat.

The political program of the PZPR under Jaruzelski is set within an ideologically rigid framework that on the national level allows neither doctrinal nor permanent institutional concessions to social democracy. The intention to preserve a monopoly of power has been combined, for the time being, with a benevolent and carefully guarded flexibility on a number of social and economic matters as a way of releasing social pressures. It also provides for cooperation with the church as a way of gaining strength from the church's authority and popularity. At the moment, this sort of solution appears the only way to put the country in order without provoking a Soviet invasion.

In effect, General Jaruzelski has rejected the idea of a genuine dialogue with the nation in favor of meaningless consultations with the people on terms defined by the party, a classical communist procedure. Archbishop Jozef Glemp dismissed Jaruzelski's idea of compromise by saying, "It is a false dialogue when one side says it will not concede one inch" (quoted in *WP*, 7 January).

The Church. The political message of the Roman Catholic church in Poland contains the themes of victory, freedom, reconciliation, and sacrifice. For Catholics, 1983 was a year of redemption, a victory of good over evil. "Venimus, vidimus, Deus vicit"—We came, we saw, God conquered—Pope John Paul II said on his arrival in Poland, recalling the words of Jan III Sobieski, the Polish king who saved Vienna from Turkish invasion in 1683. Christianity has again been victorious in Poland, proving that the spirit of the time does not favor a second socialist construction, but a second millennium of Christianity in Poland. This is a time of renewal for the Polish nation.

The pope's summer pilgrimage (16–23 June), his second visit to Poland as pope, was an occasion to reaffirm the church's responsibility for the fate of the Polish nation. General Jaruzelski and his colleagues were instructed not to expect internal peace without "a dialogue in the national arena," "democratic observance of freedom," and without "the existence of structures that ensure the people's participation." The state of war between the nation and the authorities would never cease in the absence of honest two-way negotiations, the pope said. The principle of dialogue and reciprocity has been a fundamental part of the church's domestic policy and the time has come for the party to display a similar attitude, the pope added. (*L'Osservatore Romano*, special edition, July.)

The pope also lectured his communist audience on the nature of Poland's political tradition. He challenged the official version of Polish history (the country's independence was made possible by the Bolshevik Revolution and Soviet victory in World War II; the West systematically betrayed the Poles). Poland has always found its political inspiration in the West, the pope recalled. The country's proper place in Europe is between two segments of the continent. "It is my ardent wish that Poland always occupy the place it deserves among the nations of Europe, between the East and the West. It is my ardent wish that conditions again will come about for good cooperation with all nations of the West on our continent as well as the American continent—above all . . . the United States of North America, where so many millions of citizens are of Polish origin." (Ibid.)

Later, in the name of the church, the pope elaborated on Poland's international role, stressing the nation's loyalty to the West and its willingness to sacrifice. In a reference made to a centuries-old Promethean concept of Polish history that contends that Poland is the Christ of nations, he said that its mission is to accept pain for others. This idea was given new force by the church when, in October 1982, the pope canonized Maximilian Kolbe, a Polish priest who sacrificed his life in Auschwitz for the life of another man. According to the church, that deed represents the moral essence of Poland, a moral and spiritual triumph in the face of physical destruction.

Although cloaked in religious terms, the church's message was political. It was intended to provide comfort and meaning to the existing situation. Implicit was the conclusion that the government is ranged on the side of evil. It lacks a mandate. Its power derives from a foreign conqueror. Without the instruments of control that legitimacy provides, it rules by force. It is the church that enjoys the full confidence of the Polish people, and no one can rule Poland by consensus without the church's support. In case anyone doubted the authority of the message, it came directly from the pope.

The business side of the pope's visit involved direct negotiations with Jaruzelski, both formal and informal. The visit posed a considerable risk for the military regime since it could have incited the nation against the political authorities. Jaruzelski and his men decided to gamble, counting on the church's political prudence and hoping that the visit would enhance the regime's moral facade. It was a compromise of sorts. The church had a chance to make known its political platform, and the regime had a chance to bask in the reflected light of the church's moral prestige. The meeting between the pope and the general symbolized the possibility of a dialogue and the existence of common ground between communists and Catholics. That ground is patriotism—Polish interests regardless of mutually exclusive world views.

Church policy in 1983 was to allow the authorities to win more popular trust and self-confidence. The church-party summit was designed to give Jaruzelski added legitimacy and security and to make him more amenable to the tangible concessions required for stability. In addition to a mandate from the Kremlin, General Jaruzelski was able to add a mandate from the Vatican. But church endorsement of his government was conditioned on a prompt reopening of negotiations along the lines of the August 1980 social contract.

Yet the church did not insist on the restoration to legality of the outlawed trade union, Solidarity. It stressed the need for the release of Solidarity activists from jail, but it did not ask for inclusion of Solidarity in future negotiations. Although it publicly condemned martial law, it implicitly accepted the harsh measures of military rule as preferable to a Soviet invasion.

In addition to its efforts to improve the overall political atmosphere, the church also focused on the issue of territorial self-government. With the regime formally committed to local self-government, the church campaigned vigorously for a law granting greater political and fiscal autonomy to local people's councils. (After two years of deliberation, the parliament finally enacted the Law on the System of People's Councils' Territorial Self-Government, a major step toward decentralization. The councils were given the right to control the local economy, without interference from the center. A new electoral law was being discussed to regulate the March 1984 elections. Implementation of the statute was held in abeyance, however, and the Army Inspectorate continued to administer local affairs. [*Rzeczpospolita*, 12–13 February.] Then in November, parliament expanded the range of powers of the national defense committees and at the same time enlarged the powers of the voivodship defense committees, which by law control all the social and economic activities in every region of Poland [*Zolnierz Wolnosci*, 28 November].)

The pope's visit helped set limits for resumption of a national dialogue and promoted an evolution toward stabilization, without, however, any agreement on either a specific policy or a timetable for normalization. Because of underlying mistrust and antagonism between the church and the party, progress was limited and largely symbolic.

Like the party, the church was undergoing a factional split. Disagreement was over the proper strategy toward the communist authorities. The younger and lower-ranking clergy became discontent with what they saw as the passive and conciliatory policy of Archbishop Glemp, a prelate they taxed for being unimaginative and soft on the regime. His political philosophy entailed accepting reality "as it is." (*Los Angeles Times*, 8 December 1982.) Even some clergy in senior positions criticized the archbishop. It was well known in Poland that Franciszek Macharski, the colorful and charismatic archbishop of Krakow, was expected to be selected as primate, and that there were groups within the church trying to portray Glemp as an incompetent and indecisive leader. In a move to calm speculation that Glemp would be moved to the Vatican to make way for a more energetic primate, the pope used the visit to Poland to elevate Glemp to cardinal. (*Slowo Powszechne*, 15 February.)

Despite the pope's interest in healing the split in the church, it persists, surfacing usually at occasions associated with Solidarity anniversaries. Young priests continue to identify themselves with Solidarity. Their radicalism has two effects: the regime has begun to threaten individual priests with prosecution for "abusing religious freedom," and church authorities have felt themselves under pressure to take a harder position toward the regime. (*Rzeczpospolita*, 30 November.)

Thus the church is contributing to the political complexities. Factional disputes within the two key Polish institutions hinder real progress in political, economic, and social matters since so much energy is spent on internal quarrels, doctrinal disagreements, definition of principles, and consolidation of ranks. They also encourage mistrust and contempt between the main actors in the national dialogue, threatening national stability. In reality, Polish politics resembles some unruly multiparty system where particularism thwarts any collective effort to overcome a debilitating crisis.

Normalization. Adding to the complexity of the political situation is a crisis of confidence—a popular distrust of the regime so widespread that it paralyzes the process of recovery. It feeds the insecurity of the regime, by making it fear that concessions will be seen as a sign of weakness. Immobility at the top increases popular apathy and alienation, which in turn reinforces the authorities' suspicion of the public. The long-term effect of General Jaruzelski's state of war against the Polish nation is that of a deep cleavage between the conquerors and the conquered, the largest element of the destabilization in Poland.

According to the official view, Poland is in a "transitional" stage, an interim period expected to last until the end of 1985 (*CSM*, 13 August). The most significant development in this respect was the lifting of martial law on 22 July—independence day. (Martial law had been imposed on 13 December 1981; some of its provisions had been suspended a year later.) Implicit in the decision to end martial law was a return to the status quo ante, the legal political framework that prevailed before December 1981. But General Jaruzelski had something else in mind.

Simultaneous with the lifting of martial law came the introduction of measures that in effect incorporated martial law provisions into civil law. Until 22 July, there had been no firm constitutional grounds for imposing martial law because of an internal threat. New constitutional changes empowered Poland's collective executive, the State Council, to "introduce martial law in part of the Polish People's Republic or in the whole of it if considerations of defense or an external threat to the security of the state so require. For the same reasons, the State Council may declare partial or general mobilization." Moreover, in "urgent cases" the State Council may introduce in the entire country or part of it and for any period of time a "state of emergency" if "the state's internal security has been threatened." (*Trybuna Ludu*, 23/24 July.) In this way, General Jaruzelski set the stage constitutionally for the reimposition of martial law at any time in the future.

Concurrent with the constitutional amendments was legislation entitled Special Legal Regulations During the Period of Overcoming the Socioeconomic Crisis and on Changes in Some Laws. A draconian labor law stipulated that in enterprises classified as "fundamental . . . for the national economy or for the state's defense, in public service enterprises, and in enterprises that meet the needs of the population"—that is, practically the entire national economy—management had the right to extend the workweek from

40 to 46 hours. Management was also given the power to dissolve elected self-management committees and to reject a worker's request to quit his job. (Ibid.)

If that were not enough, Poland copied a Soviet "social parasite" statute making work an obligation instead of a right. The Council of Ministers and local executive authorities were authorized to require economic enterprises to employ "certain categories of people directed to take up jobs under compulsory recruitment" and to induce "persons who shirk work" to find employment.

Another set of regulations revoked self-management in institutions of higher education. The chairman of the Council of Ministers now has the right to invalidate any resolutions passed by academic assemblies, to "suspend for up to six months the powers of collegial bodies," and to "transfer these powers to the appropriate one-person bodies." Any student or teacher can be suspended or expelled for activities harmful to society. The right of association is restricted to approved organizations. Participation in activities of the outlawed Independent Student Union or Solidarity or participation in an unauthorized protest is punishable by up to three years in prison. (Ibid.)

A new censorship law restricted the legal activities of the press and gave the government sweeping powers to stop publication of materials considered a threat to the "state security." All publications—regardless of their affiliation—must follow the political direction set by the regime. A new Press Council under the authority of the chairman of the Council of Ministers will supervise the press. (Ibid., 15 July.)

The issue of state power over culture was dramatized by such drastic measures as the decision to dissolve the Polish Writers' Union. This "normalization"—à la Jaruzelski—of Polish literary life was motivated by the regime's determination to do away with what it could not control. At its Twenty-first Congress in December 1980, the Writers' Union was dominated by a freely elected executive fully committed to protecting the freedom of expression of writers. In the face of official pressure, the union declined to expel members openly critical of the communist system, such men as Andrzej Braun, who characterized Soviet-type socialism as a "single system of values and a single—that is, one-sided—

criterion of evaluation," a system that forced people to live "without dignity, rights, and freedoms and to suffer poverty in the bargain" (ibid., 12 September).

After the Writers' Union was suspended in December 1981 for the duration of martial law, the authorities made several attempts to impose a communist-dominated executive body on the association. A key point came in February, when communist writers held a separate national conference at which they charged the union with failing to represent a cross-section of writers in violation of an open cultural policy and of harboring an antisocialist bias. The "compromise" proposed by the rump conference was voluntary subordination to the party line by substantially increasing the membership of the union's governing bodies (Warsaw domestic service, 21 August; FBIS, 22 August). When the union rejected the ultimatum and dismissed the accusations as "untrue and in no way proved," the mayor of Warsaw dissolved the organization on 19 August. It formally ceased to exist on 9 September, when the minister of internal affairs rejected the union's appeal for reinstatement (Trybuna Ludu, 12 September).

As in so many previous instances, the regime imposed drastic and unpopular measures to safeguard its control over every aspect of Poland's social and economic life. In this case, a legal and democratic union was condemned for what the authorities said were its toleration of antisocialist political activists, its cooperation with Western "centers of political subversion," its threat to "the unity of Polish literature by taking authors and works abroad to émigré publishing centers," and its active opposition to martial law (ibid.).

For these reasons, like Solidarity, this freely constituted, self-governing union ceased to exist. In its place the authorities established a new organization in the name of respect for the law, plurality of opinions, political tolerance, and full representation of various groups of writers. At the end of 1983, the new union claimed 350 members (Polityka, 10 December).

Finally, on 22 July, the government announced a partial amnesty for political offenders. Covered by the amnesty were people guilty of violating martial law regulations and of offenses connected with strikes or protest actions. The amnesty law authorized remission of legally valid jail sentences of three years or less and provided for a 30 percent reduction of prison terms in excess of three years.

The amnesty law explicitly excluded individuals accused of attempting to overthrow the government, specifically all prominent leaders of Solidarity and the Committee for Social Self-Defense (KOR), who faced prosecution unless they agreed to leave the country. It was not a blanket amnesty; each case had to be considered individually. In all, 536 former members of Solidarity benefited from the amnesty measure (*NYT*, 1 November), which on closer scrutiny resembled probation. Anyone released under the amnesty law who committed a similar offense before the end of the "transition" period would automatically be returned to prison to serve the remainder of the original sentence. The "transition" period is expected to last until 13 December 1985. It is evident that the amnesty was designed to create an impression of flexibility and good will without restricting the regime's ability to detain groups or individuals deemed undesirable.

The manipulative, arbitrary, and highly conditional character of the amnesty reflects the provisional nature of the entire process of normalization in Poland. Already in 1982, during the first year of martial law, the regime was beginning to build a legal infrastructure for the future political order: a network of legal provisions that would guarantee far-reaching and unchecked powers in social, cultural, economic, and administrative matters. The process of incorporating key provisions of martial law into civil law was well advanced when military rule was lifted in mid-1983. Constitutional amendments and changes in the labor and penal codes were just the finishing touches to a vast program of legal revision intended to equip the regime with the power to prevail in every aspect of its relations with the citizenry. Jaruzelski's normalization has been characterized by an unyielding determination to stay in power. Advancement toward normality has been measured by the ability of the regime to impose its will on the people without the use of tear gas and truncheons. The process resembles a monologue rather than a dialogue, a process of pacification where society accepts defeat without a struggle.

It is misleading to label these developments "normalization" since they do not involve a return to the status quo ante. In fact, the last thing the regime wants is a return to the situation that existed before martial law, a period when the communist authorities faced open, organized opposition and were required to participate in a genuine dialogue, to compromise. The government of General Jaruzelski wants to determine unilaterally the direction, the pace, and the content of "normalization" and to retain practically all the powers it won in its war against the nation. As *Zolnierz Wolnosci* (20 October) pointed out, martial law was not eliminated but only "minimalized," that is, reformulated in a milder manner more acceptable to the public.

It is evident that the regime prefers to deal with the people in an arbitrary manner and with no public accountability. Like Lenin, General Jaruzelski seems fascinated by the use of physical force. He seems to make no distinction between dissolving Solidarity and motivating people to work as a way of overcoming the sociopolitical crisis. Coercion is applied equally. As a Polish journalist, a former member of Solidarity, stated, "It seems Jaruzelski doesn't understand what society's feelings are. It seems he is looking at society as a military unit; you issue a regulation, and that's that." (Quoted in *WP*, 1 August.)

Despite the restricted and conditional nature of "normalization" in Poland, there is a growing conviction there and in the West that the Jaruzelski regime is the least evil of possible alternatives. The genuine democracy favored by Solidarity is an unrealistic option in light of Soviet determination to prevent such a development by any means necessary. The only real alternative to Jaruzelski's selective and guided normalization is the one proposed by the neo-Stalinists, who prefer to resolve Poland's dilemma by means of an unconditional stress on discipline and repression. They are perfectly willing to reinstate all Stalinist methods of social control, to repeat all the old mistakes. This strategy of combat and labor camps, the equalization of poverty, makes Jaruzelski appear as a moderate, charting a careful course between East and West, the best choice under the circumstances of domestic crisis and tense U.S.-Soviet relations.

Economy. Although the consitution declares that Poland has attained the stage of a developed socialist society, the fact is the country now finds itself implementing a sui generis New Economic Policy (NEP). The private sector is in the process of expansion, and state-owned enterprises are experimenting with free-market levers to overcome stagnation if not decline. The Polish economy is multi-structured, with the public sector divided between state-owned and cooperative enterprises. The private sector consists of agencies that use state property for private use, a sphere of direct individual production by proprietors, and a capitalist segment founded on private ownership, hired labor, and quite frequently foreign capital. As in the case of Lenin's NEP, the "demon" of capitalism has been released in Poland to stimulate private initiative and cure a socialist economy.

In February 1982, the Jaruzelski regime committed itself to far-reaching economic reforms intended to transform the socialist sector from an extensive to an intensive mode of development. As in other socialist-bloc countries, notably the Soviet Union, expansion had depended largely on a continuous increase in the consumption of raw materials (especially energy) and labor. In the 1970s, an unusually high rate of growth and technological modernization was made possible due to the easy availability of hard-currency credits from Western banks and governments, but the mode of the economy remained extensive and the dependencies were structurally unchanged.

Although the first symptoms of economic crisis surfaced a decade ago, catastrophe was delayed until 1978. At that time a combination of factors—a substantial increase in raw material prices, including Soviet petroleum; renewed demands for higher wages by Polish workers; and the maturing of some Western loans—made their weight felt. The result of the crisis has been a 25 to 30 percent drop in GNP since 1978, with worse performances in selected industrial sectors: the decline in metallurgy, automobiles, and shipbuilding attained 45 percent by 1983 (*Kultura*, Paris, no. 11/434). In real terms, this has meant a return to pre-1970 levels, erasing an entire decade of national effort to place Poland among the leading industrialized states of Europe.

The Jaruzelski reforms appeared as impressive as the crisis they intended to overcome. The program is aimed at the most sacred axioms of socialist economics: centralized, command planning and centralized budgeting of economic units. Individual enterprises have been granted managerial and fiscal flexibility and added responsibilities as a substitute for administrative manipulation and control. Under the new law, an economic enterprise has the authority to determine what to produce, the quality of its production, the size of its work force, and level of wages paid (within limits). In addition, enterprises have gained a measure of financial self-sufficiency with the authority to deal directly with banks and to set their own prices. So-called "contract" prices replace the notorious system of unrealistic "regulated" prices. (*Glos Wybrzeza*, 1 September.) These measures were intended to result in substantially lower production costs by saving raw materials (energy), by rationalizing the size of the work force at each enterprise, and by raising quality. In sum, this was to be a swift transformation to intensive production under the stimulation of market forces, including the necessity of making a profit. (*Trybuna Ludu*, 19 June.)

These attempts at structural rehabilitation were made during a deep crisis, certainly a difficult time for experimentation. If executed faithfully, the reforms would deprive the political authorities of direct control over the economy, with far-reaching consequences for any communist state. The Polish state, only a short time before, had thought it necessary to militarize key components of the economy as a way of preserving the party's political hegemony. So a combination of political and economic factors work to retard change, particularly any change that would increase risk. For traditionalists, the forms of a command economy on the Soviet model appeared the most risk-free.

In practice, the reforms have resulted in little more than new methods of administrative supervision and a new round of inflation. Mandatory government contracts became the new vehicle of control, providing a shield against the impact of market forces for over 70 percent of industrial production. The system of centrally allocating basic raw materials and hard currency has not been revised, nor has the lopsided preference for heavy industry (with its military overtones) over market-sensitive light industry. The new powers of enterprises to pay higher wages were offset by introduction of a steeply progressive tax intended to cap inflationary trends. (*Rzeczpospolita*, 27 June.)

Finally, the authority of enterprises to set their own prices was introduced in an environment where normal market mechanisms, such as competition, were unavailable to check the surge in prices. The pricing reform was expected to bring greater efficiency. Instead, it enabled enterprises to raise their prices to the point where it paid to produce inefficiently. (*Trybuna Ludu*, 10 November.)

The extensive socialist portion of the Polish economy continued to rely on subsidies to operate. It is not the West, however, which has been underwriting inefficient Polish industry, but the Soviet Union, which sustains a trade deficit with Poland amounting to several billion rubles (*Ideologia i Polityka*, June). Moscow supplies Poland with essential raw materials on credit and at prices substantially below the market price, and it is the principal importer of Polish products of dubious quality. The results are an excessive dependence on the USSR and Soviet economic and political penetration facilitated by the Western embargo. While Polish authorities portray the Soviet effort to keep the Polish economy upright as a selfless and benevolent act (*Wojsko Ludowe*, April), they nevertheless must be concerned with the present trend. They have only to recall the consequences before 1956 of Soviet monopolization of Poland's foreign trade. Such a concern has been implied in some statements declaring the need to transform the structure of foreign trade despite the stability of economic relations with other CMEA states (*Glos Wybrzeza*, 1 June).

The government, meanwhile, claimed that Polish industry had overcome the crisis and would register an 8 to 9 percent growth in 1983. The forecast for the following two years, until the end of 1985, was for a further increase of 16 percent. (*Rzeczpospolita*, 20 June.) While such figures may have looked impressive, they simply meant that the Poles would have to wait until the start of 1986 before production regained its 1978 level.

In any event, disturbing signs were apparent at the end of 1983 indicating serious economic and political difficulties. The press suddenly fell silent about economic reform, and there were indications of further placement of enterprises under military control. Personnel changes indicated Jaruzelski's intention to assume direct control over the economy, especially the appointment of Manfred Gorywoda, a close associate of the general's, as head of the Planning Commission (*WP*, 23 November). New legislation submitted to parliament contradicted the spirit of the reforms by centralizing government control. And there was an ominous sign in the reorganization of the National Defense Committee. The mining and export of coal, Poland's "black gold," resumed its importance as a bulwark of the economy. One could conclude from reading the Catholic *Tygodnik Powszechny*'s discussion of macroeconomic issues that the country was in deep economic troubles and that General Jaruzelski was sharpening his sword in preparation for new outbreaks of popular discontent. The trend at the end of the year was toward a military-command economy regardless of the social economic cost. It seemed that once again in Poland's postwar history, economic reform would not be allowed to proceed beyond rhetoric. The most durable quality of the socialist economy is its resistance to change.

More than a decade ago, Poland embarked on a program of industrial modernization with the help of Western Europe and the United States. In the process, it accumulated a substantial debt, which by the end of 1983 totaled some $26 billion, with $1 billion in interest charges being added annually (*Glos Wybrzeza*, 2 August). The situation was further complicated by Western economic sanctions imposed in response to human rights offenses by the martial law regime. Sanctions curtailed Polish contacts with Western markets, and trade with the West fell at an annual rate of $2.3 billion in 1982 and 1983. Trade with Western countries amounted to $7.5 billion in 1980. (Ibid.) The Western sanctions affected the entire economy. It is estimated that their combined cost to the Polish economy has been some $12 billion (*Trybuna Ludu*, 14 June).

Particularly effective in restricting Polish access to Western markets were the drastic reduction in the availability of new Western credits and the loss of most-favored-nation status since tariffs added about 30 percent to the cost of Polish products, making them uncompetitive. In addition, in 1983, the United States blocked consideration of Poland's application for membership in the International Monetary Fund.

In 1982, Poland received slightly less than $1.5 billion in credits, instead of an expected $3 billion. The effect on food production was dramatic: poultry output fell by 74 percent and egg production by 21 percent; fisheries products dropped by 5 kilograms per capita for the year. (*Rzeczpospolita*, 4 August.) Total Western credits made available in 1983 may not exceed $600 million (Warsaw domestic service, 5 August, 3 November; *FBIS*, 5 August, 4 November). The sanctions stymied the Polish economy, leaving the country semibankrupt, with a huge debt and few resources to repay its international financial obligations.

It had been expected in Poland that sanctions would be lifted or substantially reduced in 1983. The pope's visit and the end of martial law were to satisfy Western conditions of respect for human rights and signal resumption of economic assistance. But General Jaruzelski's rewriting of martial law into civil law was far from satisfactory as a justification for lifting trade restrictions. The only tangible economic relief provided by the West was in the form of very generous supplies of food directly to Polish families and an agreement to reschedule payment of the Polish debt.

Poland was due to repay $2.6 billion in 1983, $1.5 billion in principal and $1.1 billion in interest. Western banks agreed to convert 65 percent of the interest due (about $715 million) into short-term trade credits, and 95 percent of the principal into a ten-year loan. (*WP*, 19 August.) Poland devalued the zloty against the dollar by about 9 percent in an attempt to improve its terms of trade with the West. The zloty-ruble parity remained unchanged. (*Rzeczpospolita*, 1 July.)

Amid the confusion caused by the economic reforms and the poor performance of the Polish economy in 1983, the country's standard of living declined for the fourth consecutive year. The fall in 1983 was 10 to 15 percent (author's estimate). Inflation was officially reported to be 30 percent (*WP*, 2 November), but in reality was probably twice that. The average Polish family spends about half of its monthly income on food, a disproportion that would be aggravated by further increases in the prices of basic necessities. The inflationary trend has triggered widespread fears that the government would impose a currency exchange, a fiscal measure used in the 1950s to cope with sharply rising prices.

In addition to low productivity, chronic shortages of food and consumer goods, inflation, and rationing, Poland's economic ills include speculation and an enormous black market where goods are bartered or purchased at exorbitant prices, usually payable in hard currency. These items are far beyond the reach of the average worker, certainly beyond the means of workers in the socialist sector who operate under the additional handicap of having no right to switch to a job in the private sector.

The causes of the unusually poor agricultural performance can be found in the ideologically dictated policies of 1948–1956. An attempt to copy the Soviet model brought forced collectivization that resulted in the structural disintegration of production, distribution, and financing of farming. Poland has been unable to feed itself since 1948, even though some land was returned to private cultivation after the October 1956 crisis—a move whose force was undercut by the regime's hesitation to guarantee private ownership by civil law and the omnipresent fear of recollectivization on the part of private farmers.

This is the background to General Jaruzelski's conciliatory gesture toward private farmers. A constitutional amendment that took effect 22 July offered stronger guarantees of landownership and the right to inherit agricultural enterprises. Although this long-overdue measure states that the Polish People's Republic "cares about private family farms belonging to working peasants and will guarantee the permanence of these farms," the constitution also commits the regime to support "agricultural circles and cooperatives" (*Trybuna Ludu*, 23/24 July), which long ago were recognized as a scaled-down substitute for collective farms. Still, the amendment should be considered a significant departure from previous practices, a positive move toward the full recognition of private production within a socialist economy, and a step toward greater stability and prestige for the peasantry. After 27 years, the ambivalence toward private agriculture was put to an end.

The amendment cleared the way for an agreement without precedent in any communist state: an accord between the government and the Roman Catholic church allowing the church to administer a program of direct economic assistance to private farmers. The agreement was worked out in principle between the pope and General Jaruzelski during the pope's visit. It envisions the delivery directly to farmers by church authorities of at least $2.6 billion worth of Western agricultural machinery, fertilizers, and other supplies (*Los Angeles Times*, 16 September).

Jaruzelski's acceptance of the church's taking responsibility for a sector that provides 75 percent of the nation's foodstuff (*CSM*, 23 August) testifies to the regime's incapacity to offer practical solutions. It is an admission of incompetence and an abdication of authority, explained no doubt by a fear of famine and its unwelcome political consequences. It also allowed the government to circumvent Western sanctions and to reduce hard-currency expenditures for Western agricultural products. Poland's foreign spending for food averages $1.6 billion a year, leaving few resources for the acquisition of machinery needed by industry and making repayment of the foreign debt more difficult (*WP*, 23 June). The Soviets are in a position to stimulate Poland's industrial production with low-cost raw materials, but Soviet agricultural problems and a foreign exchange shortage render the Soviets ill positioned to feed the Poles. The Soviets seemed to have no alternative other than to accept the ideologically deviant Catholic-communist alliance to boost Poland's agricultural production.

There was a delay in reaching agreement on the details of the agricultural fund because of several controversial questions. The church was willing to proceed only if it had full administrative authority over the program and assistance was limited to private farms. The regime insisted on comanagement of the fund and the eligibility of collective farms for assistance. The church refused both demands as contrary to the purpose of the fund. Negotiations proceeded slowly and were subject to frequent interruptions.

It is understandable that there would be considerable opposition among the political authorities to the concept of using Western capital to stimulate private agriculture in Poland. First of all, it would imply a revival of authentic participation by private farmers in production decisions in a way that would strengthen tendencies toward the self-managing, independent peasant movement embodied in Rural Solidarity (*Glos Szczecinski*, 12 July). In addition, the plan would increase the regime's dependence on the church and magnify the differences between the private and socialist branches of farming. The authorities feared capitalism as well as the social consequences of favoring a group that had already achieved an above-average income. (*Przeglad Techniczny*, 10 April.) Yet they appeared willing to reverse themselves and give priority to attitudes of individualism and entrepreneurship they had discredited in the past.

To avert starvation in Poland, the improvement of agricultural production is imperative. It has been estimated that in 1975 Polish agriculture was 25 years behind that of Western Europe, that by 1983 it was 30 years behind, and that if present trends continue it will be four decades behind by 1990 (*Trybuna Ludu*, 16 June). In 1983 alone, due to the shortage of fodder, the cattle herd was reduced by 5.4 percent, and there was an abrupt 20 percent drop in the number of hogs. The number of livestock was reduced to 1971 levels, but the population was greater by 4 million people. (Ibid., 26 July.)

Despite an increase in state agricultural investment, from 23 percent in 1982 to 28 percent in 1983, it is expected that annual meat consumption by 1985 will drop to 55–60 kilograms per capita, roughly half the 1978 level. The production of potatoes and cereal is expected to grow, but even under the most favorable circumstances, the plan calls for 1985 cereal imports to be twice as high as those of 1983. (Ibid., 16 June.)

The cereal harvest in 1983 was above average: the harvest exceeded 22 million tons, enabling the government to reduce imports by 20 percent (Warsaw domestic service, 2 November; *FBIS*, 2 November). But the overall results, however, were disappointing and politically destabilizing. Jaruzelski was forced to reinstate meat rationing and move ahead with another round of food price increases, always risky for public order. The regime appeared no more capable than its predecessors of devising a clear economic program, and its behavior was confusing and self-contradictory, divided as it was between talk of reform and a predilection for militarization of the economy.

The only bright spot in the otherwise gloomy Polish economy was the private industrial-services sector, especially the so-called Polania firms owned by Poles who are citizens of Western countries (usually the United States, West Germany, France, Sweden, or Austria). Between 10 million and 18 million Poles live abroad. In 1972, the government initiated a program designed to tap their economic potential (*Sprawy Miedzynarodowe*, June). The first three Polania licenses were issued in 1977, and by 1981 there were 144 such companies. The following year 230 permits were granted, increasing the total to 374. Output from these firms was worth 17.6 billion zlotys in 1982 (about $1.8 billion at the official exchange rate), and they accounted for $10 million in exports. Most production, 79 percent, is geared for the domestic market, however. (*Przeglad Tygodniowy*, 20 February.)

The size of these firms varies. Some employ more than 200 workers, have high profit margins (40 to 50 percent), and show a low ratio of managers to employees (about 5 percent). They are involved in various business activities, including construction, metallurgy, chemicals, cosmetics, advertising, and others. Since 1981, they have had the same right as government enterprises to apply for raw materials and other supplies. Another important privilege is a tax exemption good for the first three years of operation. (Ibid.)

These outposts of capitalism have become sources of economic revival and a vital channel to the West at a time of Western sanctions. They reduce imports, attract hard currency, and sometimes provide opportunities for state-owned firms to become partners in lucrative foreign ventures under a Polania firm's sponsorship. (*Rynki Zagraniczne*, 18 December 1982.)

Registration and operation of the Polania firms are handled by local authorities, which in some cases oppose the reappearance of capitalism as a troubling factor in society and competitor for scarce resources. Not only do these highly efficient and prosperous businesses contrast painfully with the sluggish socialist economy, but they serve as magnets for badly needed specialists. In light of some local opposition, more centralized control and protection of Polania firms were planned in 1983. The trend seemed to be toward more favorable treatment for these businesses, which despite five years of severe depression in the national economy were registering growth on the order of 300 percent.

Finally, small private industries and services appeared to be in good shape, although they were sometimes accused of speculation and high prices (*Trybuna Ludu*, 6/7 August; *Tygodnik Demokratyczny*, 18 September). Small industries, services, and artisans' shops were expected to increase their output by about 13.5 percent in 1983, attracting employees from the public sector, despite a decline of some 30 to 40 percent in some services such as appliance repair and automobile garages. It was expected that in 1983 about 16,000 new small businesses and 34,000 additional employees would join this private sector of the economy. These changes were encouraged by modifications in the law and the easy availability of credits. Major problems involved raw material shortages and the role of a newly established government employment agency with some authority over newly hired workers. (*Tygodnik Demokratyczny*, 6 February.) The private sector is a critical supplement to national industries and even more important as an adjunct to state-administered services. Private business has a key

role to play in Poland. Together with private agriculture, it accounts for an estimated 40 percent of Poland's GNP.

There were no major breakthroughs in 1983 in the struggle for decentralization, efficiency, and freedom from the gigantic, inert bureaucracy. Instead of modernization and revitalization, the socialist sector continued to decline, demanding increased resources and relying on Soviet subsidies and Jaruzelski's stress on martial discipline to keep going.

At the same time, the private sector showed signs of a slow expansion into domains previously reserved for socialism. The process is in its early stages, but if the church can obtain and dispense Western aid to private agriculture, Poland will have two economies of equal strength—one private, one state—a situation bound to affect the political structure. For the second straight year since the beginning of communist rule, trends in the Polish economy favored the private sector over the public sector.

The Unions. Two unions representing radically different political ideas exist concurrently in Poland. Although outlawed in 1982, Solidarity preserved a de facto entity when it moved underground and adopted a new program of action. The government-controlled trade union system set up in January to replace Solidarity is still something of a legal fiction. It exists in law only, despite a tremendous official effort to give it substance and support.

Although Solidarity was supposedly nonexistent, official polemics against the union and its individual leaders were conducted almost daily throughout 1983. At the core of the argument was who was more patriotic and more capable of representing Poland's national interest—the union or the communist authorities. The regime made a pretense of popular and growing support. It founded its legitimacy on Poland's raison d'être and, surprisingly, a willingness to live up to the spirit and the letter of the August 1980 Gdansk agreement. The entire campaign to discredit Solidarity had a pseudo-patriotic overtone that evoked the unwritten rule that domestic changes must not jeopardize national security.

Solidarity ceased to exist as a nationwide mass organization with the destruction of its infrastructure and the imprisonment and isolation of many of its leaders. It survived, however, as a clandestine but visible opposition supported by millions and as a national symbol of resistance to the communist system, which Poles see as a form of Soviet occupation. Solidarity is a memory of freedom, a dream of independence, and an active organization that assumes the government will never be able to resolve the nation's social and economic crisis and that another popular confrontation with the regime is only a matter of time. The regime, meanwhile, is busily attempting to dismantle the myth of Solidarity, a counterproductive campaign providing the union with additional attention and disproving the official claim that Lech Walesa is nothing more than a "private person." Anti-Solidarity propaganda has not inspired loyalty to the regime, nor has it bolstered credibility for the thesis that communists regard the Gdansk agreement not as a historic blunder, but as a historic opportunity that has permanently altered the fundamental character of the communist state (*Polityka*, 20 August).

Some Solidarity leaders who escaped arrest organized a Provisional Coordinating Commission (TKK), which as early as January 1983 drew up a basic outline for a resistance program aimed at perpetually isolating the military regime from the people. These new methods of struggle recognize the change in the national mood from confrontation to survival. The major points advise pressure on the authorities, but within the system, combined with the preservation of "independent forms of thinking to overcome the state's monopoly on the printed and spoken word" and a readiness to hold general strikes to keep the authorities in a "political vacuum." (*WP*, 29 January.) Workers at every factory have formed clandestine Solidarity cells to publish newspapers, organize demonstrations and other protest actions, provide support for the families of arrested members, and, above all, boycott the new unions. These are called temporary enterprise committees (TKZ), as distinct from TKK, which coordinates national strategy. ("Solidarity and the Situation in Poland," New York, Committee in Support of Solidarity, 24 May.)

This strategy had become known as "frontal refusal." It goes beyond passive resistance since it involves, according to a prominent underground Solidarity leader, "ignoring all actions of the authorities, with the exception, of course, of ones directly affecting us, such as those by the police, which have to be counteracted, and organizing various forms of independent activities in

science, education and culture, outside the influence of the authorities" (quoted in *NYT*, 19 December). This idea of an underground society recalls the organization of the Polish resistance during the Nazi occupation. The outlawed union continues to enjoy widespread political and moral support and can resurface on short notice, providing conditions are favorable. The underground union believes that only its reactivation would open a genuine dialogue between the government and the people, which is the only way of solving the nation's economic problems.

Throughout the year, the country was flooded with Solidarity leaflets and posters, and public broadcasts were sometimes interrupted by clandestine Solidarity transmissions. Street protests had limited success, but three important dates brought thousands to demonstrate in the face of the truncheons and water cannons of the mechanized units of the Citizens' Police. The occasions were May Day, 31 August (the anniversary of the Gdansk agreement), and 13 December (the day martial law was declared in 1981). The demonstrations were considered successful because, as Walesa stated, "the people responded to the call . . . everybody sees that only force prevents them from demonstrating the way they want to" (*FBIS*, 2 May). Thousands of arrests followed each demonstration (*WP*, 15 August; *NYT*, 1 September, 17 December).

For the regime the moment of greatest embarrassment and irritation in 1983 was the awarding of the Nobel Peace Prize to Lech Walesa for his "attempt to find a peaceful solution to his country's problems" and "to establish a dialogue between the organization he represents—Solidarity —and the authorities." Indeed, the political means employed by the union and the communist regime contrasted sharply. In its arsenal, Solidarity had strikes, the threat of a general strike, and appeals for elections. It never advocated or attempted the forceful overthrow of the government. It was the regime that killed hundreds of people, wounded and imprisoned thousands, and intimidated millions. The Nobel Prize changed nothing in Poland, but it did give the Poles a feeling of welcome satisfaction. As Walesa wrote in the lecture read at the Nobel Prize ceremony, it showed that the "Polish people have not been subjugated, nor have they chosen the road of violence and fratricidal bloodshed" (*NYT*, 12 December).

The regime reacted by ridiculing Walesa for

not being an intellectual, for being a worker—an odd sort of accusation for a workers' state. The prize was a trick by President Reagan, the regime said, a deliberate provocation "chosen by the experts in the anticommunist crusade." A dose of anti-Semitism was even added to attest to the worthlessness of the prize: *Zolnierz Wolnosci* (8 October) told its readers that the prize had once been awarded to Menachim Begin, the prime minister of Israel. But no propaganda or fabrication could erase the simple reality that the efforts of a common Polish worker had received prestigious international recognition and that he had joined the company of such famous Polish writers as Sienkiewicz and Rejmond who a century ago kept the Polish national idea alive.

In 1983, Poland again had trade unions that were represented by the authorities as free, independent, and self-governing. They were intended to replace Solidarity. With the new unions, the authorities employed the principle of atomization, organizing the unions along craft lines, thus precluding easy centralization of power on a local, regional, or national level. The consolidation of various professional groups had enabled Solidarity to organize strikes with cross-occupational participation and to make credible the threat of a general strike.

Multi-union association at the national level and nationwide federation of each individual craft had originally been postponed until 1985, but in an effort to stimulate interest in the new unions and give them some credibility, the government authorized given professions or branches of industry to form national organizations as of 1 January 1984. (*Rzeczpospolita*, 16–17 August). The prevailing apathy toward these organizations must have persuaded the authorities that it was politically safe and useful to stimulate their horizontal and vertical proliferation.

The autonomy of the new unions is a well-understood farce. The law founding them severely restricts their freedom of action. Court registration is mandatory and conditional on adoption of union bylaws copied from an official sample. Each individual union must pledge allegiance to the communist system, the leading role of the party, and Poland's international alliances and promise noninvolvement in political affairs. The right to strike, a union's most effective form of expression, exists in theory only, since in each case a union must obtain advance permission. A large number of key industries, crafts, and professions are denied the right altogether. (*CSM*, 11 May 1982.)

Within three months of the signing of the Gdansk agreement, Polish workers swelled Solidarity's ranks to 10 million members. The new unions have prompted mostly mistrust. Official figures, certainly exaggerated, claimed that over 17,000 individual unions had registered as of September 1983, out of about 60,000 eligible, and that membership stood at 3.7 million, or 20–30 percent of all employees (*Trybuna Ludu*, 1 September; *Sztandar Mlodych*, 11 October; PAP, 19 December; *FBIS*, 19 December). Average membership in each union is 180 workers, hardly a threat to the regime. The fact that the new unions have not become a mass organization and that they have produced no strong leaders are evidence of the effectiveness of Solidarity's underground campaign against the official unions. The authorities are attempting to show that the unions demonstrate respect for the principle of pluralism and that they have already produced tangible bread-and-butter gains for their members (*Trybuna Ludu*, 2 February; *Rzeczpospolita*, 7 November).

The regime knows it cannot recreate around its creature the euphoria that surrounded Solidarity, and indeed it may not even want to. The public in any case has withdrawn from political activity. The regime has deliberately discouraged party members from joining the new unions so as to emphasize the party's distance from the organizations and to stress the unions' nonpolitical objectives (*Zolnierz Wolnosci*, 5 October). The authorities seem convinced that their persistence and the lack of an alternative for the workers will pay off in rising membership in the new organizations.

Foreign Affairs. For Poland's communist regime, foreign affairs have special meaning. The contemporary Polish state is an outgrowth of the international system, and ever since the Yalta agreements of 1945, Poland has been compelled to live according to external requirements. Membership in the Soviet commonwealth has not automatically guaranteed security since on no less than four occasions (1948, 1956, 1970, and 1980–1981) Poland was threatened with the danger of Soviet invasion.

Although it has become an almost daily ritual in Warsaw to reassure the Soviet leadership of

Polish loyalty, Warsaw has also found it possible and useful to exercise its own discretion in foreign affairs by expanding ties with Western Europe, the United States, and Third World countries in a way that does not conflict with Soviet interests. This modest international activism has more than just a psychological importance; it has become a lever to elevate Poland's status in the Soviet camp to junior partner rather than mere satellite.

The rise of Solidarity and General Jaruzelski's coup d'etat destroyed the foreign policies—East and West—that had so carefully been constructed in the 1970s. Poland lost its credibility as an ally in Moscow, and it lost the sympathy of the West as the most independent and assertive Soviet-bloc state. Facing a hostile nation, Jaruzelski's martial law regime put itself in a precarious position between East and West, that of conflict with both blocs. Among the top priorities of the regime since the lifting of martial law has been the mending of Poland's relations with the Soviet Union and Eastern Europe followed by an attempt to end its isolation from the rest of the world.

Polish authorities explain their country's dependence on the Soviet Union as a matter of choice, rather than necessity. A communist reading of Polish history concludes that France, Great Britain, and the United States—with neither a common border nor common security interests with Poland—have taken unfair advantage of Poland's pro-Western melancholy and lack of political realism. The situation today differs little from the time of the Napoleonic wars, World War I, or World War II, in this view. President Reagan, for example, is admired in Poland— there is a Polish expression, "Reagan, our brother"—but he is no altruist championing the Polish cause; he is just another cynical Western politician interested in Polish instability as a way of affecting the global balance of power in his favor. Regime spokesmen argue that the West is using Poland as a pawn in its anti-Soviet campaign. A change in the Polish domestic system would have a domino effect in Eastern Europe. A neutral or pro-Western Poland would cost it Soviet support and would isolate East Germany, which would be absorbed by West Germany. A reunited Germany would eventually dismantle the Polish state. The alternative to communist rule is yet another partition of Poland. (*Nike*, July; *Slowo Powszechne*, 22–24 July.)

In a speech to the Sejm, Stefan Olszowski, Poland's foreign minster and the leading communist hard-liner, charted a new policy for the 1980s. In contrast to the pragmatic, businesslike analysis of foreign affairs and Poland's place in the international environment that had characterized public debate in the 1970s, Olszowski's statement was highly ideological and tough, closely resembling Soviet pronouncements. Using language reminiscent of the Cold War and frequently invoking the class struggle, Olszowski assured Moscow that Poland would have "respect for the realities of contemporary Europe" and that "allied ties of friendship and cooperation with the Soviet Union . . . [will] remain the immutable cornerstone of Polish foreign policy" (Warsaw domestic service, 31 January; *FBIS*, 1 February). The United States and the other NATO countries were accused of attempting nuclear blackmail of the socialist states.

This strongly pro-Soviet foreign policy line was no protection against public attacks from Moscow. An attack much more serious than the *Novoye vremya* incident (see above) came from the Soviet theoretical journal *Kommunist*, which questioned several aspects of Polish socialism as *Nowe Drogi*, the Polish party's theoretical journal, had described it (*NYT*, 21 May). The Soviets were disturbed by the lesser-evil justification for the political crackdown against Solidarity, an interpretation that implies that Jaruzelski shares Reagan's view of the Soviet empire as an evil worse than martial law.

The Soviets also expressed reservations about what they considered the delicate treatment of the political opposition in Poland, the partnership with the church, and, in Soviet eyes, the generally open style of political discussion. The Soviet accusations echoed what Polish hard-liners had been saying, indicating a possible Soviet preference for the neo-Stalinist faction.

These public polemics subsided when the editorial board of *Nowe Drogi* invited a delegation from *Kommunist* to Poland on a fact-finding trip, which, as *Trybuna Ludu* (7 June) reported, resulted in agreement "to continue cooperation between the two editorial boards and to continue the exchange of editors, publishers, and materials." The statement was significant in that it failed to mention any "identity of views." Presumably, the Soviet visitors continued to have serious reservations about the methods and direction of Polish socialism.

Yet Poland's foreign policy in 1983 appeared

to be based on a literal translation of the Russian text. Poland's criticism of U.S. Euromissile deployments included accusations that the United States had embarked on a dangerous militaristic course designed to raise international tensions and was involved in an attempt to push "the USSR against the wall" with first-strike weapons. The only strictly Polish theme to these outpourings was an accusation that West Germany wanted to revise the territorial status quo in Europe and restore Germany's 1937 borders (Warsaw domestic service, 16 May; *FBIS*, 17 May).

Warsaw adopted the Soviet interpretation of the Korean Air Lines incident, taking advantage of the occasion to blame President Reagan and the CIA for a cynical provocation and of using the tragedy for the "benefit of forces that do not want accord, are striving to achieve military supremacy over the socialist world, and are driving the world toward a confrontation" (*Trybuna Ludu*, 9 September).

The unusually strong pro-Soviet orientation of Polish foreign policy in 1983 colored Warsaw's rejection of the U.N. resolution based on the "Report on the Situation in Poland," by Hugo Gobbi, a deputy secretary general. The report accused the regime of serious human rights violations. The Polish government rejected both the report and the resolution as "illegal, invalid, politically harmful and morally two-faced" and of being orchestrated by Washington (Warsaw domestic service, 1 March; *FBIS*, 2 March).

This foreign policy line paid off in the form of full rehabilitation as a Soviet-bloc member in good standing. In August, an East German delegation led by Erich Honecker traveled to Warsaw, the first visit by a Warsaw Pact head of state since imposition of martial law. The visit was apparently a success. The East Germans expressed satisfaction with Poland's determination to preserve its socialist orientation and promised to invite Poland's participation in joint economic ventures. Honecker was followed by János Kádár, the Hungarian leader, who promised help to reduce the impact of Western sanctions (Warsaw domestic service, 27 October; *FBIS*, 28 October). Finally there was the visit of Gústav Husák, the hard-line Czechoslovak leader, who, like Jaruzelski, distinguished himself by "normalizing" his country. He was the most qualified to congratulate General Jaruzelski: "The great service rendered by the socialist and patriotic forces of [Poland] not merely for their own country but also for the whole socialist community and the cause of peace in Europe is that they succeeded in securing a socialist direction for emerging from the crisis and opening up for Poland a path of a new socialist development" (Prague domestic service, 30 November; *FBIS*, 1 December).

By the end of the year, Poland had regained full credibility in the Soviet bloc. The Soviet leader himself could not visit, but he sent his proconsul, the new Soviet ambassador and a former senior KGB official, Aleksandr Aksenov (Warsaw domestic service, 19 July; *FBIS*, 20 July).

Poland's attempts to break out of its isolation in the West were much less successful. No Western chief of state or head of government paid a visit, although Franz-Josef Strauss, the conservative political leader of Bavaria, did make a semiprivate visit. Warsaw used it as an opportunity to convey a message to the West that Poland's domestic situation had stabilized, that the risk of violent eruptions had passed, and instead of sending charity to the Polish people, the West should advance new credits to the Polish government (*Trybuna Ludu*, 23/24 July). The tone of Strauss's visit was cordial, but produced no direct results.

Another failure from Warsaw's point of view was a visit by a group of U.S. senators, including Christopher Dodd, a member of the Foreign Relations Committee and chairman of the International Financial and Monetary Policy Subcommittee. The Polish government wanted a lifting of the sanctions, an end to U.S. meddling in Poland's internal affairs, and acceptance of a proposal to reschedule repayment of Poland's foreign debt over a twenty-year period, with an eight-year grace period (ibid., 11 and 19 August). Finding little progress in human rights, the United States did not revise its policy toward Poland.

Besides activism within the Soviet bloc, Polish diplomacy sought political and economic support in Asia, Africa, and Latin America. Foreign Minister Olszowski visited numerous foreign countries, beaming home communiqués of friendly bilateral relations and an occasional economic or cultural agreement. These small successes were in sharp contrast to the summit visits of the 1970s, and they symbolize a decline in Poland's international status. Gone are the dreams of playing broker between East and West.

Assessment. Now that Poland has gone through its second consecutive year of martial rule, it seems appropriate to examine the prospects for stability and the essence of General Jaruzelski's model of socialism.

The most remarkable feature of Polish history since the end of World War II has been the regular cycle of sociopolitical crises (1948, 1956, 1968, 1970, 1976, 1980). These explosions of popular dissatisfaction draw attention to the repeated failure of the ruling communist party to provide competent political leadership and rational economic management. The pattern recurs regardless of what team is in control of the party apparatus. Since the war, several different kinds of communists have held sway: Stalinists, nationalists, technocrats, and now the military. So far not one of these groups has been able to fulfill the aspirations of the Polish people. There is very little likelihood that the military will fare much better.

Instability is not caused by the mishandling of the nation's affairs by one ruling group or another, it is inherent in the system itself. Poland continues to be ruled by minority governments incapable of governing by consensus, yet unwilling to open a real national dialogue. General Jaruzelski fits the mold. Under the influence of party liberals, he has made some gestures toward pluralism. He has had written into the constitution and the statute books several provisions that mark a departure from some monopolistic practices of communism. His PRON formula is significant because there is no built-in communist majority. The laws on trade unions and territorial self-government suggest a desire to create pluralistic institutions. Within limits, the press appears relatively free and argumentative; prohibited of course, are direct attacks on Jaruzelski, the Soviet Union, or the principle of socialism. The problem is that these pluralistic tendencies have not been allowed to be carried out in practice, owing to military surveillance of the civil authorities. The rule of thumb seems to be that for each concession to pluralism, there is a compensating move by the military to grasp more power.

The centralistic features of communism have been retained, especially in the economy and in spite of considerable expansion of the private sector. The changes are intended to weaken the party-government bureaucratic apparatus and to increase the influence of the military. This is not a structural redesign: it is simply a shift in the center of gravity within the same old system. General Jaruzelski has not removed the primary cause of instability, and the Polish predicament will continue. The next eruption of disorder is merely a matter of time, particularly since his cure for economic decline is to increase prices, historically the most frequent immediate cause for revolts.

Arthur R. Rachwald
U.S. Naval Academy
Annapolis

Romania

Population. 22.5 million (January 1983; *Scînteia*, 27 April)
Party. Romanian Communist Party (Partidul Comunist Român; PCR)
Founded. 8 May 1921
Membership. Over 3.3 million (ibid., 5 August)

General Secretary. Nicolae Ceauşescu

Political Executive Committee (PEC). 23 full and 19 alternate members; 13 of whom belong to the Permanent Bureau: Nicolae Ceauşescu (president of the republic), Stefan Andrei (foreign minister),* Iosif Banc, Emil Bobu (chairman, Council on Problems of Economic and Social Organization), Virgil Cazacu, Elena Ceauşescu (first deputy prime minister), Nicolae Constantin (chairman, Central Council of the General Confederation of Trade Unions), Constantin Dascalescu (prime minister), Petru Enache (vice-president, State Council),* Gheorghe Oprea (first deputy prime minister), Ion Patan (minister of technical-material supply and control of fixed assets), Gheorghe Radulescu (vice-president, State Council), Ilie Verdeţ (chairman, Central Council of Workers' Control of Economic and Social Organization); additional PEC full members: Lina Ciobanu (minister of light industry), Ion Coman, Ion Dinca (first deputy prime minister), Ludovic Fazekas (deputy prime minister), Alexandrina Gainuse (deputy prime minister), Petru Lupu (chairman, PCR Central Collegium), Manea Manescu (vice-president, State Council), Paul Niculescu, Constantin Olteanu (minister of national defense), Gheorghe Pana, Dumitru Popescu, Stefan Voitec (vice-president, State Council); additional PEC alternate members: Stefan Birlea (chairman, State Planning Committee), Miu Dobrescu, Marin Enache, Suzana Gadea (chairwoman, Council of Socialist Culture and Education), Mihai Gere (president, Council of Workers of Hungarian Nationality), Nicolae Giosan (chairman, Grand National Assembly), Constantin Leonard, Stefan Mocuţa (chairman, Committee for the Affairs of People's Councils), Ana Mureşan (chairwoman, National Council of Women), Elena Nae, Cornel Pacoste, Ion Radu, Ion Stoian, Iosif Szasz (vice-chairman, Grand National Assembly), Ion Totu (deputy prime minister), Ioni Ursu (first vice-chairman, National Council of Science and Technology), Richard Winter (minister–state secretary for technical-material supply and control of fixed assets). (*Andrei and Petru Enache are the only two members of the Permanent Bureau who are PEC alternate members.)

Secretariat. 8 members: Nicolae Ceauşescu, Iosif Banc, Emil Bobu, Ion Coman, Miu Dobrescu, Petru Enache, Gheorghe Stoica, Ilie Verdeţ

Central Committee. 250 full and 174 alternate members

Last Congress. Twelfth, 19–23 November 1979, in Bucharest; next congress scheduled for 1984. National Conference meets between congresses to review implementation of party decisions. The last conference occurred 16–18 December 1982.

Last Election. 1980, 98.5 percent, all 369 seats won by Front of Socialist Democracy and Unity

Auxiliary Organizations. Union of Communist Youth (UTC, 3.2 million members), Nicu Ceauşescu, first secretary; General Confederation of Trade Unions (7 million members), Nicolae Constantin, chairman of the Central Council; National Council of Women, Ana Mureşan, chairwoman; Councils of Workers of Hungarian and German Nationalities, Mihai Gere and Eduard Eisenburger, respective presidents.

Publications. *Scînteia*, PCR daily (except Monday); *Era Socialista*, PCR theoretical and political biweekly; *Munca de Partid*, PCR monthly for party activists; *România Libera*, electoral bloc daily (except Sunday); *Lumea*, foreign affairs weekly; *Revista Economica*, economic weekly. Agerpress is the official news agency.

Founded as the result of a split in the Romanian socialist movement in May 1921, the PCR was effectively outlawed in 1924. Completely subservient to Comintern, its leadership factious and dominated by ethnic minorities, and its policies inimical to the territorial integrity of the Romanian nation-state, the PCR was numerically weak, if sporadically disruptive, during the interwar period. Having played a subordinate and relatively minor role in the antifascist uprising of August 1944, the PCR, supported by the occupying Soviet army, engineered the assumption of power by fellow traveler Petru Groza in March 1945. In December 1947, a people's republic was established. The PCR merged with the rump Social Democratic Party in 1948, forming the Romanian Workers' Party (Partidul Muncitoresc Român; PMR). Overcoming leadership challenges from alleged Titoists (1948), Muscovite elements (1952), and intellectual Khrushchevites (1957), Gheorghe Gheorghiu-Dej directed party and state affairs until his death in March 1965. Nicolae Ceauşescu succeeded to the PMR leadership and in 1974 became president of the Socialist Republic of Romania, a name change effected in 1965 when the party reclaimed its original name.

As a consequence of its commitment to the Stalinist model of economic development, in the early 1960s the party rejected Soviet plans for bloc economic integration, embarking on an assertively national course that has often conflicted with Soviet priorities. The PCR's autonomy has been most stridently expressed in state foreign and interparty relations. Domestically, however, the PCR has maintained a rigidly orthodox Stalinist regime. Fueled by Western credits and draconian rates of capital accumulation and investments, the Romanian economy was among Europe's fastest growing between 1965 and 1975. As much a result of unfavorable international economic conditions as of administrative overcentralization and imprudent planning, the economy stagnated in the late 1970s and early 1980s. Instead of implementing genuine economic reforms, the PCR re-emphasized its Stalinist economic priorities, provoking widespread consumer privation and worker apathy.

In most respects, 1983 was a year of marginal economic recovery and relative political stability, although the PCR's priorities continued to cause friction with Romania's Warsaw Pact allies and Council for Mutual Economic Assistance (CMEA) partners.

Party Leadership and Organization. PCR membership continued to grow in 1982, reaching 3,262,125 by 31 December of that year. Representing nearly 14.5 percent of the population, 21 percent of the adult population, and 31 percent of the work force, PCR membership levels are a clear rejection of the Soviet-style "vanguard party." Of the 111,313 members added in 1982, 77,000 (69 percent) were reportedly industrial workers and 26,216 (23.5 percent) were agricultural workers. Only 10,000 (9 percent) intellectuals received party cards, a reflection, perhaps, of Ceaușescu's belief that they represented too high a proportion of party membership. Of the new total, 55.63 percent were reported to be industrial workers, 15.8 percent peasants, and 20.83 percent intellectuals, the remainder being unclassified workers and pensioners. Romania's ethnic minorities were said to be represented in proportion to their share of the overall population. Below the national level, there were 40 county PCR organizations (including Bucha-

rest), 242 municipal, 2,705 commune, and 68,493 basic organizations. (*Scînteia*, 25 and 31 March.) In August, Ceaușescu reported that there were 580,000 party activists and more than 3.3 million PCR members (ibid., 5 August).

Leadership statements at various times during 1983 stressed the need to recruit more workers, peasants, and women. Goals for workers' membership are 55–65 percent of the total and for peasants 15–25 percent, which, if maximally achieved, could reduce the intelligentsia's proportion of PCR membership to 10 percent or less (ibid., 31 March). Female membership is to rise from its current level of 30.6 percent to 50 percent (ibid.), and the number of females in PCR leadership positions from the current 6 percent to 27 percent by 1985. The percentage of women in state posts is to increase from 14.4 percent to 30 percent in the same time period (ibid., 22 June).

Nicolae Ceaușescu continued to dominate the PCR in 1983. The elaborate personality cult reached new heights, particularly during the January celebrations of Ceaușescu's sixty-fifth birthday and the questionable fiftieth anniversary of the start of his "revolutionary activity," occasions marked by mass meetings, volumes of adulatory poetry, television documentaries, art exhibits, and innumerable public testimonials to his myriad accomplishments (ibid., 18 January–15 February; *RFE Romanian Situation Report* [*RFE SR*], 29 January, 19 February; *Le Monde*, 31 January). While it never completely disappeared from the daily press, eulogistic commentary reappeared emphatically during the July commemoration of the eighteenth anniversary of the Ninth PCR Congress, the inception of the "Ceaușescu era"; in the autumn during Ceaușescu's "peace offensive"; and in December at the time of the sixty-fifth anniversary of the formation of the national unitary state. Cult propaganda focused on Ceaușescu's revolutionary activism, his ideological originality, his championing of peace and disarmament, and his patriotism. Ceaușescu's wife, Elena, was a secondary object of adulation, particularly during the January celebration of her birthday. Praised as a "remarkable politician and stateswoman, brilliant scientist, savant of world renown, [and] wife and mother who brilliantly embodies the traditional virtues of Romanian womanhood" (*Scînteia*, 8 January), Elena Ceaușescu continued to exercise penultimate authority, particularly in science and technology policy, placement of cadres, and culture. While rumors persisted that she was under esoteric attack by the artistic community and although one of her protégés, Eugen Florescu, lost his post in the central apparat (*RFE SR*, 2 May, 29 June), Elena Ceauşescu's position as the PCR's second most important leader appeared to be secure at year's end. Nicu Ceauşescu, the leading couple's youngest son, was named UTC first secretary in December. At 33, Nicu Ceauşescu is already a Central Committee member and holder of numerous PCR and state posts. His globetrotting exploits as chairman of a U.N. Youth Year commission were duly recorded by the Romanian press (e.g., *Scînteia*, 4 and 11 October). Rumors persisted that Nicu Ceauşescu was being groomed to succeed his father.

Despite its outward enthusiasm, the Romanian public is clearly tiring of the personality cult, the intensity of which seems to increase with the deepening of the economic crisis. Intellectuals, in particular, are alternately embarrassed and offended by the cult's omnipresence and its deleterious effects on rational decisionmaking and artistic creativity (*CSM*, 5 May; *Le Monde*, 31 January). While they grudgingly acknowledge Ceauşescu's restoration of national dignity and his very real diplomatic triumphs, they see Elena Ceauşescu and her protégé-son as calculating and unprincipled manipulators dedicated only to the realization of the dynastic succession. Still, the cult may serve a useful, if Machiavellian, purpose in its focused mobilization of national pride for the achievement of ambitious economic and social goals. It provides community-building rituals that symbolically unite a citizenry as yet unconvinced of the system's efficacy.

Unlike previous years, when Ceauşescu's policy of cadre rotation created something like a perpetual round of "musical chairs" among top PCR officials (*YICA*, 1983, p. 327), only a handful of leading party bureaucrats lost their jobs during 1983. Leadership stability rather than experiential broadening and cadre rejuvenation seemed to carry the day. Prime Minister Constantin Dascalescu appeared to enjoy the Ceauşescus' full confidence. He undertook a number of important diplomatic missions and delivered key economic reports. Manea Manescu, Ceauşescu's brother-in-law and a former prime minister who made a spectacular political comeback in late 1982 (ibid.), was made chairman of the National Council for the Unitary Management of Land Supply (*JPRS*, no. 83963; *Buletinul*

Oficial, 8 April) and represented Romania at the U.N. Conference on Trade and Development (UNCTAD) (*Scînteia*, 10 June). Ilie Verdeţ, the "survivor" of the 1982 "spring scandals" (*YICA*, 1983, pp. 326, 330–31), regained some of his former prominence in 1983 as a Central Committee secretary. Another secretary, Petru Enache, who, along with Miu Dobrescu represented the PCR at the March meeting of bloc ideologists in Moscow (*Scînteia*, 16 March), seems to have ceded much of his authority to Elena Ceauşescu (*RFE SR*, 2 May). Since party education and propaganda and various other ideological shortcomings were frequent targets of the general secretary's ire (e.g., *Scînteia*, 5 August), Enache's future seemed unsure.

Domestic Affairs. One cannot easily distinguish the Romanian government from the PCR. Unification of some party and state posts is legally mandated and administrative cadres regularly come and go from those that are not. All 369 members of the Grand National Assembly elected in March 1980 were candidates of the PCR's electoral front, the Front of Democracy and Socialist Unity, of which Ceauşescu is president. This unicameral parliament meets infrequently (four times in 1983), serving as a sounding board and rubber stamp for PCR policies. A more important legislative body is the 27-member State Council, over which Ceauşescu presides, which meets frequently and exercises decree power. Ceauşescu is also president of the republic and chairman of any number of party, state, and joint commissions, commands, councils, and committees. The government has 26 ministers, thirteen committee or department chairmen, three first deputy prime ministers, and five deputy prime ministers.

The economy continued to dominate domestic affairs in 1983. The report on the 1982 plan fulfillment was mixed. While the 2.6 percent increase in domestic net material product was gratifying, it represented less than half of the planned 5.5 percent growth. Among the primary economic indicators, only gross agricultural production, recording a 7.5 percent increase, was within plan parameters. Labor productivity, which was supposed to grow 7.1 percent, grew a disappointing 1.7 percent. Production costs dropped a scant 0.6 percent. Investment targets in industry and construction were not met. (Ibid., 9 February; *RFE SR*, 7 March.) The 1983 plan reflected some of the realism voiced at the December 1982 National Conference (*RFE Background Report* [*BR*], 15 March), but periodic reports and criticisms aired during the year indicated that productivity, consumption, and investment targets were not being achieved.

The most striking economic innovation of 1983 was the introduction of a new system of worker remuneration. Phased into effect starting 1 September, the plan linked wages to an enterprise's success or failure in meeting plan targets and to a worker's fulfillment of the stipulations of the obligatory labor contracts. In theory, if production exceeds plan targets, the worker will receive a bonus above the normal wage in proportion to the excess. If, however, norms are unmet, for whatever reason, then the 80 percent wage floor previously in effect no longer obtains. The hapless worker, whose purchasing power declined 8.8 percent due to 1982 price increases, is thus left at the mercy of the feckless distribution of production inputs, the renowned incompetence of Romanian managers, and the hyperbole of central planners. Western analysts agreed that the "reform," presented as a 5 percent wage increase relative to 1980 rates, would further depress workers' real income. (*Scînteia*, 5 April, 2 July, 8–10 September; *RFE SR*, 7 June, 10 October; *Economist*, London, 17 September.)

Agricultural production has lagged behind demand in recent years. In 1983, PCR leaders debated and implemented a number of programs designed to increase the amount of land in production, to increase the productivity of land already cultivated, to stabilize agricultural prices, and to increase the agricultural labor force. In March, Ceaușescu announced a State Council decree ordaining the reclamation of 84,000 hectares of the Danube Delta (*Scînteia*, 29 March). At the June Central Committee session, he called for the doubling of irrigated land to more than 50 percent of that cultivated, or about 5.5 million hectares, and for the doubling of land in soil conservation programs to some 3.7 million hectares (ibid., 1 July). The 1 November PEC meeting pinpointed a long-standing problem — speculation in and squandering of food (ibid., 2 November). Food distribution is so unpredictable that Romanians are given to hoarding food and then either turning a profit at times of scarcity or trading it on the active unofficial markets. A March State Council decree aimed at suppressing these and other inflationary practices (*RFE SR*,

18 April) seemed to have little effect. Finally, the leadership mobilized all available labor resources, including students, factory workers, and soldiers, to help with the harvest and irrigation system construction (ibid., 27 October). Despite more realistic plan targets and increased investments in agriculture, the measures to increase food production in 1983 seem to have fallen short, especially for the autumn crops (*Scînteia*, 16 November). Nonetheless, the 1984 plan calls for a 4.5–6.0 percent increase in agricultural production (ibid., 16 December).

Still another sore spot in the Romanian economy was the energy sector. Following the National Conference's resolution to supply 90 percent of energy needs domestically, the Central Committee met with mining officials in late January. In a speech to the assembly, Ceaușescu called for an increase of 40,000 tons of coal mined daily, with a target of 160,000–170,000 tons. Better machines, wage incentives, and more miners were promised. (Ibid., 30 January.) Production peaked at 157,000 tons in April, and shortfalls were noted thereafter (*RFE SR*, 10 October). Energy conservation is vigorously pursued. On 27 November, *Scînteia* published a patriotic appeal to reduce nonproductive energy consumption a further 50 percent. Among the recommended measures were a limit of one low-wattage light bulb per room; the reduction of lighted areas, the renunciation of home electric appliances such as vacuum cleaners, radios, and refrigerators; the curtailing of sporting and cultural events requiring illumination; and further reductions in home consumption of natural gas for heating and cooking. Thus, once again, the Romanian consumer, already left squinting and half-frozen by previous energy consumption reductions, will bear the burden of energy independence.

Although the food and energy shortages must have negatively affected the average Romanian's health, medical costs were to sharply increase. Following a PEC debate (*Scînteia*, 15 May), an August State Council decree stipulated the implementation of charges for some categories of medical care and hospitalization (*RFE SR*, 27 October). In a related development, the PEC, disturbed by the recent decline in the birthrate, instructed local authorities to enforce Romania's pronatalist policies strictly (*Scînteia*, 27 April).

In sum, Romania's program of economic austerity continued in 1983. While Ceaușescu proudly noted a 5 percent growth in industrial production for the first eleven months of 1983 (ibid., 16 November), the recovery has been uneven and lethargic despite the admitted sacrifices of the population (*NYT*, 26 December). While some of the blame surely rests with international economic circumstances, overcentralization, bureaucratic inertia, and worker apathy are contributing factors. Achievement of the almost 10 percent growth envisioned by the 1984 plan (*Scînteia*, 16 December) seems problematic at best.

One of the most intriguing developments of 1983 was a reported attempt at a military coup against the Ceauşescu regime (*Le Monde*, 8 February). While no official verification was forthcoming, Bucharest rumors centered on 30 January and a small group of relatively junior officers led, perhaps, by an airborne commander. Their plot uncovered by a secret police informer, the conspirators were said to have been summarily executed. Some credence was lent to the rumors by a noted increase of security precautions around the general secretary in early February and by his spirited defense of his military doctrine before PCR activists in the armed forces (*Scînteia*, 5 March). Military professionals have good reason for discontent: their equipment is antiquated and poorly maintained; military spending is frozen at 1982 levels through 1985, and, if Ceauşescu has his way, it will be reduced 20 percent thereafter; military personnel must engage in degrading labor, such as the notorious Danube–Black Sea Canal and the irrigation program; and the armed forces are obliged to share the responsibility for national defense with politicized paramilitary organizations.

The Romanian cultural establishment was considerably shaken by Ceauşescu's speech to a Central Committee meeting on 4 August. Two themes emerged, both echoes of previous cultural-ideological pronouncements most recently heard at the June 1982 Central Committee plenum. The first was a fierce cultural nationalism. The general secretary railed against the "polluting" influence of Western propaganda (i.e., culture), which encouraged nationalism, racism, and anti-Semitism—all of which, it may be observed, flourish in contemporary Romania. Art must be patriotic and revolutionary; the annual Hymn to Romania festival was the type of culture that should be encouraged. Second, art must be "socialist humanist." Positive heroes are

needed. The general secretary singled out the Romanian film industry in general and, by implication, film director Dan Pita in particular, for the harshest criticism. Films were not providing heroes worthy of the builders of Romanian socialism. (Ibid., 5 August.) During the intensive campaign that followed, the film industry engaged in the requisite self-criticism (ibid., 18 September, 20 October). The dogmatic-nationalist school of Ceauşescu sycophants in the arts reveled in their triumph. More ominously, media workers with relatives living in the West were removed from their posts, and rumors circulated predicting the virtual cessation of literary translations (*RFE SR*, 27 October). Elena Ceauşescu and her cultural operatives, Suzana Gadea and Tamara Dobrin, were given much of the credit for Romania's renewed flirtation with Zhdanovism.

Church-state relations were uneven in 1983. While some reports stressed the common ground of the major denominations and the PCR on peace issues (ibid., 28 July), the government continued a campaign of denunciation and harassment of evangelical Christians (*CSM*, 13 October). Cults were identified as being particularly pernicious (*Scînteia*, 8 July).

The "polytechnizing" of secondary and higher education continued in 1983. An April PEC decision stipulated that 92.4 percent of the graduates of the first eight years of schooling should be enrolled in vocational high schools (ibid., 27 April). The objective of the program, according to Ceauşescu's speech marking the start of the new school year, was to link education more closely to production (*FBIS*, 21 September). On the other hand, he seemed to be attempting to assuage the intelligentsia's fears that the humanities were being sacrificed when he warned of the dangers of too narrow a technical education. In keeping with the xenophobic aspects of the speech on culture, reports reached the West of drastic cutbacks in university-level language and exchange programs.

Taken in sum, the cultural, religious, and educational policies pursued by the PCR in 1983 were interpreted both in Romania and in the West as a continuation of the campaign against intellectuals, in whom the Ceauşescus perceive a threat to their authority.

Foreign Affairs. In many ways the international activities of the PCR and the Romanian government were linked to their economic priorities and Stalinist methods of political control.

Foreign Indebtedness. Fresh from its success in rescheduling the 1981 and 1982 portions of its $10 billion external debt (*YICA*, 1983, pp. 331–32), Romania followed Brazil's lead in unilaterally declaring a moratorium on the repayment of the principal due in 1983, estimated at some $1.5 billion (*WSJ*, 4 January; *Le Monde*, 5 January; *Economist*, 8 January). Romania's creditors acceded to demands that negotiations begin to reschedule the 1983 debt, encouraged by the 1982 trade surplus of $1.8 billion (*Scînteia*, 25 March), by the austerity program, by Romania's forswearing of further hard-currency loans, and by the fact that Romania was in the last year of its imprudently scheduled debt payments "hump." Two sets of negotiations took place. The first, between Romania and Western banks, reached agreement on Romania's ability to pay back some $800 million in short- and medium-term debts in 1983. The second, between Romania and Western guarantor governments, was successfully concluded after Romania and West Germany settled their dispute on emigration. (*RFE SR*, 29 June.)

Romania's improved creditworthiness was, in part, the result of the 1982 trade surplus, which had been achieved by a drastic reduction in hard-currency imports and an aggressive policy of selling Romanian products abroad. Ministry of Foreign Trade officials forecast a 1983 surplus of the same magnitude as that for 1982 (*NYT*, 26 December), giving some credence to Ceauşescu's announced goal of reducing foreign indebtedness by 25 percent in 1984 and completely eliminating it by 1988 (*Scînteia*, 16 November). During the year, stress was placed on improving the competitiveness of goods produced for export and on wage incentives for workers in the export sector (e.g., ibid., 23 September). However successful the export program, the reduction in Western imports took on potentially ominous political consequences as trade with Romania's CMEA partners increased from 38 percent of the total in 1981 to about 50 percent in 1982 (*RFE SR*, 7 March; *NYT*, 26 December), placing Bucharest at some risk of becoming more vulnerable to Soviet pressure.

The CMEA. Romania's relations with its CMEA partners reflected that fear. Bucharest had long argued for a CMEA summit in order to present its case for less expensive intrabloc energy and food prices and for more technology transfers (*Era Socialista*, 25 February). Moscow, on the other hand, had agreed to convene a summit because it hoped for greater CMEA integration, the very cause of Romania's original divergence from bloc solidarity in the early 1960s. The PEC clearly articulated the PCR position prior to the May summit: "Collaboration within the framework of CMEA...must be based on the principles of *equality* and *noninterference in internal affairs* and must assure the progress of *each national economy*" (emphasis added; *Scînteia*, 15 May). In plain language, the PCR rejected outright the Soviet designs for the summit. As a result of the Romanian-Soviet disagreement, preliminary meetings were unable to agree on an agenda, and the summit was postponed indefinitely (*Economist*, 7 May). The issues, however, were not forgotten. At the Berlin meeting of CMEA prime ministers in October, Dascalescu emphatically reiterated the Romanian position, including the necessity of a summit (*RFE BR*, 26 October; *RFE SR*, 27 October).

The West. In order to avoid knuckling under to Soviet economic pressure, Romania's commercial relations with the West needed to remain as good as the trade imbalance would allow. Maintaining such relations with Romania's two most important Western trading partners, the United States and West Germany, proved difficult. The problem arose because of a November 1982 State Council decree requiring prospective emigrants to reimburse the state in convertible currency for their education before being issued exit visas (*Scînteia*, 6 November 1982). Purportedly, the "education tax" was Ceauşescu's response to the flight of highly trained and economically valuable Romanians to the West. During the year, the media tried to dispel the myth of Western affluence. In the past few years, some 20,000 Romanians have emigrated each year (averaging 15,000 ethnic Germans to West Germany, 2,000 Jews to Israel, and 3,000 of no particular nationality to the United States). Almost immediately after the decree's publication, the United States informed Ceauşescu that implementation would result in Romania's loss of most-favored-nation (MFN) status pursuant to provisions of the Jackson-Vanik amendment to the Trade Act of 1974 (*NYT*, 28 December 1982).

A visit by Assistant Secretary of State Lawrence Eagleburger (*Scînteia*, 12 January) failed to shake Ceauşescu's determination. After unsuccessful last-minute negotiations with Deputy Foreign Minister Gheorghe Dolgu (*NYT*, 3 March), the White House announced that Romania's MFN status would expire on June 30. Bucharest reacted angrily, denouncing the decision as an unjustified and illegal interference in Romanian internal affairs (*Scînteia*, 6 March). Both sides left open the possibility for accommodation. Romania could ill afford the annual loss of $200–250 million in hard-currency trade the nonextension of MFN would entail. The Reagan administration, eager to prove itself loyal to the "policy of differentiation," wished to maintain excellent relations with the Ceauşescu regime, which had been diplomatically useful in the past. Ceauşescu blinked first. In May, Foreign Minister Stefan Andrei came to Washington and, in effect, promised that the decree would not be enforced (*NYT*, 19 May; *WP*, 19 May). On 3 June, President Reagan recommended extension of the Jackson-Vanik waiver, and thus MFN, for another year (*NYT*, 4 June). Despite some congressional resistance based on Romania's less than enviable human rights record (*RFE SR*, 16 August), Romania received MFN extension in the late summer. In September, Vice-President George Bush visited Bucharest and, while chiding Ceauşescu on human rights, praised Romania's foreign policy autonomy (ibid., 10 October; *WP*, 29 November). Although the Romanian press roundly denounced the U.S. intervention in Grenada (e.g., *Scînteia*, 27 October), the joint Romanian-American Economic Commission meeting in Bucharest resolved to restore annual bilateral trade to the $1 billion level it had reached in 1981 (*RFE SR*, 27 October).

Relations with West Germany followed a similar course. Bonn was clearly upset with Bucharest's rumored education tax "compromise," which would have increased West Germany's payment of 5,000 marks per ethnic German emigrant to 80,000 marks. Christian Democratic deputies introduced a resolution in the Bundestag calling for energetic protests in Bucharest (*Frankfurter Allgemeine Zeitung*, 5 March). As a sign of its displeasure, the West German government refused to participate in intergovernmental discussions in Paris on the rescheduling of the Romanian debt. In April, Foreign Minister Andrei quietly slipped in and out of Bavaria, where he discussed a compromise with West German officials. In late May, Bavarian premier Franz-Josef Strauss and West German foreign minister Hans-Dietrich Genscher visited Bucharest (*Scînteia*, 25 May, 1 June). A bargain was struck. For its part, Romania repeated its pledge to Washington not to enforce the decree. Bonn agreed to join the intergovernment debt-rescheduling discussions, to release frozen export credits earmarked for Romania, and to increase its payment for emigrants to 7,000–8,000 marks (*RFE SR*, 7 June).

The West German case may have been strengthened by the April visit to Bucharest of French foreign minister Claude Cheysson (ibid., 2 May; *Scînteia*, 22 April). Franco-Romanian relations hit a low ebb in 1982 as a result of the "Tanase affair" (*YICA*, 1983, p. 333) and did not improve with the revelation of Romanian espionage in France (*Le Monde*, 11 February) and further plots against Romanian émigrés (*RFE SR*, 2 May). Romanian reports on the meetings Cheysson held with Ceauşescu and Andrei glossed over the issues that had recently soured traditionally excellent bilateral relations and looked forward to increased trade between the two nations (*Scînteia*, 23 April). No other important NATO visitors paid court to Ceauşescu during 1983, reflecting his diminished esteem in Western capitals.

The Middle East. Romania continued its active diplomacy in the Middle East in 1983. Bucharest's need for Middle Eastern crude oil for its underutilized refining industry and its fear that superpower confrontation in that volatile area would require greater solidarity in the southern tier of the Warsaw Pact account for its interest. Alone among the Soviet bloc states, Romania maintains good relations with both Israel and the Palestine Liberation Organization (PLO). With only a few subtle refinements, Ceauşescu has advocated a four-point Middle East peace plan for almost a decade: Israeli withdrawal from all Arab territories occupied since 1967, including East Jerusalem and Lebanon; establishment of an independent state led by the PLO; guarantees for the security of all the region's states; and the convocation of an international peace conference, including representatives of the PLO, USSR, and United States (*RFE SR*, 6 June).

Although Ceauşescu visited only moderate

Egypt and Sudan during the year (*Scînteia*, 20 and 23 October), he received Libya's Moammar Khadafy in January (ibid., 21 January), Jordan's King Hussein while the Reagan peace plan was still under active consideration (ibid., 18 February; *RFE SR*, 17 March), a trio of important Egyptian officials — Foreign Minister Kamal Hassan Ali (*Scînteia*, 29 April), President Mohammed Hosni Mubarak (ibid., 11 June), and Prime Minister Dr. Ahmed Fu'ad Muhyi al-Din (ibid., 30 July) — and Iraqi first deputy prime minister Taha Yosin Ramadan (ibid., 12 November), as well as a number of lesser personalities and delegations from the Arab countries. As is his habit, from time to time Ceauşescu dispatched a number of his most trusted aids, including Foreign Minister Stefan Andrei, presidential counselor Florea Dumitrescu, PEC member Gheorghe Oprea, Foreign Trade Minister Vasile Pungan, and Prime Minister Constantin Dascalescu to carry personal messages to Arab leaders, most frequently to Syrian president Hafiz al-Assad (ibid., 3 May, 3 and 7 June, 25 September, 11 October; *FBIS*, 8 November; *RFE BR*, 6 June). The foremost concern was the strife in Lebanon, from which, Ceauşescu repeatedly insisted, *all* foreign troops must be withdrawn in order to facilitate national reconciliation (*Toronto Star*, 10 December). Ceauşescu's frequent messages to Damascus and his reception in Bucharest of Druze leader Walid Jumblatt (*Scînteia*, 11 October) and of the special envoy of Lebanese president Amin Gemayel (ibid., 8 July) suggested that he was intensely involved in seeking a de-escalation of the Lebanese civil war. While widely praised, there were no indications that Ceauşescu's efforts had been successful.

PLO chairman Yassir Arafat visited Bucharest three times in 1983 (ibid., 21 April, 5 June, 8 August). Alluding to Syrian-backed PLO insurgents under Abu Musa, Ceauşescu allowed that there was factional conflict within the Palestinian movement (*Newsweek*, overseas edition, 16 May) but seemed to favor Arafat during the fighting in Tripoli (*Scînteia*, 11 November). Nevertheless, he kept channels open to other Palestinian factions, dispatching PEC member Ion Coman, a former minister of defense, to the Palestinian National Council in Algiers, reveling in the appreciation of the spectrum of the PLO leadership, and hosting National Council president Khalid al-Fahhoum in Bucharest (*RFE SR*, 17 March; *RFE BR*, 6 June).

Relations with Israel were marked by visits of Labor Party leaders Shimon Peres and Victor Shemtov (*Scînteia*, 26 March, 13 August); of the director general of Prime Minister Menachim Begin's office, Mattetiahu Shmuelevich (ibid., 4 May); and of Foreign Minister Yitzhak Shamir (*RFE SR*, 10 October). While the nonimplementation of the education tax eased tension between Romania and Israel somewhat, Ceauşescu annoyed Tel Aviv by attributing the continuing Middle East stalemate to Israel's lack of Sadat-like courage (ibid.; *Newsweek*, overseas edition, 16 May). Rumors were rife that Ceauşescu was serving as Israel's conduit to the Soviet Union and was even attempting to mediate a restoration of Israeli-Soviet diplomatic relations (*RFE SR*, 10 October). Somewhat disingenuously, Ceauşescu denied these rumors but allowed that once the Palestinian question was resolved, there would be no impediments to normal relations between Israel and the Soviet bloc states (*FBIS*, 19 October). Israel rejects all four points of Ceauşescu's peace plan but continues to exploit the opportunities offered by good relations with Romania.

Finally, the Romanian leader again urged a negotiated settlement of the Persian Gulf war on the basis of a mutual withdrawal to internationally recognized borders and direct talks between Iran and Iraq (ibid.). The joint communiqué issued on the occasion of Ramadan's visit to Bucharest implied Iraq's agreement with Ceauşescu's call for negotiations (ibid., 14 November), but Stefan Andrei's earlier mission to Tehran appeared to have failed to budge the Iranian government (*Scînteia*, 7 June).

The Third World. In relations with other parts of the Third World, Ceauşescu sent Stefan Andrei as his personal representative to New Delhi for the Nonaligned Summit Conference, at which Romania enjoys permanent guest status. Ceauşescu's message to the meeting (ibid., 8 March) stressed the need for détente and for the new international economic order. It avoided any mention of the thorny issues that plagued the conference (*RFE SR*, 30 March). In July, Ceauşescu embarked on his seventh African tour since 1972, visiting Ethiopia, Zimbabwe, Mozambique, Zambia, and Somalia. In Maputo, he met with Oliver Tambo, president of the African National Congress (*Scînteia*, 20 July) and in Lusaka with Sam Nujoma, president of the South-West

Africa People's Organization (SWAPO) (ibid., 22 July). The latter visited Bucharest in October (ibid., 15 October). On several occasions during the year, PCR bodies endorsed SWAPO's struggle to liberate Namibia from South African occupation (e.g., the PEC's statement in ibid., 2 November), an expression of solidarity present in all the communiqués issued during the African tour and the handful of visits to Bucharest by African leaders.

Neighboring States and Parties. Romanian-Hungarian relations remained strained during 1983. The Hungarian government and intellectual circles viewed with concern the policy of ethnic assimilation pursued in Romania. Bucharest chafed under semiofficial Hungarian criticism of its nationalities policies and suspected Soviet manipulation of Hungarian irredentism. During the winter, Foreign Minister Stefan Andrei called on his counterpart in Budapest. Official Hungarian news releases left no doubt that the minority issue had been discussed (*RFE BR*, 7 March). In April, Ceauşescu and other PCR officials defended Romanian policies at the joint meeting of the Councils of Workers of Hungarian and German Nationalities (*Romania, Documents-Events*, nos. 21 and 24, April). Press articles echoed the same theme (e.g., *JPRS*, no. 83803; *Viaţa Studenteasca*, 6 April). In May, Budapest intellectuals responded, sharply criticizing Ion Lancranjan's *A Word on Transylvania*, a fiercely nationalistic defense of Romania's right to Transylvania published in 1982 (*RFE BR*, 7 June). The most strident defense of Romania's historical right to Transylvania was made by Ceauşescu himself on the occasion of the sixty-fifth anniversary of its union with the rest of Romania. Citing Marx, Lenin, and even Béla Kun, Ceauşescu engaged in his most nationalistic rhetoric of the year (*FBIS*, 6 December). The speech and its attendant media coverage was sure to rile Hungarian tempers.

As is their habit, Ceauşescu and Bulgarian state and party leader Todor Zhivkov exchanged visits (*Scînteia*, 25 February, 7 October). Outward agreement was reached on all matters, but differences in the published accounts of the latter visit suggested that the two leaders failed to agree on a number of East-West issues. Both leaders endorsed the idea of a Balkan nuclear-free zone. (*RFE BR*, 2 December.)

Visits to Romania by Yugoslav party Presidium president Mitja Ribičič in April and by Federal Presidium president Mika Špiljak in November revealed the harmony of Romanian and Yugoslav views on international issues (*RFE SR*, 2 May; *Scînteia*, 3–5 November). Yugoslavia also supported the idea of a Balkan nuclear-free zone (*FBIS*, 8 November).

Ceauşescu's visit to Turkey in May (*RFE SR*, 7 June) and a number of important Turkish missions to Romania (*Scînteia*, 21 January, 3 July, 5 November) failed to convince Ankara to jump on the nuclear-free zone bandwagon, perhaps because Greece favored the proposal. Romania's negative reaction to the proclamation of a Turkish Cypriot republic (ibid., 17 November) followed by only three weeks Ceauşescu's visit to the island, during which he had voiced support for a united Cyprus (ibid., 25 October).

One curious nonevent of 1983 was the failure of any important political figures from the GDR, Czechoslovakia, Poland, or Hungary to visit Bucharest.

The USSR. Romania's relations with the USSR in 1983 were inaugurated by the arrival in Bucharest of a new Soviet ambassador, Yevgeny Tyazhelnikov, formerly head of the Soviet Central Committee's Agitprop Department. A victim of Yuri Andropov's housecleaning, Tyazhelnikov's posting to Bucharest was clearly a demotion. Local wags found it perversely amusing that the former mastermind of the Brezhnev personality cult had been sent to Bucharest, the center of a personality cult of ludicrous proportions. The statements exchanged on the occasion of Ceauşescu's formal acceptance of Tyazhelnikov's credentials reflected long-standing Romanian-Soviet differences. The new ambassador stressed bilateral cooperation and the importance of the Warsaw Pact and CMEA, while Ceauşescu reiterated his foreign policy principles, which read like a litany of Romanian independence (ibid., 20 January). The evolution of Romanian-Soviet relations during 1983 focused on both European and bilateral issues.

The most important issue allegedly confounding relations was the Romanian approach to the Euromissile controversy. Since the announcement of NATO's dual-track policy in 1979, Ceauşescu has repeatedly urged the destruction of all intermediate-range nuclear forces (INF) in Europe and has closely monitored the Soviet-U.S. talks in Geneva. While the Warsaw Pact summit in Prague did not reveal any new Romanian-Soviet differences (*RFE BR*, 12 January), when the Soviet Union began to threaten a response in kind if the NATO deployment took place, Ceauşescu chided both superpowers for intransigence (*RFE SR*, 7 June; *Scînteia*, 29 May). Some Western analysts saw in the June Warsaw Pact summit's moderate pronouncement the influence of Ceauşescu's refusal to toe the Soviet line (*Economist*, 2 July). On 22 August, Ceauşescu sent letters to Presidents Reagan and Andropov deploring the Geneva impasse and making two proposals: to continue the negotiations with a postponement of new NATO deployments until at least the end of 1984 coupled with a Soviet pledge to neither deploy new missiles nor modernize existing ones while reducing the number already deployed; or, if that suggestion proved unacceptable, to at least ban deployment of new Euromissiles in the two Germanys, Czechoslovakia, and unnamed other countries while negotiations continued (*Scînteia*, 23 August; *RFE SR*, 16 September). An interesting footnote was Ceauşescu's support for the destruction of *Soviet* missiles in any European reduction, a position he apparently took with visiting Japanese foreign minister Shintaro Abe in August (*RFE SR*, 16 September) and later repeated in an interview granted to the Egyptian daily *al-Ahram* (*FBIS*, 19 October). When the Geneva INF talks broke down, the PEC and State Council issued a joint declaration profoundly regretting the cessation of negotiations without, unlike its Warsaw Pact allies, pointing an accusing finger at the United States. Urging an immediate resumption of the talks, Romania made two proposals to facilitate re-engagement. First, the United States should not assemble or deploy the Euromissiles that had been delivered, and the USSR and the United States should reciprocally reduce their in-place intermediate-range delivery systems. Or second, the United States should not deploy any new Euromissiles and the USSR should provisionally retain in its European arsenal a number of missiles equal to that deployed by France and Great Britain at a distance from West Germany equal to the distance of French and British launchers from the USSR. The declaration also urged that a superpower summit meeting and a foreign ministers meeting be convened as soon as possible. The declaration's call for a joint NATO and Warsaw Pact foreign ministers meeting to "assist" the Soviet-U.S. talks reflected Romanian frustration

with both superpowers. (*Scînteia*, 26 November; *NYT*, 26 November.) These proposals were made at the height of a "peace offensive" in Romania, leading some to speculate that the declaration was an orchestrated part of a campaign to bolster Ceauşescu's sagging popularity both at home and abroad. While some Western commentators, noting the similarities between the Romanian and Soviet positions, deduced that Ceauşescu had knuckled under to Soviet pressure (*CSM*, 23 November), the tone of the Romanian statements had little in common with those emanating from Moscow and loyalist capitals and that the Romanian proposals were a framework for negotiations, not a bargaining position. Still, there was little doubt about the issues discussed during the visits of Marshals Viktor Kulikov and Aleksei A. Yepishev to Bucharest (*Scînteia*, 19 February, 29 April, 14 October).

The Romanian-Soviet differences in INF took place during a year in which Bucharest and Moscow clashed over the agenda for a CMEA summit and in which Romania was staking out its own, un-Soviet ground at the Madrid follow-up meeting of the Conference on Security and Cooperation in Europe (CSCE). At Madrid, Romania was unusually active and successful. Chief delegate Vasile Sandu achieved his primary mission, that of convincing other participants to convene a European disarmament conference in Stockholm in early 1984. Breaking ranks with its allies, Romania supported Western amendments to the nonaligned states' draft statement. Siding with Malta on the consensus issue, Romania played a key role in the compromise eventually reached, in recognition of which Ceauşescu was grandly received in Malta in October. (*RFE SR*, 17 March, 16 July, 30 August; *Scînteia*, 19 October). The PEC gave Ceauşescu the credit for success in Madrid (*FBIS*, 13 October). Romania's maneuvering in Madrid could not but have annoyed the Soviets, who watched, lead-footed, as Sandu nimbly ingratiated himself with everyone at Moscow's expense.

Both ideological and policy disputes characterized interparty relations in 1983. The origins of the ideological dispute date back to the 1960s and were best articulated in the PMR's 1964 "declaration of independence" and the Brezhnev Doctrine in 1968. The Romanians insisted on absolute party autonomy and on the principles of equality, noninterference, and mutual respect as the basis for interparty relations. The Soviets argued for each party's responsibility to the international movement and for class solidarity ("proletarian internationalism") as the basis for interparty relations. Secondarily, Ceaușescu has argued for the continued relevance of the nation during the construction of socialism, and Andropov has called for the "merger of nations." It was on this secondary issue that the 1983 debate centered.

As in past rounds of the debate, both sides chose esoteric media in which to air their differences. Of particular importance on the Romanian side were articles published in *România Libera* and *Scînteia* (*RFE BR*, 8 February; *RFE SR*, 7 March, 24 May). On 5 February, *Scînteia* published an article by PEC member Dumitru Popescu praising Ceaușescu's corrections of erroneous (i.e., Soviet) interpretations of Romanian history. Popescu also dismissed the notions that any single party had a monopoly on Marxist-Leninist truth and that there was only one correct way to build socialism. The article left little doubt that the views Popescu was attacking were those of the Soviet party in general and of Andropov in particular. As if to emphasize the historical point, the Romanian media noted the anniversary of the union of Bessarabia with the rest of Romania (*RFE SR*, 2 May), and Ceaușescu told Italian journalists that he was concerned about Romanians living abroad (i.e., in Bessarabia; *Scînteia*, 16 April). Finally, an *Era Socialista* article (10 June) on interference in other countries' internal affairs was obviously aimed at the USSR.

The Soviet counterattack was obscure. Instead of attacking Popescu the ideologist, the Soviets attacked Popescu the novelist. The Soviet Writers' Union's weekly savagely critiqued a novel by Popescu as ahistorical and anti-Soviet. The parallel Romanian weekly responded in kind. (*Le Monde*, 14 May; *RFE SR*, 24 May.) Even more curiously, the Soviet foreign affairs weekly *Novoye vremya* (15 April) attacked the views on the contemporary importance of the nation expressed by a totally obscure writer in a secondary journal in mid-1982. The writer, Vasile Iota, defended his (i.e., Ceaușescu's) views in the Romanian media. (*RFE SR*, 7 June.)

It is noteworthy that neither side in the dispute directly addressed the central issue, the legitimacy of PCR autonomy. Furthermore, neither side committed its primary spokesmen to the fray as both had in 1968. For the time being, both the PCR and the Soviet party appear content to engage in ideological skirmishing without doing battle, a policy mutually understood and beneficial to both parties.

Still another consistent ideological deviation of the PCR was reiterated in a May *Era Socialista* article (25 May). In it, PCR Secretary Gheorghe Stoica argued for expanded party contacts with all the world's progressive forces, even if they were not avowedly Marxist-Leninist, a label, in any case, which the PCR rarely uses to describe itself. In his controversial *Scînteia* article, Dumitru Popescu had sounded a similar note, denying that communist parties had a monopoly on political legitimacy and truth. Ceaușescu's 1983 party contacts seemed to confirm this apparent attempt to heal the old split in the international workers' movement. He hosted dozens of centrist and leftist leaders from outside the socialist countries, but only one nonbloc communist leader of note, Spanish party secretary Jaime Ballesteros (*Scînteia*, 21 June). The Soviet position remains rigidly Leninist. While other progressive forces may assist in the revolutionary process, only the communist parties possess ultimate legitimacy.

Aside from the Euromissile, CMEA, and CSCE issues, the PCR remained at odds with the Soviets with regard to Afghanistan and Kampuchea. While Ceaușescu's message to the Nonaligned Summit was diplomatically mute regarding these touchy issues (ibid., 8 March), he reiterated long-standing policies on other, more politically advantageous, occasions. He told Swedish journalists that the Afghan people themselves should decide their future and that foreign (i.e., Soviet) troops should withdraw (ibid., 28 June). In a joint communiqué with the visiting prime minister of Malaysia, Ceaușescu and his guest proposed a similar formula for Kampuchea (ibid., 19 May). Romania is the only Warsaw Pact member-state unwilling to endorse the Soviet positions on these issues.

With the prolonged illness of Yuri Andropov during the last half of 1983, Romanian-Soviet polemics subsided, indicating, perhaps, that the Soviet challenge to Ceaușescu's views came from the very highest source. The two men do not get along well. Andropov is rumored to have a low tolerance for East European mavericks, and Ceaușescu reportedly backed Konstantin Chernenko at the time of Brezhnev's death. (*RFE BR*, 19 January.) The ascent of the Soviet military bodes ill for Ceaușescu, whose nationalist legitimacy would be undermined if the Soviet marshals demanded and he agreed to closer collaboration with the Warsaw Pact. While Romanian-Soviet disagreements will not soon fade, on the vast majority of international issues the Romanian and Soviet parties and governments are in complete agreement.

Asian Communist Countries. Chinese party general secretary Hu Yaobang visited Bucharest in May, returning Ceauşescu's 1982 trip to China (*YICA*, 1983, p. 335). Both parties endorsed the correctness of the other's policies. Both supported every party's right to autonomy and the principles of equality, noninterference, and mutual respect as the bases for interparty relations. Both wanted Soviet troops to get out of Afghanistan and for Vietnamese troops to leave Kampuchea. These views were reiterated during Hu's visit. (*RFE BR*, 23 June.) Economic issues were not resolved and required a visit to China by Prime Minister Dascalescu in November (*Scînteia*, 22 November.)

In June Mongolian party leader Yumjaagyin Tsedenbal paid his first visit to Romania. A treaty of friendship and collaboration was signed, and Soviet loyalist Tsedenbal and maverick Ceau-şescu glossed over their differences on major international issues (ibid., 15–19 June).

North Korean vice-president and Politburo member Pak Song-chol came to Romania in August (ibid., 21 August). Relations between Ceauşescu and Korean leader Kim Il-song are exceptionally good. Pak's visit was only one of a number by North Korean officials during the year.

Romania's international prestige had its ups and downs in 1983. The continued suppression of basic human rights in a country where typewriters must be registered with the police offsets the admiration of many for Ceauşescu's foreign policy stands. Few would deny that Ceauşescu is an able, if Byzantine, politician, but his fragile domestic support no longer rests on his now elusive international reputation. It rests, albeit shakily, on his ability to solve the profound economic problems that threaten to destroy Romanian society.

Walter M. Bacon, Jr.
University of Nebraska at Omaha

Union of Soviet Socialist Republics

Population. 272,308,000 (30 June; AP, 30 August)

Party. Communist Party of the Soviet Union (Kommunisticheskaia Partiia Sovetskogo Soiuzu; CPSU)

Founded. 1898 (CPSU, 1952)

Membership. 18,331,000; 17,571,000 full members; 760,000 candidates (*Pravda*, 26 September; *Partiinaya zhizn*, no. 15, August); 44.1 percent workers; 12.4 percent peasants; 43.5 percent technical intelligentsia, professionals, administrators, and servicemen; women, 27.6 percent of all party members, 33 percent of candidates

General Secretary. Yuri V. Andropov

Politburo. (Unless otherwise indicated, nationality is Russian.) 13 full members: Yuri V. Andropov (b. 1914, president), Geidar A. Aliev (b. 1923, Azerbaijani, first deputy chairman, Council of Ministers), Konstantin U. Chernenko (b. 1911), Mikhail S. Gorbachev (b. 1931), Viktor V. Grishin

(b. 1914, first secretary, Moscow city party committee), Andrei A. Gromyko (b. 1909, first deputy chairman, Council of Ministers, and foreign minister), Dinmukhamed A. Kunaev (b. 1912, Kazakh, first secretary, Kazakh Central Committee), Grigori V. Romanov (b. 1923), Vladimir V. Shcherbitsky (b. 1918, Ukrainian, first secretary, Ukrainian Central Committee), Mikhail S. Solomentsev (b. 1913, chairman, Party Control Committee), Nikolai A. Tikhonov (b. 1905, Ukrainian, chairman, Council of Ministers), Dimitri F. Ustinov (b. 1908, defense minister), Vitali I. Vorotnikov (b. 1927, chairman, Russian Soviet Federated Socialist Republic [RSFSR] Council of Ministers); 6 candidate members: Viktor M. Chebrikov (b. 1923, Ukrainian, chairman, Committee of State Security [KGB]), Piotr N. Demichev (b. 1918, minister of culture), Vladimir I. Dolgikh (b. 1924), Vasili V. Kuznetsov (b. 1901, first deputy chairman, Presidium of the USSR Supreme Soviet), Boris N. Ponomarev (b. 1905), Eduard A. Shevardnadze (b. 1928, Georgian, first secretary, Georgian Central Committee)

Secretariat. 11 members: *Yuri V. Andropov (general secretary), *Konstantin U. Chernenko (ideology), *Mikhail S. Gorbachev (organizational affairs and agriculture), *Grigori V. Romanov (industry), *Vladimir I. Dolgikh (heavy industry), *Boris N. Ponomarev (international affairs), Egor K. Ligachev (b. 1920, cadres), Ivan V. Kapitonov (b. 1915, organizational affairs), Konstantin V. Rusakov (b. 1909, ruling communist parties), Nikolai I. Ryzhkov (b. 1929, economy), Mikhail V. Zimianin (b. 1914, Belorussian, culture) (*member of Politburo)

Central Committee. 319 full and 151 candidate members elected at Twenty-sixth CPSU Congress; 1 November 1983: 311 full, 141 candidate members

Status. Ruling party (The CPSU is the only legal political party in the USSR.)

Last Congress. Twenty-sixth, 23 February–4 March 1981, in Moscow; next congress scheduled for 1986

Last Election. Supreme Soviet, 1979; 99.9 percent of vote for CPSU-backed candidates, all 1,500 of whom were elected; 71.7 percent of elected candidates were CPSU members.

Auxiliary Organizations. Communist Youth League (Kommunisticheskii Soyuz Molodezhi; Komsomol), 42 million members (*Komsomolskaya pravda*, 9 July), led by Viktor M. Mishin; All-Union Central Council of Trade Unions (AUCCTU), 130 million members, led by Stepan A. Shalayev; Voluntary Society for the Promotion of the Army, Air Force, and Navy (DOSAAF), more than 65 million members; Union of Soviet Societies for Friendship and Cultural Relations with Foreign Countries

Publications. Main CPSU organs are the daily newspaper *Pravda* (circulation more than 11 million), the theoretical and ideological journal *Kommunist* (appearing 18 times a year, with a circulation over 1 million), and the semimonthly *Partiinaia zhizn*, a journal of internal party affairs and organizational matters (circulation more than 1.16 million). *Kommunist vooruzhennikh sil* is the party theoretical journal for the armed forces, and *Agitator* is the same for party propagandists; both appear twice a month. The Komsomol has a newspaper, *Komsomolskaia pravda* (6 days a week); a monthly theoretical journal, *Molodoi kommunist*; and a monthly literary journal, *Molodaia gvardia*. Each USSR republic prints similar party newspapers in local languages and usually also in Russian. Specialized publications issued under supervision of the CPSU Central Committee include the newspapers *Sovetskaia rossiia*, *Selskaia zhizn*, *Sotzialisticheskaia industria*, *Sovetskaia kultura*, and *Ekonomicheskaia gazeta* and the journal *Politicheskoye samoobrazovaniie*. Tass is the official news agency.

In 1983, the CPSU was principally concerned with the necessity of coping with the legacy of the Brezhnev era. During Leonid Brezhnev's tenure as head of the party (1964–1982), the USSR consolidated its superpower position and was able to claim impressive gains in the world "correlation of forces." But growing international prestige was achieved at the price of exacerbating chronic domestic imbalances: while industrial production tripled under Brezhnev, agricultural production rose 30 to 40 percent. In 1981, Brezhnev identified agriculture as the Soviet system's "number one problem," and in 1982 a modest "food program" was adopted as a partial corrective. The success of Brezhnev's world policy was confirmed by U.S. recognition of Soviet parity and the signing of the SALT I treaty (1972), but, over the years, détente unraveled and was finally demolished with the Soviet invasion of Afghanistan (1979). Moreover, the installation of SS-20 missiles targeted against Western Europe (1979–1983) set the stage for a new confrontation with NATO. Internally, the Brezhnevian style of rule, emphasizing stability and security of cadres, compounded the problem of official corruption, which seemed to reach epidemic proportions in the early 1980s. The emphasis on stability resulted in an aging leadership: within a period of two years, the four most prominent leaders of the system departed the political scene: Aleksei Kosygin (November 1980), Mikhail A. Suslov (January 1982), Brezhnev, and Andrei P. Kirilenko (November 1982). Among the problems confronting the new leadership, bloc incohesion posed special difficulties. The crisis in Poland (1980–1983) spotlighted the economic failures of the bloc as a whole and threatened to spill over into other East European states and into the USSR.

Leadership and Party Organization. Like all new Soviet leaders, Yuri Andropov faced the necessity of consolidating his position of power, of extending his authority over the complex bureaucratic system from formal to real control. Only by asserting his personal power could Andropov restore discipline and correct the massive systemic deficiencies, which he rather frankly admitted were urgent requirements. But Andropov had three major liabilities unprecedented in a new Soviet leader. First, his age made it unlikely that he would have many years to carry out a systemic renovation. Second, his health was highly questionable, raising the possibility that political elites would perceive him as merely an interim leader. Finally, as a career party foreign affairs and security specialist, Andropov lacked an organizational "tail" in republic and regional party organizations, which complicated the task of restaffing important positions with his own followers. The last two liabilities probably accounted for the more cautious approach to party renewal than that anticipated by many Western observers. However, significant personnel changes were made. At the June Central Committee plenum, Grigori Romanov was named to the party Secretariat after thirteen years as head of the Leningrad party organization and Vitali Vorotnikov, an Andropov protégé, was elected an alternate member of the Politburo. At the subsequent session of the Supreme Soviet, An-

dropov was elected to the largely ceremonial presidency, a position that had been left vacant since the death of Brezhnev. Numerous low- and mid-level posts in both party and government changed hands. Perhaps more important, officials were put on notice that they would be held accountable for breaches of discipline and for inefficiency, and some governmental ministries and party regional organizations came under fire from the leadership.

Andropov's last public appearance of 1983 came on 18 August, when he received a visiting delegation of U.S. senators in the Kremlin (*NYT*, 19 August). Soviet officials explained Andropov's absence as due to "a cold," but unofficial sources reported that he was suffering from a serious kidney ailment (*Guardian*, London, 8 November). The Soviet leader missed both the Bolshevik Revolution anniversary celebration in the Kremlin and the traditional 7 November military parade on Red Square (*NYT*, 8 November).

During Andropov's absence, statements were frequently issued in his name, but Western officials were uncertain about the status of power relationships in the Kremlin. There was some speculation that with Andropov apparently disabled, military leaders were assuming an increasing role in the formation of foreign policy. The perception of leadership instability in the USSR complicated the development of Western policies on arms control and other issues.

The usual fall meetings of the CPSU Central Committee and the Supreme Soviet were postponed to the last week of the year, apparently because of Andropov's illness. Movement of ZIL limousines into and out of the exclusive Kuntsevo district on Moscow's outskirts added substance to reports that the Soviet leader was being treated in a sanatarium in that area (ABC News, 26 December). Speculation that Andropov might have to step down continued. When the Central Committee and Supreme Soviet sessions were held, Andropov was again absent. However, policy pronouncements and personnel changes seemed to confirm his continuing leadership.

The December Central Committee plenum promoted Party Control Committee chairman Mikhail S. Solomentsev, 70, and RSFSR premier Vitali I. Vorotnikov, 57, to full membership in the Politburo and elected Viktor M. Chebrikov, 60, head of the KGB, a candidate member of the Politburo. Egor K. Ligachev, 63, appointed head of the Central Committee Cadres Department earlier in the year was named to the party Secretariat. (*Pravda*, 27 December.) All of the new appointees were Andropov loyalists, and Vorotnikov, Chebrikov, and Ligachev qualified as protégés of the general secretary.

Andropov's message, read to the Central Committee plenum, reaffirmed the hard line on discipline and labor productivity. "A great deal has been achieved," Andropov said, "but much is still to be done." The leader displayed particular impatience with delays in the construction industry. "What is needed," he concluded, "are not explanations but real improvements." (*NYT*, 27 December.)

The December plenum had appeared to strengthen the position of Andropov loyalists, but they had insufficient time to consolidate their hold on party and government. The party leader's health continued to deteriorate; he was reportedly seriously ill with diabetes and kidney and circulatory problems. Andropov died on 9 February 1984 and was succeeded by his erstwhile opponent, Konstantin Chernenko.

The Politburo. At the outset of the year, General Secretary Andropov conveyed an image of vigorous leadership; in less than two months, he seemed to have shaken the Soviet system out of the lethargy of the late Brezhnev years. However, there were clouds on the political horizon. Not only had the Supreme Soviet missed two opportunities to name Andropov to the presidency at its November and December sessions but it had left the position vacant, the 81-year-old first deputy president Vasili Kuznetsov continuing to act as head of state. This suggested to some observers the possibility of a deadlock within the Politburo over the consolidation of power by the party leader. Further, Andropov's presumed main opponent for the general secretaryship, Konstantin Chernenko, had evidently been assigned to Mikhail Suslov's old post as overseer of the ideological and foreign affairs sectors of the Central Committee apparat and was the de facto number-two man in the Secretariat. During the first quarter of the year, entrenched party bureaucrats were reported to be rallying around Chernenko to slow the momentum of change in both personnel and policy. Further, there were persistent rumors about Andropov's precarious health. He was reportedly hospitalized for heart and kidney ailments in mid-March (AP, 17 April), and a Politburo meeting

scheduled for 17 March was apparently canceled due to his absence (UPI, 24 March).

Immediately after Andropov's reported hospitalization came a move that apparently strengthened his position in the hierarchy. On 24 March, the Presidium of the Supreme Soviet named Foreign Minister Andrei Gromyko a first deputy premier (Tass, 24 March; *Izvestiia*, 25 March). Notably, the move was made while Prime Minister Nikolai Tikhonov was away on a trip to Yugoslavia and obviously undermined his position as a foreign policy spokesman for the regime. Gromyko had reportedly been one of Andropov's closest allies in his drive toward the leadership, while Tikhonov had apparently loyally supported his fellow Brezhnev protégé Chernenko. Following Gromyko's appointment, rumors surfaced in Moscow concerning the possible political eclipse of Chernenko. After attending the 165th anniversary celebration of Karl Marx's birth on 30 March, Chernenko was not seen in public for some six weeks, and he missed the May Day parade. However, in early May, his office reported that Chernenko had been suffering from pneumonia (AP, 5 May), and he shortly resumed a full schedule of official duties. In recent years, Chernenko had maintained a reputation as the hardiest of the veteran Kremlin hierarchs.

The oldest Politburo member, Arvid I. Pelshe, 84, died 29 May, reportedly a victim of lung cancer (*Selskaya zhizn*, 31 May; *FBIS*, 31 May). The last surviving veteran of the Bolshevik Revolution among CPSU leaders, Pelshe had been head of the Party Control Committee and a full Politburo member since 1966. From 1959 to 1966, he had served as first secretary of the Latvian party. The physical debility of the octogenarian Pelshe had been widely credited for the Party Control Commission's reputation in recent years as an ineffective watchdog encouraging lax discipline within the party.

A second major post for party leader Andropov was disclosed in early May. Defense Minister Ustinov, in an article marking the thirty-eighth anniversary of the Soviet victory over Nazi Germany, identified Andropov as chairman of the Defense Council, the main supervisory agency with authority over the armed forces (*Pravda*, 9 May).

When the Supreme Soviet held its regular semiannual session in June, Andropov was elected to the presidency, presumably strengthening his authority substantially (*Izvestiia*, 17 June). However, the session evoked additional doubts about the party leader's health. He walked unsteadily to the rostrum at the opening of the meeting but delivered his acceptance speech while standing at his seat (*NYT*, 17 June). Andropov's apparent frailty was cited by some Western observers as a probable reason for the absence of a widely expected major reshuffle of the leadership at the Central Committee plenum, 14–15 June.

The full Politburo membership remained unchanged, with no replacement for Pelshe, and the number of members, eleven, was the lowest since 1971. Mikhail S. Solomentsev, premier of the RSFSR since 1971, was named Pelshe's successor as chairman of the Party Control Commission (*Pravda*, 17 June). In view of Solomentsev's reputation as a hard-driving administrator, his appointment was expected to add momentum to Andropov's anticorruption drive, with the Control Committee reasserting its assigned role as enforcer of party decisions. The failure of Solomentsev to gain full Politburo membership was widely attributed to reservations among holdover Brezhnev protégés in the ruling body. As a protégé of Frol Kozlov, Solomentsev had run afoul of the Brezhnevites, particularly Kazakhstan party chief Dinmukhamed Kunaev, in factional feuding in that republic in the mid-1960s.

A more important change was the appointment of Leningrad *obkom* first secretary Grigori V. Romanov as a member of the Central Committee Secretariat (ibid.). The transfer to Moscow put Romanov, 60, in a strategic position for a possible future bid as Andropov's successor. Notably, Romanov was the one member of the leadership who had publicly criticized the "stability of cadres" policy (in a 1972 *Kommunist* article); he was expected to provide vigorous support for Andropov in an anticipated shake-up of elite posts. The promotion of Romanov represented another setback for Ukrainian party head Shcherbitsky, again denied admission to the inner circle of leadership in Moscow. Apparently increasingly out of favor during Brezhnev's later years, he has reportedly been hampered by factional infighting in the Ukraine involving the Kharkov and Donetsk party organizations.

Another promotion at the June plenum involved one of the few Andropov protégés in prominent party "line" positions. Vitali I. Vorotnikov, 57, party first secretary for Krasnodar

krai, was elected a candidate member of the Politburo (ibid.). Vorotnikov was the first person promoted directly to Politburo rank from a regional secretaryship since Andrei Kirilenko in 1962. As expected, Vorotnikov was subsequently elected to fill the vacancy in the RSFSR premiership created by Solomentsev's transfer (see below). Usual CPSU practice for many decades has required officials to achieve high party or governmental rank prior to attainment of Politburo status; the reversal of that procedure in this case could presage early further advancement for Vorotnikov, who was clearly rewarded for his ruthless campaign against corruption in the scandal-ridden Krasnodar area. Following service as first secretary of Voronezh *obkom*, as first deputy premier of the RSFSR, and as ambassador to Cuba, Vorotnikov had been named to the Krasnodar post in July 1982, one month after Andropov's return to the Secretariat, to replace Brezhnev protégé Sergei F. Medunov. The disgraced Medunov was dropped from Central Committee membership at the June plenum, as was another former close associate of Brezhnev, ex–minister of internal affairs Nikolai A. Shchelokov (*NYT*, 16 June).

The youngest member of the Politburo, Mikhail S. Gorbachev, 52, expanded his activities considerably during the year, his political position apparently unaffected by a string of poor harvests since his appointment as party secretary for agriculture in November 1978. Gorbachev was chosen as the Lenin anniversary speaker, an honor accorded to Andropov the previous year. His speech, somewhat shorter and less polemical than the usual orations on these occasions, emphasized the growing tensions in East-West relations and the party's call for greater productivity (*Pravda*, 23 April). In his capacity as agriculture secretary, Gorbachev led a delegation to Canada in May to discuss grain sales and other trade matters. This unusual excursion by a Politburo member into NATO territory enhanced Gorbachev's prestige and resulted in a temporary mellowing of Soviet-Canadian relations. The favorable impression made by Gorbachev was demonstrated by the lavish praise accorded him by several Canadian parliamentarians, as reported in the Western press. He addressed a meeting of the parliament's foreign affairs committees and led the delegation on visits to Toronto, Windsor, and Alberta. (Ibid., 23 and 24 May; Tass, 21 May.) Gorbachev's success in

Canada was evidently duly noted in the Kremlin. During the summer, at a time when Andropov and Gromyko were both absent from Moscow, Gorbachev headed a group of top officials attending a meeting in the Soviet capital on foreign policy and trade issues; his potential rival for the leadership, Romanov, was conspicuously missing from the list of those attending the meeting (*Newsweek*, 22 August). There were also indications that Gorbachev had assumed much responsibility for personnel matters, in effect becoming party organizational secretary. In late August, Gorbachev chaired a conference on party organizational work, assisted by Central Committee secretary Ivan V. Kapitonov and new Cadres Department head Egor K. Ligachev (*Pravda*, 30 August). The conference discussed fulfillment of a Central Committee resolution "On Holding Reports and Elections in Primary, Raion, City, Okrug, Oblast, and Krai Party Organizations," issued earlier in the month (ibid., 14 August). Sharaf R. Rashidov, 65, first secretary of the Uzbekistan party and candidate member of the CPSU Politburo, died 31 October (ibid., 1 November).

The December plenum of the Central Committee made some additions to the depleted party leadership ranks, naming several Andropov supporters to key positions. Party Control Committee chairman Solomentsev was finally accorded full Politburo membership. After only six months as a candidate member, the swiftly rising newcomer Vorotnikov, RSFSR premier, was also elected a full Politburo member. KGB chairman Viktor M. Chebrikov was named as a candidate member. (Ibid., 27 December.)

Party Organizational Work and Personnel. The new emphasis on discipline and tightening the system was reflected in numerous media exhortations about the need for improving party work, unusual frankness and specificity in discussions of organizational problems, occasional praise for party organizations recognized for meritorious work, and severe criticisms for those who had failed to meet more exacting standards.

A 29 January *Pravda* leader noted that some party committees "merely call for the imposition of order and stronger discipline without reinforcing their calls with practical action" and prescribed coordinated efforts by party organizations to deal with the pressing problem of the low growth rate in labor productivity. The Tash-

kent *obkom* was singled out for its struggle against the "notorious downward revision of plans." (*FBIS*, 9 February.) A 12 May *Pravda* editorial condemned "formalism" in party work and denounced "the mania for holding meetings, low exactingness regarding assignments and the adoption of a plethora of decisions on the same questions, which in fact remain unmonitored." Sverdlovsk *obkom* was praised for its efforts to eliminate losses in production, while Gorky *obkom* was criticized for failure to fulfill targets on rural housing for the first two years of the current five-year plan (1981–1985). (*FBIS*, 23 May.)

One of the most severe condemnations of a regional organization was directed at Saratov *obkom*. A Central Committee report on that regional organization, detailed in a 7 July front-page *Pravda* article, criticized the *obkom* for failure to realize the *oblast*'s industrial, agricultural, and scientific potential, for particular deficiencies in fulfillment of the food program, for inadequate ideological work, and for shortcomings in the placement of personnel.

A "large number" of CPSU cadres and industry chiefs in the Moscow region were purged in May for violations of party discipline (AFP, Paris, 28 May; *FBIS*, 31 May). Moscow *oblast* first secretary Vasili Konotop cited several offenses by the fired officials, notably the maintenance of "preferential lists" for the allocation of apartments.

The repeated calls for tightened party discipline were almost invariably associated with discussions of problems in the economy, and in a highly publicized February article, Andropov called for more technical professionalism among party cadres (*Kommunist*, no. 3, February). The appointment of Nikolai I. Ryzhkov, first deputy head of Gosplan, to the party Secretariat in November 1982 had given an early indication of Andropov's preference for the co-option of economic specialists into key party positions, and the selection of a new leader for the Belorussian party in January seemed to confirm it. Following the death of Tikhon Y. Kiselev, Nikolai N. Slyunkov, 53, a deputy head of Gosplan and a political unknown, was elected the Belorussian first secretary (*Pravda*, 14 January).

It was notable that the number-two figure in the Belorussian hierarchy, Aleksandr N. Aksenov, 59, a former KGB official, was passed over for the republic's top party post. Six months later, Aksenov was replaced as Belorussia's prime minister by Vladimir I. Brovikov, 52, party second secretary and a career party organizational specialist; Aksenov was named ambassador to Poland (*Izvestiia*, 11 July). The reshuffle in the republic was generally regarded as reflecting Moscow's dissatisfaction with the Belorussian leadership. However, given Aksenov's background and his assignment to the critical Warsaw post, it seemed quite possible that he was being groomed as eventual successor to Konstantin V. Rusakov as party secretary for bloc affairs.

When Vitali Vorotnikov moved up to the RSFSR premiership, another governmental economic specialist was named to the Krasnodar post. G. P. Razumovsky, head of the USSR Council of Ministers Agro-Industrial Complex Department, was elected first secretary of the Krasnodar *kraikom* (*Izvestiia*, 25 July).

Two prominent party officials were named to diplomatic posts. Yevgeny M. Tyazhelhnikov, 55, who had been displaced as Central Committee Propaganda Department head by Boris I. Stukalin, 58, in late 1982, became ambassador to Romania, succeeding the deceased Vasili I. Drozdenko (Tass, 26 December 1982; *FBIS*, 28 December 1982). Vasili N. Taratuta, 53, first secretary of Vinnitsa *obkom* and long regarded as one of the more promising prospects for future leadership of the Ukrainian party, was dispatched as ambassador to Algeria (*Pravda*, 9 April).

Nikolai V. Bannikov retired as first secretary of Irkutsk *obkom* and was replaced by N. I. Sitnikov, second secretary of Kemerovo *obkom* (ibid., 29 March).

When Romanov was transferred to Moscow in June, Lev N. Zaikov, 60, chairman of the Leningrad City Soviet Executive Committee, was named his successor in the first secretaryship of the Leningrad *oblast* party organization (ibid., 22 June).

Several changes were made in the Central Committee apparatus. Georgi S. Pavlov was relieved of his post as head of the Administration of Affairs Department (ibid., 3 September). Sergei P. Trapeznikov, longtime head of the Science and Educational Institutions Department and a close associate of Brezhnev, was replaced by Vadim A. Medvedev, 54, rector of the Central Committee's Academy of Social Sciences since 1978 (ibid., 8 and 20 August). Nikolai M. Pegov, head of the Cadres Abroad Department, gave way to Stepan V. Chervonenko, 68, formerly ambassador to China, Czechoslovakia, and France (*Radio Liberty Research*, 9 September). Konstantin Chernenko yielded responsibility for the General Department to Klavdii M. Bogolyubov, 74, the department's former deputy head (*NYT*, 22 October). Egor K. Ligachev, 63, first secretary of Tomsk *obkom*, assumed the post of head of the Party Organizational Work Department, apparently as a subordinate of the former department head, cadres secretary Ivan V. Kapitonov, who reportedly was given a wider range of responsibilities (*Radio Liberty Research*, 9 September).

Government. Like most other Soviet political institutions, the Supreme Soviet concentrated on economic questions during the year. An important session of the Presidium in January was devoted largely to matters of "practical implementation" of the food program and improvements in the quantity and quality of consumer goods (Moscow domestic service, 12 January; *FBIS*, 13 January). The regular session of the Supreme Soviet in June approved a Law on Work Collectives, which provided for upgraded participation by unions in the making and implementation of management decisions and was a mild step toward economic decentralization (*Izvestiia*, 17 June).

Most government personnel changes during the year reflected dissatisfaction with economic performance. At the outset of the year, the minister and deputy minister of the textile industry in the RSFSR were publicly reprimanded for toleration of widespread theft and waste in the industry, and several officials and plant managers were fired (*Sotsialisticheskaya industriya*, 4 January; *Radio Liberty Research*, 20 January). Two weeks later, Valentin N. Makeev, 53, USSR first deputy prime minister with responsibility for light industry, including textiles, was demoted to secretary of the AUCCTU (Moscow domestic television service, 20 January; *FBIS*, 21 January). Makeev had been one of the few young party officials to overcome the obstacles of "stability of cadres" and rise to high rank at the center of the system; after four years as Viktor Grishin's chief deputy in Moscow *gorkom*, he had been named a deputy prime minister in late 1980. His firing was perhaps the clearest signal to date of Andropov's tough approach to the economy.

One day after Makeev's demotion, Aleksandr I. Struev, 77, minister of trade and a full member of the CPSU Central Committee, was relieved of his ministerial post and replaced by Grigori I. Vashchenko, 63, first deputy prime minister of the Ukraine since 1972 (Tass, 21 January; *FBIS*, 24 January). In March, Anatoly M. Yershov, first deputy minister of machine building for light industry, was dismissed amid reports of corruption in his ministry (*Pravda*, 20 March). Also in March, the Ministry of Instrument Making, Automation Equipment, and Control Systems came under fire for shortcomings in its work; one department head was sacked, and several reprimands were issued (ibid., 28 March). In this episode, media attention centered upon Deputy Minister Aleksei I. Shibaev, who had been dismissed a year earlier as head of the AUCCTU following a steady drumbeat of criticism about that organization's shortcomings.

Ignati T. Novikov, 76, first deputy prime minister responsible for construction and a former close associate of Brezhnev, was retired from his post in July. Novikov's departure closely followed strong Politburo criticism concerning delays in the construction of the Atommash nuclear plant and the town of Volgodonsk on the Don River. (*Izvestiia*, 30 July; *NYT*, 31 July.)

As expected, Vitali I. Vorotnikov was named chairman of the RSFSR Council of Ministers at the republic's Supreme Soviet session in June, succeeding Mikhail S. Solomentsev, newly appointed head of the CPSU Party Control Committee (*Izvestiia*, 25 June).

Viktor P. Nikonov, 54, was transferred from the post of USSR deputy minister of agriculture to the position of RSFSR minister of agriculture (*Sovetskaya rossiya*, 29 January).

Semyon A. Skachkov, 76, retired as chairman of the State Committee on Foreign Economic Relations and was replaced by Yakov P. Ryabov, 55, first deputy head of Gosplan since 1979 (*Pravda*, 29 May). Ryabov was one of several former associates of retired party organizational secretary Andrei Kirilenko assigned to important posts during the early months of Andropov's leadership, including new party secretary Nikolai I. Ryzhkov, who was identified as head of the Economics Department, a restyled version of the old Finance and Planning Organs Department of the Central Committee.

Former president Nikolai V. Podgorny died in January (*Izvestiia*, 14 January) and was buried with state honors, a first for a disgraced ex-leader (*WP*, 15 January). Following the laudatory treatment of Andrei Kirilenko at his retirement in November, this seemed to indicate a more delicate touch by Andropov than that exhibited by Brezhnev in the treatment of defeated politicians. However, past links to corruption called for harsher handling, as in the cases of Shchelokov and Medunov. Yuri M. Churbanov, Brezhnev's son-in-law, whose wife, Galina Churbanova, had been associated with the notorious "Boris the Gypsy" smuggling case in 1982, lost his job as first deputy head of the Ministry of Internal Affairs (MVD) and was assigned as head of the militia in Murmansk (*NYT*, 14 August). But Brezhnev's son Yuri retained his post as first deputy minister of foreign trade and signed the obituary notice of a former foreign trade minister during the spring, despite persistent rumors that he was scheduled for a demotion (*Izvestiia*, 5 May; AFP, Paris, 5 May; *FBIS*, 6 May).

Domestic Affairs. Spurred by perceptions of widespread laxity in system control during Brezhnev's later years, the CPSU accorded top priority in domestic affairs to the goal of a general restoration of discipline in the society. A spectacular crackdown on labor absenteeism was in full swing at the beginning of the year but evidently lost momentum in the following months. But the drive against corruption, featuring upgraded roles for both the KGB and a revitalized militia, was sustained. Regime leaders seemed determined to involve the public more fully in major issues confronting the society, an aim reflected in a greater openness in the dissemination of information. The Soviet press covered major events, ranging from Politburo meetings to disasters, and discussed crime, alcoholism, and other social problems in an unusually frank manner. Andropov made a highly publicized visit to a Moscow factory, evidently with the aim of dispelling somewhat the traditional image of aloofness associated with the leadership. But such indications of more flexible methods did not herald a liberalization of the regime. The commitment to restoration of discipline was wide-ranging, touching most areas of life in the USSR. The campaign against dissent continued unabated, accompanied by new evidence of hostility toward religion and all foreign influence. And the new leadership's reputation for pragmatism meshed poorly with the inordinate attention devoted to the promotion of ideological commitment and conformity.

Law and Order. Most of the various drives to restore social discipline were continuations of programs and directives initiated under Brezhnev (*Radio Liberty Research*, 21 February). However, there was a marked change in tone, and the new leadership lent credibility to its exhortations with some dramatic actions conveying an image of vigorous direction of the society. One major area of regime activity was that of "law and order." In the first few months following Andropov's accession to power, numerous arrests, dismissals of personnel, and reprimands indicated a much tougher attitude by the authorities toward deviant behavior. The transferring of KGB chairman Vitali V. Fedorchuk to the post of head of the uniformed police (MVD) in December 1982 had been widely regarded as a signal of an impending crackdown, an impression confirmed during 1983 as Fedorchuk assumed a highly visible role as chief enforcer of discipline.

Fedorchuk addressed a meeting of the Supreme Soviet on 12 January that dealt with violations of "socialist legality." Both the police and the procuracy were criticized, and Fedorchuk called for improved coordination of the work of all law enforcement agencies in the struggle against crime (Tass, 16 January; *Radio Liberty Research*, 21 February). Fedorchuk was again the principal speaker at a 25 January conference of KGB, MVD, Justice Ministry, Procuracy, and Administrative Organs Department officials in Moscow discussed means of preventing crimes against "socialist property" and approved measures to correct "deficiencies in the work of the organs of internal affairs" (*Pravda*, 26 January). The MVD itself, particularly its antifraud division (UBKhSS), had been heavily implicated in charges of corruption. As expected, Fedorchuk carried out a vigorous shake-up of the police organization and in August gave a public assurance that the UBKhSS and other sections of the MVD were being "purged of employees who are morally or ideologically immature" (*NYT*, 14 August).

The appearance of public involvement in the "law and order" campaign was clearly a high priority for the leadership, and the principal vehicle for such participation was "letters from citizens," heralded in recent years as proof of the growth of "socialist democracy." In a feature article in *Pravda* (9 January), Aleksandr Rekunkov, USSR procurator general, pointed to frequent citizen's complaints about crime and "hooliganism" and the failure of law enforcement agencies to cope with the problem. Gorky's Moskovskiy *raion* was singled out as an area where citizens had been afraid to walk the streets in the evenings due to criminal activity. According to Rekunkov, the "facts were confirmed," and responsible officials in Gorky had been punished. Rekunkov cited a Twenty-sixth CPSU Congress resolution on the right of citizens to demand proper law enforcement; the strengthening of law and order, he said, requires "both the force of the law and the force of public opinion."

The themes of citizen involvement and responsiveness by the authorities were stressed in a lengthy article in *Literaturnaya gazeta* (no. 3, 19 January) and a resulting investigation of its charges. The article detailed the harassment by local officials in Odessa of a young man who had tried to secure legal action against corruption in a merchant marine school. Fedorchuk made a personal reply in the same journal two months later, reporting that an investigation had been made, followed by severe reprimands, demotions, and dismissals for responsible militia officials (*Literaturnaya gazeta*, no. 12, 23 March; *FBIS*, 6 April). MVD personnel were also targets of the anticorruption drive in Krasnodar *krai*; the press reported in March that several militia officers in that territory had been sentenced to prison for accepting bribes and other trials were in progress (*Sovetskaya rossiya*, 22 March; *FBIS*, 6 April).

Krasnodar was also a testing ground for a scheme to promote anonymous denunciations that evoked memories of the Stalin era. Citizens were reportedly invited to send unsigned postcards to the police naming persons involved in crimes and other social offenses. The cards reportedly had been used in Kiev in the fall of 1981 and in other cities, especially Krasnodar, in 1982–1983 (*Los Angeles Times*, 4 July). Meanwhile laws against "parasitism" were apparently being more stringently enforced, especially in the RSFSR (*Sovetskaya rossiya*, 19 January; *FBIS*, 20 January).

A notable example of greater frankness in discussion of social problems was a radio broadcast by Yegeny A. Smolentsev, deputy chairman of the USSR Supreme Court, in January. "People with a positive attitude toward life are in the absolute majority," Smolentsev said. "There are, however, slackers, hooligans, drunkards, speculators, bribe-takers, plunderers and other offenders. The problem of educating people thus remains today." Further, the jurist sounded the same notes about crime and the shortcomings of the police as did Fedorchuk: "Crimes cause great damage to all of society, to the national economy and in the final analysis to each of us. It must be admitted that because of shortcomings in the work of the investigatory organs, not all crimes are as yet solved in good time." (Moscow domestic service, 24 January, *FBIS*, 25 January.)

Media. During Brezhnev's final years in office, the Soviet media had drawn criticism for its generally simplistic presentation of news. Under Andropov, objections to the level of media reporting were pressed even more strongly, with considerable self-criticism by various publications, in line with the imperative for public involvement in the drive for greater social discipline. A front-page *Pravda* editorial (18 January) utilized the familiar "letters from citizens" gambit as a prelude to its call for media improvement: "Our Soviet person is no mere consumer of news: he expects from press organs a serious, businesslike, detailed discussion of urgent topics and wants to see in every article and program not only a truthful, up-to-the-minute account of the facts but an intelligent, comprehensive study of them, sensible generalizations, and valuable conclusions."

Following *Pravda*'s cue, the media did display greater openness in communication, even touching on some previously taboo topics. Accounts of Politburo meetings regularly appeared in the press, and some disasters, such as air crashes and ships trapped in the Arctic ice, were reported. The usual media criticism of poor economic performance in selected areas was intensified, accompanied by the attacks on corrupt or incompetent law enforcement officials noted above. In one instance, there was even criticism of military commanders (see below). However, the authorities drew the line at overt criticism of regime foreign policy.

A Radio Moscow announcer, Vladimir Danchev, a native of Tashkent, created a sensation when he referred to the Soviet presence in Afghanistan as an "occupation." This departure from the official line evidently went unnoticed until discovered by BBC monitors. Following extensive Western reportage of the incident, Danchev was reportedly fired and informally exiled to Uzbekistan. (*CSM*, 10 June.)

Labor Discipline. Party leader Andropov made a much publicized visit in January to the Ordzhonikidze machine-tool plant in Moscow. He toured the shops and addressed representatives of labor and management, urging efforts for greater labor productivity (Moscow domestic service, 31 January; *FBIS*, 1 February). Andropov's conversations with ordinary workers were reported in detail, indicating a desire to alter the popular image of an aloof leadership. But the message was no doubt more important than the image; throughout the year, the leadership concentrated on the crucial problem of labor productivity. In June, a major effort to secure voluntary cooperation by workers was launched when the Supreme Soviet adopted a new law on labor collectives.

Drafting of the law had begun in 1981, spurred by labor unrest in Poland and the threat of spillover into the USSR. But its adoption had been delayed by stiff opposition from party and state bureaucracies and the trade unions, which was evidently overcome only by Andropov's strong support for the proposals. The new legislation, scheduled to go into effect 1 August, provides a role for labor collectives in shaping management policies and the right to hold management to account on the implementation of decisions (*Izvestiia*, 18 June; *WP*, 18 June).

Obviously eager to generate grass-roots support, the authorities nevertheless relied most heavily on coercion in dealing with the problem of labor discipline. The early weeks of the year saw a major drive against absenteeism and alcoholism, featuring Operation Trawl, the unleashing of police and vigilantes to search for people improperly absent from work. A sensational midday raid on the Sandunovsky Bath in Moscow reportedly netted hundreds of people, including high-ranking bureaucrats, who were unable to explain why they were not at work (*WP*, 30 January; *NYT*, 3 February).

Initially the raids evidently did have the desired effect, sharply reducing absenteeism in major cities, but the drive reportedly aroused strong resentment among citizens, shopkeepers, and some sectors of the bureaucracy, and the effort apparently lost steam within a few weeks.

During the summer, the carrot and stick approaches were combined in a Central Committee decree dealing with labor discipline. The decree provided that managers could fine employees up to one-third of their monthly wages for poor work, cut vacation time for chronic absentees, and require drunkards to pay in full for any damage they cause. On the other hand, the decree made possible the granting of two extra days of vacation each year for industrious workers and priority on lists for apartments, plus other incentives. (*Pravda*, 8 August.)

Other Economic Problems and Prospects. The first quarter economic report showed an increase in industrial production of 4.7 percent over first quarter 1982 and a rise in labor productivity of 3.9 percent (*Izvestiia*, 24 April). The improvement in productivity was generally attributed to the campaign for labor discipline. An *Izvestiia* editorial (26 April) claimed that had labor productivity remained at the previous year's level, over one million additional workers would have been required to fulfill plan requirements; the rise, said the government daily, was "the product of the struggle for the rational use of machines and equipment, material-technical resources, and work time." The first quarter rise was not matched over the subsequent two quarters, but it seemed likely that the increase in industrial production for the year would be more than double that recorded in 1982.

As usual, consumer goods production failed to match that of heavy industry, especially in quality. In Turkmenistan, consumer goods production was reportedly up 8 percent for the first quarter. Production of "cultural, food, and economic products" had reached only 80 percent of targeted levels over the previous two years. Mukhamednazar G. Gapurov, Turkmen party first secretary, said that "the quality of industrial and food products is still low" (*Turkmenistan iskra*, 19 March; *FBIS*, 14 April).

Some modest improvements were reported on the agricultural front, and during the winter, food supplies appeared to be more plentiful in major cities. The Ukraine reported first-quarter production increases of 14 percent for milk, 6 percent for meat, and 8 percent for eggs (*Pravda ukrainy*, 27 March; *FBIS*, 12 April). For the country as a whole, purchases of livestock and poultry were reportedly up 6 percent, milk 14 percent, and eggs 4 percent (*Izvestiia*, 26 April).

Some early reporting on the crop season emphasized difficulties produced by severe weather, especially in Latvia and Kazakhstan (Moscow domestic service, 27 May; *FBIS*, 31 May). For the longer run, emphasis was placed on improvements in irrigation and transportation, set forth in a government resolution on measures to increase productivity of natural hayfields and pastures (*Izvestiia*, 17 February).

The new leadership stuck doggedly to Brezhnev's food program, regarded by most Western observers as more slogan than substance, instead of initiating more fundamental reforms. Nevertheless, early indicators pointed to a substantial increase in the grain harvest, following four consecutive years of massive shortfalls.

The construction industry was spotlighted during the year as a particularly troubled area of the economy. A Central Committee resolution in February called results in housing construction "intolerable," noting two consecutive years of failure to fulfill plans. The Ministries of Heavy Industry Construction and Industrial Construction were scored for a shortfall of 2 million square meters in construction work during 1981–1982. The resolution charged that the ministries involved were "slack about dealing with housing and civic construction and do not consider it a matter of priority importance." (*Pravda*, 26 February.) Particularly embarrassing was the reported collapse of a building at the Atommash nuclear reactor building facility in Volgodonsk. Construction problems at the Atommash complex reportedly triggered the firing of Deputy Premier Novikov in July (see above).

The perennial debate on the degree of centralization in the economy continued, with Andropov evidently inclined toward decentralization measures and top-level bureaucrats resisting any erosion of their power. A *Pravda* editorial (10 January) concerning responsibility for discipline and efficiency by both labor and management pointed strongly toward economic decentralization, stressing the importance of "long and stable links between enterprises" (*FBIS*, 10 January). At a meeting of party leaders in the Kremlin in August, Andropov sought to drum up support for reforms providing for decentralization. He said that experiments in plant autonomy would be limited initially to a small fraction of enterprises but should eventually be extended to all of the country's plants. However, Andropov said that the changes would be introduced cautiously. (*Pravda*, 16 August.)

Two days after Andropov's speech, Gosplan head Nikolai K. Baibakov sounded a somewhat different note at a news conference. The planning chief said that the experimental plan to give plant managers greater leeway in matters of output, production techniques, and wages would go hand in hand with a stronger overall role for the central planning authorities. Baibakov also expressed considerable optimism about the general condition of the economy, in contrast to the gloomy assessments frequently expressed by Andropov since his assumption of the party leadership (*NYT*, 18 August).

Development of Siberia's natural resources had been a key plank in Brezhnev's economic platform; sharp criticism of responsible officials indicated that the Siberian development program had bogged down badly. Economist A. Aganbegyan, in a featured *Pravda* article (2 August), noted that poor planning and widespread inefficiency was wasting vast sums in the effort to develop the area's energy resources. Aganbegyan accused ministries supervising the steel industry, transport construction, coal, and energy of inadequate equipment purchases, slowness in building roads, and improper utilization of allocated funds. Oil exploration, he said, was hampered by the "intolerably low" quality of borings. (*NYT*, 3 August.)

Basic construction of the 2,765-mile natural gas pipeline to Western Europe was reported completed. However, pumping would not be possible until sometime in 1984 because of production problems with Soviet turbines. (*Baltimore Sun*, 16 October.)

Gosplan chairman Baibakov, at the December Supreme Soviet session, announced that labor productivity had increased 3.5 percent over 1982 figures. The coal industry was singled out for special criticism: 1983 production was reported as 718 million tons, well below the average annual target in the five-year plan. Agriculture showed improvement during the year, according to Baibakov. (*Izvestiia*, 29 December; *NYT*, 29 December.) However, for the third year in a row, no statistics on the harvest were released. The U.S. Department of Agriculture estimated the 1983 harvest at about 200 million metric tons, better than that of 1982 but well short of the 240 million ton goal set by the five-year plan (AP, 29 December).

Dissent. The lengthy campaign against dissident activity, orchestrated by Andropov during his fifteen years as head of the KGB, had resulted in the crushing of most organized efforts to criticize the regime, but there was no relaxation in the drive for conformity. Persecution of dissidents evidently became even more severe after Andropov's return to the Secretariat in May 1982, and ideological conformity was clearly regarded as an essential element of the general campaign for restoration of discipline in the society. Nevertheless, the authorities were unable to prevent the rise of new dissident groups, notably the unofficial peace movement. Two dissident leaders of the 1970s, Andrei Sakharov and Anatoly Shcharansky, were still able to attract Western attention despite their respective exile and imprisonment, and Soviet abuse of psychiatry continued to stir protests in the West.

Shcharansky's family reported in January that his life was in danger as a result of the hunger strike he had begun in September 1982 and that his mother was not allowed to see him (*WP*, 15 January). French party head Georges Marchais wrote a letter to Andropov asking for an explanation of Shcharansky's internment. In his reply, Andropov affirmed the espionage charges against Shcharansky but said that he had been allowed to see his mother, had given up his hunger strike, and was in good health (Paris domestic service, 24 January; *FBIS*, 24 January).

Sakharov appealed in January to all the signatories of the Helsinki pact for "humanitarian and legal aid" against the repressive actions against him by the authorities (DPA, Hamburg, 19 January; *FBIS*, 20 January). German author Heinrich Böll charged that the harassment of the seriously ill Sakharov posed a danger to the dissident leader's life. Böll also drew attention to the situation of author Georgi Vladimov, subjected to repeated interrogations and searches despite a serious heart condition (DPA, Hamburg, 2 February; *FBIS*, 4 February). A French professor who had talked with Yolena Bonner, Sakharov's wife, reported in May that Sakharov was not only gravely ill but also "demoralized" and affected by "psychic disturbances" due to his persecution by the police (AFP, Paris, 28 May; *FBIS*, 1 June). The campaign against Sakharov reached a new level of intensity during the summer, following his statement that the U.S. nuclear buildup might be necessary in order to produce effective negotiations with the USSR. Four Soviet scientists signed an article condemning Sakharov as a "morally degraded and vindictive" man who "in essence is urging war on his own country" (*Izvestiia*, 2 July).

Western observers regarded as ominous the harassment of historian Roy Medvedev, author of *Let History Judge* and other works published in the West. Medvedev, principal spokesman for the view that democratic reform in the USSR can eventually be achieved through the communist party, had been granted unusual freedom for a dissident and reportedly had important contacts in party and state apparats. In January, Medvedev reported that he had been summoned by the deputy chief prosecutor of the USSR and warned to "cease his activities prejudicial to the Soviet state" or be indicted (AFP, Paris, 19 January; *FBIS*, 20 January).

Religious and national dissidence and labor unrest in the Baltic states have aroused considerable concern in Moscow during recent years, with the threat of "spillover" from Poland a special worry. Events during 1983 confirmed the high priority accorded to suppression of dissent in that area. In January, it was announced that criminal charges had been instituted against Alfonsas Svarinskas, pastor of the Roman Catholic church in Vidukle, Lithuania, for "illegal anti-constitutional and anti-state activities"; the priest was said to have through his sermons "systematically instigated" believers to "go over to open struggle against the Soviet power" (Tass, 26 January; *FBIS*, 27 January). Significantly, the announcement coincided with the arrival in Rome of Riga's bishop, Julijans Vaivods, for ceremonies at which the 87-year-old Latvian was installed as a cardinal, making him the first resident Roman Catholic cardinal in the USSR since the Bolshevik Revolution (*WP*, 27 January). In May, a Lithuanian woman, Jadvyga Bieliauskiene, was sentenced to four years' deprivation of freedom and three years' exile for "slanderous attacks against Soviet officials and the socialist system" in conjunction with her work in giving religious instruction to children (Radio Vilnius, 27 May; *FBIS*, 1 June).

Estonian party first secretary Karl G. Vaino admitted in an April article that events in Poland had inspired nationalist agitation and calls for labor strikes in Estonia during the fall and winter of 1981. According to Vaino, the authorities had had to mobilize all their resources to control the unrest. (*WP*, 20 April.)

An exhibition about the peace movement in the United States was first blocked and then permitted in February, but the independent peace movement was subjected to severe reprisals.

Vladimir Brodsky, in whose apartment the exhibition was held, was beaten up by a group of six unidentified men on a Moscow street, and another member, Vladimir Fleishgakker, was sentenced to fifteen days of administrative arrest for "petty hooliganism." Fleishgakker received another fifteen-day sentence in September, and in the same month, group member Sergei Rozenoer was jailed for ten days (*Radio Liberty Research*, 3 October). Despite the persecution, by the end of February more than 900 people had signed the declaration of the Group for the Establishment of Trust Between the USSR and the U.S.A. (ibid., 27 April).

The Soviet Society of Psychiatrists withdrew from the World Association of Psychiatrists in February. Society head Professor Georgi Morozov said that the action was taken because of "groundless charges against Soviet medical workers" involving allegations about the use of psychiatry for "political purposes" (Moscow world service, 16 February; *FBIS*, 17 February). Three weeks later, Amnesty International responded with detailed information concerning Soviet abuse of psychiatry, charging that at least 300 people have been held for political reasons and treated with powerful drugs in psychiatric hospitals since 1969 (Reuters, 9 March).

Existence of another *samizdat* publication was revealed following the arrests of Sergei Grigoryants and Viktor Beskrovnykh on 25 February and Dimitri Markov on 21 March in Kaluga *oblast*. The trio was charged with slander against the Soviet system under Article 190 of the RSFSR Criminal Code for distributing copies of the *Express Information "V" Bulletin*. The publication had been in existence for several years, but open dissemination had not begun until January 1983. (*Radio Liberty Research*, 20 May.)

Six Pentecostal Christians voluntarily left the U.S. Embassy in Moscow after nearly five years spent there as refugees from the Soviet authorities. Lydia Vashchenko, one of the group that had stormed the Embassy in 1978, was allowed to emigrate to Israel, and the other six Pentecostals decided to return to their Siberian home, as she had done in 1982, and apply for exit visas (UPI, 18 April).

Georgian nationalism provided the background for a demonstration involving about one hundred people, mostly students, in Tbilisi in July. The demonstrators, five of whom were arrested, called for the release of two students imprisoned in June for urging a boycott of the celebration of the bicentennial of Georgia's incorporation into the Russian empire. (AFP, Paris, 15 July; *FBIS*, 2 August.)

Ideology. During the later years of Brezhnev's tenure, ideological laxity had been recognized and condemned, with repeated calls for improved propaganda work. As in other areas, the criticisms continued, with a tone of greater urgency, under Andropov. With former ideological overseer Andropov installed in the party leadership and with his erstwhile opponent, Konstantin Chernenko, settled into Suslov's old post, ideological conformity was emphasized as an important feature of the new drive for discipline, and Soviet failings in the competition with "imperialist propaganda" were acknowledged.

Both Andropov and Chernenko, at the June Central Committee plenum, called for a tightening of ideological control in many areas, including the arts (*Pravda*, 16 June). This followed numerous articles in the press demanding that books, plays, films, radio, television, and even popular music abandon "bourgeois" and "nihilistic" themes for a celebration of Soviet ideals (*NYT*, 17 June).

Alongside the exhortations for conformity appeared a note of ideological retrenchment, a stepping back from claims advanced earlier about the level of Soviet social development. One aspect of this was the planning of a new party program, scheduled for unveiling at the Twenty-seventh CPSU Congress in 1986, to replace the one adopted at the Twenty-second CPSU Congress in 1961. At the June plenum, Andropov said that "fundamental provisions" of the present program "are confirmed by life." But, he added, "some of its provisions, and this must be said straightforwardly, have not held up entirely against the test of time because they contained elements of separation from reality, of anticipating things, and of unwarranted detailedness." (*Pravda*, 16 June.)

The concept of "developed socialism," so much emphasized by Brezhnev, underwent something of a metamorphosis, as Andropov elaborated a view of socialist society still coping with developmental problems.

In a highly publicized February article, "The Teaching of Karl Marx and Some Questions of Building Socialism in the USSR," Andropov affirmed the validity of the concept of "developed socialism" but noted the "outstanding problems left over from yesterday" and rejected the idea of a "'ready,' accomplished socialism." Particularly, Andropov noted that "complete social equality does not come overnight and in a finished form" and stressed the importance of "material and moral incentives, combined with an efficient organization of labor" at the present stage of social development. (*Kommunist*, no. 3, February.) At the June plenum, Andropov spoke of "the process of perfecting developed socialism" and cautioned that the USSR had only entered the stage of advanced socialism; he again called for practical measures that implied a less advanced stage of development than that claimed by Brezhnev (*Pravda*, 16 June).

A *Pravda* article (3 July) by historian S. Kolesnikov spoke of "mature socialism" when summarizing Andropov's ideas advanced at the June plenum: "The concept of mature socialism elaborated by the CPSU's efforts reflects the real dynamics of our society's development and prospects. That concept shows the dialectical unity of real successes in the implementation of the many economic, social and cultural tasks of socialist building, the burgeoning shoots of the communist future and the still unresolved problems bequeathed to us from the past." (*FBIS*, 19 July.)

On the sensitive matter of integration of nationalities, Andropov took a similar tack, affirming settled long-range goals while acknowledging existing difficulties. At the celebration of the USSR's sixtieth anniversary in December 1982, he had upheld the aim of the eventual amalgamation (*sliianie*) of nations. However, both in that speech and in another delivered to the Supreme Soviet Presidium in January, he acknowledged that much remained to be done in matters of national antagonisms and warned that "legitimate national pride" must not be allowed to turn into "national conceit or arrogance." This was presumably aimed at "Great Russian chauvinism"; on the other hand, there was also a warning for minority nationalities. Andropov made it clear that there would be no toleration of "attempts to idealize outdated habits and customs which contradict a Soviet and Communist way of life." (BBC, 14 January.)

Auxiliary and Front Organizations. Among the many auxiliary organizations that constitute "transmission belts" for the CPSU, the communist youth organization, the Komsomol, appeared to attract most attention during the year.

Moreover, the regular criticism of the Komsomol by leaders and the media that had shadowed the organization during Brezhnev's later years was noticeably missing, apparently reflecting the leadership's confidence in new Komsomol chief Viktor M. Mishin, who had assumed the post at age 39 in December 1982.

The July plenum of the Komsomol Central Committee was mainly devoted to discussion of the party goals of improved labor discipline and increased productivity. Mishin reported that the Komsomol exercised "patronage" over 135 all-union construction sites and some 4,000 republic, *krai*, and *oblast* construction sites and had dispatched 50,000 volunteers to the most important shock construction sites since the beginning of the year. On the negative side, Mishin admitted that on many construction sites the Komsomol "has still not achieved the creation of stable labor collectives." (*Komsomolskaya pravda*, 9 July; *FBIS*, 28 July.)

The worldwide network of front organizations directed by the CPSU was spotlighted in a secret CIA report to the Permanent Select Committee of the U.S. House of Representatives in July 1982, which became public knowledge in December 1982 and January 1983. According to the report, the USSR annually spends $1–3 billion on "active measures" to influence public opinion and discredit the United States. Coordination of this activity is a responsibility of the CPSU Central Committee's International Department, which was said to manage or motivate more than 70 pro-Soviet communist parties, international front groups, and some national liberation movements.

The major focus of recent "active measures," according to the CIA, has been the promotion of "peace" and "disarmament" movements in the West. The CIA report noted that front organizations heavily involved in this campaign included the World Peace Council, the largest and most active Soviet front organization, with affiliates in 142 countries; the World Federation of Trade Unions; and the Women's International Democratic Federation. (*News World*, 11 February.)

International Views, Positions, and Activities. After Yuri Andropov's assumption of leadership, there were indications that Soviet world policy would be characterized both by greater flexibility and by increased activism. Andropov impressed Western observers with his apparent vigor in directing Soviet foreign policy, and at the beginning of the year, prospects seemed fairly good for splitting, or at least deflecting, the Western alliance. But, in the course of the year, the state of Andropov's health raised questions about his control of policymaking. More important, a cascade of dramatic events resulted in a general confrontational stance toward the West, and U.S.-Soviet relations plummeted to the lowest point since the Cuban missile crisis of 1962. The Soviets scored some early propaganda points on the issue of missile deployment in Western Europe, but elections in Britain and West Germany maintained conservative leaders in power and the NATO alliance held firm. Western missile deployment could not be checked by Soviet warnings of strategic reactive moves and threats to withdraw from arms control negotiations; the first cruise missiles arrived in Britain in November. The shooting-down of an unarmed Korean passenger airliner on 1 September produced almost worldwide outrage and negated most of the USSR's hard-won propaganda gains on the "peace" issue. Initially, Soviet handling of the incident was characterized by apparent confusion and inconsistency, but the leadership maintained an unyielding hard-line posture. Andropov remained in the background on the issue, and his prolonged absence from public view combined with the harsh assertiveness of the military raised troubling questions in the West about the relations between civilians and soldiers in the Soviet leadership. Meanwhile, the international activism of the Reagan administration, notably the occupation of Grenada in October and November, resulted in real losses for the USSR in the world "correlation of forces," whatever the propaganda fallout. Soviet leaders could take some satisfaction from progress on one front. After many years of hostility and bitterness, relations with China showed some improvement. But even here, outstanding issues remained unresolved and difficult, particularly the massive Soviet military presence on China's borders, the war in Afghanistan, and the USSR's role in Southeast Asia.

Flight 007. The most spectacular developments of the year involved the shooting-down of an unarmed Korean passenger plane by a Soviet pilot near Sakhalin Island on 1 September. Two hundred sixty-nine lives were lost in the destruction of Flight 007, including U.S. Representative

Larry McDonald (R-Ga.) and several other Americans. The incident had immediate international repercussions, sparking widespread demonstrations against the Soviet Union and prompting a two-week boycott of the USSR by pilots of other countries, including even those of Finland.

Official U.S. reaction was comparatively mild, perhaps because of the absence of viable alternatives for reprisal. The rhetoric of U.S. spokesmen, particularly President Reagan, was exceptionally harsh, and complaints were filed with various international bodies. A transcript of the conversation between the Soviet interceptor pilot and his ground controller was released by the United States (*NYT*, 7 September), apparently at the risk of compromising U.S. intelligence-gathering facilities. But Secretary of State George Shultz held a scheduled meeting with Soviet Foreign Minister Gromyko at a Conference on Security and Cooperation in Europe (CSCE) session in Madrid; as anticipated, the conversation between the two diplomats was extremely frosty (AP, 7 September). The United States refused Gromyko permission to land at a civilian airport for his annual visit to the United Nations, supposedly due to concern for his safety; he was given the option of landing at a U.S. military base (UPI, 16 September). This U.S. move afforded the Soviets an excuse for canceling the trip, which, in view of the sustained international outcry, might have been highly embarrassing for Gromyko.

Soviet leaders were evidently caught off-base by the crisis, and Moscow's initial moves created an impression of confusion and uncertainty. Andropov reportedly cut short a vacation to deal with the crisis but made no public appearances. Indeed, the entire Soviet political leadership maintained an extremely low profile throughout the crisis, with only Foreign Minister Gromyko speaking out publicly on the incident. At the outset, the Soviets admitted nothing and waited six days before acknowledging responsibility for shooting down the jetliner (Tass, 6 September; *Pravda*, 7 September). Thereafter, despite some inconsistencies in official explanations, the Soviets adhered to the charge that the Korean jetliner was a spy plane and affirmed their intention to maintain the "inviolability" of the USSR's "sacred frontiers."

Most remarkable was the role of Soviet military figures in the public treatment of the crisis. An authoritative article by Gen. Ivan Shkadov obliquely defended the military's actions in the affair and argued for further strengthening of the authority of local commanders (*Krasnaya zvezda*, 8 September; *Radio Liberty Research*, 22 September). On 9 September, Marshal Nikolai V. Ogarkov, army chief of staff and first deputy minister of defense, held an unprecedented press conference for Soviet and foreign newsmen, accompanied by First Deputy Foreign Minister Georgi M. Kornienko and Central Committee International Information Department head Leonid M. Zamyatin.

Ogarkov repeated the charge that the Korean 747 jetliner was a spy plane, pointing out that it was 300 miles off course, had flown directly over or near the most sensitive Soviet military installations, and appeared to be headed for Vladivostok. Further, Ogarkov noted the unusual presence of a U.S. RC 135 reconnaissance plane in the general area as tracking of the Korean aircraft began and viewed the matter as a coordinated U.S.–South Korean intelligence venture. The decision to shoot down the plane, Ogarkov said, was made by the regional air defense command in the Far East. Asked by Western newsmen about Moscow's involvement in the decision, he stated that the military authorities in the capital were informed "at the appropriate time," leaving unanswered the question whether the informing took place before or after the plane was fired on. (*NYT*, 10 September.)

As Soviet, U.S., and Japanese naval units conducted intensive and apparently unsuccessful searches for the plane's "black box," amid reports of Soviet interference with the others' search efforts, most Western observers concluded that the order to shoot had been given by local commanders. This action supposedly accorded with new instructions given to air defense forces after the 1978 penetration of a Korean airliner a thousand miles into Soviet airspace and with a law on defense of the USSR's frontiers enacted in late 1982.

Some indications of disagreement within the Soviet leadership were conveyed to foreign audiences. On a visit to Britain, *Pravda* editor Viktor G. Afanasyev criticized "our military people" for the long delay in acknowledging responsibility (BBC, 18 September; ABC, 19 September). Viktor Linnik, a commentator on foreign affairs for *Pravda*, admitted in a BBC interview that Soviet pilots were mistaken in assuming that the Korean jet was a reconnaissance plane, an admission that he subsequently sought to retract or modify (*Radio Liberty Research*, 22 September).

For the domestic audience, there was also criticism of some military personnel, but of a far different kind. Air Marshal Piotr Kirsanov, an ex-commander in the Far East and currently a counselor to Defense Minister Ustinov, indirectly criticized air defense forces in a *Pravda* article (20 September) for allowing the plane to transmit "coded intelligence data" for two hours before it was downed. Subsequently, several senior officers of the Far East military command were reportedly dismissed for the two and a half hour delay in halting the flight of the Korean plane (*WP*, 5 October).

The episode left many questions unanswered in its wake, not the least of which were those concerning the degree of independence enjoyed by the Soviet military. Whatever the domestic power relationships that provided a backdrop for the affair, it was clear that the USSR had sustained a major diplomatic defeat that entailed a serious setback in its "peace" offensive in Western Europe.

Arms Control. The United States and the Soviet Union traded arms control proposals during the year, with little or no progress toward limitation of armaments in any area. Proposals by both sides were clearly designed at least in part for their propagandistic impact on domestic and foreign audiences. The USSR seemed to be ahead on points in the propaganda war until the Flight 007 incident, which jolted the "peace" movement in the West. Activists recovered their momentum somewhat with mass demonstrations in November but were unable to affect the Western deployment schedule. The deployment of Pershing II and cruise missiles in Western Europe was, of course, the crucial issue. The United States and its allies aimed at utilizing the scheduled deployment to force bargaining concessions from the Soviets or, failing that, to establish a nuclear balance in Europe. The USSR sought to maintain its existing advantages, but if a compromise were required, the Soviets wanted to include independent British and French missiles in any agreement and to minimize the upgrading of NATO capabilities. Each side displayed some flexibility in its proposals, but these were usually a matter of public proclamation rather than quiet negotiation and became inextricably mixed with the propaganda offensives. On balance, the various arms

proposals relating to Europe appeared to lead to a heightening of international tensions rather than their diminution.

Andropov had offered to remove "dozens" of SS-20s from the European part of the USSR, leaving 162 missiles, equal to the total number of British and French missiles (*CSM*, 29 December 1982). The United States rejected that proposal, and with the evident aim of enlisting Western public pressure against the Reagan administration, Soviet officials indicated on 11 January to a visiting group of U.S. congressmen that the USSR would "consider" destroying some SS-20 missiles removed from the European part of the USSR as part of an eventual Geneva accord (ibid., 18 January). The arms control talks between the superpowers resumed in Geneva in late January, with no signs of a break in the deadlock.

Unable to shake the United States from its "zero option" negotiating position, Moscow stepped up its public relations offensive, blatantly attempting to influence the outcome of the West German elections. When that gambit failed, the Soviets threatened countermoves against the imminent NATO deployment while maintaining the main features of their "peace" offensive. On 17 April, Viktor Isakov, counselor of the Soviet embassy in Washington, said on the CBS "Face the Nation" television program that if NATO went ahead with deployment, the USSR might deploy medium-range nuclear missiles within striking distance of the United States. Isakov refused, however, to say where the USSR might place the weapons. (AP, 18 April.)

In late April, Andropov dispatched his celebrated "Dear Samantha" letter, responding to the worries about nuclear war expressed to him in a letter by Samantha Smith, a twelve-year-old from Manchester, Maine. In his letter, Andropov reaffirmed that the USSR would never be the first country to use nuclear weapons and expressed a desire to start eliminating nuclear stockpiles (Tass, 25 April; *FBIS*, 26 April). During the summer, Samantha Smith visited the USSR, with much fanfare from the Soviet media, but did not see Andropov, presumably because of his health problems. In the same week that he wrote his "Dear Samantha" letter, Andropov replied to an appeal from a group of U.S. scientists with a letter claiming Soviet leadership in the campaign for measures to prevent the militarization of outer space (Tass, 27 April; *FBIS*, 27 April). In that busy week, Andropov also gave an interview to *Der Spiegel* in which he maintained that recent alterations in U.S. proposals did not fundamentally change the earlier "zero option" approach and that, in all its proposals, the United States strove "first and foremost to inflict damage on the security of the Soviet Union, to tilt in its favor the existing balance of forces" (*Pravda*, 25 April).

Andropov offered a hint of softening in the USSR's bargaining position in a Kremlin speech in early May. He indicated that the USSR would be willing to count warheads as well as missiles in an agreement between the two sides. However, he continued to brandish the Soviet stick, warning that in the event of NATO deployment, the USSR and Warsaw Pact countries would be "compelled to take reply measures." (Ibid., 4 May.) Western observers quickly noted that Andropov's new proposal included nothing about dismantling of the highly mobile SS-20 missiles (AP, 4 May).

The fourth round of the Geneva talks on arms limitations in Europe started on 17 May, with a U.S. proposal on the table concerning limitation of nuclear warheads in Europe as an interim step toward banishment of medium-range missiles from the continent. The outlook was hardly encouraging; the Soviets had already denounced the proposal as a scheme to impose a "unilateral reduction" on the USSR (ibid., 18 May). In late May, Moscow lent some specificity to its threats, indicating that the USSR would introduce new nuclear weapons in Eastern Europe if the NATO deployment proceeded (*NYT*, 28 May).

This latest threat set off a new round of rhetorical sparring by the superpowers. As U.S. president Reagan attended the Williamsburg summit meeting of Western leaders, his press spokesman released a statement regretting the "unwarranted threats of retaliation" by the Soviet government and arguing anew for the "zero option." The statement continued: "The Soviet demands for nuclear forces as large as all countries combined is tantamount to a demand for effective military superiority and thus global hegemony." (Ibid., 29 May.)

Noting Reagan's comment at Williamsburg that there could be no progress at the Geneva arms talks unless the Soviet Union saw that "the United States was keeping to its planned schedule of deploying missiles in Western Europe," Tass denounced Reagan as "illogical and inconsistent" and said that it has always been the United States that "seeks military superiority." The statement

also repeated the warning that the USSR would take "timely and effective reply measures" to counter a NATO deployment. (UPI, 2 June.) Further warnings along these lines were issued by Defense Minister Ustinov (*NYT*, 28 June) and by Andropov at his meeting in Moscow with West German chancellor Helmut Kohl (AP, 6 July). However, Kohl reportedly gained the impression that there was still a "margin of flexibility" in Moscow's bargaining position and that Andropov was interested in reaching an agreement before the December deadline for installation of new U.S. medium-range missiles in West Germany, Britain, and Italy (*NYT*, 9 July).

Following a meeting of the NATO special consultative group in late July, Richard Burt, assistant U.S. secretary of state for European affairs, announced that the Soviets had refused "serious discussion" of a U.S. proposal for limiting medium-range nuclear warheads in Europe to 50 for each side (AP, 27 July). Meanwhile, at the Strategic Arms Reductions Talks (START) in June and July, there was some convergence on proposed ceilings on intercontinental missiles and bombers, but Washington and Moscow remained far apart on sublimits for land- and sea-based missiles for nuclear-warhead weapons (UPI, 3 August).

Andropov returned to his proposal for a ban on the militarization of space during his meeting with a delegation of nine Democratic U.S. senators in the Kremlin on 18 August. Senator Claiborne Pell (R.I.) reported that Andropov said the USSR was ready to eliminate existing antisatellite weapons and ban development of new ones. The USSR, believed to be the only nation possessing a working antisatellite system, is well ahead of the United States in this field, and the Andropov proposal was regarded in Western circles as a ploy to forestall planned U.S. tests (AP, 19 August). Tass reported that Andropov had described U.S.-Soviet relations in his talk with the senators as "tense in virtually every field" (*Pravda*, 19 August).

After Reagan spoke to the U.N. General Assembly on arms control and other matters and offered to include nuclear bombers in calculations of medium-range weapons systems and to refrain from matching global levels of Soviet warheads, Andropov responded with one of the sharpest attacks on U.S. foreign policy by a Soviet leader in years. The statement, read on Moscow television news, dismissed Reagan's proposals and accused Washington of pursuing a "militaristic course" that "raises the danger of nuclear war." Apparently stung by the furor over the Flight 007 episode, Andropov commented for the first time on the affair, charging that the United States was guilty of a "sophisticated provocation" and had used the crisis to step up the arms race. (*WP*, 29 September.)

Undeterred by the harsh Soviet rhetoric, Reagan pressed on with new proposals, launching the "build-down" concept in early October. He called on the Soviet Union to agree to a 5 percent annual cut in long-range nuclear missiles, offered to negotiate ceilings on long-range bombers and air-launched cruise missiles, and proposed that older systems be destroyed as new ones were deployed (AP, 5 October). Moscow summarily rejected the Reagan plan; an official statement said that it would only mask a nuclear weapons buildup and allow deployment of "new, upgraded systems of mass annihilation" (Tass, 5 October; *Pravda*, 6 October).

The talks on limitation of nuclear arms in Europe resumed in Geneva in October amid Soviet threats to walk out of the negotiations if NATO's scheduled deployment proceeded (AP, 12 October). However, an ambiguously worded Warsaw Pact statement called for continuing negotiations beyond the end of the year and appeared to seek a delay in the NATO deployment (ibid., 14 October). In mid-October, West German foreign minister Hans-Dietrich Genscher told Soviet Foreign Minister Gromyko that Bonn would go ahead with its deployment unless an agreement were reached at Geneva (UPI, 15 October).

In the wake of Genscher's warning, Soviet threats again took center stage. A high-ranking Soviet officer, Col. Gen. Nikolai Chervov, told the West German newsweekly *Stern* that if the NATO deployment were carried out, the USSR would build nuclear missiles that "could reach targets in America in ten minutes." Chervov denied that this meant basing SS-20 missiles in Cuba. "Of course we will take countermeasures that directly threaten U.S. territory," he said. "We would build up our intercontinental systems and balance out the short flying time of the Pershing II." (AP, 17 October.) A more immediate form of reprisal was announced a week later. The Soviet Defense Ministry said that "missile complexes of operational-tactical designation" were

being readied in East Germany and Czechoslovakia (Tass, 24 October).

As the deployment deadline neared, the United States and USSR traded further arms proposals. A statement issued in Andropov's name offered to reduce the number of SS-20s in Europe to "about 140" but continued to insist on no deployment of Pershing II and cruise missiles and the counting of British and French nuclear weapons in any negotiating tally. "The Geneva talks can be continued," he said, "if the United States does not start the actual deployment of the missiles." (*Pravda*, 27 October.)

The U.S. response was an offer presented by negotiator Paul H. Nitze in Geneva to limit the deployment of new missiles in Europe to fewer than 420 nuclear warheads if the USSR would agree to cut its overall medium-range force in Europe and Asia to 140 missiles, with a maximum of 420 warheads (*NYT*, 15 November). Moscow publicly rejected the offer. A *Pravda* editorial (18 November) said that the plan was unacceptable because it permitted NATO deployment and did not count British and French missiles. *Pravda* maintained that with British and French missiles counted, the latest U.S. proposal would give NATO twice the medium-range nuclear strength of the USSR. Meanwhile, Vadim V. Zagladin, deputy head of the Central Committee's International Department, reiterated the Soviet threat to walk out of the European nuclear arms talks if deployment proceeded and said that deployment would also have a "negative effect" on the parallel START talks (AP, 17 November).

The first U.S. cruise missiles arrived in Britain on 14 November (*NYT*, 15 November). In a last-minute effort to stave off deployment, Soviet negotiator Yuli Kvitsinsky reportedly approached Nitze in Geneva on 13 November with an offer to drop the demand that British and French missiles be counted and to reduce its warheads in Europe by about 60 percent provided that NATO abandoned deployment of new weapons. The United States promptly rebuffed the purported offer (AP, 18 November); Moscow denied that any such offer had been made (Tass, 18 November). As the arms talks impasse continued, a new element was introduced into the nuclear equation: it was reported that the USSR's version of the cruise missile would be operational in early 1984 (ABC, 16 November).

After the West German Bundestag gave final

approval for the missile deployment in November, chief Soviet negotiator Kvitsinsky announced suspension of "this round" of the intermediate-range nuclear forces talks in Geneva (*NYT*, 24 November).

Moscow subsequently displayed its opposition to the NATO deployment by putting all other arms negotiations in cold storage. On 8 December, the Soviets recessed the START talks in Geneva without setting a date for resumption, and on 15 December, Warsaw Pact delegates refused to set a new date for negotiations when the Mutual and Balanced Force Reductions talks recessed in Vienna (AP, 9 and 16 December).

Other U.S.-Soviet Relations. The United States displayed increasing concern over covert Soviet attempts to obtain Western technology useful for military purposes. The numerous Soviet diplomats expelled from Western countries during the year for espionage activities included Lt. Col. Yevgeny Barmyantsev, arrested by the FBI in April while attempting to collect films containing information about the current state of U.S. laser technology (*NYT*, 17 April).

The Office of Technology Assessment, a nonpartisan agency that advises the U.S. Congress, reported in May that the USSR was making a major effort to obtain Western technology for military purposes and that Washington had only limited power to deny the Soviets access to U.S. technology through export licenses (*Los Angeles Times*, 9 May). In November, the United States persuaded Sweden to delay temporarily the transshipment of a U.S. computer that officials in Washington said could be used in the guidance system of nuclear rockets. In November, in an attempt to restrict industrial espionage by Soviet "diplomats," the U.S. State Department barred Soviet diplomatic personnel from California's Silicon Valley and other sensitive areas, while allowing free access to such cities as Cleveland and Birmingham (*NYT*, 21 November).

The sour state of U.S.-Soviet relations was reflected in tougher attitudes by each side toward the other's diplomats. Richard Osborne, a first secretary in the economic section of the U.S. embassy in Moscow, was expelled from the USSR in March, followed by Louis Thomas, an attaché, in June; the Soviets charged that both had engaged in espionage activities (*WP*, 5 June). In an unusual move, the U.S. government in

August delayed the departure of Andrei V. Berezhkov, the sixteen-year-old son of the Soviet embassy first secretary, pending investigation; the boy had allegedly written to President Reagan and the *New York Times* (14 and 15 August) saying he did not want to go home.

Both the old and the new U.S. Embassy in Moscow were sites of controversy. Construction of the new U.S. Embassy in central Moscow was halted for a time when some 300 workers walked off their jobs after U.S. security officials used a new machine designed to discover listening devices implanted in the building (*WP*, 27 May). U.S. ambassador Arthur A. Hartmann reported that after a five-year interval, the Soviets had resumed microwave bombardment of the U.S. Embassy (*Los Angeles Times*, 11 November).

In November and December, Soviet police carried out a campaign of harassment at the U.S. Embassy, carefully screening all Muscovites who entered (UPI, 18 December).

Western Europe. Soviet espionage activities also colored relations with major West European countries. On 31 March, Britain ordered the expulsion of Col. Gennadi A. Primakov, air attaché; embassy second secretary Vladimir V. Ivanov; and journalist Igor V. Titov for "unacceptable activities" (*NYT*, 1 April). The Soviets responded by ordering a British air attaché and a journalist to leave the USSR "for activities incompatible with their status" (UPI, 8 April).

A week after the British action, Paris announced the discovery of a large Soviet spy ring. Forty-seven Soviets with diplomatic status were expelled from France, including Nikolai Chetverikov, the third-ranking embassy official, who was reportedly the head of Soviet intelligence operations in that country (*NYT*, 6 April). French counterintelligence officials claimed that Soviet spies had stolen more than 30 percent of France's technological achievements during the past decade (UPI, 8 April). Tass charged that the French action was "arbitrary" and based on "obviously fabricated pretexts that are totally at odds with reality" (*Izvestiia*, 6 April).

As in the past, such revelations scarcely slowed Soviet efforts to exert influence on "bourgeois" regimes. Moscow maintained a steady flow of top-level diplomatic exchanges and other visits, while providing covert aid and public support for West European "peace" movements. In

January, Hans-Jochen Vogel, the Social Democratic candidate for chancellor of West Germany, was warmly received in Moscow, where he met with Andropov (*Pravda*, 14 January). Foreign Minister Gromyko traveled to Bonn for conversations with Foreign Minister Genscher that dealt principally with arms control questions (ibid., 18 January).

French foreign minister Claude Cheysson visited Moscow in February and met with both Gromyko and Andropov. Cheysson signed an agreement on Soviet-French cooperation in science and technology for the period 1983–1993 (Tass, 17 February; *FBIS*, 18 February). An official Soviet statement said the talks "will give an additional impetus to diverse and fruitful ties between the Soviet Union and France in the field of economic, scientific-technical, and cultural cooperation" (*Izvestiia*, 23 February). On the more important matter of nuclear arms, the two governments remained far apart. An unnamed European diplomat briefed by Cheysson said that according to the French foreign minister, on this matter "the Soviet stand is like a block of concrete" (*WP*, 22 February).

Underscoring Moscow's hopes for influencing the leftist government of Greece and undercutting NATO's southeastern flank, Prime Minister Tikhonov visited Athens in late February, where an agreement on economic, industrial, scientific, and technical cooperation between the USSR and Greece was signed (*Pravda*, 28 February). The question of NATO's missile deployment and other matters were discussed during an April visit to Moscow by Belgian foreign minister Leo Tindemans. The Soviet press quoted Tindemans as being "very pleased" with the visit, which featured an eight-hour meeting with Gromyko (Tass, 12 April; *FBIS*, 13 April); however, there was no evident change in Belgium's positions on outstanding issues.

General elections in Britain and West Germany yielded victories for incumbent conservative governments and smashing defeats for socialist parties hostile to NATO's deployment plans. These electoral setbacks did nothing to soften Moscow's positions; indeed, the early reaction to the Christian Democratic victory in Germany was a warning to Kohl that his election did not constitute an endorsement of his support for U.S. security policies (Tass, 7 March; *Radio Liberty Research*, 8 March). Soviet attempts to influence the outcome of the West German elec-

tions had been so blatant as to elicit an official protest; nevertheless, Moscow's hostility did not impel Kohl to burn all bridges to the East. Under considerable domestic pressure despite his electoral triumph, Kohl sought to demonstrate Bonn's willingness to negotiate and desire to maintain some measure of détente. In July, Kohl visited Moscow for talks with top Soviet party and government leaders. The Soviet press noted approvingly that "trade and economic ties, resting on a solid legal base, are developing in a stable manner to the mutual advantage of the USSR and the Federal Republic of Germany" (*Pravda*, 7 July). On the vital issue of nuclear deployment, signals were somewhat mixed (see above). Subsequently, Kohl maintained his commitment to NATO plans, and in late November the Bundestag gave final approval for the missile deployment (*NYT*, 23 November). The day after the Bundestag vote, the first Pershing II missiles arrived in West Germany (ibid., 24 November).

The Italian investigation of the 1981 attempt to assassinate Pope John Paul II proceeded slowly and inconclusively. A Bulgarian defector, Yordan Mantarov, claimed that the plot had been devised by the KGB and by the Bulgarian secret service, a charge later supported by the attempted assassin, Mehmet Ali Agca (ibid., 23 March and 9 July). The USSR responded that the accusation was "threadbare propaganda" (Tass, 9 July; *NYT*, 10 July). Meanwhile, Italian investigators evidently continued to be perplexed by inconsistencies in Agca's accounts of the affair. The assassination attempt and its aftermath had produced severe strains in Soviet-Italian relations. However, in April, the two countries signed a protocol on radio and television exchanges for 1983–1984 (Moscow domestic service, 12 April; *FBIS*, 13 April).

Eastern Europe. The East European bloc countries were relatively quiet during the year, as the Polish crisis cooled and area political leaders watched for indications of the direction of the new Soviet leadership's policies. However, East Europe played a crucial role in Moscow's strategy to counter the NATO missile deployment, a role spelled out explicitly in a late November policy statement by Andropov (*Pravda*, 25 November). The annual meeting of Warsaw Pact foreign ministers in April had been used to rally East European support for Soviet policy on nuclear missiles in Europe (ibid., 8 April; *NYT*, 6–8

April). However, when it became apparent that the USSR would install missiles in East Germany and Czechoslovakia, some tension appeared in the alliance. In November, the main Czechoslovak party newspaper, *Rudé právo*, said that "some are questioning the wisdom of deployment of Soviet medium-range missiles in this country" (*NYT*, 6 November).

In regard to Poland, the Soviet leadership seemed generally amenable to a fairly wide latitude for Gen. Wojciech Jaruzelski's government as its stabilization of Poland continued. However, Soviet media pressure was evident, the most notable example being a May attack on Deputy Prime Minister Mieczyslaw Rakowski. The journal *Novoye vremya* described the attitude of the weekly *Polityka*, founded by Rakowski, as "revisionist" throughout the Polish crisis and branded the periodical "allergic to real socialism" (*CSM*, 10 May). Western observers viewed the *Novoye vremya* article as strengthening hardliners in Poland opposed to Jaruzelski's "economic reforms" (*NYT*, 10 May).

On bloc economic questions, as on many other matters, the Andropov leadership appeared to move slowly, or even to mark time. In January, the USSR signed an agreement providing for an increase in commodity turnover with Hungary during 1983 (*Izvestiia*, 24 January). The publicity surrounding this routine agreement accorded with the unusual attention paid to Hungarian economic reforms in the early months of the year. However, as Soviet domestic economic reform was slow in gaining momentum, the Soviet media's interest in Hungary's economy diminished sharply.

The Council for Mutual Economic Assistance Executive Committee session in Moscow produced no indications of bold initiatives to deal with the area's deep-seated economic problems. The discussions dealt with the production of robots and "joint measures aimed at improving the supply of. . . foodstuffs" (ibid., 26 June; Tass, 30 June; *FBIS*, 1 July).

China. Rapprochement with China would yield a valuable counterweight in the USSR's campaign against NATO; the new leadership seemed determined to pursue this course. Already, in Brezhnev's last year as leader, there had been strong signs of Soviet inclination toward détente with China. An article by Foreign Minister Gromyko in the month following Andropov's

accession to the leadership dramatically affirmed Moscow's commitment to normalization. Gromyko said that the Soviet Union "is ready to do and is doing everything it can" to promote favorable, normal relations with China and noted the recent "positive response" by the PRC to such initiatives (*Kommunist*, no. 18, December 1982).

A Soviet broadcast to China at the outset of the year carried forward the theme of normalization, claiming that the CPSU and the Soviet state had always maintained that "the fundamental and long-range interests of the Soviet and Chinese people are identical" (Radio Moscow, 2 January; *FBIS*, 3 January). Any significant normalization of relations would obviously involve hard bargaining over real conflicts of interest, and Moscow clearly intended to keep the pressure on Beijing, alternating such ambiguous olive branches with tough specific signals. In mid-January, *Novoye vremya* returned to the denunciation of Chinese territorial claims on the USSR, charging bitterly that wider circulation was being given within China to these claims, which had nothing in common "with the historical truth," while the USSR was pursuing the goal of normalization (*WP*, 14 January).

One indicator of improving relations was an upsurge in bilateral trade, which had jumped from a total of $150 million in 1981 to $300 million in 1982. Negotiations for a further increase in trade between the two countries opened in Moscow on 8 February and continued until 15 March (Tass, 15 March; *FBIS*, 15 March). Meanwhile, a Chinese delegation led by Deputy Foreign Minister Qian Qichen arrived in Moscow on 1 March for consultations aimed at improving relations (AFP, Paris, 15 March; *FBIS*, 15 March); the main topic of the discussions reportedly was Indochina, especially differences over Kampuchea. The trade talks resulted in an agreement to increase trade to a value of $800 million in 1983 (*FEER*, 24 March). At the conclusion of the political talks, Gromyko met with Qian Qichen (Tass, 21 March; *Pravda*, 22 March); apparently, the results were inconclusive. Reportedly, the USSR sought to confine the talks to the disposition of military forces on the Sino-Soviet border. While the talks were in progress, *People's Daily* (Beijing) accused Moscow of refusing to discuss Afghanistan, Kampuchea, and Soviet troops in Mongolia (*Radio Liberty Research*, 22 March). Nevertheless, Soviet officials claimed that a "substantial détente" had been achieved. One evidence of improved relations was said to be the exchange of salutes and visits by Soviet and Chinese troops along the 4,500-mile frontier (*NYT*, 20 March).

Other indications of improved relations included a visit to Beijing by the influential *Izvestiia* political commentator Aleksandr Bovin and an invitation for Soviet chess players to compete in a Beijing competition in April (*CSM*, 18 March).

Clashes between Chinese and North Vietnamese troops in April were reported by the Soviet press as "armed provocations" by China (*Izvestiia*, 18 April). Further, Moscow delivered a stinging attack on Beijing for anti-Soviet propaganda, which, it claimed, served U.S. interests; the *People's Daily* alone, said a Soviet spokesman, published between 120 and 140 anti-Soviet articles each month (ibid.; *NYT*, 19 April). Shortly before these verbal blasts, the USSR and China had signed two agreements on border trade. One agreement covered exchanges of goods across the Amur and Ussuri Rivers; the other dealt with trade between southern Siberian border areas and the northern part of Inner Mongolia (Reuters, 10 April; *NYT*, 11 April).

A move by the Soviet-dominated Mongolian People's Republic (MPR) in late spring was hardly calculated to improve the climate for negotiations. Some 8,000 Chinese citizens were forcibly expelled from the MPR and reportedly humiliated and harassed by Mongolian border guards (*FEER*, 9 June). However, Beijing presented only a mild formal protest and quietly arranged for the orderly return of Chinese nationals from the MPR. Of much greater impact was the low-key Chinese reaction to the downing of the Korean jetliner in September; China abstained on resolutions condemning the USSR in both the U.N. General Assembly and the International Civil Aviation Organization.

A round of talks in Beijing, held during October, between Soviet Deputy Foreign Minister Leonid F. Ilyichev and Qian Qichen resulted in agreements doubling the volume of trade, increasing cultural ties, and resuming technical cooperation. However, the two sides failed to resolve differences over Kampuchea, Afghanistan, and security along the Sino-Soviet border. (Ibid., 3 November.)

Afghanistan. Soviet involvement in Afghanistan continued, despite signs that the new leadership might be amenable to a political settlement that would cut Soviet losses in the four-year-old war.

The year opened with an angry Soviet blast at President Reagan for supporting the Afghan guerrillas. *Pravda* (6 January) reported that over one million people had participated in recent anti-U.S. rallies in that country and blamed Washington for organizing an undeclared war against the Kabul regime.

A more conciliatory note was sounded two weeks later in an interview with an Italian newspaper by Vadim Zagladin, first deputy head of the Central Committee's International Department, who spoke of a "new stage." "Contacts are under way between Afghanistan and Pakistan," said Zagladin, "and a political solution that ends the external intervention and allows for the withdrawal of our soldiers is possible" (*WP*, 24 January).

Such signals continued but were not followed by positive indications of progress toward a settlement. The Soviet ambassador to Afghanistan, Vitali S. Smirnov, said in a May interview that the Kabul government was willing to set a timetable for the total withdrawal of Soviet troops provided it had international guarantees against intervention from across its borders (*NYT*, 20 May). In June, Pakistani president Mohammad Zia-ul Haq said that Moscow was taking a "very positive approach" to U.N.-sponsored indirect talks in Geneva between Pakistan and Afghanistan for a political solution (ibid., 2 June).

In sharp contrast to this "peace offensive," the Soviet military seemed more determined than ever to wipe out all resistance. Several major offensives were launched, with use of unprecedented numbers of fighter-bombers and helicopter gunships to support ground attacks (*CSM*, 4 May). Meanwhile, for the first time the Soviets established a garrison in northwest Afghanistan near the Iranian border, and unconfirmed reports indicated an increase in the number of Soviet troops in the country (*NYT*, 18 May). Despite massive Soviet efforts to crush opposition, there was no apparent letup in guerrilla activity. In September, a rebel attack on two Soviet convoys south of Kabul forced the convoys to turn back, with the reported loss of 24 Soviet soldiers (ibid., 29 September). In December, at least 2,500 Soviet soldiers backed by tanks, jet fighters, and helicopter gunships launched a major offensive against Afghan rebels in the Shomali region north of Kabul (AP, 7 December).

As in other matters, the Soviet media displayed a new frankness in reporting on Afghanistan. A number of press accounts graphically depicted the hazards of the guerrilla war for Soviet troops (*Los Angeles Times*, 7 March). A Tass dispatch (19 March) reported that "thousands of peaceful Afghan citizens" had been killed in the fighting; another press report admitted that rebel attacks had damaged factories and interrupted power supplies, producing major losses for the Afghan economy (*Sovetskaya rossiya*, 19 March).

Middle East. This area provided the first test of the anticipated resurgence of Soviet activism outside Europe under the new leadership. The USSR's clients had suffered a humiliating defeat in the Lebanon war of 1982; Moscow sought to restore a credible presence in the area by stepping up its logistical and moral support for Syria. But Soviet policy was complicated by a falling out among its clients. As Palestine Liberation Organization (PLO) rebels backed by Syria made war against Yassir Arafat, on whose leadership Moscow had staked much, Soviet political difficulties mounted. Meanwhile, Soviet-Iranian relations continued to deteriorate, and Moscow tilted further toward Iraq in its continuing war with Iran.

During the early months of the year, Soviet support for Arafat appeared strong. In March, Deputy Foreign Minister Oleg Grinevsky met with Arafat in Tunis (AFP, Paris, 21 March; *FBIS*, 22 March). Arafat's second-in-command, Abu Iyad, was received in Moscow in early June, and Andropov reportedly dispatched two letters of support for the PLO leader, one to Arafat and one to Syrian president Hafiz al-Assad (*CSM*, 11 June). As tensions mounted between the Soviet clients, Moscow cooled toward Arafat and moved toward a neutral position. When Farouk Kaddoumi, PLO foreign affairs specialist, visited Moscow in July, the Soviet press report did not mention Arafat. Instead, an official statement called on the PLO to put its house in order and "strengthen cooperation" with "progressive Arab countries" (*Pravda*, 14 July; *NYT*, 15 July). The threat of Syrian domination of the PLO, with its probable consequence of weakening support for the Palestinians among moderate Arab states, subsequently nudged the Soviets back toward Arafat's corner. As PLO rebel forces closed in on Arafat's supporters in Tripoli, Syrian foreign minister Abdul Halim Khaddam visited Moscow and received a strong message of Soviet dissatisfaction with the threat to Arafat. The official communiqué spoke of a "thorough exchange of opinions" between the Syrian foreign minister and Gromyko and concluded: "The Soviet side stressed the pressing, urgent need to overcome strife and restore unity in the ranks of the Palestinian resistance movement so that it will continue to be an active and effective force in the anti-imperialist struggle in the Middle East" (Tass, 11 November; *NYT*, 12 November).

Unable to derive clear-cut benefits from the seething cauldron of Lebanon, Moscow sought other avenues of influence in the region, putting out feelers for a thaw with Saudi Arabia (*CSM*, 11 June) and taking more overt steps in regard to Egypt. A Soviet commentary described Soviet-Egyptian economic cooperation as "satisfactory" (Radio Moscow, 17 April; *FBIS*, 19 April) on the eve of a Soviet diplomatic initiative toward Egypt. Yuri Kirichenko, head of the Department of Cultural Relations of the Soviet Foreign Ministry, led a delegation for five days of talks in Cairo aimed at normalizing cultural, scientific, and technological relations (Iraqi News Agency, Baghdad, 19 April; *FBIS*, 19 April).

However troublesome the quarrel among its militant clients may have been, the most important negative factor in the regional "correlation of forces" from Moscow's standpoint was the continued presence of U.S. and other Western forces in the area. The USSR increased its logistical support for Syria and repeatedly issued rhetorical blasts against Washington. As U.S. forces became more heavily involved in the fighting in Lebanon despite apparently growing doubts about the operation among the American public, Moscow stepped up its verbal barrages. An official statement charged that the United States was planning a "massive attack" on "national-patriotic forces" in Lebanon and warned against such a move. The Soviets also maintained that the U.S. Marines were violating international law by their presence and activities in Lebanon. (Tass, 4 November; *NYT*, 5 November.)

Further to the east, Soviet-Iranian relations approached the breaking point. About seventy members of the pro-Soviet Tudeh Party, including its leader, Nureddin Kianuri, were arrested in February on charges of espionage. Moscow protested the "groundless and slanderous nature of the accusations made against the Tudeh leaders" and warned that Soviet-Iranian relations would suffer if Tehran proceeded against the Tudeh (*Pravda*, 20 February, 23 March). "It is still not too late," said *Pravda*, "to prevent the prejudiced trial on false, preposterous charges." Moscow's pressure had no effect. On 30 April, Kianuri made a "confession" on Tehran television, and on 4 May, the Iranian government banned the Tudeh Party (*CSM*, 6 May). On the same day, eighteen Soviet diplomats were expelled from Iran (*Radio Liberty Research*, 5 May). Subsequently, the Soviets reportedly increased military support for Iraq and strengthened their forces near the Iranian border of Afghanistan (see above) but proceeded with caution, apparently reluctant to add a total break with Iran to their list of complex international problems.

India. Commencement of indirect negotiations on Afghanistan apparently served to dispel New Delhi's uneasiness about the Soviet invasion of that country; otherwise, Moscow continued to maintain excellent relations with the government of Indira Gandhi. Deputy Foreign Trade Minister Ivan T. Grishin visited India in April (*Izvestiia*, 30 April), and in May First Deputy Prime Minister Ivan Arkhipov signed an agreement in New Delhi on construction of a metal plant (Tass, 12 May). Meanwhile, India considered an increase in arms purchases from the USSR to counter modernization of weaponry by China and Pakistan and to reduce a surplus of about $2 billion in trade with the Soviet bloc. However, India was reluctant to move too far from its existing policy of diversification in arms purchases, and critics in the country's military leadership pointed to the poor performance of Soviet arms in Lebanon in 1982 (*FEER*, 2 June).

Japan. Relations between Moscow and Tokyo, strained in recent years by Soviet refusal to return territory seized at the end of World War II, deteriorated further. Major points of contention were the accelerated Soviet military buildup in the Far East and Moscow's heavy-handed attempts to slow the pace of Japanese rearmament. The Japanese were concerned about the USSR's reinforcement of the Kuriles, reportedly garrisoned by a mechanized infantry division of 14,000 men (*NYT*, 30 December 1982). Even more worrisome was the Soviet nuclear presence in the Far East. The government of Prime Minister Yasuhiro Nakasone called for increased Japanese military expenditures and moved closer to the United States on security policy. When Nakasone visited Washington in January, Moscow delivered a harsh warning, saying that Nakasone envisioned Japan as "an unsinkable aircraft carrier" aimed against the USSR. "Is it not clear, however," the Soviets asked, "that in the present nuclear age, there can be no unsinkable aircraft carrier?" (Tass, 20 January.)

Tokyo protested in January, to no avail, about statements by Andropov and Gromyko concerning the possible redeployment of SS-20s from west to east of the Urals and about the Soviet military buildup in the Northern Territories (*NYT*, 26 January). Gromyko made a direct thrust against Japan in his press conference of 2 April, saying that the USSR had the right to deploy its SS-20s as required by its security interests and charging that "the Soviet Union is surrounded by a ring of military bases; Japan and waters surrounding Japan are crammed with nuclear weapons and the necessary carriers" (*Pravda*, 3 April).

Deputy Foreign Minister Mikhail S. Kapitsa sought to allay Japanese fears during an April visit to Tokyo; he said that Soviet SS-20s in Asia were targeted not on Japan but on U.S. sea-based nuclear weapons in the Pacific (*Radio Liberty Research*, 14 July). However, the Kapitsa talks yielded no palpable progress on substantive issues, and a round of talks between Shozo Kadota, head of the U.N. Bureau of the Japanese Foreign Ministry, and Soviet officials in Moscow in July (ibid.) also left the two countries at loggerheads.

Tense relations between Moscow and Tokyo were further exacerbated by the Flight 007 episode in September. Japan cooperated closely with the United States in the recovery efforts in the Sea of Japan and moved even closer to the United States on security policy, the strengthened relationship being most evident in the warm welcome accorded President Reagan during his November visit to Tokyo.

Africa. Activities of the USSR and its surrogates on this continent attracted much less attention than usual, but Moscow attempted to maintain its footholds in various areas. Amid continuing reports of Ethiopia's dissatisfaction with Soviet assistance and the possibility of a turn to the West for aid, the Soviet press lavished praise on the Ethiopian revolution on the occasion of the Second Congress of the Ethiopian party (*Pravda*, 2 January). The Soviet press also stressed the USSR's continuing role in development of the oil port of Assab on the Red Sea (ibid., 21 April).

Much publicity attended the visits of friendly African leaders to Moscow during the year. A Nigerian National Assembly delegation led by Senator O. K. Adebayo was greeted in February by First Deputy Chairman of the Supreme Soviet Presidium Vasili V. Kuznetsov and other officials (*Izvestiia*, 21 February; *FBIS*, 23 February). Mozambican president Samora Moises Machel visited Moscow in March for conversations with Andropov, Tikhonov, Gromyko, Ustinov, and Ponomarev (*Pravda*, 6 March). President José Eduardo dos Santos of Angola traveled to Moscow in May and met with Gromyko, Ustinov, and First Deputy Minister of Defense Marshal Nikolai V. Ogarkov (ibid., 16 and 18 May).

Latin America. Central America and the Caribbean were focal points of U.S.-Soviet competition, as the Reagan administration made clear its determination to resist further expansion of Moscow's influence via proxies in the Americas.

Washington expressed much concern about Cuban and Soviet efforts to destabilize the region, particularly logistical support for Nicaragua's Sandinistas, and controversy flared in the United States over the Reagan administration's activist role in Central America. Moscow emphasized its economic aid for the Managua regime, as Nicaraguan minister of planning Henry Ruiz Hernández traveled to Moscow for a conference with Gosplan head Nikolai K. Baibakov (ibid., 17 February; *FBIS*, 23 February). U.S. officials, however, contended that the Soviet thrust in the region was primarily military in character.

U.S. Defense Department sources reported in March that two Nicaraguan airfields were being improved to take Soviet jets and that a similar airfield was being constructed on the island of Grenada (*NYT*, 9 March). Two weeks later, Reagan appeared on U.S. television with a graphic presentation concerning the Soviet military buildup in Cuba, Nicaragua, and Grenada (ibid., 23 March). Grenada's Marxist government vehemently denied Reagan's charge that the airfield under construction was for military purposes, insisting that it was designed to encourage development of the island's tourist industry. In the aftermath of these charges and countercharges, Grenadian premier Maurice Bishop and foreign minister Unison Whiteman visited Moscow, where Soviet officials reaffirmed their support for Bishop and his New Jewel Movement (*Pravda*, 16 April).

Soviet construction of a drydock and floating pier to service Soviet tuna vessels on Nicaragua's west coast aroused speculation among U.S. military officials that the project was a smoke screen for further Soviet military expansion in the region (*NYT*, 15 May). The alleged Soviet military threat was again spotlighted, in June, when the Venezuelan navy found an abandoned cargo ship off Barbados carrying 5,000 crates of Soviet-made artillery shells (ibid., 20 June).

Following the angry rhetorical exchanges during the early part of the year, Grenada's prime minister gave indications of willingness for a rapprochement with Washington. But more radical elements in the Grenadian leadership overthrew Bishop in a coup, and he was subsequently killed. Grenada's leftist turn further alarmed Washington, concerned about the island's proximity to the main sea-lanes for U.S. oil imports from the Middle East and the possibility of the new airfield's servicing both Nicaragua and Cuban forces in Africa. At the request of several small Caribbean countries, U.S. forces occupied the island in October, ousting the Marxist government.

The discovery of large quantities of Soviet arms on the island, plus the presence of Soviet advisers and a contingent of Cuban "construction workers" who fought like veteran troops, led Reagan to charge that Grenada was "a Soviet-Cuban colony being readied as a major military bastion to export terror and undermine democracy" (AP, 27 October). Subsequently, the United States supervised the expulsion of all Soviet and Eastern bloc diplomats, North Korean technicians, and Cuban personnel from the island (*WP*, 5 November).

The dramatic U.S. action aroused controversy in various international forums but appeared to constitute a definite setback for the USSR in the world "correlation of forces." One largely unnoted negative effect was an apparent chilling of Moscow's relations with Venezuela, the object of a minor Soviet diplomatic offensive, featuring an exchange of visits during April. Sattar N. Imashev, deputy chairman of the Supreme Soviet Presidium, led a delegation on an official visit to

Caracas (*Izvestiia*, 14 and 19 April), and José Zambrano, Venezuela's foreign minister, visited Moscow for talks with Gromyko on a wide range of international issues (Moscow television service, 25 April; *FBIS*, 26 April).

International Party Contacts. Despite Yuri Andropov's physical problems, which inhibited and sometimes ruled out entirely an active role for him in dealings with other communist parties, the CPSU maintained extensive contacts with both ruling and nonruling parties. Where necessary, other CPSU officials substituted for Andropov, and the Soviet media avoided calling attention to the leader's absence. Indeed, the experiences of 1982–1983 suggest that during a leader's incapacitation, international party contacts may be used to divert attention from the absent leader and convey the impression of regular functioning of the Soviet system. As usual, contacts with the bloc parties of Eastern Europe were much emphasized; otherwise, relations with West European communist parties attracted the most attention, reflecting the Soviet "peace" offensive in that area. However, strains continued to be evident in relations with some of the West European parties, notably those of Spain and Italy, whose initiatives for a "new internationalism" in recent years have apparently been just as unacceptable to Moscow as was the Eurocommunism of the 1970s.

One major function attended by Andropov that attracted foreign communists was the 113th anniversary celebration of Lenin's birth. Four leaders of foreign parties were present: Khalid Bakhdash, secretary general of the Syrian party; Luís Corvalán, secretary general of the Chilean party; Rubén Darío Sousa, general secretary of the People's Party of Panama; and Michael O'Riordan, general secretary of the Irish party (Radio Moscow, 22 April; *FBIS*, 22 April).

Erich Honecker of East Germany became the first Warsaw Pact leader to pay an official visit to the USSR since Andropov's accession. He was received for four days of talks in Moscow in early May (*Izvestiia*, 8 May). A connection between Honecker's visit and the Euromissile question was suggested by the fact that his arrival in Moscow followed shortly after the announcement of the scheduled July visit of West German chancellor Helmut Kohl (*RFE Research*, 24 May). One month earlier, Soviet defense minis-

ter and Politburo member Ustinov had made an official visit to East Germany (AP, 2 April). In February, Hermann Axen, East German party secretary and Politburo member, had conferred in Moscow with CPSU secretaries Chernenko and Ponomarev concerning cooperation on Karl Marx anniversary celebrations (ADN, East Berlin, 14 February; *FBIS*, 16 February).

At the ceremonies in March on the centennial of Marx's death, the CPSU delegation was headed by Vadim A. Medvedev, director of the CPSU Central Committee Academy of Social Sciences (Moscow domestic service, 9 March; *FBIS*, 10 March). Medvedev also participated in a mass meeting at Trier, Marx's birthplace, which was attended by "prominent progressive figures" from West and East Germany, the USSR, France, and Salvador (Tass, 13 March; *FBIS*, 23 March).

The regular meeting of bloc party ideological secretaries was held in Moscow in March. The session was addressed by CPSU secretary Mikhail Zimianin and by Kurt Hager (East Germany), Marian Orzechowski (Poland), and Vu Quang (Vietnam) (Tass, 15 March; *FBIS*, 16 March). The bloc secretaries met with Andropov (Moscow domestic service, 15 March; *FBIS*, 16 March). As expected, a major feature of the conference was discussion of NATO's missile deployment plans (*Pravda*, 16 March).

Apparently eager to stabilize relations with the post-Tito leadership of Yugoslavia, the Soviets dispatched Prime Minister Tikhonov to Belgrade for a major official visit in March. Although Tikhonov was given a friendly reception, Yugoslav president Petar Stambolić pointedly observed that Soviet-Yugoslav relations "are based on the principles of equal rights and friendship" (ibid., 26 March).

A Czechoslovak party delegation was welcomed in February for the regular Prague Days in Moscow festival, presided over as usual by Moscow party first secretary Viktor V. Grishin. The Czechoslovak delegation was headed by Antonín Kapek, first secretary of the Prague party committee (Radio Moscow, 7 February; *FBIS*, 9 February). A CPSU delegation headed by A. N. Kashtanov, deputy head of the Central Committee's Agriculture and Food and Industry Section, visited Czechoslovakia in June to study the Czechoslovak party's "experience in the implementation of its agrarian policy" (*Pravda*, 12 June). In July, Gústav Husák arrived in the USSR for a "rest" at the invitation of the CPSU (Tass, 15 July; *FBIS*, 18 July), but little attention was accorded the visit by Soviet media.

In contrast to the almost unnoticed arrival of Husák, Hungarian party leader János Kádár's visit a few days later was accompanied by loud drumbeats of Soviet publicity, evidently reflecting Andropov's long-standing special connection with the Hungarian party. Kádár was greeted at the airport by Politburo members Gromyko, Aliev, and Gorbachev, and by Central Committee secretary for bloc affairs Konstantin V. Rusakov (Tass, 18 July; *FBIS*, 18 July). Kádár conferred with top CPSU officials and visited the Ukraine. Concurrent with the Kádár visit, intergovernmental talks were held in Moscow between delegations led by Hungarian premier György Lázár and Soviet first deputy premier Aliev (MTI, Budapest, 19 July; *FBIS*, 20 July). At a press conference prior to his departure, Kádár described his talks with Andropov and other Soviet officials as "exceptionally cordial" (*Pravda*, 23 July).

In accord with the new leadership's low-key approach to the situation in Poland, less attention was devoted to interparty relations than in the past. Moscow played up the thirty-eighth anniversary of the Polish-Soviet friendship treaty, claiming that Poles were "widely celebrating" it (ibid., 20 April; *FBIS*, 22 April); at the same time, a delegation of the Polish-Soviet Friendship Society was received in Moscow (*Krasnaya zvezda*, 21 April; *FBIS*, 22 April). In the same month, a delegation headed by Marian Wozniak, Warsaw city first secretary and Politburo member, met in Moscow with officials of that city's party organization (Moscow domestic service, 9 April; *FBIS*, 11 April).

CPSU relations with the Bulgarian party continued to be exceptionally close. Culture Minister and candidate Politburo member Piotr N. Demichev was welcomed to Sofia in May for talks with Bulgarian leader Todor Zhivkov (*Pravda*, 26 May).

The CPSU made notable efforts to cement relations with those parties in Western Europe that have been closest to Moscow in recent years. French Communist Party leader Georges Marchais visited Moscow in July, heading a delegation that included Politburo member Maxime Gremetz and Central Committee members Jean-François Gau and Jean-François Meyer (Tass, 13 July; *FBIS*, 14 July). A lower-level French delegation, composed of Central Committee members and secretaries of party organs, visited Uzbekistan in the same month (Tashkent international service, 25 July; *FBIS*, 1 August).

Portuguese party leader Alvaro Cunhal has been the staunchest defender of "proletarian internationalism" among the Latin parties. In June, he reaffirmed his strong commitment to that principle and to the general goals of Soviet foreign policy when he met with a visiting CPSU delegation (Tass, 23 June; *FBIS*, 27 June). The CPSU delegation was headed by Eduard A. Shevardnadze, first secretary of the Georgian party and candidate member of the Politburo, and included Aleksandr A. Khomyakov, first secretary of Tambov *obkom*, and Y. V. Zhilin, a consultant to the Central Committee's International Department (*Pravda*, 27 June).

The small Austrian party has been noted for its slavish devotion to Moscow's interests, and CPSU leaders have in return frequently bestowed on it signs of attention surpassing those accorded larger nonruling parties. This pattern was maintained during the summer when Austrian party leader Franz Muhri and Central Committee secretary and Politburo member Erwin Scharf journeyed to Moscow for a much publicized meeting with International Department head Boris N. Ponomarev and his deputy Vadim V. Zagladin. As expected, the Austrian communists issued a vigorous denunciation of NATO plans for missile deployment in Western Europe (Tass, 1 August; *FBIS*, 2 August).

Soviet media coverage of the Sixteenth Congress of the Italian Communist Party in March was sparse, reflecting continuing strains between that party and the CPSU. The CPSU delegation was headed by Viktor G. Afanasyev, editor in chief of *Pravda* (Tass, 2 March; *FBIS*, 7 March). A brief television report on the congress stressed that Italian leader Enrico Berlinguer had stressed "the Soviet peace initiatives directed at reducing the military threat in Western Europe" (Moscow domestic television service, 6 March; *FBIS*, 7 March).

The Twenty-seventh Congress of the Communist Party of Denmark in May supported Soviet positions on questions of armaments. The CPSU delegation to the Congress was led by Latvian party first secretary Avgust E. Voss (Tass, 13 May; *FBIS*, 16 May). Danish Politburo member and Central Committee secretary Poul Emanuel led a delegation that visited the USSR in June and

July and toured industrial and other installations in Uzbekistan (*Pravda*, 6 July).

Richard I. Kosolapov, editor of *Kommunist*, headed the CPSU delegation to the Twelfth Congress of the Swiss Labor Party in May (ibid., 26 May).

A delegation of the Progressive Party of the Working People of Cyprus, led by General Secretary Ezekias Papaioannou, visited Moscow in July and was welcomed by Andropov, Ponomarev, and Zagladin. The delegation joined the CPSU officials in condemning the NATO missile deployment and calling for an end to the arms race (Tass, 30 July; *FBIS*, 2 August).

The CPSU was quite active during the year in contacts with African parties, particular attention being directed toward Ethiopia, an apparently wavering Soviet ally. Gosplan head and Central Committee member Nikolai K. Baibakov visited Ethiopia in March for conversations with Mengistu Haile Mariam and inspection of projects being built with Soviet technical help (Tass, 12 March; *FBIS*, 14 March). Aleksandr V. Vlasov, first secretary of Chechen-Ingush *obkom*, led a CPSU delegation on a "working visit" to Ethiopia in the same month (Tass, 17 March; *FBIS*, 24 March). The Commission to Organize the Party of the Working People of Ethiopia (COPWE) sent delegations to the USSR in March and April. One, led by COPWE Executive Council member Berhanu Bayhi, conferred with Ponomarev and studied CPSU party work (*Pravda*, 23 March). The other COPWE delegation, headed by Lemma Gutema, first secretary of the Addis Ababa Workers' Party, visited Azerbaijan (Baku domestic service, 21 April; *FBIS*, 27 April).

Yuri N. Balandin, first secretary of Kostroma *obkom*, headed a delegation that visited Zambia in March at the invitation of the United National Independence Party's Central Committee (*Pravda*, 17 March).

Samora Moises Machel, party chairman and president of the People's Republic of Mozambique, visited Moscow in March and was greeted by Gromyko, Chernenko, Kuznetsov, and Ponomarev (Tass, 1 March; *FBIS*, 1 March). The CPSU was represented at the Mozambican party's Fourth Congress by a delegation under the leadership of Piotr N. Demichev, minister of culture and candidate Politburo member (*Pravda*, 24 and 27 April).

A delegation of the Revolutionary Party of Tanzania, headed by Politburo member P.

Sozigva, visited the USSR 13–20 February at the invitation of the CPSU Central Committee (ibid., 23 February).

The Congolese Labor Party hosted a group of CPSU party workers led by *Agitator* editor Mikhail Gabdulin that visited the People's Republic of the Congo for discussions concerning agitation and propaganda (ibid., 6 March).

Angolan party head and president José Eduardo dos Santos visited Moscow in May (see above).

Aleksei V. Romanev, chief editor of *Sovetskaya kultura*, headed the CPSU delegation at the third Congress of the Moroccan Party of Progress and Socialism (ibid., 23 March).

Karen N. Brutents, deputy head of the Central Committee International Department, led a CPSU delegation on a visit to Beirut, where talks were held with officials of the Lebanese Communist Party on the Near Eastern situation and questions of interparty ties (ibid., 3 February). There was an exchange of visits between the CPSU and the Yemen Socialist Party (YSP). A CPSU delegation, led by Aleksandr S. Dzasokhov, first deputy chairman of the Committee for Solidarity with Asian and African Peoples, visited in January (Aden radio, 25 January; *FBIS*, 26 January). A YSP delegation returned the visit in July, studying CPSU cadre work and touring the Tatar Autonomous Republic (*Pravda*, 2 July).

Rubén Darío Sousa, general secretary of the People's Party of Panama (PPP), visited Latvia in January and conferred with Latvian first secretary Avgust E. Voss and officials of the CPSU International Department on party organizational matters and international problems (Riga domestic service, 3 January; *FBIS*, 24 January).

Armando Hart, Cuban Politburo member and minister of culture, led a delegation that visited Moscow in March for talks with Chernenko and other CPSU officials (*Pravda*, 12 March). Ivan V. Arkhipov, first deputy premier and CPSU Central Committee member, led the Soviet delegation at the thirteenth session of the Cuban-Soviet Commission on Economic and Scientific-Technical Cooperation (Tass, 15 March). Cuban vice-president and Politburo member Carlos Rafael Rodríguez was honored on his seventieth birthday with the presentation of the USSR's Order of the October Revolution (*Pravda*, 8 July).

A group of ideological workers of the Argentine party visited the USSR in June. The Argentine communists had meetings with officials of the CPSU Propaganda and International departments and toured industrial and agricultural establishments in Bratsk and Irkutsk (ibid., 3 July).

Grenadian prime minister and leader of the New Jewel Movement Maurice Bishop paid his last visit to Moscow in April, on the way back from a trip to North Korea (ibid., 16 April), in the wake of President Reagan's charges about the Soviet-Cuban military presence in Grenada (see above).

Biographies. *Grigori Vasilevich Romanov.* Born 7 February 1923, at Zikhnovo, Novgorod *oblast*, Grigori Romanov is the son of a peasant. Following three years in a technical school, Romanov served in the Soviet Army, 1941–1945, and was admitted to the CPSU in 1944.

A 1953 graduate of the Leningrad Shipbuilding Institute, Romanov served as a designer at the A. A. Zhdanov ship construction complex until co-opted for party work in the mid-1950s. Thereafter, he rose steadily through the Leningrad party ranks: secretary of the Kirov *raion* party committee, 1957–1961; secretary of Leningrad city party committee, 1961–1962; secretary of Leningrad *oblast* party committee, 1962–1963; second secretary, 1963–1970.

When Vasili Tolstikov was deposed as Leningrad *obkom* first secretary in 1970, Romanov was chosen to succeed him. During his thirteen years as head of the party in Leningrad, Romanov gained a reputation as an able administrator of industry and a vigorous opponent of dissent. In 1973, he was elected a candidate member and, in 1976, after the Twenty-fifth CPSU Congress, a full member of the Politburo. In June 1983, he was transferred to Moscow as a secretary of the CPSU Central Committee.

Romanov was given responsibility for defense industries and other aspects of the economy. He has taken a prominent role in foreign affairs, attending Soviet bloc economic meetings and party conventions.

Romanov has been awarded numerous decorations, including three Orders of Lenin and the Order of the October Revolution. (Sources: Boris Lewytzkyi and Juliusz Stroynowski, eds., *Who's Who in the Socialist Countries*, Munich, 1978; *Pravda*, 17 June; *NYT*, 17 June.)

Egor Kuzmich Ligachev. Born in 1920, a Russian, Egor Ligachev became a member of the CPSU in 1944. Trained as an aircraft engineer, he graduated from the Moscow Aviation Institute in 1943 and from the Party Higher School of the CPSU Central Committee in 1951. After several years of work in industry and the Komsomol, Ligachev was assigned to full-time party organizational work in 1949, subsequently rising to the position of secretary of the Novosibirsk *oblast* party committee. In 1961, he was transferred to the RSFSR office of the CPSU Central Committee, serving first as deputy head of the Department of Agitation and Propaganda, then as deputy head (for industry) of the Department of Party Organs.

Selected as first secretary of the Tomsk *oblast* party committee in 1965, Ligachev gained a reputation as a hard-driving foe of corruption and inefficiency, attracting the favorable attention of Yuri Andropov. In the summer of 1983, Andropov installed Ligachev as head of the Cadres Department of the CPSU Central Committee. At the December 1983 plenum, Ligachev was named a secretary of the CPSU Central Committee.

Ligachev was elected a candidate member of the CPSU Central Committee in 1966 and a full member in 1976. A deputy of the USSR Supreme Soviet for more than twenty years, Ligachev has served on several standing commissions of the country's nominal parliament. (Sources: Boris Lewytzkyi and Juliusz Stroynowski, eds., *Who's Who in the Socialist Countries*, Munich, 1978; *Pravda*, 27 December; *NYT*, 27 December; *Radio Liberty Research*, 9 September.)

Mikhail Sergeevich Solomentsev. Born 7 November 1913, a Russian, Mikhail Solomentsev is from a peasant background. Trained as an engineer, he graduated from the Leningrad Polytechnic Institute in 1940 and was admitted to membership in the CPSU in the same year. Solomentsev worked as an engineer in Lipetsk and Cheliabinsk up to 1954, when he was co-opted for full-time party work. He served as secretary, then as second secretary, of the Cheliabinsk *oblast* party committee and in 1957 became chairman of the Cheliabinsk economic council.

Assigned to Kazakhstan as first secretary of the Karaganda *oblast* party committee in 1959, Solomentsev became deeply involved in the factional conflict between the adherents of Leonid Brezhnev and those of party secretary Frol Kozlov. In a shake-up of Kazakhstan's political leadership engineered by Kozlov in 1962, Solomentsev was promoted to second secretary of the republic's party organization and Brezhnev's close associate Dinmukhamed Kunaev was demoted from party first secretary to the republic's premiership. In December 1964, following Brezhnev's election as CPSU first secretary, Solomentsev was ousted from his post and Kunaev was restored to his former position. At that time, Solomentsev was assigned as party first secretary in Rostov *oblast*, a region long dominated by party secretary Mikhail Suslov.

Evidently sponsored by Suslov, Solomentsev was brought to Moscow in 1966 as head of the Heavy Industry Department and secretary of the CPSU Central Committee. In July 1971, Solomentsev was named chairman of the Council of Ministers of the RSFSR, succeeding Gennadi Voronov, and in November 1971 was elected a candidate member of the CPSU Politburo.

Promotion to full Politburo membership was precluded by the continuing hostility of the dominant Brezhnev group in the party, but Solomentsev reportedly established close working relationships with Yuri Andropov and with two of Andropov's associates, party secretary Mikhail Gorbachev and Vitali Vorotnikov (who served as Solomentsev's deputy, 1975–1979). These relationships paid off in June 1983, when Solomentsev was named head of the CPSU Party Control Committee. However, Solomentsev was again denied promotion to full Politburo membership, apparently because of opposition from the Brezhnevites, especially Kunaev. Six months later, at the December Central Committee plenum, he was finally elected to full Politburo membership, a clear signal of the dominance of Andropov and his close associates.

Solomentsev has been a member of the CPSU Central Committee since 1961 and a deputy of the USSR Supreme Soviet since 1958. He holds the following decorations: two Orders of Lenin, the Order of the Red Banner of Labor, and Hero of Socialist Labor. (Sources: Boris Lewytzkyi and Juliusz Stroynowski, eds., *Who's Who in the Socialist Countries*, Munich, 1978; *Pravda*, 17 June, 27 December; *NYT*, 17 June, 27 December.)

Vitali Ivanovich Vorotnikov. Born in 1926, a Russian, Vitali Vorotnikov became a member of the CPSU in 1947. He was trained as an aircraft engineer, graduating from the Kuibyshev Aviation Institute in 1954, and he worked in an aircraft factory in Kuibyshev, 1942–1944 and 1947–1960, rising to the post of the plant's chief controller. Co-opted into party work, he was named a secretary of the Kuibyshev *oblast* party committee in 1961 and its second secretary in 1963.

Vorotnikov served as chairman of the Kuibyshev *oblast* Soviet executive committee from 1967 to 1971, when he assumed the first secretaryship of the Voronezh party *obkom*. From 1975 to 1979, he held the post of first deputy chairman of the RSFSR Council of Ministers. From November 1976, he was also chairman of the USSR-Angolan Friendship Society, a position that led to his 1979 appointment as ambassador to Cuba.

Recalled from Cuba in July 1982, Vorotnikov was named party first secretary of the corruption-riddled Krasnodar *krai*, replacing the dismissed first secretary, Sergei Medunov, an associate of Brezhnev's. Working closely with the police, Vorotnikov initiated a vigorous drive against corruption in Krasnodar *krai* and was rewarded with election as a candidate member of the CPSU Politburo at the June 1983 Central Committee plenum. Following the plenum, Vorotnikov was named chairman of the Council of Ministers of the RSFSR, succeeding Mikhail Solomentsev, newly appointed head of the Party Control Committee.

After only six months as a candidate, Vorotnikov was elevated to full membership on the Politburo at the December 1983 Central Committee plenum. His return from Cuba in 1982 and his subsequent meteoric rise have been attributed to his close relationship with Andropov, who reportedly salvaged Vorotnikov's career after he had fallen into disfavor with Brezhnev in the late 1970s.

Vorotnikov has been decorated with the Order of the October Revolution (Sources: Boris Lewytzkyi and Juliusz Stroynowski, eds., *Who's Who in the Socialist Countries*, Munich, 1978; *Radio Liberty Research Bulletin*, 30 May 1982; *NYT*, 17 June; *Pravda*, 17 June; *Izvestiia*, 25 June.)

R. Judson Mitchell
University of New Orleans

Yugoslavia

Population. 22.6 million (mid-1983)

Party. League of Communists of Yugoslavia (Savez komunista Jugoslavije; LCY). As the only political party in the Socialist Federative Republic of Yugoslavia (SFRY), the LCY exercises power through its leading role in the Socialist Alliance of the Working People of Yugoslavia (Socijalistički savez radnog naroda Jugoslavije; SAWPY), a front organization that includes all mass political organizations as well as individuals representing various social groups.

Founded. 1920

Membership. 2.2 million (mid-1983); workers, 30.6 percent

President of Presidium. Dragoslav Marković (elected on 30 June for a 1-year term)

Secretary of Presidium. Nikola Stojanović (serving the second half of his 2-year term)

Presidium. 23 members, 3 from each republic, 2 from each of the 2 autonomous provinces, and 1 from the army. Slovenia, Mitja Ribičič, Milan Kučan, Andrej Marinc; Croatia, Jure Bilić, Dušan Dragosavac, Josip Vrhovec; Bosnia-Hercegovina, Nikola Stojanović, Franjo Herljević, Hamdija Pozderac; Montenegro, Veljko Milatović, Miljan Radović, Dobroslav Ćulafić; Serbia, Dragoslav Marković, Dobrivoje Vidić, Dušan Čkrebić; Macedonia, Dimče Belovski, Kiro Hadži-Vasilev, Krste Markovski; Kosovo, Ali Šukrija, Ilijaz Kurteši; Vojvodina, Petar Matić, Slavko Veselinov; Army, Dane Ćuić

Central Committee. 165 members

Status. Ruling party

Last Congress. Twelfth, 26–29 June 1982, in Belgrade; next congress scheduled for 1986

Auxiliary Organizations. Confederation of Trade Unions of Yugoslavia (5.5 million members claimed in 1981), League of Socialist Youth of Yugoslavia (3.8 million members claimed in 1981)

Main State Organs. The president and vice-president of the 8-member State Presidency serve 1-year terms, and the positions rotate among members. The current president is Mika Špiljak (Croatia) who assumed this duty on 16 May; the vice-president is Vidoje Žarković (Montenegro). Other members are Sergej Kraigher (Slovenia), Cvijetin Mijatović (Bosnia-Hercegovina), Lazar Koliševski (Macedonia), Petar Stambolić (Serbia), Radovan Vlajković (Vojvodina), and Fadil Hodža (Kosovo). The main administrative organ is the 29-member Federal Executive Council (FEC), theoretically chosen by and responsible to the Yugoslav Federal Assembly. FEC members serve 4-year terms. Major figures include Milka Planinc (premier); Zvone Dragan, Borislav Srebrić, Mijat Šuković (vice-premiers); the most important among the 14 federal secretaries are Lazar Mojsov (foreign affairs), Branko Mamula (defense), Stane Dolanc (internal affairs); 11 members of the FEC are ministers without portfolio.

Parliament and Elections. All candidates to the 220-seat Federal Chamber and the 88-seat Chamber of Republics and Provinces run on the ticket of SAWPY. All delegates are chosen indirectly through a multilayer process. The people vote freely for delegates only at the local level. At the provincial/republic and federal levels, voters merely confirm delegates nominated by the LCY. The last elections took place in 1982.

Publications. The main publications of the LCY are *Komunist* (weekly) and *Socijalizam* (monthly).

The major daily newspapers are *Borba* (organ of SAWPY, with Belgrade and Zagreb editions), *Politika* (Belgrade), *Vjesnik* (Zagreb), *Delo* (Ljubljana), *Oslobodjenje* (Sarajevo), *Nova Makedonija* (Skoplje). The most important weeklies are NIN (*Nedeljne informativne novine*, Belgrade), *Ekonomska politika* (Belgrade), and *Danas* (Today, Zagreb). Tanjug is the official news agency.

Due to circumstances beyond our control, there is no profile on Yugoslavia this year. The Yugoslav profile in the next edition of the *Yearbook* will cover calendar years 1983 and 1984.

Council for Mutual Economic Assistance

Despite a number of optimistic statements issued by leaders of the Council for Mutual Economic Assistance (CMEA) during 1983, the outlook for the economies of the member-states remained rather bleak. Most of the economic reforms in the individual states and measures taken for more effective cooperation within the organization failed to tackle fundamental flaws. Basic structural problems stayed unresolved. Economic recovery was spotty, with Romania and Poland still in desperate straits. There was an improvement in the balance of trade with the West, but this resulted to a large extent from the inability of the CMEA states to pay for more goods and services in hard currency and from the somewhat diminished willingness of the Western states to grant additional credits. There was, however, additionally, a recognition on the part of the CMEA states that Western goods and technology had not been integrated very effectively into their economies and that, moreover, these had increased their vulnerability. There continued to be significant disagreements among the member-states, and the postponement of an economic summit and of the thirty-seventh session of the CMEA Council was an indication of the problems among the members. Nevertheless, the Soviet Union continued to press for greater integration and for

"deeper qualitative" cooperation. Greater socialist integration, which differs in fundamental ways from Western integration (the early emphasis on bilateralism being but one characteristic of the former), was hardly welcomed by all the member-states, but the advantage continued to shift toward Moscow. The external trade of the member-states was also directed more and more toward the CMEA. Thus, despite many difficulties, Moscow's leverage over the other CMEA states grew considerably.

Background and Functions. Established in 1949, the CMEA comprises the Soviet Union, Bulgaria, Czechoslovakia, East Germany, Hungary, Poland, Romania, and the non-European states of Cuba, Mongolia, and Vietnam. Structurally, the CMEA rejects the notion of supranationality and appears to conform to the oft-declared principles of national sovereignty and equality of member-states. Unlike the European Community, it does not have an international legal personality. The powers of the CMEA Council, the chief decisionmaking forum, are strictly circumscribed, even though it is composed of the prime ministers of member-states. Its recommendations take effect only if member-governments adopt them. The unanimous vote provision incorporated into the charter continues to determine voting practice. Officially, the Executive Committee, which meets between the sessions of the Council, is the next most important organ. A Secretariat is located in Moscow. Several minor committees, commissions, and joint research institutes were created in the 1960s and 1970s. These included such entities as the Permanent Committee on Foreign Currency and Financial Matters, the Standing Commission on Cooperation in the Sphere of Standardization, the Standing Commission on the Chemical Industry, the Permanent Commission for Engineering, and the Council for Environmental Protection. In 1971, three major committees were created: the Committee for Planning and Cooperation, the Committee for Scientific and Technical Cooperation, and the Committee for Materials and Technical Supply. These committees were given the right to "influence" the work of other CMEA organs and to assign certain priorities. Nevertheless, in comparison with the European Community, the CMEA still suffers from institutional underdevelopment.

Despite the principle of equality, the CMEA was and remains a Soviet-controlled organization. Since World War II, Moscow has sought to impose general conformity in domestic and foreign policies in Eastern Europe. Initially, the motivation was largely political, and Western-style economic integration would not have been compatible with the Soviet and East Central European system of "command economies" revolving around a central plan. Genuine socialist economic integration would involve the creation of a single command economy encompassing all member-states.

Moscow has, however, made significant progress in achieving its goal of greater control over the bloc states and over the newer members outside of Europe. In 1962, it managed to push through the adoption of the "international socialist division of labor," which called for the coordination of member-states' economies and an acceleration of specialization. This attempt failed in large part because of the determined opposition of Romania (with tacit support from some of the other states). Two CMEA banks were also created: in 1964 the International Bank of Economic Cooperation, with the "convertible ruble" as its base currency, and in 1970 the International Investment Bank, as a projected multilateral clearing house. Neither was especially suc-

cessful, and the ruble continues to have only very limited convertibility. A number of multilateral projects were undertaken, including joint pipelines and joint investment in iron ore extraction. The most significant step toward integration, however, was undertaken in 1971 when the twenty-fifth CMEA Council session adopted the "comprehensive program for economic integration." This program was amplified in 1975 when the twenty-ninth Council session approved a five-year plan for further multilateral economic integration. It envisioned ten large projects, nine of which provided for closer links between the Soviet Union and the bloc states, costing 9 billion transfer rubles (U.S. $12.2 billion) (*Times*, London, 3 January 1976). In 1976, the thirtieth Council session envisioned further coordination and integration. This process has continued. The aim has been to set a "complex target program" for coordinating long-term planning to 1990, involving five "target groups": fuel and energy; machine building; agriculture and food supply; consumer goods; and transport (*RFE-RL Research*, no. 147, 16 June 1980). To achieve this goal, Soviet premier Aleksei Kosygin urged members at the thirty-second Council meeting (1978) to move decisively toward the overall integration of their individual economies (*Scînteia*, Bucharest, 28 June 1978). In 1979, at the thirty-third session, he stressed the need for joint efforts in the energy field (see *YICA*, 1980, p. 108).

More than a decade after the CMEA adopted the "comprehensive program," economic integration, defined as the free flow of commodities and harmonization of policies and the creation of a single effective market with unified prices, has been limited. Socialist integration continues to differ from that of market economies, but it is also subjected to both centrifugal and centripetal forces, both regional and global. A political commitment to socialist integration is vital, especially in the case of the preponderant power and moving force within the grouping. Shortly before his death, Brezhnev noted that "socialist economic integration has become an integral feature of the life of our community, a powerful and stable factor in the all-around progress of the fraternal countries" (*Pravda*, 15 October 1982). He had also singled out two economic tasks that should be tackled more vigorously both domestically and by the CMEA organs: the acceleration of scientific and technical progress and the organization of direct ties between sectors and enterprises (*Izvestiia*, 13 June 1982). The Andropov regime continued to recognize the broad significance of integration. At a meeting of the Political Consultative Committee of the Warsaw Treaty Organization in January, integration within the CMEA was one of the important matters under discussion (*Ekonomicheskaia gazeta*, Moscow, no. 10, p. 19). In June, Yuri Andropov declared that Moscow's aim was to reach a "qualitatively new level" of integration within the CMEA and that such integration must be "increasingly deep, comprehensive, and effective" in order to ensure a strengthening of the economies of the member-states (*Politika*, Belgrade, 21 June; *FBIS*, 23 June).

Despite these repeatedly expressed Soviet desires for greater integration within the CMEA and the possibility of enhanced leverage to achieve some of these goals, integrative progress has been hampered by economic and political difficulties. The long-awaited economic summit of the CMEA heads of parties did not take place, and the Council session that traditionally convenes in late spring or early summer did not take place until the fall, when the heads of government met in East Berlin. Nevertheless, there was a flurry of meetings throughout the year of the various lesser organs of the CMEA, which created at least the impression of momentum but at the same time revealed some of the continuing difficulties. The most significant of these were the sessions of the CMEA Executive Committee, which at least officially, is the most important body to convene between Council sessions. Still, the other gatherings also serve as useful indicators of internal CMEA developments. The meetings of the Council for Environmental Protection, or the Commission on Cooperation in the Sphere of Standardization, or of the Standing Commission for Cooperation in the Chemical Industry as well as those of the various research institutes and organizations such as the CMEA International Institute of Economic Problems of the World Socialist System demonstrate that, at the official level at least, the scope of the activities of the organization was extensive indeed.

Throughout these meetings the emphasis was on greater cooperation. The CMEA Planning Committee session in East Berlin in February stressed the need to ensure the growth of socialist economic integration and the consequent necessity to enhance the role of the committee itself (East Berlin domestic service, 24 February; *FBIS*, 24 February). At the twenty-eighth meeting of the CMEA Committee for Scientific and Technical Cooperation, held in Havana in March, the themes of the previous year's council session of helping Cuba and of improving scientific and technological cooperation in the use of industrial robots and microprocessor technology and in the economical and rational use of fuel energy and raw materials were reiterated. Nevertheless, one could also detect at these meetings some of the divergent views of the member-states as well as some of the basic difficulties and concerns of the organization. Romania, for example, emphasized its concern with cooperation in the supply of energy and downplayed socialist integration. Gheorghe Oprea, Romanian first deputy prime minister, expressed his country's eagerness to participate in the building of nuclear power stations, but as far as overall cooperation was concerned, he declared that such collaboration "should start from the technico-material base created in each of the countries," in keeping with Romania's basic foreign policy orientation (Agerpress, Bucharest, 5 April).

The four sessions of the Executive Committee seemingly dealt largely with issues carried over from the previous year, in the usual quasi-bureaucratic manner. The meetings held at the deputy premier level took up the five major long-term CMEA programs, but the nuances again provide some clue to the difficulties faced by the member-states. The 105th session, held in Moscow 18–20 January, gave particular emphasis to the issue of planning, especially in the matter of shared production of machinery and in the joint improvement in the conception of advanced manufacturing methods (*Pravda*, 22 January). These developments were viewed by Moscow, as well as by other states such as Poland, as evidence of the growing influence of the CMEA (de facto Moscow) on the process of the international division of labor (*Zycie Warszawy*, Warsaw, 24 January; *FBIS*, 1 February). But the concerns of the other states to secure supplies of energy and raw materials were also expressed in a resolution that was aimed at further pooling efforts in order to satisfy more fully member-states' long-term requirements for these resources. Still, calls for cooperation in transportation, for the further development of unified power grids, for greater integration in such chosen industries as electronic products and computers, and for an improvement of ports and airports conveyed further Soviet integrative goals, even though substantive progress in some of these areas may have been rather limited.

At the 106th Executive Committee session, held 28–30 June in Moscow, more work was done on the thirty-sixth CMEA Council's decision (in 1982) on a program for coordinating the member-countries' plans for 1986–1990. That this meeting concerned itself largely with a study of "generalities" is in itself illustrative of some of the intrinsic problems. The program is to provide organizational and methodological backup for the planned coordination. It is made up of three parts: the first sets out basic organizational and methodological provisions; the second provides a procedure and time scales; and the third lists the priorities of multilaterally coordinated planning. This is a greater departure, at least in intention, from the traditional bilateralism between the Soviet Union and the individual member-states, and if implemented, it would achieve greater multilateral integration. Soviet economist V. Kuznetsov wrote recently that the cooperation program "made the conversion of all of the fraternal countries' national planning and planned coordination into a single and interlinked process" (*Ekonomicheskaia gazeta*, no. 32, August, p. 20). But the reiteration of certain national goals of cooperation also showed some of the input of the non-Soviet states. Particular attention was to be paid to the areas of cooperation in the development and production of oil and raw materials as well as that of the production of manufactured goods.

It appears that at the 107th meeting of the Executive Committee, the non-Soviet member-states continued to press for greater cooperation in the energy and raw material fields to ensure their security of supply (PAP, 6 September; *FBIS*, 8 September). But particular attention was paid not merely to production but to possible means of reducing consumption of energy and raw materials. The session also discussed on- and off-shore exploration for fuel, including the agreement under which Petrobaltic was set up by Poland, the GDR, and the USSR. And lastly, the meeting examined the agricultural and food program, which was of particular concern for Poland (*Trybuna Ludu*, Warsaw, 7 September; *FBIS*, 13 September).

The 108th Executive Committee session was held in the latter part of October; its somewhat more nominal function was to devise the best means to implement the directives adopted by the thirty-seventh Council session. And it was this delayed Council session that was expected by some to deal more forcefully with the pressing problems faced by the member-states.

The Thirty–seventh CMEA Council Session. In lieu of the CMEA summit of party leaders that failed to materialize during the year, the Council session, attended by the heads of the member-states' governments was the most important meeting of the organization during the year. The session covered economic and politico-military concerns and chose a new secretary general for the CMEA. It appeared to be an opportunity to introduce substantive remedies or reforms. Certainly the need for such changes was evident throughout the year, and there were many signals regarding key concerns within the organization. In the spring, rumors emanating from Prague predicted a revision of the structure of the economic mechanism of mutual cooperation and a debate on the coordination of economic plans up to the year 1990 (Tanjug, Belgrade, 19 May; *FBIS*, 20 May). It was also thought possible that some steps would be taken toward the establishment of a "new economic order" within the CMEA that would give greater consideration to national interests (Tanjug, 12 April; *FBIS*, 13 April). Still, such changes, which may well have been overstated by rumors coming from Eastern Europe, would have been more likely to be introduced at a summit of the party leaders rather than one of heads of governments. But the Council session, as the only organization-wide summit, albeit of heads of government, could have substituted on several of the issues.

It was apparent at the meetings of the various CMEA suborgans that there was considerable dissatisfaction among the member-states with intra-CMEA cooperation. The supply and price of raw materials, particularly energy resources from the Soviet Union, remained an important concern. Product quality and the exchange of technologically advanced goods created additional controversy. Restrictions on credits and on high technology from the West and, perhaps more important, the threat of such restrictions were another important preoccupation of the member-states, particularly the Soviet Union. Therefore, several key issues seemed to have been mapped out for the Council session, which was held in East Berlin 18–20 October. In addition to the CMEA member-countries, Yugoslavia and Nicaragua sent delegations under agreements with the organization, and Angola, Afghanistan, South Yemen, Laos, Mozambique, and Ethiopia took part in the session as invited observers. Some important disagreements quickly became apparent in the speeches of the various leaders. Nikolai Tikhonov, chairman of the Soviet Council of Ministers, voiced optimism that the discussions would lead "to an increase in the effectiveness of the cooperation among the fraternal states and will make it possible to raise our economic integration to a qualitatively new level and to fashion it more deeply, more comprehensively and more effectively, and will ensure a reliable strengthening of the economies of the countries" (ADN, 19 October; *FBIS*, 20 October). His response to the threat of various Western economic sanctions was to push for greater "self-sufficiency" and "self-reliance" within the CMEA. Though he expressed some satisfaction with what he called the deepening of socialist integration, which found expression in joint efforts to solve such major economic problems as the supply of raw materials and of technologically advanced equipment, he also declared that this was not nearly enough (*Pravda*, 19 October). In his view, the community possessed everything it needed to ensure technical and economic invulnerability through collective efforts and that therefore it was very important that the coordination of state plans continued and grew. He contended that the USSR intended to coordinate its state plan with those of other countries in close association with the main directions of the Soviet Union's socioeconomic development for the long term. What was important was not only increasing volume but also securing "profound qualitative improvements of our cooperation." Urgent measures should be taken, according to Tikhonov, to improve the quality of products and goods subject to reciprocal deliveries. He added that it was very important that the countries' obligations stemming from the agreements reached should be fulfilled on schedule and in full. The member-states, in his view, should quickly undertake more "mutual obligations" and participate in the joint production of equipment, both for the extraction of raw materials and for conservation. (Ibid., 20 October.)

Some of these concerns had been echoed by the other participating members as well. Many of the other leaders also complained that agreements were not being fulfilled on schedule or in full. Czech prime minister Lubomír Štrougal supported Tikhonov, complaining that agreements were being signed but not implemented. He also advocated deepening the integration processes. (*Rudé právo*, Prague, 19 October; *FBIS*, 25 October.) But perhaps among the more striking aspects of Tikhonov's message were his bravado regarding CMEA "self-sufficiency" and his ominous warning to the other members regarding Soviet supplies of energy and raw materials. He declared that the Soviet ability to supply raw materials "largely depends on the extent to which the other CMEA countries are able to supply products which the USSR's national economy needs" (*Pravda*, 20 October). Thus self-sufficiency would tie the other states more closely to Moscow, and the Kremlin clearly could and very likely would use the supply of energy and raw materials as leverage, at least in order to achieve certain economic goals.

Considerable dissatisfaction with such an approach was expressed by the Romanian and the Hungarian heads of government. Romania's Constantin Dascalescu criticized cooperation within the CMEA both in general and in specific terms. He argued that had a summit on economic questions been held prior to the Council session a whole series of deficiencies in the activities of the various bodies of the organization could have been eliminated (Agerpress, 19 October). Therefore, the Romanian Communist Party insisted on calling such a summit at the earliest possible time. Furthermore, he declared that Romania considered that "the primordial problem of the present and of the more distant future is the nonsatisfaction of the CMEA member-countries' basic requirements for fuel, energy and raw materials, on the basis of national norms in levels of consumption per inhabitant, which should not differ much from one country to another." This statement in essence covered two areas of frequent criticism of the CMEA and Moscow by the Romanians. Bucharest has long contended that the gap in the development of the various states should be eliminated and that Romania, as one of the least developed states, should be helped in closing such a lag. Second, for a number of years Romania has been trying to purchase Soviet oil on a barter basis or through the use of "soft" currency. The Soviet Union has been willing to sell Romania only small quantities of oil and this for hard currency only. Dascalescu also asked for greater collaboration in helping the member-states improve the supply of foodstuffs, and he argued for an easing of the burden on some states of participation in a series of technical-scientific collaboration agreements. (Ibid.)

György Lázár, the Hungarian head of government, expressed concern with the weaknesses in the CMEA community (*Népszabadság*, Budapest, 19 October). For several years, in fact, Budapest has been advocating deep reforms within CMEA operations that would necessitate commensurate domestic changes in all the member-countries. Although Moscow has been monitoring Hungarian reforms with a somewhat benign interest, it is highly unlikely that such changes would be acceptable either at home or in the other East European states. Furthermore, some Hungarian proposals such as that to permit enterprises in all CMEA countries to trade with each other directly and independently (*Danas*, Zagreb, 17 May; *RFE Research*, 24 May, p. 2) would also be unacceptable. Lázár moreover differed with the Soviet Union on the need for CMEA "self-sufficiency." After reviewing the poor prospects for the Hungarian economy during the current year, he contended that Budapest viewed it as necessary to strive for an expansion of its trade with the developing countries and the advanced capitalist countries and not just with the socialist bloc. (Ibid.)

In view of these difficulties and disagreements, one might have expected a communiqué of some substance. What was issued, however, was a bland document, not so much a consensus at a lower level, as a sort of "holding operation" until the CMEA summit meeting of party heads. The communiqué (*Pravda*, 21 October), touted certain achievements and promised continuity with previous plans. Ambivalence and vagueness characterized much of the document. It urged greater self-reliance through a "deepening of mutually advantageous economic cooperation within the CMEA framework." At the same time, it expressed the member-countries' commitment to normal international political and economic relations with the Western states. The communiqué announced that the session had approved comprehensive measures for cooperation in the development of the branches of the agro-industrial complexes to improve the supply of foodstuffs (as a supplement to the long-term specific-purpose program of cooperation in agriculture and the food industry adopted earlier),

measures that should provide economic incentives to agricultural production. Consequent increases in mutual deliveries of foodstuffs were to be coordinated only among "interested" members. This seems more of the traditional bilateral rather than the multilateral approach that a qualitatively higher level of integration envisions. Still plans called for greater cooperation in agricultural production and for reciprocal deliveries of vegetables and fruits and the development of industrial fish breeding and the utilization of gene pools.

According to the communiqué, measures were outlined for further concentration of efforts on the solution of priority scientific and technical problems, but the nature of the agreements or the date that they would be put into effect was not clarified. Mention was made in this area of joint work on advanced equipment, including semiconductors as well as instruments and equipment to help in resource and energy conservation. Energy conservation, instead of an increase in the supply of these resources as some of the East European states had thought, was one of the chief points in the communiqué. Efforts would be made to cooperate in the "economical and rational utilization of fuel, power, and raw material resources, including secondary resources," and in the production of equipment for such conservation as well as in the exchange of information for the speedy implementation throughout the organization of new measures. These measures were to be carried out in the next few years in the subsequent five-year plan, but the communiqué also stipulated that a cooperative program in this field for the period up to the year 2000 would be worked out by the CMEA agencies. As a further palliative, the Council session instructed the CMEA's agencies to ensure the implementation of two measures for cooperation in the field of resource conservation and in the improvement of the supply of food to the population of the member-states during the coordination of the national economic plans for 1986–1990. This went hand in hand with a call for further widening and deepening of "equally and mutually advantageous cooperation within the CMEA framework." (Ibid.)

During the session, the member-states delved more deeply into politico-military matters and issued a joint statement on the threat of the deployment of U.S. missiles in Western Europe (ibid., 21 October). The statement accused the

United States and its allies of trying to achieve military superiority and concluded that the deployment of medium-range missiles would have dire consequences, the first of which would be an aggravation of the extant economic difficulties. The statement also supported the Soviet proposals at Geneva and called on the United States and its NATO allies to postpone the deployment beyond their announced deadlines, should no agreement be reached. No new threats of countermeasures were made, thus ensuring a certain degree of moderation, but it is noteworthy that Romania, which had earlier called for the elimination of all missiles (as part of a general nuclear disarmament in Europe), was among the signatories. And finally, the Council session relieved the secretary of the Council, N. V. Faddeyev, of his duties "at his request in connection with his retirement on pension" and appointed a 50-year-old Soviet specialist in the field of energy, Vyacheslav Sychev, to the post. Overall then, the session made only limited progress in dealing with the problems of economic growth, of intra-bloc trade, of the supply of energy and other raw materials, and of Western indebtedness and trade.

Economic Growth and Systemic Problems. Socialist hopes of surpassing the advanced Western nations have long given way to a struggle to prevent the existing gap from widening further. Moreover, the socialist states have come to recognize that they are not completely immune to major fluctuations in the Western economies. The impact of economic developments in the advanced industrialized states of the West on the CMEA states is often indirect, and there is but an awkward and sporadic correlation. Therefore the economic recovery in the West led by the United States is hardly likely to have a locomotive effect on the economies of the CMEA member-countries. Nevertheless, there have been some improvements in the CMEA. An increase in the overall output of the CMEA, however, is probably dependent on the performance of the Soviet economy, which contributes 80 percent of the total. Consequently Soviet assertions that gross industrial output in the organization increased by 4.3 percent in the first half of the year (*Izvestiia*, 20 October) point first of all to some recovery in the economy of the largest CMEA component, the Soviet Union.

It had been Yuri Andropov's declared goal since assuming the leadership of the Soviet party to improve the economic performance of the Soviet Union. A confidential Kremlin report leaked in August contained devastating criticisms of the Soviet economy (*Times*, London, 6 August). As a former head of the KGB, Andropov was undoubtedly well aware of the true state of the Soviet economy from the "hard" statistics that were made available to him. Both in speeches at public appearances and through letters and pronouncements after he secluded himself in August with a "cold," he waged an intensive campaign for improving economic efficiency. In the process of consolidating his power, he also cracked the whip at the endemic corruption within the Soviet system (ibid., 29 and 30 August). But the problems of the Soviet economy cannot be resolved through some fine-tuning or even a large-scale anticorruption program. Among suggestions made by Soviet economists has been an increase in the range of planning. Vasily Ivanchenko, head of the Institute of Economics at the Soviet Academy of Sciences, writing in *Voprosi ekonomiki* reported on the extensive work of Soviet experts to formulate a long-term economic development program from 1986 to the year 2000 (*Globe and Mail*, Toronto, 10 May). It would set general guidelines that would partly indicate the way the five-year plans are to be formulated rather than replace them. These guidelines would take into account more precise demographic trends, for instance, but according to Ivanchenko, this would not necessarily mean any reforms or the relaxation of planning methods.

Despite the lack of fundamental reforms, there has been some improvement in comparison with the dismal Soviet economic performance of 1982. Soviet statistics show that industrial production grew at a rate of 4.1 percent during the first eleven months of this year, a rate higher than the growth target (ibid., 24 December) yet somewhat lower than the industrial growth rate of 4.4 percent in the first four months (*Pravda*, 13 May). This suggests that even this modest growth rate was slowing during the year and that very likely it was not sustainable in the long run. A study by U.S. economists Paul Marrese and Jan Vanous shows that Soviet national income is likely to grow annually by only 2 percent—at the most 3 percent—during the rest of the 1980s (*Soviet Economy in the 1980s*, Washington,

D.C.: Joint Economic Committee). And Soviet national income grew at a slower rate than industrial production although favorable weather conditions have helped Soviet agricultural output and there has been an increase in natural gas production (*Globe and Mail*, 24 December). These modest Soviet improvements could help in the economic recovery of the other CMEA member-states, but they may also entail new Soviet demands and pressures.

Economic growth in the other CMEA member-states varied considerably. In the two worst-affected states, Poland and Romania, there was limited improvement. Production increased in both states but at a slow rate. In Poland gains in coal production were accompanied by very steep rises in the costs of extraction. In Romania the national income was to rise by 5 percent, and Bucharest planned increases of 7 percent for 1984 (ibid., 7 January 1984). It is doubtful that either of the projected figures would be reached, and shortages of a wide variety of consumer goods persisted in both Poland and Romania throughout the year. In Hungary, in many ways the socialist bloc's most successful economy, the government freely admitted that it was unlikely that the year's modest plans would be met (*Népszabadság*, 19 October). Among the difficulties cited by the Hungarian government was the failure to restructure industry sufficiently to offset difficulties caused by market factors. The national product had been slated to grow only between 0.5 and 1 percent with but a slight improvement to 1.5–2.0 percent in 1984 (*Globe and Mail*, 31 December). The Czechoslovak economy, however, performed even more poorly. In the first half of the year, the growth rate was practically zero. Even the planned industrial growth of 2.4 percent for the year, given the inflation rate of 4–5 percent, would likely lead to no real growth in that area as well (ibid., 17 December). Consequently, Czechoslovakia's substantial industrial base continued to suffer, and its competitiveness in innovation continued to fall behind international standards. The Cuban economy also merely plodded along, suffering both from shortfalls in the sugar harvests and low sugar prices on the international market. The German Democratic Republic (GDR), though, fared better than most of the other CMEA states, and it projected one of the highest economic growth rates for 1984—4.4 percent (ibid.). The East Berlin government, however, may have benefited from the largesse of Bonn in extending more credit. For instance, on 30 June, West Germany agreed to guarantee a credit of $379 million to the GDR "as an act of good faith" (*Times*, London, 30 June).

Such growth rates could hardly have been encouraging. The systemic problems of central planning can only be resolved through fundamental reforms that appear to be politically unacceptable. Among the CMEA states, economic growth continues to be extensive instead of intensive—industry tends to be overcapitalized, and there is generally lack of competition and of flexibility in the wage and price systems, coupled with risk avoidance. Not only are CMEA members finding it increasingly difficult to generate the type of high-technology industry that has been the locomotive driving the economies of the advanced industrialized Western states, but they have also demonstrated a tendency to make poor use of high technology imported from the West. The excessively long lead times and escalating investment costs are all very damaging. No transfer of technology whether from the West or among the member-states of the CMEA can be employed effectively if it takes on average seven to eight years to complete a project. And even Hungary's New Economic Mechanism is not nearly efficient enough. Moscow's solution, besides various attempts at fine-tuning, appears to be directed towards increasing trade and integration among the CMEA states and building greater self-reliance and self-sufficiency.

Trade. The exchange of goods and services among the CMEA states grew at a significantly higher rate than trade with the rest of the world throughout the year. This is a part of a general trend in the organization during the 1980s. For instance, in the case of the GDR its volume of trade with the CMEA increased from R. 16.1 billion (transfer rubles) in 1980 to R. 19.5 billion in 1982 (*Neues Deutschland*, East Berlin, 20 October; *FBIS*, 24 October). Moscow projected a significant increase in trade with its CMEA partners for the year as well, with the GDR taking up R. 13 billion, Czechoslovakia R. 10.8 billion, Bulgaria R. 10 billion, Poland R. 9.8 billion (counting Soviet credits to balance discrepancies in reciprocal deliveries), and Hungary R. 8 billion (*Izvestiia*, 15 February). Trade with Cuba increased as well, and Havana is to supply the CMEA states with 2 million tons of tropical fruit by 1990 compared with the current rate of 200,000 tons (East Berlin domestic service, 28 August; *FBIS*, 30 August). Exchanges have also increased sharply with Yugoslavia, and trade is to be expanded significantly with Nicaragua, according to an agreement signed in September.

These increases in trade were in part responsible for a growing surplus for Moscow in its exchanges with its socialist partners. Another, and perhaps even more important, element was the rise in the price of Soviet oil and gas during the year. According to the German Institute of Economic Research, the Soviet Union's cumulative trade surplus with the other six East European CMEA states rose to R. 13 billion ($17.5 billion) for the first nine months, an amount that is double the trade surplus for all of 1980 and one that exceeds the USSR's surplus for all of 1982 by R. 2 billion (*Globe and Mail*, 31 December). The increasing reorientation of trade inward among the CMEA states and the further strengthening of the already preponderant economic position of the Soviet Union within the organization as evidenced by these surpluses, some of which the Kremlin views as credits, may be perceived perhaps as progress along the road of integration mapped out by the Soviet Union.

But one should be rather cautious, for trade flows in the CMEA are a function of the central plan, and they tend to operate as limited catalysts for integration. Socialist integration as opposed to absorption or annexation is more difficult without the employment of market forces, according to many Western analysts. The Soviet leaders, however, have claimed that planned economies have the advantage because they are able to determine the main directions of economic development and plan strategies for many years ahead (*Berliner Zeitung*, East Berlin, 6 October). In practice, though, they have recognized the need to employ a multiplicity of methods and tools to achieve their notion of integration. Soviet academician Oleg T. Bogomolov, director of the Economics of the World Socialist System Institute of the Soviet Academy of Sciences, stressed the need for the extension of economic integration in the 1980s and 1990s through greater international specialization and cooperation in the production of finished products, components, and parts and by supplementing the coordination of the CMEA countries' five-year national economic plans "with coordination of their economic policy as a whole" (*Argumenty i fakty*, Moscow,

no. 4, January, p. 326). He also envisioned a greater role for the transfer ruble. Moreover, the influential Soviet economist told the Hungarians, for example, that "integration of the socialist countries imparts increasing scope for the economies of individual countries and leads their inner development to new dimensions" (*Népszabadság*, 16 April). But what Bogomolov has been saying is in line with what Andropov and other Soviet leaders have called for—a "qualitatively new level" of integration (*Politika*, Belgrade, 21 June; *FBIS*, 23 June). The Soviet leader declared that integration must be "increasingly deep, comprehensive, and effective" in order to strengthen the economies of the member-states. In practice, this has meant a quest for greater multilateral and bilateral cooperation and enhanced plan coordination. But it also hints at the readjustment of prices in intra-CMEA trade in such a way that Moscow could end what it sees as heavy subsidies to its socialist partners.

The political dangers in such "economic" developments have worried East European states, and Romania has been at the forefront in expressing its unease. Bucharest takes every opportunity to reject the possibility of supranationality in the CMEA. Writing in the Romanian Communist Party's theoretical journal *Era Socialista* (no. 23, 1982, pp. 21–24), Prof. Mihai Paraluta declared that the CMEA is not and cannot be allowed to contain any element of supranational leadership and that the current system of planned regulation of economic relations among countries could only "assume the form of coordination." He added that "joint planning" cannot be employed in the sense of a uniform plan and does not require that an international body should assume any of the prerogatives of the socialist state. It is not a dependent form of economic cooperation but rather constitutes a component of the mechanism of planning cooperation. The national planning bodies of each member-state, in his opinion, are alone responsible for organizing the planned cooperation at the bilateral and at the multilateral level.

In spite of such dissent, Moscow has pushed forward with its plans for integration (which lately have also been increasingly concerned with an improvement in the provision of foodstuffs). An entire range of integration measures has been introduced and reintroduced in the area of high technology, particularly robotics and microprocessors, and in a myriad of large and small industrial and resource extraction projects (*YICA*, 1983, p. 383). Yet Moscow has also taken a fairly sophisticated approach to coping with dissension and with the systemic difficulties of multilaterality. Even though a great many multilateral projects have been undertaken since the long-term cooperation program began, numerically the 120 multilateral agreements have been far outnumbered by the thousand or so bilateral agreements (Radio Moscow, 15 July; *FBIS*, 19 July). The greater manageability of bilateral agreements is evidenced in Moscow's relations with the GDR. The latter is assuming an increasingly larger role in the modernization of the Soviet Union's underdeveloped agriculture and food-processing industry and is to help further improve overall Soviet consumer goods production (*Globe and Mail*, 24 December). Moscow has also found it useful to operate multilateral agreements at the subgroup level. For instance, during the thirty-seventh Council session, a multilateral agreement was signed on organizing cooperation in the construction of the Krivoi Rog Mining and Concentrating Combine in the Soviet Union, which would process inferior iron ore (*Pravda*, 21 October). But only Hungary, the GDR, and Czechoslovakia (countries very anxious to receive the iron ore) would participate with the Soviet Union. And Moscow is also aware of the potential for leverage at its disposal through supplying energy and raw materials to these states at what it regards as subsidized rates.

Energy. Even though mutual trade turnover over the past few years has grown much more rapidly than the CMEA trade with external partners (in 1982, for instance, intra-CMEA trade growth was twice that of external exchanges; ibid., 19 October), the supply of energy resources from the Soviet Union to the East European states did not keep pace with demand. There is a widespread assumption among many observers both inside and outside the CMEA that over the past decade the Soviet Union has been subsidizing its partners through the supply of oil and raw materials. And such a subsidy, particularly in the case of energy resources, would function as a key variable in the integration of the socialist bloc. The extent of the subsidy is much more difficult to gauge. According to one study, Soviet subsidies to the East European and other CMEA member-states in the form of lower than world prices for energy and materials have to be bal-anced in any accounting process by the facts that Moscow has retarded technical change and its actions have been detrimental to the growth of production and income levels among its partners (Philip Hanson, "Soviet Trade in Eastern Europe," in K. Dawisha and P. Hanson, eds., *Soviet–East European Dilemmas*, London: Royal Institute of International Affairs, 1981). Officials at the U.S. Treasury and State departments, however, have estimated on the basis of available data that the Soviet foreign and raw material subsidy to Eastern Europe reached $22 billion by 1980 (*Economist*, London, 22 May 1982). A recent U.S. report also put the 1981 subsidy at $22 billion as the peak year (Marrese and Vanous, *Soviet Economy*). But the Soviets' perception of these subsidies is perhaps just as important as the actual figures, which might be difficult to ascertain. And Moscow has been freely citing the figures provided by the *Economist* as evidence of its largesse towards its socialist allies (Tass, Moscow, 13 May; *FBIS*, 16 May). The East European states have expressed their unhappiness that in the past few years, as the price of oil has fallen on the world market, the Soviet operation of the five-year sliding scale system of pricing has been working against their interests. Nevertheless, they are still very anxious to receive those supplies. Yet, should world oil prices fall further under the current scheme, Soviet oil could be more expensive for its partners than OPEC's base price. This would cause additional damage to the economies of the East European states. However, with the exception of Romania, these states still pay the USSR in rubles. From their point of view, this is still very much preferable to purchasing oil on the world market for difficult-to-obtain hard currency.

Moscow has found that its costs of extracting oil and of locating new sources have been increasing sharply. Even though the CIA may have underestimated Soviet energy resources, Soviet management suffers from such inbred deficiencies that these would largely nullify the benefits of the potential additional resources (*YICA*, 1983, p. 384). Soviet oil output for the year was targeted to increase by less than 1 percent (to 619 million metric tons). Although throughout most of the year the projected base was maintained, in October *Pravda* admitted that the oil industry had failed to reach its output quotas (*Globe and Mail*, 16 November). Soviet oil sales to CMEA partners are also complicated by Moscow's heavy dependence on its oil sales to the noncommunist world for hard-currency earnings; such sales represent well over half of its hard-currency trade earnings. Consequently Moscow has been cutting back on its supplies of oil to the East European states, with the exception of Poland, and has been pressing for new conservation measures throughout the organization. Yet despite diminishing supplies, as long as East European states can buy Soviet oil for rubles, preferably at below world market prices, they will still eagerly seek that commodity.

In contrast to difficulties in the oil industry, natural gas production increased substantially, to 487 billion cubic meters (by 7 percent) in the first eleven months (ibid., 24 December). In the first three years of the current five-year plan, the Soviet Union committed itself to deliver 92 billion cubic meters of gas to Eastern Europe (*Pravda*, 19 October); Moscow should have no difficulty in fulfilling that goal. Natural gas has become a key energy component for several East European states, particularly Hungary (*YICA*, 1983, p. 385).

Nuclear energy is still popular in the CMEA states, and it remains a variable in the process of energy-stimulated integration. Both bilateral and multilateral cooperation has been intensive in the area (ibid.). Capacity has increased from 9 million kilowatts in 1977 to 22 million kilowatts; another 23 million kilowatts are at the stage of coordination planning and construction outside the USSR (*Pravda*, 13 June). A bloc-wide electrical grid has been developed in order to improve cooperation in energy production and sharing. The network is already extensive and continues to be upgraded. *Pravda* (19 October) reported that in the first three years of the current five-year plan, the Soviet Union supplied the other CMEA states with 53 billion kilowatt-hours of electricity.

Moscow has expressed repeatedly its unhappiness with its subsidized energy and raw material sales to Eastern Europe and put its case rather bluntly during the thirty-seventh Council session. It has contended that a higher level of integration would have to mean some readjustment in prices, and Tikhonov declared that East European states will need to contribute more to integration if they are to secure continuing supplies. According to some observers, as Moscow's terms of trade with Eastern Europe improve, the value of its subsidies will decline from the peak of

1981 and are likely to fall to $17 billion by 1985 (Marrese and Vanous, *Soviet Economy*). But this seems to be a slow process. The leverage that is derived from the supply of energy and raw materials and from subsidies is likely to remain in the Soviet armory for a considerable time yet.

Western Indebtedness and Trade. Major efforts were undertaken by the CMEA states to lower or at least stabilize external debt not only out of a desire to move toward a more autarkic development in line with Soviet integration plans but also because hard-currency indebtedness has had some significantly undesirable effects on their development. The level of dependence and the burden of loan repayment varies considerably among these states. Those states where a large portion of the hard-currency debt is made up of official credits are better off since such credits are generally given for use over a longer period of time and have lower, fixed interest rates. Much of the Soviet Union's debt is made up of such official credits. On the other hand, commercial loans have floating interest rates and shorter repayment periods, thereby increasing the vulnerability of the borrower. Poland is an extreme example of the latter case; about 75 percent of its loans originate from commercial lenders (*RFE Research*, 19 August, p. 223). There is also a difference in the debt liquidation rate (that is, the percentage of foreign exchange receipts from exports annually going to pay back principle and interest in foreign currency) among the various CMEA states. These range from 18 percent for the Soviet Union to 92 percent for Poland (*Deutsche Verkehrs-Zeitung*, Hamburg, 2 October 1982). The efforts of the CMEA states, together with somewhat greater reluctance on the part of the Western nations and banks to grant additional credits, seem to be taking effect, and the size of the overall debt may be declining. According to some projections, the decline in external debt for the East European states themselves could be substantial (ranging from a 15 percent decline for Bulgaria to 43 percent for Romania). These projections of significant declines for the year may be overly optimistic, as several of the CMEA states including Poland, Romania, and Cuba have had to ask for a rescheduling of their debts (*Globe and Mail*, 3 March, 24 December). Several of the states also had to seek additional credits in order to roll over their existing debts and to maintain or increase their exports.

Strenuous efforts to increase exports and limit imports (combined with a diminished availability of Western credits) have enabled the CMEA states to increase their trade surplus with the West. In the first half of the year, the CMEA states, collectively, recorded a surplus of $2.9 billion compared with only $1.2 billion a year earlier (ibid., 26 September). Romania, which cut back its oil imports drastically, managed a hard-currency trade surplus of $1 billion in the first half of the year compared with $1.8 billion for all of 1982 (ibid., 1 October). Poland also managed to achieve a trade surplus of 60 billion zloty through renewed export of raw materials to the West during the first half of the year (*Rzeczpospolita*, Warsaw, 2 August; *RFE Research*, no. 200, 19 August).

The collapse of the Polish economy following massive borrowing in the West and the near bankruptcy of Romania have had a significant impact on the thinking of CMEA leaders. According to Zbigniew Fallenbuchl, the author of a report for the Organization for Economic Cooperation and Development entitled "Technology Transfer: Study of Poland, 1971–80," it is apparent that the hopes for a great leap forward through the infusion of Western technology bought on easy Western credit did not materialize. Central planners can easily throw their economies out of gear, and as Fallenbuchl shows, the rapid increase in imports from the West combined with the very long periods that it took to apply Western technology led to disastrous distortions of the economy. Furthermore the central planning system turned out to be singularly ill-adapted to provide a quick route to exports to hard-currency areas. Furthermore Western technical know-how failed both in Poland and throughout the CMEA states to spark indigenous innovation. And lastly, the purchase of Western investment goods and licenses created a long-term demand for Western materials, components, and spare parts, thereby increasing the dependence of these states on the West. But Western penetrations simply could not be tolerated politically. Small wonder, then, that Moscow, in particular, concluded that trade with the West was risky and greater CMEA self-sufficiency through deeper and qualitatively higher integration was necessary (*Financial Times*, London, 16 December).

Yet self-sufficiency is unlikely to be a solution. First of all, past developments do not give much cause for optimism that the CMEA states will be able to generate the kind of technological innovation that is needed to keep pace with worldwide industrial development. A certain level of trade will have to be maintained as a matter of general economic necessity. The East European states, with much smaller markets than the Soviet Union, have recognized that industrial modernization requires a substantial exchange with Western nations, even though attempts should be made to avoid Poland's mistakes. Hungary is at the forefront both in encouraging trade with the West and in pressing for market-oriented reforms within the CMEA that would facilitate such exchanges. Nevertheless, as noted, the perceptible overall trend in the CMEA seems to be of a redirection inwards.

There has been an increased wariness on the part of Western governments and banks to grant new credit to the socialist states. There has also been a great deal of concern, particularly in the United States, regarding exports of high technology that could be put to military uses. For a number of years, the Western nations have tried to coordinate their policies toward the CMEA, but with little success. Among a variety of considerations has been the unwillingness of Western nations to risk default or a cutoff in trade. To paraphrase Keynes, when debts become large enough, leverage shifts to the debtor. Despite some restrictions on credit and promises to monitor the flow of technology more carefully (*YICA*, 1983, p. 386), most West European nations were reluctant to accept the strong measures proposed by the Reagan administration. At the spring summit of the major industrialized Western states held at Williamsburg in the United States, usually hard-line British prime minister Margaret Thatcher pleaded with the United States to modify its tough proposed East-West trade bill (*Times*, London, 30 May). In July, Franz-Josef Strauss, the staunchly anticommunist Bavarian prime minister, declared that he supported the decision to grant a large amount of hard-currency credit to the GDR (ibid., 13 July). The latter's support indicates some of the political dimensions of Western trade with the CMEA states. For the Germans in particular, trade with the GDR and the granting of credits are part and parcel of maintaining political contacts and of preserving the myth of some future reunification.

Consequently, there have been and there will likely continue to be a great many disagreements between the United States and the West European states (and possibly among the latter) as to what economic measures may be taken against the socialist bloc. Even the current greater West European caution in granting credits to the East is substantially different in certain aspects from U.S. goals, and disputes such as that over the construction of the Siberian natural gas pipeline reveal the magnitude of the difficulty in arriving at any sort of effective joint Western policy.

Some of the CMEA states have been trying to take advantage of the continuing if diminished willingness of Western states to extend credit and to continue large-scale trade in high-technology manufactured goods with the socialist states. Hungary has been at the forefront in letting its larger companies do their own foreign trading as part of its market-oriented reforms. Other CMEA members have followed more reluctantly, but nevertheless several have brought about significant changes in their foreign trade organizations, including Poland, Romania, and Bulgaria. The Soviet Union, the GDR, and Czechoslovakia have been more reluctant in certain ways to allow alterations in the pricing system and greater decentralized decisionmaking. Hungary, Romania, and Poland are members of the International Monetary Fund (IMF), which facilitates securing the necessary development capital but also forces them to assume certain commitments toward the IMF that may be viewed as incompatible with some CMEA rules.

Yet, despite such reforms, the export potential of the smaller CMEA states, and in certain vital areas also that of the Soviet Union, is rather limited. Few of these states are capable of producing manufactured goods of a sufficiently high quality to be acceptable on Western markets. Even Hungary, with all its economic reforms, has had considerable difficulty. Primary products make up 70 percent of CMEA exports to the West, and manufactured goods have declined to less than a third (*Financial Times*, 2 January 1984). Of the primary products, the principal

component has been energy exports from the Soviet Union, and at least the Soviet position should be helped with the completion of the natural gas pipeline to Western Europe. In the case of some of the smaller CMEA states such as Romania, an insistence on "countertrade," which may be divided into the three categories of compensation payback, counterpurchase, and barter, has further inhibited trade. Many Canadian suppliers of nuclear power equipment in the sale of CANDU reactors to Romania have termed their experience in countertrade with Bucharest as a nightmare. There are thus two basically contradictory impulses at work within the CMEA. On the one hand, the member-states, to various degrees, recognize the need for Western credits, technology, and trade, although they want to avoid the mistakes of Poland and Romania. On the other hand, there is Soviet pressure for further integration through both bilateral and multilateral steps as well as the systemic problems within each state and within the CMEA itself that militate for a further turning inward. And the latter forces appear to be very much in ascendancy.

Biography. *Vyacheslav Sychev.* Appointed CMEA secretary general at the thirty-seventh CMEA Council session (October), Sychev was born in December 1933. He is a doctor of technical science and a professor specializing in the field of energy. He studied at the Moscow Energy Institute and worked at scientific research establishments. He has held positions as deputy director of the All-Union Scientific Research Institute of High Temperatures of the Soviet Academy of Sciences and as director of the All-Union Science and Technology Information Center of the Soviet State Committee for Science and Technology. In November 1979, he was appointed deputy chairman of the USSR State Committee for Science and Technology.

Aurel Braun
University of Toronto

Warsaw Treaty Organization

As the controversy raged between East and West over the possible and later the actual deployment of U.S. medium-range missiles on the territory of the West European NATO allies, the Soviet Union both demonstrated the potential for political support of the Warsaw Treaty Organization (WTO) and employed the dispute as an opportunity to press for closer integration within the organization. Through the various phases of reasonableness and crescendos of threats that characterized Soviet statements on the missiles, the WTO provided a chorus of support, with only occasional and limited dissent from Romania. The main thrust of the Soviet/WTO campaign was to try to influence public opinion in the West on the dangers of escalating the nuclear arms race. All potential fissures among the Western allies were explored. In concentrating on West Germany, Moscow gave the German Democratic Republic (GDR) an important role to play in the overall Soviet/WTO propaganda effort. Nor did the Soviet Union neglect the military aspects of the organization. As the predominant force and as the primary provider of external security to the regimes of the member-states, it continued its massive arms buildup. It also supplied both the conventional and nuclear military doctrines that are the de facto basis for WTO "strategy" and pursued the construction of a "greater socialist army." Furthermore, Moscow and the other WTO members also recognized the linkages between economic well-being and military strength and therefore WTO meetings touched on some economic concerns. The political dimensions of the organization, though, tended to play a more visible role than the economic one, in part because of the Western focus on the various negotiating forums in Geneva, Madrid, and Vienna. The Soviet decision to break off or suspend talks in Geneva and Vienna increased Western concern, which was then magnified further by the uncertainty over the Soviet leadership. Moscow's poor handling of the Korean Air Lines disaster and Yuri Andropov's disappearance from public view after August fueled these concerns, even though the Soviet Union went to great lengths to demonstrate the stability and continuity of its leadership.

Established on 14 May 1955, the WTO was Moscow's response to the Western decision to include West Germany in NATO. Moscow declared that the WTO's aim was to prevent the remilitarization of West Germany and to help dismantle NATO. Moscow's offer to disband the WTO if NATO is simultaneously liquidated is reiterated every year. In addition to the multilateral WTO, the Soviet Union created a network of bilateral treaties in Eastern Europe after 1955. However, a multilateral treaty provided Moscow with political, military, and juridical benefits that bilateral treaties might not have. Moreover, in certain limited ways, a multilateral forum is useful for conflict resolution among the member-states and as a safety valve for nationalistic frustrations.

Although the disparities between NATO and the WTO regarding the importance and nature of membership make dissolution of the Western alliance such a prize for Moscow that it would be worth the sacrifice of the WTO, this ultimate and often expressed Soviet goal belies the pact's growing importance. The WTO has become a useful forum for articulating policy agreement and support for Soviet proposals. A multilateral alliance is also an important asset to Moscow in its ideological confrontations with the West and the People's Republic of China. Militarily, a multilateral alliance has enhanced the ability of the Soviet Union to create more effective defensive and offensive forces in Europe. Juridically, the

WTO provided a partial legal justification for the 1968 invasion of Czechoslovakia. It is little wonder that by 1971 Brezhnev declared that the WTO was "the main center for coordinating the fraternal countries' foreign policies."

Nominally, the WTO is an organization of sovereign states (East Germany, Poland, Czechoslovakia, Hungary, Romania, Bulgaria, and the Soviet Union). Its top governing body is the Political Consultative Committee (PCC), composed of the leaders of the communist parties, heads of state, and foreign and defense ministers of the member-states. Day-to-day affairs are handled by the Joint Secretariat, which is chaired by a Soviet official and has a representative from each country. The Permanent Commission (located, as is the Secretariat, in Moscow) makes foreign policy recommendations for the WTO. Supreme military power is supposed to reside in the Committee of Defense Ministers. Created in 1969, it consists of the defense ministers of the six East European states and the Soviet Union. Chaired by the commander in chief of the WTO joint armed forces, it includes, among others, the deputy ministers of defense of the member-states. A second military body, the Joint High Command (JHC), is responsible for strengthening the WTO's defense capabilities, preparing war plans, and deciding the deployment of troops. The Military Council, chaired by the commander in chief of the WTO, advises the JHC on nonoperational matters. The Council includes, in addition to the commander in chief, the chief of staff and permanent military representative from each of the allied armed forces. There is also a Committee on Military Technology. In 1976, a Committee of Foreign Ministers and a Unified Secretariat were added. Both the commander in chief and the chief of staff have always been Soviet generals. Currently, Marshal Viktor G. Kulikov is commander in chief, and Army Gen. Anatoli I. Gribkov is first deputy commander and chief of staff. Air defense, which has a high priority in WTO and Soviet strategic planning, has always been under a Soviet commander. The Soviet Union continues to provide the bulk of WTO air defense, which consists of early radar warning systems, air defense control centers, a manned interceptor force, and surface-to-air missiles and antiaircraft artillery units. These four elements are under the command of Soviet Marshal of Aviation Aleksandr I. Koldunov, who is also a deputy commander in chief of the

WTO. The entire air defense system is integrated with that of the Soviet Union. In addition, there are common fuel pipelines, joint arms and ammunition depots, and continuous joint planning. Militarily, then, the WTO appears to be very much a Soviet creature.

Military Developments. During the 1950s, the WTO was largely dormant as an organization, with the Soviet Union relying on the geographic benefits of the East European states as a potential defensive or offensive glacis. In the early 1960s, however, Moscow decided to increase the military role of the WTO, and in October 1961 the pact held its first joint maneuvers. Greater roles were assigned to the armed forces of the bloc states, although no WTO military doctrine evolved. Soviet military strategy prevailed, and this helped lead to the evolution of a "tier" system in the bloc. Moscow came to refer to the three countries on the axis of the most likely locus of an East-West conflict—the GDR, Poland, and Czechoslovakia—as the "first strategic echelon" of the WTO. This northern tier continues to receive superior armaments from the Soviet Union and holds Moscow's primary strategic attention.

Effective military integration of the WTO forces is a vital component of Soviet strategic doctrine. The northern tier states with their superior military capabilities and more vital strategic location are especially important to Moscow. Soviet strategy calls for rapid movement of large-scale, integrated battlefield forces able to operate both in conventional and nuclear environments. This emphasis on mobility, quick response, and tremendous firepower requires an effective central command and well-equipped and highly trained forces. Greater military integration and massive modernization of equipment play key roles in shifting the battlefield and theater balance in favor of the WTO, which in turn is important for the implementation of Soviet strategic doctrine.

The Soviet forces continued to receive large infusions of modern equipment. The ground forces in Eastern Europe have been provided with T-80 main battle tanks, with new amphibious self-propelled gun/howitzers, new antitank weapons, more large trucks, and an increased number of helicopters, which include the Mi-24 Hind (International Institute for Strategic Studies, *The Military Balance, 1983–84*, London,

1983, p. 12). All these have given Soviet troops greater firepower and mobility. Furthermore, additional ground-support aircraft have been delivered, and airborne command and control continue to be upgraded. East European forces have also received new equipment, although in far more modest quantities. This has included more T-72 tanks, BRDM and BMP armored fighting vehicles, SA-9 surface-to-air missiles for Czechoslovakia, and additional MiG-23 aircraft. Romania continued production of its domestic M-77 tanks and of a small number of IAR-93 fighter/trainer aircraft. (Ibid., pp. 19–24.)

As important as these deliveries of equipment to the Soviet and to the allied member-states' armies were, they may be far outweighed as a trend indicator by the type of reorganization that has been and is likely to take place. For example, the Soviet air force has been reorganized into twenty regional commands and five air armies, and three of these armies have taken over the formal functions of the long-range air force in order to perform a strategic and strategic/tactical role. The Voyska-PVO has not only taken over the role of the air defense forces of the former PVO-Strany and of the army air defense troops, but has also taken over some of the former frontal aviation's interceptor inventory. The air armies and the Voyska-PVO will now be coordinated at the theater headquarters level, and in wartime, air and ground forces and air defense will be integrated at the theater of military operations level, thereby giving these forces new flexibility and a more effective control mechanism. This will not only enhance Soviet fighting capabilities, but since the entire air defense system of the WTO (with the exception of Romania) is controlled by the Soviet Union, this reorganization will provide for even greater military integration. (Ibid., pp. 11–12.) Rumors persist, moreover, that a doctrinal change in Soviet strategy may result in the creation of all-arms mobile forces intended to exploit any weakness in NATO defenses and to penetrate rear areas as deeply and as quickly as possible (ibid.). The establishment of such forces would mean that participating East European troops would have to be upgraded both in training and in equipment and even more completely integrated into the Soviet military machine.

Numerical assessments alone, are an inadequate gauge for comparing the military power of the WTO and NATO. Qualitative changes may be even more important than quantitative ones, and evaluations inevitably contain a large element of subjectivity. Role and mission have to be analyzed together with the numbers and types of weapons or the manpower levels. Nevertheless, there appears to be a consensus among the Western allies that the balance of power in conventional weapons between East and West is steadily, if slowly, shifting in favor of the WTO. The Danish Defense Intelligence Agency has concluded that the WTO armies continued to grow both quantitatively and qualitatively (*Berlingske Tidende*, Copenhagen, 21 May, p. 7; *JPRS*, no. 83840, 7 July). And Michael Heseltine, the British defense secretary, concluded in a White Paper issued in July that "the overall picture remains of an unremitting Soviet buildup both in nuclear and conventional capabilities. This trend has continued for well over a decade, even through those periods which we in the West regarded as the high point of détente." (*Facts on File*, 8 July, p. 510.) The tremendous efforts of the Soviets to develop extremely advanced weapons, either through indigenous innovations or through acquisition of Western high technology, have also meant that the West has largely lost the technological edge that it believed compensated for quantitative inferiority (*Air Force Magazine*, Washington, D.C., December, p. 143).

Yet the situation is not quite as bleak as these developments would tend to suggest. Despite the commonality of equipment that allows for a level of standardization in the WTO that could never be imitated by NATO or the advantages of central coordination of the WTO's logistic system and its superior mobilization rates, there are significant shortcomings. The reliability of East European forces is certainly a cause for concern for the Soviet Union. The Polish crisis has undoubtedly reduced Polish morale, and despite massive efforts on the part of the Soviet Union to ensure the full participation of Polish forces in the WTO and to increase their reliability, the reduction in morale, especially among younger officers, NCOs, and enlisted men diminishes Poland's effectiveness. In the southern tier, Romania has virtually opted out of potential WTO offensive/defensive operations vis-à-vis the West through a reorganization of its forces on the basis of a "people's war" doctrine that is similar to the Yugoslav model of territorial defense. Furthermore, there continues to be resentment throughout Eastern Europe not only against Soviet military-political domination in the WTO but also against Moscow's virtual monopoly of the design and full-scale production of main weapon systems (John Erickson, "Military Management and Modernization Within the Warsaw Pact," in Robert W. Clawson and Lawrence S. Katlan, eds., *The Warsaw Pact*, Wilmington, Del.: Scholarly Resources, 1982, pp. 213–19). Economic problems have also affected the ability of the WTO states to increase spending, and *The Military Balance, 1983–84* (pp. 150–51) suggests that defense spending among the non-Soviet WTO states has been static since 1979, with the overall increase coming largely from greater Soviet expenditures. But, given economic burdens, even the superpowers may have to concentrate on quality instead of quantity. As far as the Soviet Union is concerned, demographic trends may also present problems. Given the low birthrate of the Russian population, it is projected that by the 1990s, about 30 percent of Soviet forces will be drawn from central Asian and Muslim peoples (ibid., p. 146), which would raise further questions of political reliability. And a CIA report, released by the Joint Economic Committee of Congress in November, shows that between 1976 and 1982, due to the sluggish performance of the Soviet economy, Soviet defense expenditures grew at 2 percent per year, a slower rate than earlier assessments (*NYT*, 19 November). Therefore, the Soviet Union and its allies may not have achieved the kind of superiority that would allow them to predict with a high degree of confidence a favorable outcome in a major conflict. The International Institute for Strategic Studies has concluded that there is no mad, out-of-control arms race between the WTO and NATO and that the overall balance of forces continues to be such that military aggression is a highly risky undertaking (*The Military Balance, 1983–84*, pp. 136–37).

Although there is no immediate danger of a Soviet/WTO attack, there is still cause for considerable concern in NATO. The CIA study, for instance, also forecast a 3.5 percent growth in the Soviet economy for 1983; given Andropov's determination to maintain a favorable military balance, Soviet defense spending, by far the largest component of WTO military expenditures, is likely to increase commensurately. The CIA report also stated that despite the slowdown in spending, since 1975 Soviet forces have received about 2,000 land- and sea-based intercontinental missiles, more than 5,000 combat aircraft,

15,000 tanks, and substantial numbers of naval surface vessels and submarines (*NYT*, 19 November). Furthermore, demographic problems should be examined in the light of difficulties facing potential opponents. NATO states will also suffer from a sharp fall in the level of manpower available to the military. By 1999, the number of men between the ages of 17 and 30 will decline in West Germany from 6.5 million to 4.2 million and in Britain from 5.8 million to 4.8 million (*The Military Balance, 1983–84*, pp. 145–49).

Moreover, one should not overlook the Soviet Union's tremendous determination to preserve the efficacy of its military power, the area in which it has been most successful. Moscow's approach is a comprehensive one designed to overcome all key weaknesses at home and throughout the WTO. Shortly before his death, Brezhnev told commanders of Soviet forces that greater emphasis will be placed on raising the combat readiness of the army and navy as well as building and consolidating the material base of the armed forces. Important operational, technical, and organizational measures were being implemented in order to increase the effectiveness of the armed forces, particularly through the use of large-scale military maneuvers. (Tass, 27 October 1982; *Facts on File*, 29 October 1982, pp. 793–94.) Marshal Nikolai V. Ogarkov, chief of staff of the Soviet forces, warned the West in the wake of the June plenary session of the Soviet party that "the armed forces will even more actively master up-to-date combat equipment... and constantly maintain their combat readiness at a high level" (*Izvestiia*, 22 September). The WTO would, of course, participate in this effort to enhance combat effectiveness, and one of the primary means to achieve this would be through the use of large-scale military maneuvers. Army Gen. A. I. Gribkov, the chief of staff of the WTO's Joint Armed Forces, called joint maneuvers the supreme form of the comprehensive training of troops, commanding officers, and of staffs of the WTO. He asserted that during exercises the troops dealt with various questions of efficiency regarding combat deployment, evaluated operations and combat plans, and resolved questions of coordination of various units and subunits of the allied armies. Each exercise, he added, was a new step toward strengthening socialist internationalism. (*Sovetskaia Belorussiia*, Minsk, 14 May; *FBIS*, 27 May.) In the past, the

USSR has also employed "intimidation through maneuver" to convey strong signals to a number of East European states that dissent from Soviet policies might be unacceptable. But this quasi-political function has usually been overshadowed by military-strategic needs. And the evolution of Soviet strategic and tactical doctrines stressing firepower, mobility, and deep-penetration capabilities have made joint maneuvers an ever greater military necessity in the effective integration of WTO forces.

A number of joint maneuvers were held during the year. In January, Hungarian, Soviet, and Czechoslovak troops participated in a large-scale international military exercise, Danube-83, in Hungary. It involved aircraft, helicopters, and tanks, reservists were used in addition to regular troops, and amphibious crossings of the Danube were made (Budapest domestic service, 21 January; *FBIS*, 24 January). The exercise, which was held after the Prague summit of WTO leaders, indicated a determination to maintain the military strength of the organization. The involvement of Soviet and Czechoslovak troops also showed that Hungary, which is nominally in the southern tier, is militarily blending more and more into the northern one. On 15 February, the French news agency Agence France Presse (AFP) reported that WTO winter maneuvers were being carried out in northwest Czechoslovakia close to the East German border with contingents from the home state, the Soviet Union, and Hungary. The exercises were not officially announced, meaning that they probably involved fewer than 25,000 men. In March, another military exercise was conducted by the northern tier forces of Poland, Czechoslovakia, the GDR, and those of the Soviet Union. According to reports, they involved largely fighter aircraft and air defense forces. (*Neues Deutschland*, East Berlin, 24 March; *FBIS*, 30 March.) Polish participation was, of course, essential in order to help demonstrate the stability and reliability of the Jaruzelski regime.

Large-scale exercises were commenced at the end of May and continued into June. Code-named "Soyuz-83," the joint command and staff exercises were held in parts of the GDR, Poland, Czechoslovakia, and the southern part of the Baltic Sea from 30 May to 9 June. The maneuvers were carried out under the command of Marshal Kulikov. The official objective was to "master questions of troop command and interaction of the high commands of the allied armies and navies during the joint operation" (Tass, 10 May; *FBIS*, 11 May). The various communiqués further emphasized the integrative aspect of the maneuvers in "perfecting the interaction between the high staff, and strengthening the combat cooperation of the personnel of the fraternal armies" (Tass, 10 June; *FBIS*, 15 June). Both the GDR and Poland expressed satisfaction with the performance of the troops (ADN, 8 June; *Zolnierz Wolnosci*, Warsaw, 8 June; *FBIS*, 8 and 14 June). Warsaw's satisfaction with the effectiveness of its forces was important in at least maintaining an image of a return to normalcy, but the nature and the location of the maneuvers themselves also indicate continued WTO concentration on the northern tier of the organization. In an interview with a Swedish paper, Romanian leader Nicolae Ceauşescu criticized maneuvers as an activity that increased East-West tension (*Times*, London, 30 June). The compartmentalization of the WTO, however, has usually allowed Moscow to bypass Romanian dissent or to ignore Bucharest's concerns.

Bucharest's "dissenting" views are not new. Romania has differed with Moscow on a number of matters. Ceauşescu has opposed Moscow on the issues of raising Romania's military budget and on a number of occasions has called for withdrawal of Soviet troops from Afghanistan (ibid.). Nevertheless, Romania has remained a member of the WTO and continues to send staff officers (but not combat troops) to some maneuvers. In September, Romania dispatched staff officers (as did the other WTO states) to civil defense exercises in Hungary. These lasted one week and involved, by and large, first-aid procedures for earthquakes, large-scale railway and road accidents, and large fires. (MTI, 25 September; *FBIS*, 25 September.)

It is often difficult to distinguish the military, political, and economic dimensions of WTO activities. Given bloc economic problems and Soviet efforts to try to persuade the Western European states to reject the deployment of the U.S. medium-range missiles, the degree of overlap of these three dimensions has become even greater, with large grey areas and numerous nuances. At times, political and economic goals conflicted, as did genuine Soviet desires to achieve arms control and the temptation to score propaganda points. For some time, the Soviet military has been stressing the increasingly close interrelationship between military matters and the economy (*Krasnaia zvezda*, Moscow, 9 December 1982). And Soviet political leaders have expressed their belief that the WTO's "combat readiness" cannot be maintained or enhanced without close bloc economic integration (Tanjug, 10 May; *FBIS*, 10 May). It is difficult to compartmentalize the functions of the several meetings that the various bodies of the WTO held during the year. The session of the Military Council of the Joint Armed Forces in Bucharest 26–28 April covered both military and political matters. Chaired by Marshal Kulikov, it discussed military issues, but it also dealt with the political dimensions of the decisions made at the earlier Prague meetings of the PCC and of the Committee of Defense Ministers. (Tass, 28 April; *FBIS*, 29 April.) This regular meeting also demonstrated Romania's continued participation in the important forums of the WTO. Another regular meeting of the Military Council was held in the Soviet Union in October. It again dealt with internal military problems and the threat of the deployment of U.S. missiles in Europe.

This political and military duality was also maintained at the meetings of the Committee of WTO Defense Ministers. The first of these took place in Prague on 11 and 12 January. Originally planned for November 1982, it followed the session of the PCC of the previous week. It was supposed to discuss a number of military-defense aspects within the regular activities of the WTO and to examine the stance taken at the PCC meeting, matters that in many ways were largely political (Tanjug, 7 January; *FBIS*, 10 January). All the WTO defense ministers, Marshal Kulikov, and the chief of staff, General Gribkov, attended. On 20 October, as the deployment date for the U.S. missiles neared and as the German Bundestag was gearing up for a final debate on deployment, the WTO convened an "extraordinary" meeting of the Committee of Defense Ministers in East Berlin. It was attended by all the WTO defense ministers, including Col.-Gen. Constantin Olteanu of Romania (Tass, 20 October; *FBIS*, 21 October). The GDR's approach at the session was to combine political and military elements, thereby emphasizing high combat readiness together with a "doctrine of peace" (ADN, 20 October; *FBIS*, 21 October). The communiqué, at the end of the session, was aimed as much at internal as at external audiences. It declared that the WTO countries "have not sought and do not now seek to gain military superiority *but that in no event would they allow anyone to gain military superiority over them*" (emphasis added, *Pravda*, 22 October). A subsequent regular meeting of the Committee of Defense Ministers held in Sofia, Bulgaria, in the first week of December (following Moscow's decision to break off the Intermediate-Range Nuclear Forces [INF] talks in Geneva) discussed both internal problems and external threats. The Bulgarians, in particular, emphasized the need to strengthen the unity and cohesion of the peoples and armies of the WTO member-states (Tass, 7 December; *FBIS*, 7 December).

Sessions of the Committee of Foreign Ministers (CFM) followed a somewhat similar pattern in blending internal issues with external political concerns, but given the nature of the CFM, the political dimensions appeared much larger. At the CFM's regular meeting, held 6–7 April in Prague, the participants were to deal largely with questions connected with the implementation of the proposals and initiatives set forth by the Prague meeting of the PCC (Tass, 6 April; *FBIS*, 7 April). Although some internal military problems were discussed, the emphasis was on formulating a broader political stance against the West. This was combined with overall support for the Soviet position that the West was responsible for renewed tensions. Furthermore, according to the communiqué, the participants repeated calls for the creation of nuclear-free zones in the north of Europe and in the Balkans. (Tass, 7 April; *FBIS*, 8 April.) A nuclear-free Balkan zone has long been a plank of Romanian foreign policy. The next regular meeting of the CFM, on 13 and 14 October in Sofia, produced a relatively moderate communiqué, largely concerned with the deployment of new medium-range nuclear missiles in the NATO states (Tass, 14 October; *FBIS*, 14 October). The communiqué tried to create an impression of Soviet/WTO reasonableness but contained threats that were sufficiently ambiguous that they were likely designed to generate greater Western anxieties rather than to indicate new countermeasures. The document did state, however, that those states that allowed the stationing of the nuclear missiles "would assume grave responsibility before all peoples for the ensuing consequences for peace and tranquility in Europe, as this would precipitate another round of the nuclear arms race on the continent." This meeting was held before NATO was scheduled to begin deploying its new missiles, and the supporting WTO chorus for the Soviet position illustrates some of the broader political uses of the organization.

Political Developments. Not only are the political dimensions difficult to separate from military ones, but the former have been clearly and openly incorporated in the WTO from its very inception, thereby entailing a broad definition of security that involves both external and internal elements. General Sergei Shtemenko, the late WTO chief of staff, contended in an article (published posthumously) that a key function of the alliance was the "suppression of counterrevolution" in Eastern Europe (*Za rubezhom*, Moscow, 7 May 1976). Moscow intervened in Hungary in 1956 and in Czechoslovakia in 1968, and it supported the imposition of martial law in Poland. Brezhnev declared, shortly before his death, that "the WTO has everything necessary to firmly defend our peoples' socialist achievements, and we will do everything in our power so that this may also be true in the future" (*Rabotnichesko delo*, Sofia, 2 October 1982; *FBIS*, 6 October 1982). Soviet defense minister Marshal Dimitri Ustinov assured Poland's General Jaruzelski that Moscow would continue to back him and martial law—"the Polish People's Republic as a member-state of the WTO can be certain of the full support and help of the Soviet Union" (*Krasnaia zvezda*, 12 October 1982). And in various statements that touched on such issues, Yuri Andropov indicated that his attitude did not differ from that of his predecessor.

The concern with the cohesion of the organization was also illustrated by the frequent meetings of Marshal Kulikov with the leaders of the East European states between sessions of the various bodies of the WTO, as well as by the gatherings of the party central committee secretaries or of those of members of the parliaments of the member-states. For instance, in February Kulikov met with Hungarian leader János Kádár in Budapest and with Nicolae Ceauşescu in Bucharest. In September, the Soviet marshal visited Kádár again and saw Gustáv Husák in Prague. This not only added to the frequency of consultation among the member-states but very likely represented continued Soviet efforts to ensure that the East European states stayed in line. In the first part of March, secretaries from the central committees of the communist parties of the WTO states met in Moscow in order to discuss strengthening ideological ties (AFP, 13 March; *FBIS*, 14 March). And on 9–10 November, representatives of the parliaments of the WTO states met in Sofia, where they endorsed the 5 January Prague Declaration and the 28 June joint statement of the WTO states. They also called on parliamentarians of all countries to oppose the deployment of new U.S. missiles in Europe. (*Izvestiia*, 13 December.) Thus, there was an intensive effort throughout the year to maintain the political cohesion of the WTO. But perhaps the clearest indications of some of the political dimensions of the WTO were given at the two summits in January and June and at the various arms control talks between East and West.

The summit meeting of the PCC, held 4–5 January in Prague, set the tone for the organization's political activities vis-à-vis the West, particularly on questions of arms control. This summit, attended by a relatively vigorous looking Andropov, issued a long declaration that incorporated a great many of Moscow's previous statements on international issues together with many "motherhood" statements. In the lengthy joint declaration (*Pravda*, 7 January), the WTO proposed treaties, conventions, and further negotiations, including a treaty on the mutual nonuse of military force and on the maintenance of peace (i.e., an East-West nonaggression pact), an agreement that would not limit the legitimate right of the participants to individual and collective self-defense in accordance with Article 51 of the U.N. Charter. The treaty, according to the WTO, should be complemented by commitments to the security of international communications, by the continuation of talks on reduction of armaments, and by the undertaking of measures to avert a surprise attack. Furthermore, the WTO proposed a mutual quantitative freeze on the strategic arms of the superpowers, followed by a program of stage-by-stage nuclear disarmament. It also proposed an agreement to end the development and production of new systems of nuclear weapons and fissionable materials and the production of delivery systems. The WTO suggested that a treaty should be drawn up as soon as possible on the complete and universal prohibition of nuclear tests and expressed its belief that the best solution would be to rid Europe completely of nuclear weapons. It also reiterated proposals to establish nuclear-free zones in northern Europe and in the Balkans. Furthermore, it called for the drafting of a convention to ban neutron weapons, the elimination of chemical weapons, and the commencement of talks on the prohibition of the deployment of weapons in outer space. The participants also expressed themselves in favor of an agreement on "nonescalating military spending and on a subsequent reduction both in percent and in absolute terms." They also advocated a lowering of the level of conventional armaments and forces. The participants renewed their call for the dissolution of both NATO and the WTO and expressed their support for the Soviet arms control proposals. As part of the political, military, and economic linkages, in the joint declaration the participants also sought more political dialogue and greater business cooperation, all to be combined with the military dimension, which, as noted, would include nonaggression and non–first use of either nuclear or conventional weapons.

There was little of substance, then, that was new in the Prague Declaration. Moreover, the Western states believed that most of its proposals would merely solidify the existing Soviet/WTO military advantages. A freeze on nuclear weapons production and on deployment of new systems would lock in Soviet quantitative superiority and would prevent Western innovation that could provide a qualitative counterbalance. A ban on testing weapons in outer space would also help the Soviet Union since it is widely believed that Moscow conducted extensive antisatellite weapons tests in 1982 (*Times*, London, 27 August). WTO calls for further negotiations on several other issues were viewed as attempts to generate additional pressure on the West, particularly the United States. Consequently, most NATO leaders saw the declaration as the beginning of a vast public relations campaign on the part of the Soviet Union to win support from Western disarmament movements and governments and thereby prevent NATO from going through with plans to deploy the cruise and Pershing-II medium-range missiles. Nevertheless, given the susceptibility of Western publics to calls for peace and especially the tremendous West European concern with an increase in tensions, the NATO governments reacted cautiously and guardedly to the Prague Declaration, rather than rejecting it outright.

A second meeting of all the party leaders of the WTO states, held in Moscow on 28 June, resulted in a relatively mild statement on the organization's political position in general and its stand on the deployment of U.S. missiles in Western Europe in particular. The joint statement reaffirmed the broad program put forth in the Prague Declaration: it called for the implementation, without delay, of a freeze on nuclear arms among all nuclear powers, but most urgently by the USSR and by the United States; it sought pledges on no–first use of nuclear weapons; it called for an agreement to limit military spending at 1 January 1984 levels, which then would function as a ceiling; it asked for an examination of proposals for a treaty on mutual nonuse of military force between the WTO and NATO; and of course, it also urged that an accord be reached between East and West that would preclude the deployment of new U.S. nuclear missiles in Europe. (*Izvestiia*, 29 June.)

There was little likelihood that any of these proposals would be any more acceptable than it had been in the past. A freeze on nuclear weapons was again used as an attempt to safeguard Soviet quantitative superiority and to limit U.S. technical innovation. Limits on spending were important to both superpowers, but given the greater weakness of the Soviet economy and Soviet superiority in several categories of military resources, U.S. policymakers, in particular, viewed this proposal as an attempt to allow the Soviet Union another advantage. Yet, the joint statement was more moderate than expected in light of the threats that Moscow had been making to deter the deployment of the cruise and Pershing-II missiles. One possible explanation was that opposition to a confrontation by some of the East European states, particularly Romania, had induced further moderation in Moscow. It is a somewhat unlikely explanation, though, given Moscow's previous habit of either disregarding Bucharest or of compartmentalizing Romanian challenges. Furthermore, on closer examination, Romania's opposition to increased military spending and to deployment of additional Soviet missiles or even the continued stationing of the SS-20s has not been quite as confrontational as might at first appear. Romania's unwillingness to spend more on its defense does not prevent the Soviet Union or the other WTO members from increasing their expenditures. As far as the missiles are concerned, it should be remembered that when Romania called for a halt to the deployment on the continent of new medium-range nuclear missiles in conjunction with the destruction of the ones in place, it also declared that this should be a prerequisite for the achievement of a "nuclear-free Europe" (*Scînteia*, Bucharest, 11 January). All of these goals together do not differ very much from the Soviet position. The denuclearization of Europe, though, has been unacceptable to NATO. In messages to Andropov, Reagan, and to various European leaders in the fall, Ceauşescu again called for "a stop in the deployment of further medium-range missiles in Europe, for the withdrawal and scrapping of the ones in place, and for the elimination of *any* nuclear weapons from the continent" (emphasis added; Agerpress, 19 October; *FBIS*, 20 October).

As the two WTO summits and the various meetings of WTO organs indicated, the possibility of reaching a meaningful accord at the Madrid follow-up talks of the Conference on Security and Cooperation in Europe (CSCE), the Mutual and Balanced Force Reductions (MBFR) talks in Vienna, the Intermediate-Range Nuclear Forces (INF) talks, and at the Strategic Arms Reduction Talks (START) were rather remote. Yet at Madrid, despite fundamental differences, the parties managed in September to agree on a concluding document that contained gains for the Soviet Union and some compensation for the West. A conference on confidence- and security-building measures and disarmament in Europe, something very much favored by Moscow and its allies, was scheduled for Stockholm for 17 January 1984. On the other hand, the West also received the promise of a conference on human rights to be held in Ottawa on 7 May 1985. At the very least, then, the channels of communication remained open.

At the MBFR talks in Vienna, which have dragged on for more than a decade, the problems of data and verification remained unresolved. Soviet proposals to withdraw 20,000 soliders from Eastern Europe in exchange for U.S. reduction of 13,000 as an "initial practical step" for larger withdrawals (*Globe and Mail*, Toronto, 19 February) did not evoke a positive Western response. The NATO allies (and independent observers) believed that the Soviet Union underestimated WTO troop strength by about 160,000 men and was unwilling to agree to effective verification. In the fall the WTO states appeared willing to make some concessions on verification, but in mid-December the Soviet Union and its allies suspended the talks and refused to fix a

resumption date, ostensibly as a response to NATO's decision to deploy the medium-range missiles. Some U.S. officials consequently concluded that the WTO may have been willing to make some concessions only in the interest of appearing conciliatory before suspending the talks (*WP*, 16 December).

At the INF talks in Geneva, the various Soviet proposals, the last of which was made by Andropov in an interview in *Pravda* on 26 October, were unacceptable to the United States because they would have allowed Moscow to maintain significant numbers of missiles without a Western counterdeployment. According to U.S. statistics, the Soviet Union deployed a total of 360 SS-20s with a total of 1,080 warheads (*NYT*, 19 November), of which 243 missiles and 729 warheads were aimed at Western Europe (*Globe and Mail*, 15 November). The Soviet Union also rejected President Reagan's "zero-option" offer as well as certain variations. On 23 November, after West Germany approved the NATO deployment of missiles and Pershing-II and cruise missiles began to arrive in West Germany and Britain (respectively), Moscow suspended the INF talks. Soviet first deputy foreign minister Georgi Kornienko indicated, in fact, that these talks would not resume when he declared that the INF talks "are now a dead letter" (ibid., 6 December). Some of the announced Soviet countermeasures, though, such as the implacement of SS-21 and SS-22 missiles in Czechoslovakia and the GDR (some were supposed to have been there already) and the possibility of a more forward deployment of the SS-20s may not have much military importance but would still present Moscow with additional opportunities and justifications for a greater integration within the WTO, at least of the northern tier states.

At START, the parallel bilateral negotiations between the superpowers at Geneva, little if any progress was made during the year. Moscow rejected President Reagan's "build-down" plan. Although the START sessions continued after the suspension of the INF talks on 23 November, the Soviet Union was unwilling to merge the two. In December, it suspended these talks as well. Thus, the forthcoming Stockholm Conference on Confidence- and Security-Building Measures and Disarmament in Europe remained the only formal channel of communication on armaments between East and West. The U.S. decision to send Secretary of State George Shultz to these talks is a recognition of the importance of maintaining at least some channels of communication.

Throughout these talks and throughout the various meetings of the Warsaw Pact, particularly in the latter part of the year, one of the key questions on the minds of most observers was the health of Andropov. Every attempt was made in the Soviet Union to give the impression that Andropov could fulfill the essential party and state functions. Great emphasis was laid on continuity in the WTO, and Soviet pressure for a higher

level of integration continued. But nagging doubts persisted. And arms control talks were made even more complicated by the inability of the Soviet leader to participate in an East-West summit, if need be. Small wonder, then, that both inside and outside the WTO there were concerns about the uncertainties of a new succession.

Aurel Braun
University of Toronto

International Communist Organizations

WORLD MARXIST REVIEW

The *World Marxist Review*, as it is entitled in its English-language editions (other-language editions use the title *Problems of Peace and Socialism*), is an international, Soviet-line, ideological monthly. It has been headquartered in Prague since 1958. In a sense, it is the latter-day successor of the Comintern (1919–1938) and the Cominform (1947–1956), the only formal organization under Soviet guidance joining the world communist movement. As of late 1983, 75 national editions were printed in 40 languages and distributed in 145 countries.

Soviet control of the publication appears pervasive. The magazine's chief editor (currently Yuri A. Skhlyarov) has always been a Soviet; so has one of its two executive secretaries (currently Sergei V. Tsukasov). The other executive secretaryship has traditionally been reserved for a Czechoslovak, and the current incumbent (Pavel Auersperg) has been described by an organ of the independent Japan Communist Party as "more Soviet than the Soviets." This same organ described these three officials as "the core of the

Editorial Office" and the magazine's Editorial Board as instrumental in maintaining Soviet control of the operation. This latter statement seems plausible since even the magazine says the board "supervises the work of the editorial staff." On it are represented only fifteen communist parties, ten of which are strongly pro-Soviet (Argentine, Bulgarian, Czechoslovak, East German, Indian, Iraqi, Mongolian, Polish, Soviet, and U.S.), two of which are at least mildly so (French and Hungarian), and only three of which are independent (British, Italian, and Romanian). Also, the only time the magazine could ever have been suspected of deviating from the Soviet line came just after the 1968 Czech invasion when the magazine skipped an issue. This was also the occasion for a change of chief editors. Finally, those communist parties that have run completely afoul of the Soviets either never joined (Yugoslav) or withdrew after relations soured (Albanian and Chinese in 1962). The independent parties associated in the effort apparently do so only because they can choose the articles they publish in their own national edition.

There is evidence of direct Soviet control at

the working (as opposed to policy) level. Each of the 65 representatives on the Editorial Council apparently also sits on one or more geographical or functional commissions of the magazine, which are responsible for overseeing articles and conferences within their sphere of competence. There are ten such commissions: Problems of Socialist Construction (communist-ruled countries), Class Struggle in Capitalist Countries (developed noncommunist countries), National Liberation Struggle in Asian and African Countries, National Liberation Struggle in Latin America and the Caribbean, General Problems of Theory, Exchanges of Experience of Party Work, Problems of Peace and Democratic Movements (international communist front organizations), Problems of Science and Culture, Communist Press Criticism and Bibliography, and Scientific Information and Documents. From the little evidence that can be gleaned from the pages of the magazine, it appears that each commission has a Soviet secretary who doubles as head of a corresponding department composed entirely of Soviets. The assumption is that the departments were set up to control the commissions (and that is why the departments were not mentioned in articles describing the work of the magazine in its August and September 1981 issues).

The sponsoring or cosponsoring of thematic conferences is the other major function of the *Review*'s staff. In view of the failure since 1973 of Soviet efforts to arrange a new world conference of communist parties (due to the objections of independent parties), two of the larger cosponsored meetings (Sofia, December 1978, and East Berlin, October 1980) appeared, because of their scope, to have been intended by the Soviets as substitutes for a world conference. So also did the last of the series of conferences held to discuss the work of the magazine (Prague, November 1981), which was attended by representatives from 81 communist and nine "revolutionary democratic" parties. The leader of the Japanese delegation openly criticized Soviet domination of the magazine and later claimed that in so doing he had been explicitly supported by the British, Italian, Belgian, and Spanish delegations and implicitly supported by the Romanian and Swiss ones. At the time of the publication of the November 1983 edition, however, none of these parties had been deleted from the magazine's masthead (even though the Japan Communist

Party had called for its dissolution). The *Review* remains an important—indeed, the only—permanent institutional symbol of unity for the world's pro-Soviet and independent communist parties. (The above is an updated synopsis of an article entitled "New Head, Old 'Problems of Peace and Socialism,'" prepared by the author for the November–December 1982 issue of *Problems of Communism*, pp. 57–63.)

FRONT ORGANIZATIONS

An attempt is made below to identify the most important policymaking and working-level leaders on front "presidential boards" (an unofficial term, used here to include presidents and vice-presidents) and secretariats, respectively. Included, of course, are Soviet secretaries, generally believed to be resident controllers of their respective organizations (see *YICA*, 1983, p. 394). In their absence, the Soviet vice-presidents apparently perform the same function (see ibid.). In view of the status of the World Peace Council, the largest and most important front and coordinator of the other organizations, those front leaders who sit on the new WPC Presidential Committee, elected in June, are also noted. The relative strength of such representation, together with claimed membership figures and number of national affiliates, provides a rough approximation of each organization's relative importance. The fronts are listed in this presumed order of importance. Also noted as a measure of each organization's acceptance by and degree of involvement in U.N. programs is its consultative status with various specialized U.N. agencies (including the United Nations Education, Scientific and Cultural Organization [UNESCO], Economic and Social Council [ECOSOC], Conference on Trade and Development [UNCTAD], Industrial Development Organization [UNIDO], Children's Fund [UNICEF], Food and Agriculture Organization [FAO], and International Labor Organization [ILO]).

The latest issue of *World Marxist Review* (see above) in which a front leader has an article is also noted, as an indication of the importance of the writer involved. (In almost all cases, that person was the front's speaker before the Second U.N. Special Session on Disarmament in 1982 [ibid., p. 396] and the leader receiving the highest WPC position the following year.) Next, the most recent top meeting of each organization and major conferences during 1983 are shown; the former by and large includes election of officers, and the latter indicates the major propaganda campaigns for the year. Finally, certain related organizations are listed for each major front, with the nature of this relationship briefly described. An asterisk indicates data newly noted in 1983.

Name. World Peace Council (WPC)

Headquarters/Formation. Helsinki/1950

Claimed Strength. Affiliates in 142* countries; total membership unknown

Publications. *New Perspectives* (bimonthly), *Peace Courier* (monthly), *Disarmament Forum* (monthly)

Status with U.N. UNESCO (A), ECOSOC (Roster), UNCTAD

Presidential Board. President: (also de facto secretary general) Romesh Chandra (India); 39 vice-presidents: Severo Aguirre de Castro (Cuba), *Olga Aviles López (Nicaragua), Richard Adriamanjato (Madagascar), *Eduardo Arévalo Burgos (Colombia), *Ali Ba Dhib (South Yemen), Mohammed J. Bajbouj (Syria), Vital Balla (Congo), Freda Brown (Women's International Democratic Federation), *Martha Buschmann (West Germany), Józef Cyrankiewicz (Poland), Camara Damantang (Guinea), Jacques Denis (France), *Günther Drefahl (East Germany), *Luís Echeverria (Mexico), George Georges (Australia), Dawit Giorgis (Ethiopia), Francisco da Costa Gomes (Portugal), *Matti Kekkonen (Finland), James Lamond (U.K.), Pascual Luvualu (Angola), Khalid Muhyi-al-Din (Egypt), *John Hanley Morgan (Canada), *Gus Eugene Newport (U.S.), Alfred Nzo (South Africa), Camilio O. Pérez (Panama), Phan Anh (Vietnam), *E. M. Primakov (USSR), Nadim Abd al-Samad (Lebanon), *Ilona Sebestyén (Hungary), Blagovest Sendov (Bulgaria), Aziz Sharif (Iraq), *Filifing Sissoko (Mali), *T. B. Subasinghe (Sri Lanka), Amerigo Terenzi (Italy), *Mikis Theodorakis (Greece), *Emma Torres (Bolivia), *Tomáš Trávníček (Czechoslovakia), Alfredo Varela (Argentina), *Ibrahim Zakariya (World Federation of Trade Unions)

Secretariat. Executive secretary: *Frank Swift (U.K.); 15 secretaries: *Sana Abu Shakra (Lebanon), Daniel Cirera (France), Nathaniel Hill Arboleda (Panama), Kosta Ivanov (Bulgaria), Károly Lauko (Hungary), Karel Lukaš (Czechoslovakia), *Rolf Lutzkendorf (East Germany), Max Moabi (South Africa), Bahig Nasser (Egypt), *Ryszard Tyrluk (Poland), Arsénio Rodríguez (Cuba), *Carl Rosschou (Denmark), Mamadu Sako (Mali), Tair Tairov (USSR), Karen Talbot (U.S.)

Last WMR Article. December 1981 (Romesh Chandra)

Last Top Meeting. World Peace Council (Prague, June 1983)

Other Major 1983 Conferences. Western WPC affiliates (Moscow, January, anti–deployment of U.S. missiles); WPC vice-presidents (Prague, February, anti–deployment of U.S. missiles); International Forum on Southeast Asia (Phnom Penh, February, support of pro-Soviet Kampuchean regime); International Conference on Human Rights, Disarmament, and the Right to Life (Mexico City, March); International Conference in Solidarity with Front-Line States (Lisbon, March, cosponsored by the Afro-Asian People's Solidarity Organization [AAPSO], support to African National Congress and South-West Africa People's Organization, opposition to apartheid); Conference for Peace and Security in Asia and the Pacific (Ulan Bator, April, anti–nuclear arms race); World Assembly for Peace and Life, Against Nuclear War (Prague, June, anti–deployment of U.S. missiles, universal disarmament); International Conference on Israel–South African Alliance (Vienna, July, cosponsored by AAPSO and other organizations); International Conference for Solidarity with Cyprus (Lisbon, October); First Emergency Meeting for Peace in Central America and the Caribbean (Mexico City, November, support of Grenada and Nicaragua); WPC Presidential Committee Board (anti–deployment of U.S. missiles). The WPC was also a major participant in the Conference on Proposals to Avert the Dangers of War from Europe (Vienna, February) and the Second Vienna Dialogue–International Conference on Disarmament and Détente (November, sponsored by the WPC-related International Liaison Forum of Peace Forces [see below]).

Related Organizations. International Liaison Forum of Peace Forces (though Chandra is also its head, it involves additional and more innocuous organizations pursuing WPC aims); International Institute of Peace (research body left behind in Vienna when WPC moved to Helsinki); International Committee for European Security and Cooperation (pursues WPC aims regionally; Raymond Goor, head, is a WPC observer); Women's International League for Peace and Freedom (its secretary general, Edith Ballantyne, played a leading role in organizing and running the World Assembly for Peace and Life, Against Nuclear War; she is a vice-president of the International Liaison Forum of Peace Forces)

Name. World Federation of Trade Unions (WFTU)
Headquarters/Formation. Prague/1945
Claimed Strength. 90 affiliates in 81 countries; total claimed membership 206 million
Publications. *World Trade Union Movement* (monthly), *Flashes from the Trade Unions* (weekly)
Status with U.N. UNESCO (A), ECOSOC (I), UNCTAD, UNIDO, UNICEF, FAO, ILO
Presidential Board. President: Sándor Gáspár (Hungary); 6 vice-presidents: Indrajit Gupta (India), Elias Habre (Lebanon), Karel Hoffman (Czechoslovakia), Roberto Viega (Cuba), Romain Vilon-Guezo (Benin), Andreas Ziartidhis (Cyprus)
Secretariat. Secretary general: Ibrahim Zakariya (Sudan); 5 secretaries: *Ernesto Araneda Briones (Chile), Boris Averyanov (USSR), Jindrich Kusnierik (Poland), Jan Nemoudry (Czechoslovakia), K. G. Srivastava (India)
Last WMR Article. January 1983 (*Ibrahim Zakariya)
WPC Presidential Committee. *Ibrahim Zakariya (WPC vice-president), *Sándor Gáspár
Last Top Meeting. Tenth Congress (Havana, February 1982)
Major 1983 Conferences. Thirty-fifth General Council meeting (Nicosia, April, anti–deployment of U.S. missiles, "worker solidarity" in struggle against unemployment, traditional support for Arabs and Black South Africans and opposition to U.S. troops in South Korea and Turkish troops in Cyprus, attack on U.S. policies in Central America and the Caribbean); Ninth International Conference of Chemical, Oil and Allied Workers' Trade Union International (TUI) (Prague, May); International Trade Union Conference on Chemical Weapons (Ho Chi Minh City, May, condemned new U.S. chemical weapons); Eighth International Conference of Workers in Food, Tobacco, Hotel and Allied Industries (Moscow, September); Ninth International Conference of Agricultural, Forestry, and Plantation Workers' TUI (Budapest, October); Ninth International Conference of Building, Wood, and Building Materials Industries' TUI (Sofia, October); Thirtieth WFTU Bureau session (Damascus, October, anti–deployment of U.S. missiles, united action against transnationals, anti–arms race, support to Syrian workers and people). The WFTU also played the leading role in the International Conference on Trade Unions and Peace (Sofia, October), sponsored by the allied International Trade Union Committee for Peace and Disarmament (see below).
Related Organizations. Trade Unions International (TUIs) (coordinated by a WFTU department and represented on the WFTU Council and Bureau): Agriculture, Building Industry, Chemical Industry, Commerce, Food Industry, Metalworkers, Miners, Public Service, Teachers (World Federation of Teachers' Unions), Textile, Transport; de facto regional affiliates (high percentage of joint affiliates with WFTU): Permanent Congress of Trade Union Unity of Latin American Workers (CPUSTAL), International Confederation of Arab Trade Unions (ICATU), Organization of African Trade Union Unity (OATUU); other: International Trade Union Committee for Peace and Disarmament (many WFTU-affiliated personnel)

Name. Women's International Democratic Federation (WIDF)
Headquarters/Formation. East Berlin/1945
Claimed Strength. 131 affiliates in 116 countries; over 200 million members
Publications. *Women of the Whole World* (quarterly), *Documents and Information* (frequency unknown)

Status with U.N. UNESCO (B), ECOSOC (I), UNICEF, ILO (Special List)

Presidential Board. President: Freda Brown (Australia); 11 vice-presidents: Issam Abdul Hadi, (Palestine), Aruna Asaf Ali (India), Luisa Amorim (Portugal), Vilma Espin de Castro (Cuba), Fatima Zohra Djaghroud (Algeria), Fanny Edelman (Argentina), Fuki Kushida (Japan), Salome Moiane (Mozambique), Nguyen Thi Dinh (Vietnam), Valentina Nikolayeva-Tereshkova (USSR), Ilse Thiele (East Germany)

Secretariat. Secretary general: Mirjam Vire-Tuominen (Finland); organizing sectetary: Sabina Hager (East Germany); 17 secretaries: Mercedes Alvarez Moreno (country unknown), Evgenia Andrei (Romania), Aurora Barcena (Mexico), Hanna Busha (Iraq), Helga Dickel (West Germany), Olga Gutiérrez (Argentina), Norma Hidalgo (Chile), Valeria Kalmyk (USSR), Surjeet Kaur (India), Susan Mnumzana (South Africa), Azza al-Horr Mroueh (Lebanon), Anna Maria Navarro (Cuba), Vesselina Peytcheva (country unknown), Maria Taneva (Bulgaria), Wanda Tycner (Poland), Nancy Ruíz (Cuba), Soledad Parada (country unknown)

Last WMR Article. March 1983 (*Freda Brown)

WPC Presidential Committee. Freda Brown (WPC vice-president), Mirjam Vire-Tuominen

Last Top Meeting. Eighth Congress (Prague, October 1981)

Major 1983 Conferences. Women's Consultative Meeting (East Berlin, January, anti–deployment of U.S. missiles), WIDF Council meeting (Budapest, October, mobilization against nuclear war and for women's rights (The WIDF also played an important role in a seminar entitled "The Economic and Social Effects of the Arms Race on the Situation of Women and Their Families" in Copenhagen in April.)

Related Organizations. De facto regional affiliates (presumed joint affiliations; all participate with WIDF in WPC activities): All-African Women's Organization, Arab Women's Federation, Continental Front of Women (Against Intervention in Central America)

Name. World Federation of Democratic Youth (WFDY)

Headquarters/Formation. Budapest/1945

Claimed Strength. Over 270 affiliates in 123 countries; total membership over 150 million

Publications. *World Youth* (monthly), *WFDY News* (semimonthly)

Status with U.N. UNESCO (B), ECOSOC (I), FAO, ILO (Special List)

Presidential Board. President: Walid Masri (Lebanon); 9 vice-presidents: Khalil Elias (Sudan), Manuel Hernández Vidal (Chile), Hoang Thuy Giang (Vietnam), Alfred Junior (Angola), Kim Chang-yong (North Korea), Vsevolod Nakhodkin (USSR), Francisco Phillipe (Portugal), Jorge Prigoshin (Argentina), Pablo Reyes Dominguez (Cuba)

Secretariat. Secretary general: Miklós Barabás (Hungary): 2 deputy secretaries general: Oscar Gonzáles (Colombia), *Turay Saidu (Sierra Leone); 6 secretaries: Akira Kassai (Japan), Salim Obayid Altamini (South Yemen), *Joachim Brückner (East Germany), *Tarley Francis (Grenada), Franklin Gonzáles (Venezuela), Ivan Nicolae Joan (Romania), *Lubomír Ledl (Czechoslovakia), *Allan López (Costa Rica), Leonard Mabassy (Congo), Vesselin Mastikov (Bulgaria), Panayotis Michalatos (Greece), Thomas Borg Mogensen (Denmark), Markku Soppela (Finland), Jacek Paliszewski (Poland), Daniel Santana (Dominican Republic), Denis Sibeko (South Africa) (There are also positions for additional secretaries from France, Italy, Palestine, and the United States, but none known for the USSR. Identities of incumbents are unknown.)

Last WMR Article. None noted

WPC Presidential Committee. Miklós Barabás, *Walid Masri

Last Top Meeting. Eleventh General Assembly (Prague, June 1982)

Major 1983 Conferences. Enlarged WFDY European Commission meeting (Budapest, March, anti–deployment of U.S. missiles), WFDY Executive Committee meeting (West Berlin, April, solidarity with peoples of Lebanon, Palestine, Nicaragua, El Salvador; followed immediately by Youth Peace Conference, also in West Berlin), International Seminar on Peace and Disarmament (Vienna, October)

Related Organizations. Official subsidiaries: International Bureau of Tourism and Youth Exchange (BITEJ), International Commission of Children's and Adolescents' Movements (CIMEA), International Voluntary Service for Friendship and Solidarity of Youth (SIVSAJ); de facto regional affiliates: Arab Youth Union (presumed joint affiliations), Pan-African Youth Movement (joint affiliations)

Name. Afro-Asian Peoples' Solidarity Organization (AAPSO)
Headquarters/Formation. Cairo/1957
Claimed Strength. 87 affiliates; membership not given
Publications. *Solidarity* (monthly), *Development and Socio-Economic Progress* (quarterly)
Status with U.N. UNESCO (C), ECOSOC (II), UNCTAD, UNIDO
Presidential Board. President: Abd-al-Rahman Sharqawi (Egypt); 8 vice-presidents: Abd-al-Muhsin Abu Mayzar (Palestine), Abdul Aziz (Sri Lanka), Mirza Ibragimov (USSR), Vassos Lyssarides (Cyprus), Nguyen Thi Binh (Vietnam), Alfred Nzo (South Africa), Anahita Ratebzad (Afghanistan), Aziz Sharif (Iraq)
Secretariat. Secretary general: Nuri Abd-al-Razzaq Husayn; 4 deputy secretaries general: Facinet Bangoura (Guinea), Chitta Biswas (India), Abd-al-Galil Ghaylan (South Yemen), Abdurashid Issakhodzhayev (USSR); 11 secretaries: Dan Cindi (South Africa), Joaquim de Lemos (Angola), S. T. Haidongo (Namibia), Zubayr Sayf al-Islam (Algeria), Daniel Kouyela (Congo), Eva Ranaweera (Sri Lanka), Assim O. al-Rayah (Sudan), Joshua Siyolwe (Zambia), Muhammad Sobayh (Palestine), Tran Van Anh (Vietnam), Dieter Wagner (East Germany); assistant secretary general for technical affairs: Eduard al-Kharrat (Egypt)
Last WMR Article. August 1980 (Nuri Abd-al-Razzaq Husayn)
WPC Presidential Committee. Nuri Abd-al-Razzaq Husayn, Abd-al-Rahman Sharqawi (in addition, AAPSO Vice-Presidents Ratebzad, Sharif, and Nzo represent their respective countries on this body, the latter two as WPC vice-presidents)
Last Top Meeting. Fifth Conference (Cairo, January 1972, but extensive organizational changes took place at the Thirteenth Council Session, Aden, March 1981)
Major 1983 Conferences. AAPSO Arab affiliates (Aden, January, support of the Palestinian people), International Conference on Palestine and Lebanon (Athens, April, support of the Palestinian people)
Related Organizations. (Presumed from scope and similar involvement in leftist activities, including those of the WPC): Organization of Solidarity with the Peoples of Africa, Asia and Latin America (AALAPSO *or* OSPAAL), Afro-Asian Writers' Association

Name. International Union of Students (IUS)
Headquarters/Formation. Prague/1946
Claimed Strength. 117 affiliates in 109 countries; total membership over 10 million
Publications. *World Student News* (monthly), *IUS News Service* (fortnightly)
Status with U.N. UNESCO (B), ECOSOC (Roster)
Presidential Board. President: Miroslav Stepan (Czechoslovakia); 11 vice-presidents: Mohammed Bakir (Iraq), Leonardo Candieiro (Mozambique), José Castillo (Panama), Leszek Kaminski *or* Witold Nawrocki (Poland), Kim Guang-hub (North Korea), Ravane Kone (Senegal), Ong Dung (Vietnam), Antonio Pardo Sánchez (Cuba), Petrus Schmidt (Namibia), Aleksandr N. Zharikov (USSR), Vladimir Zlatinov *or* Dmitur Karamfilov (Bulgaria)
Secretariat. Secretary general: Srinivasan Kunalan (India); 9 secretaries: Manuel Coss (Puerto Rico), Nicolae Daravoinea (Romania), John Gallagher (Ireland), Károly György (Hungary), Gerardo Herrera (El Salvador), John Kwadjo (Ghana), Faysal al-Miqdad (Syria), Christina Valanidou (Cyprus), Ahmad Salim al-Wahishi (South Yemen)
Last WMR Article. August 1983 (*Miroslav Stepan)

WPC Presidential Committee. Miroslav Stepan
Last Top Meeting. Thirteenth Congress (East Berlin, November 1980)
Major 1983 Conferences. International Student Conference on Palestine (Athens, January, support of the Palestinian and Lebanese people), European Students' Peace Forum (Helsinki, February, peace and disarmament issues)
Related Organizations. De facto regional affiliates (presumed joint affiliations): All-African Students Union, Latin American Continental Students Organization (OCLAE)

Name. World Federation of Scientific Workers (WFSW)
Headquarters/Formation. London/1946
Claimed Strength. About 33 affiliates and members in over 70 countries; membership about 450,000
Publication. *Scientific World* (quarterly)
Status with U.N. UNESCO (A), ECOSOC (Roster)
Presidential Board. President: Jean-Marie Legay (France); 5 vice-presidents: N. G. Basov (USSR), Kiril Bratanov (Bulgaria), Pierre Biquard (France), T. Hirone (Japan), N. P. Gupta (India)
Secretariat. Secretary general: John Dutton (U.K.); deputy secretary general: M. A. Jaegle (France); organization secretary: unknown; 2 assistants to the secretary general: G. Durrafourg (France), G. Kotovski (USSR)
Last WMR Article. April 1973 (by then-president E. H. S. Burhop)
WPC Presidential Committee. No representation since January 1980 death of E. H. S. Burhop
Last Top Meeting. Thirteenth General Assembly (Paris, September)
Other Major 1983 Conferences. International Round Table on Science and the Qualitative Arms Race (East Berlin, April); Executive Council of WFSW (Prague, April, welcomed the "intensification" of the peace movement); Symposium on Science and the Crisis of Development (Paris, September, adverse economic effects of the arms race)
Related Organizations. None known

Name. International Organization of Journalists (IOJ)
Headquarters/Formation. Prague/1946
Claimed Strength. Affiliates in over 120 countries; membership over 180,000
Publications. *Democratic Journalist* (monthly), *IOJ News Letter* (semimonthly)
Status with U.N. UNESCO (B), ECOSOC (II)
Presidential Board. President: Kaarle Nordenstreng (Finland); 23 vice-presidents: Bola Adedoja (Nigeria), Viktor Afanasyev (USSR), Wieslaw Bek (Poland), Marcelo Ceballos Rosales (Ecuador), Baba Dagamaissa (Mali), Jerome Dramou (Guinea), Saber Falhout (Syria), Salah Galal (Egypt), Gerard Gatinot (France), Said Qassim Hammudi (Iraq), Eberhard Heinrich (East Germany), Kim Kwi-nam (North Korea), Teodomiro Leite de Vasconcelos (Mozambique), *Dao Tung (Vietnam), Juan Molina Palacios (Nicaragua), Tsend Namsrai (Mongolia), Efraín Ruiz Caro (Peru), Paavo Rounaniemi (Finland), Bassim Abu Sharif (Palestine), Luís Suárez López (Mexico), Shiro Suzuki (Japan), José Miguel Varas (Chile), Ernesto Vera (Cuba)
Secretariat. Secretary general: Jiří Kubka (Czechoslovakia); 7 secretaries: Kosta Andreev (Bulgaria), Miguel Arteaga (Cuba), Sergiusz Klaczkow (Poland), Boris Sakharov (USSR), Victor Stamate (Romania), Leopoldo Fernández Vargas (Colombia), Manfred Wiegand (East Germany)
Last WMR Article. December 1974 (Jiří Kubka)
WPC Presidential Committee. Jiří Kubka
Last Top Meeting. Ninth Congress (Moscow, October 1981)
Major 1983 Conferences. IOJ Presidium (Luanda, January, solidarity with people of Angola, Namibia, and South Africa; "new world information and communication order"), Fourth Consultative Meeting of Journalists (Prague, June, journalistic ethics, preservation of world peace), World Conference of Journalists Against Imperialism (Pyongyang, July, support for Korean unification), enlarged session of IOJ Presidium (Paris, November, support of Soviet peace efforts)

Related Organizations. De facto regional affiliates: Federation of Arab Journalists (presumed joint affiliations), Federation of Latin American Journalists (FELAP) (presumed joint affiliations), Union of African Journalists (joint affiliations)

Name. Christian Peace Conference (CPC)
Headquarters/Formation. Prague/1958
Claimed Strength. Affiliates in at least 80 countries; membership not given
Publications. *CPC* (quarterly), *CPC Information* (semimonthly)
Status with U.N. UNESCO (C), ECOSOC (III)
Presidential Board. President: Bishop/Dr. Károly Toth (Hungary); 9 vice-presidents: Rev. Dr. Richard Andriamanjato (Madagascar), Metropolitan/Dr. Paulos Mar Gregorios (India; elected a copresident of the World Council of Churches in August*), Prof./Dr. Gerhard Bassarak (East Germany), Prof./Dr. Sergio Arce-Martínez (Cuba), Metropolitan Nicolae Corneau (Romania), Rev. Dr. Lee Charles Gray (U.S.), General Bishop/Prof. Jan Michalko (Czechoslovakia), Bishop Pham Quang Phuoc (Vietnam), Mrs. Bernadeen Silva (Sri Lanka); Continuation Committee chairman: Metropolitan Bilaret of Kiev and Galicia (USSR)
Secretariat. Secretary general: Rev. Dr. Lubomír Mirejovsky (Czechoslovakia); 2 deputy secretaries general: Rev. Alfred Christian Rosa (Sri Lanka), Archmandrite Sergei Fomin (USSR); office director: Dr. Tibor Görög (Hungary). (The CPC does not appear to have the usual group of fulltime secretaries at its headquarters. The International Secretariat, of which Dr. Görög is a member, is apparently brought together only occasionally.)
Last WMR Article. December 1981 (Károly Toth)
WPC Presidential Committee. Károly Toth (in addition, Richard Andriamanjato also represents Madagascar as a WPC vice-president)
Last Top Meeting. Fifth All-Christian Peace Conference (Prague, June 1978)
Major 1983 Conferences. CPC International Secretariat (Prague, February, anti–deployment of U.S. missiles); Consultative Meeting on Disarmament (Budapest, May); CPC International Secretariat (West Berlin, September); CPC Working Committee (Moscow, October, disarmament)
Related Organizations. Official regional subsidiaries: African CPC, Asian CPC, CPC in Latin America and the Caribbean; complementary organizations (with different religious constituencies, they cooperate with the CPC): Berlin Conference of European Catholics, Asian Buddhists Peace Conference

Name. International Association of Democratic Lawyers (IADL)
Headquarters/Formation. Brussels/1946
Claimed Strength. Affiliates in nearly 80 countries; membership about 25,000
Publication. *Review of Contemporary Law* (semiannual)
Status with U.N. UNESCO (B), ECOSOC (II)
Presidential Board. President: Joe Nordmann (France); first vice-president: Gerhard Stuby (West Germany); 25 vice-presidents: Ahmed al-Khawaga (Egypt), Shabib al-Maliki (Iran), Abderrahmane Bouraoui (Algeria), Solange Bouvier-Ajam (France), João Cruz Pinto (Guinea), Apoliner Díaz Callejas (Colombia), Zouheir al-Midani (country unknown), Gloria Gabuardi (Nicaragua), Yang Huanan (China), V. R. Krishna Iyer (India), Igor I. Karpets (USSR), Karl J. Lang (Finland), Adam Lopatka (Poland), Josef Ondrej (Czechoslovakia), Susumu Ozaki (Japan), Stane Pavelic (Yugoslavia), John Platts-Mills (U.K.), Jean Salmon (Belgium), Jamal Sourani (Palestine), Boris Spasov (Bulgaria), Tchoe Minsin (North Korea), Umberto Terracini (Italy), Armando Uribe (Chile), Francisco Varona y Duque Estrada (Cuba), Doris Brin Walker (U.S.)
Secretariat. Secretary general: Amar Bentoumi (Algeria); 14 secretaries: Eduardo Barcesat *or* Nelly Minyerski (Argentina), Tudor Draganu (Romania), Ahmed al-Hilaly (Egypt), Lennox Hinds (U.S.), Sergio Insunza (Chile), Semyon Ivanov (USSR), Lórand Jókai (Hungary), Pierre Lavigne *or* Roland Weyl (France), Ugo Natoli (Italy), Phan Ahn (Vietnam), Kazuyoshi Saito (Japan), Jitendra Sharma (India)

Last WMR Article. None noted

WPC Presidential Committee. No representation

Last Top Meeting. Eleventh Congress (Valletta, November 1980)

Major 1983 Conferences. None. (No major IADL activity has been noted since the December 1982 International Lawyers Conference on the Mediterranean in Algiers, and the organization was apparently the only major front not to send representation to the World Assembly for Peace and Life, Against Nuclear War.)

Related Organization. De facto regional affiliate: Arab Lawyers Union (joint affiliations)

Note on the Peace Movement. Throughout 1983, the main Soviet effort vis-à-vis the peace movement as a whole was to unite its two main strands in a campaign to prevent the scheduled year-end emplacement of U.S. intermediate-range missiles in Western Europe. The problem for the USSR was that it could control only one of these strands, the bulk of those organizations affiliated with the WPC. The other strand, a more diverse and independent group of religious and secular pacifists plus environmentalists, among others, tended to place equal blame on both superpowers for the nuclear arms race. The latter called for dismantling of Soviet SS-20s as well as nondeployment of the new U.S. missiles. This second group was the more powerful in the United Kingdom, West Germany, the Netherlands, and Italy. The Campaign for Nuclear Disarmament (CND), the "Greens," the Interchurch Peace Council (IKV), and Eurocommunists are representative components (even though the Eurocommunists are formally incorporated into the WPC). This independent group also antagonized the Soviets by openly sympathizing with the "unofficial" (non-WPC-affiliated) peace groups in Eastern Europe, which combined a similarly neutralist approach to disarmament with a call for Western-style civil rights in the Soviet bloc (most notable here were Charter '77 in Czechoslovakia, Swords into Plowshares in East Germany, and the Dialogue Movement in Hungary).

During the first half of the year, a series of events occurred that caused further alienation of this independent group from the Soviets. First, the Soviet Peace Committee (chairman Yuri Zhukov) had written a letter (made public in early January) to organizers of the independents' then-projected Second European Nuclear Disarmament Conference, claiming that the independents were attempting to "split the peace movement" and that their "equal responsibility" theory attempted to "justify the aggressive, militaristic policies of the United States and NATO" (*Tages-*

zeitung, West Berlin, 4 January). The conference itself, held in West Berlin in May, had delegates neither from the official Soviet bloc peace movements (WPC affiliates that refused to attend) nor from their "unofficial" counterparts (who were prevented from attending by their respective governments) (*Tribune*, Sidney, 15 June). Members of a delegation of Greens who crossed over to East Berlin for a demonstration were arrested and sent back. Somewhat similarly, independent observers at the WPC-organized World Assembly for Peace and Life, Against Nuclear War the following month in Prague ran into police harassment when they met with Charter '77 leaders outside the assembly framework. This situation, incidentally, resulted in the premature departure of at least three Greens and two Italian communists. (*Times*, London, 27 June; *RFE Research*, 12 July.) The Prague Assembly, like its independent counterpart a month earlier, claimed over 3,000 participants (*Izvestiia*, 2 July); clearly, it was the major communist front meeting of the year.

With respect to the Prague Assembly, there is no reason to disbelieve either a Western press account that "much if not most of [its] effort was taken up with planning 'joint actions' against 'U.S. militarism' and 'imperialism' in general" (*Reformatorisch Dagblad*, Apeldoorn, 27 June) or a communist one that the majority of its representatives criticized the U.S.-Soviet "joint responsibility" theory (Tass, Prague, 26 June). It is surprising then that its Appeal, aside from having "No to *new* [italics added] missiles in Europe" as its lead slogan, went a long way toward compromise with the independent line: the United States was not singled out by name as the chief villain and the need for disarmament by both sides was stressed (ibid.). Subsequent events seemed to indicate that this reflected a change from a stick to a carrot approach by the Soviets in their efforts to influence the independent peace movement.

The first among subsequent events was the failure of Yuri Zhukov to be re-elected a WPC vice-president at the reorganizational meeting of that body, which took place the day after the Assembly had ended (*Peace Courier*, July–August), most unusual treatment for a Soviet Peace Committee chairman. Second, the influential "political observer" Aleksandr Bovin (*Izvestiia*, 2 July) described the Prague Assembly as a "dialogue" between two strands of the peace movement and characterized the "evenhanded" group as "*sincerely* [italics added] mistaken," a decided contrast with Zhukov's earlier comments. Then, the following month's *Kommunist* (no. 12) carried an unsigned editorial entitled "Peace, the Working Class, and the Communists," which again stressed the "representative nature" of the Prague Assembly and chided the narrow-minded attitude of "some comrades" toward pacifist (e.g., CND, IKV) and ecological (e.g., Greens) organizations that were "unable to see in these movements their objective allies in the struggle for peace" (*JPRS*, no. 84724, 10 November, pp. 22, 27). Finally, Boris Ponomarev, the Soviet party secretary responsible for "non-bloc" political parties, hosted a delegation of Greens in Moscow that included two of the very same leaders (Petra Kelly and General Gerd Bastian) who had been ousted from East Berlin in May (*Pravda*, 30 October). This delegation, incidentally, appears to have had an audience with East German chief Erich Honecker in East Berlin on its way home (Tass, East Berlin, 1 November).

Despite the ultimate failure to prevent deployment of the U.S. missiles, Soviet efforts were successful in uniting West European peace movements along desired lines: whatever their theoretical outlook, by late 1983, the independents had become de facto unilateralists. Perhaps the most extreme, though indirect, example was CND leader Bruce Kent's branding of both Margaret Thatcher and Ronald Reagan (but not Andropov) as "international criminals" (*Morning Star*, London, 17 November). As noted by *Pravda* (23 October), the greatest successes were in West Germany. On 22 October, a "human chain," claimed to be 250,000 strong, was strung between U.S. European Command headquarters near Stuttgart and the projected Pershing II site in Neu-Ulm. Massive demonstrations opposing deployment were held in Bonn (500,000 claimed), and in Hamburg (400,000 claimed) (see *Flashes from the Trade Unions*, Prague, 4 November; *New Age*, New Delhi, 6 November). And in November, the Social Democrats, in a possible reversal of their previous position, voted against deployment. One source states that while only 2 of some 26 diverse groups constituting the peace movement in West Germany are clearly procommunist, the German Communist Party has been able to influence the movement strongly through superior organizational skills and large-scale Soviet funding (*WSJ*, 19 October).

The capitals of the other countries facing year-end deployment also experienced massive demonstrations on 22 October at the beginning of U.N. Disarmament Week: Rome had a claimed turnout of 500,000–750,000, while London had some 500,000 (*New Age*, 6 November; *Flashes from the Trade Unions*, 4 November). While the ruling Socialists in Italy and France did not oppose the deployment, the nonruling ones in the United Kingdom and West Germany did. Soviet cultivation of the socialists on the issue of non-deployment was assiduous during the year and seems to have been successful in Scandinavia and the Low Countries in addition to those areas mentioned above (*WSJ*, 19 October). Of course, both the WPC, which has long incorporated elements of the socialist Left (see Ralph M. Goldman, ed., *Transnational Parties: Organizing the World's Precincts*, pp. 38–39, 324), and the independent peace movement had a role to play here, the former directly and the latter indirectly.

Wallace H. Spaulding
McLean, Virginia

WESTERN EUROPE

Introduction

In November 1982, the *World Marxist Review* published an article entitled "Where Is Western Europe Going?" The article stressed that "the ideas advanced by Europe's communists meet the innermost interests of peoples, for they concern a vital problem of our time. The unprecedented growth of mass anti-war actions is a product of the objective conditions of social development, that is, first of all, the greatly increased significance of foreign policy problems, above all the issue of war and peace."

During 1983, this theme received major attention from Western Europe's communist parties. This focus, however, belied more significant problems. The *World Marxist Review* also emphasized that the communist parties of Western Europe "must ensure defense of the working people's economic and political rights, help raise their class consciousness, and build up working-class influence on developments in West European countries." This would require "the cohesion of the working class, unity of action of the political parties representing it, and joint efforts to bar reaction, defend democratic achievements and open new prospects for social progress." The article concluded that "where Western Europe goes will depend on the outcome of this struggle" to accomplish "real changes in the interests of the working people."

This conclusion captured very well the problem confronting Western Europe's communist parties during the year, which will continue to have a major effect on their credibility in 1984. The conclusion drawn in 1982 by an observer of communist affairs—that "Western Europe's Communists are faltering" —has proved correct (Alberto Jacoviello, *WSJ*, 24 March 1982). The disarray in which Western Europe's communist movement found itself in 1982 became more serious during 1983. It was reflected not only in the dilemmas facing the French Communist Party, but more generally in the poor election showings of communist parties throughout Western Europe.

In Western Europe as a whole, economic problems were of paramount importance. Communist party programs were unsuccessful in achieving any significant "unity of action" to deal with them. Advocacy of democratic government, socialism in nationalistic colors, disarmament, and world peace were laudable goals, but did not provide solutions for domestic problems such as inflation and unemployment. As a consequence, 1983 witnessed further erosion of support for Western Europe's communist parties.

To detract attention from their inability to provide viable solutions for serious economic issues, the parties extolled the virtues of the "peace movement" and specifically focused on criticism of the United States for introducing improved weapons into the NATO missile force. The year 1982 had seen major demonstrations in a number of West European cities in support of nuclear disarmament and reductions in conventional weapons and forces stationed in Europe. The emphasis placed on these demonstrations was intensified during 1983.

The "peace movement" sought to unify as many Western Europeans as possible in opposition to increased defense expenditures for NATO, whose conventional and nuclear capabilities remained inferior to those of the Soviet Union. This emphasis proved unable to eclipse the failure to translate political slogans of hope and promise into political reality. Declining popularity, party strife, and factionalism among Western Europe's communist parties were the result, and this exerted a major negative impact on their activities during 1983. At the end of the year, there was every indication that this would continue to be the case in 1984 and that Western Europe's communist parties did not have any clearer idea of the direction they were taking than they had at the beginning of the year.

In 1983, 14 of Western Europe's 23 parties were represented in their respective parliaments: those of Belgium, Cyprus, Finland, France, Greece, Iceland, Italy, Luxembourg, Netherlands, Portugal, San Marino, Spain, Sweden, and Switzerland (the communist party is not represented in the legislatures of Austria, Denmark, Federal Republic of Germany, Great Britain, Ireland, Malta, Norway, Turkey, and West Berlin). In 1983, party members no longer held cabinet posts in Iceland and Finland, but did retain two cabinet positions in France.

National elections were held during the year in ten Western European countries (four were held in 1982). The parties sustained losses in nine countries (Austria, Denmark, Federal Republic of Germany, Finland, Great Britain, Ireland, Italy, San Marino, and Switzerland); in Portugal the party gained three parliamentary seats. Communist party representation continued to be largest in Italy, where the party holds slightly less than one-third of the parliamentary seats (198 of 630). Of the parties with legislative representation, Cyprus had the highest percentage of seats (34.3 percent), followed by Italy (31.4 percent), San Marino (25 percent), Portugal (17.6 percent), Iceland (16.7 percent), Finland (13.5 percent), and France (9.0 percent). The remaining parties held between 5.7 percent (Sweden) and 0.5 percent (Switzerland) of their respective parliamentary seats.

In 1982, declining popularity and party strife produced the conclusion that "the decline of the communist parties of Western Europe seems irreversible" because of "their incapacity to propose solutions acceptable to the societies in which they operate." From a realistic perspective this suggested that the traditional Marxist-Leninist "ideology" had not provided solutions for difficulties confronting the continent's industrialized countries. (Ibid.)

This dilemma did not disappear in 1983, and it is likely to become increasingly significant in 1984. Ideological solutions do not provide answers to the questions, nor do they ameliorate the magnitude of the difficulties caused by unemployment, inflation, and recession or by unprecedented Soviet military expansion.

An excellent illustration of this conclusion was provided by views and positions taken by the French Communist Party (PCF). The electoral victory of the Socialist Party (PS) and the PCF in 1981 was followed in 1982 and 1983 by growing inflation, severe weakening of the French franc, nationalization of major French banks and industries, and changes in tax policy aimed at a small minority for economically unsound and politically punitive reasons. Concern with the magnitude of Soviet military power also prompted the French government to take positions highly critical of Soviet foreign policy. These developments produced a dilemma for the PCF. The PCF found itself to an increasing degree in the position of having to choose between supporting government policies of which it disapproved or maintaining its own positions, which it was unable to implement.

In 1981, the French national elections established François Mitterrand's PS as the most powerful political party in the country. As a result of an electoral coalition, the PCF was given four ministerial posts in the cabinet: transport, civil service and administrative reform, health, and vocational training (in 1983 the Ministries of Health and Civil Service and Administrative Reform were reduced to subcabinet-level positions, but were still occupied by members of the PCF). These appointments were made on the basis of an agreement between both parties that required the PCF to pledge "entire solidarity" at all levels of government. In 1981, the Soviet party endorsed this development as "an historic event for France and all Western Europe" (*Guardian*, London, 5 July 1981). According to French political analyst Jean-François Revel, the French elections meant that "Marxism had won" and that "government by ideology" had returned to France (*Public Opinion*, August/September, 1981). This asserted success, however, did not produce broad public support as the government's domestic policies unfolded during 1982 and 1983.

Since entering the French cabinet as a junior partner of the PS, the PCF has been unable to deal with a critical political dilemma: that of remaining a loyal member of the PS-led government while maintaining sufficient independence from that party to preserve its own identity as a separate and rival force on the Left. The events of 1983 only aggravated the problems facing the PCF as a result of this predicament.

On the other hand, the PCF, headed by Secretary General Georges Marchais, remained reluctant to withdraw from the cabinet, even though the PS pursued policies that differed markedly from the PCF's stated preferences. The PCF shared massive electoral losses with the PS in the municipal elections held in the spring, primarily because of the government's economic performance. By the end of 1983, however, in spite of pressure exerted on Marchais from within the party, the PCF reaffirmed its intention to remain in the coalition government.

On the other hand, the party continued to insist on its right to assert its own views on a variety of controversial issues, even if these position conflicted with official government policy. The determination to remain a certain distance from the PS stemmed from the PCF's historic struggle with the PS for influence within the Left, and from its long-standing ties with the Communist Party of the Soviet Union (CPSU).

The consequence was an inevitable increase in uncertainty among PCF members concerning what the party's positions actually were. This led to a decrease in membership, to a decline in the readership of *L'Humanité* (the PCF's daily newspaper), and to a general malaise in the party as a whole. In addition, the defeat in the municipal elections was unprecedented since 1945. The PCF lost control of fifteen cities with populations in excess of 100,000 persons, including such long-held mayoralties as St.-Etienne and Nîmes.

At the beginning of 1984, the PCF faced a quandary. It could resign from the coalition government, or it could remain in the coalition and continue its efforts to convince an increasingly doubtful electorate of its viable contribution to French political life. Either path presented risks, and it was uncertain which path the PCF would take in the new year.

In 1983, national elections were held in Italy for the first time since 1979. Although the Italian Communist Party (PCI) lost three positions in the Italian legislature, it retained 198 of 630 seats. Unlike the PCF, however, the PCI is not represented in the Italian government.

In March, the PCI held its Sixteenth Congress, and it was marked by several unusual developments. It was attended by delegations from 80 different countries, but the only foreign guest invited to address the congress was the president of the European Parliament. In addition, the secretary of the Christian Democratic Party attended the meeting, as did leaders of several other parties, for the first time in the PCI's history. A delegation from China attended for the first time in twenty years. The PCI, together with the Spanish Communist Party, took the leading role in the Eurocommunist movement during the 1970s, and its views and positions have consistently generated widespread attention. During 1980, 1981, and 1982, the party continued to advocate independence from the CPSU as well as to exercise the prerogative of openly criticizing Soviet policy. It was joined in a more moderate fashion in this position by many of Western Europe's smaller communist parties, in addition to the Spanish party. In 1983, the magnitude of the PCI's rift with the CPSU remained significant. The CPSU sent a delegation to the PCI congress of lower rank than it had on previous occasions, and its message to the congress was very clear: "We are always willing to develop voluntary comradely cooperation and solidarity with all communist parties on the basis of the life-tested ideas of Marx-Engels-Lenin" (Tass, 1 March).

The domestic positions of the PCI during the year did not vary significantly from those taken during 1982. The party remained in opposition at the national level while sharing governmental responsibility in many regions, large cities, and municipalities. Disputes between the Socialist and the Communist parties within Italy itself, however, resulted in resignation of the communist mayors of Florence and Turin and also in a significant election loss of five percentage points in the municipal election of Naples.

Considerable attention was devoted throughout the year to the "peace movement," but the PCI did not endorse the position of the CPSU and a number of other communist parties in Western Europe. The PCI did not join the "unilateral disarmament" parades and demonstrations that enjoyed such great attention in the Netherlands, Germany, and France. At the same time, the party did not approve of the introduction of new U.S. missiles in Europe and also made it clear that the peace movement would not succeed "on the basis of complete identification with the policy of the USSR" (*L'Unità*, 9 October). The party did endorse, however, "the Kennedy-Hatfield resolution . . . that calls for a general 'freeze' of all nuclear weapons of both superpowers" (ibid., 3 March). The party strongly favored the continuation of the Soviet-U.S. negotiations on nuclear weapons, and PCI secretary general Enrico Berlinguer made it very clear that the PCI rejected "alignment for or against either of the two military blocs" (ibid.). The party also reiterated its support of the Solidarity movement in Poland and stressed that "the search for dialogue, for new forms of democracy, for a national unity based on pluralism" must be continued in that country (ibid., 3 May).

It is unclear what emphasis the PCI will give its domestic and foreign policies in 1984. The highly publicized "third way," endorsed by Berlinguer, remains too vague to win a consensus of the majority within the PCI and among Italy's electorate. If the PCI is to gain increased respect and electoral support, it must devote greater attention to defining clearly its own priorities in 1984.

The Spanish Communist Party (PCE) continued to undergo internal dissension. Legalized in 1977, the PCE very quickly became a principal advocate of Eurocommunism between 1977 and 1981 under the leadership of Santiago Carrillo. In 1982, however, Carrillo resigned as secretary general and was replaced by Gerardo Iglesias (then 37 years old). In 1983, Iglesias moved rapidly to heal the rifts within the party and to rebuild the party's influence in national affairs. At the party's Eleventh Congress in December, he was re-elected head of the party for the next three years.

Iglesias did not directly condemn Carrillo's past performance, but did attribute the PCE's loss of popularity to "errors of leadership," alienation of intellectuals, and to neglect of the "mass movement." Carrillo did not accept responsibility for the party's decline in popularity, but acknowledged that "Eurocommunist excesses" had caused serious internal damage and regretted that he had not been more decisive in dealing with divisions within the PCE. Iglesias, for his part, emphasized the need for broader participation within the party and for a Eurocommunist "renewal" stressing less authoritarian leadership.

One of the consequences of this effort was a recovery in the municipal elections held in May, which clearly established the PCE as Spain's third political force. Nearly 8 percent of the total ballot went to the PCE, double the percentage won in the devastating general elections of October 1982, resulting in the election of approximately 200 communist mayors. Iglesias asserted that the "new atmosphere" within the party accounted for this success.

The PCE, however, still remained at a significant disadvantage. It held only 4 seats in the Spanish Cortes, having lost 19 of its 23 seats in the 1982 national election. Thus, at the end of the year, the party still required a major rebuilding effort. It would have to regain the support of the Spanish electorate at a time when Spain, despite continued terrorist activity, was remarkably stable, and was ruled by a socialist government.

It is unclear how the difficulties that confronted the parties of France, Italy, and Spain during the year will affect their activities in 1984. It does seem reasonably certain, however, that in all three cases the parties, albeit for different reasons, must engage in a major effort to increase support among their respective electorate. Whether they will be successful is doubtful in view of the relatively strong position of the socialist party in each country. Whether the communist parties' declining electoral popularity reflects a "crisis of communist ideology" is an intriguing question. But of even greater importance is the steps they will take in 1984 to regain the influence they have lost during the past several years. Their success in rebuilding their credibility will have a major impact on the views and positions of Western Europe's other communist parties. This is not to suggest that the activities of communist parties elsewhere in Western Europe do not merit careful observation, but the views they support and the positions they take will be significantly influenced by the successes and failures of the communist parties of France, Italy, and Spain.

The pro-Soviet Portuguese Communist Party (PCP) is led by Alvaro Cunhal. While the party is less influential now than during the first two years following the end of the country's dictatorship in 1974, it still exercises major control in Portugal's labor unions and commands significant electoral support. In the national elections held in April, the PCP garnered 18 percent of the vote (1980, 16.7 percent) and 44 of 250 parliamentary seats in an electoral coalition of several leftist groups. Noting that the total number of seats won by the Socialist Party (101) and the PCP represented 55 percent of the electorate, Cunhal proposed formation of a coalition government by the two parties. This proposal was rejected by

Socialist Party leader Mário Soares, who formed a coalition government with the Social Democratic Party, securing a two-thirds majority with 176 seats. The PCP remained, therefore, in the opposition and devoted the remainder of the year to criticism of government policies.

In Cyprus, Greece, Turkey, Malta, and San Marino, communist party activities resulted in minimal impact on political life. In Turkey, the communist party remains proscribed and therefore did not participate in the national election held in November; it did, however, hold a party congress for the first time in more than half a century. The Communist Party of Malta, established in 1969, is without noteworthy influence, and no party member was a candidate in the national elections held in 1981. The Communist Party of San Marino won 15 of 60 parliamentary seats in the national elections held in 1983 and participates in the country's coalition government.

In Cyprus, the communist party (AKEL) draws its principal support from the Greek Cypriot majority, which comprises approximately 80 percent of the island's estimated population of 653,000. Since the establishment of the Republic of Cyprus in 1960, AKEL has enjoyed legal status.

With an estimated membership of 14,000, it is the island's best-organized political party. The party is proscribed in the Turkish Federated State of divided Cyprus. In the most recent national election (1981), AKEL received 32.8 percent of the vote and 12 of the 35 seats in the House of Representatives. Despite its strength, the party does not hold any cabinet positions. The president of Cyprus, Spyros Kyprianou, was re-elected in 1983 to a five-year term with the support of AKEL. The party was not, however, rewarded with any political appointments following the election, and therefore relations with the ruling Democratic Party became increasingly strained during the year. It remained unclear, however, which direction the party would follow in 1984.

In Greece, the party remains split into pro-Soviet and Eurocommunist factions. In the Greek parliament, the pro-Soviet faction of the party (KKE) holds 13 of 300 seats. The party's views and positions on questions of domestic and foreign policy normally parallel those of the Panhellenic Socialist Movement (PASOK), established by Andreas Papandreou in 1974; the Eurocommunist faction of the KKE failed to win a seat in the most recent national election, held in 1981. The Marxist-oriented PASOK received 48 percent of the vote, elected 172 deputies to the Greek legislature, and formed the first socialist government in Greek history. Since that election, Prime Minister Papandreou has softened his opposition to NATO, and in July Greece and the United States concluded a five-year agreement allowing the continuation of U.S. military bases on Greek soil. KKE overtures to participate in the PASOK government have not been favorably acted on, and as a consequence KKE criticism of PASOK policies has continued to mount. In 1984, the KKE is almost certain to be increasingly critical of Papandreou's "mild" policies toward the West and "timid" measures in "socializing" the economy.

In Great Britain and Ireland, both parties maintained low profiles during 1983 and have not occupied a position of significance in many years. The Communist Party of Great Britain (CPGB) has not been represented in the House of Commons since 1950; however, one member, Lord Milford, sits in the House of Lords. At the party's Thirty-eighth Congress, held in November, emphasis was given the problem posed by declining party membershp, now at its lowest point since 1945. In the general elections held in June, the CPGB's 35 candidates polled less than 12,000 votes. The party does, however, continue to play a significant role in the country's trade union movement (there are 2 members of the CPGB on the 38-member General Council of the Trades Union Congress) and takes an active part in encouraging confrontation between the British government and labor unions. The Irish Communist Party, on the contrary, plays no role whatsoever. The sole significant event of the year was the party's celebration of its fiftieth anniversary. The party supports the unification of Ireland by the means of a "working-class solidarity" that would unite both Catholics and Protestants.

No new developments of major significance were recorded in the activities of the communist parties of Belgium, Denmark, the Netherlands, and Luxembourg. The Luxembourg party continued to play a minor role in political life, and the party's organizational structure remains in control of the Urbany family.

The internal dissension that plagued the Communist party of Denmark (DKP) during 1982 continued in the new year. This was reflected in the parliamentary elections held on 10 January 1984, in which the DKP received 0.7 percent of the vote (its worst showing in postwar history). Throughout the year, the party contended for popular support with four other leftist parties, who collectively polled 14.9 percent of the vote in the January 1984 election. The DKP held its Twenty-seventh Congress in May and re-elected Jorgen Jensen party chairman.

The Communist Party of the Netherlands (CPN) received 1.9 percent of the vote in the most recent national elections (1982) and holds 3 of the 150 seats in parliament. The CPN, under its new "pluralistic" leadership headed by Elli Izeboud, concentrated almost entirely in 1983 on implementing the decisions of the Twenty-eighth Congress in November 1982. In an effort to appeal to the Left as a whole, the CPN's program emphasizes a total renewal in ideology, a complete break with "existing socialism," a de-Stalinization of the party, and editorial independence for the party newspaper, *De Waarheid*. As a consequence, the year focused on bitter and intense internal debate concerning implementation of these decisions. In view of the debilitating internal power struggle, CPN activities dealt only marginally with domestic and foreign policy issues. In 1984, the internal debate is almost certain to continue as the CPN leadership prepares a draft party program to be submitted for debate and approval in the spring.

In the Nordic countries of Iceland, Norway, Sweden, and Finland, developments of any significance were registered only in the last country. In 1982, relations between the Finnish Communist Party (SKP) and its electoral front, the Finnish People's Democratic League (SKDL), were characterized by factional strife. This rift continued in the new year. The year was marked, however, by the worst election defeat for the SKP in its history. The party was without a cabinet minister for the first time in eight years, and the SKDL lost 8 of the 35 seats it previously held in the 200-seat parliament.

The declining fortunes of the SKP resulted not only from the factionalism that has plagued the party since 1969, but also from the prosperous economy, which allows Finnish workers and farmers to compare their own standard of living with that in the Soviet Union to the latter's disadvantage. As the Twentieth Congress of the party approaches in the spring of 1984, it is very likely that the divisions between the various factions will deepen. If this occurs, disunity will continue to mark party life in the new year.

The communist party of Iceland (AB) is the third largest of six parties represented in the Icelandic parliament and holds 10 of 60 seats. During 1983, however, the Icelandic coalition government of which the AB was a part resigned, and the party was, at the end of the year, the largest opposition party and had lost its three cabinet posts (health, finance, and industry). In 1983, economic problems continued to dominate political life. The party's November congress stressed the AB's militant positions on economic issues, as well as its continued opposition to Icelandic membership in NATO.

In Sweden, the Left Party Communists (VPK) continued to play a marginal role in Swedish politics. The VPK does hold 20 of 349 parliamentary seats, but is not represented in the Swedish government. The party's goal remains "the struggle of the working class and of the people" in order to achieve "victory over capitalism." During the year, the VPK emphasized the importance of the "peace movement" and, with its counterparts in Finland, Norway, and Denmark, continued to support a nuclear-free zone for these Nordic countries. While this issue received considerable attention during the year, it nevertheless did not result in increased support for the VPK. During 1984, the party is expected to continue emphasizing domestic issues in an effort to garner support for the national elections scheduled in 1985 (the party is represented on thirteen of sixteen parliamentary committees, excluding the committees on justice, taxation, and defense).

The Norwegian Communist Party (NKP) is not represented in the country's parliament and continues to operate on the fringe of Norwegian politics. As a consequence of the party's decision not to merge with several left-socialist parties in 1975, its position has remained weak. It is staunchly pro-Soviet in orientation and supports "unity of action" in the labor movement. It did share the positions of Western Europe's other communist parties concerning opposition to the deployment of new nuclear weapons in Europe, but was unsuccessful in generating widespread support for opposition to NATO. In view of the activities of several active leftist parties in Norway, all of which compete with each other for voter attention, it is unlikely that the NKP will gain in stature in 1984.

The influence exerted during the year by the communist parties of Austria and Switzerland continued to be negligible. In the Austrian national elections in April, the party (KPO) received only 0.66 percent of the vote and no representation in parliament. Reflecting the themes of other Western European communist parties, the KPO criticized high taxes and unemployment levels and emphasized the importance of the "peace movement." As in Austria, the communist party in Switzerland suffered an electoral defeat. In national elections held in October, it lost two of its three parliamentary seats; in addition, the party received strong competition from several other leftist political parties in the country. It is unlikely that either party will enjoy increased support during 1984, but it is almost certain that both parties continue to endorse the "peace movement."

The communist party in West Berlin (SEW) does not exert any significant influence on the life of the city. The party is pro-Soviet in orientation and reflects the views and positions of its counterpart in the German Democratic Republic. In the most recent elections to the city's parliament (1981), the SEW received less than 1 percent of the vote. No leadership changes were reported during the year. The party competes with a number of leftist groups in the city whose activities attract little support in a city surrounded by the Berlin Wall and mine fields.

The German Communist Party (DKP) is pro-Soviet and maintains a highly structured organizational framework. The DKP has offices in more than 200 cities in the Federal Republic and an estimated income of 60 million marks. Its activities are very closely monitored by the communist party of the German Democratic Republic. During the year, the party focused its attention on the peace and ecological movements in an effort to stimulate and encourage "unity of action" among diverse political parties. Particular emphasis was devoted to opposing the introduction of new missiles in the Federal Republic. While the party played an active role in the "peace movement," it nevertheless was unable to increase its support at the polls during the national elections in March (the DKP received 0.2 percent of the vote). In 1984, the DKP will probably continue to focus on the "peace movement," especially in view of the fact that a conservative government was elected for the first time in more than a decade.

Dennis L. Bark
Hoover Institution

Austria

Population. 7.6 million
Party. Communist Party of Austria (Kommunistische Partei Österreichs; KPO)
Founded. 3 November 1918
Membership. 15,000 (1982 estimate)
Party Chairman. Franz Muhri (b. 1921)
Politburo. 12 members: Michael Graber (editor of *Volksstimme*), Franz Hager, Anton Hofer, Hans Kalt (secretary of Central Committee), Franz Karger, Gustav Loistl, Franz Muhri, Karl Reiter, Erwin Scharf, Irma Schwager, Walter Silbermayr, Ernst Wimmer
Central Committee. 68 members
Status. Legal

Last Congress. Twenty-fourth, 6–8 December 1980, in Vienna; next congress scheduled for January 1984 in Vienna

Last Election. Federal, 24 April, 0.66 percent (1979: 0.96 percent), no representation

Publications. *Volksstimme* (People's voice), KPO daily organ (Vienna); *Weg und Ziel* (Path and goal), KPO theoretical monthly (Vienna)

In the parliamentary elections of 24 April, the KPO slumped markedly below its recent average of 1 percent of the vote. Austrian pessimism about the economy continued, but the economy continued to perform well, with unemployment and inflation below 5 percent.

This essay benefits from a publication, in late 1982, by Anton Pelinka, the eminent Austrian political scientist ("Die KPÖ: Eine Kleinpartei in der Isolierung," in A. Kohl and A. Stirnemann, eds., *Österreichisches Jahrbuch für Politik, 1981* [Munich: Oldenbourg, 1982]; hereafter *Die KPÖ*).

Party Internal Affairs. The fifteenth plenary session of the KPO Central Committee, held in Vienna on 10 May, adopted the following four-point resolution (*Volksstimme*, 12 May): (1) the report is to be the basis for further party discussions; (2) these discussions are to result in written reports submitted by provincial secretaries to the Central Committee by June, whereupon the Politburo is to submit a document to the Central Committee; (3) the Twenty-Fifth KPO Congress is to be convened in mid-January 1984; (4) the continuing party struggle is to focus on socio-economic questions, especially tax burdens, unemployment, and the peace movement, including participation in the all-Austrian peace demonstration on 22 October in Vienna.

While the percentage of party members among party voters is still standard for Austria, it dropped from 89 percent in 1947 to 31 percent in 1977 (*Die KPÖ*, p. 148). While three of ten new members of the Central Committee elected in 1980 are women, women still make up only 8 percent of the Politburo and 13 percent of the Central Committee (ibid., pp. 149, 150). The party, in the face of nationwide losses, gained votes in Vorarlberg in 1979 due to the Eurocommunist efforts of the provincial secretary, who was later expelled from the party (ibid., p. 150). In addition to the KPO's hidden financing through Eastern trade (*YICA*, 1983, p. 405), Pelinka reports considerable income for the party through its Globus publishing house's trade with the Eastern bloc (*Die KPÖ*, p. 152).

Domestic Affairs. The parliamentary election of 24 April cost the KPO nearly one-third of its slender 1979 vote. The vote fell in every province. This was the first election in which the KPO fielded a full slate, where it failed to poll 1 percent in any province.

The KPO succeeded in polling more than 1 percent of the vote in only 19 of Austria's 121 political districts. Communist electoral strength waned in all but a couple of industrial districts.

In its federal campaign, the KPO proclaimed: "The communist party considers itself heir and continuer of the revolutionary social democracy . . . its task [is] to organize the proletariat politically, to imbue it with the consciousness of its situation, [and] to ready and maintain it psychologically and physically for the struggle" (*Salzburger Nachrichten*, 14 April). With little hope for parliamentary representation, the party participates in extraparliamentary initiatives, especially environmental issues. Party chairman Muhri said in January, "Even two communists in parliament could achieve much in the workers' interest . . . They would fulfill the task of an independent left-wing opposition." The KPO pledges to fight profits, big capital (domestic and foreign), privilege, and the rich. It attacks the Socialist (SPO) government as supporting big capital and running a bourgeois state. It also attacks Austria's social partnership, which spreads "the lie that there are between multimillionaires and pensioners common interests and that there is a balance in everyone's interest."

In a press conference following the plenary session of the KPO Central Committee, Muhri denied that "the KPO is finished" (*Wiener Zeitung*, 11 May). Communists lost votes to "Green" parties and to the Socialists because some workers feared the loss of the SPO's majority. But the party's political line, he insisted, continues to be correct.

When the budget was presented in November, Muhri demanded the taxing of profits, which had grown by more than $2 billion in 1982, instead of taking an additional $1 billion from the masses.

Hans Kalt, secretary of the KPO Central Committee, authored an article entitled "Against

Manipulating the Masses," in which he attacked Austria's mass media. He identified as "main lines of work": (1) actions for peace and disarmament, including resistance to anticommunism and the "psychological war" that reaction and its media are waging against socialist countries; (2) support for the social and economic demands of the working class and resistance to bourgeois attempts to shift the burden of the crisis onto the people's shoulders; (3) actions in defense of democracy, far greater democratic freedoms, and resistance to neo-Nazi activities; (4) exhaustive discussion of the problems and demands of new social movements; (5) popularizing the policy of the party. Kalt attacked the bourgeois "rags" and the SPO press and urged a larger readership for the KPO's *Volksstimme*. He attacked Austria's government broadcasting system for its conservative proclivities and warned of the danger of the developing cable TV systems. He reminded readers of the KPO program's demand for "establishing and making applicable the fundamental right of all citizens to objective, authentic, and comprehensive information." (*WMR*, June, pp. 28–32.)

Pelinka reported some interesting KPO election data. Between the Chamber of Labor elections of 1949 and 1979, the total KPO vote dropped from 9.7 to 1.2 percent (workers, 11.0 to 1.3 percent; employees, 5.7 to 0.9 percent; transport employees, 9.2 to 1.5 percent) (*Die KPÖ*, p. 145). He also reported KPO percentages of representatives in the Trade Union Congress (OGB), with data from 1977–1979 (ibid., p. 146): all shop stewards, 0.7 percent; municipal workers' representatives, 3.0 percent; federal and provincial workers' representatives, 0.2 percent; railroad shop stewards, 5.4 percent; post office shop stewards, 1.8 percent; delegates to OGB Congress, 2.6 percent; representatives to OGB executive, 3.7 percent. In 1980, there were 15 KPO councillors in 13 municipalities in Carinthia, 47 councillors in 35 municipalities in Lower Austria, 8 councillors in 6 municipalities in Upper Austria, 1 councillor in Salzburg, 16 councillors in 13 municipalities in Styria, and 5 borough councillors in Vienna. Of the provincial capitals, only Graz and Linz had city councillors in 1980. (Ibid., p. 147.)

International Affairs. An article, "Cooperation Among Left Forces in Europe," by Erwin Scharf, then secretary of the Central Committee

of the KPO, appeared in October 1982. Using the KPO and SPO as examples, Scharf emphasized the need for cooperation of the European Left in view of the new nuclear threat from the United States. (*WMR*, October 1982, pp. 8–14.) The 1983 conference of the working-class movement, held in Linz was devoted to the centenary of the death of Karl Marx (ibid., March, p. 43). Muhri's statement, "There are no neutrals in the fight for peace" (ibid., pp. 20–23) suggests links between the KPO and the Austrian peace movement. Finally, in an article, "Existing Socialism and the Working-Class Movement," Bruno Furch, KPO representative to the *World Marxist Review*, mocks the "third way" of Social Democrats (ibid., April, pp. 53–58).

International Party Contacts. The first half of 1983 was again an active period for KPO international contacts. Péter Várkonyi, secretary of the Central Committee of the Hungarian party, visited Vienna in January (*Volksstimme*, 22 January). On 21 February, a Soviet party delegation arrived for a visit (ibid., 22 February). In March, Michal Stefanak, a candidate member of the Czechoslovak party's Central Committee, visited Erwin Scharf (Prague domestic service, 23 March; *FBIS*, 24 March). Vadim Zagladin, first deputy chief of the Soviet Central Committee's International Department, came to Vienna in early April to visit Muhri and Scharf. The meeting dealt with peace, disarmament, and Soviet-Austrian relations (*Volksstimme*, 6 April). On 29 May, a delegation from the Romanian party arrived for a visit to Vienna and Upper Austria (ibid., 31 May).

Pelinka makes a relevant and useful conclusion: "The 'Normalization' [following a brief flirt with Eurocommunism] brought the party back into the ghetto it had escaped for a short time. This return to a normal state of isolation kept the KPO, in the years of a Socialist government, from making even slight use of the opportunities that a governing and thus necessarily pragmatic social democracy offers to a left opposition. The KPO has not succeeded in channeling, even in part, the discontent with the governing practice of the Socialists. In this situation, the KPO apparently considers it necessary to deceive itself through programmatic rhetoric. The KPO, the party of permanent lack of success, of steady decline of voters and members, of increasingly threatening aging, resolved at its Twenty-fourth Party Congress in its draft program: 'In all continents, in more than a hundred countries, under various conditions, there are revolutionary parties guided by scientific socialism. Their origin and growth confirm that the cause of the working people needs these revolutionary parties. Nothing can replace them. Such a party in our country is the KPO.'" (*Die KPÖ*, pp. 156–57.)

Frederick C. Engelmann
University of Alberta

Belgium

Population. 9.9 million
Party. Belgian Communist Party (Parti communiste de Belgique; Kommunistische Partij van Belgie; PCB/KPB)
Founded. 1921
Membership. 10,000 (estimate)
Leadership. President: Louis van Geyt; vice-presidents: Claude Renard (French-language wing), Jef Turf (Dutch-language wing); national secretary of the Central Committee: Jan Debrouwere
Politburo. 14 members: Pierre Beauvois, Marcel Couteau, Jan Debrouwere, Filip Delmotte, Robert Dussart, Roel Jacobs, Ludo Loose, Jacques Moins, Jacques Nagels, Claude Renard, Jef Turf, Louis van Geyt, Jules Vercaigne, Jack Withages
Central Committee. 72 full members: 37 in the French-language wing, 35 in the Dutch-language wing
Status. Legal
Last Congress. Twenty-fourth, March and December 1982 (two stages)
Last Election. 1981, 2.3 percent, 2 of 212
Auxiliary Organizations. Communist Youth of Belgium; Union of Belgian Pioneers; National Union of Communist Students
Publications. *Le Drapeau rouge*, daily party organ in French; *De Rode Vann*, Dutch-language weekly (circulation: 14,500 and 11,000 respectively); *Les Cahiers communistes* (PCB monthly), ideological review; *Vlaams Marxistisch Tijdschrift* (KPB quarterly)

The PCB/KPB is a minor and declining party of little significance in the political life of a small country. Its persistence in presenting itself as a "national" party two decades after progressive regionalization (in fact, federalization) of the country's institutions and the division of other parties into distinct regional entities made it increasingly difficult for the PCB/KPB to keep in touch with current domestic issues since the policy decisions and the approaches of other parties are distinctly regional. At an extraordinary congress in late 1982, the party "federalized, to be more united." The adoption of a Eurocommunist stance, the enhanced importance of the European peace movement, and particularly the prospective deployment of cruise missiles in Belgium have provided the party with new or more important issues on which to express positions distinctive in the Belgian setting and with opportunities to exert greater influence. However, a shrinking membership, declining electoral fortunes in the most recent national and local elections, and internal division have reduced its position further in recent years.

Internal Affairs. At its Twenty-fourth Congress (March 1982) the party was no longer able to sustain its attempt to retain its basically unitary structure in the context of the largely federalized Belgian state and a party system comprised of regional parties. The internal divisions were exacerbated by the increased salience of regional issues and by a split within the party between pro-Moscow and "Eurocommunist" factions. The decline in the party's electoral base (from 3.3 percent in 1978 to 2.3 percent in the election of November 1981 and setbacks in the local elections of October 1982) and loss of membership—both stimulated by Soviet operations in Afghanistan and the military government in Poland—have created a crisis atmosphere in the party. The old-line Stalinist faction, particularly strong in the Walloon city of Liege, has been reduced in strength and put on the defensive by martial law in Poland and the invasion of Afghanistan. The Eurocommunist faction has strengthened its position inside the party by reaching out to the Chinese People's Republic and by criticizing Soviet actions in Afghanistan and Poland.

The division of the party into organizationally distinct Flemish, Walloon, and Brussels-based components at the extraordinary December 1982 session of the Twenty-fourth Congress (which unfolded under the theme of "federalizing in order to struggle in a more united fashion") brought the party's formal structure into harmony with the regional organization of the country that has become progressively more pronounced during the past twenty years and with the division of the larger parties and current issues into similarly regionalized configurations. But the initial efforts to associate the regional wings of the party with regionally defined issues that often pit Flanders against Wallonia or one or both of those larger regions against the smaller Brussels region have not been notably successful.

The main consequence of the December 1982 special congress was the institutionalization of the Eurocommunist line in party doctrine. The positions adopted stress the party's independence as a national entity. References to Marxism-Leninism were dropped from party statutes, and the party's goals were defined in terms of a "democratic, pluralistic, federalist, and self-managing socialism." (*RAD Background Report*, 18 January.) "Internationalist solidarity" and cooperation with noncommunist and nonsocialist elements everywhere underline the new open tone of the party's formal positions.

Domestic Affairs. The current government of Wilfried Martens (the fifth cabinet organized by that prime minister) is pursuing a drastic austerity program to regain control of the public budget and to improve the international competitive position of the economy. The PCB/KPB has criticized those aspects of the austerity program that impinge on transfer payments to individuals and families and on the salaries and benefits of public-sector workers. The party generally supported a wildcat strike of railroad workers that grew into a comprehensive labor stoppage—lasting two weeks—among public employees in September (*Intercontinental Press*, 31 October). The party's position on issues relating to the general management of the economy continues to be presented in relatively nonspecific terms. They entail the advocacy of general economic growth to be achieved through increased "socialist self-management." The party sees the current right-of-center coalition's austerity policies as increasing rather than decreasing existing income inequality. The government's "neo-liberal" policies are condemned for increasing returns to capital at the expense of diminished incomes for and transfer payments to workers. (*Le Drapeau rouge*, 20 December 1982.)

While speaking out on domestic economic issues regularly, the party's leaders continue to distinguish it from other parties principally in terms of foreign policy and security matters. The increased salience of these in the period since the NATO "dual-track decision" of December 1979 has contributed to the formulation of domestic policy positions in terms of increased international solidarity and the definition of domestic economic problems in terms of international confrontations.

Foreign Affairs. The party has been a vocal advocate of arms limitations, nuclear disarmament, and the European peace movement for several years. The beginning of the deployment of Pershing II and cruise missiles in Western

Europe (some of the latter are destined for emplacement on Belgian territory) has served to increase its emphasis on these issues as well as its activities in various Western European peace movements. Its increasingly Eurocommunist stance has led to calls for the denuclearization of Europe—i.e., the dismantling of at least some Soviet theater nuclear weapons, as well as those of NATO.

The most notable departure for the party in the past year has been the reopening of relations with the Chinese Communist Party through visits to Beijing of PCB/KPB leaders. This "normalization" of relations, coupled with the Belgian party's condemnation of the Soviet position in Afghanistan and martial law in Poland, and its concern for mutual rather than only NATO restraint in the deployment of nuclear missiles in Europe has carried the PCB/KPB closer to its Western European sister parties along the path of Eurocommunism.

Martin O. Heisler
University of Maryland

Cyprus

Population. 653,000 (80 percent Greek; 18 percent Turkish)
Party. Progressive Party of the Working People (Anorthotikon Komma Ergazomenou Laou; AKEL)
Founded. 1922 (AKEL, 1941)
Membership. 14,000 (*WMR*, October 1982): 67 percent industrial workers and employees, 20 percent peasants and middle class, 24 percent women, 30 percent under 30 years old; 80 percent from Greek Cypriot community
General Secretary. Ezekias Papaioannou
Politburo. 13 members: Ezekias Papaioannou, Andreas Fandis, Dinos Konstantinou, G. Katsouridhis, Khambis Mikhailidhis, Andreas Ziartidhis, Khristos Petas, Kiriakos Khristou, Mikhail Poumbouris, G. Khristodoulidhis, A. Mikhailidhis, G. Sophokles, Dhonis Khristofinis
Secretariat. 3 members: Papaioannou, Fandis (deputy general secretary), Konstantinou (organizing secretary)
Status. Legal
Last Congress. Fifteenth, 13–15 May 1982
Last Election. 1981, 32.8 percent, 12 of 35 seats in House of Representatives
Auxiliary Organizations. Pan-Cypriot Workers' Federation (PEO), 45,000 members, Andreas Ziartidhis, general secretary; United Democratic Youth Organization (EDON), 10,000 members; Confederation of Women's Organizations; Pan-Cyprian Peace Council; Pan-Cyprian Federation of Students and Young Professionals; Union of Greek Cypriots in England, 1,200 members, considered London branch of AKEL
Publications. *Kharavyi* (Dawn), AKEL daily and largest paper in Cyprus; *Demokratia*, AKEL weekly; *Neo Kairoi* (New times), AKEL magazine; *Ergatiko Vima* (Workers' stride), PEO weekly; *Neolaia* (Youth), EDON weekly

The original Communist Party of Cyprus (Kommonistikon Komma Kiprou) was secretly founded in 1922 by Greek Cypriot cadres trained in mainland Greece. Four years later, the party openly held its first congress, after the island became a British crown colony. Outlawed in 1933, the party thrived as an underground movement until 1941, when it resurfaced as the AKEL. All political parties were proscribed in 1955 during the insurgency against the British led by the Greek Cypriot paramilitary group known as EOKA. AKEL leaders chose not to take up arms in that anticolonial campaign and later rationalized their inaction as "a nonviolent alternative to EOKA terrorism in the independence struggle." This peaceful policy may have been a serious miscalculation by the communists because the AKEL is criticized to this day by disaffected leftists. Since the establishment of the Republic of Cyprus in 1960, the AKEL has enjoyed legal status as the island's strongest, best-organized political party.

The AKEL claims it is "a people's party, a party of Greek and Turkish working people" (*WMR*, September 1979). While the AKEL is officially banned in the northern part of the island, which is controlled by Turkish Cypriots, the communists have never stopped trying to appeal to the island's minority population. The goal of AKEL states: "We believe the patriotic front should include, as is done in the free territory, Turkish Cypriots (Marxists and members of progressive, democratic groups living in the occupied areas)" (ibid., October 1982). Communist front groups exist in the Turkish Cypriot part of the island, and representatives of these groups attended the World Conference on Peace and Life, Against Nuclear War, held in Prague during June (*Kharavyi*, 22 June).

Party Internal Affairs. The AKEL is reputed to be a tightly controlled apparatus, and few disagreements are aired in public. Replacement of the gerontocracy that now rules AKEL will be a critical problem for younger party members as the present leaders grow older in their secure career positions. Today the AKEL attaches special importance to recruiting, training, and educating younger people. In the words of Politburo member Dhonis Khristofinis, "Leaders do not emerge overnight, as we all know; they attain maturity and are tried and tested in hard work and everyday struggle for the working people's interests. To prove their worth as new party workers and achieve tangible results, they must equip themselves with sound theoretical and political knowledge. The party sees to it that comrades receive proper Marxist-Leninist training." (*WMR*, October 1982.)

At the Fifteenth Party Congress in May 1982, attention was given to the "party and mass movement." The final communiqué hailed the "great success in the organizational sector" and referred to the various steps that had been taken to improve party work. Cited as a specific accomplishment was the vigorous effort to enlist "thousands of new members from all the strata of the people of Cyprus, so that our party consolidates itself and makes its presence felt where the people live and work, at every place of work as well as every place of residence, every village, every neighborhood." (*Kharavyi*, 30 May 1982.) Since the Fourteenth Congress, "party membership has increased by 2,479" to its present strength of "nearly 14,000 members." What is more encouraging to the AKEL leaders is that some 96,000 Cypriots voted for the party in the 1981 parliamentary elections, which "is an indication of the potentialities of increasing the party's numerical strength." (*WMR*, October 1982.)

The AKEL claims that it "uses tested forms of work among the masses" in its attempts to tell the people "the truth about what goes on in Cyprus and throughout the world." To that end, "it circulates leaflets, pamphlets, and articles dealing with topical matters and organizes lectures and talks through its political schools." In accordance with guidelines of the last congress, the AKEL Central Committee is "reorganizing and strengthening its Ideological Department which must supply its counterparts at the district level with material on current ideological and political issues." Moreover, "much will have to be done to improve party publications, increase their circulation and win a larger readership for them." The purpose of these measures "is to take the offensive on the ideological and political front and expose imperialist and reactionary schemes more effectively." (Ibid.)

Each September, the AKEL holds a "fund-raising drive to provide money for the party's normal activity" and to demonstrate "a symbolic expression of mass support for the party." Additional operating capital for the AKEL is generated "from activities under the indirect but tight control of the party in...branches of...production and distribution of goods (cooperatives, retail stores, financing enterprises, tourist agencies, export-import enterprises)." As a direct result of these commercial endeavors, the AKEL has "become probably the major employer on the island." (*Andi*, Athens, 16 January 1981.) The two best-known communist-controlled enterprises are the Popular Distiller's Company of Limassol, which produces wines and brandies for the domestic market and export, and the People's Coffee Grinding Company in Nicosia.

The AKEL's leading front group, the Pan-Cypriot Workers' Federation (PEO), the island's largest labor union, held elections to its General Council, Executive Bureau, and Executive Council. Andreas Ziartidhis, who has been in the forefront of labor affairs for four decades, was re-elected general secretary. His deputy, Pavlos Dhinglis, and his assistant, A. Lasettas, were also reinstated. (Nicosia domestic service, 26 November.)

Domestic Affairs. The re-election of President Spyros Kyprianou of the centrist Democratic Party (DIKO) on 13 February gave AKEL "serious responsibilities" because of "the confidence which the people have invested in us through their overwhelming vote for the Democratic Cooperation, the minimum program, and for the joint candidate of the cooperating AKEL-DIKO parties" (*Kharavyi*, 13 March; *WMR*, July). The post-election euphoria, however, was short-lived as tension between AKEL and the Kyprianou forces emerged over the communist demand that "the cooperating parties must work out, in close collaboration, a specific program for setting the priorities, promoting and implementing the minimum program" (*Kharavyi*, 13 March). Obviously, the AKEL wanted some rewards for backing the winning presidential candidate. While the communists did not expect a cabinet seat, Papaioannou did make a strong presentation of the long-standing communist demands for AKEL representation on such semi-governmental bodies as the Cyprus Broadcasting Corporation. But these overtures met with little success. Hence, "AKEL's efforts to penetrate the government machinery and DIKO's corresponding reaction to foil these efforts . . . cast a shadow on the cooperation between the two parties" (*I Simerini*, 6 August). The failure of AKEL to gain any political appointments was only one reason why Papaioannou commented that

"democratic cooperation between AKEL and DIKO has been enduring a great test" (*Kharavyi*, 3 October).

While AKEL and DIKO are supposedly bound by all the points included in the pre-election minimum program worked out by the two parties, "they fully maintain the inalienable right to follow their own policy on issues that are not covered by the minimum program" (ibid.). A difference arose over the U.N. secretary general's new initiative to resume stalled inter-communal talks. This dispute was soon overshadowed, however, by the Turkish Cypriots' declaration of independence. Papaioannou was a member of the official three-man Cypriot delegation that went to New York City to protest the move. The U.N. Security Council passed a resolution asking the Turkish Cypriots to withdraw their unilateral declaration of independence. The AKEL Politburo later said that the AKEL's primary duty was "to insist on the full implementation of this resolution" but only through peaceful means. "We reject every idea for military confrontation because this would bring ruin and further remove the solution of the problem confronting the Cypriot people." (Nicosia domestic service, 26 November.) The Politburo also reiterated the Soviet-inspired suggestion for a special international conference on the Cyprus problem.

President Kyprianou and the communists jointly backed a peace march in June calling for complete demilitarization of war-divided Cyprus and a ban on nuclear weapons, which was the kind of cooperation the AKEL wished for when it signed the minimum program with the DIKO prior to the 1983 election. The right-wing press claimed that the march was "organized within the framework of Moscow's international propaganda campaign" and that many DIKO members felt it was impossible for them to participate in a demonstration "which serves communist expediencies" (*I Simerini*, 3 June). For example, the AKEL injected slogans such as "Out with the British bases," which embarrassed President Kyprianou, who reportedly is not ready to raise the question of the complete dismantling of British bases in Cyprus (ibid.). Nonetheless, the march did attract some 20,000 participants, far less than the claimed 65,000 marchers in a similar 1982 protest that stretched "20 kilometers" along the road between Limassol and Akrotiri (*WMR*, October 1982).

Foreign Affairs. The AKEL's approach to key international issues was reflected in the documents of the Fifteenth Party Congress (May 1982), which stressed the importance of protecting life on earth by averting the threat of a nuclear catastrophe by opposing the "imperialist policy of gaining military superiority, the production of neutron weapons, and the NATO decision to deploy new American medium-range missiles in Western Europe." The congress expressed unreserved support for the Soviet Union's "constructive proposals intended to provide dependable safeguards against nuclear war, promote détente and lower armament levels with a view to bringing about general and complete disarmament." The final resolution of the congress emphasized "the Cypriot communists' militant solidarity with the struggle of the people of El Salvador, with revolutionary Nicaragua, socialist Cuba, the heroic Palestinian people and the progressive forces of Lebanon, the patriots of Namibia, and the fighters against South Africa's racist regime." The AKEL claims that it must help the masses "master the secrets of international politics"... [and] open their eyes to the real source of the war menace...the U.S. imperialist reaction's policy of aggression and expansion." (Ibid.)

The Cypriot communists continued their attack on the presence of British bases and other military forces on Cyprus, "which the aggressive imperialist forces want to turn into an unsinkable air carrier" (*Kharavyi*, 22 June). Papaioannou complained that the British "were not content with their profits from the 1960 agreements," which established the bases, but have forced Cyprus to "become entangled in the gears of imperialist strategy in the eastern Mediterranean." As a result, "37 percent of Cypriot territory is under Turkish occupation, the Americans have three radio monitoring stations and, in addition, four NATO countries (United States, Britain, France, and Italy) are using the Larnaca International Airport, Larnaca port, and Cypriot territorial waters to transfer Marines and war materiel to Lebanon and use them against that country's national patriotic forces." Consequently, Cypriots "stand the danger of receiving blows" from Syrian missiles that are launched against the NATO countries. With "the support of Greece and international support in general," the Cypriot people must struggle to accomplish the communist goal of "an independent, nonaligned, sovereign, integral, and demilitarized

Cyprus." (Ibid., 8 November.) To that end, the communist youth organization, EDON, staged a rally in September to denounce the military action in Lebanon, "which the Israeli Zionists started with imperialist help," and to express "unstinting solidarity with the neighboring, friendly Lebanese people, and particularly with its patriotic forces, which include the brother Lebanese Communist Party" (ibid., 16 September).

As a reaction to President Reagan's June statement on the Strategic Arms Reduction Talks (START), a communist editorial described the U.S. position as "hypocritical" and went on to endorse fully the Soviet reservations about the talks (ibid., 10 June). AKEL has consistently scored the United States for its reliance "on growing military power and its unlimited use in foreign policy" and has praised the Soviet commitment "not to be the first to use nuclear weapons" (*WMR*, October 1982).

Cypriot foreign minister Nicos Rolandhis resigned from the government in September after a domestic political disagreement with President Kyprianou. The AKEL regretted this decision of a "minister who has won the esteem and confidence of his colleagues from the nonaligned, socialist countries who support us." Moreover, the move "creates an undesirable rift in the lines of the democratic patriotic forces at a time when we all agree that there is a need for broader and greater unification and cohesion." (*Kharavyi*, 22 September.) The new minister of foreign affairs is George Iacovou, a 45-year-old former ambassador to Bonn. The communists were seemingly noncommittal about this appointment and withheld judgment.

International Party Contacts. The AKEL is known to maintain frequent and extensive relations with both ruling and nonruling communist parties, as well as with all the international front groups. On the invitation of the AKEL Central Committee, a delegation of the Lebanese Communist Party visited Cyprus in March. In the customary "cordial, comradely atmosphere," there was a frank exchange of views on the situation in their respective countries. The visit ended with an expression of their fraternal relations and a "willingness to develop these relations on the basis of Marxism-Leninism and proletarian internationalism." (Ibid., 3 April.) In September, a delegation of the Bulgarian youth union came to Cyprus to celebrate the fortieth anniversary of the founding of EDON (ibid., 23 September). The same month, an official delegation of the Soviet Foreign Ministry was in Cyprus to discuss the upcoming U.N. General Assembly meeting (ibid., 10 September). Another governmental meeting was held in October when a delegation of the Supreme Soviet paid an eight-day visit at the invitation of the Cypriot House of Representatives. The influence of AKEL was felt at the end of the visit when the House president expressed "the love and appreciation of the House of Representatives and the Cypriot people for the people of the Soviet Union" (Nicosia domestic service, 28 October; *FBIS*, 31 October). This meeting paved the way for a bilateral agreement for legal cooperation between the two countries to cover, among other things, the extradition of fugitives.

An AKEL group headed by Papaioannou attended the Prague Peace Conference in June. In July, AKEL leaders made their annual trip to the USSR, and in August a similar group went to Prague. Most of these official party visits to Soviet bloc countries are justified by AKEL members as necessary to develop further "genuinely fraternal relations." Greetings are also normally exchanged on various national holidays and celebrations. One unusual AKEL message was sent to the Central Committee of the Turkish Communist Party to commemorate "the sixty-third anniversary of its founding" and "the one-hundredth anniversary of the birth of its founder and first president, Mustafa Sufi." The AKEL also expressed gratitude for the Turkish party's "heroic stand against the invasion of Turkish troops in Cyprus." (*Kharavyi*, 10 September.)

On his seventy-fifth birthday, Papaioannou was awarded "one of the highest orders of the German Democratic Republic, the Grand Star of International Friendship...[and] praised as an outstanding representative of the international communist movement" (ADN, 8 October; *FBIS*, 11 October). About the same time, Bulgaria awarded the Georgi Dimitrov Order to the AKEL general secretary for his contribution to "the consolidation of the unity of the international communist and workers movement" (Sofia domestic service, 7 October; *FBIS*, 12 October).

Speaking at a meeting in Nicosia to mark the anniversary of the October Revolution, Soviet ambassador Sergei T. Astavin reaffirmed the USSR's position that Cyprus must remain "a unified, independent, sovereign, territorially integral, and nonaligned state." He also said that Soviet-Cypriot relations "are developing in a positive manner in all fields." (Nicosia domestic service, 7 November; *FBIS*, 9 November.)

T. W. Adams
Washington, D.C.

Denmark

Population. 5.1 million (1983 estimate)
Party. Communist Party of Denmark (Danmarks Kommunistiske Parti; DKP)
Founded. 1919
Membership. 10,000 (estimate)
Chairman. Jorgen Jensen (elected December 1977)
Executive Committee. 16 members: Jorgen Jensen (chairman), Ib Norlund (vice-chairman), Poul Emanuel (party secretary), Jan Andersen, Villy Fulgsang, Margit Hansen, Bernard Jeune, Gunnar

Kanstrup (editor of *Land og Folk*) Kurt Kristensen, Dan Lundrup, Freddy Madsen, Jorgen Madsen, Anette Nielsen, Bo Rosschou, Ole Sohn, Ingmar Wagner

Central Committee. 51 members, 15 candidate members

Control Commission. 5 members

Status. Legal

Last Congress. Twenty-seventh, 12–15 May 1983, in Brondby Strand; next congress scheduled for 1986

Last Election. 1984, 0.7 percent, no representation

Auxiliary Organizations. Communist Youth of Denmark (Danmarks Kommunistiske Ungdom; DKU), Ole Sorensen, chairman; Communist Students of Denmark (Danmarks Kommunistiske Studenter; KOMM. S.), Frank Aaen, chairman

Publications. *Land og Folk* (Nation and people), daily, circulation 13,000 weekdays and 16,000 weekends; *Tiden-Verden Rund* (Times around the world), theoretical monthly; *Fremad* (Forward), monthly

Despite the bravado of its twenty-seventh Congress in May, the DKP continued to decline throughout the year. This was confirmed in the national parliamentary elections of 10 January 1984, when the party received a scant 22,880 votes (0.7 percent), its worst showing since World War II. The DKP lost all its parliamentary seats in October 1979, when its vote share fell below the 2 percent minimum required for proportional representation in the parliament (Folketing). Its vote was down by one-third from its mediocre showing in the December 1981 parliamentary elections. In addition, internal strife continued, and the aging DKP leadership was attacked by prominent former members.

The January 1984 elections, Denmark's seventh parliamentary elections in less than thirteen years, reflect the continuing tenuous parliamentary balance. This situation has continued since the destabilizing election of December 1973. During this difficult decade, extremist parties of the Left and Right have controlled between a quarter and a third of the parliamentary seats, making it difficult for the more moderate parties to govern effectively. The current four-party coalition led by conservative Poul Schlüter failed to gain support from the reformist Social Democratic Party (SDP), which it succeeded in September 1982. Nor was the center-right government able to gain consistent parliamentary support from the other nonsocialist parties. When the critical budget act failed to win a parliamentary majority in December, Schlüter called for a new election.

Once again, the DKP had to compete with four other Marxist parties to the left of the SDP. In the past ten to fifteen years, these various leftist parties have typically captured an eighth of the national vote. In January 1984, they collectively polled 14.9 percent, and the DKP share continued to plummet. They compete for the same voters, and whenever one moves ahead, another leftist party declines. In 1981, the SDP apparently also lost votes to the leftist parties. The principal gainer has been the independent Marxist Socialist People's Party (Socialistisk Folkeparti; SF), which doubled its strength in the 1981 parliamentary elections. It held on to these gains in the 1984 election. The third leftist party with significant support is the Left Socialist Party (Venstresocialisterne; VS), a leftist fragment of the SF that enjoys substantial support from public employees (as does the SF) and students. The VS retained its five Folketing seats in 1984.

Less important are three small sects: the Communist Workers' Party (Kommunistisk Arbeiderparti; KAP), which has unsuccessfully sought a closer relationship with the VS and did not run in the January 1984 elections; the International Socialist Workers' Party (Internationalen Socialistisk Arbeiderparti; SAP), the Danish branch of the Trotskyist Fourth International, which received 2,200 votes; and a new group, the Marxist-Leninist Party (Marxistisk-Leninistisk Parti; MLP), which polled fewer than 1,000 votes in January 1984, the lowest for any registered party in recent Danish history.

Party Internal Affairs. Despite its dismal electoral performance, the DKP had an active year, in part because of its Twenty-seventh Congress in May. Once again, the DKP demonstrated its organizational conservatism. Jorgen Jensen, who succeeded to the party chairmanship on the death of Knud Jespersen in 1977, is a veteran of more than thirty years in the DKP. He was reaffirmed as chairman at the congress. Ib Norlund, the party's number-two man and chief theoretician, has been in power for decades. The same is true for the party's secretary (administrative director) Poul Emanuel. Challengers to the party leadership have been forced to leave the party either by exclusion or resignation. The party continued to feel the effects of the public attack on its leadership by Hanne Reintoft, a popular leftist and former DKP member of parliament, and several other members. After the congress, a new group of resignations, concentrated in the party's intellectual wing, were announced. The protesters' spokesman, Kjeld Ammundsen, an employee of Danish State Radio, denounced the leadership as "tired men" who had failed to respond to problems at home and in other socialist countries such as Poland (*Politiken Weekly*, 14–19 May).

The party's highest authority is the triennial congress. The Twenty-seventh met in Brondby Strand, a working class suburb of Copenhagen, in May. The Central Committee is elected at the congress, and it, in turn, elects the party's Executive Committee (politburo), chairman, secretary, and other posts. Despite the attendance of some 453 delegates at the recent congress, the DKP functions in the Leninist model of a self-perpetuating elite. In recent years, the Central Committee has met from four to six times annually. In addition, the party holds special conferences a couple of times each year as well as annual meetings in years without a congress (*Tiden-Verden Rund*, Special Issue, 1983). Nevertheless, the aging and the isolation of the core of veterans has become apparent as more energetic and pragmatic members erupt in outrage at the party's decline. Such open criticism is usually swiftly followed by resignation or expulsion (*Information*, 11 May).

The DKP is not entirely immune from change, however. Elections to the Central Committee at congresses do reflect individual popularity. Ivan Hansen, longtime Central and Executive Committee member, failed to be re-elected because of his moderation while a municipal councillor in Copenhagen prior to the 1981 municipal elections. On the other hand, Jens Peter Bonde, who is prominently anti–Common Market, was catapulted onto the Central Committee as a full member without the usual probationary period as a candidate member. Similarly, Anker Schjerning, a peace activist, received the highest number of votes, and two trade union activists outpolled Chairman Jensen. (Ibid., 16 May.)

The DKU reported that its activities continued to fall into two areas: support for radical trade union factions appealing to apprentices and young workers and mobilization and influence over younger participants in the various peace organizations. The DKU has not been successful in either area. The KOMM.S. overlaps the DKU, but concentrates its efforts on university students. Communists periodically have held high posts in the Danish National Students' Council (Danske Studerendes Faellesraad; DSF), but the DSF's strength has been uncertain in recent years. KOMM.S. maintains some organizational autonomy with its own publications, *Røde Blade* (Red leaves) and *Spartakus*, and its own meetings (Sixth Congress, October 1982).

Although the DKP has policies regarding the self-governing territories of Greenland and the Faeroe Islands, it does not have organizations in either. There was an attempt to form an autonomous Faeroese Communist Party in 1975 and later years, but it apparently failed.

Domestic Affairs. As has been the case for several consecutive years, economic recession continued to be the main item on the domestic Danish political agenda. The nonsocialist Schlüter government introduced a variety of austerity measures, most of which had to be modified to pass parliament. The large governmental deficits began to contract, as did the country's perpetual balance-of-payments deficit. Production ceased falling, and national income grew at an estimated modest rate of 2.25 percent. With the fall in interest rates, construction ceased to decline. Unemployment at 10 percent remained serious and chronic. Each year the figures edge upward as the labor force expands and the number of jobs, especially in industry, contract. The impact of unemployment continues to be especially hard on youth and women. Accordingly, the DKP and other leftist parties have pushed this issue in their domestic agitation. The moderate general collective bargaining agreements in the spring (calling for 4 percent wage increases) were in line with the government's austerity program. Although there was some disagreement with individual unions, the SDP-controlled Trade Union Confederation (Landsorganisationen) signed the agreements, and the majority of members voted in favor of ratification.

The DKP could again only comment on these issues in its press and at the Twenty-seventh Congress. The party's new manifesto, The Denmark We Want, and its action program, Our Answer, contained little that was new. There is much dissatisfaction with the Schlüter government and the national and foreign monopolies in whose interests the government is presumed to act. Well-known points are reiterated: establishment of new public enterprises, nationalization of all banks and financial institutions, close state supervision of investment, the cooperative movement, agriculture and fisheries, increases in collective housing construction, and, finally, the famous DKP proposal to reduce the workweek to 35 hours, restrict overtime, extend various leaves, etc., with no reduction in real wages.

The DKP has little influence over major trade unions, but it does have influence at various locals. The DKP has long been stronger in the labor movement than in electoral politics. Communist strength has been especially visible in the metalworkers', typographers', and maritime unions. The expulsion of Seamen's Union chief Preben Moller Hansen in 1977 weakened the DKP's hold on this powerful union. Violence during blockades and strikes by longshoremen in Jutland attracted considerable attention, but there is little evidence that communists were instrumental in that action, although the Seamen's Union did provide financial assistance (Jyllands-Posten, 3 February). With the SDP move into the official political opposition, it has become somewhat easier for SDP trade unionists to maintain their internal position within the movement (YICA, 1983, p. 414).

Foreign Affairs. The international political situation has always had a direct impact on the political fate of the DKP, often in uncertain ways. The cold war of the late 1940s quickly eroded the party's initial postwar strength. The waning of détente in the late 1970s, capped by the Soviet invasion of Afghanistan in 1979, spelled domestic disaster for the DKP. Few West European communist parties have been more steadfastly loyal to the foreign policy line of the Soviet Union than the DKP. On the other hand, the DKP has cleverly exploited international issues such as the growing unpopularity of Danish membership in the European Community (EEC) and the strong revival of the peace movement over the issue of intermediate-range nuclear missiles in Europe. Through front organizations, the DKP has been able to promote positions that would attract little attention under the DKP label.

The DKP's official foreign policy program has been rigid, but its ability to control foreign policy organizations through dedicated individuals has been notable. Newly elected Central Committee member Jens Peter Bonde is a leading figure in the broadly based Popular Movement Against the EEC (Folkebevaegelsen imod EF), sits as one of its four members in the European Parliament, and edits its weekly paper. Anker Schjerning has similarly been prominent in the peace movement. At the DKP congress, Chairman Jensen reiterated the party's goals: "The key task today," he stressed, "is to prevent the deployment of U.S. nuclear missile systems in Europe" (WMR, August). In addition, the DKP participated in the attack on long-standing U.S. installations in Greenland, repeating claims that such bases had offensive purposes (Land og Folk, 1 September).

The Euromissile issue went far beyond DKP rhetoric and loomed as a major issue in Danish foreign policy debates throughout the year. The reformist SDP and other leftist parties in parliament sought to delay the deployment until the United States and the Soviet Union had given the Geneva talks a better chance. Motions opposing the deployment of U.S. missiles in Europe were passed over the government's objections, ending the traditional consensus on security policy among the country's main political parties. (The left-centrist Radical Liberal party, reflecting traditional pacifistic and anti-NATO views, supported this effort as well.) The DKP was thus part of a larger movement, but it could not claim leadership or direction of the movement.

The peace movement, which is decentralized into several competing factions, was ambiguous about DKP participation. Revelations of infiltration and espionage by Soviet KGB agents made many wary of closer association with the DKP and elements under its control. Although the government decided for national security reasons to drop its prosecution of Danish writer Arne Herlov Petersen for espionage, it made clear that it had evidence of Soviet efforts to control the peace movement (NYT, 26 July). Similarly, continuing revelations of Soviet submarine and other military activity around the Nordic countries weakened the appeal of a Nordic nuclear-free zone, which has long been a DKP goal.

Anti-EEC sentiment remains strong in Denmark with continuing disputes over fishing quotas, farm policy, and budgetary matters. Elections to the European Parliament are due in 1984, and the DKP remains committed to the Popular Movement front.

International Party Contacts. The DKP leadership maintains close ties to other pro-Moscow communist parties, especially those in Eastern Europe. Delegations from all of the Warsaw Pact countries attended the DKP congress. The large Soviet delegation was led by Central Committee member Avgust Voss, who is also chairman of the Latvian Communist Party. East Germany sent a large delegation, headed by a candidate member of the Politburo. In all, 29 foreign communist parties and organizations were represented (*Tiden-Verden Rund*, Congress Issue).

The DKP leadership supported plans for a World Assembly for Peace and Life, Against Nuclear War scheduled for June in Prague. Chairman Jensen led a delegation to Moscow in November, where the DKP repeated its full support for every aspect of Soviet foreign and domestic policy (Radio Moscow, 22 November; *FBIS*, 22 November). In sum, the DKP courted its big brothers without visible signs of criticism from either side. Earlier there had been rumors in the Danish press that the Soviets had doubts about the effectiveness of the current communist leadership in certain Western European parties, including the DKP (*Information*, 8 March 1982). Loyalty has been an acceptable substitute for power in the DKP's relationship with the Soviet party.

Other Marxist/Leftist Groups. The DKP is only one of several left-wing parties currently active in Danish politics. The SF is by far the most powerful of these groups. The SF splintered from the DKP in 1958, when the communists expelled then chairman Aksel Larsen, who set about establishing a broadly based national Marxist party. Ever since it won its first parliamentary representation in 1960, its primary political tactic has been to push the SDP leftward. In 1966–1967 and 1971–1973, SF votes kept the Social Democrats in power. The first experiment in formal SF-SDP collaboration (the so-called

Red Cabinet) ended when the SF's left wing split off to form the VS party. In 1973, several right-wing Social Democrats abandoned their party to form the Center Democrats. Following the SF's advance in December 1981, it appeared that another effort would be made at collaboration. However, the SF and SDP did not have sufficient votes to pass legislation without additional support. The VS rejected any cooperation with the SDP. The Radicals, another traditional support party for the SDP, were willing to cooperate only on an issue-by-issue basis. Premier Anker Jorgensen found it increasingly difficult to satisfy these two parties on domestic issues, and he resigned in September 1982. The SF has little influence in opposition to the nonsocialist coalition.

The SF program is decidedly socialist and Marxian, but it emphasizes Danish origins and values and rejects foreign socialist models. The SF is explicitly non-Leninist in both its internal party governance and its attitudes toward Danish parliamentary democracy. It has had periodic internal feuds and schisms, but under the experienced leadership of its veteran chairman, Gert Petersen, the party has become a natural alternative to dissatisfied Social Democrats and other leftist voters. Despite its limited influence, the SF held its strong position following the January 1984 elections. It again received 11.5 percent of the vote and kept all of its 21 seats. Once again its Folketing delegation comprises men and women who are employed by the public sector (*Jyllands-Posten*, 13 January 1984).

The SF discussed several major policy issues at its annual convention in May. Chairman Petersen called for a united front by the labor parties. More specifically, after sharp debate the party modified its position on reduction of the workweek. It went on record as accepting a reduction without wage compensation. Bjarne Mortensen, chairman of the party's Labor Relations Committee, objected to intervention into the collective bargaining process even in favor of a six-hour day.

Foreign affairs were also discussed extensively at the annual convention, for the SF has long made its opposition to NATO and EEC membership a major point. In parliament, the SF played a role in urging the SDP to put forward its resolution against U.S. Euromissiles, despite the expiration of the original NATO deadlines on an arms-control treaty with the USSR. The party's foreign policy position, although critical of Soviet foreign policy, has been a major barrier to its full participation in coalition considerations (*Nordisk Kontakt*, no. 11). The SF has informal but close ties to analogous parties in Norway and Sweden and looser ties to the Italian Communist Party and other independent leftist parties. The SF is more than a protest party, although dissatisfaction with the DKP and SDP have accounted for some of its support. It is a haven for activists and voters who are committed to Danish Marxist and democratic socialist solutions without reference or apologies for less fortunate experiments elsewhere.

The VS is much weaker, but it kept its five Folketing seats in the January 1984 elections and holds seats on several city councils. It is a native party without significant foreign ties, but despite positive references to parliamentary democracy and civil liberties, it is ambiguous about their applicability to a revolutionary "situation." Internal party strife has been endemic in the VS, given its penchant for personality conflicts, internal secrecy, and weak organizational structure. The VS electoral achievements came despite several polls in 1983 that showed the party below the crucial 2 percent threshold and the forced resignation (because of party rules on maximum terms of office) of two popular VS parliamentarians, Preben Wilhjelm and Steen Folke. These two long-time party activists and another member of parliament, Mikael Waldorff, organized a party fraction, the VS Forum, to encourage more open debate about the party's goals and procedures (*Berlingske Tidende*, 17 February).

The KAP is the oldest of the extreme left-wing sects that garner only a few thousand votes and are always far short of winning national or local office. Danish electoral laws make it possible to run nationally for parliament with only about 20,000 signatures. A major incentive to under-take even a hopeless parliamentary campaign is the free and generous television time allowed all parties. But even this was not sufficient incentive for the KAP under its perpetual leader, Copenhagen University lecturer Benito Scocozza, to undertake another campaign. Maoist in origins, the party has bravely but forlornly stuck with the Maoist alternative even as the aging Chairman Mao and the PRC sought more pragmatic solutions. The KAP suggested that a union with the VS might be mutually advantageous, but nothing came of it. Whether the party will continue to participate in national elections remains uncertain. It has, however, continued its vehement attacks on the United States and the Soviet Union.

The SAP appeared on the ballot in the January 1984 election, but as noted, its vote remained minuscule. Its newspaper, *Klassekampen* (Class struggle), keeps Danes abreast of developments in the international Trotskyist movement. Some Trotskyists attempted their familiar infiltration tactics in a local branch of the SDP (Aarhus), but were uncovered and expelled.

Yet another leftist sect appeared on the ballots, but drew less than a thousand votes. The Marxist-Leninist Party, which sought registration as the Communist Party of Denmark—Marxist-Leninist but was denied this confusing name by the Interior Ministry, is dedicated to bringing the Albanian model to Denmark. Its close ties to the Albanian Party of Labor were demonstrated in February during a visit to Tirana by Klaus Klausen, the MLP's first secretary (Tirana domestic service, 26 February; *FBIS*, 3 March). Its influence could scarcely be more modest.

Eric S. Einhorn
University of Massachusetts at Amherst

Finland

Population. 4.9 million (*World Factbook*, 1983)
Party. Finnish Communist Party (Suomen Kommunistinen Puolue; SKP); runs as the Finnish People's Democratic League (Suomen Kansan Demokraatienen Litto; SKDL) in parliamentary elections
Founded. 1918
Membership. 50,000 claimed
Chairman. Jouko Kajanoja
Politburo. 10 members: (moderates) Jouko Kajanoja, Arvo Aalto (general secretary), Aarne Saarinen, Arvo Kemppainen, Helja Tammisola, Tutta Tallgren, (Stalinists) Veikko Alho (vice-chairman), Taisto Sinisalo, Seppo Toiviainen, Marjatta Stenius-Kaukonen
Central Committee. 50 full and 15 alternate members
Status. Legal
Last Congress. Nineteenth, 22–24 May 1981, in Helsinki; next regular congress scheduled for 1984; special congress, 14–15 May 1982, in Helsinki
Last Election. 20–21 March 1983, 14 percent (down from 18 percent in 1979), 27 of 200 seats (down from 35 in 1979)
Auxiliary Organizations. Finnish Democratic Youth League; Women's Organization
Publications. *Kansan Uutiset* (daily); *Tiedonantaja* (daily), Stalinist; *Folktidningen* (Swedish-language weekly); all published in Helsinki

In 1983, the troubled SKP suffered its worst election defeat ever. The setback left the party without a cabinet minister for the first time in eight years. The communists, who once could count on one vote out of four in national elections, received less than one out of eight in 1983.

The election setback only punctuates what has been a long decline in the fortunes of the party. One of the structural reasons for the decline has been the shrinkage of the SKP's natural constituency—workers and farmers. Industrial workers now account for only a third of the Finnish labor force, while farm workers account for less than 10 percent (*WP*, 29 May).

But even among the industrial and farm workers, the SKP is experiencing difficulties. While the SKP will always enjoy the support of a small, hard-core group of industrial and farm workers, the reform-minded Social Democrats have effectively co-opted a large segment of what had previously been the SKP's natural constituency. A harmonious blend of the welfare state and a prosperous economy has given many Finnish workers and farmers a stake in the existing Social Democratic political economy, thus taking the edge off any socioeconomic grievances the SKP might otherwise exploit. The concomitant lack of enthusiasm of these workers for disrupting the existing political economy is reinforced whenever they contrast it with the failing Soviet economy across the border.

Of course, the declining fortunes of the SKP (and its electoral front, the SKDL) also result from the factionalism and disunity that have plagued the party for a decade and a half. The origin of SKP factionalism dates back to 1969 when the pro-Soviet Stalinist minority wing of the party (led by Taisto Sinisalo) took issue with the reforms being adopted by the more liberal, or Eurocommunist, majority wing of the party. Factionalism increased when the SKDL socialists and Eurocommunists participated in a number of

Finnish coalition governments, over heated protests from the Stalinists.

Events outside of Finland have also deepened divisions in the SKP and sapped its strength. Tension in the party increased following the 1968 Soviet invasion of Czechoslovakia—an event criticized by the Eurocommunists but supported by the Stalinists. This led to a decision by the Stalinists to walk out of the party congress in 1969 and brought the SKP to the brink of a formal split. Only Soviet pressure averted it.

Factionalism and disunity in the SKP became so intense during 1982 that a special party congress was called in May in an attempt to reconcile the two wings. But on the eve of the congress, a strong Soviet statement of support for the Stalinists (whom Moscow felt were being threatened) inflamed the situation even more. And at a two-day conference in Moscow, Soviet Politburo member Arvid Pelshe read a letter attacking the Eurocommunists for their anti-Sovietism and witch-hunts against the Stalinists.

Far from unifying the party, the Soviet campaign fanned the fires of factionalism. Retiring SKP chairman Aarne Saarinen delivered a blunt rejoinder at the party congress to the Soviet letter, rejecting the charges leveled against the Eurocommunists by the Communist Party of the Soviet Union (CPSU). For his efforts, Saarinen won the applause of the congress as a whole. Many of Moscow's favorite Stalinists saw their positions weakened, including Taisto Sinisalo, who lost the post of vice-chairman. Most disturbing to the Stalinists was their loss of three seats on the SKP Central Committee. This prompted a new crisis when the Stalinists threatened to boycott the SKP leadership bodies.

An uneasy compromise was worked out, only to be overtaken by another Stalinist complaint, this time over SKDL and Eurocommunist support for a government that pushed through a devaluation in October 1982.

With general parliamentary elections less than four months away, the SKP-dominated SKDL broke up Finland's four-party coalition government on 29 December 1982 by voting against a proposed defense allocation. In an attempt to revive its electoral support, which has been declining for years, the SKDL decided to go into opposition to promote itself as a party of peace and to strengthen party unity in preparation for the parliamentary elections on 20 and 21 March (*NYT*, 30 December).

Curiously enough, the SKDL opposition to a modest increase in the defense budget meant that the SKDL was, by definition, also opposed to buying Soviet arms. This position was ironically counter to the post-WWII foreign policy line of friendship with the Soviet Union, which virtually all the other Finnish political entities accept. In fact, the SKDL was alone in opposing a deal that the Soviet Union readily accepted since it served to reduce Finland's large trade surplus with the Soviets.

Moreover, the SKDL's "disarmament" position also created still further confusion and disorder within the SKP. While the Stalinist wing of the SKP had always been against cooperation with the government, it would have preferred to see the SKDL leave the government over the government's decision in 1982 to devalue the Finnish mark by 10 percent (when the SKDL abstained in the voting and remained in the government coalition, despite noisy criticism from the Stalinists) (*Tiedonantaja*, 14 October 1982).

In any event, the SKDL's decision to leave the government was little help to its political fortunes. The SKP suffered a severe setback in the March elections when the SKDL lost 8 of the 35 seats it previously held in the 200-member parliament. In addition, half of the SKDL incumbents were not re-elected. While most electoral observers had expected the SKP to lose votes, the size of the flight from the SKDL—over 100,000 votes or 18.5 percent less than in 1979—surprised almost all political analysts.

The SKDL electoral defeat clearly reflected voter dissatisfaction with the internal squabbling within the SKP. In addition to the chronic issues dividing the party, a new one began in September 1982, when the Eurocommunists in the Central Committee of the SKP pushed through a decision to reissue party membership cards, a move that would fan still further the ever-present fires of discord between the Stalinist and Eurocommunist wings of the SKP on the eve of the election. (See *Kansan Uutiset*, 9 November 1982.)

This move to exchange the ten-year SKP membership books for new party books has been something the Eurocommunists have wanted for some time. In the eyes of the Eurocommunists, the Stalinists have been deliberately falsifying the old party books in order to increase their strength. In many areas, for instance, the Stalinists allegedly retained deceased persons on party rolls and cast votes in their names at party elections. In addition, the majority moderates felt that the exchange of party books would help to improve the weak financial status of the SKP. Many SKP members would now be required to pay back dues assessed on the basis of their actual income.

A study by Risto Sankiaho, a leading Finnish expert on elections, attributes the SKDL setback to two other factors. First, the SKDL failed to exploit public dissatisfaction with the government's 1982 decision to devalue the Finnish mark by 10 percent. Second, the SKDL's tactical decision to withdraw from the government coalition in December 1982 and strengthen party unity in preparation for the March elections backfired. The SKDL's last-minute departure from the government did not give the SKDL enough time to explain its "peace" issue to the voters prior to the election. To some would-be SKDL supporters, leaving the government over a small defense spending issue was contrived, transparent electoral politics.

The election defeat polarized the different factions within the SKDL. Noncommunist SKDL leaders delivered speeches and statements threatening to destroy the SKDL unless SKP factional activity stopped. Many noncommunist SKDL leaders, in fact, believe that a formal split is not only unavoidable but necessary if the SKDL ever wants to play a significant role in another government coalition. They would like to see the Stalinists leave the SKDL and allow a more politically homogeneous SKDL composed of the Eurocommunists and left-socialists. In essence, such a restructured SKDL without the Stalinists would, of course, strengthen the authority of the left-socialists within the SKDL and thus discourage them from leaving the SKDL.

The other option would be for the left-socialists in the SKDL to break away and form a new party that would aim at encouraging defections by left-wing social democrats as well as by the communists. In fact, the left-socialists have been organizing at the grass-roots level. The socialists in the SKDL began building their own organization within the SKDL in December 1982. And in May 1983, the SKDL socialists held an unprecedented two-day convention in Helsinki. They decided that in the future they would emphasize the fact that they are socialists, not communists, while at the same time remaining in the SKDL. This new SKDL socialist organization may be an omen of a complete break with the SKP at some point in the future, however. (*Kansan Uutiset*, 25 April, 24 May; *Tiedonantaja*, 24 May; *Helsingin Sanomat*, 23 May.)

In the eyes of many observers, the SKDL has always been unduly controlled by the SKP and thus unduly influenced by the Stalinists and the CPSU. For instance, while the SKDL has over 40,000 members, only about a fifth are communists, yet about two-thirds of the members of the decisionmaking organs are communist.

The Eurocommunists are also critical of SKP Chairman Jouko Kajanoja and his conciliatory policy toward the Stalinists. In militant Eurocommunist eyes, Kajanoja's weak and ineffective leadership—and his desire to accommodate the Stalinists in the name of party unity—has contributed in no small way to the electoral demise of the SKDL. Increasingly, the Eurocommunists have been working through General Secretary Arvo Aalto, the arch-Eurocommunist who represents them and the real power in the SKP.

While the SKDL (and the SKP within the SKDL) suffered a devastating electoral setback, the Stalinist wing of the SKP actually improved its relative position vis-à-vis the Eurocommunist majority in the SKP. The March election left the Stalinists with 9 out of the 27 SKDL seats, compared with 11 out of 35 before the election.

Threats from the left-socialists to leave the SKDL and the increasing strength of the Stalinists within the SKDL at a time of overall voter flight from the SKDL opened the door to even more intraparty factionalism and dissension after the election. In particular, the proportionally greater losses sustained by the Eurocommunists prompted Eurocommunist and left-socialist leaders to adopt a more hard-line attitude and to be less amenable to compromise than in the past. In essence, the results were a catalyst to those in the SKDL who wanted to resolve SKP factionalism by either "disciplining" the Stalinists to conform to the views of the Eurocommunist majority, or else purge the SKP (and the SKDL) of the Stalinist minority altogether.

Leadership and Organization. The SKP Central Committee met in late March to decide how to regroup following the dismal electoral showing of the SKDL earlier in the month. The Central Committee called for prompt and decisive action to end factionalism within the SKP. In particular, the Eurocommunists in the Central Committee pushed through a proposal (31–16, with three abstentions) calling for the Politburo to set up a task force to draft concrete recommendations to eliminate factional activity and to improve unity by 22 April.

The anti-Stalinist crusade in the SKP Central Committee was led by Arvo Aalto. Also recommending harsh action against the Stalinists were former party chairman Aarne Saarinen, defeated member of parliament Mikko Ekorre, and the acknowledged leader of the anti-Stalinist northern rebellion, Arvo Kemppainen.

The election results also contributed to heated charges and countercharges at the SKDL parliamentary caucus during 4 to 7 April. The SKP rift widened further at the caucus when the Stalinists walked out after the Eurocommunists refused membership in the caucus to one of the Stalinists. The Stalinists thereupon departed en masse, calling the exclusion of one of their members "immoral" and pledging to boycott future meetings until their delegate was invited back.

Following the Central Committee meeting, the Eurocommunists in the SKP took the lead and pushed ahead with two attacks on Stalinist interests. First, the Eurocommunists called for the closing of the Stalinist newspaper *Tiedonantaja* and the creation of a new party newspaper to replace it and the Eurocommunist *Kansan Uutiset*. Since *Tiedonantaja* presently serves as a vital organizational vehicle for the Stalinist wing of the SKP, the Stalinists viewed this move as a transparent way to weaken their ranks. Second, the Eurocommunists recommended the expulsion of Stalinist dissidents in the SKP who defied party district committees and ran as independent candidates. One such dissident was Esko-Juhani Tennila, a member of parliament from Lapland, who was re-elected even though he had been removed from the official SKDL list of candidates. On 16 April, the local party organization in Lapland, supported by Aalto and Eurocommunist leaders at the national level, expelled Tennila, his campaign manager, and almost a hundred other communists from the Lapland party (*Hufvudstadsbladet*, 17 April).

The Politburo's recommendations for resolving the crisis were scheduled to be considered at the 22 April meeting of the SKP Central Committee. However, the task force was unable to arrive at recommendations in time. Soviet intervention was probably the major factor inhibiting the Eurocommunists' anti-Stalinist moves at the meeting (see below).

Besides the major role of the CPSU, the failure of the Central Committee to resolve the differences and problems in the SKP was also due, in part, to the inability of the majority Eurocommunists to agree among themselves. The non-Stalinists in the SKP can be divided into at least three groups: those who favor closer ties with noncommunist left-socialist groups within the SKDL; those who supported hard-line measures against the Stalinists such as those taken in the Lapland district; and those (the so-called Third Line) who advocate making every effort to reach a modus vivendi with the Stalinists in the interests of party unity. This Third Line element consists of young people and women exasperated by the inability of old-guard leaders to achieve unity in the SKP. Just as these Third Liners wielded the balance of power at the May 1982 party congress, so did they play a significant role at the 22 May meeting, making every effort to find a compromise that would keep the party together.

The stop-gap measures taken at the Central Committee meeting were essentially a compromise between those anxious to take harsh action against the Stalinists and the fence-straddlers who sympathized with the hard-liners but who were timid about rocking the boat. This loose partnership was able to push through a watered-down attack against the Stalinists in the committee by majority vote.

On 22 April, the Central Committee tabled a final decision on how to deal with "parallel organizations" (for example, Stalinist groups) within the SKP until the party congress in May 1984. The Central Committee also backed off from its threat to discipline the minority Stalinists and close *Tiedonantaja*. While Eurocommunists were still critical of *Tiedonantaja*, they decided to set up a committee to study what should be done about the Stalinist newspaper. This move preserved *Tiedonantaja*'s subsidy as a newspaper of the SKP.

By August, it was clear that the "axing policy advocates" (militant Eurocommunists who resent the Soviet hold on the party) were losing out to pragmatists in the SKP who favored unifying the SKP along the lines of the Stalinists and returning it to a strongly Soviet-oriented party. The firing of Uolevi Mattila, an axing policy advocate, from the Information Section of the SKP Central Committee attests to the new winds blowing through the SKP. (JPRS, no. 84460, 3 October.)

The apparent influence of the CPSU on the

SKP printing shop and certain newspapers (such as the financially troubled *Kansan Uutiset*) probably contributes to the increasingly pro-Soviet and Stalinist direction of the SKP. For instance, the Yhteistyo Company's printing shop reportedly provides the SKP income of 3 million markka each year. Almost certainly, this funding comes from the CPSU. The fact that the SKDL-owned *Kansan Uutiset* is hopelessly in debt to the presumably Soviet-financed Yhteistyo printing shop makes the SKDL socialists and Eurocommunists dependent on the CPSU and the Stalinists.

In addition, the defeat of the SKDL in the parliamentary elections brought with it a reduction of some 9 million markkas in party press subsidies (*Uusi Suomi*, 7 June). Since *Tiedonantaja*'s financial support from the CPSU was unaffected by the election setback, the Stalinists were in a far better position to strengthen their relative position in the SKP than were the Eurocommunists supporting *Kansan Uutiset*. Nowhere was the financial muscle of the Stalinists better shown than in the bitter press fight between the Stalinists and the Eurocommunists.

The economic strength of the Stalinists became more evident following the 11 September decision by the SKP Central Committee—by a vote of 46 to 3—to begin publishing a new weekly newspaper. Beginning in January 1984, this new newspaper will replace the theoretical journal *Kommunisti* and the already discontinued internal information organ, *Paivan Posti*. In addition, the SKP Politburo has proposed that the weekly be changed into a daily, which would in turn be merged with *Tiedonantaja* into a newspaper that would be published four times weekly. (JPRS, no. 84676, 3 November.)

Thus, when the SKP convenes its congress in May 1984, it must decide whether to implement the Politburo's proposal to publish a new newspaper for the party. That decision will go a long way in defining the future path of the SKDL as well as the SKP.

Many of the socialists and Eurocommunists in the SKDL share the fear that the press settlement will strengthen Stalinist minority positions and increase the danger of SKDL disintegration (ibid.) According to these officials, the purpose of the Politburo's solution was to weaken the position of *Kansan Uutiset* and to make *Tiedonantaja* the official organ of the SKP.

The Stalinists and the Eurocommunists have also been fighting over who would replace Stalinist Christina Porkkala as general secretary of the Finnish-Soviet Friendship Society. That matter was dealt with in early September when Erkki Kauppila, the chief editor of *Kansan Uutiset*, the newspaper of the SKP and SKDL, was designated the new secretary general of the society by the SKP. In a vote taken in the SKP Politburo, Kauppila won over Stalinist Timo Karvonen, the education secretary of the society, by a vote of 6–3. (Ibid., no. 84460, 3 October.)

At a meeting of the society's Presidium, Center Party representatives apparently concluded that the SKP had to find a candidate acceptable to the Stalinists as well as the Eurocommunists. Erkki Kivimaki, the veteran managing editor of the SKDL and SKP publication, *Yhteistyo*, somewhat more agreeable to the Stalinists, was introduced as a compromise candidate. The Stalinists, however, seemed to be more interested in Finnish Broadcasting Corporation's Moscow correspondent, Beijo Nikkila, who is no ally of the Eurocommunists.

International Views, Positions, and Party Contacts. The new leadership in Moscow showed early signs of flexibility in its policy toward the SKDL. In contrast to the previous Soviet policy of allowing only SKP members in SKDL delegations to the Soviet Union, Moscow allowed a noncommunist member to join an official SKDL delegation visiting Moscow 26–29 January.

Since almost all political groups in Finnish politics now accept the foreign policy line of friendship with the Soviet Union, it made little difference to the Soviets who won the elections; nor did it matter much to the Soviet Union how many votes the SKP received.

What did matter to Moscow, however, was making sure the Stalinists remained solid and influential in the SKP and, indirectly, in the SKDL. In this way, the CPSU could still use the Stalinists as surrogates to advance Soviet policy while keeping all Finnish political entities deferential and protective of Soviet interests in the region.

The convergence of de facto Soviet assets among Finnish noncommunist and communist groups was apparent when Finland's "bourgeois" press warned the militant Eurocommunists that harsh attacks against the Stalinists and a split in the SKP was ill-advised since it would not be in the best interests of overall Finnish-Soviet relations.

What was disturbing to Moscow, however, was the beginning of an anti-Stalinist campaign led by the militant Eurocommunists, shortly after the SKDL election setback. By April, Moscow had moved away from its early position of support for all elements of the SKDL. The anti-Stalinist activities of the SKP Eurocommunists and some of the socialists provoked the CPSU to step into the fray between the two wings of the SKP. Moscow came down wholeheartedly on the side of the Stalinists—as it had a year earlier when it wrote a letter blasting several Eurocommunists on the eve of the May 1982 extraordinary party congress.

This time Soviet intervention on behalf of the Stalinists was even more direct. On 7 April, CPSU Politburo member Grigori V. Romanov delivered a speech in Finland to the SKP, severely critical of the militant Eurocommunists for their anti-Stalinist actions. Romanov called former SKP chairman Aarne Saarinen, SKP secretary general Arvo Aalto, and Kalevi Kivisto, the noncommunist chairman of the SKDL, "dispersionists" (that is, those who wanted to purge or "ax" the Stalinists from the SKP and the SKDL) (*FBIS*, 7 April).

Romanov also stressed the need for party unity in the SKP, as did Soviet diplomats who spoke to Jouko Kajanoja at the Soviet Embassy a few days before the Central Committee meeting. In addition, Romanov warned that if the Eurocommunists purged the party of the Stalinists, the CPSU would recognize a new party formed by the Stalinist minority faction as the sole "legitimate" communist party of Finland.

Moscow followed Romanov's unambiguous warning with a 21 April *Pravda* article, on the eve of the Central Committee meeting, again warning the SKP not to expel the Stalinists from the SKP. The article blasted Eurocommunists in the SKP Lapland district for expelling Esko Tennila and the other Stalinists. The Soviets coupled this demand with a telegram to the Lapland district expressing a strong vote of confidence for the Stalinist minority there on the eve of a Lapland District Committee meeting. The *Pravda* article also attacked Arvo Aalto for his involvement in the "repressions" against the Stalinists. Aalto, in his defense, stated that Moscow had misunderstood the situation in Lapland, that he had actually tried to prevent the Lapland district

from dismissing Tennila. The SKP Central Committee, while not rejecting the *Pravda* attack on Aalto explicitly, upheld Aalto by a vote of 31 to 18.

These Soviet activities put a damper on the anti-Soviet activities of the Central Committee task force. In fact, the balance of power in the SKP began to turn away from the militant Eurocommunists. The moderate Eurocommunists could not agree on stronger measures against the Stalinists because of the importance they attached to traditional SKP-CPSU ties and the knowledge that Moscow was willing to sever ties in the event the Stalinists were kicked out.

But while the Soviet actions effectively arrested any strong anti-Stalinist actions by the Eurocommunists, it did not prevent the liberals from complaining about Soviet heavy-handedness. Former SKP chairman Aarne Saarinen said that the *Pravda* article dealing with the Lapland district would harm endeavors to achieve unity in the party (*Hufvudstadbladet*, 24 April). Later in the year, Saarinen candidly chided the CPSU for its "continuous . . . open and emphatic interference in the internal affairs" of the SKP (*FBIS*, 8 December).

The Eurocommunists were also quick to point out that the Soviet actions constituted a breach of the agreement worked out at the Conference of European Communist and Workers' Parties in East Berlin in 1976 regarding noninterference in one another's internal affairs. But no matter what their opinion of the CPSU or the Stalinists, most of them could not face the thought of being isolated from the international communist movement. Romanov clearly warned them that if the party split, it would be the Stalinists who would be welcome in Moscow, not the Eurocommunists or socialists. Thus, the specter of being isolated externally brought most of the moderate Eurocommunists back into line.

A move against the Stalinists would also have isolated the SKP internally. Since all other Finnish parties have had to cultivate relations with the CPSU over the years (including the conservatives), none of them could afford cooperation with a SKP considered "anti-Soviet." Thus, not only would the expulsion of the Stalinists have precipitated an open break between the SKP and the CPSU, it would also have contributed to a deterioration of overall Soviet-Finnish diplomatic relations, thus leaving the SKP out in the cold domestically.

On 26 April, *Pravda* supported the decision of the special SKP plenum (called to reconcile the differences between the Stalinists and the Euro-communists) to postpone a decision on a formal SKP split. But *Pravda* also charged that the problems in the SKP were not organizational, but ideological and political in nature, thus implicitly supporting the Stalinist wing of the party and warning the Eurocommunists not to bring about a change in policy. (*FBIS*, 26 April.)

Leif Rosenberger
Washington, D.C.

France

Population. 55.6 million (1982 census)
Party. French Communist Party (Parti communiste français; PCF)
Founded. 1920
Membership. 710,000 (Report to the Central Committee, 3 February 1982); 27,500 cells
Secretary General. Georges Marchais
Politburo. 22 full members: Georges Marchais (secretary general), Gustave Ansart (chairman of the Central Commission on Political Control), Mireille Bertrand (health), Jean Colpin (assistance with the advancement of members), Charles Fiterman (minister of transport), Maxime Gremetz (foreign policy), Jean-Claude Gayssot (party activity in businesses), Guy Hermier (editor of *Révolution*), Philippe Herzog (economics), Pierre Juquin (propaganda), Henri Krasucki (secretary of the General Confederation of Labor), André Lajoinie (chairman of the PCF group in the National Assembly), Paul Laurent (party organization), Francette Lazard (director of the Institute of Marxist Studies), René Le Guen (science and technology), Roland Leroy (editor of *L'Humanité* and *L'Humanité dimanche*), Gisèle Moreau (party activity among women), René Piquet (chairman of PCF delegation in the European Assembly), Gaston Plissonier (coordination of work by the Politburo and Secretariat), Claude Poperen (liaison with party federations), Louis Viannet (Mail Workers Federation), Madeleine Vincent (local communities, elections)
Secretariat. 7 full members: Fiterman, Gremetz, Lajoinie, Laurent, Marchais, Moreau, Plissonier
Central Committee. 145 full members
Central Commission for Financial Control. 5 members
Status. Legal
Last Congress. Twenty-fourth, 3–7 February 1982; next congress planned for 1986
Last Election. 1981, 16.2 percent, 44 of 491 seats
Auxiliary Organizations. General Confederation of Labor (CGT), Georges Séguy, secretary general; World Peace Council, Michel Langignon, secretary; Movement of Communist Youth of France (MCJF); Committee for the Defense of Freedom in France and the World; Association of Communist and Republican Representatives
Publications. *L'Humanité*, Paris, daily national organ, circulation 130,000; *L'Humanité dimanche*, Paris, Sunday newspaper, circulation 360,000; three regional dailies; *Cahiers du communisme*, official monthly theoretical journal; *Révolution*, weekly, official publication of the Central Committee; Editions Sociales, PCF publishing house, Paris

Since entering the French cabinet as a junior partner of the Socialist Party (PS) in the spring of 1981, the PCF has had to confront a critical political dilemma: that of remaining a loyal member of the PS-led government while maintaining sufficient independence from the PS to preserve its own identity as a separate, and indeed rival, force on the Left. The events of 1983 only aggravated the problems facing the PCF as a result of this predicament.

On the one hand, the party leadership, headed by Secretary General Georges Marchais, remained reluctant to withdraw from the cabinet, even though government policy continued to be set largely by the PS and President François Mitterrand. In 1983, in both the domestic and international arenas, Mitterrand pursued policies that differed markedly from the PCF's stated preferences. Moreover, the PCF and the PS suffered massive electoral losses in municipal elections in March and subsequent months, as voter dissatisfaction with the government's performance (especially in economic matters) intensified. In the face of these setbacks, and in spite of pressure on Marchais from within the party to change course, the PCF in late 1983 once again confirmed its intention to stay in the government.

On the other hand, the party continued to insist on its right to assert its own views on a variety of controversial issues, even when these positions clashed with the official policies of Mitterrand and the PS government. In large measure, this determination to keep a certain distance from its coalition partners stemmed from the PCF's historic struggle with the PS for influence within the Left's traditional constituencies and from the PCF's long-standing ties with the Soviet Union. In both instances, this fierce independence is rooted in the PCF's very identity as a communist party, an identity that party leaders believe it can preserve only by reaffirming its claims to being the sole authentic representative of the interests of the French working class and its allies.

Leadership and Party Organization. The frustrations resulting from the municipal elections and the PCF's subordinate role in the government led some communists to question the wisdom of supporting the government's policies. Marchais himself admitted that certain party activists had advised against voting in favor of a package of new austerity measures unveiled by Mitterrand in March (*L'Humanité*, 22 April). In late April, the secretary general acknowledged receipt of an open letter to the Central Committee by Jeannette Thorez-Vermeersch, the widow of former PCF chief Maurice Thorez (1900–1964). The letter was reportedly critical of the PCF leadership's decision to remain in the government (ibid., 21 April; *WP*, 24 April). There were also disagreements over the leadership's foreign policies. In November, a group of left-leaning party members known as the Southeast Communist Group voiced disapproval of Marchais's condemnation of terrorist attacks on Israeli forces in Lebanon, accusing him of siding with Israel (*Le Monde*, 9 November). From the right wing of the party came criticisms of the leadership's pro-Soviet stance on such issues as Poland and Afghanistan. Here the assault on party policy was led by the dissident group that publishes *Rencontres communistes*, many of whose leaders, such as Henri Fiszbin, had in previous years been eased out of their official positions within the party. These dissidents were also critical of the PCF's refusal to allow wider internal debate (Serge Briand, "They Are Already Talking About It," *Rencontres communistes hebdo*, 1 July; *JPRS*, 3 October). In some constituencies, the *Rencontres communistes* group fielded candidates for municipal office in opposition to PCF candidates, and Marchais at one point charged that the dissidents were garnering the support of local PS functionaries (*L'Humanité*, 6 January).

Reports that Marchais himself was encountering opposition within the PCF Central Committee and might be forced to step down also circulated (*Le Figaro*, 22 April). The substance of these discussions within the party leadership remained for the most part veiled in secrecy, however, and in late 1983 Marchais confidently asserted that his position as party leader was not in jeopardy (*Le Monde*, 22 November).

Other signs of uncertainty and malaise within the PCF included a reduction in the number of party activists and a decline in the circulation of party periodicals. Although PCF officials continued to contend that party membership numbered around 700,000 (Paul Laurent, "The Communist Party We Need Now," *Cahiers du communisme*, July–August; *JPRS*, 11 October), various outside estimates placed the number of militants at no more than 80,000, with perhaps as few as 25,000 (*Time*, 26 September; AFP, Paris, 6 April; *FBIS*, 7 April). Paul Laurent, the Politburo's specialist on party organization, admitted that many party members had not renewed their membership and noted that "a lot" of party sections had fewer than fifty members, while 20 percent of the party cells had not held public rallies (*JPRS*, 11 October). While party officials stated that upwards of 42,000 new members had joined the PCF in 1983, they offered no firm figures on the number of dropouts (*L'Humanité*, 22 September). The readership of *L'Humanité*, the national PCF daily newspaper, had dropped to 130,000 by the end of 1982, a decline of nearly 14 percent (*Time*, 26 September). Support for the CGT, the party's trade union affiliate, also continued to decline (*Le Monde*, 1 August). While the official figures put CGT membership at approximately 2 million, unofficial estimates place it at 1.5 million (*Financial Times*, London, 1 February 1984).

On 15 February, former PCF chief Waldeck Rochet (b. 1905) died after a protracted illness. Rochet, who assumed the party leadership in 1964 on the death of Thorez, had not been seen in public since 1969, after reportedly suffering a cerebral hemorrhage. Details as to the precise nature of his illness remained shrouded in mystery until recently, and he was not formally replaced as secretary general until 1972, when Marchais assumed the post (Kevin Devlin, "The Second Death of Waldeck Rochet," *RFE/RL*, 24 February).

Domestic Affairs. The PCF's steady decline was most graphically demonstrated by the results of the municipal elections. Held in over 36,400 cities and towns throughout France on 6 and 13 March, the elections were a major disappointment for the governing parties. In contrast to their triumphs in the municipal elections of 1977, the PS and PCF lost control of 31 cities having a population of over 100,000. (PS leaders had earlier indicated that a loss of 10–15 major cities would be "normal" [*Le Monde*, 11 January].) The PCF lost 15 of these large cities, including such long-held mayoralties as St.-Etienne and Nîmes. Even more alarming to PCF leaders were the unprecedented losses the party suffered in the working-class suburbs of Paris, traditionally known as the "Red Belt." Prior to 1983, the PCF administered 119 of these municipalities. Following the March elections, the number fell to 86 (*Est & Ouest*, April). This figure was reduced even further in the fall, when new elections were mandated in four Red Belt cities following the

cancellation of earlier results by French courts owing to charges of election fraud and corruption on the part of local PCF officials. One of these towns, Aulnay-sous-Bois, had been a PCF stronghold for eighteen years. In all, at the end of 1983, the PCF governed approximately 180 towns having a population of over 9,000, as compared with 225 prior to the elections. The party gained only 10–15 percent of the vote in parts of the Red Belt (AFP, Paris, 15 March; *FBIS*, 16 March), and it was estimated that the PCF's share of the national electorate had dwindled to perhaps 10 percent (*WP*, 24 April), a postwar nadir amounting to less than half of its percentage of the vote prior to 1968.

This long-term secular decline in the PCF's electoral fortunes was no doubt accelerated by the party's role as a coalition partner of the PS. Inevitably, the communists were regarded by many voters as sharing responsibility for the government's inability to make good on its promises of substantial improvements in economic and social welfare. In certain constituencies, particularly in the Red Belt, the PCF may also have suffered defections by traditional communist voters who turned to extreme right-wing candidates hostile to the immigrant populations of these communities. The essential problem for the PCF leadership, however, was that a withdrawal from the cabinet at this time could conceivably exacerbate these downward tendencies. By mid-November, polls showed that a majority of PCF voters still wanted the party to stay in the government (*Le Monde hebdomadaire*, 1–7 December).

The disappointing election returns were soon followed by additional indications of the PCF's waning influence. On 22 March, Mitterrand reorganized the cabinet, reducing its membership from 44 to 15. Two of the four PCF cabinet ministers were demoted to subcabinet ministerial positions. (Charles Fiterman remained in the cabinet as minister of transportation, and Marcel Rigout retained his post as minister of vocational training. Those demoted were Jack Ralite, the former minister of health, who became minister-delegate for social affairs and national solidarity in charge of employment, and Anicet Le Pors, the former minister of civil service and administrative reform, who became secretary of state in charge of the public sector and administrative reform.

Mitterrand's decision to shuffle the cabinet foreshadowed a major shift in the government's economic policy. In the context of mounting trade deficits, continuing inflation, and a further devaluation of the franc, Mitterrand on 25 March announced a new austerity program that veered sharply from the leftist government's original emphasis on reducing unemployment and redistributing income. Although the PCF had opposed austerity policies in previous years, the party leadership decided to approve the new measures, although PCF spokesmen preferred to use the term "stringency" rather than "austerity" when referring to them. Fully cognizant of the unpopularity of the stringency program among leftist voters, Marchais and other party leaders initially objected to certain of its proposed provisions and extracted from Mitterrand certain modifications before voting for it in the National Assembly. Meanwhile, the PCF's rhetoric remained critical, warning the PS against straying too far from the Left's earlier pledges to reform the French economy by attacking the capitalist system. The PCF leadership was clearly trying to position the party to take political advantage of popular discontent with the austerity program evident among supporters of the leftist parties.

International Activities. International issues also contributed to the strains in the PCF's relationship with the PS. As in previous years, the PCF in 1983 largely accepted the Soviet Union's rationale for such events as the invasion of Afghanistan and the imposition of martial law in Poland (*L'Humanité*, 23 July; Paris domestic service, 26 September; *FBIS*, 27 September). While calling on the Soviets to provide more information in the wake of the downing of the Korean jetliner in September, PCF leaders reserved their most critical comments for the Reagan administration's reactions to the incident (*L'Humanité*, 8 September). The PCF's views contrasted sharply with the Mitterrand administration's more critical attitude toward the Soviets on these issues.

The PCF and Mitterrand also differed on the question of France's role in the controversy surrounding the deployment of intermediate-range nuclear forces (INF) in Europe. Early in the year, Marchais seemed to share Mitterrand's view that French nuclear forces should not be included in the overall calculations of the INF balance in Europe, as demanded by the Soviet Union. In February, he came close to adopting President Reagan's "zero option" plan, calling for the elim-

ination of Soviet SS-20 missiles in exchange for cancellation of NATO plans to install new Pershing II and cruise missiles in Western Europe (*NYT*, 23 February). In June, however, Marchais severely criticized Mitterrand's renewed support at the Williamsburg summit meeting for the NATO deployment plans, adding that the French nuclear force could no longer be excluded from the INF negotiations between the superpowers in Geneva (*L'Humanité*, 3 June). The PCF at this time also called for the inclusion of all the states of Europe in the Geneva talks (ibid., 1 June). A further evolution in Marchais's position occurred in mid-July and was accompanied by a bizarre incident while the PCF leader was in Moscow on a hastily scheduled visit. On 13 July, *L'Humanité* reported that the Soviet press, in its initial accounts of the PCF-Soviet talks, had neglected to take note of Marchais's insistence on the need for "balanced arms reductions" and had falsely attributed to Marchais statements he had never made. (According to the first Tass report on the meetings, Marchais had allegedly described "the main danger" as stemming from the projected U.S. INF deployments [*WP*, 13 July].) Subsequent Soviet press accounts, as well as the communiqué issued at the conclusion of the talks, rectified these errors, according to both PCF and Soviet spokesmen (*L'Humanité*, 15 July; Paris domestic service, 13 July; *FBIS*, 14 July). The PCF leader now came out explicitly in favor of including French forces in the determination of the existing East-West INF balance, while at the same time asserting that French forces should not at the present time be reduced. The PCF-Soviet communiqué, and subsequent statements by PCF and Soviet officials, confirmed Moscow's agreement with both of these positions (Tass, 12 and 15 July; *FBIS*, 13 and 15 July; *L'Humanité*, 20 July).

The Moscow meeting evoked varying interpretations in France, with some analysts stressing PCF-Soviet differences and others suggesting that the dispute was largely contrived to camouflage Marchais's acceptance of the Soviet position on France's inclusion in the INF balance (*WP*, 17 and 25 July). Soviet foreign policy specialists, such as Boris Ponomarev and Vadim Zagladin, acknowledged the existence of differences with the PCF on the INF question (*Le Monde*, 25 October), but it appeared that these differences derived mainly from the PCF's unwillingness to place the blame for the missile controversy exclusively on the United States and NATO and from the PCF's appeals for "balanced" reductions in the number of Soviet SS-20s. For his part, Marchais stated that the Soviets did not as yet agree with his proposal to open the Geneva INF talks to other states (*L'Humanité*, 14 July).

Meanwhile, the PCF continued to voice support for the West European peace movement and criticized U.S. efforts to proceed with deployment of the new missiles on schedule. In October, the PCF and the CGT participated in peace demonstrations aimed primarily against the U.S. missiles, but sparse crowds in Paris and other cities attested to Mitterrand's success in building a national consensus around his defense policies (*Le Monde*, 25 October).

As in domestic policy, however, the PCF did not seek a rupture with the PS over international issues. In late November, Marchais affirmed the PCF's "almost total accord" with Mitterrand's foreign policy (ibid., 22 November). The PCF approved the government's decision in August to send French paratroopers to Chad, but warned against a direct combat role (ibid., 26 August). The party also approved of French military retaliation against Syria following a terrorist attack on French forces in Lebanon in October, but called for a negotiated accord among the Lebanese factions that would allow the repatriation of the French troops (ibid., 22 November). Party leaders declined to take a firm position on the expulsion of 47 Soviet officials from France for espionage. In addition, the PCF reiterated its 1977 position in favor of maintaining and modernizing French military forces. It voted for the government's military budget in June and confirmed its support for the construction of France's seventh nuclear submarine and for the current military draft law (*L'Humanité*, 24 January). The party restated its acknowledgment of France's membership in the Atlantic Alliance, but affirmed its continuing opposition to France's reintegration into NATO's military command and its preference for an "omnidirectional" defense policy (ibid., 8 June; *Le Monde*, 22 November).

International Party Contacts. During 1983, the PCF maintained high-level contacts with a number of ruling and nonruling communist parties. Ties with the Communist Party of the Soviet Union (CPSU) received particular attention. Marchais met with Andropov during his Moscow visit in July, and prominent Soviet officials, in-

cluding Zagladin and Anatoli S. Chernayev, deputy head of the International Department of the CPSU Central Committee, came to Paris. Although the PCF supported Soviet policies in a number of areas, party leaders on occasion insisted that PCF policy was fashioned in complete independence from the Kremlin. Examples of PCF foreign policy positions that diverged from Soviet views included the party leadership's criticisms of the SS-20 missiles, its support for the French military presence in Lebanon and Chad, and its opposition to what Marchais called "Syria's criminal aggression" against the Palestine Liberation Organization (PLO) (*L'Humanité*, 5 November). At times PCF leaders demonstrably played up their alleged differences with the USSR, as when Marchais told a Catholic newspaper on his return from Moscow that the PCF "rejected the idea that Europe's fate could be decided by the two superpowers. I categorically stated this to Yuri Andropov!" (*Témoignage chrétien*, 30 July.) Nevertheless, the PCF supported Moscow's positions on such sensitive questions as Poland, Afghanistan, and, increasingly, the INF controversy.

Meanwhile, the PCF continued to develop its relationship with the Chinese Communist Party, which was rekindled during Marchais's visit to Beijing in October 1982. Two delegations led by members of the Chinese Secretariat visited France in 1983; the editor of China's *People's Daily* attended *L'Humanité*'s annual fair; PCF Politburo member and *L'Humanité* editor Roland Leroy led a group of journalists to China; and PCF Central Committee members met with Chinese leaders while vacationing in the PRC. Although Marchais spoke of the PCF's wish "to extend cooperation" with the Chinese party, it was doubtful that any future collaboration would come at the expense of the PCF's links with the Soviet Union. In this respect, it was interesting that a CPSU delegation headed by Chernayev was in Paris at the same time as a Chinese group led by party secretary Xi Zhongxun (*Pravda*, 29 November; *L'Humanité*, 3 December; NCNA, 6 December; *FBIS*, 6 December).

The PCF also extended its contacts with the communist parties of Southeast Asia. Maxime Gremetz, the Politburo's foreign affairs specialist, journeyed to Vietnam, Kampuchea, and Laos in April (see his account of the trip in *L'Humanité*, 27 May), and a Vietnamese delegation visited France in late September (ibid., 8

October). The PCF reaffirmed its support of the Vietnamese involvement in Kampuchea and called on the French government to cooperate with that country's Vietnamese-backed government (ibid., 27 May). The PCF maintained routine contacts with the ruling parties of the Warsaw Pact states, highlighted by Marchais's talks with Todor Zhivkov in Bulgaria in August.

The most important meetings with nonruling communist parties were with the Greek and Italian parties. In March, Marchais visited Athens for talks with Greek party leader Kharilaos Florakis (*Rizospastis*, Athens, 30 March; *FBIS*, 1 April). In October, he went to Rome for talks with Italian secretary general Enrico Berlinguer. In their public statements, the leaders of the two largest communist parties of Western Europe did not dwell on their differences, but stressed their basic agreement on such issues as Lebanon and INF (*L'Unità*, 6 October; *FBIS*, 21 October). The PCF also held meetings with representatives of the communist parties of Israel (*L'Humanité*, 7 May) and Lebanon (ibid., 13 June).

In addition, the PCF pursued its own diplomacy in the Third World. Marchais visited Algeria for talks with leading government officials in April (ibid., 28 April) and in October went to Africa for discussions with the leaders of Benin, the Congo, and Angola (ibid., 25 and 31 October). PCF leaders also met with representatives of the PLO (*Volksstimme*, Vienna, 15 March; *FBIS*, 16 March), the South West Africa People's Organization (*L'Humanité*, 27 April), the Democratic Revolutionary Front of El Salvador (ibid., 14 April), the government of Nicaragua (ibid.,

15 September), and other Third World governments or political movements. The PCF's Central American policy continued to be based on support for the Sandinista regime in Nicaragua and for the Franco-Mexican statement of August 1981 calling for a negotiated settlement in El Salvador.

Conclusion. Despite continuing tensions between the PCF and the PS, symbolized by the decision of the communist director of the French Coal Board, Georges Valbon, to quit his post in mid-November to protest the government's coal policies, the year ended on a positive note. A PCF-PS summit meeting was held on 1 December. The Joint Declaration released by the two parties contained compromise formulas on economic priorities but defended the Mitterrand regime's stringency measures. It also highlighted areas of agreement on foreign policy while avoiding mention of well-known disagreements. (Paris domestic service, 2 December; *FBIS*, 2 December.) By the end of 1983, the PCF was still committed to remaining in the government, a decision that Marchais labeled "a principled stand" that would remain in force through the next presidential and legislative elections (*FBIS*, 27 September). The events of 1983 had shown, however, that this policy was fraught with risks for the PCF. By the same token, party leaders seemed to realize that a premature break with the PS might prove even riskier.

Michael J. Sodaro
George Washington University

Germany:
Federal Republic of Germany

Population. 61.5 million (1980)
Party. German Communist Party (Deutsche Kommunistische Partei; DKP)
Founded. 1968
Membership. 48,856 (claimed by the DKP in May 1981)
Chairman. Herbert Mies
Presidium. 17 members: Herbert Mies, Hermann Gautier, Jupp Angenfort, Kurt Bachmann, Martha Buschmann, Werner Cieslak, Gerd Deumlich, Kurt Fritsch, Willi Gerns, Erich Mayer, Ludwig Müller, Georg Polikeit, Rolf Priemer, Max Schäfer, Karl Heinz Schröder, Werner Stürmann, Ellen Weber
Secretariat. 11 members: Herbert Mies, Hermann Gautier, Vera Achenbach, Jupp Angenfort, Gerd Deumlich, Kurt Fritsch, Willi Gerns, Josef Mayer, Ludwig Müller, Karl Heinz Schröder, Wilhelm Spengler
Executive. 91 members
Status. Legal
Last Congress. Sixth, 29–31 May 1981, in Hanover
Last Election. 1983, 0.2 percent, no representation
Auxiliary Organizations. Socialist German Workers Youth (Sozialistische Deutsche Arbeiter Jugend; SDAJ), ca. 16,000 members (SDAJ claim: 35,000), Werner Stürmann, chairman; Marxist Student Union–Spartakus (Marxistischer Studentenbund; MSB-Spartakus), ca. 6,500 members, Uwe Knickrehm, chairman; Young Pioneers (Junge Pioniere; JP), ca. 4,000 members
Publications. *Unsere Zeit* (Our time), Düsseldorf; DKP daily organ, circulation ca. 50,000 copies; *elan*, SDAJ monthly organ; *rote blätter* (Red leaves), MSB-Spartakus monthly organ

The pro-Soviet DKP is the successor to the Communist Party of Germany (Kommunistische Partei Deutschlands; KPD), which was founded on 31 December 1918. The KPD was the third-largest political party in the Weimar Republic. Under Hitler, the KPD was outlawed and became an ineffective underground party. During the Allied occupation following World War II, the KPD was reactivated. In the Soviet-occupied zone, the KPD and Social Democratic Party of Germany (Sozialdemokratische Partei Deutschlands; SPD) were forced by the Soviets to merge and adopted the name Socialist Unity Party of Germany (Sozialistische Einheitspartei Deutschlands; SED). In the first national elections in the Federal Republic of Germany (FRG) in 1949, the

KPD received 5.7 percent of the vote and fifteen seats in the Bundestag. In the next elections in 1953, the KPD vote decreased to 2.2 percent, below the 5 percent required by German law for representation in the federal legislature. In August 1956, the Federal Constitutional Court outlawed the KPD for pursuing unconstitutional objectives. The KPD continued its activities as an underground party, led by Max Reimann, who resided in East Berlin. The party lost most of its members despite continued substantial financial and operational support from the SED.

In September 1968, the DKP was founded as a result of SPD Chancellor Willy Brandt's concession made to Leonid Brezhnev. Most of the "new" party's leaders had been officials in the illegal

KPD, which at that time had about 7,000 members. In 1971, the Federal Security Service (BVS) stated that the DKP, which emphasizes it is part of the international communist movement and the only legitimate heir to the KPD, was the successor of the outlawed party.

According to the annual report of the BVS, there are two orthodox communist organizations (membership: 44,500), with thirteen affiliated organizations (27,000) and 50 organizations influenced by communists (70,000). In addition, there are 23 basic organizations of the dogmatic New Left (3,900), with eleven affiliated organizations (1,100) and eighteen organizations (4,300) in which these groups have some influence, as well as 55 undogmatic organizations of the New Left. After deducting for membership in more than one organization, the BVS concluded that membership in these organizations totaled 60,150 and membership in organizations influenced by these groups 55,700. (Bundesministerium des Innern, *Verfassungsschutz 1982*, Bonn, April 1983, p. 21.)

Party Internal Affairs. No changes in the leadership were reported in 1983. The party received more than 60 million marks in direct financial assistance from the SED of the German Democratic Republic (GDR) (Radio Free Europe Research, *RAD Background Report/58*, 16 March). The DKP denies this and claims that all of its income of 16.5 million marks derives from membership dues (6.2 million marks), inheritances (about 300,000 marks), and donations (*Frankfurter Allgemeine Zeitung* [*FAZ*], 15 November). The amount reported by the party does not suffice to pay for the several hundred full-time party workers or for the expenses of the party headquarters in Düsseldorf and the over 200 local offices. The party also supports the Karl Liebknecht School in Leverkusen, the Marx-Engels Foundation, and the Institute for Marxist Studies and Research (IMSF). Additional funds are needed for the DKP's publications such as the party organ *Unsere Zeit*, which has five editions per week with about 25,000 copies. The Friday and weekend edition has about 50,000 copies, and those published for special events have up to 400,000 copies. (*Deutscher Informationsdienst* [*DI*], July.) The DKP publishes about 400 factory newspapers (ibid., 2 May/1 June) and about 530 local papers. Not included in the 60 million marks is the cost of the schooling of DKP functionaries at the SED school Franz Mehring in Berlin-Biesdorf (East), which has a permanent teaching staff of 30 and several times as many support personnel, where so far more than 3,000 DKP cadres have been trained. The courses last one month, three months, or a year. Also the expenses of an ambitious delegation program sponsored by the SED are not included in the transfer of funds to the DKP either via couriers or through the communist-controlled network of firms in the FRG. At present, there are about 600 delegations a year with nearly 10,000 members. (*FAZ*, 20 December; *Die Welt*, 10 December.) In addition, some 4,000 children from the FRG are sent each year to holiday camps in the GDR (*RAD Background Report/58*, 16 March). There is no other communist party in a Western country that is as dependent and strictly controlled by a foreign party as the DKP is by the SED. The West Department within the SED Central Committee is charged with the direction and control of the DKP (*FAZ*, 20 December).

The organizational structure of the DKP follows the typical communist party model. The more than 1,400 primary party organizations are subordinated to the about 200 county organizations, which in turn are under the twelve district organizations.

The exchange of party membership books, scheduled to take place every fourth year, was to be carried out at the beginning of 1983 (*DI*, December 1982). The party also prepared for the Seventh Party Congress, planned for 6–8 January 1984 in Nuremberg (ibid., 15 March, 2 May/1 June).

The Fourth Youth Festival, sponsored by the SDAJ and MSB, was held on 17–19 June in Dortmund. Representatives of 94 organizations from 64 countries participated. Romesh Chandra, president of the World Peace Council and a member of the Indian Communist Party, was the most prominent guest. (Ibid., 2 May/1 June.)

A number of pro-Moscow communist-led organizations continued to assist the DKP in carrying out its "unit of action" program, particularly in increasing DKP influence in the peace and ecological movements. (For details of these organizations, see *YICA*, 1983, p. 431.) The Association of Victims of the Nazi Regime/League of Antifascists (VVN/BdA) held its national congress in May, attended by 334 delegates and guests from thirteen countries. The congress was addressed by the governing mayor of Hamburg,

Klaus von Dohnany (SPD), as well as by representatives of the DKP, SDAJ, Young Socialists (Jusos), Young Democrats, Green Party, and German Peace Society/United War Service Resisters (DFG/VK). The new "orientation and action program" reflects the same objectives as those of the DKP and the other communist-led organizations, such as the fight against implementation of the NATO dual-track decision to station 572 Pershing II and cruise missiles in Europe. Several DKP members serve on the newly elected directorate of the VVN/BdA. The Presidium consists of 86 members, representing ten provincial (*Länder*) organizations and affiliated organizations. (*DI*, 2 May/1 June.) The DFG/VK held its Third Congress "Youth Against War Service," 17–19 June, in Hamm and participated in the mobilization against the visit of Vice-President George Bush on 25 June to Krefeld (ibid., 15 March). The collection of signatures for the Krefeld Appeal, which demands that the German government rescind its agreement to station NATO missiles on German soil, continued during 1983 and was vigorously supported by the DKP and other pro-Soviet organizations. The German Peace Union (DFU)–sponsored Third Forum of the Krefeld Initiative was held on 18 September in Bad Godesberg. It was asserted that 5 million signatures had been collected. More than 20 speakers addressed the forum, among them members of the SPD, Green Party, DKP, and U.S. Nobel laureates Linus Pauling and George Wald. (*FAZ*, 19 September.) These events reflect the DKP "alliance policy," directed in particular toward the "peace movement." Issues such as the communists' loyalty to Moscow are de-emphasized, and common objectives such as the rejection of NATO missiles are accentuated.

The DKP utilizes left-extremists among foreign workers. The Federal Security Service reported that at the end of 1982 about 122,000 of the 4.7 million foreigners in the FRG belonged to extremist groups. About 3.5 million are over sixteen years of age. Of those, 3.5 percent are in organizations responsible for activities detrimental to German security. Following are membership numbers and percentages of left-extremists among some of the ethnic groups: Arabs 3,000, 3.9 percent; Iranians 2,600, 9.5 percent; and Turks 53,750, 5.2 percent. Pro-Moscow groups account for 65,100. About 24,000 belong to the New Left. (*Verfassungsschutz 1982*, pp.

159–62.) The Turkish Workers' Associations (FIDEF) are directed by the Communist Party of Turkey (outlawed in Turkey) and collaborate closely with the DKP. The FIDEF's Seventh Congress, in Essen, attacked "U.S. imperialism," supported the "peace policy of the socialist countries," and promised to intensify support for the Krefeld Appeal and to fight the stationing of new U.S. nuclear missiles. (Ibid., p. 175; *DI*, 14 April.)

Ideological education of party members remained a high priority of party work. The DKP "education year" added the topic "Are today's workers still revolutionary?" The text prepared for this topic answers this question in the affirmative and restates the role of the working class as the determining factor of history. (*DI*, December.) The Marxist Workers' Education (MAB) elected a new directorate at its annual conference of delegates, held at the Marx-Engels Center in Wuppertal. The directorate comprises representatives from the DKP, SDAJ, MSB, IMSF, the publishing company Marxistische Blätter, Free Thinkers' Association, and regional offices of the MAB and the Marxist Workers' Schools. (Ibid., 31 October.)

Domestic Attitudes and Activities. Federal elections were held on 6 March. The DKP continued its downward trend, receiving 65,789 votes (0.2 percent) compared with 71,600 (0.2 percent) in 1980 (*FAZ*, 8 March). Of the 402 communist candidates, 87 percent were members of trade unions, including a good number of shop stewards (*DI*, 11 February). In *Land* elections in Schleswig-Holstein, Rhineland-Palatinate, and Hesse, the DKP polled at most 0.3 percent. In Bremen, the DKP did not run at all. (*FAZ*, 12 and 27 September.)

The party's "alliance policy" appeared to be far more successful than its capability to obtain votes. On the occasion of the fiftieth anniversary of Hitler's rise to power, demonstrations and rallies were held in several German cities. The organizer was the VVN/BdA, supported by the DKP and several other communist-led organizations. The appeal "Never again fascism—never again war" was also signed by SDP organizations, trade unionists, theologians, and academicians. (*radical info*, no 1.)

The most important objective of communist action was the struggle against the stationing of new U.S. missiles in the FRG. Friedrich Zimmermann, the federal minister of the interior, stated that the apparatus for the fall action against NATO was 75 percent in the hands of the DKP (*Rheinischer Merkur/Christ und Welt*, 13 May). The security service in Schleswig-Holstein reported that the real managers of many actions of the peace movement were the communists even though they represented only 3 to 5 percent of the potential membership of the movement. However, they achieved control by occupying key positions and constituted a majority on the preparatory committees. At a conference in Hanover to prepare demonstrations in the area of Bremen and Hamburg, the communists had a two-thirds majority. (*FAZ*, 31 August.)

The central information office for the Easter marches was the Hesse regional office of the DFU. Also the contact addresses for most of the protest demonstrations were all either DFU offices or DKP members. The DFU openly stated its role in the Easter marches and claimed to be a recognized partner of the peace movement. About 250,000 persons participated throughout the FRG in the demonstrations, including blockades of military installations. (*DI*, 2 May/1 June; *radical info*, no. 2, p. 2.) *Unsere Zeit* (20 April) reported that the Easter marches proved the strength of the peace movement since communists, Social Democrats, trade unionists, Greens, Christians, and Liberals could make common cause. DKP chairman Herbert Mies declared that the communists of the FRG participated actively together with all peace forces in the preparation and holding of the Easter marches (Tass, 4 April; *FBIS*, 5 April).

Several orthodox communist groups, supported by representatives of democratic parties, youth organizations, and "autonomous groups," organized a demonstration against the visit of Vice-President Bush to Krefeld on 25 June on the occasion of the tricentennial of the first immigrants from Krefeld. The Arbeitskreis (working group) Krefeld Peace Weeks consisted of 24 citizens of Krefeld, among them Social Democrats, Jusos, Greens, and members of the DKP. The local SPD declared its willingness to participate in the activities. (*DI*, 2 March/1 June.) The high point of the fight against the NATO dual-track decision was planned for the "action week" 15–22 October. This included demonstrations, blockages of U.S. military installations, and a mass rally in Bonn.

During 1983, the DKP, which for many years

favored large-scale demonstrations, became more involved in violent activity. Pastor Konrad Luebbert, an official of the communist-led Committee for Peace, Disarmament, and Cooperation (KFAZ), who is also a member of the Presidium of the Moscow-controlled World Peace Council, stated that what had to be done "legitimately" against NATO policy could "no longer always" be carried out "legally" (*Rheinischer Merkur/ Christ und Welt*, 13 May). The DKP and the SDAJ included in their actions the blocking of supply shipments to NATO bases and the establishment of a network of informers to conduct "peace espionage" (*Die Welt*, 24 May). The SDAJ called for "resistance in the schools" on 20 October and for "peace actions" (*DI*, 15 September).

Communist infiltration of the trade unions pursues the objective of capturing the unions' bureaucracy by means of an effective alliance and personnel policy. The concept of "class autonomy" is intended to achieve political independence for the trade unions from political parties and public institutions and to lead them toward antagonistic relations with the democratic state. This policy enjoyed noted successes, such as the closer approximation between many trade union officials and the peace movement, the condemnation of Solidarity in Poland by several union officials, attacks against anticommunist trade unionists, and a willingness to join "unity of actions" launched by communists. (*FAZ*, 5 October.)

International Views and Party Contacts. The foreign policy statements of DKP functionaries are almost identical with those made by Moscow and East Berlin. DKP chairman Herbert Mies welcomed the visit of West German chancellor Helmut Kohl to the Soviet Union and urged him to assure Moscow that the FRG will remain free of U.S. intermediate-range missiles. According to Mies, Kohl missed a great opportunity, however, to guarantee peaceful and friendly relations with the Soviet Union. His commitment to "Reagan's ideas" will make the FRG "a launching site for first-strike nuclear weapons against the USSR." (*Neues Deutschland*, 9–10 July.) Mies stressed that the DKP will tirelessly demand from the West German government that it contribute to disarmament by canceling its consent to the deployment of Pershing II and cruise missiles and declaring the FRG a nuclear-free zone. The DKP supports the proposals of the socialist states spelled out in the Prague Political Declaration urging conclusion of a treaty on mutual nonuse of military force and maintenance of peace between the states of the Warsaw Pact and NATO. Mies also demanded that the West German government develop relations with the nonaligned countries and support anti-imperialist, national-liberation movements. (Tass, 21 March; *FBIS*, 23 March.)

The aim of the DKP is to destabilize NATO and have the FRG declare neutrality (*FAZ*, 25 March). The DKP "revealed" that the U.S. army had utilized the German Bayer chemical concern to develop nerve gas and had decided to begin production. The German communists demanded a ban on the production of chemical weapons and the liquidation of all stocks in the FRG. (Tass, 17 August; *FBIS*, 18 August.) The DKP Presidium protested against the United States' armed interference in Lebanon and accused the "right-wing" government in Bonn of being a loyal vassal of Reagan (Tass, 22 September; *FBIS*, 23 September).

Contacts were maintained with many communist parties, especially with those of the Soviet Union and GDR. Mies emphasized "that a positive attitude toward the Soviet Union and the Communist Party of the Soviet Union is the criterion of a genuine communist" (*radical info*, no. 1, p. 2), recalling a very similar statement made by Ernst Thälmann, the leader of the KPD in the Weimar Republic. At the occasion of the sixty-sixth anniversary of the October Revolution, 86 editors in chief of communist and "revolutionary-democratic" newspapers and magazines met in Moscow. *Unsere Zeit* was represented by deputy editor Günther Hänsel. (*DI*, 1 November.)

Herbert Mies and Erich Honecker, secretary general of the SED, met several times during 1983. At a September meeting, both stressed that in the interest of the socialist countries' security and the defense of world peace, NATO must not be allowed to achieve military superiority. They also welcomed Yuri Andropov's recent "constructive initiatives." (*Pravda*, 23 September; *FBIS*, 30 September.) The three communist parties "on German soil," the SED, DKP, and Socialist Unity Party of West Berlin (SEW), published an "Appeal to parties of the working-class movement, trade unions, and youth organizations and all people in Europe who want to live in peace." It called on them to prevent the deployment of new U.S. nuclear missiles in Western Europe and to organize campaigns for nuclear-free zones. (*Neues Deutschland*, 27 September.) Mutual visits of DKP and SED delegations coordinated both parties' propaganda efforts.

In June, Martha Buschmann, member of the DKP Presidium and of the Bureau of the KFAZ, was elected a vice-president of the communist-front organization World Peace Council (*DI*, 15 September).

Other Leftist Groups. Numerous parties, associations, action groups, and revolutionary organizations of the New Left remained active during 1983. The ever-changing organizations and splinter groups pursued different revolutionary concepts but shared a rejection of pro-Soviet orthodox communism. The New Left comprises various dogmatic Marxist-Leninists and Trotskyists, anarchists, "autonomists," and antidogmatic social revolutionaries. The dogmatic Marxist-Leninist organizations (K-groups) continued to decline (from 5,300 to 3,900 members). The followers of the antidogmatic groups increased slightly in number (from 3,200 to 3,700). (*Verfassungsschutz*, p. 21.) The "autonomous" anarchist groups were mainly responsible for violence against the state. They were repeatedly the initiators of violent fights by the so-called squatters and formed the militant core of the new protest movement directed against the "imperialist preparation for war." Like the terrorist Revolutionary Cells, their militant actions included bombings and arson.

The dogmatic New Left includes five Marxist-Leninist parties (K-groups) and eleven Trotskyist organizations. The Marxist-Leninist Party of Germany (Marxistisch-Leninistische Partei Deutschlands; MLPD), formed in 1982 by members of the now defunct Communist Workers' League of Germany is, with about 900 members, the strongest of the K-groups. The MLPD regards itself as the avant-garde of the working class of the FRG and West Berlin. The party's objective is the overthrow of monopoly capitalism and the establishment of the dictatorship of the proletariat. The MLPD's headquarters in Essen oversees the activities of more than 80 local groups, organized in eleven districts. The official party organ is the weekly *Rote Fahne* (about 8,000 copies). Affiliated organizations are the Revolutionary Youth League of Germany (publisher of *Rebell*), the Communist Student

Groups (publisher of *Roter Pfeil*), and the League of Communist Intellectuals.

The pro-Albanian Communist Party of Germany (Marxist-Leninist) (Kommunistische Partei Deutschlands [Marxisten-Leninisten]; KPD-ML) was able to maintain its membership of about 500. Its weekly paper, *Roter Morgen*, has a circulation of about 6,000. The party held its Fifth Party Congress in November and after adjournment reconvened in December. (*DI*, 1 November.) Its youth organization is the Communist Youth of Germany (KJD) with about 250 members; its monthly publication, *Roter Rebell*, has a circulation of 3,000 copies. The KJD conducted a propaganda campaign against NATO and for a neutralized Germany. It also recommended that leftists join the German military in order to learn how to shoot. (Ibid., 14 October.) The affiliated student organizations are the Communist University Groups (KHG) (organ: *zwischenruf links*). The KHG's objective is to organize the revolutionary students under one working group. The KPD-ML, the Maoist League of West German Communists, the Communist League, and the anarchist Free Workers' Union (FAU) are represented in the working group. (Ibid.) KPD-ML mass organizations are the Revolutionary Trade Union Opposition (RGO) with about 1,300 members (publication: *RGO-Nachrichten*) and the People's Front Against Reaction, Fascism, and War (*Volksfront*). The public was excluded from the Third Volksfront Congress, held in Frankfurt on 26–27 November. (Ibid.) A KPD-ML delegation, headed by Ernst August, chairman of the party, visited Albania in March (Albanian Telegraphic Agency, Tirana, 31 March; *FBIS*, 1 April). The KPD-ML and the Maoist League of West German Communists (Bund Westdeutscher Kommunisten; BWK) decided on joint lists of candidates for the federal elections in March (*DI*, 15 January). The KPD-ML and the BWK also planned a joint meeting of their central committees in November in order to examine a possible merger and the founding of a party of revolutionary socialists (ibid.). The meeting was later postponed until January 1984.

The BWK has about 500 followers, organized in seven regional groups. Its biweekly publications are *Politische Berichte* (about 1,500 copies) and *Nachrichtenhefte* (about 1,250 copies). The BWK also publishes about 35 newspapers (mostly quarterlies) for specific factories, uni-

versities, and military installations (total of over 32,000 copies). The BWK was founded in 1982 by about 600 disillusioned members of the Communist League of West Germany.

The Maoist-oriented Communist League of West Germany (Kommunistischer Bund Westdeutschlands; KBW) continued to lose members and now has about 500. Defections included KBW leaders, who recommended the dissolution of the party. Most of the KBW offices were reduced in size or closed and publications discontinued, although a new monthly *Kommune*, started in 1983. Affiliated organizations also ceased to exist.

The Communist League (Kommunistischer Bund; KB) has about 500 members (300 of them in Hamburg). Its central organ is the monthly *Arbeiterkampf* (about 6,000 copies). At the end of 1979, the KB split, and about 200 followers founded the Center Faction (Zentrumfraktion; Gruppe Z). Group Z has about 150 members, most of them in Hamburg. Group Z dominates the Green Party in Hamburg, while the KB supports and controls the Green Alternative List in that city.

The Workers League for the Reconstitution of the KPD, with about 300 members, operated mostly in Rhineland-Westfalia and Bavaria. It is of no significance.

The eleven Trotskyist groups, having a total of about 600 members, advocate "permanent revolution" and the "dictatorship of the proletariat." The Group of International Marxists is the German section of the Fourth International in Brussels and has about 200 members. It publishes the biweekly *Was tun* (2,000 copies). The League of Socialist Workers is the German section of the International Committee of the Fourth International in London and together with its youth organization, the Socialist Youth League, has about 150 members. Its weekly, *neue Arbeiterpresse*, appeals to the young unemployed. The Trotskyist League of Germany has 80 followers, pursues a pro-Soviet course, and condemns the Polish trade union Solidarity as counterrevolutionary.

The numerous groups of the antidogmatic New Left, totaling more than 3,000 followers, provided the dominant force of the contemporary militant struggle against the democratic state. Frequently, these groups are short-lived and of local character. Among them are advocates of social-revolutionary or anarchist concepts. They all reject Marxist-Leninist dogma and rigid organizational structures. They emphasize the need for flexibility in their "confrontation with the system." Their aim is the destruction of the "system" and the creation of a society free of suppression. The first generation of the antidogmatic New Left developed in the 1960s when the Socialist German Student League dissolved. The second generation was formed after 1977 by disillusioned followers of K-groups at various universities. The third generation has emerged since 1980 and developed among militant opponents of nuclear power plants, radicals engaged in house occupations, and adherents of the peace movement. Antidogmatists formed occasional local and temporary action groups. The so-called alternative press—numerous, mostly local or regional people's newspapers—is an important medium for the exchange of views among the antidogmatists. The *tageszeitung*, for example, is distributed throughout the FRG and publishes appeals and reports about developments within the antidogmatic camp. Among the irregularly published local papers are *Vorwarnzeit* (Hamburg), *Putz* (Bochum), *Kriegsratinfo* (Karlsruhe), and *Der Schwarze Kanal* (Berlin). The anarchist magazine *883* (3,000 copies) made a comeback in 1983 after it had been discontinued for about three years. (*DI*, 1 November.) Antidogmatists also made use of illegal radio transmitters for the dissemination of current information and to mobilize and direct demonstrations.

The anarcho-syndicalist Initiative Free Workers' Union (I.FAU) with twelve groups and support bases (organ: *direkt aktion*) and the Free Workers' Union (FAU) (monthly publication: *direkte Aktion*)—the latter separated from the I.FAU in 1980 and has about 25 local groups and 200 members—espouse antiparliamentarism, direct democracy, and anarchy. The local FAU publication *grosse freiheit* (Hamburg) called for actions against U.S. ammunition transports and demanded the withdrawal of U.S. troops from West Germany. (Ibid., 19 August.)

The Federation of Violence-free Action Groups—Grass-roots Revolution, formed in 1980, has over 50 groups and 600 followers (monthly publication: *Graswurzelrevolution*, output 4,500 copies).

The "autonomous" scene comprises diffuse groupings, totaling several thousand followers, mostly among the young. These groupings have not been able to organize regional associations or decide on a common strategy in their struggle against the "pig system" and the democratic state. They participated actively in "peace demonstrations" against NATO and "U.S. imperialism."

The Socialist Buro (SB) is an antidogmatic group in the tradition of the protest movement of 1968. Its membership has fallen to about 900. It publishes the monthly *links* (7,000 copies). The SB's goal is to provide initiatives for common political actions for the revolutionary change of society. The SB supported its members within the Green Party, the Democratic Socialists, trade unions, and the social movements.

The Marxist Group (MG) occupies a special position within the New Left because of its hierarchical structure, strict discipline, intensive schooling, and secrecy. The MG has about a thousand members, mostly students and academicians, and several thousand sympathizers organized in plenums. MG organs are *Marxistische Studentenzeitung* and the *Marxistische Arbeiterzeitung*. In addition, the MG publishes university newspapers with editions of up to 14,000 copies and factory and local papers. The MG can mobilize several thousand participants for demonstrations against "NATO imperialism."

The borderline between the autonomous groups and left-extremist terrorists is difficult to determine. Most of the bombing attacks and arson cases were the work of the Revolutionary Cells (RZ) and were directed against military installations, nuclear power plants, and public offices (*FAZ*, 25 August). The RZ attacked the "imperialist" policy of NATO countries as well as the invasion of Warsaw Pact troops in Czechoslovakia and of Soviet troops in Afghanistan (*DI*, 1 November).

The Young Socialists (Jusos), the official youth organization of the SPD, as well as other socialist youth, student, and women's organizations, generally not perceived as left-radical organizations, share many objectives with the extreme left and have increasingly participated in unity of actions with communists and other leftists. Their anti-NATO and anti-U.S. policy and their support of Moscow's arms control proposals provide the basis for cooperation.

WEST BERLIN

West Berlin is still under "occupation" by the forces of the United States, Britain, and France. The 1971 Quadripartite Agreement concerning

Berlin confirmed its "special status," based on previous agreements in 1944 and 1945, declaring that the former German capital is not part of the FRG. Even though the 1971 agreement was meant to cover the area of Greater Berlin, the Soviet-occupied eastern sector of the city has been completely integrated into East Germany and has been declared the capital of the GDR. The Western powers have encouraged the FRG to maintain close ties with West Berlin. The population declined from 2.3 in 1959 to 2.0 million in 1983.

Berlin's special status made it possible for the SED to set up a subsidiary in West Berlin. In 1959, an "independent" organizational structure was introduced for the West Berlin section of the SED. In 1962, the party was renamed Socialist Unity Party of Germany—West Berlin; in 1969, the present designation, Socialist Unity Party of West Berlin (Sozialistische Einheitspartei Westberlin; SEW), was introduced in order to create the impression that the party is a genuine, indigenous political party.

The SEW, like the DKP, is a pro-Soviet party and depends financially on the SED. Its statements are identical with the ideological and political views of the East German and Soviet parties. SEW membership is about 4,500. In the last elections (1981) for the city's House of Representatives, the SEW obtained 8,216 votes, or 0.7 percent, compared with 1.1 percent in 1979. No changes in the SEW leadership were reported in 1983. Horst Schmitt remains SEW chairman and Dietmar Ahrens deputy chairman. The SEW has a 17-member Executive (Buro), a 7-member Secretariat, and a 47-member Presidium. The SEW's official organ, *Die Wahrheit*, has a circulation of 13,000 copies.

The communist youth organization in West Berlin is the Socialist Youth League Karl Liebknecht (Sozialistischer Jugendverband Karl Liebknecht), with about 700 members, 250 of them children in the Pioneer organization. The SEW–University Groups have about 400 members and the SEW-influenced Action Group of Democrats and Socialists about 500 members. Other SEW-led organizations include the Democratic Women's League Berlin (about 600 members), the Society for German-Soviet Friendship (about 500 members), the Association of Victims of the Nazi Regime West Berlin/League of Anti-fascists (about 300 members).

The SEW and its affiliated organizations cooperated actively with the peace movement in the anti-NATO missiles campaign. The West Berlin communists were able to participate in several "peace initiatives," such as Information Circle Peace (Coordination), and collaborated with democratic and church organizations. Another propaganda topic was the problem of mass unemployment.

The SEW maintained contacts in 1983 with the international communist movement by means of mutual visits, especially with the SED.

Many New Left groups and left-extremist terrorists operate in West Berlin. House occupations and mass demonstrations offer opportunities for militant actions.

Eric Waldman
University of Calgary

Great Britain

Population. 56 million
Party. Communist Party of Great Britain (CPGB)
Founded. 1920
Membership. Under 16,000
Secretary General. Gordon McLennan
Political Committee. 16 members: including Gordon McLennan, Peter Carter, Ian MacKay, Nina Temple, Maggie Bowden, Gerry Pocock
Executive Committee. 42 members
Status. Legal
Last Congress. Thirty-eighth, 12–15 November 1983
Last Election. June 1983, 0.03 percent, no representation
Auxiliary Organizations. Young Communist League (YCL); Liaison Committee for the Defence of Trade Unions (LCDTU)
Publications. *Morning Star*, *Marxism Today*, *Communist Focus*, *Challenge*, *Spark*, *Link*, *Our History Journal*, *Economic Bulletin*, *Medicine in Society*, *Education Today and Tomorrow*

The CPGB is a recognized party that contests local and national elections. It does not operate in Northern Ireland, which it does not recognize as British territory. The party has had no members in the House of Commons since 1950, but has one member, Lord Milford, in the nonelected House of Lords.

Leadership and Party Organization. The CPGB is divided into four divisions: the National Congress, the Executive Committee and its departments, districts, and local and factory branches. Constitutionally, opposition is rare, and the biennial National Congress is the party's supreme authority. Responsibility for party activities rests with the 42-member Executive Committee, which meets every two months. The Executive Committee comprises members of special committees, full-time departmental heads, and the 16-member Political Committee, the party's innermost controlling conclave.

Party leaders remain deeply preoccupied by the continuing decline in support for the party. Membership has continued to fall and is now under 16,000, its lowest point since World War II. Only about half of these have paid their fees. YCL, with only 623 members, is now close to collapse. The decline in electoral support was emphasized in the June general elections when the party's 35 candidates polled only 11,598 votes.

However, the poor showing of the CPGB at the polls belies the party's strength in the trade union movement. Although the party does not control any individual trade union, it is represented on most union executives and has played a major role in most government-union confrontations in recent years. The CPGB's success is partly attributable to low turnouts in most union elections, to the fact that it is the only party seeking to control the outcome of these elections, and to its close interest in industrial affairs, which ensures support from workers who might not support other aspects of the party's program. There are 2 members of the CPGB on the 38-member General Council of the Trades Union Congress: Mick McGahey of the National Union of Mineworkers and Ken Gill of the Technical and Supervisory Section of the Amalgamated Union of Engineering Workers. In addition, CPGB ideas exercise a considerable influence on other trade union executives and on a few Labour Party members of parliament.

Domestic Party Affairs. In 1983, the CPGB's Eurocommunist-inclined leadership was under attack from the party's hard-line left. The conflict centered on a dispute between the party's Executive Committee and its chief theoretical journal, *Marxism Today*, on the one hand, and the *Morning Star*, on the other. The *Morning Star*, although nationally recognized as the party's daily paper, is technically owned by the People's Press Printing Society (PPPS). Throughout 1983, the PPPS was in the hands of opponents of the Executive Committee's policies. The editor of the *Morning Star*, Tony Chater, warned that the paper would not tolerate interference from an "outside body," namely, the party's Executive Committee. The *Morning Star* group has been joined by Michael Costello, a former party industrial organizer, and has denounced the party leadership and *Marxism Today* for moving from an emphasis on strike activity toward more fashionable causes such as feminism and ecology.

Opposition to the party leadership came to a head during the party's Thirty-eighth Congress in November. The official list of candidates for the 42-member Executive Committee was endorsed by a considerably smaller margin than usual. The leadership was relieved to win the congress's approval for its muted criticism of Poland's martial law regime by a vote of 143 to 101 in spite of fierce criticism and arguments that Polish leaders were forced to impose martial law "legitimately and constitutionally and in order to avoid open civil war" and that the crisis was a struggle between "the forces of peace and socialism on the one hand and the forces of counterrevolution on the other." The CPGB leadership was certain, however, that it had to support the right of Polish workers to form independent trade unions just as strongly as it supported their formation in Britain. However, the platform emphasized that CPGB support of Solidarity did not presuppose full agreement with all of Solidarity's views.

The other main point of contention concerned *Marxism Today*, the party's theoretical journal, which under the editorship of Martin Jacques has massively increased its sales but at the cost of losing its clear-cut pro-Soviet image. The jour-

nal's wide range of contributors has angered the party's traditionalists. Articles written by Soviet dissidents and others denouncing the shop stewards' movement were explicitly condemned by delegates at the congress. The opposition's censure motion claimed that *Marxism Today* had become indistinguishable from the "quasi-sociological anticommunist material that appears in the capitalist-controlled media and academic texts." This motion was defeated by a small majority on a show of hands.

Further evidence of strong opposition to party leaders was provided at the congress by the appearance of a dissident manifesto in defiance of party discipline. The paper, distributed in plain brown envelopes, called for the dismissal of the leadership, a return to absolute pro-Sovietism, and the rebuilding of a Leninist revolutionary organization. Dissident groups also emerged at many regional meetings before the National Congress. In Glasgow, a party discussion became so heated that the police had to be called in to stop the fighting.

The Thirty-eighth National Congress also attracted much publicity because it was addressed by Monsignor Bruce Kent, general secretary of the Campaign for Nuclear Disarmament (CND). Kent, the first prominent Catholic cleric to address the communists, was given a warm reception. In a much criticized speech, Kent said "I am honored to be where I am. I am very proud to have been invited and glad to have been able to accept."

Domestic activities remained much the same as in 1982. Opposition to the policies of the Conservative government, sharpened by the continuing rise in unemployment, remained the party's principal activity. In particular, the party sponsored and participated in a series of protest demonstrations against unemployment and the government's proposed changes in trade union legislation, which are widely seen among left-wing activists as an attack on trade union rights. The party was an active supporter of the CND and bitterly denounced the stationing of U.S. cruise missiles at Greenham Common in November. The CPGB supports unilateral nuclear disarmament by the United Kingdom.

Auxiliary Organizations. CPGB activity in industry centers on its approximately 200 workplace branches. Its umbrella organization is the LCDTU. The YCL is the youth section of the party but has barely 600 members. The party retains a number of financial interests, including Central Books, Lawrence and Wishart Publishers, Farleigh Press, London Caledonian Printers, Rodell Properties, the Labour Research Department, and the Marx Memorial Library.

International Views. The CPGB retained its customary support for the Soviet Union. Generally this took a predictable course. In European affairs, the party favored arms reduction talks with the USSR and opposed the deployment of U.S. cruise and Pershing II missiles in Europe. The CPGB sought Britain's withdrawal from NATO and the European Community. The party is critical of Israel and seeks the recognition of the Palestine Liberation Organization. Predictably, the party is opposed to the multinational peacekeeping force in Lebanon and is especially critical of the U.S. role there. The CPGB remained hostile to the South African regime and to South Africa's continuing incursions into Angola; it supports the black African National Congress.

There are only three areas where CPGB views differ from those of the USSR. The party continues to favor the recognition of Solidarity while being careful not to support all statements issued by Solidarity. The party originally opposed the Soviet invasion of Afghanistan and has not revised that position. However, it supports the incumbent government in Kabul and has refrained from calling for the withdrawal of Soviet forces. Similarly, the CPGB originally opposed the Soviet invasion of Czechoslovakia in August 1968 but sometimes betrays signs of being a prisoner of that decision. Persecution of dissidents in Czechoslovakia is still quietly criticized.

Other Marxist Groups. Besides the CPGB, several small, mostly Trotskyist, groups are active on the left-wing extreme. Very active

throughout the 1970s despite their small memberships, their influence is now waning, probably because of the adoption by the Labour Party of more hard-line policies, which is encouraging extremists to join the Labour Party rather than revolutionary groups.

Probably the most important of the Trotskyist groups is Militant, which derives its name from its paper of the same name. Militant claims to be merely a loose tendency of opinion within the Labour Party, but there is little doubt that Militant possesses its own distinctive organization and for some years has been pursuing a policy of entryism (the tactic of penetrating the larger, more moderate Labour Party). Militant controls about 50 Labour Party constituencies. Despite repeated criticism of Militant by right-wing Labour Party members, there seems little likelihood of any firm steps being taken against it. However, by the end of the year, former Labour prime minister Lord Harold Wilson had reopened the issue with some trenchant criticisms.

The other significant Trotskyist organizations are the Socialist Workers' Party (SWP) and the Workers' Revolutionary Party (WRP). The SWP has won most of its attention because of its publicity-seeking ventures in the anti-unemployment campaign. It has played a major organizing role in marches for jobs, often through its trade union organization, the Rank and File Movement. The WRP's activities are more secretive but are known to be primarily located in the engineering, mining, theater, and auto industries.

Another significant Trotskyist group is the Socialist League (SL), formerly the International Marxist Group. The SL is most notorious for its activity at British Leyland. The company dismissed thirteen of its employees in August for membership in this disruptive organization.

Richard Sim
London

Greece

Population. 9.9 million (*World Factbook*, 1983)
Party. Communist Party of Greece (Kommunistikon Komma Ellados; KKE)
Founded. 1921
Membership. 27,500 (estimate)
Secretary General. Kharilaos Florakis
Politburo. 9 regular members: Kharilaos Florakis, Nikos Kaloudhis, Grigoris Farakos, Kostas Tsolakis, Roula Kourkoulou, Loula Logara, Dimitris Gondikas, Andonis Ambatielos, Dimitris Sarlis; 2 candidate members: Takis Mamatsis and Orestis Kolozov
Status. Legal
Last Congress. Eleventh, 14–19 December 1982, in Athens
Last Election. 1981, 10.9 percent, 13 of 300 seats
Publications. *Rizospastis*, daily; *Kommunistiki Epitheorisi* (*KOMEP*), monthly review

During the 1920s, the KKE remained small and ineffectual, suffering a series of internal splits. In 1931, it was reorganized under a Comintern-imposed Stalinist group headed by N. Zakhariades. Five years later, the party was forced to go underground by the Metaxas dictatorship, which very effectively infiltrated party ranks and undermined its organization. The party regrouped its forces and gained extensive influence behind the patriotic mantle of the resistance organization known as the National Liberation Front (EAM) during the Nazi occupation of Greece. After the German withdrawal, an attempt by the KKE-controlled guerrilla forces (ELAS) to seize power in Athens was defeated by the British. A protracted guerrilla campaign (1946–1949) was crushed by the Greek army with U.S. aid. The party remained outlawed between 1947 and 1974. Currently, the KKE enjoys all the rights and privileges of a legitimate political party in Greece. From 1952 to 1967, the communist left was represented by the United Democratic Left (EDA). During the military dictatorship (1967–1974), the KKE split into two factions (KKE-Exterior and KKE-Interior). The KKE-Exterior, the pro-Moscow faction, eventually emerged as the official KKE. The KKE-Interior adopted a more independent and moderate view and has become the representative of Eurocommunism in Greece.

In the 1982 municipal elections, KKE-sponsored candidates received approximately 20 percent of the total vote, a significant increase from the 12.23 percent received in the October 1981 parliamentary election by the two communist parties combined. To assess the real meaning of this substantial shift, one must recall that in the 1981 parliamentary election, the Marxist parties—the Panhellenic Socialist Movement (PASOK), the KKE, and the KKE-Interior—together received 60.2 percent of the total vote. In the municipal elections, PASOK and KKE candidates again received a combined total of approximately 60.2 percent. The shift is likely to prove temporary. In the next parliamentary election, the KKE vote share is not expected to exceed 15 percent.

Leadership and Organization. The KKE is organized along traditional communist party lines. Party cells are found in factories, in villages, and in other "collectives." Major cities such as Athens have a city party organization and communist base organizations, which coordinate the activities of the local "cells" and "aktivs." The party also has branch organizations in professional and labor groups. A party congress is normally convened every four years. The most recent congress, the Eleventh, met in December 1982. The congress reduced the membership of the Politburo from sixteen to eleven members, of whom nine are regular and two are candidate members. Dropped from the Politburo were full members Kostas Loules, D. Tsiambis, and Mina Yiannou and candidate members Gerasimos Georgatos and Nikos Kyriakidis. The removal of these individuals does not seem to have major political significance for the party.

Party Internal Affairs. The Eleventh Congress attracted delegations from many communist parties throughout the world. The Communist Party of the Soviet Union was represented by Boris Ponomarev, Soviet Politburo candidate member and secretary in charge of relations with nonruling communist parties, and Vadim V. Zagladin, deputy head of the Soviet Central Committee's International Department. The congress held no surprises. The party program, as summarized by Secretary General Florakis, included the familiar objectives of (1) abolishing the privileges of foreign and domestic monopolies, (2) having the government advance productive public investments, (3) nationalizing the strategic branches of the national economy, (4) withdrawing from the military wing of NATO as a prelude to complete disengagement from the alliance, (5) defining a brief and specific timetable for the complete removal of the U.S. bases, and (6) beginning Greece's disassociation from the "European Community of the monopolies."

A major issue for the party during 1983 was the signing by Greece and the United States of an agreement providing for a five-year extension of the U.S. bases in Greece. Florakis's mild opposition following the signing of the agreement in July—in spite of previous strong statements against the "bases of death"—prompted a mini-crisis within the party. Florakis immediately called an extraordinary session of the Central Committee, which endorsed his policy on this matter. Florakis's stand reflected an equally mild reaction to the bases agreement by the Soviet Union. The agreement was eventually ratified by the Greek Chamber of Deputies in November 1983 without the votes of the thirteen KKE deputies.

Another important issue for the party was the decision of the PASOK government to allow the unrestricted repatriation from the Soviet Union and Eastern Europe of KKE partisans who had fled Greece in 1949 when the guerrilla campaign ended in defeat. The KKE welcomed the measure in the expectation that these individuals would strengthen party ranks. Subsequent comments in KKE publications indicate that some of the repatriates are reluctant to join the party actively. The most prominent among the repatriates is Markos Vafiades, the leader of the guerrilla army in 1946–1949. Now in his seventies, Vafiades is not taking a vigorous role in party affairs.

Domestic and International Views and Positions. During 1983, the KKE was preoccupied with its relations with the governing PASOK. PASOK does not oppose in principle any of the objectives included in the KKE platform as approved by the Eleventh KKE Congress. In fact, PASOK's "anti-imperialist" rhetoric and some of the positions taken by the Greek government on international issues such as the deployment of Pershing II and cruise missiles in Europe, a nuclear-free zone in the Balkans, or the downing of the Korean airliner, were indistinguishable from those of the KKE. As a result, the KKE has concentrated its criticism on the pace of implementation by the PASOK government of the so-called socialist transformation that PASOK had promised prior to the 1981 parliamentary election. The KKE, however, has been rather circumspect in its criticism of PASOK, apparently for two reasons. One is the friendly attitude of the Soviet government toward the PASOK government; the second is the anticipation that in the next parliamentary election, cooperation with PASOK may be necessary in the interest of both parties. During the year, the KKE made veiled overtures for participation in the PASOK government, but these were ignored because the PASOK government has a comfortable parliamentary majority in the legislature and has no need to invite communists into the Cabinet. Currently, the KKE is working diligently to attract to its ranks those PASOK followers who are dissatisfied with what they consider the slow pace of the socialist transformation as pursued by the PASOK government.

In international affairs, the party has supported every Soviet initiative in the area of arms control, has been active in "peace movement" activities, has continued its opposition to Greece's participation in the European Economic Community, and has remained steadfast in its belief that Turkish policies regarding the Aegean are instigated by the United States. The KKE appeared to be supportive of the initiative of U.N. secretary general Javier Pérez de Cuellar in the summer of 1983 designed to break the deadlock in Cyprus. In this, the KKE's stand was in line with that of the Cypriot communist party. Both Moscow-oriented parties reflected in their policies the Soviet view that in the absence of a compromise solution, the Turkish-occupied area in the northern part of the island may be declared an independent state. Such a move could extend the NATO area to Cyprus. On the five-year extension of U.S. bases in Greece, the KKE continues to press PASOK and the government of Andreas Papandreou to live up to their promise that the five-year extension is "terminal" and that their objective is to eliminate, if in office five years from now, the bases.

In the past two years, the party has benefited from the anti-U.S., anticapitalist, and pro-Marxist rhetoric used by PASOK and by a significant portion of the daily press and the government-controlled media. Views and arguments that in earlier years were voiced only in the communist press now appear routinely on information channels enjoying traditional legitimacy. Because of this, the KKE finds inflammatory rhetoric on its part unnecessary.

The KKE-Interior has remained a marginal political force because a moderate, Eurocommunist approach has little appeal for Marxist-Leninists. The declaration of the KKE-Interior in October 1982 that it favors pluralism did not contribute to its popularity among the supporters of the extreme left in Greece. In many ways, the rhetoric of KKE-Interior is less strident than that of PASOK. The KKE-Interior is associated with the daily *Avgi*, which lately has been in serious financial trouble.

International Party Contacts. The KKE continued its contacts with East European communist parties. A KKE delegation headed by Politburo member A. Ambatielos visited Bulgaria in March 1983. Another delegation under KKE secretary general Florakis visited Bucharest and East Germany in May.

In spite of its limited political support within Greece, the KKE-Interior has actively maintained contacts with foreign parties. In March, KKE-Interior leaders met with a delegation of the Italian Communist Party. During the same period, a KKE-Interior delegation visited Belgrade for talks with leaders of the League of Yugoslav Communists. During the year the leadership of KKE-Interior exchanged friendly messages with the communist parties of Yugoslavia, Italy, France, and Algeria.

Other Marxist-Leninist Organizations. The Revolutionary Communist Party of Greece and the Marxist-Leninist Communist Party of Greece espouse more extremist and dogmatic views, but their minuscule followings appear to have declined even more in the year under review.

D. G. Kousoulas
Howard University

Iceland

Population. 235,000 (1 December 1982)
Party. People's Alliance (Althydubandalagid; AB)
Founded. 1968
Membership. 3,000 (estimate); mostly workers and intellectuals, located primarily in Reykjavik and
   eastern fjords
Chairman. Svavar Gestsson
Executive Committee. 10 members: Svavar Gestsson (chairman), Vilborg Hardardottir (deputy
   chair), Helgi Gudmundsson (secretary), Margret Frimannsdottir (treasurer) and six others
Central Committee. 42 regular members, plus Executive Committee ex officio; 15 deputy members
Status. Legal
Last Congress. November 1983, Reykjavik; next congress due in 1985
Last Election. Third largest of six parties represented in Althing; 1983, 17.3 percent, 10 of 60 seats.
Auxiliary Organizations. Organization of Base Opponents (OBO), organizer of peace demonstra-
   tions against U.S.-NATO bases
Publications. *Thjodviljinn*, daily (Reykjavik); at least two weeklies, *Verkamadhurinn* (Akureyri) and
   Mjolnir (Siglufjordhur)

The AB is the successor to a line of leftist parties
dating back to 1930, when the Icelandic Communist Party (Kommunistaflokkur Islands) was established by a left-wing splinter from the Labor
Party. In 1938, the Social Democratic Party,
another left-wing group, splintered from the Labor Party and joined with the communists to
create a new party, the United People's Party–
Socialist Party (Sameiningar flokkur althydu-
Sosialista flokkurinn; UPP-SP). Patterned on the
Norwegian Labor Party, the UPP-SP based its
ideology on "scientific socialism–Marxism," but
had no organizational ties to Moscow. Its main
political goal in the early years was the complete
independence of the country. Home rule had
been granted in 1918, but complete independence
was not achieved until 1944. By this time, the
other political parties had accepted the UPP-SP
as a responsible democratic party, and it had
participated in governing coalitions. In 1956, the
UPP-SP formed an electoral alliance with still
another group of left-wing social democrats and
the small, isolationist National Preservation

Party. This coalition assumed the name People's
Alliance. In 1968, the UPP-SP dissolved itself
into the AB, which then formed itself into the
present national Marxist party. It has participated
regularly in coalition governments, most recently joining the Progressive (agrarian liberal)
Party in a coalition headed by maverick Gunner
Thoroddsen, formerly of the Independence (conservative) Party. The Thoroddsen government
resigned in April after the constituent parties
suffered severe electoral reverses in the national
elections of 23 April. The AB held three cabinet
posts: social and health affairs (Svavar Gestsson), finance (Ragnar Arnalds), and industry
(Hjörleifur Guttormsson). It is now the largest
opposition party.

Participation in the government during a
severe economic recession hurt the AB and
clearly cost it votes in the April general elections.
Falling fish catches, continuing stagnation in
international trade, and soaring inflation (which
reached an unprecedented 159 percent annual
rate in the late spring) had already forced the

Thoroddsen government, with AB participation, to introduce economic austerity measures that brought about a decline in real wages. Despite these economic hardships, unemployment in Iceland remained remarkably below that in other Western countries.

While in the government, the AB had blocked conclusion of a much-needed agreement to modernize facilities at the Keflavik International Airport, which is shared by civilian and U.S./NATO operations. Following the elections, the Independence Party, whose vote share rose 3.3 percentage points, for a gain of two seats, formed a majority coalition with the Progressives, whose share fell 6.4 percentage points, for a loss of three seats. The new government concluded an agreement with the United States in July that provides for extensive modernization of both civilian and military facilities at Keflavik. Nearly all of the initial costs will be borne by the United States. (*Nordisk Kontakt*, no. 12.)

Party Internal Affairs. The end of the AB's participation in the center-left coalition government in April eased internal party tensions. The inevitable necessity of compromise and pragmatism incumbent on a governing party displeased many AB ideological purists. A return to the opposition is likely to permit a more militant stand and thus defuse some of the discontent in the party's left wing. At the party's National Congress in Reykjavik in mid-November, former social minister Svavar Gestsson was re-elected party chairman. Vilborg Hardardottir of Reykjavik was elected the new deputy chairman, and Helgi Gudmundsson of Akureyri, the new party secretary; neither faced opposition. Margret Frimannsdottir overwhelmingly won a contested election for party treasurer. (*Thjodviljinn*, 18 November.)

Domestic Affairs. It was a tumultuous year for Icelandic politics as economic problems and the question of how to respond to them paralyzed the Thoroddsen government and dominated the general elections. Efforts to brake the accelerating wage-price spiral, which reached an annual rate of 60 percent and was running at twice that rate by early 1983, placed severe strains on the coalition when Thoroddsen sought to modify the complex Icelandic indexing system. The AB opposed such measures and threatened to leave the government. (*Nordisk Kontakt*, no. 4.) These halfhearted measures antagonized labor and the AB, but failed to halt inflation. Iceland has long had inflation of Latin American proportions, but simultaneously has had reasonable economic growth (led by rising exports) and full employment. Unfortunately, a sharp drop in the fish catch and the global recession slowed Icelandic growth. In 1981, maritime products accounted for 78 percent of Icelandic exports while aluminum, Iceland's principal nonmaritime export, amounted to 9.5 percent (*News from Iceland*, January). Although there is little any Icelandic government can do about fishing conditions or global demand, the AB took a militant stand toward the Icelandic Aluminium Company, which is owned by a Swiss concern. Industry Minister Guttormsson proposed significant increases in the price of electricity provided to the aluminum smelter in Straumsvik. The company resisted these moves, and the AB's coalition partners sought to avoid a showdown. (*Nordisk Kontakt*, nos. 3 and 5.)

The aluminum issue reflected a major point in the AB's domestic program: militant national control of economic resources. In early 1983, the government proposed state ownership of all resources on the continental shelf (ibid., no. 2). As the parliamentary elections approached, no final action was taken, but the AB stressed the aluminum and resource issue in the ensuing campaign.

The AB suffered a notable setback in the 23 April elections. It received 22,489 votes (a loss of 2,000), which amounted to 17.3 percent of the vote, a loss of 2.4 percentage points, and its parliamentary delegation was reduced to ten, a loss of one seat. The AB parliamentary group leader, Olafur R. Grimsson, lost his seat in the Reykjavik constituency. The other main governing party, the centrist Progressive Party, fared even worse; it lost three seats and 6.4 percentage points, but it remained the second-largest party with fourteen seats. The reformist Social Democratic Party also lost ground, receiving 11.7 percent and six seats, down from 17.4 percent and ten seats. The Social Democrats were directly affected by a schism that established a new Social Democratic Federation Party (Bandalag jafnadarmanna), which polled 7.3 percent of the vote and won four seats. The new socialist party remained reformist and committed to continued Icelandic membership in NATO. Finally, a left-centrist Women's Party (Samtök um kvennalista) won 5.5 percent of the vote and elected three women to the Althing. (Ibid., no. 8.)

The fractioning of parliament led to protracted negotiations on possible governing coalitions. During the month-long effort, AB chairman Svavar Gestsson attempted to put together a broad coalition of all parties except the Independence Party, which had been one of the election winners, with 23 seats (a gain of 2) and 38.7 percent of the vote (a gain of 3.3 percentage points). This effort failed, and in late May, Progressive Party chairman Steingrimur Hermannsson assembled a coalition with the Independence Party. The center-right government could count on 37 of the Althing's 60 seats. (Ibid., no. 11.)

With inflation soaring at an annual rate of 159 percent, national income plunging, and foreign indebtedness rising, the new government immediately undertook drastic measures. The currency was devalued 14.6 percent, and a freeze was placed on wage indexes. The AB could now protest these measures from the opposition benches, which it did with characteristic energy. The labor movement, which is mainly controlled by Social Democrats, but in which the AB has influence, also protested these measures. During the summer, petitioners against the wage freeze collected some 34,000 signatures, but despite AB protests, the new government refused to call an extraordinary summer session of parliament to debate the issue. In November, however, the government relaxed the measures somewhat, particularly for low wage earners. (Ibid., nos. 13, 14, and 15.) By the end of the year, the inflation rate fell to a more normal 30 percent, and the government forecast a 10 percent rate by the end of 1984. Nevertheless, national income fell by some 10 percent from 1982 to 1983 and was expected to fall another 2.5 percent in 1984.

Freed of the responsibilities of coalition government, the AB stressed its militant positions on economic matters at its November congress. The government had already achieved a compromise on the aluminum power issue, and with some luck with the fishing catch and global economic recovery, the Icelandic economy could recover quickly. (Ibid., no. 16.) Such a recovery would not aid the AB's efforts to regain its electoral losses in the last two parliamentary elections.

Foreign Affairs. Domestic political turmoil did not restrain the well-established AB foreign policy line. It is still vigorously opposed to the U.S./NATO bases at Keflavik and elsewhere in Iceland as well as the country's membership in NATO. The coalition government of Thoroddsen sidestepped some of these issues, but the revision of the Keflavik Airport agreement, in connection with planned physical improvements, required governmental action. The shared civilian and military facilities were convenient for neither user. In principle, the United States agreed to pay most of the costs connected with modernization of the airport. As part of its historic opposition to the Keflavik base, the AB stalled government action. The Thoroddsen government had agreed at the outset that no changes would be made in foreign and security policy without unanimity within the coalition.

The departure of the AB from the government in April opened the way for speedy conclusion of the Keflavik modernization agreement in July. The United States has agreed to pay nearly all of the initial costs, even though freight and civilian passenger traffic will benefit greatly from the improvements. As the project continues through 1987, Icelandic expenditures will more closely match the U.S. figures (*News from Iceland*, August). Foreign Minister Geir Hallgrimsson also announced a modernization of two radar stations operated by the U.S. Icelandic Defense Force. As an opposition party, the AB could do little but protest. Opposition to the U.S./NATO bases at Keflavik and elsewhere and to Icelandic membership in NATO remains a central part of the AB's political catechism. Nevertheless, it appears that the AB can no longer make political gains on this issue alone. A public opinion poll indicated that among those expressing an opinion, continued NATO membership was supported by more than three to one, and the U.S. military presence was supported two to one (ibid, December). The Euromissile issue attracted considerable political attention in Iceland, although NATO plans do not involve Icelandic territory for either cruise or Pershing II missiles. In December, a motion was introduced into parliament, with support of all political parties except the Independence Party, calling for an agreement not to introduce more nuclear weapons into Europe. It was directed at the Soviet Union as well as the United States. (*Nordisk Kontakt*, no. 16.) Earlier there had been questions from the AB concerning a report commissioned by the U.S. Defense Department discussing the possibility of deploying missiles in Iceland. Foreign Minister Hallgrimsson stressed that fears about such a change in policy were "totally groundless" and that the report was not official U.S. policy. Iceland has full power to decide the nature and quantity of military equipment in the country. (*News from Iceland*, December.)

There was no change in Iceland's extensive commercial arrangement with the Soviet Union regarding Icelandic exports of fish products and import of Soviet petroleum. About 7.5 percent of Icelandic export earnings came from sales to the Soviet Union, but the United States remains Iceland's largest customer. There has been some discussion of diversifying Iceland's oil supplies away from the Soviet Union, although the latter has never successfully applied economic pressure on Iceland. There is broad Icelandic consensus on separating foreign economic affairs from conventional foreign policy. (*Morgunbladid*, 30 July.)

International Party Contacts. The AB has remained aloof from the international communist movement. It has tended to identify more closely with democratic socialist parties, particularly those with strong leftist and pacifist positions. It interacts informally but regularly with the Socialist Left Party of Norway and the Socialist People's Party in Denmark. Official visits are not frequent, but the annual meetings of the Nordic Council as well as the council's extensive committee work provide ample opportunity for interaction. The AB leadership and press are regularly critical of Soviet political behavior, although more passion is unleashed at the misdeeds of the United States and multinational corporations.

In sum, the AB continues to reflect the personal, passionate, and idiosyncratic nature of Icelandic politics. Radical in program, but often pragmatic in practice, xenophobic by habit, but cosmopolitan in spirit, the AB remains a colorful but not currently influential element. The international situation and the domestic economic crisis may give it future opportunities. The April election showed continued decline, but freed from the responsibilities of government and faced with the continuing disintegration of the weak social democratic parties, the AB may be able to recoup the losses of recent years.

Eric S. Einhorn
University of Massachusetts at Amherst

Ireland

Population. 3.5 million (Republic); 1.5 million (Northern)
Party. Communist Party of Ireland (CPI)
Founded. 1933
Membership. 500 (estimate)
Secretary General. Michael O'Riordan
National Political Committee. Includes Michael O'Riordan, Andrew Barr, Sean Nolan, Tom Redmond, Edwina Stewart, Eddie Glackin
Status. Legal
Last Congress. Eighteenth, 14–16 May 1982, in Dublin
Last Election. 1982; no representation
Auxiliary Organizations. Connolly Youth Movement
Publications. *Irish Socialist, Irish Workers' Voice, Unity, Irish Bulletin*

The CPI was founded in 1921, when the Socialist Party of Ireland expelled moderates and decided to join the Comintern. During the Civil War, the party became largely irrelevant and virtually disappeared, although very small communist cells remained intact. The CPI was refounded in June 1933, the date the communists now adopt as the founding date of their party. In 1983, the party celebrated its fiftieth anniversary. The party organization was disrupted during World War II because of the belligerent status of the North and the neutrality of the South. In 1948, the communists in the south founded the Irish Workers' Party and those in the north the Communist Party of Northern Ireland. At a specially convened "unity congress" held in Belfast on 15 March 1970, the two groups reunited.

The CPI is a recognized political party on both sides of the border and contests both local and national elections. It has, however, no significant support and no elected representatives.

Leadership and Organization. The CPI is divided into two geographical branches corresponding to the political division of the country. In theory, the congress is the supreme constitutional authority of the party, but in practice it simply endorses the decisions of the national executive. The innermost controlling body is the National Political Committee.

Domestic Party Affairs. The main event of the year for the CPI was the celebration of its golden jubilee, with commemorative events in Dublin, Belfast, Cork, and Sligo. The highlight was an exhibition of party history at Connolly House, Dublin.

The continuing political division of the country remained a vital issue in 1983. The party continued to call for the creation of a single, united, socialist Ireland. The party holds that the principal obstacle to unification is the United Kingdom, which is seen as deliberately using all its powers to keep Ireland subordinate. The CPI is, however, opposed to violence and denounces the use of force by paramilitaries on both sides of the communal divide. The party believes Irish unification can be achieved through working-class solidarity, thus uniting Catholics and Protestants.

One of the main political events of the year was the 7 September referendum on a constitutional amendment designed to reduce existing rights to contraception. The CPI played a vigorous role in opposing the amendment, but its position was soundly defeated. The party also led an unsuccessful propaganda campaign against the government's Criminal Justice Bill, which gave the police greater powers.

A parliamentary by-election, which underlined the party's lack of electoral support, was held in Dublin in November. Although the CPI ran a strong campaign in support of its candidate, Eddie Glackin, a CPI National Executive member, the party polled only a discouraging 243 votes.

International Views. The CPI is totally subservient to Moscow and has never expressed any criticism of Soviet policy. The party, for example, supported the Soviet invasion of Afghanistan and favors military rule in Poland. In general, its foreign policy pronouncements are predictable, differing little from year to year. It is virulently anti-American and strongly castigates U.S. policy in Central America, Grenada, and Lebanon. The party also maintained its traditional hostility to Irish membership in the European Economic Community, which it sees as a device to draw Ireland into NATO planning.

In April, a high-level delegation of the Communist Party of Great Britain met representatives of the CPI in Belfast. The Irish delegation consisted of Michael O'Riordan, James Stewart, and Tom Redmond. They issued a joint statement calling for British withdrawal from Northern Ireland and the establishment of a unified Irish state.

Other Marxist Groups. There are numerous Marxist groups in Ireland, most of them commanding greater support than the minuscule CPI. The most important are Sinn Fein—The Workers' Party, the Irish Republican Socialist Party, and the Provisional Sinn Fein.

Richard Sim
London

Italy

Population. 57.3 million (estimate)
Party. Italian Communist Party (Partito Comunista Italiano; PCI)
Founded. 1921
Membership. 1.67 million at the end of 1982 (ANSA, 1 March) including members of Communist Youth Federation
Secretary General. Enrico Berlinguer
Secretariat. 9 members: Enrico Berlinguer, Gerardo Chiaromonte, Adalberto Minucci, Giancarlo Pajetta, Ugo Pecchioli, Alfredo Reichlin, Adriana Seroni, Aldo Tortorella, Renato Zangheri
Directorate. 33 members
Central Control Commission. 57 members: Allessandro Natta, chairman
Central Committee. 180 members
Status. Legal
Last Congress. Sixteenth, 2–6 March 1983, in Milan
Last Election. June 1983, 29.9 percent of the vote, 198 seats in the 630-seat lower house and 107 of 315 seats in the Senate
Auxiliary Organizations. Communist Youth Federation, National League of Cooperatives
Publications. *L'Unità*, official daily published in Rome and Milan, Emanuele Macaluso, editor, Romano Ledda, co-editor; *Rinascita*, weekly, Giuseppe Chiarante, editor; *Critica Marxista*, theoretical journal, Aldo Tortorella, editor; *Politica ed Economia*; *Riforma della Scuola*; *Democrazia e Diritto*; *Donne e Politica*; *Studi Storici*; *Nuova Rivista Internazionale*

The PCI was established in 1921 when a radical faction of the Italian Socialist Party (PSI), led by Amedeo Bordiga, Antonio Gramsci, and Palmiro Togliatti, seceded from the PSI. Declared illegal under the fascist regime, the PCI went underground and the party headquarters was moved abroad. It reappeared on the Italian scene in 1944 and participated in governmental coalitions in the early postwar years. Excluded from office in 1947, it has remained in opposition since then, except for a brief period (summer 1976 to January 1979) when it became part of a governmental coalition but without holding cabinet posts. At the local level, the PCI has been in power in a large number of municipalities, especially in Emilia-Romagna, Tuscany, and Umbria. Alone or in coalition with the PSI, the PCI controls the administration of most major cities.

Internal Party Affairs. The Sixteenth National Congress was held in Milan on 2–6 March. It was preceded by a widespread debate at the local and federation level that lasted over three months. According to some observers, it was the "most open and undogmatic debate in the history of the party." (*La Repubblica*, 21 February.) Others noted that the discussions held at different levels "presented an unprecedented picture of dissent and disagreement openly expressed through voting and amendments to the policy document of the leadership" (*RFE Research*, 25 February).

The congress was attended by over 1,200 delegates representing different areas of the country and by 140 delegations of political parties from 80 different countries. As in past congresses, most of these foreign delegations represented communist parties, with the notable addition of the Chinese Communist Party (CCP), which for the first time in 20 years sent a delegation. Foreign attendance also included a large number of delegations of socialist and social democratic parties from Belgium, France, the Netherlands, Greece, Sweden, Spain, Norway, and others. Interestingly, none of the foreign communist delegates was invited to address the congress, but an invitation was extended to Piet Dankert, Dutch socialist leader and president of the European Parliament. Another novelty of the congress was the presence, for the first time in Italian history, of the secretary of the Christian Democratic Party, Ciriaco De Mita, who attended the meeting with leaders of several other parties.

A large number of parties sent messages to the PCI on the occasion of the congress. Notable among these messages was one sent by the CCP that stressed "traditional friendship" and the "new developments of the past few years," a clear reference to the rapprochement between the two parties that has taken place in recent times (NCNA, 1 March). The message from the Communist Party of the Soviet Union (CPSU) was considerably cooler: "We are always willing to develop voluntary comradely cooperation and solidarity with all communist parties on the basis of the life-tested ideas of Marx-Engels-Lenin" (Tass, 1 March). The coolness between the two parties that has characterized their relations for the past three years was also underscored when the CPSU sent a delegation of lower rank than had been the case on past occasions.

Unlike other national congresses, the sixteenth was characterized by a challenge to the top leadership coming from a member of the Directorate, Armando Cossutta. His criticisms began to surface at the beginning of 1982, shortly after the PCI's strong denunciation of the military takeover in Poland. Arguing that the official position taken by the party represented a break with tradition and a "rejection of socialism," Cossutta expressed his "fundamental disagreement" with the statement made by the leadership (L'Unità, 6 January 1982). Cossutta quickly became identified as the leader of a pro-Soviet faction, even though he was to state later that "the Soviet system has never been a model for me" (ibid., 19 February). Although Cossutta's position appeared to be an isolated one among higher party officials, there were reasons to suppose that he had some support at the grass-roots level and that

dissent from the official party line would become visible during the debates held in preparation for the congress. Accordingly, when in November 1982 the Central Committee prepared the theses for the Sixteenth Congress, Cossutta and Guido Cappelloni, another member of the committee, presented a number of amendments designed to tone down criticisms of the USSR contained in the document and to limit the extent of the break between the PCI and the CPSU. These amendments were overwhelmingly defeated in the Central Committee, but they were published in the PCI daily and thus served as a rallying point for those members who shared a critical attitude toward the leadership and its positions. Precongressional debates held in late 1982 and early 1983 revealed, however, that sentiments in favor of Cossutta's positions were far less widespread than had been thought. Despite pro-Soviet activities by other groups outside the party and not directly connected with internal dissenters (for example, the Italian edition of Novoe Vremya, the pro-Soviet magazine Interstampa, and the pro-Soviet peace movement Struggle for Peace), the theses proposed by the PCI leadership were approved in local and federation congresses by over 96 percent of those voting (ANSA, 1 March). Nor did the challenge mounted by Cossutta fare any better during the congressional debates. Moreover, other amendments that were implicitly an expression of pro-Soviet sentiment were also soundly defeated. Among these was one proposed by the Lucca Federation that called for Italy's withdrawal from NATO. It was overwhelmingly rejected with only 26 votes in favor and 34 abstentions out of over 1,100 votes cast. In the last session of the congress, Cossutta and Cappelloni withdrew the amendments they had submitted a few months before. They argued that "these amendments had fulfilled a useful function and had stimulated reflection but that with the debate over, there was no point in maintaining them" (L'Unità, 6 March). In the end, this episode of dissent turned out to be far less crucial than many observers had originally anticipated. Nor did the dissenters pay any particular price for their opposition. Both were re-elected to the Central Committee, and Cossutta was re-elected a member of the Directorate as well.

But this did not mean that Cossutta had fully accepted the party line. In October, after a brief visit to the USSR, he accused PCI leaders of having failed to mobilize the masses against the installation of U.S. missiles in Italy. This was the result, he argued, of the PCI notion that both superpowers were responsible for the growth of international tensions. (*Panorama*, 10 October.) In response, leaders close to Berlinguer argued that the peace movement could not gain ground "on the basis of a complete identification with the policy of the USSR and the positions of Soviet diplomacy" (*L'Unità*, 9 October).

Shortly after the conclusion of the congress, leadership posts in the party were reassigned. Berlinguer was confirmed as secretary general and, to dispel rumors that had circulated about his replacement, declared that while he was not "secretary general for life," he had a mandate from the entire party. He added that prior to the congress an extensive inquiry had been made among all important national and regional party leaders and that the sentiment was overwhelmingly in favor of endorsing him as leader of the party. (Ibid., 18 March.) The Secretariat was expanded from seven to nine members, and former Secretariat member Alessandro Natta was appointed chairman of the 57-member Central Control Commission. The addition of Renato Zangheri, former mayor of the city of Bologna, was thought to be an indication that he might be in line to replace Berlinguer.

The PCI posted a deficit of 5.6 billion lire for fiscal 1982. Party leaders blamed the deficit on the persistent high inflation rate, the high cost of borrowing money, and the serious financial situation of the party's press, which was burdened by exorbitant costs. The report accompanying the budget pointed out that the share of public funds had dropped from 45 percent of all income in 1974 to 31 percent in 1982. Concern with the state of party finances led the Directorate to draw up an economic and financial plan, covering several years, designed to eliminate the deficit, which in previous fiscal years had reached 14.6 billion lire and at the end of 1982 was over 20 billion lire. Major sources of income for 1982 were membership dues and portions of the salaries of communist members of parliament (27.8 billion); public financing (23.3 billion); and receipts from *L'Unità* festivals, donations, and press subscriptions (21.7 billion). Major expenditures included 46.4 billion distributed by party headquarters to peripheral organizations and 16.4 billion for publications, mostly operating expenses of the PCI daily. (Ibid., 30 January.) A proposal for restructuring the operations of the

newspaper to reduce its cost met with strong resistance on the part of workers affected, and a strike was called. Continuing difficulties for the daily were reported at the end of the year.

In contrast to the difficult position of the party's newspaper, the PCI publishing house, Editori Riuniti, celebrated its thirtieth anniversary in good financial health. Created in 1953 with little capital and for the purpose of reprinting the works of classic Marxist thinkers, Editori Riuniti has grown into a major publishing enterprise with sales of 11 billion lire, with publications in a wide variety of fields and several specialized magazines and journals. According to President Roberto Bonchio, Editori Riuniti is not just an appendix to the party but a self-sufficient entity (*Panorama*, 4 July).

Toward the end of the year, there was a reshuffling of some high party officials. On 25 November, the Central Committee and the Central Control Commission announced that Achille Occhetto had been appointed to the Secretariat, with responsibility for the Propaganda and Information Department. Adalberto Minucci was given the Cultural Activities and Education Department, and Aldo Tortorella assumed general coordination functions. Antonio Bassolino, who had served in the Naples area as a regional official, was promoted to head of the Southern Italy Section. (*L'Unità*, 25 November.)

Domestic Affairs. The domestic strategy and posture of the PCI in 1983 resembled those of the preceding two years. The party remained in opposition at the national level while sharing governmental responsibility in many regions, large cities, and municipalities. While PCI strategy between 1975 and 1980 had envisaged a broad coalition of all major political groups, in late 1980 the party moved to the democratic alternative line—a government based on a coalition with the PSI, with help from other leftist and center-left parties. Arguing that this formula was already working well at the local level, PCI leaders continued to press other parties in this direction but without much success. Toward the end of 1982, the PSI joined another center-left coalition led by Christian Democrat Amintore Fanfani, and the PCI confirmed its opposition. In early 1983, it became clear that the Fanfani experiment would not last long and that a new parliamentary election might be called in late spring. According the some observers, PCI leaders looked with some apprehension at the possibility of an early election and would have preferred that the electoral contest be held at its scheduled time in 1984.

Elections for the Chamber of Deputies (630 seats) and the Senate (315 seats) were held on 26 and 27 June. The returns in the race for the lower house gave the PCI 29.9 percent of the vote, down half a percentage point from 1979, and a loss of 3 seats. The returns for the Senate were similar: 30.8 percent and 107 seats (down 0.6 of a point and 2 seats). Coming on the heels of a campaign conducted on the defensive and dominated by the rivalry between the PSI and the Christian Democratic Party (DC), these results did not look bad at all. Although the PSI improved its position marginally, it did not achieve the decisive boost it had expected. The Christian Democrats, the target of PCI attacks in recent years, suffered a disastrous blow. There were thus ample reasons for Berlinguer's satisfaction with the results, even though the PCI itself had not done particularly well. As he pointed out, "The PSI did not assert itself as the most dynamic and modern party, as the party of the so-called emergent social sectors . . . The PSI had a modest improvement that cannot be brandished as a strategic success since it failed to achieve the goal of 'an adjustment of the balance on the Left,' namely an advance at the PCI expense." As for the DC, "its losses are on such a scale that a democratic majority without the DC is numerically possible in the new parliament." (Ibid., 18 July.) The fact that the parliamentary strength of the two major parties had become more equal (32.9 for the DC and 29.9 percent for the PCI) undoubtedly constituted an additional element of satisfaction.

By themselves, electoral returns could not, however, open the door to PCI participation in a new government. The democratic alternative scenario requires the cooperation of the PSI and other center-left groups, and in the aftermath of the election, there was no sign that these parties were moving in the direction desired by the PCI. In August, a new center-left coalition led, for the first time in Italian history, by the PSI was inaugurated. The PCI promptly announced its opposition to the new experiment. The PCI labeled the program presented by Bettino Craxi, the new prime minister, "vague and inconsistent," the coalition as "the umpteenth rehash of the five-party formula," and the foreign policy lines presented by the prime minister "disappointing and worrisome" (ibid., 10 and 11 August). In his closing remarks in parliament during the debate on the vote of confidence for the new Craxi government, Berlinguer stated: "The alternative is not only indispensable, it is possible and attainable. We make this assertion on the basis of two convictions. One is based on the intrinsic weakness of the government's solution, which does not have the prerequisites, capacity, and will to tackle the roots of modern development problems in a country like Italy. In addition, we do not really believe that it will be possible to overcome the conflict of directions inherent in the five-party coalition, conflicts that seem doomed to become more acute rather than to disappear. And we will certainly not stand idly by." (Ibid.)

Polemical exchanges between the PCI and PSI, already frequent during the first part of the year, continued and intensified after the inauguration of the Craxi government. One bone of contention was the balance of power between the two parties in local governments. In January, the PSI withdrew from a leftist coalition in the city of Florence, provoking the downfall of PCI mayor Elio Gabuggiani, who had been in office since 1976. Later in the year, a rift between the two major parties of the Left brought to a standstill the administration of the city of Turin, and communist mayor Diego Novelli was forced to resign.

Local elections were held in November in a number of municipalities and in the northern provinces of Trento and Bolzano. The returns for the communal councils were generally negative for the PCI, although the losses in most cases were minor. One major exception was the election in the city of Naples, where the PCI has shared power with the PSI since the mid-1970s. In Naples, the PCI lost 5 percentage points and five seats. In the city of Reggio Calabria and in the provinces of Trento and Bolzano, PCI losses were less pronounced (−1.4, −0.3, and −1.4 percentage points, respectively).

Foreign Affairs. Throughout the year, PCI officials voiced their concern over the worsening international situation, repeatedly stressed that the blame did not rest with one side only, and advanced proposals for reducing international tensions. While PCI leaders were often critical of the policies of the Reagan administration, their proposals were very similar to those advanced in Europe by socialists and social democrats and in the United States by certain segments of Congress. On the issue of arms reduction, for example, the party stated: "We fail to understand how it is possible to pursue a balance of forces at a higher level unless, in fact, one is pursuing not balance but superiority . . . One must acknowledge the correctness of another position, namely the one proposed by the Kennedy-Hatfield resolution . . . that calls for a general 'freeze' on all nuclear weapons by both superpowers." (Ibid., 3 March.)

As could be expected, the PCI criticized U.S. policies in Latin America ("U.S. military threats, economic boycotts, and political stances against Nicaragua and other Central American countries are creating a critically dangerous situation regarding those peoples' independence and the future of world peace" [ibid., 31 July]) and severely condemned the U.S. military intervention in Grenada (ibid., 26 October). But the USSR also came under fire for the downing of the Korean airliner: "A careful reading of the Tass communiqué . . . has consolidated the painful conviction that we are dealing with a crime against innocent victims and world peace and order . . . we are distressed over the enormity of the crime . . . no defense doctrine and no shortcoming in international law could give any semblance of acceptability to what has occurred . . . it cannot escape the Soviet leaders' attention that international relations have suffered a serious blow." (Ibid., 3 September.) Armando Cossutta took a very different stance. Asked if the pro-Soviet faction shared the condemnation, he replied: "I do express the firmest condemnation—but against those U.S. intelligence services that sent so many innocent victims to such an atrocious fate" (Panorama, 10 October).

Berlinguer summarized the PCI's position on the question of Euromissiles in a report to the Central Committee and the Central Control Commission: "We think that in the short term it is necessary (1) that the Geneva negotiations be continued, if necessary beyond the 1983 date, without any deployment of missiles while the negotiations are under way . . . that the Italian government should decide not to deploy the missiles this year, should suspend preparatory work at the Comiso base, and should refer the whole question to parliament for debate" (L'Unità, 19 July).

Finally, on the Lebanon crisis and the presence of Italian troops in the multinational peacekeeping force, the PCI position was that in order to avoid becoming involved in acts of war, the troops should be pulled out. Explained Berlinguer, "Our support for the parliamentary decision to send in an Italian army contingent came in the wake of the massacres of Sabra and Shatila, but today the situation has changed radically" (ibid., 19 September).

International Party Contacts. In 1983, the relationship between the PCI and the CPSU and other Eastern European communist parties continued to remain cool. Although polemical exchanges were not as frequent and as intense as in previous years, both sides voiced reciprocal criticisms on a number of occasions. An article in the Czech ideological journal Tribuna (29 December 1982) attacked the tendency of "Italian revisionists" to misuse the work of Gramsci "in order to sanctify the theory of the so-called third path and to make him the father of Eurocommunism." The article accused these revisionists of erroneously linking Gramsci with the theories of Eduard Bernstein, Herbert Marcuse, Theodor Adorno, Austro-Marxism, and Eurocommunism, and it argued that the founder of the PCI was instead a true Leninist. "Gramsci's work demonstrates that there has not been and there cannot be any 'third path' in the era of imperialism. There is only one solution, well tried in theory and practice: the dictatorship of the proletariat [moving] toward the classless communist society."

Although Berlinguer's report to the Congress did not deal extensively with relations with other communist parties, some of his remarks showed that the party had not changed its opinion of the Soviet Union. Berlinguer repeated that the forward thrust of the Soviet model had petered out and that "the military intervention in Afghanistan —to cite only the most serious example—has shown that the Soviet Union, too, has adopted and can adopt forms of conduct typical of power politics and carry out actions contrary to détente and without respect for popular sovereignty and independence. These are the reasons . . . that prompt us to reject the identification of the peace struggle with an alignment for or against either of the two military blocs. (L'Unità, 3 March.) Immediately after the PCI congress, members of the Soviet delegation expressed their disagreement with parts of the document adopted at the meeting, especially with the theses that the Soviet Union had lost "its propulsive force" and that the two blocs were equally responsible for the crisis in détente. The Soviet delegates argued that the blocs "reflected the existence of two antagonistic forces, the force of progress and peace on one side and that of imperialism and international reaction on the other. Every communist must make a choice between these antagonistic forces." (Ibid., 7 March.)

On 10 April, the PCI daily reacted sharply to the publication in *Voprosi istorii KPSS* (Problems in the history of the CPSU) of an article praising former Italian communist leader Palmiro Togliatti for the way in which he had stressed in his writings the primary need of solidarity with the Soviet Union. In response, *L'Unità* argued that this praise constituted an indirect attack on the present leadership of the PCI, as well as a falsification of the position taken by Togliatti, who had expressed reservations about the Soviet regime in the Yalta memorandum in which he spoke of "the suppression of democratic and individual freedoms" under Stalin.

In April, Aldo Tortorella of the PCI Secretariat attended the international conference on Marxist thought held in East Berlin under the auspices of the East German party. In contrast to the orthodox statements of most participants, Tortorella referred to the Soviet intervention in Afghanistan as a "gravely negative development," argued that the peace movement should not identify itself with one bloc against the other, and maintained that contradictions existed not only in capitalist countries but also in socialist states. Finally, he suggested that the crisis that had surfaced in some communist societies was due to the failure to give the workers real participation in decisionmaking. (*Neues Deutschland*, East Berlin, 15 April.) On 3 May, *L'Unità* strongly condemned the "brutal" repression by Polish police of the May Day pro-Solidarity demonstrations. After noting that "the police struck workers on the day that is the symbol of their struggle for emancipation and liberation," the editorial went on to say: "The tragic epilogue of the Polish May Day is but the latest link in a chain of events that since the coup of December 1981 has further deepened the rift between the regime and the people." It concluded that "the search for dialogue, for new forms of democracy, for a national unity based on pluralism remains more than ever on the agenda of Polish life."

Another episode that was likely to irritate the communist parties of Eastern Europe was the publication by Editori Riuniti of a book by exiled Polish economist Wlodzimierz Brus, sharply criticizing the Soviet and other Eastern European regimes. Moreover, the book was given considerable publicity, and a debate was held in Rome at the PCI's Gramsci Institute on the occasion of the publication of the volume. PCI leaders and party experts attending the meeting raised probing questions on the reasons behind the economic failures of these systems and stressed the need to tackle them through political reform. (*L'Unità*, 21 May.)

On 21 August, on the fifteenth anniversary of the Warsaw Pact invasion of Czechoslovakia, *L'Unità* published an article by Adriano Guerra, one of the party's Eastern European experts, arguing that the policy of "normalization" had not solved any of the problems that had emerged in the 1968 crisis. Normalization, stated Guerra, had in fact blocked the demands for reform within the system, and stagnation had resulted. On 24 August, an angry reply appeared in *Rudé právo*, the Czechoslovak party daily. After noting that Western assessments of Czechoslovakia are usually inspired by the CIA, the author accused the PCI of assessing "the post-August developments in our fatherland in the same way and spirit . . . By its attitude toward the Czechoslovak Socialist Republic, *L'Unità* has objectively placed itself on the side of the enemies of socialism. Possibly it will earn an appreciative clap on the back from the bourgeois communication media and politicians for its 'independence' and 'autonomy.'" A short rejoinder by the PCI daily (25 August) dismissed the Czech statement as being "conspicuous for its crudity and disinformation. Only invectives and no argument."

Polemics between the PCI and other communist parties are by no means confined to the parties of Eastern Europe. Largely because of the positions adopted by the PCI in recent years, the party finds itself in disagreement over major issues with some of the Western European parties, especially those closely aligned with Moscow. One such major difference emerged in the late summer when the PCI strongly backed a proposal by Altiero Spinelli, a former European commissioner elected to the European Parliament as an independent representative on the PCI list, for strengthening Western European integration. The Spinelli proposal, adopted by a large majority of the European Parliament on 16 September, would lead to the creation of a European Union with the power, among other things, to levy taxes, conduct collective foreign policy, and negotiate on the international level. In contrast to the PCI, the French communist newspaper *L'Humanité* (16 September) basically ignored it and defined it a "dangerous utopia." Other differences between the two parties were in evidence during the meeting between Berlinguer and French party leader Georges Marchais, held in Rome in early October. Poland and Afghanistan were not discussed; Berlinguer spoke of an excess of Soviet missiles, but Marchais made no reference to Moscow's SS-20s (ANSA, 5 October).

The PCI has traditionally maintained extensive contacts with other parties at the international level, and this practice continued in 1983. From 5 through 7 January, International Department chief Giancarlo Pajetta visited Yugoslavia as a guest of the League of Communists and met with party president Mitja Ribičič (*L'Unità*, 9 January). In late May, Berlinguer, Pajetta, and foreign affairs expert and Central Committee member Antonio Rubbi met in Rome with the secretary general of the Spanish Communist Party, Gerardo Iglesias (ibid., 26 May). In June, Antonio Rubbi met in Frankfurt with Karsten Voigt, International Bureau chief of the West German party. In early August, George Hawi, secretary of the Lebanese Communist Party, traveled to Rome for a meeting with Berlinguer. The two leaders agreed "on the need for the withdrawal of all foreign troops from Lebanon" (ANSA, 2 July). Other contacts involved the representative in Italy of the Palestine Liberation Organization (12 August), Somali president Mohamed Siad Barre (7 October), and Andreas Papandreou, secretary general of the Greek Panhellenic Socialist Movement (21 November). During his visit to Greece, Secretariat member Giancarlo Pajetta also met with delegations of both factions of the Greek Communist Party (*L'Unitá*, 21 November).

Of greater significance was Berlinguer's visit to the People's Republic of China in the middle of August. Billed as a vacation (Berlinguer traveled with members of his family), the trip received considerable attention on the part of observers. Berlinguer had traveled to Beijing in April 1980 to normalize relations between the two parties. Berlinguer's 1983 visit involved long discussions with party chairman Hu Yaobang, Foreign Minister Wu Xueqian, and other important Chinese leaders. The Chinese leaders chose the occasion

to republish a statement made by Deng Xiaoping three years earlier on the occasion of Berlinguer's first visit, which contained a reference to "the CPSU behaving like a patriarchal party and practicing big-nation chauvinism" (*Beijing Review*, 22 August). At the conclusion of his trip, Berlinguer pointed out that relations between the two parties had developed in a very positive way and would be developed further. Lest his trip be interpreted as a sign that a special relation was being created, Berlinguer added: "I would like to stress that criteria of autonomy, respect, and independence also govern the relations that the PCI maintains with communist, socialist, and social democratic parties and Third World national and liberation movements. In our view, these are the principles on which a new internationalism among the worldwide progressive forces can be developed." (*L'Unità*, 28 August.)

In the first part of December, a PCI delegation composed of directorate members Gerardo Chiaromonte, Gianni Cervetti, and Napoleone Colajanni traveled to Moscow at the invitation of the CPSU Central Committee. This was the first high-level Italian delegation to visit the USSR since the strong denunciation of aspects of Soviet foreign policies by the PCI. The purpose of the trip was ostensibly to hold talks on international issues and economic problems. But observers believed that the conversations of the PCI delegation with Boris Ponomarev and Vadim Zagladin included discussions about a possible meeting between Soviet leader Yuri Andropov and PCI secretary Berlinguer. Delegation member Gianni Cervetti stated that no specific dates had been discussed and that it was a question of determining "the time and the manner of the visit so that it might be profitable to the cause of disarmament and peace." As for relations between the two parties, the Italian delegation pointed out that these were not at the focus of the discussions, that each side had explained clearly its position to the other, and that the discussions had taken place in a "pretty normal" atmosphere. (*Corriere della Sera*, 11 December.)

In mid-December, Berlinguer embarked on a tour of Eastern Europe in an attempt to reopen the dialogue between East and West. He first visited Romania and held talks with Nicolae Ceauşescu and then traveled to East Berlin for conversations with Erich Honecker (ibid., 12 December). From 21 to 23 December, Berlinguer also visited Yugoslavia for talks with President Mika Špiljak and party leader Dragoslav Marković. (ANSA, 21 December).

Other Communist Groups. The Party of Proletarian Unity for Communism (PDUP) and Proletarian Democracy (DP) are composed largely of former communists and left-wing socialists and are generally regarded as competing with the PCI on the left wing of the political spectrum. In the June parliamentary election, the DP, which had no representatives in the outgoing parliament, received 1.5 percent of the vote and seven seats. The DP also has a seat in the European Parliament. On the other hand, the PDUP, which had six members of parliament from 1979 to 1983, did not compete in the June elections but presented some of its candidates on the PCI lists.

Terrorist Groups. Episodes of terrorism carried out by self-styled "true communist" groups, which have plagued Italy since the mid-1970s, declined sharply in 1983. During the year, a number of alleged terrorists were arrested, and many of those arrested in previous years were brought to trial. In January, 32 members of the Red Brigades were sentenced to life imprisonment for the kidnapping and murder of former prime minister Aldo Moro in 1978 (*NYT*, 25 January). In April, over eighty members of the radical guerrilla band Prima Linea were sentenced to prison terms after a six-month trial (ibid., 25 April). In August, a Sardinian court convicted several members of a Red Brigade terrorist cell. Finally, in November, a Milan court convicted the members of a terrorist group responsible for the murder of well-known journalist Walter Tobagi. In accordance with a recent law aimed at fighting terrorism, the court gave light sentences to several defendants who, after their arrest, had collaborated with the police and had contributed to the dismantling of a number of terrorist organizations. The release of some well-known political assassins who had turned state's evidence provoked a bitter debate.

Giacomo Sani
Ohio State University

Luxembourg

Population. 366,000
Party. Communist Party of Luxembourg (Parti communiste luxembourgeois; CPL)
Founded. 1921
Membership. 600 (estimate)
Chairman. René Urbany
Honorary Chairman. Dominique Urbany
Executive Committee. 10 members: Aloyse Bisdorff, Jos Grandgenet, François Hoffmann, Jacques Hoffmann, Fernand Hübsch, Marianne Passeri, Marcel Pütz, Dominique Urbany, René Urbany, Jean Wesquet
Central Committee. 28 full, 6 candidate, and 7 honorary members
Secretariat. 2 members: René Urbany, Dominique Urbany
Finance Control Commission. 3 members: Jorry Leick, Walter Stefanetti, Jacqueline Urbany
Status. Legal

Last Congress. Twenty-third, 31 May–1 June 1980
Last Election. 1979, 5.0 percent, 2 of 59 seats
Auxiliary Organizations. Jeunesse communiste luxembourgeoise; Union des femmes luxembourgeoises
Publications. *Zeitung vum Lëtzeburger Vollek*, official CPL organ, daily, 1,000–1,500 copies (CPL's claim: 15,000–20,000)

The pro-Soviet CPL played a minor political role in Luxembourg prior to World War II. After 1945, the CPL's position improved. Communists were elected to serve in parliament and in several communities. From 1945 to 1947, Luxembourg's cabinet included one communist minister. The best election results were achieved in 1968. In elections in 1974 and 1979, the communist vote declined steadily. In 1979, the CPL received 5 percent of the vote. In the first elections to the European Parliament on 10 June 1979, the CPL obtained 5.1 percent. In municipal elections in 1981, the CPL received 7.2 percent, compared with 16 percent in 1975.

The party leadership is dominated by the Urbany family. Party chairman René Urbany succeeded his father, Dominique, at the first meeting of the Central Committee after the Twenty-second Party Congress in 1977. Dominique Urbany is presently honorary chairman of the CPL. Members of the Urbany family hold many key positions in the party and its auxiliaries. René Urbany is also director of the party press. His brother-in-law, Central Committee member François Frisch, heads the organization of former resistance fighters and is also secretary of the Luxembourg Committee for European Security and Cooperation. His father-in-law, Executive Committee member Jacques Hoffmann, serves on the executive board of the communist printing company Cooperative ouvrière de press et d'édition (COPE).

The CPL, like the other communist parties in Western Europe, supported Soviet foreign policy objectives in its "mass publications" and its effort to promote "joint actions against the threat of war." François Hoffmann stated the party's "four main lines": "First, explanation of the USSR's peace-loving policy and its constructive initiatives. Second, presentation of the catastrophic consequences of a nuclear war for humankind. Third, exposure of the aggressive nature of impe-rialism and the Pentagon's attempts to turn Europe into an area for exchange for nuclear strikes. And fourth, demonstration of the absurdity of the arms race." The CPL claimed credit for the increased activities of the "anti-war movement." (*WMR*, October 1982.)

Contacts with fraternal parties were maintained during 1983. Honorary Chairman Dominique Urbany was awarded the Order of Lenin for his "active participation in the struggle against fascism" (Tass, 28 March; *FBIS*, 31 March). A Soviet delegation, headed by G. F. Sizov, chairman of the Soviet party's Auditing Commission, visited Luxembourg (27 March–2 April) at the invitation of the CPL Central Committee (*Pravda*, 28 March; *FBIS*, 29 March). A CPL delegation, led by Executive Committee member Fernand Hübsch, visited the Soviet Union from 30 April to 7 May and participated in the May Day celebrations (*Pravda*, 8 May; *FBIS*, 26 May). Another party delegation, headed by party chairman René Urbany, visited Bulgaria (16–21 May). The CPL delegation reported on their fight against the deployment of U.S. missiles in Western Europe and the "militarization of the country." Together with their Bulgarian comrades, they "condemned . . . U.S. imperialism, [which is] aimed at confrontation," and declared their "solidarity with the struggle of the peoples of Asia, Africa, and Latin America for national independence and social progress." (*Rabotnichesko Delo*, Sofia, 22 May; *FBIS*, 25 May.)

COPE, the CPL's publishing company, prints the French edition of the *World Marxist Review*. COPE's new and modern technical equipment and production facilities, which exceed local requirements by far, serve communist parties and organizations in several other countries.

Eric Waldman
University of Calgary

Malta

Population. 364,000
Party. Communist Party of Malta (Partit Komunista Malti; CPM)
Founded. 1969
Membership. 145 (estimate)
Secretary General. Anthony Vassallo
Leading Organs. Membership not available (see text for leading personalities)
Status. Legal
Last Congress. Second, February 1979
Last Election. 1981 (CPM did not participate)
Auxiliary Organizations. Malta-USSR Friendship and Cultural Society, Anton Cassar, president; Peace and Solidarity Council of Malta, Joseph V. Muscat, president; Communist Youth League (CYL)
Publications. *Zminijietna* (Our times), monthly tabloid, partly in Maltese and partly in English; *Il Bandiera l-Hamra* (Red flag), issued by CYL in Maltese; *Bridge of Friendship and Culture, Malta-USSR*, issued by Malta-USSR Friendship and Cultural Society, quarterly, in English

The CPM was founded in 1969, five years after the island gained independence from the United Kingdom. The founders were former members of the leftist Malta Labor Party (MLP), who had united for the country's anticolonial struggle even though they used communist slogans and did not hide their true colors during the period. From its initial congress in the Maltese town of Gwardamangia, the CPM's leading personality has been Anthony Vassallo, then as now the party's secretary general. Legal since its inception, the CPM describes itself as a "voluntary organization made up of the most politically conscious members of the workers' class, together with others, who are determined to found a Socialist Malta" (*Proletarjat*, no. 1, 1977). The current strength of the CPM is estimated to be some 145 active members, not including representatives of various communist front groups.

Malta's government is led by Bulgarian-born Dominic Mintoff, leader of the MLP, who has held the prime minister's job since 1971. The MLP regained control of the 65-member parliament in the December 1981 elections, with full support of the CPM, over the church-dominated Nationalist Party and the more conservative Christian Democratic Party.

Leadership and Organization. The CPM is headed by a Central Committee elected at a secret party congress held every three or four years. A report from the Second Congress (1979) mentioned the following officials: Chairman Anthony Balsacchino, who is a shipwright and General Workers' Union steward at the Malta Drydocks; Secretary General Anthony Vassallo, who is a career official in the CPM; international secretary Paul Agius, who is the first vice-president of the Malta-USSR Friendship and Cultural Society and general secretary of the Malta Peace Committee; education and propaganda secretary Mario Vella Macina, who is former head of the Communist Youth League (CYL) and an economist at the government's Malta Development Corporation; documentation secretary Lilian Sciberras, who was international secretary of the CYL and is currently an assistant librarian at the University of Malta; and John Agius, Philip

Bugeja, Renald Galea, Mario Mifsud, John Muscat, and Paul Muscat.

It is widely believed that a substantial number of communists are also crypto-members of the MLP despite the latter's policy of prohibiting such dual memberships. The MLP rests its philosophy on a social democratic basis, which the CPM openly opposes. In addition, CPM operatives have infiltrated the government-controlled General Workers' Union, which includes more than 50 percent of all organized workers. In the early 1970s, the CPM also established the League of Social Justice in a largely unsuccessful effort to appeal to students at the country's two universities. Under the auspices of the Malta-USSR Friendship and Cultural Society, a number of Maltese students have been sent to Eastern bloc universities. In 1982, for instance, twelve scholarships were offered by the USSR alone, but this number was cut to only four in 1983. Typically such awards cover tuition, a monthly allowance, and free medical care. The area of study is fairly wide. The first graduate of a Russian university in 1981, Guzeppi Schembri, is now employed at the Maltese Foreign Office.

Party Internal Affairs. The leadership of the CPM is stable, supported by loyal and obedient party members. While the communists have often declared their intention to field their own candidates in parliamentary elections, no CPM member ran under the party's banner in the 1981 contests. Instead the CPM tries to exercise its influence through the ruling MLP government "primarily toward improving the working and living conditions of the working people" (*Népszabadság*, Budapest, 14 July 1982). In order "to prevent a division of the democratic forces," the CPM chooses not to "take away votes" from the majority MLP. Thus, a major problem of the CPM is maintaining its identity while being an operational adjunct of Prime Minister Mintoff's forces, whom the CPM openly abjures. Apparently, the CPM leadership has decided to work behind the scenes toward its goals rather than to engage in fruitless polemics with the other political parties. The government acknowledged the CPM's role, nonetheless, in the 1981 trade agreements signed between the USSR and Malta. Also, the CPM met with obvious success in its efforts to establish a Soviet embassy in Malta, which is now the island's largest. If there have been any disagreements or purges within the CPM organization in the fourteen years since its founding, little publicity has been given them.

Domestic Affairs. A major goal of the CPM is "to oppose the concessions being made to domestic and foreign capital and to resolve the country's social problems on the basis of socialist concepts" (ibid.). Despite substantial economic progress since independence, unemployment is one of Malta's nagging problems. While the CPM was successful in helping to eliminate the British military presence when the base agreements expired in 1979, the accomplishment resulted in the gradual loss of 11,000 well-paying jobs for Maltese workers and the ending of an annual $33 million British subsidy for the use of the island's port facilities. Even though Soviet ships gained the use of former NATO oil bunker operations in 1981, they resigned the agreement in 1983, and the benefit to indigenous labor has been slight. The Soviets also have the use of the Malta Drydocks for ship repair, but during 1983 a total of only ten Russian ships were serviced, with an income to the Maltese government of some $7 million dollars, far below optimistic estimates (*Sunday Times*, Malta, 23 October). As a consequence of unresolved economic problems, the CPM claimed that the MLP "lost voters among the workers and small artisans, as well as working people employed in the service sectors," to the Nationalist Party in the 1981 elections (*Népszabadság*, 14 July 1982).

One standard suggestion the CPM seems to offer the government to ease its economic ills is to seek cooperative agreements with Eastern bloc countries. While Malta does have some sort of trade relationship with all the Eastern bloc countries, its total exports to the entire Soviet bloc area in 1982 were less than the total registered in 1979, and its 1982 imports from the Eastern bloc surpassed those for 1981 (*Sunday Times*, Malta, 11 September). Seemingly to try to redress the trade imbalance, a Soviet delegation headed by K. Vitaly, deputy chief of the Soviet planning agency, Gosplan, visited Malta in March to discuss joint ventures and "spectacular trade deals which have yet to materialize" (ibid.). In November, the General Workers' Union and the Central Council of the Czechoslovak Trade Unions signed an agreement of cooperation, which provided for "an exchange of delegations and for training courses in trade-unionism and related subjects" (ibid., 19 November). Without offering statistical evidence, the CPM claims that such a broad range of economic activity with the Soviet bloc does "guarantee employment for a considerable number of Maltese workers . . . [and] this is the fruit of neutrality and friendship amongst nations with different social systems" (*Bridge of Friendship and Culture, Malta-USSR*, April–June).

A significant new law was proposed and debated in June. The Devolution of Certain Church Property Act, 1983 would allow the government sweeping rights over church-owned property, which is a measure endorsed by the CPM. In addition, the law would force the Roman Catholic church to allocate some of its profits from land sales to provide free education in its traditionally fee-paying schools (Reuters, 28 June). Catholicism is the dominant religion in Malta, and the CPM has refrained from any overt attacks on historic church practices in its effort to appeal to pious Maltese citizens.

Foreign Affairs. The CPM generally supports the government's handling of foreign affairs and concurs with "the policy of nonalignment, which is the most consistent with the country's interests." Also, the CPM believes that relations with the European countries are very important to solving the problems that ensued in Malta "following the departure of the British, the economic transformation . . . [and] the crises besetting the world economy." However, nothing is more important to Maltese communists "than preserving peace and security." As for tensions in the Mediterranean area and the Middle East, the CPM supports "the struggle of the people of Cyprus against military bases, as well as that of the Italian working people against the establishment of missile bases in Sicily . . . and the struggle of the Palestinian people for their own homeland and human rights." Moreover, the CPM condemns "Israel's Lebanon aggression" and renounces "a military solution of disputed issues" (*Népszabadság*, 14 July 1982).

The CPM uses the phrase "obstructionist misuse of the consensus principle" to refer to the Maltese government's initial effort to prevent approval of the final document of the European Security and Cooperation Conference in September (*Zminijietna*, October). The CPM was also extremely critical of the instruction given to the Maltese ambassador to walk out of the U.N. Geneva conference on the problem of Palestine because of an "allegation of an Arab boycott on a Maltese company for trading with Israel" (ibid.). On the downing of the South Korean plane by the USSR, the CPM termed Malta's support of the United States' resolution as "a somewhat slavish position" (ibid.). Anthony Vassallo, in a departure from past tradition, summarized the foreign policy of Malta for the year as pure Machiavellianism and not reflective of "true nonalignment."

International Party Contacts. While the CPM claims extensive "international relations" and "regular bilateral meetings" with communist parties of the socialist countries, it still looks for "additional opportunities to develop further relations" (*Népszabadság*, 14 July 1982). Regarding disputes among and within communist parties, the CPM leadership states that these "must be constructive, avoiding any intervention in other parties' internal affairs." Furthermore, "the unity and collaboration of the communist and workers' parties constitute an indispensable prerequisite for preserving the security of mankind and world peace" (ibid.). In marking the twenty-fifth anniversary of the founding of the *World Marxist Review*, *Zminijietna* (September) carried a long editorial extolling the *Review* for its success in "spreading knowledge of the fraternal parties' strategy and tactics" among its other accomplishments.

Communist publications are available at the offices of the Progressive Bookshop and Progressive Tours, which are owned by Paul Agius. These enterprises also represent Eastern bloc commercial interests and help provide the CPM with operating funds.

T. W. Adams
Washington, D.C.

Netherlands

Population. 14.4 million
Party. Communist Party of the Netherlands (Communistische Partij van Nederland; CPN)
Founded. 1909
Membership. 14,000 (estimate)
Chairperson. Elli Izeboud
Executive Committee. 10 members: Elli Izeboud, Ina Brouwer, Jaap Wolff, John Geelen, Karel Hoogkamp, Boe Thio, Simone Walvisch, Frank Biesboer, Ton van Hoek (one vacancy due to resignation of Bart Schmidt)
Secretariat. 3 members
Central Committee. 55 members (John Geelen, secretary, Ton van Hoek, spokesman)
Status. Legal
Last Congress. Twenty-eighth, 26–28 November 1982; next congress scheduled for 4–5 February 1984
Last Election. 1982, 1.9 percent, 3 of 150 seats; CPN also holds 2 of 75 seats in upper house, which is indirectly elected.
Auxiliary Organizations. General Netherlands Youth Organization, Netherlands Women's Movement, People's Congress Committee, Stop the N-Bomb/Stop the Nuclear Arms Race, Women Against Nuclear Weapons, CPN Youth Platform
Publications. *De Waarheid* (Truth), official daily, circulation 16,000 copies; *CPN–Leden krant*, published 10 times yearly for CPN members; *Politiek en Cultuur*, theoretical journal published 10 times yearly; *Komma*, quarterly, issued by CPN's Institute for Political and Social Research. CPN owns Pegasus Publishers.

The CPN was founded in 1909 as the Social Democratic Party (Sociaal-Democratische Partij) by radical Marxists. It assumed the name Communist Party of Holland (Communistische Partij Holland) in 1919 when the party affiliated with the Comintern. The present name dates from 1935. Except during World War II, the party has always been legal.

The CPN, under its new "pluralistic" leadership headed by Chairperson Elli Izeboud, concentrated almost entirely in 1983 on implementing the new party line as laid down by the Twenty-eighth Congress in November 1982 and on initiating a discussion within the party on a draft party program, which will be presented to 750 voting delegates and 50 nonvoting delegates at an extraordinary congress on 4–5 February

1984. In view of the radical change brought about at the Twenty-eighth Congress by the younger members of the CPN, the new party line became the focus of bitter and intense internal debate. A rearguard action against party "renewal" is being fought by the older orthodox members of the CPN who formed the Horizontal Consultation of Communists (HOC) in 1982.

The new party line, accepted by a majority vote at the Twenty-eighth Congress, consists of a total renewal in ideology, a complete break with "existing socialism," a de-Stalinization of the party, and editorial independence for the party newspaper, *De Waarheid*. The focal point of the debate has been, in large part, the attempt of the editors of *De Waarheid* to develop an editorial strategy whereby the paper, and therefore the

CPN, would appear acceptable to the whole of the Left, including the Labor Party, and to various social movements, especially the peace movement.

The results thus far of this new coalition policy have been meager, although agreement was reached, after laborious discussions, with four other progressive parties on 26 November on a joint election list for the European Parliament elections in 1984. The CPN will join with the Pacifist Socialist Party (PSP), the Political Radical Party (PPR), the Evangelical People's Party (EVP), and the Green Platform, in supporting a common program. The CPN increased its representation in the first chamber of parliament by the election of Henk Hoekstra by members of the provincial legislatures on 31 August. Hoekstra will join Kees IJmker in the First Chamber. The CPN representation in the second chamber of parliament remains at three (Ina Brouwer, Evelien Eshuis, and Marius Ernsting, who replaced Gijs Schreuders).

In view of the debilitating internal power struggle, CPN political activities in 1983 have been marginal and have succeeded only when widespread support was found on particular issues, such as the 29 October peace demonstration in The Hague. Although the Central Committee has expressed support for the policy of renewal, both at a Central Committee meeting in June and by the acceptance of a definitive draft party program drawn up by a special commission appointed by the Central Committee and headed by Marcus Bakker, the attempt of the Executive Committee to mediate between the reformers and the HOC has weakened and demoralized many within the reform wing of the party. Whether the impetus for party renewal witnessed at the Twenty-eighth Congress will be retained during the extraordinary congress remains to be seen. It is highly unlikely, however, that the party will return to its Stalinist character of the past as demanded by many within the HOC, although a split within the party is likely if the draft party program is accepted as now written. Should a split occur, the CPN would most likely be reduced to the orthodox communists in the HOC. It would thereby become a sectarian party of minimal importance in Dutch politics. The majority, that is, those belonging to the reform movement in the party, would either leave the party altogether or attempt to form a new party with progressives on the Left.

Party Internal Affairs. In accordance with the mandate of the Twenty-eighth Congress, the Central Committee appointed in 1983 an eleven-member program-drafting commission to stimulate discussion on and draw up a draft program. On 1 October, the CPN published the program, with an introduction by Elli Izeboud. The purpose of the new program is "to develop in the Netherlands a socialism that is peaceloving, humanitarian, and freedom-loving." The principal stands and goals of the CPN, according to the draft program, are to strive for "freedom, democratic participation, equality, self-determination, and socialism." The draft is critical of the "Stalinistic pattern," which "prevents effective progressive coalitions." While socialism will nationalize the means of production, the CPN accepts that "socialism and democracy are inseparable." In order to change society, however, broad public support must be sought through a policy of coalition politics with other progressive parties. Parliamentary democracy is accepted as the legitimate form for change. The program will use Marxist ideas as a source of inspiration, but rejects democratic centralism in favor of majority rule in decisionmaking.

In 1983, the orthodox members in the CPN, dissatisfied with the process of renewal, founded a monthly bulletin, *Manifest*. The editors and leaders of this group are Tom Boekman, Piet van Kalken, and Laurens Meerten. In opposition to the CPN party leadership, Laurens Meerten published an article in this bulletin (no. 9, November) containing minimal demands of the HOC for the CPN party program. The CPN must be a party based on Marxist-Leninist recognition of the fundamental nature of the class struggle and the role of the working class, solidarity with the socialist states, the objective of overcoming capitalism by any means, and recognition of the class nature of the struggle for peace and of the organizational principle of democratic centralism.

The polarity within the CPN originated with the influx of youth during the late 1960s and 1970s, largely in the CPN district of Amsterdam, which comprises one-third of CPN membership. In elections for provincial legislatures on 24 March 1982, 13.2 percent of the vote in Amsterdam went to the CPN. There are six CPN members on the Amsterdam city council, two of whom are orthodox communists. This is roughly the division between reform and orthodox communists in Amsterdam. The other major CPN stronghold is the CPN district of Groningen, where the party captured 6.8 percent of the vote in the provincial elections in 1982 and took four seats in the provincial legislature.

The two factions have concentrated their struggle on the editorial policy of *De Waarheid*, as this reflects the course of the CPN. Thus far, the reform wing of the party has been successful in deflecting the HOC's bitter attacks, but not without considerable losses. This polarity was manifested most clearly by the attempt of the editors of *De Waarheid* to implement the resolution accepted at the Twenty-eighth Congress directing the paper to follow an independent editorial policy by making it accessible to non-CPN readers. The CPN reform activists also created a newspaper, *Doorbraak*, to enlist support among non-CPN members for *De Waarheid* and to increase the circulation of the paper. This policy was strongly attacked by the HOC and was complicated by a cool relationship between the editors and party leaders. This, in turn, was aggravated by the financial position of the paper, which had suffered a loss of *f*800,000 in 1981 and was subsequently forced to borrow *f*200,000 in 1982 (*NRC Handelsblad*, 18 January). The editors of the paper believed it was essential to renew the format of the paper, to extend its readership to all leftists, and to include non-CPN journalists if the paper were to continue in existence. The HOC believed this would be disastrous for the CPN, as it then would no longer be "the megaphone of the leadership." As a consequence of this debate, both Bart Schmidt, the editor in chief of the paper, and Elsbeth Etty, adjunct editor in chief, resigned. Schmidt also left the Executive Committee. On the other hand, a leading HOC exponent, Laurens Meerten, resigned his Amsterdam city council seat in early January because of what he termed "personal attacks" on him in an article by Susan Legêne in the paper that suggested that his refusal to sign an open letter from the city council of Amsterdam to the city council of Moscow appealing for clemency for Anatoly Shcharansky was symptomatic of the lack of support among communists for the victims of anti-Semitism in socialist countries (*Het Parool*, 11 January).

A leadership meeting on 15 June decided to support *De Waarheid* and its opening to the Left, but held that the position of the CPN leadership must be recognizable in the paper (ibid., 16 June; *De Waarheid*, 16 June). The Executive Com-

mittee also decided to postpone a decision on whether to include non-CPN members on the board governing the Foundation for the Promotion of the Press for the Working Class of the Netherlands (Bepenak—the publisher of *De Waarheid* and the administrative organ of CPN property, originally founded in the 1950s in order to guarantee the existence of *De Waarheid* should the CPN be declared an illegal party; its relationship to the CPN printing company, Dijkman & Co., is unknown) (*Vrij Nederland*, 27 August). Bepenak appointed Constant Vecht, 35, former head of the General Student Union of Amsterdam and for seven years parliamentary journalist of *De Waarheid*, as editor in chief of the paper in early November.

By attempting to mediate between those supporting the policy of renewal and the orthodox communists, the Executive Committee contributed to the internal debate by giving tacit support to the demands of the orthodox communists. The orthodox communists in Groningen, drawing conclusions from this tacit support, supported the CPN section in Beerta (the only municipality in the Netherlands with a CPN mayor), which had denounced the new party line. Fré Meis, the leader of the CPN district in Groningen, justified this by stating it was time to turn the CPN into a real communist party, *De Waarheid* must again become a party paper, and the party must concentrate on the class struggle. In complete opposition to the party line, which had distanced the CPN from the communist parties in the socialist countries, a CPN delegation from Groningen paid a visit to the Soviet Embassy in The Hague ostensibly to discuss possible financial support for the district. The visit, however, occurred shortly before a much disputed trip to Moscow by a CPN delegation. (*De Groene Amsterdammer*, 31 August.)

Domestic Affairs. The highest priority of the CPN in 1983 was the campaign against the stationing of cruise missiles in the Netherlands. A ten-member CPN commission on peace and security decided to promote this campaign by participating in the peace movement umbrella organization, the National Consultation Organ of Peace Organizations (LOVO), which was planning actions against the possible stationing of cruise missiles in the Netherlands. The CPN delegation to the first meeting of LOVO on 5 February was headed by Truus Divendal, but another

CPN-sponsored organization, Stop the N-Bomb/ Stop the Nuclear Arms Race, led by G. Vonderführ, was also present (*NRC Handelsblad*, 7 February). The LOVO, led primarily by the Interchurch Federation under M. J. Faber, held a massive peace demonstration on 29 October in The Hague involving 600,000 people. The Amsterdam district of the CPN issued a publication entitled *Het Wapen van Woensdrecht* in support of the demonstration (*CPN–Leden krant*, no. 6, September). The name of the publication refers to a possible base in the Netherlands for the cruise missiles should the Christian Democratic Appeal/People's Party for Freedom and Democracy (liberal-conservative) coalition government decide in favor of the NATO decision. The CPN also organized a discussion dealing with the question of illegal activities should the government begin stationing the missiles. In connection with an action against the use of the Lauwers Lake area in Friesland for military maneuvers, a three-member CPN front organization, the People's Congress Committee, cooperated with the National Union for the Protection of the Wadden Sea (*Trouw*, 29 January).

On the domestic economic front, the CPN continued its efforts to influence the position of trade unions and other progressive parties, social groups, and movements by participating in a congress, Stop the Policy of Division, For a Progressive Alternative, on 22 January sponsored by the Dialogue of Driebergen. The purpose of the congress was to see what "the progressive camp is able to do in opposition against the present policies of the cabinet" (*De Tijd*, 28 January). The congress concluded that the progressive parties must join with extraparliamentary groups in combating the conservative policies of the government, but that such an alternative offers little real chance of success under present circumstances. The CPN vigorously supported the trade union stop-and-go strike action in the fall, but again with little success. In terms of policy, the CPN urged the adoption of a shorter workweek, but differences within the party on corresponding pay reductions prevented a clear policy on this issue. The party leadership, in response to the position of orthodox CPN members in industry, reassured them, in contrast to demands from the reformists to subordinate CPN interests to those of the trade unions and to stress further democratization within industrial concerns, that the CPN

leadership would strengthen the position of traditional communist working groups.

The third strategic policy emphasized by the CPN on the domestic front in 1983 was to exert greater efforts to realize the new coalition policy with political parties to the left of the Labor Party (PvdA). The new coalition policy has taken two forms: first, the Consultation of Progressive Parties, a broad coalition of all the Left, and second, a more narrow coalition limited to the PSP and PPR. The PvdA distrusts the CPN in terms of party organization and strategy and refused to participate in any form of coalition with the CPN. The only successful result of the new coalition policy began on 3 May and lasted until late November when agreement was reached on a common election list with PPR, PSP, EVP, and the Green Platform (Green Progressive Accord) for the elections to the European Parliament in the spring of 1984. A CPN party conference on 26 November approved the agreement by a vote of 123 to 11.

Foreign Affairs and International Party Contacts. CPN foreign activities in 1983 were sharply curtailed due to the internal party conflict. Although Ton van Hoek of the Executive Committee traveled to East Berlin in May to attend the Marx conference, it was not until Ina Brouwer, the chairman of the CPN Second Chamber delegation, and Jaap Wolff, a member of the Executive Committee, made a controversial trip to Moscow on 25–30 August that contact was made with the international communist movement. The visit resulted in the resignation from the Second Chamber of Gijs Schreuders (replaced by Marius Ernsting, the treasurer of the CPN). According to Schreuders, the trip was made without adequate preparation and discussion within the party leadership. Schreuders, a member of the reform wing, believed the trip was intended to strengthen the position of the orthodox communists within the party because the level of reception in Moscow could only signal Soviet support for the HOC. Brouwer and Wolff met with, among others, Mikhail V. Ziminan, a secretary of the Central Committee of the Communist Party of the Soviet Union, and with Vadim Zagladin, deputy head of the International Department of the Central Committee. According to Brouwer, the trip took place in the context of a White Paper drawn up by the CPN Central

Committee commission on peace and security that accorded with a resolution accepted at the Twenty-eighth Congress. Brouwer also defended the trip on the basis of adequate discussion within the party leadership and with Schreuders. The content of the discussion dealt primarily with the Geneva arms talks, the peace movement and its relationship to a breakthrough in questions of military balance, and the existence of autonomous peace movements beside "official" organizations. (*CPN–Leden krant*, no. 7, September.)

In the context of the peace and security White Paper, other trips abroad included one to Romania in September by John Geelen, a member of the Executive Committee, and to East Germany in September by Rinus Haks, CPN member of the provincial legislature of North Holland; Hanneke Jagersma, the mayor of Beerta; and Tineke van den Klinkenberg, an Amsterdam alderman. CPN delegations also traveled to Bulgaria, Yugoslavia, and Hungary. The CPN, in view of its break with the communist parties of Poland and Czechoslovakia, made no contact with these parties. Some informal contacts between adherents of the HOC were made with the East German party, which hopes to influence CPN politics in favor of the HOC (*Vrij Nederland*, 27 August).

Robert I. Weitzel
Amsterdam

Norway

Population. 4.1 million (*World Factbook*, 1983)
Parties. Norwegian Communist Party (Norges Kommunistiske Parti; NKP); Socialist Left Party (Sosialistisk Venstreparti; SV); Workers' Communist Party (Arbeidernes Kommunistiske Parti; AKP), runs as Red Electoral Alliance (Rod Valgallians; RV) in elections
Founded. NKP: 1923; SV: 1976; AKP: 1973
Membership. NKP: 500 (estimate); SV: 2,000 (estimate); AKP: 1,000 (estimate)
Chairman. NKP: Hans I. Kleven; SV: Theo Koritzinsky; AKP: Paal Steigan
National Board (NKP). 16 full members: Hans I. Kleven, Arne Jorgensen (vice-chairman, editor of *Friheten*), Trygve Horgen (deputy vice-chairman), Odd S. Karlsen (organizing secretary), Martin Gunnar Knutsen (past chairman), Asmund Langsether, Rolf Dahl, Gunnar Wahl, Rolf Galgerud, Bjarne Baltzersen, Grete Johansen, Kare Andre Nilsen, Berit Federiksen, Bjorn Kjenong, Arvid Borglund, Asbjorn Furali; 9 alternate members
Status. Legal
Last Congress. NKP: Seventeenth, 4–6 December 1981, in Oslo; SV: 11–13 March 1983, in Oslo; AKP: Third, RV, April 1983, in Oslo
Last Election. 1981, NKP: 0.3 percent, no representatives; SV: 4.9 percent, 4 of 155 representatives; AKP: 0.7 percent, no representatives
Auxiliary Organizations. NKP: Norwegian Communist Youth League (NKU)
Publications. NKP: *Friheten* (Freedom), semiweekly; AKP: *Klassekampen* (Class struggle), daily

Until 1979, the Norwegian Labor Party (Det Norske Arbeiderparti; DNA)—a moderate social-democratic reform movement—dominated postwar Norwegian politics. During this era, the DNA was the main governing party and the strongest political party in Norway and all but monopolized the Left in Norwegian politics. Three obscure, almost forgotten, political dwarfs have operated as Marxist parties to the left of the DNA: the pro-Soviet NKP and SV and the Maoist AKP, which has campaigned in the last three parliamentary elections as the RV.

The DNA was strong enough to ignore both this Marxist fringe and conservative groups for most of this period. In the 1970s, the DNA was able to utilize the rich Norwegian oil revenues to build a social welfare state that was the envy of nearly every other West European country. But in 1981, the DNA was abruptly shoved into the opposition by a conservative coalition led by Kaare Willoch. In this new, unfamiliar role, the DNA can no longer afford the luxury of ignoring either of its political flanks. On balance, Willoch's conservative coalition has tended to push the DNA further to the left, forcing it to look for new issues and allies to boost its sagging political standing.

In the security area, for example, the DNA in power pursued resolutely pro-U.S. policies; the DNA out of power has discovered new popularity from identifying with the peace movement in Western Europe, which is at least partially anti-U.S. In a 21 November debate in the Norwegian parliament on the new NATO nuclear missiles in Western Europe, the DNA backed a proposal that Norway should *not* support their deployment. The Norwegian parliament rejected the proposal by a single vote (78 to 77)—hardly an overwhelming mandate for a continuation of the postwar security policies of the DNA itself.

In addition, the DNA is beginning to find political support by criticizing the economic policies of the Willoch government. While oil revenues are certain to keep the Norwegian economy in the black for years to come, there are still severe economic problems. In 1982 and 1983, Norwegians faced record unemployment (though the current level of 3.3 percent is the envy of other West Europeans).

If the results from local elections in September are any indication, Norwegian voters do not agree that Prime Minister Willoch's austerity policy is the proper medicine for a sluggish economy. Results from Norway's local elections showed a swing to the left and an apparent rejection of the belt-tightening economics of Willoch's Conservative Party, which was the biggest loser at the polls (receiving only 26.1 percent of the vote, a drop of 5.5 points from its 1981 total). At the same time, the DNA increased its share of the vote (by 2 percentage points over 1979).

The DNA appears to be riding a wave of public opinion that is moving to the left; at least two of the Marxist parties have direct or indirect ties to the DNA now. In the September local elections, for example, the SV was a parliamentary ally of the DNA and captured 5.2 percent of the vote. In addition, new SV chairman Theo Koritzinsky began discussing the possibility of cooperating with the NKP. These latest moves may well be an aberration that will soon be corrected. Nevertheless, questions about the nature of the far left in Norwegian politics are now being raised.

The Norwegian Communist Party. The NKP began as a small splinter group of radical trade unionists and politicians who left the DNA in 1923. The NKP experienced many lean years until after World War II, when NKP support for the war effort against Nazi Germany and the Soviet liberation of northern Norway boosted NKP popularity at the polls (eleven seats in the first postwar parliament). But NKP fortunes began to plummet with the onset of the cold war.

The electoral weakness of the NKP is due, in large part, to its decision to remain a staunchly pro-Soviet, Stalinist party in 1975. Its numbers and popularity dwindled when Reidar Larsen, its then chairman, and several other leaders left the NKP and formed the SV.

While differences still exist between the NKP and the SV, NKP chairman Hans I. Kleven responded favorably to SV chairman Theo Koritzinsky's call for a broad united front of left-wing parties in Norway. Kleven mentioned that it was especially important to establish unity of action in the labor movement, both in the unions themselves as well as in the political parties of the labor movement—the DNA, SV, and NKP.

In addition, Kleven supported Koritzinsky's proposal for electoral cooperation between the NKP and the SV. Kleven suggested running SV and NKP candidates on joint election lists. Kleven also backed Koritzinsky's proposal for the NKP and SV to cooperate on specific issues in order to reshape Norwegian society in a socialist direction, rather than merely trying to improve the electoral fortunes of an individual leftist party at the expense of another leftist party.

The NKP continues to be one of the weakest communist parties in all of Western Europe. The NKP received a dismal 7,025 votes (0.3 percent) in the last parliamentary elections in September 1981, far short of the number needed to win a seat. And in the September local elections, the NKP captured only 0.4 percent of the vote.

The Nuclear Issue. In 1983, the NKP continued to pursue the peace offensive it had formally adopted at the 1981 congress. The essence of this policy was the abortive struggle against the deployment of new nuclear weapons in Europe and for a nuclear-free northern Europe. The party also continued to advocate a nuclear-free zone encompassing Norway, Sweden, Denmark, and Finland, formalized by a treaty guaranteed by the great powers. (*WMR*, April.)

In this regard, the NKP supported the No to Nuclear Arms movement, which claims to comprise diverse social forces but be neutral in party politics. The platform of the movement espouses a reduction of nuclear armaments in East and West, a ban on deployment of nuclear weapons in Norway in both peace and wartime, and the creation of a nuclear-free zone in northern Europe. The NKP advocated joining with other social and political forces to advance the cause of this movement.

The NKP does not view the struggle against nuclear weapons as solely a communist struggle; rather, it sees the peace offensive as being of vital importance to the whole labor movement. It urges Norwegian trade unions to become more involved in foreign policy issues. (Ibid.)

The NKP was active in preparations for the twenty-day Peace March 1983, which began on 10 July from Eidsvoll in the south and finished in the northern city of Trondheim. The slogans were predictably "No to nuclear weapons in Norway" and "No to the deployment of new missiles in Europe." NKP-affiliated sponsors of the march included the Women's Committee for Peace (which also organized antiwar marches in Europe in 1981 and 1982) and the Norwegian Peace Committee. (Ibid.)

Domestic Activities. While the NKP is unlikely to forgive the December 1979 parliamentary vote in support of the NATO decision to deploy new U.S. nuclear missiles in Europe, the positions on this issue of the DNA and the NKP seem to be moving closer. In fact, the NKP fully supported the October 1982 vote by the social democrats against appropriations needed to prepare for the siting of the new missiles. (Ibid.)

As part of the NKP policy of bringing diverse social and political forces into the peace movement, the NKP also had kind words for some of the January 1983 findings of the DNA commission that was studying that party's armaments policy. The DNA commission opposed the deployment of U.S. Pershing II and cruise missiles in Western Europe. The NKP also praised the DNA commission for its support of a nuclear freeze and the establishment of nuclear-free zones in northern Europe. (Ibid.)

Nevertheless, the pro-Soviet NKP is critical of the DNA call for reductions in Soviet medium-range missiles. The NKP maintains that the DNA position that the two superpowers are equally dangerous, while a welcome change from its pro-U.S. position of 1979, is an inaccurate reading of the international situation. The NKP wants the DNA to say that the United States is endangering peace while the Soviet Union is defending it. (Ibid.)

In addition, in 1983 the NKP continued to support the Warsaw Pact's proposal for a treaty with the NATO countries renouncing military force. The NKP also backed the ongoing appeal by the socialist countries to the United States and other nuclear powers to follow the Soviet example and commit themselves to no–first use of nuclear weapons. (Ibid.)

The NKP continued to push an October 1982 directive from the Central Board of communists in the trade unions to link the struggle for better working and living conditions with demands for cuts in military spending. The NKP advocated switching funds earmarked for military purposes to civilian needs. The party line was that the arms race does not help create jobs; rather it leads to greater unemployment. (Ibid.)

In early March, the NKP National Executive Committee held a special meeting. At a press conference following the meeting, NKP chairman Hans I. Kleven bemoaned the lack of members and influence of the NKP. In a formal NKP statement following the meeting, Kleven advocated taking "direct action" to assure jobs. In the security area, Kleven warned that the Willoch government's defense policy was adversely affecting relations between Norway and the Soviet Union. (*Aftenposten*, 9 March; *JPRS*, 20 April.)

International Views. The NKP continued to be critical of the December 1979 vote by the DNA government for the NATO decision to deploy U.S. nuclear missiles in Europe. According to the NKP, the Conservative Party, which took power in 1981, continued and even accentuated the pro-U.S. trend in foreign affairs. In essence, the NKP feels that the Conservative Party has made Norway an even greater puppet of the United States. (*WMR*, April.)

The NKP claims that Norway plays a very important role in U.S. nuclear strategy because of its geographic location and its shared border with the Soviet Union. NKP chairman Kleven criticized the Norwegian government for allowing airfields, radio direction-finding stations, and submarine bases on Norwegian territory, as well as the arrival in central Norway of the first shipments of heavy U.S. military hardware to be used by U.S. marines in the event of a major conflict. Kleven charged that decisions on using Norwegian territory for military purposes are made in Washington and the Brussels headquarters of NATO, and not in Oslo. (Ibid.)

Predictably, the NKP opposed the 1983 Norwegian military budget, which was up 4 percent over the 1982 figure. The NKP alleged that the increase indicated that Norway was contributing to tension in northern Europe and not to détente. The NKP continued to support resistance "to the escalation of war preparations" in Norway and involvement in "U.S. militarist plans." The NKP publicly favored an "independent security and defense policy." (Ibid.)

International Contacts. NKP chairman Hans I. Kleven attended the Karl Marx anniversary celebrations in East Berlin in April and delivered a speech (*Neues Deutschland*, East Berlin, 12 April). A delegation headed by First Vice-Chairman Arne Jorgensen made an official visit to Poland 24–28 January. The delegation was received by Polish leader Wojciech Jaruzelski and met with a number of senior party officials. (*PAP*, 28 January; *FBIS*, 28 January.)

The Socialist Left Party. The SV is easily the strongest Marxist party to the left of the DNA. In 1981, it received 4.9 percent of the vote

—up 0.8 percent from 1977—and four seats—up two from 1977. As stated earlier, the SV campaigned as a parliamentary ally of the DNA in the September local elections. It received 5.2 percent of the vote, a slight increase over 1981.

Leadership and Organization. In January, party leader Berge Furre was replaced by Theo Koritzinsky, who had been chairman of the Socialist Youth League. The SV congress in March produced almost a completely new leadership. Theo Koritzinsky was confirmed as chairman of the party. Tora Houg and Einar Nyheim were unanimously selected to be the new deputy chairmen. Erik Solheim will continue as party secretary.

In addition, a new Executive Committee was formed. The committee now consists of three veterans—Finn Gustavsen, Hanna Kvanmo, and Berge Furre—as well as Hilde Bojer, Bitte Vadtvedt, Svein Bolton, Bjorg Ofstad, Arna Eggesvik, and Frank Kristoffersen.

Views and Activities. In January, newly elected SV chairman Theo Koritzinsky came out in favor of broad case-by-case cooperation by the Left, especially between the SV and the NKP. Koritzinsky would like to see cooperation among peace, environmental, women's, and labor union groups. Koritzsinky stresses, however, that any such cooperation must be under the control of local party groups and must not be aimed at party unifications. (*Friheten*, 26 January; *JPRS*, 3 March.)

Unlike the more radical NKP, however, the SV favors reforms rather than total rejection of current institutions. Nonetheless, Koritzinsky stresses that these reforms must be structural in nature, with a transfer of power to popularly elected delegates and organized labor. This means increased municipal and county authority and stronger company democracy. Koritzinsky says that the SV is considering the concept of wage-earner funds, which could give the unions and elected delegates more control over capital. (*Friheten*, 28 January; *JPRS*, 3 March.)

Earlier in January, then party leader Berge Furre presented the SV Executive Committee's draft for a working program for the 1980s. The program calls for stronger state power, increased state subsidies, and a further expansion of the public sector. It demands higher taxes and wages, and more housing, as well as nationalization, "self-sufficiency," and increased "power for the workers." In short, the "new" working program appears to be little more than a repackaging of old ideas. (*Aftenposten*, 29 January; *JPRS*, 23 February.)

In spite of the similarities between the old SV working program and the new one, Koritzinsky is determined to make the SV a livelier party. In July, he indicated that the SV had become too far removed from the people. Koritzinsky stated that SV party work can no longer be "sheets of paper and words." The SV must "appeal to the emotions" of the people. With this in mind, he spent the summer on an unofficial election campaign (for the municipal and county board elections), animating it with carnivals, action theater, and music. (*Aftenposten*, 29 July; *JPRS*, 31 August.)

The SV congress in March passed a resolution urging SV members throughout Norway to take part in local peace marches against several airports in Norway that the SV claims are a part of U.S. nuclear strategy, "so that the civilian population in the districts concerned understand the dangers they are exposed to" (*Aftenposten*, 14 March; *JPRS*, 20 April). The congress focused on two other tasks: the struggle against growing unemployment in Norway and the struggle for the equality of women (Tanjug, 11 and 13 March; *FBIS*, 14 March).

In addition, considerable criticism was leveled against the editorial staff of the party newspaper, *Ny Tid*, during the congress. When Steinar Hanssan of the editorial staff was given only three minutes to defend himself against this criticism, he marched out in protest. When he returned the next day, he was greeted with flowers and applause. No new editor was chosen to replace him. (*Aftenposten*, 14 March; *JPRS*, 20 April.)

The proposal by Executive Committee member Hanna Kvanmo to reduce the value-added tax to 16 percent received almost unanimous approval at the congress. The SV believes that a reduction in the tax would cost the Norwegian government 3.7 billion kroner, and this figure does not include the reduction in payments to the unemployment fund. Together with other measures, the SV thinks that a reduction in this tax would assure 20,000 jobs. (*Aftenposten*, 19 January; *JPRS*, 3 March.)

Several delegates brought up the SV's relationship with the Trade Union Federation. The consensus was that SV members should organize in the Trade Union Federation and not in other unions. According to a survey conducted at the congress, 53.7 percent of SV members were part of the Trade Union Federation. Also, 45.8 percent of the SV delegates were women, and the average age of the delegates was about 37. (*Aftenposten*, 19 January; *JPRS*, 3 March.)

On the international front, the SV, in a strongly worded statement, condemned the Soviet war in Afghanistan. But there was disagreement in the congress over what relationship the SV ought to have with the Afghanistan committee. Many SV members felt that the committee is too strongly dominated by Marxist-Leninists. There also are differences in the SV regarding some of the liberation movements in Afghanistan. The national congress agreed to support the work of the Afghanistan committee, but only by the slim margin of 115 to 92 votes. (*Aftenposten*, 14 March; *JPRS*, 20 April.)

The Workers' Communist Party. The AKP began in the late 1960s as an amalgam of various Maoist organizations disenchanted with the Soviet economic model and Soviet foreign policy and behavior. The AKP was founded as a formal organization in 1973. In recent years, the AKP's enthusiasm for China has cooled somewhat as changes have occurred in Chinese politics and foreign policy.

The AKP's electoral front, the RV, has not fared well. In the 1981 parliamentary elections, the RV captured 17,593 votes (0.7 percent), far short of the amount necessary for a seat in parliament, although slightly better than the vote share of the NKP.

The Red Electoral Alliance. The RV is no longer simply an offshoot of the AKP. It is now a coalition of the AKP and independent socialists. The RV now has 25 elected representatives on municipal and county councils. The third annual RV congress was held in Oslo in April.

The debate at the congress over the shape of socialism after the revolution is nothing new in RV circles. A definitive resolution of the debate was postponed until the AKP's next congress, scheduled for 1984 (*Aftenposten*, 18 April).

The independent socialists in the RV and some AKP members pushed through a resolution guaranteeing "real, not just formal" democratic rights for working people after the revolution. The electoral manifesto of the RV, written by Kjersti

Ericsson, now states that a postrevolutionary socialist government must allow "freedom of speech and organization, independent trade unions, the right to strike, legal protection and control by the workers over state and production organs." (Ibid.)

On the question of security policy, a debate developed in the congress over Norway's membership in NATO. Some members strongly supported a motion calling for Norwegian withdrawal from NATO, arguing that Norway had become too obsequious to the alliance. Others argued that Norwegian membership in NATO was necessary to deter Soviet aggression and expansionism. However, while Norway should continue its political participation in NATO, it ought to withdraw from military cooperation in NATO. The motion on withdrawal from NATO was defeated by a vote of 54 to 35. (Ibid.)

As part of its manifesto, the RV agreed on a plank calling for strengthening the conventional defenses of Western Europe as well as building a strong independent defense system outside NATO. The RV argued that "the prospect of being rescued from across the Atlantic is more than doubtful. For this reason, the RV proposes that Norway must get out of NATO's integrated military cooperation." (Ibid., 16 April.)

The RV charges that the Soviet "guarantee" not to use nuclear arms against the Nordic region is worthless. The RV also warns against relying on Soviet advocacy of arms reduction and argued for strong international pressure on the Soviet Union to force the Kremlin to destroy its SS-20 missiles under international supervision. (Ibid.)

The RV manifesto is critical of both superpowers and their quest for world supremacy. But the RV came down harder on the Soviet Union.

According to the RV, the most aggressive superpower is the Soviet Union. Soviet power and aggressiveness are on the rise, and the United States is on the decline. Thus, with no counterforce to Soviet muscle and combativeness, the threats of Soviet occupation and world war are becoming more likely. (Ibid.)

The RV manifesto maintains that the working class must fight each step of the way, that real socialism can be introduced only through a socialist revolution in which the working class assumes state power. The RV is, therefore, ultimately a revolutionary rather than a reform-minded party. Thus, while it participates in elections, it maintains that Norway "will never get socialism through the ballot box." The RV does value election campaigns, however, because they provide a platform in municipal and county councils for the RV to reveal who is served by capitalism and who is exploited by it. (Ibid., 13 April.)

Finally, in 1983 scholars of Norwegian Marxism were treated to a rare glimpse of life in the AKP. In *High School Teacher Pedersen's Account of the Big Political Revival in Our Country*, AKP member Dag Solstad describes the total immersion of AKP loyalists in a world of radical political and social ideas.

Constant squabbling has been the rule for the AKP during the early 1980s, according to Solstad. The AKP seems to be seeking in vain for some sense of purpose and direction. This may mean an inevitable period of AKP decline and ultimately a collapse in the near future.

Leif Rosenberger
Washington, D.C.

Portugal

Population. 10.05 million
Party. Portuguese Communist Party (Partido Comunista Português; PCP)
Founded. 1921
Membership. 187,000 claimed
Secretary General. Alvaro Cunhal, since 1961
Secretariat. 8 full members: Alvaro Cunhal, Carlos Costa, Domingos Abrantes, Blanqui Teixeira, Joaquim Gomes, Jorge Araujo, Octavio Pato, Sergio Vilarigues; 2 alternate members: Jaime Felix, Luisa Araujo
Central Committee. 165 members
Status. Legal
Last Congress. Tenth, 8–11 December 1983, in Oporto
Last Election. April 1983, United People's Alliance (communist coalition), 18 percent, 44 of 250 seats
Auxiliary Organizations. General Confederation of Portuguese Workers (Confederação Geral de Trabalhadores Portugueses—Intersindical Nacional), Portugal's largest labor grouping, including some 1.7 million of the 2 million unionized workers (*WMR*, January); National Confederation of Farmers (Confederação Nacional de Agricultores), comprising 400 peasant organizations (ibid.); Popular Democratic Movement (Movimento Democrático Popular; MDP), a communist-front "satellite"; the Greens (Os Verdes), a communist-front pacifism-ecology-oriented party founded in 1982 (*A Tarde*, 8 February; *NYT*, 25 April); People's Forces—25th of April, allegedly an underground terrorist tool of the communists (*NYT*, 22 November)
Publications. *Avante!*, weekly newspaper; *O Militante*, theoretical journal; and *O Diário*, semiofficial daily newspaper (all published in Lisbon)

Directing the communist movement in Portugal is Western Europe's most Stalinist, most pro-Soviet party. Less influential now than during the first two years after the 1974 ousting of the dictatorship, it still controls most of the labor unions and commands significant electoral support, although it has been excluded from the government since a frustrated 1976 coup attempt. Numerous radical-left groups, chiefly Maoist and Trotskyist splinterings who in the 1960s rejected the more moderate policies of the "revisionist" pro-Moscow communists, flourished after 1974 but have languished in recent years.

Leadership and Party Organization. At its Tenth Congress, held 8–11 December in Oporto,

the PCP renamed Alvaro Cunhal secretary general, reaffirmed its pro-Soviet commitment, and pledged "social resistance" to the policies of the government coalition. The party enlarged its Central Committee from 72 to 165 members and its policymaking Secretariat from 7 to 10 members. For the first time, it elected a woman, Luisa Araujo, to the Secretariat. (*NYT*, 19 December.)

There were reports early in the year of a conflict concerning the eventual successor to Cunhal. One faction was said to be loyal to the orthodox and uncompromising Carlos Costa, number two in the PCP hierarchy, while a "liberal" wing favored the more open Carlos Brita, number three, as a more likely renovator of the party. The struggle came to light when some "liberal" members complained privately that they had been removed from the electoral lists for parliament; official spokesmen dismissed as "perfectly ridiculous" the suggestion that the exclusions had political motives. (*Expresso*, 12 March; *JPRS*, 20 April.)

Domestic Party Affairs. PCP strength was boosted in the April general elections from 16.7 (in 1980) to 18 percent of the vote, thereby confirming, according to the PCP, the party's "great influence" in national life (*Avante!*, 29 April; *FBIS*, 11 May; *NYT*, 19 December). Anticipating a decisive defeat for the ruling center-right Democratic Alliance (Aliança Democrática; AD), the PCP eagerly supported President Antonio Ramalho Eanes's decision in February to dissolve parliament and to call for a general election. The PCP and the Socialist Party (PS) insisted that a new cabinet proposed by the AD coalition could not survive. (*NYT*, 24 January, 5 February.) AD Prime Minister Francisco Pinto Balsemão had resigned in December 1982 (see *YICA*, 1983, p. 469).

The president did not heed communist demands for the appointment of a caretaker government representing all political parties in order to end "the abuse of power" by a "reactionary" lame-duck government and "to guarantee democratic elections" (*Diário de Notícias*, 30 January; *FBIS*, 10 February). Communists were nonetheless elated that "demagogy, manipulation, and discrimination" by the AD did not prevent the "democratic forces" from scoring a major victory (*Avante!*, 29 April; *FBIS*, 11 May, 23 August). Noting that the total number of seats won by the PS (101) and by the communist bloc (44) represented 55 percent of the electorate, Cunhal called for the formation of a coalition government by the two parties. As expected, PS leader Mário Soares rejected the overture, saying he could not understand how the communists could "call us agents of the CIA in Portugal one day and dear friends the next." (*FBIS*, 23, 28, and 29 April.)

Since the PS lacked an absolute majority, Soares was forced to form a cabinet alliance with the Social Democratic Party (Partido Demócrata Social; PDS), thereby securing a two-thirds majority with 176 seats (*WP*, 5 June). Cunhal was outraged at this "complete disregard" for the will of the electorate, which had rejected the AD parties and, therefore, the coalition's principal

constituent, the PDS, by awarding them only 40 percent of the vote. The new government, he said, was bound to perpetuate AD policies and further exacerbate the nation's economic, social, and political crises. (*Avante!*, 12 May; *IB*, July.) He failed to note that even though the PDS lost seats and the PCP gained three, the latter's total was still significantly exceeded by the PDS's 75 (*O Jornal*, 29 April; *FBIS*, 10 May; *JPRS*, 25 May).

When Soares took office in June as prime minister, the PCP launched a two-pronged attack —through the unions and in parliament—on his coalition government's blueprints for economic recovery. The communist-led unions called brief transportation strikes to protest government plans to streamline bloated and inefficient nationalized sectors and to seek a "social pact" among workers, employers, and government to contain wage and price rises. PCP deputies denounced a quickly approved four-year austerity program as a policy of "cudgels for the workers and prizes, convenience, and protection for big business." Seven bills—to abolish wage ceilings, legalize abortion, and similar proposals—represented the communist prescription for recovery. Some observers suggested that an apparent aim was also to provoke disagreement over the measures between the PS and PDS parliamentary groups, thereby undermining government harmony. (*Diário de Notícias*, 2 and 7 June; *WP*, 10 June; *NYT*, 26 June; *JPRS*, 11 and 12 July.)

Soares denounced the "destabilizing" tactics of the communists and suggested they should study Poland and Cuba "where there are no great economists but where there are long lines and difficulties" (*NYT*, 26 June). The PCP countered that it was the government that was destabilizing the national economy "through its restrictive policy of stagnation aimed not at emerging from the crisis but at restoring big capital's power" (*Avante!*, 11 August; *FBIS*, 18 August).

The PCP charged that the government was also seeking to destabilize the armed forces by proposing the dismissal of Army Chief of Staff Gen. Garcia dos Santos, the only remaining high-level officer connected with the military operations of the 25 April uprising of 1974. In this way, the military power of the president would be further eroded, permitting the armed forces to be placed more readily at the service of the government's "anti-people" policy. (*Avante!*, 28 July;

FBIS, 9 August.) Soares expressed his own concern that the communists, lacking the support for a power bid through the ballot or through street demonstrations, had infiltrated and were seeking to manipulate the army with organized cells (*NYT*, 22 November).

Auxiliary and Front Organizations.

During the parliamentary election campaign, the MDP joined the PCP in a coalition called the United Popular Alliance. The MDP won 3 of the coalition's 44 seats (Lisbon domestic service, 9 May; *FBIS*, 10 May). Also participating in the campaign were various minor Maoist, Trotskyist, and Marxist-Leninist parties — radical-left groups that regard the PCP as a "parliamentary bourgeois party"—but they gained no seats in the legislature (EFE, Madrid, 4 April; *FBIS*, 5 April; *JPRS*, 7 April; *Diário de Notícias*, 15 May). The Popular Democratic Union (União Democrática Popular) lost its single parliamentary seat (Lisbon domestic service, 26 April; *FBIS*, 26 April).

Prime Minister Soares charged the communists with trying to disrupt the country and sow fear through an underground terrorist organization called People's Forces—25th of April. Its targets, he said, were businessmen and directors of state-owned and private enterprise. (*NYT*, 22 November.)

International Views, Positions, and Activities.

The PCP denounced a Soares visit to the United States in February as an "obvious electioneering" ploy—"to seek support to offset the lack of real popular support in the country." It was also cited as further evidence of the PS leader's subservience to U.S. imperialism. (*Avante!*, 3 March; *FBIS*, 17 March.)

PCP delegations visited Italy, Yugoslavia, Hungary, Bulgaria, the Soviet Union, and Ethiopia during 1983. In Ethiopia, the visitors expressed support for the Ethiopian revolution and its "significant contribution" to the change in the world balance of power (*Avante!*, 24 February; *FBIS*, 3 March). Portuguese communists refused to attend an International Parliamentary Union conference in Seoul, claiming that holding an international meeting in South Korea would sanction and solidify the artificial division of that country (Lisbon domestic radio, 25 August; *FBIS*, 29 August). Traveling to Portugal were communist officials from the Soviet Union, Czechoslovakia, and Spain. Cunhal met in Lisbon with Spanish communist leader Gerardo Iglesias with the aim of improving the strained relations between the two parties (*Mundo Obrero*, 15–21 July; *FBIS*, 26 July).

H. Leslie Robinson
Elbert Covell College
University of the Pacific

San Marino

Population. 22,000
Party. Communist Party of San Marino (Partido Comunista de San Marino; CPS)
Founded. 1941
Membership. 300 (estimate)
Secretary General. Ermenegildo Gasperoni

Status. Legal
Last Congress. 1980, Tenth
Last Election. 1983, 24.3 percent, 15 of 60 seats

The CPS was founded in 1921 as a section of the Italian Communist Party (PCI) and in 1941 became an independent party. Although the CPS has an independent status vis-à-vis the PCI and maintains direct relations with other communist parties, its political positions over the years have been affected by the presence and the policies of its Italian counterpart.

Following World War II, the CPS entered a coalition government with the Socialist Party of San Marino that lasted until 1957. Excluded from office in that year, the CPS remained in the opposition until the spring of 1978.

In the elections of 28 May 1978, the CPS received 25 percent of the vote and sixteen seats. Following that election, a new leftist coalition of communists, socialists, and left-wing social democrats was formed. It ruled San Marino for five years.

On 29 May 1983, the voters of the tiny city-state elected the 60 members of the Great and General Council. The returns did not change the balance of forces appreciably. The Christian Democrats, who had made a determined effort to unseat the ruling coalition, remained the largest party with 42 percent of the vote and 26 seats. But this was not enough to replace the Left in power. The CPS lost a fraction of a percentage point and obtained 15 seats (one less than it had before). However, the loss was compensated by the gains of the CPS coalition partners. The Socialist Party obtained 9 seats and the Socialist Unity Party 8 seats, giving the Left a total of 32 seats. A new coalition was formed after the election, and unless a shift in alliances occurs, the CPS should remain in power until the election of 1988.

The CPS maintains friendly relations with a number of communist parties and is on good terms with both the Soviet and the Chinese parties. In January, CPS chairman Ermenegildo Gasperoni and party secretary Umberto Barulli traveled to Moscow and held talks with Soviet official Boris Ponomarev. According to Tass (4 January) "The exchange of opinions demonstrated the coincidence of views on the present-day international situation." In February, a CPS delegation headed by party secretary Barulli traveled to Beijing for talks with high-ranking party officials of the PRC. In March, the Chinese returned the visit. Hu Qili, a member of the Chinese party's Secretariat was a guest of CPS leaders in San Marino (NCNA, 9 March).

At the beginning of October, Renzo Renzi, a communist, and Germano De Biagi, a socialist, were installed as captains-regent of the small republic. The captains-regent are rotated every six months among officials of the parties in the ruling coalition.

Giacomo Sani
Ohio State University

Spain

Population. 38.2 million
Party. Spanish Communist Party (Partido Comunista de España; PCE)
Founded. 1920

Membership. 84,000 (*La Vanguardia*, 6 December; *FBIS*, 9 December); down from 200,000 in 1977, though still exceeding the 1976 total of 15,000; pre–civil war membership, 300,000
Secretary General. Gerardo Iglesias
President. Dolores Ibárruri (legendary La Pasionaria of civil war days)
Secretariat. 11 members: Jaime Ballesteros, Andreu Claret, José María Coronas, Enrique Curiel, Gerardo Iglesias, Juan Francisco Pla, Adolfo Pinedo, Francisco Romero Marín, Simón Sánchez Montero, Francisco Palero, Eulalia Vintró
Executive Committee. 24 members
Central Committee. 102 members
Status. Legal
Last Congress. Eleventh, 14–18 December 1983, in Madrid
Last Elections. 1982, 4 of 350 seats
Auxiliary Organization. Workers' Commissions (Comisiones Obreros; CC OO), Marcelino Camacho, chairman; 897,000 members, compared with 806,000 in unions affiliated with the Socialist Party (*El País*, 29 November 1982)
Publications. *Mundo Obrero* (Labor world), weekly; *Nuestra Bandera* (Our flag), bimonthly ideological journal; both published in Madrid

Although it survived the Franco dictatorship as a major potential force, the communist movement in Spain fragmented into numerous dissident groups, and in recent years, its membership and national impact have declined. The weakening of the main communist party led to the replacement of its secretary general in 1982. Marxist Basques, said to have foreign communist backing, and a few other left-wing extremists continue to terrorize the country.

Leadership and Party Organization. During his first year as secretary general, 38-year-old Gerardo Iglesias moved quickly to try to heal the rifts in the PCE and to regain some of the party's lost influence in national affairs. As evidence of progress achieved, he exulted in February about an "already more unified and expanding party" and in May over some improvement in the party's electoral support in municipal elections. He maneuvered to undermine the remaining party leverage of his predecessor and former mentor, Santiago Carrillo, whom he replaced in November 1982 and bested in December in a showdown for party support at the Eleventh Congress. He was re-elected, 69–31, to head the party for the next three years. Limited shifts in the Secretariat, which he made in January, helped to reinforce his position. (*RFE Research*, 26 January; *El País*, 26 January; *JPRS*, 28 February; *Mundo Obrero*, 20–26 May; *FBIS*, 31 May; *NYT*, 19 December.)

Early in his tenure, Iglesias made it clear he was not disposed to be Carrillo's "puppet," although he avoided direct public criticism of the latter (*Tiempo*, 7–14 February; *JPRS*, 22 March;

NYT, 17 December). He did attribute the PCE's downturn to "errors of leadership," alienation of intellectuals, and the party's post-Franco tendency to neglect the "mass movement." He also blamed the transfer of many communists to the larger Socialist Party in order to assure a leftist victory over an invigorated right wing. (*RFE Research*, 26 January; *Bohemia*, Havana, 8 July; *JPRS*, 23 August.)

Two former party officials, Fernando Claudín and Manuel Azcárate, published far more scathing analyses of Carrillo's "autocratic" leadership. Claudín charged the former secretary general with failure to overhaul communist theory and practice along genuine Eurocommunist lines; Azcárate wrote that Carrillo had misjudged the strength of the party, had ignored the reality of an increasingly affluent and growing middle class, and had failed to perceive the potential growth of the Socialist Party. (*WP*, 20 March.) Carrillo refused to accept any responsibility for the party's setback, although he did admit in a new book that "Eurocommunist excesses" had inflicted serious internal damage. He mostly blamed the 1981 coup attempt and the restricted "political space" available to the PCE after Franco's death. He also acknowledged the role of internal squabbles, precipitated because some party members were never really communists or had stopped being communists. The only valid reproach to his leadership, he said, was perhaps that he had not been decisive enough in dealing with divisive tendencies. (*La Vanguardia*, 11 March; *JPRS*, 28 April; *Los Angeles Times*, 17 November.)

The prescription for recovery advanced by the new secretary general called for a Eurocommunist "renewal" of the party structure and more internal democracy without factionalism. Disavowing reports of a Catalonian-Asturian split within the Secretariat, he suggested that "neither iron discipline nor the appearance of factions is productive." His principal thesis touched on the need for broader participation and more open-mindedness in debates so as to make "thinking men" feel at home in the party. (*RFE Research*, 26 January; *El País*, 26 January; *Mundo Obrero*, 1–7 July; *FBIS*, 15 July; *Bohemia*, 8 July; *JPRS*, 28 February, 23 August.) He clearly hoped to recover many militants who had been purged or had abandoned communist ranks (*Tiempo*, 7–14 February; *JPRS*, 22 March). Iglesias also recommended increased attention to mass movements along with "critical support" (i.e., only "moderate" and "constructive" criticism) of the government of Felipe González of the Socialist Party (EFE, Madrid, 27 June; *FBIS*, 28 June; *Economist*, London, 10 December).

In direct confrontation with Iglesias, Carrillo argued for more vigorous criticism of the González government and opposed reconciliation with former rebellious PCE militants. He was apparently bidding for the support of the party's "old guard" as he shifted during the year to a somewhat more hard-line and pro-Moscow position. (*RFE Research*, 7 October; *Economist*, 10 December; *NYT*, 17 December.) Nonetheless, he was re-elected to the Central Committee in December with only 396 votes out of 797; Iglesias received 413 (*NYT*, 19 December). Close to half the membership clearly held no brief for either the old or the new leader, although the popular Dolores Ibárruri helped to shore up Iglesias by siding with him against "any division in our ranks." Meanwhile, veteran official Ignacio Gallego quit the Executive and Central committees and launched a rival pro-Moscow party in January 1984. (*RFE Research*, 29 October; *NYT*, 17 December.)

Domestic Party Affairs. Iglesias hailed the communists' "considerable recovery" in the May municipal elections, which, he said, "clearly" established the PCE as Spain's third political force. Nearly 8 percent of the total ballot went to the party, double the percentage won in the devastating general elections of October 1982, though still less than the 10.8 percent scored in 1979 local elections. Voted in were some 200 communist mayors, two-thirds of the 1979 figure. Control of Barcelona's industrial suburbs, the so-called Red Belt, was lost to the Socialist Party, which swept to a decisive victory in most of Spain's towns and cities; however, the PCE was cheered by a spectacular communist win—by a huge majority—in Córdoba, its only triumph in a major provincial capital. (*CSM*, 10 May; *Mundo Obrero*, 20–26 May; *FBIS*, 31 May.)

The "new atmosphere" in the party accounted for the communist rebound, Iglesias claimed. He also suggested that the communist image as a "different Marxist left" gained credibility by the "intelligent balance" struck between a constant attack on the right-wing Popular Alliance (Alianza Popular; AP) and "responsible" criticism—as distinguished from "hounding and harassing" —of the most negative aspects of the González government. (*FBIS*, 31 May.) The latter's "clearly bourgeois" policies, he said, were "constantly more rightist"—in some cases more so— than those of the previous conservative governments (*Bohemia*, 8 July; *JPRS*, 23 August; *ABC*, 20 and 22 September; *JPRS*, 26 and 27 October). Specific official aims criticized by the party were a reduction in public spending, emphasis on indirect taxes, and limitations on collective bargaining—"a stabilization plan rather than a plan of solidarity against unemployment" (*El País*, 18 February; *JPRS*, 22 March). Iglesias indicated that the communists were pressuring not so much because things were not being done quickly enough but because "genuine atrocities" were being committed as the economy moved backward rather than forward (*Mundo Obrero*, 25 February–3 March; *FBIS*, 10 March).

The PCE further charged that the Socialist Party was tackling the country's problems on the basis of a permanent resolve to intensify the two-party system. They displayed the "refinement," Iglesias complained, of designating as opposition leader the AP's Manuel Fraga Iribarne even as they leveled "excessive and false" accusations against the PCE, thereby implying that "only the right" was entitled to conduct critical opposition. (*El País*, 19 September; *FBIS*, 29 September.) The Socialist Party dismissed PCE scolding as merely an effort to divert the attention of its militants from the problems and disorders of the party's own leadership (*Ya*, 22 February; *JPRS*, 21 March).

Carrillo, increasingly acerbic in his attacks,

contended in a new book, *Memorandum of the Transition*, that it was a "dangerous political joke" to label the González government left wing. He concluded that Spain would be condemned to poverty unless the state carried out an industrial and social revolution. Private enterprise has neither the means, capacity, nor will to make the needed changes he said. He also argued that democracy in Spain could not be regarded as secure so long as it hinged on a balance maintained by King Juan Carlos between parliament and "coercive state apparatuses." (*Los Angeles Times*, 17 November.)

Auxiliary Organizations. Clashes between the government and the CC OO loomed as authorities sought to restrain wage increases below the projected inflation rate for 1984 and to overhaul job-inflated state-run industries. A national strike was averted in September when the government agreed to reinstate dismissed workers in a Valencia iron and steel plant. Carrillo commented that the dismissal was a surprising action for a socialist government, which was "acting in a capitalistic way." Labor conflict also seemed likely over pending legislation to make it easier for private companies to hire and fire, thereby allowing them to respond more readily to market conditions. (*NYT*, 25 September, 16 October.)

The most serious challenge to the government was an upsurge of bombings, assassinations, and kidnappings by the terrorist Basque group, Basque Homeland and Liberty (ETA). The interior minister said that ETA had killed 20 people during the Franco dictatorship and 500 since then (*CSM*, 26 October). Additional agitation was created by the ETA's political arm, Herri Batasuna (People's Unity Party), which organized a rash of flag burnings and demonstrations against the flying of the Spanish flag (*NYT*, 22 August). Basque intrigue in Central America also came to light as Costa Rican authorities arrested an ETA member and uncovered a plot to kill Nicaraguan rebel leaders (*ABC*, 26 December 1982; Managua international service, 21 September; *FBIS*, 13 January, 22 September).

Official negotiations to make peace with the Basque terrorists collapsed early in the year, the latter insisting that the González government was just as much its enemy as other governments (*NYT*, 12 February). González then vowed to use "all the legal machinery" of the state to prosecute the "antidemocratic" and "Nazi-like" terrorists.

He tried unsuccessfully to prevent abductions by forbidding payment of ransom. He sought to upgrade police methods and in November announced tough new measures, saying the door to negotiations was now definitely closed. The government called for stiffer penalties, especially for attacks on the armed forces, and declared that, if necessary, authorities would outlaw any political organization—an obvious reference to Herri Batasuna—that supported the guerrillas. (Ibid., 20 January, 22 August, 4 November; *El País*, 7 November.) Efforts were made to improve the morale of policemen by publicly praising their courage (*NYT*, 12 February). González emphatically instructed the army, which leaked reports about plans to create an independent antiterrorist command, that it was not to intervene in any way in what was the responsibility of democratic institutions (*CSM*, 31 October). Dismissed from his command in September was a senior general who expressed support for the 1981 coup plotters and who belittled government antiterrorist measures and "lenient" treatment of Basque flag-burners (*NYT*, 16 September).

In a December meeting with French president François Mitterrand, González also discussed ways of dealing with Basque terrorists who take refuge on the French side of the border. He had said he would pressure France to consider such exiles criminals rather than political refugees. (*CSM*, 31 October; *NYT*, 22 December.) Four Spanish police officers were arrested in southern France in October after a bungled attempt to kidnap an ETA leader (*CSM*, 26 October). A new organization called the Group for Anti-Terrorism and Liberation claimed to have killed a Basque separatist in a Bayonne bar and promised further action against ETA (*NYT*, 22 December).

Basques were increasingly outspoken in their criticism of the violence. Huge throngs demonstrated against ETA in the Basque area and throughout Spain, and Basque deputies in parliament supported the tough new government measures announced in November (ibid., 12 February; *CSM*, 26 October; *El País*, 7 November). While the PCE continued to condemn terrorism, the Basque Communist Party charged that the González government was not showing any willingness to further the cause of Basque autonomy (*Mundo Obrero*, 25–31 March, 22–28 July; *JPRS*, 2 May, 31 August).

Another minor source of guerrilla activities

was the October First Antifascist Resistance Group (Grupo de Resistencia Antifascista Primero de Octubre; GRAPO). In early January, it announced a resumption of its resistance after a two-month-long "truce" since it was clear that the González government was "the same old dog, wearing another tag." This followed the death of the group's leader in a police shoot-out in Barcelona (see *YICA*, 1983, p. 475), leaving an estimated twelve members. In eight years, GRAPO was said to have carried out 424 attacks and killed 55 persons. (*FBIS*, 12 January, 10 August; EFE, 9 August.)

International Views, Positions, and Activities. One of the principal issues exploited by the PCE during the municipal election campaign was the government's failure to call the promised national referendum on the question of Spanish membership in NATO. Citing polls that indicated over 70 percent of the Spanish population did not want to join, Iglesias decried the Socialist Party's "lack of political will" and announced a PCE campaign to demand a referendum. In December, however, a parliamentary committee rejected a communist proposal to call for a vote before the end of the year (*Mundo Obrero*, 28 January–3 February, 1–7 April; *FBIS*, 10 February, 2 December; *JPRS*, 4 May; *NYT*, 15 March.)

Communists insisted that Spain was actually entering the NATO military structure through a "false door" by agreeing in May to continue leasing military bases to the United States (*Mundo Obrero*, 29 April–5 May; *JPRS*, 6 June). Iglesias cited this, along with González's support for missile deployment in Europe, as further evidence that the government was throwing Spain into the arms of President Reagan, "the crazy cowboy" (*Mundo Obrero*, 20–26 May; *FBIS*, 31 May, 5 July). A May rally in Zaragoza, "completely supported" by the PCE, demanded the dismantling of all U.S. military bases in Spain and the rest of Europe (*Egin*, 25 May; *JPRS*, 12 July). Meanwhile, Carrillo questioned the validity of Spanish claims to Gibraltar—which the government was evidently pressing in conjunction with discussions about NATO—so long as Spain continued to occupy the North African enclaves of Ceuta and Melilla (*Los Angeles Times*, 17 November).

Iglesias declared in March that communists had found virtually no opportunities for supporting Spain's foreign policy. He criticized steps taken to recognize Israel, González's lack of support for the Polisario Front in North Africa, and his condemnation of the armed struggle in Central America. (*Mundo Obrero*, 18–24 March; *El Nuevo Diário*, Managua, 16 June; *FBIS*, 31 March, 5 July.) The PCE also protested U.S. "aggression" in Central America and the "brutal" intervention in Grenada (*Mundo Obrero*, 29 July–4 August, 18–25 November; *FBIS*, 11 August, 30 November).

Following a customary Eurocommunist line, Iglesias found occasion to denounce both the United States and the Soviet Union, as, for example, in connection with the "inadmissible" shooting-down of a South Korean airliner by a Soviet fighter. At the same time, the party condemned U.S. "use of civil aircraft for espionage." Carrillo, on the other hand, departed from his previous practice and sided fully with the Soviets, blaming "American provocation" for the tragedy. "I have never been, and never will be, anti-Soviet," he said. (*RFE Research*, 7 October; *Economist*, 10 December.)

Iglesias and other Spanish communists visited Hungary, Bulgaria, Romania, Italy, Portugal, Cuba, Nicaragua, and China and received Bulgarian, Polish, Portuguese, and Chinese delegations in Spain. The Spanish and Chinese conferees made special mention, now a rigorous formality, of each party's independence and lack of interference in each other's affairs (*Mundo Obrero*, 9–15 September; *FBIS*, 19 September). Iglesias attended the congress of the Italian Communist Party, which he praised as a model for the PCE because the Italians had a great knack for resolving major disagreements without tension or rigid attitudes (*Mundo Obrero*, 15–21 July; *FBIS*, 26 July). In a meeting with Alvaro Cunhal in Lisbon, he sought "better relations" with the Portuguese Communist Party, with which dealings have been strained over the issue of loyalty to Moscow (*FBIS*, 26 July).

H. Leslie Robinson
Elbert Covell College
University of the Pacific

Sweden

Population. 8.3 million
Party. The Left Party Communists (Vänsterpartiet Kommunisterna; VPK)
Founded. 1921 (VPK, 1967)
Membership. 17,500, principally in the far north, Stockholm, and Göteborg
Chairman. Lars Werner
Executive Committee. 9 members: Lars Werner, Eivor Marklund (vice-chairman), Bo Hammar (secretary), Lennart Beijer, Viola Claesson, Bror Engström, Kenneth Kvist, Bertil Mabrink, Margo Ingvardsson
Party Board. 35 members
Status. Legal
Last Congress. Twenty-sixth, 20–24 November 1981
Elections. 1982, 5.6 percent, 20 of 349 seats
Auxiliary Organizations. Communist Youth (KU), Communist Women's Organization
Publications. *Ny Dag* (New day), semiweekly; *Socialistisk Debatt* (Socialist debate), monthly; both published in Stockholm

The ancestor of the VPK, Sweden's Communist Party (Sveriges Kommunistiska Partiet), was established in 1921, but a number of divisions adversely affected it in the 1920s. Its greatest moment came right after World War II in local elections, when it obtained 11.2 percent of the vote. This result was largely due to the popularity of the Soviet Union at the end of the war. Since then, the communist party has usually garnered around 4–5 percent of the vote. The Swedish communist party has had a marginal influence in Swedish politics. It has never made a truly major contribution to communist history. Perhaps its most important role has been to allow the Social Democrats to govern during much of Sweden's recent history. During the last half century, the Social Democrats have been Europe's most dominant social democratic party, and during many of the years that the Social Democrats have formed the government, they have relied on a combined majority with the communists in the parliament (Riksdag). The communists have, however, never been part of the government.

In Sweden, a party has to clear a 4 percent threshold in order to be represented in parliament, and after the bitter reaction to the Soviet invasion of Czechoslovakia in 1968, the VPK went under the 4 percent mark and was not represented. In the 1970 and 1976 elections, it received 4.8 percent, and in 1979 and 1982, 5.6 percent of the vote. The next election is scheduled for 1985.

The communists changed both the name and the direction of the party at a party congress in 1967. Blue-collar workers constituted the majority of the communist electorate in previous years, but increasingly the VPK is attracting white-collar workers and younger people. Voting studies indicate no significant age differentials among the voters of various parties, except for the VPK. In the 1979 election, approximately half of the VPK voters were under the age of 30. Most of the party's new white-collar supporters are in cultural, educational, and health-related occupations.

The VPK projects a Marxist image, even though it has disassociated itself from Moscow and is generally regarded as one of the more moderate Western European communist parties. Its program states: "The party's foundation is scientific socialism, the revolutionary theory of Marx and Lenin. It seeks to apply this theory, develop it, infuse it with the struggle of the Swedish working class. The party's goal is to have the struggle of the working class and of the people, guided by the ideas of revolutionary socialism, lead to victory over capitalism and to a classless society."

The year under review saw the VPK concentrating on economic issues and on associating itself with the peace movement and also trying to avoid any backlash from the well-publicized sightings of presumed Soviet submarines in Swedish waters.

Party Internal Affairs. At the end of 1982, Tore Forsberg, who had been party secretary for thirteen years, stepped down because of illness and was succeeded by Bo Hammar. Hammar is a journalist, employed by the party newspaper, *Ny Dag*. Previous to his succeeding Forsberg, he had served as the VPK international secretary. The VPK Executive Committee decided that during the last months of 1982 and throughout 1983, the party should concentrate on unemployment, distribution policy, and the questions of peace and disarmament. The Executive Committee drew up guidelines for an ideological campaign to counteract the "reactionary" propaganda of the Conservative (Moderata) Party and the Swedish Employers' Confederation (SAF) and "to strengthen the position of socialism." (*Ny Dag*, 16 November 1982.) The campaign began in the spring with studies and was followed in the fall with propaganda activity.

A minor ripple in VPK politics was caused in November 1982, when the party branch in Skara in central Sweden decided to leave the party and join the Socialist Party (formerly the Communist Workers' Association). *Dagens Nyheter* (18 November 1982) reported that the Skara group was bolting the party because, according to a spokesman for the defectors, "The VPK is on the side of the oppressors against the East European and Soviet workers." The spokesman further explained that the defecting group was upset because, among other things, the VPK decided not to support the Solidarity movement in Poland.

At the May convention of the KU, the youth group took a position on Soviet rearmament different from that of the VPK, reflected in a head-line in *Gnistan* (30 June) "The VPK's Youth Federation Attacks the Mother Party." Maria Bruun, a defecting member of the KU Executive Committee, said, "The KU does not want to take a position against the Soviet Union's rearmament in the same way as the VPK" (ibid.). At the congress, a proposal that the KU should demand the dismantling of the Soviet SS-20 missiles was defeated 95–54. This contrasted with the VPK's somewhat more critical attitude of Soviet rearmament.

Domestic Affairs. A public opinion poll released on 27 December showed the VPK receiving 0.1 percentage point less than it had in the 1982 election (5.5 percent). In the 1982 elections, the combined Social Democratic Party–VPK total was 51.5 percent, compared with 45.1 percent for the three so-called bourgeois parties. The December poll indicated a combined Social Democratic–VPK total of 46.5 percent versus 51 percent for the more conservative parties. The most notable change was the gain for the Conservative Party (6.4 percentage points) and the drop for the Social Democrats (4.9 percentage points).

The most controversial issue in Swedish domestic politics in 1983—one that may help explain the figures above—was employee (or wage-earner) funds, under which elected committees of trade unionists buy shares in private industry. Opponents claimed that the unions would eventually take over the companies. Assar Lindbeck, the Social Democrats' leading economist, resigned from the party in 1982, claiming that the fund would lead to the "collectivization of society." Opposition to the "fund" was massive and well-financed, as was apparent at a huge rally in Stockholm in October.

VPK chairman Lars Werner was also critical of the wage-earner fund, but from a different vantage point. He thought it was a step in the right (socialist) direction, but that it was too watered down from the original proposal. He stressed that the new version served the purpose of increasing investment in companies in the short run. According to Werner, "The discussion of power within companies should start at the beginning." (*Dagens Nyheter*, 28 July.)

An important editorial in the conservative Stockholm daily *Svenska Dagbladet* (22 July) speculated on a question that a number of other observers have pondered—why the VPK continues to draw as much support as it still does.

Because of the Soviet Union's suppression of Solidarity in Poland, its continuing occupation of Afghanistan, and its submarine activity in Swedish waters, one might imagine a significant decrease in support for the VPK. As the editorial pointed out, however, "The VPK is in the best of health. The old communist party is no longer regarded—at least by its voters and sympathizers—as a traditional communist party. The old workers' party has become a party for environmentalists, first-time voters, intellectuals, and the new class of bureaucrats. Soviet communism has been exchanged for a general left-wing opportunism that is often pursued very skillfully." The editorial noted, however, that there was a possible cost for the VPK in transforming itself from "a class party for aware workers into a fad party for unaware students." Workers concerned with the "class struggle" tend to be more stable in their political loyalties than voters temporarily attached to a particular issue. The editorial concluded that an unusually large number of VPK voters in the 1982 elections were first-time voters. In other words, the question that numerous observers, in addition to the editorial writer, have raised is whether a party that, from a class-based party is becoming a more politically opportunistic leftist party, can convince its first-time voters to become permanent adherents.

The influential Stockholm daily *Dagens Nyheter* (17 December 1982), in an editorial entitled "Palme in the Communist Cage," expressed the opinion that "there is not a single precedent for the agreement that has now been reached between the Social Democrats and the VPK on the increased value-added tax, the study of a differentiated value-added tax, higher tobacco taxes, and higher food subsidies." The paper pointed out that the two longtime Social Democratic prime ministers, Per Albin Hansson and Tage Erlander, never negotiated with the communists. The editorial writer and others have speculated that although the communists have never been part of a Social Democratic government, that perhaps they now have a bit more leverage with the Social Democrats.

In May, the Social Democrats received the support of the Center and Liberal parties for funding an increased budget to pay for chasing submarines in Swedish waters by increasing the oil tax. Then, within a day, the government went to the VPK for support for increasing payroll taxes. (*Dagens Nyheter*, 26 May.)

During the last months of 1982 and throughout 1983, the VPK, for the first time, was represented on the Riksdag's Foreign Affairs Committee, which has to read many classified documents. The Conservative Party was highly critical of this Social Democratic move. The VPK is now represented on thirteen parliamentary committees, but not on the Justice, Taxation, and Defense committees. (Ibid., 7 October 1982.)

Foreign Affairs. The most-discussed issue affecting Swedish-Soviet relations during 1983 was the continued sightings of Soviet submarines in Swedish territorial waters. There has been no repetition of the dramatic 1981 incident in which a Soviet Whisky-class submarine ran aground near the naval base of Karlskrona in southern Sweden, resulting in banner headlines in the Swedish and international press. On 26 April, a Swedish official commission charged that the USSR had deployed six submarines inside Swedish waters in October 1982 in "gross violation" of Swedish territory. The commission stated that six submarines—including three manned midgets with a "bottom-crawling capacity of a hitherto unknown character"—were near the coast in October. It said that three of the submarines evaded an extensive search in Horsfjärden Bay, where a naval base is situated, and the other three remained just outside the bay in the archipelago. The imprints left by the submarines were photographed by Swedish divers and displayed as part of the commission report.

The commission noted that at least 40 submarine intrusions had been noted in 1982, a significant increase over past years. Moreover, the intrusions were marked by increasingly "provocative behavior." "It is essential," the commission said, "that both alliances [NATO and the Warsaw Pact] have confidence in Sweden's resolve and ability to guarantee both in peacetime and in war that no foreign power will be allowed to take advantage of Swedish territory." (*WP*, 27 April.)

The plethora of newspaper and television stories about the submarines have been notably anti-Soviet. Both before and especially since the commission report, the public has assumed that any submarine sighting involves a Soviet sub. Prime Minister Olof Palme has displayed considerable anger at the wide scope and "effrontery" of the submarine intrusions, and Swedish antisubmarine defenses were more heavily funded during 1983. The Swedish ambassador to Moscow did not take part in the Soviet May Day celebration, and the Swedish government is discouraging high-level official visits.

VPK chairman Werner agreed with the commission's conclusion that the submarines were Soviet ones, but since the VPK has tried to distance itself from the Soviet party, it is not clear what long-term impact the Soviet incursions will have on the political fortunes of the VPK.

There were other strains in Soviet-Swedish relations in 1983. The "Where is Raoul Wallenberg?" question continued to surface in Swedish and foreign media. Wallenberg was the Swedish diplomat in Budapest who saved thousands of Jews from the Nazis. He was seized by Soviet forces after the Soviets occupied Hungary in 1945 and three weeks later was in Moscow's Lubyanka prison. There have been reports in recent years that he is still alive and in prison in the Soviet Union, although the Soviets say that Wallenberg died in 1947.

Other sources of friction were the expulsion of three Soviet citizens, two of them diplomats, for spying (*Dagens Nyheter*, 15 January) and the reported harassment of two Swedish defense attachés during a car trip in the Soviet Union by a group of unknown men (Stockholm international service, 22 April; *FBIS*, 25 April).

The VPK took an active role in demonstrations against the positioning of U.S. missiles in Europe, but it also pressured the Soviet Union to reduce its missiles. The VPK members of parliament wrote a letter to the Soviet party, proposing that the Soviet Union unilaterally begin reducing the number of its SS-20 missiles and appealing to the Soviets for "concrete new initiatives for continued negotiations in Geneva that could prevent the deployment of new nuclear missiles in Europe."

In a 10 November press conference commenting on the letter, Chairman Werner said, "The superpowers' disarmament negotiations in Geneva are in the process of breaking down. We see it as a problem in that the small states directly affected by the deployment of the superpowers' nuclear arms have no say in the matter. It would not be a weakness if the Soviet Union were to begin unilateral reductions of its missiles." (*Dagens Nyheter*, 11 November.)

International Party Contacts. Party Secretary Bo Hammar implied that the VPK had been in touch with other European communist parties that have also appealed to the Soviet Union to reduce its missiles (ibid.).

A KU committee met with Chinese Communist Party and Chinese Communist Youth League officials in June. Also in June, Werner and a delegation of VPK officials traveled to Bucharest to meet Nicolae Ceauşescu, general secretary of the Romanian Communist Party, to exchange views on collaboration between Sweden and Romania in political, economic, technical, and cultural areas.

A delegation of the VPK went to East Berlin in June to hear the German Democratic Republic "peace policy" explained by Ingeborg Lange, a secretary of the German Central Committee. According to the GDR domestic service (9 June; *FBIS*, 10 June), "The two sides agreed that in view of the aggravated confrontation and arms buildup policy of the most aggressive forces of the United States and NATO, there is no more important task than protecting the peoples from a devastating nuclear war."

Rival Communist Groups. The pro-Soviet Communist Workers' Party (Arbetarpartiet Kommunisterna; APK) was founded in 1977. APK chairman Rolf Hagel told the party's Twenty-seventh Congress in Stockholm that the Soviet Union and other socialist countries were the main force in the struggle for peace. *Norskenflamman* (Northern lights) is the party paper. In 1982, the party won 0.1 percent of the vote and twelve local government seats, mainly in the north of Sweden. The APK claims 5,000 members.

The pro-Chinese Sweden's Communist Party (Sveriges Kommunistiska Partiet) was founded as the Communist League of Marxists-Leninists (KFML) in 1967 and was especially vocal during the Vietnam war. It changed its name in 1969. Its chairman is Roland Pettersson, and it publishes *M-L Gnistan* (The spark). It won eight seats in local elections in 1982.

The pro-Albanian Marxist-Leninist Communist Party, Revolutionary (Kommunistiska Partiet Marxist-Leninisterna, Revolutionerna) was founded in 1970 because its members perceived the KMFL as not being radical enough. Its chairman is Frank Baude. The party issues the weekly *Proletären*. It won three seats in the 1982 local elections.

The Socialist Party (Socialistiska Partiet) was

founded in the early 1970s as the Communist Workers' League and changed to its present name in 1982. It is the Swedish section of the Trotskyist Fourth International and is directed by the Executive Committee of the International. It publishes *Internationalen*. It received about 3,900 votes in the 1982 election but won no seats.

Peter Grothe
Monterey Institute of International Studies

Switzerland

Population. 6.5 million
Party. Swiss Labor Party (Partei der Arbeit der Schweiz/Parti suisse du travail/Partito Svizzero del Lavoro; PdAS)
Founded. 1921
Membership. 5,000 (estimate)
Secretary General. Armand Magnin
Politburo. 14 members
Secretariat. 5 members
Central Committee. 50 members
Status. Legal
Last Congress. Twelfth, 21–22 May 1983
Last Election. 1983, 0.9 percent, 1 of 200
Auxiliary Organizations. Communist Youth League of Switzerland (KVJS), Marxist Student League, Swiss Women's Organization for Peace and Progress, Swiss Peace Movement, Swiss-Soviet Union Society, Swiss-Cuban Society, Central Sanitaire Swiss
Publications. *Voix Ouvrière* (Geneva), daily, circulation 7,000 copies; *Vorwärts* (Basel), weekly, circulation 6,000 copies; *Il Lavatore*, Italian-language edition; *Zunder*, KVJS organ

---

The pro-Soviet PdAS is the oldest communist party in Switzerland. It was founded on 5 March 1921 as the Swiss Communist Party. The party was outlawed in 1940 and re-established on 15 October 1944 under its present name. It has regional organizations in fifteen cantons.

The Twelfth Party Congress (21–22 May 1983) elected the Central Committee, Politburo, and Secretariat. It re-elected Armand Magnin as secretary general. The congress was attended by delegates from all linguistic areas of Switzerland and from a number of fraternal parties. The Soviet delegation was headed by Richard Kosola-

pov, a member of the Central Committee. (Tass, 21 and 23 May; *FBIS*, 25 May.) Secretary General Armand Magnin announced that the "Swiss appeal for peace, against nuclear death" had obtained 170,000 signatures. The foreign policy statements made at the congress, such as those condemning new U.S. medium-range missiles in Europe, Israel's invasion of Lebanon, South Africa's "provocations" in Angola, and U.S. foreign policies in Central America, followed those of Moscow.

In the 23 October elections for the 200-member lower house (Nationalrat), the PdAS lost two of its three seats. Magnin lost his seat in Geneva, once a communist stronghold. (*NYT*, 25 October.) The PdAS obtained 0.9 percent of the vote compared with 2.1 percent in 1979.

During the 1960s, followers of the New Left who refused to join the PdAS founded several Marxist parties, such as the Progressive Organizations Switzerland (POCH), the Revolutionary Marxist League (RML; presently the Swiss Socialist Workers' Party; SAP), the Autonomous Socialist Party (PSA), and the various Maoist parties.

As a result of the rejection of strict organizational forms by many young adherents of the protest movement, numerous so-called alternative and ideologically diffuse groups emerged. These collaborated with the political parties of the Left for progressive, revolutionary objectives such as liberation, antinuclear, ecological, peace, and women's issues.

The POCH (Progressive Organisationen Schweiz) was founded in 1972 by student dissidents from the PdAS who rejected that party's adherence to the world communist movement and were opposed to the sterile policies of the old party. In spite of POCH's emphasis on its independence, it pursues pro-Soviet policies. During its founding phase, the Progressive Organization Basel occupied the leadership position; however, since 1973, the party's secretariat has been located in Zurich. The POCH's membership is estimated at 10,000. It publishes *POCH-Zeitung*.

In the October elections, the POCH increased its representation from two to three seats. Its vote share increased from 1.7 percent in 1979 to 2.2 percent. (*Frankfurter Allgemeine Zeitung*, 29 October.)

A POCH subsidiary, the Organization for Women's Affairs, is the most important women's group in Switzerland. It emerged from the Progressive Women Switzerland. The organization's magazine is the weekly *Emanzipation*. Other organizations affiliated with POCH are the Solidarity Committee for Africa, Asia, and Latin America and the Swiss Society for Social Health.

The SAP (Sozialistische Arbeiterpartei/Parti socialiste ouvrière) adopted its new name at the Fifth Congress of the Revolutionary Marxist League (LMR) in 1980. The LMR was founded in 1969 by a group of young Trotskyists who left the PdAS. The SAP is the Swiss section of the Fourth International (Trotskyist), which is head-

quartered in Brussels. The party emphasizes the revolutionary class struggle in production centers. Its goal is the eventual capture of the control of enterprises, a policy resembling former revolutionary syndicalism. Its leading theoretician is Fritz Osterwalder. Membership is about 500. The youth organization of the SAP, Maulwurf ("mole"), disbanded in the late 1970s. In 1983, it was reinstated as the Revolutionary Socialist Youth Organization. SAP publications include *Bresche* (German), *La Brèche* (French), *Rosso* (Italian), and *Rojo* (Spanish).

The PSA (Autonome Sozialistische Partei/ Parti socialiste autonome/Partito Socialista Autonomo) is the outcome of a split within the Socialist Party of the canton of Tessin in 1960. Even though the dissidents obtained the support of a majority at the party congress in 1966, they were not able to assert themselves against the entrenched leadership and, in April 1969, founded the PSA. Its membership is about 1,000. The PSA's influence is limited to the Italian section of Switzerland. The party considers itself an autonomous component of the communist world movement and rejects social democracy, Trotskyism, and spontaneity. In the October elections, the PSA received 10 percent of the vote in Tessin, giving it one seat in the lower house. This brought the strength of the PdAS/POCH/PSA parliamentary fraction to five seats. The PSA publishes *Politika Nuova*.

The Communist Party of Switzerland Marxist-Leninist (KPS/ML), founded on 2 January 1972, has about 200 members and a thousand sympathizers. The KPS/ML is the only pro-Chinese party that survives of the several Maoist organizations that emerged following the Sino-Soviet split. The party considers itself a part of the international communist movement and maintains close relations with the Chinese Communist Party, the Albanian Party of Labor, and other Marxist-Leninist parties. The Workers' and Soldiers' Organization Offensive is an affiliated and Maoist-oriented organization that favors a strong Swiss military establishment and opposes Soviet aspirations for hegemony. The KPS/ML publishes *Oktober* (in various languages).

In addition, there are numerous unstructured left-extremist groups, holding views from radical socialism to anarchism. Some of their followers are known as "chaoists" and advocate direct and violent action against the state and its institutions.

Many originally peaceful demonstrations conducted for various objectives have turned violent as a result of the chaoists' activities.

The left wing of the Socialist Party of Switzerland as well as a number of trade unions cooperate with communists. In 1983, Moscow-directed front organizations, such as the Novosti Press Agency and the World Peace Council demonstrated their marked influence on Swiss organizations (e.g., the Swiss Peace Council, Swiss Peace Movement, Christian Peace Service, and others) and their activities.

At the end of April, the office of Novosti was closed by orders of the Swiss government and its director, Alexei Dumov, expelled. Dumov, together with two Swiss collaborators who were members of the PdAS, was engaged in extensive propaganda and subversive activities, such as organizing and supporting demonstrations, influencing so-called peace activities, and spreading disinformation. (Informationsgruppe Schweiz, *Kommunistische Organisationen und revolutionäre Bewegungen in der Schweiz*, November 1983.)

The activities of the peace movement climaxed on 5 November in a mass meeting in Bern directed against the new medium-range NATO missiles. The event was supported by 80 organizations and groups.

Eric Waldman
University of Calgary

Turkey

Population. 45 million
Party. Turkish Communist Party (Türkiye Komünist Partisi; TCP)
Founded. 1920
Membership. Unknown
Secretary General. Haydar Kutlu
Central Committee. (Incomplete listing): Nahit Sargin, Mehmet Karace, Kemal Daysal, Ferzo Solt, Veysi Sarisözen, Alp Otman
Status. Illegal
Last Congress. Fifth, October or November 1983
Last Election. Not applicable
Auxiliary Organizations. None known
Publications. Party statements are broadcast over Our Radio, which is based in East Berlin.

The major political event of 1983 in Turkey was the parliamentary election of 6 November. It was the focus of political activity for both the government and nongovernmental groups, for it marked the culmination of the planned transition from military to civilian rule. Previous steps in this transition consisted of the ratification of a new constitution in November 1982 and the promulgation of new laws regulating political parties and elections in the spring of 1983. The military junta kept close control of the process, exercising veto powers over leadership cadres and candidates of the parties in the fall election campaign. As a result, only three parties were able to compete in the election: the conservative Nationalist Democracy Party (NDP) led by Turgut Sunalp, a retired general; the Motherland Party, also conservative, led by former deputy prime minister Turgut Ozal; and the moderate leftist Populist Party, led by retired civil servant Necdet Calp. Two important parties (the Right Way Party and the Social Democratic Party) were unable to qualify. These two parties were widely viewed as successor parties to the outlawed conservative Justice Party and the social-democratic Republican People's Party, respectively. President Kenan Evren made it clear that he would not tolerate the return of the old parties in any guise since he held them primarily responsible for the anarchy and political stalemate that had brought on the military coup of 12 September 1980. To reinforce this determination, he detained fourteen leaders of the old parties (including former acting president Ihsan Sabri Çaglayangil, former prime minister Süleyman Demirel, and former minister of finance Deniz Baykal) for most of the election campaign and banned yet another party that he contended was controlled from behind the scenes by Demirel and his associates. In addition, several prominent newspapers were shut down without explanation for varying periods of time.

Thus, the election could hardly be characterized as fully free. Aside from the limitations noted above, it was widely understood that the regime favored the NDP; indeed, on the eve of the election, President Evren made that preference explicit in a radio/TV address to the nation. The mildly social-democratic Populist Party was expected to emerge as the opposition party. Turgut Ozal's Motherland Party was in the race partly because it initially appeared that it would be overshadowed by the officially favored NDP and partly because the junta could not outlaw Ozal's minions without embarrassment since he had served the regime as deputy prime minister from September 1980 until the summer of 1982. The regime was embarrassed anyway since Ozal managed not only to stay in the race, but to establish a clear image of dynamism and independence of official control. The election results constitute a tribute to his political skill. He garnered 45 percent of the vote and an absolute majority of the 400 seats in the new parliament (the first absolute majority won by any party in fourteen years). The officially favored NDP did not even qualify as the leading opposition party, coming in a poor third with only 23 percent of the vote and 71 seats. The poorly organized and poorly financed Populist Party received 30 percent of the vote and 117 seats. Unquestionably, the election results were a major disappointment to the Evren regime. Many observers concluded that the Turkish voter had graphically demonstrated a strong streak of independence and sophistication.

Although the transition to civilian rule thus appears complete, the military junta is not out of the picture. Under the 1982 constitution, President Evren, the leader of the junta, retains important powers for the remainder of his seven-year term and may be eligible for re-election. His four colleagues on the now dissolved National Security Council (the official name of the junta) have become a presidential advisory council for the remainder of the president's first term. The precise manner in which he and his advisers, relying on extensive powers granted them under the constitution, will interact with the prime minister, Turgut Ozal, who relies on majority support in the newly elected parliament, remains to be seen.

While these important developments were unfolding, significant changes were also occurring on the extreme left. The TCP remains illegal, as has been the case since shortly after its inception in the early days of the Turkish republic some sixty years ago. Nevertheless, it appears to have been singularly active during 1983. For one thing, it held a congress for the first time in more than fifty years. The congress re-elected the party's two top officials, I. Bilen as chairman and Haydar Kutlu as secretary general (his real name is Nabi Yagci, according to *Tercuman*, 28 April; *JPRS*, 6 June). The younger Kutlu dominated the party's radio broadcasts throughout most of the year, and in any event, Bilen reportedly died on 18 November at the age of 81. He had been chairman for ten years and was hailed by the Central Committee as "a great party founder who raised the TCP to a new stage in all aspects and who played a key role in the creation of an entirely new generation in the ranks of the Turkish communist movement" (Our Radio, 24 November; *FBIS*, 2 December).

According to the conservative Istanbul daily *Tercuman*, Kutlu was selected as secretary general at a plenary session of the party's Central Committee on 2 April. *Tercuman* maintained that this signified a takeover of the TCP by leaders of the Turkish Workers' Party, which had been established in 1961 and had succeeded in electing fourteen members to the Turkish Parliament in 1965. That party was later outlawed by the Constitutional Court. Some of its leaders, particularly Behice Boran, left the country after the military takeover of 1980, presumably to avoid detention and trial on charges of sedition. In fact, *Tercuman* alleged that the new secretary general of the TCP was still closely associated with Boran. *Tercuman* also alleged that the change in TCP leadership was linked with the succession of Yuri Andropov to the leadership of the Soviet Union. (*JPRS*, 6 June.)

Both the Central Committee meeting in April and the party congress later in the year produced extensive statements on Turkish affairs, although no clear new direction for the TCP was indicated. In the eyes of the TCP, Turkey had been brought to an "impasse" by the military junta. Realizing that it can no longer "maintain control on the basis of bayonets," the junta purportedly proposed to transform itself into "a new reactionary, militarist and police regime with a civilian facade, under the guise of a transition to democracy." (*FBIS*, 25 April.) The TCP dismissed the November election as a charade, particularly in view of the strict limits imposed on the process. The outcome would not change the basic balance of forces either internally within Turkey or internationally. Under the circumstances, the TCP urged Turkish voters to manifest their resistance to the regime by spoiling their ballots (abstention was not advised as voting was compulsory). Official election results indicate that this advice was massively ignored (only 5 percent of the votes were invalid, about normal for Turkish elections). The TCP accused the regime of falsifying this figure to hide the true extent of disaffection, but that accusation lacked credibility since the outcome of the election was not exactly what the Evren regime had hoped for.

The military regime continued to apprehend small groups of alleged communists and other leftists, as well as occasional rightists and religious militants. Late in the year, it was announced that a major trial of the communist detainees would begin on 20 December. Other trials proceeded during the year, and sentences were announced from time to time. Human rights organizations continued to express concern for both the condition of the large number of imprisoned and the appropriateness of the sentences in many cases. One of the most prominent cases involved a group of respected professionals and academics who had been leaders of a peace society. Another *cause célèbre* was created by a hunger strike staged by political prisoners throughout the prison system to protest the conditions under which they were held. Although the TCP claimed that 6,000 individuals had participated in the strike, the *New York Times* (29 July) estimated that approximately 1,800 prisoners were involved. Amnesty for those accused of political crimes became a lively topic of discussion after the inauguration of the civilian Ozal government in December, but the newly appointed prime minister made it clear that on this issue, as on other politically sensitive matters, he would proceed with considerable caution.

Frank Tachau
University of Illinois at Chicago

Select Bibliography, 1982–83

GENERAL

Alexandrova, Liliana, ed. *Programme on History of the International Workers', Communist, and National Liberation Movement*. Sofia: Bulgarian Communist Party, Central Committee, Academy of Social Sciences and Social Management, 1982. 35 pp.

Broadhurst, Arlene Idol. *The Future of the European Alliance Systems: NATO and the Warsaw Pact*. Boulder, Colo.: Westview Press, 1982. 316 pp.

Callinicos, Alex. *Marxism and Philosophy*. New York: Oxford University Press, 1983. 177 pp.

Carver, Terrell. *Marx's Social Theory*. New York: Oxford University Press, 1982. 296 pp.

Copper, John F., and Daniel S. Papp, eds. *Communist Nations' Military Assistance*. Boulder, Colo.: Westview Press, 1983. 201 pp.

Cornell, Richard. *Revolutionary Vanguard: The Early Years of the Communist Youth International, 1914–1924*. Toronto: University of Toronto Press, 1982. 353 pp.

Debray, Regis. *Critique of Political Reason*. New York: Schocken Books, 1983. 361 pp.

Dunayevskaya, Raya. *Rosa Luxembourg: Women's Liberation and Marx's Philosophy of Revolution*. Sussex, U.K.: Harvester, 1982. 234 pp.

duToit, Pieter. *Reflections on Marxism*. Pretoria: J. L. van Schaik, 1982. 283 pp.

Fischer, Norman, et al., eds. *Continuity and Change in Marxism*. Atlantic Highlands, N.J.: Humanities Press, 1982. 249 pp.

Goldman, Ralph M., ed. *Transnational Parties: Organizing the World's Precincts*. Lanham, Md.: University of America Press, 1983. 360 pp.

Gurley, John G. *Challenges to Communism*. Stanford, Calif.: Stanford Alumni Association, 1982. 174 pp.

Hook, Sidney. *Marxism and Beyond*. Totowa, N.J.: Rowman and Littlefield, 1983. 225 pp.

Janke, Peter. *Guerrilla and Terrorist Organizations: A World Directory and Bibliography*. New York: Macmillan, 1983. 531 pp.

Jessop, Bob. *The Capitalist State: Marxist Theories and Methods*. New York: New York University Press, 1982. 296 pp.

Kende, Pierre, et al., eds. *Le Système communiste: Un monde en expansion*. Paris: IFRI, 1982. 287 pp.

Knoche, Hansjürgen. *Von Marx bis Paulus*. Munich: Meta A. Behrendt, 1983. 162 pp.

Langguth, Gerd. *Protest-bewegung: Die neue Linke seit 1968*. Cologne: Berend von Nottbeck, 1983. 374 pp.

Larrain, Jorge. *Marxism and Ideology*. Atlantic Highlands, N.J.: Humanities Press, 1983. 263 pp.

Lopata, P. *Communism as a Social Formation*. Moscow: Progress, 1983. 182 pp.

Löw, Konrad. *Warum fasziniert der Kommunismus? Eine systematische Untersuchung*. Cologne: Deutscher Instituts-Verlag, 1983. 380 pp.

Mahlou, Bruno, and Harald Neubert. *Die Kommunisten und ihr Zusammenwirken*. East Berlin: Dietz Verlag, 1983. 240 pp.

McFadden, Charles Joseph. *Christianity Confronts Communism*. Chicago: Franciscan Herald Press, 1982. 423 pp.

Meisner, Maurice J. *Marxism, Maoism, and Utopianism: Eight Essays.* Madison: University of Wisconsin Press, 1982. 255 pp.

Munroe, Trevor. *The Working Class Party Principles and Standards.* Kingston, Jamaica: Vanguard Publishers, 1982. 211 pp.

Nelson, Daniel N., ed. *Communism and the Politics of Inequalities.* Lexington, Mass.: Lexington Books, 1983. 291 pp.

Parkinson, G. H. R. *Marx and Marxisms.* New York: Cambridge University Press, 1982. 268 pp.

Ponomarev, Boris N. *Communism in a Changing World.* New York: Sphinx Press, 1983. 266 pp.

Potichnyj, Peter J., and Jane Shapiro Zacek, eds. *Politics and Participation Under Communist Rule.* New York: Praeger, 1983. 282 pp.

Silberner, Edmund. *Kommunisten zur Judenfrage: Zur Geschichte von Theorie und Praxis des Kommunismus.* Opladen: Westdeutscher Verlag, 1983. 402 pp.

Sleeper, Raymond S., ed. *A Lexicon of Marxist-Leninist Semantics.* Alexandria, Va.: Western Goals, 1983. 362 pp.

Solnemann, K. H. Z. *The Manifesto of Peace and Freedom: The Alternative to the Communist Manifesto.* Freiburg/Br.: Mackay Gesellschaft, 1983. 234 pp.

Szajkowski, Bogdan. *The Establishment of Marxist Regimes.* London: Butterworth & Co., 1982. 173 pp.

Union of International Associations. *Yearbook of International Organizations, 1983/84.* 20th ed. New York: K. G. Saur, 1983. Vol 1. 911 pp.

Wesson, Robert, ed. *Yearbook on International Communist Affairs, 1983.* Stanford, Calif.: Hoover Institution Press, 1983. 590 pp.

Whetten, Lawrence L., ed. *The Present State of Communist Internationalism.* Lexington, Mass.: Lexington Books, 1983. 272 pp.

White, Gordon, et al., eds. *Revolutionary Socialist Development in the Third World.* Lexington: University of Kentucky Press, 1983. 278 pp.

Zagladin, V. V. *Za prava trudiashchikhsia za mir i bezopasnost' narodov: Kommunisticheskii avangard rabochego dvizheniia v nachale 80-kh godov.* Moscow: Mysl', 1982. 291 pp.

Zwick, Peter. *National Communism.* Boulder, Colo.: Westview Press, 1983. 260 pp.

AFRICA AND THE MIDDLE EAST

Abd-Allah, Umar F. *The Islamic Struggle in Syria.* Berkeley, Calif.: Mizan Press, 1983. 300 pp.

Africa South of the Sahara, 1982–83. 12th ed. London: Europa Publications, 1983. 1399 pp.

Albright, David E. *The USSR and Sub-Saharan Africa in the 1980's.* New York: Praeger, 1983. 129 pp.

Arlinghaus, Bruce E., ed. *Arms for Africa: Military Assistance and Foreign Policy in the Developing World.* New York: D. C. Heath, 1982. 233 pp.

Bidwell, Robin. *The Two Yemens.* Boulder, Colo.: Westview Press, 1983. 350 pp.

Chabal, Patrick. *Amilcar Cabral: Revolutionary Leadership and People's War.* New York: Cambridge University Press, 1983. 272 pp.

Damis, John. *Conflict in Northwest Africa.* Stanford, Calif.: Hoover Institution Press, 1983. 173 pp.

Denisova, T. S. *Rabochii klass sovremennoi Nigerii.* Moscow: Nauka, 1983. 166 pp.

Devlin, John G. *Syria: Modern State in an Ancient Land.* Boulder, Colo.: Westview Press, 1983. 140 pp.

Dudley, Billy. *An Introduction to Nigerian Government.* London: Macmillan, 1982. 367 pp.

Erlich, Haggai. *The Struggle over Eritrea, 1962-1978: War and Revolution in the Horn of Africa.* Stanford, Calif.: Hoover Institution Press, 1983. 155 pp.

Firebrace, James. *The Hidden Revolution: An Analysis of Social Change in Tigray (Ethiopia) Based on Eyewitness Accounts.* London: War on Want, 1982. 92 pp.

First, Ruth. *Black Gold: The Mozambican Miner, Proletarian and Peasant.* New York: St. Martin's Press, 1983. 255 pp.

FRELIMO. *IV Congress Held in Maputo from 26–30 April 1983.* Maputo: FRELIMO, 1983. 3 vols.

Gann, Lewis H. *Africa Between East and West*. Cape Town: Tafelberg, 1983. 132 pp.

Gilmour, David. *Lebanon: The Fractured Country*. New York: St. Martin's Press, 1983. 228 pp.

Gordon, David C. *The Republic of Lebanon: Nation in Jeopardy*. Boulder, Colo.: Westview Press, 1983. 171 pp.

Gromyko, Andrei A., et al. *The USSR and Africa*. Moscow: *Social Sciences Today* Editorial Board, 1983. 205 pp.

Hooglund, Eric J. *Land and Revolution in Iran, 1960–1980*. Austin: University of Texas Press, 1982. 191 pp.

Israeli, Raphael. *PLO in Lebanon: Selected Documents*. Jerusalem: Hebrew University, 1983. 316 pp.

Jurquet, Jacques. *Mouvement communiste et nationaliste en Algérie*. Paris: Presse d'Aujourd'hui, 1982. 186 pp.

Katsikas, Suzanne. *The Arc of Socialist Revolutions: Angola to Afghanistan*. Cambridge, Mass.: Schenkman, 1982. 332 p.

Keddie, Nikki R., ed. *Religion and Politics in Iran: Shi'ism to Quietism to Revolution*. New Haven, Conn.: Yale University Press, 1983. 258 pp.

Kirk-Greene, Anthony, and Douglas Rimmer. *Nigeria Since 1970: A Political and Economic Outline*. New York: Holmes & Meier, 1982. 161 pp.

Mallakh, Ragaei el. *Saudi Arabia: Rush to Development*. Baltimore, Md.: Johns Hopkins University Press, 1982. 474 pp.

The Middle East and North Africa, 1982–83. 29th ed. London: Europa Publications. 1983. 1013 pp.

Mortimer, Edward. *Faith and Power: The Politics of Islam*. New York: Vintage Books, 1982. 432 pp.

Movimento Popular de Libertação de Angola–Partido do Trabalho. *1980 Angola Special Congress: Report of the Central Committee of the MPLA–Workers' Party presented by Jose Eduardo dos Santos, President, Luanda, 17–23 December 1980*. London: Mozambique, Angola and Guinea Information Centre, 1982. 93 pp.

Munslow, Barry. *Mozambique: The Revolution and Its Origins*. New York: Longmans, 1983. 195 pp.

Nelson, Harold D., ed. *Sudan: A Country Study*. 3rd ed. Washington, D.C.: American University Foreign Area Studies, 1983. 365 pp.

Nwafor, Azinna. *FRELIMO and Socialism in Mozambique*. Roxbury, Mass.: Omenana Books, 1983. 46 pp.

Nyrop, Richard F., ed. *Egypt: A Country Study*. 4th ed. Washington, D.C.: American University Foreign Area Studies, 1983. 362 pp.

Sadovskaia, L. *Sotsial-reformizm v. Afrike*. Moscow: Profizdat, 1983. 117 pp.

Sauldie, Madan M. *Ethiopia: Dawn of the Red Star*. New York: Apt Books, 1982. 241 pp.

Shaw, Tim M., ed. *Alternative Futures for Africa*. Boulder, Colo.: Westview Press, 1982. 365 pp.

Spencer, John. *James Beuttah: Freedom Fighter*. Nairobi: Stellascope, 1983. 118 pp.

Talili, al-Bashir. *Nationalismes, socialismes et communismes dans la Tunisie de l'entre deux guerres (1919–1934)*. Tunis: Faculté de lettres et sciences humaines, 1983. n.p.

Tamene, Bitima. *Die ungelöste national Frage in Äthiopien: Studie zu den Befreiungsbewegungen der Oromo und Eritreas*. Frankfurt/Main: P. Lang, 1983. 226 pp.

Tronje, Rüdiger H. *SWAPO: Die Geisel Südwestafrikas*. Berg am See: Vowinckel, 1983. 157 pp.

Usman, Yusufu Bala, ed. *Political Repression in Nigeria*. Kano, Nigeria: Bala Mohammed Memorial Committee, 1982. Vol. I.

Vanneman, Peter. *Soviet Foreign Policy in Southern Africa: Problems and Prospects*. Pretoria: Africa Institute of South Africa, 1982. 57 pp.

Wei, Liang-Tsai. *Peking Versus Taipei in Africa, 1960–1978*. Taipei: Asia and World Institute, 1982. 457 pp.

THE AMERICAS

Arevalo, Oscar. *El Partido Comunista*. Buenos Aires: Centro Editor de America Latina, 1983. 158 pp.

Arico, José. *Marx y America Latina*. 2nd ed. Mexico City: Alianza Editorial Mexicana, 1982. 242 pp.

Bekarevich, A. D., ed. *Kuba: Stroitel'stvo sotsializma*. Moscow: Nauka, 1983. 287 pp.

Blasier, Cole. *The Giant's Rival: The U.S.S.R. and Latin America*. Pittsburgh: University of Pittsburgh Press, 1983. 213 pp.

Campodónico, F., ed. *El pensamiento comunista, 1917–1945*. San Isidro, Peru: Mosca Azul Editores, 1982. 228 pp.

Carim, Enver, and Catherine Fear, eds. *Latin America and the Caribbean, 1983*. 4th ed. New York: Ballantine Books, World of Information, 1983. 270 pp.

Castro, Fidel. *La crisis economica y social del mundo*. Havana: Oficina de Publicaciones del Consejo de Estado, 1983. 238 pp.

Colectivo Nacional de Dirigentes Comunistas. *Os Comunistas e a questão da mulher*. São Paulo: Editora Novos Rumos, 1982. 90 pp.

Dias, Giocondo. *Os objectivos dos comunistas: Artigos, entrevistas e um depoimento político*. São Paulo: Editora Novos Rumos, 1983. 164 pp.

Dobbs, Farrell. *Revolutionary Continuity: Birth of the Communist Movement, 1918–1922: Marxist Leadership in the U.S.* New York: Monad Press, 1983. 240 pp.

Donno, Antonio. *La questione comunista negli Stati Uniti: Il communist party dal fronte popolare alla guerra fredda (1935–1954)*. Lecce, Italy: Milella, 1983. 207 pp.

Dulles, John W. F. *Brazilian Communism, 1935–1945*. Austin: University of Texas Press, 1983. 289 pp.

Ermolaev, Vasilii I. *Iz istorii rabochego kommunisticheskogo dvizheniia v Latinskoi Amerike*. Moscow: Mysl', 1982. 252 pp.

Fava, Athos. *Qué es el partido comunista?* Buenos Aires: Editorial Sudamericana, 1983. 239 pp.

———, and Jorge Pereyra. *Declaración del partido comunista*. Buenos Aires: Editorial Anteo, 1983. 30 pp.

Field, Frederick Vanderbilt. *From Right to Left: An Autobiography*. Westport, Conn.: Lawrence Hill, 1983. 321 pp.

Ghioldi, Orestes. *Nuestra lucha consecuente por una nueva Argentina: El partido comunista cumple 65 años*. Buenos Aires: Editorial Anteo, 1982. 29 pp.

Gillespie, Richard. *Soldiers of Peron: Argentina's Montoneros*. New York: Oxford University Press, 1982. 310 pp.

Gornov, M. F., ed. *Kommunisticheskie partii Latinski Ameriki*. Moscow: Nauka, 1982. 363 pp.

Hopkins, Jack W., et al., eds. *Latin America and the Caribbean Contemporary Record, 1981–82*. Vol. 1. New York: Holmes & Meier, 1983. 892 pp.

Horowitz, Irving L., ed. *Cuban Communism*. 5th ed. New Brunswick, N.J.: Transaction Books, 1984. 688 pp.

Klehr, Harvey. *The Heyday of American Communism*. Buffalo, N.Y.: Prometheus Books, 1983. 450 pp.

LaFeber, Walter. *Inevitable Revolutions: The United States in Central America*. New York: W. W. Norton, 1983. 357 pp.

Levine, Barry B., ed. *The Cuban Presence in the Caribbean*. Boulder, Colo.: Westview Press, 1983. 274 pp.

Lyons, Paul. *Philadelphia Communists, 1936–1956*. Philadelphia: Temple University Press, 1982. 244 pp.

Marcos Lozza, Arturo. *Viaje por el partido de los comunistas*. Buenos Aires: Editorial Anteo, 1983. 109 pp.

McMichael, R. Daniel, and John D. Paulus, eds. *Western Hemisphere Stability: The Latin American Connection*. Pittsburgh: World Affairs Council of Pittsburgh, n.d. 138 pp.

Merrill, Andrea T., ed. *Chile: A Country Study*, 2nd ed. Washington, D.C.: American University Foreign Area Studies, 1982. 296 pp.

Moraes, Denis de. *Prestes, lutas e autocriticas*. Petropolis, Brazil: Vozes, 1982. 227 pp.

Naison, Mark. *Communism in Harlem During the Depression*. Urbana: University of Illinois Press, 1983. 355 pp.

Noticias de Venezuela: Facsimil del organo de los desterrados venezolanos el Partido Comunista en Mexico. Caracas: Centauro, 1983. n.p.

Os comunistas de Pernambuco e as eleições de 1982. [Brasilia]: Editora Novos Rumos, 1983. 46 pp.

Paquin, Lyonel. *The Haitians: Class and Color Politics.* New York: Lyonel Paquin, 1983. 275 pp.

Partido Comunista de la Argentina. *Comunistas argentinos desaparecidos.* Buenos Aires: Apoderados del Partido Comunista, 1982. 55 pp.

_____. *Plataforma Nacional del Partido Comunista: Elecciones nacionales del 30 de octubre de 1983.* Buenos Aires: Editorial Anteo, 1983. 30 pp.

_____. *Primera asamblea nacional de abogados comunistas.* [Buenos Aires]: Partido Comunista, [1983]. 32 pp.

_____. Comisión Nacional de Educación del Partido Comunista. *Escuela de primer nivel el Partido Comunista: Su programa, su linea, su organización.* 7th ed. Buenos Aires: Editorial Anteo, 1983. 46 pp.

_____. Congreso Nacional. *Todos juntos, por la liberación contra la dependecia: Peronistas, comunistas, fuerzas del pueblo.* Buenos Aires: Editorial Anteo, 1983. 90 pp.

Partido Comunista Peruano. *Hacía un gobierno popular por el camino de la izquierda unida y de la acción de masas: VIII congreso nacional extraordinário del P.C.P., Lima, 27–31 enero 1982.* Lima: P.C.P., Comisión Nacional de Propaganda, 1982. 55 pp.

Partido Comunista Revolucionario [Peru]. *Democracia, Frente Unico y violencia en el marxismo y en el Peru actual: La reunificación del PCR/Partido Comunista Revolucionario.* Lima: Comisión de Prensa Nacional, 1982. 115 pp.

Prado Redondez, Raimundo. *El marxismo de Mariátegui.* Lima: Amaru Editores, 1982. 109 pp.

Robbins, Carla Anne. *The Cuban Threat.* New York: McGraw-Hill, 1983. 351 pp.

Rudolph, James D., ed. *Nicaragua: A Country Study.* 2nd ed. Washington, D.C.: American University Foreign Area Studies, 1982. 278 pp.

Sarkis, Charles, ed. *What Went Wrong? Articles and Letters on the U.S. Communist Left in the 1970's.* New York: United Labor Press, 1982. 152 pp.

Shields, Art. *My Shaping-Up Years.* New York: International Publishers, 1983. 240 pp.

Wesson, Robert, and David V. Fleischer. *Brazil in Transition.* New York: Praeger, 1983. 197 pp.

ASIA AND THE PACIFIC

Amin, Samir. *The Future of Maoism.* New York: Monthly Review Press, 1983. 128 pp.

An, Tai Sung. *North Korea in Transition.* Westport, Conn.: Greenwood Press, 1983. 213 pp.

Arnold, Anthony. *Afghanistan's Two-Party Communism.* Stanford, Calif.: Hoover Institution Press, 1983. 246 pp.

Bradsher, Henry. *Afghanistan and the Soviet Union.* Durham, N.C.: Duke University Press, 1983. 324 pp.

Bunge, Frederica M., ed. *Japan: A Country Study.* 4th ed. Washington, D.C.: American University Foreign Area Studies, 1983. 494 pp.

Chandler, David P. *A History of Cambodia.* Boulder, Colo.: Westview Press, 1983. 195 pp.

_____, and Ben Kiernan, eds. *Revolution and Its Aftermath in Kampuchea.* New Haven, Conn.: Yale University, Southeast Asia Studies, 1983. 319 pp.

Communist Party of India (Marxist). *Documents of the Eleventh Congress of the CPI (M), Vijayawada, 26–31 January 1982.* New Delhi: Communist Party of India (Marxist), [1982]. 408 pp.

_____. *Political-Organisational Report of the Eleventh Congress of the CPI (M).* New Delhi: Communist Party of India (Marxist), 1982. 201 pp.

Communist Party of India (Marxist-Leninist). *Towards a New Phase of Spring Thunder: Evaluation of the CPI (ML) in Its Historical Background.* [India]: Central Reorganization Committee, 1982. 164 pp.

Corsino, Macarthur F. *Communist Revolutionary Movement as an International State-Actor: A Case of the PKI-Aidit.* Singapore: Maruzen Asia, 1982. 229 pp.

Davis-Friedman, Deborah. *Long Lives: Chinese Elderly and the Communist Revolution*. Cambridge, Mass.: Harvard University Press, 1983. 140 pp.

Diamond, E. Grey. *Inside China Today: A Western View*. New York: W. W. Norton, 1983. 272 pp.

Duiker, William J. *Vietnam: Nation in Revolution*. Boulder, Colo.: Westview Press, 1983. 171 pp.

The Far East and Australasia, 1982–1983. 14th ed. London: Europa Publications, 1982. 1410 pp.

Feigon, Lee. *Chen Duxiu: Founder of the Chinese Communist Party*. Princeton, N.J.: Princeton University Press, 1983. 279 pp.

Gasster, Michael. *China's Struggle to Modernize*. New York: Knopf, 1983. 212 pp.

Gatu, Dagfinn. *Toward Revolution: War, Social Change, and the Communist Party in North China, 1937–45*. Stockholm: Stockholm University, Institute of Oriental Studies, 1983. 353 pp.

Ho, Chih-cheng. *Fourth Constitution of Communist China*. Republic of China: World Anti-Communist League, China Chapter, 1983. 72 pp.

Hsu, Immanuel C. Y. *China Without Mao: The Search for a New Order*. New York: Oxford University Press, 1983. 212 pp.

Hu, Chi-hsi. *L'Armée rouge et l'ascension de Mao*. Paris: Editions de l'Ecole des Hautes Etudes en Sciences Sociales, 1982. 272 pp.

Huynh, L'am. *Le Viet-Nam à l'heure communiste*. Paris: Pensée Universelle, 1982. 222 pp.

Isaacs, Arnold R. *Without Honor: Defeat in Vietnam and Cambodia*. Baltimore, Md.: Johns Hopkins University Press, 1983. 559 pp.

Ishida, Takeshi. *Japanese Political Culture: Change and Continuity*. New Brunswick, N.J.: Transaction Books, 1983. 173 pp.

Kapur, Jagdish C. *India: An Uncommitted Society*. New Delhi: Vikas, 1982. 229 pp.

Kim, C. I. Eugene, and B. C. Koh, eds. *Journey to North Korea: Personal Perceptions*. Berkeley: University of California, Institute of East Asian Studies, 1983. 164 pp.

Kodikara, Shelton U. *Foreign Policy in Sri Lanka: A Third World Perspective*. Atlantic Highlands, N.J.: Humanities Press, 1982. 224 pp.

Lee, Chong-Sik. *Revolutionary Struggle in Manchuria: Chinese Communism and Soviet Interest, 1922–1945*. Berkeley: University of California Press, 1983. 219 pp.

Lim, Un (pseud.). *The Founding of a Dynasty in North Korea*. Tokyo: Jiyusha, 1982. 329 pp.

MacFarquhar, Roderick. *The Origins of the Cultural Revolution: The Great Leap Forward, 1958–1960*. New York: Columbia University Press, 1983. Vol. 2. 170 pp.

Mackerras, Colin. *Modern China: A Chronology from 1842 to the Present*. San Francisco: Freeman, 1982. 703 pp.

Mathews, Jay, and Linda Mathews. *One Billion: A China Chronicle*. New York: Random House, 1983. 383 pp.

Morse, Ronald A., ed. *The Limits of Reform in China*. Boulder, Colo.: Westview Press, 1983. 155 pp.

Mosher, Steven. *Broken Earth: The Rural Chinese*. New York: Free Press, 1983. 317 pp.

Mukerjee, H. *Under Communism's Crimson Colors: Reflections on Marxism, India and the World Scene*. New Delhi: People's Publishing House, 1982. 329 pp.

Nee, Victor, and David Mozingo, eds. *State and Society in Contemporary China*. Ithaca, N.Y.: Cornell University Press, 1983. 303 pp.

Nossiter, Thomas J. *Communism in Kerala: A Study of Political Adaptation*. Berkeley: University of California Press, 1982. 426 pp.

Peng, Shu-tse. *L'Envol du communisme en Chine: Mémoires de Peng Shuzhi*. Paris: Gallimard, 1983. 490 pp.

Scalapino, Robert A., and Jun-yop Kim, eds. *North Korea Today: Strategic and Domestic Issues*. Berkeley: University of California, Institute of East Asian Studies, 1983. 370 pp.

Srivastava, M. P. *The Korean Conflict*. New Delhi: Prentice-Hall of India, 1982. 120 pp.

Thaxton, Ralph. *China Turned Right Side Up: Revolutionary Legitimacy in the Peasant World*. New Haven, Conn.: Yale University Press, 1983. 286 pp.

Thomas, Raju G. C., ed. *The Great-Power Triangle and Asian Security*. Lexington, Mass.: Lexington Books, 1983. 200 pp.

U.S. Central Intelligence Agency. Directorate of Intelligence. *Directory of Chinese Officials: Provincial Organizations.* Washington, D.C.: National Technical Information Service, August 1983. 254 pp.

———. *Directory of Officials of the Democratic People's Republic of Korea.* Washington, D.C.: National Technical Information Service, September 1983. 124 pp.

Van Canh, Nguyen. *Vietnam Under Communism, 1975–1982.* Stanford, Calif.: Hoover Institution Press, 1983. 328 pp.

Van Dyk, Jere. *In Afghanistan: An American Odyssey.* New York: Coward McCann, 1983. 253 pp.

Wang Kao et al. *Advising the Chinese Communists to Abandon Communism.* Taipei: Kuang Lu Publishing Service, 1983. 113 pp.

Wedel, Yuangrat. *The Thai Radicals and the Communist Party.* Singapore: Maruzen Asia, 1983. 87 pp.

Weiner, Myron. *India at the Polls, 1980: A Study of the Parliamentary Elections.* Washington, D.C.: American Enterprise Institute, 1983. 198 pp.

Yahuda, Michael. *Towards the End of Isolationism: China's Foreign Policy After Mao.* London: Macmillan Press, 1983. 279 pp.

EASTERN EUROPE

Albright, Madeline K. *Poland: The Role of the Press in Political Change.* New York: Praeger, 1983. 147 pp.

Ash, Timothy. *Und willst du nicht mein Bruder sein? Die DDR heute.* Hamburg: Spiegel Verlag, 1982. 207 pp.

Baichinski, Kostadin. *Georgi Dimitrov on the Leading Role of the Working Class and the Communist Party.* Sofia: Sofia Press, 1982. 95 pp.

Bailey, Anthony. *Along the Edge of the Forest: An Iron Curtain Journey.* New York: Random House, 1983. 332 pp.

Banac, Ivo, ed. *The Effects of World War I. The Class War After the Great War: The Rise of Communist Parties in East Central Europe, 1918–1921.* Boulder, Colo.: Social Science Monographs, 1983. 282 pp.

Belousova, R. A., and G. B. Khromushinal, eds. *Kollektivnyi opyt sovershenstvovaniia upravleniia sotsialisticheskoi ekonomikoi: Po materialam s'ezdov kommunisticheskikh i rabochikh partii.* Moscow: Ekonomika, 1983. 231 pp.

Bolgarska Komunisticheska Partiia. Kongres (12th, 1981, Sofia). *XII s'ezd Bolgarskoi kommunisticheskoi partii: Sofia, 31 marta–4 aprelia 1981 goda.* Moscow: Politizdat, 1982. 239 pp.

Brumberg, Abraham, ed. *Poland: Genesis of a Revolution.* New York: Random House, 1983. 322 pp.

Carlton, David, and Carlo Schaerf. *South-Eastern Europe After Tito: A Powder-Keg for the 1980s?* New York: St. Martin's Press, 1983. 211 pp.

Childs, David. *The GDR: Moscow's German Ally.* London: Allen & Unwin, 1983. 346 pp.

Clissold, Stephen. *Djilas: The Progress of a Revolutionary.* New York: Universe Books, 1983. 352 pp.

Csaba, László. *Economic Mechanism in the GDR and in Czechoslovakia.* Budapest: Hungarian Scientific Council for World Economy, 1983. 140 pp.

Curry, Jane L., ed. *Dissent in Eastern Europe.* New York: Praeger, 1983. 227 pp.

Dahm, Helmut. *Der gescheiterte Ausbruch: Entideolisierung und ideologische Gegenreformation in Osteuropa (1960–1980).* Baden-Baden: Nomos, 1982. 938 pp.

Erbe, Günter. *Arbeiterklasse und Intelligenz in der DDR.* Berlin: Westdeutscher Verlag, 1982. 224 pp.

Fehér, Ferenc, and Agnes Heller. *Hungary 1956 Revisited.* Winchester, Mass.: Allen & Unwin, 1983. 174 pp.

Futaky, István. *Ungarn: Ein kommunistisches Wunderland?* Reinbek bei Hamburg: Rowohlt Taschenbuch Verlag, 1983. 187 pp.

Honecker, Erich. *Entwickelter Sozialismus und Gewerkschaften: Aus Reden und Schriften, 1971–82.* East Berlin: Verlag Tribüne, 1982. 368 pp.

Jelinek, Yeshayahu A. *The Lust for Power: Nationalism, Slovakia, and the Communists, 1918–1948.* Boulder, Colo.: East European Monographs, 1983. 185 pp.

Keefe, Eugene K., ed. *East Germany: A Country Study.* 2nd ed. Washington, D.C.: Government Printing Office, 1982. 348 pp.

Kemp-Welch, A. *The Birth of Solidarity: The Gdánsk Negotiations, 1980.* New York: St. Martin's Press, 1983. 213 pp.

Khadzhinikolov, Veselin, et al. *Georgi Dimitrov: Biograficheski ocherk.* Moscow: Progress, 1982. 413 pp.

Lewis, William J. *The Warsaw Pact: Arms, Doctrine and Strategy.* New York: McGraw-Hill, 1982. 471 pp.

Lueers, Hartwig. *Das Polizeirecht in der DDR.* Cologne: Verlag Wissenschaft und Politik, 1982. 156 pp.

Michev, Dobrin, et al. *Georgi Dimitrov: Biografiia.* Sofia: Partizdat, 1982. 663 pp.

Mihajlov, Mihajlo. *Underground Notes.* 2nd rev. ed. New Rochelle, N.Y.: Caratzas Brothers, 1982. 206 pp.

North Atlantic Treaty Organization. *The CMEA Five-Year Plans (1981–1985) in a New Perspective: Planned and Non-planned Economies*: Brussels: NATO Economics and Information Directorates, 1983. 309 pp.

Osadczuk, Bogdan. *Weisser Adler, Kreuz, und rote Fahne.* Zurich: *Neue Zürcher Zeitung*, 1982. 203 pp.

Radde, Jürgen. *Die Aussenpolitische Führungselite der DDR.* Cologne: Verlag Wissenschaft und Politik, 1982. 240 pp.

Sanford, George. *Polish Communism in Crisis.* New York: St. Martin's Press, 1983. 250 pp.

Schönburg, K.-H., ed. *Errichtung des Arbeiter- und Bauern-Staates der DDR, 1945–1949.* East Berlin: Staatsverlag der DDR, 1983. 297 pp.

Sodaro, Michael J., and Sharon L. Wolchik, eds. *Foreign and Domestic Policy in Eastern Europe in the 1980s.* New York: St. Martin's Press, 1983. 192 pp.

Sozialistische Einheitspartei Deutschlands. *Die Herausbildung der Kommunistischen Partei Deutschlands im Kampf gegen Imperialismus und Krieg.* East Berlin: Dietz Verlag, 1983. 228 pp.

———. *Wörterbuch des wissenschaftlichen Kommunismus.* East Berlin: Dietz Verlag, 1982. 421 pp.

———. Institut für Marxismus-Leninismus beim ZK d. SED. *Dokumente und Materialen der Zusammenarbeit zwischen der Sozialistischen Einheitspartei Deutschlands und der Kommunistischen Partei Tschechoslowakei, 1976 bis 1981.* East Berlin: Dietz Verlag, 1982. 274 pp.

Surman, Rolf. *Die Münzenberg-Legende.* Cologne: Böhlau Verlag, 1983. 307 pp.

Staar, Richard F. *La Europa comunista: Economia y sociedad.* Madrid: Editorial Playar, 1983. 324 pp.

Szajkowski, Bogdan. *Next to God . . . Poland: Politics and Religion in Contemporary Poland.* New York: St. Martin's Press, 1983. 258 pp.

Tampke, Jürgen. *The People's Republics of Eastern Europe.* New York: St. Martin's Press, 1983. 178 pp.

Touraine, Alain, et al. *Solidarity. The Analysis of a Social Movement: Poland.* New York: Cambridge University Press, 1983. 203 pp.

U.S. Central Intelligence Agency. *Directory of Officials of the Hungarian People's Republic.* Washington, D.C.: National Foreign Assessment Center, 1982. 154 pp.

Wädekin, Karl Eugen. *Agrarian Policies in Communist Europe.* Totowa, N.J.: Allanheld, Osmun, 1982. 324 pp.

Weydenthal, Jan B. de; Bruce D. Porter; and Kevin Devlin. *The Polish Drama, 1980–1982.* Lexington, Mass.: Lexington Books, 1983. 351 pp.

Winkler, Karl. *Made in the GDR: Jugendszenen aus Ost-Berlin.* West Berlin: Oberbaum Verlag, 1983. 202 pp.

Woodall, Jean, ed. *Policy and Politics in Contemporary Poland: Reform, Failure, Crisis.* London: Frances Pinter, 1982. 200 pp.

Zhivkov, Todor. *Osnovni polozheniia na partiinata kontseptsiia za noviia Kodeks na truda: Utvurdeni ot plenuma na TSK na BKP, sustoial se na 29 i 30 noemvri 1982 godina.* Sofia: Partizdat, 1982. 142 pp.

USSR

Andropov, Yuri. *Izbrannye rechi i statii.* Moscow: Politizdat, 1983. 320 pp.

Arbatov, Georgi A., and Willem Oltmans. *The Soviet Viewpoint.* New York: Dodd, Mead, 1983. 219 pp.

Barron, John. *KGB Today: The Hidden Hand.* New York: Reader's Digest Press, 1983. 489 pp.

Beichman, Arnold, and Mikhail S. Bernstam. *Andropov: New Challenge to the West.* New York: Stein and Day, 1983. 264 pp.

Bergson, Adam, and Herbert S. Levine, eds. *The Soviet Economy: Toward the Year 2000.* Winchester, Mass.: Allen & Unwin, 1983. 452 pp.

Bogorad, V. A., ed. *Kommunisty i trudiashchiesia krupnykh gorodov v borb'e za sotsial'nyi i nauchno-tekhnicheskii progress.* Moscow: Nauka, 1982. 462 pp.

Brown, Archie, and Michael Kaser, eds. *Soviet Policy for the 1980s.* Bloomington: Indiana University Press, 1983. 282 pp.

Byrnes, Robert F., ed. *After Brezhnev: Sources of Soviet Conduct in the 1980's.* Bloomington: Indiana University Press, 1983. 457 pp.

Chernenko, K. U. *Avangardnaya rol' partii kommunistov.* Moscow: Mys'l, 1982. 463 pp.

Cockburn, Andrew, *The Threat: Inside the Soviet Military Machine.* New York: Random House, 1983. 338 pp.

Dunlop, John B. *The Faces of Contemporary Russian Nationalism.* Princeton, N.J.: Princeton University Press, 1983. 361 pp.

Ebon, Martin. *The Andropov File.* New York: McGraw-Hill, 1983. 284 pp.

Edmonds, Robin. *Soviet Foreign Policy: The Brezhnev Years.* New York: Oxford University Press, 1983. 285 pp.

Gélard, Patrice. *Le Parti communiste de l'Union soviétique.* Que sais-je? no. 2016. Paris: Presses Universitaires de France, 1982.

Goldman, Marshall I. *USSR in Crisis: The Failure of an Economic System.* New York: W. W. Norton, 1983. 210 pp.

Golitsyn, Anatoliy. *New Lies for Old: The Communist Strategy of Deception and Misinformation.* New York: Dodd, Mead, 1983.

Grigorenko, Petr G. *Memoirs.* New York: W. W. Norton, 1982. 462 pp.

Hansson, Carola, and Karen Liden (interviewers). *Moscow Women.* New York: Pantheon, 1983. 194 pp.

Hayward, Max. *Writers in Russia, 1917–1978.* San Diego: Harcourt Brace Jovanovich, 1983. 340 pp.

Hill, Ronald J., and Peter Frank. *The Soviet Communist Party.* 2nd ed. London: Allen & Unwin, 1983. 168 pp.

Hoffman, Eric P., and Robbin F. Laird. *The Scientific Technological Revolution and Soviet Foreign Policy.* Ithaca, N.Y.: Cornell University Press, 1982. 215 pp.

Hosmer, Stephen, and Thomas Wolfe. *Soviet Policy and Practice Towards Third World Conflicts.* Lexington, Mass.: Lexington Books, 1983. 318 pp.

Kauppi, Mark V., and R. Craig Nation. *The Soviet Union and the Middle East in the 1980s.* Lexington, Mass.: Lexington Books, 1983. 292 pp.

Kerblay, Basile. *Modern Soviet Society.* New York: Pantheon, 1983. 321 pp.

Klimov, Iu. *Stories About the Party of Communists.* Moscow: Progress, 1982. 118 pp.

Kommunisticheskaiia Partiia Sovetskogo Soiuza. *KPSS o formirovanii novogo cheloveka: Sbornik dokumentov i materialov, 1965–1981.* 2nd rev. ed. Moscow: Politizdat, 1982. 686 pp.

Kopelev, Lev. *East My Sorrows: A Memoir.* New York: Random House, 1983. 256 pp.

Laqueur, Walter. *The Pattern of Soviet Conduct in the Third World.* New York: Praeger, 1983. 250 pp.

Luttwak, Edward N. *The Grand Strategy of the Soviet Union*. New York: St. Martin's Press, 1983. 242 pp.

Mace, James E. *Communism and the Dilemmas of National Liberation: National Communism in Soviet Ukraine, 1918–1933*. Cambridge, Mass.: Harvard Ukrainian Research Institute, 1983. 334 pp.

Matveeva, G. S., ed. *Mongol'skii revoliuts'ionnii soyuz molodezhy*. Moscow: Nauka, 1983. 248 pp.

Medvedev, Roy. *Khrushchev: A Biography*. New York: Doubleday, 1983. 292 pp.

Medvedev, Zhores A. *Andropov*. New York: W. W. Norton, 1983. 227 pp.

Misiunas, Romauld J., and Rein Taagepera. *The Baltic States: Years of Independence, 1940–1980*. Berkeley: University of California Press, 1983. 334 pp.

Moreton, Edwina, and Gerald Segal, eds. *Soviet Strategy Toward Western Europe*. Winchester, Mass.: Allen & Unwin, 1983. 240 pp.

Okladnikov, A. P., et al., eds. *Istoriia Mongol'skoi Narodnoi Respubliki*. 3rd rev. ed. Moscow: Nauka, 1983. 661 pp.

Parrott, Bruce. *Politics and Technology in the Soviet Union*. Cambridge, Mass.: MIT Press, 1983. 428 pp.

Radziejowski, Janusz. *The Communist Party of Western Ukraine, 1919–1929*. Edmondon, Alberta: Canadian Institute of Ukrainian Studies, 1983. 224 pp.

Razumov, YE. Z. *Problemy kadrovoi politiki KPSS*. Moscow: Politizdat, 1983. 192 pp.

Romanov, G. V. *Izbrannye rechi i statii*. Moscow: Politizdat, 1983. 640 pp.

Schmid, Karin, et al., eds. *Sowjetunion, 1982/83: Ereignisse, Probleme, Perspektiven*. Munich: Carl Hanser Verlag, 1983. 366 pp.

Solovyov, Vladimir, and Elena Klepikova. *Yuri Andropov: A Secret Passage into the Kremlin*. New York: Macmillan, 1983. 320 pp.

The Soviet Union: Socialist or Social Imperialist? Essays Toward the Debate on the Nature of Soviet Society (compiled by the editors of *Communist*). Chicago: RCP Publications, 1983. 210 pp.

Suvorov, Viktor. *Inside the Soviet Army*. New York: Macmillan, 1982. 296 pp.

———. *The "Liberators": My Life in the Soviet Army*. New York: W. W. Norton, 1983. 202 pp.

Toman, B. A. *Istoriografiia istorii Kommunisticheskoi Partii Latvii*. Riga: Avots, 1983. 324 pp.

Tuominen, Arvo. *The Bells of the Kremlin: An Experience in Communism*. Hanover, N.H.: University Press of New England, 1983. 333 pp.

Tumarkin, Nina. *Lenin Lives! The Lenin Cult in Soviet Russia*. Cambridge, Mass.: Harvard University Press, 1983. 315 pp.

Ulam, Adam. *Dangerous Relations: The Soviet Union in World Politics, 1970–1982*. New York: Oxford University Press, 1983. 325 pp.

Ustinov, D. F. *Serving the Country and the Communist Cause*. New York: Pergamon Press, 1983. 114 pp.

Valenta, Jiri, and W. C. Potter, eds. *Soviet Decisionmaking for National Security*. Winchester, Mass.: Allen & Unwin, 1983. 400 pp.

Valkenier, Elizabeth Kridl. *The Soviet Union and the Third World: An Economic Bind*. New York: Praeger, 1983. 188 pp.

Vigor, P. H. *Soviet Blitzkrieg Theory*. New York: St. Martin's Press, 1983. 218 pp.

Zemtsov, Ilya. *Andropov*. Jerusalem: Israel Research Institute of Contemporary Society, 1983. 252 pp.

WESTERN EUROPE

Alba, Victor. *The Communist Party in Spain*. New Brunswick, N.J.: Transaction Books, 1983. 475 pp.

Anderson, Gerald D. *Fascists, Communists, and the National Government: Civil Liberties in Great Britain, 1931–37*. Columbia: University of Missouri Press, 1983. 243 pp.

Aragon, Louis. *Les Communistes*. Paris: Messidor/Temps Actuels, 1982. 2 vols.

Arangueren, José Luís L. *España: Una meditación política*. Barcelona: Editorial Ariel, 1983. 138 pp.

Bahne, Siegfried, ed. *Les Partis communistes des pays latins et l'Internationale communiste dans les années 1923–1927.* Boston: D. Reidel, 1983. 703 pp.

Barbieri, Orazio. *La fede e la ragione: Ricordi e riflesioni di un comunista.* Milan: La Pietra, 1982. 357 pp.

Beaunez, Roger. *Les Municipales: Lois nouvelles, élections et organisation communale.* Paris: Syros, 1983. 192 pp.

Belligni, Silvano. *La giraffa a il licorno: Il PCI dagli anni '70 al nuovo decennio.* Milan: Agneli, 1983. 382 pp.

Berlinguer, Enrico, et al. *PCI e la cultura di massa.* Rome: Savelli, 1982. 147 pp.

Boltanski, Luc. *Les Cadres: La Formation d'un groupe social.* Paris: Editions de Minuit, 1982. 523 pp.

Boris, Peter, ed. *Die sich lossagten: Stichworte zu Leben und Werk von 461 ex-Kommunisten.* Cologne: Markus Verlag, 1983. 314 pp.

Calabro, Gian Pietro. *Antonio Gramsci: La "transizione" politica.* Naples: ESI, 1982. 110 pp.

Claudin, Fernando. *Santiago Carrillo.* Barcelona: Planeta, 1983. 387 pp.

Coudou, Roger. *La Cabochard: Mémoires d'un communiste, 1925–82.* Paris: La Découverte/Maspero. 1983. 241 pp.

Elwell, Charles. *Tracts Beyond the Times: A Brief Guide to the Communist or Revolutionary Marxist Press.* London: Social Affairs Unit, 1983. 32 pp.

Esteban, Jorge de. *Los partidos políticos en la España actual.* Barcelona: Planeta, 1982. 229 pp.

Estruch, Tobella Joan. *El PCE en la clandestinidad, 1939–56.* Madrid: Siglo XXI, 1982. 258 pp.

Flores d'Arcais, Paolo. *Il dubbio e la certezza. Nei dintorni del marxismo e oltre (1971–1981).* Milan: Sugarco, 1982. 270 pp.

Fredet, Jean-Gabriel. *Les Patrons face à la gauche.* Paris: Editions Ramsay, 1982. 430 pp.

Gallagher, Tom. *Portugal: Twentieth Century Interpretation.* Manchester: Manchester University Press, 1983. 278 pp.

Galluzzi, Carlo. *La Svolta: Gli anni crucial del Partito Comunista Italiano.* Milan: Sperling & Kupfer, 1983. 263 pp.

Giglio, Tommaso. *Berlinguer o il potere solitario.* Milan: Rizzoli, 1982. 218 pp.

Graham, Lawrence, and Douglas L. Wheeler, eds. *In Search of Modern Portugal: The Revolution and Its Consequences.* Madison: University of Wisconsin Press, 1983. 380 pp.

Hamon, Hervé. *Le Deuxième gauche: Histoire intellectuelle et politique de la CFDT.* Paris: Editions Ramsay, 1982. 446 pp.

Käselitz, Hella. *Kommunistische Parteien in der Hauptländern des Kapitals (1944/45–1969/70).* East Berlin: Dietz Verlag, 1982. 316 pp.

Kelly, Petra, and Joe Leinen. *Prinzip Leben, Oekopax: Die neue Kraft.* West Berlin: Verlag Olle & Wolter, 1982. 160 pp.

La Torre, Pio. *La ragioni di una vita.* Bari: De Donato, 1982. 235 pp.

Lefranc, George. *Visages du mouvement ouvrier français.* Paris: Presses Universitaires de France, 1982. 232 pp.

Lemaître, Maurice. *Journal d'un militant.* Paris: Lemaître/Les Lettres Libres, 1982. 260 pp.

Levin, I. B. *Robochee dvizheniie v Italii, 1966–1976 gg.* Moscow: Nauka, 1983. 336 pp.

Llorens Castillo, Carlos. *Antieurocomunismo: Sobre el X⁰ Congreso del PCE.* Valencia: Autor, 1981. 231 pp.

Machin, Howard, ed. *National Communism in Western Europe: A Third Way to Socialism?* New York: Methuen, 1983. 232 pp.

Maren-Griesbach, Manon. *Philosophe der Grünen.* Munich: Olzog, 1982. 134 pp.

McHale, Vincent E., and Sharon Skowronski, eds. *Political Parties of Europe.* 2 vols. Westport, Conn.: Greenwood Press, 1983. 1297 pp.

Mujal-Leon, Eusebio. *Communism and Political Change in Spain.* Bloomington: Indiana University Press, 1983. 288 pp.

Nyrop, Richard F., ed. *Federal Republic of Germany: A Country Study.* 2nd ed. Washington, D.C.: American University Foreign Area Studies, 1983. 454 pp.

Padovani, Marcelle. *Vivre avec le terrorisme: La Modèle italien.* Paris: Calmann-Lévy, 1982. 252 pp.

Pansa, Giampaolo. *Ottobre, Addio: Viaggio fra i communisti italiani.* Milan: Arnoldo Mondadori, 1982. 303 pp.

Parti Communiste Français. *Construire le socialism aux couleurs de la France.* Paris: Editions Sociales, 1982. 229 pp.

Partito Comunista Italiano. *Economia, stato, pace: L'iniziativa e le proposte del PCI.* Rome: Editore Riuniti, 1983. 172 pp.

―――. *PCI-PCUS: Due mesi di polemiche.* Milan: Teti, 1982. 240 pp.

Piccone, Paul. *Italian Marxism.* Berkeley: University of California Press, 1983. 206 pp.

Priester, Karin. *Hat der Eurokommunismus eine Zukunft?* Munich: H. C. Beck, 1982. 236 pp.

Pronier, Raymond. *Les Municipalités communistes.* Paris: Editions Balland, 1983. 475 pp.

Ramsay, Robert. *The Corsican Time-Bomb.* Manchester: Manchester University Press, 1983. 245 pp.

Raufer, Xavier. *Terrorisme: Maintenant la France? La Guerre des partis communistes combattants.* Paris: Garnier, 1982. 336 pp.

Robrieux, Philippe. *Histoire intérieure du Parti communiste, 1972–1982.* Paris: Fayard, 1982. 544 pp.

Ronchey, Alberto. *Chi vincerà in Italia? La democrazia bloccata, i comunisti e il "fattore K."* Milan: Arnoldo Mondadori, 1982. 190 pp.

Rosenhaft, Eve. *Beating The Fascists? The German Communists and Political Violence, 1929–1933.* New York: Cambridge University Press, 1983. 273 pp.

Rubenstein, W. D. *The Left, the Right and the Jews.* London: Croom Helm, 1982. 234 pp.

Sagnes, Jean. *Le "Midi Rouge": Mythe et réalité.* Paris: Editions Anthropos, 1982. 310 pp.

Saligue, Marc P. *Principe autonome: Au-dela du principe communiste pour l'abolition de l'esclavage salarie.* Paris: Les Cahiers Marx Envers et Contre Marx, 1983. 109 pp.

Salsano, Alfredo. *Comunismo e socialdemocrazia.* Bari: Laterza, 1982. 819 pp.

Salzman, Mojshe. *Als Mojshe Kommunist war.* Darmstadt: Darmstädter Blätter, 1982. 401 pp.

Santen, J. van. *Weimar, 1933: Demokratie tussen fascisme en kommunisme.* Nijmegen: SUN, 1983. 232 pp.

Shipley, Peter. *The Militant Tendency: Trotskyism in the Labour Party.* Surrey, U.K.: Foreign Affairs Publication, 1983. 179 pp.

Sobreques i Callico, Jaime. *El pactisme a Catalunya.* Barcelona: Ediciones 62, 1983. 123 pp.

Souchy, Agustín B. *With the Peasants of Aragon: Libertarian Communism in the Liberated Areas.* Orkney, U.K.: Cienfuegos, 1982.

Spriano, Paolo. *I comunisti europei e Stalin.* Turin: G. Einaudi, 1983. 303 pp.

Stöss, Richard, ed. *Parteien Handbuch: Die Parteien der Bundesrepublik Deutschland, 1945–1980.* Opladen: Westdeutscher Verlag, 1983. Vol. 1. 1310 pp.

Strübel, Michael. *Neue Wege der italienischen Kommunisten: Zur Aussen- und Sicherheitspolitik der KPI.* Baden-Baden: Nomos, 1982. 424 pp.

Thompson, Wayne C. *Western Europe, 1982.* Washington, D.C.: Stryker-Post Publications, 1982. 404 pp.

Townshend, Charles. *Political Violence in Ireland: Government Resistance Since 1848.* New York: Oxford University Press, 1984. 454 pp.

Turban, Manfred. *Die wirtschaftspolitischen Vorstellungen der Französischen Kommunistischen Partei in den siebziger Jahren.* West Berlin: Osteuropa Institut, 1983. 276 pp.

Verdes-Leroux, Jeanine. *Le Parti communiste, les intellectuels et la culture (1944–1956).* Paris: Fayard, 1983. 585 pp.

Wall, Irwin M. *French Communism in the Era of Stalin.* Westport, Conn.: Greenwood Press, 1983. 268 pp.

Weber, Hermann. *Kommunismus in Deutschland, 1918–1945.* Darmstadt: Wissenschaftliche Buchgesellschaft, 1983. 187 pp.

Wilson, Frank L. *French Political Parties Under the Fifth Republic.* New York: Praeger, 1982. 285 pp.

Index of Biographies

Alia, Ramiz	Albania	1983, pp. 247–48
Aliev, Geidar A.	USSR	1983, p. 364
Andropov, Yuri V.	USSR	1983, p. 364
Bakhdash, Khalid	Syria	1984, pp. 68–69
Berlinguer, Enrico	Italy	1983, pp. 454–55
Bishop, Maurice	Grenada	1982, p. 106
Borge Martínez, Tomás	Nicaragua	1982, pp. 129–30
Brezhnev, Leonid I.	USSR	1983, pp. 365–66
Çarçani, Adil	Albania	1983, pp. 248–49
Carrillo, Santiago	Spain	1983, p. 474
Cayetano Carpio, Salvador	El Salvador	1983, pp. 89–90
Chandra, Romesh	India	1979, p. 449
Chebrikov, Viktor M.	USSR	1983, p. 366
Chernenko, Konstantin U.	USSR	1979, p. 450
Deng Xiaoping	China–PRC	1983, pp. 168–69
Dolanc, Stane	Yugoslavia	1979, p. 450
Dolgikh, Vladimir I.	USSR	1983, p. 365
Fedorchuk, Vitali V.	USSR	1983, pp. 366–67
Fuwa, Tetsuzo	Japan	1983, pp. 182–83
Gorbachev, Mikhail S.	USSR	1980, p. 449
Grabski, Tadeusz	Poland	1983, pp. 318–19
Handal, Shafik Jorge	El Salvador	1983, p. 90
Heng Samrin	Kampuchea	1980, p. 449
Herrmann, Joachim	GDR	1979, p. 451
Hu Yaobang	China–PRC	1981, pp. 464–65
Iglesias, Gerardo	Spain	1983, p. 475
Jaruzelski, Wojciech	Poland	1982, pp. 449–50
Kania, Stanislaw	Poland	1981, p. 463
Karmal, Babrak	Afghanistan	1980, p. 450

Kim Chong-Il	Korea	1981, p. 465
Kim Il-song	Korea	1983, p. 191
Kiselev, Tikhon Y.	USSR	1981, pp. 463–64
Langer, Felicia	Israel	1984, p. 34
Ligachev, Egor K.	USSR	1984, p. 401
Machel, Samora Moises	Mozambique	1982, p. 42
Marchais, Georges	France	1983, pp. 427–28
Mengistu Haile Mariam	Ethiopia	1982, pp. 17–18
Muhyi al-Din, Khalid	Egypt	1984, pp. 20–21
Ortega Saavedra, Daniel	Nicaragua	1982, p. 130
Ortega Saavedra, Humberto	Nicaragua	1982, p. 130
Petkoff, Teodoro	Venezuela	1982, pp. 151–52
Pol Pot	Kampuchea	1979, p. 451
Romanov, Grigori V.	USSR	1984, p. 401
Santos, José Eduardo dos	Angola	1983, pp. 9–10
Solomentsev, Mikhail S.	USSR	1984, pp. 401–2
Sychev, Vyacheslav V.	USSR (CMEA)	1984, p. 416
Tikhonov, Nikolai A.	USSR	1980, pp. 450–51
Truong, Chinh	Vietnam	1984, pp. 285–86
Vorotnikov, Vitali I.	USSR	1984, p. 402
Wheelock Román, Jaime	Nicaragua	1982, pp. 130–31
Zhao Ziyang	China–PRC	1981, p. 464

Index of Names

Aaen, Frank, 453
Aalto, Arvo, xxi, 458–63 *passim*
Aarons, Eric, 197
'Abassi, 'Abd al-Wahhab, 69
Abbas, Mahmud, 36
Abbud, Ibrahim, 62
Abdallah, Amir, 28
Abdullah, Abu, 55
Abdullah, C. D., 253, 254
Abe, Shintaro, 310, 370
Abrantes, Domingos, 511
Abrasimov, Piotr, 332
Abu Bakar, Dewa, 255
Abu Mayzar, Abd-al-Muhsin, 431
Abu Shakra, Sana, 428
Achenbach, Vera, 470
Aczél, György, 334, 336, 337, 341, 342
Adebayo, O. K., 397
Adedoja, Bola, 432
Adhikari, Man Mohan, xviii, 257, 258
Adjibade, Tiamiou, 14
Adjitorop, Jusuf, xvii, 226
Adorno, Theodor, 493
Adriamanjato, Richard, 428, 433
Adyaa, Gelegiyn, 255
Afanasyev, Viktor G., 387, 399, 432
Afzali, Bahram, 27
Aganbegyan, A., 383
Agca, Mehmet Ali, 306, 307, 392
Agius, John, 498
Agius, Paul, 498, 500
Aguadelo Ríos, John, 104
Aguilar Mora, José Manuel, 153
Aguilar Talamantes, Rafael, 152
Aguirre de Castro, Severo, 428
Ahmadi, Mohammad, 24
Ahmar, Abdullah al-, 36, 67, 68
Ahrens, Dietmar, 477
Aikpe, Michel, 14
Ajajai, Yusuf al-Hassan al-, x, 12
Aksenov, Aleksandr, N., 359, 377, 378
Alayza, Ernesto, 168

Alende, Oscar, 82
Alexandrov, Chudomir, 302
Alfaro, Eloy, 119
Alfonsín, Raúl, 82, 83, 115, 177
Alho, Veikko, 458
Ali, Aruna Asaf, 430
'Ali, Bashir Hadj, 7
Ali, Kamal Hassan, 368
Ali, Salim, 55
Alia, Ramiz, 293–301 *passim*
Aliev, Geidar A., 218, 372, 399
Alladaye, Michel, 14
Allende, Andres Pascal, 96
Allende, Salvador, 142
Almeida, Eduardo de, 90
Almeida, Roberto de, 9, 10, 11
Almeidau, Freddy, 118
Almeyda, Clodomiro, 96, 97
Alocer Villanueva, Jorge, 149, 150
Aloma, Ernesto, 24
Altamini, Salim Obayid, 430
Altamirano, Eli, 154
Altangerel, Bat-Ochirym, 255
Alva, César, 164
Alva Orlandini, Javier, 216
Alvarales, Andrés, 103
Alvarez, Vladimiro, 119
Alvarez Fiallo, Efraín, 118
Alvarez Martínez, Gustavo, 142
Alvarez Moreno, Mercedes, 142, 428
Amaya, René Barrios, 122
Amazonas, João, 90
Ambatielos, Andonis, 481, 483
Amin, Hafizullah, 187
Amir, Izz-al Din Ali, 61
Ammundsen, Kjeld, 454
Amorim, Luisa, 430
Amu'i, Mohammad Ali, 24
An Sung-hak, 237, 239
Anaya Montes, Mélida, 81, 121
Andersen, Gordon Harold, 259, 261, 262
Andersen, Jan, 452
Andrade, Antonío Torres, 164
Andrade, Costa, 9

Andrade, Joaquim Pinto de, 9
Andrade, Mario de, 8
Andreev, Kosta, 432
Andrei, Evgenia, 430
Andrei, Stefan, 342, 361, 367, 368, 369
Andriamanjato, Richard, 433
Andropov, Yuri V., xx, 113, 207, 216, 224, 225, 265, 287–92 *passim*, 307, 313, 318, 319, 342, 369–402 *passim*, 406, 410, 412, 417, 423, 425, 426, 468, 474, 495
Angenfort, Jupp, 470
Anitnov, Vlady, 192
Anozie, Chaika, 6, 52
Ansart, Gustave, 464
Ant, Clara, 90
Antar, Ali Ahmad Nasir, 72
Anthony, Spiro, 200
Antonov, Sergei, 306, 307
Aquino, Benigno S., Jr., 267, 270
Arafat, Yassir, 2, 33, 35, 41, 42, 257, 309, 368, 395
Araneda Briones, Ernesto, 429
Araujo, Jorge, 511
Araujo, Luísa, 511
Araujo, Raul, 9
Arauz, Virgilio, 160
Arbenz, Jacobo, 131
Arboleda, Nathaniel Hill, 160
Arboleda, Pedro León, 104
Arce Castano, Bayardo, 154, 157
Arce-Martínez, Sergio, 433
Archimède, Gerty, 130
Ardón, Sergio Erich, 106, 108
Arenas, Jacobo, 99
Arévalo Burgos, Eduardo, 428
Arias Londoño, Gustavo, 103
Arismendi, Rodney, xvi, 177, 311
Arkhipov, Ivan V., 255, 396, 400
Armstrong, Warwick James, 261
Arnalds, Ragnar, 484
Arokov, Vlado, 192
Arteaga, Miguel, 432

Arthit Kamlangek, 278, 279
Arthur, David George, 261
Ary Yee Chong Tchi-Kan, 53, 54
As'ad, Nasir al-, 44
Asfaw, Legesse, 21, 23
Ashhab, Na'im Abbas, 34–38
    passim
Assad, Hafiz al-, 2, 29, 66, 67,
    368, 395
Assad, Rif'at al-, 67
Assogba, Janvier, 14
Astavin, Sergei T., 452
Atanasov, Atanas, 303
Atanasov, Georgi, 302
Auersperg, Pavel, 426
August, Ernst, 301, 475
Augusto, José Cesar, 10
Aurich, Eberhard, 322
Austin, Hudson, 124, 126
Avakian, Bob, 175
Avanesian, Gagig, 24
Averyanov, Boris, 429
Aviles López, Olga, 428
Awdah, Dhamin, 34
Axen, Hermann, 322, 333, 398
Ayo, Eleanor Matilda, 261
Azcárate, Manuel, 515
Azim, Mohammed Abdul, 192
Aziz, Abdul, 431
Aziz Mohamed, Nazri, 255
Azonhiho, Martin, 14, 15

Baba, Sayed, 187
Babikar, Ali al-Tijani Al-Tayyib,
    61
Bachmann, Kurt, 470
Ba Dhib, Ali Abd al-Razzaq, 73,
    428
Baibakov, Nikolai, K., 382, 383,
    397, 400
Bain, Fitzroy, 125
Bain, Norris, 124, 125
Bains, Hardial, 91
Bajbouj, Mohammed J., 428
Bajbuj, Jabir, 68
Bakhdash, Khalid, xii, 29, 41,
    65–69 passim, 311, 398
Bakin, Boris V., 265
Bakir, Mohammed, 431
Bakker, Marcus, 502
Bakr, Ibrahim, 65, 68
Balaguer, Joaquín, 117
Balandin, Yuri, N., 400
Baldrige, Malcolm, 216, 219,
    341
Balev, Milko, 302, 303, 311
Balla, Vital, 428

Ballantyne, Edith, 429
Ballesteros, Jaime, 371, 515
Balsacchino, Anthony, 498
Balsemão, Francis Pinto, 512
Baltzersen, Bjarne, 505
Baluku, Beqir, 298
Balweg, Conrado, 273
Banana, Canaan S., 216
Banc, Iosif, 361
Bandaranaike, Sirimavo, 275
Bangoura, Facinet, 431
Banias, Yiannis, xxii
Bannikov, Nikolai V., 378
Banzar, Jambalyn, 257
Baquisa, Pedro, 270
Barabás, Miklós, 200, 430
Barcena, Aurora, 430
Barcesat, Eduardo, 433
Barcikowski, Kazimierz, 343
Barmyantsev, Yevgeny, 391
Barnes, Jack, 175
Bárnica, Edgardo Paz, 143
Barr, Andrew, 487
Barrantes Lingán, Alfonso,
    164–69 passim
Barrenechea, Ramiro, 86
Barret, Gervais, 53, 54
Barulli, Umberto, 514
Baryalai, Mahmoud, 186, 188
Baryshev, Viktor, 280
Barzani, Mustafa, 28
Basavapuniah, A., 222, 223
Basir, Isahak, 138
Basov, N. G., 432
Bassarak, Gerhard, 433
Bassolino, Antonio, 491
Bastian, Gerd, 331, 435
Basu, Jyoti, 223
Bateman Cayón, Jaime, 103
Batmonkh, Jambyn, 225, 257
Bator, Damdiny Sukhe, 256
Bauer, Tamás, 338
Bauer País, A., 135
Bayhi, Berhanu, 21, 22, 400
Baykal, Deniz, 526
Baylosis, Rafael, xix, 266, 268
Bazzaglio Recinos, Rogelio A.,
    121
Beauvois, Pierre, 446
Bechetti, Arnold, 173
Begin, Menachim, 2, 32, 357,
    368
Beheshti, Mohammad, 25
Behzadi, Manuchehr, 24, 27
Beijer, Lennart, 519
Bejger, Stanislaw, 343
Bek, Wieslaw, 432
Bekteshi, Besnik, 293, 301

Belaúnde Terry, Fernando,
    164–69 passim
Belchev, Belcho, 308
Belgrave, Cyril, 138
Belovski, Dimče, 403
Benitez, Luís, 164
Benjedid, Chadli, 4, 7, 45
Benke, Valéria, 334
Beňo, Mikuláš, 312
Bentoumi, Amar, 433
Berezhkov, Andrei V., 391
Berlinguer, Enrico, xxii, 216,
    399, 440, 469, 489–95 passim
Bernales, Enrique, 165
Bernstein, Eduard, 493
Berrios Martínez, Ruben, 170
Bertrand, Mireille, 464
Beskrovnykh, Viktor, 384
Betancur, Belisario, 100, 102,
    103
Betancur, Jaime, 103
Bhagwan, Moses, 138
Bhutto, Murtaza, 264
Bhutto, Zulfikar Ali, 264
Biagi, Germano De, 514
Bieliauskiene, Jadvyga, 384
Biesboer, Frank, 501
Bil'ák, Vasil, 90, 312, 321
Bilaret (metropolitan), 433
Bilen, I., 526
Bilić, Jure, 403
Biquard, Pierre, 432
Bird, Vere Cornwall, 216
Birendra (king), 258, 259
Birlea, Stefan, 361
Bisdorff, Aloyse, 496
Bishop, Maurice, xiv, xxvi, 79,
    110, 114, 124–29 passim,
    172, 180, 241, 330, 397, 401
Bishop, Rupert, 124
Bismarck, Otto von, 329
Biswas, Chitta, 431
Biton, Charlie, 30
Bittel, Deolindo, 83
Blanco, Hugo, 165
Blanco, Salvador Jorge, 116
Blears, Betty, 197
Bo Yibo, 209
Boatswain, Ernest Albert, 199
Bobu, Emil, 361
Boekman, Tom, 502
Bogolyubov, Klavdii M., 378
Bogomolov, Oleg T., 412
Bohley, Bärbel, 324
Bojer, Hilde, 508
Boksteen, Lothar, 171
Bolanos Sánchez, Bolívar, 118
Böll, Heinrich, 383

Bolton, Svein, 508
Bonchio, Roberto, 491
Bond, Julian, 174
Bonde, Jens Peter, 454, 455
Bonev, Stanish, 304
Bongo, Hadj Omar, 216
Bonino, Carlos, 164
Bonner, Yolena, 383
Bopage, Lionel, 276
Boran, Behice, 527
Bordiga, Amedeo, 489
Borge Martínez, Tomás, 154–58
    passim
Borglund, Arvid, 505
Borsányi, György, 337
Bosque, Juan Almeida, 110
Bou Thang, 235, 236
Boumediene, Houari, 4, 7
Bouraoui, Abderrahmane, 433
Bourguiba, Habib, 4, 70
Bouterse, Desi, 114, 172
Bouvier-Ajam, Solange, 433
Bovin, Aleksandr, 394, 435
Bowden, Maggie, 478
Bozhinov, Todor, 302
Brahim, Ahmed, 69
Brandt, Willy, 470
Bratanov, Kiril, 432
Braun, Andrzej, 349
Brezhnev, Leonid, xxv, 224, 225,
    287–91 passim, 332, 368,
    371, 372, 373, 378–86 pas-
    sim, 393, 401, 402, 405, 470
Brezhnev, Yuri L., 379
Briand, Serge, 465
Brita, Carlos, 511
Brodie, Ben, 146
Brodsky, Vladimir, 384
Brouwer, Ina, 501–5 passim
Brovikov, Vladimir I., 378
Brown, Freda, 428, 430
Brückner, Joachim, 430
Bruera, Leopoldo, 177
Bruun, Maria, 520
Brus, Wlodzimierz, 494
Brutents, Karen, 43, 151, 400
Bugeja, Philip, 489, 498
Bukhali, Larbi, 7
Bulányi, György, 340
Burbano Burbano, Ghandi, 118
Burhop, E. H. S., 432
Burnham, Forbes, 139, 140
Burnstein, David, 30
Burt, Richard, 389
Buscayno, Bernabe, 268
Buschmann, Martha, 428, 470,
    474
Bush, George, 300, 311, 340,
    341, 367, 472, 473

Busha, Hanna, 430

Caamaño Deño, Francisco, 117
Cabaco, José Luís, 47
Caballero Méndez, Asunción,
    164
Çaglayangil, Ihsan Sabri, 526
Calderón, Rafael, 105
Calero, Adolfo, 155, 156
Calp, Necdet, 526
Camacho, Marcelino, 515
Camacho Aguilera, Julio, 110
Çami, Foto, 293
Campa Salazar, Valentin, 150
Candieiro, Leonardo, 431
Capgras, Emile, 148
Čapka, Miroslav, 313
Capo-Chici, Gratien, 14
Cappelloni, Guido, 490
Caraballo, Francisco, 102
Çarçani, Adil, 293
Cardenas, Oswaldo, 172
Cardona, Ramón, 131, 149
Cardona Hoyos, José, 101
Cardoza Aguilar, José, 135
Cariou, Kimball, 92
Carney, James, 142, 143
Carranza, Mario Aguiñada, 120,
    123
Carrillo, Santiago, 440, 515–18
Carrión, Carlos, 154
Carrión Cruz, Luís, 154
Carter, Jimmy, 124, 162
Carter, Peter, 478
Casaroli, Agostino, 317
Casas, Julio, 179
Casey, William, 306
Cassar, Anton, 499
Castillo, Alfredo, 118
Castillo, Eduardo, 165
Castillo, José, 431
Castillo, Nelly, 154
Castillo Figueroa, Fabio, 120
Castillo Martínez, Herberto, 151
Castro, Antonio, 135, 136, 137
Castro Ruz, Fidel, xiv, xxvi, 79,
    80, 81, 87, 107, 110–15 pas-
    sim, 125, 128, 157, 170
Castro Ruz, Raúl, 110, 113, 114
Caycedo, Jaime, 99
Cayetano Carpio, Salvador, 80,
    81, 121
Cazacu, Virgil, 361
Ceaușescu, Elena, 361–65 passim
Ceaușescu, Nicolae, xx, 308,
    342, 361–72 passim, 421,
    423, 425, 495, 522
Ceaușescu, Nicu, 361, 363

Ceballos Rosales, Marcelo, 432
Cela, Aranit, 297
Céleste, Christian, 130
Çeliku, Hajredin, 293
Cepeda, Manuel, 99, 102
Çerava, Vangjel, 293, 296–99
    passim
Černík, Oldřich, 313
Cervetti, Gianni, 495
Césaire, Aimé, 148
Chae Hui-chong, 237, 239
Chalista, Marcos, 103
Chaljub Mejía, Rafael, 116
Chan Phin, 235, 236
Chan Si, 235, 236, 247
Chand, Lokendra Bahadur, 258
Chandarpal, Indra, 139
Chandarpal, Navin, 139
Chandra, Romesh, 428, 429, 471
Chang Marin, Carlos, 158
Chapman, Frank, 474
Chater, Tony, 479
Chea Sim, 235
Chea Soth, 235, 236
Chebrikov, Viktor M., 307,
    373–77 passim
Checa, Victor, 164
Chen Muhua, 209
Chen Pixian, 209
Chen Yun, 209, 214
Chennault, Anna, 216
Chernayev, Anatoli S., 468
Chernenko, Konstantin U., 43,
    44, 158, 288, 289, 307,
    371–75 passim, 378, 385,
    398, 400
Chervonenko, Stepan V., 378
Chervov, Nikolai, 390
Chetverikov, Nikolai, 391
Cheysson, Claude, 367, 392
Chiarante, Giuseppe, 489
Chiaromonte, Gerardo, 489, 495
Chin Peng, xviii, 249, 251, 253
Chin Xindong, 169
Chin-a-sen, Henk, 172
Chipande, Alberto, 47
Chipenda, Daniel, 9
Chissano, Joaquim Alberto, 47,
    48, 216
Chňoupek, Bohuslav, 317, 319
Cho Se-ung, 237
Choe Chae-u, 237
Choe Kwang, 237
Choe Yong-nim, 237, 239
Choijilsuren, 255
Chon Ha-chol, 239
Chon Mun-sop, 237
Chon Pyong-ho, 237
Chong Chun-ki, 237

Chong Kyong-hui, 237
Chu Huy Man, 280
Chun Doo-Hwan, 240, 241, 244
Churbanov, Yuri, M., 379
Churbanova, Galina, 379
Cid, Carlos del, 162
Cienfuegos, Fermán, 121
Cienfuegos Gorrián, Osmany, 110
Cieslak, Werner, 470
Cindi, Dan, 431
Ciobanu, Lina, 361
Ciosek, Stanislaw, 342
Cirera, Daniel, 428
Císař, Čestmír, 313
Cissoko, Seydou, xii, 56
Čkrebić, Dušan, 403
Claesson, Viola, 519
Clancy, Patrick Martin, 198, 199
Claret, Andreu, 515
Clark, William, 129
Claudín, Fernando, 515
Coard, Bernard, 79, 114, 124–27 passim
Coard, Phyllis, 125, 127
Colajanni, Napoleone, 495
Collymore, Clinton, 138
Colotka, Petr, 312
Colpin, Jean, 464
Coman, Ion, 34, 361, 368
Constantin, Nicolae, 361
Contreras, Manuel, 135
Conyers, John, 174
Cordera Campos, Rolando, 149
Cordero, Asdrúbal, 181
Córdova Rivas, Rafael, 154
Cordovez, Diego, 193, 195, 265
Corneau, Nicolae, 432
Coronas, José, María, 515
Corvalán, Luís, xiii, 95, 96, 398
Coss, Manuel, 431
Cossutta, Armando, 490, 493
Costa, Carlos, 511
Costa Gomes, Francisco da, 428
Costello, Michael, 479
Couteau, Marcel, 446
Craxi, Bettino, 158, 492
Creft, Jacqueline, 124, 125
Cristina, Orlando, 49
Croes, Hemmy, 179
Cruickshank García, Jorge, 152
Cruz, Viriato da, 8
Cruz Pinto, Joąo, 433
Csoóri, Sándor, 339, 340
Cuadro Chamorro, Joaquín, 154
Cubas, Edgardo, 165
Cuca, Pablo, 154
Cuculiza, Mirko, 165
Ćuić, Dane, 403

Çuko, Lenka, 293
Ćulafić, Dobroslav, 403
Cunhal, Alvaro, xiii, 321, 399, 440, 511, 512, 513, 518
Çuri, Vitoria, 298
Curiel, Enrique, 515
Cyrankiewicz, Józef, 428
Czechowski, Tadeusz, 343
Czyrek, Jozef, 343

Dadoo, Yusef, 5, 58, 59, 60
Dagamaissa, Baba, 432
Dahl, Rolf, 505
Dam, Kenneth, 129
Damantang, Camara, 428
Damdin, Paavangiyn, 255
Dammert, Manuel, 164
Danchev, Vladimir, 381
Danesh, Mohammed Ismail, 186
Dang Quoc Bao, 280
Dange, S. A., 225
Daninthe, Guy, xiv, 129, 130
Dankert, Piet, 490
Dansoko, Amath, 56
Dao Tung, 432
Daoud, Mohammed, 187
Darag, Sudi, 62
Daravoinea, Nicolae, 431
Dario Paredes, Rubén, 159, 160, 162
Darwish, Yusuf, 18, 20
Dascalescu, Constantin, 216, 308, 361, 363, 366, 368, 372, 408
Dash, Sam, 171
David, V., 255
Davies, Sonya, 262
Davis, Angela, xxvi, 173
Daysal, Kemal, 525
Debrouwere, Jan, 446
Dejid, Bujyn, 255
De Leon Espinoza, César Agusto, 158
Delmotte, Filip, 446
del Valle Jimenez, Sergio, 110
Demichev, Piotr N., 51, 306, 373, 399, 400
Demirel Süleyman, 526
Demszky, Gábor, 339
Deng Liqun, 209, 214
Deng Xiaoping, 183, 184, 209–14 passim, 219, 242, 243, 495
Deng Yingchao, 209, 210, 215
Denis, Jacques, 428
Deras, Herminio, 142
Desta, Fisseha, 21, 23
Deumlich, Gerd, 470

Devandas, Mario, 106
Dewhurst, Alfred, 92
Dhinglis, Pavlos, 450
Dias, Giacondo, xiii, 88, 89, 90
Diawara, Ange, 16
Díaz, Carmelo, 137
Díaz Callejas, Apoliner, 433
Díaz Martínez, Emilio Antonio, 168
Dickel, Helga, 430
Dimitrov, Georgi, 68, 303, 307
Dinca, Ion, 361
Diouf, Abdou, 56
Dishoni, Sharif, 62
Divendal, Truus, 503
Dixon, Felix, 158
Dixon, Graciela J., 160
Djaghroud, Fatima Zohra, 430
Do Muoi, 280
Dobraczynski, Jan, 346
Dobrescu, Miu, 361, 363
Dobrin, Tamara, 365
Dodd, Christopher, 359
Dode, Piro, 298
Dohlus, Horst, 322, 323, 330
Dohnany, Klaus von, 472
Dolanc, Stane, 403
Dolgikh, Vladimir I., 373
Dolgu, Gheorghe, 367
Domic, Marco, 86
Dong Sy Nguyen, 280
Dorticós Torrado, Osvaldo, 111
Dost, Shah Mohammed, 190–94 passim
Douglas, Kenneth George, 261, 262
Doynov, Ognyan, 302, 310
Dragan, Zvone, 403
Draganu, Tudor, 433
Dragoicheva, Tsola, 302
Dragosavac, Dušan, 403
Dramou, Jerome, 432
Drefahl, Günther, 428
Drozdenko, Vasili I., 378
Duarte, Efraín, 142
Dubček, Alexander, 313, 321
Dubs, Adolph, 194
Dumitrescu, Florea, 368
Dumov, Alexei, 525
Duncan, D. K., 144
Duray, Miklós, 314, 339, 342
Durbridge, Rob, 197, 198
Durrafourg, G., 432
Dussart, Robert, 446
Dutton, John, 432
Duvalier, François, 141
Duvalier, Jean-Claude, 141
Dyulgerov, Petur, 302, 303, 306
Dzantav, Lhaghbajabyn, 256

Dzasokhov, Aleksandr S., 400
Dzhurov, Dobri, 302, 309

Eagleburger, Lawrence, 367
Eanes, Antonio dos Santos
    Ramalho, 512
Ebion, Robert, 148
Ebrahimi, Anushirvan, 24
Echeverria Alvarez, Luís, 152,
    428
Edelman, Fanny, 430
Eggesvik, Arna, 508
Egusquiza, Miguel Cavero, 167
Eisenburger, Eduard, 361
Ekorre, Mikko, 461
Ekwueme, Alex I., 216
Elezi, Mehmet, 293, 297
Elias, Khalil, 430
Emanuel, Poul, xxi, 399, 452,
    454
Enache, Marin, 361
Enache, Petru, 361, 363
Engström, Bror, 519
Enrile, Juan Ponce, 273
Ericsson, Kjersti, 509, 510
Erlander, Tage, 521
Erlich, Wolf, 30, 32
Ernsting, Marius, 502, 504
Ershad, Hussain Mohammed, 202
Escalona, Julio, 181
d'Escoto Brockman, Miguel, 116,
    154, 157, 158
Eshuis, Evelien, 502
Eskandari, Iraj, 25
Espin de Castro, Vilma, 430
Espinoza Montesinos, Gustavo,
    164
Espriella, Ricardo de la, 159, 160
Esquivel, José Renan, 160
Estimé, Dumarsais, 141
Etty, Elsbeth, 503
Evren, Kenan, 526, 527

Faber, M. J., 504
Faddeyev, N. V., 410
Fahhoum, Khalid al-, 368
Falhout, Saber, 432
Fallenbuchl, Zbigniew, 415
Fandis, Andreas, 448
Fanfani, Amintore, 491
Fang Yi, 209
Farakos, Grigoris, 481
Farhad, Muhammed, xvii, 202,
    203
Faría, Jesús, xvi, 177, 178, 179
Farsetti, Paolo, 310
Fatogun, (Idi)dapo, xi, 52

Fava, Athos, xiii, 82, 83, 84
Fayad, Alvaro, 103
Faysal, Yusuf, 65, 67, 68
Fazekas, Ludovic, 361
Federiksen, Berit, 505
Fedorchuk, Vitali, V., 380
Fedosor, Vladimir, 200
Fejti, György, 334, 340
Felfe, Werner, 322, 323, 332
Felix, Jaime, 511
Ferede, Tamirat, 22
Fernández, Freddy, 106
Fernández Vargas, Leopoldo, 432
Ferrao, Valerino, 51
Ferreira Aldunate, Wilson, 117
Ferreto, Arnaldo, 106–9 passim
Ferro, Rodolfo Quente, 10
Figueiredo, João, 89
Figueres, José, 105
Figueroa, Enrique, 155
Figueroa, Jaime, 164
Filatov, Anatoly, 169
Filho, David Capistrano, 89
Filipov, Grisha, 302, 304, 308
Filomena, Alfredo, 164
Fischer, Oscar, 332
Fiszbin, Henri, 465
Fiterman, Charles, 464, 466
Fitte-Duval, Solange, 149
Fleishgakker, Vladimir, 384
Florakis, Kharilaos, xxii, 469,
    481, 482, 483
Florent, Hervé, 149
Florescu, Eugen, 363
Fojtík, Jan, 312
Fokin, Yuri, 158
Folke, Steen, 457
Fomin, Sergei, 433
Forero, Teofilo, 99
Forsberg, Tore, 520
Fraga Iribarne, Manuel, 516
Francis, Tarley, 430
Francisco, Agostinho Miguel, 9
Franjiyah, Suleiman, 41
Fraser, Malcolm, 196
Frati, Regis, 88
Frimannsdottir, Margret, 484,
    485
Frisch, François, 497
Fritsch, Kurt, 470
Fuentes, Antonio, 135
Fulgsang, Villy, 452
Furali, Asbjorn, 505
Furch, Bruno, 445
Furre, Berge, 508
Fuwa Tetsuzo, xvii, 230, 234

Gabdulin, Mikhail, 400

Gabuardi, Gloria, 433
Gabuggiani, Elio, 492
Gadea, Suzana, 361, 365
Gainuse, Alexandrina, 361
Gairy, Eric, 124
Galal, Salah, 432
Galavish, Ali, 24
Galea, Renald, 499
Galgerud, Rolf, 505
Gallagher, John, 431
Gallagher, Norm, 197
Gallardo Meltiz, Rincon Gilberto,
    149, 150
Gallego, Ignacio, xxiii, 516
Gallegos Mancera, Eduardo, 178
Gamarra, Isidoro, 164–68 passim
Gamboa, Francisco, 107
Gandhi, Indira, 194, 220–25
    passim, 310
Gandhi, Rajiv, 225
Gapurov, Mukhamednazar G.,
    382
Garaycoa Ortíz, Xavier, 118
García, Alán, 165
García, Edgardo, 154
García, José Guillermo, 122
García Ferand, Galo, 119
García Frías, Guillermo, 110
García Ponce, Guillermo, 180
García Solis, Ivan, 149
Gascon Mercado, Alejandro, 151
Gaspar, Carlos, 271, 272
Gáspár, Sándor, 334, 428
Gasperoni, Ermenegildo, xxiii,
    513, 514
Gatinot, Gerard, 432
Gau, Jean-François, 399
Gautier, Hermann, 470
Gayssot, Jean-Claude, 464
Gear, Eddy, 143
Geelen, John, 501, 505
Gelfand, Alan, 175
Gemayel, Amin, 368
Gemayel, Bashir, 41
Génies, Daniel, 130
Genscher, Hans-Dietrich, 310,
    319, 341, 367, 390, 392
Georgatos, Gerasimos, 482
Georges, George, 428
Georgiev, Georgi, 304
Gere, Mihai, 361
Gerganov, Penko, 304, 307
Gerns, Willi, 470
Gerö, Ernö, 335
Gerson, Si, 173
Gestsson, Svavar, xxi, 484, 485,
    486
Ghaylan, Abd-al-Galil, 431
Gheorghiu-Dej, Gheorghe, 361

Ghiyasi, Burhan, 186
Gill, Ken, 478
Gillespie, Richard Edward, 261
Giorgis, Dawit, 428
Giosan, Nicolae, 361
Girón, Lourdes, 154
Giscard d'Estaing, Valéry, 290
Gjegprifti, Llambi, 293
Glackin, Eddie, 487, 488
Glemp, Jozef, 346, 348
Glowczyk, Jan, 343
Gobbi, Hugo, 359
Goldman, Marshall I., 288, 289
Goma, Sylvain, 16
Gombojav, Damdiny, 255
Gomes, Artur Vidal, 10
Gomes, Joaquim, 511
Gómez, Angel, 159
Goméz Alvarez, Pablo, xv, 149, 150, 151
Gondikas, Dimitris, 481
Gonen, Benjamin, 30, 32
Gong Dafei, 11
Gonzáles, Franklin, 430
Gonzáles, Oscar, 430
González, Adelso, 181
Gonzalez, Andrea, 175
González, Carlos, xv, 135, 136, 137
González, Felipe, 158, 516, 517, 518
González, Leonel, 121
González Ramírez, Eduardo, 150
González Torres, Pedro, 135
Goodluck, Wahab, 52
Goor, Raymond, 429
Gorbachev, Mikhail S., 92, 342, 372, 373, 376, 377, 399, 402
Göring, Hermann, 207
Görög, Tibor, 433
Gorywoda, Manfred, 343, 352
Goulart, João, 89
Graber, Michael, 443
Gramsci, Antonio, 489
Grandgenet, Jos, 496
Gray, Lee Charles, 433
Gregorios, Paulos Mar, 433
Grekov, Leonid, 307
Gremetz, Maxime, 399, 464, 468
Gribkov, Anatoli I., 418, 420, 422
Grigoryants, Sergei, 384
Grimsson, Olafur Ragnar, 485
Grinevsky, Oleg, 395
Grishin, Ivan T., 396
Grishin, Viktor V., 372, 378, 398
Gromyko, Andrei A., 128, 291, 319, 373, 375, 377, 387, 390, 392, 396–400 passim

Groza, Petru, 361
Grzyb, Zofia, 343
Gu Mu, 209
Guaraca, Jaime, 99
Guardado y Guardado, Facundo, 120
Gudmundsson, Helgi, 484, 485
Guebuza, Armando Emilio, 47
Guerra, Adriano, 494
Guevarra, Ernesto "Che," 81, 85, 117
Gueye, Semy Pathe, 56
Gulabzoy, Sayed Mohammed, 191
Gunasekara, D. E. W., 275, 276
Gunawardene, Leslie, 275
Gungunhana, 51
Guo Qingshi, 216
Gupta, Indrajit, 428
Gupta, N. P., 432
Gupta, Pramode Das, 222
Gurumu, Taye, 22
Gustavsen, Finn, 508
Gutema, Lemma, 400
Gutiérrez, Olga, 430
Gutiérrez, Rodrigo, 105
Guttormsson, Hjörleifur, 484
Gúzman, Abimael, 117, 166
Gyenes, András, 342
György, Károly, 431

Haakmat, Andre, 172
Habash, George, 67
Habibi, Emile, 30
Habre, Elias, 429
Habyarimana, Juvenal, 216, 241
Hadi, Issam Abdul, 430
Hadjares, Sadiq, 7
Hadži-Vasilev, Kiro, 403
Haferkamp, Wilhelm, 341
Hagel, Rolf, xxiii, 522
Hager, Franz, 443
Hager, Kurt, 322, 329, 398
Hager, Sabina, 430
Haidongo, S. T., 431
Hájek, Jiří, 318
Hajji, Salah al-, 69
Haks, Rinus, 505
Halevi, Ilan, 33
Hall, Gus, xvi, xxvi, 173, 174
Hallgrimsson, Geir, 486, 487
Haman, Josef, 312
Hamid, Salim, 55
Hamid, Sulayman, 61
Hammami, Khalid, 65, 67
Hammar, Bo, 519–22 passim
Hammer, Armand, 311
Hammudi, Said Qassim, 432

Han Guang, 209, 213
Han Tianshi, 209
Handal, Shafik Jorge, xiv, 121, 123
Hänsel, Günther, 474
Hansen, Ivan, 454
Hansen, Margit, 452
Hansen, Preben Moller, 455
Hanssan, Steinar, 509
Hansson, Per Albin, 521
Hao Jianxiu, 209
Hardardottir, Vilborg, 484, 485
Harmel, Muhammad, xii, 69, 70
Hart Davalos, Armando, 110, 400
Hartmann, Arthur A., 391
Harun, Shihata, 19
Hassan (king), 7, 45
Hatch, Orrin, 216
Hatfield, Mark, 439, 493
Hatim, Abu, 36
Haughton, John, 146
Hauswald, Harald, 324
Havasi, Ferenc, 334, 338, 341
Havel, Václav, 318
Havlín, Josef, 312
Hawi, George, xi, 39–44 passim, 67, 311, 495
Haydar, Muhammad, 67
Hayes, Charles, 174
Hazbiu, Kadri, 294–98 passim
Hazboun, George, 35
Heinrich, Eberhard, 432
Hekmatyar, Gulbuddin, 193
Heng Samrin, xviii, xxvii, 235, 247, 285
Hepburn, Mavis Laura, 261
Herder, Gerhard, 330
Herljević, Franjo, 403
Hermannsson, Steingrimur, 486
Hermier, Guy, 464
Hermlin, Stephan, 329
Hernández, Miguel, 143
Hernández, Pablo, 135
Hernández Colón, Rafael, 171
Hernández Tellez, Sabino, 149, 150
Hernández Vidal, Manuel, 430
Herrera, Gerardo, 431
Herrera, Guillermo, 164
Herrera, Leticia, 154
Herrera Campins, Luís, 180
Herrmann, Joachim, 322
Herzog, Philippe, 464
Heseltine, Michael, 419
Hidalgo, Norma, 430
Hilaly, Ahmed al-, 433
Hill, Edward Fowler, 196, 197
Hill Arboleda, Nathaniel, 428

Hinds, Lennox, 433
Hirone, T., 432
Hitler, Adolf, 470, 472
Ho Chi Minh, 247, 283, 285
Ho Chong-suk, 237
Ho Tam, 237, 239
Hoang Quoc Viet, 284
Hoang Thuy Giang, 200, 430
Hoang Tung, 280
Hoarau, Elie, 53, 54
Hoarau, Mario, 5, 54
Hoarau, Roger, 53, 54
Hodža, Fadil, 403
Hoekstra, Henk, 502
Hofer, Anton, 443
Hoffman, Karel, 312
Hoffmann, François, 496, 497
Hoffmann, Jacques, 496, 497
Hoffmann, Heinz, 322, 326, 329
Honecker, Erich, xx, 23, 90,
    179, 322–33 passim, 359,
    398, 435, 474, 495
Hong Song-nam, 237
Hong Song-yong, 237, 239
Hoogkamp, Karel, 501
Höpcke, Klaus, 328
Hořeni, Zdeněk, 313
Horgen, Trygve, 505
Horn, Gyula, 337
Houg, Tora, 508
Hoxha, Enver, xix, 293–300
    passim
Hoxha, Nexhmije, 295, 298
Hrušković, Miloslav, 312, 316
Hrůza, Karel, 316
Hu Jiwei, 184, 215
Hu Na, 218
Hu Qiaomu, 209
Hu Qili, 514
Hu Yaobang, xvii, 183, 184, 209,
    211, 215, 216, 223, 242, 243,
    372, 495
Huaman Centero, Adrian, 168
Huang Huoqing, 212
Huang Kecheng, 209
Hübsch, Fernand, 496, 497
Huerta Montalvo, Francisco, 119
Hůla, Václav, 312
Hummel, Arthur, 219
Hun Sen, 235
Hurtado, Hernando, 99
Hurtado, Jaime, 119
Hurtado, Jorge, 164
Hurtado, Pedro, 154
Husák, Gústav, xx, 23, 67, 311,
    312, 313, 317, 318, 319, 332,
    359, 398, 399, 423
Husayn, Nuri Abd-al-Razzaq,
    431

Husayn, Saddam, 3, 29
Husayni, Hatem, 33
Hussein (king), 37, 216, 368
Huynh Tan Phat, 280, 284
Hwang Chang-yop, 237, 239
Hyon Mu-kwang, 237

Iacovou, George, 451
Ibarbaru, Rita, 177
Ibárruri, Dolores, 515, 516
Ibragimov, Mirza, 431
Ibrahim, Fatimah, 63
Ibrahim, Mohammed, 193
Ibrahim, Muhsin, 39, 44
Ibrahimi, Ahmed Taleb, 11
Ichikawa, Shoichi, 233
Iglesias, Gerardo, xxiii, 440,
    495, 513–18 passim
IJmker, Kees, 502
Illyés, Gyula, 340
Ilón, Gaspar, 133
Ilyichev, Leonid F., 218, 394
Imashev, Sattar N., 397
Indra, Alois, 312, 317
Ingvardsson, Margo, 519
Inoue, Kiyoshi, 234
Insunza, Sergio, 433
Iota, Vasile, 371
Irge, Yehoshua, 30
Irrizarry, Franklin, xvi
Isa Conde, Narciso, xiv, 116
Isai, Hekuran, 293
Isakov, Viktor, 388
Iscaro, Rubens, 82, 83
Ishibashi, Masashi, 216
Islam, Zubayr Sayf al-, 431
Issa, Farouq Abu, 63
Issakhodzhayev, Abdurashid, 431
Ivanchenko, Vasily, 410
Ivanov, Kosta, 428
Ivanov, Semyon, 433
Ivanov, Vladimir, 391
Iyer, V. R. Krishna, 433
Izaguirre, Julio César, 168
Izeboud, Elli, xxii, 442, 501

Jacinto, Antonio, 9
Jackson, George Edward, xviii,
    259, 261, 262–63
Jackson, Henry, 219
Jackson, James, 173, 174
Jackson, Jesse, 174, 175
Jacobs, Roel, 446
Jacques, Martin, 479
Jadambaa, Buralyn, 256
Jaegle, M. A., 432
Jagan, Cheddi, xv, 138, 139, 140

Jagan, Janet, 138, 139
Jagersma, Hanneke, 505
Jagvaral, Nyamin, 255, 257
Jahangiri, Shahrokh, 24
Jakeš, Miloš, 312
Jalalandoni, Luís, 269
Jalalar, Mohammad Khan, 191
Jalan-Aajav, Sampilyn, 184, 255,
    256
Jan, Pehalawan Mohammed, 193
Jankú, Vladimír, 316
Jaramillo Flores, Roberto, 151
Jarowinsky, Werner, 322
Jarpa, Sergio Onofre, 97
Jaruzelski, Wojciech, xx, 319,
    343–55 passim, 358, 359,
    360, 393, 421, 423, 508
Jayasena, A. G., 275
Jayeskara, Peter, 275
Jayewardene, J. R., 275, 276
Jensen, Jorgen, 442, 452–56
    passim
Jespersen, Knud, 453
Jeune, Bernard, 452
Ji Pengfei, 23, 197
Jiang Hua, 212
Jiang Qing, 211
Jijón Saavedra, Milton, 118
Jiménez, Lucio, 154
Joan, Ivan Nicolae, 430
Johansen, Grete, 505
John XXIII (pope), 317
John Paul II (pope), 290, 306,
    310, 321, 346, 392
Johnston, Elliot Frank, 197
Jókai, Lóránd, 433
Jonathan, Joseph Lebua, 241, 310
Jorgensen, Anker, 456
Jorgensen, Arne, 505, 508
Juan Carlos (king), 517
Jugnauth, Aneerood, 216
Jumblatt, Walid, 368
Junior, Alfred, 430
Juquin, Pierre, 464

Kabrhelová, Marie, 312
Kádár, János, xx, 319, 332–35
    passim, 340, 341, 342, 359,
    399, 423
Kaddoumi, Farouk, 395
Kadota, Shozo, 396
Kajanoja, Jouko, 458, 460, 463
Kalin, Ivan P., 87, 169
Kalinin, Arnold Ivanovich, 10
Kalkus, Stanislaw, 343
Kalmyk, Valeria, 430
Kaloudhis, Nikos, 481
Kalt, Hans, 443, 444, 445

Kamal, Michel, 3, 18, 19, 20
Kamal, Najib, 18
Kaminski, Leszek, 431
Kang Hui-won, 237
Kang Keqing, 209, 215
Kang Song-san, 237
Kang Yang-uk, 239
Kangleon, Edgardo, 273
Kanstrup, Gunnar, 452–53
Kant, Hermann, 328
Kapek, Antonín, 312, 398
Kapitonov, Ivan V., 373, 377, 378
Kapitsa, Mikhail S., 218, 229, 396
Kapo, Hysni, 295
Kapo, Vito, 295
Karace, Mehmet, 528
Karadzhov, Velichko, 303
Karakowsky, José Woldenberg, 150
Karamanlis, Constantin, 309
Karamfilov, Dmitur, 431
Karger, Franz, 443
Karim, Ahmad, 7
Karlsen, Odd S., 505
Karmal, Babrak, xvii, 26, 183, 186, 187–88, 191, 257, 265
Károlyi, Mihály, 334
Karpets, Igor D., 433
Karran, Ram, 138, 139
Karvonen, Timo, 462
Karwal, Mir Saheb, xxvii, 186
Kashtan, William, xiii, 91, 92
Kashtanov, A. N., 398
Kassai, Akira, 430
Katali, François, 16
Katsouridhis, G., 448
Kauppila, Erkki, 462
Kaur, Surjeet, 430
Kawawa, Rassidi Mfaume, 216
Kawayana, Eusi, 138
Kaysone Phomvihan, xviii, 246, 247
Kazdaghli, Habib, 69
Kekkonen, Matti, 428
Kelly, Petra, 331, 435
Kempný, Josef, 312
Kemppainen, Arvo, 458, 461
Kennedy, Edward, 439, 493
Kent, Bruce, 435, 478
Kerekou, Mathieu, x, 14, 15
Keshtmand, Sultan Ali, 186–91 passim, 194
Keuneman, Pieter, 275
Khadafy, Moammar, 45, 46, 309, 368
Khaddam, Abdul Halim, 395
Khalilullah (general), 187

Khamene'i, Sayed Ali, 27
Khamis, Saliba, 30
Khamtai, Siphandon, 246
Khan, Fatayab Ali, 264
Khan, Meraj Mohammad, 264
Khan, Yaqub, 194
Kharkabi, Zahi, 30, 33
Kharrat, Eduard al-, 431
Khavari, Ali, 24, 27
Khawaga, Ahmad al-, 432
Khayri, Zaki, 28
Khenin, David, 30, 33
Khieu Samphan, 216, 236
Khin Maung Gyi, 204, 205
Khomeini, Ruhollah, 1, 3, 24–29 passim, 174, 193
Khomyakov, Aleksandr, 399
Khristodoulidhis, G., 448
Khristofinis, Dhonis, 448, 449
Khristou, Kiriakos, 448
Khristov, Khristo, 308
Khudadad (colonel), 193
Kianuri, Nureddin, xi, 3, 24–27 passim, 395, 396
Kidan, Tesfaye Gebre, 21
Kim Chang-yong, 430
Kim Chong-il, 184, 237–42 passim
Kim Chung-nin, 237
Kim Guang-hub, 431
Kim Hwan, 237
Kim Il, 237
Kim Il-song, xviii, 84, 237–43 passim, 372
Kim Il-tae, 239
Kim Kwang-hwan, 237
Kim Kwi Nam, 237
Kim Nam-yun, 239
Kim Pok-sin, 237, 239
Kim Pyong-il, 241
Kim Tu-man, 237
Kim Yong-nam, 237
Kimba, Evaristu Domingos, 10
King, Mel, 174
Kirichenko, Yuri, 395
Kirilenko, Andrei P., 374, 376, 379
Kirsanov, Piotr, 388
Kiselev, Tikhon Y., 377
Kissinger, Henry, 127, 288
Kiszczak, Czeslaw, 343
Kivimaki, Erkki, 462
Kivisto, Kalevi, 463
Kjenong, Bjorn, 505
Klaczkow, Sergiusz, 432
Klausen, Klaus, 457
Kleiber, Günther, 322
Kleven, Hans I., xxii, 505–8 passim

Klibi, Chedli, 309
Knickrehm, Uwe, 470
Knox, Walter James, 262
Knutsen, Martin Gunnar, 505
Koçallari, Sotir, 293, 299
Kohl, Helmut, 389, 392, 398, 473
Kolbe, Maximilian, 347
Koldunov, Aleksandr, 418
Kolesnikov, S., 385
Kolingba, André, 216
Koliševski, Lazar, 403
Kolle Cueto, Jorge, xiii, 85, 86
Kolozov, Orestis, 481
Kone, Ravane, 431
Kong Chin-tae, 237
Konotop, Vasili, 377
Konrád, György, 339
Konstantinou, Dinos, 448
Korčák, Josef, 312
Koritzinsky, Theo, 505–9 passim
Kornidesz, Mihály, 337
Kornienko, Georgi M., 387, 425
Korom, Mihály, 334, 336
Kosev, Kiril, 308
Kosolapov, Richard I., 400, 523
Kostadinov, Penyu, 311
Kosygin, Aleksei, 374, 405
Kotovski, G., 432
Kourkoulou, Roula, 481
Kouyela, Daniel, 431
Kozlík, Jan, 318
Kozlov, Frol, 376
Kraigher, Sergej, 403
Krasucki, Henri, 464
Krenz, Egon, 322
Kriangsak Chamanan, 249, 277
Krishna, N. K., 224, 225
Kristensen, Knut, 452
Kristoffersen, Frank, 508
Křížková, Maria Rut, 318
Krolikowski, Herbert, 332
Krolikowski, Werner, 322
Kruglova, Zinaida, 11
Kubadinski, Pencho, 302
Kubiak, Hieronim, 343
Kubka, Jiří, 432
Kučan, Milan, 403
Kudachkin, Mikhail F., 151
Kulikov, Viktor G., 291, 342, 370, 418, 421, 422, 423
Kulin, Ferenc, 339
Kun, Béla, 334, 337, 369
Kunaev, Dinmukhamed A., 373, 376, 402
Kunalan, Srinivasan, 431
Kuno, Chiyi, 244
Kurin, Konstantin N., 151
Kurteši, Ilijaz, 403

Kushida, Fuki, 430
Kusnierik, Jindrich, 429
Kutlu, Haydar (Nabi Yagci),
    xxiii, 525, 526
Kux, Ernst, 288
Kuzichkin, Vladimir, 26, 373
Kuznetsov, V. (economist), 407
Kuznetsov, Vasili V. (CPSU
    Politburo member), 375, 397,
    400
Kvanmo, Hanna, 508, 509
Kvist, Kenneth, 519
Kvitsinsky, Yuli, 390, 391
Kwadjo, John, 431
Kyaw Mya, 204, 205
Kyaw Zaw, 205
Kye Ung-tae, 237
Kyin Maung, 204, 205
Kyprianou, Spyros, 441, 450,
    451
Kyriakidis, Nikos, 482

Laborit, Carmelo, 181
Laeq, Suleiman, 189
Lagadinova, Elena, 303
Lairet, Germán, 180
Lajoinie, André, 464
Lallemand, Daniel, 53, 54
Lalov, Nano, 303
Lamond, James, 428
Lancranjan, Ion, 342
Landazábal Reyes, Fernando,
    100, 104
Lang, Karl J., 433
Lange, Ingeborg, 322, 522
Langenier, Lucet, 54
Langer, Felicia, 34
Langignon, Michel, 464
Langsether, Asmund, 505
Lantos, Tom, 340
Lara, Lucio, 9
Lara, Ruth, 9
Lara, Vantagem, 9
Larrazábal, Radamés, 178
Larsen, Aksel, 456
Larsen, Reidar, 506
Lasettas, A., 450
Lauko, Károly, 428
Laurent, Paul, 464, 465
Lava, Jose, 268
Lavigne, Pierre, 433
Lawrence, Chris, 144
Lázár, György, 330, 334, 341,
    342, 399, 409
Lazard, Francette, 464
Le Duan, xix, 247, 280, 281, 282
Le Duc Anh, 280
Le Duc Tho, 280, 281

Le Quang Dao, 280
Le Van Luong, 282
Lechin, Juan, 86
Ledda, Romano, 489
Ledesma, Genaro, 164
Ledl, Lubomír, 430
Lee Kuan Yew, 251
Legay, Jean-Marie, 432
Legêne, Susan, 503
Le Guen, René, 464
Leick, Jorry, 496
Leite de Vasconcelos,
    Teodomiro, 432
Lékai, László, 341
Lemoine, Georges, 130
Lemos, Joaquim de, 431
Lenárt, Jozef, 312
Lenin, V. I., 168, 240, 350, 351,
    369, 398, 520
Leonard, Constantin, 361
Le Pors, Anicet, 466
Leroy, Roland, 464
Li Chang, 209
Li Desheng, 209, 212
Li Ji, 216
Li Weihan, 209
Li Xiannian, 209, 212, 214, 234
Li Zhuang, 215
Liao Chenghzi, 209
Liberda, Vladimír, 318
Liehm, Antonín, 321
Ligachev, Egor K., 373–78
    passim, 401
Lilov, Alexander, 303, 311
Lindbeck, Assar, 520
Ling Yun, 212
Lingán, Alfonso Barrantes, 164
Lini, Walter Hadye, 216
Linnik, Viktor, 387
Lis, Ladislav, 318
Liska, Tibor, 338
Lo Hsing-han, 205
Logara, Loula, 481
Loginov, Vadim Petrovich, 10
Loistl, Gustav, 443
Lombardo de Silva, Adriana, 152
Lombion, Jean-Claude, 130
Lon Nol, 236
Loose, Ludo, 446
Lopatka, Adam, 433
López, Allan, 430
López, Fernando, 142
López, Julián, 113
López, Raul, 142
Lorscheider, Ivo, 88
Losonczi, Pál, 334
Louison, George, 124
Loules, Kostas, 482
Lowry, Joseph, 174

Lublitz, Ruth, 30
Lucas García, Romeo, 134–35,
    137
Lucio, Ramiro, 103
Luder, Italo, 83
Luebbert, Konrad, 473
Lukanov, Andrey, 302
Lukaš, Karel, 428
Lukoki, Ambrosio, 9
Lumpkin, John, 174
Lundrup, Dan, 453
Lupu, Petru, 361
Luther, Martin, 324, 326, 329
Lutzkendorf, Rolf, 428
Luvsangombo, Sonomyn, 255
Luvsantseren, 255
Luvualu, Pascal, 10, 11, 428
Lyssarides, Vassos, 431

Ma Guorui, 209
Mabassy, Leonard, 430
Mabhida, Moses, xii, 5, 57–61
    passim
Mabote, Sebastião Moses, 47
Mabrink, Bertil, 519
Macaluso, Emanuele, 489
Macapagal, Felicismo C., xix,
    266, 268, 270
Machado, Gustavo, 178
Machado Ventura, José Ramón,
    110
Macharski, Franciszek, 348
Machel, Samora Moises, xi,
    47–51 passim, 397, 400
Machungo, Mario de Graça, 47
Macina, Mario Vella, 478
MacKay, Ian, 478
Madrid, Miguel de la, 157, 158
Madsen, Freddy, 452
Madsen, Jorgen, 453
Magallona, Merlin, 268
Magnin, Armand, xxiii, 523, 524
Mahathir Mohamed, Datuk, 250,
    252, 254
Mahjub, Abd al-Khaliq, 63
Mahjub, Mohammad, 64
Mahmud, Aziz, 4, 12, 13
Mahsud, Ahmad Shah, 192
Mai Chi Tho, 282
Maichantan, Sengmani, 246
Maidana, Antonio, xv, 162, 163
Maidar, Damdinjavyn, 255
Makeev, Valentin N., 378
Maléter, Pál, 340
Maliki, Shahib al-, 433
Malile, Reiz, 299, 300, 301
Malina, Salomão, 88
Malki, 'Ali, 7

Mamatsis, Takis, 481
Mamula, Branko, 403
Manandhar, Bishnu Bahadur, 257
Maneiro, Alfredo, 178
Manescu, Manea, 361, 363
Mangaljavyn, 255
Mangueira, Manuel Alves dos
    Passos Barroso, 9
Manik, Saifuddin Ahmed, 203
Manley, Michael, 144, 145, 146
Manov, Stefan, 304
Mansur, Muhammad Ibrahim
    Nugud, xii, 61
Mantarov, Yordan, 306, 392
Mao Zedong, 184, 215, 260, 457
Marchais, Georges, xxi, 12, 43,
    311, 383, 399, 439, 464–69
    passim, 495
Marcos, Ferdinand, 267–74
    passim
Marcuse, Herbert, 493
Marcy, Sam, 175
Mari Bras, Juan, xvi, 170
Marín, Conrado, 103
Marinc, Andrej, 403
Marino Ospina, Iván, 103
Marjai, József, 341, 342
Marklund, Eivor, 519
Marko, Rita, 293
Markov, Dimitri, 384
Marković, Dragoslav, 403, 496
Markovski, Krste, 403
Maróthy, László, 334
Márquez, Pompeyo, 179
Marrese, Paul, 410
Marshall, Scott, 174
Marston, John Leslie, 261
Martens, Wilfried, 447
Martí, Farabundo, 120
Martín, Américo, 178, 180
Martínez, Ana Guadalupe, 120,
    121
Martínez, Teofilo, 143
Martínez Cuenca, Alejandro, 154
Martínez Verdugo, Arnaldo, 149,
    152
Marulanda Vélez, Manuel, 99,
    100
Marvanová, Anna, 318
Marx, Karl, 2, 3, 5, 6, 13, 20,
    28, 33, 36, 52, 55, 60, 63, 68,
    148, 162, 168, 200, 211, 227,
    262, 276, 311, 369, 375, 385,
    398, 445, 504, 508, 520
Masire, Quett K. J., 216
Masri, Walid, 430
Massemba Debat, Alphonse,
    15, 16
Massie, Gordon, 92

Mastikov, Vesselin, 430
Mas'udi, Mahdi, 69
Matamoros, Marta, 160
Matić, Petar, 403
Matsinhe, Mariano de Araujo, 47
Mattila, Uolevi, 461
Mauge, René, xiv, 118, 119
Mauroy, Pierre, 130, 141, 341
May, Karl, 316
Mayer, Erich, 470
Mayer, Josef, 470
Mayzar, Muhammad Abu, 38
Mbaye, Makhtar, 56
McDonald, Larry, 387
McDonald, Tom, 198
McGahey, Mick, 478
McLennan, Gordon, xxi, 478
McNulty, Francis Edward, 261
McPhail, Donald, 125
McPhillips, John Leslie, 196–99
    passim
Mecklenburg, Ernst, 330
Medunov, Sergei F., 376, 379,
    402
Medvedev, Roy, 384
Medvedev, Vadim A., 378, 398
Meerten, Laurens, 502, 503
Méhes, Lajos, 334
Mehr, Bram, xvi, 171
Meis, Fré, 503
Mejía Victores, Oscar Humberto,
    132–37 passim
Meléndez, Segundo, 180
Mello, Teodoro, 88
Melo Dias Flora, Jorge Henriques
    Varrela de, 9
Mendes, Luciano, 89
Mendis, M. G., 275
Mengistu Haile Mariam, xi, 4,
    21, 22, 23, 115, 241, 319, 400
Messner, Zbigniew, 343
Mestre, Francia, 10
Meyer, Jean-François, 399
Meyers, George, 173
Meza, Salom, 181
Mezzich, Julio César, 168
Miah, Malik, 175
Michalatos, Panayotis, 430
Michalek, Zbigniew, 343
Michalko, Jan, 433
Midani, Zouheir al-, 433
Mielke, Erich, 322
Mies, Herbert, xxi, 311, 470,
    473, 474
Mifsud, Mario, 499
Mihali, Qirjako, 293
Mijatović, Cvijetin, 403
Mikhailidhis, A., 448
Mikhailidhis, Khambis, 448

Mikhailov, Ivan, 304
Mikhailov, Stoyan, 302
Milatović, Veljko, 403
Milewski, Miroslaw, 343
Milford (lord), 441, 478
Milian, Arnaldo, 111
Miller, Alan, 196, 199, 200
Mindszenty, József, 335
Mino, Rrapo, 297
Mintoff, Dominic, 498, 499
Minucci, Adalberto, 489, 491
Minyerski, Nelly, 433
Miqdad, Faysal al-, 431
Mirejovsky, Lubomír, 433
Miret Prieto, Pedro, 110
Mishev, Misho, 302
Mishin, Viktor M., 373, 386
Mishka, Pali, 293, 296
Misuari, Nur, 272
Mita, Ciriaco De, 490
Mitchell, Charlene, 173, 174
Mittag, Günter, 322, 332
Mitterrand, François, 148, 216,
    290, 341, 438, 465–69 pas-
    sim, 517
Miyagawa, Torao, 234
Miyamoto, Kenji, 230, 231, 233
Mizani, Farajollah, 24
Mladenov, Petur, 302, 309, 310
Mnumzana, Susan, 430
Moabi, Max, 428
Mocuţa, Stefan, 361
Mogensen, Thomas Borg, 430
Mohamed, Feroze, 138
Mohammadzadeh, Raf'at, 24
Mohmand, Niaz Mohammed, 186
Moiane, Salome, 430
Moins, Jacques, 446
Mojsov, Lazar, 403
Mokrzyszczak, Wlodzimierz, 343
Moleiro, Moisés, 180
Molina, Juan, 432
Molom, Tsendiin, 256
Molomjamts, Demchigiyn, 255
Mondlane, Eduardo, 47
Monge, Luís Alberto, 107, 109
Monsanto, Pablo, 133
Montana Oropesa, Jesús, 110
Monteiro, Armand, 14
Monteiro, Jose Oscar, 47, 48
Montero, Pedro, 119
Montero Mejía, Alvaro, 106
Monterrey, Glenda, 154
Montes Manzano, Eduardo, 149
Mora Valverde, Eduardo, 105–9
    passim
Mora Valverde, Manuel, 105,
    106, 107
Morales, Horatio "Boy," 269

Morales, William, 170
Morán, Rolando, 137, 138
Moreau, Gisèle, 464
Moreno, Carmen, 154
Morgan, John Hanley, 92, 428
Moro, Aldo, 496
Morozov, Georgi, 384
Mortensen, Bjarne, 456
Morvan, Claude, 130
Mosquera, Alvaro, 99
Mosquera, Francisco, 103
Mossadegh, Mohammed, 25
Moussa, Baba, 14
Moutoussamy, Ernest, 129, 131
Mroueh, Azza al-Horr, 430
Mrue, Abdel Karim, 44
Mubarak, Hamad, 55
Mubarak, Mohammed Hosni, 20,
    21, 68, 216, 241, 368
Mückenberger, Erich, 322
Mudhawi, Aziz Ahmad, 12
Mugabe, Robert, xiii, 5, 75, 76,
    77, 319, 332, 341
Mugoša, Dušan, 294
Muhajid, Farid, x
Muhammad, Abdullah, 55
Muhammad, Abu al-Qasim (Gas-
    sim), 61
Muhammad, Ali Nasir, xiii, 44,
    67, 71, 72, 309
Muhammad, Aziz, x, 28, 29, 67
Muhammad, Jasim, 12
Muhammad, Nasir, 55
Muhri, Franz, xxi, 399, 443,
    444, 445
Muhyi-al-Din, Ahmed Fu'ad, 368
Muhyi al-Din, Khalid, 19, 20–21,
    428
Muhyi al-Din, Zakariya, 21
Mujica, Felipe, 179
Mujica, Hector, 178
Mukherjee, Biswanath, 225
Muldoon, Robert David, 262,
    341
Müller, Ludwig, 470
Müller, Margarete, 322
Mundey, Judy, xvii, 196
Munir, Sjahrul, 227
Munro, Trevor, xv, 144, 145,
    146
Mura, Prokop, 296, 299
Murad, Yusuf, 66
Mureşan, Ana, 361
Murrugarra, Edmundo, 164
Mursi, Fu'ad, 20
Murtopo, Ali, 228
Muruwwah, Karim, 42
Musa, Abu, 368
Musa, Hamid Majid, 30

Musa, Hitam Datuk, 250, 254
Musa, Jamal, 30
Musavi, Mir Hossein, 25, 241
Muscat, John, 499
Muscat, Joseph V., 498, 499
Muscat, Paul, 499
Mustafa, 'Abd al-Hamid ben, 69
Muteka, Fernando Faustino, 10
Muttetuwegama, Sarath, 275, 276
Muzenda, Simon, 75
Muzorewa, Abel, 76
Myerson, Michael, 174
Myftiu, Manush, 293
Myo Myint, 204, 205
M'zali, Muhammad, 70

Naarendorp, Edward, xvi, 171
Nadra, Fernando, 82
Nae, Elena, 361
Nafa'a, Muhammad al-, 69
Nagels, Jacques, 446
Nagib, Muhammad, 21
Nagin, Rick, 173
Nagy, Imre, 335, 340
Nagy, Richárd, 337
Nahra, Maurice, 44
Najibullah (Dr.), 186, 190
Najjab, Sulayman al-, 34
Nakasone, Yasuhiro, 185, 232,
    233, 244, 319, 396
Nakodkin, Vesvolod, 430
Namboodiripad, E. M. S., xvii,
    216, 220–23 passim
Namsrai, Tsend, 432
Nanayakkara, V., 276
Naqqash, Farida, 19
Nashshab, Sulayman al-, 34
Nasir, Khadir, 62
Nasser, Bahig, 428
Nasser, Gamel Abdul, 21, 69
Nateq-Nuri, Ali-Akbar, 25
Natoli, Ugo, 433
Natta, Alessandro, 489, 491
Naumann, Konrad, 322
Na'us, Khalil, 41
Navarro, Anna Maria, 430
Nawrocki, Witold, 431
Nazish, Ali, xix, 263, 264
Ne Win, 206, 207
Nedev, Vasil, 304
Neilly, Warwick, 197
Nejezchleb, Richard, 319
Németh, Károly, 334, 338
Nemoudry, Jan, 429
Neto, Agostinho, 8, 9
Neugebauer, Bernhard, 330
Neumann, Alfred, 322
Newport, Gus Eugene, 174, 428

Ngouabi, Marien, 16, 17
Nguyen Co Thach, 280
Nguyen Duc Tam, 280, 282
Nguyen Lam, 280
Nguyen Thanh Binh, 280
Nguyen Thi Binh, 431
Nguyen Thi Dinh, 430
Nguyen Van Linh, 282
Ni Zhifu, 209, 215
Nicolas, Armand, xv, 147, 148,
    149
Nicolescu, Paul, 361
Nie Rongzhen, 209
Niehous, William, 181
Nielsen, Anette, 453
Nieves, David, 181
Nieves, Elias, 154
Nikaido, Susumu, 216
Nikkila, Reijo, 462
Nikolayeva-Tereshkova, Valen-
    tina, 430
Nikonov, Viktor P., 379
Nilsen, Kare Andre, 505
Ni'mah, Daniel, 65, 66
Niño, Avelino, 103
Nishizawa, Tomio, 244
Nitze, Paul H., 390
Nixon, Richard, 289
Nkomo, Joshua, 5, 75, 77
Noel, Vincent, 125
Noel y Moral, Roberto Clemente,
    167, 168
Nokta, Harry Persaud, 138
Nolan, Sean, 487
Noma, Hiroshi, 234
Nordenstreng, Kaarle, 432
Nordmann, Joe, 433
Noriega, Manuel Antonio, 161,
    162
Norlund, Ib, 454
Norodom, Sihanouk, 216, 236
Nosaka, Koken, 244
Nosaka, Sanzo, 230
Nouhak, Phoumsavan, 246
Novelli, Diego, 492
Novikov, Ignati T., 379, 382
Nujoma, Sam, 333, 368
Numeiri, Jaafar, 4, 62–65 passim
Núñez Téllez, Carlos, 154, 155
Nur Ahmad Nur, 186, 188
Nyers, Rezsö, 336, 343
Nyheim, Einar, 508
Nze, Pierre, 16
Nzeyimana, Laurent, 216
Nzo, Alfred, 431

O Chin-u, 237
O Kuk-yol, 237

O Paek-yong, 237
Obando y Bravo, Miguel, 155
O'Brien, Bernard Noel, 261
Obzina, Jaromír, 313
Occhetto, Achille, 491
Ochoa, Arnaldo, 114
Ofstad, Bjorg, 508
Ogarkov, Nikolai V., 387, 397, 420
Olalia, Felixberto, 269
Olavarría, Jorge, 178
Olivera, Isaac, 181
Olszowski, Stefan, 342, 343, 358, 359
Olteanu, Constantin, 361, 422
Omawale, Walter, 138
Ondrej, Josef, 433
Ong Dung, 431
Opalko, Stanislaw, 343
Opango, Yhombi, 16
Oprea, Gheorghe, 361, 368, 406
O'Riordan, Michael, xxii, 398, 487
Orlandini, Javier Alva, 169, 216
Orrega, Eduardo, 169
Ortega Saavedra, Daniel, 154, 169, 257
Ortega Saavedra, Humberto, 154, 155, 156
Orzechowski, Marian, 343, 346, 398
Osborne, Richard, 391
Osman, Abdul Magid, 49
Osorio, Roso, 99
Osterwalder, Fritz, 524
Osunde, Lasisi A., 52
Otman, Alp, 525
Ott, Harry, 330
Ould Haidalla, Mohamed Khouna, 310
Óváry, Miklós, 334
Owens, Major, 174
Ozaki, Susumu, 433
Ozal, Turgut, 526, 527

Pabón Pabón, Rosemberg, 103
Pacho, Valentín, 164, 165, 166
Pacoste, Cornel, 361
Padilla, Hernán, 170, 171
Padilla Rush, Rigoberto, xv, 141, 142, 143
Paek Hak-im, 237
Pagmadula, 255
Pahlavi, Shah Reza, 3, 25
Pajetta, Giancarlo, 489, 495
Pak Song-chol, 238, 372
Pak Song-pong, 239
Palero, Francisco, 515

Paliszewski, Jacek, 430
Pallejo, Bux, 264
Palme, Olof, 123, 521
Pana, Gheorghe, 361
Panditha, L. W., 275, 276
Panguene, Armando, 47
Panjsheri, Ghulam Dastigir, 186
Papaioannu, Ezekias, xxi, 311, 400, 448–52 passim
Papajorgji, Harilla, 295
Papandreou, Andreas, 300, 307, 309, 341, 441, 495
Papazov, Nacho, 307
Papazov, Tencho, 303
Parada, Soledad, 430
Paraluta, Mihai, 412
Pardo Sánchez, Antonio, 431
Pascual Moncayo, Pablo, 149–50
Passent, Daniel, 345
Passeri, Marianne, 496
Pastora, Edén, 108, 114, 156, 157
Patan, Ion, 361
Pato, Octovio, 511
Pauling, Linus, 472
Paulo, Simao, 9
Pavelic, Stane, 433
Pavlov, Georgi S., 378
Pavlov, S. P., 256
Payet, Bruny (Ary), 5, 53, 54
Paz Estenssoro, Víctor, 87
Paz Galarraga, Angel, 181
Paz Zamora, Jaime, 85, 87
Pe Tint, 204, 205
Pecchioli, Ugo, 489
Peci, Shefqet, 293
Pegov, Nikolai M., 378
Pelikán, Jiří, 321
Pelinka, Anton, 444, 445
Pell, Claiborne, 389
Pelshe, Arvid I., 375, 376, 459
Pen Sovan, 235
Peña Gómez, José Francisco, 116
Peng Chia-Shin (Fung Kya-Shin), 205, 206
Peng Zhen, 209, 212, 213, 214, 242
Percovitch, Luí, 167
Percy, Jim, 196, 201
Pereira, Jorge, 82
Perera, J. A. K., 275
Peres, Shimon, 368
Pérez, Camilio O., 428
Pérez, Humberto, 112, 113
Pérez, Pástor, 99
Pérez, Sigifredo Ochoa, 122
Pérez Arreola, Evaristo, 150
Pérez de Cuellar, Javier, 193, 194, 265, 319, 483

Pérez Herrero, Antonio, 110
Peristeri, Pillo, 294
Perlo, Victor, 173
Perrott, Kenneth William, 261
Persaud, Narbata, 138
Persaud, Rohit, 138
Persaud, Rupu Daman, 138
Petas, Khristos, 448
Petersen, Arne Herlov, 455
Petersen, Gert, 456
Petkoff, Teodoro, 178, 179
Petrov, Lazar, 303
Pettersson, Roland, 522
Peytcheva, Vesselina, 430
Pham Hung, 280, 281, 282
Pham Quang Phuoc, 433
Pham Van Dong, 247, 280, 281, 284
Phan Anh, 428, 433
Phillipe, Francisco, 430
Phoumi Vongvichit, 246
Phoun Sipaseut, 246, 248
Picado, Teodoro, 105
Pinchinte, José Leoncio, 120
Pinedo, Adolfo, 515
Pinochet, Augusto, 81, 96, 97
Pinto, Tirso, 179
Piot, Hippolite, 53
Piquet, René, 464
Pita, Dan, 365
Pitra, František, 312
Pittman, John, 173
Pla, Juan Francisco, 515
Plana, Alfonso, 99
Planinc, Milka, 403
Platts-Mills, John, 433
Pliaka, Sokrat, 300, 301
Plissonier, Gaston, 464
Pocock, Gerry, 478
Podgorny, Nikolai V., 379
Pol Pot, xviii, 235, 236, 249
Poledník, Jindřich, 312
Polikeit, Georg, 470
Ponama, Jean-Baptiste, 53, 54
Ponomarev, Boris N., 43, 44, 373, 397–400 passim, 435, 467, 482, 495, 514
Popa, Agim, 301
Poperen, Claude, 464
Popescu, Dumitru, 361, 371
Popović, Miladin, 294
Poppe, Ulrike, 324
Porcella Peña, Miguel Antonio, 158
Porebski, Tadeusz, 343
Porkkala, Christina, 462
Posadas Segura, Marcos Leonel, 150
Poumbouris, Mikhail, 448

Pozderac, Hamdija, 403
Pozsgay, Imre, 336
Prado, Jorge del, xvi, 164
Prem Tinsulanond, 277, 278
Prestes, Luiz Carlos, 89
Priemer, Rolf, 470
Prigoshin, Jorge, 430
Primakov, E. M., 428
Primakov, Gennadi A., 391
Puerta Aponte, Gabriel, 181
Puja, Frigyes, 337, 341
Puku, Mariano Garcia, 10
Pungan, Vasile, 368
Purdeli, Abdus Sattan, 186
Pütz, Marcel, 496

Qader, Abdul, 186, 187, 188,
    191
Qa'empanah, Gholamhassan, 24
Qasim, Abu al-, 61
Qasim, Salih Muslih, 72
Qian Liren, 197
Qian Qichen, 218, 332, 343, 393,
    394
Qiao Shi, 209
Qin Chuan, 215
Qin Jiwei, 209
Quiñónez, Francisco, 123

Rabbani, Burnhanuddin, 193
Rabbuh, Yasir Abd, 67
Rácz, Sándor, 337
Radix, Kendrick, 124
Radović, Miljan, 403
Radu, Ion, 361
Radulescu, Gheorghe, 361
Rafi, Mohammed, 186, 188
Ragchaa, Tumenbayaryn, 255,
    256, 257
Rahman, Abdur, 203
Rahman, Matiur, 203
Rahman, Zia-ur, 203
Raimajhi, Keshar Jung, 257
Rajaratnam, S., 254
Rajavi, Massoud, 27
Rajk, László (father), 335
Rajk, László (son), 339, 340
Rákosi, Mátyás, 334, 335
Rakowski, Mieczyslaw, 342,
    344, 393
Ralite, Jack, 466
Ramadan, Taha, Yosin, 368
Ramazandideh, Asef, 24
Ramdhanny, Lyden, 126
Ramili, Bu Jama'a, 69
Ramin, Julien, 53, 54

Ramírez Cuellar, Héctor, 153
Ramírez Mercado, Sergio, 154,
    158, 257
Ramos, Alberto, 120
Ramos, Fidel, 274
Ranaweera, Eva, 431
Rangel, José Vicente, 178–81
    passim
Rao, C. Rajeswara, xvii, 220,
    223, 224, 225
Rapela, Julio, 176
Rasadi, Ahmad Ali, 24
Rashid, Abdallah, Ali al-, 4, 12,
    13
Rashidov, Sharaf R., 23, 377
Ratebzad, Anahita, 186, 188,
    191, 431
Rathenau, Walter, 329
Ratnaweera, H. G. S., 275, 276
Rayah, Assim O. al-, 431
Raziq, Husayn Abd al-, 19
Razmjo, Abdul Zahoor, 186
Razumovsky, G. P., 378
Razzak, Abdur, 203
Reagan, Ronald, 20, 33, 36, 39,
    77–81 passim, 106, 111–16
    passim, 124, 134, 140, 174,
    218, 219, 234, 290, 357, 358,
    359, 367–70 passim, 387–91
    passim, 394–97 passim, 401,
    425, 435, 451, 467, 473, 518
Rebelo, Jorge, 47
Redmond, Tom, 487, 488
Reichlin, Alfredo, 489
Reimann, Max, 470
Reintoft, Hanne, 454
Reiter, Karl, 443
Rejmond, Wladyslaw, 357
Rekunkov, Aleksandr, 380
Renard, Claude, 446
René, France Albert, 216, 241
Rényi, Péter, 339
Renzi, Renzo, 514
Revel, Jean-François, 438
Rexha, Lumturi, 293, 296
Reyes, Rodrigo, 154
Reyes, Román, 99
Reyes Dominguez, Pablo, 430
Reyes Matos, José María, 142,
    143
Reza'i, Mohsen, 26
Ribičič, Mitja, xx, 369, 403, 495
Richard, Christian Remi, 319
Riddell, John, 91
Riggs, Chris (Kojo) de, 124, 128
Rigout, Marcel, 466
Ríos, John Agudelo, 104
Ríos, Daniel, 135

Ríos Montt, Efraín, 131, 132,
    135, 137
Risquet Valdés, Jorge, 110
Rivas, Eduardo, 156
Rivera, Juanito, 266, 268
Rizo Alvarez, Julián, 110
Roa, Emilio, 163
Robelo, Alfonso, 108, 156
Roca, Roberto, 121
Roca Calderío, Blas, 110
Rochet, Waldeck, 466
Rodríguez, Ana María, 142
Rodríguez, Anastacio E., 158
Rodríguez, Arsénio, 428
Rodríguez, Carlos Rafael, 80,
    110–15 passim, 400
Rodríguez, Dimos, 121
Rodríguez, Irene, 82, 83
Rodríguez, Mario, 143
Rodríguez Bautista, Nicolás, 104
Rodríguez dos Santos, Geraldo,
    88
Rodríguez Ruiz, José Napoleón,
    120
Rojas, Roberto, 164
Rojas Niño, German, 103
Rolandhis, Nicos, 451
Romanev, Aleksei, V., 45, 46,
    400
Romanik, Jerzy, 343
Romanov, Grigori V., 288, 311,
    373–77 passim, 401, 463
Romero, Carlos, 99
Romero Barceló, Carlos, 170,
    171
Romero Marín, Francisco, 515
Roopharine, Rupert, 138
Rosa, Alfred Christian, 433
Rose, Fred, 92
Rosen, Frank, 174
Rosenthal, Joseph, 18
Rosschou, Bo, 428, 453
Rosschou, Carl, 428
Roumain, Jacques, 141
Rounaniemi, Paavo, 432
Royo, Aristides, 159
Rozenoer, Sergei, 384
Rubbi, Antonio, 495
Ruiz, Nancy, 430
Ruiz Caro, Efraín, 432
Ruiz Hernández, Henry, 154,
    157, 158, 397
Rusakov, Konstantin V., 373,
    378, 399
Rusev, Svetlin, 306
Ryabov, Yakov P. 379
Ryzhkov, Nikolai I., 373, 377,
    379

Saadi, Vicente Leonidas, 84
Saarinen, Aarne, xxviii, 458–63
    passim
Sadat, Anwar al-, 18, 20, 21
Sadeqi, Mohammed Yaseen, 186
Sa'id, Rif'at al-, 19
Said Barre, Mohamed, 495
Saidu, Turay, 430
Saito, Kazuyoshi, 433
Sakharov, Andrei, 383
Sakharov, Boris, 432
Sakik, Hisham, 69
Sako, Mamadu, 428
Salam, Abdur, 203
Salamat, Hasim, 272
Salas, Luís, 181
Salas, Rodolfo, 266, 268
Salgado Tamayo, Manuel, 119
Sali Vongkhamsao, 246
Salibi, Maurice, 65, 68
Salih, Abd-al-Rahman, xii, 55
Salim, Ahmad, 62–65 passim
Salmon, Jean, 433
Samad, Nadim 'Abd al-, 41–44
    passim, 428
Samayoa, Salvador, 120, 123
Samhoun, Rafic, 40, 43
Samon, Vi-gnaket, 246
San Yu, 206
Sánchez, Juan, 164
Sánchez, Luís, xv, 154
Sánchez, Mario, 135
Sánchez, Otto, 135, 137
Sánchez Montero, Simón, 515
Sánchez Rebolledo, Adolfo, 150
Sandu, Vasile, 370
Sankatsingh, Glenn, 171
Sankiaho, Risto, 460
Santana, Daniel, 430
Santos, Garcia dos, 512
Santos, José Eduardo dos, x,
    5–11 passim, 397, 400
Santos, Manuel dos, 51
Santos, Marcelino dos, 47, 48
Sargin, Nahit, 525
Sarisözen, Veysi, 525
Sarlis, Dimitris, 481
Sarlós, István, 334
Sassou Ngouesso, Denis, x,
    16, 17
Savary, Alain, 341
Savola, Helui, 173
Šavrda, Jaromír, 318
Say Phuthang, 235
Sayyaf, Abdul, 193
Schabowski, Günter, 322, 333
Schäfer, Max, 470
Scharf, Erwin, 399, 443, 445
Scheidler, Kurt, 11

Schembri, Guzeppi, 499
Scheufelberger, Albert, 122
Schjerning, Anker, 454, 455
Schlüter, Poul, 453, 455
Schmidt, Bart, 501
Schmidt, Petrus, 431
Schmitt, Horst, xxiii, 477
Schreuders, Gijs, 502–5 passim
Schröder, Karl Heinz, 470
Schürer, Gerhard, 322
Schwager, Irma, 443
Sciberras, Lilian, 498
Scocozza, Benito, 457
Scoon, Paul, 127
Seaga, Edward, 144, 145, 146
Seagree, Clifton, 146
Sebestyén, Ilona, 428
Seghers, Anna, 329
Seguel, Rodolfo, 97
Séguy, Georges, 464
Selassie, Haile, 22
Selenica, Eleni, 296
Sen, Mohit, 223
Sendov, Blagovest, 428
Serafim (archbishop), 300
Sereenendorj, N., 256
Serra, Julián, 164
Seroni, Adriana, 489
Shagari, Alhaji Shehu, 6
Shakak, Abd-al-Majid, 62
Shalayev, Stepan A., 373
Shaltuki, Reza, 24
Shamir, Yitzhak, 32, 368
Sharif, Aziz, 428, 431
Sharif, Bassim Abu, 432
Sharif, Mahir al-, 34, 36
Sharkey, Stan, 198
Sharma, Jitendra, 433
Sharma, Yogendra, 223, 224
Sharqawi, Abd-al-Rahman, 431
Shawi, Niqula al-, 40
Shcharansky, Anatoly, 383
Shchelokov, Nikolai A., 376, 379
Shcherbitsky, Vladimir V., 373,
    376
Shefqet, Musaraj, 293
Shehu, Feçor, 294, 298
Shehu, Fiqret, 294
Shehu, Mehmet, 294–98 passim
Shemtov, Victor, 368
Sheppard, Barry, 175
Shevardnadze, Eduard A., 373,
    399
Shibaev, Aleksei, I., 379
Shiga, Yoshio, 234
Shioya, Kazuo, 244
Shkadov, Ivan, 387
Shmuelevich, Mattetiahu, 368
Shopova, Stanka, 303

Shtemenko, Sergei, 423
Shultz, George, 216–19 passim,
    341, 387, 425
Siba'i, Umar, 65
Sibeko, Denis, 430
Sid, Hassan Gassim al-, 62
Sienkiewicz, Henryk, 357
Silbermayr, Walter, 443
Siles Suazo, Hernán, 81, 85,
    86, 87
Silva, Bernadeen, 433
Silva, Jayetilleke de, 275
Silva, Kattorge P., xix, 275, 276
Silva, Lindolfo, 88
Silva, Luis Inácio da, 89
Silva, Luis Tenorio de, 88
Sindermann, Horst, 322
Singh, Ganesh Man, 258
Singh, Moni, 203
Singh, Natwar, 194
Sinha, Indradeep, 223
Sinisalo, Taisto, 458, 459
Sinuraya, Tomas, 229
Siqueira, Givaldo, 88
Sisavat Keobounphan, 246
Sisomphon Lovansai, 246
Sison, José Maria, 268
Sissoko, Filifing, 428
Sithole, Ndabaningi, 75
Sitnikov, N. I., 378
Sitthi Sawetsila, 279
Siwak, Albin, 343
Siwicki, Florian, 343
Siyolwe, Joshua, 431
Sizov, G. F., 497
Skachkov, Semyon A., 379
Skhlyarov, Yuri A., 426
Skilton, Aubrey Bruce, 261
Slovo, Joe, 59
Slyunkov, Nikolai N., 377
Small, Hugh, 144
Smirnov, A. I., 256
Smirnov, Vitali S., 394
Smith, Ian, 75
Smith, Jackson, 261, 262
Smith, Samantha, 388
Smolentsev, Yevgeny A., 380
So Chol, 237
So Kwang-hui, 237
So Yun-sok, 237
Soares, Mário, 441, 512, 513
Sobayh, Muhammad, 431
Sobieski, Jan III (king), 346
Sohn, Ole, 453
Sokolov, S. L., 195
Solheim, Erik, 508
Solís Castro, José, 118
Solomentsev, Mikhail S., 373–79
    passim, 401–2

Solomon, Mark, 174
Solstad, Dag, 510
Solt, Ferzo, 525
Somoza Debayle, Anastasio, 81, 154
Son Sann, 216, 236
Son Song-pil, 239
Song Renqiong, 209
Sophokles, G., 448
Soppela, Markku, 430
Sorensen, Ole, 453
Sosa Castro, Jesús, 150
Soto Prieto, Lionel, 110
Soubanh Srithirath, 248, 249
Souk Vongsak, 246
Souphanouvong, 246, 247
Sourani, Jamal, 433
Sousa, Manuel Bernarde de, 10
Sousa, Rubén Darío, xv, 158, 161, 162, 398, 400
Souvanna Phouma (prince), 246
Souza Batista, Clito Manuel, 158
Sozigva, P., 400
Spasov, Boris, 433
Spengler, Wilhelm, 470
Špiljak, Mika, 369, 403, 495
Spiller, Herbert Leonard, 261
Spinelli, Altiero, 494
Srebrić, Borislav, 403
Srivastava, K. G., 429
Stalin, Joseph, 246
Stamate, Victor, 432
Stambolić, Petar, 300, 398, 403
Stanishev, Dimitur, 302
Stankov, Georgi, 304
Stauffenberg, Claus von, 329
Steele, James, 174
Stafanak, Michal, 445
Stefanetti, Walter, 496
Stefani, Simon, 293, 297
Steigan, Paal, xxii, 505
Stenius-Kaukonen, Marjatta, 458
Stepan, Miroslav, 431, 432
Stephens García, Manuel, 149, 150
Stewart, Edwina, 487
Stewart, James, 488
Stoian, Ion, 361
Stoica, Gheorghe, 361, 371
Stojanović, Nikola, 403
Stone, Richard, 80, 123, 132, 157
Stoph, Willi, 322, 332
Strachan, Selwyn, 124
Strauss, Franz-Josef, 327, 330, 359, 367, 415
Stroessner, Alfredo, 163
Štrougal, Lubomír, 312, 313, 408

Struev, Aleksandr, 378
Stuby, Gerhard, 433
Stukalin, Boris, I., 378
Šturcl, Michal, 314
Stürmann, Werner, 470
Suárez Lopéz, Luís, 432
Suazo Córdova, Roberto, 142
Subasinghe, D. W., 428
Subasinghe, T. B., 275
Sudiman, Satiadjaya, 226, 227
Sudomo (admiral), 227
Sufi, Mustafa, 452
Suhail, 'Abd al-Wahid, 45
Suharto (president), 227, 228
Su'id, Muhammad, 69
Sukhai, Pariag, 138
Šuković, Mijat, 403
Šukrija, Ali, 403
Sulayman, Muhammad Ahmad, 61, 63
Sunalp, Turgut, 526
Sunmonu, Hassan, 52
Supple, Clement Thomas, 198
Surjeet, H. S., 223
Surya, Mera, 227
Suslov, Mikhail A., 374, 375, 402
Suwardi, S. P., 227
Suzuki, Shiro, 432
Svarinskas, Alfonsas, 384
Švestka, Oldřich, 313
Svoboda, Stanislav, 319
Swift, Frank, 428
Swirgon, Waldemar, 343
Sychev, Vyacheslav, 410
Symon, Peter Dudley, xviii, 196–200 passim
Szasz, Iosif, 361
Szürös, Mátyás, 334, 337, 341

Tabari, Ehsan, 24
Tabrizi, Musavi, 25
Tadioli, Pedro, 82
Taft, Mark, 197
Taik Aung, 206
Tairov, Tair, 428
Talas, Mustafa, 309
Talbot, Karen, 428
Tallgren, Tutta, 458
Tambo, Oliver, 59, 368
Tammisola, Helja, 458
Tan Zhenlin, 209
Tanada, Lorenzo, 274
Tanaka, Kakuei, 185, 231
Tanchev, Petur, 303
Taneva, Maria, 430
Tanov, Georgy, 22

Tarabulsi, Fawaz, 44
Taraki, Nur Mohammed, 186, 187
Taratuta, Vasili N., 378
Tardos, Márton, 338
Tarigo, Enrique, 176
Tariki, 'Abd al-Majid, 69
Tavárez, Claudio, 116
Tawil, Suhayl, 43
Taylor, Sid, 173
Tchoe, Minsin, 433
Tedlay, Addis, 21
Teixeira, Blanqui, 511
Teixeira, Gail, 139
Tejera Gómez, Luís, 134
Tekere, Edgar, 75
Tekeze-Shoa, Aytenfiso, 23, 319
Teklu, Zaudi, 23
Téllez, Dora Maria, 154
Temple, Nina, 478
Tennila, Esko-Juhani, 461, 463
Terenzi, Amerigo, 428
Terracini, Umberto, 433
Tetényi, Pál, 337
Thaim, Maguette, 56
Thaim, Samba Dioulde, 56
Thakin Ba Thein Tin, xvii, 204, 205, 206
Thälmann, Ernst, 474
Thapa, Surya Bahadur, 258
Thatcher, Margaret, 415, 435
Thawadi, Ahmad Ibrahim Muhammad al-, 12
Theodorakis, Mikis, 428
Théodore, René, xv, 140, 141
Thiele, Ilse, 322, 430
Thio, Boe, 501
Thomai, Themie, 300
Thomas, Clive, 138
Thomas, Louis, 391
Thomas Trottman, Ruperto Luther, 158, 160
Thorez, Maurice, 465, 466
Thorez-Vermeersch, Jeannette, 465
Thoroddsen, Gunner, 484, 485, 486
Thystere Tchikaya, Jean-Pierre, 16
Tikhonov, Nikolai A., 292, 300, 373, 375, 392, 397, 398, 408
Tikhvinsky, S. L., 218
Tin U, 206, 207
Tin Yee, 204, 206
Tindemans, Leo, 210, 392
Tirado López, Víctor Manuel, 154
Tisch, Harry, 322

Tito, Josip Broz, 294
Titov, Igor V., 391
To Huu, 280
Tobagi, Walter, 496
Todorov, Stanko, 302
Togliatti, Palmiro, 489, 494
Toiviainen, Seppo, 458
Toledo Plata, Carlos, 103
Tolstikov, Vasili, 401
Tolubeyev, Nikita, 307, 311
Tomášek, František, 317, 321
Torres, Emma, 428
Torres, Marcelo, 103
Torrijos, Omar, 159–62 passim
Tortoló Comas, Pedro, 114
Tortorella, Aldo, 489, 491, 494
Tóth, Dezsö, 339, 340
Tóth, Károly, 433
Totu, Ion, 361
Touré, Ahmed Sékou, 14, 310
Toussaint L'Overture, Pierre Do-
    minique, 141
Tran Kien, 280
Tran Van Anh, 431
Tran Xuan Bach, 280
Trapeznikov, Sergei P., 378
Travaliaris, Triantafyllos, 200
Trávníček, Tomáš, 318, 428
Traykov, Boyan, 307
Trevisin, Gabriella, 310
Trudeau, Pierre, 92, 93
Trumka, Richard, 174
Truong Chinh, 280, 281, 285,
    286
Tsanov, Vasil, 302
Tsedenbal, Yumjaagyin, xviii,
    255, 256, 257, 311, 372
Tsiambis, D., 482
Tsiba, Florent, 16
Tsolakis, Kostas, 481
Tsukasov, Sergei V., 426
Tubi, Tawfiq, 30–33 passim
Tucker, Marilyn Gay, 261
Tucker, Mike, 260
Tudev, Lodongiyn, 255
Tu'ma, Emile, 30
Tunnerman Bernheim, Carlos,
    154, 155, 158
Tupaz, Bonafacio, 269
Turf, Jeff, 446
Turk, Riyad al-, 66
Turzo, Eugen, 313
Tyazhelhnikov, Yevgeny M.,
    369, 378
Tycner, Wanda, 430
Tyner, Jarvis, 173
Tyrluk, Ryszard, 428

U Bo Ni, 206, 207
Udom Srisuwan, 278
Ueda, Koichiro, 230
Ulanfu, 209
Ulbricht, Walter, 323
Ulhoa, Benedito, 89
Ulusu, Bülent, 341
Ulyanovsky, Rostislav A., 223,
    224
Ungo, Guillermo Manuel, 120,
    123
Unzueta Lorenzana, Gerardo, 150
Upegui, Mario, 99
Urbany, Dominique, 496, 497
Urbany, Jacqueline, 496
Urbany, René, xxii, 496, 497
Uribe, Armando, 433
Ursu, Ion, 361
Urzua, Carlos, 96
Ustinov, Dimitri F., 307, 311,
    373, 375, 388, 397, 398, 423
Uthman, Al-Gazuli (Jizuli) Said,
    61
Uti, Abdul Aziz al-, 39

Vadtvedt, Bitte, 508
Vafiades, Markos, 483
Vaidyalingam, A., 275
Vaino, Karl G., 384
Vaivods, Julijans, 384
Valanidou, Christina, 431
Valbon, Georges, 469
Valdés Menéndez, Ramiro, 110
Valencia Rodríguez, Luís, 216,
    333
Vallejo Martínez, Demetrio, 151
Van Tien Dung, 247, 280
van Geyt, Louis, xxi, 446
van Hoek, Ton, 501, 504
van Kalken, Piet, 502
Vanous, Jan, 410
Varas, Miguel, 432
Varela, Alfredo, 428
Varga, Pál, 337
Vargas, Damaso, 154
Vargas Carbonell, Humberto,
    xiv, 105, 106, 107
Várkonyi, Péter, 337, 341, 342,
    445
Varona y Duque Estrada, Fran-
    cisco, 433
Vashchenko, Grigori I., 379
Vashchenko, Lydía, 384
Vásquez, Alvaro, 99
Vásquez Castaño, Fabio, 103
Vassallo, Anthony, xxii, 498, 500

Vatikiotis, P. J., 21
Vecht, Constant, 503
Vega Imbert, Augusto, 116
Vegh Villegas, Alejandro, 177
Veiga, Roberto, 112
Velarde, Mario, 86
Velasco Muñoz, Miguel Angel,
    150
Velásquez, Andrés, 178
Vellayati, Ali Akbar, 216
Veloso, Jacinto Soares, 47
Ver, Fabian C., 274
Vera, Ernesto, 432
Vercaigne, Jules, 446
Verdeţ, Ilie, 361, 363
Veress, Miklós, 339
Veress, Péter, 341, 343
Vergès, Laurence, 53, 54
Vergès, Paul, xii, 53, 54
Verner, Paul, 322
Veselinov, Slavko, 403
Viana, Gentil, 9
Viannet, Louis, 464
Vides Casanova, Carlos Eugenio,
    122
Vidić, Dobrivoje, 403
Viega, Roberto, 429
Vieira, Gilberto, xiii, 98–102
    passim
Vila, Olivera, 164
Vilariques, Sergio, 511
Villacorta, Jorge, 123
Villalobos, Joaquín, 121, 122
Villegas, Jesús, 99
Vilner, Mier, xi, 2, 30–33
    passim, 36
Vilon-Guezo, Romain, 429
Vincent, Madeleine, 464
Vintró, Eulalia, 515
Vire-Tuominen, Mirjam, 430
Vitaly, K., 499
Vladimov, Georgi, 383
Vlajković, Radovan, 403
Vlasov, Aleksandr, 400
Vo Bam, xxvii
Vo Chi Cong, 280–83 passim
Vo Nguyen Giap, xxvii
Vo Van Kiet, 280, 282
Vogel, Hans-Joachim, 392
Voigt, Karsten, 495
Voitec, Stefan, 361
Volio, Fernando, 108, 109
Volio, Jorge, 105
Vonderführ, G., 504
Voronov, Gennadi, 402
Vorotnikov, Vitali I., 373–79
    passim, 402

Vos, Peter de, 51
Voss, Avgust E., 399, 400, 456
Vrhovec, Josip, 403
Vu Quang, 398

Wadijimbi, Manuel Miguel Car-
    velho, 9
Wagner, Dieter, 431
Wagner, Ingmar, 453
Wahishi, Ahmad Salim al-, 431
Wahl, Gunnar, 505
Wajed, Sheikh Hasina, 203
Wald, George, 472
Walde, Werner, 322
Waldorff, Mikael, 457
Walesa, Lech, 175, 321, 356
Walker, Doris Brin, 433
Wallenberg, Raoul, 522
Walsch, Sam, 92
Walvisch, Simone, 501
Wan Li, 209
Wang Bingqian, 209, 212
Wang Congwu, 209
Wang Heshou, 209
Wang Ruoshi, 184
Wang Zhaoguo, 209, 215
Wang Zhen, 209
Warrad, Faik (Faiq), xi, 2, 37,
    38, 39
Warren, Mac, 175
Washington, Harold, 174
Watanjar, Mohammed Aslam,
    186
Waters, Mary-Alice, 175
Wazzan, Shafiq, 41
Webb, Sam, 173
Weber, Ellen, 470
Wei Guoqing, 209
Weinberger, Caspar, 216, 219,
    243
Weir, John, 92
Werner, Lars, xxiii, 216, 519,
    520, 522
Wesquet, Jean, 496
West, James, 173
Wetherborne, Egbert, 160
Weyl, Roland, 433
Whaley Martínez, Leopoldo
    Arthur, 150
Wheelock Román, Jaime, 154
Whiteman, Unison, 124, 125,
    397
Wiegand, Manfred, 432
Wijeweera, Rohan, 276
Wilcox, V. G., 260
Wilhjelm, Preben, 457
Williams, David, 301

Willoch, Kaare, 506, 507
Wilson, Charles, 173
Wilson, Harold, 480
Wimmer, Ernst, 443
Winsor, Curtin, 109
Winston, Henry, 173
Winter, Helen, 173
Winter, Richard, 361
Withages, Jack, 446
Wogderess, Fikre-Selassie, 21, 22
Wolfe, Richard C., xviii, 259,
    260
Wolff, Jaap, 501
Wozniak, Marian, 343, 399
Wu Jinhua, 51
Wu Xueqian, 209, 217, 219, 242,
    495

Xi Zhongxun, 209, 468
Xoxe, Koce, 294
Xu Shiyou, 209
Xu Xiangqian, 209
Xuan Thuy, 11

Yadav, Shyam Lal, 319
Yagci, Nabi, 526
Yamanu, Hailu, 23
Yang Dezhi, 209
Yang Huanan, 433
Yang Hyong-sop, 239
Yang, Jimmy, 205
Yang Jingren, 215
Yang Shangkun, 209, 212
Yang Yichen, 212
Yang Yong, 209
Yankov, Asen, 303
Yao Yilin, 209, 211, 216
Yat Kong, 252
Yata, 'Ali, 4, 45
Ye Jianying, 209, 211, 214
Yepishev, Aleksei A., 370
Yershov, Anatoly M., 379
Yi Chong-ok, 237
Yi Kun-mo, 237
Yi Song-sil, 237
Yi Won-kyung, 241
Yi Yong-ik, 239
Yiannou, Mina, 482
Yim Chun-chu, 237, 239
Yo Yong-ku, 239
Yon Hyong-muk, 237
Yoneda, Togo, 244
Yorck von Wartenburg, Hans,
    329

Yordanov, Georgi, 302, 306
Yotov, Yordan, 308
Yu Qiuli, 209, 212
Yun Ki-pok, 237, 239

Zagarell, Mike, 173
Zagladin, Vadim V., xxv, 390,
    394, 399, 400, 445, 467, 468,
    482, 495, 504
Zahir Shah (king), 193
Zahram, Ali Sa'id, 19
Zaikov, Lev N., 378
Zakariya, Ibrahim, 62, 428, 429
Zakhariades, N., 481
Zambrano, José, 398
Zamora Rivas, Rubén Ignacio,
    120, 123
Zamyatin, Leonid M., 387
Zangheri, Renato, 489, 491
Zarev, Kiril, 302
Žarković, Vidoje, 216, 403
Zarshenas, Kiumars, 24
Zaw Mai, 205
Zayyad, Tawfiq, 31
Zayyat, M. al-, 19
Zeary, Saleh Mohammed, 186
Zhang Chunqiao, 211
Zhang Tingfa, 209
Zhang Wenjin, 219
Zhao Ziyang, 183, 184, 209–16
    passim, 219, 242
Zharikov, Aleksandr N., 431
Zheng Tianxiang, 212
Zhilin, Y. V., 399
Zhivkov, Todor Khristov, xix,
    67, 302–11 passim, 332, 343,
    399, 469
Zhivkov, Vladimir, 304, 306
Zhivkova, Liudmila, 304
Zhou Yang, 214–15
Zhu Liang, 197
Zhuang Zedong, 211
Zhukov, Yuri, 434, 435
Zia, Begum Khalida, 203
Ziartidhis, Andreas, 429, 448
Zia-ul Haq, Mohammad, 263,
    264, 265, 394
Ziçishti, Llambi, 294
Zimiamin, Mikhail V., 373, 398,
    504
Zimmermann, Friedrich, 472–73
Zlatinov, Vladimir, 431
Zorinsky, Edward, 216
Zucolillo, Aldo, 163
Zuken, Joe, 92
Zúñiga, Antonio, 165
Zvěřina, Josef, 317

Index of Subjects

Discussions that can be readily located under the subheadings within each profile are not indexed here. A reader interested in Soviet foreign relations, for example, should first consult the "Foreign Affairs" section of the USSR profile. Listed here under "USSR, foreign relations" is information on this subject that occurs in other profiles.

Afghanistan: and Iran, 26, 27; Soviet troops in, 183, 290, 394; concern with cadres, 183, 184; treaties with Mongolia, 257; and Pakistan, 264, 265; trade agreement with Bulgaria, 310; and CMEA, 408; Radio Moscow error; 381; and USSR, 394–95
—CPs approving Soviet invasion: Réunion, 54; Yemen, 73; Bolivian, 86; Mexican, 150, 152
—CPs criticizing Soviet invasion: Burmese, 208; Albanian, 302; Romanian, 371; British, 408; Italian, 493, 494; Norwegian, 509
—effect of invasion on CPs: Belgian, 447, 448; Danish, 455; French 465, 467, 468
Afghanistan, People's Democratic Party of, 51, 183, 186–89, 311
Africa: and China, 216. *See also individual countries by name*
Africa, Horn of: U.S. involvement in, 23
African National Congress, 5, 49, 50, 57, 58–59, 368
Afro-Asian Peoples' Solidarity Organization, 3, 55, 72–73, 255, 431
Agriculture: in Agnola, 10; in Mozambique, 48, 49–50; in Zimbabwe, 76; in Cuba, 112, 113; collectivization, 113, 155, 247, 281; in Grenada, 127; in Nicaragua, 155; land reforms and problems in Afghanistan, 190, 191; in Laos, 247; in Mongolia, 255, 256; in Vietnam, 281, 282; in Albania, 299; in Bulgaria, 304, 305; in Czechoslovakia, 315; in Hungary, 336, 338; in Poland, 352, 353–54; in Romania, 363, 364; Soviet, under Brezhnev, 373; problems of Soviet, 378, 382, 383; CMEA cooperation in, 409; GDR help to Soviets, 413
Albania: trade, 298–301 *passim*; trade agreement with Bulgaria, 380
—pro-Albanian CPs: Brazil, 88, 302; Canada, 91, 94; Dominican Republic, 116; Peru, 164; Suriname, 171; New Zealand, 259, 260; FRG, 301, 302, 475; Great Britain, 301, 302; Portugal, 302; Denmark, 457; Sweden, 522
Albanian Party of Labor, 293–96, 302, 426
Algeria: and Angola, 11; and Morocco, 45; and French CP, 469
Algerian Communist Party, *see* Socialist Vanguard Party
Alliance for the Unity of the People (Venezuela), 178, 180
Angola: and Congo, 17; Cuban troops in, 115; and China, 216; cultural agreement with Mongolia, 275; guerrillas in, 290; kidnapping of Czechoslovaks, 319; and USSR, 397; and CMEA, 408; and French CP, 469
Angola, National Front for the Liberation of, 8
Angola, National Union for the Total Independence of, 5, 8, 11
Angola, Popular Movement for the Liberation of–Labor Party, 5–6, 8–9, 10, 12; and CPSU, 400
Antigua and Barbuda: and China, 216
Arab League: and Bulgaria, 309
Arab Socialist Union (Egypt), 18, 19, 21
Arab Socialist Work Party (Saudi Arabia), 55
Argentina: and Cuba, 115; and Uruguay, 177
Argentina, Communist Party of, 81, 82–84; and Moroccan CP, 45; and *World Marxist Review*, 426; and CPSU, 400–401
Armed Forces: CP infiltrates in Iran, 25, 26, 27; Mozambique, 48–49; Grenada, 124, 126; Nicaragua, 156; Afghanistan, 187, 188, 189; China, 210–14 *passim*; USSR, 289, 374; Albania, 296, 297; Bulgaria, 309; GDR, 326–27; Romania, 365; Soviet, and Korean Air Lines incident, 387–88; Soviet buildup in Far East, 396. *See also* Warsaw Treaty Organization
Armed Forces of National Resistance (El Salvador), 121
Armed Forces of National Revolution (Puerto Rico), 170

Armed People's Organization (Guatemala), 133–34
Armed Revolutionary Movement (Puerto Rico), 171
Arms control negotiations: Soviet positions and proposals, 289, 290, 388–91; suspension of, 290; Romanian calls for bilateral disarmament, 369–70; ban on weapons in space, 388, 389; and WTO, 417, 421–26 *passim*; French CP on inclusion of French missiles, 467; French CP's calls for balanced reductions, 467, 468; Italian CP on, 493
Association of Southeast Asian Nations, 229, 235, 247, 252, 254, 285
Australia, 185; and China, 216
Australia, Communist Party of, 195, 196–97
Australia, Communist Party of (Marxist-Leninist), 195, 196, 197
Australia, Socialist Party of, 195–200 *passim*
Australia and New Zealand, Spartacist League of, 195, 196, 200
Australian Marxist Forum, 196, 198
Austria: trade agreement with Albania, 299, 301
Austrian Communist Party, 438, 442–43, 443–46; and CPSU, 399
Autonomous Socialst Party (Switzerland), 524

Bahrain: and Yemen, 73
Bahrain, Popular Front for the Liberation of, 13
Bahrain National Liberation Front, 1, 3–4, 12–13; and Saudi CP, 55
Baluchi People's Liberation Front (Pakistan), 264
Bangladesh, Communist Party of, 185, 202–3
Basque Communist Party (Spain), 517
Basque Homeland and Liberty (Spain), 517; active in Costa Rica, 180
Ba'th Party (Iraq), 28, 29
Ba'th Party (Syria), 1–2, 66, 67; and Palestine CP, 36; and Mongolia, 257
Belgian Communist Party, 438, 446–48; and *World Marxist Review*, 427; and French CP, 469
Belgium: and El Salvador, 123; and China, 216; trade agreement with Albania, 299, 301; and USSR, 392
Benin, People's Revolutionary Party of, 6, 13–15; and Bulgarian CP, 311
Black Panthers (Israel), 30,32
Bolivia: and Cuba, 113; and North Korea, 241
Bolivia, Communist Party of, 81, 85–87
Bolivia, Marxist-Leninist Communist Party of, 85, 87
Bolivia, Socialist Party of, 85, 87
Bolivian Workers, Revolutionary Party of, 85
Botswana: and China, 216
Brazil: and Suriname, 172
Brazil, Communist Party of, 88, 89, 90
Brazilian Communist Party, 88–90; and Czechoslovak CP, 321
Brezhnev Doctrine, 291

Broad Left Front (Ecuador), 119
Bulgaria: supports Iranian CP, 27; advisers in Grenada, 79; economic aid to Mongolia, 256; foreign trade, 308, 309, 310, 411, 415; military aid to Yemen, 309; and WTO, 422; and Cypriot CP, 452;
—agreements and treaties: media, with Zimbabwe, 76; military, with Grenada, 79; trade, with Albania, 308; trade, with Romania, 309; scientific and cultural, with Greece, 309; scientific and cultural, with Rwanda, 309; friendship and cooperation, with Libya, 309; trade, with Lesotho, 310; scientific and cultural, with Lesotho, 310; economic, with Guinea, 310; economic, with Mauritania, 310; trade, with India, 310; trade, with Vietnam, 310; trade, with Afghanistan, 310; trade, with Cuba, 310; trade, with Great Britain, 310; cultural exchange, with Ecuador, 310; finance and credit, with France, 310; fishing, with U.S., 311
—foreign relations: Angola, 11; Albania, 301; GDR, 332; Hungary, 343; Romania, 369
Bulgarian Agrarian National Union, 303, 305, 306
Bulgarian Communist Party, 302–6, 311; and *World Marxist Review*, 426
—relations with other CPs: Israeli, 32; Lebanese, 43, 44; Syrian, 67–68; Panamanian, 162; Soviet, 399; French, 469; Greek, 483; Luxembourgeois, 497; Netherlands, 505; Portuguese, 513; Spanish, 518
Burma: and North Korea, 241, 242
Burmese Communist Party, 185, 204–8; and Thai CP, 279
Burundi: and China, 216

Cadres: concern of Chinese CP with, 183, 184, 211, 213; concern of Afghan CP with, 183, 184; Vietnamese rectification campaign, 282–83; training of, in Vietnam, 283; problems with, in Vietnam, 283–84; in Albania, 296, 297, 299; stability of, in USSR, 376; Soviet calls for professionalism, 377
Camilo Torres Revolutionary Committee (Dominican Republic), 117
Campaign for Nuclear Disarmament (U.K.), 434, 435, 479
Canada: and USSR, 376–77
Canada, Communist Party of, 91, 92–93
Canada, Communist Party of (Marxist-Leninist), 91, 93–94
Caribbean Community, 126
Central African Republic: and China, 216
Central America: and Cuba, 115
Central American Revolutionary Workers' Party (El Salvador), 121
Chad: and Benin, 15; Guadeloupe CP on, 131; Martinique CP on, 149; French CP on, 468

Charter '77, 317, 318, 321, 342, 434

Chile, 81

Chile, Communist Party of, 81, 95–98; and Moroccan CP, 45; and Bulgarian CP, 311; and CPSU, 398

China: polemics against, 5; aid to Congo, 17; trade with Argentina, 83; and Lebanese CPs, 43, 44; aid to Zimbabwe, 75, 77; trade with Cuba, 115; creation of Ministry of State Security, 184; aid to Thai guerrillas, 185, 278; economic and military aid to Bangladesh, 204; aid to Burmese CP, 207–8; foreign trade, 216, 217, 219; economic aid to Nepal, 259; economic aid to Pakistan, 266; trade agreement with Albania, 299–300, 301; trade agreement with Czechoslovakia, 320; toursim agreement with Hungary, 343; trade and trade agreements with USSR, 393–94

—foreign relations: Angola, 11; Benin, 15; Congo, 15; Ethiopia, 23; Peru, 169; Indonesia, 228–29; North Korea, 242, 243; Laos, 248, 249; Malaysia, 250, 254; Singapore, 254; Mongolia, 256–57; Pakistan, 265–66; Vietnam, 281, 282, 285; Albania, 299–300, 301; GDR, 331–32; Hungary, 343; Romania, 372

—pro-Chinese parties: Sudan, 63; Bolivia, 85; Canada, 91; Colombia, 99, 102–3; Dominican Republic, 117; Ecuador, 118; Peru, 164; U.S., 175; Australia, 196; Burma, 204–5, 208; Indonesia, 226–27; Malaysia, 251, 254; Nepal, 257, 258; New Zealand, 259, 260; Pakistan, 263, 264; Philippines, 266, 267; Denmark, 457; Norway, 509; Portugal, 511; Sweden, 522; Switzerland, 524

Chinese Communist Party, 209–10; concern with cadres, 183, 184, 211, 213; factions, 184; purification campaign, 211, 213, 214; campaign against foreign influences, 214–15; and *World Marxist Review*, 426

—relations with other CPs: Mozambican, 51; Mexican, 151; Australian, 197; Indian, 222–23, 225; Japanese, 234; East German, 332; Belgium, 447, 448; French 468; Italian, 439, 490, 495; San Marinan, 514; Spanish, 518; Swedish, 522

Christian Peace Conference, 433

Church-state relations: Nicaragua, 155, 156, 157; Philippines, 273; Czechoslovakia, 316–17; GDR, 324–26; Hungary, 340; Poland, 344–48 *passim*, 353–54, 358; Romania, 365; USSR, 384

CMEA, *see* Council for Mutual Economic Assistance

Colombia, Communist Party of, 98–102, *passim*

Colombia, Communist Party of, Marxist-Leninist, 99, 102–3

Colombia, Marxist-Leninist League of, 102

Colombia, Revolutionary Armed Forces of, 99–101, 104

Committee for International Trade Union Unity, 199, 262

Committee for Social Self-Defense (Poland), 350

Committee for the Defense of Unjustly Persecuted Persons (Czechoslovakia), 318

Committee of Patriotic Unity (Guatemala), 134

Communist League (FRG), 475

Communist Libertarian Movement (Mexico), 150

Communist parties. *See individual parties by name*

—aging leaderships in: Iraqi CP, 28; Tunisian CP, 70; Costa Rican CP, 105, 107; Cuban CP, 111; New Zealand CP, 261; Philippine CP, 268; Vietnamese CP, 281; CPSU, 374, 375; Cypriot CP, 448; Danish CP, 454

—decline in support for: Finnish CP, 458; French CP, 465–66; British CP, 478

—Eurocommunism, 439, 441; Mexico, 150, 151; Australia, 196; Japan, 230; and peace campaign, 434, 435; Austria, 444, 445; Belgium, 446, 447, 448; Finland, 458–64 *passim*; U.K., 479; Greece, 481, 483; Spain, 515, 516, 518

—factionalism in: Syrian CP, 66; Australian CP, 198; Indian CP, 224; Thai CP, 278; Vietnamese CP, 281–82; Polish CP, 345; in Western Europe, 438–42 *passim*; Belgian CP, 447; Danish CP, 454; Finnish CP, 458–64 *passim*; French CP, 465; British CP, 479; Italian CP, 489, 490–91; Netherlands CP, 501–3; Portuguese CP, 511–12; Spanish CP, 515–516

—income of: Austrian CP, 444; Cypriot CP, 449–50; Finnish CP, 462; West German CP, 471; British CP, 480; Italian CP, 491; Maltese CP, 500

—membership composition, Czechoslovak CP, 314; Hungarian CP, 334; Polish CP, 343; Romanian CP, 362; CPSU, 372; Cypriot CP, 448

—participation in cabinets in: Iran, 25; Bolivia, 81; Suriname, 171; Western Europe, 438–39; France, 465, 466; Iceland, 484–85; San Marino, 514

—pro-Albanian: Brazil, 88, 302; Canada, 91, 94; Dominican Republic, 116; Peru, 164; Suriname, 171; New Zealand, 259, 260; FRG, 301, 302, 475; U.K., 301, 302; Portugal, 302; Denmark, 457; Sweden, 522

—pro-Chinese: Sudan, 63; Bolivia, 85; Canada, 91; Columbia, 99, 102–3; Dominican Republic, 117; Ecuador, 118; Peru, 164; U.S., 175; Australia, 196; Burma, 204–5, 208, Indonesia, 226–27; Malaysia, 251, 254; Nepal, 257, 258; New Zealand, 259, 260; Pakistan, 263, 264; Philippines, 266, 267; Denmark 457; Norway, 509; Portugal, 511; Sweden, 522; Switzerland, 524

—recruitment: Albanian CP, 296; Hungarian CP, 335; Romanian CP, 362; Cypriot CP, 449

Communist Party/Marxist-Leninist (Panama), 160

Communist Party (Marxist-Leninist) (U.S.), 175

Communist Workers Nucleus (Dominican Republic), 117

Communist Workers' Party (Denmark), 453, 457

Communist Workers' Party (Sweden), 522

Comoros: and North Korea, 242

Conference on Security and Cooperation in Europe, 341, 370, 425, 500

Congo: treaty with USSR, 6; and Mongolia, 275; and French CP, 469

Congolese Labor Party, 6, 16–17; and Angolan party, 11; and CPSU, 400

Consumer goods: Czechoslovakia, 315; USSR, 378, 382

Contadora group, 102, 123, 152, 157, 162, 169, 179

Corruption: Angola, 9; Congo, 17; Vietnam, 282, 283; USSR, 288; Czechoslovakia, 314; Hungary, 335; Soviet anticorruption drive, 376, 378–79, 380

Costa Rica: and Nicaragua, 80; and North Korea, 242; Basque terrorists in, 517

Costa Rican Communist Party, see Popular Vanguard Party

Costa Rican Socialist Party, 105–6

Council for Mutual Economic Assistance (CMEA), 291–92; aid to Afghanistan, 190; aid to Mongolia, 256; trade with Mongolia, 256; and Bulgaria, 309, intra-bloc integration, 309, 332, 405–6, 407, 412–13, 415; and Czechoslovakia, 320; and Hungary, 341; and Poland, 344; and Romania, 366, 370; Soviet control of, 405; intra-bloc coordination, 405, 409; multilateral projects, 405–9 passim, 412, 413; scientific and technical cooperation, 406; reform of, 407, 409, 411, 415; dissatisfactions with, 407, 408–9; disagreements among members, 408; self-sufficiency, 408, 415; on NATO missiles, 409–10; impact of non-CMEA economies, 410; economic performance, 410–11; intra-bloc trade, 411–13; integration and energy, 413; foreign debt, 414–15; trade surplus with West, 415; trade with West, 415–16; export potential of, 416; use of countertrade, 416

Counterinsurgency campaigns: Ecuador, 119; El Salvador, 121–23; Guatemala, 131–32; Honduras, 142–43; Nicaragua, 156–57; Peru, 167–68; Afghanistan, 192–93, 195; Burma, 207–8; Malaysia, 252; Philippines, 267, 271–72, 273–74; Thailand, 277–78, 279

CPSU, see Soviet Union, Communist Party of the

Crime: Chinese campaign against, 213–14; in Albania, 297–98; in Czechoslovakia, 314, 315–16; in USSR, 380–81

Cuba: aid to Angola, 8; aid to Ethiopia, 23; economy, 80, 411; aid to Grenada, 80, 114, 124, 128; and Colombian CP, 102; and Costa Rican CP, 107; military aid, 114; on overthrow

of Maurice Bishop, 128; and Haitian CP, 141; aid to Honduran Left, 143; and Puerto Rican Left, 170; possible basing of Soviet missiles in, 390; Soviet military aid to, 397; trade with CMEA, 411–12

—advisers, 111–15 passim; military and medical, in Yemen, 3; in Angola, 5, 80; military, in Congo, 17; military, medical, and educational, in Ethiopia, 23; military and civilian, in Grenada, 79, 128; military and civilian, in Nicaragua, 80, 156, 157; civilian, in Jamaica, 145

—agreements and treaties: military, with Grenada, 79, 128; trade, with Peru, 169; trade, with Albania, 299; trade, with Bulgaria, 310

—foreign relations: Angola, 10, 11; Benin, 15; Ethiopia, 23; Mozambique, 51; Suriname, 79, 172; USSR, 80; Latin America, 81; El Salvador, 81, 82; Argentina, 84; Bolivia, 87; and Costa Rica, 109; Dominican Republic, 116; Ecuador, 120; Grenada, 124, 125; Jamaica, 144–45, 146; Nicaragua, 157, 158; Laos, 247; Mongolia, 257; Vietnam, 285

—pro-Cuban parties: Ecuador, 118; Suriname, 171; New Zealand, 259, 260

Cuba, Communist Party of, 110–11; and Suriname, 172; and Indian CPs, 223; and Bulgarian CP, 311; and CPSU, 400

Culture: liberalization and crackdown, in Bulgaria, 303, 306; repression of, in Czechoslovakia, 316, 318; repression of, in GDR, 328; use of historical figures in GDR, 329; Hungarian CP criticisms, 328; repression of, in Hungary, 339–40; state control of, in Poland, 349; in Romania, 365; repression of, in USSR, 385

Cyprus: and Bulgaria, 309; Romanian position on, 369

Cyprus, Communist Party of, see Progressive Party of the Working People

Czechoslovakia: nationals kidnapped in Angola, 11; deployment of Soviet missiles in, 290, 393, 425; social malaise in, 314, 318; trade balances, 315, 320; exports, 315, 320; and CMEA, 408; economic performance, 411; trade with USSR, 411; joint CMEA projects, 413; trade with West, 416; and WTO, 421, 423; unofficial peace movement, 434

—agreements and treaties: friendship and cooperation, with Ethiopia, 23; military, with Grenada, 79; trade, with Nepal, 259; trade, with CMEA partners, 320

—foreign relations: Angola, 11; Ethiopia, 23; Grenada, 125; GDR, 332; Poland, 359; Romania, 369; Malta, 499

Czechoslovakia, Communist Party of, 312–14, 321; and World Marxist Review, 426

—relations with other CPs: Syrian, 67, 68; Argentine, 84; Brazilian, 90; Bulgarian, 311; CPSU, 398–99; Austrian, 445; Cypriot, 452; Italian, 493, 494; Netherlands, 505; Portuguese, 513

Da'wah, al- (Iraq), 3, 29
Decentralization: Hungary, 336, 338; Poland, 347, 349, 351, 355. *See also under* Economy
Democratic Front Against Repression (Guatemala), 134, 135
Democratic Front for Peace and Equality (Israel), 30, 31
Democratic Kampuchea, Coalition Government of, 235, 236; and China, 216
Democratic Kampuchea, Communist Party of (Khmer Rouge), 184, 235; and China, 216
Democratic National Front (Iraq), 3, 28, 29
Democratic Popular Movement (Ecuador), 118
Democratic Revolutionary Front (El Salvador), 120, 123, 130, 131; and Martinique CP, 149; and French CP, 469
Demographic problems: Bulgaria, 304
Denmark: trade agreement with Albania, 299
Denmark, Communist Party of, 438, 441–42, 252–56; and Bulgarian CP, 311; and CPSU, 399–400
Dialogue Movement (Hungary), 434
Directorate of the National Committee of Labor Unity (Guatemala), 134
Dissent: in Angola, 9, 12; in Czechoslovakia, 317–18; in GDR, 323, 324, 325; in Hungary, 339–40; in Poland, 356; in USSR, 379, 383–85
Dominican Communist Party, 116, 117
Domincan Left Front, 116
Dominican People's Movement, 117
Dominican Republic, Communist Party of the, 116
Dominican Republic, Labor Communist Party of the, 116
Dominican Revolutionary Party, 116
Dominican Workers Party, 117

Eastern Caribbean States, Organization of, 126
Eastern Europe: and USSR, 291–93; economic problems, 292, trade agreements with Albania, 299; and Albania, 301, 302
Economic performance: Mozambique, 4, 48, 49–50; Angola, 5, 10; Zimbabwe, 76, 77; Cuba, 110–11, 112, 411; Grenada, 126–27; Nicaragua, 155; Afghanistan, 188, 190; China, 212; Mongolia, 256; Vietnam, 281–82; USSR, 288–89, 377, 382–83, 410–11; Albania, 295, 298–99; Bulgaria, 304–5; Czechoslovakia, 315–16, 411; GDR, 327–28, 411; Hungary, 335–38, 411; Poland, 350–55, 411; Romania, 363–65, 411; USSR, under Brezhnev, 373; USSR, under Andropov, 378–79; CMEA, 410–11
Economic plans: Cuba, 112–13; Afghanistan, 190; North Korea, 239–40; Bulgaria, 304–5; Czechoslovakia, 315; Hungary, 338; Romania, 363–64
Economy. Decentralization of: Czechoslovakia, 315; Poland, 351, 352, 355; USSR, 378, 382–83

—mixed: Benin, 15; Cuba, 112; Grenada, 126, 127; Afghanistan, 190; Hungary, 335, 336, 338; Poland, 350–51, 354–55
—reform of: USSR, 288; CMEA, 292, 407, 409, 411; Bulgaria, 305; Czechoslovakia, 315–16; Hungary, 335, 336, 338; Poland, 344, 350, 351, 352
Ecuador: and China, 216; and Bolivia, 310; and GDR, 333
Ecuador, Communist party of, 118, 119–20
Ecuador, Communist Party of, Marxist-Leninist, 118
Ecuador, Revolutionary Socialist Party of, 118, 119
Ecuador, Socialist Party of, 119
Ecuadorean People's Party, 119
Education: of Angolans in USSR, 10; of Ethiopians in Cuba, 23; of foreign youth in Cuba, 111; of Grenadians in USSR, GDR, and Cuba, 129; of Surinamese in Cuba, 172; of Indonesians in China, 227; problems in Czechoslovakia, 316; state control of, in Poland, 349; in Romania, 365; of Maltese in USSR, 499
Egypt: persecution of communists, 3; Jordanian CP criticisms, 38; Sudanese CP criticisms, 65; and China, 216; and North Korea, 241; and Nepal, 259; and Romania, 368; and USSR, 395
Egyptian Communist Party, 1, 3, 18, 19–20; and Palestine CP, 36; and Moroccan CP, 45
Egyptian Communist Party–8 January, 18
Egyptian Communist Workers' Party, 18–19
Egyptian Socialist Party, 18
8 October Revolutionary Movement (Brazil), 88, 90
Elections (1983): Réunion, 53–54; Argentina, 81, 82–83; Guadeloupe, 81, 129, 130; Martinique, 81, 147, 148; Peru, 81, 164, 165, 168–69; Venezuela, 81, 178; Canada, 91, 92; Jamaica, 144; 146; Japan, 185, 231, 233; Australia, 196, 198, 200, 201; India, 220, 221; Sri Lanka, 275; Bulgaria, 305–6; in Western Europe, 438, 440; France, 439, 465, 466; Italy, 439, 489, 492, 496; Spain, 440, 516; Portugal, 440, 511, 512, 513; San Marino, 441, 514; U.K., 441, 478; Denmark, 442, 453, 456; Finland, 442, 458, 459–60; Austria, 442, 444, 445; Switzerland, 443, 523–34; FRG, 443, 470, 472, 475; Cyprus, 450; Iceland, 484, 485–86; Ireland, 488; Netherlands, 502; Norway, 506–9 *passim*; Turkey, 525–26
Electoral alliances (CPs and leftist parties): Réunion, 53–54; Syria, 66–67; Yemen, 71; Argentina, 81, 83, 84; Peru, 81, 164; Bolivia, 85–86; Brazil, 90; Canada, 92; Costa Rica, 105–6; Dominican Republic, 116, 117; Ecuador, 118, 119; Guadeloupe, 130; Mexico, 153; Venezuela, 178; India, 220–21, 222; Japan, 231, 233; Cyprus, 450; France, 465, 469; Italy, 491, 492; Netherlands, 502, 504; Norway, 506, 508; Portugal, 513, San Marino, 514
Electoral reforms: Hungary, 336; Poland, 344

El Salvador, 80, 81–82; and Honduran Left, 142, 143

El Salvador, Communist Party of, 120, 121, 123

Emigration: from USSR, 288, 384; from Bulgaria, 309; from Romania, 366–67

Energy: Soviet supplies to CMEA partners, 292, 413; in Czechoslovakia, 315, 320; in Hungary, 339; Soviet exports to Hungary, 342; in Romania, 364, 406, 408–9; in USSR, 383; CMEA cooperation in, 407, 409; USSR uses to control CMEA, 408

Enterprise management: in Hungary, 338; in Poland, 344, 351; in USSR, 378, 381

Environmental groups and issues: in Czechoslovakia, 314–15, 318; in Austria, 444; in Portugal, 511

Eritrea, 23–24

Espionage: Cuban, in U.S., 113; Soviet, in Jamaica, 146; Soviet, in Thailand, 185; U.S., in Afghanistan, 194; Soviet, in Indonesia, 229; North Korean, in South Korea, 240; Soviet, in Thailand, 280; Bulgarian, in U.S., 311; Romanian, in France, 367; Soviet, in U.S., 391; U.S., in USSR, 391; Soviet, in U.K., 391; Soviet, in France, 391, 468; Soviet, in Denmark, 455; Soviet, in Sweden, 522; Soviet, in Switzerland, 525

Ethiopia: and Sudanese CP, 63; and Yemen, 72; Cuban troops in, 115; and North Korea, 241; and Czechoslovakia, 319; and Romania, 368; and USSR, 396–97, 400; and CMEA, 408

Ethiopia, Commission to Organize the Party of the Working People of, 4, 21–23; and Bulgarian CP, 311; and CPSU, 400; and Portuguese CP, 513

Ethnic minorities: and Sudanese CP, 5, 64, 65; in Congo, 16; in Zimbabwe, 76; and Indian CPs, 221–22, 224; and Sri Lankan CP, 275–76; Greek, in Albania, 295, 298, 300; Albanian, in Yugoslavia, 300; Macedonian, in Yugoslavia, 308; Turkish, in Bulgaria, 309; Hungarian, in Czechoslovakia, 314, 342; gypsies, in Czechoslovakia, 314; Hungarian, in neighboring countries, 335, 337, 339; Hungarian, in Romania, 340, 342, 361, 369; Hungarian, in Yugoslavia, 342; Germans, in Romania, 361; Georgians, in USSR, 384–85; Andropov on, 385; and Cypriot CP, 449; and Belgian CP, 447

Eurocommunism, 439, 441; Mexico, 150, 151; Australia, 196; Japan, 230; and peace campaign, 434, 435; Austria, 444, 445; Belgium, 446, 447, 448; Finland, 458–64 passim; U.K., 479; Greece, 481, 483; Spain, 515, 516, 518

European Economic Community: aid to Ethiopia, 22; trade with Hungary, 341; Danish CP opposition to, 454, 455, 456; Greek CP opposition to, 483; Irish CP opposition to, 488; Italian CP on, 494–95

Faeroese Communist Party, 454

Farabundo Martí Front of National Liberation, 80, 81–82, 121, 122, 123, 181

Fatah, al- (Palestine), 35

Fedayin-e Khalq (Iran), 25, 27

Federation of Violence-free Action Groups–Grassroots Revolution (FRG), 476

Finland: and North Korea, 243; agreements with Albania, 299, 301; and Hungary, 341; pilots boycott USSR, 387

Finnish Communist Party, 438, 442, 458–64

Finnish People's Democratic League, 458–64 passim

Food imports: Czechoslovakia, 315; Poland, 354

Foreign indebtedness: Cuba, 112, 414; Nicaragua, 155; Peru, 165, 169; China, 212; North Korea, 240; Czechoslovakia, 320; GDR, 327; Hungary, 337–38; Poland, 352–53, 414; Romania, 366, 414; USSR, 414; Bulgaria, 414

Forward Readers Group (Canada), 91, 95

Fourth International, 94, 95, 174, 453, 475, 524

Fourth International, International Committee, 94, 196, 200, 475

Fourth International, United Secretariat of, 87, 196

France: and Benin, 15; and Congo, 17; and El Salvador, 123; Guadeloupan CP criticisms of, 130, 131; Haitian CP criticisms of, 141; Martinique CP criticisms of, 148, 149; arms sales to Nicaragua, 156; and Nicaragua, 158; and China, 216; and North Korea, 243; and Nepal, 259; and USSR, 290, 392, 438; trade agreement with Albania, 299, 301; and Hungary, 341; and Poland, 358; and Romania, 367; missiles and arms control talks, 388, 390; Soviet spies in, 391; USSR and Mitterrand government, 438–39; and Spain, 517

Free Workers' Union (FRG), 475, 476

French Communist Party, 438–39, 440, 464–69; and El Salvador, 123; protest to CPSU, 383; and World Marxist Review, 426

—relations with other CPs: Angolan, 12; Lebanese, 43; Moroccan, 45; Réunion, 53; Argentine, 84; Guadeloupan, 129, 130; Martinique, 147, 148, 149; Bulgarian, 311; CPSU, 383, 399; Greek, 483; Italian, 495

FRG, see Germany, Federal Republic of

Front of the Popular Left (Argentina), 84

Gabon: and China, 216

Gang of Four, 211, 214, 223

GDR, see German Democratic Republic

German Communist Party (FRG), 438, 443, 470–74; and Bulgarian CP, 311; and German peace campaign, 435; and Italian CP, 495

German Democratic Republic (GDR): and South African CP, 5, 60, 61; military advisers in Congo, 17; treaty on cooperation with Ethiopia,

23; and Iranian CP, 25, 26–27; media agreement with Zimbabwe, 76; advisers in Grenada, 79; aid to Grenada, 128, 129; and Venezuelan CP, 179; deployment of Soviet missiles in, 290, 425; foreign trade, 327–28; economic and cooperation agreement with Zimbabwe, 333; economic performance, 411; CMEA trade, 411; trade with USSR, 411; aid to Soviet agriculture, 413; joint CMEA projects, 413; trade with West, 416; and WTO, 421, 422; unofficial peace movement, 434; and Greens (FRG), 434, 435; and Cypriot CP, 452
—foreign relations: Angola, 11; Benin, 15; Ethiopia, 23; Iran, 27; Indonesia, 229; Laos, 247; Mongolia, 257; Bulgaria, 309; Poland, 358, 359; Romania, 369
Germany, Communist Party of (Marxist-Leninist) (FRG), 475
Germany, Federal Republic of (FRG): and Benin, 15; and El Salvador, 123; and USSR, 290, 389, 390, 392; and Albania, 301; and Bulgaria, 310; and Czechoslovakia, 319; loans to GDR, 326, 328, 331, 411, 415; and GDR, 330–31; and Hungary, 341; and Poland, 359; and Romania, 366; Soviet attempts to influence election, 388, 392; trade with GDR, 415; target of Soviet peace campaign, 417; peace campaign in, 434, 435
Germany, Marxist-Leninist Party of (FRG), 474–75
Germany, Socialist Unity Party of (GDR), 322–23, 332, 333; and *World Marxist Review*, 426
—relations with other CPs: Brazilian, 90; New Zealand, 263; Bulgarian, 311; CPSU, 398; Danish, 456; West German, 470, 471, 474; West Berlin, 477; Greek, 483; Italian, 495; Netherlands, 505; Swedish, 522
Germany, Trotskyist League of (FRG), 475
Germany, Workers' League for the Reconstitution of the Communist Party of (FRG), 475
Ghana: and Benin, 15
Great Britain: aid to Zimbabwe, 5; aid to Ethiopia, 22; and China, 216; and North Korea, 243; and USSR, 290; and Albania, 301; and Hungary, 341; and Poland, 358; missiles and arms control talks, 388, 390; Soviet spies in, 391; elections' effect on USSR, 392; and East-West trade, 415; peace campaign in, 434, 435
Great Britain, Communist Party of, 438, 441, 478–80; and East German CP, 333; and *World Marxist Review*, 426, 427; and Irish CP, 488
Greece: trade agreements with Albania, 299; and Albania, 300; Balkan nuclear-free zone, 307–8, 341; and Bulgaria, 309; scientific and technological agreement with Bulgaria, 309; and Hungary, 341; and USSR, 392; and Italian CP, 495
Greece, Communist Party of, 438, 440, 481–83; and Australian CP, 200; and Bulgarian CP, 313; and French CP, 469; and Italian CP, 495

Greece, Communist Party of, Interior, 481, 483; and Italian CP, 495
Greece, Marxist-Leninist Communist Party of, 483
Greece, Revolutionary Communist Party of, 483
Green Party (FRG), 472–76 *passim*; and GDR, 331; and peace campaign, 434, 435
Green Star Movement (Thailand), 279
Grenada: and U.S., 79, 397; evidence of communist involvement, 79; communist advisers in, 79, 241; military agreements with communist-ruled states, 79, 241, 397; and Cuba, 114; and Suriname, 172, and North Korea, 241; and Laos, 247; and USSR, 397
Groupe socialiste des travailleurs (Canada), 91, 94
Group of International Marxists (FRG), 475
Guadeloupe, 81
Guadeloupe, Communist Party of, 129–31; and Martinique CP, 149
Guatemala, 80
Guatemalan National Revolutionary Unity, 132, 134, 136, 138
Guatemalan Party of Labor, 131, 133, 135–37
Guatemalan Party of Labor–Leadership Nucleus, 135
Guerrilla Army of the Poor (Guatemala), 134, 137–38
Guerrillas: South Africa, 5, 58; Angola, 5, 290; Ethiopia, 22, 23–24; Mozambique, 49; Zimbabwe, 76, 77; Nicaragua, 80, 155, 156–57, 290; El Salvador, 80, 121–23; Guatemala, 80, 131–35, 137–38; Peru, 80–81, 166–69; Bolivia, 85; Colombia, 99–104 *passim*; Costa Rica, 107–8; Dominican Republic, 116; Ecuador, 119; Honduras, 142–43; Puerto Rican, in U.S., 170; Puerto Rico, 170, 171; Venezuela, 178, 181; Afghanistan, 183, 187–93 *passim*, 394; Kampuchea, 184, 290; Burma, 185, 205, 207–8; Thailand, 185, 277, 278, 279; Philippines, 185, 267, 271–73; North Korean aid to, 241; Malaysia, 250–53 *passim*
Guinea: and Bulgaria, 310, 311
Guyana, Communist Party of, *see* People's Progressive Party

Haitian Communists, Unified Party of, 140–41
Honduran Communist Party, 141, 142, 143
Honduran Revolutionary Movement, 141, 142
Honduras: and Nicaragua, 80, 156
Hong Kong, 216
Horizontal Consultation of Communists (Netherlands), 501–5 *passim*
Housing: in Bulgaria, 305; in Hungary, 338; in USSR, 377, 382
Human rights: under Andropov, 288; violations in Albania, 298, 300
Hungarian Socialist Workers' Party, 334–37, 341–43; and *World Marxist Review*, 426
—relations with other CPs: Bulgarian, 311; CPSU,

Hungarian Socialist Workers' Party (*continued*)
399; Austrian, 445; Netherlands, 505; Portuguese, 513; Spanish, 518

Hungary: trade, 337, 338, 341, 342, 343, 411, 415, 416; economic and technical cooperation agreement with France, 341; economic and technical cooperation agreement with Greece, 341; economic agreements with USSR, 342; trade protocol with Poland, 342; economic aid to Poland, 343; tourism agreement with China, 343; and CMEA, 409; economic performance, 411; joint CMEA projects, 411; imports of Soviet natural gas, 414; unofficial peace movement in, 434; and WTO, 421, 423

—foreign relations: Grenada, 129; Albania, 301; Bulgaria, 309; Czechoslovakia, 314, 319; GDR, 332; Poland, 359; Romania, 369; USSR, 393, 399

Icelandic Communist party, *see* People's Alliance

Ideological work: in USSR, 288, 385; among GDR youth, 326–27; in Hungary, 335, 336–37; in Poland, 344, 345, 346

Income (personal): in Bulgaria, 304; in Hungary, 338; in Romania, 364

Independence and Labor Party (Senegal), 6, 56

Independent Liberal Party (Nicaragua), 154

Independent Revolutionary Workers' Movement (Colombia), 103

India, 185; and Cuba, 113; and Afghanistan, 194; and Bulgaria, 310; and Czechoslovakia, 319–20; and Hungary, 341; and USSR, 396

India, All-India Communist Party of, 255

India, Communist Party of, 220, 221, 223–25; and *World Marxist Review*, 426; and West German CP, 471

India, Communist Party of–Marxist, 220, 221–23, 226; and China, 216

India, Communist Party of–Marxist-Leninist, 226

India, Unity Committee of the Communist Revolutionaries of, 226

Indochina: meeting of foreign ministers (July), 247, 248, 285

Indonesia, 185

Indonesian Communist Party, 226–29

Initiative Free Workers' Union (FRG), 476

Institutional Revolutionary Party (Mexico), 152

In Struggle (Canada), 95

Intelligentsia: Hungarian CP recruitment of, 335; Hungarian CP criticisms of, 339; Romanian CP recruitment of, 362; Romanian CP campaign against, 362, 365

Interchurch Peace Council, 434, 435

International Association of Democratic Lawyers, 433–34

International Labor Organization: and Czechoslovakia, 314, 318

International meetings: Arab CPs (June), 1, 20, 29, 30, 36, 55, 67; USSR 60th anniversary, 20, 32, 36, 55, 56, 68, 200, 262, 276; Latin American CPs (November 1982), 87, 89–90, 119–20, 163; Central American CPs (June), 102, 109, 179; Latin American CPs (February), 152; peace and security in Asia (April), 263; against chemical and biological weapons (May), 263. *See also* Marx centenary; World Assembly for Peace and Life, Against Nuclear War

International Monetary Fund: loan to Zimbabwe, 77; and Hungary, 337; and Poland, 352

International Organization of Journalists, 153, 432–33

International Socialist Workers' Party (Denmark), 453, 457

International Spartacist Tendency, 196

International Union of Students, 12, 160, 269, 431–32

International Workers' League (Puerto Rico), 170

Intransigence and Mobilization movement (Argentina), 84

Intransigent Party (Argentina), 82, 84

Iran: expels Soviet envoys, 3; links with Iraqi CP, 29–30; and Syria, 67; Afghan refugees in, 189; and Afghan talks, 193–94; and Afghanistan, 194; and China, 216; and North Korea, 241; and Muslim dissidents in Malaysia, 250; and Romania, 368; and USSR, 395–96

Iran, Communist Party of, 25

Iran, Union of Communists in, 25

Iranian Communist Party, 27. *See also* Tudeh Party

Iran-Iraq war, 26, 28, 29, 38

Iraq: and Romania, 368; and USSR, 396

Iraqi Communist Party, 1, 3, 28–30; and Syrian parties, 66, 67, 68; and Czechoslovak CP, 321; and *World Marxist Review*, 426

Ireland, Communist Party of, 438, 441, 487–88; and CPSU, 398

Irish Republican Socialist Party, 488

Islamic dissidence: Indonesia, 228; Malaysia, 250–54 *passim*; Philippines, 272–73

Islamic Brotherhood Party (Malaysia), 249, 254

Islamic Republican Party (Iran), 3, 25, 27

Islamic Unification Movement (Lebanon), 2, 43

Israel: and Romania, 367, 368

Israel, Communist Party of, 2, 30–33; and Palestine CP, 36; and Bulgarian CP, 311; and French CP, 469

Israeli Socialist Organization, 33

Italian Communist Party, 438, 439–40, 489–96; and *World Marxist Review*, 426, 427; and Danish Left, 457

—relations with other CPs: Lebanese, 44; Moroccan, 45; Guadeloupan, 130; Australian, 197; Chinese, 216; Bulgarian, 311; Czechoslovak, 321, CPSU, 399, 439; French, 469; Greek, 483; Portuguese, 513; San Marinan, 514; Spanish, 518

Italy: and Nicaragua, 158; agreements with Albania, 299, 300; and Bulgarian involvement in attempted assassination of pope, 306–7, 310; and Czechoslovakia, 319; and USSR, 392; peace campaign in, 434, 435
Ivory Coast: and China, 216

Jamaica, Workers' Party of, 144–47
Jamaican Communist Party, 144–47
Janatha Vimukthi Peramuna (Sri Lanka), 275, 276
Japan: and China, 216; and North Korea, 243–44; and USSR, 290, 396; and Bulgaria, 310; and Czechoslovakia, 319; and Romania, 370
Japan Communist Party, 185, 230–34; and Guadeloupan CP, 130; and North Korea, 244; and *World Marxist Review*, 426, 427
John Paul II: Soviet and Bulgarian involvement in attempted assassination of, 306–7, 310, 392; visit to Poland, 320–21, 346–47, 353
Jordan: and China, 216; and Romania, 368
Jordan, Communist Party of, 1, 2, 35, 37–39; and Moroccan CP, 45

Kachin Independence Organization (Burma), 207–8
Kampuchea: and Vietnam, 184, 281, 285; and Laos, 248; and Malayan CP, 254; friendship treaty with Mongolia, 257; and Thai CP, 278; guerrillas in, 290; Romanian position on, 371
Kampuchean People's Revolutionary Party, 235–36; and Indian CPs, 223
Kenya: and China, 216
KGB, 374, 379; in Iran, 25, 26; in Thailand, 280; role under Andropov, 287, 288, 289; and attempted assassination of pope, 307, 392
Khmer Rouge, *see* Democratic Kampuchea, Communist Party of
Komeleh Party (Iran), 27
Korea, North: and Benin, 15; and Ethiopia, 23; military aid to Zimbabwe, 77; advisers in Grenada, 79, 241, 397; military agreement with and aid to Grenada, 79, 128, 241; economic aid to Grenada, 129, 241; and Nicaragua, 158; succession, 184, 238, 239; Rangoon bombing incident, 184, 240–45 *passim*; Japan CP censures for Rangoon bombing, 231, 234; aid to Third World guerrillas, 241; trade agreement with Mongolia, 257; trade agreement with Albania, 299; and Romania, 372
Korea, South: and China, 216, 242; and North Korea, 240, 241, 242
Korean Air Lines incident, 185; Zimbabwe supports USSR, 77; Martinique CP supports USSR, 149; Panamanian CP supports USSR, 162; CPUSA supports USSR, 174; U.S. CPs on, 175; Japan CP on, 231, 233; North Korea supports USSR, 242–43; and Thai-Soviet relations, 280; effect on USSR, 290, 386–88;

Poland supports USSR, 359; Chinese reaction, 394; and Japanese-Soviet relations, 390; French CP on, 467; Greece supports USSR, 482; Italian CP on, 493; Maltese CP supports USSR, 500; Spanish CP on, 518
Korean Workers' Party, 237–39; and Australian CP, 197; and Indian CPs, 223; and Albanian CP, 302; and Bulgarian CP, 311
Kurdish Democratic Party (Iran), 27
Kurdish Democratic Party (Iraq), 3, 28, 29
Kurdish national liberation movements: Arab CPs support, 1, 3; and anticommunist factions in Iraq, 3; links with Iranian CP, 27; links with Iraqi CP, 28; opposition to Iraqi CP, 28
Kurdistan, Patriotic Union of (Iraq), 3, 28, 29
Kurdistan, United Socialist Party of (Iraq), 28

Labor Alignment (Israel), 31, 32, 34
Labor discipline: USSR, 288, 375, 379, 381–82, 386; Bulgaria, 305
Labor force: Albania, 299; Bulgaria, 304; Czechoslovakia, 315; Hungary, 338
Labor Party (Argentina), 84
Labor unions. In communist-ruled states: Cuba, 110, 112; Afghanistan, 186; China, 209, 215; North Korea, 237; Mongolia, 255; Albania, 293; Bulgaria, 303, 306; Czechoslovakia, 312; GDR, 322; Hungary, 334, 338; Poland, 355–57; Romania, 361; USSR, 373, 378, 381; Yugoslavia, 403
—CP-controlled, in non-communist-ruled states: Bahrain, 12, 13; Congo, 17; Ethiopia, 22; Iran, 24; Réunion, 53, 54; Sudan, 62, 63, 64; Brazil, 88–89, 90; Canada, 91; Chile, 96, 98; Colombia, 98, 99; Costa Rica, 105; Ecuador, 118; Grenada, 122; Guadeloupe, 130; Guatemala, 135; Guyana, 139–40; Jamaica, 144; Martinique, 147, 148; Mexico, 150, 152; Panama, 158, 159, 160; Peru, 164–68 *passim*; U.S., 173, 174; Venezuela, 178, 179, 180; Bangladesh, 202; India, 220, 222; Indonesia, 227; Philippines, 266–70 *passim*; Sri Lanka, 275; Portugal, 440, 511, 512; Cyprus, 448, 450; France, 464, 466, 467; FRG, 475, U.K., 478, 479, 480; Spain, 515, 517
—communist influence in noncommunist: Algeria, 8; Benin, 15; Lebanon, 39, 40; Nigeria, 52; South Africa, 57; Argentina, 83; Bolivia, 86, 87; Canada, 92–93; Guatemala, 133; Honduras, 143; Nicaragua, 154; Australia, 185, 196–201 *passim*; New Zealand, 185, 259–62 *passim*; Austria, 445; Belgium, 447; Denmark, 454, 455; FRG, 473; U.K., 478–79; Greece, 482; Malta, 499; Netherlands, 504; Norway, 507, 509
Labor unrest: in USSR, 384
Labour Party (U.K.): and Bulgarian CP, 311
Lanka Sama Samaja Party (Sri Lanka), 275, 276

Lao People's Revolutionary Party, 246–48

Laos: Vietnamese control of, 184; and Indian CPs, 223; consular agreement with Mongolia, 257; and Thai CP, 278; and Thai guerrillas, 279; and CMEA, 408

Latin America: and Cuba, 115

Latin American Solidarity Organization, 81, 117

Latin American Trade Union Unity, Permanent Committee for, 152, 153

League of Socialist Workers (FRG), 475

Lebanese Communist Party, 1, 2, 39–44; and Moroccan CP, 45; and Syrian Ba'th Party, 67; and Bulgarian CP, 311; and CPSU, 400; and Cypriot CP, 451; and French CP, 469; and Italian CP, 495

Lebanese People's Party, 40

Lebanon: peacekeeping forces in, 1, 2; Israeli forces in, 1, 2; Muslim fundamentalism in, 2; Romanian attempts to mediate crisis, 368

Lebanon, Progressive Independent Union of, 42

Left Party Communists (Sweden), 438, 442, 519–22; and China, 216

Left Socialist Party (Denmark), 453, 456, 457

Lesotho: and China, 216; and North Korea, 241; and Bulgaria, 310

Libelu (Brazil), 88, 90

Liberal Party (Egypt), 20

Libya: and Benin, 6, 15; and Congo, 17; and Morocco, 45, 46; and Tunisia, 70; and Yemen, 72; advisers in Grenada, 79; and Argentina, 84; aid to Nicaragua, 156; support for Philippine Muslims, 273; and Bulgaria, 309, 311; and Czechoslovakia, 319; and Romania, 368

Living standards: Bulgaria, 304; Poland, 353, 354; Romania, 364

Lorenzo Zelaya People's Revolutionary Front (Honduras), 142, 143

Luxembourg, Communist Party of, 438, 441, 496–97; and Bulgarian CP, 311

Madagascar: and Czechoslovakia, 319

Maghreb, 1, 7

Malaya, Communist Party of, 249–55, 279

Malaya, Communist Party of, Marxist-Leninist, 251, 252, 253

Malaya, Malay Nationalist Revolutionary Party of, 249, 253–54

Malayan National Liberation Army, 253

Malayan People's Army, 249, 252, 253

Malaysia: and Romania, 371

Malta: and North Korea, 241; trade agreement with Albania, 301; and Bulgaria, 309; and Romania, 370

Malta, Communist Party of, 438, 440, 498–500

Maritime Unions Socialist Activities Association (Australia), 196, 198

Martinique, 81

Martinique Communist Party, 147–49

Marx centenary (East Berlin, April). Delegations from: Israel, 2, 33; Middle East, 2, 3; Africa, 5, 6; Angola, 10; Bahrain, 13; Egypt, 20; Palestine, 36; Nigeria, 52; Saudi Arabia, 55; Senegal, 56; South Africa, 60–61; Sudan, 63, 65; Syria, 68; Mexico, 152; Panama, 162; Australia, 200; Indonesia, 227, 229; New Zealand, 262–63; Sri Lanka, 276; Bulgaria, 311; USSR, 398; Italy, 494; Netherlands, 504; Norway, 508

Marxist Group (FRG), 476

Marxist-Leninist Communist Party, Revolutionary (Sweden), 522

Marxist-Leninist Party (Denmark), 453, 457

Marxist National Socialist Council (India), 226

Marxist Revolutionary Workers'–Socialist Workers' Party (Peru), 164, 165

Mauritania: and Bulgaria, 310

Mauritius: and China, 216

May 19th Communist Organization (U.S.), 175

Media: Western, in Albania, 299, 300; state control of, in Poland, 349; in USSR, 381; and Italian CP, 491, 494; and Luxembourgeois CP, 497; and Netherlands CP, 501–2, 503

Mexican Communist Party, 150, 151, 152. See also Mexico, Unified Socialist Party of

Mexican People's Party, 150, 151, 152

Mexican Workers' Party, 151–52, 153

Mexico: and Nicaragua, 157, 158

Mexico, Unified Socialist Party of, 149–53, 156; and Bulgarian CP, 311

Militant (U.K.), 480

M-19 (Colombia), 99, 101, 103, 104

Mojahedin-e Khalq (Iran), 3, 27

Mongolia: and USSR, 184; and Afghanistan, 191; and China, 217; and Laos, 248; friendship treaty with Romania, 372; and Sino-Soviet relations, 394

Mongolian People's Revolutionary Party, 255–57; and Bulgarian CP, 311; and World Marxist Review, 426

Montoneros (Argentine), 84

Morazanista Front of Honduran Liberation, 142

Moroccan Communist Party, see Party of Progress and Socialism

Morocco: and Bulgaria, 309

Moro National Liberation Front (Philippines), 272–73

Mouvement Démocratique de Libération Nationale (Egypt), 18, 21

Movement for Socialism (Dominican Republic), 117

Movement of Revolutionary Unity (Honduras), 142

Movement of the Revolutionary Left (Bolivia), 85

Movement Toward Socialism (Argentina), 84

Movement Toward Socialism (Venezuela), 81, 82, 178, 179–80

Mozambique: economic problems, 4; and China, 216; and Mongolia, 257; and Romania, 368; and

USSR, 397; and CMEA, 408
Mozambique, Front for the Liberation of, 4,
47–51; and Angolan party, 11; and Bulgarian
CP, 311; and CPSU, 400
Mozambique National Resistance, 49
Muslim Brethren, 66
Muslim fundamentalism: Lebanon, 2, 43; in Iraq,
3, 29

Namibia, 50, 54
National Council of Resistance (Iran), 27
National Democratic Front (Philippines), 266, 267,
269, 272, 273, 274
National Democratic Union (El Salvador), 120, 121
Nationalism, see Ethnic minorities
National Joint Action Committee (Trinidad and
Tobago), 149
National Liberation Army (Bolivia), 85
National Liberation Army (Colombia), 99, 103–4,
181
National Liberation Front (Algeria), 7, 8
National Liberation Front (Tunisia), 4
National Patriotic Committee (Costa Rica), 108
National Popular Alliance (Colombia), 99, 103
National Progressive Front (Syria), 1, 66–67
National Progressive Unionist Group (Egypt),
19, 21
National Progressive Unionist Party (Egypt), 19
National Revolutionary Movement (El Salvador),
120
NATO: compared to WTO, 419; Cypriot CP
criticisms, 451; French CP on, 468; Italian CP
on, 490; Spanish CP on, 518
—deployment of new missiles, 289–90, 291; Bulgaria on, 306; Czechoslovakia on, 313, 319,
321; GDR on, 323–31 passim; Poland on, 359;
Romania on, 369–70; and USSR, 388–92 passim; and WTO, 422, 423, 424; opposition to, in
Western Europe, 437–38; Italian CP on,
439–40, 491, 493; Scandinavian CPs on, 442;
West German CP on, 472–74; British CP on,
479, 480; Greece on, 482; Icelandic Left on,
486; opposition to, in Netherlands, 503–4;
opposition to, in Norway, 506, 507, 508, 510;
opposition to, in Sweden, 522. See also Peace
campaign
Natural gas: Soviet pipeline to Western Europe,
383; Soviet sales to CMEA partners, 412,
413–14
Neighborhood associations: Ethiopia, 22; Cuba,
111, 113; Nicaragua, 154
Nepal, Communist Party of, 257–58
Nepotism: Bulgaria, 304; Romania, 262–63
Netherlands: peace campaign in, 434
Netherlands, Communist Party of the, 438, 442,
501–5; and Bulgarian CP, 311
New Alternative (Venezuela), 178, 180
New Jewel Movement (Grenada), 79, 122–27; and

Martinique CP, 149; and CPSU, 401
New People's Army (Philippines), 266, 269–74
passim
New Zealand, 185; and China, 216; and Hungary,
341
New Zealand, Communist Party of, 259, 260
New Zealand, Preparatory Committee for the
Formation of the Communist Party of, 259, 260
Nicaragua, 79–80; Lebanese CP on, 44; Cuban
advisers in, 113–14, 115; Cuban military aid to,
114; and Honduran Left, 142, 143; contras,
142, 143, 290; and Martinique CP, 149; and
CMEA, 408, 412; and French CP, 469; and
Spanish CP, 518
—foreign relations: Ethiopia, 24; U.S., 79–80; El
Salvador, 82, 121, 123; Argentina, 84; Costa
Rica, 108–9; Cuba, 114; Dominican Republic,
116; Peru, 169, Laos, 247; Mongolia, 257;
USSR, 397
Nicaragua, Communist Party of (Trotskyist), 154
Nicaraguan Communist Party, see Nicaraguan So-
cialist Party
Nicaraguan Socialist Party, 154; and Bulgarian CP,
311
Nigeria: and China, 216; and USSR, 397
Nigerian Communist Party, see Socialist Working
People's Party
Nonaligned movement: and Argentina, 83, 84; and
Colombia, 102; and Cuba, 113; and Grenada,
128; and Nicaragua, 157; and Afghanistan, 191,
and India, 221, 222; and North Korea, 241-42;
and Laos, 247; and Romania, 368
North Kalimantan, Communist Party of (Malaysia),
251
Norwegian Communist Party, 438, 442, 505,
506–8; and Bulgarian CP, 311
Nuclear energy: in Czechoslovakia, 315; in Hungary, 339; in USSR, 382; in CMEA, 414
Nuclear-free zones: Balkans, 300, 307–8, 369,
422, 423, 482; northern Europe, 422, 423, 507,
510

October First Antifascist Resistance Group (Spain),
518
Oil: Hungarian consumption, 339; Soviet exports to
Hungary, 342; Soviet exports to Poland, 351; in
USSR, 383; Soviet exports to CMEA partners,
412, 413, 414
Oman: and South Yemen, 72, 73, 74
Organization of African Unity, 23, 45, 46, 78
Organization of Communist Action (Lebanon), 39,
42, 44
Ottawa Committee for Labour Action (Canada), 95

Pakistan: Afghan refugees in, 189; and Afghan
talks, 193, 194; Afghan attacks on, 194; and
North Korea, 242; and Nepal, 259

Pakistan, Communist Party of, 185, 263, 264
Pak Mai (Thailand), 249, 279
Palestine, Democratic Front for the Liberation of, 35, 44
Palestine, Popular Front for the Liberation of, 35, 37
Palestine Communist Organization (Jordan), 37
Palestine Communist Party (1922–1948), 31, 35
Palestine Communist Party (1982–), 1, 2, 18, 20, 34–36; and Israeli CP, 32, 33, 36; and Jordanian CP, 37, 38; supports Syria, 66, 67; and Syrian CP, 67, 68; and CPSU, 151
Palestine Liberation Organization, 1, 31, 35; and Syria, 2; and Jordanian CP, 2, 38; and Israeli CP, 32–33; at Marx centenary, 36; and Lebanese CP, 41, 42, 43; and Moroccan CP, 45; and Réunion CP, 54; and Syrian CP, 68; and Yemen, 72; and Malaysia, 254; and Mongolia, 254; and Bulgaria, 309; and Czechoslovakia, 319; and Romania, 367, 368; and USSR, 395; and French CP, 469; and Italian CP, 495
Palestine National Front, 37, 38
Palestinian Communist Organization (Lebanon), 35
Palestinian National Council: and Romania, 368
Panamanian Communist Party, see Panamanian People's Party
Panamanian People's Party, 158–62; and CPSU, 398, 400
Paraguayan Communist Party, 162–63
Paramilitary organizations: Benin, 15; Zimbabwe, 75; Bulgaria, 303; Czechoslovakia, 312; USSR, 373
Party of Progress and Socialism (Morocco), 1, 4, 45–46; and CPSU, 400
Party of Proletarian Unity for Communism (Italy), 496
Party of the National Left (Argentina), 84
Party of the Revolutionary Left (Bolivia), 85
Patriotic Movement of National Rebirth (Poland), 345–46
Patriotic Revolutionary Front (Nicaragua), 154
Peace campaign: Canada, 92, 93; and Mexican CP, 151; and Australian CPs, 199, 200; and Japan CP, 232; unofficial, in Czechoslovakia, 318; unofficial, in GDR, 323–31 passim; unofficial, in Hungary, 340; unofficial, in USSR, 383, 384; Soviet orchestration of, 386, 388–89, 391, 398; and WTO, 417, 424; Soviet use of noncommunist organizations in West, 434, 435; Soviet problems with independent groups, 434–35; in Western Europe, 437–38; and Italian CP, 439–40, 491, 494; in Scandinavia, 442; in West Germany, 443, 472–74; and Austrian CP, 444; and Belgian CP, 447–48; and Cypriot CP, 450, 451; and Danish CP, 455, 456; and French CP, 468; in West Berlin, 477; and British CP, 479, 480; and Greek CP, 482–83; in Netherlands, 502, 503–4; and Norwegian Left, 506, 507,
509; and Spanish CP, 518; Switzerland, 525
Peace organizations (CP-controlled): Bahrain, 13; Réunion, 53, 54; Saudi Arabia, 55; Sudan, 62; Yemen, 73; Argentina, 82; Canada, 91; Costa Rica, 105, 109; Grenada, 128; Mexico, 152; Panama, 158, 159–60; U.S., 173, 174; Australia, 196, 197, 199–200; India, 222; Japan, 230; New Zealand, 259, 262; Philippines, 266, 270; Albania, 293; Czechoslovakia, 312, 317; Hungary, 340; Cyprus, 448; France, 464; FRG, 471–73; Italy, 490; Luxembourg, 497; Malta, 498; Netherlands, 501, 503–4; Norway, 507; Switzerland, 523, 525
Peasants' organizations (CP-controlled): Ethiopia, 22; Colombia, 98, 99, 101; Costa Rica, 105, 108; Cuba, 110; Grenada, 122; Honduras, 143; Mexico, 150; Nicaragua, 154, Peru, 164; Bangladesh, 202, 203; India, 220, 222; North Korea, 237; Czechoslovakia, 312; Portugal, 511
People Advance, The (Venezuela), 178
People's Alliance (Iceland), 438, 442, 484–87
People's Democratic Union (Yemen), 3, 71, 72, 73; and Moroccan CP, 45
People's Forces—25th of April (Portugal), 511, 513
People's Liberation Army (Colombia), 99, 102–3, 104
People's Nationalist Party (Jamaica), 144, 146
People's Progressive Party (Guyana), 138–40; and Martinique CP, 149
People's Vanguard Party (Costa Rica), 179
Personality cults: China, 213; North Korea, 238–39; Romania, 362–63
Peru, 80–81; and China, 216
Peruvian Communist Party, 163–66
Peruvian Communist Party–Red Fatherland, 164
Peruvian Communist Party–Red Flag, 164, 166
Philippine Liberation Movement, 273
Philippines, Communist Party of the, 266–71 passim
Philippines, Communist Party of the (Marxist-Leninist), 266–74 passim
Poland: and Mexican CP, 150, 152; visit of pope, 290; and Brezhnev Doctrine, 291; and Albania, 301; and Czechoslovakia, 319, 320–21, 369; and GDR, 332; trade protocol with Hungary, 342; trade with Hungary, 343–44; trade with USSR, 352, 411; and USSR, 393, 399; economic performance, 411; Soviet exports of energy to, 414; trade with West, 415, 416; and WTO, 419, 421; and Belgian CP, 447, 448; and French CP, 465, 467, 468; and Italian CP, 490, 494
Polisario Front, 45
Polish United Workers' Party, 343–46; and World Marxist Review, 426
—relations with other CPs: Argentine, 84; Australian, 200; Bulgarian, 311; CPSU, 398; Netherlands, 505; Norwegian, 508; Spanish, 518

Politico-Military Organization (Paraguay), 163
Popular Action Movement (Mexico), 150
Popular Action Movement (Nicaragua), 154
Popular Christian Socialist Party (Nicaragua), 154
Popular Democratic Union (Ecuador), 118
Popular Democratic Union (Peru), 164
Popular Leagues of 28 February (El Salvador), 120, 121
Popular Liberation Forces (El Salvador), 81–82, 121
Popular Liberation Movement (El Salvador), 120, 121
Popular Liberation Movement ("Cinchoneros," Honduras), 142, 143
Popular Revolutionary Army (El Salvador), 121
Popular Revolutionary Bloc (El Salvador), 120, 121
Popular Social Christian Movement (El Salvador), 120
Popular Socialist Party (Argentina), 84
Popular Socialist Party (Mexico), 152
Popular Vanguard Party (Costa Rica), 105–9
Portugal: and Mozambique, 51; and El Salvador, 123
Portuguese Communist Party, 438, 440–41, 511–13; and Bulgarian CP, 311; and Czechoslovak CP, 321; and East German CP, 333; and CPSU, 399; and Spanish CP, 518
Price increases: Cuba, 112; Bulgaria, 315; Czechoslovakia, 315; Hungary, 338; Poland, 351–52; Romania, 364
Prima Linea (Italy), 496
Productivity: USSR, 288, 377, 381, 382, 383, 386; Albania, 298, 299; Bulgaria, 304; Czechoslovakia, 315; Hungary, 335; Poland, 353; Romania, 363
Progressive Organizations Switzerland, 524
Progressive Party of the Working People (Cyprus), 438, 440, 448–52; and Palestine CP, 36; and Bulgarian CP, 311; and CPSU, 400
Progressive Socialist Party (Lebanon), 2, 42
Proletarian Democracy (Italy), 496
Provisional Sinn Fein (Ireland), 488
Psychiatry: misuse in USSR, 288, 383, 384
Puerto Rican Communist Party, 170
Puerto Rican Socialist League, 170
Puerto Rican Socialist Party, 170
Purges: in Angola, 6, 8–9; in Benin, 14; in Congo, 16; in Ethiopia, 22; in Albania, 294, 298; in Bulgaria, 303

Radical Cause (Venezuela), 178
Rationing: in Cuba, 112; in Nicaragua, 155; in Poland, 354
Rebel Armed Forces (Guatemala), 133, 137
Red Brigades (Italy), 496
Red Electoral Alliance (Norway), 505, 506, 509–10
Red Flag (Venezuela), 178, 181
Red Pa-O (Burma), 207

Religiosity: in Czechoslovakia, 316–17
Réunion Communist Party, 5, 53–54; and Martinique CP, 149
Revolutionary Action Group (Venezuela), 178
Revolutionary Armed Forces (Guatemala), 133
Revolutionary Cells (FRG), 476
Revolutionary Communist League (Israel), 33
Revolutionary Communist Party (Argentina), 84
Revolutionary Communist Party (Peru), 164
Revolutionary Communist Party (U.S.), 175
Revolutionary Coordination of the Masses (El Salvador), 120, 121
Revolutionary Current (Egypt), 18
Revolutionary Left Movement (Venezuela), 178, 179, 180
Revolutionary Movement of the Left (Peru), 164
Revolutionary Organization of the People (Colombia), 99
Revolutionary Party of Central American Workers (Honduras), 141, 142, 143
Revolutionary People's Movement (Costa Rica), 106
Revolutionary People's Party (Suriname), 171
Revolutionary Political Organization (Marxist-Leninist) (U.S.), 175
Revolutionary Socialist Party (Mexico), 150, 151
Revolutionary Socialist Party (Peru), 164
Revolutionary Vanguard (Peru), 164
Revolutionary Workers' League (Canada), 91, 94, 95
Revolutionary Workers' Party (Bolivia), 85, 87
Revolutionary Workers' Party (Dominican Republic), 116, 117
Revolutionary Workers' Party (Mexico), 153
Revolutionary Workers' Party (Peru), 164, 165
Romania: and Angola, 11; and China, 216; economic aid to Mongolia, 256; friendship treaty with Mongolia, 257, 372; and Albania, 301; nuclear-free zone in Balkans, 308, 422; and Bulgaria, 308–9; trade agreement with Bulgaria, 309; and Hungary, 342; trade with U.S., 367; and CMEA, 405, 406, 408, 412; on NATO missiles, 401; economic performance, 411; Soviet energy supplies to, 413; trade with West, 415, 416; and WTO, 417–25 passim
Romanian Communist Party, 360–63, 371; and Israeli Left, 34; and World Marxist Review, 426, 427
—relations with other CPs: Jordanian, 39; Syrian, 68; Indian, 223; Austrian, 445; Greek, 483; Italian, 495; Netherlands, 505; Spanish, 518; Swedish, 522
Rural Solidarity (Poland), 354
Rwanda: and China, 216; and North Korea, 241

Samizdat publications: in Czechoslovakia, 316; in Hungary, 339; in USSR, 384

Sandinista Front of National Liberation (Nicaragua), 154–56
San Marino, Communist Party of, 438, 440, 511–12
Saudi Arabia: and USSR, 395
Saudi Arabia, Communist Party of, 1, 3, 13, 55
Security forces: Afghan, 190; Chinese, 212–13, 214; Albanian, 295, 297
Sendero Luminoso (Peru), 80–81, 119, 166–69, 181
Senegal, Communist Party of, *see* Independence and Labor Party
Seychelles: and China, 216; and North Korea, 241
Shan State Army (Burma), 207
Shan State Nationalities Liberation Organization (Burma), 207
Shan United Revolutionary Army (Burma), 207
Sheli Party (Israel), 34
Singapore, 185, 251, 252; and North Korea, 242. *See also* Malaya, Communist Party of
Singapore People's Liberation Organization, 249
Sinn Fein–The Workers' Party (Ireland), 488
6 April Liberation Front (Philippines), 273
Slovakia, Communist Party of, 312
Socialist Action and Unity Movement (Mexico), 150
Socialist Action League (New Zealand), 259, 260
Socialist Bloc (Dominican Republic), 117
Socialist Buro (FRG), 476
Socialist Challenge Organization (Canada), 95
Socialist International, 34, 116, 170
Socialist Labor League (Australia), 195, 196, 200
Socialist Labor Party (Egypt), 20
Socialist League (U.K.), 480
Socialist League (Venezuela), 178, 181
Socialist Left Party (Norway), 487
Socialist Party (Dominican Republic), 117
Socialist Party (Senegal), 6
Socialist Party (Sweden), 522–23
Socialist People's Party (Denmark), 453, 456–57, 487
Socialist Union of Popular Forces (Morocco), 45, 46
Socialist Unity Movement (Dominican Republic), 117
Socialist Unity Party (New Zealand), 259, 260–63
Socialist Vanguard Party (Algeria), 1, 4, 7–8; and Greek CP, 483
Socialist Workers' Movement (Dominican Republic), 117
Socialist Workers Party (Australia), 195, 196, 200–1, 260
Socialist Workers' Party (Mexico), 152
Socialist Workers' Party (Panama), 160
Socialist Workers' Party (U.K.), 480
Socialist Workers' Party (U.S.), 174–75
Socialist Working People's Party (Nigeria), 1, 52
Socialist Youth Foundation (Brazil), 88, 90

Solidarity (Poland), 344, 347–50 *passim*, 355–57; unofficial Hungarian praise of, 339; Italian CP support of, 440; West German unionists' condemnation of, 473, 475; British CP support of, 479; and Swedish CP, 520
Somalia: and Ethiopia, 23; and Romania, 368; and Italian CP, 495
South Africa: and Angola, 10, 115; and Mozambique, 49, 50–51
South African Communist Party, 5, 57–61
Southeast Communist Group (France), 465
South-West African People's Organization, 78, 115, 333, 368–69, 469
Soviet Union, Communist Party of the, 372–78; purge of ranks, 289; control of CPs, 386; and *World Marxist Review*, 426
—relations with other CPs: Ethiopian, 22, 23; Lebanese, 43; Moroccan, 45; Mozambican, 51; Syrian, 68; Argentine, 84; Canadian, 92; Guadeloupan, 130; Mexican, 151; Palestine, 151; Australian, 198; Indian, 223, 224, 225; Japan, 233–34; Mongolian, 256; New Zealand, 263; Bulgarian, 311; Italian, 439; Austrian, 445; Cypriot, 452, Danish, 456; Finnish, 459–64 *passim*; French, 467, 468; West German, 474; Greek, 482, Italian, 490, 493–94, 495; Luxembourgeois, 497; Netherlands, 504–5; Portuguese, 513; San Marinan, 514; Swiss, 523
Spain: and Nicaragua, 156–57; and Nepal, 259
Spain, Communist Party of, 438, 439, 440, 514–18; and *World Marxist Review*, 427
—relations with other CPs: Moroccan, 45; Bulgarian, 311; Czechoslovak, 321; Romanian, 371; Italian, 495; Portuguese, 513
Sparticist League (U.S.), 175
Sri Lanka, Communist Party of, 185, 275–76
Student organizations (CP-controlled): Bahrain, 12; Sudan, 62, 64; Costa Rica, 106; Ecuador, 118; Guatemala, 133, 135; Panama, 158, 160; Venezuela, 179; Bangladesh, 202, 203; India, 220, 222; Japan, 230; Nepal, 258; Pakistan, 264; Philippines, 266, 269–70; Belgium, 446; Cyprus, 448; Denmark, 453, 454; FRG, 470, 474, 475, 476; Malta, 499; Switzerland, 523
Sudan: and Romania, 368
Sudan Socialist Union, 62
Sudanese Communist Party, 1, 4–5, 61–65
Supreme Council of the Islamic Revolution (Iraq), 3, 29
Suriname: and Cuba, 79, 114
Suriname, Communist Party of, 171
Sweden: and El Salvador, 123; and Albania, 300; and U.S.-USSR, 391
Sweden's Communist Party, 522
Swedish Communist Party, *see* Left Party Communists
Swiss Communist Party, *see* Swiss Labor Party
Swiss Labor Party, 438, 443, 523–25; and Bul-

garian CP, 311; and CPSU, 400; and *World Marxist Review*, 427
Swiss Socialist Workers' Party, 524
Switzerland, Communist Party of, Marxist-Leninist, 524
Swords into Plowshares (GDR), 434
Syria: Arab CPs support, 1, 2; Soviet military aid to, 1, 395: anti-Arafat moves, 2, 395; supports Iraqi CP, 3, 29, 30; Lebanese CP supports, 42, 43; and Yemen, 72; and USSR, 291, 395; and Bulgaria, 309; and Romania, 368
Syrian Communist Party, 1–2, 65–69; and Iraqi CP, 29, 30; and Palestine CP, 36; and Lebanese CP, 41–42; and Bulgarian CP, 311; and CPSU, 398

Tanzania: and Angola, 11
Tanzania, Revolutionary Party of: and China, 216; and CPSU, 400
Technology transfers: to Hungary, 342; to USSR, 391; to CMEA members, 411, 415
Thailand: and USSR, 185; and North Korea, 242; and Laos, 248–49; and Malaysian communists, 253
Thailand, Communist Party of, 185, 277–79; and Laos, 249
31 January People's Front (Guatemala), 135
Trade unions, *see* Labor unions
Trotskyist League (Canada), 94–95
Trotskyist parties and groups: Argentina, 84; Bolivia, 85; Brazil, 88, 89, 90; Canada, 91, 94–95; Colombia, 99; El Salvador, 121; Mexico, 153; Nicaragua, 154; Panama, 160; Peru, 164, 165; Puerto Rico, 170; U.S., 174, 175; Australia, 196, 200–201; Burma, 204; New Zealand, 259, 260; Sri Lanka, 275, 276; Denmark, 453, 457; FRG, 474, 475; U.K., 480; Portugal, 511; Sweden, 523; Switzerland, 524
Tudeh Party (Iran), 1, 3, 24–27; CPUSA on, 174; Soviet protests against suppression, 395–96
Tunisia, 1, 4, 69–70; and Moroccan CP, 45; and Bulgaria, 309; and Czechoslovak CP, 321
Tupamaros (Uruguay), 181
Turkey: military actions against Iraqi CP, 3, 29; and Albania, 300, 301; and Balkan nuclear-free zone, 308; and Bulgaria, 309; and Hungary, 341; and Romania, 369
Turkish Communist Party, 438, 441, 525, 526–27; and Cypriot CP, 452; activities in FRG, 472
Turkish Workers' Party, 527

Umkhonto we Sizwe (South Africa), 58, 59
Unified Egyptian Communist Party, 18
Unified Popular Action Front (El Salvador), 120, 121
Unified Revolutionary Directorate (El Salvador), 121

Union of Soviet Socialist Republics: supports Iranian CP, 27; and Colombian CP, 102; and Dominican CP, 116; on overthrow of Maurice Bishop, 128–29; reaction to U.S. invasion of Grenada, 129; and Martinique CP, 149; and Panamanian CP, 162; Peruvian debt to, 169; military buildup in Asia, 185; military in Afghanistan, 192, 195, 290; Burmese CP criticisms of, 208; funds Philippine CP, 267; funds Thai guerrillas, 279; record of Andropov era, 287–91, 292–93; installation of Andropov loyalists, 287; CPSU criticisms of society, 288; ideological struggle, 288; Stalinism in, 288; economy, 288–89, 410–11; foreign policy, 289–91; and NATO deployment of missiles, 290, 291; missile deployments in Czechoslovakia, 319, 321; missile deployments in GDR, 324, 325; Romanian position on Soviet missiles, 369–70; Andropov's consolidation of power, 374–76, 378; crackdown on bureaucrats, 375, 380; discipline campaign, 379–81, 383, 385, 395; greater openness, 379, 380–81; citizen involvement, 380; Andropov on "developed socialism," 385; arms control proposals, 388–91, 425–26; new missiles in Eastern Europe, 392–93, 425; support for Arafat, 395; arms sales to India, 396; control and uses of CMEA, 405, 408, 414; joint CMEA projects, 413; uses of WTO, 417, 420; military budget, 420; peace campaign in West, 434–35; Italian CP on, 493–94, 495; use of Malta drydocks, 499; Norwegian leftists oppose Soviet missiles, 510; Swedish CP opposes Soviet missiles, 520, 522; submarines in Swedish waters, 521–22
—advisers: in Angola, 10; in Congo, 17; military, in Syria, 67; in Yemen, 73; military and civilian, in Grenada, 79, 128; military, in Vietnam, 185; in SE Asia, 280
—agreements and treaties: friendship, with Congo, 6, 17; fishing, with Angola, 10; friendship and cooperation, with Angola, 10; economic, scientific, and technological cooperation, with Ethiopia, 23; friendship, with Iraq, 29; trade, with Mozambique, 51; friendship, with Yemen, 73, 74; media, with Zimbabwe, 76; military and economic, with Grenada, 79, 128; trade, with Afghanistan, 190, 191; trade and economic, with Bangladesh, 203–4; trade, with China, 217, 393, 394; trade and cultural, with Pakistan, 265; on economic development, with Vietnam, 284–85; economic, with Hungary, 342; scientific and technological cooperation, with France, 392; economic and scientific cooperation, with Greece, 392; trade, with Hungary, 393; trade, with Malta, 499
—foreign aid: military, to Syria, 1, 67, 395; military, to Iraq, 3; military and economic, to Yemen, 3; to Angola, 8; civilian and military, to Ethiopia, 22, 23; military, to Iraq, 29; eco-

USSR foreign aid (*continued*)
nomic, to Yemen, 74; civilian and military, to Cuba, 80, 110–11, 112, 397; economic, to Argentina, 83; economic, to Bolivia, 87; to Grenada, 124, 128, 397; economic and military, to Nicaragua, 155, 156, 397; economic, to Afghanistan, 190, 191; economic, to India, 225, 396; economic, to Mongolia, 256; economic, to Pakistan, 265; to SE Asia, 280; economic, to Vietnam, 284, 285; to CMEA partners, 413
—foreign relations: Iran, 3, 26; Angola, 6, 10–11, 12; Benin, 15; Ethiopia, 23; Iran, 26, 27; Jordan, 37; Mozambique, 51; Yemen, 72, 73–74; Zimbabwe, 77; Cuba, 80, 113; Latin America, 81; Argentina, 83–84; Bolivia, 87; Grenada, 125, 128; Jamaica, 144, 145, 146; Nicaragua, 157, 158; Peru, 169; Suriname, 171; Venezuela, 176; Mongolia, 184, 256; Thailand, 185; Afghanistan, 187, 190, 191, 195; Bangladesh, 203; China, 217–18; India, 225; Indonesia, 229; North Korea, 242–43; Laos, 247; Malaysia, 250–51; ASEAN states, 254; Pakistan, 264, 265; Thailand, 279–80; Vietnam, 284–85; U.S., 289–91; Western Europe, 290, 291; U.K., 290; FRG, 290; Japan, 290; France, 290; Syria, 291; Eastern Europe, 291; Albania, 301–2; Bulgaria, 307; Czechoslovakia, 319, 320, 321; GDR, 332; Hungary 337–42 *passim*; Poland, 344–45, 354, 357–59; Romania, 369–72; under Brezhnev, 373–74; under Andropov, 386; Cyprus, 452; Finland, 459, 462, 463, 464; Greece, 482; Malta, 499
—oil: to Cuba, 80; to Argentina, 83; to Czechoslovakia, 319; to CMEA partners, 413–14, 416; to Iceland, 487
—trade: with Argentina, 83, 84; with Cuba, 113; with Afghanistan, 190; with U.S., 289; with GDR, 327–28, 411; with Hungary, 342, 411; with Poland, 352, 411; with Canada, 376; with India, 396; with CMEA partners, 411, 412; with Czechoslovakia, 411; with Bulgaria, 411; with West, 416; with Iceland, 487
Union of the Revolutionary Left (Peru), 164, 165
Unions, *see* Labor unions
United Communist Vanguard (Venezuela), 178, 180
United Nations: aid to Ethiopia, 22; Afghan talks, 191, 193–94, 265; resolution calling for withdrawal of Soviet troops from Afghanistan, 194; PRC participation in organs, 217; and North Korea, 245; and Poland, 359; and front organizations, 427–34
United Revolutionary Front (Guatemala), 134
United States: joint exercises with Somalia, 23; aid to Nicaraguan guerrillas, 79, 156; aid to El Salvador, 80, 122; Australian demonstrations against port calls, 200; trade with China, 219; military sales to China, 219; problem of Taiwan, 219; New Zealand demonstrations against port

calls, 262; trade with Hungary, 340, 341; trade with Romania, 367; Korean Air Lines incident, 387; arms control negotiations, 388–91; Soviet spies in, 391; Soviet moves against Middle East position, 395; and USSR in Latin America, 397–98
—foreign relations: Zimbabwe, 5, 77; Angola, 10; Egypt, 20; Ethiopia, 22, 23; Mozambique, 49, 51; Grenada, 79, 124, 127, 129; Nicaragua, 79, 157; El Salvador, 80, 123; Argentina, 83; Costa Rica, 109; Cuba, 111–15 *passim*; North Korea, 243, 244–45; Laos, 248; Nepal, 259; Philippines, 268, 270; USSR, 289–91, 388–91, 395, 397–98; Albania, 301; Bulgaria, 310–11; Hungary, 340–42; Poland, 358, 359; Romania, 366–67
United States League of Revolutionary Struggle, 175
United Workers' Party (Israel), 34
Upper Volta: and Benin, 15
Uruguay, Communist Party of, 177; and Bulgarian CP, 311; and Czechoslovak CP, 321
USA, Communist Party, 5, 81, 173–74; and South African CP, 61; and Puerto Rican Left, 170; and Bulgarian CP, 311; and *World Marxist Review*, 426

Vanuatu: and China, 216
Vatican: and Czechoslovakia, 317
Venezuela, 81, 82; and Nicaragua, 158; and USSR, 397–98
Venezuela, Communist Party of, 177, 178–79
Vietnam: control of Laos and Kampuchea, 184; aid to Thai guerrillas, 185, 279; Burmese CP criticisms, 208; troops and advisers in Kampuchea, 235; Vietnamese settlers in Kampuchea, 236; Vietnamese troops in Laos, 247; trade agreement with Mongolia, 257; and Thai CP, 278; trade agreement with Albania, 299, 301; cultural agreement with Albania, 301; trade agreement with Bulgaria, 310
—foreign relations: Angola, 11; Grenada, 129; China, 216, 218; Laos, 247, 249; ASEAN states, 254; Albania, 296, 301, 302
Vietnamese Communist Party, 280–84; factional infighting, 184
—relations with other CPs: Ethiopian, 23; Guadeloupan, 130; Indian, 223; Albanian, 302; Bulgarian, 311; CPSU, 398; French, 446–69

Wages: in Bulgaria, 304; in Romania, 364
Warsaw Treaty Organization, 291; and Bulgaria, 309; Prague meeting (January), 318–19; and Hungary, 342; and Poland, 344; and Romania, 370; Soviet use of, 393, 417–18; economic dimensions of, 417, 420, 421–22; structure, 418; joint maneuvers, 418, 420–21; northern

tier, 418; military integration, 418; weaponry, 418–19; command reorganization, 419; compared with NATO, 419; shortcomings, 419–20; used to suppress counterrevolution, 423; political dimensions of, 423–24

West Bank Communist Organization (Jordan/ Israel), 35

West Berlin, Socialist Unity Party of, 438, 443, 474, 476–77

Western Europe: and USSR, 290

Western Sahara, 4, 20, 45, 46

Western Samoa: and North Korea, 242

West German Communists, Marxist League of, 475

West Germany, Communist League of, 475

Women's International Democratic Federation, 429–30; Panamanian affiliate, 160; New Zealand affiliate, 262; and USSR, 386

Women's organizations (CP-controlled): Bahrain, 12, 13; Benin, 15; Congo, 17; Ethiopia, 22; Iran, 24; Mozambique, 47, 48; Réunion, 53; 54; Canada, 91; Cuba, 110; Grenada, 122; Guadeloupe, 130; Guyana, 139; Jamaica, 144; Martinique, 147; 148–49; Nicaragua, 154; Panama, 158, 160; Afghanistan, 186, 188; China, 209, 215; Japan, 230; Kampuchea, 235; Korea, 237; Mongolia, 255; New Zealand, 259, 262; Philippines, 266, 270; Sri Lanka, 275; Albania, 293, 296; Bulgaria, 303; Czechoslovakia, 312; GDR, 322; Romania, 361; Finland, 458; Cyprus, 448; West Berlin, 477; Luxembourg, 497; Netherlands, 501; Sweden, 519; Switzerland, 523, 524

Worker, Peasant, Student, and People's Front (Peru), 164

Workers' and Soldiers' Organization Offensive (Switzerland), 524

Workers Communist League (New Zealand), 259, 260

Workers' Communist Party (Norway), 505, 506, 509–10

Workers Communist Party (Marxist-Leninist) (Canada), 91, 93, 95

Workers League (U.S.), 175

Workers' Party (Brazil), 89, 90

Workers' Revolutionary Party (Panama), 160

Workers' Revolutionary Party (U.K.), 480

Workers' Self-Defense Movement (Colombia), 99

Workers World Party (U.S.), 175

Working People's Alliance (Guyana), 138, 140

World Assembly for Peace and Life, Against Nuclear War (Prague, June), 255, 317–18, 434, 435; Bahrain delegation, 13; Arab CP delegations, 55; Afghan delegation, 191; Australian delegation, 200; Indonesian delegation, 227; New Zealand delegation, 263; Philippine delegation, 270; Cypriot delegation, 449, 452; Danish delegation, 456

World Federation of Democratic Youth, 430; Bahrain affiliate, 12; Saudi affiliate, 55; Guyanese affiliate, 139; Mexican affiliates, 152, 153; Panamanian affiliate, 160; Australian affiliate, 200

World Federation of Scientific Workers, 432

World Federation of Trade Unions, 429; and USSR, 386

—affiliates: Réunion, 54; Sudan, 62; Colombia, 99; Guatemala, 135; Mexico, 152, 153; Panama, 160; Australia, 198, 199; Indonesia, 227; New Zealand, 262; Philippines, 267, 269

World Marxist Review, 7, 62, 98, 200, 227, 426–27, 497

World Peace Council, 428–29; and USSR, 386; and Soviet peace campaign, 434, 435

—members and affiliates: Yemen, 3, 73; Bahrain, 13; Jordan, 37; Lebanon, 40, Réunion, 54; Saudi Arabia, 55; Sudan, 62; Grenada, 128; Mexico, 152, 153; Panama, 159, 160; U.S., 174; Australia, 199; Indonesia, 227; Malaysia, 255; New Zealand, 262; Philippines, 270; FRG, 471, 473, 474; Switzerland, 525

WTO, *see* Warsaw Treaty Organization

Yemen, South: cooperates with Ethiopia, 3; Soviet and Cuban advisers in, 3; and Lebanese CP, 43; unification talks, 71; and Bulgaria, 309; Bulgarian military aid to, 309; and CMEA, 408

Yemeni Communist Party, *see* People's Democratic Union

Yemen Socialist Party, 3, 70–74; and Lebanese Organization of Communist Action, 44; and Syrian CP, 67; and CPSU, 400; and Bulgarian CP, 311

Youth: outlook of, in Czechoslovakia, 316; in Hungary, 335, 337

Youth organizations (CP-controlled): Algeria, 8; Angola, 11; Bahrain, 12, 13; Benin, 15; Congo, 17; Iran, 24; Israel, 30, 32; Mozambique, 47; 48; Réunion, 53, 54; Saudi Arabia, 55; Sudan, 62, 64; U.S., 81, 173–74; Argentina, 82; Bolivia, 85; Canada, 91; Chile, 96; Colombia, 98, 99; Cuba, 110; Grenada, 124; Guadeloupe, 130; Guatemala, 135; Guyana, 139; Jamaica, 144; Mexico, 150, 152; Nicaragua, 154; Panama, 158, 160; Venezuela, 178; Afghanistan, 186, 188; Australia, 196, 199, 200; China, 209, 215; Kampuchea, 235; Korea, 237; Laos, 247; Mongolia, 255; New Zealand, 259, 263; Philippines, 266; Sri Lanka, 275; Vietnam, 280, 284; Albania, 293, 296–97; Bulgaria, 303, 305; Czechoslovakia, 312; GDR, 322, 323; Hungary, 334, 340; Romania, 361; USSR, 373, 385–86; Yugoslavia, 403; Belgium, 446; Cyprus, 448, 451, 452; Denmark, 453, 454; Finland, 458; France, 464; FRG, 470, 471, 474, 475; West Berlin, 477; U.K., 478, 479–80; Ireland, 487; Italy, 489; Luxembourg, 497; Malta, 498; Netherlands, 501; Norway, 505; Sweden, 519, 520, 522; Switzerland, 523

Yugoslavia: and Angola, 11; and Grenada, 129; and Nicaragua, 158; and China, 216; and Albania, 295, 300; trade agreements with Albania, 299, 300; and Balkan nuclear-free zone, 308; and Bulgaria, 308; trade with Bulgaria, 308; and GDR, 332; and Hungary, 342; and Romania, 369; and USSR, 398; and CMEA, 408, 412
Yugoslavia, League of Communists of, 403–4; and *World Marxist Review*, 426
—relations with other CPs: Lebanese, 43, 44; Indian, 223; Korean, 243; Bulgarian, 311; Czechoslovak, 321; Greek, 483; Italian, 495, 496; Netherlands, 505; Portuguese, 513

Zambia: and Romania, 368; and CPSU, 400
Zimbabwe: and China, 216; and Czechoslovakia, 319; and GDR, 332–33; and Hungary, 341; and Romania, 368
Zimbabwe African National Union, 5, 75–77
Zimbabwe African People's Union, 5, 75, 77
Zones of peace: Indian Ocean, 54